INTRODUCTION TO
Criminal
Justice

FIFTH EDITION

To my wife Janet and my children, Joseph, Peter, Stephen, and Christian.

J.J.S

To my wife Therese J. Libby and my children, Rachel, Eric, and Andrew.

L.J.S.

Contents

Preface

We originally wrote *Introduction to Criminal Justice* out of the conviction that students needed to have a well-rounded, objective text that set out the basic concepts and processes of the justice system. As two professors who had taught introductory classes in a large criminal justice program, we recognized the need for a book that provided a solid review of the field's existing policies and practices. We also wanted to supply the most current information possible so that students and instructors would feel confident that the text they were using was on the cutting edge of the discipline. At the time the first edition was published in 1978 most criminal justice texts were stodgy and boring, so we wanted to create a book that was fun to read and interesting as well as informative and scholarly.

Over the years many of the professors who adopted our book told us that our original instincts were correct. They liked *Introduction to Criminal Justice* because it was comprehensive and detailed yet written in an interesting fashion. Most adopters also liked the fact that our writing style tends to be balanced and objective. Our objectivity is not serendipitous. We actually want it to be difficult for the reader to guess our political orientation and/or beliefs about criminal justice. We try to present both sides of every issue and give "equal time" to each major policy. However, in conclusion, we try to assess where the weight of the evidence falls.

Most of the instructors who use our book also like the idea that each new edition is not simply the same old words with a new cover. In fact, it takes us far longer to prepare each new edition than it did to write the original text. The study of criminal justice is a dynamic field of scientific inquiry. Keeping up with new concepts, ideas, and research is a full-time task but one that we enjoy doing.

■ The Changing Field of Criminal Justice

In some academic disciplines a textbook's fifth edition must be a difficult book to produce: after all, how many times can you rework the same material? This is not the case in criminal justice. The field is changing so rapidly that new editions are an absolute necessity if students are to keep up with the developments that are taking place. In fact, we try to change the book almost up to the day it is published (our nickname at West is "stop the presses").

It is sometimes difficult to comprehend the changes that have occurred in the field since the first edition of *Introduction to Criminal Justice* was published. At that time, the prevailing view in criminal justice was that criminal defendants' civil liberties were of predominant importance from the time of their arrest to their final release from prison. Rehabilitation and treatment were thought to be the true goals of the justice system. The death penalty was in disuse and on the way out. Since people who broke the law were "products of their social environment," it was up to the justice system to compensate for the bad hand dealt them by society. An even better strategy than rehabilitating offenders was to divert them from the justice system so they could avoid the stigma of negative social labels.

Little more than a decade later, this picture of criminal justice has changed dramatically. The general public has become more conservative and the justice system has followed suit. Offenders' civil liberties are no longer a burning social issue; victims' rights are now of greater concern. Correctional policy favors incapacitation and protection of society over rehabilitation. Capital punishment has become so commonplace that executions often go unreported in the media. The criminal offender is no longer viewed as a victim of society. Crime experts boldly assert that criminal tendencies may be inherited or even a matter of personal choice; such beliefs, if anybody held them, were only whispered among friends 12 years ago.

Considering these radical changes, it is easy to see why *Introduction to Criminal Justice* has been updated and changed. Our aim is to reflect what is going on today and show where the field is headed in the 1990s. We are excited to bring this information to you because we want to be part of the evolution of criminal justice, and educating its future leaders and policymakers is an important part of that change.

■ The Fifth Edition

The fifth edition of *Introduction to Criminal Justice* provides a framework for the study of criminal justice by analyzing and describing the agencies of justice and the procedures they use to identify and treat criminal offenders. It covers what most experts believe are the critical issues in criminal justice and analyzes their impact on the justice system. This edition continues to focus on policy issues in the criminal justice system. We explore the real impact such proposed and actual changes as bail reform, gun control, electronic monitoring, the operation of correctional institutions by private firms, community policing, and determinate sentencing have or will have on the operations of the justice system.

In writing this new edition, we have the following goals:

1. To provide students with a thorough knowledge of the criminal justice system
2. To be as comprehensive and up-to-date as possible
3. To be objective and unbiased
4. To describe current methods of social control and to analyze their strengths and weaknesses

We have tried to provide a text that is both scholarly and informative, comprehensive yet interesting, well organized and objective, yet provocative and thought provoking.

The fifth edition of *Introduction to Criminal Justice* has been thoroughly revised and reorganized to incorporate the changes in the criminal justice system. The evolution of crime control policy has been treated by updating the discussion of the criminal justice system with recent court decisions, legislative changes, and theoretical concepts that reflect the changing orientation of the field. In addition, some significant changes have been made in the organization of the text:

Chapter 1, The Study of Criminal Justice, has been completely rewritten and now contains a detailed description of the agencies and processes of justice. Chapter 2, The Nature of Crime and Victimization, and Chapter 3, The Causes of Crime and Victimization, now contain expanded coverage of victim data and trends and theories of victimization in order to provide more information on the important field of victimology.

Chapter 4 has also been radically changed. It now combines in one chapter analysis of procedural and substantive criminal law and their influence on the justice system. It contains material on legal issues that were covered in two separate chapters (4 and 6) in earlier editions.

Chapter 5 now covers the most important perspectives and goals of the criminal justice system and shows how it operates as a social control agency. It discusses such issues as electronic surveillance and efforts to combat the drug trade. A new section looks at the relationship between criminal justice and the victim.

The coverage of law enforcement has been expanded to four chapters in order to provide additional material on this critical area of criminal justice. Chapter 6 covers the emerging use of technology in police work and also discusses the important concept of community policing. We have broadened the discussion of police roles and updated the legal issues in policing.

The coverage of the judicatory process contained in Chapters 10 through 14 has also undergone major reorganization. The first two chapters in the section cover court organization and personnel: Chapter 10 discusses the court system and the judiciary, while Chapter 11 deals with the prosecution and defense. Chapters 12 through 14 focus more directly on the court process: the pretrial, trial, and sentencing stages of justice. We have tried to update these chapters to include such emerging issues as preventive detention and bail reform, sentencing guidelines, court technology, and changes in indigent defense systems.

The correctional area has also undergone major revision. Chapter 15 now covers probation and intermediate sanctions such as electronic monitoring and house arrest. Chapter 17, Living in Prison, now includes material on prisoners' rights that had formerly been contained in a separate chapter. Chapter 18, Returning to Society, looks at the problems faced by inmates in the outside world and the probability of their successful adjustment.

Chapter 19, Juvenile Justice, now contains an analysis of recent changes in the death penalty for minors, the rise of teenage gangs, and drug use among American youth.

■ Learning Tools

The text contains the following features designed to help students learn and comprehend the material:

1. Each chapter begins with an outline and list of key terms used throughout the chapter. Every effort has been made to include the key terms within the glossary that concludes the book.
2. The book contains more than 200 photos, tables, and charts that dramatize the events that take place in the criminal justice system and help students visualize its processes. Many of these are now in full color.
3. Every chapter contains Criminal Justice in Review boxes that highlight intriguing issues concerning criminal justice policy or processes. By reading these boxed inserts, the student will discover whether criminal behavior is actually influenced by police presence, how much the criminal justice system costs, how many people are under its control, how prisons are making use of private prison enterprise, and if offenders can be monitored by computers in their own home. The boxes are designed to give the reader a more realistic perspective on the operations of the system.
4. As in previous editions, the major U.S. Supreme Court decisions that influence and control the justice system are examined in some detail in the Law in Review boxes. Cases include *Tennessee v. Garner*, on the police use of deadly force, and *United States v. Salerno*, on the use of preventive detention.
5. A glossary that defines the key terms used in the text is included at the end of the book.

Since we believe that criminal justice is a fascinating area of study, we hope that these materials will help the reader generate the same interest in the field that we have maintained for over 20 years.

■ Acknowledgments

The preparation of this text would not have been possible without the aid of our colleagues who helped by reviewing the text and giving us material to use in its preparation. They include

William Ashlen
David Barger
Cathy C. Brown
Steve Brown

George S. Burbridge
Nicholas Carimi, Jr.
Kathy Lynn Cook
Steven G. Cox
Robert Culbertson
Gerhard Falk
Steven Gilham
Kathryn Golden
Peter Grimes
Ed Grosskopf
Earl Hamb
John P. Harlan
Donald Harrelson
William Hobbs
Robert G. Huckabee
Barton Ingraham
Michael Israel
Dorothy K. Kagehiro
James M. Knight, Sr.
Robert Lockwood
Thomas McAninch
Tom Mieczowski
Frank Morn
Anthony T. Muratore
Michael Neustrom
Robert Page
Helen S. Ridley
Ronald Robinson
Rudy SanFillipo
William Selke
Gayle Shuman
Mark Tezak
Howard Timm
Donald Torres
Laurin A. Wollan, Jr.
Kevin Wright

A number of other friends and colleagues made helpful suggestions and provided material. They include Mark Blumberg, James Byrne, Frank Cullen, Edward Donovan, Lee Ellis, Chris Eskridge, Chuck Fenwick, Edith Flynn, James A. Fox, James Fyfe, James Garafalo, Gilbert Geis, John Goldkamp, Jack Greene, Dennis Hoffman, James Kane, Pete Kuchel, Steven Lagoy, Bob Langworthy, Edward Latessa, John Laub, Alan Lincoln, Edward McGarrell, Arthur Miller, Michael Odawa, Janet Porter, Spencer Rathus, Robert Regoli, Frank Schubert, Marty Schwartz, Bill Wakefield, Sam Walker, Gennaro Vito, Marvin Zalman, the staff at the Institute for Social Research at the University of Michigan, the Hindelang Research Center at SUNY-Albany, the National Center for State Courts, the Criminal Justice Research Center at the University of Lowell, and Kristina Rose and Janet Rosenbaum of the National Criminal Justice Reference Service.

And, of course, our colleagues at West Publishing did their usual outstanding job of aiding us in the preparation of the text. Mary Schiller, our senior executive editor, did her typical superb job in helping, inspiring, and encouraging us in our efforts. Laura Mezner Nelson, our production editor on the project, was always there with thoroughly professional advice and technical skills.

The Nature of Crime, Law and Criminal Justice

1

The Concept of Criminal Justice

The nature and control of criminal behavior are topics that have always fascinated the American public. At some time in their lives, most people have been tantalized and enthralled, or conversely horrified and repelled, by some well-publicized criminal event; a man shoots four boys who attack him on a New York subway; a mentally deranged man brings an automatic rifle to the public school he attended as a child and kills five schoolchildren; a millionaire stockbroker is indicted for insider trading; a high-ranking government official is accused of taking bribes; a serial killer is executed for slaying more than 30 young women.

The proper means of controlling criminal behavior is also a lively topic for debate: Should drugs be legalized? Should convicted murderers be executed? Does insanity excuse criminal conduct? Should police be allowed to shoot at fleeing criminals? Questions such as these often come up whenever people get together to discuss intriguing social issues. But whereas most people attempt to satisfy their curiosity about crime-related issues in their spare time or through casual observation, **criminal justice** experts make the study of crime and its control their lifework.

Interest in criminal justice has reached unprecedented levels; it has become a political "hot potato." Crime was a major issue when presidential candidates George Bush and Massachusetts governor Michael Dukakis squared off in the 1988 presidential campaign. Some commentators felt that a major factor in the Dukakis loss was his failure to respond affirmatively during the second presidential debate when he was asked if he would support the use of the death penalty if his wife Kitty had been raped and murdered; others believed that his advocacy of gun control and prison furlough programs cost him the deciding votes. Even the victorious Bush took a political pounding because he had led the Reagan administration's ineffective efforts to deal with international drug trafficking. A previously obscure first degree murderer named Willy Horton became a major figure in the presidential contest when the nation was told how he had escaped from a Massachusetts prison furlough program and raped a Maryland woman and assaulted her husband. For many voters, the Horton case came to symbolize Dukakis's unpopular liberal approach to crime.

The degree of attention paid by national political candidates to what are essentially local and state issues underscores the importance of crime to the American public and demonstrates why criminal justice has become such an important and popular area of study.

This text serves as an introduction to the study of criminal justice. The first chapter introduces some basic issues. After defining the concept and study of criminal justice, the chapter introduces the major components and processes of the criminal justice system so that students can develop an overview of how the system functions. Finally, careers in criminal justice are discussed in order to connect the study of criminal justice to future professional employment choices.

■ The Concept of Criminal Justice

The term *criminal justice* refers to an area of knowledge concerned with controlling crime through the scientific administration of police, court, and correctional agencies. It is an interdisciplinary field that draws upon the knowledge bases of sociology, psychology, law, public policy, and other related fields.

KEY TERMS

Criminal justice
Law Enforcement Assistance
    Administration (LEAA)
Patterned social regularities
System
Process
Probable cause
In-presence requirement
Lineup
Bill of indictment
Information
Arraignment
Appeal
Nolle prosequi
Courtroom work group
Pro bono

The origins of the scientific study of criminal justice as a social control agency are usually traced to the mid-eighteenth century when Italian social thinker Cesare Beccaria published a famous treatise on crime and punishment in which he made a convincing argument against torture and for the use of the minimum amount of punishment necessary to control crime.[1] Ever since Beccaria's work was published, experts have sought to find the formula for a social policy that would simultaneously control crime, treat criminals, protect victims, and benefit society as a whole. Nevertheless, until fairly recently there was little effort to study the agencies of criminal justice in a systematic fashion. In fact, not until 1919 did a criminal justice system in the United States come under rigorous study. In that year the *Chicago Crime Commission*, a professional association funded by private contributions, was created.[2] This organization, which acted as a citizen's advocate group, monitored the ongoing activities of local justice agencies. The commission still carries out its work today.

The pioneering work of the Chicago group was soon copied in other jurisdictions. In 1922, the Cleveland Crime Commission provided a detailed analysis of local criminal justice policy and uncovered the widespread use of discretion, plea bargaining, and other practices unknown to the public. Some commentators believe the Cleveland survey was the first to treat criminal justice as a people processing system, an approach that is still widely used.[3] Similar projects were conducted by the Missouri Crime Survey (1926) and the Illinois Crime Survey (1929).

In 1931 then President Herbert Hoover appointed the National Commission of Law Observance and Enforcement, which is commonly known today as the *Wickersham Commission*. This national study group made a detailed analysis of the American justice system and helped usher in the era of treatment and rehabilitation in the U.S. correctional system. The study revealed in great detail the myriad rules and regulations that govern the system and exposed the problems its legal and administrative complexity pose for justice personnel.[4]

The modern era of criminal justice study began in 1967 when the President's Commission on Law Enforcement and Administration of Justice (the *Crime Commission*), which had been appointed by Lyndon Johnson, published its final report entitled *The Challenge of Crime in a Free Society*.[5] This group of practitioners, educators, and attorneys had been charged with creating a comprehensive view of the criminal justice process and providing recommendations for its reform. Concomitantly, Congress passed the Omnibus Crime Control and Safe Streets Act of 1968, which provided federal funds for state and local crime control efforts.[6] This act helped launch a massive campaign to restructure the justice system by funding the **Law Enforcement Assistance Administration (LEAA),** an agency that provided hundreds of millions of dollars in aid to local and state justice agencies. Federal intervention through LEAA ushered in a new era in research and development in the criminal justice system.

Since that time, other national groups and agencies, including the American Bar Association and the National Advisory Commission on Criminal Justice Standards and Goals, have also explored the American criminal justice system in depth.[7] Many of their major recommendations have been implemented. On the state level, numerous jurisdictions have reformed their criminal codes. In addition, police, court, and correctional agencies have implemented hundreds of new crime control and offender treatment programs. Although commentators disagree about the effectiveness of such efforts, they have promoted a new era of concern and interest in the operations of the criminal justice system.

■ The Study of Criminal Justice

As a result of these efforts, an interdisciplinary field of criminal justice has come into being. Nearly every federal, state, and local crime control program refers to the "criminal justice system." Rather than being treated as thousands of independent institutions, police, court, and correctional agencies are commonly viewed as components in a large integrated "people processing system" that manages law violators from the time of their arrest through trial, punishment, and release. To study criminal justice and train students for management roles in the justice-related agencies, more than six hundred departments or colleges of criminal justice have been developed in institutions of higher education. Academic institutions have become a major resource for those trying to find solutions to the crime problem; university involvement in problems of criminal justice has provided needed resources and authenticity to a relatively new field.

Criminal justice is truly an interdisciplinary field in that it draws upon a number of academic disciplines to develop insights into the causes and prevention of criminal behavior. Sociologists have long studied the social and environmental factors associated with crime and delinquency. Psychologists have conducted research that seeks to determine if the typical offender's criminal behavior is symptomatic of some emotional or mental health problem. Legal scholars have focused on such issues as the effect of legal rule changes on the justice process and the relationship between social control and civil liberties. For example, what is the effect on police behavior of a Supreme Court decision prohibiting the shooting of unarmed suspects who are fleeing arrest?[8]

A variety of other disciplines also contribute to the field of criminal justice. Historians examine the historical context of the law and the development of early justice agencies. Political scientists explore the role of federal and state governments in dealing with urban problems, analyze political parties and pressure groups, examine legislation, and study how government influences the justice system. Using economic theory to analyze crime, some economists have suggested that people commit crime after conducting a cost-benefit analysis of the gains they may make from a criminal act compared to the losses they may suffer if they are apprehended by the police.

Even physical scientists have become active in criminal justice. For example, forensic chemists work closely with police agencies to develop scientific techniques for analyzing evidence. Biologists and medical doctors have conducted studies on the biochemical and physical bases of criminal behavior and the effect of diet and medication on the treatment of known offenders.[9]

Thus, a great deal of information has been taken from various disciplines and consolidated to serve as the knowledge base for the new area of study. Understanding the various areas of knowledge that are represented in this field helps us to reach a working definition of criminal justice study:

> The study of criminal justice may be defined as the application of the scientific method to the administration, procedures, and policies of those agencies of government charged with the enforcement of law, the adjudication of crime, and the correction of criminal conduct. The study of criminal justice involves analysis of how these institutions influence human behavior and how they are in turn influenced by law and society.

Note that this definition recognizes that criminal justice is essentially a *social control* institution. Its study involves analysis of how the justice system responds to social norms and trends and how its operations have a reciprocal influence on societal behavior and values.

As social scientists, criminal justice experts try to bring carefully controlled scientific methods, such as surveys and experiments, to bear on their subject matter whenever possible. Using these methods, they focus on the inner processes of the agencies of justice: police and law enforcement organizations, courts and related institutions such as the district attorney's office; and correctional agencies such as jails, prisons, and parole authorities. Thus, in addition to studying the role of crime in society, criminal justice analyzes the formal processes and social agencies that have been established for crime control.

The Goals of Criminal Justice Study

What are the goals of criminal justice study? Like other social scientists, criminal justice scholars seek to *explain, predict, and influence* the events they encounter, including the operations of the agencies of justice. They look for **patterned social regularities** (behaviors that occur over and over again) in the organizations and processes they study. Their goal is to determine whether any distinct patterns of behavior exist that will improve their understanding of the operations of the justice system. For example, scholars may study activities within a correctional facility to determine the effect of overcrowding on prisoner behavior. If overcrowding is generally related to violence or unrest among the prison population, it follows that reducing the number of inmates in a correctional institution can help reduce tension.

When possible, these findings are interwoven into theories of behavior that can be used to explain the operations of the criminal justice system on a broader level. Observations of a particular agency can be used to help explain similar phenomena in agencies not yet examined. For example, a study of overcrowding and its relationship to prison violence in a single institution can be used to make general assumptions about prison conditions throughout the United States.

Using their research findings and conclusions, criminal justice scholars also attempt to predict future occurrences within the system. They may wish to show police executives what will happen if the number of patrol cars on the street is doubled or help correctional authorities determine the probability of success if inmates are released early from prison on parole. One of the most important recent developments in the criminal justice field is the attempt to predict which offenders are likely to become chronic career criminals and to impose prison sentences that are severe enough to control their behavior. Some experts criticize such efforts on the ground that punishing individuals on the basis of predictions of their future criminality is unfair because no one's future behavior can be known with absolute certainty.

Finally, justice scholars attempt to influence the operations of the criminal justice system. All scholars have a particular point of view or philosophy that they would like to see implemented. Some view the justice system as a purely social control force and therefore advocate policies that they believe will help attain that goal—long prison sentences for serious offenders, aggressive police patrol, abolition of the insanity defense, and so on. Others who take a more liberal stance lobby for more rehabilitation-oriented programs, such as the diversion of young offenders into community-based treatment programs in lieu of prison sentences. Such diverse opinions make for many lively debates over what form the justice system should take and what directions its policies should follow.

In addition to their political orientations, criminal justice scholars can be classified on the basis of their goals. Some scholars believe their primary role is to be social thinkers and commentators who serve as watchdogs over the criminal justice system and its policies. Prominent among this group are such conservative thinkers as James Q. Wilson and Earnest Van Den Haag as well as more liberal observers such as Samuel Walker, Francis Cullen, and Karen Gilbert.[10] Other criminal justice experts are more concerned with working directly with the agencies of justice in order to understand and improve their operations. For example, research conducted by police expert James Fyfe on the use of deadly force has significantly influenced the way law enforcement officers are permitted to use their weapons against suspected criminals who resist arrest.[11]

Another way of looking at this distinction is to say that some criminal justice experts view crime and justice as abstract social issues whereas others are interested in more practical applications of their efforts. Whereas the former seek to define such concepts as fairness, justice, due process, and social control, the latter might offer ways to make police patrol more effective or devise a way of effectively processing cases through the criminal courts. In such a diverse field as criminal justice, there is room for both types of orientation, and some experts have been able to make contributions in both areas of analysis.

■ Governmental Structure and Criminal Justice

Before describing the criminal justice system and its components, it is essential to explain how the criminal justice system fits into our governmental structure.

The legislative, judicial, and executive branches of the government provide the basic framework of the American criminal justice system. Legal authority to establish crime control programs rests initially within this governmental structure. The legislature defines the law by determining what conduct is prohibited, establishing penalties for criminal violation and rules for criminal procedure; the appellate courts interpret the law and determine whether it meets constitutional requirements; the executive branch plans programs, appoints personnel, and exercises administrative responsibility for criminal justice agencies.

Criminal justice agencies can be created by legislative acts, executive orders, or constitutional requirements. The legislature establishes and controls the authority and discretion of certain administrative organizations, such as state corrections departments; other organizations, such as local police departments, fall under the authority of locally elected officials such as the mayor and/or city council. Some agencies, such as parole boards, often have broad discretion and delegated authority to provide services for convicted offenders; others, such as trial courts, are generally given greater legislative directions. Nevertheless, all criminal justice agencies have authority within the law to develop rules and regulations that control operational policies and procedures.

Because the legislature defines criminal behavior, it is often perceived as playing a more important role in the criminal justice system than the judicial and executive branches. This perception of the criminal justice power structure is not entirely correct. Rather than functioning independently, all three branches and the governmental bureaucracy generally work together to influence the operation of the criminal justice system. For example, when the legislature passes a criminal statute establishing a one-year mandatory sentence for persons convicted of possession of a handgun, both the judicial and executive branches share in the implementation of the statute and its effect on the criminal justice system. Such a law may have been proposed by the executive branch, subject to legislative approval and judicial review. The trend toward court intervention in the operational procedures of police agencies and the constitutional safeguards established by the courts are other examples of the interrelationship of the legislative, judicial, and executive functions. Similarly, the sentencing process involves all three branches of government: criminal sanctions are created by legislators, imposed and reviewed by the judiciary, and carried out by the executive branch. Thus, in order to understand how criminal justice works, one must examine the legislative, judicial, and executive systems as well as the administrative agencies, which are often collectively referred to as the fourth branch of government.

Legislature

The primary role of legislatures in the criminal justice system is to define criminal behavior and establish criminal penalties. To carry out these functions, legislatures enact laws on the basis of authority granted to them by the Federal or state constitutions.

The initiative to pass a law, such as a new capital punishment bill, may come from a legislator, the executive, a criminal justice agency, a public official, or a group of citizens. The issue is first studied by a legislative committee, where lobbyists and outside interest groups may present their views on the proposed bill. If the committee approved the bill, it is sent to the legislative houses for a vote. If both houses do not pass the legislation in its initial form, it is given to a joint committee composed of members of both houses, which drafts a compromise bill that is eventually voted on by both bodies. When the bill has been passed, it is given to the chief executive for his or her signature. If signed, the bill becomes a law. If vetoed, the bill may be dropped or referred back to the legislature for reconsideration (see Figure 1.1).

When a statute defining criminal behavior is passed, the courts require that it be sufficiently definite and clear. When offenses such as disorderly conduct, juvenile delinquency, and morality crimes involving drunkenness, gambling, obscenity, and sexual misconduct are not defined precisely, the vagueness of the law creates uncertainty for police and judicial enforcement practices. Thus, laws prescribing substantive crimes must be clearly stated.

In addition to establishing definitions of crimes, legislatures also pass laws involving criminal procedures. These include rules and regulations concerning arrests, search warrants, bail, trial court proceedings, and sentencing. Although much criminal procedure in recent years has resulted from leading constitutional cases relating to the investigation and prosecution of crime, such rules are also often enacted as statutes.

Besides defining crimes and fixing sentences, the legislature also provides financial support for crime control programs. Availability of funds for such programs remains one of the major concerns of the criminal justice system. Criminal justice agencies often lack financial support for facilities, adequate staff, and programs. In many cases, police courts and correctional agencies compete with one another for the same tax dollars.

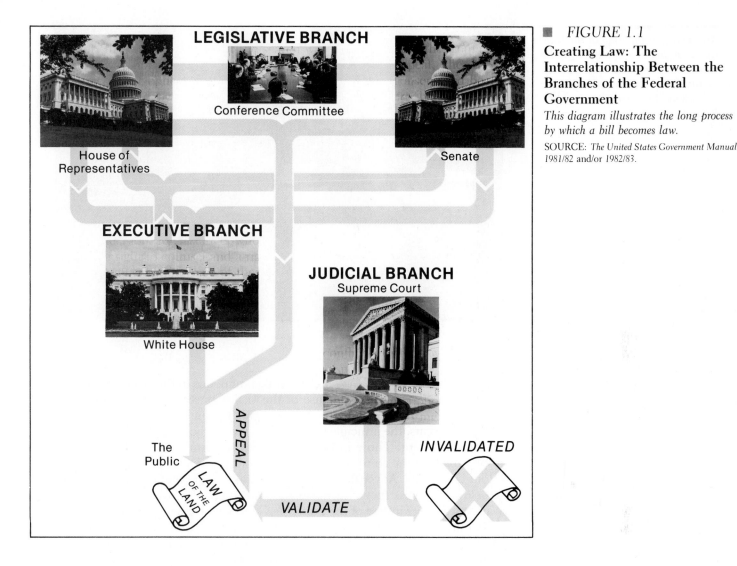

■ *FIGURE 1.1*

Creating Law: The Interrelationship Between the Branches of the Federal Government

This diagram illustrates the long process by which a bill becomes law.

SOURCE: *The United States Government Manual 1981/82 and/or 1982/83.*

Other important functions of the legislature include acting as a forum for the public expression of views on criminal justice issues and investigating potential criminal activity (e.g., the Iran-Contra hearings in 1988).

Judiciary

Although the legislature enacts laws, most criminal procedures are established by the appellate courts. The United States has a dual system of courts. Each state has a court system that interprets the state's laws, while the federal judiciary interprets federal laws.

Each system includes both trial and appellate courts. Trial courts conduct criminal trials and impose sentences on guilty offenders, whereas appellate courts interpret the law in light of constitutional standards. These courts, the most important of which is the U.S. Supreme Court, issue legal decisions about how laws should be applied. Were it not for the power of judicial review which was established within the federal system in the case of *Marbury v.*

An important function of the legislature is acting as a forum for public opinion and investigating ongoing criminal activity. Here a legislative sub-committee conducts a public hearing.

Madison, the courts would exert only limited influence in the criminal process. In addition, the supremacy clause of the U.S. Constitution has allowed the Supreme Court to declare state and local laws unconstitutional.[12]

Over the years, the principle of judicial review has been applied both actively and with restraint. Those in favor of judicial activism maintain that it is the responsibility of the courts to monitor and control governmental infringement of our civil rights. Advocates of judicial restraint argue that the courts should uphold laws unless they clearly violate constitutional provisions. When Earl Warren was chief justice of the Supreme Court (the *Warren Court*) in the 1960s, the Court took an activist position, issuing many decisions in many criminal cases that expanded individual rights. In recent years under the leadership of Chief Justices Warren Burger and William Rehnquist, the Court has taken a more conservative view of criminal justice issues.

Executive

The third major governmental authority with functions related to criminal justice is the executive branch. Executive power is vested in such public officials as the president, governors, and mayors. Today's officials are often actively involved in criminal justice issues. Many have extensive powers of appointment; they appoint judges and heads of administrative agencies such as police chiefs, commissioners of corrections, and executive directors of criminal justice planning agencies. They also have the authority to remove administrative personnel. Another important executive function involves the power to grant pardons for crimes. President Gerald Ford's pardon of Richard Nixon for his involvement in the Watergate scandal is a controversial example of this power.

Executives also play an important leadership role in criminal justice matters. For example, through the submission of programs to the legislature, executive persuasion, and party politics, a governor can influence others to follow his or her suggestions. A governor can also use the veto power to nullify legislation, thus maintaining a system of checks and balances within the governmental structure. In addition, each chief executive has a staff to develop programs and at least theoretically direct the operations of the various criminal justice departments and agencies. Thus a president, governor, or mayor is both a chief executive and the administrative head of a segment of the governmental bureaucracy.

■ The Criminal Justice System

The contemporary criminal justice system within the United States is monumental in size. It includes more than 55,000 public agencies; has a total annual budget of over $50 billion for police, court, and correctional operations; and maintains a staff of almost 1.4 million people.[13] There are approximately 18,000 police agencies, nearly 17,000 courts, over 8,000 prosecutorial agencies, approximately 5,700 correctional institutions, and over 3,500 probation and parole departments; the number of people processed through these agencies each year is equally enormous. In recent years, police have made over 12 million arrests annually, including more than 2 million for serious felony offenses.[14] In addition, almost 1 million juveniles were handled by the juvenile courts.[15] The average daily population of state and federal prisons and jails is approximately 850,000 inmates; more than 1.8 million offenders are thought to be under probation supervision and about 275,000 are on parole.[16] It costs approximately $70,000 to build a prison cell, and about $15,000 dollars per year is needed to keep an inmate in prison; juvenile institutions cost about $25,000 per year per resident (see "The Costs of Justice" in the Criminal Justice in Review). The magnitude and complexity of agency services in crime control have led to the development of what experts term the "criminal justice system."

The idea that these agencies of justice actually form a "system" is still open to debate. Theoretically, the term **system** refers to an organized and integrated array of diverse parts or elements that function as an interrelated group or unit. The systems approach to criminal justice presupposes a functional interrelationship among all those agencies concerned with the prevention of crime in our society and assumes that change in one part or agency of the system will effect change in the others. It implies that a closely knit coordinated structure of organizations exists among the various components of the system. Unfortunately, this approach exists more in theory than in practice. The various elements of the criminal justice system—such as police, courts, and corrections—are all related, but only to the degree that they are influenced by the others' policies and practices; they have not yet become so well coordinated that they can be described as operating in unison. Beyond these problems, the justice systems of the various states and federal government do not cooperate as closely as could be desired, nor are their justice practices and policies closely coordinated or compatible. "Fragmented," "divided," and "splintered" continue to be the adjectives most commonly used to describe the American system of criminal justice, prompting one commentator to label it the "criminal justice non-system."[17]

Yet, there is enough similarity in the agencies of justice and their operations to make criminal justice a feasible area of study. That is, despite all the apparent organizational differences that exist among the agencies of justice, it has proven possible to develop a body of knowledge that is applicable to criminal justice in jurisdictions across the nation.

The Costs of Justice

What is the cost of the criminal justice system to American taxpayers? Current estimates put the cost of operating the criminal justice system at more than $50 billion per year. This figure includes over $22 billion for police and law enforcement services, $10 billion for the courts, and $13 billion for the correctional system. These figures include the cost of police who investigate crimes and appear in court, public defenders who represent indigent offenders, and judges and juries who conduct trials. Correctional costs include providing inmates with medical care, educational programs, and vocational rehabilitation as well as light, heat, and food. It is not surprising that, as old correctional hands are likely to say, "it costs twice as much to send someone to the "State Pen" as to Penn State." You also must remember that many criminal justice agencies such as police departments, jails, and prisons operate on a 24-hour basis requiring three shifts of workers.

Table A shows the estimated costs for such activities as apprehending criminals, prosecuting cases, and incarcerating convicted criminals; Table B shows the overhead cost for building a new prison cell or buying a police car.

TABLE A ■ The Costs of Justice

Victim compensation (1980 and 1981)		
Average maximum award	$18,000	per award
Average award	$3,000	per award
Investigative and court costs		
A state or federal wiretap (1986)	$35,508	per wiretap
To protect a federal witness (1986)	$118,200	per year
Juror payment (1986)		
State	$10	per day
Federal	$30	per day
Court case (1982)		
California Superior court	$5	per minute
Florida Circuit Court	$4	per minute
Washington State Superior Court	$4	per minute
U.S. District Courts	$9	per minute
To arrest, prosecute, and try a robbery case in New York City (1981)		
With guilty plea and sentencing day after arrest	$851	per case
With guilty plea after indictment and sentencing 68 days after arrest	$6,665	per case
With trial disposition and sentencing 250 days after arrest	$32,627	per case
Most frequently assigned counsel hourly rate (1982)		
Out-of-court	$20–30	per hour
In court	$30–50	per hour
Average indigent defense case (1982)	$196	per case
Corrections operations costs		
For one adult offender		
In a federal prison (1986)	$13,162	per year
In a state prison (1984)	$11,302	per year
In a state-operated, community-based facility (1984)	$7,951	per year
In a local jail (1983)	$9,360	per year
On federal probation or parole (1986)	$1,316	per year

■ Components of Criminal Justice

The control and prevention of criminal activity and the treatment and reform of criminal offenders are carried out by the government agencies described in the next sections.

Police

Police departments are those public agencies that have been created to maintain order, enforce the criminal law, provide emergency services, keep the streets and highways moving freely, and develop a sense of community safety.

TABLE A ■ The Costs of Justice—*continued*

On state probation (1985)	$584 per year
On state parole (1985)	$702 per year
For housing	
An unsentenced federal prisoner in a local jail (1986)	$36 per day
A sentenced federal prisoner	
In a local community treatment center (1986)	$30 per day
In a jail (1986)	$33 per day
One resident in a public juvenile facility (1985)	$25,200 per year
Prison industry wage (1985)	$0.24–1.02 per hour

TABLE B ■ New Construction Costs in Criminal Justice

New correctional facility construction costs	
Maximum security state prison (1985)	$70,768 per bed
Medium security state prison (1985)	$53,360 per bed
Minimum security state prison (1985)	$29,599 per bed
"Constitutional" jail (1982)	$43,000 per bed
Juvenile facility (1985)	$26,470 per bed
Average remodeling for additions to prisons (1985)	$19,944 per bed
New courthouse construction costs (1982)	$54–$65 per sq. ft.
Police car costs	
Average purchase price (1981)	$8,000 per car
To equip a new police car	
Police radio (1981)	$2,000 per car
Siren and light bar (1981)	$800 per car
Other (1981)	$300 per car
To maintain and operate (not including patrol salary) (1981)	$6,000 per year
Resale value (1981)	$1,000 per car

These figures should be adjusted upward because of the effects of inflation.

At a time when heavy federal and state budget deficits have led to calls to reduce government spending, the spiraling costs of justice have put an overwhelming strain on the criminal justice system. Understaffed police forces, backlogged courts, and overcrowded prisons are the result. Yet the public seems willing to spend money on apprehending, trying, and incarcerating criminals while at the same time calling for cuts in welfare spending and care for the noncriminal poor. One might argue, however, that as the federal, state, and local governments cut back on welfare, medical, and educational programs, the long-term costs of funding a rapidly expanding correctional system will far outstrip the immediate costs of providing social services. In other words, should we pay now or pay later? ■

SOURCE: Bureau of Justice Statistics, *Report to the Nation on Crime and Justice* (Washington, D.C.: Bureau of Justice Statistics, 1988); Sue Lindren, *Justice Expenditures and Employment, 1985* (Washington, D.C.: Bureau of Justice Statistics, 1987).

The system and process of criminal justice depend on effective and efficient police work, particularly in the areas of preventing and detecting crime and apprehending and arresting criminal offenders. As our society becomes more complex, new and additional functions are required of the police officer. Today, police officers work actively with the community to prevent criminal behavior; they help divert members of special needs populations, such as juveniles, alcoholics, and drug addicts, from the criminal justice system; they participate in specialized units such as the Juvenile Aid Bureau and drug prevention squads; they cooperate with public prosecutors to initiate investigations into organized crime and drug trafficking; they resolve neighborhood and family conflicts; and they provide emergency services, such as preserving civil order during strikes and political demonstrations.

Because of these expanded responsibilities, the role of the police officer has become more professional. The officer must not only be technically competent to investigate crimes but must also be aware of the rules and procedures associated with arrest, apprehension, and investigation of criminal activity. The police officer must be aware of the factors involved in the causes of crime

Chapter 1

The Concept of
Criminal Justice

Police departments maintain public order, enforce the criminal law and provide emergency services. This photo shows a police raid on a "crack house" in Florida.

in order to screen and divert offenders who might be better handled by other, more appropriate agencies. The officer must also be part community organizer, social worker, family counselor dispute resolver, and emergency medical technician.

The police officer's role is established by the boundaries of the criminal law. Although the officer sets the criminal justice system in motion by using the authority to arrest, and this authority is vested in the law, it is neither final nor absolute. The police officer must exercise discretion on numerous matters dealing with a variety of situations, victims, criminals, and citizens. The officer must determine when an argument becomes disorderly conduct or criminal assault; whether it is appropriate to arrest a juvenile or refer him or her to a social agency; and when to assume that probable cause exists to arrest a suspect for a crime. Former Chief Justice Warren Burger stressed the importance of individual decision making and discretion when he stated:

> The policeman (or woman) on the beat, or in the patrol car, makes more decisions and exercises broader discretion affecting the daily lives of people every day and to a greater extent, in many respects, than a judge will ordinarily exercise in a week.[18]

Thus, the actions of police officers represent the exercise of discretionary justice.

Courts

Many commentators regard the criminal court as the core element in the administration of criminal justice:

> It is [the] part of the system that is the most venerable, the most formally organized, and the most elaborately circumscribed by law and tradition. It is the institution

around which the rest of the system has developed and to which the rest of the system is in large measure responsible. It regulates the flow of the criminal process under governance of the law. . . . It is expected to articulate the community's most deeply held, most cherished views about the relationship of individual and society.[19]

The criminal court houses the process that determines the criminal responsibility of defendants accused of violating the law. Ideally, it is expected to convict and sentence those found guilty of crimes while ensuring that the innocent are freed without any consequence or burden. The court system is formally required to seek the truth, to administer fair and evenhanded justice in a forum of strict impartiality and fairness, and to maintain the integrity of the rule of law. However, overcrowded courtrooms are often the scene of informal "bargain justice," designed to conclude the case as quickly as possible and at the least possible cost. Under the system of bargain justice, defendants are encouraged to plead guilty. This means that most criminal defendants do not go to trial but instead "work out a deal" with the prosecutor in which they agree to plead guilty as charged in return for a more lenient sentence, the dropping of charges, or some other considerations. Critics have tried to limit plea bargaining in recent years, but controlling it remains difficult.

In the event that the defendant is found guilty at the conclusion of the adjudication, either by an admission of guilt or by a decision made by a judge or jury, the criminal court judge is responsible for sentencing the offender. The sentence imposed by the court may serve not only to rehabilitate the offender but also to deter others from crime. Once sentencing is accomplished, the corrections component of the criminal justice system begins to function.

The entire criminal court process is undertaken with the recognition that the rights of the individual should be protected at all times. These rights, which are determined by federal and state constitutional mandates, statutes, and case laws, include such basic concepts as the right to an attorney, the right to a jury trial, and the right to a speedy trial. A defendant also has the right to be given due process, or to be treated with fundamental fairness. This includes the right to be present at trial, to be notified of the charge(s), to have an opportunity to confront hostile witnesses, and to have favorable witnesses appear. In addition, the Supreme Court has mandated tht indigent criminal defendants must be provided with legal counsel in any case where the possibility of incarceration exists.[20] Such practices are an integral part of a process that seeks to balance the interests of the individual and the state.

The court system administering the criminal process includes lower criminal courts, superior courts, and appellate courts. Each state has its own independent court structure unique to that particular jurisdiction, as does the federal government. When a crime is a violation of state law, it is ordinarily prosecuted in the state court; offenses against federal laws are generally handled by the federal court system.

The lower criminal courts of any state, variously called police courts, district courts, or recorder's courts, deal with the largest number of criminal offenses. Referred to as the people's courts, they are scattered throughout the state by county, town, or geographic district. They daily handle a large volume of criminal offenses, including such crimes as assault and battery, disorderly conduct, breaking and entering, possession of drugs, petty larceny, traffic violations, and juvenile offenses. Many cases are disposed of without trial, either because the defendant pleads guilty or because the circumstances of the offense do not warrant further court action. When trials are required in the lower courts, they often occur before a judge rather than a jury, because defendants frequently waive their constitutional right to a jury trial. Lower criminal courts, although primarily responsible for misdemeanor offenses, also process the first stage of felony offenses by holding preliminary hearings, making bail decisions, and conducting trials of certain felonies where they have jurisdiction as defined by statute.

In sum, the lower criminal courts often dispense routine and repetitious justice and are burdened with a heavy responsibility they are generally not equipped to fulfill. Characterized by cramped courtrooms, limited personnel, and a tendency to rely on bargain justice (plea bargains), they remain a critical problem area in criminal justice administration.

The superior courts, or major trial courts, have general jurisdiction over all criminal offenses but ordinarily concentrate on felony offenses. They conduct jury trials with much formality and with strict adherence to the defendant's constitutional rights. In addition to conducting trials, these courts accept guilty pleas, generally give offenders longer sentences because of the more serious nature of their crime, and in certain instances review sentences originally imposed by lower courts.

The highest state court is a supreme, or appeals, court whose functions are similar to those of the U.S. Supreme Court in the federal judicial system. State supreme courts are primarily appellate courts that do not conduct criminal trials. Appellate courts deal with procedural errors in the lower courts, such as the admission of illegal evidence, that violate rights guaranteed by the state constitution and/or the U.S. Constitution. Questions of fact that were decided in the original trial are not ordinarily reviewed in the appellate process. The appellate court has the authority to affirm, modify, or reverse decisions of the lower criminal court.

Corrections

Following a criminal trial that results in conviction and sentencing, the offender enters the correctional system. After many years of indifference, public interest in corrections has become widespread as a result of well-publicized prison riots, such as the riot at Attica in 1971, and the alleged inability of the system to rehabilitate offenders.

In the broadest sense, corrections involve community supervision or probation (more than 1.7 million people are on probation today!), various types of incarceration (including jails, houses of correction, community correctional centers, and state prisons), and parole programs for both juvenile and adult offenders. Corrections ordinarily represent the postadjudicatory care given to offenders when a sentence is imposed by the court and the offender is placed in the hands of the correctional agency.

Complicating this system is the expected dramatic population explosion in prisons. Most recently, the nation's prison population contained over 600,000 inmates; more than 30 states are under court order to reduce prison crowding.[21]

Despite its tremendous size and cost, the performance record of the correctional system has been extremely poor. It has been able neither to protect the public nor to rehabilitate criminal offenders effectively. It is often plagued with high recidivism rates (many offenders return to crime shortly after incarceration).[22] High recidivism rates are believed to result from the lack of effective treatment and training programs within incarceration facilities, poor physical environments and health conditions, and the fact that offender populations in many institutions are subjected to violence from other inmates and guards.

Despite these problems, corrections play a critical role in the criminal justice system. By exercising control over those sentenced by the courts to incarceration or community supervision, the system acts as the major sanctioning force of the criminal law. As a result, the corrections system has many responsibilities, including protecting society, deterring crime, and—equally important—rehabilitating offenders. The achievement of both proper restraint and effective reform of the offender is the system's most frustrating yet awesome goal. Some of the major components of correction are discussed in the next sections.

■ Justice System Unification

All of the major agencies and subagencies in the criminal justice system are functionally and administratively independent from each other. Their inability to work together effectively has been a major concern of criminal justice policymakers. It has resulted in disorganized and fragmented delivery of justice services. In a classic article, Daniel Skoler described the criminal justice "non-system." He identified the following causes of the system's fragmentation: (1) the constitutional separation of powers between the executive, legislative, and judicial branches of government; (2) the predominantly local character of police and prosecutorial agencies; (3) the elective nature of the attorney general's office in most jurisdictions; (4) the states' tendency to place adult and juvenile social services in human service agencies rather than criminal justice agencies.[23] Skoler proposed the formation of a "superagency" to administer the criminal justice system.[24] Such an approach would provide more efficient services to local agencies while simultaneously encouraging efforts at regionalization and coordination. The state police, the prosecutor's office, adult corrections, and the state public defender's office would all be included in this superagency. Along these lines, Alaska has a unified criminal justice system in which all its crime control agencies, except municipal law enforcement, are under the authority of the state government.

Even gaining intra-agency cooperation within a state jurisdiction can prove to be a difficult task. Law enforcement agencies are usually cool to the idea of a unified system of justice for several reasons: (1) law enforcement has traditionally been administered at the local level of government; (2) most people are skeptical about the creation of broad-based police agencies, because they fear that such agencies would be the first step toward the creation of a police state; and (3) the large size of many police departments makes it difficult for them to work together as a system.[25]

In contrast, state judicial systems have generally experienced some success in unifying the trial courts into a central administrative structure. Statewide centralized court administration permits uniform court procedures and allows for relocation of judicial personnel to meet changing workloads. Many states have already made substantial progress in this area of court reform.[26]

A few states have created unified correctional systems. Some actually use a "superagency" concept that combines adult and juvenile correctional facilities, social service components, and mental health divisions. This model places all state human service under the administration of a single agency. Unification of correctional agencies is often difficult, however, because although prisons, probation, and parole are all parts of the same process, each agency has its own vested interests.

Even if direct unification of criminal justice services is never achieved, interagency cooperations and interface are likely to increase in the future. A number of developments may encourage better working relationships: (1) the influence of higher education; (2) the development of shared information systems on local, state, and federal levels; (3) the establishment of joint training activities; (3) the creation and dissemination of criminal justice standards; and (4) the creation of statewide planning units to coordinate the operations of local criminal justice agencies. Intra-agency cooperation will be improved in the future if the directors of criminal justice agencies share similar educational experiences, belong to the same groups, and are accredited by the same standard-setting agencies.

■ The Formal Criminal Justice Process

Criminal justice refers to a **process** as well as to a system of agencies and organizations. This process involves a reasonably well-defined series of steps, beginning with the arrest of an offender and concluding with the offender's reentry into society (see Figure 1.2). The emphasis throughout the process is on the offender and the various sequential stages that person passes through. When criminal justice is viewed as a system, the various crime control organizations are the major concern; the process approach concentrates instead on the movement of individual cases through criminal justice decision points. The process normally includes the following steps:

1. *Initial contact.* The initial contact stage involves an act or incident that makes a person the subject of interest to the agencies of justice. In most instances, initial contact is a result of a police action: police officers on patrol observe a person acting suspiciously and conclude the suspect is under the influence of drugs; a victim reports a robbery, and police officers respond by going to the scene of the crime; an informer tells police about some ongoing criminal activity in order to receive favorable treatment. In some instances initial contact occurs because the police department is responding to a request by the mayor or other political figures to control an ongoing social problem such as gambling, prostitution, or teenage loitering.

2. *Investigation.* The purpose of the investigatory stage of the justice process is to gather enough evidence to identify the perpetrators, justify their arrest, and bring them to trial. Some investigations take only a few minutes, as when police officers see a crime in progress and apprehend the suspect within minutes. Others, including such famous cases as the Atlanta child killings and the Hillside Strangler in Los Angeles, take many months and involve hundreds of police officers.

3. *Arrest.* Arrests occur when the police take persons into custody, and the suspects believe that they have lost their liberty. An arrest is considered legal when all the following conditions exist: (a) the police officer believes that there is sufficient evidence, referred to as **probable cause,** that a crime is being or has been committed and that the suspect is the perpetrator; (b) the officer deprives the individual of freedom; (c) the suspect believes that he or she is now in the custody of the police. The police officer is not required to use the word arrest or any similar term to initiate an arrest, nor does the officer have to take the suspect to the police station. In order to make an arrest in a misdemeanor, the

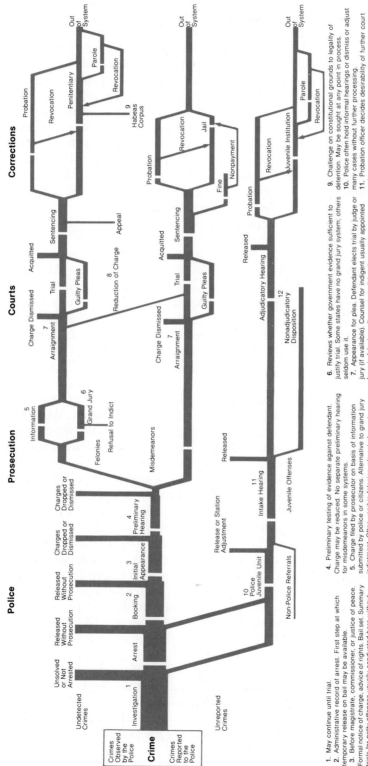

■ *FIGURE 1.2*

Movement of Cases Through the Criminal Justice System*

*This chart presents a simple yet comprehensive view of the movement of cases through the criminal justice system. Procedures in individual jurisdictions may vary from the pattern shown here. The differing weights of line indicate the relative volumes of cases disposed of at various points in the system, but this is only suggestive, since no nationwide data of this sort exists.

SOURCE: President's Commission of Law Enforcement and Administration of Justice, *The Challenge of Crime in a Free Society* (Washington, D.C.: U.S. Government Printing Office, 1967)

1. May continue until trial.

2. Administrative record of arrest. First step at which temporary release on bail may be available.

3. Before magistrate, commissioner, or justice of peace. Formal notice of charge, advice of rights. Bail set. Summary trials for petty offenses usually conducted here without further processing.

4. Preliminary testing of evidence against defendant. Charge may be reduced. No separate preliminary hearing for misdemeanors in some systems.

5. Charge filed by prosecutor on basis of information submitted by police or citizens. Alternative to grand jury indictment. Often used in felonies, almost always in misdemeanors.

6. Reviews whether government evidence sufficient to justify trial. Some states have no grand jury system; others seldom use it.

7. Appearance for plea. Defendant elects trial by judge or jury (if available). Counsel for indigent usually appointed here in felonies, often not at all in other cases.

8. Charge may be reduced at any time prior to trial in return for plea of guilty or for other reasons.

9. Challenge on constitutional grounds to legality of detention. May be sought at any point in process.

10. Police often hold informal hearings or dismiss or adjust many cases without further processing.

11. Probation officer decides desirability of further court action.

12. Welfare agency, social services, counseling, medical care, etc., for cases where adjudicatory handling not needed.

officer must have witnessed the crime personally; this is known as the **in-presence requirement.** A felony arrest can be made on the basis of the statement of a witness or victim.

4. *Custody.* The moment after an arrest is made, the detained suspects are considered to be in police custody. At this juncture, the police may wish to search the suspects for weapons or contraband, interrogate them in order to gain more information, find out if they had any accomplices, or even encourage them to confess to the crime. The police may wish to search a suspect's home, car, or office for further evidence. Similarly, the police may want to bring witnesses to identify the suspect in a **lineup** or in a one-to-one confrontation. During custody the police will obtain personal information from the suspect, such as his or her name, address, fingerprints, and photograph. Because these procedures are so crucial and can have a great bearing on a later trial, the U.S. Supreme Court has granted suspects in police custody protection from the unconstitutional abuse of police power, such as illegal searches and intimidating interrogations.

5. *Charging.* If sufficient evidence exists to charge a person in police custody with a crime, the case will be turned over to the prosecutor's office for additional processing. If the case involves a misdemeanor, the prosecutor will file a document, generally called a "complaint," before the court that will try the case. If the case involves a felony, the prosecutor must decide whether to bring the case forward to either a grand jury or a preliminary hearing, depending on the procedures used in the jurisdiction and the nature of the crime (see below). In either event, the decision to charge the suspect with a specific criminal act involves many factors including the sufficiency of the evidence, the seriousness of the crime, the prosecutor's caseload, and political issues.

6. *Preliminary hearing/grand jury.* Since there are great financial and personal costs when a person is forced to stand trial for a felony, the U.S. Constitution mandates that the government must first prove that there is probable cause that the accused committed the crime he or she is charged with and that a trial is warranted under the circumstances. In about 15 states and the federal system, this decision is rendered by a grand jury composed of a group of citizens. The grand jury considers the case in a closed hearing where only the prosecutor presents evidence. If the evidence is sufficient, the grand jury will issue a **bill of indictment,** which specifies that the accused must stand trial for a particular crime. The remaining states have replaced the grand jury with a preliminary hearing. In these jurisdictions, a charging document called an **information** is filed before a lower trial court, which then conducts an open hearing on the merits of the case. This procedure is sometimes called a probable cause hearing. The defendant and the defense counsel may appear at this hearing and dispute the prosecutor's charges. If the prosecutor's evidence is accepted as factual and sufficient, the suspect will be called to stand trial for the crime.

7. *Arraignment.* Before the trial begins, the defendant will be arraigned or brought before the court that will hear the case. At the **arraignment** the formal charges will be read; the defendant will be informed of his or her constitutional rights (for example, the right to be represented by legal counsel); an initial plea (not guilty or guilty) will be entered in the case; a trial date will be set, and bail issues will be considered.

8. *Bail/detention.* Bail is a money bond, the amount of which is set by judicial authority. The purpose of bail is to allow criminal defendants pretrial freedom

to prepare their defense while ensuring that they will return for trial. Defendants who do not show up for trial forfeit their bail. Persons who cannot afford to post bail or who cannot borrow sufficient funds remain in state custody prior to trial. In most instances this means an extended stay in a county jail or house of correction. Most jurisdictions have developed programs that allow defendants awaiting trial to be released on their own recognizance (promise to the court), without bail, if they are stable members of the community and have committed nonviolent crimes.

9. *Plea bargaining.* Soon after an arraignment, if not before, defense counsel will meet with the prosecution to see if the case can be concluded without the necessity of a trial. In some instances, this can involve filing the case while the defendant participates in a community-based treatment program (this might entail entering a detoxification unit or receiving psychiatric care at the local medical center). Most commonly, the defense and prosecution will discuss a possible guilty plea in exchange for reducing or dropping some of the charges or agreeing to a request for a more lenient sentence. Almost 90 percent of all cases brought before the criminal justice system end in a plea bargain rather than a criminal trial.

10. *Adjudication.* If an agreement cannot be reached or if the prosecution does not wish to arrange a negotiated settlement of the case, a full-scale inquiry into the facts of the case will commence. The criminal trial is held before a judge or jury who will decide whether the evidence against the defendant is *sufficient beyond a reasonable doubt*. The defendant may be found guilty or not guilty as charged. Sometimes in a jury trial, a decision cannot be reached (a deadlocked or "hung jury"), leaving the case unresolved and open for a possible retrial.

11. *Disposition.* An accused who has been found guilty as charged at a criminal trial will be returned to court for sentencing. Possible dispositions include a fine, probation, a period of incarceration in a penal institution, or some combination of these. In cases involving first degree murder, approximately 38

A criminal trial is a full scale formal hearing into the facts of a case in order to determine whether the evidence against the defendant is sufficient beyond a reasonable doubt. This photo was taken during the trial of Klaus von Bulow who was charged with the poisoning of his socialite wife.

Chapter 1

The Concept of Criminal Justice

New correctional models are constantly being tried. The Alternative Incarceration Unit at the Burgess Training Center in Forsyth, Georgia uses a high intensity short term "boot camp" approach with young offenders.

states and the federal government make it possible to sentence the offender to death.

Dispositions are usually made after the probation department conducts a presentence investigation in which the defendant is evaluated. The investigators try to determine whether a period of community supervision or secure confinement is more likely to lead to the defendant's successful rehabilitation. Sentencing is a key decision point in the justice system because in many jurisdictions judicial discretion can result in people receiving vastly different sentences even though they have committed the same crime.

12. *Postconviction remedies.* Convicted criminal defendants who believe they were not treated fairly by the justice system may **appeal** the conviction before an appellate court. An appeals court reviews the procedures used during the processing of the case. It considers such questions as the following: Was the evidence presented properly? Did the judge conduct the trial in an approved fashion? Was the jury selected in a representative manner? Did the attorneys in the case act appropriately? If the court rules that the appeal has merit, it can hold that the defendant be given a new trial or, in some instances, be released outright. Outright release can be ordered when the state prosecuted the case in violation of the double jeopardy clause of the U.S. Constitution or when it violated the defendant's right to a speedy trial.

13. *Correctional treatment.* After sentencing, the defendants may be placed under the jurisdiction of state or federal correctional authorities. They may serve a probationary term, be placed on a community correctional facility, serve a term in a county jail, or be housed in a prison. During this stage of the criminal justice process, offenders may be asked to participate in rehabilitation programs designed to help them make a successful readjustment to society.

14. *Release.* Upon completion of the sentence, the convicted offender will be free to return to society. Release may be earned by serving the maximum sentence imposed by the court or through an early release mechanism such as parole or pardon. Most inmates do not serve the full term to which they were sentenced for their crimes. Offenders sentenced to community supervision simply finish their term and resume their lives in the community.

15. *Postrelease.* After the termination of the correctional treatment, the convicted offenders will have to make a successful return to the community. Their adjustment is usually aided by members of the corrections department who attempt to counsel them through their period of reentry into society. They may be asked to spend some time in a community correctional center, which acts as a bridge between a secure treatment facility and absolute freedom. They may find that their conviction has cost them some personal privileges such as the right to hold certain kinds of employment. These may be returned by court order once the offenders have proven they are trustworthy and willing to adjust to society's rules.

Criminal Justice Assembly Line

The image that comes to mind is an assembly line conveyor belt down which moves an endless stream of cases, never stopping, carrying them to workers who stand at fixed stations and who perform on each case as it comes by the same small but essential operation that brings it one step closer to being a finished product, or to exchange the metaphor for the reality, a closed file. The criminal process is seen as a screening process in which each successive stage—pre-arrest investigation, arrest, post-arrest investigation, preparation for trial, trial or entry of plea, conviction, disposition—involves a series of routinized operations whose success is gauged primarily by their tendency to pass the case along to a successful conclusion.[27]

Thus Herbert Packer describes the criminal justice process. According to this view, each of the 15 stages described above is actually a decision point through which cases flow. For example, at the investigator stage, police must decide whether to pursue the case or terminate involvement because the evidence is insufficient to identify a suspect, the case is considered trivial, the victim decides not to press charges, and so on. At the bail stage, a decision must be made whether to set bail so high that the defendant remains in custody, set a reasonable bail, or release the defendant on his or her own recognizance without requiring any monetary bail at all. Each of these decisions can have a critical effect on the defendant, the justice system, and society. If an error is made, an innocent person may suffer, or a dangerous individual may be released to continue to prey upon society.

Figure 1.3 illustrates the approximate number of offenders removed from the criminal justice system at each stage of the process. As the figure shows, relatively few suspects who suffer arrest are bound over for trial, convicted, and sentenced to prison. Some are released before trial because of a procedural error, evidence problems, or other reasons that result in a ***nolle prosequi,*** the decision of a prosecutor to drop the case. Though most cases that go to trial wind up in a conviction, others are dismissed by the presiding judge because a witness fails to appear or because of procedural irregularities. Thus the justice process can be viewed as a funnel, which holds many cases at its "mouth" and relatively few at its end.

Theoretically, individual cases should be disposed of as quickly as possible at nearly every stage of the process. The criminal justice process is slower and more tedious than could be desired, however, because of congestion, inadequate facilities, limited resources, inefficiency, and the nature of governmental bureaucracy. When defendants are not processed smoothly, often because of the large caseloads and inadequate facilities that exist in many urban jurisdictions, the procedure breaks down, the process within the system fails, and the ultimate goal of a fair and efficient justice system cannot be achieved.

■ The Informal Justice System

The traditional model of the criminal justice system outlined above depicts the legal process as a series of decision points through which cases flow. Each stage of the system, beginning with investigation and arrest and ending after a sentence has been served, is defined by time-honored administrative procedures and controlled by the rule of law. The public's perception of the system, fueled by the media, is that it is manned by daredevil, crime-fighting police officers (who never ask for overtime or sick leave), crusading district attorneys (who stop at nothing to send Mr. Big "up the river"), wily defense attorneys (who never seem to ask their clients for cash upfront), no-nonsense judges (who maintain strict decorum in the courtroom), and tough wardens (who rule the "yard" with an iron hand). This "ideal" model of justice still merits concern and attention, but it would be overly simplistic to assume that the system works this way for every case. Although a few cases do receive a full measure of rights and procedures, many are settled informally between the major actors in the justice process. For example, police may be willing to make a "deal" with suspects in order to gain their cooperation; the prosecutor "bargains" with the

Chapter 1

The Concept of
Criminal Justice

■

23

FIGURE 1.3 The Criminal Justice Funnel

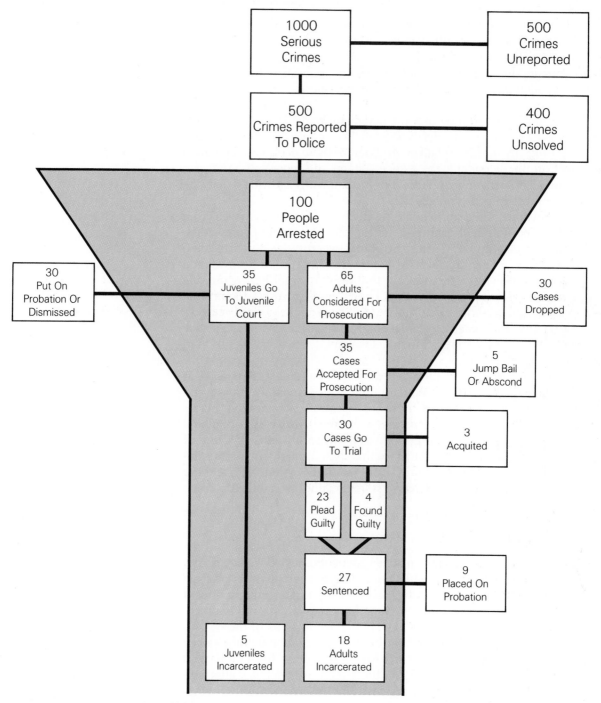

SOURCE: Edward Lisefski and Donald Manson, *Tracking Offenders, 1984* (Washington, D.C.: Bureau of Justice Statistics, 1988); Patrick Langan, *Felony Sentences in State Courts, 1986* (Washington, D.C.: Bureau of Justice Statistics, 1989).

defense attorney to gain a plea of guilty as charged in return for a promise of leniency. Law enforcement agents and court officers are allowed tremendous discretion in their decision to make an arrest, bring formal charges, handle a case informally, substitute charges, and so on. Crowded courts operate in a spirit of settling the matter quickly and cleanly rather than engaging in long drawn-out criminal proceedings with an uncertain outcome.

Although the traditional model regards the justice process as an adversary proceeding in which the prosecution and defense are combatants, the majority of criminal cases are actually cooperative ventures in which all parties get together to work out a deal; this is often referred to as the **courtroom work group**.[28] This group, made up of the prosecutor, defense attorney, judge, and other court personnel, functions to streamline the process of justice through the extensive use of plea bargaining and other alternatives. Rather than looking to provide a spirited defense or prosecution, these legal agents, who attended the same schools and have known each other and worked together for many years, try to resolve a case to their own advantage through an informal legal process that sometimes disregards the interests of the defendant and the public. In most criminal cases, cooperation between prosecution and defense rather than conflict appears to be the norm. Only in a few widely publicized "heavy" criminal cases involving rape or murder is the adversarial process called into play. Consequently, upward of 80 percent of all felony cases and over 90 percent of misdemeanors are settled without trial.

What has developed is a system in which the criminal courts can be viewed as a training ground for young defense attorneys looking for seasoning and practice, a means for newly established lawyers to receive government compensation for cases taken to get their practice going, or an arena in which established firms can place their new associates for experience before they are assigned to paying clients. Similarly, successful prosecutors can look forward to a political career or a high-paid partnership in a private firm. To further their career aspirations, prosecutors must develop and maintain a winning "track record" in criminal cases. No district attorney wants to become a "Hamilton Burger," the fictional prosecutor who loses every case to legendary defense attorney Perry Mason.

Although the courtroom work group limits the constitutional rights of defendants, it may be essential to keeping our overburdened justice system afloat. Moreover, it is not absolutely certain that informal justice is inherently unfair to both victim and offender. Research shows that the defendants who commit the least serious crimes benefit the most from informal court procedures while the more chronic offenders gain relatively little.[29]

The "Wedding Cake" Model of Justice

Samuel Walker, a justice historian and scholar of some renown, has devised a rather dramatic way of describing this informal justice process: he compares it to the four-layer cake depicted in Figure 1.4.[30]

The top layer of Walker's model is made up of celebrated cases involving wealthy and powerful defendants, such as Ivan Boesky, Patty Hearst, Claus von Bulow, and John De Lorean, or the not so powerful who victimize a famous person, such as John Hinckley who shot President Ronald Reagan or Sirhan Sirhan who assassinated Robert Kennedy. Other cases fall into the first layer because they became media events, such as the case of Robert Chambers who

The top layer of the criminal justice "wedding cake" is made up of celebrated cases which receive media attention. Here, Hedda Nussbaum gives testimony in the widely publicized case in which attorney Joel Steinberg was convicted of killing his adopted daughter Lisa.

■ *FIGURE 1.4*

The Criminal Justice "Wedding Cake"

SOURCE: Based on Samuel Walker, *Sense and Nonsense about Crime* (Monterey, Calif.: Brooks/Cole, 1985).

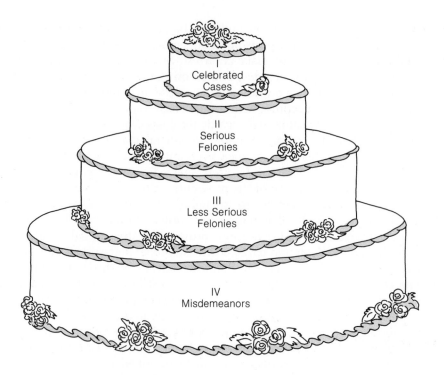

strangled his teenage lover Jennifer Levin in what became known as the "preppie" murder case or attorney Joel Steinberg, a cocaine addict and wife batterer, who was convicted of killing his illegally adopted daughter. Also included within this category are cases involving unknown criminals that become celebrated either because they become the subject of major Supreme Court decisions on procedural irregularities, such as the cases of Ernesto Miranda and Clarence Gideon, or because they involve some hideous event such as the murder of 45 boys in Chicago by Wayne Gacy.

People in the first layer of the criminal justice wedding cake attract a great deal of public attention, and their cases usually receive the full panoply of criminal justice procedures including famous defense attorneys, jury trials, and elaborate appeals. There are also allegations that prosecutors are more than willing to try such cases because they attract the media attention needed to launch political careers. When Bess Myerson, a former Miss America and New York City's cultural affairs commissioner, was acquitted of fraud, bribery, and obstruction of justice on 23 December 1988, her attorney Michael Feldberg claimed that the charges were fueled by her fame:

> There's a mentality that a lot of prosecutors have of, if the target is prominent, it helps you in deciding you want to bring a case.[31]

Because the public hears so much about these cases, they are regarded as the norm, but in reality such cases are not representative of the system as a whole.

The second and third layers of the cake are made up of serious felonies, such as robberies, burglaries, rapes, and homicides, that occur daily in urban jurisdictions throughout the United States. Those that fall into the second layer do so by virtue of their seriousness, the prior record of the defendant, and the defendant's relationship to the victim. For example, a million dollar burglary is treated quite differently from a simple break-in that netted the burglar a stereo. Similarly, criminal justice decision makers perceive a rape involving a stranger as being quite different from one in which the victim had known the offender previously. Crimes that result from personal disagreements or are committed by first-time offenders are relegated to the third layer of the system. These may be dealt with by an outright dismissal, a plea bargain, reduction in charges, or a probationary sentence.

The fourth layer of the cake is made up of millions of misdemeanors such as disorderly conduct, shoplifting, public drunkenness, and minor assault. These are handled by the lower criminal courts in assembly line fashion. Few defendants insist on exercising their constitutional rights because this would delay matters and cost them valuable time and money. Since the typical penalty is a small fine, everyone wants to get the case over with and move on to other matters. Malcolm Feeley's study of the lower court in New Haven, Connecticut, shows that in a sense the experience of going to court is the real punishment in a misdemeanor case. Few (4.9 percent) of the cases involved any jail time.[32]

The informal justice system model depicts the justice system in political terms. Cases that are "important" because they involve people or events with media interest go to the top of the pile. In contrast, cases in which the poor victimize one another get little formal attention from the justice system. The typical criminal case is handled as if it were a civil complaint or law suit: a settlement agreeable to all parties involved—defendant, victim, attorney, police, and prosecutor—seems the best course of action.

The informal, "wedding cake" model of justice is an intriguing alternative to the traditional criminal justice flowchart. Criminal justice officials do handle individual cases quite differently. Yet particular types or classes of cases are dealt with in a highly consistent manner in every legal jurisdiction. That is, police and prosecutors in Los Angeles, Boston, New York, and San Antonio will all handle the murder of a prominent citizen in a similar fashion. They will also deal with the death of an unemployed street person killed in a brawl in a similar manner. Yet, in each jurisdiction, the two cases will be handled very differently from one another. The celebrity killer will receive a full-blown jury trial (with details on the 6 o'clock news); the drifter's killer will receive a quick plea bargain.

■ Criminal Justice as a Career

The criminal justice system offers numerous career opportunities. The preceding sections have already identified some of the different roles and career lines that fit into the justice process. Some who choose to go into the field are motivated by the desire to help people and are attracted to social service work. Others are more interested in law enforcement and policing. Others choose teaching and research, while other want to supplement their criminal justice education with legal studies in order to become defense attorneys, prosecutors, or magistrates. Of course, some enterprising people are able to fill a number of these different roles during their criminal justice career: a police officer earns a Ph.D. and embarks on a teaching career; a probation officer goes to law school and becomes a prosecutor; a professor is appointed head of a state corrections department, and so on. Let us now examine some of the specialties within the field of criminal justice to demonstrate what some of the career alternatives actually are.

Law Enforcement

Over half a million people are employed in policing and law enforcement in the United States. The following sections describe just a few of the career opportunities that involve the enforcement of the criminal law.

MUNICIPAL POLICE OFFICER. The majority of people who go into law enforcement work for city police departments. Of course, the work of the patrol officer, traffic cop, and detective is familiar to anyone who watches television or goes to movies (though the accuracy of those entertainment vehicles is highly suspect). Beyond these familiar roles, however, police work also involves a great many administrative and service jobs such as training officers, communications experts, records and purchasing, and so on. A student interested in a police career but not necessarily excited by the idea of roaming the streets chasing bad guys will find that police work has many other opportunities to offer.

STATE AND COUNTY LAW ENFORCEMENT. In addition to city police agencies, state and county governments also provide career opportunities in law enforcement. The state police and county sheriff's department do much the same work as city police agencies—traffic, patrol, and investigation—depending on their area of jurisdiction. Ordinarily, these agencies take on a greater law enforcement role in more rural areas and provide for ancillary services such as running the local jail or controlling traffic in urban centers.

FEDERAL LAW ENFORCEMENT. The federal government also employs thousands of law enforcement personnel in such agencies as the Federal Bureau of Investigation, Drug Enforcement Agency, Secret Service, and so on. These agencies are often considered the elite of the law enforcement profession, and standards for entry are quite high. The duties of federal agencies include upholding federal laws such as those controlling counterfeiting, terrorism, espionage, bank robberies, and the importation and distribution of controlled substances.

PRIVATE SECURITY. In addition to public police agency work, the field of private security offers many career opportunities. Some positions are in large security companies such as Pinkertons or Wackenhut. Others are in company security forces such as those maintained by large retail chains, manufacturing companies, railroads, and so on. Public institutions such as hospitals, airports, and port facilities also maintain security teams.

Social Service Work

A significant number of people who work in the field of criminal justice become involved in its social service side. Social service offers many opportunities to provide direct service to people before they actually become involved with the law or after their case comes to the attention of criminal justice agencies.

PROBATION OFFICER. Probation officers supervise offenders who have been placed under community supervision by the criminal court. Their duties include counseling clients to help them adjust to society. This may include family counseling, individual counseling, and group sessions. Probation officers are trained to use the resources of the community to help their clients. Their work involves them with the personal, family, and work problems of their clients.

CORRECTIONAL COUNSELOR. Although some may believe that correctional work is simply a matter of guarding incarcerated inmates, that narrow view is far from accurate. Correctional treatment staff engage in such tasks as vocational and educational training, counseling, recreational work, and so on. Almost every correctional institution has a social service staff that helps inmates adjust to the institution and prepare for successful reentry into the outside world.

COMMUNITY CORRECTIONAL COUNSELOR. There are thousands of community-based correctional facilities in operation around the country. These house nonviolent criminals serving out their prison sentences and inmates from high security institutions who have been transferred near the completion of their prison terms; there are also separate facilities for juvenile offenders. These facilities provide ample opportunity for direct service work since the overwhelming majority of programs emphasize the value of rehabilitation and treatment. Some of the most innovative treatment techniques used in the criminal justice system are provided in the community-based corrections setting.

PAROLE AND AFTER CARE. Parole and after-care workers supervise offenders upon their release from correctional treatment. This involves helping them find jobs, helping them achieve their educational objectives, assisting them in sorting out family problems, and so on. Parole officers employ various counseling techniques to help clients clarify their goals and find ways of surmounting obstacles so that they can make a successful readjustment to the community.

Law and the Courts

The criminal justice system provides many opportunities for people interested in working in the law, the legal system, and the courts. Of course, in most instances these careers require postgraduate education such as a law degree or a course in court management.

PROSECUTOR. Prosecutors represent the state in criminal matters. They bring charges against offenders, engage in plea bargaining, conduct trials, and help determine sentences. Prosecutors work at the local county, state, and federal levels of government. For example, an assistant U.S. attorney general would prosecute violations of federal law in one of the 91 U.S. District Courts.

DEFENSE COUNSEL. All criminal defendants are entitled to legal counsel. Therefore agencies such as the public defenders have been created to provide free legal services to indigent offenders. In addition, private attorneys often take on criminal cases without compensation as a gesture of community service or are assigned cases by the court for modest compensation (referred to as a **pro bono** case). Defense attorneys help clients gather evidence to support their innocence; represent them at pretrial proceedings, at trial, and at sentencing hearings; and serve as their advocate if an appeal is filed upon conviction.

JUDGE. Judges carry out many different functions during the trial stage of justice. They help in jury selection, oversee the admission of evidence, and control the flow of the trial. Their most important duty is to ensure that the trial is conducted within the boundaries of legal fairness. Although many criminal defense attorneys and prosecutors aspire to become judges, few are actually chosen for this honor.

COURT MANAGER. Most court jurisdictions maintain an office of court administration. Court administrators help in case management and ensure that the court's resources are used in the most efficient manner. Court administrators are usually required to obtain advanced education at programs specializing in court management, such as those at the University of Southern California and at American University in Washington, D.C.

Research, Administration, and Teaching

In addition to careers within the agencies of justice themselves, criminal justice also offers opportunities in teaching, research, and administration.

PRIVATE SECTOR RESEARCH. A number of private sector institutes and research firms, such as the Rand Corporation (Santa Monica, California), Abt Associates (Cambridge, Massachusetts), and the Battelle Institute (Seattle, Washington), employ scientists who conduct research on criminal justice topics. In addition, a number of private nonprofit organizations are devoted to the study of criminal justice issues; these organizations include the Police Executive Research Forum (PERF), the Police Foundation, and the International Association of Chiefs of Police (IACP), all located near Washington, D.C.; the National Council on Crime and Delinquency (NCCD) with offices in San Francisco, California; and the Vera Foundation in New York City. All of these organizations employ staff members who conduct criminal justice research and prepare policy studies.

In addition to these independent organizations, many universities maintain research centers that have maintained ongoing efforts in criminal justice often with funding from the government and private foundations. For example, the Institute for Social Research at the University of Michigan (ISR) has conducted an annual survey of teenage substance abuse; the Hindelang Research Center at SUNY-Albany produces the *Sourcebook of Criminal Justice Statistics*, an invaluable research tool; the National Neighborhood Foot Patrol Center at Michigan State University conducts research on community policing; and the Criminal Justice Research Center at the University of Lowell is involved in measuring the effectiveness of probation supervision.

Most people who work for these research centers hold advanced degrees in criminal justice or other applied social sciences. Some of the projects carried out by these centers, such as the study of career criminals conducted by Rand Corporation scientists and the Police Foundation's study of the deterrent effect of police patrol, have had a profound effect on policy making within the justice system.

PUBLIC SECTOR RESEARCH. Most large local, state, and federal government agencies contain research arms that evaluate ongoing criminal justice programs and plan for the development of innovative efforts designed to create positive change in the system. For example, state corrections departments have planning and research units that monitor the flow of inmates to and from the prison system and help evaluate the effectiveness of prison programs such as work furloughs. On a local level, larger police departments often employ civilian research coordinators who analyze police data in order to improve the effectiveness and efficiency of police services.

The most significant contribution to criminal justice research made by the public sector probably comes from the federal government's Bureau of Justice Statistics (BJS) and National Institute of Justice (NIJ), which are the research and data collection arms of the U.S. Justice Department. In recent years, these agencies have supported some of the most impressive and important of all research on criminal justice issues such as sentencing, plea bargaining, and victimization.

SYSTEM ADMINISTRATION. Many states and the Federal government also maintain central criminal justice planning offices that are responsible for setting and implementing criminal justice policy or distributing funds for its implementation. For example, the National Institute of Justice (NIJ) sets priorities for criminal justice research and policy on an annual basis and then distributes funds to local and state applicants who are willing to establish and evaluate demonstration projects. Recently the NIJ targeted the following areas: apprehension, prosecution and adjudication of criminal offenders; public safety and security; punishment and control of offenders; victims of crimes; white-collar and organized crime; criminal careers; drugs and alcohol and crime; forensic science; offender classification; and violent criminal behavior.[33]

A number of states also maintain statewide criminal justice administration agencies that set policy agendas and coordinate state efforts to improve the quality of the system.

COLLEGE TEACHING. More than 600 programs offer criminal justice education in the United States. These include specialized criminal justice programs, programs where criminal justice is combined with another department such as sociology or political science, and programs that offer a concentration in criminal justice as part of another major.

Criminal justice educators have a career track similar to most other teaching specialties. Whether they teach at the associate, baccalaureate, or graduate level, their course load will reflect the core subject matter of criminal justice, including courses on policing, the courts, and the correctional system.

■ Financial Rewards in Criminal Justice

Many people believe that a criminal justice career is limited financially because it involves working for local, state, or federal governments. However, a great many careers within the criminal justice system offer substantial salaries and financial benefits. Table 1.1 lists the typical salaries paid to criminal justice

TABLE 1.1 ■ Financial Rewards in Criminal Justice

Position	Average annual salary*
Law enforcement officers (1985 and 1986)	
City police officer (entry level)	$18,913
City police officer (maximum)	24,243
City police chief	33,158
County sheriff patrol officer	Not available
State trooper (entry level)	18,170
State trooper (maximum)	28,033
Deputy U.S. marshal	19,585
U.S. border patrol agent	23,058
U.S. immigration inspector	24,719
U.S. immigration agent	34,259
Federal drug agent	36,973
FBI agent	40,321
Prosecutors (1986)	
State and local prosecution personnel	Not available
Federal prosecutor	$53,027
Defenders (1986)	
State and local defense personnel	Not available
Federal defender	$43,582
Court personnel (1986 and 1987)	
State court administrator	$59,257
State general jurisdiction trial court judge	60,697
State intermediate appellate court justice	67,172
State associate supreme court justice	67,434
State supreme court justice	70,161
U.S. Magistrate	72,500
U.S. Bankruptcy Court Judge	72,500
U.S. Court of Claims Judge	82,500
U.S. Court of International Trade Judge	89,500
U.S. District (trial) Court Judge	89,500
U.S. Circuit (appellate) Court Judge	95,000
U.S. Supreme Court Associate Justice	110,000
U.S. Supreme Court Chief Justice	115,000
Correctional officers (adult facilities, 1986)	
Local jail officer (entry level)	$16,939
State correctional officer (entry level)	14,985
State correctional officer (maximum)	16,427
State director of corrections	59,947
Federal correctional officer	22,857
Probation and parole officers (adult clientele, 1986 and 1987)	
Local probation officer	Not available
State probation officer (entry level)	$19,402
State parole officer (entry level)	19,986
State chief probation officer	28,600
State chief parole officer	31,233
State parole board member	43,429
State parole board chairman	46,100
Federal probation officer (entry level)	22,458
Federal parole case analyst	22,458– 42,341
Federal parole hearing examiner	38,727–59,488
Federal regional probation/parole administrator	53,830–69,976
U.S. Parole Commissioner	72,500

*There are jurisdictions where the salaries are higher or lower than these averages.

SOURCE: Bureau of Justice Statistics, 2d ed. (Washington, D.C.: Bureau of Justice Statistics, 1988), *Report to the Nation on Crime and Justice*, p. 126.

personnel. As you can see, a number of positions such as federal law enforcement agent, federal prosecutor, federal judges, and state and federal court personnel receive fairly substantial salaries. It is important to note that these salary data were collected in 1986 and 1987 and should be adjusted upward from 10 to 20 percent, figuring a modest 4 percent annual increase in salary. Similarly, the data do not include salary adjustments such as overtime, education benefits, and promotions. For example, police officers in Boston receive a starting salary of almost $40,000. Overtime and special detail pay can add to this sum. In 1988, 75 uniformed Boston police officers earned more than $80,000, and 7 topped $100,000 (the highest being a patrolman who earned $118,472.[34] Although people should consider a career in criminal justice for reasons other than financial rewards, an individual can do quite well while working within the justice system.

■ SUMMARY

The term *criminal justice* first became prominent around 1967 when the President's Commission on Law Enforcement and Administration of Justice began a study of the crime problem in the United States. Since then, criminal justice has emerged as a field of study that uses knowledge from various disciplines in an attempt to learn why people commit crimes and how to deal with the crime problem. Thus criminal justice consists of the study of crime and of the agencies concerned with its prevention and control.

Criminal justice is both a system and a process. As a system, it ideally functions as a cooperative effort among the primary agencies—police, courts, and corrections. In contrast, the process consists of the actual steps the offender takes from the initial investigation through trial, sentencing, and appeal.

In many instances the criminal justice system works informally to expedite the disposal of cases. Criminal acts that are very serious or notorious may receive the full complement of criminal justice processes, from arrest to trial. Less serious cases, however, are often settled when the prosecution and the defense reach a bargain.

Many careers are open to people interested in working within the criminal justice system. Among the options are police work, social service, research, administration, and teaching.

■ QUESTIONS

1. Discuss the interrelationship of the executive, legislative, and judicial branches of government in the decision to institute and implement capital punishment.
2. What role can the fields of sociology, biology, and psychology play in the field of criminal justice?
3. What is meant by the "wedding cake" model of justice? Discuss its various "layers."
4. To what does the term "criminal justice assembly line" refer?
5. Discuss the various career opportunities in the criminal justice system. Which has the most appeal to you? Which has the least appeal?

■ NOTES

1. Cesare Beccaria, *On Crimes and Punishments* (1764, reprint ed.; Indianapolis: Bobbs-Merrill Co., 1963).
2. Samuel Walker, *Popular Justice* (New York: Oxford University Press, 1980).
3. Ibid.
4. Ibid.
5. President's Commission on Law Enforcement and the Administration of Justice, *The Challenge of Crime in a Free Society* (Washington, D.C.: U.S. Government Printing Office, 1967).
6. See Public Law 90–351, Title I—Omnibus Crime Control Safe Streets Act of 1968, 90th Congress, June 19, 1968.
7. American Bar Association, *Project on Standards for Criminal Justice* (New York: Institute of Judicial Administration, 1968–1973); National Advisory Commission on Criminal Justice Standards and Goals, *A National Strategy to Reduce Crime* (Washington, D.C.: U.S. Government Printing Office, 1973).

8. Frank Zarb, "Police Liability for Creating the Need to Use Deadly Force in Self-Defense," *Michigan Law Review* 86 (1988): 1982–2009.

9. See, for example, Stephen Schoenthaler and Walter Doraz, "Types of Offenses Which Can Be Reduced in an Institutional Setting Using Nutritional Intervention," *International Journal of Biosocial Research* 4 (1983): 74–84.

10. James Q. Wilson, *Thinking about Crime* (New York: Basic Books, 1975); Ernest Van Den Haag, *Punishing Criminals: Concerning a Very Old and Painful Question* (New York: Basic Books, 1975); Samuel Walker, *Sense and Nonsense about Crime* (Monterey, Calif.: Brooks Cole, 1985); Francis Cullen and Karen Gilbert, *Reaffirming Rehabilitation* (Cincinnati, Ohio: Anderson, 1982).

11. James Fyfe, *Shots Fired: An Examination of New York City Police Firearm Discharges* (Ann Arbor, Mich.: University Microfilms, 1978). For similar research, see Peter Scharf and Arnold Binder, *The Badge and the Bullet: Police Use of Deadly Force* (New York: Praeger, 1983).

12. *Marbury v. Madison*, 1 Cranch 137 (1803).

13. Sue Lindren, *Justice Expenditures and Employment, 1985* (Washington, D.C.: Bureau of Justice Statistics, 1987).

14. Federal Bureau of Investigation, *Crime in the United States, 1987* (Washington, D.C.: U.S. Government Printing Office, 1988).

15. Ibid., 240.

16. Bureau of Justice Statistics, *Report to the Nation on Crime and Justice* 2d ed. (Washington, D.C.: Bureau of Justice Statistics, 1988), p. 102.

17. Daniel Skoler, "Antidote for the Non-System: State Criminal Justice Superagencies," *State Government* 46 (Winter, 1976): 1–23.

18. From an address by former Chief Justice Warren Burger, U.S. Supreme Court, as reported in *Criminal Law Reporter* (1972): 305.

19. President's Commission on Law Enforcement and the Administration of Justice, *Challenge of Crime*, p. 125.

20. *Powell v. Alabama* 287 U.S. 45, 53 S.Ct. 55, 77 L.Ed. 158 (1932); *Gideon v. Wainwright*, 372 U.S. 335, 83 S.Ct. 792, 9 L.Ed.2d 799 (1963);

Argersinger v. Hamlin, 407 U.S. 25, 92 S.Ct. 2006, 32 L.Ed.2d 530 (1972).

21. See Bureau of Justice Statistics, *Report to the Nation*, pp. 108–9.

22. See generally Gray Cavender, *Parole: A Critical Analysis* (Port Washington, N.Y.: Kennikat Press, 1982).

23. Skoler, "Antidote for the Non- System," p. 2.

24. Ibid.

25. U.S. Department of Justice, LEAA, National Institute of Law Enforcement, *Recent Criminal Justice Unification, Consolidation, and Coordination Efforts: An Exploratory National Survey* (Washington, D.C.: U.S. Government Printing Office, 1976).

26. National Commission on Criminal Justice Standards and Goals, *Report on Courts*, standard 8.1 (Washington, D.C.: U.S. Government Printing Office, 1976), p. 164.

27. Herbert L. Packer, *The Limits of the Criminal Sanction* (Stanford, Calif.: Stanford University Press, 1975), p. 21.

28. James Eisenstein and Herbert Jacob, *Felony Justice* (Boston: Little, Brown, 1977); Peter Nardulli, *The Courtroom Elite* (Cambridge, Mass.: Ballinger, 1978); Paul Wice, *Chaos in the Courthouse* (New York: Praeger, 1985); Marcia Lipetz, *Routine Justice: Processing Cases in Women's Court* (New Brunswick, N.J.: Transaction Books, 1983).

29. Douglas Smith, "The Plea Bargaining Controversy," *The Journal of Criminal Law and Criminology* 77 (1986): 949–67.

30. Walker, *Sense and Nonsense about Crime.*

31. Judie Glave, "Case against Myerson was weak, jurors say," *Boston Globe*, 24 December 1988, p. 3.

32. Malcolm Feeley, *The Process Is the Punishment* (New York: Russell Sage Foundation, 1979).

33. National Institute of Justice, *Research Program Plan Fiscal Year 1989* (Washington, D.C.: National Institute of Justice, 1988).

34. Brian Mooney, "Salaries of 7 Boston officers topped $100,000," *Boston Globe*, 2 February 1989, p. 21

Chapter 1

**The Concept of
Criminal Justice**

2

The Nature of Crime and Victimization

Part One

The Nature of Crime,
Law and Criminal Justice

Crime is a familiar and disturbing aspect of life in the United States. Surveys indicate that many people fear crime and believe that the criminal justice system can do little to reduce its incidence; most Americans respond positively when asked if "the crime rate in my area has been increasing."[1] This should not come as a surprise considering the daily barrage of newspaper stories, magazine articles, television series, and films that have crime as their principal topic or theme. The salience of crime in American life, its impact on lifestyles and behavior, and the widespread belief that something should be done to reduce the crime rate have probably all contributed to the popularity of programs in criminal justice on the nation's college campuses.

If the criminal justice system is to become an effective instrument to reduce or control criminal behavior, administrators and policymakers must have up-to-date, accurate information about the nature and extent of crime. The policies and procedures of the justice system cannot exist in an informational vacuum. Without accurate information about crime, we can never determine whether a particular policy, process, or procedure has the effect its creators envisioned. For example, a state may enact a new law establishing a mandatory prison sentence for anyone who uses a firearm to commit a crime. Such a law is aimed directly at reducing the incidence of violent crimes such as murder, armed robbery, and assault. The state cannot demonstrate that the law has met its objective unless it can show that the use of firearms actually declined after the law was instituted and, concomitantly, show that crimes involving knives or other alternative weapons did not increase. Without accurate measurements of crime, understanding its causes or planning its elimination would be impossible.

This chapter discusses some of the basic questions raised by the study of crime and justice: How is crime defined? How is crime measured? How much crime is there, and what are its trends and patterns? How many people become victims of crime, and under what circumstances does victimization take place?

■ The Concept of Crime

The study of criminal justice is bound up with the concept of crime. To most people, the term **crime** evokes such familiar images as a bank robbery, an auto theft, or an assault. Legal scholars, however, have long wrestled with the problem of defining crime so that it can be more easily studied. Currently, there are three distinct views on the subject.

One approach is the **consensus view** of crime. According to the consensus view, crimes are behaviors that (1) are essentially harmful to a majority of citizens living in society and (2) have been controlled or prohibited by the existing **criminal law**. The term "consensus view" means that most people agree that the behaviors prohibited by the criminal law are generally harmful to the well-being of society. The consensus position is that the criminal law is a set of rules that express the norms, goals, and values of a majority of society. Consequently, the criminal law, and the justice system that upholds it, has a **social control** function; it restrains those who would take advantage of others' weakness for their own personal gain, thereby endangering the social framework. Although differences in behavior can be tolerated within a properly functioning social system, behaviors that are considered inherently destructive and dangerous are outlawed to maintain the social fabric and ensure the peaceful functioning of society.

The second approach to crime is the **interactionist view.** Proponents of the interactionist view agree that the criminal law defines crime, but they challenge the belief that the law represents the will and opinion of a majority of citizens. Instead, the interactionist view holds that the criminal law is influenced by people who hold social power and use it to mold the law to reflect their way of thinking. For example, various groups have recently tried to influence laws regulating the possession of handguns, the use of drugs and alcohol, and the availability of abortions. According to Howard Becker, these **moral entrepreneurs** use their economic, social, and political influence to impose their definition of right and wrong on the rest of the population. Becker's classic statement on crime and deviance is probably the most important expression of the interactionist position:

> Social groups create deviance by making the rules whose infraction constitutes deviance, and by applying those rules to particular people and labeling them as outsiders. From this point of view, deviance is not a quality of the act the person commits, but rather a consequence of the application by others of rules and sanctions to an "offender."[2]

Those who hold a **conflict view** of crime maintain that the true purpose of the criminal law is to protect the power of the upper classes at the expense of the poor. The conflict approach depicts society as a collection of diverse groups—owners, workers, professionals, students, minority groups, and so on—who are in conflict with one another over a number of issues. Groups able to assert their political and economic power use the law and the criminal justice system to advance their own causes. Criminal laws, therefore, are viewed as acts created to protect the "haves" from the "have nots."[3]

Despite the obviously wide theoretical gulf separating these views of crime and criminality, they do share some common ground. All three link crime to the existing legal code; agree that the law is constantly changing and evolving; conclude that social forces mold the definition of crime; and view the criminal justice system as responsible for carrying out the criminal law's **social control** function. Since these concepts of crime overlap, it is possible to use elements from each view to create an integrated definition that incorporates aspects of all three positions:

> Crime is a violation of societal rules of behavior as interpreted and expressed by a criminal code created by people holding social and political power. Its content may be influenced by prevailing public sentiments, historically developed moral beliefs and the need to protect public safety. Individuals who violate these rules may be eligible for sanctions administered by state authority, which include social stigma, and loss of status, freedom, and even on occasions one's life.

Our working definition of crime links criminal behavior to law violation and also to the beliefs and actions of political power groups. Later this book discusses the nature, properties, and extent of the criminal law. For now, it will suffice to say that the criminal law is a legal code that represents (in part) the influence of a number of sources—including traditionally proscribed types of behavior (common law), public opinion, the will and power of the state and its representatives, and the influence of pressure groups or lobbies (e.g., pro- or anti-abortion lobbies), private enterprise, and the clergy—each of which attempts to control public behavior through control of the law. Most of the time, the criminal law is in accord with the attitudes of the majority of citizens. On other occasions, lifestyles and attitudes change so rapidly that the law seems out of step with the public's behavior. When a situation like this arises, change may be literally forced on the legal system. For example, the public's fear of drug use in the 1980s led states and the federal government to pass new laws that significantly increased penalties for the importation and sale of narcotics. It is easy to see why a definition of crime with the criminal law as its source is liable to have different meanings, interpretations, and impacts at different times and in different jurisdictions. The flexibility built into the nature of the law does seem to move the concept of crime away from configuration of immorality and deviance and into the realm of public opinion and political policy. The status quo, the inability to change legal definitions quickly, and the maintenance of personal power all work to control the substance of the legal code and thus to determine what constitutes crime and criminality. In this sense, crime is a constantly changing concept, and behavior that is considered a breach of public morality in one generation may be found acceptable and commonplace in another. But regardless of its scope and content, crime is the focal concern of the criminal justice system.

■ How Crime is Measured

Crime and its consequences are among the social problems most often discussed in the United States today. It is therefore ironic that no one is sure how much crime actually occurs, where and when it takes place, or how many criminals and victims exist nationwide. The public is likely to get information about these matters secondhand, from newspaper and television news, for example; these sources often dwell on the sensational and lurid and are therefore inadequate for the serious student of criminal justice. The day-in, day-out varieties of criminal behavior well known to police and court personnel are usually hidden from the public view. How then can one discover the truth about the extent of the crime problem? Some tentative answers to these questions may be found in the statistical data currently being compiled by state and federal agencies concerned with accurately measuring criminal activity. These sources of statistics are by no means perfect; in fact, they have become a popular target for criticism by law enforcement experts who have raised questions about their validity. Despite the astuteness of these critics, official crime statistics do provide a valuable tool with which to estimate the amount and type of current criminal behavior, the number of annual arrests, the number of incarcerated felons, and so on. Some of the major sources of crime data will be discussed in this section.

Survey Data

Survey data is comprised of information obtained from people on their behaviors, attitudes, beliefs, and abilities. For example, criminal justice experts survey teenagers in order to record the nature and frequency of their drug and alcohol use; a telephone survey can be used to determine how many people favor capital punishment.

Most survey data comes from **probability samples,** drawn from populations (all those individuals who share at least one similar trait—for example, rapists, schoolteachers, and so on).[4] In a probability sample, a limited number of subjects are randomly selected from the larger population; ideally, every individual in the population has an equal chance of being selected for the study. For example, the Nielsen survey, which evaluates American television-viewing habits, involves a relatively small group of people who are randomly drawn from the millions of television watchers in the United States. Probability sampling assumes that the characteristics of the small, select sample group mirror or are similar to those of the larger population from which the sample group is drawn; thus, the criminologist who utilize statistics gathered in probability sampling can develop generalizations from information collected from a few people and apply them to the behavior of millions.

Criminological surveys provide a valuable source of information on a number of topics. They are most valuable for gathering information on particular crime problems, such as drug use, which are rarely reported to police and may therefore go undetected. Victim surveys have been an invaluable source of information on the nature and extent of crime victimization, where crime takes place, how it harms victims, and so on.

Surveys are usually conducted by means of mailed or personally distributed questionnaires that participants are asked to complete and return. Sometimes surveyors also interview subjects, in person or over the telephone, about their attitudes and behavior; occasionally, both questionnaires and interviews are used.

Aggregate Record Data

A significant proportion of criminal justice data involves the compilation and evaluation of official records. The records may be acquired from a variety of sources, including schools, courts, police departments, social service centers, and correctional agencies.

Records can be used for a number of purposes. Prisoners' files can be analyzed in an effort to determine what types of inmates can adjust to prison and what types tend to be disciplinary problems or suicidal. Parole department records are evaluated to determine the characteristics of inmates who successfully adjust to the outside and the characteristics of those who fail. Educational records are important indicators of IQ, academic achievement, school behavior, and other information that can be related to delinquent behavior patterns. The most important sources of crime data, however, are those records compiled by police departments that are annually collected and analyzed by the Federal Bureau of Investigation (FBI); these are referred to as the **official crime statistics.**

Other Sources of Crime Data

There are a variety of other sources of crime information in addition to surveys and record data. For example, the systematic **observation,** recording, and deciphering of types of behavior within a sample or population is another popularly used method of criminal justice data collection. Some observation studies are conducted in the field, where the researcher observes subjects in their normal environment; other observations take place in a contrived, artificial setting or laboratory. Still another type of observation study is called participant observation. In this type of research, the observer joins the group being studied and behaves as a member of the group. It is believed that participation enables the scientist to better understand the subjects' motives for their behavior and attitudes. Participation also helps the researcher develop a frame of reference similar to that of the subjects and allows the researcher to better understand how the subjects interact with the rest of the world. Classic participant observation studies have been conducted by William F. Whyte on the lives of young lower-class youth (*Street Corner Society*) and Laud Humphreys on homosexual behavior in public places (*Tearoom Trade*).[5]

Observation is a time-consuming way to conduct research and occasionally involves some ethical risks, such as when the subjects engage in deviant behavior during the data-gathering stage of the research and the observer is faced with the decision of whether to betray their trust or let a criminal act go unreported. Participant observation studies, however, do allow the researcher to gain insights into behavior that might never be available otherwise. In addition, since observation studies depend more on actual behavior than on surveyed opinions, the researcher can be fairly sure of the validity of the information because it will be more difficult for subjects to give false impressions or responses. It is difficult if not impossible to standardize the conditions or replicate the results of observation studies; thus they usually stand as unique and valuable contributions of concerned scientists and scholars.

Another fascinating technique of criminal justice data collection is the **life history.** This method utilizes personal accounts of individuals who have had experience in crime, deviance, law enforcement, and other related areas. Diaries or autobiographies can be used; sometimes an account is given to a second party to record "as told to." Recent examples of this approach are contained in two important works by Carl Klockars and Darrell Steffensmeir on the lives of criminal "fences" (people who buy and sell stolen merchandise).[6]

Life histories provide insights into the human condition that other less personal research methods cannot hope to duplicate. They are sometimes moving, often revealing individual testimonies of the feelings, beliefs, values, and attitudes of convicts, delinquents, and criminals. Of course, life histories do not represent the average criminal. Most life histories are provided by talented, artistic individuals who eventually successfully readjust to society. Nevertheless, their stories often illustrate the conditions they had to overcome and the strengths they had to call upon in order to reenter society.[7]

■ The Nature and Extent of Crime

Each crime data source has value and makes a unique contribution to our understanding of the crime problem. However, the national **crime rate** is usually equated with the amount and trends in crime contained in the aggregate criminal incidence data collected by the FBI from police departments around the United States.

Prepared by the FBI, the **Uniform Crime Reports (UCR)** are the best known and most widely cited source of criminal statistics.[8] The FBI receives and compiles reports from over 16,000 police departments serving a majority of the population of the United States. The reports are analyzed largely in terms of the **index crimes:** murder and nonnegligent manslaughter, forcible rape, robbery, aggravated assault, burglary, larceny-theft, arson, and motor vehicle theft (see Table 2.1). The FBI tallies and annually publishes the number of reported offenses by city, county, standard metropolitan statistical area (SMSA), and geographical division of the United States. In addition to these statistics, the UCR provides information on the number and characteristics of individuals who have been arrested and the number and location of assaults on police officers.

In the following sections we will review the methods the FBI uses to prepare the UCR, discuss some recent trends in crime statistics, and examine the criticisms of the UCR.

UCR Reporting Procedures

Law enforcement agencies tabulate the number of index offenses on a monthly basis (see Table 2.1).[9] A count of these crimes, which are also known **as Part I offenses,** is taken from records of all complaints of crime received by law enforcement agencies from victims, officers who discovered the infractions, or other sources. Whenever investigation reveals that complaints of crime are unfounded or false, they are eliminated from the actual count. The number of "actual offenses known" in Part I is reported to the FBI whether anyone is arrested for the crime, whether the stolen property is recovered, or whether prosecution is undertaken. In addition, each month law enforcement agencies report the total number of these crimes cleared. Crimes are "cleared" in one of two ways: (1) when at least one person is arrested, charged, and turned over to the court for prosecution; or (2) when some element beyond police control precludes the physical arrest of an offender (for example, if the suspect dies). Data on the number of clearances involving only the arrest of offenders under the age of 18, the value of property stolen and recovered in connection with Part I offenses, and detailed information pertaining to criminal homicide are also reported.

Arrest data, which include the age, sex, and race of persons arrested, are reported monthly for both Part I and Part II offenses, by crime category. **Part**

TABLE 2.1 ■ **UCR Crimes and Definitions**

Homicide	Causing the death of another person without legal justification or excuse. Negligent manslaughter, suicide, and deaths due to accident are excluded.	**Burglary**	Unlawful entry of any fixed structure, vehicle, or vessel used for regular residence, industry, or business, with or without force, with the intent to commit a felony or larceny.
Rape	Unlawful sexual intercourse with a female, by force or without legal or factual consent. Assaults or attempts to commit rape by force or threat of force are included; statutory rape without force and other sex offences are excluded.	**Larceny (Theft)**	Unlawful taking or attempted taking of property other than a motor vehicle from the possession of another, by stealth, without force and without deceit, with intent to permanently deprive the owner of the property. It includes pocket-picking, purse-snatching, theft from motor vehicles.
Robbery	Unlawful taking or attempted taking of property that is in the immediate possession of another, by force or threat of force, or by putting the victim in fear.	**Motor Vehicle Theft**	Unlawful taking or attempted taking of a motor vehicle owned by another, with the intent of depriving the owner of it permanently. It includes theft of cars, trucks, buses, motorcycles, and scooters.
Assault	Unlawful intentional inflicting, or attempted inflicting, or injury upon the person of another. *Aggravated assault* is the unlawful intentional inflicting of serious bodily injury or unlawful threat or attempt to inflict bodily injury or death by means of a deadly or dangerous weapon with or without actual infliction of injury. *Simple assault* is the unlawful intentional inflicting of less than serious bodily injury without a deadly or dangerous weapon or an attempt or threat to inflict bodily injury without a deadly or dangerous weapon	**Arson**	Intentional damaging or destruction, or attempted damaging or destruction, by means of fire or explosion of the property without the consent of the owner, or of one's owner, or of one's own property or that of another by fire or explosives with or without the intent to defraud.

Source: Adapted from Federal Bureau of Investigation, *Uniform Crime Report,* 1987.

JUDGE TERRY SLAPS JUSTICE FIELD IN THE FACE AND IS SHOT DEAD BY DEPUTY MARSHAL NEAGLE, AT LATHROP, AUGUST 14, 1889. TERRY SAT AT THE EAST END OF THE FIFTH TABLE, SAME ROW.

II offenses, while excluding traffic violations, include all other crimes except those classified as Part I, for example, drug offenses, liquor law violations, sex offenses, juvenile offenses (runaways), and weapons offenses.

Data on law enforcement officers assaulted or killed are collected on a monthly basis. Other law enforcement employee data, specifically the number of full-time sworn officers and other personnel, are reported as of October 31 of each calendar year.

The UCR employs three methods of expressing crime data. First, the number of crimes reported to the police and the number of arrests made are expressed as raw figures (for example, 517,704 robberies occurred in 1987). Second, percentage changes in the amount of crime between years are computed (for example, robbery decreased 4.6 percent between 1986 and 1987). Third, the crime rate per 100,000 people is computed; that is, when the UCR indicates that the robbery rate was 212 in 1987, it means that about 212 people in every 100,000 fell victim to robbery between January 1 and December 31 of 1987. The following equation is used:

$$\frac{\text{Number of reported crimes}}{\text{Total U.S. population}} \times 100{,}000 = \text{Rate per 100,000}$$

of the most significant trends reported by the UCR.

Crime Trends

Crime is not just a twentieth-century phenomenon.[10] Studies have shown that a gradual increase in the crime rate, especially in the area of violent crime, occurred from 1830 to 1860. Following the Civil War, this rate increased significantly for about 15 years. Then, from 1880 until World War I, with the possible exception of the years immediately preceding and following the war, the number of reported crimes decreased. After a period of readjustment, the crime rate steadily declined until the depression (about 1930), whereupon another general increase, or crime wave, was recorded. Crime rates increased gradually following the 1930s until the 1960s, when the growth rate became much greater. The homicide rate, which had actually declined from the 1930s to the 1960s, also began a period of sharp increase that continued through the 1970s. In 1981 the number of index crimes peaked at about 13.4 million and then began a consistent decline to 1984 when 11.1 million crimes were recorded by police. Unfortunately, beginning in 1985, the crime rate started to move upward. Although there has not been a major new "crime wave," as Table 2.2 indicates, both the number of offenses known to the police and the rate of crime per 100,000 citizens have increased measurably.[11] Thus, after two decades of governmental efforts to deter, prevent, and otherwise eliminate crime, these data suggest that neither has an effective crime control policy been found nor has criminal behavior ceased being a major social problem.

Violent Crime Trends

The violent crimes reported by the FBI include murder, rape, assault, and robbery. In 1988, some 1,560,000 violent crimes were reported to police, a rate of 637 per 100,000. The number of violent crimes increased another 5.5 percent between 1987 and 1988; violence in the United States has increased dramatically in the past 10 years. The number of reported violent acts increased about 40 percent between 1978 and 1988, while the violence rate increased more than 22 percent. Though the murder rate has actually declined during the past decade, the rate of rapes, robbery, and assaults increased dramatically: the police received 67,610 reports of rape in 1978, by 1988 the number was about 92,000; reported assaults jumped from 571,460 in 1978 to about 910,000 in 1988.

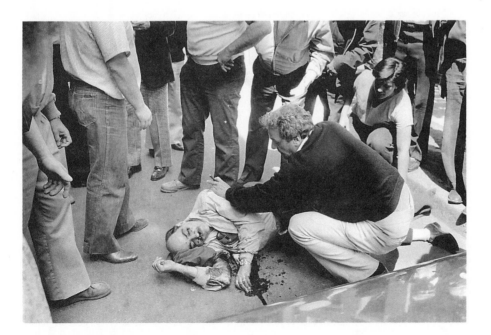

About 1.5 million violent crimes are reported to the police each year.

Chapter 2

The Nature of Crime and Victimization

TABLE 2.2 ■ Index of Crime, United States, 1977–1988

Population[1]	Crime Index Total[2]	Violent Crime[3]	Property Crime[3]	Murder and Nonnegligent Manslaughter	Forcible Rape	Robbery	Aggravated Assault	Burglary	Larceny-Theft	Motor Vehicle Theft
Number of offenses										
1978—218,059,000	11,209,000	1,085,550	10,123,400	19,560	67,610	426,930	571,460	3,128,300	5,991,000	1,004,100
1979—220,099,000	12,249,500	1,208,030	11,041,500	21,460	76,390	480,700	629,480	3,327,700	6,601,000	1,112,800
1980—225,349,264	13,408,300	1,344,520	12,063,700	23,040	82,990	565,840	672,650	3,795,200	7,136,900	1,131,700
1981—229,146,000	13,423,800	1,361,820	12,061,900	22,520	82,500	592,910	663,900	3,779,700	7,194,400	1,087,800
1982—231,534,000	12,974,400	1,322,390	11,652,000	21,010	78,770	553,130	669,480	3,447,100	7,142,500	1,062,400
1983—233,981,000	12,108,600	1,258,090	10,850,500	19,310	78,920	506,570	653,290	3,129,900	6,712,800	1,007,900
1984—236,158,000	11,881,800	1,273,280	10,608,500	18,690	84,230	485,010	685,350	2,984,400	6,591,900	1,032,200
1985—238,740,000	12,430,400	1,327,770	11,102,600	18,980	87,670	497,870	723,250	3,073,300	6,926,400	1,102,900
1986—241,077,000	13,210,800	1,488,140	11,722,700	20,610	90,430	542,780	834,320	3,241,400	7,257,200	1,224,100
1987—243,400,000	13,508,700	1,484,000	12,027,700	20,096	91,111	517,704	855,088	3,236,184	7,499,851	1,288,674
Percentage change: number of offenses										
1988/1987	+3.0	+5.5	+2.8	+3.0	+1.0	+4.0	+7.0	-1.0	+2.0	+11.0
1987/1986	+2.2	-.3	+2.6	-2.5	-.4	-4.6	+2.5	-.2	+3.3	+5.3
1986/1982	+1.8	+12.5	+.6	-1.9	+14.8	-1.9	+24.6	-6.0	+1.6	+15.2
1986/1977	+20.3	+44.5	+17.8	+7.8	+42.4	+31.5	+56.1	+5.5	+22.9	+25.2
Rate per 100,000 inhabitants										
1978	5,140.3	497.8	4,642.5	9.0	31.0	195.8	262.1	1,434.6	2,747.4	460.5
1979	5,565.5	548.9	5,016.6	9.7	34.7	218.4	286.0	1,511.9	2,999.1	505.6
1980	5,950.0	596.6	5,353.3	10.2	36.8	251.1	298.5	1,684.1	3,167.0	502.2
1981	5,858.2	594.3	5,263.9	9.8	36.0	258.7	289.7	1,649.5	3,139.7	474.7
1982	5,603.6	571.1	5,032.5	9.1	34.0	238.9	289.2	1,488.8	3,084.8	458.8
1983	5,175.0	537.7	4,637.4	8.3	33.7	216.5	279.2	1,337.7	2,868.9	430.8
1984	5,031.3	539.2	4,492.1	7.9	35.7	205.4	290.2	1,263.7	2,791.3	437.1
1985	5,206.7	556.2	4,650.5	7.9	36.7	208.5	302.9	1,287.3	2,901.2	462.0
1986	5,479.9	617.3	4,862.6	8.6	37.5	225.1	346.1	1,344.6	3,010.3	507.8
1987	5,550.0	609.7	4,940.3	8.3	37.4	212.7	351.3	1,329.6	3,081.3	528.4
Percentage change: rate per 100,000 inhabitants										
1987/1986	+1.4	-1.3	+1.6	+3.5	-1.3	-5.5	+1.5	-1.1	+2.4	+4.3
1986/1982	-2.2	+8.1	-3.4	-5.5	+10.3	-5.8	+19.7	-9.7	-2.4	+10.7
1986/1977	+7.9	+29.7	+5.7	-2.3	+27.6	+18.0	+40.1	-5.3	+10.3	+12.4

[1]Populations are Bureau of the Census provisional estimates as of July 1, except April 1, 1980, preliminary census counts, and are subject to change.
[2]Because of rounding, the offenses may not add to totals.
[3]Violent crimes are offenses of murder, forcible rape, robbery, and aggravated assault. Property crimes are offenses of burglary, larceny-theft, and motor vehicle theft. Data are not included for the property crime of arson.
All rates were calculated on the offenses before rounding.

SOURCE: Federal Bureau of Investigation, *Crime in the United States, 1987*, (Washington, D.C.: U.S. Government Printing Office, 1988), p. 41, updated.

Property Crime Trends

The property crimes reported in the UCR include burglary, larceny, motor vehicle theft, and arson. In 1988, 12,360,000 property crimes were reported, an increase of 2.6 percent from the preceding year. This represented a crime rate of 5,027 per 100,000 population. In 1988 the overall property crime rate increase (2.8 percent) was led by motor vehicle theft (+ 11 percent) and larceny (+ 2.0 percent). The property crime rate has remained relatively stable during the past decade. The actual number of theft-related offenses increased about 19 percent (half that of violent crimes) while the property crime *rate* increased about 6 percent (as compared to the violent crime rate increase of 22 percent). However, the rates of two crimes in the group, motor vehicle theft and larceny, have both experienced appreciable gains over the past decade.

Arrest Trends

The FBI also records the number of people arrested in the United States each year for both index and nonindex crimes. In 1987 almost thirteen million (12,711,600) arrests were recorded, including 2,646,00 for index crimes; this represented a rate of 5,330 per 100,000, a slight increase over the preceding year (5,230).

In the past 10 years the annual number of arrests has increased by almost 2,000,000. The number of violent crime arrests has increased 25 percent, and property crime arrests have increased 16 percent. The increase can be attributed to major crackdowns on crimes involving substance abuse: drunk driving arrests increased 25 percent; liquor law violation arrests jumped 62 percent; and drug abuse violations rose 55 percent. Arrests for other crimes also showed major increases: rape and larceny arrests were both up 30 percent; assault arrests increased 37 percent; and the catchall "all other offense" category jumped a significant 55 percent.

CRIMES CLEARED The FBI also tallies **crimes cleared by arrest** (reported crimes in which at least one person is arrested and turned over for prosecution). The police cleared about 21 percent of all crimes reported to them. Clearances were much higher for violent crimes (47 percent) than they were for property offenses (18 percent). Both the overall clearance rate and the rate for individual crime patterns have remained very stable over time.

The differences between the clearance rates for violent crime and property crime can be attributed to three factors: (1) the victims of violent crime are much more likely to be able to describe or identify their assailant; (2) the perpetrator of violent crime is likely to be a friend, acquaintance, or relative of the victim; and (3) police are more likely to devote resources to violent crimes than to property offenses. In either event, the data show that police are able to "solve" only one in five reported crimes.

▪ Explaining Crime Trends

How can we account for the recent patterns in the crime rate? There are a number of possible answers to this question. When crime rates skyrocketed between 1965 and 1980, some commentators placed the blame on such targets as a large, alienated teenage population who did nothing but disobey their parents and listen to rock 'n' roll music; urban decay; racial disharmony; the rise of a drug culture; and the erosion of middle class values. According to this view, it was not surprising that the postwar generation brought up under the permissive rules of Dr. Spock, weaned on violent television shows and Elvis Presley, and later influenced by urban riots and the war in Vietnam, would increasingly turn to crime and violence.[12]

When crime rates declined in the mid-1980s, experts believed that the decline in the U.S. birthrate had resulted in a smaller number of people in the most crime-prone age bracket, 18 to 25 years old.[13] As we shall see, young people maintain the highest overall crime rate, and some experts believed that the crime rate had declined concomitantly with the "greying" of society.

Another popular explanation was that the "get tough" crime control policy that held sway during the Reagan administration helped deter criminal behavior. As the prison and jail population skyrocketed and judges put a greater percentage of convicted criminals behind bars, it stood to reason that the crime rate should go down. It was also claimed that the "law and order" philosophy met with a great deal of public approval and that the resulting increase in police-community cooperation helped stem the crime rate. Finally, the improved economy and low unemployment rate in the mid-1980s may have helped to stabilize crimes rates.

How can the more recent crime rate increases be explained since the unemployment rate remains low, the number of teenagers in the population has not expanded, citizens have not stopped cooperating with the police, and the incarceration rate continues to climb? One explanation is that the improving economy has actually helped *increase* the crime rate by creating greater opportunities to commit crime. Since an improved economy means that there are more people with money and goods, (so called "suitable targets"), the opportunities to commit crime may have increased.[14] At the same time the gulf between the wealthiest and poorest members of society has widened, a fact that some crime experts fear produces criminal behavior. Although the overall economy has done well, the level of poverty and unemployment among youths in the nation's largest cities remains shockingly high; there is evidence that the economic gap between black and white citizens is growing.[15] A number of studies have shown that the crime rate is extremely high when people who live in close proximity to one another do not share equal economic conditions.[16] Although an improving economy should reduce the crime rate, the structure of American society, which separates citizens into "haves" and "have nots," may reduce the positive influences of prosperity.

Another explanation for the change in crime rates has been the influence of drug use on crime. A number of research efforts have shown that a single drug user commits an enormous amount of crime annually and that a significant number of all arrested criminals have recently used drugs.[17] Although the overall rate of drug use has not increased dramatically in recent years, the problem of teenage cocaine and crack use in inner city areas may have accentuated the crime problem.[18] The addition of even a relatively few hard-core drug users to the population can result in a significant increase in the crime rate.[19]

Finally, the evidence that "get tough" policies alone can control the crime rate is at best inconclusive. Although some research links the level of punishment to crime rates, other evidence suggests that the link is rather feeble.[20]

It is also important to realize that any change or movement in the crime rate may be more a matter of law enforcement reporting practices than actual fluctuations in criminal behavior. The UCR is dependent on accurate crime reporting and uniformity in the way crimes are defined and tallied. A reduction in the crime rate may reflect the desire of the nation's police departments to show they are on top of the crime problem: they can record a burglary as a breaking and entering and avoid counting it as an index crime; the value of a larceny can be underestimated so that the crime is not counted. In contrast, crime rate increases may reflect confidence in the police and the willingness of victims to report criminal events. Therefore it is possible that changes in the overall crime rate may reflect the way citizens report crime to the police and the way police departments record the results, rather than any actual change in the amount or rate of criminality.

In the following sections some of the specific patterns identified in the UCR will be examined more closely.

■ Patterns of Crime

Part I and Part II (arrest) data are both major sources of information about the patterns of crime in the United States.[21] Some of the most important issues are discussed in the next sections.

Ecological Differences

As Table 2.3 indicates, there is a distinct relationship between crime rates and urbanization. Areas with rural and suburban populations are more likely to have much lower crime rates than larger urban areas. This finding, consistent over many years, suggests that the crime problem is linked to the social forces operating in the nation's largest cities—overcrowding, poverty, social inequality, narcotics use, racial conflict, and so on. UCR data also indicate that crime rates are highest in the summer months probably because teenagers are out of school, people spend so much time outdoors and are less likely to secure their homes. Crime rates also vary regionally. The West and South have significantly higher rates than the Middle West and New England.

TABLE 2.3 ■ **Reported Crime Rate per 100,000 Inhabitants by Geographic Area**

Geographic Area	Total Crimes	Violent Crimes	Property Crimes
Total United States	5,550	609	4,940
Large cities (over 50,000)	6,294	720	5,574
Smaller cities (under 50,000)	4,898	351	4,547
Rural areas	1,900	178	1,722

SOURCE: Federal Bureau of Investigation, *Uniform Crime Report, 1987* (Washington, D.C.: U.S. Government Printing Office, 1988).

Gender and Crime

UCR arrest data consistently show that males have a much higher crime rate than females. The overall arrest ratio is about 4:1 and for violent crimes approaches 8:1. In the past decade, however, the female arrest rate for all crimes has risen at a faster rate than that of males (33 percent versus 23 percent); the same trend exists for felony arrests (see Table 2.4). Some experts attribute this trend to the emergence of a "new female criminal" whose criminal activity mirrors the changing role of women in modern society.[22] Other experts disagree and find that female emancipation has had relatively little influence on criminality. They hold that women are arrested more often today simply because police are more willing to arrest and formally process female offenders, a result of the feminist movement's call for equal treatment for men and women.[23]

Race and Crime

UCR arrest statistics also indicate that minority citizens are overrepresented in the official arrest statistics for many serious crime categories. As Table 2.5 shows, the black arrest rate for such crimes as murder and rape is higher than their relative representation in the population, and an absolute majority of people arrested for robbery are black. Overall about 30 percent of all people arrested are black, and 69 percent are white with the remainder split between native Americans, Alaskans, Asians, and Pacific Islanders.

These data have proved controversial, because they can either reflect racial differences in the crime rate or differential law enforcement practices. In other words, blacks may show up in arrest statistics because they are the victims of

TABLE 2.4 ■ Felony Arrest Trends by Sex, 1978–1987

	Male Percentage Change	Female Percentage Change
Murder	+7.7	−15.0
Rape	+30.0	+7.5
Robbery	+5.0	+17.0
Assault	+38.0	+36.0
Burglary	−15.0	+5.0
Larceny	+31.0	+27.0
Auto theft	+10.0	+23.0
Arson	−4.0	+14.0
Violent	+25.0	+28.0
Property	+13.0	+25.0
Total	+16.0	+26.0

SOURCE: Federal Bureau of Investigation, *Crime in the United States, 1987* (Washington, D.C.: U.S. Government Printing Office, 1988), p. 169.

TABLE 2.5 ■ Felony Arrests by Race

	White	Black	Total	Percentage Black	Percentage White
Murder	7,642	8,746	16,678	52	46
Rape	15,652	15,106	31,208	48	50
Robbery	43,899	77,957	123,152	63	36
Assault	174,317	121,528	300,652	40	58
Burglary	250,844	117,553	374,079	31	67
Larceny	825,786	401,692	1,254,559	32	66
Auto Theft	87,240	56,531	146,535	39	69
Arson	11,017	3,857	15,116	26	73
Violent	241,510	223,337	471,690	47	51
Property	1,174,887	579,633	1,790,289	32	65
Total	2,416,397	802,970	2,261,979	35	63

SOURCE: Federal Bureau of Investigation, *Crime in the United States, 1987* (Washington, D.C.: U.S. Government Printing Office, 1988), pp. 182–83.

discrimination on the part of law enforcement officials or perhaps because they live in areas that receive more intensive police supervision. In contrast, some experts view the official crime statistics as an accurate reflection of the black crime rate. They believe that the black experience in the United States, which has been one of racism, differential opportunity, powerlessness, and other social disabilities, has resulted in a higher black crime rate as an expression of anger and frustration.[24]

Social Class and Crime

Researchers have used the UCR data in conjunction with census data to determine whether crime is closely linked to poverty, unemployment, and membership in lower class society.[25] Though the class-crime relationship has been the subject of almost constant research, the true association between them is far from established. Although some research efforts do show a strong class-crime relationship, they are matched by others that indicate the relationship between poverty and crime is weak or nonexistent. There is evidence that middle-class youths are just as crime-prone as those in the lower class. Lower crime rates in middle-class areas may be more a function of lax law enforcement than the absence of crime.[26]

Measuring the relationship between social class and crime has proven to be a very complex problem. Researchers have had difficulty agreeing on the variables used to measure lower-class status, and different studies employ a variety of measures, such as being a welfare recipient, average income, being unemployed, and so on. The resulting confusion may mask the true relationship between crime and lower-class status.[27]

Despite these problems, the weight of the most recent research does seem to indicate that crime rates are highest in deprived, inner city slum areas, and that those who believe that poverty does not produce crime or that the middle and upper classes are equally as crime-prone as the lower class are just wishful thinkers.[28]

How can the relationship be crime and poverty be explained? One view is that it is not poverty per se that is related to crime but **social inequality.** That is, in areas where the disadvantaged and the wealthy live side by side, social differences are magnified, and the result is a higher crime rate.[29] Other studies indicate that the social forces existing in high-risk, disorganized neighborhoods—poverty, dilapidated housing, poor schools, broken families, drugs, and street gangs—significantly increase the likelihood that residents will engage in criminality.[30] Rodney Stark argues that as the social system breaks down and the rule of law becomes a distant threat, slum areas begin to attract criminals and deviants who find the environment suitable for their law-violating behavior; the moral vacuum acts as a magnet for undesirables, and conditions steadily worsen.[31]

Age and Crime

As Table 2.6 illustrates, UCR arrest data consistently show that there is a significant relationship between age and crime: young people between the ages of 15 and 25 are responsible for an overwhelming number of all arrests; the

TABLE 2.6 ■ **Arrests by Age Distribution in the United States**

Age	Percentage of Population	Percentage of Index Arrests	Percentage of All Arrests
Under 10	15.0	1.0	0.4
10–12	4.0	3.0	1.3
13–14	3.0	7.0	3.5
15	1.5	5.3	3.0
16	1.5	6.4	3.9
17	1.5	6.4	4.5
18	1.5	5.7	4.7
19	1.6	4.9	4.6
20	1.7	4.3	4.4
21	1.7	7.0	4.4
22	1.7	3.8	4.4
23	1.7	3.6	4.3
24	1.8	3.5	4.3
25–29	9.0	14.8	18.3
30–34	8.0	10.7	13.1
35–39	7.0	6.6	8.4
40–44	6.0	3.5	4.9
45–64	18.0	4.8	7.9
Over 65	12.0	0.8	0.8

SOURCE: Federal Bureau of Investigation, *Uniform Crime Reports, 1987* Washington, D.C.: U.S. Government Printing Office, (1988); U.S. Dept. of Commerce, Census Data, 1987.

elderly, those aged 60 and over, are relatively crime-free. The peak age for property crime is about 16, and for violence the modal age is 18. In 1987 about 45 percent of all arrests involved people aged 24 and under; 17 percent were for youths under 18 years of age. In contrast, people over 45 accounted for only about 8.7 percent of all arrests.

Despite such overwhelming evidence, the true relationship between age and crime has proven to be one of enduring controversy. Some experts hold that all people commit less crime as they age. That is, regardless of race, sex, or class, younger people commit more crime than older ones.[32] How can this phenomenon be explained? One factor involves lifestyle; many young people are part of a youth culture that favors risk taking, short-run hedonism, and other forms of behavior that can lead to trouble with the law. Another factor is that youths have few legitimate ways of obtaining desired funds other than by resorting to theft and other illegal means. The high-risk lifestyle of most youths ends as they enter the work force.[33] A more simple explanation is biological: young people have the energy, strength, and physical skill needed to commit crime, and these erode with age (as well we know!).[34]

Not all crime experts agree with this view. Some, including David Greenberg and Alfred Blumstein, argue that although most offenders do reduce their criminal activity as they age, there is a group of high-rate offenders who embark on a life of crime early in their adolescence and maintain a high rate of criminal violations throughout their lifespan. These **chronic offenders** are immune to both the ravages of age and the punishments of the justice system. More important, this small group may be responsible for a significant portion of all serious criminal behavior.[35] The concept of the chronic offender is discussed more fully in the following Criminal Justice in Review.

Those supporting each side of this argument have engaged in some lively academic debates. At the time of this writing neither side seems willing to concede defeat.

Analysis of the UCR

Unquestionably, the FBI and many of its contributing law enforcement agencies have made a serious attempt to measure the incidence and amount of crime and delinquency in the United States. Nevertheless, a great deal of criticism has been directed at the actual validity of the national crime statistics and official statistics in general. Methodological problems have compelled some experts to advocate total abandonment of the use of official crime statistics in criminal justice research.

The issues that most disturb critics may be divided into two main categories: (1) the fact that many citizens neglect or refuse to report delinquent and criminal acts to police and (2) the problems caused by variations in police reporting practices. Because each of these issues is important, they will be discussed separately below.

REPORTING INFLUENCES. American citizens are believed to report less than half of all criminal and delinquent acts to police. The reasons for this are varied. Many individuals in lower-class areas neglect to carry property insurance and therefore believe it is useless to report theft-related offenses to police since "nothing can be done." In other cases the victims may fail to notify police because they fear reprisals from friends or relatives of the offenders.

The Chronic
Offender

One of the most dramatic developments in the study of crime and delinquency has been the "discovery" of the chronic criminal offender. There is growing recognition among researchers that a relatively few delinquent offenders commit a significant percentage of all serious crimes in the community, and that these same offenders grow up to become chronic adult criminals who contribute a significant share to the total adult crime rate.

Chronic offenders can be distinguished from conventional criminals. The latter category contains law violators who are apprehended for a single instance of criminal behavior, usually of relatively minor seriousness—shoplifting, simple assault, petty larceny, and so on. The chronic offender is one who has serious and persistent brushes with the law, who is building a career in crime, and whose behavior may be excessively violent and destructive.

The concept of the chronic career offender is most closely associated with the research efforts of **Marvin Wolfgang** and his associates at the University of Pennsylvania. In 1972, Wolfgang, Robert Figlio and Thorsten Sellin published a landmark study, *Delinquency in a Birth Cohort*, that has had a profound influence on the very concept of the criminal offender.

Wolfgang, Figlio, and Sellin used official records to follow the criminal careers of a **cohort** of 9,945 boys, born in Philadelphia, Pennsylvania, in 1945, until they reached 18 years of age in 1963.

About two-thirds of the cohort (6,470) never had a contact with police authorities, while the remaining 3,475 were arrested at least once during their minority; they were responsible for a total of 10,214 arrests.

The cohort data indicated that 54 percent (1,862) of the offenders were **persisters** (repeat offenders) and 46 percent (1,613) were **desisters** (one-time offenders). The persisters could be further divided into **nonchronic recidivists** and **chronic recidivists**. The former consisted of 1,235 youths who had been arrested more than once but less than five times whereas the latter were a group of 627 boys arrested *five times or more*. About 18 percent of all arrestees and 6 percent of the total sample of 9,945 were considered chronic recidivist offenders (hence their designation as "the chronic 6 percent").

Chronic offenders were responsible for 5,305 *arrests, 51.9 percent of the total.* Even more striking was the involvement of chronic offenders in serious criminal acts. Of the entire sample, they committed 71 percent of the homicides, 73 percent of the rapes, 82 percent of the robberies, and 69 percent of the aggravated assaults. Arrest and punishment did little to deter the chronic offenders. In fact, punishment was inversely related to chronicity—the stricter the sanctions they received, the more likely they

In a study conducted by the National Crime Survey (NCS), a large, nationally drawn sample of citizens was used to determine the factors that influence the reporting or nonreporting of criminal activity.[36] (See The Nature and Extent of Victimization later in this chapter for a more detailed discussion of the NCS.) The NCS data reveal that the reasons given for not reporting crime vary according to the type of criminal behavior. Rape and attempted-rape victims said they did not report crime because it was a "private matter" (27 percent) and because they "feared reprisals" (12 percent). Assaults remained unreported because people felt they were "a private matter" (32 percent). For the most part, however, people did not report crimes such as robbery, burglary, and larceny because they believed "nothing could be done" and because the victimization was "not important enough."

The fact that under 50 percent of all victimizations are eventually reported to the police makes the accuracy of the UCR highly uncertain.

ADMINISTRATIVE INFLUENCES. The way police departments record and report criminal and delinquent activity also affects the validity of UCR statistics. The manner in which police interpret the definitions of index crimes

were to engage in repeated criminal behavior.

Wolfgang and his associates later followed a 10 percent sample of the original cohort (974 subjects) through their adulthood to age 30. They found that those classified as chronic juvenile offenders in the original birth cohort had an 80 percent chance of becoming adult offenders and a 50 percent chance of being arrested four or more times as adults. The former chronic delinquents were involved in 74 percent of all arrests and 82 percent of all serious crimes, such as homicide, rape, and robbery.

Wolfgang and his colleagues conducted a second birth cohort study, this time with a group of 27,160 boys and girls born in Philadelphia in 1958 and again found the presence of a chronic, persistent offender. Subsequent studies in other areas of the country have substantiated Wolfgang's original findings.

The chronic offender concept has significant implications for the criminal justice system. If a relatively few offenders commit a significant amount of all serious crime, then it follows that their early identification, capture, and incapacitation should measurably re-duce the crime rate. In addition, since persisters are unaffected by punishment, keeping them out of circulation seems to be the best approach to crime control. This strategy, referred to as **selective incapacitation,** requires the enactment of special laws that escalate prison sentences for multiple offenders. This approach has been recently adopted by the federal government and other legal jurisdictions.

The record number of inmates currently in prison and jail reflects the justice system's effort to curb career offenders and the steps taken to "lock'em up and throw away the key." This solution is troubling to civil libertarians because it involves the prediction of a person's future behavior. Is it not possible that some people will be unfairly punished because their background characteristics mistakenly indicate they are chronic offenders? Conversely, might not some serious offenders be overlooked because they have a conventional background? No prediction method is totally accurate, and error can significantly infringe upon a person's civil rights.

Despite the problems civil libertarians may have with the concept of the chronic career offender, it has already had a profound influence on the daily operations of the criminal justice system. It has strengthened the position of conservative policymakers who call for a "get tough" approach to crime control. It makes both economic and practical sense to incarcerate the few chronic offender who are responsible for most of the crime problem. It is safe to say that the discovery of the chronic offenders has helped shift criminal justice philosophy away from the liberal orientation that predominated in the 1960s and early 1970s toward the more conservative, social control orientation that exists today. ■

SOURCE: Marvin Wolfgang, Robert Figlio, and Thorsten Sellin, *Delinquency in a Birth Cohort* (Chicago: University of Chicago Press, 1972); Marvin Wolfgang, "Delinquency in Two Birth Cohorts," in *Perspective Studies of Crime and Delinquency,* Katherine Teilmann Van Dusen and Sarnoff Mednick, eds. (Boston: Kluwer-Nijhoff, 1983), pp. 7–17; Lyle Shannon, *Assessing the Relationship of Adult Criminal Careers to Juvenile Careers: A Summary* (Washington, D.C.: U.S. Department of Justice, 1982); Donna Hamparian, Richard Schuster, Simon Dinitz, and John Conrad, *The Violent Few* (Lexington, Mass.: Lexington Books, 1978).

may affect reporting practices. For example, one study found that Boston police reported only completed rapes to the FBI, while those in Los Angeles reported completed rapes, attempted rapes, and sexual assaults. Reporting practices helped account for the fact that the rape rate is far higher in Los Angeles than in Boston.[37] A more recent study by Lawrence Sherman and Barry Glick for the Police Foundation found that local police departments make systematic errors in UCR reporting.[38] All 196 departments surveyed counted an arrest only after a formal booking procedure, although the UCR requires arrests to be counted if the suspect is released without a formal charge; 29 percent did not include citations and 57 percent did not include summonses, though the UCR requires it. An audit of arrests found an error rate of about 10 percent in every Part I offense category. Similarly, Patrick Jackson found that the FBI's newest crime category, arson, may be seriously underreported because many fire departments do not report suspicious fires to the UCR and those that do exclude many fires that are probably set by arsonists.[39]

More serious are allegations that police officials deliberately alter reported crimes in order to put their departments in a more favorable light with the public. Some critics have suggested that police administrators interested in lowering the crime rate and thus improving their department's image may

Chapter 2

The Nature of Crime and Victimization

■

falsify crime reporting by deliberately undervaluing the cost of stolen goods so that an index larceny will be relegated to a nonreportable offense category.[40] Thus, political issues may help to raise or lower crime rates.

Finally, increased police efficiency and professionalism may actually increase crime rates. As more sophisticated computer-aided technology is developed for police work and as the education and training of police employees increase, so too might their ability to record and report crimes, producing higher crime rates.

Rethinking the UCR

Methodological issues continue to cloud the validity of the UCR. Leonard Savitz has collected a list of 20 irksome problems that have yet to be addressed; included among them are the following:

1. No federal crimes are reported.
2. Reports are voluntary and vary in accuracy and completeness.
3. Not all police departments submit reports.
4. The FBI uses estimates in its total crime projections.
5. If an offender commits multiple crimes, only the most serious is recorded. Thus, if a narcotics addict rapes, robs, and murders a victim, only the murder is recorded as a crime.
6. For some crimes, each act is listed as a single offense. Thus, if a man robs six people in a bar, it is listed as one robbery; but if he assaulted them, it would be listed as six assaults.
7. Uncompleted acts are lumped together with completed ones.
8. Important differences exist between the FBI's definition of a crime and the definitions used in a number of states. Some crime categories such as rape may contain acts that by some states' definitions would be molestation or assault, while burglary can include illegal trespass or breaking and entering.[41]

Because of these and other problems, it has become commonplace for justice experts to question the validity of the UCR as a source for criminal justice research. Yet, despite these criticisms, a great deal of criminal justice research still relies heavily on the UCR. Such faith may yet prove not to have been misplaced. A number of important research efforts indicate that the UCR may be more accurate than previously believed.[42] In a significant analysis of the existing evidence on the subject, Walter Gove, Michael Hughes, and Michael Geerken found evidence that the UCR is a valid indicator of serious crime.[43] Although it is true that many crimes are not reported to the police, Gove and his colleagues found the nonreported crimes to be generally less serious ones that may not even satisfy the legal requirements of criminality. They found evidence that citizens and police are in general agreement about what a serious crime entails: it results in bodily injury or a significant amount of lost property; it is committed by a stranger; it involves breaking and entering. When a criminal act meets these criteria, it has a good chance of being reported to the FBI.

The generally favorable "reviews" given the UCR by Gove and his colleagues have been reinforced by other research studies.[44] Nevertheless, some researchers still believe the UCR is so flawed that it should not be considered a valid indicator of the crime rate.[45] To help improve the quality of UCR statistics, the FBI is currently revising their form and content. First, the definitions of many crimes will be revised. For example, rape will now be defined in sexually neutral terms:

> The carnal knowledge of a person, forcibly and/or against that person's will; or not forcibly or against the person's will where the victim is incapable of giving consent because of his/her temporary or permanent mental incapacity.

Secondly, an effort will be made to obtain more detailed information on individual criminal incidents. Instead of submitting statements of the kinds of crime that individual citizens reported to the police and summary statements of resulting arrests, local police agencies will be asked to provide at least a brief account of each incident within the existing Part I crime categories. In addition, agencies serving more than 100,000 people, and a sample of smaller departments, will submit detailed reports, including incident, victim, and offender information, on 23 crime categories. These expanded crime categories will include numerous additional crimes, such as blackmail, embezzlement, drug offenses, and bribery. This will allow a national data base on the nature of crime, victims, and criminals to be developed. Finally, more stringent auditing techniques will be used to ensure that material submitted by the police is accurate and complete.[46]

When implemented, the new UCR program may result in more uniform cross-jurisdictional reporting and more accurate official crime data.

■ Self-Report Data

In addition to its methodological problems, the UCR cannot accurately determine the prevalence of such important criminal behavior as drug use, nor does it provide much information about individual criminals. Consequently, another method of collecting crime data called *self-reports* has been developed. These ask offenders to tell about their own criminal activities. Self-reports have two main advantages: (1) they measure the so-called dark figures of crime—acts such as drug use, gambling, and alcohol abuse, which often go unreported to the police, and (2) they can be used to collect personal information from offenders such as age, race, IQ, attitudes, values, and income.

Typically, self-report surveys are distributed to groups of people in order to guarantee the anonymity of respondents. Self-reports have often been used in schools to measure the delinquent activity of youths, but they may also be used with adults, such as prison inmates, to measure their criminal behaviors.

A typical self-report instrument will provide a list of criminal acts and ask the subjects to tell how often in the past year (or lifetime) they participated in each act. Sometimes in a single study, self-reports will be distributed to thousands of people chosen randomly in various sites around the United States.

What do self-report studies tell us? Overall, they reinforce the view that crime is much more common than the UCR indicates.[47] Samples of youths have reported significant and widespread involvement in delinquent activity. Many self-report studies indicate that youth crime is spread evenly through the social structure. In other words, middle-class youths are as likely to use drugs, engage in theft, and damage property as lower-class youths.[48] Though this issue has not yet been fully resolved, there is growing evidence that the crimes self-reported by middle-class youths are less serious than those of the lower class—shoplifting versus armed robbery, for example.[49]

Self-Reported Drug Use

One of the most important uses of self-reports has been in the effort to monitor drug use by the nation's youth. The most comprehensive research in this area is being carried out by the Institute For Social Research (ISR) of the University of Michigan. ISR researchers have conducted surveys of about 17,000 high school seniors each year since 1975. The trends in the lifetime use of drugs self-reported by those students are illustrated in Table 2.7. Although these data show a disturbingly extensive pattern of teenage drug use, it is also evident that usage rates have been in decline for a decade. Despite growing national concern, the ISR's most recent (1988) annual survey found that drug use declined once again.[50] The number of youths who reported ever using drugs dropped to about 54 percent, the lowest level since 1975. In 1979, about 11 percent of seniors reported using marijuana everyday; in 1988 only 2.7 percent reported daily usage. What is especially encouraging is that the use of both cocaine and its potent derivative "crack" has declined between the two most recent surveys (1987–1988).

The ISR's research on drug use illustrates how self-report surveys can be used to collect important information on criminal behavior that would otherwise be unavailable.

■ The Nature and Extent of Victimization

On the receiving end of crime are its victims. For many years, victims and victimization were not considered an important topic for criminal justice study. Victims were viewed as the passive receptor of a criminal's anger, greed or frustration; they were simply in the wrong place at the wrong time. In the late 1960s a number of pioneering studies found that victims actually could tell us a great deal about the crime problem and that contrary to popular belief victims play an important role in the crime process.[51] This early research encouraged the development of the most widely used and most extensive victim survey to date, the **National Crime Survey (NCS)**.[52]

The National Crime Survey is conducted by the U.S. Bureau of the Census in cooperation with the Bureau of Justice Statistics of the U.S. Department of Justice. In the national surveys, samples of housing units are selected on the basis of a complex, multistage sampling technique.

The total annual sample for the most recent national survey included about 49,000 households, containing about 100,000 individuals over 12 years of age. The total sample is composed of six independently selected subsamples, each containing about 8,000 households and 16,000 individuals. Each subsample is interviewed twice a year about victimizations suffered in the preceding six months. For example, in January, 16,000 individuals are interviewed. In the following month—and in each of the four succeeding months—an independent probability sample, the same size as the subsample, is interviewed. In July, the housing units originally interviewed in January are revisited, and interviews are repeated; likewise, the original February sample units are revisited in August, the March units in September, and so on. Each time they are interviewed, respondents are asked about victimizations suffered during the six months preceding the month of interview. The crimes they are asked about include personal and household larcenies, burglary, motor vehicle theft, assaults, robberies, and rape.

TABLE 2.7 ■ Trends in Lifetime Prevalence of Eighteen Types of Drugs

Percent Ever Used

	Class of 1975 (9,400)	Class of 1976 (15,400)	Class of 1977 (17,100)	Class of 1978 (17,800)	Class of 1979 (15,500)	Class of 1980 (15,900)	Class of 1981 (17,500)	Class of 1982 (17,700)	Class of 1983 (16,300)	Class of 1984 (15,900)	Class of 1985 (16,000)	Class of 1986 (15,200)	Class of 1987 (16,300)	Class of 1988 (16,300)	1987–1988 change
Approx. N =															
Marijuana/Hashish	47.3	52.8	56.4	59.2	60.4	60.3	59.5	58.7	57.0	54.9	54.2	50.9	50.2	47.2	−3.0
Inhalants	NA	10.3	11.1	12.0	12.7	11.9	12.3	12.8	13.6	14.4	15.4	15.9	17.0	16.7	−0.3
Inhalants adjusted	NA	NA	NA	NA	18.2	17.3	17.2	17.7	18.2	18.0	18.1	20.1	18.6	17.5	−1.1
Amyl & butyl nitrites	NA	NA	NA	NA	11.1	11.1	10.1	9.8	8.4	8.1	7.9	8.6	4.7	3.2	−1.5s
Hallucinogens	16.3	15.1	13.9	14.3	14.1	13.3	13.3	12.5	11.9	10.7	10.3	9.7	10.3	8.9	−1.4s
Hallucinogens adjusted	NA	NA	NA	NA	17.7	15.6	15.3	14.3	13.6	12.3	12.1	11.9	10.6	9.2	−1.4s
LSD	11.3	11.0	9.8	9.7	9.5	9.3	9.8	9.6	8.9	8.0	7.5	7.2	8.4	7.7	−0.7
PCP	NA	NA	NA	NA	12.8	9.6	7.8	6.0	5.6	5.0	4.9	4.8	3.0	2.9	−0.1
Cocaine	9.0	9.7	10.8	12.9	15.4	15.7	16.5	16.0	16.2	16.1	17.3	16.9	15.2	12.1	−3.1
"Crack"	NA	NA	NA	NA	NA	NA	NA	NA	NA	NA	NA	NA	5.6	4.8	−0.8
Other cocaine	NA	NA	NA	NA	NA	NA	NA	NA	NA	NA	NA	NA	14.0	12.1	−1.9
Heroin	2.2	1.8	1.8	1.6	1.1	1.1	1.1	1.2	1.2	1.3	1.2	1.1	1.2	1.1	−0.1
Other opiates	9.0	9.6	10.3	9.9	10.1	9.8	10.1	9.6	9.4	9.7	10.2	9.0	9.2	8.6	−0.6
Stimulants	22.3	22.6	23.0	22.9	24.2	26.4	32.2	35.6	35.4	NA	NA	NA	NA	NA	NA
Stimulants adjusted	NA	NA	NA	NA	NA	NA	NA	27.9	26.9	27.9	26.2	23.4	21.6	19.8	−1.8
Sedatives	18.2	17.7	17.4	16.0	14.6	14.9	16.0	15.2	14.4	13.3	11.8	10.4	8.7	7.8	−0.9
Barbiturates	16.9	16.2	15.6	13.7	11.8	11.0	11.3	10.3	9.9	9.9	9.2	8.4	7.4	6.7	−0.7
Methaqualone	8.1	7.8	8.5	7.9	8.3	9.5	10.6	10.7	10.1	8.3	6.7	5.2	4.0	3.3	−0.7
Tranquilizers	17.0	16.8	18.0	17.0	16.3	15.2	14.7	14.0	13.3	12.4	11.9	10.9	10.9	9.4	−1.5
Alcohol	90.4	91.9	92.5	93.1	93.0	93.2	92.6	92.8	92.6	92.6	92.2	91.3	92.2	92.0	−0.2
Cigarettes	73.6	75.4	75.7	75.3	74.0	71.0	71.0	70.1	70.6	69.7	68.8	67.6	67.2	66.4	−0.8

SOURCE: Institute for Social Research, Press Release, 24 February 1989.

Chapter 2

The Nature of Crime
and Victimization

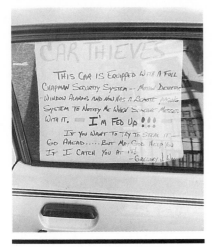

An estimated 35 million Americans will become crime victims this year. This one has issued a warning to would-be criminals.

The data reported represent estimates of crimes occurring in the United States, based on weighted sample data. It is possible to make these estimates because a probability sample of respondents was surveyed. The interview completion rate in the national sample is about 95 percent or more of those selected to be interviewed in any given period; hence population estimates are relatively unbiased.

General Victimization Patterns

How many people report being the victims of crime? According to the most recently available NCS data, some 35.9 million personal crimes occurred in 1988, marking the second time in 5 years that victimization increased. Table 2.8 and Figure 2.1 indicate, however, that although NCS data are relatively stable, there has been a decrease in the total number of victimizations and the victimization rate for the past 10 years. Though the overall number of victimizations increased in 1988, the total was still 16 percent less than the highwater mark of 41.5 million crimes recorded in 1981; in the past year the victim rate did increase slightly.[53]

The number of crimes recorded by the NCS is considerably larger than that reported by the FBI. For example, whereas the NCS estimated that 167,000 rapes occurred in 1988, the UCR reported a little more than 90,000 cases. Similarly, whereas the UCR recorded 855,088 aggravated assaults, the NCS estimates that about 1.7 million actually occurred. The reason for such discrepancies is that fewer than half the violent crimes, less than one-third the personal theft crimes such as pocketpicking, and less than half the household thefts are reported to police. The reasons most often given by victims for not reporting crime include the belief that nothing can be done, that the crime was a private matter, or that they did not want to get involved. If we are to believe NCS findings, the official statistics do not provide an accurate picture of the crime problem because many crimes go unreported to the police.

TABLE 2.8 ■ **The Number and Rate of Victimization, 1980–1988**

Year	Total number of victimizations[a]	Violent Crimes Number[a]	Violent Crimes Rate[b]	Personal Theft Number[a]	Personal Theft Rate[b]	Household Crimes Number[a]	Household Crimes Rate[b]
1980	40,252	6,130	33.3	15,300	83.0	18,821	227.4
1981	41,454	6,582	35.3	15,863	85.1	19,009	226.0
1982	39,756	6,459	34.3	15,553	82.5	17,744	208.2
1983	37,001	5,903	31.0	14,657	76.9	16,440	189.8
1984	35,544	6,021	31.4	13,789	71.8	15,733	178.7
1985	34,864	5,823	30.0	13,474	69.4	15,568	174.4
1986	34,118	5,515	28.1	13,235	67.5	15,368	170.0
1987	35,336	5,796	29.3	13,575	68.6	15,966	173.9
1988	35,989	6,025	30.2	13,584	68.1	16,386	175.5

a. The number of victimizations is in thousands.
b. The rate is the number of victimizations per 1,000 persons age 12 and older or per 1,000 households.

SOURCE: United States Dept. of Justice, Press Release, April 9, 1989.

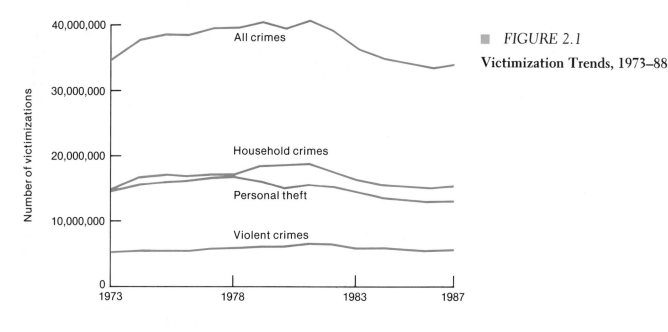

Victim Characteristics

The NCS provides information on the background characteristics of the victims of crime. Sex is related to one's chances of being a victim. Men are about twice as likely as women to be victims of robbery and assault. Women, as might be expected, are far more likely to be rape victims. However, although the rape rate for women is about 10 times that of men, it is estimated that thousands of males are rape victims each year. Women are also much more likely to be the victims of personal larcenies with contact due to the inclusion of purse snatching in that category.

Racial characteristics also influence a person's chances of being a crime victim. Blacks experience violent crimes at a higher rate than other groups, a condition mostly attributable to the number of robberies perpetrated against black male victims.

The NCS data also show that members of the lowest income categories (less than $3,000) were by far the most likely to be victims of violent crimes and most personal theft crimes. One important pattern emerges: although blacks as a group are much more likely to be victims than whites, there is relatively little difference between racial groups in the lowest income category. Thus, whether they are black or white, the economically deprived are more likely to be the victims of crime.

The Social Ecology of Victimization

The NCS data also provide information about the ecology of victimization—where, when, and how it takes place. Of offenses included in the survey, most occurred in the evening hours (6 P.M. to 6 A.M.); only personal larcenies with contact, such as purse snatchings and pocketpickings, predominated during

Chapter 2

The Nature of Crime and Victimization

■

daytime hours. Crimes of violence occurred more often at night. Generally, the more serious forms of these crimes took place after 6 P.M.; the less serious, before 6 P.M. For example, the majority of aggravated assaults took place at night, while simple assaults occurred during the day.

The most likely site for each crime category was an open, public area such as a street, park, or field. Only the crimes of rape and simple assault with injury were at all likely to occur in the home. Nevertheless, a significant number of rapes, robberies, and aggravated assaults occurred in public places.

An overwhelming number of victimizations involved a single person. Most victims report that their assailant was not armed. In the robberies and assaults involving injury, however, a majority of the assailants were reported armed. Guns and knives were used almost equally, and no pattern in which a particular weapon was used for a particular crime could be discerned.

The Likelihood of Victimization

In addition to general victim and offense characteristics, the NCS data also reveal that about 20 million American households experience some form of criminal activity each year. Because of this high incidence of crime, Americans maintain a significant chance of becoming a victim sometime during their lifetime. The probability of the average 12 year old being the victim of violent crime sometime during his or her life is about 83 percent; 25 percent of all American citizens will experience violence three or more times. Even more startling is the fact that 99 percent of the U.S. population will experience personal theft and that 87 percent will become a theft victim three or more times.[54]

Victims and Their Criminal

The NCS data can also be used to obtain information about the characteristics of people who commit crime. Of course, this information is available only on criminals who actually came in contact with the victim through such crimes as rape, assault, or robbery.

Most offenders and victims did not know one another; about 65 percent of all violent crimes are committed by strangers, and that number has remained stable for the past 10 years. Women, however, seem much more likely than men to be victimized by acquaintances. In fact, a majority of female assault victims knew their assailants.

Victims reported that a majority of crimes were committed by a single offender over age 20. About one-quarter of the victims indicated their assailant was a young person 12 to 20 years of age. This may reflect the criminal activities of youth gangs and groups in the United States.

Whites were the offenders in the majority of single-offender rapes and assaults, but the majority of robberies were carried out by blacks; this pattern held true for crimes involving multiple offenders.

The NCS has recently begun to ask victims if their assailants were under the influence of drugs or alcohol. Victims reported that substance abuse was involved in 36 percent of violent crime incidents, including 46 percent of the rapes.[55]

Crime and Victimization

Both NCS and UCR data can be interpreted as suggesting that the risk of being a crime victim is a function of personal characteristics and lifestyle. Victimization risk can be increased by going out in public places in urban areas late at night. It can also be increased by living in a large household in an urban environment. Conversely, one's chances of victimization can be reduced by staying home at night, moving to the country, staying out of public places, earning more money, and getting married. The important point is that crime is not a haphazard occurrence that is independent of the actions of victims. Crime and victimization seem to exist in a symbiotic relationship in which the probability of the former occurring is dependent on the activities of the latter. This has led to the development of a **routine activities** approach to criminal behavior.[56] This view holds that the incidence of criminal activity is related to the nature of normal, everyday patterns of human behavior. Put another way, crime occurs because people place themselves in jeopardy. The crime rate is a function of victim behavior: if households filled with expensive goods are left unguarded, the crime rate will increase; crime rates would decline if households contained little of value and were defended like forts by well-armed guards.

Critique of the NCS

Like the UCR data, the findings of the NCS and all other victim surveys must be interpreted with caution because they suffer from some methodological problems, including the following:

1. Overreporting due to victims' misinterpretation of events. For example, a lost wallet may be reported as stolen, or an open door may be viewed as a burglary attempt.
2. Underreporting due to the embarrassment of reporting the crime to interviewers, fear of getting in trouble, or simply forgetting an incident.
3. Inability to record the personal criminal activity of those interviewed, such as drug use or gambling.

■ Major Forms of Crime

The three main sources of criminal statistics have been used to identify trends and patterns in the major forms of criminal behavior. Though an exhaustive evaluation of all criminal behaviors is impossible here, some of the most important features of common illegal activities are outlined in the next sections.

Violent Crimes

The violent crime that has plagued American society includes such offenses as murder, robbery, rape, and assault. Fear of violence has provoked such incidents as Bernhard Goetz shooting four would-be muggers on a New York City subway, an incident that received national attention and was the subject of much debate.

RAPE. Rape—the carnal knowledge of a female forcibly and against her will—is a frightening and misunderstood crime because the victim's character and behavior are often put on trial alongside the accused.[57] Since consent is an issue in many rape cases and usually the only witness is the victim, a conviction can hinge on whether a judge or jury believes the victim's story. In other words, victims of burglary or assault never have to prove in court that they did not encourage their assailant to rob or beat them; a rape victim might have to convince a jury she did not encourage her attacker to have sexual relations. This is the major reason only about half of the estimated 167,000 annual rapes are reported to police. To improve the justice system's handling of rape cases, states have implemented some important changes in rape laws. Some have replaced rape with sexually neutral **sexual assault** laws. Others have implemented shield laws that protect women from being questioned about their sexual history.[58] Another change has been to remove the **marital exemption** to rape; this had previously prevented husbands from being charged with raping their wives.[59] In addition, rape crisis centers have been developed around the country to help victims deal with their trauma.[60] Perhaps these changes explain the recent increase in the percentage of rapes reported to the police; rape is one of the few index crimes that has undergone a significant increase in the past few years.

MURDER. About 20,000 people are the victims of murder each year. Most murders, an estimated 85 percent, involve people who knew each other—wives, husbands, children, neighbors, friends, lovers. For example, it has become common for women battered by their spouses to kill if they believe their lives are in imminent danger. A study of big city domestic homicides by Coramae Richey Mann indicates that women's role in domestic homicides may be changing: in contrast to the past, women who kill their mates are more likely to be the "victors" in a domestic battle than victims who are fighting back merely to survive.[61]

Not all murders involve people who knew each other. Research by Marc Reidel and by Margaret Zahn and Philip Sagi has shown that stranger homicides, such as those committed during robberies or random killings, may be on the rise.[62] **Serial murder** involves killers who roam cities preying on large numbers of unrelated victims. Some serial killers like Theodore Bundy travel the country, killing as they go; Bundy was executed in 1989. Others like Albert DeSalvo, the "Boston Strangler," can terrify an entire city. Though we are not sure of the motivations of these people, they are most likely to be white males who manifest antisocial or sociopathic personality disorders.[63]

ROBBERY. Robbery is the taking of another's property through force or threat. Approximately 500,000 robberies are reported to the police each year. According to FBI arrest statistics, the typical robber is an urban black male living in the northeast. The average value of property taken during a robbery is about $630, though bank robberies netted criminals an average of $3,000. All told, robberies result in a national loss of about $327 million dollars. Why do people commit robbery? According to John Conklin, robbers can be divided into four categories: professionals who earn the bulk of their living from theft; opportunists who steal when a vulnerable target presents itself; addicts who steal to support their drug habits; and alcoholics whose robberies are related to their excessive consumption of alcohol.[64]

Police escort Albert DeSalvo, center, also known as the Boston Strangler, to the police station in Lynn, Massachusetts. DeSalvo was convicted of murder in 1967 and sentenced to life imprisonment. A year later he received an additional ten-year sentence after he escaped from prison and was recaptured. DeSalvo was later killed in prison.

SERIOUS ASSAULT. Serious assault (about 850,000 were reported to police in 1987) exhibits much the same pattern as murder: an intraracial crime, committed by young male offenders in urban areas during the summer months. It can almost be regarded as an incomplete killing. A trend of the 1980s has been the recognition that a significant—and disturbing—number of assaults occur in the home. It has been estimated that almost 2 million children are subject to **child abuse** in a given year.[65] A survey conducted by Diana Russell found that 38 percent of women in the United States may have been the victims of family-centered **sexual abuse** when they were children.[66] In addition, some estimates indicate that almost 260,000 people experience **spouse abuse** annually.[67] Efforts on a national scale are now being undertaken to help curb these examples of domestic violence. Every state now requires teachers, physicians, and others who regularly come into contact with youth to report cases of suspected child abuse to the police or welfare authorities.

Economic and Property Crimes

As a group, economic and property crimes can be defined as acts in violation of the criminal law designed to bring financial reward to the perpetrator. In our society the scope of economic crime is tremendous, ranging from multimillion dollar computer fraud schemes to a teenager shoplifting from a record store. Most economic crimes are committed by amateurs who are motivated by a short-run need to solve a financial problem or other personal matters. In contrast, are the professional criminals who earn a significant portion of their income from economic crime. Though their numbers are relatively small, professionals engage in crimes that produce the greatest loss to society. These include the resale of stolen merchandise (fence), shoplifting (booster), pocketpicking (cannon), substituting fake jewelry for real (pennyweighter), burning structures for profit (torch), stealing goods in transit (hijacker), and other crimes that require skill and cunning rather than fear and violence.

COMMON THEFT OFFENSES. Included within the general theft category are many common crimes that involve economic loss to the victim. **Larceny** involves the illegal taking and carrying away of the property of another. Falling within this category are such acts as shoplifting, stealing cars, pocketpicking, passing bad checks, and using credit cards illegally. Although most of the 7.5 million larcenies and 1.3 million car thefts recorded annually are the work of amateurs, professional pickpocket, car theft, and stolen credit card rings are not uncommon.

Another common theft offense is **fraud,** which occurs when a wrongdoer misrepresents fact to cause a victim to willingly give his or her property away. For example, an unscrupulous art dealer who sells copies as original paintings commits fraud. Similarly, an **embezzlement** occurs when a person, such as a bank teller or stockbroker, who has temporary custody of money or property keeps it for his or her own purposes. In some jurisdictions fraud and embezzlement are separate crimes, while in others they have been combined with larceny into a general theft offense category.

About 3.2 million **burglaries** are committed annually according to the FBI; victimization data indicate that the actual number is closer to 6 million. Burglary is probably most often committed by occasional criminals, though some professionals are active in the trade. Research has shown that the

A store security guard, right, watches a shoplifter before apprehending him in order to catch the shoplifter with incriminating evidence. Because false arrest, a type of false imprisonment, is a tort, some states have passed statutes that allow store officials to detain suspected shoplifters for a reasonable amount of time without being liable to prosection.

professional burglar is particularly interested in commercial establishments such as supermarkets that handle a great deal of cash.[68]

The FBI also records about 100,000 arsons per year. Although many of these begin as pranks by wayward teenagers (the percentage of teens arrested for arson [43 percent] is greater than for any other serious crime), quite a few are the work of professional arsonists or **torches**.[69] The torch finds work when a business or landlord wants to get rid of outdated merchandise, needs insurance money, wants to get rid of a competitor, and so on.

WHITE-COLLAR CRIMES. Included within the category of white-collar offenses are all crimes that involve a business, government agency, or other institution. White-collar crime involves the illegal activities of people and organizations whose acknowledged purpose is legitimate enterprise. In some instances, white-collar crimes involve individuals who misuse their place of trust in an organization for their own benefit. Such criminal acts include insider trading by an individual who uses nonpublic information about a company to buy and sell stock in it, bribe taking by government officials, or conversely, the giving or taking of **kickbacks** by business executives to secure favored treatment from a client. Other types of white-collar crime involve businesses set up solely for the purposes of crime, such as bogus land companies and phony oil deals.

White-collar crime can also involve the illegal activities of executives of large businesses whose actions are designed to benefit the market position of the company; this is sometimes referred to as **corporate crime.** Illegal restraint of trade, false advertising, environmental pollution, price fixing, and large-scale bribery are examples of corporate crimes that can cost the taxpayers millions of dollars in lost revenues and higher prices.

It is commonly believed that white-collar crimes are rarely and leniently punished. For the most part, penalties are economic and only amount to a slap on the wrist for large corporations or wealthy executives. The government has begun to tighten up on white-collar crime. In a well-publicized Wall Street **insider trading** scandal, financier Ivan Boesky was fined over $100,000,000 and sentenced to three years in prison.[70] Similarly, corporate executives have been found guilty of murder when an employee died in a business-related incident that was attributed to corporate neglect.[71] This was the first case in which corporate executives were personally blamed for a wrongful death caused by a company-related policy. Thus, although many people consider "real crime" to be rape, robbery, and burglary, white-collar crimes can account for considerably more loss in terms of economic damage and physical suffering than the average street crime and are beginning to be punished accordingly.[72]

Organized Crime

Organized crime involves the illegal activities of people and organizations whose acknowledged purpose is illegitimate gain through illegal enterprise. Organized crime provides goods and services that are outlawed by the criminal law yet demanded by the public: prostitution, narcotics, gambling, loan sharking, pornography, and untaxed liquor and cigarettes. In addition, organized criminals infiltrate legitimate organizations such as unions in order to drain off their funds and profits for illegal purposes.[73]

For a long time, organized crime was equated with the secret activities of close-knit groups of Italian immigrants, variously called the Mafia or La Cosa Nostra. Many law enforcement officials including the U.S. Justice Department still equate organized crime with these "families" located in large cities such as New York, Chicago, and Cleveland. Criminologists refer to this as the **alien conspiracy theory.** Another view is that rather than being run by an all-powerful group or syndicate that oversees operations and settles disputes, organized crime is a series of groups made up of members of different ethnic and racial backgrounds competing with each other for power and profit.[74]

Some organized gangs are referred to as **enterprise groups.** These provide illegal goods and services such as prostitution, gambling, and pornography. Other gangs are organized as **power groups,** which provide no tangible goods or services but instead prey upon the public and also upon other criminals through fear, violence, and extortion. Power groups sell protection, demand a percentage of the profits of legitimate businesses, muscle in on unions and other organizations, and carry out large-scale burglaries and robberies.

Though federal and state agencies have been dedicated to wiping out organized crime, and some well-publicized arrests have been made, it seems unlikely that the organized crime problem will ever be solved. As long as profits can be made from the sale of narcotics, prostitution, pornography, gambling, and other illegal enterprises, people will be willing to sell and distribute them. Although many of the "traditional" ethnic gang leaders have been given long prison sentences, the result may not be the destruction of organized crime but the emergence of new groups to fill the vacuum created by federal prosecutors.[75]

Public-Order Crimes

Public-order crimes do not involve a victim per se, although one could argue that all society is victimized by these acts. They include prostitution, illegal sexual acts, obscenity, gambling, and substance abuse. These so-called **victimless crimes** are prohibited because society believes it has a duty to outlaw behaviors that can erode the moral fabric and create social harm. Even if a direct victim cannot be identified, as in the case of pornography, such acts are generally shunned because they conflict with our moral beliefs and values. In the case of drug abuse, the perpetrators themselves can be viewed as long-term victims who deserve protection from harm.

SEX FOR PROFIT. State jurisdictions have specific laws prohibiting sexual practices that are considered improper or harmful. These include prostitution, sale of pornographic material, and deviant sexual acts such as homosexual relations. These laws are often highly controversial because they outlaw behavior freely engaged in by consenting adults. Moreover, the line between legal and illegal behavior is often a fine one. For example, who is to say what is obscene and what isn't? How do we distinguish an openly sold adult publication such as *Playboy* from a legally objectionable porno magazine?[76] Why should a sexual act between two adult gays be considered illegal? Should police officers actively work to arrest prostitutes by posing as clients? These are only a few of the questions that arise when crimes involving sexual behavior are

Drug-Involved Youth

One of the most significant problems facing the criminal justice system is how to deal with the violence and social unrest linked to youth gangs who deal and use controlled substances. The reading below discusses the lifestyle of drug-involved youth and shows the problem they present for the criminal justice system.

ADOLESCENTS WHO DISTRIBUTE DRUGS AND COMMIT MANY OTHER TYPES OF CRIMES

By far the most serious adolescent dealers are those who use multiple substances and commit both property and violent crimes at high rates. Only about 2 percent of all adolescents pursue serious criminality *and* use multiple types of illicit drugs. Such youths commit over 40 percent of the total robberies and assaults by adolescents. Additionally, they are responsible for over 60 percent of all teen-age felony thefts and drug sales. They are more likely than any other type of juvenile offender to continue committing crimes as young adults. Among multiple drug users, girls are as likely as boys to become high-rate persistent drug-involved offenders, whites as likely as blacks, and middle-class adolescents raised outside cities as likely as lower-class city children.

Most research has focused on boys in cities. Seriously delinquent drug-involved city boys are frequently hired by adult or older adolescent street drug sellers as runners. Loosely organized into crews of 3 to 12, each boy generally handles relatively small quanities of drugs—for example, two or three packets or bags of heroin. They receive these units "on credit," "up front," or "on loan" from a supplier and are expected to return about 50 to 70 percent of the drug's street value.

In addition to distributing drugs, these youngsters may act as lookouts, recruit customers, and guard street sellers from customer-robbers. They typically are users of marijuana and cocaine, but not heroin. Moreover, in some cities, dealers and suppliers prefer to hire distributors who do not "get high" during an operation. But their employment as runners is not generally steady; it is interspersed with other crimes including robbery, burglary, and theft. When involved in selling drugs, they generally work long hours and facilitate many small transactions. They are rarely arrested for these activities since, when police approach, they and other runners flee in all directions.

A relatively small number of youngsters who sell drugs develop excellent enterpreneurial skills. Their older contacts come to trust them, and they parlay this trust to advance in the drug business. By the time they are 18 or 19 they can have several years of experience in drug sales, be bosses of their own crews, and handle more than $500,000 a year. However, there is a high level of violence associated with the position of crew boss. Violent tactics are used both by and against crew bosses to regulate the trade. But given the rewards, youngsters who achieve this position find the risk worthwhile.

For example, Darryl, a youngster in Harlem, started as a runner when he was 9 and was part of a clique of older major dealers before he was 19. He was the boss of a crew that sold heroin and cocaine. His income allowed him to indulge his taste for expensive clothes and cars; he simultaneously owned a Mercedes, BMW, and Cadillac.

Youngsters like Darryl earn great respect among the other drug-involved adolescents in their community. Many work for him and dream of having his clothes, cars, and customers. However, most other youngsters who are integral to the street drug trade do not have the skills to succeed, and most either stop or become so dependent on drugs that they have continuing contacts with the justice system. ■

SOURCE: Marcia Chaiken and Bruce Johnson, Characteristics of Different Types of Drug-Involved Offenders (Washington, D.C.: National Institute of Justice, 1988), pp. 12–13 (Footnotes omitted).

---

discussed. Despite questions over their propriety, laws restricting sexuality lead to the arrest of about 200,000 people for sex-for-profit crimes each year.

SUBSTANCE ABUSE. The United States is currently the scene of a multibillion dollar drug trade. Despite local, state, and federal efforts to control drug sales and use, business continues to flourish. The most commonly used

Chapter 2

The Nature of Crime and Victimization

■

drugs include marijuana, cocaine, anesthetics like PCP, narcotics such as morphine and heroin, amphetamines such as methadrine, and hallucinogens such as LSD. Though drug use appears to have declined in the past two years, there are still a reported 500,000 to 750,000 heroin addicts in the United States, and about half of all high school seniors have reported using drugs sometime in their lives.[77] In addition, the FBI reports that about 1,000,000 drug-related arrests are made each year. There is growing evidence that drug abuse is related to a significant amount of all criminality and that drug abusing youth represent a major portion of all serious chronic offenders (see the Criminal Justice in Review on drug use among youth on page 67.)

Drug use is a particularly serious problem because of the social harm it causes society. In addition to the human misery it produces, there is a great deal of evidence that drug users commit a significant percentage of all crimes. In one study conducted in New York City, heroin users were found to commit an average of 225 crimes per year, including robbery, burglary, fraud, fencing, and shoplifting. The addicts also were involved in 823 drug-related crimes, for a total of 1,048 crimes per year![78] This shocking evidence gives weight to the problem of substance abuse in the United States.

■ SUMMARY

Crime has become a familiar and disturbing fact of life in the United States. When we speak about crime, we refer to a violation of existing societal rules of behavior that are expressed in the criminal code created by those holding political power. Individuals who violate these rules are subject to state sanctions.

Today, information on crime is available from a number of different sources. One of the most important is the Uniform Crime Reports (UCR), compiled by the FBI. This national survey of serious criminal acts reported to local police departments indicates that about 13 million index crimes (murder, rape, burglary, robbery, assault, larceny, motor vehicle theft) occurred in 1987. This figure represents a steady increase in the crime rate, beginning in the mid-1980s.

Critics have questioned the validity of the UCR. They point out that many people fail to report crime to police because of fear, apathy, or lack of respect for law enforcement. In addition, questions have been raised about the accuracy of police records and reporting practices.

To remedy this situation, the federal government has sponsored a massive victim survey designed to uncover the true amount of annual crime. The National Crime Survey (NCS) reveals that about 34 million serious crimes are committed every year and that the great majority are not reported to police. Other forms of justice information include self-report surveys, which ask offenders to tell about their criminal behaviors.

The various sources of criminal statistics provide extensive information about the nature and patterns of crime. Crime appears to be related to demographic conditions as well as to race, sex, age, and socioeconomic status. These patterns, especially the relationship between socioeconomic status and crime, are still the subject of considerable debate, however.

Criminal statistics can also tell us a great deal about other crime patterns including the major forms of crime, such as organized crime, public order offenses, and violence and theft-related offenses.

■ QUESTIONS

1. Why are crime rates higher in the summer than during other periods?

2. Have you been a victim of crime? Did you report it to the police? If not, why?

3. Why would a police department report more serious crimes than actually took place?

4. Would you answer a self-report survey honestly? Do you think such data are valid?

■ NOTES

1. The Harris Survey, cited in Timothy Flanagan and Katherine Jamieson, *Sourcebook of Criminal Justice Statistics—1987* (Washington, D.C.: U.S. Government Printing Office, 1988), p. 123.

2. Howard Becker, *Outsiders*, 2d ed. (New York: Macmillan Co., 1972).

3. For a general discussion of Marxist thought, see Michael Lynch and W. Byron Groves, *A Primer in Radical Criminology* (New York: Harrow and Heston, 1986), pp. 6-26.

4. For an important discussion of how survey techniques are used (and abused) in criminological research, see Travis Hirschi and Hannon Selvin, *Principles of Survey Analysis* (New York: Free Press, 1973); see also Earl Babbie, *Survey Research Methods* (Belmont, Calif.: Wadsworth Publishing Co., 1973).

5. William F. Whyte, *Street Corner Society: The Social Structure of an Italian Slum* (Chicago: University of Chicago Press, 1955); Laud Humphreys, *Tearoom Trade: Impersonal Sex in Public Places*, rev. ed. (Chicago: Aldine Publishing Co., 1975).

6. Carl Klockars, *The Professional Fence* (New York: Free Press, 1976); Darrell Steffensmeir, *The Fence: In the Shadow of Two Worlds* (Totowa, N.J.: Rowman and Littlefield, 1986).

7. See, for example, Harry King and William Chambliss, *Box Man: A Professional Thief's Journey* (New York: Harper & Row, 1972), p. 24.

8. At the time of this writing, the latest volume of the UCR was the Federal Bureau of Investigation's *Crime in the United States, 1987* (Washington, D.C.: U.S. Government Printing Office, 1988). Wherever possible, statistics in this volume will be supplemented by estimates based on data from the 1988 crime survey.

9. Adapted from Federal Bureau of Investigation, *Crime in the United States, 1987*, pp. 2–3.

10. Clarence Schrag, *Crime and Justice: American Style* (Washington, D.C.: U.S. Government Printing Office, 1971), p. 17.

11. Federal Bureau of Investigation, *Crime in the United States, 1987*, p. 43.

12. James Gilbert, *A Cycle of Outrage: America's Reaction to the Juvenile Delinquent in the 1950s* (New York: Oxford University Press, 1986).

13. Michael Gottfredson and Travis Hirschi, "Science, Public Policy and the Career Paradigm," *Criminology* 26 (1988): 37–57.

14. Marcus Felson, "Routine Activities and Crime Prevention in the Developing Metropolis," *Criminology* 25 (1987): 911–31.

15. Daniel Lichter, "Racial Differences in Underemployment in American Cities," *American Journal of Sociology* 93 (1988): 771–92.

16. Robert Sampson and John Wooldredge, "Linking the Micro- and Macro-Level Dimensions of Lifestyle–Routine Activity and Opportunity Models of Predatory Victimization," *Journal of Quantitative Criminology* 3 (1987): 371–93; Judith and Peter Blau, "The Cost of Inequality: Metropolitan Structure and Violent Crime," *American Sociological Review* 47 (1982): 114–29.

17. Eric Wish, *Drug Use Forecasting: New York 1984 to 1986* (Washington, D.C.: National Institute of Justice, 1987).

18. Marcia Chaiken and Bruce Johnson, *Characteristics of Different Types of Drug-Involved Offenders* (Washington, D.C.: National Institute of Justice, 1988).

19. Chaiken and Johnson, *Characteristics of Different Types of Drug-Involved Offenders*, pp. 5–7. See also M. Douglas Anglin, Elizabeth Piper Deschenes, and George Speckart, "The Effect of Legal Supervision on Narcotic Addiction and Criminal Behavior," paper presented at the American Society of Criminology meeting, Montreal, Canada, November 1987.

20. Raymond Paternoster, "Examining Three-Wave Deterrence Models: A Question of Temporal Order and Specification," *Journal of Criminal Law and Criminology* 79 (1988): 135–79. See also Lonn Lanza-Kaduce, "Perceptual Deterrence and Drinking and Driving among College Students," *Criminology* 26 (1988): 321–41; Raymond Paternoster, "The Deterrent Effect of the Perceived Certainty and Severity of Punishment," *Justice Quarterly* 4 (1987): 173–217.

21. The findings in this section are based on 1987 UCR statistics.

22. Freda Adler, *Sisters in Crime* (New York: McGraw-Hill, 1975); Rita James Simon, *The Contemporary Woman and Crime* (Washington, D.C.: U.S. Government Printing Office, 1975).

23. Joseph Weis, "Liberation and Crime: The Invention of the New Female Criminal," *Crime and Social Justice* 1 (1976): 17–27; Steven Box and Chris Hale, "Liberation/Emancipation, Economic Marginalization or Less Chivalry," *Criminology* 22 (1984): 473–78.

24. See, for example, James Comer, "Black Violence and Public Policy," in *American Violence and Public Policy*, Lynn Curtis, ed. (New Haven, Conn.: Yale University Press, 1985).

25. Emilie Andersen Allan and Darrell Steffensmeier, "Youth, Underemployment and Property Crime: Differential Effects of Job Availability and Job Quality on Juvenile and Young Adult Arrest Rates," *American Sociological Review* 54 (1989): 107–23.

26. Michael Hindelang, Travis Hirschi, and Joseph Weis, *Measuring Delinquency* (Beverly Hills, Calif.: Sage Publications, 1981).

27. Colin Loftin and Robert Nash Parker, "An Errors-In-Variable Model of the Effect of Poverty on Urban Homicide Rates," *Criminology* 23 (1985): 269–87.

28. For a general view, see James Byrne and Robert Sampson. *The Social Ecology of Crime* (New York: Springer-Verlag, 1985).

29. Blau, "The Cost of Inequality: Metropolitan Structure and Violent Crime," pp. 114–29.

30. Douglas Smith and G. Roger Jarjoura, "Social Structure and Criminal Victimization," *Journal of Research in Crime and Delinquency* 25 (1988): 27–52; Janet Heitgerd and Robert Bursik, Jr., "Extracommunity Dynamics and the Ecology of Delinquency," *American Journal of Sociology* 92 (1987): 775–87; Ora Simcha-Fagan and Joseph Schwartz, "Neighborhood and Delinquency: An Assessment of Contextual Effects," *Criminology* 24 (1986): 667–703.

31. Rodney Stark, "Deviant Places: A Theory of the Ecology of Crime," *Criminology* 25 (1987): 893–910.

32. Travis Hirschi and Michael Gottfredson, "Age and the Explanation of Crime," *American Journal of Sociology* 89 (1983): 552–84.

33. Herman and Julia Schwendinger, "The Paradigmatic Crisis in Delinquency Theory," *Crime and Social Justice* 18 (1982): 70–78.

34. Michael Gottfredson and Travis Hirschi, "The True Value of Lambda Would Appear to Be Zero: An Essay on Career Criminals, Criminal Careers, Selective Incapacitation, Cohort Studies and Related Topics," *Criminology* 24 (1986): 213–34; further support for their position can be found in Lawrence Cohen and Kenneth Land, "Age Structure and Crime," *American Sociological Review* 52 (1987): 170–83.

35. Arnold Barnett, Alfred Blumstein, and David Farrington, "Probabilistic Models of Youthful Criminal Careers," *Criminology* 25 (1987): 83–107; David Greenberg, "Age, Crime and Social Explanation," *American Journal of Sociology* 91 (1985): 1–21.

36. NCS data come from Flanagan and Jamieson, *Sourcebook of Criminal Justice Statistics—1987*, pp. 131–76.

37. Duncan Chappell, et al., "Forcible Rape: A Comparative Study of Offenses Known to the Police in Boston and Los Angeles," in *Studies in the Sociology of Sex*, James Henslin, ed. (New York: Appleton-Century-Crofts, 1971), pp. 169–93.

38. Lawrence Sherman and Barry Glick, "The Quality of Arrest Statistics," *Police Foundation Reports* 2 (1984): 1–8.

39. Patrick Jackson, "Assessing the Validity of Official Data on Arson," *Criminology* 6 (1988): 181–95.

40. David Seidman and Michael Couzens, "Getting the Crime Rate Down: Political Pressure and Crime Reporting," *Law and Society Review* 8 (1974): 457.

41. Leonard Savitz, "Official Statistics," in *Contemporary Criminology*, L. Savitz and N. Johnston, eds. (New York: John Wiley & Sons, 1982), pp. 3–15.

42. Hindelang, Hirschi, and Weis, *Measuring Delinquency*.

43. Walter Gove, Michael Hughes, Michael Geerken, "Are Uniform Crime Reports a Valid Indicator of the Index Crimes? An Affirmative Answer with Minor Qualifications," *Criminology* 23 (1985): 451–501.

44. John Braithwaite, "The Myth of Social Class and Crime Reconsidered," *American Sociological Review* 46 (1981): 35–58.

45. Scott Decker, David Shichor, and Robert O'Brien, *Urban Structure and Victimization* (Lexington, Mass.: Lexington Books, 1982).

46. U.S. Department of Justice, *The Redesigned UCR Program* (Washington, D.C.: U.S. Department of Justice, N.D.).

47. For example, the following studies have noted the great discrepancy between official statistics and self-report studies: Maynard Erickson and LaMar Empey, "Court Records, Undetected Delinquency, and Decision-making," *Journal of Criminal Law, Criminology, and Police Science* 54 (1963): 456–69; Martin Gold, "Undetected Delinquent Behavior," *Journal of Research in Crime and Delinquency* 3 (1966): 27–46; James Short and F. Ivan Nye, "Extent of Unrecorded Delinquency, Tentative Conclusions," *Journal of Criminal Law, Criminology, and Police Science* 49 (1958): 296–302; David Farrington, "Self-reports of Deviant Behavior: Predictive and Stable?" *Journal of Criminal Law and Criminology* 64 (1973): 99–110.

48. Charles Tittle, Wayne Villemez, and Douglas Smith, "The Myth of Social Class and Criminality: An Empirical Assessment of the Empirical Evidence," *American Sociological Review* 43 (1978): 643–46.

49. Michael Hindelang, Travis Hirschi, and Joseph Weis, "Correlates of Delinquency: The Illusion of Discrepancy between Self-Report and Official Data," *American Sociological Review* 44 (1979): 995–1014. See also John Braithwaite, "The Myth of Social Class and Crime Reconsidered," pp. 35–58; Terence Thornberry and Margaret Farnworth, "Social Correlates of Criminal Involvement: Further Evidence on the Relationship between Social Status and Criminal Behavior," *American Sociological Review* 47 (1982): 505–18.

50. Lloyd Johnston, Patrick O'Malley, and Jerald Bachman, *Drug Use among American High School Students, College Students, and Other Young Adults* (Washington, D.C.: U.S. Department of Health and Human Services, 1988). Updated with press release, 10 March 1989.

51. Philip Ennis, *Criminal Victimization in the United States*, Field Survey 2 (Washington, D.C.: Report on a National Survey by President's Commission on Law Enforcement and Criminal Justice, 1967).

52. Data in these sections come from three Bureau of Justice Statistics reports: *Criminal Victimization 1987* (Washington, D.C.: Bureau of Justice Statistics, 1988); *Households Touched by Crime, 1987* (1988); "Criminal Victimization 1988," preliminary report, 9 April 1989, news release.

53. Ibid.

54. Bureau of Justice Statistics, *Households Touched by Crime, 1987*.

55. Catherine Whitaker, *The Redesigned National Crime Survey: Selected New Data* (Washington, D.C.: Bureau of Justice Statistics, 1989).

56. Lawrence Cohen and Marcus Felson, "Social Change and Crime Rate Trends: A Routine Activities Approach," *American Sociological Review* 44 (1979): 588–608; L. Cohen, James Kleugel, and Kenneth Land, "Social Inequality and Predatory Criminal Victimization: An Exposition and Test of a Formal Theory," *American Sociological Review* 46 (1981): 505–24; Steven Messner and Kenneth Tardiff, "The Social Ecology of Urban Homicide: An Application of the 'Routine Activities' Approach," *Criminology* 23 (1985): 241–67.

57. Kenneth Polk, "Rape Reform and Criminal Justice Processing," *Crime and Delinquency* 31 (1985): 191–206.

58. Comment, "The Rape Shield Paradox: Complainant Protection amidst Oscillating Trends of State Judicial Interpretation," *The Journal of Criminal Law and Criminology* 78 (1987): 644–98.

59. Susan Estrich, *Real Rape* (Cambridge, Mass.: Harvard University Press, 1987), pp. 72–79.

60. Janet Gornick, Martha Burt, and Karen Pittman, "Structure and Activities of Rape Crisis Centers in the Early 1980s," *Crime and Delinquency* 31 (1985): 247–68.

61. Coramae Richey Mann, "Getting Even? Women Who Kill in Domestic Encounters," *Justice Quarterly* 5 (1988): 31–51.

62. Marc Reidel, "Stranger Violence: Perspectives, Issues, and Problems," *The Journal of Criminal Law and Criminology* 78 (1987): 223–58; Margaret Zahn and Philip Sagi, "Stranger Homicides in Nine American Cities," *The Journal of Criminal Law and Criminology* 78 (1987): 337–97. See also Marc Reidel and Margaret Zahn, *The Nature and Pattern of American Homicide* (Washington, D.C.: U.S. Government Printing Office, 1985).

63. Jack Levin and James Alan Fox, *Mass Murder* (New York: Plenum Press, 1985).

64. John Conklin, *Robbery and the Criminal Justice System* (New York: J. B. Lippincott Co., 1972).

65. Richard Gelles and Murray Straus, "Violence in the American Family," *Journal of Social Issues* 35 (1979): 15–39.

66. Diana Russell, *Sexual Abuse* (Beverly Hills, Calif.: Sage Publications, 1985).

67. Patsy Klaus and Michael Rand, *Family Violence* (Washington, D.C.: Bureau of Justice Statistics, 1984).

68. John Gibbs and Peggy Shelly, "Life in the Fast Lane: A Retrospective View by Commercial Theives," *Journal of Research in Crime and Delinquency* 19 (1982): 229–330.

69. Leigh Edward Somers, *Economic Crime* (New York: Clark Boardman, 1984).

70. Tim Metz and Michael Miller, "Boesky's Rise and Fall Illustrate a Compulsion to Profit by Getting Inside Track on Market," *Wall Street Journal*, 17 November 1986.

71. Bill Richards and Alex Kotlowitz, "Judge Finds 3 Corporate Officials Guilty of Murder in Cyanide Death of Worker," *Wall Street Journal*, 17 June 1985, p. 2.

72. Laura Schrager and James Short, "Toward a Sociology of Organizational Crime," *Social Problems* 25 (1978): 415–25.

73. See generally, Jay Albanese, *Organized Crime in America*, 2d ed. (Cincinnati, Ohio: Anderson Publishing, 1989).

74. Alan Block, *East Side/West Side* (New Brunswick, N.J.: Transaction Books, 1983).

75. Albanese, *Organized Crime in America*, p. 167.

76. Pauline Bart, "Pornography: Hating Women and Institutionalizing Dominance and Submission for Fun and Profit: Response to Alexis M. Durham," *Justice Quarterly* 3 (1986): 103–5.

77. Johnston, O'Malley, and Bachman, *Drug Use among American High School Students, College Students, and Other Young Adults*.

78. Bernard Gropper, "Probing the Links between Drugs and Crime," *NIJ Reports* (National Criminal Justice Reference Service, November 1984), pp. 6–7.

3

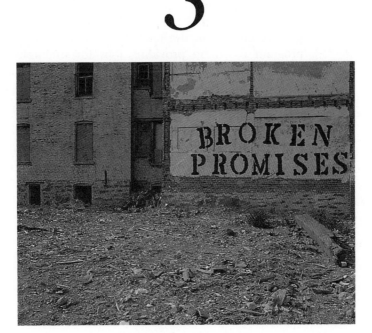

Understanding Crime and Victimization

Part One

The Nature of Crime,
Law and Criminal Justice

72

One of the most important goals of the study of criminal justice is to understand and improve the operations of the justice system. In order to meet this goal, it is necessary to develop an understanding of the nature and causes of crime and victimization. Unless we know why crime occurs, we cannot create effective crime control and prevention programs. We will never be sure that our efforts are aimed at the proper audience, or, if they are, whether they are the programs most likely to cause positive change in the target population. For example, a crime prevention program based on providing jobs for unemployed teenagers will only be effective if a link between crime and unemployment exists. Similarly, a plan to reduce prison violence by reducing the sugar intake of inmates is feasible only if research shows that biochemical factors are actually related to antisocial behavior.

In addition to understanding the nature and causes of criminal behavior, criminal justice policymakers must also study and understand the role of victims in the crime process. Such knowledge is essential for developing strategies to reduce the probability of predatory crime and provide self-help information that people can use to decrease the likelihood that they will become the target of criminals.

■ Theories of Crime Causation

Pinpointing or even suggesting the underlying causes of crime has proven difficult. Early scholars attempted to identify singular factors whose presence or absence would predispose individuals toward criminality. Physical factors, such as body build, and psychological, genetic, social, political, and economic influences were each at one time or another thought to be the single most important cause of crime. Almost unanimously, early crime experts believed that one fundamental factor could be identified as the primary underlying determinant of criminal behavior. Unfortunately, the single controlling cause of criminality has proved as illusory for criminologists as the fountain of youth was for the early explorers. There are too many different, complex individuals committing too many crimes for far too many reasons to allow for a single element to be responsible for them all.

Many competing single-factor theories flourished simultaneously, with each theorist contradicting the others. As soon as one theory of the cause of crime appeared on the scene, it was almost inevitable that another criminologist would refute and replace it. Theoretical models were criticized as too broad or too narrow, overly simplistic or too complex.

Today, the single-factor approach to the cause of crime has been rejected in favor of less dogmatic multiple-cause theories. These models portray individual crime patterns (e.g., lower-class gang delinquency) as products of a variety of independent or related influences. Although the effects of any single factor are not considered sufficient to account for crime as a whole, a number of these individual influences working together are believed to be significant enough to cause criminal behavior. Today, each individual criminal act is seen as a function of a varied number of social, psychological, or environmental factors, with no two sets of factors necessarily being exactly alike.

Unfortunately, multiple-cause theories are beset by some of the same problems that plague single-cause approaches. Regardless of how broad a theory's explanation of criminality is meant to be, critics can always identify some criminal types whose behavior patterns seem to fall outside the theory's suggested framework. Broadening a theory's scope to accommodate these deviant cases often makes it overly complex and burdensome.

In the next sections, the most important theoretical perspectives in criminology are described.

◼ Choice Theory

One prominent view of criminality is that people *choose* to commit crime after weighing both the *benefits and consequences* of their actions. For example, before concluding a drug sale, a dealer will balance the chance of making a large profit with the consequences of being apprehended and punished. If the potential profits are great enough and the chances of apprehension minimal, the crime will be committed. If, however, the dealer believes that the transaction will bring him only a small profit and carries with it a large risk of apprehension and punishment, his enthusiasm for crime will be dampened.

The origins of this rational approach to crime causation developed in the mid-eighteenth century, in what is known today as **classical theory.** The main principles of the classical approach are as follows:

1. All people can choose of their own free will between conventional or criminal behaviors.
2. For some people, criminal solutions are more attractive because they require less effort for greater gain.
3. People will refrain from antisocial acts if they believe that the punishment or pain they will receive for their actions will be greater than any potential gain.
4. The punishments threatened by the existing criminal law are the primary **deterrent** to crime.

According to classical criminology, all people have the potential to engage in criminal activity, but the majority are kept in check by their fear of criminal sanctions. This relationship is controlled by three factors: the severity of punishment, the certainty of punishment, and the celerity (speed) of punishment. For punishment to deter crime, it must be severe enough to outweigh any benefits of law violation. For example, a 30-year prison sentence should deter potential bank robbers, regardless of the amount of money kept in the bank's vault. No matter how severely the law punishes a criminal act, however, it will have little deterrent effect if potential law violators believe they have hardly any chance of being caught or that the wheels of justice are slow and inefficient. Consequently, punishment must be fast, certain, and severe if it is to be effective.

The principles of classical theory were first set down by the moral philosophers Cesare Beccaria and Jeremy Bentham, who opposed the uniformly harsh punishments of the eighteenth century. They argued that, to be effective, punishment need only be sufficient to deter crime.[1] Excessive force and punishment might actually increase the chances that people would commit serious crimes, since after their first offenses they would have nothing more to lose. In a famous statement on the matter, Beccaria said:

> In order for punishment not to be in every instance an act of violence of one or many against a private citizen, it must be essentially public, prompt, necessary, the least possible in the given circumstances, proportionate to the crimes, dictated by the laws.[2]

Beccaria's principles of justice have continued to influence criminological thinking for two hundred years.

Rational Choice and Routine Activities

Though classical theory was formulated in the eighteenth century, it is still a powerful influence on both criminological theory and criminal justice policy. In recent years classical principles have been reformulated by a number of modern criminological thinkers. For example, Lawrence Cohen and Marcus Felson's routine activities theory holds that crime rates are the product of three elements: motivated offenders (such as teenagers who are looking for marketable merchandise); suitable targets (goods that have value and can be easily transported); and absence of capable guardians (such as police and security forces or even adults who guard a home).[3] According to this approach, crime rates are a function of both conventional, everyday behavior and criminal motivation. For example, if family incomes increase because more women are employed in the work force, and consequently the average family is able to afford more luxury goods such as televisions and VCRs, we might expect a comparable increase in the crime rate because the number of suitable targets has expanded while the number of capable guardians left to protect the home has been reduced. People who engage in such routine behaviors as consuming large amounts of alcohol or spending weekend nights away from home help make themselves "crime-prone."[4]

The concept that crime is a function of the choices made by motivated criminals has received additional support from such prominent social scientists as Philip Cook, Ronald Clarke, and Derek Cornish.[5] They argue that law-violating behavior should be viewed as events that occur when offenders decide to take the chance of violating the law after considering their own personal situation (need for money, personal values, learning experiences, and so on) and situational factors (how well the target is protected, whether people are at home, how wealthy the neighborhood is). Accordingly, entry into a criminal lifestyle and the decision to commit a specific type of crime are matters of personal decision making, based on a weighing of available information.

Lawrence Cohen and Richard Machalek have conceptualized the decision to commit crime as a matter of devising strategies to get ahead by beating the system. For example, the decision to sell drugs may be based on the observation that "dealing" is an easier and safer way of making extra money than working overtime at the plant or getting a part-time job.[6] Life circumstances may influence the probability that an individual will "choose crime." If resources are lacking, the choice is motivated by survival instincts. Even if resources such as wealth and education are available, criminal solutions may still be chosen because the individuals believe they can (1) "get away with murder" because of their social standing or (2) use their position to take advantage of an unusual opportunity, e.g., insider trading on the stock market. Conversely, the decision to forgo crime may not be based on the fear of apprehension and punishment, but on the perception that economic benefits can be gained by legal strategies.[7]

Principles of Choice Theory

If crime is a matter of choice, it follows that it can be controlled by convincing criminals that breaking the law is indeed a bad or dangerous choice to make.

This central premise has suggested a number of crime control policies to those who embrace choice theory. Crime control policy and choice theory are so tightly linked that it is often hard to separate the principles of the theory from its suggested practices. In the next sections the most important principles/policies of choice theory are discussed in some detail.

GENERAL DETERRENCE. Choice theories suggest that if people believe that they are certain to be apprehended by the police, quickly tried, and severely penalized, they will most likely forgo any thought of breaking the law.[8] In other words, people will not choose crime if they fear legal punishment. This principle is referred to as **general deterrence.**

If the justice system could be made more effective, those who care little for the rights of others would be deterred by fear of the law's sanctioning power.[9] "What the laws prohibit because disadvantageous to society can be advantageous to some individuals; or they may think it is," argues Ernest Van Den Haag. "Society must try to make prohibited acts clearly disadvantageous to all if its laws are to be heeded."[10] Van Den Haag argues that even if every criminal were incarcerated or successfully rehabilitated, the crime problem would not be halted; new criminals would simply take their place. Only by reducing the benefits of crime through sure, swift, and certain punishment can society be sure that a group of new criminals will not emerge to replace the ones who have already been dealt with.[11]

In some instances the law's deterrent power can be focused on total elimination of an act. For example, narcotics control laws are designed to eliminate illegal sale and use of such drugs as heroin and cocaine; this is known as **absolute deterrence.** In contrast, lawmakers may simply wish to control or limit a behavior. Laws restricting alcohol use are designed to limit consumption to adults but not ban the sale of alcoholic beverages outright; this is called **partial deterrence.**

Criminologists also recognize that some crimes may be more susceptible to deterrence than others. William Chambliss distinguishes between expressive and instrumental crimes.[12] **Expressive crimes** are generated by some personal, inner need of the offender (for example, killing someone in a fight). **Instrumental crimes** are designed to bring a reward or goal that may then be used for another purpose (for example, drug sales, burglary, or theft). It is generally believed that instrumental crimes are a better target for deterrence than expressive crimes because they are motivated by the desire for material gain, which can be more easily offset by "costly" punishments.

The general deterrence concept has had an increasingly important influence on criminal justice policy making. Fear of crime, coupled with the increasingly conservative views of the nation's lawmakers, has led to the development of mandatory prison sentences that guarantee that convicted offenders will spend time behind bars. Furthermore, capital punishment is now employed in most states, and over 3,000 people are currently on "death row."

IS DETERRENCE EFFECTIVE? Despite its impact, research on deterrence has provided little hard evidence that deterrent measures can actually achieve their desired effect. With few exceptions, studies examining the relationship between sanctions and crime rates have failed to generate data sufficient to demonstrate that increasing penalties will always decrease criminal behaviors.[13] Similarly, studies measuring people's perceptions of the consequences of criminal acts have failed to prove that fear of the law can itself deter crime.[14] In fact, a number of research efforts seem to show that fear of informal sanctions, such as parental and peer disapproval, are more important deterrents than fear of the law; this suggests that socialization and upbringing and not the threat of legal punishment are the key to crime control.[15] Although there is some indication that increases in criminal penalties are related to lower crime rates, the relationship is far from perfect, and research in the area has been criticized for using unsound methods.[16]

What factors inhibit the deterrent power of the criminal law? For one thing, the efficiency of the justice system is highly suspect, which significantly affects the certainty of punishment. According to the UCR only about 20 percent of serious reported crimes result in an arrest.[17] If white-collar or public-order crimes are considered, the chance of apprehension is even smaller. There is reason to believe that people who engage in repeated criminal activity are well acquainted with these facts and consequently believe that the certainty of punishment, a key element in deterrence, is low.

Similarly, the elaborate arrray of legal rights guaranteed to people accused of crime reduces the efficiency of the legal system and helps weaken any direct link between crime and punishment. Furthermore, to increase efficiency, most local prosecutors engage in plea bargaining—reducing charges in exchange for an offender's plea of guilty. Plea bargaining and other legal maneuvers help limit the deterrent power of the criminal law.

Finally, the concept of general deterrence assumes rationality on the part of offenders—that they carefully weigh and balance the pains and benefits of the criminal act. But there is some question whether potential offenders actually engage in such a thoughtful analysis of the dangers associated with law violation. Studies of arrestees show that a significant majority were under the influence of drugs or alcohol at the time of their detention, and surveys of incarcerated inmates find that more one-third report being intoxicated before committing the crime for which they were convicted and 25 percent reported drinking heavily each day during the year preceding their crimes.[18] It is likely that many offenders are physically or mentally incapable of having the rational thought patterns that the theory of general deterrence demands.

INCAPACITATION. Incapacitation refers to the belief that dangerous criminal offenders should be locked away for long periods of time. If crime is a matter of choice, it follows that (1) people will not choose to commit crime if they face long periods of incapacitation and (2) incapacitated criminals are in no position to choose to prey on the public. At the heart of the incapacitation concept is the belief that relatively few people commit a great number of criminal offenses and that if they are put out of circulation, their absence will have a significant impact on the crime rate.[19] The overall purpose of incapacitation is to protect the law-abiding members of society by limiting the activities and freedom of known criminals.

Although the concept of incapacitation seems to have inherent logic, there is actually little evidence that putting large numbers of convicted criminals in prison can lower the crime rate.[20] Consider a case in point: crime rates increased from 1985 to 1988, the same period in which judges were putting record numbers of convicted offenders behind bars. How can this puzzling phenomenon be explained? One reason may be that the economic benefits of crime actually increase as more criminals are incarcerated. Gary Becker has shown that people will commit crime when they perceive it will benefit them economically.[21] Even if all currently active criminals were incarcerated, equal numbers of new offenders would take their place in order to take advantage of the wide open criminal opportunities.[22] It would be the same as having all the video stores in your neighborhood suddenly go out of business. Since people still want to rent videos and will now be willing to pay a premium for them, renters can get top dollar; it might pay for you to quit school and go into the video business yourself. By analogy, if every drug dealer were put in prison, the price of drugs would skyrocket, and people would be encouraged to get into drug dealing.

Another flaw in the logic of incapacitation as a crime control mechanism is the high recidivism (repeat offense) rate of convicted offenders. One recent study of young parolees, aged 17 to 22, found that 69 percent were rearrested within six years of their release from prison; 53 percent were convicted for a new offense; and 49 percent were returned to prison.[23] Putting people in prison may encourage or expand the incidence of their criminal behavior once they are released. Regardless of its benefit, incapacitation has become an established social policy—upward of 600,000 people are currently incarcerated in the nation's prisons.

SPECIFIC DETERRENCE. If crime is a matter of choice, then it should follow that if punishment were severe enough, convicted criminals would never dare repeat their offense. This view is known as **specific deterrence.** Prior to the twentieth century, specific deterrence was a motive for the extremely harsh tortures and physical punishments commonly inflicted on convicted criminals. By physically breaking the convicts' spirit, legal authorities hoped to control their behavior.[24]

Although our more enlightened society no longer uses such "cruel and unusual punishments," we do employ long prison sentences in dangerous and forbidding prisons as a substitute. Yet such measures do not seem to deliver the promise of crime control. Research indicates that a majority of inmates repeat their criminal acts soon after returning to society and that most incarcerated inmates had previously served time.[25]

Why have our efforts to use legal punishments such as prison failed to convince offenders not to repeat their criminal acts? The liberal explanation is that our current system of justice appears inconsistent and arbitrary, creating a sense of injustice in the inmate population; punishment may increase rather than diminish the offender's motivation to commit crime. Nor would it be wise to increase legal sanctions sufficiently to control crime: Who would want to live in a society in which punishments are so brutal that fear of them is sufficient to control crime?

The conservative view is that our system of punishment is currently too lenient to support specific deterrence. Defendants often plea bargain for a reduced sentence, including probation for felony offenses; those sent to prison rarely serve their entire sentence before being granted parole or some other early release mechanism.[26] Rather than producing a specific deterrent effect, the correctional process enhances it by reducing both the certainty and severity of punishment.

It is also possible that the failure of the legal system to attack the root causes of crime, whether they be political, economic, social, psychological, or physical, is responsible for the failure of specific deterrence. Recidivism is high because the original motives to commit crime remain after a penal sentence is served.

Choice Theory and Criminal Justice Policy

In recent years, choice theory has had considerable impact on criminal justice policy. It has been used to justify the "get tough" law and order approach to crime control that was predominant in the 1980s and continues into the 1990s. Concepts such as deterrence and incapacitation have been the cornerstone of federal and state criminal code revision. They have resulted in the adoption of such policies as the resumption of the use of the death penalty, the development of mandatory prison sentences for certain crimes, such as those involving handguns, and legislation designed to allow state jurisdictions to act more firmly with serious delinquent youths. In addition, choice theory principles influence the day-to-day operations of justice system agencies. Police have employed strategies such as arresting abusive husbands in domestic violence cases on the grounds that such formal action (arrest) can have a specific deterrent effect.[27]

Another vivid example of the influence of choice theory on criminal justice policy is the efforts being made to toughen penalties for repeat offenders. Since Marvin Wolfgang first identified the chronic offender in his 1972 cohort study,[28] it has been commonplace for law enforcement agencies to devise task forces to locate and apprehend them and for state legislative bodies to enact sentencing laws that provide long prison sentences for recidivists. Harsh penalties are believed to be the best way to keep repeaters incarcerated and protect the general public.

Although a get tough policy designed to control chronic recidivists may seem attractive to conservative policymakers, it is not without costs. The nation's prison system is now filled to capacity, and active incarceration policy would merely strain it further.[29] One approach is to restrict severe punishments to the most serious repeat offenders.[30]

■ Trait Theory

As the twentieth century began, some criminologists postulated that crime was caused not so much by human choice but by human **traits:** intelligence, body build, size and shape, mental state, and so on. Those holding such views were known as **positivists**—scientists who believe that human behavior is controlled by physical, mental, and social processes and interactions. Positivists argue that all behavior is *determined* by who we are and the world we live in.

The origins of this view of crime causation are found in the biophysical theories of Cesare Lombroso (1835–1909). Lombroso, an Italian army physician fascinated by human anatomy, became interested in learning what motivated criminals to commit crimes. He physically examined hundreds of prison inmates and other criminals in order to discover any similarities between them. On the basis of his research, Lombroso proposed that criminals manifest **atavistic** or **degenerate anomalies;** in other words, the active criminal is a physical and biological throwback to early stages of human evolution who adjusts poorly to modern society and is thrust into criminal activities. Careful physical measurement of hundreds of convicted criminals led Lombroso to catalog attributes that denoted criminality: an asymmetric face or excessive jaw, eye defects, large eyes, a receding forehead, prominent cheekbones, long arms, a twisted nose, and swollen lips.[31]

With Lombroso's work as their focal point, a number of other early criminologists continued to search for a biological basis for crime. Raffaele

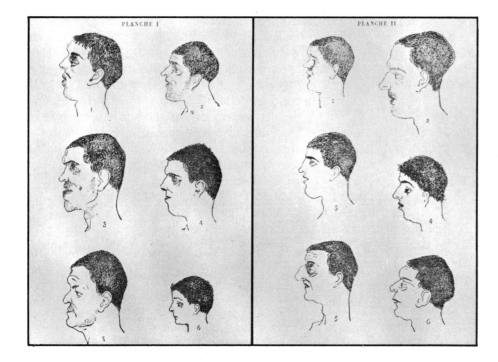

These drawings by Cesare Lombroso, a nineteenth-century Italian criminologist, were used to illustrate his theory that criminals are a special subgroup within the human race who can be distinguished by their physical and psychological characteristics. According to Lombroso, these "criminal types" are born with a propensity toward criminal behavior and should therefore receive different punishment from a person who is forced into crime by adverse circumstances.

Garofalo (1851–1934) found that criminals lacked compassion for others, a condition he attributed to organic problems and inherited instincts.[32] Similarly, Enrico Ferri (1856–1929) attempted to identify the biological, social, and organic factors associated with crime and delinquency.[33] As late as 1939, Ernest Hooton argued that criminals suffered from biological and social inferiority.[34] Another early branch of biological criminology, inheritance theory, focused on the family trees of criminal offenders and attempted to show that a propensity for crime was an inherited characteristic passed down from one generation to the next.[35] Today, trait theory can be separated into biological and psychological branches.

■ Biological Theory

Biological theories of crime causation fell out of favor in the mid-twentieth century when their methodologies were questioned and their assumptions challenged. A majority of criminologists embraced sociological or psychological explanations of crime (discussed in the following sections). However, with the publication of Edward O. Wilson's book *Sociobiology: The New Synthesis* in 1975,[36] interest was renewed in linking biological explanations to human social behavior. Sociobiology differs from earlier theories of behavior in that it focuses on an evolutionary explanation of human behavior. It assumes that social behavior has evolved as part of a genetic adaptation. For example, sociobiology maintains that the dominant members of each species will be the most likely to survive, and therefore the need to dominate others is bred into the human species. Sociobiology also stresses that biological and genetic conditions affect perception and learning of social behavior, which in turn are linked to existing environmental structures.

Chapter 3

Understanding Crime and Victimization

■

The popularity of sociobiology spurred a number of criminologists to look once again at the biological underpinnings of crime. For the most part, their efforts have involved explaining violence. It is believed that three elements of a person's biological makeup are responsible for aggressive antisocial behavior: biochemical, neurological, and genetic factors.[37] But biocriminologists hold that no one factor absolutely controls behavior and that a deficiency in one area may be compensated for by increased efforts in another. For example, a youth with a learning deficiency can be given special corrective care to compensate for the learning problems, or a youth whose violent acts can be attributed to a chemical imbalance may be put on medication (or even vitamins) to correct biological deficiencies.

Today biocriminologists are attempting to link physical traits with tendencies toward violence, aggression, and other antisocial behavior. Their work, which is still in the early stages of development, can be categorized in three broad categories: biochemical factors, neurological studies, and genetic influence.

Biochemical Factors

One major area of modern biocriminology involves identifying the influence of biochemical factors on behavior. Areas of concern include diet, environmental contaminants, and allergies.[38] Some research efforts have linked vitamin and mineral deficiencies to antisocial behavior. Research focusing on the behavior of jailed inmates has shown that subjects who maintain high levels of sugar and caffeine in their diet are more likely to engage in antisocial behavior than control-group subjects.[39] A number of research efforts have concluded that hypoglycemia, a lack of blood sugar, may contribute to outbursts of antisocial behavior and violence.[40] Similarly, allergic reactions to such common foods as milk, chocolate, and corn have been associated with hyperactivity and aggression in children.[41]

Neurological Studies

Another area of interest to biocriminologists is the relationship of brain activity to behavior. It is believed that people with minimum brain dysfunction (an abnormal cerebral structure) may experience periods of explosive rage.[42] Research has shown that learning-disabled children are more likely to become involved with the juvenile court than non-learning-disabled youths, though the link between learning disabilities and crime has been the subject of debate.[43]

Biocriminologists have also used the electroencephalogram (EEG) to record the electrical impulses given off by the brain. Preliminary studies indicate that whereas 5 to 15 percent of non-law-violating youths have abnormal EEG ratings, 50 to 60 percent of those with behavior disorders display abnormal recordings.[44] Studies of problem children have found that almost half have abnormal EEG ratings; studies using adult subjects have found that abnormal EEG patterns are associated with hostile, nonconforming, and impulsive behavior.[45] Tests of convicted murderers show that a disproportionate number manifest abnormal EEG ratings.[46]

Violent behavior has also been linked to brain tumors, brain injuries, and other central nervous system diseases.

Genetic Factors

Although the earliest biological studies of crime tried and failed to discover a genetic basis for criminality, modern biocriminologists are still concerned with the role heredity plays in producing crime-prone people. Interest in this area was spurred in the late 1960s when Richard Speck, convicted killer of eight nurses in Chicago, was found to have an abnormal chromosome structure. He carried an extra male sex chromosome, a condition known as the **47XYY syndrome.** However, a great deal of research in this area has produced little evidence that 47XYY males are more dangerous than those with the normal 46 XY configuration.[47]

More recent research efforts have focused on the behavior of twins. If inherited traits are related to criminality, one would expect that twins would be similar in their antisocial activities. Since most twins are brought up together, however, it is difficult to determine whether behavior is a function of environmental influences or genetic influences. To overcome this dilemma, biocriminologists usually compare identical MX (monozygotic) twins with fraternal DZ (dizygotic) twins of the same sex. Since MZ twins are genetically identical, their behavior would be expected to be more similar than that of DZ twins. Preliminary studies have shown that the criminal behavior of MZ twin pairs is indeed more similar than that of DZ pairs. For example, Karl Christiansen studied the criminal behavior patterns of 3,586 male twin pairs and found a 52 percent similarity between MZ twins and only a 22 percent similarity between DZ twins.[48] A more recent evaluation of twin behavior by David Rowe found that the criminality of youths was better explained by their shared genetic makeup than by social or environmental variables.[49]

Another approach has been to evaluate the behavior of adopted children. If a child's criminal behavior is more similar to that of his or her biological parents than that of the adopted parents, it would be strong evidence to support a genetic basis for crime. Preliminary studies conducted in Europe have indicated that the criminality of the biological father is a strong predictor of a child's law-violating behavior.[50] Moreover, when both sets of parents exhibit criminality, the probability that the youth will engage in crime greatly increases.

■ Psychological Views

The view that criminals may be suffering from psychological abnormality or stress has also had a long history and is experiencing current popularity. One of the earliest advocates of psychological theory, Henry Maudsley (1835–1918), a British psychologist, believed that criminals were **morally insane** and that moral insanity was an inherited quality; his theoretical statements implied that criminals are "born and not made."[51] According to Maudsley, crime was a way for the criminal to express or alleviate pathological urges inherited from mentally or morally deficient ancestors.[52]

Today, psychological views of crime can be divided into four significant areas of study, described below.

Psychoanalytic Theory

Psychoanalysis, the creation of Viennese doctor Sigmund Freud (1856–1939), still holds a dominant position in psychological thought.[53] Freud believed the human personality is divided into three areas that make up the unconscious part of the mind. The *id* is the primitive aspect of personality that is present at birth; it demands instant gratification (known as the *pleasure principle*). The *ego* develops when the infant learns that its wishes cannot always be gratified and that it must cope with the practical and conventional standards of society; the ego operates on the *reality principle*. The *superego* incorporates the moral standards and values of parents and others; it forms our *conscience*. Freud also postulated the existence of two basic instinctual human drives present at birth, sex and aggression, which are normally repressed into unconsciousness and channeled into productive modes of behavior—career motivation, artistic endeavors, and so on.

According to Freud and his followers, some people encounter problems during their early development that cause an imbalance in their personality to develop. *Neurotics* are people who are extremely anxious and fear that repressed unacceptable impulses may break through and control their behavior. **Psychotics** are people whose primitive id functions actually control their personality. One type of psychosis is **schizophrenia,** a condition marked by incoherent thought processes, lack of insight, hallucinations, feelings of persecution, and so on.

A number of prominent psychoanalysts believe that many law violators may suffer from some sort of personality disorder. They may have damaged egos or superegos that make them powerless to control their primitive impulses and urges. They may suffer delusions and feel persecuted, worthless, and alienated.[54] David Berkowitz, known as the "Son of Sam," and John Hinckley, Jr., who attempted to assassinate President Reagan, are examples of people suffering from severe character disorders. However, even nonviolent criminals may be motivated by a lack of insight and control caused by personality disorders.[55] As a result, they seek immediate gratification of their needs without consideration of right and wrong or the needs of others. However, there is little clear-cut evidence that mentally ill people are any more criminal than the rest of us. Studies focusing on the personality traits of known criminals and the criminal activity of known mental patients have failed to establish a clear link between crime and psychiatrically diagnosed problems.[56]

Behavioral Theory

A second branch of psychological theory believes behavior is learned through interactions with others. Simply put, behavior that is rewarded becomes habitual; behavior that is punished disappears. One branch of behaviorism of particular relevance to criminology is called **social learning theory.** According to social learning theorists, such as Albert Bandura, people learn to act aggressively as children when they model their behavior after the violent acts of adults.[57] Later in life, these violent behavior patterns persist in social relationships.

Social learning theorists conclude that the antisocial behavior of potentially violent people can be triggered by a number of different influences: verbal taunts and threats; the experience of direct pain; and perceptions of relative social disability, such as poverty and racial discrimination. Those who have learned violence and have seen it rewarded are more likely to react violently under these stimuli than those who have not.

One area of particular interest to social learning theorists is whether the media can influence violence. Studies have shown that youths exposed to aggressive, antisocial behavior on television and in the movies are likely to copy that violent behavior. Laboratory studies generally conclude that direct viewing of violence on television can lead to aggressive behavior by children and teenagers who watch such programs.[58] Whether the evidence obtained in controlled laboratory studies can be applied to the "real world" is still an issue of debate. A number of studies, including nationally publicized research conducted by Richard Kania, have found little evidence of a link between the amount of violence depicted on television and crime rates.[59] Although Kania's research seems to indicate that there has been an association between the frequency of violent crime shows and the crime rate during certain periods (1962–1974, for example), the relationship is absent during other periods. Considering that the average child watches more than 20 hours of television a week, more research is needed on this crucial issue.

Other areas of concern include whether abused children grow up to be violent and abusive themselves and whether reading pornography laced with violence can cause some people to be violent toward women.

Cognitive Theory

Cognitive psychologists are concerned with the way people perceive and mentally represent the world they live in. Some cognitive psychologists focus on information processing; that is, how people process and store information. They view the operation as analogous to the way computers function as information processors. Another prominent area of cognitive psychology is **moral (or intellectual) development theory.** According to this approach, people go through a series of moral stages beginning early in childhood and continuing through their adult years.[60] Each stage is marked by a different view of right and wrong. For example, a child may do what is right simply to avoid punishment and censure. Later in life, the same person will develop a sensitivity to others' needs and do "what is right" to avoid hurting others. On reaching a higher level of moral maturity, the same person may behave in accordance with his or her perception of universal principles of justice, equality, and fairness.

According to one pioneering developmental psychologist Lawrence Kohlberg, criminals may be significantly lower in their moral judgment than noncriminals of the same social background.[61] Whereas a majority of criminals report that their outlooks are characterized by self-interest, those who engage in conventional behavior are more likely to consider the rights of others and are concerned with maintaining the rules of society. Kohlberg and his associates linked criminality to impaired moral development.

Another cognitive view is that aggressive people actually base their behavior on faulty information processing. They perceive other people as more aggressive than they actually are and are consequently more likely to be vigilant, on edge, or suspicious. When they attack victims, they may believe they are actually defending themselves even though they are simply misreading the situation.[62]

Physiological Theory

Physiological or biopsychologists search for relationships between physical properties such as brain cell activity or biochemical reactions, mental processes, and behavior. In many respects their work is similar to that of the biocriminologists discussed earlier.

One area of physiological psychology that is of particular interest to criminology is the identification of the **psychopathic** (or **sociopathic**) personality. Psychopaths are believed to be dangerous, aggressive, antisocial individuals who act in a callous manner. They neither learn from their mistakes nor are deterred by punishments.[63] Although they may appear charming and have at least average intelligence, psychopaths lack emotional depth, are incapable of caring for others, and maintain an abnormally low level of anxiety. The concept of the psychopathic personality is important for criminology because it has been estimated that between 10 and 30 percent of all prison inmates can be classified as psychopaths or sociopaths or have similar character disorders.[64] Psychopathy has also been linked to the phenomenon of serial murderers—people who roam a city or even the entire nation killing at random.[65]

Some psychologists suspect that psychopathy is a function of physical abnormality, especially the activity of the autonomic nervous system (ANS). The ANS mediates activities associated with emotions, such as heartbeat, blood pressure, muscle tension, and respiration. Studies measuring the physical makeup of clinically diagnosed psychopaths indicate that such persons react differently to pain and have lower arousal levels to noise and environmental stimuli than control subjects. Researchers have also found that clinically defined psychopaths who have had their levels of arousal increased through injections of the hormone adrenalin begin to respond as normal subjects do. It is possible that psychopaths are thrill seekers who engage in high-risk, antisocial activities to raise their general neurological level to a more optimal rate.[66] Another view, advanced by psychiatrists Samuel Yochelson and Stanton Samenow, is that the psychopathic personality is imprinted at birth and is relatively unaffected by socialization.[67]

Trait Theory and Justice Policy

Biological and psychological explanations of some crimes—specifically irrational, violent, and antisocial criminal acts—have recently received increased attention. Most research efforts, however, have suffered from inadequate scientific methodology and nonrepresentative sampling. Modern trait theory is still in its infancy. One reviewer has noted:

> These new approaches to the theoretical understanding of criminal behavior may be little more than a momentary flicker from the dying embers of Lombrosian criminology. Or, they may be the kindling out of which some fundamental changes will gradually arise to engulf the behavioral sciences. . . . I suspect the latter.[68]

There have been some well-publicized attempts to use biological and psychological approaches in the treatment of criminal offenders. For example, a number of prisons and jails have instituted programs to change the diet of inmates in order to reduce levels of antisocial behavior. In another well-known program the state of Texas provides plastic surgery for inmates who suffer from physical problems that are believed to contribute to their antisocial behavior. About 150 prisoners are treated each year in an effort to correct physical conditions such as facial deformities that may have led them to retaliate against society.[69] Similarly, correctional administrators have begun to adjust the diet of inmates with an idea of controlling their biochemical intake.[70]

Judges almost always order that offenders who seem to be manifesting personality problems be given a psychological evaluation by local social service agencies, which may or may not be part of the criminal justice system. The evaluation may come right after arrest or at some time during the trial or sentencing stages. Almost all people sent to prison are evaluated at classification centers in order to assess the dimension of their personality. Thereafter psychological treatment of various types becomes a routine part of their correctional rehabilitation.

The fact that criminal justice agencies are willing to spend time and money treating offenders for psychological problems and assessing their diet and other biological needs suggests that policymakers are willing to acknowledge that personal traits can be a contributing cause of criminality.

■ Sociological Theories of Crime

Official, self-report, and victim data all indicate that there is a relationship between the crime rate and social factors, such as sex, income, race, age, domicile, and lifestyle. Thus, it would appear that social forces influence criminality. Because of this apparent relationship, sociological explanations of crime have predominated since the 1930s.

Sociological criminology can be said to have originated in the works of early European social thinkers such as Aldophe Quetelet (1796–1874) and, later, Émile Durkheim (1858–1917). Quetelet, supported by statistics gathered in France and Belgium, discovered that many personal phenomena such as marriage, divorce, suicide, birth, and crime were influenced by social circumstances and that the study of crime in the mass (i.e., criminal statistics) could lead to the development of social laws to explain the occurrence of crime.[71]

Durkheim also viewed crime as a social phenomenon.[72] In his formulation of the theory of anomie and his analysis of the division of labor, Durkheim concluded that crime is an essential part of society and a function of its internal conflict. As he used the term, **anomie** means the absence or weakness of rules and social norms in any person or group; the lack of these rules or norms may lead an individual to lose the ability to distinguish between right and wrong.

As the field of sociological criminology emerged in the twentieth century, greater emphasis began to be placed on environmental conditions, while the relationship between crime and physical and/or mental traits was neglected. Equating the cause of criminal behavior with socially derived pressures or other societal factors was instrumental in the development of treatment-oriented crime prevention techniques. For if criminals are, in fact, "made and not born"—if they are forged in the crucible of societal action—then it logically follows that crime can be eradicated by the treatment and eventual elimination of the responsible social elements. Consequently, the focus of crime prevention shifted from the individual to the social forces causing criminal behavior.

We now turn to some of the most important criminological theories that have a sociological basis.

■ Social Structure Theory

Social structure theories maintain that crime is a function of a person's place in the social structure. According to this view the United States is a *stratified society*. Social strata are created by the unequal distribution of wealth, power, and prestige. Social classes are segments of the population whose members have relatively similar attitudes, values, and norms, and share an identifiable

Unemployment and Crime

The social structure approach indicates that there is a strong relationship between poverty and crime. It follows then that the crime rate will increase during times of high unemployment. The following reading by Richard McGahey discusses the relationship between jobs and crime.

In discussing the relationships between crime and economic distress, it is important to be specific about the type of crime, the type of potential crime, and the specifics of any policy aimed at reducing crime. There has been a substantial amount of research on the relation between unemployment and crime. Some of it analyzes statistics on national crime rates and the business cycle. Some of it focuses on the effects of experiments in which employment opportunities are made available to offenders or ex-prisoners. All of this research provides important sources of information about the relationship between economic conditions and crime; none of it is definitive.

1. *Aggregate studies.* Many studies on crime and the economy have examined aggregate national crime rates and economic indicators such as the unemployment rate. Scholars looking for consistent and reliable connections or correlations between such rates use a variety of complex statistical techniques. Unfortunately, the results are ambiguous. Some researchers find consistent relations between economic distress and crime, but many others have been unable to confirm such findings. Studies vary in the type of data they use, the time periods and geographic areas studied, and the statistical techniques they employ, which makes it hard to compare their findings. But the lack of consistent confirmation of even general trends has caused many scholars to be skeptical about an automatic relationship between economic distress and criminality.

2. *Experimental programs.* A second source of information comes from evaluations of programs that have been organized primarily for the purpose of studying the relations between crime and unemployment. In such programs various target groups, such as ex-offenders, unemployed youth, single parents on welfare, and ex-addicts, are given job experience, training, and support services such as counseling. To make the findings of the studies more reliable, some people are assigned randomly to the program, while others continue their regular street life. The experiences of the two groups are then compared to see if the program has had any discernible effect.

One major federal program, the "supported work" program of the Manpower Development Research Corporation, had disappointing results in terms of reducing crime for ex-offenders and unemployed youth, and

lifestyle. In U.S. society it is possible to identify an upper, middle, and lower class, with a broad range of economic variations existing within each group.

The contrast between the lifestyles of the wealthiest members of the upper class and the poorest segment of the lower class is striking. A recent study found that the number of families living in poverty doubled between 1978 and 1988. The research also found that there are approximately 20 million high school dropouts and graduates under the age of 25 who face dead-end jobs, unemployment, and social failure.[73] Because of their meager economic resources, lower-class citizens are often forced to live in slum areas beset by substandard housing, inadequate health care, poor educational opportunities, underemployment, and despair. Many families are fatherless and husbandless, headed by a female who is the sole breadwinner and who is often forced to go on welfare and receive ADC (Aid to Dependent Children).

The problems of lower-class culture are particularly acute for racial and ethnic minorities. Black citizens have an income level significantly lower than that of whites and an unemployment rate almost twice as high. This crushing economic burden results in the development of stable slum areas, which are

some success with the ex-addict group. Other programs have had similar disappointing results, with the exception of the Job Corps, a program for disadvantaged youth that seems to have reduced crime among its participants. But, as with the aggregate studies, the overall research results have been inconsistent and hard to interpret.

3. *Studies of individuals.* These studies are another source of information and have been of two types: statistical studies of ex-offenders, arrestees, and inner city youth; and "ethnographic" field studies, conducted by urban anthropologists, of small groups of "high risk" youth.

The statistical studies do not point to any consistent relationship between unemployment and crime. For certain types of offenders, especially older ones, there may be a direct relationship between crime and unemployment. Inner city youth who have high expectations about potential income from crime report more criminality than those who do not. The ethnographic studies, while not statistical in nature, provide rich detail about the lives of young people in urban areas, and they show a variety of relationships between unemployment and crime.

Part of the problem in trying to link crime and unemployment is that each is a very complicated subject. Many factors besides the economy can influence crime. Crime patterns may be tied to deterrence from police, courts, and prisons; to differences in families and neighborhoods; and to other unobserved factors. Economic conditions, in turn, are influenced by relationships among international competition, government policy, and personal and structural factors. Sorting out the effects of these many factors is extremely difficult.

4. *Research: a summary.* Any broad assertion about *the* relationship between economic distress and crime is likely to be misleading. A critical observer asks which types of crime are at issue. What are the specific effects being proposed and how would they work? What other unobserved factors might cause the same effects? Does the alleged relationship make sense in light of other information that is available?

This may help clarify . . . the question, "Is there any connection between general economic conditions and the crime rate?" . . . Some analysts claim that the economy has a consistent, measurable impact on crime; for every percentage point rise in unemployment, crime goes up by some stated percentage.

Such broad claims are not well supported by the findings of empirical research. However, there is . . . evidence that certain types of crime, notably robbery and burglary, appear to increase during recessions and economic slumps. . . . While economic downturns may have no impact on many crimes—murder, for instance—they may have an influence on the number of burglaries and robberies. Although these findings are tentative, they are based on research that specifies the type of crime in question and provides a focused explanation. Since robbery and burglary are income-oriented crimes, it is plausible that such crimes would be influenced by economic conditions. ■

SOURCE: Adapted from Richard McGahey, *Jobs and Crime* (Washington, D.C.: National Institute of Justice, 1988).

the scene of what Oscar Lewis has described as a **culture of poverty.**[74] This lifestyle contains elements of apathy, cynicism, helplessness, and mistrust. Moreover, it is passed from generation to another so that slum dwellers become part of a permanent *underclass.*[75]

Considering the social disabilities suffered by lower-class slum dwellers, it is not surprising that their socioeconomic condition is regarded as a primary source of criminal behavior. The social structure view is that a significant majority of people who commit violent crimes and serious theft offenses come from lower-class backgrounds. Research shows that a number of known (official) criminals come from poor, lower-class backgrounds and that a majority of all crimes occur in inner city areas. When members of the middle or upper classes commit crime, it is usually of the nonserious variety.

There have been a number of attempts to explain the relationship between social class and crime. Some criminologists hold that poverty causes crime because lower-class people form their own culture whose norms and values place them in conflict with conventional society. Another view is that poverty causes frustration or *strain*, which in turn causes lower-class people to lash out

Chapter 3

Understanding Crime and Victimization

■

against society or form their own **subcultures.** A more modern view is that crime flourishes in deteriorated, disorganized slums that serve as a breeding ground for crime.

Cultural Deviance Theory

Cultural deviance theory suggests that slum dwellers violate the law because they hold to an independent value system that is unique to urban slum areas. This value system places young, lower-class males in conflict with middle-class rules and norms. These substitute values applaud such behaviors as being tough and cool, never showing fear, being disrespectful to authority, living for today, seeking excitement, respecting "street smarts," and scoffing at formal education. Unconventional values have been passed down from one lower-class generation to the next in a process known as **cultural transmission.** Consequently, each generation of slum dwellers has a ready supply of recruits for the teenage gangs and groups that rule the streets.

The concept of cultural transmission was formulated by famed University of Chicago sociologists Clifford R. Shaw and Henry D. McKay.[76] Their research indicated that the inner city was a breeding ground for juvenile gangs and adult criminality. They viewed crime as a product of decaying **transitional neighborhoods,** which manifest social disorganization and maintain conflicting values and social systems. Transitional neighborhoods are undergoing successive changes in the composition of their population—from purely residential to a mixture of commercial, industrial, transient, and residential. Their existing culture is disintegrating, providing a diffusion of cultural standards. Residents in these areas often develop norms and values that are in conflict with the rules and laws of conventional society.[77] Sociologist Walter Miller identified the unique values present in lower-class areas (which he labels **focal concerns**), such as the need for excitement, independence, and trouble, which produce conflict between their residents and the agents of conventional society.[78]

In sum, cultural deviance theory holds that the burden of poverty and urban decay in lower-class areas produce a unique set of values that conflict with conventional rules and laws. Obeying the demands of their immediate culture places the residents in conflict with conventional society and results in their being branded as criminals.

Strain Theory

Strain theories view crime and delinquency as a result of the frustration and anger people of limited means experience over their inability to achieve legitimate social and financial success. Strain theorists disagree with the subcultural view that lower-class people have a unique value system that is in opposition to conventional society. Instead they maintain that all people desire the same things, but the ability to achieve them is stratified by socioeconomic class. Members of the upper classes can achieve legitimate success through their control of the marketplace and their ability to use the institutions of society for their own benefit. In lower-class slum areas strain or **status frustration** occurs because legitimate avenues for success are all but closed. With no acceptable means open for obtaining success, people may either use deviant methods for obtaining their goals or reject socially acceptable goals, (i.e., a good education), and substitute others for them (i.e., a tough reputation). Thus strain theorists do not believe that criminals have substituted deviant values for conventional ones. They believe that crime occurs when individuals simply cannot fulfill their ambitions and dreams because they come from a poor background and see no way out.

Strain theory can be traced to the pioneering work of famed sociologist **Robert Merton.** Merton applied the concept of *anomie* to the study of crime and deviance.[79] He used this term to refer to a condition of **normlessness** that occurs when the means for achieving success that individuals have at their disposal are insufficient to achieve culturally defined goals. Although almost all people in American society are aware that desirable goals include a nice home, good car, and plenty of money in the bank, only members of the middle and upper classes have the means to achieve these legitimately. For example, most middle-class college students hope to get a share of American prosperity by attending school, getting a good job, and saving their wages. Those who believe they have little chance for conventional success because of their position in the social structure will use illegitimate means to achieve the same results. For example, they may steal, sell drugs, gamble, and so on. Merton referred to this state of adaptation as *innovation*—using innovative but illegal means and devices to achieve success when legitimate means are closed off because of one's social status or class position.

The Subcultural View

Following Merton, a number of prominent criminologists further developed strain theory. Albert Cohen described the conflict between lower-class youths and the agents of conventional society (teachers, employers, police).[80] A primary cause of this conflict is the use of what Cohen refers to as "middle-class measuring rods"—judging lower-class kids on the basis of middle-class values and social skills. Failing to measure up condemns the lower-class youth to a marginal economic and social existence in a menial job, or for the more angry and frustrated slum dweller, a life of crime. Few lower-class boys have the social and educational skills it takes to escape the limited boundaries of their lives.

In a similar vein, Richard Cloward and Lloyd Ohlin found that not only are legitimate opportunities closed to lower-class youth, but so too are the more lucrative forms of criminal activity such as organized crime and professional theft.[81] The perception that the system is not fair and/or that they cannot better their position through conventional means leads lower-class youth to either "drop out" (become an addict or substance abuser), join a violent gang, or get involved in theft-related activity.[82]

Both Cohen and Cloward and Ohlin projected the development of deviant subcultures, small reference groups that provide members with a unique set of values, beliefs, and traditions. Within the subculture, lower-class youth could achieve success unobtainable within the larger culture, while gaining a sense of identity and achievement. Such subcultures are best exemplified by the teenage gangs that have been a fixture of American culture since the 1940s. Although gang culture seemed to be on the wane in the 1960s and 1970s, drug-oriented groups like the "Crips" and "Bloods" in Los Angeles now contain thousands of members. Whereas gangs in the 1940s and 1950s defended their neighborhood "turf" and provided a sense of belonging for their members, today's gangs seem to be more involved with the commercial aspects of the drug trade than with honor or tradition.[83]

Ecological Theory

A number of modern scholars have sought to identify the social forces that contribute to high crime rates in urban areas. One important factor is **social disorganization**—the inability of local communities to express the common values of their residents or solve common problems.[84] Social disorganization occurs when communities experience high rates of population turnover and have difficulty understanding or assimilating their newest members. Indicators of social disorganization include high population density, large numbers of single parent households and homes with unrelated people living together, lack of employment opportunities, and significant levels of fear of crime, alienation, and social dissatisfaction.[85] For example, Leon Pettiway's research on the ecological causes of arson in Houston, Texas, indicated that arson rates may be a consequence of economic and racial segregation. Areas that experience a high rate of housing abandonment, neighborhood decline, increased population density, and urban growth also experience an increased likelihood of arson.[86] Research by Roland Chilton has shown that homicide and robbery trends are linked to changing neighborhood composition; Chilton concludes that

> the major obstacles to increased public safety in older urban areas are the poverty and demoralization of their black populations, which themselves are the result of a subtle and prevasive racism that continues to divide the U.S. population into two separate and unequal societies.[87]

A second ecological view is that crime is related to **relative deprivation:** when "haves" and "have nots" live in close proximity to one another, comparative economic disadvantages produce a sense of social injustice, leading to a state of anger and frustration.[88] The effects of relative deprivation have also been associated with neighborhoods undergoing **gentrification**—the upward transformation that occurs when professional or upper-class families

Crime rates are consistently higher in socially disorganized, physically deteriorated urban areas.

move into a formerly lower-class area and renovate the existing property.[89] Income inequality is most apparent in such urban areas as Los Angeles, New York, and Chicago where deprived teenagers witness luxury firsthand but cannot partake in it through conventional means. It is no wonder that making several thousand dollars a week selling "crack" seems more attractive than earning $4.50 an hour at the local fast food restaurant.[90]

Social Structure and Social Policy

Social structure theory has played a prominent role in criminology and has had an important influence on criminal justice policy making for most of the twentieth century. The belief that the lower-class slum is the breeding ground of serious crime has prompted the development of community action programs designed to give members of the lower class opportunities to succeed legitimately. The Chicago Area Project developed by Clifford Shaw was the forerunner of numerous attempts to marshal the resources of a community to improve the lives of its citizens. More recent efforts include Project Head Start, various community action projects (CAP) around the country, and the Job Corp.

Of course, reducing crime rates by revitalizing the community is extremely difficult because the problems of decayed, transitional neighborhoods are so overwhelming that any individual effort is dwarfed by the social problems ingrained in these areas. In addition, in the 1980s budget deficits have severely curtailed the funds available for serious community development projects. Consequently, crime control efforts have shifted their focus from the community to the individual offender.

■ Social Process Theory

Not all criminologists agree that the culture of poverty is the root cause of crime. They point to self-report studies that indicate that many middle- and upper-class youths commit serious criminal acts.[91] Furthermore, they find that the social structure approach fails to account for the fact that many people who live in even the worst slum areas hold conventional values and forgo any criminal activity. Consequently, they conclude that the forces that determine whether a person will become involved in criminal activity must be operating in all strata of society.

The resulting theoretical perspective is commonly referred to as social process theory. As a group these theorists hold that people commit crime as a result of their **socialization** experiences with the various organizations, institutions, and processes of society. People are most strongly influenced toward criminal behavior by poor family relationships, peer group pressures, educational failure, problems with agents of the justice system, and so on. Although lower-class citizens have the added burdens of poverty and blocked opportunities, even middle-class or upper-class citizens may turn to crime if their socialization is poor or destructive.

Social process theorists point to research efforts linking family problems to crime as evidence that socialization, and not social structure, is the key to understanding the onset of criminality. At one time most criminologists believed that living in a broken home was a strong predictor of delinquency. Today, the quality of family life is considered to be at least as important as its structure in determining the behavior of youths.[92] Among the most important studies are those that show that inconsistent discipline, poor supervision, and lack of warm parent-child relationships are closely related to a child's deviant behavior. Of recent interest have been the studies that show that child abuse is related both to delinquency and to later instances of family abuse. In other words, abused children grow up to become child abusers themselves.

In addition to the family, educational experience has been found to have a significant impact on behavioral choices. Schools help contribute to criminality when they set problem youths apart by creating a track system that labels some students as college-bound and others as academic underachievers. Studies show that children who do poorly in school, lack educational motivation, and feel alienated are those most likely to engage in antisocial behavior. One study by Terence Thornberry, Melanie Moore, and R. L. Christenson presented evidence showing that school dropouts are more likely to become involved in crime than those who complete their education.[93]

In a similar vein, studies of prison inmates show that their prior relationships with the institutions of society are less than adequate. Inmates tend to grow up in single parent households, have relatives who served time in prison, be single or divorced but still have dependent children, have a dropout rate three times the national average, and be educational underachievers.

In sum, social process theorists find that the direction and quality of human interaction and relationships influence control over criminal behavior. However, there is some disagreement over the direction this influence takes. Some believe it involves learning criminal techniques and attitudes from close and intimate relationships with peers and family members. Others view it as a function of breaking of one's ties or bonds to society, while still others view crime as a product of labeling and stigmatization. Each of these three branches of social process theory is described below.

Learning Theories

Learning theories hold that people enter into a life of crime when they are taught from a very young age the attitudes, values, and behaviors that support a criminal career. They may learn the techniques of crime from peers, neighbors, family, and so on.

The best known example of learning theory is Edwin Sutherland's **differential association theory**; its major premises are outlined in Table 3.1.[94] Sutherland's theory has had considerable influence on American criminology. His learning theory both accounts for the disproportionate amount of crime in lower-class areas and explains middle- and upper-class crime. After all, even in these areas people can be exposed to a variety of pro-crime definitions from such sources as opportunistic parents and friends.

Sutherland's learning approach has been adopted by a number of other criminologists. For example, Ronald Akers translated it into terms of operant conditioning, popularized by behavioral psychologists such as B. F. Skinner.[95] Another variation is **neutralization theory,** formulated by sociologist David Matza and his associate Gresham Sykes.[96] According to this view, youths become involved in criminality when they learn to throw off the moral constraints of society. To do this, they must adopt as a personal code a series of justifications for crime that free them to *drift* between illegal and conventional behavior. The most widely used techniques of neutralization include

TABLE 3.1 ■ Principles of Differential Association Theory

1. Criminal behavior is learned. In this respect crime is similar to all other forms of social behavior. Crime is neither inherited, nor is it invented by unsophisticated persons.

2. Criminal behavior is learned as a result of the communication that occurs in social interaction, and this communication is most effective in primary groups that are characterized by intimacy, consensus, and shared understandings. Impersonal communications, in general, are less effective.

3. When criminal behavior is learned, the learning includes both the techniques that are necessary to commit the crime and the motives, rationalizations, and social definitions that enable an individual to utilize criminal skills. In some situations (societies, neighborhoods, families, groups, and so on), an individual is surrounded by people who almost invariably define the laws as rules to be observed, while in other situations the individual encounters many persons whose definitions are favorable to law violations. Although the relative numbers of people who endorse criminal and noncriminal definitions may vary in time, place, and other circumstances, it seems almost inevitable that there will be some conflict over the efficacy and the morality of legal codes, especially in pluralistic societies.

4. More specifically, criminal behavior is learned when the definitions favoring law violations an individual encounters exceed those that support conformity. This is the basic principle of differential association. It refers to the counteracting influences of both criminal and noncriminal contacts, and it maintains that the probability of criminal behavior varies directly with the number of criminal definitions. Hence the generic formula for criminal behavior may be written as follows:

$$\text{Probability of crime} = \frac{\text{Definitions favorable to violations}}{\text{Definitions opposed to violations}}$$

5. Differential association with criminal and noncriminal behavior patterns may vary in frequency, duration, priority, and intensity. Frequency refers to the number of contacts during a given interval of time. Duration indicates the length of time during which a pattern of contacts is maintained. Priority designates an individual's age at the time of establishing contact with distinctive behavior patterns or developing certain modes of response. Intensity is not precisely defined but deals with such things as the prestige of the carriers of social norms or the affective attachments that may be generated among individuals involved in certain contact patterns.

blaming the victim ("they had it coming"), denial of responsibility ("they made me do it"), denial of injury ("they have insurance"), condemnation of condemners ("why pick on me—cops and judges take bribes"), and appeal to higher loyalties ("I had to protect my buddies"). Sykes and Matza suggest that by learning these justifications youths can free themselves from the constraints of social mores and participate in criminal behavior. Later adults can use similar neutralizations to justify such crimes as tax evasion, drunk driving, and drug use: After all, everyone is doing it, and it does not really hurt anyone.

Control Theories

Control theories hold that all people have the propensity to commit crime, but that most are held in check by their relationships to conventional institutions and individuals such as the family, school, and peer group. Travis Hirschi's **social bond theory** is probably the best known and widely studied control theory.[97] According to Hirschi, most individuals have the potential for committing crime but are kept in check by their equally potent commitment to the rules, controls, values, and conditions of the society in which they live. When their "bond" to society is weakened or broken, however, they are free to engage in deviant acts they would otherwise avoid.

Hirschi postulates that a person's bond to society is predicated on a number of different elements:

1. *Attachment.* Means caring for and valuing relationships with others, including parents, friends, and teachers. A person with a strong sense of attachment will seek out the advice of teachers, associate with friends, and maintain strong ties with family members; these activities are believed to shield a person from criminal temptations.

According to learning theory, youth acquire deviant attitudes and behavior from family and peers.

Chapter 3

Understanding Crime and Victimization

■

2. *Commitment.* Involves the time, energy, and effort expended in the pursuit of conventional lines of action. Commitments may embrace such activities as spending time in school or working to save money for the future. The more commitment one has, the less chance there is of engaging in criminal activity.

3. *Involvement.* Means an individual's participation in conventional activities such as school, recreation, church, family, or hobbies. The youth who is always active will not have time for delinquent acts.

4. *Belief.* Reflects a person's accepting commonly held moral values such as sharing, sensitivity to others, obeying the law, and refraining from hurting others.

Hirschi maintains that people with a strong social bond are unlikely to engage in criminal misconduct because they have a strong stake in society. Those whose social bond is weakened are much more likely to succumb to the temptations of criminal activity. After all, crime does offer rewards, such as excitement, action, material goods, and pleasures. Although Hirschi does not give a definitive reason for why a person's social bond may weaken, it seems likely that the process has two main sources: disrupted home life and poor school ability (leading to subsequent school failure and dislike of school).

Control theory as articulated by Hirschi has become one of the preeminent social theories of crime. With few exceptions its major premises have been upheld by a number of important research efforts.[98] It has been used to clarify the importance of the family, school, and peer group in the onset of criminality.

Labeling Theory

According to the **labeling** approach, society creates crime through a system of social control agencies, such as courts and prisons, which define people as criminals and permanently label them as stigmatized individuals who are outside the normal social order. The determination of which acts will be considered criminal or deviant and which people will be so labeled and punished is made subjectively; the decisions reflect current opinion, norms, and the existing power structure.

The apprehended "criminal" is made to feel like an **outsider** who should be avoided by the upstanding members of society. In time, the stigmatized person begins to believe that the label is accurate, assumes it as a personal identity, and eventually enters into a deviant or criminal career. For example, students put in special education classes begin to view themselves as "stupid" or "backward," mental patients accept society's view of them as "crazy," and convicted criminals consider themselves "dangerous" or "wicked."

Accompanying the criminal label are a variety of degrading social and physical restraints—handcuffs, incarceration, a criminal record, bars, cells, and so on—that leave an everlasting impression on the accused. Moreover, labels and sanctions work to define the whole person, meaning that a label evokes stereotypical conceptions of the criminal that carry over to other aspects of character. Thus the negatively labeled person may be regarded as evil, cruel, or untrustworthy and prevented from reentering the legitimate social order.

Faced with such condemnation, the negatively labeled person may see no alternative but to find others who are similarly stigmatized; with them the labeled offender will enjoy equal status, but is also likely to be prompted to commit other deviant acts. If apprehended again and subjected to even more severe negative labels, the offender may be transformed into a "real" deviant—one whose self-image is in direct opposition to conventional society. The deviant label may become more comfortable and personally acceptable than any other social status, and the individual whose original crime may have been relatively harmless may be transformed by societal action into a career deviant.

Despite its widespread initial acceptance, labeling theory has been subjected to quite a bit of scholarly criticism. Among its alleged failures is its inability to distinguish precisely between deviance and legitimate behavior—that is, to specify the conditions that must occur before an act or individual is considered deviant. It has also been criticized on the grounds that it views criminals as passive actors in crime, which is actually controlled by agents of the justice system.[99] However, with the realization that punishing criminals has little effect on their future behavior, and that some heavily sanctioned people become chronic, repeat offenders, there may be renewed interest in the labeling approach: It is logical that repeated arrest, conviction, and punishment simply drives home the point that "you're bad, everyone knows it, why even try to change?"[100]

Policy Implications of Social Process Theory

Social process theories have had a great deal of influence on criminal justice policy making. As a group they shift the focus of crime prevention toward efforts to help potential and known offenders avoid social interactions that produce criminal behavior. Each branch of social process theory—learning, control, and labeling—has made a valuable contribution to formulating programs to reduce the crime rate. For example, learning theory–based programs have been designed to present alternative values and lifestyles to youths who have bought into a delinquent way of life. These programs often use group process and counseling to attack the criminal-behavior orientations of their clients.

Control theories have been the basis of numerous community-based programs designed to strengthen a young person's bond to society. These involve family development and counseling programs and school-based prevention programs. In addition, the various state youth and adult correctional authorities maintain treatment programs that stress career development, work and educational furloughs, and self-help groups, all designed to reestablish social bonds.

Labeling theory principles have been used to design programs that limit an offender's interface with the criminal justice system. The idea behind these programs is that any sort of official contact can only help promote the stigma that locks a young offender into a life of crime. Among the most prominent policy efforts based on the labeling approach have been efforts that *divert* first offenders away from the normal justice process and into treatment programs; order offenders to pay *victim restitution* rather than enter into the justice process; and *deinstitutionalize* noncriminal youth from the juvenile justice system (that is, removing runaways, truants, and incorrigible youth from secure lockups that also contain criminal youth).

So although conservative views seemed dominant in the 1980s, there still remains an ongoing effort to produce treatment and rehabilitation programs, many of which are described in the remainder of this text. More often than not, these are based on social process theory principles.

■ Social Conflict Theory

Social conflict theory views the economic and political forces operating in society as a fundamental cause of criminality.[101] It regards the criminal law and criminal justice system as vehicles for controlling the poor, have-not members of society. According to this view, the criminal justice system helps the rich and powerful impose their particular morality and standards of good behavior on the entire society while the system protects their property and physical safety from the "have nots" of the lower class, even at the expense of their legal rights. Those in power control the content and direction of the law and legal system. Crimes are defined in accordance with the needs of the ruling classes. The theft of property worth five dollars by a poor person may be punished much more severely than the misappropriation of millions by a large corporation. The middle classes are drawn into this pattern of control because they are led to believe they too have a stake in maintaining the status quo and should support the views of the upper-class owners of production.[102]

Social conflict theory can be divided into two separate branches. One approach—known as conflict criminology—views crime as a product of the class conflict that can exist in any society.[103] The second subbranch—called critical, radical, *or* Marxist criminology—focuses on the evils of capitalism and attempts to expose the crime-producing forces inherent in the free enterprise system.[104] Both branches agree that the legal and justice systems are mechanisms used by those in power to control the "have-not" members of society.

Conflict theorists of both branches devote their research efforts to exposing discrimination and class bias in the application of laws and justice. They trace the history of criminal sanctions to show how those sanctions have corresponded to the needs of the wealthy. They attempt to show how police, court, and correctional agencies have served as tools of the upper classes. Their goal is **praxis**—the transformation of the current arrangements and relationships in society through writings, discussion, or social action.

How have social conflict theorists reacted to the conservative trend in the United States? In an important paper Anthony Platt, one of the best known Marxist scholars, has called for a reevaluation of conflict principles.[105] Platt argues that conflict theorists must become more realistic and propose programs that can help lower the crime rate, rather than blaming capitalism for all of society's ills. He feels it is time for radicals, liberals, and progressives to bury the hatchet and join forces to fight the right wing.

Policy Implications of Conflict Theory

Social conflict theorists have tried to make criminal justice policymakers aware of the inequities inherent in the criminal justice system, especially the plight of the poor when they confront the agencies of the justice system. Consequently, we have seen the development of such institutions as free legal services for indigent offenders and ombudsmen to oversee the operations of police and correctional authorities.

Other efforts to increase fairness in the justice system involve the enforcement of laws prohibiting the crimes of the rich and powerful. There is little question that greater attention is being paid to *white-collar* crimes such as price-fixing and stock fraud than ever before. Although these acts are rarely punished in proportion to their seriousness, law enforcement officials are now being forced by public opinion to give them increased attention.

■ Theories of Female Criminality

No discussion of criminal behavior theories would be complete without mention of female criminality. Although some of the previously mentioned theories can be applied to women and girls, it is probably true that the majority of criminological theories are directed toward males.[106] The role of women in crime is usually treated as a unique and independent topic.

Early criminologists traditionally devoted little time or effort to studying female criminality for several possible reasons: the female crime rate was significantly lower than the male crime rate; the types of crime women committed were considered nonserious; and criminologists were generally males who had little interest in the problems of women.

At one time the female criminal was regarded as an oddity. Pioneer criminologists such as Cesare Lombroso noted the physiobiological differences between men and women and suggested that those differences were responsible for woman's passive, law-abiding nature.[107] Women were believed to be less "primitive" than men and thus less likely to be violent or offensive. The rare woman who did commit criminal acts was viewed as being more masculine in personality and demeanor than her law-abiding sisters, or she was considered sexually maladjusted or otherwise psychologically unfit. Explanations of feminine crime by criminologists such as Otto Pollak were often based on the widely held belief that women engaged in crimes that were amoral or sexual in nature rather than violent or motivated by profit.[108]

In the 1950s and 1960s, it was popular to portray female crime as a function of emotional disturbance. The psychosocial disturbance school is best illustrated by the works of Gisela Konopka, who suggests that the conflict found in the role of today's female—her need for emotional support and understanding and her consequent frustrations when these are not met—is a cause of crime.[109] Often, when support from her family, loved ones, or society is not forthcoming, the troubled female suffers from a low self-image and depression and turns to criminal behavior or sexual promiscuity. Sources of conflict include overpowering or absent parents, lack of outlets for frustration (boys can fight or play football while girls can't), and the persistent double standard that labels women and girls deviant if they engage in or submit to sexual activity outside marriage, although such behavior is acceptable among young males.

Recent Theories of the Female Offender

In recent years, criminologists have expressed renewed and greater interest in the female criminal. In the 1970s, social scientists, influenced by the rise of feminine consciousness, began to accord more significance to the role of women in society, and criminal activity was one aspect of that role that was of particular importance. Women were simply committing more crimes, and the rise in their arrest and incarceration rates justified increased academic concern.

A sociopolitical view of female criminality was developed, which suggested that the women's movement had had an appreciable effect on the crime rate. As a result of women's economic emancipation, the social forces that play a strategic role in the behavior of males were believed to be having a similar effect on female criminality. Commenting on the "new" female (with regard to youth crime), Freda Adler stated:

> The emancipation of women appears to be having a two-fold influence on female juvenile crimes. Girls are involved in more drinking, stealing, gang activity and fighting—behavior in keeping with their adoption of male roles.
>
> We also find increases in the total number of female deviancies. The departure from the safety of traditional female roles and the testing of uncertain alternative roles coincide with the turmoil of adolescence creating crimogenic risk factors which are found to create this increase.[110]

Adler substantiated her claims by noting that while the arrest rate for male delinquents rose 82 percent between 1960 and 1972, it rose 306 percent for female delinquents. This dramatic increase suggested that female delinquents and criminals were rapidly intensifying their overall participation in the American crime scene.

Those scholars who heralded the discovery of the "new" female criminal also detected trends in the UCR data that showed a remarkable increase in the number of women arrested for white-collar crimes, such as embezzlement, larceny, and forgery, and a comcomitant stabilization in the rate of moral and sexual offenses. Roy Austin found evidence that feminine participation in serious theft-related behavior can be traced to the onset of the women's movement.[111]

Furthermore, self-report data uncovered in the 1970s indicated that the relationship between male and female delinquency was closer than previously believed and that although overall boys are more delinquent than girls, males and females generally engage in the same types of delinquent behavior.[112] Rita Simon, a noted expert on gender differences in the crime rate, stated that emerging economic and legal rights, such as simplified divorce and abortion, and a new sense of group identification via the women's movement meant that women will be less likely to be "victimized, dependent, and oppressed" by the men in their lives.[113] As a consequence, the liberated woman may also be less likely to engage in violent acts out of frustration and despair, and more likely to become involved in business-related crimes.

There is still much debate over whether the economic opportunities provided by the women's liberation movement have influenced female crime trends. Some authorities argue that the gender differences in the crime rate have not changed and that any increases in the female rate can be attributed to changes in the way agents of the justice system treat women; police may be more likely to arrest women than ever before, and courts more likely to convict them. Those who dispute the analysis of Simon and Adler talk about the "invention of the new female criminal."[114]

Other scholars such as Meda Chesney-Lind find that much female criminality can be linked to sexual and physical abuse. She argues:

> Young women, a large number of whom are on the run from homes characterized by sexual abuse and parental neglect, are forced by the very statutes designed to protect them into the lives of escaped convicts. Unable to enroll in school or take a job to support themselves because they fear detection, young female runaways are forced into the streets. Here they engage in panhandling, petty theft, and occasional prostitution in order to survive. Young women in conflict with their parents (often for very legitimate reasons) may actually be forced by present laws into petty criminal activity, prostitution, and drug use.[115]

Chesney-Lind's conclusions are in accord with other research showing that female offenders grew up in dysfunctional homes without adequate love, protection, and nurturing.[116] Other studies have shown that alcohol and substance abuse problems play a major role in determining the behavior choices of female offenders.[117] Thus although economic factors may explain some elements of female criminality, there is still evidence that family life and socialization play an important role in shaping the behavior of female offenders.[118]

■ Theories of Victimization

For many years criminological theory focused on the actions of the criminal offender; the role of the victim was virtually ignored. Then a number of scholars found that victims were not passive targets for crime but persons whose behavior could influence their own fate.

Hans Von Hentig was one of the first scholars to suggest that victims were an important part of the crime process. Writing in the 1940s, he portrayed the crime victim as someone who "shapes and molds the criminal."[119] The criminal might be a predator, but the victim may contribute by becoming a willing prey. Stephen Schafer continued this approach by focusing on the victim's responsibility in the "genesis of crime."[120] Schafer accused some victims of violating the principle that one should do nothing to provoke the criminal to do harm.

These early works helped focus attention on the role of the victim in the crime problem and led to further research efforts that have sharpened the image of the crime victim.

Victim Precipitation

One view of the victim's role in the criminal event is the concept of **victim precipitation.** This refers to the belief that many victims may have actually initiated the confrontation that led to their injury or death: the "victim" provoked the person who was later identified as the "criminal" to commit an act of violence that he or she might not have engaged in otherwise. The victim may have threatened the criminal, used "fighting words," or even attacked first. The spotlight was first placed on victim-precipitated crime by Marvin Wolfgang in his 1958 study of criminal homicide. Wolfgang found that crime victims were often intimately involved in their demise and that as many as 25 percent of all homicides could be classified as victim precipitated.[121] Wolfgang's argument was extended to the crime of rape by Menachem Amir who suggested female victims often contributed to their attacks through a relationship with the rapist.[122]

The concept of victim precipitation implies that in some but not all crimes the victim provoked or instigated the crime: the crime could not have taken place unless the victim actually cooperated with the criminal.

The concept of victim precipitation is most often on display in rape cases where courts continue to return "not guilty" verdicts if the rape victim's actions can in any way be construed as giving consent to the crime. For example, "date rapes," which start out as voluntary relationships but end in violence, often go unpunished.[123]

As law professor Susan Estrich claims in her book *Real Rape*:

> . . . the force standard continues to protect, as "seduction," conduct which should be considered criminal. It ensures broad male freedom to "seduce" women who feel

Many people believe that rape is a victim precipitated crime. This theme was explored in the movie The Accused *in which Jodie Foster played a rape victim and Kelly McGillis her attorney. The film was based on an actual barroom assault which took place in New Bedford, Massachusetts.*

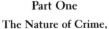

themselves to be powerless, vulnerable, and afraid. It effectively guarantees men freedom to intimidate women and exploit their weakness and passivity, so long as they don't "fight" with them, and it makes clear that the responsibility should be placed squarely on the women.[124]

Lifestyle Theories

A more current view of victimization links the chances of becoming a victim to lifestyle and activities. As we pointed out in Chapter 2, people who behave in certain ways (going out late at night) or live in certain areas (urban rather than rural) increase their chances of becoming victims. These patterns which are culled from the NCS data have led to the development of a *routine activities* approach to victimization. This view holds that the incidence of criminal activity is related to the nature of normal everyday patterns of human behavior. According to Lawrence Cohen and Marcus Felson and their associates, predatory crime is a function of three events: an offender motivated to commit the violation; a suitable target to be victimized by the offender; and the absence of crime prevention or control influences.[125]

The *routine activities* view of victimization suggests that people risk criminal behavior in proportion to their daily activities (e.g., whether they stay close to home) and the existence of personal characteristics correlated with victimization risk (e.g., being young, a minority group member, living in an urban area).[126] The routine activities approach seems a promising way of understanding crime and victimization patterns and predicting the probability of victim risk.

The Proximity Hypothesis

The national victimization data show that the people most likely to become crime victims share many personal characteristics and traits, including gender, race, age, class, and environment, with those who are most likely to be arrested for criminal offenses. One reason is that both groups live in close physical proximity to each other and criminals tend to select victims who share their backgrounds and circumstances.

The **proximity hypothesis** is based on the fact that victims and criminals live in the same environment and engage in similar routine activities. People who live in high crime areas, spend time in public places, go out late at night, and so on are the ones most likely to interact with lawbreakers who have similar lifestyles. In other words, crime is an inevitable consequence of having potential victims in close proximity to motivated offenders.

The Equivalent Group Hypothesis

Another explanation of why victims and criminals share similar characteristics is that they are not in reality separate groups. This argument is supported by research that shows that crime victims report significant amounts of criminal behavior themselves. For example, Joan McDermott found that the young victims of school crime were likely to strike back at other students in order to

Some victims may commit criminal acts out of a sense of rage and frustration. In his defense for shooting four would-be robbers on a subway in New York, Bernhard Goetz said he was a traumatized crime victim. He indicated that the extreme fear he felt may have caused his body to go on "automatic pilot." The jury believed Goetz acted reasonably and acquitted him of all charges except that of possessing an illegal handgun.

regain lost possessions or recover their self-respect.[127] In another study Simon Singer found that victims of violent assault commonly become offenders themselves later.[128] And a number of studies show that the victims of child abuse are quite likely to later victimize their own children and families.[129] Gary Jensen and David Brownfield conclude:

> . . . for personal victimizations, those most likely to be the victims of crime are those who have been most involved in crime; and the similarity of victims and offenders reflects that association.[130]

Consequently, it may be foolish to divide criminals and victims into separate categories; the conditions that create criminality may be present in all people at some time in their lives.

The true nature of the victim-criminal relationship is complex and far from certain. Some victims may commit criminal acts out of a sense of rage and frustration; some, such as abused children, may have learned antisocial behavior as a consequence of their own experiences; others may engage in law-violating behaviors such as violence as a means of revenge, self-defense, or social control. Nevertheless, it is important to note that not all victims become criminals nor have all criminals experienced victimization. Recent research by Jeffrey Fagan and his associates indicates that although a relationship between victimization and criminality exists, the social processes that produce both events are not identical.[131] Further research is needed to clarify this important interrelationship.

■ The Future of Crime Theory

A recent development in criminological theory that will probably continue to influence the field in years to come is the increasing acceptance of the fact that serious predatory crime is not spread evenly throughout the social structure: deviant individuals and deviant places do exist.[132] The concept of a career criminal who is a persistent offender living in an ecologically deteriorated neighborhood is now a familiar concept in criminology.[133]

This social fact has caused criminologists to expand their horizons and produce integrated theoretical models that combine personal, social, physical, and economic concepts and borrow elements from all the various branches of social, trait, and choice theories.[134]

It is evident that integrated theoretical models will be used more often in the future. It is also likely that they will combine social as well as psychological and biological variables as James Q. Wilson and Richard Herrnstein have done in their highly controversial book *Crime and Human Nature*.[135] They argue that biological and psychological factors such as body build, IQ, and personality disorders interact with social variables such as family problems and poverty to produce crime. People with physical abnormalities will be the ones most likely to succumb to the crime-producing influences in the environment. Even such highly repsected social thinkers as Travis Hirschi and Michael Gottfredson embrace a biological cause of crime when they maintain that all people commit less crime as they age. If, as they maintain, growing older, weaker, and more tired causes one to desist from crime, then it follows that such physical factors as youthful strength, vigor, energy, and pep are a cause of crime![136]

TABLE 3.2 ■ Theories of Criminology: A Review

Theory	Major premise	Strengths	Unanswered Questions and Other Weaknesses
Choice Theory	People commit crime when they perceive that the benefits of law violation outweigh the threat and pain of punishment.	Explains how crime can be deterred. Can be empirically tested.	Assumes that crime is a rational choice. Does not explain why people break the law though harsh punishments exist.
Biological	People commit crime because of genetic, biochemical, or neurological deficiencies.	Explains the onset of criminality. Explains why crime is found in all levels of society. Explains why irrational violence occurs.	Does not account for geographic crime patterns. Has not been tested with adequate samples. Does not explain why the crime rates are linked to age, sex, race, income, etc.
Psychological			
Psychoanalytic	People commit crime because of personality imbalances developed early in childhood.	Explains the onset of crime. Explains middle- and upper-class crime.	Does not account for crime rates and patterns. Does not explain why juvenile delinquents do not necessarily become adult criminals.
Social learning	People commit crime when they model their behavior after others they see being rewarded for the same acts.	Explains such patterns as child abuse and family violence.	Does not account for the fact that many who are exposed to violence do not become violent themselves.
Social structure			
Cultural deviance theory	Citizens who obey the street rules of lower-class life (focal concerns) find themselves in conflict with the dominant culture.	Identifies more coherently the elements of lower-class culture that push people into committing street crimes.	Does not provide empirical support for the existence of a lower-class culture. Does not account for middle-class influence. Does not explain upper-class crime.
Strain theory	People who adopt the goals of society but lack the means to attain them seek alternatives such as crime.	Points out how competition for success creates conflict and crime. Suggests that social conditions and not personality can account for crime. Can explain middle- and upper-class crime.	Does not explain why people choose the crime patterns they do. Does not account for violent and senseless acts.
Subcultural theories			
Cohen's theory of delinquent gangs	Status frustration of lower-class boys, created by their failure to achieve middle-class success, causes them to join gangs.	Shows how the conditions of lower-class life produce crime. Explains violence and destructive acts. Identifies conflict of lower class with middle class.	Does not account for middle-class crime. Reseaarch efforts have been inconclusive. Ignores delinquency that is rational and profitable.
Cloward and Ohlin's theory of opportunity	Blockage of conventional opportunities causes lower-class youths to join criminal, conflict, or retreatist gangs.	Shows that even illegal opportunities are structured in society. Indicates why people become involved in a particular type of criminal activity. Presents a way of preventing crime.	Does not account for middle-class crime. Assumes that lower-class citizens have the same values as the middle class. Gang surveys indicate that delinquent gang boys do not specialize in one type of crime.

TABLE 3.2 ■ (*Continued*)

Theory	Major premise	Strengths	Unanswered Questions and Other Weaknesses
Social ecology theories			
Relative deprivation	Crime occurs when the wealthy and poor live in close proximity to one another.	Explains high crime rates in deteriorated inner city areas.	Does not account for noncriminals in poor areas. Is limited to explaining urban crime rates.
Social disorganization	The conflicts and problems of urban social life and communities control the crime rate.	Accounts for urban crime rates and trends.	Is limited to urban crime rates. Does not account for individual differences.
Social process			
Social learning theories			
Differential association theory	People learn to commit crime from exposure to antisocial definitions.	Explains onset of criminality. Explains the presence of crime in all elements of social structure. Explains why some people in high-crime areas refrain from criminality. Can apply to adults and juveniles.	Where do antisocial definitions originate? How can we measure antisocial definitions or prove that someone has been exposed to an excess of them? Fails to explain illogical acts of violence and destruction. Fails to discuss how to test theory adequately.
Neutralization theory	Youths learn ways of neutralizing moral restraints and periodically drift in and out of criminal behavior patterns.	Explains why many delinquents do not become adult criminals. Explains why youthful law violators can participate in conventional behavior.	Fails to show whether neutralizations occur before or after law violations. Does not explain why some youths drift and others do not. Cannot explain self-destructive acts such as heroin addiction.
Control theories			
Social bond theory	A person's bond to society prevents him or her from violating social rules. If the bond weakens, the person is free to commit crime.	Explains onset of crime; can apply to both middle- and lower-class crime. Explains its theoretical constructs adequately so they can be measured. Has been empirically tested.	Fails to explain differences in crime rates. Fails to show whether a weakened bond can be strengthened. Does not distinguish the importance of different elements of the social bond—for example, is attachment more important than commitment?

■ SUMMARY

This chapter has reviewed some of the most important theoretical models in criminology. As we have stressed, there is more than one approach to understanding the causes of crime and its consequences. Many questions are still the subject of debate: Is crime a social, economic, psychological, biological, or personal problem? Is it a matter of free choice or the product of uncontrollable social and personal forces? Can it be controlled by the fear of punishment or the application of rehabilitative treatment? Consequently, there are a number of different schools of criminological theory, some of which focus on the individual while others view social factors as the most important element in producing crime.

TABLE 3.2 ■ (*Continued*)

Theory	Major premise	Strengths	Unanswered Questions and Other Weaknesses
Social conflict			
Conflict theory	People commit crime when the law, controlled by the rich and powerful, defines their behavior as illegal. The immoral actions of the powerful go unpunished.	Helps explain the historical development of law and social control. Draws attention to the inequality in the law.	Has not been adequately tested. Cannot explain laws banning corrupt business practices that benefit the rich. Does not explain legal protections for the poor, such as public defenders, paid for by wealthy taxpayers.
Integrated	Youths who grow up in lower-class cultures are more likely to have weakened bonds to society and suffer other socialization problems.	Combines the strength of social process and social structure theory. Can account for higher crime rates in lower-class areas.	Has not been empirically tested.
Cohen and Felson's routine activities theory	Crime is a function of the availability of the victim, the presence of an offender, and the absence of an effective guardian.	Can explain fluctuation in crime rates; draws attention to the role of social control agencies in producing crime.	Does not explain individual motivations for committing crime.
Wilson and Herrnstein's human nature theory	People choose to commit crime when they are biologically and psychologically impaired.	Shows how physical traits interact with social conditions to produce crime. Can account for noncriminal behavior in high-crime areas.	Has not been empirically tested and relies on secondary sources. Does not adequately explain crime rates and trends.

Recent conceptualizations have tried to integrate a number of different views into a complex theory of crime causation. For example, James Q. Wilson and Richard Herrnstein have proposed a theory of criminality that holds that crime is a matter of personal choice (classical approach) influenced by a person's physical traits (biological theory) and family life (social process theory). Other sociologists have attempted to combine elements of the social learning, social structure, and social process theories.

The various theories of crime causation have all had an important influence on criminal justice policy. Each has been used to formulate criminal justice policy and can be linked to one of the various perspectives in criminal justice.

■ QUESTIONS

1. Have you ever been a victim of crime? Did you take your frustration out on others?

2. Should prior victimization ever be a defense to a criminal charge? What about battered wives who kill their husbands?

3. Do the residents of lower-class slum areas possess unique values? Do most poor people reject middle-class norms and beliefs?

4. What aspects of socialization are most likely to produce crime and delinquency?

5. To what does the term anomie refer? Have you ever felt anomie?

■ NOTES

1. Cesare Beccaria, *On Crimes and Punishments*, 6th ed., Henry Paolucci, trans. (Indianapolis: Bobbs-Merrill Co., 1977). Jeremy Bentham, *A Fragment on Government and an Introduction to the Principles of Morals and Legislation*, Wilfred Harrison, ed. (Oxford: Basil Blackwell, 1967).

2. Beccaria, *On Crimes and Punishments*, p. 99.

3. Lawrence Cohen, Marcus Felson, and Kenneth Land, "Property Crime Rates in the United States: A Macrodynamic Analysis, 1947–1977, with Ex-ante Forecasts for the Mid-1980s," *American Journal of Sociology* 86 (1980): 90–118.

4. James Lasley and Jill Leslie Rosenbaum, "Routine Activities and Multiple Personal Victimization," *Sociology and Social Research* 73 (1988): 47–48.

5. Philip Cook, "The Demand and Supply of Criminal Opportunities," in Michael Tonry and Norval Morris, eds., *Crime and Justice* vol. 7 (Chicago: University of Chicago Press, 1986), pp. 1–28; Ronald Clarke and Derek Cornish, "Modeling Offender's Decisions: A Framework for Research and Policy," in Michael Tonry and Norval Morris, eds., *Crime and Justice*, vol. 6 (Chicago: University of Chicago Press, 1985), pp. 147–87; Morgan Reynolds, *Crime by Choice: An Economic Analysis* (Dallas: The Fisher Institute, 1985).

6. Lawrence Cohen and Richard Machalek, "A General Theory of Expropriative Crime: An Evolutionary Ecological Approach," *American Journal of Sociology* 94 (1988): 465–501.

7. Ibid.

8. James Q. Wilson, *Thinking about Crime* (New York: Basic Books, 1975); Ernest Van den Haag, *Punishing Criminals* (New York: Basic Books, 1975).

9. Herbert Packer, *The Limits of the Criminal Sanction* (Stanford, Calif.: Stanford University Press, 1968).

10. Van Den Haag, *Punishing Criminals*, p. 20.

11. Ernest Van Den Haag, "Could Successful Rehabilitation Reduce the Crime Rate?" *Journal of Criminal Law and Criminology* 73 (1985): 1022–35.

12. William Chambliss, "The Deterrent Influence of Punishment," *Crime and Delinquency* 12 (1966): 70–75.

13. Alfred Blumstein, Jacqueline Cohen, and Daniel Nagen, *Deterrence and Incapacitation: Estimating the Effects of Legal Sanctions on Crime Rates* (Washington, D.C.: National Academy of Science, 1978).

14. Linda Anderson, Theodore Chiricos, and Gordon Waldo, "Formal and Informal Sanctions: A Comparison of Deterrent Effects," *Social Problems* 25 (1977): 103–14.

15. Charles Tittle, *Sanctions and Social Deviance* (New York: Praeger Publishers, 1980).

16. Raymond Paternoster et al., "Perceived Risk and Deterrence: Methodological Artifacts in Perceptual Deterrence Research," *Journal of Criminal Law and Criminology* 73 (1982): 1238–58.

17. Federal Bureau of Investigation, *Crime in the United States, 1987* (Washington, D.C.: U.S. Government Printing Office, 1988).

18. Eric Wish, *Drug Use Forecasting, New York, 1984 to 1986* (Washington, D.C.: National Institute of Justice, 1987); U.S. Department of Justice, *Crime and Alcohol* (Washington, D.C.: U.S. Government Printing Office, 1983).

19. Peter Greenwood, *Selective Incapacitation* (Santa Monica, Calif.: Rand Corporation, 1982).

20. See, generally, Blumstein, Cohen, and Nagen, *Deterrence and Incapacitation*.

21. Gary Becker, "Crime and Punishment: An Economic Approach," *Journal of Political Economy* 76 (1968): 174–82.

22. Charles Silberman, *Criminal Violence, Criminal Justice* (New York: Vintage Books, 1980), pp. 245–62.

23. Allen Beck and Bernard Shipley, *Recidivism of Young Parolees* (Washington, D.C.: Bureau of Justice Statistics, 1987).

24. Michel Foucault, *Discipline and Punish* (New York: Random House, 1978).

25. Beck and Shipley, *Recidivism of Young Parolees*.

26. Joan Petersilia, Susan Turner, James Kahan, and Joyce Peterson, *Granting Felons Probation: Public Risks and Alternatives* (Santa Monica, Calif.: Rand Corporation, 1985).

27. Lawrence Sherman and Richard Berk, "The Specific Deterrent Effects of Arrest for Domestic Assault," *American Sociological Review* 49 (1984): 375–94.

28. Marvin Wolfgang, Robert Figlio, and Thorsten Sellin, *Delinquency in a Birth Cohort* (Chicago: University of Chicago Press, 1972).

29. Samuel Walker, *Sense and Nonsense about Crime* (Monterey, Calif.: Brooks Cole, 1988).

30. Greenwood, *Selective Incapacitation*.

31. See, generally, Cesare Lombroso, *Crime, Its Causes and Remedies* (Montclair, N.J.: Patterson Smith, 1968).

32. Raffaele Garofalo, *Criminology*, Robert Miller, trans. (Boston: Little, Brown & Co., 1914).

33. Enrico Ferri, *Criminal Sociology* (New York: D. Appleton & Co., 1909).

34. Ernest Hooton, *The American Criminal* (Cambridge, Mass.: Harvard University Press, 1939).

35. Henry Goddard, *The Kallikak Family: A Study in the Heredity of Feeble Mindedness* (New York: Macmillan Co., 1927); Richard Dugdale, *The Jukes: A Study in Crime, Pauperism, Disease, and Heredity* (New York: G. P. Putnam, 1910); Arthur Estabrook, *The Jukes in 1915* (Washington, D.C.: The Carriage Institute of Washington, 1916).

36. Edward O. Wilson, *Sociobiology: The New Synthesis* (Cambridge, Mass.: Harvard University Press, 1975).

37. C. Ray Jeffrey, "Criminology as an Interdisciplinary Behavioral Science," *Criminology* 16 (1978): 161–62.

38. Leonard Hippchen, "Some Possible Biochemical Aspects of Criminal Behavior," *Journal of Behavioral Ecology* 2 (1981): 1–6.

39. B. D'Asaro, C. Grossback, and C. Nigro, "Polyamine Levels in Jail Inmates," *Journal of Orthomolecular Psychiatry* 4 (1975): 149–52.

40. J. A. Yaryura-Tobias and F. Neziroglu, "Violent Behavior, Brain Dysrhythmia, and Glucose Dysfunction, a New Syndrome," *Journal of Orthopsychiatry* 4 (1975): 182–88.

41. Ray Wunderlich, "Neuroallergy as a Contributing Factor to Social Misfits: Diagnosis and Treatment," in *Ecologic-Biochemical Approaches to Treatment of Delinquents and Criminals*, Leonard Hippchen, ed. (New York: Van Nostrand Reinhold Co., 1978), pp. 229–53.

42. R. R. Monroe, *Brain Dysfunction in Aggressive Criminals* (Lexington, Mass.: D. C. Heath Co., 1978); L. T. Yeudall, *Childhood Experiences as Causes of Criminal Behavior* (Senate of Canada, issue no. 1, Thirteenth Parliament, Ottawa, Canada, 1977).

43. Charles Murray, *The Link between Learning Disabilities and Juvenile Delinquency* (Washington, D.C.: U.S. Government Printing Office, 1976), p. 65. See also B. Claire McCullough, Barbara Zaremba, and William Rich, "The Role of the Juvenile Justice System in the Link between Learning Disabilities and Delinquency," *State Court Journal* (1979): 45.

44. D. Williams, "Neural Factors Related to Habitual Aggression—Consideration of Differences between Habitual Aggressives and Others Who Have Committed Crimes of Violence," *Brain* 92 (1969): 503–20.

45. R. S. Aind and T. Yamamoto, "Behavior Disorders of Childhood," *Electroencephalography and Clinical Neurophysiology* 21 (1966): 148–56.

46. Z. A. Zayed, S. A. Lewis, and R. P. Britain, "An Encephalographic and Psychiatric Study of 32 Insane Murderers," *British Journal of Psychiatry* 115 (1969): 1115–24.

47. T. R. Sarbin and L. E. Miller, "Demonism Revisited: The XYY Chromosome Anomaly," *Issues in Criminology* 5 (1970): 195–207.

48. See S. A. Mednick and Karl O. Christiansen, eds. *Biosocial Bases of Criminal Behavior* (New York: Gardner Press, 1977).

49. David Rowe and D. Wayne Osgood, "Heredity and Sociological Theories of Delinquency: A Reconsideration," *American Sociological Review* 49 (1984): 526–40.

50. B. Hutchings and S. A. Mednick, "Criminality in Adoptees and Their Adoptive and Biological Parents: A Pilot Study," in Mednick and Christiansen, eds., *Biosocial Bases of Criminal Behavior.*

51. See Peter Scott, "Henry Maudsley," in *Pioneers in Criminology,* Hermann Mannheim, ed. (Montclair, N.J.: Patterson Smith, 1970), p. 212.

52. Traditionally, the law has recognized that some offenders are mentally ill and should therefore be excused from criminal responsibility. However, *insanity* is a legal, not psychological, term and will therefore be discussed in Chapter 3, where we review the criminal law.

53. For an analysis of Freud, see Spencer Rathus, *Psychology* (New York: Holt, Rinehart & Winston, 1988), pp. 412–20.

54. August Aichorn, *Wayward Youth* (New York: Viking Press, 1965).

55. Seymour Halleck, *Psychiatry and the Dilemmas of Crime* (New York: Harper & Row, 1967), pp. 99–115.

56. John Monahan and Henry Steadman, *Crime and Mental Disorder* (Washington, D.C.: National Institute of Justice Research Brief, September 1984); David Tennenbaum, "Research Stuuies of Personality and Criminality," *Journal of Criminal Justice* 5 (1977): 1–19.

57. This discussion is based on three works by Albert Bandura: *Aggression: A Social Learning Analysis* (Englewood Cliffs, N.J.: Prentice-Hall, 1973); *Social Leaarning Theory* (Englewood Cliffs, N.J.: Prentice-Hall, 1977); "The Social Learning Perspective: Mechanisms of Aggression," in *The Psychology of Crime and Criminal Justice,* H. Toch, ed. (New York: Holt, Rinehart & Winston, 1979), pp. 198–326.

58. Department of Health and Human Services, *Television and Behavior* (Washington, D.C.: U.S. Government Printing Office, 1982).

59. Richard Kania, "T.V. Crime and Real Crime: Questioning the Link," paper presented at the annual meeting of the American Society of Criminology, Chicago, Ill., November 1988.

60. See, generally, Jean Piaget, *The Moral Judgement of the Child* (London: Kegan Paul, 1932).

61. Lawrence Kohlberg et al., *The Just Community Approach in Corrections: A Manual* (Niantic, Conn.: Connecticut Department of Corrrections, 1973).

62. J. E. Lockman, "Self and Peer Perception and Attributional Biases of Aggressive and Nonaggressive Boys in Dyadic Interactions," *Journal of Consulting and Clinical Psychology* 55 (1987): 404–10.

63. See, generally, Albert Rabin, "The Antisocial Personality—Psychopathy and Sociopathy," in *The Psychology of Crime and Criminal Justice,* H. Toch, ed. (New York: Holt, Rinehart & Winston, 1979), pp. 236–251.

64. Ibid.

65. Jack Levin and James Alan Fox, *Mass Murder* (New York: Plenum Books, 1985).

66. Rathus, *Psychology,* p. 546.

67. Samuel Yochelson and Stanton Samenow, *The Criminal Personality* (New York: Jason Aronson, 1977).

68. Lee Ellis, "Genetics and Criminal Behavior," *Criminology* 20 (1982): 59.

69. "A. P. Prison Surgeons Reshape Faces, Futures," *Omaha World Herald,* 13 January 1986, 25.

70. Paul Boccomini, Bill Strum, and Alexander Schauss, "Sub-Clinical Thiamine Deficiency and Behavior Disorders: Case History," *Journal of Behavioral Ecology* 2 (1981): 5–6.

71. L. A. J. Quetelet, A *Treatise on Man and the Development of His Faculties* (Gainesville, Fla.: Scholars' Facsimilies and Reprints, 1969).

72. Émile Durkheim, *The Division of Labor in Society* (New York: Free Press, 1964); *Rules of the Sociological Method,* S. A. Solvay and J. H. Mueller, trans. G. Catlin, ed. (New York: Free Press, 1966).

73. William T. Grand Foundation, *The Forgotten Half* (Cambridge, Mass.: 1988).

74. Oscar Lewis "The Culture of Poverty," *Scientific American* 215 (1966): 19–25.

75. Ken Auletta, *The Under Class* (New York: Random House, 1982).

76. Clifford R. Shaw and Henry D. McKay, *Juvenile Delinquency and Urban Areas,* rev. ed. (Chicago: University of Chicago Press, 1972).

77. Thorsten Sellin, *Culture Conflict and Crime,* Bulletin no. 41 (New York: Social Science Research Council, 1938).

78. Walter Miller, "Lower Class Culture as a Generating Milieu of Gang Delinquency," *Journal of Social Issues* 14 (1958): 5–19.

79. Robert Merton, "Social Structure and Anomie," in *Social Theory and Social Structure* (Glencoe, Ill.: Free Press, 1975).

80. Albert Cohen, *Delinquent Boys* (New York: Free Press, 1955).

81. Richard Cloward and Lloyd Ohlin, *Delinquency and Opportunity* (Glencoe, Ill.: Free Press, 1960).

82. Ronald Simons and Phyllis Gray, "Perceived Blocked Opportunity as an Explanation of Delinquency among Lower-Class Black Males: A Research Note," *Journal of Research in Crime and Delinquency* 26 (1989): 90–101.

83. George Hackett and Michael Lerner, "L.A. Law: Gangs and Crack," *Newsweek* 27 April 1987, pp. 35–36.

84. Robert Bursik, "Social Disorganization and Theories of Crime and Delinquency: Problems and Prospects," *Criminology* 26 (1988): 519–51 at 521.

85. Robert Sampson, "Structural Sources of Variation in Race-Age-Specific Rates of Offending across Major U.S. Cities," *Criminology* 23 (1985): 647–73; Janet Heitgerd and Robert Bursik, Jr., "Extracommunity Dynamics and the Ecology of Delinquency," *American Journal of Sociology* 92 (1987): 775–87; Ora Simcha-Fagan and Joseph Schwartz, "Neighborhood and Delinquency: An Assessment of Contextual Effect," *Criminology* 24 (1986): 667–703.

86. Leon Pettiway, "Urban Spatial Structure and Incidence of Arson: Differences between Ghetto and Nonghetto Environments," *Justice Quarterly* 5 (1988): 113–29.

87. Roland Chilton, "Twenty Years of Homicide and Robbery in Chicago: The Impact of the City's Changing Racial and Age Composition," *Journal of Quantitative Criminology* 3 (1987): 195–213.

88. Richard Rosenfeld, "Urban Crime Rates: Effects of Inequality, Welfare Dependency, Region and Race," in James Byrne and Robert Sampson, *The Social Ecology of Crime* (New York: Springer-Verlag, 1985), pp. 116–30; Leo Carroll and Pamela Irving Jackson, "Inequality, Opportunity, and Crime Rates in Central Cities," *Criminology* 21 (1983): 178–94.

89. Ralph Taylor and Jeanette Covington, "Neighborhood Changes in Ecology and Violence," *Criminology* 26 (1988): 553–89.

90. Judith and Peter Blau, "The Cost of Inequality: Metropolitan Structure and Violent Crime," *American Sociological Review* 147 (1982): 114–29; Richard Block, "Community Environment and Violent Crime," *Criminology* 17 (1979): 46–57.

91. Charles Tittle, Wayne Villemez, and Douglas Smith, "The Myth of Social Class and Criminality: An Empirical Assessment of the Evidence," *American Sociological Review* 43 (1978): 643–56.

92. Lawrence Rosen, "Family and Delinquency: Structure or Function?" *Criminology* 23 (1985): 553–73.

93. Terence Thornberry, Melanie Moore, and R. L. Christenson, "The Effect of Dropping Out of High School on Subsequent Criminal Behavior," *Criminology* 23 (1985): 3–18.

94. Edwin Sutherland and Donald Cressey, *Criminology* (Philadelphia: J. B. Lippincott Co., 1970), pp. 71–91.

95. Ronald Akers, *Deviant Behavior: A Social Learning Approach*, 2d ed. (Belmont, Mass.: Wadsworth, 1977).

96. David Matza, *Delinquency and Drift* (New York: John Wiley & Sons, 1964); Gresham Sykes and David Matza, "Techniques of Neutralization: A Theory of Delinquency," *American Sociological Review* 22 (1957): 664–70; see also M. William Minor, "The Neutralization of Criminal Offense," *Criminology* 18 (1980): 103–20; Robert Regoli and Eric Poole, "The Commitments of Delinquents to Their Misdeeds: A Reexamination," *Journal of Criminal Justice* 6 (1978): 261–69.

97. Travis Hirschi, *Causes of Delinquency* (Berkeley: University of California Press, 1969).

98. See, for example, Randy La Grange and Helen Raskin White, "Age Differences in Delinquency: A Test of Theory," *Criminology* 23 (1985): 19–45; Marvin Krohn and James Massey, "Social Control and Delinquent Behavior: An Examination of the Elements of the Social Bond," *Sociological Quarterly* 21 (1980): 529–44.

99. Ronald Akers, "Problems in Sociology of Deviance: Social Definitions and Behavior," *Social Forces* 46 (Spring 1968): 463; David Bordua, "On Deviance," *Annals* 111 (1967): 121; Clarence Schrag, *Crime and Justice: American Style* (Washington, D.C.: U.S. Government Printing Office, 1971), pp. 89–91; see also William Pelfrey, *The Evolution of Criminology* (Cincinnati, Ohio: Anderson Publishing Co., 1980), pp. 47–48.

100. Charles Tittle, "Two Empirical Regularities (Maybe) in Search of an Explanation: Commentary on the Age/Crime Debate," *Criminology* 26 (1988): 75–85.

101. For the most thorough view of conflict theory, see Ian Taylor, Paul Taylor, and Jock Young, *The New Criminology—For a Social Theory of Deviance* (New York: Harper & Row, 1973).

102. W. Byron Groves and Robert Sampson, "Critical Theory and Criminology," *Social Problems* 33 (1986): 58–80.

103. Gresham Sykes, "The Rise of Critical Criminology," *Journal of Criminal Law and Criminology* 65 (June 1974): 206.

104. John Braithwaite, "Retributivism, Punishment and Privilege," in W. Byron Groves and Graeme Newman, eds., *Punishment and Privilege* (Albany, N.Y.: Harrow and Heston, 1986), pp. 55–66.

105. Anthony Platt, "Criminology in the 1980s: Progressive Alternatives to Law and Order," *Crime and Social Justice* 21–22 (1985): 191–99.

106. Meda Chesney-Lind, "Girl's Crimes and Woman's Place: Toward a Feminist Model of Female Delinquency," *Crime and Delinquency* 35 (1989): 5–29.

107. Cesare Lombroso and William Ferrero, *The Female Offender* (New York: D. Appleton & Co., 1899).

108. Otto Pollak, *The Criminality of Women* (New York: A. S. Barnes & Co., 1950).

109. Gisela Konopka, *The Adolescent Girl in Conflict* (Englewood Cliffs, N.J.: Prentice-Hall, 1966).

110. Freda Adler, *Sisters in Crime: The Rise of the Female Criminal* (New York: McGraw-Hill, 1975). p. 95.

111. Roy Austin, "Women's Liberation and Increase in Minor, Major, and Occupational Offenses," *Criminology* 20 (1982): 407–30.

112. Gordon Barker and William Adams, "Comparison of the Delinquencies of Boys and Girls," *Journal of Criminal Law, Criminology, and Police Science* 53 (1962): 470–75; Michael Hindelang, "Age, Sex, and the Versatility of Delinquency Involvements," *Social Forces* 14 (1971): 525–34; John Clark and Edward Haurek, "Age and Sex Roles of Adolescents and Their Involvement in Misconduct: A Reappraisal," *Sociology and Social Research* 50 (1966): 495–508; Gary Jensen and Raymond Eve, "Sex Differences in Delinquency: An Examination of Popular Sociological Explanations," *Criminology* 13 (1976): 427–48; Rachelle Canter, "Sex Differences in Self-reported Delinquency," *Criminology* 20 (1982): 373–94.

113. Rita James Simon, "Women and Crime Revisited," *Social Science Quarterly* 56 (March 1976): 658.

114. Joseph Weis, "Liberation and Crime: The Invention of the New Female Criminal," *Crime and Social Justice* 1 (1976): 17–27.

115. Chesney-Lind, "Girl's Crime and Woman's Place: Toward a Feminist Model of Female Delinquency," p. 24.

116. Jill Leslie Rosenbaum, "Family Dysfunction and Female Delinquency," *Crime and Delinquency* 35 (1989): 31–44.

117. Brenda Miller, William Downs, and Dawn Gondoli, "Delinquency, Childhood Violence, and the Development of Alcoholism in Women," *Crime and Delinquency* 35 (1989): 94–108.

118. John Hagan, John Simpson, and A. R. Gillis, "Class in the Household: A Power-Control Theory of Gender and Delinquency," *American Journal of Sociology* 92 (1987): 788–816.

119. Hans Von Hentig, *The Criminal and His Victim: Studies in the Sociobiology of Crime* (New Haven, Conn.: Yale University Press, 1948), p. 384.

120. Stephen Schafer, *The Victim and His Criminal* (New York: Randon House, 1968), p. 152.

121. Marvin Wolfgang, *Patterns of Criminal Homicide* (Philadelphia: University of Pennsylvania Press, 1958).

122. Menachem Amir, *Patterns in Forcible Rape* (Chicago: University of Chicago Press, 1971).

123. Susan Estrich, *Real Rape* (Cambridge, Mass.: Harvard University Press, 1987).

124. Ibid., p. 69.

125. Lawrence Cohen and Marcus Felson, "Social Change and Crime Rate Trends: A Routine Activities Approach," *American Sociological Review* 44 (1979): 588–608; Cohen, Felson, and Land, "Property Crime Rates in the United States: A Macrodynamic Analysis, 1947–1977, with Ex-ante Forecasts for the Mid-1980s." For a review, see James LeBeau and Thomas Castellano, "The Routine Activities Approach: An Inventory and Critique" (Center for the Studies of Crime, Delinquency and Corrections, Southern Illinois University-Carbondale, Ill. 62901: Unpublished, 1987).

126. Steven Messner and Kenneth Tardiff, "The Social Ecology of Urban Homicide: An Application of the 'Routine Activities' Approach," *Criminology* 23 (1985): 241–67; Cook, "The Demand and Supply of Criminal Opportunities"; Clarke and Cornish, "Modeling Offender's Decisions: A Framework for Research and Policy."

127. Joan McDermott, "Crime in the School and in the Community: Offenders, Victims and Fearful Youth," *Crime and Delinquency* 29 (1983): 270–83.

128. Simon Singer, "Homogeneous Victim-Offender Populations: A Review and Some Research Implications," *Journal of Criminal Law and Criminology* 72 (1981): 779–99.

129. Ross Vasta, "Physical Child Abuse: A Dual Component Analysis," *Developmental Review* 2 (1982): 128–35.

130. Gary Jensen and David Brownfield, "Gender, Lifestyles and Victimization: Beyond Routine Activities," *Violence and Victims* (1986): 85–101.

131. Jeffrey Fagan, Elizabeth Piper, and Yu-Teh Cheng, "Contributions of Victimization to Delinquency in Inner Cities," *Journal of Criminal Law and Criminology* 78 (1987): 586–613.

132. Lawrence Sherman, Patrick Gartin, and Michael Buerger, "Hot Spots of Predatory Crime: Routine Activities and the Criminology of Place," *Criminology* 27 (1989): 27–56.

133. Rodney Stark, "Deviant Places: A Theory of the Ecology of Crime," *Criminology* 25 (1987): 893–911.

134. Delbert Elliott, David Huizinga, and Suzanne Ageton, *Explaining Delinquency and Drug Use* (Beverly Hills, Calif.: Sage Publications, 1985).

135. James Q. Wilson and Richard Herrnstein, *Crime and Human Nature* (New York: Simon and Schuster, 1985); see also Frank Pearson and Neil Alan Weiner, "Toward an Integration of Criminological Theories," *Journal of Criminal Law and Criminology* 76 (1985): 116–50, at 150.

136. Michael Gottfredson and Travis Hirschi, "The True Value of Lambda Would Appear to Be Zero: An Essay on Career Criminals, Criminal Careers, Selective Incapacitation, Cohort Studies and Related Topics," *Criminology* 24 (1986): 213–34.

Chapter 3

Understanding Crime and Victimization

■

4

Criminal Law:
Substance and Procedure

A t the heart of the criminal justice system stands the rule of law. The criminal law defines crimes, dictates punishments, and controls the procedures used to process criminal offenders through the justice system.

This chapter focuses on the basic principles of the **substantive criminal law**, which regulates conduct in our society. In addition, constitutional **criminal procedure,** the law that governs judicial process, will be discussed to show how the rules of procedure, laid out in the U.S. Constitution and interpreted over time by the Supreme Court, control the operations of the justice system.

The substantive criminal law defines crime in American society. Each state government, and the federal government as well, has its own criminal code, developed over many generations and incorporating moral beliefs, social values, political and economic matters, and other societal concerns. The criminal law is a living document, constantly evolving to keep pace with society and its needs.

The rules designed to implement the substantive law are known as **procedural law.** It is concerned with the criminal process—the legal steps through which an offender passes—commencing with the initial criminal investigation and concluding with release of the offender. Some elements of the law of criminal procedure are the rules of evidence, the law of arrest, the law of search and seizure, questions of appeal, and the right to counsel. Many of the criminal rights that have been extended to offenders over the past two decades lie within the field of procedural law.

A working knowledge of the law is critical for the criminal justice practitioner. In our modern society the rule of law governs almost all phases of human enterprise, including commerce, family life, property transfer, and the regulation of interpersonal conflict. It contains elements that control personal relationships between individuals, and public relationships between individuals and the government. The former is known as **civil law** while the latter is criminal law (see the following Criminal Justice in Review for more on this distinction). Since the law defines crime, punishment, and procedure, which are the basic concern of the criminal justice system, it is essential for students to know something of the nature, purpose, and content of the substantive and procedural criminal law.

■ Historical Development of the Criminal Law

The roots of the criminal codes used in the United States can be traced back to such early legal charters as the Babylonian Code of Hammurabi (2000 B.C.), the Mosiac Code of the Israelites (1200 B.C.), and the Roman Twelve Tables. During the sixth century, under the leadership of the Byzantine emperor Justinian, the first great codification of law in the western world was prepared. Justinian's *Corpus Juris Civilis,* or body of civil law, summarized the system of Roman law that had gradually developed for over a thousand years. Rules and regulations to ensure the safety of the state and the individual were organized into a code and served as the basis for future civil and criminal legal classifications. Centuries later, the French emperor Napoleon created the French civil code, using Justinian's code as a model. France and the other countries that have modeled their legal systems on French and Roman law have what are known as civil law systems.

A more immediate source than Roman law for much U.S. law, however, is the English system of jurisprudence.[1] Prior to the ratification of the U.S.

■   ■   ■

KEY TERMS

Substantive criminal law
Criminal procedure
Procedural law
Civil law
Torts
Intent
Common law
False pretenses
Law of precedent
Stare decisis
Folkways
Mores
Ex post facto laws
Bills of attainder
Substantive due process
Procedural due process
Mala in se
Mala prohibitum
Felony
Misdemeanor
Corpus delicti
Actus reus
Mens rea
Criminal negligence
General or specific intent
Transferred intent
Strict liability
Insanity
M'Naghten rule
Durham rule
Substantial capacity test
Self-defense
Entrapment
Double jeopardy
Preventive detention
Separation of powers
Bill of Rights
Due process of law
Exclusionary rule
Self-incrimination
Incorporation
Theory of selective incorporation
Fundamental fairness

Criminal Law and Civil Law

In modern American society, law can be divided into two broad categories: criminal law and civil law. All law other than criminal law is known as civil law; it includes tort law (personal wrongs and damages), property law (the law governing the transfer and ownership of property), and contract law (the law of personal agreements).

SIMILARITIES AND DIFFERENCES

The differences between criminal law and civil law are very significant because, in our legal system, criminal proceedings are completely separate from civil actions.

The major objective of the criminal law is to protect the public against harm by preventing criminal offenses. The primary concern of the civil law—in the area of private wrongs or **torts,** for example—is that the injured party be compensated for any harm done. The aggrieved person usually initiates proceedings to recover monetary damages. In contrast, when a crime is committed, the state initiates the legal process and imposes a punishment in the form of a criminal sanction. Fur-

thermore, in criminal law the emphasis is on the **intent** of the individual committing the crime; a civil proceeding gives primary attention to affixing the blame each party deserves for producing the damage or conflict.

Despite these major differences, criminal and civil law share certain features. Both areas of the law seek to control people's behavior by preventing them from acting in an undesirable manner, and both impose sanctions on those who commit violations of the law. The payment of damages to the victim in a tort case, for example, serves some of the same purposes as the payment of a fine in a criminal case. The criminal law sentences offenders to prison, while the civil law also imposes confinement on such in-

dividuals as the mentally ill, alcoholics, and the mentally defective. In addition, many actions, such as assault and battery, various forms of larceny, and negligence, are the basis for criminal as well as civil actions. Table A summarizes the similarities and differences between the criminal law and tort law.

In summary, the criminal law usually applies in an action taken by the local, state, or federal government against an individual who has been accused of committing a crime. The civil law comes into effect when an individual or group seeks monetary recompense for harmful actions committed by another individual or group. ■

TABLE A ■ **A Comparison of Criminal and Tort Law**

Similarities

Both criminal and tort law seek to control behavior.
Both laws impose sanctions.
Similar areas of legal action exist; for example, personal assault and control of white-collar offenses such as environmental pollution.

Differences

Criminal Law	Tort Law
Crime is a public offense.	Tort is a civil or private wrong.
The sanction associated with criminal law is incarceration or death.	The sanction associated with a tort is monetary damages.
The right of enforcement belongs to the state.	The individual brings the action.
The government ordinarily does not appeal.	Both parties can appeal.
Fines go to the state.	The individual receives damages as compensation for harm done.

SOURCE: Joseph Senna & Larry Siegel, *Introduction to Criminal Justice*, 4/e (St. Paul, West Publishing Company, 1987).

Constitution in 1788 and the development of the first state legal codes, formal law in the original colonies was adopted from existing English law, which is known today as the **common law.** Common law first came into being during the reign of King Henry II (1154–89) when royal judges were appointed to travel to specific jurisdictions to hold court and represent the crown. The royal judges began to replace local custom with a national law that was followed in courts throughout the country—thus, the law was "common" to the entire nation. The common law developed when English judges actually created many crimes by ruling that certain actions were subject to state control and sanction. The most serious offenses such as murder, rape, treason, arson, and burglary, which had hitherto been viewed largely as personal wrongs (torts for which the victim received monetary compensation from the offender), were redefined by the judges as offenses against the state, or crimes.

The English common law evolved constantly to fit specific incidents that the judges encountered. In fact, legal scholars have identified specific cases in which judges created new crimes, some of which exist today. For example, in the "Carrier's" case (1473) an English court ruled that a merchant who had been hired to transport merchandise was guilty of larceny (theft) if he kept the goods for his own purposes.[2] Prior to the "Carrier's" case, the common law had not recognized a crime when people kept something that was voluntarily

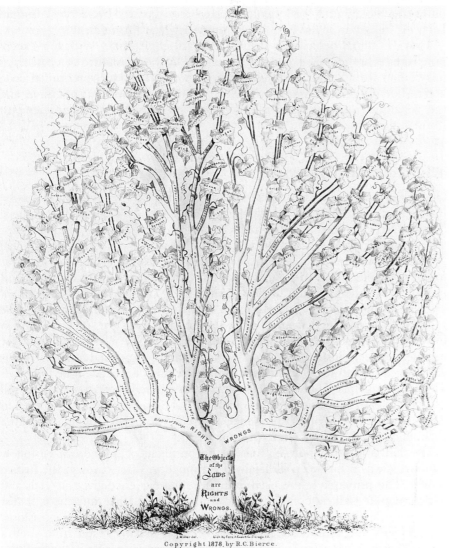

Copyright 1878, by R.C. Bierce.

The Common Law---In the Similitude of a Tree. By R.C. Bierce, Counselor at Law.

This lithograph from 1878 uses the metaphor of a tree to demonstrate the organic structure and relationships of the common law.

Chapter 4

Criminal Law: Substance and Procedure

113

placed in their possession, even if the rightful owner had only given them temporary custody of the merchandise. Breaking with legal tradition, the court recognized that the commercial system could not be maintained unless the law of theft were changed. Thus, larcenies defined by separate and unique criminal laws, such as embezzlement, extortion and false pretenses, came into existence.

Prior to the American Revolution the common law was the law of the land in the colonies. The original colonists abided by the various common law rulings and adapted them to fit their needs, making extensive changes in them when necessary. After the War of Independence, most state legislatures incorporated the common law into standardized legal codes. Over the years, some of the original common law crimes have changed considerably due to revisions. For example, the common law crime of rape originally applied only to female victims. This has been replaced in a number of jurisdictions by general sexual assault statutes that condemn sexual attacks against any persons, regardless of whether they are male or female. Similarly, statutory offenses such as those banning the sale and possession of narcotics or outlawing the pirating of videotapes have been passed to control human behavior unknown at the time the common law was formulated.

Today, criminal behavior is defined primarily by statute. With few exceptions, crimes are removed, added, or modified by the legislature of a particular jurisdiction. In addition, many states have both a substantive criminal code and a code of criminal procedure that separates the definitions of crimes and the penalties from the various procedures used to process the defendant through the justice system.

The Principle of *Stare Decisis*

One of the principal components of the common law was its recognition of the **law of precedent.** Once a decision had been made by a court, that judicial decision was generally binding on other courts in subsequent applicable cases. This principle is based on judge-made, or case, law created by judicial decisions. For example, if a homeowner who killed an unarmed intruder was found not guilty of murder on the ground that he had a right to defend his property, that rule would be applied in subsequent cases involving the same set of facts. In other words, a decision on the issue of self-defense in that case would be followed in that jurisdiction by the same court or a lesser court in future cases presenting the same legal problem. Since the common law represented decisions handed down by judges, as distinguished from law that is determined by statutes, it was essential that the rule of precedent be followed. This legal principle, known as *stare decisis,* originated in England and is still used as the basis for deciding future legal cases.[3] *Stare decisis* is firmly rooted in our American system of jurisprudence and serves to furnish the courts with a clear guide for the adjudication of similar issues.

The courts are generally bound by the principle of *stare decisis* to follow criminal law as it has been judicially determined in prior cases in the justice system. This principle is also used in interpreting evidence given in trials and in determining trial outcomes. The advantage of this legal doctrine is that it promotes stability and certainty in the process of making legal decisions. Predictability and uniformity in judicial decision making result from such a policy. However, where sufficient reason exists for varying from precedent, the court need not follow previous case decisions. For example, in the case of *Gideon v. Wainwright*, the U.S. Supreme Court ruled that a defendant in a felony case had the legal right to an attorney, although previous courts had decided such a right existed only in capital cases.[4] In other words, when a principle of law established by precedent is no longer appropriate because of changing economic, political, and social conditions, courts can redefine legal traditions and overrule precedent.[5] Because of this flexibility, the principle of *stare decisis* remains firmly embedded in our legal system.

■ Purposes of the Criminal Law

Today, the criminal law serves a number of different purposes, five of the most important of which are discussed here. Underlying these broad purposes is the desire to prevent and control unacceptable behavior and protect the interests of society and its citizens.

1. *Identification of Public Wrongs.* One major purpose of the substantive criminal law is the identification of conduct that society deems unjustifiable. Such conduct inflicts or threatens to harm individuals or the public interest.[6] Conversely, acts that are not identified by the criminal law as crimes are protected from state sanction. In some instances, the law seeks an outright ban on acts such as murder, rape, and arson. In other situations, the law seeks to create boundaries of acceptable behavior. For example, consider the 55-mile-per-hour speed limit, 21-year-old drinking age, or government lotteries in jurisdictions that prohibit other types of gambling.

2. *Exertion of Social Control.* The criminal law allows the state to control and sanction those people who commit crime. This distinguishes crimes from the unwritten rules of conventional society: ordinary customs and conventions referred to as **folkways,** and universally followed behavior norms and morals known as **mores.** Whereas crime brings the offender into confrontation with the state and its authorities, infringement of unwritten rules is subject only to social disapproval and individual expressions of scorn.

3. *Deterrence of Antisocial Behavior.* Society must give fair warning of the nature of forbidden conduct and describe the sanctions associated with the outlawed behaviors. The well-publicized punishments connected to criminal law violations serve to deter potential criminals from carrying out their illegal plans and schemes. It is believed that if punishments of adequate severity are swiftly given, and if criminals believe they are likely to be caught, the threat of the criminal law should be sufficient to deter crime.

4. *Regulation of Punishments.* The criminal law spells out the punishments given to law violators. In so doing, it safeguards offenders against excessive, disproportionate, or arbitrary punishments.[7] In an ideal world offenders who have similar criminal backgrounds and who commit similar crimes would receive identical sanctions. Of course, this does not always work in practice, but the criminal law attempts to regulate punishment or at least keep penalties within an acceptable range. In creating punishments, the framers of the criminal law should take into account such issues as public opinion about the crime's social harm, the ability of the justice system to carry out sanctions, and the latest scientific views on the prevention of crime and treatment of offenders. For example, society would be appalled if shoplifters were punished as severely as rapists, or if traffic offenders were regularly sentenced to prison.

5. *Maintenance of the Social Order.* An underlying principle of all legal systems is to support and maintain the boundaries of the social system they serve. In medieval England the law protected the feudal system by defining an orderly system of property transfer and ownership. Similarly, the legal systems in communist or socialist countries are designed to curtail profiteering and private ownership of production. The American free enterprise system is maintained by the power of the criminal law to protect the marketplace and allow commerce to exist. For example, if it were not for the various laws of theft—larceny, burglary, robbery—businesspeople would be prevented from accumulating large sums of money that they do not have in their direct possession. The banking system could not exist, nor could credit be extended. Thus, the criminal law is tailored to fit the social and economic system it serves.

■ Sources of the Criminal Law

The five major sources of the criminal law are (1) common law, (2) statutes, (3) case decisions, (4) administrative rules and regulations, and (5) constitutional law.[8]

Common Law and Statutes

The common law crimes adopted into state codes form one major source of the substantive criminal law today. At common law, crimes had a general meaning, and everyone basically understood the definition of such actions as murder, larceny, and rape. Today, statutes, enacted by state and federal legislative bodies, have built on these common law meanings and often contain more detailed and specific definitions of the crimes. Statutes are thus a way in which the criminal law is created, modified, or expunged.

Case Decisions

Case law and judicial decision making also change and influence laws. For example, a statute may define murder as the "unlawful killing of one human being by another with malice." Court decisions might help explain the meaning of the term "malice" or clarify whether "human being" includes a fetus. A judge may rule that a statute is vague or deals with an act no longer of interest to the public or is an unfair exercise of state control over an individual. Conversely, some judges may interpret the law so that behaviors that were previously acceptable become outlawed. For example, judges in a particular jurisdiction might find all people who sell magazines depicting nude men and women guilty of the crime of selling obscene material, whereas in the past obscenity was interpreted much more narrowly. Or, some courts might consider drunken driving a petty crime, while others might interpret the driving under the influence (DWI) statute more severely.

Administrative Rulemaking

Administrative agencies with rule-making authority also develop measures to control conduct in our society.[9] Some agencies regulate taxation, health, environment, and other public functions; others control drugs, illegal gambling, or pornographic material. The listing of prohibited drugs by various state health boards, for example, is an important administrative control function. Parole boards are administrative agencies that implement the thousands of parole regulations that govern the conduct of criminal offenders after their release from prison. Such rules are called administrative rules with criminal sanctions, and the agency decisions about these rules have the force and authority of law.

Constitutional Law and its Limits

Regardless of its source, all criminal law in the United States must conform to the rules and dictates of the U.S. Constitution.[10] In other words, any criminal law that conflicts with the various provisions and articles of the Constitution will eventually be challenged in the appellate courts and stricken from the legal code by judicial order (or modified to adhere to constitutional principles). As Chief Justice John Marshall's opinion in *Marbury v. Madison* indicated, "If the courts are to regard the constitution and the constitution is superior to any ordinary act of the legislature, the constitution and not such ordinary act must govern the case to which they apply."[11]

Among the general limitations set by the Constitution are those that forbid the government to pass **ex post facto laws.** Such laws create crimes (or penalties) that can be enforced retroactively (though civil penalties such as tax laws can be retroactive). The Constitution also forbids **bills of attainder,** legislative acts that inflict punishment without a judicial trial. In addition, criminal laws have been interpreted as violating constitutional principles if they are too vague, or overbroad, to give clear meaning of their intent. For example, a law forbidding adults to engage in "immoral behavior" could not be passed because it does not use clear and precise language nor give adequate notice as to which conduct is forbidden.[12] The Constitution also forbids laws that make a person's status a crime. For example, addiction to narcotics cannot be made a crime, though laws can be passed forbidding the sale, possession, and manufacture of dangerous drugs.

In general, the Constitution has been interpreted to forbid any criminal law that violates a person's right to be treated fairly and equally; this principle is referred to as **substantive due process.** Usually, this means that, before a new law can be created, the state must show that there is a compelling need to protect public safety or morals. However, a law that unfairly penalizes a particular group of people would be considered unconstitutional. Therefore, laws requiring drivers to buckle their seat belts to protect their physical well-being are considered a reasonable exercise in public safety; in contrast, a law requiring all people to attend church every Sunday to protect their moral well-being would be considered an infringement of the personal freedom guaranteed by the First Amendment.

By the same token, constitutional provisions can be used to strike down administrative or judicial rules and regulations that do not meet the requirements of **procedural due process.** This means that the Constitution guarantees fairness and justice in such proceedings. The hearing must be fair; defendants must have the opportunity to defend themselves; the hearing must be held before an impartial tribunal, and so on. In this and subsequent chapters, the due process guarantees of criminal procedure will be discussed in detail.

■ How Crimes are Classified

The decision of how a crime should be classified rests with the individual jurisdiction. Each state has developed its own body of criminal law and consequently determines its own penalties for the different crimes. Thus, the criminal law of a given state defines and grades offenses, sets levels of punishment, and classifies crimes into different categories. Over the years, crimes have been generally grouped into the following classifications: (1) felonies, misdemeanors, and violations; and (2) other statutory classifications such as juvenile delinquency, sex offender categories, and multiple- or first-offender classifications.

The Concepts of *Mala in se* and *Mala Prohibitum*

In the early twentieth century, such terms as *mala in se* and *mala prohibitum* were also used to describe categories of crime.[13] **Mala in se** crimes were basically those that appeared inherently wrong or evil by their nature. Crimes involving gross immorality or depravity—such as murder, armed robbery, kidnapping, and rape—are all essentially evil and are considered *mala in se* offenses. Common law crimes were generally considered to be *mala in se* because the common law concerned itself with actions wrong in themselves and not with crimes forbidden by statutory law.

 Mala prohibitum offenses were those that were sanctioned because they were prohibited by statute; that is, they had been defined as crimes by the penal code. The question of immorality does not exist in *mala prohibitum* crimes because these crimes are created by legislative enactment for the well-being of society. Such crimes included speeding, driving under the influence of alcohol, going through a red light, being disorderly or vagrant, and other similar breaches of the public peace.

 Over the years, this historic distinction between *mala in se* and *mala prohibitum* offenses has been a useful reference for legislative substantive law revisions, particularly when they involve issues of criminal intent and liability. Practically speaking, however, such distinctions have little bearing on the classification of crimes today.

 Crimes can also be grouped according to the harm done. Who and what is the legislature trying to protect from injury is the basic question with regard to this kind of classification. Some crimes, such as murder, manslaughter, rape, assault, and robbery, are classified offenses against a person. Other crimes, such as arson, burglary, and larceny, are classified as offenses against property to protect the home and the interest in personal property. Offenses against authority in the administration of justice include many public welfare crimes and serious offenses such as perjury and treason. Crimes are categorized in this fashion in almost every state penal code. Such a classification helps the legislature locate particular crimes within the penal code and develop comparable sentences for the various offenses.

Felonies and Misdemeanors

The most common classification in the United States is the division between felonies and misdemeanors.[14] This distinction is based primarily on the degree of seriousness of the crime.

Distinguishing between a **felony** and a **misdemeanor** is sometimes difficult. Simply put, a felony is a serious offense and a misdemeanor a less serious one. *Black's Law Dictionary* defines the two terms as follows:

> A felony is a crime of a graver or more atrocious nature than those designated as misdemeanors. Generally it is an offense punishable by death or imprisonment in a penitentiary. A misdemeanor is lower than a felony and generally punishable by fine or imprisonment otherwise than in a penitentiary.[15]

Each jurisdiction in the United States determines by statute what types of conduct constitute felonies or misdemeanors. The most common definition for a felony is that it is a crime punishable in the statute by death or imprisonment in a state prison. In Massachusetts, for example, any crime that a statute punishes by imprisonment in the state prison system is considered a felony, and all other crimes are misdemeanors.[16] Another way of determining what category an offense falls into is by providing in the statute that a felony is any crime punishable by imprisonment for more than one year. In the former method, the place of imprisonment is critical; in the latter, the length of the prison sentence distinguishes a felony from a misdemeanor.

In the United States today, felonies include serious crimes against the person such as criminal homicide, robbery, and rape, or crimes against property such as burglary and larceny. Misdemeanors include petit (or petty) larceny, assault and battery, and the unlawful possession of marijuana. The least serious, or petty, offenses, often involving criminal traffic violations, are called infractions.

The felony-misdemeanor classification has a direct effect on the offender charged with the crime. A person convicted of a felony may be barred from certain fields of employment or from entering some professional fields of study, such as law or medicine. A felony offender's status as an alien in the United States might also be affected, or the offender might be denied the right to hold public office, vote, or serve on a jury.[17] These and other civil liabilities exist only when a person is convicted of a felony offense, not a misdemeanor.

Whether the offender is charged with a felony or a misdemeanor also makes a difference at the time of arrest. Normally, the law of arrest requires that if the crime is a misdemeanor and has not been committed in the presence of a police officer, the officer cannot make an arrest. This is known as the in-presence requirement. However, the police officer does have the legal authority to arrest a suspect for a misdemeanor at a subsequent time by the use of a validly obtained arrest warrant. In contrast, an arrest for a felony may be made regardless of whether the crime was committed in the officer's presence, as long as the officer has reasonable grounds to believe that the person has committed the felony.

Another important effect of this classification is that a court's jurisdiction often depends on whether a crime is considered a felony or a misdemeanor. A person charged with a felony must be tried by a court that has jurisdiction over the type of offense. Similarly, some states prosecute felonies only on indictment. This means that a person accused of a felony ordinarily has a legal right to a preliminary hearing and presentment of the charges by indictment of a grand jury or information.

In addition to serious felony crimes and less serious offenses labeled misdemeanors, some jurisdictions also have a third category of least serious offenses called violations. These violations, ordinarily of town, city, or county ordinances, are regulatory offenses that may not require *mens rea* (criminal intent). Examples include health and sanitary violations, unlawful assembly, public disturbances, and traffic violations.

Behavioral Classifications

In addition to the felony-misdemeanor classifications, crimes may be classified according to the characteristics of the offender. All states, for example, have juvenile delinquency statutes that classify children under a certain age as juvenile delinquents if they commit acts that would constitute crimes if committed by adults. Some states have special statutory classifications for sex offenders, multiple offenders, youthful offenders, and first offenders. Generally, no special statutory classification exists for white-collar crimes, which usually involve nonviolent conduct such as embezzlement, fraud, and income tax violation.

■ The Legal Definition of a Crime

There is no single universally accepted legal definition of crime. Because the determination of what constitutes a crime rests with the individual jurisdiction, the federal government and each of the states have their own body of criminal law. Most general legal definitions of a crime are basically similar in nature, however. A crime can be defined as follows:

> A crime is (1) a legal wrong (2) prohibited by the criminal law (3) prosecuted by the state (4) in a formal court proceeding (5) in which a criminal sanction or sentence may be imposed.

As determined by most legal systems, crime can result from the commission of an act in violation of the law or from the omission of a required legal act. For example, a crime can be an intentional act of striking another person or of stealing someone else's property. A crime can also involve the failure of a person to act, such as the failure to file an income tax return, a parent's failure to care for a child, the failure to report a crime, or the failure to report an automobile accident.

The legal definition of a crime involves the elements of the criminal acts that must be proven in a court of law if the defendant is to be found guilty. For the most part, common criminal acts have both mental and physical elements, both of which must be present if the act is to be considered a legal crime. The following definition of the crime of burglary in the nighttime, as stated in the Massachusetts General Laws, is an example of the mental and physical elements of the substantive criminal law:

> Whoever breaks and enters a dwelling house in the nighttime, with intent to commit a felony, or whoever, after having entered with such intent, breaks such dwelling house in the nighttime, any person being lawfully therein, and the offender being armed with a dangerous weapon at the time of such breaking or entry, or so arming himself in such house or making an actual assault on a person lawfully therein, (commits the crime of burglary).[18]

The elements of the crime are

1. Nighttime
2. Breaking and entering, or breaking or entering
3. A dwelling house

4. Being armed, or arming the self after entering, or committing an actual assault on a person lawfully therein
5. Intent to commit a felony

Notice how certain basic elements are required in order for an act to be considered a crime. For the crime of burglary, the state must prove that the defendant actually entered a home by force and was not invited in, that the defendant carried an identifiable weapon, that the crime occurred after sundown, and that the act was intentional. These elements form what is known as the **corpus delicti,** or "body of the crime." Often, the term *corpus delicti* is misunderstood. Some people, for instance, wrongly believe that it refers to the body of the deceased in a homicide. *Corpus delicti* describes all the elements that together constitute a crime; it includes (1) the *actus reus,* (2) the *mens rea,* and (3) the combination of *actus reus* and *mens rea.*

Actus Reus

The term **actus reus,** which translates as "guilty act," refers to the forbidden act itself. The criminal law uses it to describe the physical crime and/or the commission of the criminal act (or omission of the lawful act). In *Criminal Law,* Wayne LaFave and Austin Scott state:

> Bad thought alone cannot constitute a crime, there must be an act, or an omission to act where there is a legal duty to act. Thus, the criminal law crimes are defined in terms of act or omission to act and statutory crimes are unconstitutional unless so defined. A bodily movement, to qualify as an act forming the basis of criminal liability, must be voluntary.[19]

The physical act in violation of the criminal statute is usually clearly defined within each offense. For example, in the crime of manslaughter, the unlawful killing of a human being is the physical act prohibited by a statute; in burglary, it is the actual breaking and entering into a dwelling house or other structure for the purpose of committing a felony.

Regarding an omission to act, many jurisdictions hold a person accountable if a legal duty exists and the offender avoids it. In most instances the duty to act is based on a defined relationship such as parent-child or on a contractual duty such as lifeguard-swimmer. The law, for example, recognizes that a parent has a legal duty to protect a child. When a parent refuses to obtain medical attention for the child and the child dies, the parent's actions constitute an omission to act, and that omission is a crime.

Finally, the *actus reus* must be a measurable act; thought alone is not a crime. However, planning, conspiring, and soliciting for criminal purposes are considered an *actus reus* even if the actual crime is never carried out or completed.

Mens Rea

The second element basic to the commission of any crime is the establishment of the **mens rea,** translated as "guilty mind." *Mens rea* is the element of the crime that deals with the defendant's intent to commit a criminal act and also includes such states of mind as concealing criminal knowledge (scienter), recklessness, negligence, and criminal purpose.[20] A person ordinarily cannot be convicted of a crime unless it is proven that he or she intentionally, knowingly, or willingly committed the criminal act.

The following case illustrates the absence of *mens rea*. A student at a university took home some books, believing them to be her own, and subsequently found that the books belonged to her classmate. When she realized that the books did not belong to her, she returned them to their proper owner. The student could not be prosecuted for theft because she did not intend to steal the books in the first place; she did not knowingly take the books and therefore lacked sufficient knowledge that her act was unlawful.

Another case that illustrates a lack of criminal intent, but one in which actual harm occurs, is that in which a pedestrian is accidentally killed in an automobile accident. At the time of the accident, the driver is operating the motor vehicle legally and with appropriate care, but the victim steps out in front of the car and is struck and killed. The driver cannot be convicted of manslaughter unless evidence can be found that some intent or gross criminal negligence existed at the time of the accident. This situation would be considered in a completely different legal light if it could be proved that the driver actually intended to hit the pedestrian or had been driving the car in a willful and reckless manner, indicating criminal negligence.

Ordinary negligence is any conduct that falls below the normal standard established by law for the protection of others against unreasonable risk. **Criminal negligence,** on the other hand, exists where actions show a significant degree of carelessness that results in a culpable disregard for the safety of others. Thus, in order for an individual to be found guilty of committing most crimes, it must be proved that he or she committed the physical act itself and that he or she intended to do so with full awareness of the consequences of the act.

Other variations on the concept of criminal intent exist. Different degrees of intent are used to determine the mental state necessary for an individual to commit a particular crime. Where a criminal homicide occurs, it may be necessary to prove that a mental state of premeditation and malice existed in the accused before a judgment of first-degree murder can be reached; for a judgment of second-degree murder, it may be necessary to prove malice; and for a judgment of third-degree murder, it may be necessary to prove guilty knowledge or criminal negligence.

Mens rea conditions also differ among the types of crime when considering whether a **general** or **specific intent** to commit the crime exists. For most crimes, a general intent on the part of the accused to act purposefully or to accomplish a criminal result must be proved. A specific intent requires that the actor intended to accomplish a specific purpose as an element of the crime. Burglary, for example, involves more than the general intent of breaking and entering into a dwelling house; it usually also involves the specific intent of committing a felony, such as stealing money or jewels. Many other crimes such as robbery, larceny, assault with intent to kill, false pretense, and even kidnapping may require a specific intent.

Relationship of *Mens Rea* and *Actus Reus*

The third element needed to prove the *corpus delicti* of a crime is the relationship of the act to the criminal intent or result. The law requires that the offender's conduct must be the approximate cause of any injury resulting from the criminal act. If, for example, a man chases a victim into the street intending to assault him and the victim is struck and killed by a car, the accused could be convicted of murder if the court felt that his actions made him responsible for the victim's death. If, however, a victim dies from a completely unrelated illness after being assaulted, the court must determine whether the death was a probable consequence of the defendant's illegal conduct or whether it would have resulted even if the assault had not occurred.

In addition, to prove a crime, the state must show that the external physical act and the internal mental state were in some way connected to one another. For example, if a man breaks into another person's house to escape a violent storm and while in the home notices some jewels and steals them, he cannot be found guilty of the crime of burglary since he did not intend to commit a crime at the time he broke into the house. Nevertheless, he could be convicted of larceny and criminal trespass, since he had the necessary intent at the time he committed these crimes. However, evil intent and the act it produces do not necessarily have to take place at the same time. If a terrorist plants a bomb in an airport, but it does not go off until three weeks later, that would still be considered murder—assuming people are killed.

Criminal liability, as previously explained, cannot be imposed for simply having had bad thoughts about the victim at a previous time. Thus, a concurrence of act and intent—*actus reus* and *mens rea*—must be present if a crime is to occur. However, cases do exist where one person intends criminal action against another but harms a third party instead; for example, the accused intends to shoot one person but misses and shoots another. In this instance, the law transfers the original criminal intent to the innocent bystander. Under the legal doctrine of **transferred intent,** the accused would be considered criminally responsible for transferring wrongful intent to the other person.

Most environmental protection laws involve strict liability. To be found guilty of violating a statute prohibiting illegal dumping of dangerous chemicals, it is not essential to show mens rea.

Strict Liability

Existence of a criminal intent and a wrongful act must both be proved before an individual can be found guilty of committing a crime. However, certain statutory offenses exist in which *mens rea* is not essential. These offenses fall within a category known as public welfare, or **strict liability,** crimes. A person can be held responsible for such a violation independent of the existence of intent to commit the offense. Strict liability criminal statutes generally include narcotics control laws, traffic laws, health and safety regulations, sanitation laws, and other regulatory statutes. For example, a driver could not defend himself against a speeding ticket by claiming that he was unaware of how fast he was going and did not intend to speed, nor could a bartender claim that a juvenile to whom she sold liquor looked quite a bit older. No state of mind is generally required in such instances, where a strict liability statute is violated.[21]

The general purpose of such laws is to protect the public and to provide the prosecution with an opportunity to convict offenders of crimes that would ordinarily be difficult to prove in court. Over the years, most legal commentators have been critical of strict liability offenses because it seems unfair to punish a person without referring to that person's state of mind when committing the crime.[22] However, these statutes still remain part of the legal codes in many jurisdictions.

Table 4.1 presents some categories of major substantive crimes common to all jurisdictions. The basic elements of each crime are contained within its definition.

TABLE 4.1 ■ Common Law Crimes

Crimes Against the Person	Examples
First-degree murder. Unlawful killing of another human being with malice aforethought and with premeditation and deliberation.	A woman buys some poison and pours it into a cup of coffee her husband is drinking, intending to kill him. The motive—to get the insurance benefits of the victim.
Second-degree murder. Unlawful killing of another human being with malice aforethought but without premeditation and deliberation.	A man intending to greatly harm his friend after a disagreement in a bar hits his friend in the head with a baseball bat, and the victim dies as a result of the injury. Hitting someone hard with a bat is known to cause serious injury. Because the act was committed in spite of this fact, it is second-degree murder.
Voluntary manslaughter. Intentional killing committed under extenuating circumstances that mitigate the killing, such as killing in the heat of passion after being provoked.	A husband coming home early from work finds his wife in bed with another man. The husband goes into a rage and shoots and kills both lovers with a gun he keeps by his bedside.
Involuntary manslaughter. Unintentional killing, without malice, that is neither excused nor justified, such as homicide resulting from criminal negligence.	After becoming drunk, a woman drives a car at high speed down a crowded street and kills a pedestrian.
Battery. Unlawful touching of another with intent to cause injury.	A man seeing a stranger sitting in his favorite seat in the cafeteria goes up to that person and pushes him out of the seat.
Assault. Intentional placing of another in fear of receiving an immediate battery.	A student aims an unloaded gun at her professor who believes the gun is loaded. She says she is going to shoot.
Rape. Unlawful sexual intercourse with a female without her consent.	After a party a man offers to drive a young female acquaintance home. He takes her to a wooded area and despite her protests forces her to have sexual relations with him.
Statutory rape. Sexual intercourse with a female who is under the age of consent.	A boy, aged 18, and his girlfriend, aged 15, have sexual relations. Though the victim voluntarily participates, her age makes her incapable of legally consenting to have sexual relations.
Robbery. Wrongful taking and carrying away of personal property from a person by violence or intimidation.	A man armed with a loaded gun approaches another man on a deserted street and demands his wallet.

■ Criminal Responsibility

The idea of criminal responsibility is also essential to any discussion of criminal law. The law recognizes that certain conditions of a person's mental state might excuse him or her from acts that otherwise would be considered criminal. These factors have been used in legal defenses to negate the intent required for the commission of a crime. For example, a person who kills another while insane may argue in court that he or she was not responsible for criminal conduct. Similarly, a child who violates the law may not be treated as an adult offender. Three major types of criminal defense are detailed in this section.

Insanity

Criminal **insanity** is a legal defense involving the use of rules and standards to determine if a person's state of mental balance negates criminal responsibility. Insanity is a legal concept and not one coined by the mental health field. Consequently, there are no standard symptoms of insanity or any specific behaviors that determine its existence. Instead, each legal jurisdiction defines

TABLE 4.1 ■ *(continued)*

Inchoate (Incomplete) Offenses	Examples
Attempt. An intentional act for the purpose of committing a crime that is more than mere preparation or planning of the crime. The crime is not completed, however.	A person intending to kill another places a bomb in the second person's car so that it will detonate when the ignition key is used. The bomb is discovered before the car is started. Attempted murder has been committed.
Conspiracy. Voluntary agreement between two or more persons to achieve an unlawful object or to achieve a lawful object using means forbidden by law.	A drug company sells larger-than-normal quantities of drugs to a doctor, knowing that the doctor is distributing the drugs illegally. The drug company is guilty of conspiracy.
Solicitation. Efforts by one person to encourage another person to commit or attempt to commit a crime by means of advising, enticing, inciting, ordering, or otherwise.	A person offers another a hundred dollars to set fire to a third person's house. The person requesting that the fire be set is guilty of solicitation, whether the fire is set or not.
Burglary. Breaking and entering of a dwelling house of another in the nighttime with the intent to commit a felony.	Intending to steal some jewelry and silver, a young man breaks a window and enters another's house at 10 P.M.
Arson. Intentional burning of a dwelling house of another.	A secretary, angry that her boss did not give her a raise, goes to her boss's house and sets fire to it.
Larceny. Taking and carrying away the personal property of another with the intent to steal the property.	While a woman is shopping, she sees a diamond ring displayed at the jewelry counter. When no one is looking, the woman takes the ring and walks out of the store.
Embezzlement. Fraudulent appropriation of another's property by one already in lawful possession.	A bank teller receives a cash deposit from a customer and places it in the cash drawer with other deposits. A few minutes later, he takes the deposit out of the cash drawer and keeps it by placing it in his pocket.
Receiving stolen goods. Receiving of stolen property with the knowledge that the property is stolen and with the intent to deprive the owner of the property.	A "fence" accepts some television sets from a thief with the intention of selling them, knowing that the sets have been stolen.

insanity as it sees fit and then, at trial, attempts to determine whether the defendant meets the standards set forth in the state's criminal code. Usually, people who claim they are insane are examined by psychologists and psychiatrists who will then testify at trial on the defendant's mental condition. This procedure is often unsatisfactory because members of the mental health profession will disagree sharply on their diagnosis, and their conflicting opinions only serve to confuse the judge and jury.

STAGES OF INSANITY. If a person is declared insane at the time he or she committed a criminal act, a judgment of *not guilty by reason of insanity* is entered. The person is then held in an institution for the criminally insane until found to be sane and eligible for release. Defendants may also be incompetent to stand trial because of their mental condition. In this instance they would be held in a mental institution until ready to stand trial. If after a reasonable period of time they are still unable to stand trial, the state might move to have them committed to an institution under civil commitment procedures. On rare occasions, a person who was insane or temporarily insane at the time of committing a crime is treated successfully before coming to trial.

Under those circumstances the state would have no choice but to find the person not guilty and release him or her into the community, since psychiatric care is no longer needed.

LEGAL DEFINITION OF INSANITY. Over the years, the legal system has struggled to define the rules relating to the use of insanity as a defense in a criminal trial. The different tests for criminal responsibility involving insanity followed by United States courts are (1) the *M'Naghten rule*; (2) the *irresistible impulse test*; (3) the *Durham rule*; and (4) the *substantial capacity test*.

The **M'Naghten rule,** or the right-wrong test, is based on the decision in the *M'Naghten* case.[23] In 1843, Daniel M'Naghten shot and killed Edward Drummond, believing Drummond to be Sir Robert Peel, the British prime minister. M'Naghten was prosecuted for murder. At his trial he claimed that he was not criminally responsible for his actions because he suffered from delusions at the time of the killing. M'Naghten was found not guilty by reason of insanity. Because of the importance of the case and the unpopularity of the decision, the House of Lords reviewed the decision and asked the court to define the law with respect to crimes committed by persons suffering from insane delusions. The court's answer became known as the M'Naghten rule and has subsequently become the primary test for criminal responsibility in the United States. The M'Naghten rule can be stated as follows:

> A defendant may be excused from criminal responsibility if at the time of the committing of the act the party accused was labouring under such a defect of reason, from a disease of the mind, as not to know the nature and quality of the act he was doing, or if he did know it, that he did not know that he was doing what was wrong.

Thus, according to the M'Naghten rule, a person is basically insane if he or she is unable to distinguish between right and wrong as a result of some mental disability.

Over the years, the courts have become critical of the M'Naghten rule. Many insane individuals are able to distinguish between right and wrong. Also, a clear determination by the courts of terms such as "disease of the mind," "know," and "the nature and quality of the act" has never been made. As a result, many jurisdictions that follow the M'Naghten rule have supplemented it with the **irresistible impulse test.** This rule excuses from criminal responsibility a person whose mental disease makes it impossible to control personal conduct. The criminal may be able to distinguish between right and wrong but may be unable to exercise self-control because of a disabling mental condition. Approximately 20 states use a combined M'Naghten rule–irresistible impulse test.

Another rule for determining criminal insanity is the **Durham rule.** Originally created in New Hampshire in 1871, the Durham rule was reviewed and subsequently adopted by the Court of Appeals for the District of Columbia in 1954, in the case of *Durham v. United States.*[24] In that opinion, Judge David Bazelon rejected the M'Naghten formula and stated that an accused is not criminally responsible if the unlawful act was the product of mental disease or defect. This rule, also known as the *products test*, is based on the contention that insanity represents many personality factors, all of which may not be present in every case. It leaves the question of deciding whether a defendant is insane in the hands of jurors.

The Durham rule has been viewed with considerable skepticism, primarily because the problem of defining "mental disease or defect" and "product" does not give the jury a reliable standard by which to make its judgment. Consequently, it has been dropped in the jurisdictions that experimented with it and is used in only New Hampshire today. Nevertheless, the Durham rule was probably the most important factor in stimulating rethinking of the entire insanity issue, and it revolutionized the law of insanity in the United States. It opened up the insanity defense to the urban poor, desegregated mental hospitals, and helped bring legal psychiatric services to the needy.

Another test for criminal insanity, which has become increasingly popular with many courts, is the **substantial capacity test.** In summary, as presented in § 4.01 of the American Law Institute's Model Penal Code, this test states:

> A person is not responsible for criminal conduct if at the time of such conduct as a result of mental disease or defect he lacks substantial capacity whether to appreciate his criminality (wrongfulness) of his conduct or to conform his conduct to the requirements of law.[25]

This rule is basically a broader restatement of the M'Naghten rule–irresistible impulse test. It rejects the Durham rule because of its lack of standards and its inability to define the term "product." The most significant feature of this test is that it requires only a lack of "substantial capacity" rather than complete impairment of the defendant's ability to know and understand the difference between right and wrong. Twenty-four states use the substantial capacity test as defined by the American Law Institute.[26]

For a summary of various rules for determining criminal insanity, see Table 4.2. In reality, only a small number of offenders actually use the insanity defense because many cases involving insane offenders are processed through civil commitment proceedings.

TABLE 4.2 ■ **Various Insanity Defense Standards**

Test	Legal Standard Because of Mental Illness	Final Burden of Proof	Who Bears Burden of Proof
M'Naghten	"didn't know what he was doing or didn't know it was wrong"	Varies from proof by a balance of probabilities on the defense to proof beyond a reasonable doubt on the prosecutor	
Irresistible Impulse	"could not control his conduct"		
Durham	"the criminal act was caused by his mental illness"	Beyond reasonable doubt	Prosecutor
Substantial Capacity	"lacks substantial capacity to appreciate the wrongfulness of his conduct or to control it"	Beyond reasonable doubt	Prosecutor
Present Federal Law	"lacks capacity to appreciate the wrongfulness of his conduct"	Clear and convincing evidence	Defense

SOURCE: National Institute of Justice, *Crime Study Guide: Insanity Defense* by Norval Morris (Washington, D.C.: U.S. Department of Justice, 1986), p. 3.

DEBATE OVER THE INSANITY DEFENSE. The insanity defense has been controversial for many years. It has been criticized on the grounds that it (1) spurs crime, (2) releases criminal offenders, (3) requires extensive use of expert testimony, and (4) commits more criminals to mental institutions than to prisons.[27] In addition, according to Norval Morris, a University of Chicago law professor, defendants end up with a double stigma—namely, that they are "bad and mad" when they are found not guilty by reason of insanity.[28]

The case of John Hinckley, Jr., further heightened the debate over the insanity plea.[29] Hinckley was charged with the attempted murder of President Ronald Reagan in 1981. At his criminal trial, expert testimony was offered to show that Hinckley suffered from a serious form of schizophrenia that grew worse with age. This caused Hinckley to be criminally insane. He was unable to appreciate his actions or control himself because he had a serious disease of the mind. The government, on the other hand, was required to show that Hinckley was sane beyond a reasonable doubt and responsible for his behavior at the time of the crime. After the trial, the general public, legal commentators, and experts in the criminal justice system were shocked at the jury decision that Hinckley was not guilty by reason of insanity.

Consequently, many prosecutors, judges, and even mental health experts feel that changes are needed in the insanity plea. Two law scholars, Charles Nesson of the Harvard Law School and Norval Morris of the University of Chicago Law School, suggest that the Hinckley verdict points up the need for a new verdict of *guilty but insane*.[30] Under this procedure, if a person uses the insanity defense but a judge or jury finds the evidence insufficient to find for legal insanity, a verdict of guilty but mentally ill can be reached. This indicates the defendant is suffering from an emotional disorder severe enough to influence behavior but insufficient to render him or her insane. Consequently, after such a finding the court can impose any sentence it could have used on the crime charge. The convicted defendant is sent to prison where the correctional authorities are required to provide therapeutic treatment. If the mental illness is cured, the offender is returned to the regular prison population to serve out the remainder of the sentence. Currently, 12 states provide for a verdict of guilty but mentally ill.[31]

Another approach is to ban from court all evidence of mental illness, as was recently done in Montana, Idaho, and Utah (Idaho does allow psychiatric evidence on the issue of intent to commit crime).[32] Some commentators suggest more moderate changes, such as eliminating pleas involving "diminished capacity," where defendants lack the ability to premeditate the crime, and limiting the role of expert witnesses at trial.

Lastly, the federal government and one jurisdiction, the state of Indiana, have adopted a new test of criminal responsibility known as the appreciation test. It resembles the M'Naghten test by relying on cognitive incapacity and differs from the substantial capacity test in that the defendant is not required to show lack of control regarding behavior. It also shifts the burden of proof to the defense.[33]

Intoxication

As a general legal rule, intoxication, which may include drunkenness or being under the influence of drugs, is not considered a defense. In the highly publicized 1989 criminal homicide child abuse case of Joel Steinberg in New York City, the court rejected the defense of drug use, when it was shown that such behavior was voluntary on the defendant's part. However, a defendant who becomes involuntarily intoxicated under duress or by mistake may be excused for crimes committed. Voluntary intoxication may also lessen the degree of a crime—for example, a judgment may be decreased from first- to second-degree murder because the defendant may use intoxication to prove the lack of critical element of *mens rea*, or mental intent. Thus the effect of intoxication upon criminal liability depends upon whether the defendant uses the alcohol or drugs voluntarily. For example, a defendant who enters a bar for a few drinks, becomes intoxicated, and strikes someone can be convicted of assault and battery. On the other hand, if the defendant ordered a nonalcoholic drink, but it was "spiked" by someone else, the defendant may have a legitimate legal defense.

Given the frequency of crime-related offenses with drugs and alcohol, the impact of intoxication on criminal liability is a frequent issue in the criminal justice system. The connection between drug use, alcoholism, and violent street crime has been well documented. Although those in law enforcement and the judiciary tend to emphasize the use of the penal process in dealing with problems of chronic alcoholism and drug use, others in corrections and crime prevention favor approaches that depend more on behavioral theories and the social sciences. For example, in the case of *Robinson v. California*, the U.S. Supreme Court struck down a California statute making addiction to narcotics a crime on the ground that it violated the defendant's rights under the Eighth and Fourteenth Amendments to the U.S. Constitution.[34] On the other hand, however, the landmark decision in *Powell v. Texas*, which is highlighted in the Law in Review on page 130, placed severe limitations on the behavioral science approach in *Robinson*, when it rejected the defense of chronic alcoholism of a defendant charged with the crime of public drunkenness.[35]

Age

The law holds that a child is not criminally responsible for actions committed at an age that precludes a full realization of the gravity of certain types of behavior. Under common law, there is generally a conclusive presumption of incapacity for a child under age 7; a reliable presumption for a child between the ages of 7 and 14; and no presumption for a child over the age of 14. This generally means that a child under 7 years old who commits a crime will not be held criminally responsible for these actions, and that a child between 7 and 14 may possibly be held responsible. These common law rules have been changed by statute in most jurisdictions. Today, the maximum age of criminal responsibility for children ranges from 14 to 17, while the minimum age may be set by statute at 7 or under 14.[36] In addition, every jurisdiction has established a juvenile court system to deal with juvenile offenders and children in need of court and societal supervision. Thus, the mandate of the juvenile justice system is to provide for the care and protection of children under a given age established by state statute. In certain situations a juvenile court may transfer a child or young adult to the adult criminal court where an effort is made to deal with a more serious chronic youthful offender. The juvenile court system is discussed in detail in Chapter 18.

Powell v. Texas (1968)

The decision in *Powell v. Texas* placed significant constitutional limitations on the ruling in *Robinson v. California*, which had held unconstitutional a 90-day sentence for the crime of being addicted to the use of narcotics. In *Powell*, the U.S. Supreme Court rejected the defense of chronic alcoholism claiming that persons inflicted with the disease cannot use their disease as a defense to a criminal charge.

FACTS

In December 1966, the defendant in *Powell* was arrested and charged with being found in a state of intoxication in a public place in violation of the Texas Penal Code, which reads as follows: "Whoever shall get drunk or being found in a state of intoxication in any public place shall be fined not exceeding $100."

The defendant was tried in the Austin, Texas Corporation Court, found guilty, and fined $20. A *de novo* trial was subsequently held where the defense attorney argued that the defendant was afflicted with the disease of chronic alcoholism and that his public drunkenness was not of his own volition, and that to punish him criminally would be cruel and unusual punishment in violation of the Eighth and Fourteenth Amendments to the U.S. Constitution. The trial judge ruled that chronic alcoholism was not a defense to the charge of public drunkenness and found the defendant guilty as charged. The case was subsequently appealed to the U.S. Supreme Court.

Testimony given during the trial of the defendant indicated that he was a chronic alcoholic who was unable to control his intoxication and had an uncontrollable compulsion to drink. Psychiatric testimony was also admitted to indicate that the defendant had no willpower to resist the excessive consumption of alcohol. Based on such expert testimony, the trial court agreed (1) that chronic alcoholism was a disease; (2) that a chronic alcoholic does not appear in public by his own volition but under a compulsion symptomatic of the disease of chronic alcoholism; and (3) that Leroy Powell was in fact a chronic alcoholic afflicted with such disease.

But, in light of the uncertain medical knowledge at this time, it appears that chronic alcoholics do not necessarily suffer from an irresistible compulsion to drink and to get drunk in public, nor are they utterly unable to control their actions.

DECISION

The Supreme Court was asked to decide whether alcoholism was a condition of such an involuntary nature that to punish an individual for public in-

■ Criminal Defense: Justification and Excuse

Criminal defenses may also be based on the concept of justification or excuse. In other words, certain defenses allow for the commission of a crime to be justified or excused on grounds of fairness and public policy. In these instances, defendants normally acknowledge that they committed the act but claim that they cannot be prosecuted because they were justified in doing so. The following major types of criminal defenses involving justification or excuse are explained in this section: (1) consent, (2) self-defense, (3) entrapment, (4) double jeopardy, and (5) mistake, compulsion, and necessity.

Consent

As a general rule, the victim's consent to a crime does not justify or excuse the defendant who commits the action. The type of crime involved generally determines the validity of consent as an appropriate legal defense. Crimes such as common law rape and larceny require lack of consent on the part of the victim. In other words, a rape does not occur if the victim consents to sexual relations. In the same way, a larceny cannot occur if the owner voluntarily

toxication would be cruel and unusual punishment under the Eighth and Fourteenth Amendments to the U.S. Constitution. Prior to this case, the Court had ruled in *Robinson v. California* that a state statute making it a crime to be addicted to the use of narcotics was unconstitutional. On its face, however, according to the Court, the *Powell* case did not fall within that same meaning, since the defendant was convicted not of being a chronic alcoholic, but of being in public while drunk on a particular occasion. According to the Court, this is a far cry from convicting someone for being an addict, being mentally ill, or being a leper. Although *Robinson* forbade punishing a person for being afflicted with any disease or predisposition, Powell was a chronic alcoholic who was prosecuted for being drunk in a public place, not for being an alcoholic per se. According to the majority, if Leroy Powell could not be convicted of public intoxication, it was difficult to see how a state could convict an individual for murder, if that individual while exhibiting normal behavior suffers

from a compulsion to kill, which is an exceedingly strong but not overpowering influence.

Therefore, the Supreme Court concluded that Powell was not convicted for being a chronic alcoholic but for being drunk in public. His actions did not fall within the ruling of *Robinson*, which held that conviction for being a drug addict alone is cruel and unusual punishment. In *Powell* the conviction protected public safety and health and was constitutionally permissible.

SIGNIFICANCE OF THE CASE

Although the decision in *Robinson v. California* supported the position that a chronic alcoholic with a compulsion to consume alcohol should not be punished for drinking per se, the defendant in *Powell* was convicted for the crime of being drunk in a public place. Even though the defendant showed that he was compelled to drink, medical evidence and testimony does not indicate whether alcoholism as a dis-

ease is physically addicting or psychologically habit forming. Given the state of the record and current medical knowledge, the public has an interest in controlling behavior and actions that result from public intoxication that violates criminal laws. Consequently, a conviction for public drunkenness must be sustained even where the defendant is a chronic alcoholic whose alcoholism resulted in his being intoxicated in public, the crime for which he was arrested. The decision in *Powell* makes clear, however, that punishment for a status is particularly obnoxious and in many instances is cruel and unusual because it involves punishment for a mere propensity and desire to commit a crime, and the mental element, or *mens rea*, is not part of the criminal activity. Chronic alcoholism, even defined as a disease, however, is not a defense to being found intoxicated in a public place if such behavior violates a legitimate public intoxication statute. ■

consents to the taking of the property. Consequently, in such crimes, consent is an essential element of the crime, and it is a valid defense where it can be proven or shown that it existed at the time the crime was committed. In statutory rape, however, consent is not an element of the crime and is considered irrelevant, because the state presumes that young people are not capable of providing consent.

Consent is also not an appropriate defense in cases involving assault and battery, mayhem, or homicide, or in any crime where serious harm can come to a person. In addition, regardless of whether both parties consent to a fight, if there is a likelihood of serious bodily injury, mutual consent is not a valid defense.

Self-Defense

In certain instances the defendant who admits to the acts that constitute a crime may claim to be not guilty because of an affirmative **self-defense.** In order to establish the necessary elements to constitute self-defense, the defendant must have acted under a reasonable belief that he or she was in danger of death or great harm and had no means of escape from the assailant.

As a general legal rule, however, a person defending himself or herself may use only such force as is reasonably necessary to prevent personal harm. A person who is assaulted by another with no weapon is ordinarily not justified in hitting the assailant with a baseball bat. A person verbally threatened by another is not justified in striking the other party. If a woman hits a larger man, generally speaking the man would not be justified in striking the woman and causing her physical harm. In other words, to exercise the self-defense privilege, the danger to the defendant must be immediate. In addition, the defendant is obligated to look for alternative means of avoiding the danger such as escape or retreat, or looking for assistance from others.[37]

The 1984 case of Bernhard Goetz, the celebrated "subway shooter," is a much publicized example of legal self-defense versus unlawful vigilantism in an urban setting.[38] Goetz, a 37-year-old businessman, shot four black teenagers on a New York subway train after being asked for five dollars. Three of the teens were carrying sharpened screwdrivers and had prior arrest records; they had allegedly threatened Goetz. New York state law allows a victim to shoot in self-defense only if there is reasonable belief that the assailant will use deadly force and if the victim cannot escape.

After a much publicized refusal by a first grand jury to indict Goetz for attempted murder, Goetz was subsequently indicted, tried, and acquitted in 1987 of attempted murder and assault, but convicted of illegal possession of an unlicensed concealed handgun. Goetz claimed he shot the four youths in self-defense because he feared he was about to be robbed. This bitter and controversial case involving urban crime finally came to an end in January 1989 when Goetz was given a one-year jail sentence for the illegal handgun charge. According to the prosecution, Goetz had taken the law into his own hands. Goetz himself maintained that society needs to be protected from criminals.

The elements that constitute self-defense are also applicable to the defense of another and to the defense of one's property. The right to defend another is based on the responsibility of a citizen to use force to exercise a citizen arrest and to defend members of a family group. The right to defend one's property is dependent on the exercise of reasonable force to retain property or to remove a trespasser. Most jurisdictions use the "reasonableness" test determined by the facts of the action to decide what constitutes an appropriate defense of property. In some other jurisdictions, force has been accepted as a reasonable way to prevent a burglary. Generally speaking, however, force is ordinarily an acceptable means of protecting property only when it is used as a last resort when the police are unavailable or when reasonable requests to control trespass or unlawful action have been ignored.[39]

Entrapment

The term **entrapment** refers to an affirmative defense in the criminal law that excuses a defendant from criminal liability when law enforcement agents use traps, decoys, and deception to induce criminal action. It is generally legitimate for law enforcement officers to set traps for criminals by getting information about crimes from informers, undercover agents, and codefendants. Police officers are allowed to use ordinary opportunities for defendants to commit crime, and to create these opportunities without excessive inducement and solicitation to commit and involve a defendant in a crime. However, when the police instigate the crime, implant criminal ideas, and coerce individuals into bringing about a crime, defendants have the defense of entrapment available to them. Entrapment is not a constitutional defense but has been created by court decision and statute in most jurisdictions.

The degree of government involvement in a criminal act leading to the entrapment defense has been defined in a number of U.S. Supreme Court decisions beginning in 1932. The majority view of what constitutes entrapment can be seen in the 1932 case of *Sorrells v. United States*.[40] During Prohibition, a federal officer passed himself off as a tourist while gaining the defendant's confidence. The federal agent eventually enticed the defendant to buy illegal liquor for him. The defendant was then arrested and prosecuted for violating the National Prohibition Act. The Supreme Court held that the officer used improper inducements that amounted to entrapment. In deciding this case, the Court settled on the "subjective" view of entrapment, which means that the predisposition of the defendant to commit the offense is the determining factor in entrapment. Following the *Sorrells* case, the Supreme Court stated in *Sherman v. United States* that the function of law enforcement is to prevent crime and to apprehend criminals, and not to implant a criminal design, which originates with the officials of the government, in the mind of an innocent person.[41]

In 1973, the U.S. Supreme Court ruled on the entrapment case of *United States v. Russell*.[42] In this case an agent of the Federal Bureau of Narcotics offered to supply defendants with ingredients necessary to manufacture the drug "speed." The defendants showed the agent the laboratory where the speed was produced. The agent eventually obtained a search warrant and arrested the defendants for the unlawful manufacture, sale, and delivery of drugs. Defendant Russell raised the defense of entrapment in his criminal trial. The Court ruled that the participation of the narcotics agent was not entrapment in this case and rejected the "objective" test of entrapment, which looks solely to the police conduct to determine if a law-abiding citizen has been persuaded to commit crime.

In a 1976 case, *Hampton v. United States*, the Court ruled that the defendant's predisposition rendered the entrapment defense unavailable to him even when a federal informant had provided the heroin that the defendant was charged with selling.[43] According to Justice Rehnquist, "the police conduct in *Hampton* no more deprived the defendant of any right secured to him by the U.S. Constitution than did the police conduct in *Russell* deprive Russell of any rights."[44]

Consequently, the major legal rule today considers entrapment primarily in light of the defendant's predisposition to commit a crime. A defendant with a criminal record would have a tougher time of it than one who had never been in trouble before. In the recent *DeLorean* case, automobile manufacturer John DeLorean was acquitted, even though the jury was shown video tapes of DeLorean freely engaging in the sale of narcotics. The jury felt that a well-respected businessman would never have gotten involved in such a crime without government entrapment.

Over the last decade, the defense of entrapment has resulted in a great deal of litigation concerning undercover police work and criminal liability. Sting and scam operations are often employed to obtain evidence on burglars, drug manufacturers, and corrupt public officials. The "Abscam" operation, for example, in which FBI agents paid bribes to government officials resulted in the conviction of several congressmen. And Operation Greylord uncovered attorneys, judges, and older court personnel "on the take" in the Chicago court

The television monitor shows automaker John DeLorean and an undercover FBI agent looking at a suitcase, purportedly containing cocaine. The jury believed DeLorean was entrapped by the FBI.

system.[45] "Governmental activity in the criminal enterprise," a phrase used in the decision in *United States v. Russell* has become an increasingly commonplace tool in the justice system.[46]

Double Jeopardy

By virtue of the Fifth Amendment, "no person shall be subject for the same offense to be twice put in jeopardy of life or limb."[47] The objective of this constitutional protection is to prohibit the reprosecution of a defendant for the same offense by the same jurisdiction. Thus, a person who has been tried for armed robbery in the state of Massachusetts by a judge or jury may not be tried again in that state for the same incident.

A review of the **double jeopardy** question involves a number of issues: (1) Does prosecution for the same or similar offenses by the state and federal governments constitute double jeopardy? (2) When does double jeopardy attach in a criminal prosecution? (3) What effect does the double jeopardy clause have on sentencing provisions?

The issue of federal versus state prosecutions arises from the existence of offenses that are crimes against the state as well as against the federal government. The U.S. Supreme Court has held, in the case of *Bartkus v. Illinois* (1959), and in numerous other cases, that both state and federal prosecutions against a defendant for the same crime are not in violation of the Fifth Amendment.[48] The Court reasoned that every citizen is a citizen of the United States and of a state. Consequently, either or both jurisdictions can try to punish an offender.

On the other hand, a state can try an accused only once. The state has the responsibility either to convict the defendant legally or to acquit the defendant on all charges. The Fifth Amendment prohibits a second prosecution, unless there has been an appeal by the defendant. The state may obtain a second trial in cases involving a mistrial, a hung jury, or some other trial defect.

With regard to when double jeopardy attaches, the general rule is that the Fifth Amendment applies when a criminal trial begins before a judge or jury. In the case of *Benton v. Maryland* (1969), the U.S. Supreme Court held the double jeopardy provisions of the Fifth Amendment applicable to the states.[49] The accused has the right to be tried until a final determination of the case is made. Jeopardy may exist when a jury is selected and sworn or even when a defendant is indicted for a crime. However, in the case of *Illinois v. Somerville* (1973), the double jeopardy clause did not bar the retrial of a defendant where a mistrial was caused because of a fatal defect in the government's indictment.[50] Also, a dismissal that occurs prior to jeopardy attaching does not prohibit a second prosecution under the Fifth Amendment. In other words, double jeopardy normally does not apply until after a criminal trial has started; thus early pretrial dismissals do not bar further prosecutions.

In terms of the sentence itself, the double jeopardy clause does not restrict the court's decision with regard to the length of the sentence imposed on a defendant in a second trial. However, the court is required to sentence fairly in accordance with due process of law. Vindictiveness or harshness against a defendant for being successful in overturning the first conviction is not appropriate grounds for imposing a sentence in the second trial. Thus, although the double jeopardy clause does not prevent or restrict harsh sentences on retrial, the case of *North Carolina v. Pearce* (1969) makes clear that sentences on retrial must be realistic and in accordance with fair principles of law and procedure.[51]

Pearce was convicted of assault with intent to commit rape in North Carolina. He was given a sentence of 12 to 15 years in prison. After a reversal of his conviction, Pearce was retried, convicted, and sentenced to a term that amounted to a longer sentence than originally imposed. The Court made clear that, although the double jeopardy clause is not an absolute bar to a more severe sentence, vindictiveness against a defendant can play no part in the new sentence.[52]

Mistake, Compulsion, and Necessity

Mistake or ignorance of the law is generally no defense to a crime. According to the great legal scholar William Blackstone, "Ignorance of the law, which everyone is bound to know, excuses no man."[53] Consequently, a defendant cannot present a legitimate defense by saying he or she was unaware of a criminal law, had misinterpreted the law, or believed the law to be unconstitutional.

On the other hand, mistakes of fact, such as taking someone else's coat that is similar to your own, may be a valid defense. If the jury or judge as trier of fact determines that criminal intent was absent, such an honest mistake may remove the defendant's criminal responsibility.

Compulsion or coercion may also be a criminal defense under certain conditions. In these cases the defendant is forced into committing a crime. In order for this defense to be upheld, a defendant must show that the actions were the only means of preventing death or serious harm to self or others. For example, a bank employee might be excused from taking bank funds if she can prove that her family was being threatened and that consequently she was acting under duress. But there is widespread general agreement that duress is no defense to an intentional killing.

Closely connected to the defense of compulsion is that of necessity. According to the Model Penal Code, "necessity may be an acceptable defense, provided the harm to be avoided is greater than the offense charged."[54] In other words, the defense of necessity is justified when the crime was committed because other circumstances could not be avoided. For example, a husband steals a car to bring his pregnant wife to the hospital for an emergency delivery, or a hunter shoots an animal of an endangered species that was about to attack her. The defense has been found inapplicable, however, where defendants sought to shut down nuclear power plants or abortion clinics, or sought to destroy missile components under the belief that the action was necessary to save lives or prevent a nuclear war. Even those who use a controlled substance such as marijuana for medicinal purposes often cannot claim vindication based on medical necessity, although some courts have viewed this as a legitimate defense.[55]

In sum, affirmative defenses—consent, self-defense, entrapment, and double jeopardy—refer primarily to situations where the defendants admit that they committed the act but claim that they should not be punished. Such is the case when a person exercises proper self-defense, when the police deliberately entice a defendant to commit a crime, or when someone is tried twice for the same offense.

◼ Reform of the Substantive Criminal Law

In recent years many states and the federal government have been examining and revising their substantive and procedural criminal codes. An ongoing effort has been made to update legal codes so that they provide an accurate reflection of public opinion, social change, technological innovation, and other important social issues.

What was a crime 30 years ago—such as performing an abortion—may no longer be a crime today. In this instance clouds of protest continue to surround the issue as pro-life and pro-choice groups argue the merits of such decisions by the government. Conversely, what was unregulated behavior in the past, such as using children to pose for so-called adult publications, may be outlawed because of public concern and outrage.[56]

One aspect of criminal law reform involves weeding out laws that seem archaic in light of what is now known about human behavior. For example, alcoholism is now considered a disease that should be treated, not an offense that should be punished. Many experts believe that offenses like drunkenness, disorderly conduct, vagrancy, gambling, and minor sexual violations are essentially social problems and should not be dealt with by the criminal justice system.

The RICO Statute

Other criminal law revisions reflect increasing awareness about problems that confront American society. As mentioned previously, a number of states have eliminated traditional rape laws and replaced them with sexually neutral assault statutes that recognize that men as well as women can be the victim of rape. Most jurisdictions have adopted laws that require people in certain occupations, such as teachers and doctors, to report suspected cases of child abuse to the proper authorities. In an effort to control organized crime, the federal government passed the Racketeer Influenced and Corrupt Organization Act (RICO). This law prevents people from acquiring or maintaining an interest in an ongoing enterprise, such as a union or legitimate business, with funds derived from illegal enterprises and racketeering activities.[57]

RICO did not create new categories of crime, but it did create new categories of offenses in racketeering activity, which it defined as involvement in two or more acts prohibited by 24 existing federal statutes and eight state statutes. The offenses listed in RICO include state-defined crimes such as murder, kidnapping, gambling, arson, robbery, bribery, extortion, and narcotic violations; and federally defined crimes such as bribery, counterfeiting, transmission of gambling information, prostitution, and mail fraud.

RICO is designed to limit "patterns" of organized criminal activity by defining racketeering as an act intended to

■ Derive income from racketeering or the unlawful collection of debts and to use or invest such income.
■ Acquire through racketeering an interest in or control over any enterprise engaged in interstate or foreign commerce.
■ Conduct business enterprises through a pattern of racketeering.
■ Conspire to use racketeering as a means of generating income, collecting loans, or conducting business.

An individual convicted under RICO is subject to 20 years in prison and a $25,000 fine. Additionally, the accused must forfeit to the U.S. government any interest in a business in violation of RICO. These penalties are much more potent than simple conviction and imprisonment.

Using RICO, the U.S. attorneys for New York, Boston, and Chicago attacked the leadership of major organized crime families and obtained convictions of high-ranking mafiosi during the late 1980s. In 1986–1987, in a trail-breaking case, the U.S. attorney for New York used language in the Securities and Exchange Act of 1934 to prosecute and convict Ivan Boesky and others for insider trading crimes.[58] Boesky agreed to pay a $100 million penalty for trading on inside stock information supplied by others and was subsequently sentenced to three years in prison. Although slow to respond to such criminal violations over the years, the federal government now admits that insider trading violations will receive full attention in the future. With such activities as "junk" bond underwriting, mergers and acquisitions, and venture capital investing, the number of people exposed to confidential information has increased enormously. In addition, the number of people able to reap huge potential profits illegally has resulted in a proliferation of insider trading abuses. Although it may seem astonishing that for decades the stock market remained unscathed by criminal prosecutions, the government's ability to use RICO and other such statutes will further increase the number of prosecutions in this area.

Movement for Legislative Reform

There have been a number of ongoing efforts to help states make changes in their criminal laws. The Model Penal Code of the American Law Institute offers a comprehensive model of the substantive criminal law and serves as a guide for the elimination of outdated laws. Comprehensive revisions of criminal legislation have been undertaken in numerous states since the establishment of the Model Penal Code.

One of the most significant criminal law revisions in the last decade was the 1984 Federal Crime Bill.[59] This legislation reforms a code that has been criticized for its complexity and inconsistency. Among the most important changes is the treatment of the insanity defense. In the past, federal prosecutors had the burden of proving that a defendant was sane. Now the burden of proof for insanity has shifted to the defendant. In addition, the new federal code eliminates parole and requires that criminal punishments be imposed more fairly and evenhandedly. Another important provision allows judges to detain offenders in jail prior to their trials if they are considered a danger to the community and themselves. **Preventive detention** is a significant change in the nation's bail system. Despite these changes, in comparison with the revisions that have taken place in many states, the federal criminal law has not been extensively overhauled.

In addition, amid much national concern about drugs, the Congress passed the Omnibus Drug Bill of 1988.[60] Earmarking over $2 billion for antidrug activities, the law calls for increased drug education and treatment programs and broader federal drug interdiction efforts. Some of its major provisions include (1) the establishment of an office of national drug control policy headed by a drug czar to coordinate a national drug policy; (2) increased funding for school drug abuse and mental health programs; (3) more funding for drug abuse education throughout the country; (4) increased efforts in dealing with international narcotic problems; and (5) stricter criminal sanctions including the use of the death penalty for major drug traffickers who intentionally kill someone as part of their drug-related transactions. Although opponents of the death penalty say its imposition has no deterrent value even in controlling drugs, proponents argue that it reflects a determination on the part of our society to be tough on major drug suppliers.

■ Constitutional Criminal Procedure

Whereas substantive criminal law primarily defines crime, the law of criminal procedure consists of the rules and procedures that govern the pretrial processing of criminal suspects and the conduct of criminal trials. As codified in the modern Federal Rules of Criminal Procedure, such rules provide for the "just and fair determination of all criminal proceedings."[61] The principles that govern criminal procedure flow from the relationship between the individual and the state and include (1) a belief in the presumption of innocence; (2) the right to a defense against criminal charges; and (3) the requirement that the government should act in a lawful manner. In general, these policies are mandated by the provisions of state constitutions. A sound understanding of criminal procedure requires an awareness of constitutional law.

The U.S. Constitution

The U.S. Constitution has played and continues to play a critical role in the development of the criminal law used in the criminal justice system. The forerunner of the present federal Constitution was the Articles of Confederation, adopted by the Continental Congress in 1781. The Articles were found to be generally inadequate as the foundation for effective government because they did not create a proper balance of power between the states and the central government. As a result, in 1787 the Congress of the Confederation adopted a resolution calling for a convention of delegates from the original states. Meeting in Philadelphia, the delegates' express purpose was to revise the Articles of Confederation. The work of that convention culminated in the drafting of the Constitution; it was ratified by the states in 1788 and put into effect in 1789.

In its original form, the Constitution consisted of a preamble and seven articles. The Constitution divided the powers of government into three independent but equal parts: the executive, the legislative, and the judicial branches. The purpose of the **separation of powers** was to ensure that no single branch of the government could usurp power for itself and institute a dictatorship. The measures and procedures initiated by the Framers have developed over time into the present form of government.

How does the Constitution, with its formal set of rights and privileges, affect the operations of the criminal justice system? One way is to guarantee that no one branch of government can in and of itself determine the fate of those accused of crimes. The workings of the criminal justice process illustrate this principle. A police officer, who represents the executive branch of government, makes an arrest on the basis of laws passed by the legislative branch, and the accused is subsequently tried by the judiciary. In this way, offenders are protected from the arbitrary abuse of power by any single element of the law.

The Bill of Rights

In addition to providing protection by ensuring a separation of powers within the government, the Constitution also controls the operations of the criminal justice system. It does this by guaranteeing individual freedoms in the 10 amendments added to it in 1791, which are collectively known as the Bill of Rights.

The **Bill of Rights** was added to the Constitution to prevent any future government from usurping the personal freedoms of citizens. In its original form, the Constitution contained few specific guarantees of individual rights. The Founders, aware of the past abuses perpetrated by the British government, wanted to ensure that the rights of citizens of the United States would be safe in the future. The Bill of Rights was adopted only to protect individual liberties from being abused by the national government, however, and did not apply to the actions of state or local officials. This oversight resulted in abuses that have been rectified only with great difficulty and even today remain the subject of court action.

Over the last three decades, the U.S. Supreme Court's interpretation of the Constitution has served as the basis for the creation of legal rights of the accused. The principles that govern criminal procedure are required by the U.S. Constitution and Bill of Rights. Of primary concern are the Fourth, Fifth, Sixth, and Eighth Amendments, which limit and control the manner in which the federal government operates the justice system. In addition, the due process clause of the Fourteenth Amendment has helped define the nature and limits of governmental action against the accused on a state level. Because these key amendments furnish the basis for our system of criminal procedure, they are examined carefully.

THE FOURTH AMENDMENT. The Fourth Amendment to the U.S. Constitution provides some of the major limits on police behavior. It states:

> The right of the people to be secure in their persons, houses, papers, and effects, against unreasonable searches and seizures, shall not be violated, and no warrants shall issue, but upon probable cause, supported by oath or affirmation, and particularly describing the place to be searched, and the persons or things to be seized.

The Framers of the Constitution were greatly concerned about the power of the central government to interfere in personal matters. After all, the Constitution's authors had just engineered a revolution against a government they viewed as tyrannical and opposed to individual freedom. In addition, the predominant philosophical movement of the time, known today as the Enlightenment, stressed limitations on the state's power to interfere with the rights of its citizens. Issues such as liberty and privacy were of central concern when the Bill of Rights was formulated. Considering these goals, it is not surprising that the Fourth Amendment is designed to protect citizens from unnecessary intrusions by the government into their private affairs. The Fourth Amendment is especially important for the criminal justice system because it means that police officers cannot indiscriminately use their authority to investigate a possible crime or arrest a suspect unless either or both actions are justified by the law and the facts of the case. Stopping, questioning, or searching an individual without legal justification represents a serious violation of the Fourth Amendment right to personal privacy.

The right to privacy is not unlimited, however, because it must be properly balanced against the need for public protection. The police can search and seize evidence under certain circumstances with a properly authorized *search warrant*, issued when a magistrate has been presented with sufficient evidence to convince him or her that a crime has been committed and that the place to be searched contains seizable evidence. The police can also perform a search without a warrant under special circumstances such as when they have legally arrested a person and wish to search him or her for weapons or contraband.

Because the police are constantly involved in street encounters with suspects, Fourth Amendment issues are always before the courts. For example, a person accused of a crime who believes that an illegal search was conducted can have an attorney file a motion before the court to suppress any evidence obtained during that search. Federal courts have formulated the rule that any evidence seized by authorities in violation of the Fourth Amendment cannot be used against suspects in a court of law; this is known as the **exclusionary rule.** A large body of complex legal decisions, known as the law of *search and seizure*, deals with the rights protected by the Fourth Amendment. These issues will be discussed in detail in Chapter 9.

In addition, the U.S. Supreme Court has extended Fourth Amendment privacy protections to such diverse areas as wiretapping and issues involving criminal abortion statutes. In 1973 the constitutionally derived right to privacy was made explicit by the Supreme Court in *Roe v. Wade*, where the Court declared unconstitutional a Texas statute that made it a crime to procure an abortion.[62] In this case the Court held that a person's body is private and that the government therefore cannot make laws to control it.

THE FIFTH AMENDMENT. Limiting the admissibility of confessions that have been obtained unfairly is another method of controlling police behavior.

The right against self-incrimination is frequently asserted by a defendant in an effort to exclude confessions or admissions that might be vital to the government's case. In such instances, the meaning of the Fifth Amendment to the U.S. Constitution is critical. The amendment states:

No person shall be held to answer for a capital, or otherwise infamous crime, unless on a presentment or indictment of a grand jury, except in cases arising in the land or naval forces, or in the militia, when in actual service in time of war or public danger; nor shall any person be subject for the same offense to be twice put in jeopardy of life or limb; nor shall be compelled in any criminal case to be a witness against himself, nor be deprived of life, liberty, or property, without due process of law, nor shall private property be taken for public use, without just compensation.

It was a common practice in Europe to subject people awaiting trial to horrible tortures designed to elicit confessions and implicate co-conspirators. Often a trial became superfluous when suspects had already been broken on the rack or had their arms and shoulders dislocated on the strappado. To prevent such practices from continuing in the United States, the Framers of the Constitution added the rights contained in the Fifth Amendment.

One of the primary purposes of the Fifth Amendment is to prevent torture and coercion of suspects by providing that no person shall be compelled to be a witness against himself or herself. This protection has two separate parts: First, the witness has the right not to answer questions that would tend to be self-incriminating. A witness can claim the Fifth Amendment right against **self-incrimination** in a congressional investigation, grand jury proceeding, or criminal trial. This privilege normally extends to all kinds of proceedings, including those of a civil as well as a criminal nature. Second, under the Fifth Amendment the defendant has the right not to take the stand in a criminal trial. If the defendant decides not to testify, the prosecution cannot comment on the silence or infer in any way that failure to testify is evidence of guilt.

The Fifth Amendment has had a tremendous impact on the American criminal justice system. In 1966, in the landmark case of *Miranda v. Arizona*, the

Miranda's successful appeal against a rape-kidnap conviction prompted the Supreme Court to establish the "Miranda warning" requiring that criminal suspects be told of their rights when taken into custody.

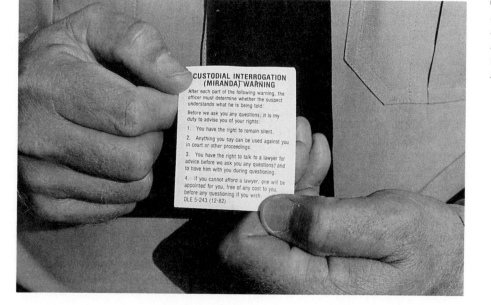

Police carry cards printed with the Miranda warning so that they can inform suspects of their rights to obtain counsel and remain silent during investigations.

Chapter 4
Criminal Law:
Substance and Procedure

U.S. Supreme Court held that a person accused of a crime has the right to refuse to answer questions when placed in police custody.[63] As a result of the *Miranda* case, which is discussed in Chapter 9, the Supreme Court developed a set of rules with which the police must comply when questioning a suspect prior to trial.

The Fifth Amendment right against self-incrimination does not stand alone but is often combined with the Fourth Amendment protections against unreasonable searches and seizures. For example, when the police investigate a crime and make an arrest, or when they question a suspect to obtain a confession or admission, they may use information obtained from the defendant to locate incriminating evidence. An illegal interrogation can result in an improper search for evidence; an illegal search can trigger an arrest and subsequent interrogation. Thus, in each step of the criminal justice process, the police must respect the rights accorded to every individual under the law. Since constitutional violations against both amendments are often present in the same case, the amendments represent a dual constitutional protection against governmental intrusions.

In addition to the prohibition against forcing people to incriminate themselves, the Fifth Amendment forbids the government from trying people more than one time on the same charge—double jeopardy. The amendment also establishes the concept of **due process of law,** or the right of people to be treated fairly and openly when they are confronted by state authority.

THE SIXTH AMENDMENT. The Sixth Amendment states:

> In all criminal prosecutions, the accused shall enjoy the right to a speedy and public trial, by an impartial jury of the state and district wherein the crime shall have been committed, which district shall have been previously ascertained by law, and to be informed of the nature and cause of the accusation; to be confronted with the witnesses against him; to have compulsory process for obtaining witnesses in his favor, and to have the assistance of counsel for his defense.

One of the goals of the Framers of the Constitution was to ensure that criminal defendants received a fair trial. Their concern stemmed from the abuses to human rights that had occurred in England and other European nations prior to the revolution. For example, in the seventeenth century an English court known as the Star Chamber tried persons charged with political crimes in secret and passed judgment upon them with little regard to fairness or due process of law. To protect American citizens from such practices, the Sixth Amendment set out rights guaranteed to all people facing criminal charges.

The Sixth Amendment guarantees the defendant the right to a speedy and public trial by an impartial jury, the right to be informed of the nature of the charges, and the right to confront any prosecution witnesses. This amendment has had a profound effect on the treatment of persons accused of crimes and has been the basis for numerous significant Supreme Court decisions that have increased the rights of criminal defendants. Regarding the right to a speedy trial, the Sixth Amendment demands that a defendant be brought to trial within a reasonable time following accusation without undue delay by the prosecution. The Sixth Amendment has also been interpreted to mean that a defendant must be given a trial by a jury of his or her peers in all criminal cases where imprisonment for more than six months may be authorized. The right to a trial by an impartial jury means that the jury must be free from any prejudice, bias, or preconceived notions of the defendant's guilt. The right to a public trial protects the accused from being tried secretly or in a closed trial.

Many Supreme Court decisions regarding the Sixth Amendment have also concerned the individual's right to counsel. The right of a defendant to be represented by an attorney has been extended to numerous stages of the criminal justice process, including pretrial custody, identification and lineup procedures, preliminary hearing, submission of a guilty plea, trial, sentencing, and postconviction appeal. The major legal decisions and statutes involving the right to jury trial, counsel, self-representation (the right to represent oneself), and speedy and public trial are examined in Chapter 13.

THE EIGHTH AMENDMENT. According to the Eighth Amendment,

Excessive bail shall not be required, nor excessive fines imposed, nor cruel and unusual punishments inflicted.

Bail is a money bond put up by the accused in order to attain freedom between arrest and trial. Bail is meant to ensure a trial appearance, since the bail money is forfeited if the defendant misses the trial date.

The Eighth Amendment does not guarantee a constitutional right to bail but rather prohibits the exactment of excessive bail. Nevertheless, since many state statutes place no precise limit on the amount of bail a judge may impose, many defendants who cannot make bail are often placed in detention while awaiting trial. It has become apparent over the years that the bail system is discriminatory in that a defendant who is financially well-off is more likely to be released on bail than one who is poor. In addition, placing a person in jail results in serious financial burdens on local and state governments—and, in turn, taxpayers—which must pay for the cost of confinement. These factors have given rise to bail reform programs that depend on the defendant's personal promise to appear in court for trial (recognizance) rather than on the financial ability to meet bail (see Chapter 12). Despite reforms that have enabled many deserving but indigent offenders to go free, another trend has been to deny people bail on the grounds that they are a danger to themselves or others in the community. Although the Supreme Court has not dealt with this issue with respect to adults, the Court has ruled that the preventive detention of minors is permitted to promote public safety.[64]

The Eighth Amendment restriction on excessive bail may also be interpreted to mean that the sole purpose of bail is to ensure that the defendant returns for trial; bail may not be used as a form of punishment, nor may it be used to coerce or threaten a defendant.

Another goal of the Framers was to curtail the use of torture and excessive physical punishment. In the early history of Europe, convicted criminals were often subjected to bizarre and cruel methods of execution including burning, being slowly crushed with heavy objects, and even being pulled apart by wild horses. Consequently, the prohibition against cruel and unusual punishment was added to the Eighth Amendment. This prohibition has affected the imposition of the death penalty and other criminal dispositions and has become a guarantee that serves to protect the accused and convicted offenders from actions regarded as unacceptable by a civilized society. Many prison reforms—such as those moderating prison discipline, isolation, and segregation, and allowing prisoners to express grievances—have resulted from litigation based on the prohibition against cruel and unusual punishment. Nevertheless, the Supreme Court has not outlawed the use of physical punishment per se, since it has upheld the use of *capital punishment* and the use of physical discipline in schools. It has, however, banned the use of force in a discriminatory or excessive fashion.

■ Limitations on State Actions in the Criminal Justice System

The Fourteenth Amendment has been the vehicle most often used to apply the protections of the Bill of Rights to the states. The Fourteenth Amendment states:

> All persons born or naturalized in the United States, and subject to the jurisdiction thereof, are citizens of the United States and of the state wherein they reside. No state shall make or enforce any law which shall abridge the privileges or immunities of citizens of the United States; nor shall any state deprive any person of life, liberty, or property, without due process of law; nor deny to any person within its jurisdiction the equal protection of the laws.

As we have seen, the first 10 amendments came into being in 1791. As the years passed and the new republic grew, however, it became apparent that in spite of the Bill of Rights many oppressive conditions remained. Slavery existed in many states, while some men were forced into military service and others worked for the state without pay. The states confiscated land and property and frequently denied rights guaranteed by the Bill of Rights to individuals and their families.

At the conclusion of the Civil War, the Thirteenth Amendment (abolishing slavery) was added to the Constitution. Because other substantial infringements of individual rights continued to exist, the Fourteenth Amendment was adopted in 1868. The most important aspect of this amendment is the clause that says no state shall "deprive any person of life, liberty, or property, without due process of law." This meant that the same general constitutional restrictions previously applicable to the federal government were to be imposed on the states. It is essential to keep the following constitutional principles in mind while examining the Fourteenth Amendment:

1. The first 10 amendments, ordinarily referred to as the Bill of Rights, originally applied only to the federal government. They were designed to protect citizens against injustices inflicted by federal authorities. The Bill of Rights restricts the actions of the federal government and does not apply to the states.
2. The Fourteenth Amendment's *due process* clause applies to state governments. It has been used to provide individuals in all states with the basic liberties guaranteed by the Bill of Rights.
3. The U.S. Supreme Court has expanded the right of defendants in the criminal justice system by interpreting the due process clause to mean that the states must be held to standards similar to those applicable to the federal government by the Bill of Rights.

Application of the Bill of Rights to the States

From its inception until about the middle of the twentieth century, the Bill of Rights had little bearing on the state criminal justice process. Individuals charged with federal crimes were guaranteed rights under the Fourth, Fifth, and Sixth Amendments, but defendants charged with criminal acts in state cases were denied similar treatment. The fact that the Bill of Rights was originally designed to govern the relationship between the individual and the federal government was pointed out by Chief Justice John Marshall in the case of *Barron v. Baltimore* in 1833.[65] In *Barron*, Justice Marshall rejected the claim that the Fifth Amendment was applicable to the states and held that the Constitution was binding only on the federal government. The question of whether the Bill of Rights was applicable to the states was further explored by the U.S. Supreme Court in 1884 in the case of *Hurtado v. California.*[66] This case raised the question of whether the due process clause of the Fourteenth Amendment contains the liberties expressed in the Bill of Rights. The Court held that the provisions of the Bill of Rights were not binding on the states through the Fourteenth Amendment.

Theories of Incorporation

Gradually, however, through a long series of decisions the Supreme Court has held that the guarantees of the First, Fourth, Fifth, Sixth, and Eighth Amendments apply to the states as well as to the federal government. The movement to make the Bill of Rights applicable to the states has gained impetus during the latter half of the twentieth century. It is based on a number of legal theories that describe the relationship of the Bill of Rights to the Fourteenth Amendment. The first theory, known as the **incorporation** theory, states that all the provisions of the Bill of Rights are incorporated into the Fourteenth Amendment's due process clause. Thus, such fundamental rights as freedom from unreasonable search and seizure, the right to jury trial, and the right to counsel are all considered binding on the states through the Fourteenth Amendment. The idea of total incorporation has never received majority support in any Supreme Court decision, however, nor has it been accepted in any substantial way by legal scholars or historians. Those supporting total incorporation argue that an individual is a citizen of both the federal government and a state government and should receive similar protections from each, while those arguing against this position suggest that the states should be allowed to develop their own criminal procedures.

The most widely recognized theory of constitutional responsibility is the **theory of selective incorporation,** which states that the Bill of Rights does apply to the states through the due process clause of the Fourteenth Amendment but only on a case-by-case basis. Advocates of this theory believe that some of the provisions of the Bill of Rights may be binding on the states—such as the right to a jury trial or the right to be free from self-incrimination—but that these should apply only after a careful consideration of the facts, or merits, of each case.

One way of determining which federal rights must be incorporated into the states' criminal justice systems was set forth in the decision in *Palko v. Connecticut* in 1937.[67] That case questioned whether the defendant's second trial for a state crime constituted double jeopardy and violated the due process clause of the Fourteenth Amendment. The U.S. Supreme Court decided that the defendant's due process rights were "not" violated because the Fourteenth Amendment applied to the states only those aspects of the Bill of Rights "which are the very essence of a scheme of ordered liberty."[68] Double jeopardy was not considered "fundamental" or "so rooted in the traditions and conscience of our people" that it should apply to the states as well as to the federal government.

Clarence Earl Gideon's appeal of his burglary conviction to the Supreme Court in 1963 established an indigent defendant's right to counsel in felony cases.

From the Supreme Court decisions such as *Palko* evolved a new legal theory called **fundamental fairness.** If the Supreme Court decided that a particular guarantee in the Bill of Rights was "fundamental" to and "implicit" in the American system of justice, it would hold that right applicable to the states. This became the method by which states could be held to the same standards of criminal due process as the federal government.

Using the formula derived from the *Palko* case, the incorporation of the provisions of the Bill of Rights into the Fourteenth Amendment moved forward slowly on a case-by-case basis, accelerating in 1953 when Earl Warren became chief justice of the U.S. Supreme Court. Under his leadership, the due process movement reached its peak. The Court decided numerous landmark cases focusing on the rights of the accused and brought about a revolution in the area of constitutional criminal procedure. The Warren Court granted many new rights to those accused of crimes and went so far as to impose specific guidelines on the policies of police, courts, and correctional services that ensured that due process of law would be maintained.

Today, the Fourteenth Amendment's due process clause has been interpreted by the U.S. Supreme Court to mean that an accused in a state criminal case is entitled to the same protections available under the federal Bill of Rights. Some of the major Supreme Court decisions making the Bill of Rights applicable to the states have been *Mapp v. Ohio* (1961),[69] which guaranteed the right of an individual to be free from unreasonable searches and seizures and to exclude the illegally seized evidence from criminal trials; *Malloy v. Hogan* (1964),[70] which guaranteed the right of an individual to be free from forced self-incrimination; *Gideon v. Wainwright* (1963),[71] which guaranteed the right to counsel; and *Klopfer v. North Carolina* (1967),[72] which overturned *Palko v. Connecticut* and guaranteed the right to be free from double jeopardy. These are some of the pertinent decisions that grant similar rights to an accused person on both state and federal levels. A schematic diagram of the relationship between the Bill of Rights and the Fourteenth Amendment is presented in Figure 4.1.

■ Procedural Due Process of Law

The concept of due process has been used as a basis for incorporating the Bill of Rights into the Fourteenth Amendment. Due process has also been used to evaluate the constitutionality of legal statutes and to set standards and guidelines for fair procedures in the criminal justice system.

Due process has often been divided into its substantive and procedural areas. The substantive aspects of due process are generally used to determine whether a statute is a fair, reasonable, and appropriate use of the legal power of the legislature. The concept of substantive due process was used extensively in the 1930s and 1940s to invalidate minimum wage standards, price-fixing, and employment restriction statutes. Today, substantive due process is used relatively sparingly; it is employed occasionally, however, to hold that a criminal statute—such as an act prohibiting disorderly conduct, imposing capital punishment, or banning pornography—is unconstitutional because it is arbitrary or unreasonable.

Much more important today are the procedural aspects of due process of law. In seeking to define the meaning of the term, most legal experts believe that it refers to the essential elements of fairness under law.[73] *Black's Law Dictionary* presents an elaborate and complex definition of due process:

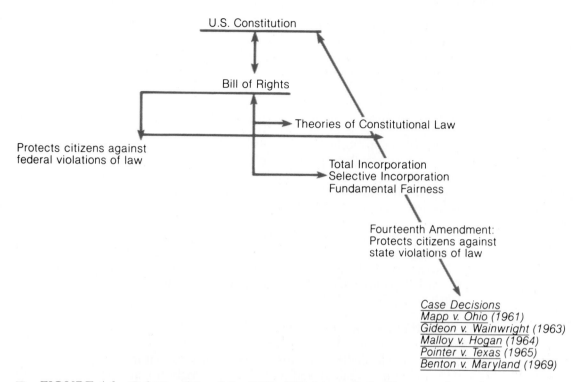

U.S. Constitution

Bill of Rights

Theories of Constitutional Law

Protects citizens against
federal violations of law

Total Incorporation
Selective Incorporation
Fundamental Fairness

Fourteenth Amendment:
Protects citizens against
state violations of law

Case Decisions
Mapp v. Ohio (1961)
Gideon v. Wainwright (1963)
Malloy v. Hogan (1964)
Pointer v. Texas (1965)
Benton v. Maryland (1969)

■ *FIGURE 4.1* **Relationship of the Bill of Rights and the Fourteenth
Amendment to the Constitutional Rights of the Accused**

> Due process of law in each particular case means such an exercise of the powers of
> government as the settled maxims of law permit and sanction, and under such
> safeguards for the protection of individual rights as those maxims prescribe for the
> class of cases to which the one in question belongs.[74]

This definition basically refers to the legal system's need for rules and
regulations that protect individual rights. The actual objectives of due process
help define the term even more explicitly. Due process seeks to ensure that no
person will be deprived of life, liberty, or property without notice of charges,
assistance from legal counsel, a hearing, and an opportunity to confront those
making the accusations. Basically, due process is intended to guarantee that
fundamental fairness exists in each individual case. This doctrine of fairness as
expressed in due process of law is guaranteed under both the Fifth and
Fourteenth Amendments.[75] Abstract definitions are only one aspect of due
process. Much more significant are the procedures that give meaning to due
process in the everyday practices of the criminal justice system. In this regard,
due process provides numerous procedural safeguards for the offender,
including the following:

1. Notice of charges
2. A formal hearing
3. The right to counsel or some other representation
4. The opportunity to respond to charges
5. The opportunity to confront and cross-examine witnesses and accusers
6. The privilege to be free from self-incrimination
7. The opportunity to present one's own witnesses

Chapter 4

**Criminal Law:
Substance and Procedure**

■

8. A decision made on the basis of substantial evidence and facts produced at the hearing
9. A written statement of the reasons for the decision
10. An appellate review procedure

Nature of Due Process

Exactly what constitutes due process in a specific case depends on the facts of the case, the federal and state constitutional and statutory provisions, previous court decisions, and the ideas and principles that society considers important at a given time and in a given place.[76] Justice Felix Frankfurter emphasized this point in *Rochin v. California* (1952):

> Due process of law requires an evaluation based on a disinterested inquiry pursued in the spirit of science on a balanced order of facts, exactly and clearly stated, on the detached consideration of conflicting claims . . . on a judgment not ad hoc and episodic but duly mindful of reconciling the needs both of continuity and of change in a progressive society.[77]

Both the elements and the definition of due process seems to be flexible and constantly changing. For example, at one time the concept of due process did not require a formal hearing for parole revocation, but it does today. Prior to 1968, juvenile offenders did not have the right to an attorney at their adjudication; counsel is now required in the juvenile court system. Prior to 1972, defendants were often unable to receive a speedy trial because of court delays. Today, state and federal laws safeguard the defendant's right to a speedy trial. In the 1970s and 1980s, the secrecy of the grand jury proceeding was a matter of much controversy. Recent reforms provide new due process protections that open the proceeding to outside review. Thus, the interpretations of due process of law are not fixed but rather reflect what society deems fair and just at a particular time and place. The degree of loss suffered by the individual (victim or offender) balanced against the state's interests also determines which and how many due process requirements are ordinarily applied. When a person's freedom is at stake in the criminal justice system, he or she is usually granted all applicable due process rights; in other cases, due process may be circumscribed.

Due process has been increasingly applied to protect individual rights when the government seeks to deprive a person of life, liberty, or property. The trend toward a wider use of procedural safeguards to prevent abuses of power has spread to many fields, including criminal justice, public welfare, mental health, juvenile delinquency, and public education. More than ever before, due process of law based on the Fifth and Fourteenth Amendments is used to challenge various types of arbitrary actions, such as the termination of aid by welfare officials or the imposition of punishment on prison inmates. Consistent judicial intervention has made these and other fields more responsive to reform through the application of constitutional rights.

■ Future Directions in Criminal Law and Procedure

Despite present problems with the criminal justice system, much progress has been made in the field of criminal law and constitutional procedure over the past 25 years. The future direction of the criminal law in the United States remains unclear. Yet there seems to be less tolerance for government corruption, more public interest in fixed sentences and capital punishment, and more conservative decision making by our judicial bodies. Attention probably will be paid to the substantive nature of criminal law in the future particularly where it is important in the preservation of American society. Special prosecutors, for example, using criminal statutes involving conspiracy, perjury, and fraud were able to uncover the illegal operations in the Nixon administration of the 1970s and to examine the Reagan administration's activities in the Iran-Contra affair in the 1980s. The criminal law system has demonstrated amazing resilience in its ability to prosecute public officials whose behavior has damaged the very government they work so hard to promote.

Both an expansion and a contraction of the criminal law itself can also be anticipated. Areas of expansion probably will include a greater emphasis on controlling chronic career criminals. Laws making it easier for states to punish serious juvenile offenders and incarcerate them in secure adult institutions will probably be passed. More attention will be given to white-collar crimes, as well as to drug-related crimes and terrorism. Corporations are almost certainly going to be held accountable for their illegal acts, especially those that result in physical as well as economic harm. Stock market and computer activities will receive close scrutiny by law enforcement agencies. In addition, there are likely to be greater efforts to sever the link between organized crime and legitimate businesses, similar to the efforts being made to stop banks from laundering illegal cash.

Lastly, the legal system will also be faced with difficult legal challenges involving the AIDS (acquired immune deficiency syndrome) disease. Currently, there are no criminal laws that specifically attempt to control the activities of prisoners, prostitutes, and drug users who may be spreading the AIDS virus.[78]

Other offenses such as those involving the use of some controlled drugs (most likely marijuana) and petty criminal offenses may be reduced in importance or removed entirely from the criminal law system. To make criminal sentencing fairer and more certain for the justice system, the public, and the offender, a system of judicially fixed sentences—and possibly the further abolition of parole in some jurisdictions—will continue to become more commonplace.

Regardless of what changes occur in the future, the criminal law system will continue to be faced with four fundamental problems: (1) defining and classifying antisocial behavior; (2) establishing appropriate criminal sanctions or punishments; (3) applying the proper degree of criminal responsibility; and (4) determining what departures from due process of law safeguards may require the reversal of a conviction.

■ SUMMARY

The criminal justice system is basically a legal system. Its foundation is the criminal law, which is concerned with people's conduct. Its purpose is to regulate behavior and maintain order in society. What constitutes a crime is defined primarily by the state and federal legislatures and reviewed by the courts.

What is considered criminal conduct changes from one period to another. Social norms, values, and community beliefs play major roles in determining what conduct is antisocial. Crimes are generally classified as felonies or misdemeanors, depending on their seriousness. Since a crime is a public wrong against the state, the criminal law imposes sanctions in the form of fines, probation, or imprisonment on a guilty defendant.

Under the criminal law, all adults are presumed to be aware of the consequences of their actions, but the law does not hold an individual blameworthy unless that person is capable of intending to commit the crime of which he or she is accused. Such factors as insanity, a mental defect, or age mitigate a person's criminal responsibility.

States periodically revise and update the substantive criminal law and the procedural laws in their penal codes; the latter deals with the rules for processing the offender from arrest through trial, sentencing, and release. An accused must be provided with the guaran-tees of due process under the Fifth and Fourteenth Amendments to the U.S. Constitution.

The U.S. Supreme Court has held that the due process clause protects citizens against two basic types of state intrusion. One involves substantive due process that "shocks the conscience" of society.[79] The second deals with the implementation of fair and just procedures—often referred to as procedural due process. Both principles hold the government responsible when an individual's liberty is at stake.

■ QUESTIONS

1. What are the specific aims and purposes of the criminal law? To what extent does the criminal law control behavior?
2. What kinds of activities should be labeled criminal in contemporary society? Why?
3. What is a criminal act? What is a criminal state of mind? When are individuals liable for their actions?
4. Discuss the various kinds of crime classifications. To what extent or degree are they distinguishable?
5. In recent years, numerous states have revised their penal codes. What are some of the major categories of substantive crimes you think should be revised?
6. Entrapment is a defense when the defendant was entrapped into committing the crime. To what extent should law enforcement personnel induce the commission of an offense?
7. What legal principles can be used to justify self-defense? Considering that the law seeks to prevent crime, not promote it, are such principles sound?
8. What are the minimum standards of procedure required in the criminal justice system?
9. Discuss the relationship between the U.S. Constitution and the Bill of Rights. What particular provisions does the incorporation theory involve?

■ NOTES

1. See E. Allan Farnsworth, *An Introduction to the Legal System of the United States* (New York: Oceana Publications, 1963), chapter 1; see also B. Gavit, *Introduction to the Study of Law* (New York: Foundation Press, 1951).
2. *Carriers Case Yearbook*, 13 Edward IV 9.pL.5 (1473).
3. 372 U.S. 335, 83 S.Ct. 792, 9 L.Ed.2d 799 (1963).
4. 372 U.S. 335, 83 S.Ct. 792, 9 L.Ed.2d 799 (1963).
5. T. Maltz, "The Nature of Precedent," *North Carolina Law Review* 66 (1988): 367–93.
6. *Robinson v. California*, 370 U.S. 660, 82 S.Ct. 1417 8 L.Ed.2d 758 (1962); see also American Law Institute, *Model Penal Code* (Philadelphia: American Law Institute, 1962), § C.
7. American Law Institute, *Model Penal Code*, § C.
8. See, generally, Wayne R. LaFave and Austin W. Scott, *Criminal Law* (St. Paul, Minn.: West Publishing Co., 1972).
9. E. Gellhorn, *Administrative Law and Process* (St. Paul, Minn.: West Publishing Co. Nutshell Series, 1981).
10. See John Weaver, *Warren—The Man, the Court, the Era* (Boston: Little, Brown & Co., 1967); see also "We the People," *Time*, 6 July 1987.
11. *Marbury v. Madison*, 1 Cranch 137, 2 L.Ed. 60 (1803).
12. Thomas Gardner, *Criminal Law* (St. Paul, Minn.: West Publishing Co., 1985), pp. 15–18.
13. See *State v. Horton*, 139 N.C. 588, 51 S.E. 945 (1905).
14. See American Law Institute, *Model Penal Code*, § 1.04.
15. Henry Black, *Black's Law Dictionary*, rev. 5th ed. (St. Paul, Minn.: West Publishing Co., 1979), pp. 744, 1150.
16. Mass. Gen. Laws, Chap. 274, Sec. 1.
17. Sheldon Krantz, *Law of Corrections and Prisoners' Rights, Cases and Materials* (St. Paul, Minn.: West Publishing Co., 1982), p. 702; Barbara Knight and Stephen Early, Jr., *Prisoners' Rights in America* ((Chicago: Nelson-Hall, 1986), chapter 1; see also Fred Cohen, "The Law of Prisoners' Rights—An Overview," *Criminal Law Bulletin* 24 (1988): 321–49.
18. See Mass. Gen. Laws Ann. Chapter 266, Sec. 14.
19. Wayne R. LaFave and Austin W. Scott, Jr., *Criminal Law*, 2d ed. (St. Paul, Minn.: West Publishing Co., 1986), p. 177; see, generally, Frank Miller, Robert Dawson, George Dix, and Raymond Parnas, *Cases and Materials on Criminal Justice Administration*, 3d ed. (New York: Foundation Press, 1988).
20. See American Law Institute, *Model Penal Code* (Philadelphia: American Law Institute, 1985), § 2.02; see also *United States v. Bailey*, 444 U.S. 394, 100 S.Ct. 624, L.Ed.2d 575 (1980).
21. See *United States v. Balint*, 258 U.S. 250, 42 S.Ct. 301, 66 L.Ed. 604 (1922); see also *Morissette v. United States*, 342 U.S. 246, 72 S.Ct. 240, 96 L.Ed. 288.288 (1952).
22. See Henry Hart, "The Aims of the Criminal Law," *Law and Contemporary Problems* 23 (1956): 402.
23. 8 English Reporter 718 (1943).
24. 94 U.S. App.D.C. 228, 214 F.2d 862 (1954).

25. American Law Institute, *Model Penal Code*, § 4.01. Copyright 1962 by the American Law Institute. Reprinted with the permission of the American Law Institute.

26. See Bureau of Justice Statistics, *Report to the Nation on Crime and Justice*, 2d ed. (Washington, D.C.: Bureau of Justice Statistics, U.S. Department of Justice, 1988), p. 87.

27. "The Insanity Defense: Should It Be Abolished?" *Newsweek*, 24 May 1982, pp. 56–70; "Hinckley Bombshell—End of Insanity Plea?" *U.S. News and World Report*, 5 July 1982, pp. 12–14.

28. See, generally, Norval Morris, *Madness and the Criminal Law* (Chicago: University of Chicago Press, 1982), chapter 2; see also Rita Simon and David Aaronson, *The Insanity Defense: A Critical Assessment of Law and Policy in the Post-Hinckley Era* (New York: Praeger, 1988), p. 45.

29. Joseph di Genova and Victoria Toensing, "Bringing Sanity to the Insanity Defense," *American Bar Association Journal* 69 (1983): 467.

30. "Hinckley Decision Points Up Need for New Verdict," *New York Times*, 1 July 1982; "It's a Mad, Mad Verdict," *New Republic*, 12 July 1983, pp. 13–19; "Straight Talk about the Insanity Defense," *The Nation*, 24 July 1982, pp. 70–72.

31. Bureau of Justice Statistics, *Report to the Nation on Crime and Justice*, p. 87.

32. "The Insanity Defense: Should It Be Abolished," pp. 56–60. For excellent references on crime and insanity, see Katherine Ellison and Robert Buckhout, *Psychology and Criminal Justice: Common Grounds* (New York: Harper & Row, 1982); Willard Gaylin, *The Killing of Bonnie Garland: A Question of Justice* (New York: Simon & Schuster, 1982); Abraham Goldstein, *The Insanity Defense* (Westport, Conn.: Greenwood Press, 1980); William Winslade and Judith Wilson, *The Insanity Plea* (New York: Scribner, 1983).

33. Comprehensive Crime Control Act of 1984. Title 18; see also B. McGraw et al., "The Guilty But Mentally Ill Plea and Verdict: Current State of the Knowledge," *Villanova Law Review* (1985): 30.

34. 370 U.S. 660. 82 S.Ct. 1417, 8 L.Ed.2d 758 (1962).

35. 392 U.S. 514, 88 S.Ct. 2145, 20 L.Ed.2d 1254 (1968).

36. Samuel M. Davis, *Rights of Juveniles: The Juvenile Justice System* (New York: Boardman, 1974), chapter 2; Larry Siegel and Joseph Senna, *Juvenile Delinquency: Theory, Practice and Law* (St. Paul, Minn.: West Publishing Co., 1988).

37. See Thomas Gardner and Victor Manian, *Criminal Law—Principles, Cases, and Readings* (St. Paul, Minn.: West Publishing Co., 1975), p. 144.

38. *People v. Goetz*, 68 N.Y.2d 96, 497 N.E.2d 41, 506 NYS2d 18 (1986); see also "New York Court Upholds Goetz Gun Conviction," *Boston Globe*, 23 November 1988, p. 5.

39. See the interesting case of *Katko v. Brinwy*, 183 N.W.2d 657, which deals with the question of whether an owner may protect personal property in an unoccupied farmhouse against trespassers by a spring gun capable of inflicting death.

40. 287 U.S. 435, 53 S.Ct. 210, 77 L.Ed. 413 (1932).

41. 356 U.S. 369, 78 S.Ct., 819, 2 L.Ed.2d 848 (1958).

42. 411 U.S. 423, 93 S.Ct. 1637, 36 L.Ed.2d 366 (1973).

43. 425 U.S. 484, 96 S.Ct. 1646, 48 L.Ed.2d 113 (1976).

44. Ibid., 489.

45. Thomas Gardner, *Criminal Law Principles and Cases*, 3d ed. (St. Paul, Minn.: West Publishing Co., 1985), p. 133; see also James Tuohy

and Rob Warden, *Greylord: Justice Chicago Style* (New York: Putnam Press, 1989).

46. 411 U.S. 423, 93 S.Ct. 1637, 36 L.Ed.2d 366 (1973).

47. See U.S. Constitution, Fifth Amendment.

48. 359 U.S. 121, 72 S.Ct. 676, 3 L.Ed.2d 684 (1959).

49. 395 U.S. 784, 89 S.Ct. 2056, 23 L.Ed.2d 707 (1969).

50. 410 U.S. 458, 93 S.Ct. 1066, 35 L.Ed.2d 425 (1973).

51. 395 U.S. 711, 89 S.Ct. 2072, 23 L.Ed.2d 656 (1969).

52. Ibid., 721.

53. William Blackstone, *Commentaries on the Law of England*, Vol. 1, ed. Thomas Cooley (Chicago: Callaghan, 1899) pp. 4, 26. Blackstone was an English barrister who lectured on the English common law at Oxford University in 1753.

54. American Law Institute, *Model Penal Code*, § 2.04.

55. *Commonwealth v. Benyon*, 509 Pa. 118, 501 A.2d 226 (1985); see also *State v. Tate* 102 N.J. 64, 505 A.2d 941 (1986).

56. In *New York v. Ferber*, 50 l.w.5077 (1982), the Supreme Court upheld state laws that ban the use of children in sexually explicit publications even if they are not legally obscene.

57. 18 U.S.C. 1961–1968 (1970). Enterprise includes both legitimate and illegitimate associations.

58. See John Brooks, *The Takeover Game* (New York: E. P. Dutton 1987), p. 319.

59. Comprehensive Crime Control Act of 1984, Title 18, U.S.C.; also Albert P. Melone, "The Politics of Criminal Code Revision," 15 *Capital U.S. Review* 191 (1986).

60. Omnibus Drug Law, H5210, *Congressional Quarterly*, 29 October 1988, p. 3145.

61. Federal Rules of Criminal Procedures, Rule 11.

62. 410 U.S. 113, 93 S.Ct. 705, 35 L.Ed.2d 147 (1973).

63. 384 U.S. 436, 86 S.Ct. 1602, 16 L.Ed.2d 694 (1966).

64. *Schall v. Martin*, 467 U.S. 253, 104 S.Ct. 2403, 81 L.Ed.2d 207 (1984).

65. 32 U.S. (7 Peters) 243, 8 L.Ed. 672 (1833).

66. 110 U.S. 506, 4 S.Ct. 111, 28 L.Ed. 232 (1884).

67. 302 U.S. 319, 58 S.Ct. 149, 82 L.Ed. 288 (1937).

68. Ibid., at 325.

69. 367 U.S. 643, 81 S.Ct. 1684, 6 L.Ed.2d 1081 (1961).

70. 378 U.S. 1, 84 S.Ct. 1489, 12 L.Ed.2d 1081 (1964).

71. 372 U.S. 335, 83 S.Ct. 792, 9 L.Ed.2d 799 (1963).

72. 386 U.S. 213, 87 S.Ct. 988, 18 L.Ed.2d (1967).

73. See *Time*, 26 February 1973, p. 95.

74. Henry Black, *Black's Law Dictionary*, p. 449.

75. See, generally, Joseph J. Senna, "Changes in Due Process of Law," *Social Work* 19 (1974): 319; see also the interesting student rights case, *Goss v. Lopez*, 419 U.S. 565, 95 S.Ct. 720, 42 L.Ed.2d 725 (1975).

76.. 342 U.S. 165, 72 S.Ct. 205, 95 L.Ed. 183 (1952).

77. Ibid., at 172.

78. See Alan Dershowitz, *Taking Liberties—A Decade of Hard Cases, Bad Laws, and Bum Raps* (Chicago: Contemporary Books, 1988, p. 148; see also Theodore Hammett, *AIDS in Correctional Facilities—Issues and Options* (Washington, D.C.: U.S. Department of Justice, 1986).

79. See *Rochin v. California*, 342 U.S. 165, 72 S.Ct. 205, 95 L.Ed. 183 (1952).

5

Perspectives on Criminal Justice and Victimization

Now that some understanding of the agencies and processes of justice, the nature and causes of crime, and the functions of the criminal law has been developed, it is time to examine some of the major issues and perspectives that apply to the system as a whole. By introducing some of the most critical issues and perspectives that confront the field of criminal justice, this chapter serves as an introduction to the remainder of the book, which focuses more directly on the major institutions of justice—police, courts, and correctional agencies.

More than twenty years have passed since the field of criminal justice came to be the subject of both serious academic study and attempts at unified policy formation. As you may recall, the modern study of criminal justice can be traced back to the efforts of the federal government to create an umbrella agency that would fund and guide policy development in criminal justice. In 1967 the President's Commission on Law Enforcement and the Administration of Justice recommended the development of a federal assistance program to improve the nation's crime control efforts. Congress responded in 1968 by creating the *Law Enforcement Assistance Administration (LEAA)* within the Department of Justice under Title I of the **Omnibus Crime Control and Safe Streets Act.**[1]

Over the next 14 years the majority of federal funds that were allocated to the states in the area of criminal justice were provided by the LEAA.[2] It required each state to establish a State Criminal Justice Planning Agency (SPA) for the purpose of developing an annual comprehensive criminal justice plan and then funneled development and operating funds to the state for law enforcement purposes. From 1969 to 1980, the LEAA gave over $7.7 billion to state and local criminal justice agencies. On April 15, 1982, the LEAA came to an end when Congress failed to provide further funding.

During its lifetime the LEAA was widely and validly criticized for failing to provide sufficient funds to have substantial impact on rising crime rates and for allowing its policies to be influenced by political pressure from the White House and Congress. High staff turnover, lack of leadership, and shifting priorities also contributed to the public's negative image of the LEAA.

Despite its well-documented failures, the LEAA helped "invent" the field of criminal justice. Federal funds inspired institutions of higher education to develop academic programs in criminal justice. The LEAA provided millions of dollars in scholarship money for the education of in-service police officers and other criminal justice personnel. Without federal money the most important graduate programs in criminal justice would probably not have been implemented, and many of the professors teaching this course today might have gone into other fields of study. In addition, federal research money helped fund some of the most important research and demonstration projects of the 1960s and 1970s, which are mentioned throughout this text. Although the LEAA can no longer influence policy or fund research, the federal government continues to fund such agencies as the National Institute of Justice (NIJ), the National Institute of Corrections (NIC), and the Office of Juvenile Justice and Delinquency Prevention (OJJDP), which play a more limited role in supporting criminal justice research and development.

After 20 years of government-sponsored research and policy analysis, it is clear that criminal justice is far from a unified field. Practitioners, academics, and commentators alike have experienced irreconcilable differences concerning its goals, purpose, and direction. Several philosophical perspectives compete within the field with the result that considerable controversy has arisen over such important social control issues as the use of electronic surveillance,

Omnibus Crime Control and Safe
    Streets Act
Crime control
Rehabilitation
Nonintervention
Radical nonintervention
Decriminalization
Deinstitutionalization
Pretrial diversion
Widening the net
Desert-based sentences
Reintegration
Community crime prevention
American Bar Association (ABA)
National Council on Crime and
    Delinquency (NCCD)
National Advisory Commission on
    Criminal Justice Standards and
    Goals
Accreditation
Commission on Accreditation for
    Law Enforcement Agencies
Decriminalization
Overcriminalization
Methadone maintenance
Surveillance
Victimization
Victim compensation

Chapter 5

Perspectives on Criminal
Justice and Victimization

the elimination of the drug trade, and gun control. Since there is no "correct" way to resolve these issues, it should not be surprising that criminal justice policy debates are both frequent and heated.

This chapter will review the major perspectives on criminal justice and examine some of the critical issues facing the field. It focuses on the diversity of opinion over what criminal justice is and should be and how these diverging views influence major issues.

■ Perspectives on Justice

Considering the complexity of criminal justice, it should not come as a surprise that no single view or concept dominates the field. Criminal justice practitioners often hold widely different perspectives on how the justice system works and how it should operate in the future. In fact, intra-agency conflict sometimes results when people holding opposing opinions share the same job responsibilities or duties. In academic departments, debates over the nature and purpose of justice can set off long-running feuds and lead to acrimonious faculty meetings.

This section brings together and summarizes the ideas that form the foundation of the dominant perspectives in criminal justice today: crime control, rehabilitation, due process, nonintervention, and justice.

Crime Control Perspective

One of the first approaches to criminal justice was the **crime control** perspective which is still a dominant force today. Its roots can be traced to the eighteenth century when philosophers such as Cesare Beccaria and Jeremy Bentham argued that the proper amount of legal punishment should alone be sufficient to deter crime.

The heart of the crime control perspective today is that the proper role of the justice system is to prevent crime through the judicious use of criminal sanctions. If the justice system operated effectively, potential criminals would be deterred from committing law violations. Those who are not deterred by the threat of punishment should, upon their apprehension and conviction, be sanctioned so severely that they will never attempt to violate the law again.

According to the crime control perspective, the focus of justice should be on the victim of crime and not the criminal; it assumes that the ultimate goal of the criminal justice system is to protect innocent people from the ravages of crime. This objective can be achieved through more effective police protection, mandatory sentences for convicted felons, prisons designed to incapacitate hardened criminals safely, liberal use of the death penalty, and so on.

Crime control enthusiasts believe in swift, sure justice. They do not want legal technicalities to tie the hands of justice and help the guilty go free. They lobby for the abolition of legal restrictions on the ability of police officers to search for evidence and interrogate suspects. They oppose judges who let obviously guilty people go free because a law enforcement officer made an unintentional procedural error. Overzealous, publicity-seeking defense lawyers who specialize in freeing notorious killers and rapists on legal technicalities or the insanity defense are the subject of unrestrained scorn.

Advocates of the crime control perspective are also skeptical of the criminal justice system's ability to rehabilitate offenders. They believe most treatment programs are ineffective because the justice system is simply not equipped to

treat people who have a long history of antisocial behavior. From both a moral and a practical standpoint, the role of criminal justice should be the control of antisocial people. If not to the justice system, then to whom can the average citizen turn for care and protection from society's criminal elements?

Crime Control Today

The crime control perspective exerts a powerful influence on criminal justice policy. Much recent legislation on the state and federal levels has enacted law-and-order-oriented programs such as mandatory prison sentences for those convicted of violent crimes. The Supreme Court with its conservative Reagan and Nixon appointees has generally eased restrictions on police operations. And a quick survey of the literature in the field of crime and justice reveals a decided slant toward the crime control perspective.

Nowhere can the influence of the crime control perspective be seen more clearly than in the continued employment of capital punishment statutes by a majority of states and the federal government. Crime control advocates argue that, because the state has a duty to protect the lives of its citizens, the death penalty is morally justified if there is any evidence that executing convicted killers will lead to a decline in the murder rate. As another argument in favor of the death penalty, crime control advocates point to research showing that convicted killers who are sent to prison often serve a small percentage of their sentence in confinement and that people on death row today had prior convictions for murder.[3] Capital punishment is also a reflection of the public will since citizens increasingly favor the death penalty for convicted murderers.

Rehabilitation Perspective

Whereas proponents of the crime control perspective view the justice system in terms of protecting the public and controlling criminal elements, those who

Chapter 5

Perspectives on Criminal
Justice and Victimization

■

Those who hold to the rehabilitation philosophy believe that criminals can be effectively treated within the criminal justice system. Here a prison inmate studies for an institution administered training program.

advocate the **rehabilitation** perspective see the justice system as a means of caring for and treating people who cannot manage themselves. They view crime as an expression of the offenders' frustration with their place in society and their inability to do anything to improve it through conventional means.

The rehabilitation philosophy holds that people are at the mercy of social, economic, and interpersonal conditions and interactions. Criminals themselves are the victims of racism, poverty, lack of hope, alienation, family disorganization, and other social problems. It is the duty of society to help them compensate for their social problems. Crime can be controlled by helping people find legitimate ways of obtaining wealth, power, and prestige and by enabling them to cope with their life situations. This can involve job training, psychological counseling, education, and the like. It is far cheaper, more efficient, and humane to treat young offenders and help them become established in the community than to punish them with a prison sentence and lock them into a life of crime.

The rehabilitation perspective places its emphasis on the criminal offender in contrast to the crime control perspective's emphasis on punishment and control. Rehabilitation advocates maintain that even if every criminal were apprehended and incarcerated, destructive social conditions in the nation's ghettos and poverty areas would create a new generation of law violators. Society has a choice: pay now, by funding treatment and educational programs, or pay later, when disenfranchised youth enter costly correctional facilities.

Rehabilitation advocates reject the concept of punishment because of its inherent brutality and futility. Its use signifies that society has given up on the offenders and precludes the hope they can ever be turned into law-abiding members of society. For example, those who call for the liberal use of the death penalty conjure up images of maniacal killers who must be executed to protect innocent children, while in truth the typical person sentenced to death is a young man who kills someone during an armed robbery. The mass murderer is actually rarely sentenced to death. Hasn't society progressed beyond the cruel punishments used by earlier civilizations?

The Rehabilitation Perspective Today

The rehabilitation view was extremely influential in the mid-1960s and 1970s when the government's ability to devise programs to counteract crime was viewed with optimism. Leading academic figures like Lloyd Ohlin and Richard Cloward were asked to advise government programs designed to provide direct services at the grass-roots level. Large-scale anti-crime and delinquency prevention programs were implemented that emphasized community development, job training, educational enrichment, and political organizing. In addition, a multitude of programs were created at every level of government to offer social services to known offenders who desired to "go straight."

In the more conservative 1980s the rehabilitation view fell into disfavor with both the public and the professional community. A series of research studies seemed to show that programs designed to rehabilitate known offenders did not work as well as expected. The failure of rehabilitation programs to receive unqualified support eroded confidence in the ability of the justice system to improve the lives of known criminals and offer alternatives to potential offenders. The cost of funding effective rehabilitation efforts, coupled with the public's fear of violent crime, helped erode the dominance of the rehabilitation philosophy in the criminal justice system.

Although questions about rehabilitation remain, the justice system has by no means terminated its efforts to treat offenders. Numerous treatment-oriented programs continue to exist in the various criminal justice agencies around the United States.[4] Most long-term correctional facilities maintain counseling services, educational programs, and job training courses. Probation departments operate a full range of community-based programs for offenders who are not in need of secure confinement. The juvenile justice system in most jurisdictions remains committed to a rehabilitation course. And although some critics may be skeptical about the success of rehabilitation programs, some new evidence suggests that correctional programs can achieve significant success with selected offender populations.[5]

Due Process Perspective

In *The Limits of the Criminal Sanction* Herbert Packer contrasted the crime control perspective with a view that he called the *due process model*.[6] According to Packer, due process combines elements of the liberals' concern for the individual with the concept of legal fairness guaranteed by the U.S. Constitution.

Advocates of the due process perspective argue that the justice system should be primarily concerned with prociding fair and equitable treatment to those accused of crime. This means providing fair and impartial hearings, competent legal counsel, equitable treatment, and reasonable sanctions. It follows that the use of discretion within the justice system should be strictly monitored to ensure that no one suffers from racial, religious, or ethnic discrimination.

Those who advocate the due process orientation are quick to point out that the justice system remains an adversary process that pits the forces of an all-powerful state against a solitary individual accused of crime. Without a fundamental concern for justice and fairness, the defendant who lacked resources could easily be overwhelmed. They point to miscarriages of justice such as the Gary Dotson case as examples of what can happen if our vigilance is relaxed for a moment. As you may recall, Dotson was the young man imprisoned for rape only to be released years later when his accuser recanted her testimony.[7] Similarly, there have been charges that more than 350 innocent people have been convicted of murder and that more than 20 have been executed.[8] Since such mistakes can happen, even the most apparently guilty offender deserves all the protection the justice system can offer.

The Due Process Perspective Today

Like the rehabilitation model, the due process orientation has not fared well in recent years. The movement to expand the legal rights of criminal defendants has been undermined by Supreme Court decisions increasing the police officer's ability to search and seize evidence and to question suspects. Similarly, the movement between 1960 and 1980 to grant prison inmates an ever-increasing share of constitutional protections was curtailed in the 1980s. There is growing evidence that the desire to protect the public has overshadowed concern for the rights of criminal defendants. And although most of the important legal rights won by criminal defendants in the 1960s and 1970s remain untouched (for example, the right of indigent defendants to be represented by counsel in criminal trials), there was little urgency to increase the scope of these rights in the more conservative 1980s. As the 1990s begin, it appears unlikely that this conservative trend will end. As the more liberal justices on the Supreme Court retire and are replaced by conservatives, it is likely that due process considerations will be placed further back on the burners of justice. Nevertheless, concerned legal scholars such as Victor Streib, who has led the fight to prohibit the execution of juvenile offenders, will continue to carry the torch of due process.[9]

Nonintervention Perspective

The fourth approach to criminal justice is known as the **nonintervention** perspective. Those who espouse this model of justice hold that criminal justice agencies should limit their involvement with criminal defendants when at all possible. Regardless of whether intervention is designed to punish or treat people, its ultimate effect is often harmful. In other words, any program that involves people with a social control agency, such as the police, department of mental health, correctional system, or criminal court, will have long-term negative effects. Thereafter, criminal defendants may be regarded with suspicion, they may be considered dangerous and untrustworthy, and they may develop a lasting record with negative connotations. Eventually, they may even come to believe their official record and view themselves as bad, evil, outcasts, troublemakers, or "crazy."

The noninterventionist philosophy was highly influential throughout the 1970s when mistrust of government cast doubt on any effort that bore the stamp of "big brother." Leading criminal justice commentators such as Edwin Schur and Edwin Lemert called for a doctrine of **radical nonintervention** that would limit the government's ability to take control of the lives of people, especially minors, who ran afoul of the law.[10] They called for the **decriminalization** of nonserious **victimless crimes** such as the possession of marijuana and violations of vagrancy laws. Noninterventionists also called for the removal of nonviolent offenders from the nation's correctional system, a policy referred to as **deinstitutionalization.** They also believed that first offenders who committed minor crimes should be removed from the formal trial process and placed in informal community-based treatment programs, a process known as **pretrial diversion.** Each of these initiatives is designed to help people avoid the stigma associated with contact with the criminal justice system.

The Nonintervention Perspective Today

The rush to place a barrier between the defendant and the criminal justice system slackened in the 1980s. Little evidence was offered to show that noninterventionist efforts work any better than the formal justice system. In fact, in an important study entitled *Beyond Probation*, Charles Murray and Louis Cox found that punishment-oriented programs may actually have more beneficial long-term effects on serious (juvenile) offenders than innovative community-based efforts founded on the principles of deinstitutionalization.[11]

Critics have also charged that efforts designed for nonintervention actually enmesh those accused of crime more firmly within the grasp of the agencies of justice, a process called **widening the net.**[12] For example, nonintervention programs may substitute a treatment-oriented label such as "mentally unstable" for a criminally oriented one such as "criminal defendant." Similarly, some treatment-oriented diversion programs actually produce greater intervention than a trial because they require the client to participate in a long-term treatment program rather than paying a fine or being placed on probation.

Despite such criticism, the nonintervention philosophy is alive and well. Efforts continue to be made to keep as many young offenders as possible out of secure detention facilities, prisons, and jails. Nevertheless, the conservative sentiments toward crime control in the 1980s have caused the prison admission rate to soar. So although efforts to remove the nonserious offender from the justice system still exist, there is also an ongoing effort to incapacitate serious offenders whenever possible.

Justice Perspective

The justice perspective combines both liberal and conservative views of justice. On the conservative side, it stresses that the purpose of the justice system is to control crime and punish those who violate the law. On the liberal side, it stresses fairness, equality, and strict control of discretion.

The justice perspective holds that it is futile to rehabilitate criminals through correctional treatment efforts. Especially suspect are prison-based programs. Correctional institutions are places of punishment and confinement and therefore cannot serve as rehabilitation-dispensing service centers. Any effort to individualize treatment and distinguish between criminal offenders will create a sense of unfairness that can interfere with an offender's readjustment to society. If two people commit the same crime but receive different sentences due to treatment considerations, the injustice will increase frustration and anger among the inmate population.

The criminal justice system must increase fairness by reducing discretion and unequal treatment. Law violators should be evaluated on the basis of their current behavior and not on how their treatment will influence others. The justice model holds that the deterrent effects of a criminal sentence should not be considered because it is unfair to punish someone solely to prevent others from committing crimes. Nor should criminals be incapacitated because they are believed to be dangerous; it is unfair to incarcerate someone based on often misguided predictions of their future behavior. The core principle of the justice model is that the treatment of criminal offenders must be based solely on their behavior: people are entitled to receive only the punishment they deserve for their acts.[13]

The Justice Perspective Today

The justice model plays an extremely influential role in the criminal justice system today. Led by its most important advocates, including Richard Singer, David Fogel, and Andrew Von Hirsch, it has been instrumental in changing the face of the American justice system. One result has been the creation of determinate sentencing models, which authorize similar sentences for every offender convicted of a particular crime category. Furthermore, justice perspective influence has caused some states to abolish parole (early release from prison) in an effort to ensure that all inmates serve the full sentence they received at trial. It is common today to see state sentencing commissions be established to create **desert-based sentences;** the new federal criminal code mandates that judges use sentencing guidelines to control their decision making and reduce discretion. In sum, efforts are now ongoing to take the discretion out of the justice system and reduce the disparity with which people are treated.

Radical Perspective

The radical view of criminal justice regards the justice system as a state-supported effort to control the "have-not" members of society and keep power in the hands of a relatively few influential individuals. Since modern society is dominated by inter- and intragroup conflict, the criminal justice system has assumed the role of power broker for the wealthy. It serves as an instrument of control that keeps workers in their place and allows capitalists to accumulate an unequal distribution of the nation's wealth. An example of this control can be found in the efforts of law enforcement agencies to infiltrate and compromise radical groups. Similarly, the lenient treatment given white-collar criminals in the nation's courts is contrasted with the harsh punishments meted out to lower-class property offenders.

According to the radical perspective, the role of the scholar in the criminal justice system involves *praxis*, the transformation of the current arrangements and relationships in society through writings, discussion, or social action. To this end, radical criminal justice scholars have tried to promote change in the system of justice by pointing out such problems as discrimination and inequality in the way the law is enforced.[14]

The Radical Perspective Today

In the conservative 1980s, radical views of justice were countered by a return to a law and order view of justice. In fact, one of the best known radical thinkers, Anthony Platt, published a paper challenging radical thinkers to get in touch with the mood of the nation and abandon some of their more utopian ideals.[15] Such a compromise by a leading radical scholar was unheard of in the late 60s and 70s.

Though it is difficult to see a direct connection between radical thought and current criminal justice doctrine, there seems to be little question that policymakers are more sensitive today than ever to issues that are of considerable importance to radical thinkers: misuse of power; discrimination by government officials; unfair application of the law; and the disadvantages suffered by the poor. Sensitivity to problems such as these has been translated into efforts to correct some of the major abuses. For example, indigent offenders are now entitled to free legal counsel; police officers are being strictly scrutinized when they use their weapons; the government has pledged to prosecute business executives who commit corporate or *white-collar crimes*. In our post-Watergate, post-Iran-Contra society, where suspicion of the government is not uncommon, some major radical propositions appear to be attracting increased public interest.

Perspectives in Perspective

Each of the various perspectives on criminal justice has its supporters who lobby diligently for their particular position. Although this multiplicity of viewpoints may seem chaotic, you should realize that most academic and professional disciplines contain a variety of different perspectives or positions. Sociology has functionalist, interactionist, and conflict theorists; psychology contains the behaviorist, psychoanalytic, cognitive, and physiological branches, and so on. Thus it is not unusual that an interdisciplinary field as complex as criminal justice contains a diversity of opinion on its basic functions and processes.

Each perspective has influenced the current justice system. During the past decade, the crime control and justice models have been predominant. Laws have been toughened, the rights of the accused curtailed, the prison population has grown, and the death penalty has been employed against convicted murderers. In the mid-1980s when the crime rate was dropping, these policies seemed to be effective. "Get tough" policies may be questioned now that rates have once again begun to rise.

Although the general public still favors punitive policies, efforts to rehabilitate offenders, to provide them with elements of due process, and give them the least intrusive treatment possible still apply. Police, court, and correctional agencies supply a wide range of treatment and rehabilitation programs to offenders at all stages of the criminal justice system. Whenever possible, those accused of crime are treated informally in nonrestrictive, community-based programs, and the effects of stigma are guarded against. The legal rights of offenders are closely scrutinized by the courts, and although the march toward increasing civil liberties has been somewhat curtailed, the basic constitutional rights of the accused such as freedom from self-incrimination have been ingrained in the American conscience.

In sum, to understand the justice system today requires analysis of a variety of occupational roles, institutional processes, legal rules, and administrative doctrine. Each of the predominant views of criminal justice provides a vantage point for understanding and interpreting these rather complex issues. No single view is the right one or the correct one. Individuals may choose the perspective that best fits their own ideas and judgment, or they may discard them all and substitute their own views.

■ The Goals of Justice

There is little question that bringing about positive change in the criminal justice system is a formidable task because it is comprised of an extremely complex set of institutions and processes. It is also difficult to effect reform because the basic goals and objectives of justice remain unclear. Criminal justice has neither a commonly agreed-on philosophical center nor an accepted direction. At one extreme are those experts who view the justice system as a giant social control agency that should punish the wicked and protect the innocent; at the other are those who regard it as a type of "superparent" that dispenses care and protection to needy dependents.

There have been a number of coordinated efforts to define the goals of criminal justice. In 1967 the President's Crime Commission emphasized the need for greater research efforts in criminal justice, use of the systems approach and systems analysis to study the field, upgrading the educational standards of criminal justice practitioners, and a reliance on treatment programs to rehabilitate criminal offenders.[16] With regard to the latter goal, the Crime Commission advocated the development of community-based programs that would replace large fortress-like prisons and the use of pretrial diversion for first offenders and nonserious criminals.[17]

In its report, A *National Strategy to Reduce Crime* (1973), the National Advisory Commission on Criminal Justice Standards and Goals, which had been appointed by then President Richard Nixon, identified the reduction in the rates of five major crimes—homicide, forcible rape, aggravated assault, robbery, and burglary—as a major goal of the criminal justice system. The Commission suggested four priorities for reducing such offenses:[18]

- Prevention of juvenile delinquency
- Improvement of delivery of social services
- Reduction in delays in the criminal justice process
- Provision for greater citizen participation in the criminal justice system

In the 1980s the stated goals of criminal justice seemed to shift away from rehabilitation and treatment toward those that emphasized concern for the victims of crime and the control of dangerous criminals. For example, in the mid-1970s, the major policy initiatives of the federal government's Office of Juvenile Justice and Delinquency Prevention (OJJDP), were to (1) remove all juveniles from adult jails and (2) prohibit states from housing noncriminal runaways and truants with delinquent youth.[19] In the 1980s, a more conservative OJJDP shifted its goals to the early identification of chronic delinquent youth and the formulation of plans to restrict their activities. Thus, the federal agency with primary concern for juvenile justice policy making shifted its major goal from treating youths in the least restrictive way possible to indentifying and incapacitating serious offenders.

In sum, the goals of the justice system can be both abstract and pragmatic. They can also be characterized as multipurpose, ever-changing, and deeply influenced by the prevailing social and political climate. Moreover, goal conflict can exist in a single criminal justice agency or be a function of interagency disagreements.

Recent Goals

It is possible to identify enduring themes in criminal justice that have served as goals for a broad spectrum of agencies across the country. Some of these are fairly abstract while others represent more practical considerations. The most important theoretical and pragmatic goals of the system are discussed next.

PREVENTION. Crime prevention efforts attempt to reduce the need to commit crime by providing potential offenders with noncriminal opportunities for success and achievement. Building stronger family units, providing counseling in schools, and developing better environmental conditions are all examples of the kind of prevention efforts that have been common in the United States.

Criminal justice agencies have long participated in prevention efforts by establishing programs that encourage law-abiding behavior among young people. For example, many larger police departments have special units that cooperate with school officials in anti-drug abuse and other education programs designed to prevent crime. Another recent approach involves experiments with community policing strategies such as foot patrols and the organization of anti-crime community groups to improve police relations with the citizens they serve. Some recent evidence suggests that these efforts can pay dividends in reduced crime rates and improved police-community relations.[20]

DETERRENCE. Deterrence strategies are designed to lower the crime rate by convincing potential criminals that (1) their risk of apprehension is great and that (2) their punishment will nullify any potential benefits they gain from crime. To effect the goal of deterrence, law enforcement agencies have conducted publicized crusades against criminals. Specific targets include international and domestic drug dealers, organized crime figures, drunk drivers, and pornographers. Prosecutors impanel grand juries to investigate criminal conspiracies; they may also demand severe punishments to make an example of those who defy the power of the law. Legislators attempt to deter crime by enacting laws that impose extremely harsh penalties such as the death penalty or mandatory life sentences.

Though there have been numerous attempts to demonstrate that the justice system can actually deter crime, there is still relatively little evidence that crime can be deterred though the fear of punishment alone.

DIVERSION. Diversion refers to the efforts made by criminal justice agencies to exclude individuals from the formal system of justice and place them in nonpunitive treatment-oriented programs such as a community detoxification unit. Diverting offenders at any stage of the justice process is designed to help the offender avoid the stigma associated with official processing by the criminal justice system, as well as the expense and trauma of a criminal trial. At the same time, diversion helps the justice system save the cost of a trial and subsequent period of correction. Diversion is usually aimed at a select type of offender, such as minor noncriminal delinquents and adult offenders who might be more appropriately handled by social agencies. The goal of diverting offenders represents a policy of using the least restrictive or intrusive method possible of treating known criminals. It is a direct offshoot of the noninterventionist perspective on justice.

REHABILITATION. Though the goal of rehabilitation has come under attack, it remains a common objective in many agencies of the criminal justice system. In fact, in most states, juvenile offenders are required by law to receive rehabilatory treatment if they are going to be confined for their offenses. Similarly, almost every prison and correctional institution maintains a wide variety of treatment approaches that are made available to inmates. Thus, although rehabilitation of criminal offenders may be less popular than it was in the 1960s, it remains a viable goal of the justice system today.

REINTEGRATION. The justice system is also dedicated to the **reintegration** of offenders into society at the conclusion of their interaction with the correctional components of the system. This can mean helping former prison inmates readjust to society after their incarceration has been completed. It can also involve helping alcoholic offenders "stay dry" after their court-ordered treatment is terminated. Finding the key to successful reintegration is an extremely important goal for the justice system because so many offenders recidivate and become reinvolved with the justice system.

PROTECTION. A stated goal of many criminal justice agencies is the protection of the public they serve. This can be accomplished through the related goals of controlling known criminals and preventing and deterring crime. In addition, justice-related agencies provide services to the victims of crime, ranging from witness assistance to monetary grants to replace crime-related losses. Criminal justice personnel engage in many non-crime-related activities, such as traffic control and emergency medical services, which help secure public safety.

The goal of community safety has not been met in localities where high crime rates have produced a fearful population and deteriorated neighborhood conditions. In response, there has been a movement to supplement the criminal justice system with **community crime prevention** programs in which citizens engage in neighborhood patrols, block watches and other self-help programs.[21]

INNOVATION. Another goal of the justice system is to adopt the most innovative methods and techniques for its component agencies. In recent years, this has meant the use of electronic data processing systems for such operations as record keeping and case processing in the court system, criminal identification in law enforcement, and the management of correctional institutions. An ongoing effort has been made to borrow methodologies from such diverse fields as economics and systems analysis in order to help the justice system achieve its goals of effective and efficient operations. Some of the most innovative justice programs, such as the electronic monitoring of offenders by computers, reflect the influence of our "high tech" society. Other programs, such as foot patrol and neighborhood policing strategies, are evidence that the lessons of the past have not been forgotten.

FAIRNESS. All persons processed through the criminal justice system should be treated fairly and uniformly. No distinctions should be made on the basis of race, class, or gender. Due process safeguards should be present in all aspects of the criminal justice system. The methods and techniques implemented in the areas of arrest, sentencing, and incarceration must be consistent with our democratic ideals and frame of government.

EFFICIENCY. Criminal justice agencies must develop efficient organization and management principles. The effectiveness of the justice system is compromised if law enforcement, courts, and correctional agencies fail to utilize their personnel and resources optimally. Efficient operations require qualified personnel, adequate organizational framework, sound fiscal planning, and the development of successful programs of crime control.

Efficiency also requires that the justice system agencies actually carry out their stated tasks. For example, does the new treatment program actually rehabilitate offenders? Does the new "get tough" policy actually deter crime? Does the antidrug campaign reduce student narcotics use?

■ Criminal Justice and Social Control

Considering the multiplicity of perspectives and goals that confront the criminal justice system, it should come as no surprise that scholars and practitioners disagree about the direction criminal justice policy should take and the role the system should play in controlling criminal behavior. Should the justice system play a more aggressive role in shaping conduct and morality or become involved in only the most serious breaches of the criminal law?

Should it initiate criminal investigations or wait until a complaint is made by an injured party? Should it control noncriminals who have shown only the "potential" to become persistent law violators? Should the use of goods and services, such as drugs and guns, that many Americans desire to use or own be controlled? These are but a few of the issues that face the justice system in the 1990s. In the following sections, some of the most important issues and trends in social control will be identified and discussed.

The Scope of Social Control

What behaviors should the criminal justice system control with a firm hand and which should remain beyond the grasp of the law? In recent years the justice system has made a measurable effort to increase its control over both the behavior that is considered a threat to the general public and the people who engage in that behavior. Yet, despite this trend, there are a few examples where some effort has been made to limit the power of the justice system to regulate human interaction.

The efforts to extend social control most often reflect society's current concern about particular offense patterns. As you may recall, the federal government's new drug control legislation significantly extends its grasp over drug importers and distributors. Many states have passed legislation toughening penalties for drunk drivers. New Hampshire, for example, now requires that offenders convicted of a second DWI offense spend three days in a county jail and seven days in a rehabilitation center.[22] There has been a crackdown on the sale of pornography, and efforts are underway to close down big city red light districts such as New York's Time Square area and Boston's Combat Zone even if it means the city must buy out or condemn adult theaters and book stores.[23] Increasing the scope of social control means that more than three million people are under state control, more than ever before (see the Criminal Justice in Review).

Although the scope of social control has increased in some areas of the law, many experts in criminal justice, law, and the social sciences have suggested that certain offenses be removed from the criminal statutes. These include drugs and narcotics, public drunkenness, pornography, vagrancy, gambling, the use of marijuana, prostitution, and sexual acts between consenting adults in private. The reduction or elimination of legal penalties for such acts is known as **decriminalization;** in contrast, **overcriminalization** involves the misuse of the criminal sanction.[24] Advocates of the decriminalization approach suggest that the criminal law is overextended when it invokes criminal sanctions for social and moral problems; they believe that the primary purpose of criminal law should be to control serious crimes affecting persons and property. As a result, they argue that these "victimless" crimes, as they are often called, should be the responsibility not of the criminal justice system but of mental health or other social-service-type agencies.

Decriminalization efforts have been initiated in order to make the criminal law reflective of current social values and attitudes while at the same time allowing the overburdened criminal justice system to concentrate on more serious criminal offenses. The decriminalization process has also been aided by legal change. For example, the movement to decriminalize the behavior of chronic alcoholics was originally influenced by two federal court decisions, *Easter v. District of Columbia*[25] and *Driver v. Hinnant*,[26] which held that a chronic

The Effects of Social Control

A conservative American public seems squarely behind efforts to increase the scope of the criminal justice system. What is the price for our national desire for legal protection? One outcome has been an ever-increasing number of people under state control. As Table A indicates, more than three million people are now on probation, in prison or jail, or on parole. These figures do not include approximately 100,000 incarcerated juvenile offenders as well as juveniles and adults in alcohol, drug, and mental health treatment centers. As Table A also shows, the number of people under state control has increased 500,000 since 1983, despite the fact that the crime rate has remained stable. These data indicate that the grasp of social control is increasing. Though the costs of justice now exceed $50 billion, the price of controlling society's deviant members does not seem to be a deterrent to its expansion. ■

SOURCE: Thomas Hester, *Probation and Parole, 1987* (Washington, D.C.: Bureau of Justice Statistics, 1988).

TABLE A ■ **Correctional Populations, Percentage of Adult Population Under Sanction, and Percentage Change, 1983–87**

	Correctional Populations Total	Probation	Jail	Prison	Parole
1983					
Number	2,475,100	1,582,947	221,815	423,898	246,440
Percentage*	1.44%	.92	.13	.25	.14
1984					
Number	2,684,222	1,740,948	233,018	448,264	266,992
Percentage*	1.55%	1.00	.13	.26	.15
1985					
Number	3,011,494	1,968,712	254,986	487,593	300,203
Percentage*	1.71%	1.12	.15	.28	.17
1986					
Number	3,239,631	2,114,821	272,736	526,436	325,638
Percentage*	1.82%	1.19	.15	.30	.18
1987					
Number	3,460,960	2,242,053	294,092	562,623	362,192
Percentage*	1.92%	1.25	.16	.31	.20
Percentage Increase in Correctional Populations (1983–87)	39.8%	41.6	32.6	32.7	47.0

*Percentage of Adult Population

alcoholic could not be found guilty of the crime of public intoxication. In 1968, in *Powell v. Texas*, the U.S. Supreme Court recognized the criminal justice system's inability to provide rehabilitation for the alcoholic.[27]

The move to decriminalize victimless crimes received a setback in 1986, when the Supreme Court, in *Bowers v. Hardwick*, upheld a Georgia statute making sexual relations between consenting adults of the same sex a crime (sodomy).[28] In deciding the case, the majority reasoned that because homosexuality has long been condemned in Western society, it is within the state's interest to limit homosexual activity. The *Bowers* decision disappointed civil liberties groups who had hoped the Court would decriminalize homosexual behavior in the same manner as it had decriminalized other sexual matters such as the use of contraceptives.

Sexually related behavior has always presented a dilemma for law makers, however. For example, all states continue to ban obscene magazines and films even though there is no clear-cut evidence that sexually related material is related to violent crimes and the definition of obscenity is still open to debate.[29]

The two most significant battlegrounds for extending the scope of social control are drugs and guns. Advocates argue that these two items should be strictly controlled, opponents argue that it is futile to prohibit them so legalization may be a better course of action. The following sections explore these issues in greater detail.

Controlling the Drug Trade

Although the scope of social control is still at issue, there is little question that attempts at controlling drug use have taken on the trappings of a crusade. For legal, political, and social reasons, there has been a massive and concerted effort to control the flow of narcotics into the United States. Significant evidence indicates that narcotics use is closely associated with criminality. One study found that about 75 percent of all arrestees test positively for drug use.[30] Other research indicates that narcotics addicts are responsible for a significant amount of all criminal activity.[31] Drug use among poor urban teenagers has been linked to gang violence and a sense of hopelessness in the nation's inner cities.[32]

The effort to control the drug trade has been carried out on a number of different levels. One approach has been to stop the flow of drugs as it enters the United States from Latin America, Europe, and Asia. Federal enforcement agencies, the military, and the Coast Guard have been involved in surveillance and seizure operations. Some foreign governments have cooperated by arresting drug smugglers and destroying supplies. A survey prepared for the U.S.

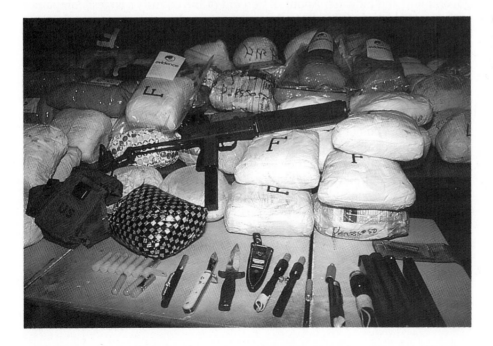

More than six billion dollars are spent annually on drug enforcement programs. These weapons and drugs were seized in a police raid.

Customs Bureau found that state, local, and federal law enforcement agencies spent $6.2 billion on controlling the drug trade (1988). State and local government agencies spent an additional $4.9 billion or 18 percent of their operating budgets on drug enforcement efforts.[33] The Bush administration has vowed to use the U.S. military in a campaign against drug dealers and has appointed a "drug czar" to coordinate the antidrug effort.[34]

Despite this massive campaign, efforts to stem the supply of drugs such as heroin, marijuana, and cocaine have not proven successful. The United States has over 12,000 miles of coastline that must be patrolled. Smugglers use ships, airplanes, and automobiles to smuggle. Despite increased funds and high tech vigilance, the amount of drugs seized is only a small portion of the total.

An attempt has also been made to destroy the raw materials for heroin, cocaine, and marijuana, in the countries in which they are grown—Turkey, Afghanistan, Thailand, Burma, Columbia, Peru, Mexico, and Jamaica. Source control is hard to achieve, however. The governments of countries that supply drugs are often unwilling to cooperate. Though some South American and Asian governments have entered the fight against the drug trade, under-developed nations actually have an economic incentive to allow this lucrative cash crop to flourish. If drug crops are destroyed, their national economies will lose millions of dollars in foreign currency, and their governments will face the displeasure of suddenly unemployed farmers. If the United States helps compensate for the losses, other nations will be encouraged to enter the drug-producing business to cash in on U.S. aid. The political scandal involving General Noriega of Panama, a national figure indicted for drug smuggling, highlights the problem.

Identifying and treating drug users has also been tried as a control technique, but it presents very difficult problems. In the United States and elsewhere, the drug user can be viewed more as a victim than a culprit. Many come from disturbed homes and suffer from depression, alienation, and other indicators of social maladjustment. There is no known long-term "cure" for drug addiction. Another problem is identifying drug users in the first place. Identification has been facilitated by mandatory drug testing programs in government and industry. About 25 percent of the country's largest companies including IBM and AT&T test job applicants for drugs.[35] After identification, a number of different treatment strategies have been employed. In the United States, **methadone maintenance** has been used to treat drug addicts. Methadone is a drug similar to heroin, which blocks the effect of heroin on the brain so that users no longer feel high or euphoric. Addicts can be treated at clinics where they receive methadone under controlled conditions. However, most methadone programs have long waiting lists and are costly: the average cost of maintaining an addict on methadone is $18,000 per year.[36]

The overwhelming problem associated with drug control is the enormous profits involved in the drug trade: 500 kilos of coca leaves worth $4,000 to a grower yield about 8 kilos of street cocaine valued at $500,000. A drug dealer who can move 100 pounds of coke into the United States can make $1.5 million on one shipment. An estimated 60 tons of cocaine with a street value of $17 billion are imported into the country each year. Government crackdowns simply serve to drive up the price of drugs and encourage more illegal entrepreneurs to enter the market. For example, the Hell's Angels motorcycle club has become one of the primary distributors of cocaine and amphetamines in the United States. Movies and television shows such as "Miami Vice," which depict the rise and fall of cocaine dealers, may be viewed as a warning to potential drug traffickers that "crime doesn't pay," but they also show the lavish lifestyles and unlimited cash supplies associated with life in the drug trade. The immense profits to be made in the drug trade can even lead "respectable" businessmen like John DeLorean to get involved in drug trading as a quick cash fix for their ailing businesses (though, of course, DeLorean was acquitted on the defense of entrapment).[37]

In sum, the tremendous profits in the drug trade, coupled with the emotional needs of users, make the control of illegal drugs an ongoing criminological dilemma.

To remedy this situation, the federal government has begun to make the arrest and conviction of drug traffickers a top priority. A recent survey found that between 1980 and 1986 the number of drug-related convictions in federal courts more than doubled, from 5,244 in 1980 to 12,285 in 1986. This 134 percent increase was significantly higher than the 27 percent increase in convictions for other federal crimes. In addition, the percentage of convictees receiving a prison sentence increased from 71 percent to 77 percent, and the average sentence increased from four to five years.[38]

These data indicate that despite a spate of "get tough" rhetoric by politicians on both the state and national levels, narcotics dealers are treated relatively leniently. Though it is often difficult to gain convictions in narcotics cases, many defendants receive probation or a short prison sentence. Nevertheless, the federal data seem to indicate a trend toward toughening criminal justice sentencing policy in an effort to limit the drug trade by incapacitating known suppliers and deterring potential ones.

Another approach to drug control that has been suggested is to legalize or decriminalize controlled substances and thereby remove them as a law enforcement issue. Legalization would diminish the cost of drugs and reduce the criminal activity of drug users who resort to crime to finance their habits. This policy has been attempted in England where private physicians and government-run clinics have the power to legally prescribe heroin. Although some experts view the English approach as a viable solution to the heroin problem in the United States, James Inciardi proclaims it a failure because the addiction rate has risen in England whereas it has actually declined in the United States (although there is no evidence that dispensing heroin in itself caused the addiction rate to rise in England).[39] Efforts to supply users with substitute drugs such as methadone have met with qualified success because addicts often supplement their supply with illegal drugs or sell the substitutes on the illegal market; it also means substituting one addiction for another. Furthermore, making narcotics more easily available might encourage the spread of AIDS, which is linked to needle sharing by intravenous drug users.[40] Thus, although fighting drug use by limiting the scope of social control may provide food for thought, it may carry with it enough social baggage to rule out legalization as a near-term solution.

Controlling Handguns

Another social control issue that has long perplexed criminal justice policy-makers is the control of handguns. On the one hand, gun control advocates point to the significant number of crimes committed with unregistered handguns and the ease with which handguns can be legally purchased. The FBI usually finds that about half of all murders and a third of all rapes and robberies are committed with a handgun. Handguns are the cause of death for two-thirds of all police killed in the line of duty.

One of the problems of controlling handguns are their easy availability and relatively low cost.

On the other hand, those in favor of permitting citizens to freely purchase and carry handguns argue that the right to bear arms is guaranteed by the U.S. Constitution and that an armed citizenry is a free one. They also argue that victims have the right to protect themselves from armed intruders and criminals. They point to studies such as the one conducted by Gary Kleck, which found that each year between 1,500 and 2,800 predatory criminals are killed by gun-wielding crime victims and that between 8,700 and 16,000 are wounded.[41] Instead of advocating controls on handguns, conservatives call for strict punishments for the use of handguns during the commission of a crime.

Efforts to control handguns take many different forms. Each state and many local jurisdictions have laws banning or restricting the sale or possession of guns. Others regulate dealers who sell guns. For example, the Federal Gun Control Act prohibits dealers from selling guns to minors, ex-felons, drug users, and so on. In addition, each dealer must keep detailed records of who purchases guns. Unfortunately, only meager resources are available to enforce this law.[42]

Do strict gun control laws make a difference in the violent crime rate? The jury is still out on this issue. The most famous attempt to regulate handguns is the Massachusetts Bartley-Fox Law, which provides a mandatory one-year prison term for possession of a handgun (outside the home) without a permit. A detailed analysis of violent crime in Boston in the years after the law's passage found that the use of handguns in robberies and murders did decline substantially (robbery 35 percent, and murder 55 percent in a two-year period). However, these optimistic results must be tempered by two facts: rates for similar crimes dropped significantly in comparable cities that did not have gun control laws; the use of other weapons, such as knives, increased.[43]

Another gun control method is to add an extra punishment for any crime involving a handgun. A well-known example is Michigan's Felony Firearm Statute, which requires that an additional two years be tacked on to the sentence of anyone convicted of a crime in which a handgun was used. An analysis by Colin Loftin and his associates found that the Michigan law had (1) little effect on the sentence given to convicted offenders and (2) little effect on violent crime in Detroit.[44] Similarly, in a study evaluating the handgun laws of all 50 states, David Lester found little evidence that strict handgun laws influence homicide rates.[45]

The use of handguns in political crimes, such as the Robert Kennedy assassination and the shooting of President Ronald Reagan and his press secretary James Brady, has spurred a majority of Americans to advocate controls on the sale of handguns and a ban on cheap "Saturday Night Specials." Nonetheless, gun control efforts may have little effect on violence.[46] There are so many guns in the United States today, a conservative estimate is 30–50 million illegal handguns, that banning their manufacture would have a relatively small effect for years to come.[47] Furthermore, if the value of handguns is increased by banning their manufacture or sale, illegal importation of guns might increase, as it has for another controlled substance—narcotics. Increasing penalties for gun-related crimes has also met with limited success, since judges may be reluctant to alter their sentencing policies to accommodate legislators. Regulating dealers is difficult and would only encourage private sales and bartering. Nevertheless, some combination of control and penalty may prove useful, and efforts should be made to discover, if at all possible, whether handgun control could indeed reduce violent crime rates.

Controlling the Chronic Offender

In the 1960s and into the 1970s, it was generally agreed that crime was a social phenomenon. Most crime experts linked criminal activity to deteriorated neighborhoods, families in turmoil, lack of jobs and economic opportunities, and other social factors. The general belief was that if environment and family life could be improved most criminals would forgo law violations and become productive citizens. Federal and state governments funded numerous programs to improve conditions in the inner city and provide legitimate alternatives to crime.

The identification of the chronic, career criminal has challenged this view of crime and correction and thereby presents an intriguing dilemma for the social control efforts of the justice system. As you may recall, Marvin Wolfgang and his colleagues at the University of Pennsylvania uncovered the existence of the chronic offender in a series of cohort studies conducted in Philadelphia. They used the term to refer to a small group of offenders who were arrested five or more times as juveniles. Whereas most offenders "age out" of crime, chronic offenders continue their criminal careers as adults and may be responsible for a significant amount of all criminality.[48]

Recognition of the chronic offender has certainly seemed to have an effect on the justice system's crime control efforts. It challenges the belief that convicted criminals should be incarcerated until they have been reformed and are competent to function in society. Traditional correctional treatment philosophy favors helping offenders alter their behavior by equipping them with marketable job skills, upgrading their educational level, and providing counseling. The current system is not prepared to deal with the implications of research that shows that such efforts may have relatively little effect on chronic offenders who will offend at a constant and persistent pace throughout their lifecycle.

The discovery of the chronic offender has supported the crime control view of the justice system. It has been interpreted to mean that crime rates could be significantly reduced if chronic offenders were taken out of circulation. The chronic offender concept has inspired a nationwide policy of incapacitation, which has been manifested in the development of mandatory prison sentences for certain crimes, as well as a concerted effort to place multiple offenders in secure confinement. It has inspired special prosecutorial task forces whose mission is specifically to indict and incarcerate chronic offenders. It has also prompted a number of different plans to get tough with multiple offenders by incarcerating them for as long as possible without the hope of parole or early release.

These plans are not without their detractors. It has been suggested that a social control policy that concentrates on punishing people because they are chronic offenders is wrong for two reasons: (1) it is based on predicting what people will do in the future and not on their current crime, and (2) no criminal prediction device has ever proven accurate. Consequently, some offenders, especially minorities, will be punished more than they deserve, a violation of their civil rights.[49]

Despite such concerns, the justice system has adopted numerous policies designed to expand the control over chronic offenders, and these policies have helped increase the correctional population to over three million.

Technology and Social Control

Another justice system concern that is closely intertwined with the scope of social control is the use of new technology to monitor suspected and convicted criminals. The new **surveillance** techniques operate on a number of different levels. Computers are now used in extensive data retrieval systems to cross-reference people and activities. Information now available on national and local data bases includes credit ratings, bank holdings, stock transfers, medical information, loans outstanding, and so on.

Computer networks also contain criminal justice system information. The most well-known network is the National Crime Information Center (NCIC), operated by the Justice Department, which houses an extensive collection of arrest records; these enable local police departments to determine instantly whether a suspect has an outstanding record.

Technology has also been improved in the area of visual and audio surveillance. The FBI has made national headlines filming and taping drug deals and organized crime connections. Hundreds of high tech, space age devices are available that have not only increased police ability to listen and watch but are also virtually self-sufficient. For example, audio listening devices now use lasers that permit eavesdropping from outside windows without the necessity of entering a home or securing a warrant. Airborne cameras can monitor human movement from 30,000 feet and help spot fields used to grow marijuana and other illegal drugs.

Also in use is electronic equipment that monitors offenders in the community. Instead of a prison or jail sentence, convicted offenders are placed under "house arrest" and kept under surveillance by a central computer. A government agency, most typically the probation department, keeps track of the offenders by requiring them to wear a nonremovable ankle or neck device that signals a computer if they move from their home without permission.

The dangers represented by the new electronic surveillance are the subject of an important book by sociologist Gary Marx.[50] He lists the following characteristics of the new surveillance techniques that set them apart from traditional methods of social control:[51]

In 1961, this law enforcement officer uses an electronic device to listen to a conversation in the distance. At that time such practices did not violate the Fourth Amendment prohibition of unreasonable searches and seizures because there was no physical trespass on constitutionally protected property. However, in 1967, the Supreme Court ruled that citizens are entitled to a reasonable expectation of privacy. Today, some uses of listening devices violate this expectation and may be considered unreasonable even though no physical trespass occurs.

Part One

The Nature of Crime,
Law and Criminal Justice

1. The new surveillance transcends distance, darkness, and physical barriers.
2. It transcends time; its records can be stored, retrieved, combined, analyzed, and communicated.
3. It has low visibility or is invisible.
4. It is often involuntary.
5. Prevention is a major concern.
6. It is capital-intensive rather than labor-intensive.
7. It involves decentralized self-policing.
8. It triggers a shift from targeting a specific suspect to categorical suspicion of everyone.
9. It is more intensive.
10. It is more extensive.

According to Marx, the use of electronic eavesdropping and other modern surveillance methods has changed the relationship between police and the public. New techniques have overcome the physical limitations that existed when surveillance was a function of human labor. Today's electronic devices never rest, are undetectable, and can store information forever. People may now be required to assist in their own monitoring by wearing devices that keep them under scrutiny; electronic devises can follow suspects everywhere, can gather extensive information on them, and can include thousands in the information "net." As Marx puts it:

> Between the camera, tape recorder, the identity card, the metal detector, the tax form, and the computer, everyone becomes a reasonable target.[52]

Marx warns that the dangers of the new surveillance may include a redefinition of the concept of "invasion of privacy" in that almost any personal information is open to scrutiny, "fishing expeditions" in which the government

Chapter 5

Perspectives on Criminal Justice and Victimization

■

can do a general check on a citizen without a court order, and the danger that machine error will destroy the lives of innocent people. He cautions us:

> The first task of a society that would have liberty and privacy is to guard against the misuse of physical coercion on the part of the state and private parties. The second task is to guard against "softer" forms of secret and manipulative control. Because these are often subtle, indirect, invisible, diffuse, deceptive, and shrouded in benign justifications, this is clearly the more difficult task.[53]

It seems evident that agents of the justice system must confront the issue of social control in the 1990s: How much control is needed? What should be its most important targets? What are the most effective and efficient social control strategies? How can the need for control be balanced with concern for civil rights and personal liberty?

■ Criminal Justice and the Victim

In addition to establishing the boundaries of social control, another critical issue facing the criminal justice system is its relationship with the victims of crime.[54] Criminal justice experts and legal commentators have long been aware of the suffering associated with **victimization.** Victim surveys indicate that almost every American age 12 and over will one day become the victim of crime.[55] For example, Dean Kilpatrick and his associates interviewed 391 adult females in a southern city and found that 75 percent had been victimized by crime at least once in their lives, including being raped (25 percent) and experiencing sexual molestation (18 percent). Disturbingly, 25 percent of the victims developed post-trauma stress syndrome, and their psychological symptoms lasted for more than a decade after the crime occurred.[56]

Crime victims suffer financial problems, mental stress, and physical hardship.[57] Assisting the victim in dealing with these problems is the responsibility of all of society and, specifically, the criminal justice system. Law enforcement agencies, courts, and correctional systems have come to realize that due process and human rights exist for both the defendant and the victim of criminal behavior.

Problems of Crime Victims

Being the target of rape, robbery, or assault is itself a terrible burden and one that can have considerable long-term consequences.[58] The FBI estimates that victims lose about $8 billion dollars a year in property.[59] However, the loss of wealth is only a small part of the cost of being victimized. In an important analysis, Mark Cohen used jury awards in civil personal injury cases involving acts similar to crimes in order to estimate the "real cost" of crime to victims.[60] As Table 5.1 shows, a crime such as rape cost its victim an average of $51,058 including $4,617 in direct losses, $43,651 for pain and suffering, and $2,880 for the risk of death. In other words, Cohen estimates that if a rape victim sued her attacker for damages, the jury award would amount to about $51,000.

In contrast to the FBI statistics, Cohen estimates that the cost of crime is a staggering *$92.6 billion annually!*

The problems of crime victims do not end when their attacker leaves the scene of the crime. After the crime has been reported to the authorities, they may be in store for further "victimization" at the hands of the justice system.

TABLE 5.1 ■ Average Cost of Crime to the Victim

Crime	Cost	Crime	Cost
Kidnapping	$110,469	Assault	$12,028
Rape	$51,058	Car theft	$3,127
Arson	$33,549	Burglary	$1,372
Bank Robbery	$18,810	Larceny	
Robbery	$12,594	Personal	$181
		Household	$173
Bombing	$77,123		

SOURCE: Adapted from Mark Cohen, "Pain, Suffering, and Cost Jury Awards: A Study of the *Law and Society Review* Cost of Crime to Victims," 22 (1988): 547.

While the crime is still fresh in their minds, they may have to endure any or all of the following:

■ The police may question the victim insensitively.

■ There may be innuendos or suspicion that the victim was somehow at fault.

■ The victim may have difficulty learning what is going on in the case.

■ Property is often kept for a long time as evidence and may never be returned.

■ Wages may be lost for time spent testifying in court.

■ Time may be wasted when a victim appears in court only to have the case postponed or dismissed.

■ Victims may find that the authorities are indifferent to their fear of retaliation if they cooperate in the criminal's prosecution.

■ Victims may be fearful of testifying in court and being embarrassed by defense attorneys.[61]

It should not come as a surprise that the National Crime Survey (NCS) data show that one of the reasons victims choose not to report crime to the police is because they believe that the "police would not want to be bothered" or that they would be "inefficient, ineffective or insensitive."[62]

The Criminal Justice Response

In 1982, because of public concern over violent personal crime, President Ronald Reagan created a Task Force on Victims of Crime.[63] This group was to undertake an extensive study on crime victimization in the United States to determine how victims of crime could be given assistance. It found that crime victims had been transformed into a group of citizens burdened by a justice system that had been designed for their protection. Their participation both as victims and as witnesses was often overlooked, and more emphasis was placed on the defendant's rights than on the victim's. The task force suggested that a balance be achieved between recognizing the rights of the victim and providing for due process for the defendant. Its most significant recommendation was that the Sixth Amendment to the Constitution be augmented by the following statement: "In every criminal prosecution, the victim shall have the right to be present and to be heard at all critical stages of the judicial proceedings."[64] Other recommendations included protecting witnesses and victims from intimidation, requiring restitution in criminal cases, developing guidelines for fair treatment of crime victims and witnesses, and expanding programs of victim compensation.[65]

Consequently, the Justice Department provided research funds to create and expand victim-witness programs, which identified the needs of victims and witnesses who were involved in a criminal incident. In addition, the Omnibus Victim and Witness Protection Act required the use of victim impact statements at sentencing in federal criminal cases, greater protection for witnesses, more stringent bail laws, and the use of restitution in criminal cases. In 1984 the Comprehensive Crime Control Act and the Victims of Crime Act authorized federal funding of state victim compensation and assistance projects.[66] With this legislation the federal government began to take steps to aid victims and make their assistance an even greater concern of the public and the justice system.

As a result of these efforts, an estimated 2,000 victim-witness assistance programs have been developed in the United States. A survey of 25 programs found that 80 percent provided the services listed in Table 5.2.[67]

Victim-witness programs are organized on a variety of governmental levels, serve a variety of clients, and provide all or some of the programs listed in Table 5.2. Table 5.3 describes three such programs operating in the United States.

Victim Compensation

High on the agenda of victim advocates has been the enactment of legislation establishing crime victim compensation programs.[68] As a result of such legislation, the victim ordinarily receives compensation from the state to pay for damages associated with the crime. Rarely are two compensation schemes alike, however, and many state programs suffer from lack of adequate funding and proper organization within the criminal justice system. The victim assistance projects that have been developed seek to help the victim learn about **victim compensation** services and related programs. The upcoming Criminal Justice in Review discusses the current state of victim compensation programs.

TABLE 5.2 ■ **Victim-Witness Program Services**

Emergency services
Medical care
Shelter or food
Security repair
Financial assistance
On-scene comfort

Counseling
24-hour hotline
Crisis intervention
Follow-up counseling
Mediation

Advocacy and support services
Personal advocacy
Employer intervention
Landlord intervention
Property return
Intimidation protection
Legal/paralegal counsel
Referral

Claims assistance
Insurance claims aid
Restitution assistance
Compensation assistance
Witness fee assistance

Court-related services
Witness reception
Court orientation
Notification
Witness alert
Transportation
Child care
Escort to court
Victim impact reports

Systemwide services
Public education
Legislative advocacy
Training

SOURCE: Peter Finn and Beverly Lee, *Establishing and Expanding Victim-Witness Assistance Programs* (Washington, D.C.: National Institute of Justice, 1988).

TABLE 5.3 ■ Victim-Witness Programs

Alameda County

The Alameda County District Attorney Victim/Witness Assistance Program in Oakland, California, serves a population of slightly over 1 million, 18 police departments, and 8 courts. With an annual budget of nearly $331,000, offices in 2 locations, and 10 full-time staff members, the program focuses exclusively on victims, even though it is administered by the district attorney.

Program staff identify more than 80 percent of their clients from prosecutor charging sheets that are routinely delivered to the program. Police reports on all incidents involving sexual assault, child molestation, homicide, and domestic violence are automatically forwarded to the program.

Police and prosecutors also call the program directly with requests for assistance. Staff is available during working hours for telephone or walk-in consultation whenever victims require emotional support. Staff members also visit the homes of elderly victims and children.

Victim notification and orientation consists of explaining, by letter and telephone, each stage of the litigation process. Staff members may also meet with victims before a court session, show them the physical layout of the courtroom, explain the upcoming proceedings, and escort the victim during hearings and trials.

Scottsdale, Arizona

The Police Crisis Intervention Unit in Scottsdale, Arizona, is a police-based program operating in a city of 112,000. The city funds the program as part of the Scottsdale police budget. Funding in 1985 was $188,000, which supports a full-time staff of four. The program serves no witnesses, but in addition to helping victims, the staff also assists many people who are not victims of crime, including accident victims, families of runaways, and disoriented individuals.

Police referrals account for 80 percent of the unit's caseload. Officers drop off police reports with a request for assistance, and they bring victims to see the program specialists at the station. After working hours, police can still refer victims by telephoning the specialists at home or paging them on beepers. Most of the remaining caseload is the result of direct calls from victims and walk-ins.

The program's principal services are 24-hour crisis intervention, referrals, orientation to court procedures, and transportation. The staff also provides emotional support to many victims during municipal court proceedings, and city judges often call the unit when victims become upset in court.

Greenville County

The Greenville County, South Carolina, Victim/Witness Assistance Unit is a small program run by the District Attorney. The program has two full-time and five part-time paid staff, and a budget of $101,000. The program serves a 2-county area of almost 300,000 people.

The program identifies 90 percent of the unit's caseload from a daily offense bulletin forwarded by the city and county police departments. Police also call the program two or three times a day for help in calming a disturbed victim, interviewing a child, locating a missing witness, or answering questions from victims and families of homicide victims.

The program's major services are witness notification, short-term counseling, victim advocacy, and orientation to the criminal justice system. The unit often helps prosecutors in witness management, such as securing the addresses and phone numbers of key witnesses, handling arrangements for out-of-state witnesses, and coordinating witness and victim arrival, transportation, and escort.

Finally, the unit acts as a buffer between prosecutors and victims who have questions or complaints about a case.

SOURCE: Peter Finn and Beverly Lee, *Establishing and Expanding Victim-Witness Assistance Programs* (Washington, D.C.: National Institute & Justice, 1988).

Victims' Rights

In addition to victim compensation and victim service programs, some criminal justice practitioners suggest that victims have implicit rights under the Constitution that are not being provided to them. In an important article, Frank Carrington suggested that crime victims have rights that should assure that they receive basic services within the criminal justice system.[69] According to Carrington, just as the justice system must guarantee such rights as the right to counsel and a fair trial to the offender, society has the obligation to ensure

*CRIMINAL JUSTICE
IN REVIEW*

Victim Compensation

The following reading discusses the growth of victim compensation programs in the United States.

VICTIM COMPENSATION PROGRAMS ARE STILL RELATIVELY NEW

Programs to assist crime victims and witnesses have been established in almost all states over the past 5 years. In general, the programs—

■ provide financial assistance to victims and witnesses
■ protect the rights of victims and witnesses
■ complement existing efforts to aid special categories of victims, such as rape victims and victims of family abuse.

Victim/witness services may also be provided by noncriminal justice agencies (for example, state or local departments of health or human resources). Many private organizations have also developed programs such as rape crisis centers to assist victims and witnesses.

MOST STATE VICTIM COMPENSATION PROGRAMS HELP TO RECOVER MEDICAL COSTS AND LOST EARNINGS

Forty-four states, the District of Columbia, and the Virgin Islands provide compensation for medical bills and lost wages for victims. In general, awards may be made to persons injured as a direct result of the crime (Table A).

If the victim dies, payments to cover burial and related expenses are generally available to dependent survivors. In many cases, "good samaritans"— persons injured while trying to prevent a crime or apprehend an offender— are also eligible for payment.

Most states establish upper limits on payments and do not provide compensation for property losses. In general, payment can be made whether or not the offender has been apprehended or convicted, but most states require that the crime be reported to proper authorities.

State compensation programs are funded with state-administered funds. The 1984 Federal Victims of Crime Act also provides for federal grants to assist states that have established qualifying victim compensation programs.

Victims must be notified of case progress— A large number of states require that—

■ victims be notified at key decision points in the trial and sentencing of the offender
■ victims be notified upon release or escape of an offender

■ victims and witnesses be advised of scheduling changes and of available funds to cover court appearances, victim compensation, etc.

Victims may participate in sentencing, parole, or other custody decisions—"Victim impact statements," which describe the financial and emotional impact of the crime on the victim (and may also include victim comments on proposed sentences) are now required in many federal and state cases to be submitted to the court at time of sentencing, parole, or other custody decisions. Victim impact statements are generally included as part of the presentence investigation report.

A COMPREHENSIVE VICTIMS' BILL OF RIGHTS IS INCLUDED IN SOME STATE LAWS

Comprehensive Victims' Bill of Rights laws—

■ protect victims against intimidation
■ ensure that victims receive notice and are allowed to participate in various stages in the case against the accused offender.

Such laws may also—

■ ensure the victim's right to continued employment
■ provide medical or social support services
■ require the appointment of an "ombudsman" to protect the rights of the victim during the trial period. ■

TABLE A ■ 44 States, the District of Columbia, and the Virgin Islands Have Compensation Programs to Help Victims of Violent Crime

State	Victim Compensation Board Location[a]	Financial Award	To qualify, victim must		
			Show financial need	Report to police within	File claim within
Alabama	Alabama Crime Victim Compensation Commission	$0–10,000	No	3 days	12 mos.
Alaska	Department of Public Safety	$0–40,000	Yes	5	24
Arizona	Arizona Criminal Justice Commission	**	Yes	3	**
California	State Board of Control	$100–46,000	Yes	*	12
Colorado	Judicial district boards	$25–10,000	No	3	6
Connecticut	Criminal Injuries Compensation Board	$100–10,000	No	5	24
Delaware	Violent Crimes Board	$25–20,000	No	*	12
D.C.	Office of Crime Victim Compensation	$100–25,000	Yes	7	6
Florida	Department of Labor and Employment Security, Workmen's Compensation Division	$0–10,000	Yes	3	12
Hawaii	Department of Corrections	$0–10,000	No	*	18
Idaho	Industrial Commission	$0–25,000	No	3	12
Illinois	Court of Claims	$0–25,000	No	3	12
Indiana	Industrial Board	$100–10,000	No	2	24
Iowa	Department of Public Safety	$0–20,000	No	1	6
Kansas	Executive Department	$100–10,000	Yes	3	12
Kentucky	Victim Compensation Board	$0–25,000	Yes	2	12
Louisiana	Commission on Law Enforcement	$100–10,000	No	3	12
Maryland	Criminal Injuries Compensation Board	$0–45,000	Yes	2	6
Massachusetts	District court system	$0–25,000	No	2	12
Michigan	Department of Management and Budget	$200–15,000	Yes	2	12
Minnesota	Crime Victims Reparation Board	$100–50,000	No	5	12
Missouri	Division of Workmen's Compensation	$200–10,000	No	2	12
Montana	Crime Control Division	$0–25,000	No	3	12
Nebraska	Commission on Law Enforcement and Criminal Justice	$0–10,000	Yes	3	24
Nevada	Board of Examiners and Department of Administration	$0–15,000	Yes	5	12
New Jersey	Executive Branch	$0–25,000	No	90	24
New Mexico	Executive Branch	$0–12,500	No	30	12
New York	Executive Department	$0–30,000+	Yes	7	12
North Carolina[b]	Department of Crime Control and Public Safety	$100–20,000		3	24
North Dakota	Workmen's Compensation Bureau	$0–25,000	No	3	12
Ohio	Court of Claims Commissioners	$0–25,000	No	3	12
Oklahoma	Crime Victims Board	$0–10,000	No	3	12
Oregon	Department of Justice/Workmen's Compensation Board	$250–23,000	No	3	6
Pennsylvania	Crime Victims Board	$0–35,000	No	3	12
Rhode Island	Superior court system	$0–25,000	No	10	24
South Carolina	Crime Victims Advisory Board	$100–3,000	No	2	6
Tennessee	Court of Claims Commission	$0–5,000	No	2	12
Texas	Industrial Accident Board	$0–25,000	No	3	6
Utah	Department of Administrative Services	$0–25,000	**	7	12
Virgin Islands	Department of Social Welfare	Up to $25,000	No	1	24
Virginia	Industrial Commission	$0–15,000	No	5	24
Washington	Department of Labor and Industries	$0–15,000+	No	3	12
West Virginia	Court of Claims Commissioner	$0–35,000	No	3	24
Wisconsin	Department of Justice	$0–40,000	No	5	12

[a]If location of the board is not indicated in the state statute, the board itself is noted.
[b]North Carolina's program is administratively established but not funded.
*Must report but no time limit specified.

**No reference in statute.
+Plus unlimited medical expenses.

SOURCE: Bureau of Justice Statistics, Report to the Nation on Crime and Justice, (Washington, D.C.: Bureau of Justice Statistics, 1988), p. 37

basic rights for law-abiding citizens. These rights range from adequate protection from violent crimes under the law to victim compensation and assistance from the criminal justice system.

Other suggested changes that might enhance the relationship between the victim and the criminal justice system include the following:

- Liberal use of preventive detention (pretrial jailing without the right to bail) for dangerous criminals who are awaiting trial.
- Elimination of delays between arrest and the initial hearing and between hearings and the trials. This would limit an offender's opportunity to intimidate victims or witnesses.
- Elimination of plea bargaining, or if that proves impossible, allowing victims to participate in the plea negotiations.
- Control over the defense attorney's cross-examination of victims.
- Allowing hearsay testimony by police at the preliminary hearing instead of requiring the victim to appear.
- Abolition of the exclusionary rule, which allows the guilty to go free on technicalities.
- Allowing victims to participate in sentencing.
- Creation of minimum sentences that convicted offenders must serve for crimes.
- Denial of furloughs and parole to murderers with life sentences.
- Making criminals serve time for each crime for which they are convicted and reducing the use of concurrent sentences, which allow convicted offenders to serve time simultaneously for multiple crimes.
- Tightening the granting of parole and allowing victims to participate in parole hearings.
- Full restitution and/or compensation to victims in all crimes.[70]

Some of these suggestions seem to be reasonable policy alternatives, but others, such as the abolition of the exclusionary rule, may be impossible to achieve since they would violate offenders' due process protections. Some jurisdictions have actually incorporated some of these proposals into their legal codes. For example, California has adopted a Victim's Bill of Rights that provides, among other things, that "restitution shall be ordered . . . in every case, regardless of the sentence or disposition imposed . . . unless compelling and extraordinary reasons exist to the contrary."[71]

■ SUMMARY

The criminal justice system is an extremely complex organization with multiple goals and perspectives. Its goals, which include fairness, protection, deterrence, rehabilitation, and diversion, are both pragmatic and idealistic. The multiple goals of the criminal justice system often lead to inefficiency as agencies try to do more than they are able to accomplish effectively. Consequently, national organizations have created standards for justice; these are sets of rules that can be adopted by local agencies. If followed, these standard procedures would narrow the focus of justice and provide for more uniform services. Among the groups that have created standards are the National Council on

Crime and Delinquency, the American Bar Association, and the American Law Institute.

The diversity in the justice system is also heightened by the various perspectives with which people regard crime and justice. According to one view, the true purpose of criminal justice is to control the dissident members of society; another view maintains that the criminal justice system should concentrate on rehabilitating offenders, and still other philosophies stress fairness, due process, and nonintervention.

The criminal justice system faces a number of important dilemmas as it attempts to control criminal behavior. They include the growing problem of drug trafficking and its relationship to criminality, the use of handguns, the increased use of electronic monitoring, and the problem of the chronic offender.

The justice system also must make provision for dealing with the victims of crime. This includes the development of compensation and other programs designed to ease the burdens of victims. Some advocates argue that victims should have an active voice in decisions such as sentencing and parole and that the civil rights of victims should be at least as important as those of the offender.

■ QUESTIONS

1. Should law enforcement agents be given a free hand to "bug" the homes and telephones of known organized crime figures?
2. What is the most important goal of the criminal justice system? Should it concentrate on rehabilitating criminals or protecting society?
3. What strategy holds the most hope for controlling the drug trade? How can the number of drug users best be reduced?

4. Should handguns be strictly controlled? Does every American have the right to bear arms without governmental intrusion?
5. Should victims be consulted when criminals are sentenced or paroled?

■ NOTES

1. Public Law 90–351, 90th Congress, 19 June 1968.
2. U.S. Department of Justice, Law Enforcement Assistance Administration, *A Partnership for Crime Control* (Washington, D.C.: U.S. Government Printing Office, 1976).
3. Lawrence Greenfeld, *Capital Punishment, 1987* (Washington, D.C.: Bureau of Justice Statistics, 1988).
4. Paul Gendreau and Robert Ross, "Revivification of Rehabilitation: Evidence from the 1980's," *Justice Quarterly* 4 (1987): 349–407.
5. Carol Garrett, "Effects of Residential Treatment on Adjudicated Delinquents: A Meta-Analysis," *Journal of Research in Crime and Delinquency* 22 (1985): 287–308.
6. Herbert Packer, *Limits of the Criminal Sanction* (Stanford, Calif.: Stanford University Press, 1968).
7. "Woman Urges Dotson's Release," *New York Times*, 25 April 1985, p. 3.
8. Hugo Adam Bedeau and Michael Radelet, "The Myth of Infallibility: A Reply to Markman and Cassell," *Stanford Law Review* 42 (1988): 161–70.
9. Victor Streib, *The Death Penalty for Children* (Bloomington, Indiana University Press, 1987).
10. Edwin M. Lemert, "The Juvenile Court—Quest and Realities", in President's Commission on Law Enforcement and the Administration of Justice, *Task Force Report: Juvenile Delinquency and Youth Crime* (Washington, D.C.: U.S. Government Printing Office, 1967); Edwin Schur, *Radical Nonintervention* (Englewood Cliffs, N.J.: Prentice-Hall, 1973).
11. Charles Murray and Louis Cox, *Beyond Probation: Juvenile Corrections and the Chronic Delinquent* (Beverly Hills, Calif.: Sage Publications, 1979).
12. James Austin and Barry Krisberg, "The Unmet Promise of Alternatives to Incarceration," *Crime and Delinquency* 28 (1982): 3–19; for an alternative view, see Arnold Binder and Gilbert Geis, "Ad Populum Argumentation in Criminology: Juvenile Diversion as Rhetoric," *Criminology* 30 (1984): 309–33.
13. See, David Fogel, *Justice As Fairness* (Cincinnati: Anderson, 1980).
14. Michael Lynch and W. Byron Groves, *A Primer In Radical Criminology* (New York: Harrow and Heston, 1986).

15. Anthony Platt, "Criminology in the 1980's: Progressive Alternatives to 'Law and Order' " *Crime and Social Justice* 18: 191–199 (1985).
16. President's Commission on Law Enforcement and the Administration of Justice, *The Challenge of Crime in a Free Society*, (Washington, D.C.: U.S. Government Printing Office, 1967).
17. Ibid., p. 159.
18. National Advisory Commission, *A National Strategy to Reduce Crime* (Washington, D.C.: U.S. Government Printing Office, 1973), pp. 34–40.
19. See U.S. Department of Justice, Bureau of Justice Statistics, *Justice Agencies in the United States, Summary Report* (Washington, D.C.: U.S. Government Printing Office, 1981), p. 7.
20. Mark Moore, Robert Trojanowicz, and George Kelling, *Crime and Policing* (Washington, D.C.: National Institute of Justice, 1988).
21. Dennis Rosenbaum, "Community Crime Prevention: A Review and Synthesis of the Literature," *Justice Quarterly* 5 (1988): 323–95.
22. N. H. Law R.S.A. 265:82 (1988).
23. John King, "N.Y. to buy out theater leases in Times Square cleanup bid," *Boston Globe*, 7 March 1989, p. 8.
24. See Norval Morris and Gordon Hawkins, *The Honest Politician's Guide to Crime Control* (Chicago: University of Chicago Press, 1970).
25. 361 F.2d 50 (D.C. Cir. 1966).
26. 356 F.2d 761 (4th Cir. 1966).
27. 392 U.S. 514, 88 S.Ct. 2145, 20 L.Ed.2d 1254 (1968).
28. _____ U.S. _____, 106 S.Ct. 2841, 92 L.Ed.2d 140 (1986).
29. See Edward Donnerstein, Daniel Linz, and Steven Penrod, *The Question of Pornography* (New York: Free Press, 1987).
30. Eric Wish, *Drug Use Forecasting: New York, 1984–1986* (Washington, D.C.: National Institute of Justice, 1987).
31. See Marcia Chaiken and Bruce Johnson, *Characteristics of Different Types of Drug-Involved Offenders* (Washington, D.C.: U.S. Government Printing Office, 1988).
32. Ibid., pp. 12–14.
33. Mark Matthews, "Bush says he might use military in drug war," *Boston Globe*, 7 March 1989, p. 9.
34. Ibid.
35. (Palo Alto, Calif.: Mayfield, 1986).

36. "Program Called Feasible in New York," *New York Times* 3 March 1989, p. A16.

37. Mary Graham, *Controlling Drug Abuse and Crime: A Research Update* (Washington, D.C.: U.S. Department of Justice, 1987), p. 6.

38. Jan Chaiken and Douglas McDonald, *Federal Drug Law Violators* (Washington, D.C.: Bureau of Justice Statistics, 1988).

39. James Inciardi, *The War on Drugs*, (Palo Alto, Calif.: Mayfield, 1986), pp. 155–156.

40. Lawrence Altman, "U.S. to Ease Methadone Rules in Bid to Curb AIDS in Addicts," *New York Times*, 3 March 1989, p. 1.

41. Gary Kleck, "Crime Control Through the Private Use of Armed Force," *Social Force* 35 (1988): 1–21.

42. Franklin Zimring, "Firearms and Federal Law: The Gun Control Act of 1968", *Journal of Legal Studies* 4 (1975): 133–98.

43. Glenn Pierce and William Bowers, "The Bartley-Fox Gun Law's Short-Term Impact on Crime," *The Annals* 455 (1981): 120–37; Samuel Walker, *Sense and Nonsense about Crime 2nd ed.* (Monterey, Calif.: Brooks Cole, 1988), pp. 70–71.

44. Colin Loftin, Milton Heumann, and David McDowall, "Mandatory Sentencing and Firearms Violence: Evaluating an Alternative to Gun Control," *Law and Society Review* 17 (1983): 287–319.

45. David Lester, *Gun Control* (Springfield, Ill.: Charles Thomas, 1984).

46. See, generally, James Wright, Peter Rossi, and Kathleen Daly, *Under the Gun: Weapons, Crime and Violence in America* (New York: Aldine, 1983).

47. Walker, *Sense and Nonsense about Crime*, p. 152.

48. Marvin Wolfgang, Robert Figlio, and Thorsten Sellin, *Delinquency in a Birth Cohort* (Chicago: University of Chicago Press, 1972); see also Paul Tracy and Robert Figlio, "Chronic Recidivism in the 1958 Birth Cohort," Paper presented at the American Society of Criminology meeting, Toronto, Canada, October 1982; Marvin Wolfgang, "Delinquency in Two Birth Cohorts," in Perspective Studies of Crime and Delinquency, Katherine Teilmann Van Dusen and Sarnoff Mednick, eds. (Boston: Kluwer-Nijhoff, 1983), pp. 7–17.

49. Lawrence Rosen, Leonard Savitz, and Michael Lalli, "Issues in the Prediction of Adult Criminality," *International Journal of Sociology and Social Policy* 12 (1988): 18–37.

50. Gary Marx, *Undercover, Police Surveillance in America* (Berkeley: University of California Press, 1988).

51. Ibid., pp. 217–19.

52. Ibid., p. 219.

53. Ibid., p. 233.

54. See, generally, William F. McDonald, ed., *Criminal Justice and the Victim: An Introduction* (Beverly Hills, Calif.: Sage Publications, 1976); American Bar Association, *Reducing Victim-Witness Compensation* (Chicago: American Bar Association, 1979).

55. Herbert Koppel, *Lifetime Likelihood of Victimization* (Washington, D.C.: Bureau of Justice Statistics, 1987).

56. Dean Kilpatrick, Benjamin Saunders, Lois Veronen, Connie Best, and Judith Von, "Criminal Victimization: Lifetime Prevalence, Reporting to Police, and Psychological Impact," *Crime and Delinquency* 33 (1987): 479–89.

57. Patricia Resnick, "Psychological Effects of Victimization: Implications for the Criminal Justice System," *Crime and Delinquency* 33 (1987): 468–78.

58. Arthur Lurigio, "Are All Victims Alike? The Adverse, Generalized, and Differential Impact of Crime," *Crime and Delinquency* 33 (1987): 452–67.

59. Federal Bureau of Investigation, *Crime in the United States, 1987* (Washington, D.C.: U.S. Government Printing Office, 1988), p. 152.

60. Mark Cohen, "Pain, Suffering, and Cost Jury Awards: A Study of the Cost of Crime to Victims," *Law and Society Review* 22 (1988): 537–55.

61. Peter Finn, *Victims* (Washington, D.C.: Bureau of Justice Statistics, 1988), p. 1.

62. Timothy Flanagan and Katherine Jamieson, *Sourcebook of Criminal Justice Statistics* (Washington, D.C.: U.S. Government Printing Office, 1988), p. 218.

63. U.S. Department of Justice, *Report of the President's Task Force on Victims of Crime* (Washington, D.C.: U.S. Government Printing Office, 1983).

64. Ibid., p. 115.

65. Ibid., pp. 2–10; and "Review on Victims—Witnesses of Crime," *Massachusetts Lawyers Weekly*, 25 April 1983, p. 26.

66. Robert Davis, *Crime Victims: Learning How to Help Them* (Washington, D.C.: National Institute of Justice, 1987).

67. Peter Finn and Beverly Lee, *Establishing and Expanding Victim-Witness Assistance Programs* (Washington, D.C.: National Institute of Justice, 1988).

68. Randall Schmidt, "Crime Victim Compensation Legislation: A Comparative Study," *Victimology* 5 (1980): 428–37.

69. See Frank Carrington, "Victim's Rights Litigation: A Wave of the Future," in *Perspectives on Crime Victims*, Burt Galaway and Joe Hudson, eds. (St. Louis: C.V. Mosby Co., 1981).

70. Adapted from Emilio Viano, "Victim's Rights and the Constitution: Reflections on a Bicentennial," *Crime and Delinquency* 33 (1987): 438–51.

71. California Penal Code § 1191.1 (West Supp. 1985).

Part One

**The Nature of Crime,
Law and Criminal Justice**

PART TWO

The Police and Law Enforcement

6

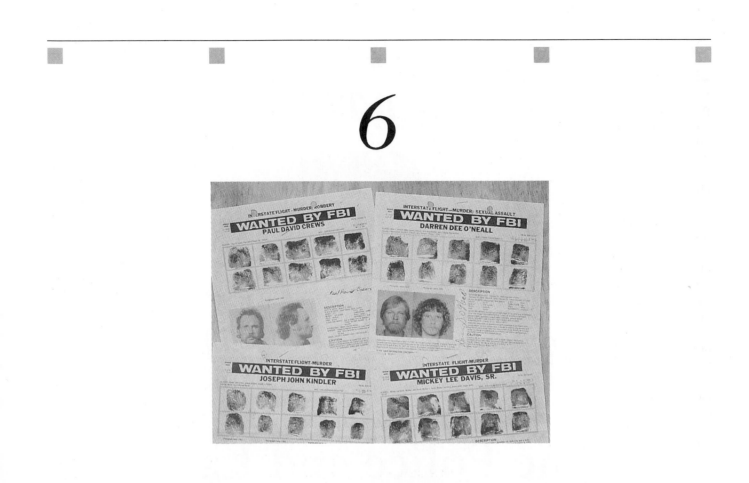

The History and Structure of American Law Enforcement

Law enforcement and police agencies and their sworn personnel—police, sheriffs, state troopers, and federal agents—are the most numerous and visible elements of the criminal justice system. Citizens who may never knowingly interact with judges, prosecutors, wardens, or prison guards are keenly aware when they are in the presence of law enforcement officers.[1] Consequently, people are more personally affected by and concerned about police behavior than any other aspect of the criminal justice system. When police pursue their job too vigorously, citizens are quick to protest against a "police state" atmosphere. If police fail to control crime effectively, the same citizens will decry the "fear stalking the city" and call for increased police protection. When scandal rocks a police department, the very essence of the justice system comes under siege: If the keepers are imperfect, how can we blame the kept?

Sometimes public ambivalence toward the police is translated into acts of open hostility and violence. For example, a poll taken in 1988 found that the average New Yorker considered police officers "too violent"; black respondents were three times as likely as whites to say that police use "too much force." In light of these responses, it is not surprising that New York has experienced an upswing in police-citizen violence: In 1985 not a single New York City police officer was killed in the line of duty; after three years of police-community conflict, seven officers were killed in 1988.[2] The "damned if you do, damned if you don't" attitudes of many citizens and public officials have caused dissatisfaction among police officers; job stress is a major concern in police departments today.

Despite such setbacks, the police are held in surprisingly high regard by the public they serve: public opinion polls show that 90 percent of the general public consider police officers honest and ethical.[3] Career interest in police work and policing is also at an all-time high. Metropolitan police departments are swamped with applications from job seekers who value an exciting, well-paid job that also offers the opportunity to provide valuable community service. Thus, while American police agencies are still trying to identify their role and effectively marshal their resources, they continue to be held in high esteem by the public they serve.

In these four chapters we will evaluate the history, role, organizational issues, and procedures of police agents and agencies.

■ The History of Police

Like the criminal law, the origins of American police agencies can be traced back to early English society.[4] Before the Norman Conquest, there was no regular English police force. Every person living in the villages scattered throughout the countryside was responsible for aiding neighbors and protecting the settlement from thieves and marauders. This was known as the **pledge system.** People were grouped in collectives of 10 families, called **tithings,** which were expected to police their own minor problems. When trouble occurred, the citizen was expected to make a **hue and cry**—that is, to sound the alarm and pursue the suspect. Ten tithings were grouped into a **hundred,** whose affairs were supervised by a **constable** appointed by the local magnate. The constable, who might be considered the first real police officer, dealt with more serious breaches of the law.[5]

Shires resembling the counties of today were controlled by the **shire reeve** appointed by the crown or local landowner to supervise the territory and

Pledge system
Tithing
Hue and cry
Hundred
Constable
Shires
Shire reeve
Watch system
Justice of the peace
Sir Robert Peel
Vigilantes
Wickersham Commission
International Association of Chiefs of Police (IACP)
August Vollmer
O. W. Wilson
Sheriff
State police
U. S. Department of Justice
Civil Rights Division
Tax Division
Criminal Division
Federal Bureau of Investigation (FBI)
Drug Enforcement Administration (DEA)
Proprietary security
Contractual services
Target hardening
Teleconferencing
DNA fingerprinting
Police-community relations (PCR)
Broken windows
Community policing
Foot patrol
Problem-oriented policing

Chapter 6

The History and Structure of American Law Enforcement

ensure that order would be kept. The shire reeve, forerunner of today's sheriff, soon began to pursue and apprehend law violators as part of his duties.

In the thirteenth century, during the reign of King Edward I, the **watch system** was created to help protect property in England's larger cities and towns. Watchmen patrolled at night and helped protect against robberies, fires, and disturbances. They reported to the area constable, who became the primary metropolitan law enforcement agent. In larger cities such as London, the watchmen were organized within church parishes; those applying for the job were usually members of the parish they protected.

In 1326, the office of **justice of the peace** was created to assist the shire reeve in controlling the county. Eventually, the justices took on judicial functions in addition to their primary duty as peacekeeper. A system developed in which the local constable became the operational assistant to the justice of the peace, supervising the night watchmen, investigating offenses, serving summonses, executing warrants, and securing prisoners. This working format helped delineate the relationship between the police and the judiciary that has existed intact for 500 years.

At first, the position of constable was an honorary one given to a respected person in the village or parish for a one-year period. Since these men were often wealthy merchants who had little time for their duties, they commonly hired assistants to help them fulfill their obligations, thereby creating another element of a paid police force. Thus, by the seventeenth century the justice of the peace, the constable, his assistants, and the night watch formed the nucleus of the local metropolitan justice system. (The sheriff's duties lay outside the cities and towns.)

Eighteenth-Century Developments

At the end of the eighteenth century, the industrial revolution lured thousands of people from the English countryside into the larger factory towns. The swelling population of urban poor, whose minuscule wages could hardly sustain them, heightened the need for police protection. Henry Fielding, the author of *Tom Jones*, organized the Bow Street Runners of London; the Runners were one of the first local police agencies to investigate crimes and attempt to bring offenders to justice.

In response to pressure from established citizens, the government passed statutes creating new police offices in London. These offices employed three justices of the peace who were each authorized to employ six paid constables. Law enforcement began to be more centralized and professional, but many parishes still maintained their own foot patrols, horse patrols, and private investigators.

In 1829, **Sir Robert Peel,** England's home secretary, guided through Parliament an "Act for Improving the Police in and near the Metropolis." The Act established the first organized police force in London. Composed of over 1,000 men, the London police force was structured along military lines. Its members wore a distinctive uniform and were led by two magistrates, who were later given the title of commissioner. However, the ultimate responsibility for the police fell to the home secretary and consequently to Parliament.

The London experiment proved so successful that the metropolitan police soon began sending aid to outlying areas that requested assistance in law enforcement matters. Another act of Parliament allowed justices of the peace to establish local police forces, and by 1856, every borough and county in England was required to form its own police force.

The Early American Experience

Law enforcement in colonial America paralleled the British model. In the colonies, the county sheriff became the most important law enforcement agent. In addition to peacekeeping and crime fighting, the sheriffs collected taxes, supervised elections, and handled a great deal of other legal business.

The colonial sheriff did not patrol or seek out crime. Instead, he reacted to citizens' complaints and investigated crimes that had already occurred. His salary was related to his effectiveness. Sheriffs were paid by the fee system and received a fixed amount for every arrest made. Unfortunately, their tax-collecting chores were more lucrative than crime fighting, so law enforcement was not one of their primary concerns.

In the cities, law enforcement was the province of the town marshal, who was aided, often unwillingly, by a variety of constables, night watchmen, police justices, and city council members. Local governments had little power of administration, however, and enforcement of the criminal law was largely an individual or community responsibility.

In rural areas in the South, "slave patrols" charged with recapturing escaped slaves were an early if reprehensible form of law enforcement.[6] In the western territories, individual initiative was encouraged by the practice of offering rewards for the capture of felons. If trouble arose, the town "vigilance committee" might form a posse to chase offenders. These **vigilantes** attempted to "eradicate" social problems such as cattle rustling through force or intimidation; the Criminal Justice in Review on page 188 discusses the San Francisco Vigilance Committee's activities in the mid-nineteenth century.

By the middle of the nineteenth century, such informal arrangements were no longer satisfactory. As the cities grew, local leaders found it increasingly difficult to step in and organize citizens' groups. Moreover, the early nineteenth century was an era of widespread urban unrest and mob violence. Local leaders began to realize that a more structured police function was needed to control demonstrators and keep the peace.

Early Police Agencies

The modern police department was born out of urban mob violence that wracked the nation's cities in the nineteenth century. Boston created the country's first formal police department in 1838. New York established its police department in 1844; Philadelphia, in 1854. The new police departments replaced the night-watch system and relegated constables and sheriffs to serving court orders and running the jail.

The first urban police departments inherited the functions of the older institutions they replaced. For example, Boston police were charged with maintaining public health until 1853, and the New York police were responsible for street sweeping until 1881.

Politics dominated the departments and determined which new officers would be recruited and which supervisors promoted. An individual with the right connections could be hired despite a lack of qualifications. "In addition to the pervasive brutality and corruption," writes justice historian, Samuel

Law enforcement officials filled in this record of arrest for Butch Cassidy when he was apprehended in Fremont County, Wyoming, for grand larceny.

Chapter 6

The History and Structure of American Law Enforcement

CRIMINAL JUSTICE IN REVIEW

San Francisco Vigilance Committees of 1851 and 1856

 As a result of the Treaty of Guadalupe Hidalgo in 1848, which concluded the Mexican War, the United States acquired a vast territory in the Southwest including California and New Mexico. After gold was discovered at Sutter's Mill in 1848, thousands of gold hunters flocked into northern California. Many of the gold rush towns where the immigrants settled had been little more than villages before the gold rush and lacked the municipal institutions that were needed to cope with the rapidly expanding populations. As government and law enforcement became increasingly disorganized and chaotic, vigilance committees were formed in many towns. The San Francisco Vigilance Committees of 1851 and 1856 provide two of the most famous examples of vigilante activity.

Before gold was discovered in 1848, the population of San Francisco had been around 800 persons. By 1851, nearly 25,000 gold seekers had arrived, most of whom settled in or near the city. Crime quickly became a problem. In 1856, a Sacramento newspaper claimed that there had been 1,400 murders in San Francisco in the last six years and that only three murderers had been hanged.

In 1851, a group of citizens, including a large number of businesspersons, under the leadership of Sam Brannan, formed the first San Francisco Vigilance Committee. The city government had failed to curb gangs of outlaws known as the "Regulators" or "Hounds," who preyed upon the inhabitants of the city and were suspected of having set a series of fires that had destroyed much of the city. The committee promptly sought out several of the alleged outlaws and sentenced them to death, deportation, or whipping.

In 1856, after a county supervisor named James P. Casey killed newspaper editor James King, the committee came back into existence under the leadership of William T. Coleman to combat lawlessness among the general population and corruption and mismanagement in the city government. The committee began by trying and executing Casey and Charles Cora, a notorious criminal. Next the committee barricaded the streets in an area where the crime rate was high and captured and punished all the criminals it could find within the barricades.

In the meantime, other citizens including a number of city officials and attorneys had formed the "Law and Order" faction to oppose the vigilantes. David Smith Terry, a justice of the California Supreme Court, tried to prevent one of the vigilantes from arresting a certain Reuben Maloney on the ground that the committee had no legal authority to conduct arrests. A fight ensued in which Terry stabbed Sterling A. Hopkins, the vigilante. Although Terry was imprisoned for a few weeks, the vigilantes' attempt to put him on trial failed, and the committee disbanded a short time later. By that time, it had lost most of its supporters and its power had waned.

Although the committees declared that the safety of the public was their purpose, the committees ignored the principles of government on all levels. Their trials did not follow standard procedures, but used only a skeletal version of established legal practices. ■

SOURCE: *The Guide to American Law*, Vol. 9 (St. Paul, Minn.: West Publishing Co., 1985), p. 101.

Walker, "the police did little to effectively prevent crime or provide public services. . . . Officers were primarily tools of local politicians; they were not impartial and professional public servants."[7]

In the late nineteenth century, police work was highly desirable because it paid more than most other blue-collar jobs. By 1880 the average factory worker earned $450 a year, while large cities paid police $900 annually. For immigrant groups, having enough political clout to be appointed to the police department was an important step up the social ladder.[8] Job security was uncertain, however, because it depended on the local political machine's staying in power.

Police work itself was primitive. There were few of the technological aids common today, such as radios or centralized record keeping. Most officers patrolled on foot, without backup or the ability to call for help. Officers were often taunted by local toughs and just as frequently responded in kind with force and brutality. The long-standing conflict between police and the public had its origins in the difficulties that untrained, unprofessional officers faced as they patrolled the streets of nineteenth-century cities and broke up and controlled labor disputes. Police were not "crime fighters" as we know them today. Their major role was keeping the peace and maintaining order. Nevertheless their power was almost unchecked. As historian Dennis Rousey found in his study of police in nineteenth-century New Orleans, the average officer had little training, no education in the law, and a minimum of supervision, yet he was a virtual judge of law and fact with the ability to exercise unlimited discretion.[9]

In the mid-nineteenth century, the Boston police became the first to add a detective bureau to their department. Until then, "thief taking" had been the province of amateur bounty hunters, who hired themselves out to victims for a price. When professional police departments replaced bounty hunters, the close working relationships that developed between police detectives and their underworld informants produced many scandals and consequently high personnel turnover.

Police during the nineteenth century were generally incompetent, corrupt, and disliked by the people they served. The police role was only minimally directed at law enforcement. Its primary functions were serving as the enforcement arm of the reigning political power, protecting private property, and maintaining control over the ever-rising numbers of foreign immigrants.

Twentieth-Century Reform

Police agencies evolved slowly through the latter half of the nineteenth century and into the twentieth century. Uniforms were introduced in 1853 in New York. The first technological breakthroughs in police operations came in the area of communications. Precincts linked to central headquarters by telegraph appeared in the 1850s. In 1867 the first telegraph police boxes were installed; an officer could turn a key in a box, and his location and number would automatically register at headquarters. Additional technological advances were made in the area of transportation. The Detroit police department outfitted some of its patrol officers with bicycles in 1897. By 1913 the motorcycle was being employed by departments in the eastern part of the nation. The first police car was used in Akron, Ohio, in 1910, and the police wagon became popular in Cincinnati in 1912.[10] Nonpolice functions such as care of the streets began to be abandoned after the Civil War.

Despite these improvements, big city police were not respected by the public, were not successful in their role as crime stoppers, and were not involved in progressive activities. The control of police departments by local politicians impeded effective law enforcement and fostered an atmosphere of graft and corruption.

In an effort to control police corruption, civic leaders in a number of jurisdictions created police administrative boards to reduce the control local officials exercised over police. These tribunals were given the responsibility to appoint police administrators and control police affairs. In many instances, these measures failed because the private citizens appointed to the review boards lacked expertise in the intricacies of police work.

In another attempt at reform, state legislators took over some big city police agencies. Although police budgets were funded by local taxes, rural politicians in the state capitals usurped control over the police. Not until the first decades

A rare nineteenth-century daguerreotype shows a police officer making an arrest.

of the twentieth century did the cities regain control of their police forces. New York City is an example of a jurisdiction that temporarily lost contol of its police force.

The Boston police strike of 1919 heightened interest in police reform. The cause of the strike was police officers' dissatisfaction with their status in society. While other professions were unionizing and improving their standards of living, police salaries lagged behind. The Boston police officers' organization, the Boston Social Club, voted to become a union affiliated with the American Federation of Labor (AFL). The officers struck on September 9, 1919. Rioting and looting broke out, resulting in Governor Calvin Coolidge's mobilization of the state militia to take over the city. Public support turned against the police, and the strike was broken. Eventually, all the striking officers were fired and replaced by new recruits. The Boston police strike ended police unionism for decades and solidified power in the hands of reactionary, autocratic police administrators.

In the aftermath of the strike, crime commissions on the local, state, and national level began to investigate the extent of crime and the ability of the justice system to deal with it effectively. As you may recall, the **Wickersham Commission** was created by President Herbert Hoover to study the criminal justice system on a national scale. In its 1931 report, the commission found that the average police supervisor's term of office was too short and that his responsibility to political officials made his position insecure. The commission also said that there was a lack of effective, efficient, and honest patrolmen. It found that no intensive effort was being made to educate, train, and discipline prospective officers or to eliminate those who were incompetent. The Wickersham Commission concluded that, with few exceptions, police forces in cities with populations above 300,000 had neither adequate communications systems nor the equipment necessary to enforce the law effectively. According to the commission, the difficulty of the police task, was compounded by the excessively rapid growth of U.S. cities in the past half century and by the tendency of ethnic groups to retain their languages and customs in large cities. Finally, said the commission, too many duties were cast on each officer and patrolman.[11] The Missouri Crime Commission reported that in a typical U.S. city the police were expected to be familiar with and enforce 30,000 federal, state, and local enactments.[12] However, with the onset of the Great Depression, justice reform became a less important issue than economic revival, and for many years the nature of policing saw little change.

The Emergence of Professionalism

In the early part of the twentieth century, a number of nationally recognized leaders called for measures to help improve and professionalize the police field. In 1893 a professional society, the **International Association of Chiefs of Police (IACP)**, had been formed. Under the direction of its first president (Washington, D.C., Chief of Police Richard Sylvester), the IACP became the leading voice for police reform during the first two decades of the twentieth century. The IACP called for the creation of a civil service police force and for the removal of political influence and control. It also encouraged police departments to centralize their organizational structure and record keeping in order to curb the power of politically aligned precinct captains. Still another reform aimed at professionalism was the creation of specialized units, such as delinquency control squads.

The most famous reformer was **August Vollmer.** While serving as police chief of Berkeley, California, Vollmer instituted university training as an important part of his development of young officers. He also helped develop the School of Criminology at the University of California at Berkeley, which became the model for justice-related programs throughout the United States. Vollmer's disciples included **O. W. Wilson,** who pioneered the use of advanced training for officers when he took over and reformed the Wichita, Kansas, police department in 1928. Wilson was also instrumental in applying modern management and administrative techniques to policing. His text, *Police Administration*, became the single most influential work on the subject. Wilson eventually took over as dean of the School of Criminology at Berkeley and ended his career in Chicago when Mayor Richard J. Daley asked him to take over and reform the Chicago police department in 1960.

Through the 1960s, police professionalism was interpreted in terms of a tough, highly trained, rule-oriented law enforcement department organized along militaristic lines. The most respected department was that of Los Angeles, under the leadership of its no-nonsense chief, William Parker. It is not merely coincidence that two of the most popular police television shows of the period, "Dragnet" and "Adam-12," stressed the high motivation, competence, and integrity of Los Angeles police officers. The Los Angeles style emphasized police as incorruptible crime fighters who would not question the authority of Parker's central command. Later the Los Angeles police would be severely criticized for their allegedly brutal treatment of minority citizens.

Policing: 1960–1980

Police work underwent a period of turmoil and crisis in the 1960s and 1970s for several reasons. First, the Supreme Court handed down a number of decisions designed to control police operations and procedures. Police agents were forced to adhere to strict legal guidelines when questioning suspects, conducting searches, wiretapping, and so on. Police complained they were being handcuffed by the courts.

During the 1960s the civil rights movement produced a growing tension between black citizens, who were demanding increased rights and freedoms, and the police, who often saw their role in terms of maintaining security and preserving the status quo. When riots broke out in New York, Detroit, Los Angeles, and other cities between 1964 and 1968, the spark that ignited conflict was often an incident involving the police. And when students across the nation began marching in anti–Vietnam War demonstrations, it was the local police departments who were called in to restore order. Consequently, a growing and open resentment developed between the police and a whole generation of young minorities and antiwar college students. Ill-equipped and poorly trained to deal with these social problems, the police engaged in a number of bloody confrontations with the public in the late 1960s.

Compounding these problems was a rapidly growing crime rate. Both the violent and property crime rates expanded rapidly during the 1960s. Similarly, drug addiction and abuse became a growing national concern. Urban police departments seemed ill-equipped to deal with crime in a manner the public expected, and police officers resented the demands placed on them by dissatisfied citizens.

The 1970s witnessed many structural changes in police agencies themselves. The end of the war in Vietnam significantly reduced tensions between police agencies and the university community. Police departments began to reexamine their relations with the minority community. Public service officers, sensitivity training, and community advisory boards became standard features in most large police departments. Special police services for juveniles, rape victims, crime prevention, and community relations were created.

Increased federal government support for criminal justice greatly influenced police operations. During the 1970s, the Law Enforcement Assistance Administration (LEAA) devoted a significant portion of its funds to police agencies. Although a number of police departments used funds to purchase little-used hardware, such as antiriot gear, federal money helped support much innovative research on police work as well as the advanced training of police officers. In perhaps the most significant development, LEAA's Law Enforcement Education Program (LEEP) helped support thousands of officers who wished to further their college education. Hundreds of criminal justice programs were developed on college campuses around the country, providing an available pool of highly educated police recruits.

The 1970s also saw increased recruitment of women and minority police officers. Affirmative action programs helped change, albeit slowly, the ethnic, racial, and sexual composition of American policing.

Policing: 1980–1990

During the 1980s, the police role seemed to be undergoing significant change. The central issue that emerged was the very nature of the police role. A number of experts acknowledged that the police were not simply crime fighters and called for them to develop greater awareness of community issues; this resulted in the emergence of a "community policing" concept.

Technological innovations, especially the utilization of computers, transformed the way police keep records, investigate crimes, and communicate with one another. State training academies improved the way police learn to deal with such issues as job stress, community conflict, and interpersonal relations.

Police unions, which first began to increase in number in the late 1960s, continued to have a great impact on departmental administration in the 1980s. Unions fought for, and won, increased salaries and benefits for their members; starting salaries of $35,000 or higher are not uncommon in metropolitan police agencies. In many instances, unions eroded the power of the police chief to make unquestioned policy and personnel decisions. During the 1980s, it became common for chiefs of police to consult with union leaders before making major decisions concerning departmental operations.

Although police operations improved significantly in the 1980s, police departments were also beset by problems that impeded their effectiveness. When the Reagan administration restructured the federal budget, state and local budgets were cut back, putting financial pressure on police agencies. The federal government, which had been a major source of funding for innovative police programs in the 1960s and 1970s, severely curtailed its interest in local police operations with the demise of LEAA.

While the effectiveness of crime fighting was not the major issue among police experts in the 1980s, the relationship between the police and the community took on even more importance. The Miami riots of 1980, 1982, and 1989 and the destruction of the MOVE headquarters by Philadelphia police in 1985, which left 11 people dead and caused millions of dollars in damage, illustrate the continuing tensions between police and minority groups.[13] These events were mirrored by other revelations such as the use by New York City police of a 50,000-volt electric stun gun to obtain confessions from minority males and the killing during a robbery attempt of a young black honors student home on vacation from an Ivy League school.[14] Incidents such as these triggered a public outcry and skepticism about the police role, especially in inner city neighborhoods. The clash between the police and the minority community in New York became a matter of public debate when Larry Davis, who admittedly *shot six police officers* trying to arrest him on drug charges, became a "folk hero" and was acquitted when he claimed to have acted in self-defense. One white officer wounded in the case called the jury decision "racist" after Davis, who is black, was acquitted by a predominantly black Bronx jury (Davis was later convicted and sent to prison on gun possession charges).[15]

Toward the end of the decade, a number of police experts decreed that the nation's police forces should be evaluated not on their crime-fighting ability but on their courtesy, deportment, and helpfulness.[16] There was renewed interest in reviving an earlier style of police work featuring foot patrols and increased citizen contact. In the 1980s our view of the police and the police view of themselves underwent significant change.

■ Law Enforcement Today

There are approximately 18,000 law enforcement agencies in the United States (see Table 6.1). They include

- 3,080 sheriff's departments
- 11,989 municipal police agencies
- 79 county police agencies
- 1,819 township police agencies
- 49 state police agencies (all states except Hawaii)
- 965 special police agencies, including park rangers, harbor police, and transit police
- 50 federal law enforcement agencies[17]

The FBI estimates that, in total, these agencies employ over 640,000 people including 480,000 officers and 161,000 civilians, or about 2.8 employees per 1,000 people.[18]

The following sections examine the operations and functions of these agencies in greater detail.

Metropolitan Police

City police comprise the majority of the nation's authorized law enforcement personnel. Metropolitan police departments range in size from the New York City policy department with its approximately 33,000 employees to the police departments in Eutawville, South Carolina, and Bertram, Texas, each of which maintains a staff of one police officer. In all, an estimated total of 493, 930 officers and civilians work in the nation's city police agencies.[19]

Regardless of how large or small an individual metropolitan police department is, almost all such departments perform the same set of functions and tasks and provide similar services to the community. These include apprehend-

TABLE 6.1 ■ Profile of State and Local Law Enforcement Agencies

A recent national survey of state, county, and local police agencies conducted by the Bureau of Justice Statistics found that these agencies employ over 750,000 people and cost $28 billion each year to operate; some of the most important survey findings are listed below:

- Local police agencies, sheriffs' agencies, and state police agencies collectively employed 757,508 persons during fiscal year 1987 (including 555,364 sworn officers) and had operating and capital expenses totaling more than $28 billion.
- About 24% of local police employees were civilians. The percentage of civilian employees in sheriffs' agencies and state police agencies was even higher, about 32% in each.
- An estimated 12.5% of the sworn employees in sheriffs' agencies were female, compared to 7.6% in local police agencies and 4.2% in state police agencies.
- Sworn personnel in local police agencies were 85.4% white (non-Hispanic), 9.3% black, and 4.5% Hispanic; for sheriffs' agencies, the proportions were 86.6% white, 8.3% black, and 4.3% Hispanic; for state police, 88.7% white, 6.5% black, and 3.8% Hispanic.
- All state police agencies and almost all local police (99.7%) and sheriffs' agencies (97.5%) with 135 or more sworn personnel required new officer recruits to have at least a high school diploma. About 10% of state and local police agencies and about 6% of sheriffs' departments required at least some college education.
- Thirteen of the almost 12,000 local police agencies in the nation served populations of 1,000,000 or more, but the great majority (89%) served jurisdictions with populations under 25,000.
- Thirty-four local police agencies employed over 1,000 sworn officers each during fiscal year 1987, but more than half had fewer than 10 sworn officers and 987 employed just 1 full-time sworn officer.
- Twelve sheriffs' agencies employed over 1,000 sworn officers each, and 27 sheriffs' agencies served populations of 1,000,000 or more.
- The main state police agency in each state had an average of 1,031 full-time sworn employees, ranging in size from slightly over 100 to nearly 6,000, and had average expenditures of over $65 million.
- Two-thirds of local police agencies authorize collective bargaining by employees.
- Approximately 88% of sworn officers in large local police agencies worked in field operations, 6% in technical support, and 5% in administration.
- The average starting salary for an entry level officer in local police departments ranged from $13,768 in jurisdictions under 2,500 people to $22,930 in jurisdictions with populations of 1 million or more. Average starting salaries for sergeants ranged from $17,464 in the smallest jurisdictions to $35,273 in the largest. Police chiefs in cities with a population of 1,000,000 or more had an average starting salary of $72,821 and an average maximum salary of $87,048.

SOURCE: Brian Reaves, *Profile of State and Local Law Enforcement Agencies, 1987* (Washington, D.C.: Bureau of Justice Statistics, 1989).

ing and convicting law violators, arbitrating neighborhood and family disputes, patrolling the area, enforcing traffic laws, and recovering stolen property. Municipal police departments also provide such personal services as giving directions and tourist information, providing crowd control at public events, and issuing licenses and permits. Larger police departments often maintain specialized services such as vice control divisions, detective bureaus, juvenile squads, and tactical patrol forces. These will be discussed in more detail in a later section.

While many municipal police departments maintain jurisdiction over law enforcement matters in their home districts, they are often assisted by a number of local auxiliary agencies. The Boston police department is a good example of this type of arrangement. In addition to maintaining the normal complement of internal bureaus, agencies, and services, the department is aided in the municipal police role by a number of independent agencies. The capitol police have special police powers and are charged with protecting the grounds and persons of the Massachusetts state government on Capitol Hill in

Boston. The transit system in Boston is policed by its own force. Like various railroad police agencies and the New York City Transit Authority force, the Massachusetts Bay Transit Authority (MBTA) police have special police powers that allow them to provide services at stations and along the railway.

The parks, beaches, and parkways in the city of Boston and its environs are patrolled by the Metropolitan District Commission (MDC) police, whose duties are similar to those of city park police in New York, Washington, D.C., and other cities. The MDC is responsible for protecting persons visiting public park facilities, maintaining public property, and overseeing private businesses and homes in the vicinity of the parks.

The Boston police are also assisted by the Massachusetts state police in carrying out traffic duties on expressways and state roads leading into and out of the city. Finally, colleges and universities in the area maintain private police forces that patrol and supervise activities at local institutions and have the power of arrest.

These are only a few examples of the multiplicity of police agencies that exist today in some of the larger urban areas. Often jurisdictional disputes arise between these agencies, and information and duties that should be shared are not. Whether unification of smaller police agencies into "super agencies" would improve services is an often debated topic among police experts. Smaller municipal agencies can provide important specialized services that might have to be relinquished if these agencies were combined and incorporated into larger departments.

City police comprise a majority of the nation's authorized law enforcement personnel.

County Law Enforcement

Most of the nation's county police departments and their 189,000 employees are independent agencies whose senior officer, the **sheriff,** is usually an elected political official (in all states except Rhode Island and Hawaii). The county sheriff's role has evolved from that of the early English sheriff, whose main duty was to assist the royal judges in trying prisoners and enforcing sentences. During the opening of the American West and until municipal departments were developed, the sheriff often acted as the sole legal authority over vast territories.

The duties of a county sheriff's department vary according to the size and degree of urban development of the county in which it is located. Officials within the department may serve as coroners, tax assessors, tax collectors, overseers of highways and bridges, custodians of the county treasury, keepers of the county jail, court attendants, and executors of criminal and civil processes; in years past, sheriff's offices also conducted executions. Many of the sheriff's law enforcement functions today are restricted to unincorporated areas within a county, and the sheriff is called on only when a city department requests aid in such matters as patrol or investigation.

There are different types of sheriff's departments. Some are exclusively law enforcement oriented (e.g., Multnomah County, Oregon); some carry out court-related duties only (e.g., those in Connecticut and Rhode Island); some deal exclusively with correctional and judicial matters and do not get involved in law enforcement (e.g., San Francisco); a majority are full-service programs that carry out judicial, correctional, and law enforcement activities.[20]

In the past, sheriff's salaries were almost always based on the fees they received for the performance of official acts. They received fees for every summons, warrant, subpoena, writ, or other process they served; they were also compensated for summoning juries or locking prisoners in cells. Today, almost all sheriffs are salaried in order to avoid conflicts of interest.

State Police

Unlike municipal police departments, which developed through historical necessity, **state police** were legislatively created to deal with the growing incidence of crime in nonurban areas, a consequence of the increase in population mobility and the advent of personalized mass transportation in the form of the automobile. County sheriffs—elected officials with occasionally corrupt or questionable motives—had proved ineffective in dealing with the wide-ranging criminal activities that developed during the latter half of the nineteenth century. In addition, most local police agencies were ineffective at preventing criminal activity by highly mobile lawbreakers who randomly struck at cities and towns throughout a state. In response to citizens' demands for effective and efficient law enforcement, state governors began to develop plans for police agencies that would be responsible to the state instead of being tied to local politics and corruption.

The Texas Rangers, created in 1835, were one of the first state police agencies to be formed. Essentially a military outfit that patrolled the Mexican border, they were followed by the Massachusetts state constables in 1865 and the Arizona Rangers in 1901. Pennsylvania formed the first truly modern state police in 1905.[21]

Today, about 23 state police agencies have the same general police powers as municipal police and are territorially limited in their exercise of law enforcement regulations only by the state's boundaries. In some jurisdictions, state

State police agencies were created to deal with crime in non-urban areas, the growing use of the automobile to commit crime, and the desire to have a police force unaffected by local politics.

police are also given special police powers. New York, Pennsylvania, and West Virginia employ their state police as fire, fish, and game wardens. In Michigan, state police may be required to execute civil process in actions to which the state is a party, while in Connecticut and Pennsylvania they conduct road tests for those desiring motor vehicle licenses. The remaining state police agencies are primarily responsible for highway patrol and traffic law enforcement. For example, the California state police specialize in protecting motorists and concentrate on enforcing traffic laws.

Most state police organizations are restricted by legislation from becoming involved in the enforcement of certain areas of the law. In Connecticut, Pennsylvania, New York, and New Hampshire, for example, state police are prohibited from entering incorporated areas to suppress riots or civil disorders except when directed by the governor or by a mayor with the governor's approval. In some states, such as Massachusetts and Colorado, state police are prohibited from becoming involved in strikes or other labor disputes unless violence erupts.

The nation's 74,344 state police employees (50,613 officers and 23,731 civilians) are not only involved in law enforcement and highway safety, but also carry out a variety of multiservice functions for local police agencies.[22] In Iowa, for example, state police maintain a training academy for both state and municipal law enforcement officers. A crime laboratory helps local departments investigate crime scenes and analyze evidence. The Iowa state police also provide special services and technical expertise in such areas as bomb-site analysis and homicide investigation. Other state police departments, such as California's, are involved in highly sophisticated traffic and highway safety programs, including the use of helicopters for patrol and rescue, the testing of safety devices for cars, and the conducting of postmortem examinations to determine the causes of fatal accidents.

Federal Law Enforcement Agencies

The federal government has within its jurisdiction a number of law enforcement agencies designed to protect the rights and privileges of U.S. citizens; no single agency has unlimited jurisdiction, and each has been purposely created to enforce specific laws and cope with particular situations. Federal police agencies have no particular order of rank or hierarchy of command or responsibility; each reports to the specific department or bureau to which it is responsible. The most important of these agencies are described in the next paragraphs.

THE DEPARTMENT OF JUSTICE. The **U.S. Department of Justice** is the legal arm of the U.S. government. Headed by the attorney general, it is empowered to (1) enforce all federal laws, (2) represent the United States when it is party to a court action, and (3) conduct independent investigations through its law enforcement services.

The Department of Justice maintains several separate bureaus that are responsible for enforcing federal laws and protecting U.S. citizens. The **Civil Rights Division** proceeds legally against violators of federal civil rights laws; such laws protect citizens from discrimination on the basis of their race, creed, ethnic background, or sex. Areas of greatest concern include discrimination in education (e.g., school busing), fair housing laws, and job discrimination, including affirmative action cases. The **Tax Division** brings legal actions against tax violators. The **Criminal Division** prosecutes violations of the Federal Criminal Code. Its responsibility includes enforcing statutes relating to bank robbery (because bank deposits are federally insured), kidnapping, mail fraud, interstate transportation of stolen vehicles, narcotics and drug trafficking, and so on.

The Justice Department also maintains administrative control over a number of independent investigative and enforcement branches, described below.

THE FEDERAL BUREAU OF INVESTIGATION. The Department of Justice first became involved in law enforcement when the attorney general hired investigators to enforce the Mann Act (forbidding the transportation of women between states for immoral purposes). Later in 1908 Justice Department investigators were formalized into a distinct branch of the government, the Bureau of Investigation. This agency was later reorganized as the **Federal Bureau of Investigation (FBI)** under the direction of J. Edgar Hoover (1924–1972).

Today, the FBI is not a police agency but an investigative agency, with jurisdiction over all matters in which the United States is, or may be, an interested party. It limits its jurisdiction, however, to federal laws including all federal statutes not specifically assigned to other agencies. These include espionage, sabotage, treason, civil rights violations, murder and assault of federal officers, mail fraud, robbery and burglary of federally insured banks, kidnapping, and interstate transportation of stolen vehicles and property.

The FBI has been our most glamorous and widely publicized law enforcement agency. In the 1920s and 1930s, its agents pursued gangsters such as Dillinger, Mad Dog Coll, Bonnie and Clyde, Machine Gun Kelly, and Pretty Boy Floyd. During World War II, they hunted Nazi agents and prevented any major sabotage from occurring on American military bases. After the war they conducted a crusade against Russian KGB agents and investigated organized crime figures. They have been instrumental in cracking tough criminal cases, which has won them enormous public respect.

After J. Edgar Hoover's death, the agency was subjected to public criticism concerning its alleged role in harassing civil rights leader Martin Luther King, Jr., its questionable investigation practices with subversives and antiwar activists, and its failure to investigate white-collar and organized criminals.[23] In the post-Watergate era, however, the FBI, under the leadership of William H. Webster and current director William Sessions, has attempted to steer a new course. Executive control over domestic intelligence operations has increased, and enforcement has been concentrated on white-collar and organized crime violations and the control of terrorist groups. There have been a few recent troublespots, including the five-year probe of the Committee in Solidarity with the People of El Salvador (CISPES), a group opposed to the Reagan administration's Latin American policies in the 1980s. The bureau was accused of illegally investigating CISPES and working with the Salvadoran National Guard to identify their opponents.[24] Nevertheless, the FBI seems to have returned to its image of incorruptible, efficient law enforcement.

The FBI offers a number of important services to local law enforcement agencies. Its identification division, established in 1924, collects and maintains a vast fingerprint file that can be used for identification purposes by local police agencies. Its sophisticated crime laboratory, established in 1932, aids local police in testing and identifying evidence such as hairs, fibers, blood, tire tracks, and drugs. The Uniform Crime Reports is another service provided by the FBI. As discussed in Chapter 2, the UCR is an annual compilation that includes crimes reported to local police agencies, arrests, police killed or wounded in action, and other information. Finally, the National Crime Information Center (NCIC) is a computerized network linked to local police departments by terminals. It makes information on stolen vehicles, wanted persons, stolen guns, and so on readily available to local law enforcement agencies. Today, the FBI is one of the few federal agencies that is slated to undergo expansion. The FBI currently employs about 21,500 people, and the number should increase by almost 1,000 in the next few years. Similarly, the agency will be spending millions on artificial intelligence models that combine investigation techniques with computer systems in order to develop leads in criminal cases.[25]

THE DRUG ENFORCEMENT ADMINISTRATION. Government interest in drug trafficking can be traced back to 1914, when the Harrison Act established federal jurisdiction over the supply and use of narcotics. A number of drug enforcement units, including the Bureau of Narcotics and Dangerous Drugs, were originally charged with enforcing drug laws. In 1973, however, these agencies were combined to form the **Drug Enforcement Administration (DEA).**

Agents of the DEA assist local and state authorities in their investigation of illegal drug use and conduct independent surveillance and enforcement activities to control the importation of narcotics. For example, DEA agents work with foreign governments in cooperative efforts aimed at destroying opium and marijuana crops at their source—hard-to-find fields tucked away in the interiors of Latin America, Asia, Europe, and Africa. Undercover DEA agents infiltrate drug rings and simulate narcotics buying in order to arrest drug dealers.

The DEA maintains regional laboratories that perform essential tests on seized drugs so that accurate records and measures can be presented at the trials of drug offenders. The DEA also has an Office of Intelligence, which coordinates information and enforcement activities with local, state, and foreign governments. Recently, the DEA has been instructed to share some of its duties with the FBI, and the two agencies now share similar administrative controls.

OTHER DEPARTMENT OF JUSTICE AGENCIES. Other federal law enforcement agencies under the direction of the Justice Department include U.S. marshals, the Immigration and Naturalization Service, and the Organized Crime and Racketeering Unit. The U.S. marshals are court officers who help implement federal court rulings, transport prisoners, and enforce court orders. Their Fugitive Investigative Strike Team (FIST) is a specialized unit that removes dangerous fugitives from the community and helps local law enforcement agencies track down known offenders.[26] The Immigration and Naturalization Service is responsible for the administration, exclusion, and deportation of illegal aliens and the naturalization of aliens lawfully present in the United States. This service also maintains border patrols to prevent illegal aliens from entering the United States. The Organized Crime and Racketeering Unit, under the direction of the U.S. attorney general, has coordinated federal efforts to curtail organized crime and prosecute members of the alleged national criminal syndicate; RICO legislation is the unit's main method of attack.

THE TREASURY DEPARTMENT. The U.S. Treasury Department maintains the following enforcement branches:

■ *The Bureau of Alcohol, Tobacco, and Firearms.* The Bureau of Alcohol, Tobacco, and Firearms helps control sales of untaxed liquor and cigarettes and, through the Gun Control Act of 1968 and the Organized Crime Control Act of 1970, has jurisdiction over the illegal sale, importation, and criminal misuse of firearms and explosives.

■ *The Internal Revenue Service.* The Internal Revenue Service (IRS), established in 1862, enforces violations of income, excise, stamp, and other tax laws. Its Intelligence Division actively pursues gamblers, narcotics dealers, and other violators who do not report their illegal financial gains as taxable income. For example, the career of Scarface Al Capone, the famous 1920s gangster, was brought to an end by the efforts of IRS agents.

■ *The Customs Bureau.* The Customs Bureau guards points of entry into the United States and prevents the smuggling of contraband into (or out of) the country. The bureau ensures that taxes and tariffs are paid on imported goods and helps control the flow of narcotics into the country.

■ *The Secret Service.* The Secret Service was originally charged with enforcing laws against counterfeiting. Today, the Secret Service is also accountable for the protection of the president and the vice president and their families, presidential candidates, and former presidents. The Secret Service maintains the White House Police Force, which is responsible for protecting the executive mansion, and the Treasury Guard, which protects the mint.

■ Private Policing and Security

No discussion of current law enforcement organizations would be complete without mention of the emergence of the private security industry. In recent years private sector policing has grown more rapidly than public policing. It is now estimated that more money is spent (an estimated $41 billion in 1989) on private protection than on state-sponsored law enforcement agencies.[27] Over one million people work in the private security area, a number that far exceeds the total number of sworn police officers.

A national study of private policing, known as the *Hallcrest Report*, found that two main types of private security are used.[28] **Proprietary security** is undertaken by an organization's own employees and includes both plainclothes and uniformed agents directed by the organization's head of security. The second type of private security involves **contractual services,** such as guards, investigators, armored cars, and so on, which are provided by private companies such as Wackenhut and Pinkertons. Also included within the category of contractual security are a wide variety of security products such as safes, electronic access control devices, and closed-circuit television. About 450,000 people are employed in proprietary programs while about 640,000 work in contract services.

Private security forces appear to be increasingly willing to assume responsibilities that heretofore were the domain of local police agencies. These include responding to burglar alarms, investigating misdemeanors, enforcing parking regulations, and maintaining court security. In some small towns private police may even replace the town police force. Reminderville, Ohio, experimented with an all-private police force and found that it resulted in a great saving in cost without any decline in service.

The Limits of Private Security

The expanded role of private security is not without its perils. Many law enforcement executives are critical of the quality of private security and believe it has little value as a crime control mechanism. One complaint heard by the Hallcrest researchers was the lack of training and standards in the profession. Still another source of contention between private security and local police agencies is the increasing number of police calls that are a function of private security measures. It is estimated that 10 to 12 percent of all police calls are false burglar alarms. In a sense, the local police are carrying out the job of the private security firm.

The *Hallcrest Report* recommends a number of strategies to improve the quality of private security in this country: upgrade employee quality; create statewide regulatory bodies and enact statutory controls for security firms; impose mandatory training; increase police knowledge of private security; expand interaction between police and private security, such as sharing information; and transfer some police functions, such as burglar alarm checking, to the private sector.

Private Employment of Public Police

In addition to full-time private security officers, an estimated 150,000 police officers moonlight as private security agents.[29] This raises questions of liability and conflict of interest. For example, if an off-duty police officer uses a firearm while working a security detail, is the local department responsible if a lawsuit is filed? Can a conflict of interest arise if police serve private rather than municipal purposes? Should the public pay for sick leave if an officer is injured while working privately? What happens if an officer is permanently injured while working a security detail and is forced to retire? Despite these problems, the private employment of public police continues to grow. The topic is discussed in the Criminal Justice In Review on page 202.

■ Community Self-Protection

Although the general public generally approves of the police, fear of crime and concern about community safety have prompted people to become their own "police force" and take an active role in community protection and citizen crime control groups.[30] Research indicates that a significant number of crimes may not be reported to police simply because victims prefer to take matters into their own hands.[31]

One way this trend has been manifested is through **target hardening**, the process of making one's home and business crimeproof through locks, bars, alarms, and other devices.[32] A Victimization Risk Survey administered to over 21,000 people residing in about 11,000 households across the United States found that substantial numbers of Americans have taken specific steps to secure their homes or place of employment.[33] One-third of the households

Private Employment of Public Police

Police officers have been hired by civilians to serve as security workers in ever-increasing numbers. Law enforcement authority Albert Reiss discusses this trend in the following reading.

In recent decades, private security has outstripped the growth of the public police; more people are now working in private security than in public policing. Yet this comparison fails to reflect another recent trend: The substantial growth in off-duty employment of uniformed police officers by private employers.

Today, in some police precincts on the day or evening shift, the actual number of uniformed officers performing police functions off duty exceeds those officially on duty. Such work—off duty but in uniform—swells the availability and visibility of police officers.

Seattle reports that 47 percent of its 1,002 police officers had work permits in 1982; Colorado Springs issued permits to 53 percent of its 426 sworn officers in 1985; they worked 20,000 off-duty hours in uniform in 1986, earning an average of $1,333 per officer. The Metro Dade Police Department in Florida estimates that payment for uniformed off-duty service exceeded $4 million in 1986.

These figures reflect a significant, but largely unremarked, shift in police department policy. Until the 1950s, most departments prohibited any private off-duty employment that required officers to work in uniform for a private employer or to exercise police powers on that employer's behalf.

Such prohibitions were grounded in concerns over conflict of interest and potential misuse of police authority to serve private, at the expense of public, ends. The pressure for change, and the resulting growth in uniformed off-duty employment, came from three areas of demand:

■ Private demand for uniformed service that the department could not meet, fueled by escalating crime rates of the 1960s and 1970s.
■ Demand for protection of persons and properties in private workplaces.
■ Demand by police officers for increased compensation, which could be met in part by off-duty employment.

The concerns underlying the original prohibitions, however, remained—along with others about department image, officer injury, potential corruption, legal liability, and public perceptions. As departments relaxed prohibitions on uniformed off-duty employment, they began, independently, to evolve policies and procedures to regulate it.

Among the types of police activity most often sought by private employers are traffic control and pedestrian safety; order maintenance at major events; security and protection of private persons and property; routine law enforcement for public housing, parks, and airports, and plainclothes details.

reported taking one or more crime prevention measures including having a burglar alarm (7 percent), participating in a neighborhood watch program (7 percent), or engraving valuables with an identification number (25 percent). Other commonly used crime prevention techniques include a fence or barricade at the entrance; a doorkeeper, guard, or receptionist in an apartment building; an intercom or phone to gain access to the building; surveillance cameras; window bars; warning signs; and watchdogs. The use of these measures was inversely proportional to people's perception of neighborhood safety: those who feared crime were more likely to use crime prevention techniques. Though the true relationship is still unclear, some evidence suggests that people who engage in household protection are less likely to be victimized by property crimes.[34]

In addition to target hardening, citizens are arming themselves in record numbers and are fighting back against crime. Douglas Smith and Craig Vchida find that citizens are willing to buy guns to defend themselves if they perceive a strong risk of crime, have been a victim in the past, and consider police to be ineffective.[35] Fear of crime has also prompted citizens to take courses in firearm training; there is some evidence that these measures are associated with lower crime rates.[36]

Private business is not the only source of extra-duty employment. Each major employment sector—government, private not-for-profit, and private for-profit—has need of uniformed services.

Ordinarily, assignment is to a specific post, not general patrol.

Three different ways in which the private employment of police is administered are summarized in Table A. ■

SOURCE: Albert Reiss, *Private Employment of Public Police* (Washington, D.C.: National Institute of Justice, 1988), pp. 1–3.

TABLE A ■ Three Management Models for the Private Employment of Police

Officer contract model
- Each officer finds own secondary employment.
- Officer independently contracts conditions of work, hours, pay.
- Officer then applies for permission to accept off-duty job.
- Department grants permission provided job meets minimum standards.
- Employer pays officer in cash (work is called "cash detail").
  Departments in Atlanta, Charlotte, Cincinnati, Minneapolis, and Omaha generally follow this model, differing on what work is permitted. Arlington County permits uniformed employment only by permission of the police chief and only at activities funded or sponsored by the county, state, or U.S. government. In Peoria, most secondary employment is independently contracted, but the department itself contracts for civic center jobs and permits officers and department heads to broker work. In Cincinnati, work for private parties is independently contracted, but the department contracts for city, county, or state agencies.

Union brokerage model
- Union, guild, or association finds paid details.
- Union assigns officers who have volunteered.
- Union sets assignment conditions for paid details.
- Union bargains with the department over status, pay, and conditions of paid details.
  Most off-duty employment of Seattle police is coordinated by the Seattle Police Officers' Guild, although the officers act as independent contractors. For privately sponsored special events at the Seattle Center complex, off-duty officers are employed by the center's security officer and paid through an outside accounting firm.

Department contract model
- Police agency contracts with employers.
- Agency assigns officers and pays them from reimbursements by employers.
- Agency assigns an off-duty employment coordinator to receive employer requests, issue work permits, and assign officers to paid details.
- Agency negotiates with union or guild on pay and job conditions.
  Boston, Colorado Springs, New Haven, and St. Petersburg fit this model. Metro-Dade contracts for police-related work (including, unlike most departments, work for private security firms), but lets officers contract for nonpolice jobs, each of which requires a permit.

Recent victimization data indicate that each year victims take self-protective measures in about 73 percent of violent personal crimes.[37] About three-fifths of the victims who took self-protective measures reported that their actions had a positive effect on the outcome of the crime, such as helping them avoid injury; 7 percent reported that fighting back actually made matters worse. About 3 percent of the victims attacked the offender with a weapon. Figuring about 6 million violent victimizations annually, this means that about 200,000 criminals were attacked with a weapon. It is not surprising that an estimated 1,500 to 2,800 felons are killed each year by gun-wielding civilians.[38] Other evidence suggests, however, that using guns for self-protection increases the probability that the victim will suffer serious injury.[39] The buildup of firearms in the United States has not been limited to handguns: more than 100,000 semiautomatic assault rifles have been imported each year. In 1989 the U.S. government moved to reduce the use of such guns for both criminal and self-protection purposes by banning the importation and sale of automatic assault rifles, a move voluntarily followed by some U.S. manufacturers.[40]

Citizens have also been working independently and in cooperation with local police agencies in neighborhood patrol and block watch programs. These

Chapter 6

The History and Structure of American Law Enforcement

■

Public concern over violent crime and community safety has prompted people to become more active in self-protection either by joining a self-help group or employing private security measures.

programs organize local citizens in urban areas to patrol neighborhoods, watch for suspicious people, help secure the neighborhood, lobby for improvements such as increased lighting, report crime to police, put out community newsletters, conduct home security surveys, and serve as a hotline for crime information or tips.[41] Table 6.2 describes the activities of one block watch program operating in Philadelphia.[42] Although such programs are welcome additions to police services, there is little evidence that they have an appreciable effect on the crime rate. There is also concern that they are less effective in low-income, high-crime areas, which are most in the need of crime prevention assistance.[43] Block watches and neighborhood patrols seem to be more successful when they are part of a general-purpose or multi-issue community group than when they focus solely on crime problems.[44]

In sum, community crime prevention programs, target hardening, and self-defense measures are flourishing around the United States. They are a response to the fear of crime and the perceived inability of police agencies to ensure community safety. Along with private security and the private employment of public police, they represent attempts to supplement municipal police agencies and expand the "war on crime" to the personal, neighborhood, and community levels.

■ The Future of Policing: Computers and Community

What changes can we expect in American police agencies during the 1990s? Two trends seem to be dominating American policing: (1) the use of technology to increase the effectiveness and efficiency of police work and (2) the attempts of local departments to gain public confidence and cooperation.

TABLE 6.2 ■ **Activities Engaged in by Neighborhood Watch Programs (Based on Program Survey Responses)**

Activity	
Neighborhood watch only	Crime-related
Crime prevention specific	Crime tip hotline
Project Operation Identification	Victim-witness assistance
Home security surveys	Courtwatch
Streetlighting improvement	Telephone chain
Block parenting	Child fingerprinting
Organized surveillance	
Traffic alteration	Community-oriented
Emergency telephones	Physical environmental concerns
Project Whistle Stop	Insurance premium deduction survey
Specialized informal surveillance	Quality of life
Escort service	Medical emergency
Hired guards	
Environmental design	
Lock provision installation	
Self-defense rape prevention	

SOURCE: Peter Finn, *Block Watches Help Crime Victims in Philadelphia* (Washington, D.C.: National Institute of Justice, 1986), p. 6.

Technology and Policing

In no area of policing will change be more apparent than in the use of technology, especially, electronic data processing. In 1964 only one city, St. Louis, had a police computer system; by 1968, 10 states and 50 cities had state-level criminal justice information systems; today, almost every city with a population of more than 50,000 has some sort of computer support services.[45] In the future, computers will link neighboring agencies, enabling them to share information on cases, suspects, warrants, and so on. One such system already in use is the Police Information Network, which electronically links the 93 independent law enforcement agencies in the San Francisco area. On a broader jurisdictional level, the FBI implemented the National Crime Information Center (NCIC) in 1967. This system makes possible the rapid collection and retrieval of data about persons wanted for crimes anywhere in the 50 states.

Some programs already appear to be highly successful. For example, the police department in St. Petersburg, Florida, has equipped all of its officers with portable computers, which has significantly cut down the time needed to write and duplicate reports.[46] The local police are developing the St. Petersburg Accident Data Acceleration System (SPADAS) to allow for more efficient collection and processing of information about automobile accidents. Police can also use their terminals to draw accident diagrams and communicate with the city traffic engineers. St. Petersburg's Paperless Information System Totally On Line (PISTOL) allows police officers to merge their incident reports into other data bases.

In Los Angeles, police are using computer-accessed data bases to identify criminal suspects. Investigators can call up suspect files by cross-referencing information (e.g., all files on suspects who own brown Chevrolets and have facial scars) without having to go through the files manually.[47] In New York City the Computer-Assisted Terminal Criminal Hunt (CATCH) is an automated mug-shot file. A witness who can remember a few details (e.g., a gold tooth or a scar on the cheek) or the way a crime was committed will only be shown pictures of known suspects who have such characteristics; this saves countless hours of looking through old-fashioned mug-shot books. CATCH can also check for fingerprints on file and match them to prints found at the scene of the crime.

The use of automated fingerprint systems is growing throughout the United States. Using mathematical models, the computerized systems automatically classify a fingerprint and identify up to 250 characteristics (minutiae) of the print.[48] These automated systems use high-speed silicon chips to plot each point of minutiae and count the number of ridge lines between that point and its four nearest neighbors; such systems are substantially faster and more accurate than earlier systems. Some police departments, such as Washington, D.C.'s, report that computerized print systems are enabling them to make over 100 identifications a month from fingerprints taken at a crime scene. Other successful systems are being used in Minneapolis, Minnesota, Houston, Texas, and San Jose, California.

In the future, computers will be relied on more heavily for record keeping and information processing. They may be used to analyze evidence and compile a list of suspects ranked in order of the probability of their guilt. Computers will certainly be used in officer training, including learning, performance evaluation, and field testing.[49] Departments are already using computer simulations to train officers in the use of deadly force.[50]

In addition to computer-driven information systems, future police technology will involve more efficient communications systems. Even today, some departments are using cellular phones in their police cars to facilitate communications with victims and witnesses.[51] Departments that cover wide geographical areas and maintain independent precincts and substations are experimenting with **teleconferencing** systems that provide both audio and video linkages. Police agencies may use advanced communications gear to track stolen vehicles. Car owners will be able to buy transmitters that emit a signal that beams a message to a satellite or other listening device, which can then be monitored and tracked by the specially equipped patrol cars; the system is currently at the testing stage.[52] Finally, some departments are interfacing advanced communications systems with computers: the police in Vancouver, British Columbia, are using a highly effective mobile digital communications system that allows patrol officers to personally access remote law enforcement data files without having to go through dispatch personnel at central headquarters.[53]

Another area of high tech development will be the use of new forensic methods of identification and analysis. One approach is **DNA fingerprinting**. This technique allows suspects to be identified on the basis of the genetic material found in hair, blood, and other bodily tissues and fluids. In the future, genetic samples may be taken from every infant at birth and their unique patterns kept on computer files for instant identification in the future.[54] Recently, the California Attorney General's office decided to use DNA fingerprinting as evidence in criminal trials.[55] Leading the way in the development of the most advanced forensic techniques is the Forensic Science Research and Training Center operated by the FBI in Washington, D.C., and Quantico, Virginia; the lab provides information and services to over 300 crime labs throughout the United States.[56]

In the future, police departments will rely more heavily on the new technologies for investigation efficiency and record keeping. The use of improved computer-based files and long-range electronic surveillance devices may pit modernized police agencies against civil libertarians who fear such technological developments will increase the power of police to intrude into the private lives of citizens.[57]

Community Policing

"A quiet revolution is reshaping American policing."[58] For the past 20 years, police agencies have made an effort to gain the cooperation and respect of the communities they serve or, in other words, to improve **police-community relations (PCR)**. Initial efforts to promote PCR focused on efforts at the station house and departmental levels designed to make citizens more aware of police activities, alert them to methods of self-protection, and improve general attitudes toward policing. In the socially turbulent 1960s, many larger departments instituted PCR units to pursue the improvement of community attitudes toward police. Others established specialized programs to improve PCR such as neighborhood watch programs, which instructed citizens in home security measures and enlisted their assistance in watching neighborhood homes. In Operation ID, which was first implemented in Monterey Park, California, in 1963, police officers passed out engraving tools with which citizens could mark their valuables for easy identification if they were stolen. Local police agencies also donated tags that, when placed on the front of a home, alerted potential thieves that valuables had been marked. Other early PCR programs included crime prevention clinics, citizen's police alert programs, and similar efforts to help citizens and police identify suspicious characters in their neighborhoods.

To some observers these early efforts to improve PCR could be classified as noble failures. Programs were criticized for their "band-aid" approach to overwhelming social problems; there was little evidence that they either improved police effectiveness or raised the public's opinion of police departments. Coupled with their less than overwhelming success at lowering the crime rate, the inability of local police agencies to win citizen cooperation troubled many police leaders. Although many of these programs remain in operation, fiscal belt-tightening in the 1990s threatens their existence.[59]

The second wave of police-community cooperation has now arrived. In a critical 1982 paper, two justice policy experts, George Kelling and James Q. Wilson, articulated a new approach to improving police relations in the community that has come to be known as the **"broken windows"** model.[60] Kelling and Wilson made three points:

A neighborhood where housing is deteriorated and broken windows left unrepaired gives out crime-promoting signals.

1. Neighborhood disorder creates fear. Urban areas filled with street people, youth gangs, prostitutes, and the mentally disturbed are the ones most likely to maintain a high degree of crime.
2. Neighborhoods give out crime-promoting "signals." A neighborhood where housing has deteriorated, broken windows are left unrepaired, and disorderly behavior is ignored emits crime-promoting signals. Honest citizens live in fear in these areas, and predatory criminals are attracted to them.
3. Community policing is essential. If police are to reduce fear and successfully combat crime in these urban areas, they must rely on the cooperation of citizens for support and assistance.

According to Kelling and Wilson, community relations and effective crime control cannot be the province of a few specialized units within a traditionally organized police department. Instead, they argue, the core police role must be altered if community involvement is to be achieved and maintained. To accomplish this goal, urban police departments should return to an earlier style of policing in which the officers on the beat had intimate contact with the people they served. In the modern age, the patrol car has removed patrol officers from the mainstream of the community, alienating people who might otherwise be potential sources of information and help for the police. According to the "broken windows" approach, police administrators would be well advised to deploy their forces where they can do the most good to promote public confidence and feelings of safety as well as elicit cooperation from citizens. Community preservation, public safety, and order maintenance, not crime fighting, should become the primary focus of patrol. Put another way, just as physicians and dentists practice preventive medicine and dentistry, police should help maintain an intact community structure instead of simply fighting crime.

COMMUNITY POLICING IN ACTION. The community policing concept has been put in operation in a number of innovative demonstration projects. The various **foot patrol** programs that have been established around the country are a direct offshoot of the community policing philosophy. Foot patrol has been used in select areas of cities such as Flint, Michigan, and Newark, New Jersey, to determine its effect on crime rates and citizen perceptions. One study of foot patrol, conducted by the Police Foundation, focused on efforts in 27 New Jersey cities, with emphasis on Newark and Elizabeth.[61] The research showed that although foot patrol did not influence the crime rate to any significant degree, residents in areas where foot patrol was added felt safer and were less afraid of crime. Though foot patrol did not deter crime per se, it helped improve citizens' attitudes toward the efforts of police.

The well-documented Flint, Michigan, foot patrol experiment has produced similar findings.[62] This carefully monitored study evaluated the effects of community policing in 14 areas of Flint, which included about 20 percent of the city's population. The Flint experiment has yielded data indicating that foot patrol, as a supplement to motor patrol, can pay dividends in terms of greater citizen cooperation, increased officer satisfaction, and reduced calls for service and assistance.

Another approach has been the development of decentralized, neighborhood-based precincts that serve as "storefront" police stations. One well-known plan is the Detroit Mini-station Program, which established over 36 such stations around the city. At first the community did not accept the program because the officers assigned to the ministations seemed to lack commitment. Since 1980 officers have been chosen for mini-station duty on the basis of their community relations skills and crime prevention ability, and the program has met with much greater community acceptance.[63]

Another community policing strategy is the development of **problem-oriented policing**. Instead of responding to calls for help, problem-oriented police identify particular community problems—street-level drug dealers, prostitution rings, gang hangouts—and develop strategies to counteract them.[64] An evaluation of such an approach by police in Newport News, Virginia, found that it was effective in reducing theft from cars, problems associated with prostitution, and household burglaries.[65]

REDUCING COMMUNITY FEAR. One of the more important goals of community policing is to develop strategies designed to reduce the level of fear in the community. Fear reduction is viewed both as an important aspect of police service to the community and as a means of increasing citizen cooperation with police officers.[66] To accomplish this goal, the National Institute of Justice funded two experimental programs in Newark, New Jersey, and Houston, Texas. Both projects involved a series of community policing models designed to improve each police department's working relationship with its community by assuring citizens that the local department cared about the quality of their lives. For example, the Houston program contained the following elements:

1. A police-community newsletter designed to give accurate information to citizens.
2. A community-organizing response team designed to build a community organization in an area where none had previously existed.
3. A citizen contact program in which individual officers remained in the same area of the city, enabling them to make individual contacts with community residents.
4. A program in which officers recontacted victims soon after their victimization to reassure them of police action in the case.
5. A police-community contact center established and staffed by two patrol officers, a civilian coordinator, and three police aids. The program included a

school component aimed at reducing truancy and a park element designed to reduce vandalism.[67]

The most successful programs gave officers time to meet with local residents to talk about crime in the neighborhood and to use personal initiative to solve problems. The police in Newark went so far as to set up a neighborhood cleanup program for juveniles who might ordinarily have little interest in civic affairs. In one neighborhood, police officers were given time to visit 500 businesses and homes to see if there were any problems the police should know about. Although not all the programs worked (police-community newsletters and cleanup campaigns did not seem to do much good), the overall impression was that patrol officers can actually reduce the level of fear in the community.[68]

What does the future hold for community policing? A survey by Robert Trojanowicz and Hazel Hardin found that over 140 communities are now experimenting with community policing concepts. Although the majority employ foot patrol, other kinds of community policing include park and walk models, team policing, horse patrol, auxiliary or reserve police, volunteers, neighborhood response units, and similar strategies.[69]

PROBLEMS OF COMMUNITY POLICING. Although many police experts and administrators have embraced the community policing concept as a revolutionary revision of the basic police role, it is not without its critics. Jack Greene, for example, has argued that the most significant problem in community policing strategies is to define "community" accurately. Greene finds that in most community policing projects, the concept of "community" is defined in terms of administrative areas traditionally used by police departments to allocate patrols. Police departments rarely define "community" in terms of an ecological area defined by common norms, shared values, and interpersonal bonds.[70] According to Greene, this oversight is vital to the future success of community policing. After all, the main focus of community policing is to activate the community norms that make neighborhoods more crime-resistant. To do so requires a greater identification with ecological areas: if community policing projects cross the boundaries of many different neighborhoods, any hope of learning and accessing community norms, strengths, and standards will be lost. Recent research by Roger Dunham and Geoffrey Alpert shows that residents of different neighborhoods have distinct views of the police role and that no single approach to community policing can possibly be correct for all areas.[71]

In addition to understanding and identifying "natural" areas, police departments must also establish the precise role of community police agents. How should they integrate their activities with those of regular patrol forces? For example, should foot patrols have primary responsibility for policing in an area, or should they coordinate their activities with officers assigned to patrol cars? Should community police officers be solely problem identifiers and neighborhood organizers, or should they also be expected to be law enforcement agents who get to the crime scene rapidly and later do investigative work?

Community police activists also assume that citizens actually *want* increased police presence in their neighborhoods. This assumption ignores the fact that the same citizens who fear crime may also fear the police.[72] A recent analysis of a victim callback program, established by the Houston police department, found that the program, which was originally designed to provide aid and support for victims, had a generally negative effect on some minority groups (Asians and Hispanics) whose members may have been suspicious of the police department's intentions.[73] Another program in Detroit also produced disappointing results.[74] Similarly, police officers have learned to be mistrustful of the general public. Police have often been described as being isolated from and suspicious of the people they serve.[75] Since the community policing model calls for a revision of the police role from law enforcer to community organizer, police training must now be revised to reflect this new mandate. If community policing is to be adopted on a wide scale, a whole new type of police officer must be recruited and trained in a way that has heretofore been unknown.

Although these criticism may have validity, there is little question that community policing will have a long-term influence on American policing. Herman Goldstein summarizes its most important benefits as follows:

1. A more realistic acknowledgment of police functions
2. Recognition of the interrelationship between and among police functions
3. An acknowledgment of the limited capacity of the police to accomplish their job on their own and of the importance of an alliance between the police and the public
4. Less dependence on the criminal justice system and more emphasis on new problem-solving methods
5. Greatly increased use of knowledge of assigned areas
6. More effective use of personnel
7. An increased awareness of community problems as a basis for designing more effective police responses[76]

Although police agencies in the 1990s will be using a diverse array of technological innovations, they may also be rethinking their role and relationships to the community. There seems to be little question that the core concept of police work is changing as administrators recognize the limitations and realities of police work in modern society. The oft-repeated charge that police catch relatively few criminals and have little deterrent effect has had a tremendous influence on police policy initiatives.

■ SUMMARY

Present-day police departments have evolved from early European and American crime control forces. Today, most police agencies operate in a quasi-military fashion; policy generally emanates from the top of the hierarchy, and it is difficult for both police officers and the public to understand or identify the source of orders and directives. Most police officers therefore use a great deal of discretion when making on-the-job decisions.

Many different types of organizations are involved in law enforcement activities; these agencies are organized on the local, state, and federal levels of government. The most visible law enforcement agencies, however, are local police departments, which conduct patrol, investigative, and traffic functions, as well as many different support activities. Police departments have

also been concerned with developing proper techniques for training their leaders, recruiting new officers, promoting deserving veterans, and developing technical expertise.

In addition to public law enforcement agencies, a large variety of private policing enterprises have developed. These include a multibillion dollar private security industry, the private employment of public police, and citizen self-help groups.

The future of policing may involve two separate developments. One is the increased use of technology to aid investigation, communication, and record keeping. The other is community policing, in which police agencies and citizen groups create a partnership to fight crime.

■ QUESTIONS

1. What does the term "vigilante" mean, and how does its current usage differ from its original meaning?

2. Should there be a national police force that combines all existing law enforcement agencies into one agency? What are the advantages and disadvantages of this approach?

3. Should police officers moonlight as private security guards? How can this trend prove damaging?

4. Can the police and community ever form a partnership to fight crime? Does the community policing model remind you of early forms of policing?

■ NOTES

1. Edward Zamble and Phyllis Annesley, "Some Determinants of Public Attitudes toward the Police," *Journal of Police Science and Administration* 15 (1987): 285–91.

2. Karen Polk, "New York Police: Caught in the Middle and Losing Faith," *Boston Globe*, 28 December 1988, p. 3.

3. Gallup Poll results cited in Timothy Flanagan and Katherine Jamieson, *Sourcebook of Criminal Justice Statistics* (Washington, D.C.: U.S. Government Printing Office, 1988), p. 134.

4. This section relies heavily on Daniel Devlin, *Police Procedure, Administration, and Organization* (London: Butterworth, 1966); Robert Fogelson, *Big City Police* (Cambridge, Mass.: Harvard University Press, 1977); Roger Lane, *Policing the City, Boston 1822–1885* (Cambridge, Mass.: Harvard University Press 1967); Roger Lane, "Urban Police and Crime in Nineteenth Century America," in *Crime and Justice*, vol. 2, N. Morris and M. Tonry, eds. (Chicago: University of Chicago Press, 1980), pp. 1–45; J. J. Tobias, *Crime and Industrial Society in the Nineteenth Century* (New York: Schocken Books, 1967); Samuel Walker, *A Critical History of Police Reform: The Emergence of Professionalism* (Lexington, Mass.: Lexington Books, 1977); Samuel Walker, *Popular Justice* (New York: Oxford University Press, 1980); President's Commission on Law Enforcement and the Administration of Justice, *Task Force Report: The Police* (Washington, D.C.: U.S. Government Printing Office, 1967), pp. 1–9.

5. Devlin, *Police Procedure, Administration, and Organization*, p. 3.

6. Phillip Reichel, "Southern Slave Patrols as a Transitional Type," *American Journal of Police* 7 (1988): 51–78.

7. Walker, *Popular Justice*, p. 61.

8. Ibid., p. 8.

9. Dennis Rousey, "Cops and Guns: Police Use of Deadly Force in Nineteenth-Century New Orleans," *American Journal of Legal History* 28 (1984): 41–66.

10. Law Enforcement Assistance Administration, *Two Hundred Years of American Criminal Justice* (Washington, D.C.: U.S. Government Printing Office, 1976).

11. National Commission on Law Observance and Enforcement, *Report on the Police* (Washington, D.C.: U.S. Government Printing Office, 1931), pp. 5–7.

12. Preston William Slossom, *A History of American Life*, vol. 12, *The Great Crusade and After, 1914–1929*, Arthur M. Schlesinger and Dixon Ryan Fox, eds. (New York: Macmillan Co., 1931), p. 102.

13. Frank Tippett, "It Looks Just Like a War Zone," *Time*, 27 May 1985, pp. 16–22.

14. "San Francisco, New York Police Troubled by Series of Scandals," *Criminal Justice Newsletter* 16 (1985): 2–4.

15. Karen Polk, "New York Police: Caught in the Middle and Losing Faith," *Boston Globe*, 28 December 1988, p. 3.

16. See James Q. Wilson and George Kelling, "Broken Windows: The Police and Neighborhood Safety," *Atlantic Monthly* 249 (March 1982): 29–38.

17. Bureau of Justice Statistics, *Report to the Nation on Crime and Justice* (Washington, D.C.: Bureau of Justice Statistics, 1988), p. 63.

18. Brian Reaves, *Profile of State and Local Law Enforcement Agencies, 1987* (Washington, D.C.: Bureau of Justice Statistics, 1989); see also Federal Bureau of Investigation, *Crime in the United States, 1987* (Washington, D.C.: U.S. Government Printing Office, 1988), p. 233. (Note that the FBI estimate of 640,000 law enforcement personnel is about 100,000 less than the BJS estimate.)

19. Reaves, *Profile of State and Local Law Enforcement Agencies, 1987*, p. 1.

20. Lee Brown, "The Role of the Sheriff", in *The Future of Policing*, Alvin Cohn, ed. (Beverly Hills, Calif.: Sage Publications, 1978), pp. 237–40.

21. Bruce Smith, *Police Systems in the United States* (New York: Harper & Row, 1960), p. 72.

22. Reaves, *Profile of State and Local Law Enforcement Agencies, 1987*, p. 2.

23. Tony Poveda, "The FBI and Domestic Intelligence: Technocratic or Public Relations Triumph?" *Crime and Delinquency* 28 (1982): 194–210.

24. Ross Gelbspan, "FBI Misled Congress on Its Latin Inquiry," *Boston Globe*. 2 January 1989, p. 5.

25. "New Budget Builds Up, FBI, DEA, Prisons, Marshals; Cuts Grants," *Criminal Justice Newsletter*, 18 February 1986, p. 1.

26. Howard Safir, "United States Marshals Service Fugitive Investigative Strike Teams," *Police Chief* 50 (1983): 34–37.

27. National Institute of Justice, *Research Program Plan, Fiscal Year 1989* (Washington, D.C.: National Institute of Justice, 1988), p. 3.

28. William Cunningham and Todd Taylor, *The Growing Role of Private Security* (Washington, D.C.: U.S. Government Printing Office, 1984).

29. Albert Reiss, *Private Employment of Public Police* (Washington, D.C.: National Institute of Justice, 1988).

30. This section relies on an excellent review of this topic, Dennis Rosenbaum, "Community Crime Prevention: A Review and Synthesis of the Literature," *Justice Quarterly* 5 (1988): 323–95.

31. Leslie Kennedy, "Going It Alone: Unreported Crime and Individual Self-Help," *Journal of Criminal Justice* 16 (1988): 403–13.

32. Ronald Clarke, "Situational Crime Prevention: Its Theoretical Basis and Practical Scope," in Michael Tonry and Norval Morris, *Annual Review of Criminal Justice Research* (Chicago: University of Chicago Press, 1983).

33. Catherine Whitaker, *Crime Prevention Measures* (Washington, D.C.: Bureau of Justice Statistics, 1986).

34. Rosenbaum, "Community Crime Prevention," p. 347.

35. Douglas Smith and Craig Uchida, "The Social Organization of Self-Help: A Study of Defensive Weapon Ownership," *American Sociological Review* 53 (1988): 94–101.

36. Gary Kleck and David Bordua, "The Factual Foundation for Certain Key Assumptions of Gun Control," *Law and Policy Quarterly* 5 (1983): 271–98.

37. Catherine Whitaker, *The Redesigned National Crime Survey: Selected New Data* (Washington, D.C.: Bureau of Justice Statistics, 1989).

38. Gary Kleck, "Crime Control through the Private Use of Armed Force," *Social Problems* 35 (1988): 1–21.

39. Rosenbaum, "Community Crime Prevention," p. 337.

40. Stephen Kurkjian and Walter Robinson, "Colt halts US sales of assault weapons," *Boston Globe*, 16 March 1989, p. 1.

41. James Garofalo and Maureen McLeod, *Improving the Use and Effectiveness of Neighborhood Watch Programs* (Washington, D.C.: National Institute of Justice, 1988).

42. Peter Finn, *Block Watches Help Crime Victims in Philadelphia* (Washington, D.C.: National Institute of Justice, 1986).

43. Ibid.

44. Garofalo and McLeod, *Improving the Use and Effectiveness of Neighborhood Watch Programs*, p. 1.

45. Mark Birchler, "Computers in a Small Police Agency," *FBI Law Enforcement Bulletin* (1989): 7–9.

46. Brewer Stone, "The High-Tech Beat in St. Pete," *Police Chief* 55 (1988): 23–28.

47. Kristen Olson, "LAPD's Newest Investigative Tool," *Police Chief* 55 (1988): 30.

48. William Stover, "Automated Fingerprint Identification—Regional Application of Technology," *FBI Law Enforcement Bulletin* 53 (1984): 1–4.

49. Paul Smith, "Inservice Training for Law Enforcement Personnel," *FBI Law Enforcement Bulletin* 57 (1988): 20–21.

50. John LeDoux and Henry McCaslin, "Computer-Based Training for the Law Enforcement Community," *FBI Law Enforcement Bulletin* 57 (1988): 8–10.

51. Stone, "The High-Tech Beat in St. Pete," p. 24.

52. Mark Thompson, "Police Seeking Radio Channel for Stolen Auto Tracking System," *Criminal Justice Newsletter*, 15 March 1989, p. 1.

53. James McRae and James McDavid, "Computer-based Technology in Police Work: A Benefit-Cost Analysis of a Mobile Digital Communications System," *Journal of Criminal Justice* 16 (1988): 47–55.

54. Matt Rodriguez, "The Acquisition of High Technology Systems by Law Enforcement," *FBI Law Enforcement Bulletin* 57 (1988): 10–15.

55. "California Attorney General Endorses DNA Fingerprinting," *Criminal Justice Newsletter*, 1 March 1989, p. 1.

56. Colleen Wade, "Forensic Science Information Resource System," *FBI Law Enforcement Bulletin* 57 (1988): 14–15.

57. Office of Technology Assessment, *Criminal Justice: New Technologies and the Constitution* (Washington, D.C.: U.S. Government Printing Office, 1988).

58. George Kelling, "Police and Communities: The Quiet Revolution," *Perspectives on Policing* (Washington, D.C.: National Institute of Justice, 1988).

59. Brent Steel and Nicholas Lovrich, "Police Community Relations Programs in U.S. Cities: Did They Survive the Termination of LEAA and the Fiscal Crisis of the 1980's?" *American Journal of Police* 7 (1988): 53–80.

60. Wilson and Kelling, "Broken Windows: The Police and Neighborhood Safety," pp. 29–38.

61. *The Newark Foot Patrol Experiment* (Washington, D.C.: Police Foundation, 1981).

62. Robert Trojanowicz, *An Evaluation of the Neighborhood Foot Patrol Program in Flint, Michigan* (National Neighborhood Foot Patrol Center, Michigan State University, undated).

63. Lawrence Holland, "Police and the Community—the Detroit Experience", *FBI Law Enforcement Bulletin* 54: 1–6 (1985).

64. John Eck and William Spelman, "Who Ya Gonna Call? The Police as Problem-Busters", *Crime and Delinquency* 33 (1987): 31–52; see also John Eck and William Spelman, *Solving Problems: Problem-Oriented Policing in Newport News* (Washington, D.C.: Police Executive Research Forum, January 1987).

65. Mark Moore and Robert Trojanowicz, *Policing and the Fear of Crime*" (Washington, D.C.: National Institute of Justice, 1988), p. 5.

66. George Kelling, *What Works—Research and the Police* (Washington, D.C.: National Institute of Justice, 1988), p. 3.

67. Police Foundation, *The Effects of Police Fear Reduction Strategies: A Summary of Findings from Houston and Newark* (Washington, D.C.: Police Foundation, 1986).

68. Ibid.

69. Robert Trojanowicz and Hazel Hardin, *The Status of Contemporary Community Policing Programs* (National Neighborhood Foot Patrol Center, Michigan State University, 1985).

70. Jack R. Greene, "The Effects of Community Policing on American Law Enforcement: A Look at the Evidence," paper presented at the International Congress on Criminology, Hamburg Germany, September 1988, p. 19.

71. Roger Dunham and Geoffrey Alpert, "Neighborhood Differences in Attitudes toward Policing: Evidence for a Mixed-Strategy Model of Policing in a Multi-Ethnic Setting," *Journal of Criminal Law and Criminology* 79 (1988): 504–22.

72. Jack Greene and Ralph Taylor, "Community-Based Policing and Foot Patrol: Issues of Theory and Evaluation," in *Community Policing, Rhetoric or Reality*, Jack Greene and Stephen Mastrofski, eds. (New York: Praeger, 1988).

73. Wesley Skogan and Mary Ann Wycoff, "Some Unexpected Effects of a Police Service for Victims," *Crime and Delinquency* 33 (1987): 490–501.

74. Dennis Rosenbaum, "Coping with Victimization: The Effects of Police Intervention on Victims' Psychological Readjustment," *Crime and Delinquency* 33 (1987): 502–19.

75. See, for example, Gary Cordner, "Fear of Crime and the Police: An Evaluation of a Fear-Reduction Strategy," *Journal of Police Science and Administration* 14 (1986): 223–28.

76. Herman Goldstein, "Toward Community-Oriented Policing: Potential, Basic Requirements, and Threshold Questions," *Crime and Delinquency* 33 (1987): 6–30, at 27–28.

Part Two

The Police and Law
Enforcement

■

7

The Police: Organization, Role, and Function

Most American municipal police departments are independent agencies, operating without specific administrative control from any higher governmental authority. On occasion, police agencies will cooperate and participate in mutually beneficial enterprises, such as sharing information on known criminals or helping federal agencies in interstate criminal investigations. Aside from such cooperative efforts, police departments tend to be functionally independent organizations with unique sets of rules, policies, procedures, norms, budgets, and so on. The unique structure of police agencies has a great deal of influence on their function and effectiveness.

This chapter describes the organization of police departments and their various operating branches: patrol, investigation, and service and administration. It discusses the realities and ambiguities of the police role and examines the ways in which the use of discretion influences police functions. The chapter concludes with a brief overview of some of the most important administrative issues confronting American law enforcement agencies.

■ Police Organization

Most larger urban police agencies are organized in a quasi-military, hierarchical manner, as illustrated in Figure 7.1. Within this organizational model, each element of the department normally has its own chain of command. For example, in a large municipal department, the **detective bureau** might have a captain as director of a particular division (e.g., homicide), while a lieutenant oversees individual cases and acts as liaison with other police agencies, and sergeants and inspectors carry out the actual field work. Smaller departments may have a captain as head of all detectives while lieutenants supervise individual subsystems (e.g., robbery or homicide). At the head of the organization is the chief who sets policy and has general administrative control over all of the department's various operating branches.

Most police agencies also follow a quasi-military system in promoting personnel within the ranks; at an appropriate time a promotion test may be given, and, based on scores and other recommendations, an officer may be advanced in rank. This organizational style discourages some police officers from furthering their education, since a college or advanced degree may have little direct impact on their promotion or responsibilities. Furthermore, some otherwise competent police officers are unable to increase their rank due to their inability to perform well on tests.

Police departments typically employ a **time-in-rank** method for determining promotion eligibility. This means that before moving up the administrative ladder, an officer must spend a certain amount of time in the next lowest rank. Put another way, a sergeant cannot become a captain without serving an appropriate amount of time as a lieutenant. Although this system is designed to promote fairness and limit favoritism, it also restricts administrative flexibility. Unlike the private sector where talented people can be pushed ahead in the best interests of the company, the time-in-rank system prohibits rapid advancement. For example, a police agency would probably not be able to hire a computer systems expert with a Ph.D, and place him or her in charge of the data analysis section. Instead the agency might be forced to hire the expert as a civilian employee under the command of a ranking senior officer who may not be as technically proficient. Similarly, under the police rank-structure system, once a title is earned, it can rarely be taken away or changed. This is often frustrating for police administrators because it means that qualified

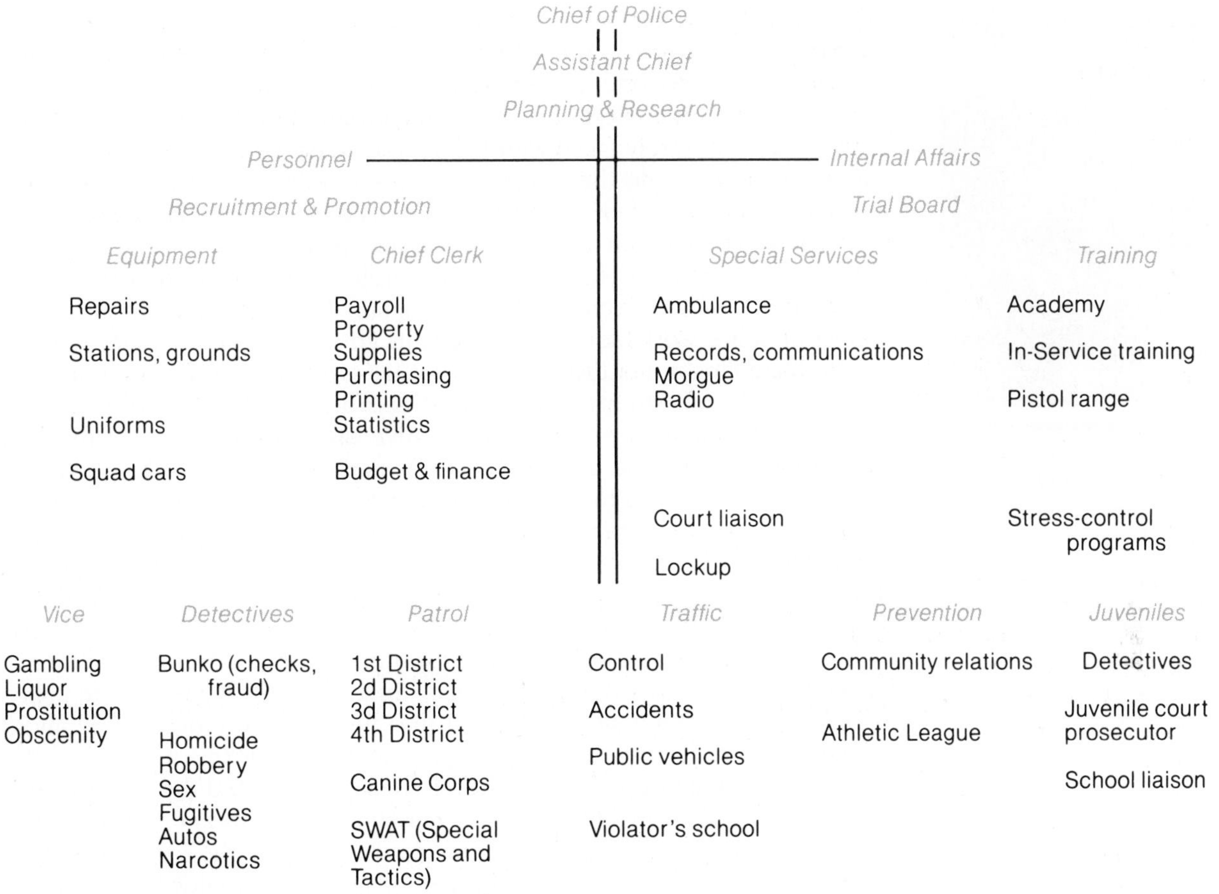

Chief of Police
Assistant Chief
Planning & Research

Personnel —————————————— Internal Affairs
Recruitment & Promotion   Trial Board

Equipment
Repairs
Stations, grounds
Uniforms
Squad cars

Chief Clerk
Payroll
Property
Supplies
Purchasing
Printing
Statistics
Budget & finance

Special Services
Ambulance
Records, communications
Morgue
Radio
Court liaison
Lockup

Training
Academy
In-Service training
Pistol range
Stress-control
programs

Vice
Gambling
Liquor
Prostitution
Obscenity

Detectives
Bunko (checks, fraud)
Homicide
Robbery
Sex
Fugitives
Autos
Narcotics

Patrol
1st District
2d District
3d District
4th District
Canine Corps
SWAT (Special Weapons and Tactics)

Traffic
Control
Accidents
Public vehicles
Violator's school

Prevention
Community relations
Athletic League

Juveniles
Detectives
Juvenile court prosecutor
School liaison

■ **FIGURE 7.1 Organization of a Metropolitan Police Department**

SOURCE: Adapted from Clarence Shrag, *Crime and Justice: American Style* (Washington, D.C.: U.S. Government Printing Office, 1971), p. 143.

junior officers cannot easily be promoted or reassigned to appropriate positions. The inability to achieve high rank has caused numerous officers to seek private employment.

A number of additional problems are associated with the typical police department's organizational structure. First, the overlapping assignments between the top administrators (chief and assistant or deputy chief) make it difficult for citizens to determine who is actually responsible for the department's policies and operations. Second, the large number of operating divisions and the lack of any clear relationship among them almost guarantees that the decision-making practices of one branch will be unknown to another; two divisions may unknowingly compete with each other over jurisdiction on a particular case. Even where cooperation is assured, the absence of a close working relationship among the various divisions of a department often causes inefficiency in the allocation and use of resources.[1]

■ The Police Role

Countless books, movies, and television shows have presented a romanticized view of policing in which police officers are invariably fearless crime fighters

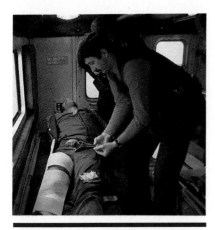

A significant portion of a police officer's time is spent on non-law enforcement duties such as emergency medical care.

who think little of their own safety as they engage in daily shootouts with Uzi-toting drug runners, psychopathic killers, and organized crime hitmen. Occasionally, but not often, do fictional patrol officers or detectives seem aware of departmental rules, legal decisions, citizen groups, civil suits, or physical danger. They are rarely faced with the economic necessity of moonlighting as security guards; nor do they worry about an annual pay raise or gripe when someone else is promoted ahead of them for political reasons. How close is this portrayal of selfless crime fighters to "real life" police work?

Not very accurate according to most research efforts, which show that police officers' crime-fighting activities are only a small part of their overall duties. Studies of police work indicate that a significant portion of an officer's time is spent on handling minor disturbances, service calls, and administrative duties.

For example, in a study of patrol activities in a city of 400,000, John Webster found that social service and administrative tasks consumed 55 percent of police officers' time and accounted for 57 percent of their calls.[2] Activities involving crime fighting took up only 17 percent of patrol time and amounted to about 16 percent of the activity calls. Similarly, Robert Lilly found that of 18,000 calls to a Kentucky police department made over a four-month period, 60 percent were for information and 13 percent concerned traffic, while 2.7 percent were about violent crime and 1.8 percent were about theft.[3] Similar findings were uncovered by Michael Brown in California, Norman Weiner in Kansas City, and Albert Reiss in Chicago.[4] In a survey of 26,000 calls to police in 21 different jurisdictions, George Antunes and Eric Scott found that only 20 percent involved the report of a criminal activity.[5] Nor is this service orientation limited to a few departments. Steven Meagher analyzed the job functions of 531 police officers in 249 municipal departments and found that regardless of size most police agencies and officers do pretty much the same thing.[6]

These results are not surprising in light of the data contained in the UCR: each year about 500,000 police officers make 2.5 million serious crime arrests or about 5 each. If all arrests are considered, each officer makes about 25 arrests per year (including DUI, vagrancy, runaways, and drug abuse violations). Assuming an even distribution of arrests, it is evident that the average police officer is making 2 arrests per month and 1 felony arrest every two months. (If the geographic distribution of crime is considered, urban police make significantly more arrests than suburban or rural officers). Thus, unlike their fictional counterparts who arrest 10 people per hour (and shoot about 5), many "real life" police officers rarely spend their days "crime fighting."

The evidence shows that the **police role** involves a preponderance of non-crime-related activities and that this role is similar in both large and small departments. Although officers in large urban departments may be called on to handle more felony cases than small town police officers, it seems likely that they too, like it or not, will engage in activities that they feel uncomfortable with or consider trivial. In fact, during the 1990s police officers will spend more of their time dealing with social tragedies such as finding and caring for missing children.[7] More attention will also be paid to **special needs populations:** the homeless, the mentally ill, and alcoholics.[8]

In light of this expanded view of the police role, "good" police officers might be described as follows:

The good police officer has the qualities required for policing. These include common sense, mature judgment, and reacting quickly and effectively to problem situations. The good police officer is able to adopt the appropriate role of policing. These involve the role of law enforcer, the role of maintaining social order, and the role of public servant. Finally, the good police officer has the appropriate concepts of policing. These concepts guide and prioritize role selection. They involve the conception of police work as an effort to improve the welfare of the community and the conception of individuals as deserving of respect for their rights, worth, and dignity.[9]

Police Role Conflict

There is little question that many police officers feel unappreciated by the public they serve. This less-than-enthusiastic reception is probably due to the underlying conflicts contained within the police role. Police may want to be **proactive** crime fighters who initiate actions against law violators rather than **reactive** agents who respond when a victim or witness initiates the call. Yet, the desire for direct action is often blunted because police are expected to perform many civic duties that in earlier times were the responsibility of every citizen: keeping the peace, performing emergency medical care, and dealing with civil emergencies. Today, we leave those tasks to the police. Although most of us agree that a neighborhood brawl must be broken up, that the homeless family must be found shelter, or the drunk taken safely home, few of us want to jump personally into the fray; we'd rather "call the cops." The police role has become that of a "social handyman" called in to fix up societal problems that the average citizen wishes would simply go away. As sociologist Egon Bittner argues, police work has, from its earliest origins, been a "tainted occupation":

> The taint that attaches to police work refers to the fact that policemen are viewed as the fire it takes to fight fire, that in the natural course of their duties they inflict harm, albeit deserved, and that their very existence attests that the nobler aspirations of mankind do not contain the means necessary to insure survival.[10]

Notice how Bittner identifies the inherent role conflict faced by the modern police officer. The public needs the police to perform those duties the general public finds distasteful or dangerous, for example, breaking up a barroom brawl. At the same time, the public resents the power the police have to use force, to arrest people, and to deny people their vices. Put another way, the average citizen wants the police to control undesirable members of society while excluding their own, sometimes law-violating, behavior from legal scrutiny.

Because of this natural role conflict, the relationship between the police and the public has aroused a great deal of concern. Many Americans seem to feel rather uncertain about police effectiveness, courtesy, honesty, and conduct. Consequently, some citizens are unlikely to go to police for help, report crimes, step forward as witnesses, or cooperate and aid police. Victim surveys indicate that many citizens have so little faith in the police that they will not report even serious crimes to them. In some communities, citizen self-help groups, such as the "Guardian Angels," have sprung up to supplement police protection.[11] In return, police officers often feel ambivalent about the public they are sworn to protect.

◼ Police Discretion

No aspect of the police role is more important than its reliance on granting individual officers a tremendous amount of personal **discretion** in carrying out their daily activities. Discretion can involve the selective enforcement of the law, as when a vice squad plainclothes officer decides not to take action against a tavern that is serving drinks after hours. The use of discretion is also evident when patrol officers decide to arrest one suspect for disorderly conduct while escorting another one to his home.

Most scholars have concluded that few police officers do not use a high degree of personal discretion in carrying out daily tasks. Jerome Skolnick has termed the exercise of police discretion a prime example of low visibility decision making in criminal justice.[12] This statement suggests that, unlike members of almost every other criminal justice agency, police are neither regulated in their daily procedures by administrative scrutiny nor subject to judicial review (except when their behavior clearly violates an offender's constitutional rights). The following sections describe the factors that influence police discretion and review suggestions for its control.

Environment and Discretion

The extent of police discretion officers will exercise is at least partially defined by their living and working environment.[13] The community culture in which police officers work or live may either tolerate eccentricities and personal freedoms or expect extremely conservative, professional, no-nonsense behavior from its civil servants. The police officer who resides in either a liberal or conservative environment is probably strongly influenced by and shares a large part of the community's beliefs and values and is likely to be sensitive to and respect the wishes of neighbors, friends, and relatives. Conflict may arise, however, when the police officer commutes to an assigned area of jurisdiction, as is often the case in inner city precincts. The officer who holds personal values that are not shared by the residents of the precinct may exercise discretion in such a way as to conflict with the community and result in ineffective law enforcement.

Dennis Powell has found that a community's racial makeup may influence police discretion.[14] After studying five adjacent police jurisdictions, Powell found that police in a predominantly black urban community demonstrated the highest use of discretion and were more punitive toward whites than toward blacks. Conversely, police in predominantly white areas were significantly more punitive to black offenders than whites. In a similar study, Douglas Smith and Jody Klein found that the socioeconomic status of the neighborhood had a great deal of influence on a police officer's use of discretion in domestic abuse cases. Police were much more likely to use formal arrest procedures in lower-class than in middle- and upper-class neighborhoods. Smith and Klein also found that income level influenced whether police officers would be willing to take citizens' complaints seriously.[15]

A final environmental factor affecting the police officer's performance is his or her perception of community alternatives to police intervention or processing. A police officer may exercise discretion to arrest an individual in a particular circumstance if it appears that nothing else can be done even if the officer doesn't believe that an arrest is the best possible example of good police work. In an environment where a proliferation of social agencies exist—detoxification units, drug control centers, and child-care services, for example—a police officer will obviously have more alternatives to choose from in the decision-making process. In fact, referring cases to these alternative

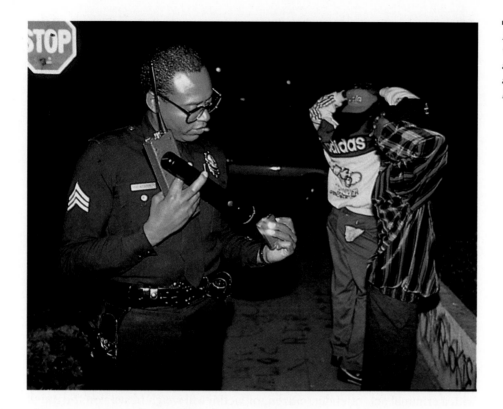

Police discretion is influenced by the working environment, community attitudes, departmental practices, and situational factors such as the location of the crime.

agencies saves the officer both time and effort—records do not have to be made out and court appearances can be avoided. Thus social agencies provide for greater latitude in police decision making.

Departmental Influences

The policies, practices, and customs of the local police department provide another influence on discretion. These conditions vary from department to department and strongly depend on the judgment of the chief and others in the organizational hierarchy. For example, departments can issue directives intended to influence police conduct. Patrol officers may be asked to issue more tickets and make more arrests, or to refrain from arresting under certain circumstances. Occasionally, a directive will instruct officers to be particularly alert for certain types of violations or to make some sort of interagency referral when specific events occur. These factors affect the decisions of the police officer who must produce appropriate performance statistics by the end of the month or be prepared to justify following a course of action other than that officially prescribed.

The ratio of supervisory personnel to subordinates may also influence discretion: departments with a high proportion of sergeants to patrol officers may experience fewer officer-initiated actions than one in which there are fewer eyes observing the action in the streets. The size of the department may also affect the level of police discretion. In larger departments looser control by supervisors seems to encourage a level of discretion unknown in smaller more tightly run police agencies.[16]

Police discretion is also subject to peer pressure.[17] Police officers suffer a degree of social isolation for two reasons. On the one hand, the job itself involves strange working conditions and hours and requires that the officer be subject to 24-hour call; on the other hand, their authority and responsibility to enforce the law cause embarrassment during social encounters. At the same time, officers must deal with irregular and emotionally demanding encounters involving the most personal and private aspects of people's lives. As a result, police officers turn to their peers both for on-the-job advice and for off-the-job companionship, essentially forming a subculture that provides status, prestige, and rewards.

The peer group affects how police officers exercise discretion on two distinct levels. In an obvious, direct manner, other police officers dictate acceptable responses to street-level problems by displaying or withholding approval in office discussions. The officer who takes the job seriously and desires the respect and friendship of others will take their advice and abide by their norms and will seek out the most experienced and most influential patrol officers on the force and follow their behavior models.

Situational Influences on Discretion

The situational factors attached to a particular crime provide another extremely important influence on police actions and behavior. Regardless of departmental or community influences, the officer's immediate interaction with a criminal act, offender, citizen, or victim will weigh heavily on the use of discretionary powers.

Although it is difficult to catalog every situational factor influencing police discretion, a few factors stand out as having major significance. Studies have found that police officers rely heavily on **demeanor** (the attitude and appearance of the offender) in making decisions. Some early research efforts by Nathan Goldman,[18] Aaron Cicourel,[19] and Irvin Piliavin and Scott Briar[20] all reached that conclusion. These studies found that if the offender was surly, talked back, or otherwise challenged the officer's authority, formal action was more likely to be taken.

Another set of situational influences on police discretion concerns the manner in which a crime or situation is encountered. If, for example, a police officer stumbles on an altercation or break-in, the discretionary response may be quite different from a situation in which the officer is summoned by police radio. If official police recognition has been given to an act, police action must be taken or an explanation made as to why it was not. Or, if a matter is brought to an officer's attention by a citizen observer, the officer can ignore the request and risk a complaint or take discretionary action. When an officer chooses to become involved in a situation, without benefit of a summons or complaint, maximum discretion can be used. Even in this circumstance, however, the presence of a crowd or witnesses may contribute to the officer's decision making.

And, of course, the officer who acts alone is affected by personal matters— physical condition, mental state, police style, whether there are other duties to perform, and so on.

Extralegal Factors and Discretion

An often-debated question is whether police take race, class, and sex into account when making arrest decisions. At issue is whether police discretion works against the young, males, the poor, and minority group members and favors the wealthy, the politically connected, and majority group members. Research has uncovered evidence that supports both sides of this argument. For example, Dale Dannefer and Russell Schutt found that racial bias was often present in the patrol officer's decision to process youths to juvenile court.[21] Dennis Powell found that police consider the race of the offender and the type of offense when using their discretion.[22] Christy Visher found that police were more likely to arrest women whose attitude and actions deviated from the stereotype of "proper" female behavior.[23] Visher found that older, white female suspects were less likely to be arrested than their younger, black, or hostile peers. And a study of 24 police departments by Douglas Smith and Christy Visher found that race (and demeanor) did in fact play an important role in police discretion. Surprisingly, Smith and Visher also found that males and females were equally likely to be arrested and formally processed for law violations.[24]

The belief that police are more likely to use formal sanctions against minority citizens has not been consistently supported by research. A number of studies have produced data indicating that racial bias does not influence the decision to arrest and process a suspect.[25] However, racial influences on police decision making are often quite subtle and hard to detect. For example, there are some indications that the victim's race and not the criminal's is the key to racial bias: police officers are more likely to take formal action when the victim of crime is white than they are when the victim is a minority group member.[26] For example, Cecil Willis and Richard Wells found that police are more likely to report child abuse cases involving white families than those involving black families.[27] The inference Willis and Wells draw from their data is either that (1) police officers view a case involving a white victim as more deserving of official attention and action than one involving a black child or that (2) the officers hold negative stereotypes of black family life including the perception that violence is normal in black families. These data suggest that any study of police discretion must take into account both victim and offender characteristics if it is to be truly valid.

These studies should not be interpreted as meaning that most police officers operate in an unfair and unjust manner. Nor can most police departments be labeled as biased. There is evidence that the influence of race on police discretion varies from jurisdiction to jurisdiction and may be a function of the professionalism of the individual department.[28] Similarly, there is evidence that sex bias, while still present, has been decreasing in recent years.[29]

Police discretion is one of the most often debated aspects of the police role. On its face, the unequal enforcement of the law smacks of unfairness and violates the Constitution's doctrines of due process and equal protection. Yet, unless some discretion is exercised, police would be forced to function as automatons merely following the book. Administrators have sought to control discretion so that its exercise may be both beneficial to citizens and nondiscriminatory. The following section discusses some of the management techniques used by police supervisors to limit discretion.

Controlling Police Discretion

The management of police behavior and discretion is one of the most difficult tasks facing law enforcement administrators. The chief and other police managers must ensure that the officers under their command do not arrest the wrong people for the wrong reasons or practice racial, sex, or class discrimination. At the same time, the administrators must inspire the officers' interest in community affairs and encourage them to maintain their vigilance against actually dangerous crimes. These combined tasks have proven to be complex and involve more than merely stating the rules or telling subordinates to play it by the book or face departmental punishment or sanctions. Police administrators must create a climate that both inspires patrol officers and encourages them to exercise their discretion properly.

One suggested approach to managing police behavior involves requiring obedience to a formal set of policies or guidelines that can ensure the just administration of the law.[30] When laws are unclearly written or police officers are unfamiliar with the application of some statute, guidelines provided by police legal counsel are useful.[31] When the effect of policy is to inform officers of a new legal tool to use in disposing of cases (e.g., the "Miranda warning"), written guidelines may publicize the availability and utility of the device. Similarly, written departmental policies can help police officers determine whether their responses to street encounters fall within the boundary of acceptable behavior. For example, New York City's written policy on the use of firearms has proved effective in limiting the use of deadly force.

A number of internal techniques have proved to be of some value to the police administrator in managing the behavior of officers; one such technique is the development of interagency and intra-agency cooperation. By setting up a specialized unit for juvenile crime prevention, rape, or vice, an administrator may shift the department's focus and the type of services provided to the community. On the other hand, the elimination or curtailment of a unit might be used to diminish interest in a particular area of policing. To be effective, such measures usually require high morale and cooperation from within the department.[32]

Another administrative technique the police supervisor may use to direct police behavior successfully is the establishment of departmental norms—sometimes known as the **"numbers game"**—for arrests, tickets, and other activities. These quotas, which may be interpreted as criteria for promotion or other forms of approval within the department, have been found by John Gardiner to actually affect police practices without the necessity of creating a specialized unit.[33]

Today, no clear answer to the management of police discretion exists. Advocates of specialized units, policy statements, legal mandates, and other approaches can only assume that the officer in the field will comply with the intent and spirit of the administrator's desire. Little knowledge is currently available concerning the specific influence any particular legal or administrative measure will have on policy discretion; that is, whether it will affect all officers equally, or why some officers react one way while others respond in an opposite fashion. Michael Brown argues that discretion is an important and necessary part of policing and should only be tampered with carefully. "We should be less concerned with worrying about how much discretion patrolmen have and searching for ways to eliminate it . . ." he argues, "than with trying to enlarge their qualities of judgment and making them responsive to the people they serve."[34]

■ Police Functions

As Figure 7.1 indicates, large metropolitan police departments carry out a wide variety of tasks and maintain a number of highly specialized roles. In keeping with their multifunction purpose, most metropolitan police departments have developed different specialized units, described below.

Patrol Function

Patrol officers are the backbone of the police department, usually accounting for about 60 percent of a department's personnel. In fact, they are the most highly visible components of the entire criminal justice system. They are charged with patrolling specific areas of their jurisdiction, called "beats," on foot, in a patrol car, or by motorcycle, horse, helicopter, or even boat. Each beat has different shifts, so that the area is covered 24 hours a day. The major purposes of patrol are (1) to deter crime by maintaining a visible police presence, (2) to maintain public order (order maintenance or "peacekeeping") within the patrol area, (3) to enable the police department to respond quickly to law violations or other emergencies, (4) to identify and apprehend law violators, (5) to aid individuals and care for those who cannot help themselves, (6) to facilitate the movement of traffic and people, and (7) to create a sense of security in the community.[35]

Patrol officers' responsibilities are immense; they may suddenly be faced with an angry mob, an armed felon, or a suicidal teenager and be forced to make split-second decisions on what action to take. At the same time, they must be sensitive to the needs of citizens living in their jurisdiction who are often of diverse racial and ethnic backgrounds.

To meet these obligations, police departments are now using computer-based crime forecasts to allocate patrol cars based on the need for service calls. Accurate prediction of the demand for service allows police managers to allocate patrol units in synch with citizen needs; two-person patrol cars can be used in high-crime areas and reserve units held out for special emergencies.[36]

PATROL ACTIVITIES. For many years, the major role of police patrol was considered to be law enforcement, but research conducted in the 1960s and 1970s showed that very little of a patrol officer's time was spent on crime-fighting duties. For example, Albert Reiss found that the typical tour of duty does not involve a single arrest.[37] Egon Bittner concluded that patrol officers average about one arrest per month and only three Index Crimes per year.[38] Although arrests alone cannot be equated with law enforcement duties, they do give some indication of the activities of patrol officers. Consequently, most experts today agree that the great bulk of police patrol efforts are devoted to what has been described as **order maintenance,** or **peacekeeping.**[39]

Order maintenance functions fall on the borderland between criminal and noncriminal behavior. The patrol officer's discretion often determines whether a noisy neighborhood dispute involves the crime of disturbing the peace or whether it can be controlled with street corner diplomacy and the combatants sent on their way. Similarly, the teenagers milling in the shopping center parking lot can be brought in and turned over to the juvenile authorities or "handled" in a less formal and often more efficient manner.

James Q. Wilson's pioneering work, *Varieties of Police Behavior*, was one of the first to view the major role of police as "handling the situation." Wilson believed that police encounter many troubling incidents that need some sort of "fixing up."[40] Enforcing the law might be one tool a patrol officer uses; threats, coercion, sympathy, understanding, and apathy might be others. Most impor-

Chapter 7

The Police: Organization, Role, and Function

■

223

tant is "keeping things under control so that there are no complaints that he is doing nothing or that he is doing too much."[41]

In sum, American police actually practice a policy of selective enforcement, concentrating on some crimes but handling the majority in an informal noncriminal manner. A patrol officer is supposed to know when to take action and when not to, whom to arrest and whom to deal with by issuing a warning or some other informal action. If a mistake is made, the officer may come under fire from his or her peers and superiors, as well as from members of the general public. Consequently, a patrol officer's job is extremely demanding and often unrewarding and unappreciated. It is not surprising that the attitudes of police officers toward the public have been characterized by ambivalence, cynicism, and tension.[42]

TRAFFIC CONTROL. Although the popular image of the police officer is that of a "crime fighter," patrol officers spend a great deal of their time dealing with that other major social problem: traffic. This involves such activities as intersection control (directing traffic), traffic law enforcement, radar operations, parking law enforcement, and accident investigations.

Traffic control is a complex daily task involving thousands or even millions of motor vehicles within a single police jurisdiction. Consequently, police departments use selective enforcement in their maintenance of traffic laws. Police departments neither expect nor wish to punish all traffic law violators. A department may set up traffic control units only at particular intersections, though its traffic coordinators know that many other areas of the city are experiencing violations. Manpower may be allocated to traffic details on the basis of accident or violation expectancy rates, determined by analysis of previous patterns and incidents.

Some officers will use wide discretion when enforcing traffic laws, allowing many violations to go unchecked or merely issuing violators a warning, while giving citations to others who commit similar violations. Other officers "play it by the book" and sanction by citation or arrest all traffic law violations. Almost all citizens who drive have turned an anxious, sorrowful face to a stern police officer while the latter decides whether to write them up or give them a break. The latter action always seems to elicit feelings that police are really doing a good job and are a fair bunch.

How and why traffic laws are enforced can have a serious effect on the way citizens view police work, and may even influence more important police-citizen contacts, such as reporting crime to police, aiding police in trouble, or stepping forth as witnesses.

PATROL EFFECTIVENESS. For many years, preventive police patrol has been considered one of the greatest deterrents of criminal behavior. The visible presence of patrol cars on the street and the rapid deployment of police officers to the scene of a crime were viewed as particularly effective law enforcement techniques. However, recent research efforts have questioned these basic assumptions. The most widely heralded attempt at measuring patrol effectiveness was undertaken in Kansas City, Missouri, under the sponsorship of the Police Foundation.[43]

To evaluate the effectiveness of patrol, 15 independent police beats or districts were divided into three groups: one group retained normal police patrol; the second ("proactive") set of districts were supplied with two to three times the normal amount of patrol forces; in the third ("reactive") group, preventive patrol was entirely eliminated, and police officers responded only when summoned by citizens to the scene of a particular crime.

Data from the **Kansas City study** indicated that these variations in patrol techniques had little effect on the crime patterns in the 15 separate locales. The presence or absence of patrol did not seem to affect residential or business burglaries, auto thefts, larcenies involving auto accessories, robberies, vandalism, or other criminal behavior.[44] Moreover, variations in police techniques appeared to have little effect on citizen attitudes toward the police, their satisfaction with police, or their fear of future criminal behavior.[45]

THE EFFECTIVENESS OF PROACTIVE PATROL. The Kansas City project, though subject to criticism because of its research design, has had a considerable influence on the way police experts view the effectiveness of patrol. Its rather lukewarm findings set the stage for new policing models that stress social service over crime deterrence. Nevertheless, the role of police as crime stoppers should not be abandoned. Although the mere presence of police may not be sufficient to deter crime, the manner in which they approach their task may make a difference. In an important paper, James Q. Wilson and Barbara Boland found that police departments that use a proactive, aggressive law enforcement style may help reduce crime rates. Jurisdictions that encourage patrol officers to stop motor vehicles to issue citations and to aggressively arrest and detain suspicious persons experience lower crime rates than jurisdictions that do not follow such proactive policies.[46] In a more recent analysis of police activities in 171 American cities, Robert Sampson and Jacqueline Cohen found that departments that more actively enforced disorderly conduct and traffic laws also experienced lower robbery rates.[47]

Like Wilson and Boland before them, Sampson and Cohen find it difficult to determine why proactive policing works so effectively. It may have a direct deterrent effect: aggressive policing increases community perception that the police arrest a lot of criminals and that most violators get caught. Its effect may be indirect: aggressive police departments arrest more suspects, and their subsequent conviction gets them off the street; fewer criminals produce lower crime rates.

Before a general policy of vigorous police work is adopted, the downside of aggressive tactics must be considered. Proactive police strategies breed resentment in minority areas where citizens believe they are the target of police suspicion and reaction.[48] There is evidence that such aggressive police tactics as stop and frisks and rousting teenagers who congregate on street corners are the seeds from which racial conflict grows.[49]

In sum, although the Kansas City study questioned the value of police patrol as a crime deterrent, later research suggests that it may be a more effective, albeit socially costly, crime suppression mechanism than was earlier believed.

THE SPECIFIC DETERRENT EFFECT OF ARREST. If the Kansas City study found that the mere presence of police patrol officers cannot reduce crime rates, what is the effect of formal police contact such as an arrest? For quite some time it was believed that police action had little deterrent effect or, if it did, that the effect was short-lived and temporary.[50] There is some indication, however, that contact with the police will cause some offenders to forgo repeat criminal behavior; that is, formal patrol activities such as arrest

There is evidence that proactive aggressive patrol tactics have the ability to significantly lower crime rates.

may have a specific deterrent function. In a study using data acquired in Scandinavia, Perry Shapiro and Harold Votey found that an arrest for drunk driving can actually reduce the probability of offender recidivism. An arrest apparently increases people's belief that they will be rearrested if they drink and drive and also heightens their perception of the unpleasantness associated with an arrest.[51] Similarly, Douglas Smith and Patrick Gartin's research shows that getting arrested reduces the likelihood that a novice offender will repeat the criminal activity and also indicates that experienced offenders will reduce future offending rates after an arrest.[52] Other evidence suggests that an increase in the arrest rate has an immediate influence on the overall crime rate.[53]

One of the most significant tests of the deterrent effect of police arrest was conducted by the research team of Lawrence Sherman and Richard Berk.[54] Sherman and Berk examined the effect of police action on domestic dispute cases in Minneapolis, Minnesota, by having police officers use random approaches in dealing with the domestic assault cases they encountered on their beat. One approach was to give some sort of advice and mediation, another was to send the assailant from the home for a period of eight hours, and the third was to arrest the assailant. Sherman and Berk found that where police took formal action (arrest), the chance of recidivism was substantially less than when the police took less punitive measures such as warning offenders or ordering them out of the house for a cooling-off period. A six-month follow-up found that only 10 percent of the arrested group repeated their violent behavior, whereas 19 percent of the advised group and 24 percent of the sent-away group repeated their offenses.

To supplement the official police data, Sherman and Berk interviewed 205 of the victims in a six-month follow-up. The victims also indicated that an arrest was the most effective way of controlling domestic assaults. Whereas 19 percent of the wives of men who were arrested reported their mates had assaulted them again, 37 percent of the advised group and 33 percent of the sent-away group reported that further assaults had taken place. If, in addition to arresting the assailant, the police took the time to listen to the victim, the reported assault rate declined to 9 percent. These results were only for nonlethal, misdemeanor assault cases and did not include life-threatening situations. In sum, Sherman and Berk found that a formal arrest was the most effective means of controlling domestic violence regardless of what happened to the offender in court.[55]

These studies deem to indicate that although the presence of patrol officers cannot reduce crime rates per se, actual contact with police and the use of formal actions may have a specific deterrent effect on future crime. Atlanta, Chicago, Dallas, Denver, Detroit, New York, Miami, San Francisco, and Seattle are among the cities that have adopted policies encouraging arrests in domestic violence cases. Other jurisdictions have insisted that patrol officers become more aggressive in their operations and concentrate on investigating and deterring crimes. Los Angeles and Portland, Oregon, have encouraged patrol initiative by decentralizing authority in their police departments and creating autonomous, regional police bureaus that operate almost independently in their areas of jurisdiction.[56]

Despite the evidence linking formal action to improved crime control, some police experts still question whether the relationship is valid. Some victims may be reluctant to report further abuse to police because they fear reprisals.

Possibly, offenders who suffer arrest are more likely to threaten their mates with reprisals, thereby reducing the likelihood of subsequent calls for service.[57]

Even if the relationship is valid, police chiefs may find it difficult to convince patrol officers to make more arrests. Research efforts indicate that departmental directives to make more arrests in domestic disputes have relatively little effect on police behavior.[58] Some recent research by Kathleen Ferraro shows that despite departmental directives to be more active, police are reluctant to make formal arrests in domestic disputes; she found that only 18 percent of assault cases involving intimate partners resulted in arrest.[59] So, although some police departments have encouraged aggressive patrol tactics as a way of controlling the crime rate, influencing actual police activities in the field may prove a more difficult task.

If police activities do make a difference in the crime rate, it stands to reason that increasing the number of patrol officers should reduce the incidence of serious crimes. The Criminal Justice in Review on page 228 discusses this important topic.

Investigation Function

Since the first independent detective bureau was established by the London Metropolitan Police in 1841, criminal investigators have been romantic figures vividly portrayed in novels, motion pictures such as *Beverly Hills Cop* and the "Dirty Harry" series, and television shows such as "Columbo," "Hunter," and "Cagney and Lacey."[60] The fictional police detective is usually depicted as a loner, willing to break departmental rules, perhaps even violate the law, in order to capture the suspect. The average fictional detective views departmental policies and U.S. Supreme Court decisions as unfortunate roadblocks to police efficiency. Civil rights are either ignored or actively scorned.[61]

Although it is likely that every police department has a few "hell-bent for leather" detectives who take matters into their own hands at the expense of citizens' rights, a more accurate picture of the modern criminal investigator is that of an experienced civil servant, trained in investigatory techniques, knowledgeable about legal rules of evidence and procedure, and at least somewhat cautious about the legal and departmental consequences of his or her actions.[62] Though detectives are often handicapped by time, money, and resources, they are certainly aware of how their actions will one day be interpreted in a court of law. Police investigators are sometimes accused of being more concerned with the most recent court decisions on search and seizure and custody interrogation than they are with shoot-outs and suspected felons.

Detectives are probably the elite of the police force: they are usually paid more than patrol officers, engage in more interesting tasks, wear civilian clothes, and are subject to less stringent departmental control than patrol officers.[63]

Detectives investigate the causes of crime and attempt to identify the individuals or groups responsible for committing particular offenses. They may enter a case subsequent to an initial contact by patrol officers, as when a patrol car interrupts a crime in progress and the offenders flee before they can be apprehended. They may also investigate a case entirely on their own, sometimes by following up on leads provided by informants.[64]

Does Adding Police Lower the Crime Rate?

The Uniform Crime Reports reveal that police solve about 20 percent of the serious crimes reported to them by victims or witnesses. There is also a direct relationship between the seriousness of a crime and the probability that it will be solved by police. In other words, murders, rapes, and serious assaults have a far greater chance of getting solved than burglaries or larcenies. Considering these findings, would increasing the number of police in a given jurisdiction increase the likelihood that serious crimes will be solved?

A government study on the level of police expenditures sheds some light on this issue. Conducted by Craig Uchida and Robert Goldberg, the study examined police expenditures in 88 American cities between 1938 and 1982. Uchida and Goldberg found that

	Per Capita Adjusted Spending			
Cities with the:	1960	1970	1980	Percentage Increase, 1960–1980
Highest crime rate	$13.82	$26.16	$38.33	180%
Next to highest	11.14	18.45	28.47	157
Next to lowest	9.14	16.54	22.50	146
Lowest	10.12	14.33	22.08	120

TABLE A ■ Per Capita Adjusted Police Expenditures for 88 Cities by Crime Rate, 1960–1980

Note: Cities were ranked by Index Crime rate for each year, derived from the FBI's Uniform Crime Reports, and divided into groups of equal size. For 1960 data are available for only 80 cities. Figures are in constant 1967 dollars, adjusted for changes in the Consumer Price Index.

between 1938 and 1982 spending for police services increased 37-fold; adjusted for inflation, cities spent 5.5 times as much on police services in 1982 as they did in 1938. This spending increase means that after adjusting for inflation the per capita cost of police services quadrupled in the 44-year period.

What was the relationship between police spending and crime rates? As the table indicates, cities with the highest crime rates also spent the most on police services. High-crime-rate cities also had the greatest increase in police spending between 1960 and 1980. The ratio of police spending between the high- and low-crime-rate areas was 1.7:1 in 1980.

The research by Uchida and Goldberg indicated that the amount of

money spent on police services has little effect on the crime rate. After reviewing the literature on the subject, Colin Loftin and David McDowall also concluded that the number of law enforcement officers in a jurisdiction has little to do with the crime rate in the area. Thus, there appears to be little factual evidence that by simply adding to the numbers of police or paying more for their services, the crime rate can be lowered. The solution to the crime problem seems to be much more elusive. ■

SOURCE: Craig Uchida and Robert Goldberg, *Police Employment and Expenditure Trends* (Washington, D.C.: Bureau of Justice Statistics, 1986); Colin Loftin and David McDowall, "The Police, Crime, and Economic Theory: An Assessment," *American Sociological Review* 47 (1982): 393–401.

Detective divisions are typically organized into sections or bureaus such as homicide, robbery, or rape. Some jurisdictions maintain morals or vice squads, which are usually staffed by plainclothes officers and/or detectives specializing in victimless crimes such as prostitution or gambling. In this latter capacity, **vice squad** officers may set themselves up as customers for illicit activities in order to make arrests. For example, undercover detectives may frequent public men's rooms and men who proposition them are arrested for homosexual soliciting. In other instances, female police officers may pose as prostitutes. These covert police activities have often been criticized as violating the personal rights of citizens, and their appropriateness and fairness have been questioned.

Detectives investigate the causes of crime and attempt to identify the individuals or groups responsible for committing particular offenses.

EFFECTIVENESS OF INVESTIGATION. A great deal of criticism has been leveled at the nation's detective forces for being bogged down in paperwork and relatively inefficient at clearing cases. In 1975, a study of 153 detective bureaus conducted by the Rand Corporation found that much of a detective's time was spent in nonproductive work and that investigative expertise did little to solve cases; the Rand researchers estimated that half of all detectives could be replaced without negatively influencing crime clearance rates.[65] The Rand survey's findings were duplicated in a study of detective work by Mark Willman and John Snortum who analyzed 5,336 cases reported to a suburban police department. They found that the majority of cases were solved when the perpetrator was identified at the scene of the crime and that scientific detective work was rarely called for. Willman and Snortum concluded, however, that detectives do make a valuable contribution to police work because their skilled interrogation and case processing techniques are essential to eventual criminal conviction.[66]

The effectiveness of detectives is also called into question by data gathered by the Police Executive Research Forum (PERF). These data disclosed that if a crime is reported while in progress, the police have about a 33 percent chance of making an arrest; the arrest probability declines to about 10 percent if the crime is reported 1 minute later and to 5 percent if more than 15 minutes elapse before the crime is reported. In addition, as time elapses between the crime and the arrest, the chances of a conviction are reduced, probably because the ability to recover evidence is lost. Once a crime has been completed and the investigation is put in the hands of detectives, the chances of identifying and arresting the perpetrator diminish rapidly.[67] Put another way, the probability that a crime will be solved is more a function of the victim's reaction than investigatory effectiveness.

IMPROVING INVESTIGATIVE EFFECTIVENESS. A number of efforts have been made to revamp and improve investigation procedures. One practice has been to give patrol officers greater responsibilities to conduct preliminary investigations at the scene of the crime. In addition, the old-fashioned precinct detective has been replaced by specialized units, such as homicide or burglary squads, which operate over larger areas and can bring specific expertise to bear on a particular case.

Another approach is suggested by data gathered by PERF researchers on 3,360 burglary and 320 robbery cases committed in DeKalb County, Georgia, St. Petersburg, Florida, and Wichita, Kansas. The data included a wide range of information on the crime, the investigation, and the outcome of the investigation. The research contained a number of key findings:

■ *Unsolved cases.* Almost 50 percent of the burglary cases were screened out before the remainder were assigned to a detective for follow-up investigation. Of those assigned, 75 percent were dropped after the first day of follow-up investigation. Although all robbery cases were assigned to detectives, 75 percent of them were also dropped after one day of investigation.

■ *Length of investigation.* The vast majority of cases were investigated for no more than four hours stretching over a 3-day period. An average of 11 days elapsed between the initial report of a crime and suspension of investigative activity.

■ *Sources of information.* Early in an investigation, the focus is on the victim; as the investigation is pursued longer, emphasis shifts to the suspect. The information most critical in determining case outcome is the name of the suspect, his or her description, and related crime information. Victims are most often the source of information; unfortunately, witnesses, informants, and members of the police department are consulted far less often. However, when these sources are consulted, they are likely to produce useful information.

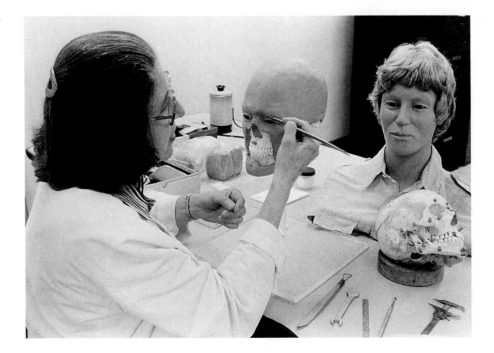

Successful investigations often depend on an efficient crime lab. Sometimes the bodies of murder victims have decomposed beyond recognition. Here an artist works modeling clay on the skull of one of John Gacy's murder victims. A photograph of the reconstructed head was later released to the media in an attempt to identify the victim. To the artist's right stands a completed reconstruction.

CRIMINAL JUSTICE IN REVIEW

Undercover Work

 One police investigation technique that has received widespread notoriety is undercover work, the subject of an important book by sociologist Gary Marx. According to Marx, undercover work can take a number of forms. A lone agent may infiltrate a criminal group or organization in order to gather information on future criminal activity. For example, a DEA agent may go undercover to gather intelligence on drug smugglers. Undercover officers may also pose as victims in order to capture predatory criminals who have been conducting street robberies and muggings.

Another approach to undercover work, commonly called **sting operations,** involves organized groups of detectives who deceive criminals into openly committing illegal acts or conspiring to engage in criminal activity. There have been numerous sting operations aimed at capturing professional thieves and seizing stolen merchandise. Undercover detectives, posing as fences, set up their own ongoing fencing operations and encourage thieves to sell them stolen merchandise. Transactions are videotaped to provide prosecutors with strong cases. One study of sting operations conducted in 40 jurisdictions over a seven-year period found that 9,970 criminals were arrested and $300 million in stolen property was recovered at a cost of $30 million.

Although undercover work can be vital to police operations, it is not without its drawbacks. By its very nature, it involves deceit by police agents that often comes close to entrapment. Sting operations may encourage criminals to commit new crimes because they have a new source for fencing stolen goods. Innocent people's reputations may be damaged because they bought merchandise from a sting operation even though they had no idea the items they purchased were originally stolen.

Undercover work also presents significant problems for the police agent. Police officers may be forced to engage in illegal or immoral behavior to maintain their cover. Furthermore, playing the role of a criminal and dealing with mobsters, terrorists, and drug dealers can be physically dangerous. In far too many cases, undercover officers are mistaken for "real" criminals and injured by other law enforcement officers or private citizens trying to stop a crime. Arrest situations involving undercover officers may also provoke violence when suspects do not realize they are in the presence of police and therefore violently resist arrest.

Undercover officers also experience psychological problems. Being away from home, keeping late hours, and always worrying that their identity will be uncovered creates enormous amounts of stress. An unexpected turn of events has been the post-undercover stress experienced by some officers. They have had trouble at work and in many instances have ruined their marriages and careers, botched prosecutions, and even turned to crime themselves.

The FBI is taking this situation quite seriously and now monitors undercover work very closely. They ask veteran agents to interview former undercover agents four to six months after they have left the field and have even retained a team of psychologists to deal with the problem.

Examples of undercover officers who succumbed to the stress of their work are legion. Dan Mitrione, an FBI agent, got so caught up in his undercover drug dealing that he took $850,000 in drug profits himself. Robert Delaney, a New Jersey state police officer, became so involved in his role as "Robert Alan Covert," a fence, that he could not shake his underground identity. His private life suffered as he reverted to the lifestyle of the mobster that he had successfully adopted for two years. And Patrick Livingstone, who participated in the pornography business for nearly three years under the alias "Pat Salamone," continued to visit his old bars, bookmakers, and criminal associates after the investigation he conducted was over. He maintained a bank account in his alias's name, used his old driver's license, and was happy to be known as Pat Salamone. When he was arrested on a shoplifting charge, defense attorneys representing the pornographers he helped identify used his tainted character as reason to have some charges dismissed and appeal the entire investigation.

Thus, despite its glamor, undercover work has many drawbacks. Sting operations have been accused of being lures that encourage people to commit crime. By putting the government in the fencing business, they blur the line between law enforcement and criminal activity. Undercover work also involves a great deal of stress for detectives and can lead to identity problems and death. Nevertheless, the FBI reports that as many as 600 agents are on a waiting list to be placed undercover. ■

SOURCE: See, generally, Gary Marx, *Undercover Police Surveillance in America* (Berkeley, Calif.: University of California Press, 1988); C. Cotter and J. Burrows, *Property Crime Program, a Special Report: Overview of the STING Program and Project Summaries* (Washington, D.C.: U.S. Department of Justice, 1981); Anthony DeStefano, "Undercover Jobs Carry Big Psychological Risk after the Assignment," *Wall Street Journal*, 4 November, 1985, p. 1.

■ *Effectiveness.* Preliminary investigations by patrol officers and follow-ups by detectives are equally important for solving crimes. Even in situations where the preliminary investigation by patrol officers did not develop information on the suspect, detectives were able to make an identification in about 14 percent of the cases and an arrest in 8 percent.[68]

Unlike earlier studies the PERF research found that detectives do make a meaningful contribution to the solution of criminal cases. To improve investigatory effectiveness, PERF recommends that greater emphasis be placed on collecting physical evidence at the scene of the crime, identifying witnesses, checking departmental records, and using informants. The probability of successfully settling a case is improved if patrol officers carefully gather evidence at the scene of a crime and effectively communicate it to the detectives working the case. Moreover, police managers should pay more attention to the screening of cases, monitoring case flow and activity, and creating productivity measures to ascertain if individual detectives and detective units are meeting their goals. Also recommended is the concept of targeted investigations, which direct attention at a few individuals, such as career criminals, who are known to have engaged in the behavior under investigation. Such individuals are often the target of undercover agents as discussed in the Criminal Justice in Review on page 231.

Support and Administrative Functions

As the model of a typical police department in Figure 7.1 indicates, not all members of a police department engage in what the general public regards as "real police work"—patrol, detection, and traffic control. A large part of police resources is actually devoted to the support and administrative functions, which maintain and control police services. Space limitations preclude a detailed discussion of all these services, but the most important include the following:

■ *Personnel.* Many police departments maintain their own personnel service, which recruits new police officers, devises entrance and other exams, and designs and implements promotions and transfers. Later in this chapter we will discuss in more detail the specific problems and issues associated with the complex task of creating adequate entrance exams.

■ *Internal affairs.* Larger police departments often maintain an internal affairs branch, which is charged with "policing the police." Internal affairs officers process citizen complaints of police corruption, investigate possible incidents of unnecessary use of force by police officers, or even investigate police participation in actual criminal activity, such as burglaries or narcotics violations. In addition, internal affairs bureaus may assist police management personnel when disciplinary action is brought against individual subordinate officers.

Internal affairs is a controversial function since its investigators are feared and mistrusted by their fellow police officers. Nevertheless, rigorous self-scrutiny is the only way police departments can earn the respect of citizens within their jurisdiction.

■ *Budget and finance.* Many police departments are responsible for the administration and control of departmental budgets and financial management. This involves managing the payroll, purchasing equipment and services, planning budgets for future expenditures, and auditing departmental financial records.

Smaller police departments have been plagued by the fact that police chiefs and other officers in charge of budgetary matters often lack the requisite skill to manage police finances accurately and effectively. In recent years, police managers seeking to maximize the growth and efficiency of their departments have turned to a Planning-Programming Budgeting System (PPBS) to improve their financial operations. This method requires police administrators to identify goals and objectives by systematically allotting available funds to them.[69] Use of PPBS and similar modern management techniques may significantly improve police operations during the coming decade.

■ *Records and communication.* Police departments maintain separate units that are charged with maintaining and disseminating information on wanted offenders, stolen merchandise, traffic violators, and so on. Modern data management systems enable police to use their records in a highly sophisticated fashion. For example, a patrol car that spots a suspicious vehicle can instantly receive a computer-based rundown on whether it has been stolen. Or if stolen property is recovered during an arrest, police can determine who reported the loss and arrange for its return.

Another important function of police communication is the effective and efficient dispatching of police patrol cars. Again, modern computer technologies have been used to maximize the benefits of available resources. For example, the computer-assisted 911 emergency number has been instituted in most large cities.[70]

■ *Training.* In many departments, training is carried out on a continuous basis throughout an officer's career. Training usually begins at a preservice police academy, which may be run exclusively by one large department or be part of a regional training center that services various smaller governmental units.

After assuming their police duties, new recruits are assigned to field training officers who break them in on the job. Training does not stop here, however. On-the-job training is a continuous process in the modern police department and includes such areas as weapons skills, first aid, crowd control, and community relations. Some departments use **roll-call training,** in which superior officers or outside experts address police officers at the beginning of the workday. Other departments allow police officers time off to attend annual training sessions to sharpen their skills and learn new policing techniques.

The amount and nature of police training vary widely. For example, Arizona requires 560 hours of preservice training while some states limit it to 220 hours. Before 1969, however, only 10 states required any preservice training at all.[71] Most training programs stress the "nuts and bolts," technical aspects of police work, such as weapons training, legal subjects, and patrol procedures. Some department curricula include community relations, sensitivity training, emergency medical training, and minimizing the use of deadly force. Currently, the Washington-based Commission on Accreditation of Law Enforcement is testing 1,000 training procedures in order to develop a standardized national police training curriculum.[72]

■ *Community relations.* Police departments provide emergency aid to the ill, counsel youngsters, speak to school and community agencies on safety and drug abuse, and provide countless other services designed to improve citizen-police interactions.

■ *Crime prevention.* Larger police departments maintain specialized units that help citizens protect themselves from criminal activity. For example, they advise citizens on effective home security techniques or conduct "Project ID" campaigns—engraving valuables with an identifying number so that they can be returned if they are recovered after a burglary.

■ *Laboratory.* Police agencies maintain (or have access to) forensic laboratories that identify substances to be used as evidence, aid in investigations, classify fingerprints, and so on.

■ *Planning and research.* New programs are designed to increase police efficiency and develop strategies to test program effectiveness. Police planners monitor recent technological developments and institute programs to adapt them to ongoing police services.

■ *Property.* Among other things, police handle evidence such as weapons and narcotics seized during investigations; hold stolen property recovered by investigators; and maintain prisoners' personal effects, lost property, and abandoned or towed motor vehicles.

■ *Detention.* Police stations maintain detention facilities for the temporary custody of suspects after their arrest.

■ Police Administration and Management

For the past 25 years, there has been a major effort to professionalize American police forces. The growth of administrative and management skills has improved the quality of policing and paved the way for reform in management and administration. Orlando Wilson's classic text, *Police Administration*, provided early guidance for police administrators attempting to improve their department's management.[73] Wilson stressed the need for a rational organizational framework that encouraged the free flow of communication, a clear chain of command, and a strict set of controls on officers' conduct backed up by written guidelines. Wilson's efforts have been furthered by such groups as the International Association of Chiefs of Police (IACP), the Police Executive Research Forum, and the Police Foundation.

The modern police department is now a civil service institution, usually overseen by a civilian board that sets criteria for hiring, promotion, discipline, and appeals. Civil service has helped remove much of the politics from policing. Although some departments, usually smaller ones, are still run by an authoritarian chief who personally controls all departmental policies and actions, most larger departments use more sophisticated management techniques.

Modern police chiefs rely on the advice of a large number of ranking officers who have authority over specific areas of the department. Some chiefs have experimented with advisory boards, made of up police officers of all ranks, that consult with them on policy and procedural problems. An effort has also been made to democratize many police departments and to consider the needs and ideas of even the lowest-ranking patrol officers. Police unions have had a hand in changing management's operational procedures, but the impetus for change has also come from management studies, which stress the utility of teamwork and group decision making. Although a truly democratic police department probably does not exist, experts and reformers such as John Angell have consistently called for the end of the military model of policing.[74]

Although an entire text could be devoted to the subject of police personnel administration and the management of a modern department, this section will focus on only a few of the more important issues in this area.

Management by Objectives

One change in police administration has been the adoption of the **management by objectives (MBO)** technique. Originated in the business community by management experts such as Peter Drucker, MBO is a process in which individual managers identify specific objectives (usually a year at a time) and then periodically review the progress they and their subordinates have made in reaching their performance targets.[75] The objectives can vary according to departmental needs:

■ *Process objectives.* These include activities that improve police efficiency. For example, patrol units in Newport News, Virginia, were asked to "identify two problem areas in their districts from weekly administrative analysis reports and develop a plan to address the problems."

■ *Outcome objectives.* These focus on particular performance initiatives such as "cut response time to in-progress burglaries to under five minutes."

■ *Cost and efficiency objectives.* These focus on containing or reducing departmental fiscal expenditures on vehicle maintenance, sick leave, communication services, and the like. For example, police in Compton, California, have created such objectives as "reduce sick and injury time by 20 percent" and "reduce the previous year's expenditures on fuel and utilities by 10 percent."[76]

A national survey of police administrative styles found that almost half of the 300 police departments contacted had adopted MBO programs. The survey concluded:

> MBO surveys appears to have considerable potential for helping police departments motivate management personnel to improve both service outcomes and service delivery efficiency.[77]

Recruitment and Selection Techniques

In recent years, the quality of police recruitment has improved due to a number of economic, political, and social factors. The depressed labor market and the scarcity of good jobs have made the security of a police career seem particularly inviting; the end of the military draft has increased the pool of eligible candidates; and the growing numbers of criminal justice programs in colleges have produced a pool of educated young people with law enforcement degrees. Equally important has been the development of a competitive salary structure in larger communities, which, with the addition of educational pay incentives, provides patrol officers with annual salaries in the neighborhood of $30,000 and up.

Most police departments have specific criteria for selection.[78] For example, only 14 percent require some form of college education; the overwhelming majority still demand only a high school diploma or less.[79] In addition, most police departments employ all or some of the following criteria: written tests; oral interviews; psychiatric/psychological appraisals; polygraphs; physical fitness, height, weight, and strength requirements; background investigations; biographical data; and medical exams. Larger police departments often use such sophisticated screening devices as the Wechsler Adult Intelligence Scale-Revised (WISC-R) to measure intelligence, and the California Test of Personality, Minnesota Multiphasic Personality Inventory (MMPI), and the Inwald Personality Inventory (IPI) to evaluate personality structure and determine whether recruits have any disorders that would impede their functioning.[80] Research indicates that these tests, taken independently or in conjunction with clinical interviews, can often be valid predictors of future police performance.[81]

Almost all departments will disqualify a candidate with an adult or juvenile felony conviction, but only about half disqualify people with misdemeanor convictions. Most metropolitan police departments place heavy emphasis on written examinations administered by the departments themselves or by state civil service commissions. These range from tests measuring reading and verbal comprehension similar to the SATs to examinations based on the department's operating manual with which the recruit is required to be familiar.

In recent years, minority group leaders have charged that these tests are designed in such a fashion as to be discriminatory and biased. Model tests have been created that contain culturally equivalent terms comparable to those found on standardized tests; when the model tests were administered to groups of black and white police officers, blacks performed better than on the standard tests by as much as 30 percent. Those questioning the validity of written police tests also point to studies that show the tests do not actually predict effective police performance in the field. To find a middle ground in the testing controversy, some departments have attempted to gear entrance exams away from the standard intelligence test format. Experts have created job-related examinations that measure a candidate's ability to take quick and reasonable action in stress situations. A sample question of this type might read:

> While on patrol, you find a panicked group of people standing at the shore of a frozen lake, staring helplessly at a youth, 15 feet off-shore, who has fallen through the ice. You would:
> a. Dash across the ice to rescue the boy
> b. Radio headquarters for help and wait by the lake
> c. Try to form a "human chain" to attempt a rescue
> d. Proceed with patrol since this is not a criminal matter

The candidate is asked to rank the answers according to their accuracy. The "correct" answers in this type of test are determined by analyzing responses made by experienced, qualified police officers. Tests such as these have been successfully challenged in the courts on the grounds that using only the "best" officers to test the items is unfair and nonrepresentative of the general police department.

Other departments have employed both individual and group simulation models. The former provide candidates with materials familiar to police agencies (police blotters, logs, memorandums, and the like) and ask them to make mock decisions on the basis of the information provided. Group simulation allows candidates to interact with one another in a problem-solving situation. For example, candidates may be asked to role-play a conflict situation that has little to do with police work to see if they have general problem-solving and leadership skills; one test included the question "I want you to imagine you are a lifeguard and an individual is running on the pool deck in violation of the rules. How would you stop him?" Verbal skills, interpersonal relations, sensitivity, and other qualities can all be assessed using this method.

In recent years, there has been a shift from reliance on physical requirements and cognitive ability to the use of intelligence and personality test measures. Instead of height and weight requirements, departments now rely more often on body proportion levels. Similarly, more than half of all police departments require psychological testing of candidates. Unfortunately, some of the limitations of this type of testing have recently been exposed. A number of research efforts indicate that while psychological tests are valid, there is a tendency for their predictive value to diminish over time.[82] A review of the literature by Elizabeth Burbeck and Adrian Furnham found not only significant methodological problems in the administration of psychological tests but also that most have little success in distinguishing between good and bad police officers. Burbeck and Furnham conclude that psychological testing may have some value in screening out candidates with mental problems but their ability to select successful police candidates is less than impressive.[83] Consequently, some critics such as Robin Inwald have called for the development of guidelines to ensure that psychological profiles are used fairly and equitably.[84]

Predicting Good Performance

The real purpose of selection criteria is to choose police recruits who will eventually turn into effective and efficient officers. There have been a number of efforts to determine the specific selection criteria that predict future police performance, including a comprehensive analysis by Allan and Norma Roe.[85] The Roes' data were reanalyzed and simplified in a subsequent study by criminologists Bernard Cohen and Jan Chaiken.[86] Interestingly, Cohen and Chaiken found that recruits' performance on written civil service tests was the best predictor of subsequent arrest activity, investigative skills, evidence gathering, and crime scene management, and was associated with supervisory ratings and career advancement. Their findings give valuable support to the predictive value of tests that measure the capacity to know, perceive, and think. Other factors that predict above average performance are oral interviews, prior work experience, numerical ability, IQ, age, and education. Conversely, unsatisfactory performances were turned in by officers with low educational levels, prior work problems, and poor probationary periods. Among the other important findings were that shorter officers were more likely to become assault victims; single and highly educated officers were more likely to resign their jobs, probably because they maintain greater mobility.[87]

Developing Effective Police Managers

A difficult task facing police administrators is developing effective leaders and selecting them for promotion to leadership positions.

One aspect of this problem is the mechanism for selecting senior officers. No single criterion is used for promotion, but most departments use a combination of oral and written tests, seniority, and supervisory ratings and evaluations. A few departments give credit for educational achievement, but these are still a distinct minority.

Promotional tests usually measure the candidate's knowledge of law, administration, and police tactics. Some departments have attempted to devise methods to make the promotion process fairer. For example, to aid in their promotion tests, the Washington, D.C., police identified the following qualities and abilities a senior officer should have: leadership, judgment, decisiveness, sensitivity, initiative, written communication, oral communication, and stress tolerance. Written and oral promotion tests were then based on these criteria. The following is an example of an oral test question:

> As a platoon leader, you have reviewed a disciplinary report submitted to you by a sergeant. The report has been meticulously prepared and you are impressed with the sergeant's effort. However, you disagree with his conclusion and recommendation. You have noticed that the report omitted some basic points in an investigation. Further, you know that this report is the first disciplinary report from this sergeant. How would you handle this situation?[88]

Despite such efforts, minority group members have questioned promotion tests because of their alleged failure to ensure proportionate racial representation within all police ranks.

Another issue related to the development of competent police managers is the use of available resources to improve and promote their leadership qualities. National, state, and local agencies have developed both in-service and preservice training programs. The FBI provides training at the National Police Academy in Quantico, Virginia. Though this program is primarily intended to teach the fundamentals of police work, it can also help trainees develop the confidence necessary for effective leadership. On a local level, colleges and universities have sponsored training courses in police executive development. One example is the Southern Police Institute at the University of Louisville, which offers a 14-week course directed at improving police executive qualities and features classroom sessions, seminars, and small-group interaction. On a state level, training academies (some run under the auspices of the civil service and others controlled by the state police) provide regular career development sessions for improving police leadership skills. A similar program, the Police Executive Training Institute (POLEX) has been in operation at Penn State University since the early 1970s.

These leadership training efforts stress many qualities, including the ability to communicate effectively with subordinates and understand their needs, the ability to organize and manage tasks of great complexity, and the capacity to analyze situations and make intelligent, rational decisions. Often leadership training borrows techniques from the business world; tomorrow's police executives may be quite similar to their corporate counterparts.

Improving Police Productivity

Government spending cutbacks, forced by inflation and legislative tax-cutting measures, have prompted belt-tightening in many areas of public service. Police departments have not been spared the budgetary pinch caused by decreased government spending. To combat the probable damage that would be caused by police service cutbacks, police administrators have sought to increase the productivity of their line, support, and administrative staff.

As used today, the term **police productivity** refers to the amount of actual order maintenance, crime control, and other law enforcement activities provided by individual police officers and concomitantly by police departments as a whole. By improving police productivity, a department can keep the peace, deter crime, apprehend criminals, and provide useful public services without necessarily increasing its costs. This goal is accomplished by having each police officer operate with greater efficiency, thus using fewer resources to achieve greater effectiveness.

Confounding the situation and heightening its importance has been the dramatic increase in the cost of maintaining police personnel, including such items as salaries, fringe benefits, and retirement plans. Moreover, the modern police department depends on expensive electronic gear, communications systems, computers, weapons, and transportation, and the cost of basic supplies from gasoline to paper is constantly increasing. It has been estimated that the cost of running U.S. police departments has increased to almost $14 billion annually.[89]

Despite the oft-stated desire to increase police effectiveness, serious questions have been raised about how the police accomplish their assigned tasks. As previously mentioned, the Rand Corporation study of police detective services strongly assailed the productivity of investigators.[90] Patrol forces have also been concerned about their productivity. One basic complaint has been that the average patrol officer spends relatively little time on what is considered "real" police work. More often than not, highly skilled police officers can be found writing reports, waiting in court corridors, getting involved in domestic disputes, and handling what are generally characterized as "miscellaneous noncriminal matters."

PRODUCTIVITY MEASURES. How have police administrators responded to the challenge of improving police productivity? As mentioned previously, applying modern technology to information, communication, and record-keeping systems has helped police improve their ability to respond to calls in a more effective fashion. For example, the 911 emergency code has been used in many cities to improve police response time.

Another productivity improvement measure has been simply to ask individual police officers to shoulder a greater workload. Many jurisdictions have decreased the number of officers in patrol cars from two to one, saving approximately $100,000 per beat annually (since three shifts are assigned to each patrol area). Research indicates that officers in one-person cars are as safe and productive as officers in two-person cars.[91]

Another move to increase police efficiency has involved consolidating police services. This means combining small departments (usually with under 10 employees) in adjoining areas into a superagency that services the previously fragmented jurisdictions. **Consolidation** has the benefit of creating departments large enough to utilize expanded services such as crime labs, training centers, communication centers, and emergency units, which are not cost-effective in smaller departments. This procedure is controversial, since it demands that existing lines of political and administrative authority be drastically changed. Nevertheless, consolidation of departments or special services (such as a regional computer center) has been attempted in California (Los Angeles sheriff's department), Massachusetts, New York, and Illinois.[92]

Some popular police department consolidation and productivity improvement techniques are listed below:[93]

1. *Informal arrangements.* **Informal arrangements,** are unwritten cooperative agreements between localities to perform a task collectively that would be mutually beneficial (e.g., monitoring neighboring radio frequencies so that needed backup can be provided). For example, the Metro Task Force program implemented in New Jersey committed state troopers to help local police officers in urban areas for limited periods and assignments.[94]

2. *Sharing.* This refers to the provision or reception of services that aid in the execution of a law enforcement function (e.g., the sharing of a communications system by several local agencies).

3. *Pooling.* This involves the combining of resources by two or more agencies to perform a specified function under a predetermined, often formalized arrangement with direct involvement by all parties (e.g., the use of a city-county law enforcement building or training academy, or the establishment of a crime task force such as those used in St. Louis, Kansas City, Topeka, Tuscaloosa, and Des Moines). In Phoenix, Arizona, the police department and the Phoenix South Community Mental Health Center have a shared relationship called the Family Stress Team. The two-person teams conduct on-site crisis intervention and attempt to stabilize family disputes in order to prevent repeated requests for police services. An evaluation indicates that the project has been a major labor-saving device.[95]

4. *Contracting.* Contracting is a limited and voluntary approach in which one government enters into a formal, binding agreement to provide all or certain specified law enforcement services (e.g., communications, patrol service) to another government for an established fee. Many communities that contract for full law enforcement service do so at the time they incorporate to avoid the costs of establishing their own police capability.

5. *Police service districts.* These are areas, usually within an individual county, where a special level of service is provided and financed through a special tax or assessment. In California, residents of an unincorporated portion of a county may petition to form such a district to provide more intensive patrol coverage than is available through existing systems. Such service may be provided by a sheriff, another police department, or a private person or agency. This system is used in Contra Costa and San Mateo counties in California and Suffolk and Nassau counties in New York State.

6. *Civilian employees.* Another practice used to increase police productivity is the employment of civilians in administrative support or even in some line activities. Their duties have included operating communications gear; performing clerical work, planning, and research; and staffing traffic control ("meter maids"). The use of civilian employees can be a considerable savings to taxpayers because their salaries are lower than those of regular police officers. In addition, they allow trained, experienced officers to spend more time on direct crime control and enforcement activities. It is not surprising that the FBI estimates that today almost 20 percent of police employees are civilians.[96]

7. *Multitasking.* Multitasking involves training police officers to carry out other functions of municipal government. For example, in Kalamazoo and Grosse Point, Michigan, the roles of fire fighters and police officers have been merged into a job called a public safety officer. The idea is to increase the number of people trained in both areas of expertise in order to have the potential for putting more cops at the scene of a crime or more fire fighters at a blaze than was possible when the two tasks were separated. The system provides greater coverage at far less cost. Although employees resisted the project at first, it seems to have become established as a labor- and cost-saving device.[97]

8. *Use of technology.* As you may recall, police agencies have embraced the computer revolution in order to improve their overall efficiency and effectiveness. Computers are not the only technology that can improve productivity. For example, Raymond Surette has described the use of video patrol to improve police surveillance of downtown shopping districts without increasing manpower costs. This project entailed the use of 100 video housings on traffic light poles, which actually housed 21 television cameras manned round the clock by volunteers. An ongoing evaluation found the program helped reduce crime in the area while increasing citizens' sense of security.[98]

9. *Special assignments.* It is also possible to increase productivity and reduce costs by training officers for special assignments and using them only when the occasion arises. For example, the Special Enforcement Team in Lakewood, Colorado, receives training in a variety of police tasks such as radar operation, surveillance, traffic investigation, and criminal investigations; they specialize in tactical operations such as crowd control and security. Use of the high impact team where needed has helped save thousands of dollars that had previously gone for overtime pay.[99]

10. *Budget supplementation.* Forced to stay within the confines of a limited budget, some police departments have looked for innovative sources of income to supplement their budget. Police in Chicago instituted a private fund drive that raised over $1.5 million to purchase protective clothing, and other departments have created ongoing private foundations to raise funds to support police-related activities. In New York City, $1.3 million was raised in one year for scholarships, health care, and training. Other schemes include the sale of property seized in crime-related activity such as drug smuggling. The Fort Lauderdale, Florida, police raised $5.5 million in three years by selling forfeited goods. Other budget-supplementing activities have included conducting fund-raising events, using traffic fines for police services, and the enactment of special taxes that go directly for police or services.[100]

THE LIMITS OF PRODUCTIVITY. Although most experts agree that efforts to improve police productivity are useful, police administrators must also be aware of the potential hazards of placing too much emphasis on constantly increasing performance. Justice experts Mark Moore and George Kelling question the wisdom of administrators who emphasize the technological aspects of police productivity at the expense of public service.[101] They state:

> The enormous investment in telephones, radios, and cars that now allow the police to respond to crime calls in under five minutes (often with more than one car) has bought little crime control, no greater sense of security, and has prevented the police from taking order maintenance and service functions seriously.[102]

Moore and Kelling believe that a truly productive police department will be more concerned with public well-being and security than with a futile effort to control crime. They suggest an increase in foot patrols in order to promote a sense of public security; the use of special decoys and stakeouts designed to prevent particular kinds of crime, such as muggings; the development of intelligence networks to combat street crimes; and concentration on the relatively small numbers of chronic criminal offenders. Moore and Kelling also call for a general reorganization of police departments. They feel that police should be organized along geographical lines, with local commanders given control over all police activities (patrol, detection, traffic, and so on) in their area of jurisdiction. Moore and Kelling believe that this will improve community relations and encourage community participation in police work, the single most important aspect of improving police productivity.

These views are shared by David Farmer in his important book on police resource management. According to Farmer, police agencies must emerge from the isolation that has characterized them since the concept of professional policing replaced old-style machine politics. He calls for a new form of police agency characterized by capability in three new areas of expertise. First, to increase productivity, these new agencies must be able to work with other public agencies to develop plans and policies that can identify optimum levels of law, order, and justice. Secondly, police agencies must assume a new position of leadership that can help mobilize other agencies and individuals to achieve social order. Finally, police agencies must make an ongoing effort to utilize research findings and technological innovations in their daily activities.[103]

■ SUMMARY

Present-day police departments operate in a quasi-military fashion; policy generally emanates from the top of the hierarchy, and it is difficult for both police officers and the public to understand or identify the source of orders and directives. Most police officers therefore use a great deal of discretion when making daily on-the-job decisions.

The most common law enforcement agencies are local police departments, which conduct patrol, investigative, and traffic functions, as well as many different support activities. Many questions have been raised about the effectiveness of police work, and some research efforts seem to indicate that police are not effective crime fighters. There are indications, however, that aggressive police work, the threat of formal action, and cooperation within departments can have a measurable impact on crime.

Police departments have also been concerned with developing proper techniques for training their leaders, recruiting new officers, promoting deserving veterans, and developing technical expertise.

■ QUESTIONS

1. Should the primary police role be law enforcement or community services?
2. Should a police chief be permitted to promote an officer with special skills to a supervisory position, or should all officers be forced to spend "time in rank"?
3. Do the advantages of proactive policing outweigh the disadvantages?

4. Should all police recruits take the same physical tests, or are different requirements permissible for male and female applicants?
5. Would you like to live in a society that abolished police discretion and used a full enforcement policy?

■ NOTES

1. Clarence Schrag, *Crime and Justice: American Style* (Washington, D.C.: U.S. Government Printing Office, 1971), pp. 142–50.

2. John Webster, "Police Task and Time Study," *Journal of Criminal Law, Criminology, and Police Science* 61 (1970): 94–100.

3. J. Robert Lilly, "What Are the Police Now Doing," *Journal of Police Science and Administration* 6 (1978): 51–53.

4. Michael Brown, *Working the Street* (New York: Russell Sage Foundation, 1981); Albert J. Reiss, *The Police and the Public* (New Haven, Conn.: Yale University Press, 1971); Norman Weiner, *The Role of Police in Urban Society: Conflict and Consequences* (Indianapolis: Bobbs-Merrill Co., 1976).

5. George Antunes and Eric Scott, "Calling the Cops: Police Telephone Operations and Citizen Calls for Service," *Journal of Criminal Justice* 9 (1981): 165–74.

6. Steven Meagher, "Police Patrol Styles: How Pervasive Is Community Variation?" *Journal of Police Science and Administration* 13 (1985): 36–45.

7. Cheryl Maxson, Margaret Little, and Malcolm Klein, "Police Response to Runaway and Missing Children: A Conceptual Framework for Research and Policy," *Crime and Delinquency* 34 (1988): 84–102.

8. Peter Finn and Monique Sullivan, *Police Response to Special Populations* (Washington, D.C.: National Institute of Justice, 1988).

9. George Pugh, "The Police Officer: Qualities, Roles and Concepts," *Police Science and Administration* 14 (1986): 1–6.

10. Egon Bittner, *The Functions of Police in Modern Society* (Cambridge, Mass.: Oelgeschlager, Gunn & Hain, 1980), p. 8; see also James Q. Wilson, "The Police in the Ghetto," in *The Police and the Community*, Robert F. Steadman, ed. (Baltimore: Johns Hopkins University Press, 1974), p. 68.

11. George Kelling, *Police and Communities: The Quiet Revolution* (Washington, D.C.: National Institute of Justice, 1988).

12. Jerome Skolnick, *Justice without Trial* (New York: John Wiley & Sons, 1966).

13. Gregory Howard Williams, *The Law and Politics of Police Discretion* (Westport, Conn.: Greenwood Press, 1984).

14. Dennis Powell, "Race, Rank, and Police Discretion," *Journal of Police Science and Administration* 9 (1981): 383–89.

15. Douglas Smith and Jody Klein, "Police Control of Interpersonal Disputes," *Social Problems* 31 (1984): 468–81.

16. Allan Meyers, Timothy Heeren, Ralph Hingson, and David Kovenock, "Cops and Drivers: Police Discretion and the Enforcement of Maine's 1981 DUI Law," *Journal of Criminal Justice* 15 (1987): 362–68; Stephen Mastrofski, R. Richard Ritti, and Debra Hoffmaster, "Organizational Determinants of Police Discretion: The Case of Drinking and Driving," *Journal of Criminal Justice* 15 (1987): 387–401.

17. William Westly, *Violence and the Police: A Sociological Study of Law, Custom, and Morality* (Cambridge: Mass.: M.I.T. Press, 1970).

18. Nathan Goldman, *The Differential Selection of Juvenile Offenders for Court Appearance* (New York: National Council on Crime and Delinquency, 1963).

19. Aaron Cicourel, *The Social Organization of Juvenile Justice* (New York: John Wiley & Sons, 1968).

20. Irvin Piliavin and Scott Briar, "Police Encounters with Juveniles," *American Journal of Sociology* 70 (1964): 206.

21. Dale Dannefer and Russell Schutt, "Race and Juvenile Justice Processing in Court and Police Agencies," *American Journal of Sociology* 87 (1982): 1113–32.

22. Powell, "Race, Rank, and Police Discretion."

23. Christy Visher, "Arrest Decisions and Notions of Chivalry," *Criminology* 21 (1983): 5–28.

24. Douglas Smith and Christy Visher, "Street-Level Justice: Situational Determinants of Police Arrest Decisions," *Social Problems* 29 (1981): 167–177.

25. See, generally, William Wilbanks, *The Myth of a Racist Criminal Justice System* (Monterey, Calif.: Brooks-Cole Publishing Co., 1987); see also Smith and Klein, "Police Control of Interpersonal Disputes."

26. Douglas Smith, Christy Visher, and Laura Davidson, "Equity and Discretionary Justice: The Influence of Race on Police Arrest Decisions," *Journal of Criminal Law and Criminology* 75 (1984): 234–49.

27. Cecil Willis and Richard Wells, "The Police and Child Abuse: An Analysis of Police Decisions to Report Illegal Behavior," *Criminology* 26 (1988): 695–716.

28. See, for example, James Q. Wilson, *Varieties of Police Behavior: The Management of Law and Order in Eight Communities* (Cambridge, Mass.: Harvard University Press, 1968). James Fyfe has found that the relationship between police use of deadly force and race differs between departments; see James Fyfe, "Blind Justice? Police Shootings in Memphis," paper presented at the Academy of Criminal Justice Sciences, Philadelphia, March 1981.

29. Marvin Krohn, James Curry, and Shirley Nelson-Kilger, "Is Chivalry Dead? An Analysis of Changes in Police Dispositions of Males and Females," *Criminology* 21 (1983): 417–37.

30. National Advisory Council on Criminal Justice Statistics and Goals, *Police* (Washington, D.C.: U.S. Government Printing Office, 1976), pp. 21–22.

31. David Aaronson, Michael Musheno, and Thomas Dienes, *Public Policy and Police Discretion* (New York: Clark Boardman, 1984).

32. Wayne Hanewicz, Christine Cassidy-Riske, Lynn Fransway, and Michael O'Neill, "Improving the Linkages between Domestic Violence Referral Agencies and the Police," *Journal of Criminal Justice* 10 (1982): 497–504.

33. John Gardiner, *Traffic and the Police: Variations in Law Enforcement Policy* (Cambridge, Mass.: Harvard University Press, 1969).

34. Brown, *Working the Street*, p. 290.

35. American Bar Association, *Standards Relating to Urban Police Function* (New York: Institute of Judicial Administration, 1974), standard 2.2.

36. Edward Ammann and Jim Hey, "The Discretionary Patrol Unit," *FBI Law Enforcement Bulletin* 58 (1989): 19–22.

37. Reiss, *The Police and the Public*, p. 19.

38. Bittner, *The Functions of Police in Modern Society*, p. 127.

39. See the analysis of the police role earlier in this chapter.

40. Wilson, *Varieties of Police Behavior*.

41. Ibid., p. 31.

42. See Harlan Hahn, "A Profile of Urban Police," in *The Ambivalent Force*, A. Niederhoffer and A. Blumberg, eds. (Hinsdale, Ill.: The Dyrden Press, 1976), p. 59.

43. George Kelling et al., *The Kansas City Preventive Patrol Experiment: A Summary Report* (Washington, D.C.: Police Foundation, 1974).

44. Ibid., pp. 3–4.

45. Ibid.

46. James Q. Wilson and Barbara Boland, "The Effect of Police on Crime," *Law and Society Review* 12 (1978): 367–84.

47. Robert Sampson and Jacqueline Cohen, "Deterrent Effects of the Police on Crime: A Replication and Theoretical Extension," *Law and Society Review* 22 (1988): 163–91.

48. Lawrence Sherman, "Policing Communities: What Works," in Crime and Justice, vol. 8, A. J. Reiss and Michael Tonry, eds. (Chicago: University of Chicago Press, 1986), pp. 366–79.

49. Ibid., p. 368.

50. H. Lawrence Ross, *Detering the Drunk Driver: Legal Policy and Social Control* (Lexington, Mass.: D.C. Heath, 1982); Samuel Walker, *Sense and Nonsense about Crime* (Monterey, Calif.: Brooks/Cole, 1985), pp. 82–85.

51. Perry Shapiro and Harold Votey, "Deterrence and Subjective Probabilities of Arrest: Modeling Individual Decisions to Drink and Drive in Sweden," *Law and Society Review* 18 (1984): 111–49.

52. Douglas Smith and Patrick Gartin, "Specifying Specific Deterrence: The Influence of Arrest on Future Criminal Activity," *American Sociological Review* 54 (1989): 94–105.

53. Mitchell Chamlin, "Crime and Arrests: An Autoregressive Integrated Moving Average (ARIMA) Approach," *Journal of Quantitative Criminology* 4 (1988): 247–55.

54. Lawrence Sherman and Richard Berk, "The Specific Deterrent Effects of Arrest for Domestic Assault," *American Sociological Review* 49 (1984): 261–72; Richard Berk and Phyllis J. Newman, "Does Arrest Really Deter Wife Battery? An Effort to Replicate the Findings of the Minneapolis Spouse Abuse Experiment," *American Sociological Review* 50 (1985): 253–62.

55. See also Richard Berk, Gordon Smyth, and Lawrence Sherman, "When Random Assignment Fails: Some Lessons from the Minneapolis Spouse Abuse Experiment," *Journal of Quantitative Criminology* 4 (1988): 209–16.

56. Gerald Carden, *Police Revitalization* (Lexington, Mass.: Lexington Books, 1977), pp. 275–76.

57. Simon Singer, "The Fear of Reprisal and the Failure of Victims to Report a Personal Crime," *Journal of Quantitative Criminology* 4 (1988): 289–302.

58. Frances Lawrenz, James Lembo, and Thomas Schade, "Time Series Analysis of the Effect of a Domestic Violence Directive on the Number of Arrests per Day," *Journal of Criminal Justice* 17 (1989): 493–99.

59. Kathleen Ferraro, "Policing Woman Battering," *Social Problems* 36 (1989): 61–74.

60. See Belton Cobb, *The First Detectives* (London: Faber & Faber, 1957).

61. See, for example, James Q. Wilson, "Movie Cops—Romantic vs. Real," *New York Magazine*, 19 August, 1968, pp. 39–41.

62. For a view of the modern detective, see William Sanders, *Detective Work: A Study of Criminal Investigations* (New York: Free Press, 1977).

63. James Ahern, *Police in Trouble* (New York: Hawthorn Books, 1972), pp. 83–85.

64. James Q. Wilson, *The Investigators: Managing FBI and Narcotics Agents* (New York: Basic Books, 1978), pp. 21–23.

65. Peter Greenwood and J. Petersilia, *The Criminal Investigation Process*, vol. 1., *Summary and Police Implications* (Santa Monica, Calif.: Rand Corporation, 1975).

66. Mark Willman and John Snortum, "Detective Work: The Criminal Investigation Process in a Medium-Size Police Department," *Criminal Justice Review* 9 (1984): 33–39.

67. Police Executive Research Forum, *Calling the Police: Citizen Reporting of Serious Crime* (Washington, D.C.: Police Executive Research Forum, 1981).

68. John Eck, *Solving Crimes: The Investigation of Burglary and Robbery* (Washington, D.C.: Police Executive Research Forum, 1984).

69. For a more complete description of these functions, see Robert Sheehan and Gary Cordner, *Introduction to Police Administration* 2d ed. (Reading, Mass.: Addison-Wesley, 1986).

70. See, for example, Richard Larson, *Urban Police Patrol Analysis* (Cambridge, Mass.: M.I.T. Press, 1972).

71. Samuel Walker, *The Police in America* (New York: McGraw-Hill, 1983), p. 265.

72. Personal communication, National Commission on Accreditation for Law Enforcement, 11 January 1989.

73. Orlando M. Wilson, *Police Administration*, 2d ed. (New York: McGraw-Hill, 1963).

74. John Angell, "Toward an Alternative to the Classic Police Organizational Arrangements: A Democratic Model," *Criminology* 9 (1971): 185–206.

75. Peter F. Drucker, "What Results Should You Expect? A User's Guide to MBO," *Public Administration Review* 36 (1970): 12–19.

76. Harry Hatry and John Greiner, *Improving the Use of Management by Objectives in Police Departments* (Washington, D.C.: National Institute of Justice, 1986), p. 1.

77. Ibid., p. 73.

78. This section leans heavily on Alan Brenner, "Psychological Screening of Police Applicants," in *Critical Issues in Policing*, Roger Dunham and Geoffrey Alpert, eds (Prospect Heights, Ill.: Waveland Press, 1989), pp. 72–87; Elizabeth Burbeck and Adrian Furnham, "Police Officer Selection: A Critical Review of the Literature," *Journal of Police Science and Administration* 13 (1985): 58–69; George Hargrave and Deirdre Hiatt, "Law Enforcement Selection with the Interview, MMPI, and CPI: A Study of Reliability and Validity," *Journal of Police Science and Administration* 15 (1987): 110–14; Jack Aylward, "Psychological Testing and Police Selection," *Journal of Police Science and Administration* 13 (1985): 201–10.

79. David Carter and Allen Sapp, *The State of Police Education: Critical Findings* (Washington, D.C.: Police Executive Research Forum, 1988).

80. George Pugh, "The California Psychological Inventory and Police Selection," *Journal of Police Science and Administration* 3 (1985): 172–77; Charles Bartel, "Psychological Characteristics of Small Town Police Officers," *Journal of Political Science and Administration* 10 (1982): 58–63.

81. See, generally, Hargrave and Hiatt, "Law Enforcement Selection with the Interview, MMPI, an CPI"; Aylward, "Psychological Testing and Police Selection."

82. Benner, "Psychological Screening of Police Applicants"; Hargrave and Hiatt, "Law Enforcement Selection with the Interview," MMPI and CPI," pp. 110–13.

83. Burbeck and Furnham, "Police Officer Selection: A Critical Review of the Literature," p. 66–68.

84. Robin Inwald, "Administrative Legal and Ethical Practices in the Psychological Testing of Law Enforcement Officers," *Journal of Criminal Justice* 13 (1985): 367–72.

85. Allan Roe and Norma Roe, *Police Selection: A Technical Summary of Validity Studies* (Ogden, Utah: Diagnostic Specialists, Inc., 1982).

86. Bernard Cohen and Jan Chaiken, *Investigators Who Perform Well* (Washington, D.C.: National Institute of Justice, 1987), pp. 16–20.

87. Ibid., p. 20.

88. R. Crytzer et al., "Promotion Process," *Police Chief* 48 (January 1981): 41–47.

89. Bureau of Justice Statistics *Report to the Nation on Crime and Justice*, (Washington, D.C.: U.S. Government Printing Office, 1988), p. 36.

90. Greenwood and Petersilia, *The Criminal Investigation Process*; Peter Greenwood et al., *The Criminal Investigation Process*, vol. 3, *Observations and Analysis* (Santa Monica, Calif.: Rand Corporation, 1975).

91. George Kelling, *What Works—Research and the Police* (Washington, D.C.: National Institute of Justice, 1988).

92. Thomas McAninch and Jeff Sanders, "Police Attitudes toward Consolidation in Bloomington/Normal, Illinois: A Case Study," *Journal of Police Science and Administration* 16 (1988): 95–105.

93. Adapted from Terry Koepsell and Charles Gerard, *Small Police Agency Consolidation: Suggested Approaches* (Washington, D.C.: U.S. Government Printing Office, 1979).

94. James Garofalo and Dave Hanson, *The Metro Task Force: A Program of Intergovernmental Cooperation in Law Enforcement*, (Washington, D.C.: National Institute of Justice, 1984, unpublished).

95. Thomas Jahn and Maryann Conrad, "The Family Stress Team Approach in Curbing Domestic Violence," *Police Chief* 52 (1985): 66–67.

96. Federal Bureau of Investigation, *Uniform Crime Reports, 1987* (Washington, D.C.: U.S. Government Printing Office, 1988), p. 236.

97. AP, " 'Firecops' Do Double Duty in Some Towns," *Omaha World Herald*, 2 March 1986, p. 13-a.

98. Raymond Surette, "Video Street Patrol: Media Technology and Street Crime," *Police Science and Administration* 13 (1985): 78–85.

99. Kenneth Perry, "Tactical Units Reduce Overtime Costs," *Police Chief* 52 (1985): 57–58.

100. Lindsey Stellwagen and Kimberly Wylie, *Strategies for Supplementing the Police Budget* (Washington, D.C.: National Institute of Justice, 1985).

101. Mark Moore and George Kelling, "To Serve and Protect: Learning from Police History," *The Public Interest* 70 (1983): 49–65.

102. Ibid., p. 62.

103. David Farmer, *Crime Control: The Use and Misuse of Police Resources* (New York: Plenum, 1984).

8

Issues in Policing

For the past three decades, the function of police in society has aroused considerable public interest. Americans appear to be genuinely concerned about the quality and effectiveness of their local police. On the one hand, most people approve of the police and hold generally favorable attitudes toward them; one national survey found that about 60 percent of all Americans believe that police do a good job against crime.[1] On the other hand, such approval is far from universal: only 39 percent of black citizens hold positive attitudes toward police, and one national survey of high school students found that about 30 percent consider police dishonest and immoral.[2] It is not surprising therefore that people are arming themselves in record numbers, depending on private security forces, and organizing self-help groups to reduce their fear of crime.

Concern about police attitudes and behavior is not limited to the general public. Police administrators and other law enforcement experts have focused their attention on issues that may influence the effectiveness and efficiency of police performance in the field. Some of their concerns are an outgrowth of the professionalization of policing: Does an independent police culture exist? If so, what are its characteristics? Do police officers develop a unique "working personality," and, if so, does it influence their job performance? Do police officers develop "styles" that make some officers too aggressive while others remain passive and inert? Is policing too stressful an occupation?

Another area of concern is the social makeup and composition of police departments: Who should be recruited as police officers? Are minorities and women being attracted to police work? If so, what have been their experiences on the force? Should police officers have a college education?

In addition to these issues, important questions are being raised about the problems police departments face in their interface with the society they are entrusted with supervising: Are police officers too forceful and brutal? Do they discriminate in their use of deadly force? Are police officers corrupt, and how can police deviance be controlled?

The Police Profession

All professions have distinct aspects that distinguish them from other occupations and institutions. Policing is no exception. Police experts have long sought to understand the unique nature of the police experience in order to determine how the challenges of police work shape the field and mold its employees. This section examines some of the factors that make policing unique.

Police Culture

It has been suggested that the experience of becoming a police officer and the nature of the job itself cause most officers to band together in a **police subculture,** characterized by clannishness, secrecy, and isolation from others in society (the so-called **blue curtain**). Police officers tend to socialize together and believe that their occupation cuts them off from relationships with civilians. Joining the police subculture means always having to stick up for fellow officers against outsiders, maintaining a tough "macho" exterior personality, and being mistrustful of the motives and behavior of outsiders to the police field.[3]

While the general public holds positive attitudes toward the police, support is less favorable in urban inner city areas.

It is generally believed that the forces that support a police culture develop from on-the-job experiences. Most officers, both male and female, originally join police forces because of a desire to help people, fight crime, and engage in an interesting, exciting, prestigious career with a high degree of job security.[4] They often find the social reality of police work does not mesh with their original career goals. In a well-respected work, *Working the Street*, Michael K. Brown argues that police officers create their own culture to meet the recurring anxiety and emotional stress that are part of police work.[5] The culture encourages decisiveness in the face of uncertainty and the ability to make split-second judgments that may later be subject to extreme criticism. Brown finds that the police culture is grounded on three principles: honor, loyalty, and individualism. Honor is given and received for risk-taking behavior, such as facing an armed assailant, that a "civilian" could never fully understand or appreciate. To be honored, the officer must be loyal to partner and peers. Loyalty demands secrecy and the belief that a police officer's most important obligation is to back up and support fellow officers. At the same time, the police culture idealizes the individualistic officer who is autonomous, aggressive, and capable of taking charge of any situation. Brown finds that individualism is compatible with loyalty, however, because police officers will need the backup and support of their partners when they take action that does not conform to accepted police procedures.

The police culture has developed in response to the insulated, dangerous lifestyle of police officers. As Egon Bittner plainly states, "Policing is a dangerous occupation and the availability of unquestioned support and loyalty is not something officers could readily do without."[6]

Police Personality

It has become commonplace to argue that being a member of the police subculture causes many police officers to develop unique personality traits that set them apart from the average citizen. The typical police personality is thought to include such traits as **authoritarianism,** suspicion, racism, hostility, insecurity, conservatism, and **cynicism**.[7] Such values and attitudes are believed to produce what William Westly calls the "blue curtain," a barrier that isolates police officers from the rest of society.[8]

In a similar vein, Jerome Skolnick has observed that the police officer's "working personality" is shaped by constant exposure to danger and the need to use force and authority to reduce and control threatening situations.[9] Police are suspicious of the public they serve and defensive about the actions of their fellow officers.

There are two opposing views on the cause of this phenomenon. One position holds that police departments attract recruits who are by nature cynical, authoritarian, secretive, and so on. Other experts maintain that police officers develop these character traits through their socialization and experience on the police force itself.[10] Since research has produced evidence supportive of both viewpoints, the question of how the police personality develops, if indeed one actually exists, is unresolved.

A number of researchers have attempted to describe the development of the police personality. One of the most influential early studies was conducted by social psychologist Milton Rokeach with police officers in Lansing, Michigan. Rokeach found some significant differences when he compared police officers' personality traits with those of a national sample of private citizens: police officers seemed more oriented toward self-control and obedience than the average citizen; in addition, police were more interested in personal goals, such as "an exciting life," and less interested in social goals, such as "a world at peace."[11] When the values of veteran officers were compared with those of recruits, Rokeach and his associates found evidence that police officers' on-the-job experience did not significantly influence their personalities, leading him to conclude that most police officers probably had a unique value orientation and personality when they first embarked on their career in the police force.

Since the Rokeach research was published, there have been numerous efforts to determine whether typical police recruits do indeed possess a "unique" personality that sets them apart from the average citizen. The results have been a mixed bag. While some studies conclude that police values are different from those of the general adult population, other studies reach an opposing conclusion; some researchers have found that police officers are actually psychologically healthier than the general population, less depressed and anxious and more social and assertive.[12]

There is probably more evidence that a police personality is developed through the ongoing process of doing police work. In his study of one urban police department, John Van Maanen found that the typical police recruit is a sincere individual motivated to join the force for reasons of job security and salary, the belief that the job will be interesting and flexible, and the desire to enter an occupation that can benefit society.[13] Van Maanen argues that the police personality is developed through the experience of becoming an officer of the law. At the police academy, highly idealistic recruits are first taught to have a strong sense of camaraderie with fellow rookies. They begin to admire the exploits of the experienced officers who serve as their instructors. From them the police trainee learns when to play it by the book and when to ignore departmental rules and rely on personal discretion.

When rookies are finally assigned street duty, their **field training officer** teaches them the ins and outs of police work, helping them through the rite of passage of becoming a "real cop." As the folklore, myths, and legends surrounding the department are communicated to recruits, they begin to understand the rules of police work. Van Maanen suggests that "the adjustment of a newcomer in police departments is one which follows the line of least resistance."[14] By adopting the sentiments and behavior of their peers, recruits avoid censure by their department, their supervisor, and, most important, their colleagues. Thus young officers adapt their personality to that of the "ideal cop."

George Kirkham, a professor who also became a police officer, has described how the explosive and violent situations he faced as a police officer changed his own personality:

> As someone who had always regarded policemen as a "paranoid" lot, I discovered in the daily round of violence which became part of my life that chronic suspiciousness is something that a good cop cultivates in the interest of going home to his family each evening.[15]

Egon Bittner concludes that an "esprit de corps" develops in police work as a function of the dangerous and unpleasant tasks police officers are required to do. Police solidarity, a "one for all, and all for one" attitude, is one of the most cherished aspects of the police occupation.[16]

THE CYNICISM FACTOR. In what is probably the best known study of police personality, *Behind the Shield*, Arthur Niederhoffer examined the assumption that most police officers develop into cynics as a function of their daily duties.[17] William Westly had earlier maintained that police officers learn to mistrust the citizens they protect as a result of being constantly faced with keeping people in line and believing that most people are out to break the law or harm a police officer.[18] Niederhoffer tested Westly's assumption by distributing a survey measuring attitudes and values to 220 New York City police officers. Among his most important findings were that police cynicism did increase with length of service, that patrol officers with college educations become quite cynical if they are denied promotion, and that quasi-military police academy training caused new recruits to quickly become cynical about themselves. For example, Niederhoffer found that nearly 80 percent of first-day recruits believed that the police department was an "efficient, smoothly operating organization"; two months later, less than a third held that belief. Similarly, half the new recruits believed that a police superior was "very interested in the welfare of his subordinates"; two months later, that number declined to 13 percent.[19]

The development and maintenance of negative attitudes and values by police officers may have an extremely detrimental effect on their job performance. In a review of police literature, Robert Regoli and Eric Poole found evidence that a police officer's feelings of cynicism intensify the need to maintain respect and increase the desire to exert authority over others.[20] Unfortunately, as police escalate the use of authority, citizens learn to mistrust and fear them. In turn the citizens' feelings of hostility and anger create feelings of potential danger among police officers, resulting in "police paranoia."[21] Regoli and Poole also found that maintaining negative attitudes contributes to the police tendency to be very conservative and resistant to change, factors that interfere with the efficiency of police work.[22]

Although cynicism may hurt the relationship between police and the public, it might actually help the police officer's career within the department. In a longitudinal study of police officers in Georgia, Richard Anson and his associates found that those exhibiting the most cynical attitudes were the most likely to receive high supervisory ratings. They conclude:

> Cynicism is a valued quality of the personality of the police officer and is positively evaluated by important individuals in police organizations.[23]

It should be noted, however, that a number of researchers have found little evidence that a "typical" police personality actually exists. Studies by sociologists Larry Tifft,[24] David Bayley and Harold Mendelsohn,[25] and Robert Balch[26] indicate that even experienced police officers are quite similar to the average citizen. Nevertheless, the weight of existing evidence generally points to the existence of a unique police personality.

Police Officer Style

Policing involves a multitude of diverse tasks, including peacekeeping, criminal investigation, traffic control, and providing emergency medical services. Part of one's socialization as a police officer is developing a working attitude, or *style*, that is used to confront and interpret these various aspects of policing. For example, some police officers may view their job as a well-paid civil service position that stresses careful compliance with written departmental rules and procedures. Other officers may see themselves as part of the "thin blue line" that protects the public from wrongdoers. They will use any means to "get their man," even if it involves such "cheating" as planting evidence on an obviously guilty person who so far has escaped detection. Should the police bend the rules in order to protect the public? Carl Klockars has referred to this dilemma as the **"Dirty Harry Problem,"** after the popular Clint Eastwood movie character who routinely (and successfully) violates all known standards of police work.[27]

Several studies have attempted to define and classify police styles into behavioral clusters. These classifications, called typologies, attempt to categorize law enforcement agents by groups, each of which has a unique approach to police work.[28] The purpose of such classifications is to demonstrate that the police are not a cohesive, homogeneous group, as many believe, but rather are individuals with differing approaches to their work. Police administrators and other individuals who wish to modify or improve police performance should be aware of the nature and extent of these stylistic undercurrents.[29] Do all officers within their jurisdiction operate with similar, unique, or conflicting styles? Is one style more effective than another? Does the existence of numerous styles within a single jurisdiction detract from good police work?

An examination of the recent literature suggests that the current behavior patterns of most police agents fall into the following four styles of police work: the Crime Fighter, the Social Agent, the Law Enforcer, and the Watchman.

THE CRIME FIGHTER. To the **Crime Fighter,** the most important police work consists of investigating serious crimes and prosecuting criminals. This type of police officer believes that murder, rape, and other serious personal crimes should be the prime concerns of police agencies. Such officers regard property crimes as less significant and believe matters such as misdemeanors, traffic control, and social service functions would be better handled by other agencies of government. These police officers believe that the ability to

The crime fighter stresses investigating serious crimes and prosecuting criminals. Actor Clint Eastwood's character "Dirty Harry" Callahan has personified this style of police work in a series of popular films.

investigate criminal behavior that poses a serious threat to life and safety, combined with the power to arrest criminals, separates the police department from other municipal agencies. Diluting these functions with minor social service and nonenforcement duties is viewed as harmful to police efforts to create a secure society.

Crime Fighters are primarily interested in dealing with hard crimes; on patrol, their senses are attuned to assaults, rapes, burglaries, and the like, and they interpret the relative importance of situations in terms of these crimes. Some occurrences that others consider appropriate occasions for police intervention (such as minor traffic violations or requests for enforcement of nonemergency situations) may be ignored or brushed off by the Crime Fighter on the grounds that they are relatively unimportant and undeserving of the police officer's time and attention.

A number of police experts have recognized the existence of the Crime Fighter type. William Muir labels them "enforcers"—supercops who lack sympathy for the common citizen.[30] Michael Brown calls them "old-style crime fighters," who use force and violence to maintain control of the streets.[31]

THE SOCIAL AGENT. In sharp contrast to the Crime Fighter is the sort of police officer one can describe as the **Social Agent.** Defenders of this type of officer note that police departments are merely part of a larger organization of several government agencies; they believe that officers are responsible for a wide range of duties other than crime fighting. They argue that police could better spend their time trying to do well those things that have to be done rather than attempting to limit police contacts with the public to crime-related events. Proponents of the Social Agent approach argue that establishing new governmental agencies or modifying existing ones to perform the duties relinquished by the Crime Fighter would create an exorbitant drain on municipal resources.

The Social Agent believes that police should become involved in a wide range of activities, without regard for their connection to law enforcement. The Social Agent does not believe enforcement is the essence of policing and may point out that the word "police" is commonly used in contexts that have at best only a tenuous relation to law enforcement (e.g., in such phrases as "the state's police powers" and "police the parade grounds"). The Social Agent who is well versed in the history of the American police will note, for example, that the Boston police department was developed in the early nineteenth century as much in response to a health and sanitary crisis as for criminal apprehension needs.

Rather than viewing themselves as criminal catchers, Social Agents consider themselves problem solvers. They are troubleshooters who keep busy patching holes that appear where the social fabric wears thin. Social agents would fit well within the new community policing models.

THE LAW ENFORCER. Like the Crime Fighter, the **Law Enforcer** tends to emphasize the detection and apprehension aspects of police work. Unlike the Crime Fighter, this police officer does not distinguish between major and minor crimes. Although a Law Enforcer may prefer working on serious crimes—they are more intriguing and rewarding in terms of achievement, prestige, and status—he or she sees the police role as one of enforcing all statutes and ordinances. According to this view, the police officer's duty is clearly set out in law, and the Law Enforcer stresses playing it by the book. Since the police are specifically charged with apprehending all types of lawbreakers, they are viewed in this typology as generalized law enforcement agents. They do not perceive themselves as lawmakers or as judges of whether existing laws are fair; quite simply, legislators legislate, courts judge, and police officers detect violations, identify culprits, and take the lawbreakers before a court.

THE WATCHMAN. James Q. Wilson's study of interdepartmental differences in police orientations provides the fourth major typology.[32] Wilson observed three general departmental styles, which he related to different demographic characteristics of American cities. One of the styles Wilson noted, the Service Type, was similar to the Social Agent, while a second, the Legalist, seemed to resemble parts of the Crime Fighter and the Law Enforcer. A third orientation, which Wilson called the **Watchman,** was characterized by an emphasis on the maintenance of public order as the police goal rather than law enforcement or general service. Police in Watchman-type departments choose to ignore many infractions and requests for service unless they believe that the social or political order is being jeopardized:

> Juveniles are "expected" to misbehave, and thus infractions among this group—unless they are serious or committed by a "wise guy"—are best ignored or treated informally. . . .
> Motorists . . . will often be left alone if their driving does not endanger or annoy others. . . . Vice and gambling are . . . problems only when the currently accepted standards of public order are violated. . . . Private disputes—assaults among friends or family—are treated informally or ignored unless the circumstances . . . require an arrest. . . . The police are watchmanlike not simply in emphasizing order over law enforcement but also in judging the seriousness of infractions less by what the law says about them than by their immediate and personal consequences. . . . In all cases, circumstances of person and condition are taken seriously into account.[33]

The Watchman type of police officer appears similar to Muir's concept of the "avoider" and to one of the groups Brown labels the "service style."[34]

DO POLICE STYLES EXIST? As you may recall, the police role involves spending a great deal of time in noncrime, service-related activities, ranging from providing emergency medical care to directing traffic. Although officers who admire one style of policing may emphasize one area of law enforcement over another, it is likely that their daily activities will require them to engage in police duties they consider trivial or unimportant. Although some pure types exist, it is unlikely that any officer can "specialize" in one area of policing while ignoring the others.

Support for this position comes from two studies. One, by Ellen Hochstedler, found that police officers in Dallas could not easily be categorized into one of the popular police styles described above.[35] Similarly, Kathryn Golden has shown that pre–law enforcement students are well aware that the police role stresses such diverse activities as crisis intervention and general service activities, and they do not join the force expecting to be the next "Hunter" or "Dirty Harry."[36] Though further research is needed to clarify this issue, it is possible that today's police officer is more of a generalist than ever before and that future police recruits understand they will be required to engage in a great variety of police tasks.

The Stress Factor

The complexity of the police role, the need to exercise prudent discretion, the threat of using violence and having violence used against them, and their isolation from the rest of society, all take a toll on law enforcement officers. It is not surprising then that police undergo tremendous **stress,** a factor that leads to alcoholism, divorce, depression, and even suicide. One commentator suggests, "It would be difficult to find an occupation that is subject to more consistent and persistent tension, strain, confrontations and nerve wracking than that of the uniform patrolman."[37] Even civilian employees such as dispatchers have been found to exhibit elevated stress levels.[38]

A number of factors have been suggested as causes of police stress. Mary Hageman suggests that the pressure of being on duty 24 hours a day leads to stress and that police learn to cope with the stress of their job by becoming emotionally detached from their work and the people they serve.[39] In contrast, William Kroes and his associates argue that police become accustomed to the harsh conditions of their job and cope with them as any professional would.[40] They find that police stress is related to internal conflict with administrative policies that deny them support and a meaningful role in decision making. Francis Cullen, Terrence Lemming, Bruce Link, and John Wozniak found that the stress associated with police work can be conceptualized as falling into two different dimensions, that involving work and that which affects the officer's personal life. They found that work stress was most significantly influenced by perceptions of dangerousness and could be counteracted by effective supervisory support. Life stress was influenced by perceptions of dangerousness and also by other problems associated with the job including shift changes and problems caused by new court rulings. Support from one's family and educational attainment tended to counteract life stress.[41] Subsequent studies have shown that the more support police officers experience in the workplace, the lower their feelings of stress and anxiety.[42]

Other stressors encountered in the literature include poor training; substandard equipment; poor pay; lack of opportunity; role conflict; exposure to brutality; fears about job competence, individual success, and safety; and job

Police work is a stressful occupation. Here a group of officers attend a stress reduction counseling session.

dissatisfaction.[43] Police psychologists have divided stressors into four distinct categories:

1. Stressors external to the police department such as verbal abuse from the public, system inefficiency, and liberal court decisions that favor the criminal.
2. Stressors associated with police organizations such as low pay, excessive paperwork, arbitrary rules, and limited opportunity for advancement.
3. Stressors connected with police duties such as rotating shifts, work overloads, boredom, fear, and danger.
4. Stressors particular to the individual officers such as being a member of a minority group, marital difficulties, and personality problems.[44]

The effects of stress can be shocking. Police work has been related to both physical and psychological ailments. Police have a significantly high rate of premature death caused by such diseases as coronary heart disease and diabetes. They also experience a disproportionate number of divorces and other marital problems. There is also evidence that police officer suicide rates are much higher than would be expected.

Police departments around the nation have attempted to combat job-related stress by training officers to cope with its effects. Today, stress training includes information on diet, biofeedback, relaxation and meditation, and exercise. Keeping this in mind, the Dallas police department studied the effects of physical fitness on overall officer performance and subsequently instituted an exercise program and developed fitness standards to ensure higher performance levels. Attacking the stress problem from another perspective, the Kansas City, Missouri, police department implemented the Marriage Partner Program, designed to involve police spouses in the effort to reduce stress.[45] In Minnesota, the Couple Communications Program works with officers and their spouses to identify issues in their relationship that might produce on-the-job stress.[46] In Indiana, the state police initiated the Employee Assistance Program (EAP), designed to help employees and their families deal with alcoholism, drug dependency, and emotional problems by referring them to a chemical dependency treatment center in Indianapolis. Referral has no effect on the officer's seniority.[47] Although attempts to reduce the stress created by family disruption are important, some studies have found that positive marital relations alone do not serve as a mediating variable to police officer stress.[48] Thus, stress-control training must have a multidirectional emphasis and include family, work, and self-related components if it is to be effective.

■ Social Factors in Policing

As the 1990s begin, important questions remain to be answered about the composition of the nation's police forces. Traditionally, police agencies were comprised of white males with a high school education who viewed policing as a secure position that brought them the respect of their family and friends and a step up the social ladder. It was not uncommon to find police families in which one member of each new generation would enter the force.[49] This picture has been changing and will continue to change. As criminal justice programs turn out thousands of graduates every year, an increasing number of police officers have received at least some college education. In addition, affirmative action programs have made the racial composition of police departments more reflective of their communities. One recent survey found that large, urban police agencies contain about 12 percent black officers and 6 percent Hispanic officers, numbers that are close to their actual representation in the U.S. population (12 percent and 7 percent, respectively). And although the gender gap is still present, about 12 percent of the sworn officers were female.[50] The following sections explore these changes in more detail.

Police Education

Many police experts have argued that incoming police officers should have a college education. This conclusion is not unexpected, since national commissions on policing have been recommending higher education for police officers since 1931.[51] Though the great majority of American police departments do not require their recruits to have a college education, the trend for police officers to have post–high school training has been spurred on by the development of law enforcement and criminal justice academic programs.[52]

What are the advantages of higher education for police officers? Among other things, education is believed to promote better communication with the public, especially minority and ethnic groups. As might be expected, educated officers demonstrate the ability to write more fluently and more clearly and are more likely to be promoted. Police administrators believe that education enables officers to perform more effectively, receive fewer citizen complaints, show more initiative, and generally be more professional. In addition, educated officers are less likely to have disciplinary problems and are viewed as better decision makers.[53]

Considering its advantages, what is the status of higher education in policing today? To answer this question, on behalf of the Police Executive Research Forum, David Carter and Allen Sapp conducted a 1988 survey of all state and local police agencies serving populations of more than 50,000.[54] Of the 699 agencies that responded to Carter and Sapp, 62 percent had at least one formal policy in support of officers pursuing higher education, and 58 percent required that coursework be "job related." Although the concept of job-related education included a variety of subjects, about half (49 percent) of the surveyed departments expressed a preference for criminal justice majors, most often because of their enhanced knowledge of the entire criminal justice system and issues in policing. Another promising trend: 82 percent of the departments, while not requiring college credits for promotion, recognize that college education is an important element in promotion decisions.

In some respects the findings of the Carter and Sapp survey can be considered disappointing. Only 14 percent of the departments had a formal college requirement for employment, and 75 percent reported they had no policy or practice requiring college education for promotion. In addition, most (75 percent) of the departments that supported in-service higher education did not require that the coursework be part of a degree program.

DOES HIGHER EDUCATION MATTER? Despite the growth of educational opportunities for police, the issue of higher education for police officers is not a simple one. A number of factors have impeded police departments from requiring aspiring officers to attain college credits. The most often cited reason is that many potential candidates, especially those in the minority community, would be dissuaded from police work if a college degree were required. In addition, a college-educated police force would be more costly to recruit and, assuming they would want higher salaries than a less-educated force, more costly to maintain.

Still another factor hindering the growth of educational requirements is the lack of clear-cut evidence that college education enables police to perform their daily activities more effectively.[55] The diverse aspects of the police role, the need for split-second decision making, and the often boring and mundane tasks police are required to do have all been cited as reasons why formal education for police officers may be a waste of time.[56]

In addition, there is little agreement as to which education model is the most effective for training the modern police officer. For example, liberal arts may be too general, criminal justice too focused, and law enforcement too technical to be of use to the "street" cop. This important issue was addressed by the report of the National Advisory Commission on Higher Education for Police Officers (commonly called the **Sherman Report**).[57] The *Sherman Report* examined the findings of a national study of existing college curriculum and educational delivery systems for police education in the United States and recommended that prospective police officers should receive a liberal education and that criminal justice courses and course materials should emphasize ethical considerations and moral values in law enforcement, not the nuts and bolts of police procedures.

Although the jury is still out on the value of police education, a number of research efforts have indicated that a college education does have a beneficial influence on police performance. Studies have shown that college-educated police officers receive fewer citizen complaints and have better behavioral and performance characteristics than their less-educated peers.[58] Higher levels of education have been associated with fewer on-the-job injuries, fewer injuries by assault and battery, fewer disciplinary actions from accidents, fewer sick days per year, and fewer physical force allegations.[59] Other research has shown that higher education results in higher aspirations; decreased dogmatism, authoritarianism, rigidity, and conservatism; fewer disciplinary problems; fewer citizen complaints; increased promotions; greater acceptance of minorities; decreased use of discretionary arrests; increased perception of danger; and better ability to tolerate job-related excitement.[60] The Criminal Justice in Review on page 258 discusses the benefits of requiring higher education for law enforcement officers.

Despite the general recognition that education is of benefit to law enforcement officers, public finances and the ability to recruit college-educated recruits will probably determine whether police departments will increase their educational requirements. One promising sign is that some cities, such as San Diego, San Jose, and Sacramento, California, and Tulsa, Oklahoma, and state police agencies such as New York's and Minnesota's, have recently adopted measures requiring police recruits to have at least two years of college education.[61]

Minority Representation in the Police

For the past two decades, American police departments have made a concerted effort to attract minority police officers. The reasons for this recruitment effort are varied. Viewed in its most positive light, police departments recruit minority citizens to field a more balanced force that truly represents the community it serves. A heterogeneous police force can be instrumental in

Higher Education for Police Officers

David Carter, Allen Sapp, and Darrel Stephens have studied the benefits and drawbacks of higher education for police officers. Their research has led them to develop the following list of 18 advantages a college education can provide for police officers:

1. It develops a broader base of information for decision making.

2. It allows for additional years and experiences for maturity.

3. Course requirements and achievements inculcate responsibility in the individual.

4. Both general education courses and coursework in the major (particularly a criminal justice major) permit the individual to learn more about the history of the country, the democratic process and an appreciation for constitutional rights, values and the democratic form of government.

5. College education engenders the ability to flexibly handle difficult or ambiguous situations with greater creativity or innovation.

6. In the case of criminal justice majors, the academic experience permits a better view of the "big picture" of the criminal justice system and both a better understanding and appreciation for the prosecutorial, courts and correctional roles.

7. Higher education develops a greater empathy for minorities and their discriminatory experiences through both coursework and interaction within the academic environment.

8. A greater understanding and tolerance for persons with differing lifestyles and ideologies which can translate into more effective communications and community relationships in the practice of policing.

9. The college-educated officer is assumed to be less rigid in decision-making in fulfilling the role of the police while balancing that role with the spirit of the democratic process in dealing with variable situations; a greater tendency to wisely use discretion to deal with the individual case rather than applying the same rules to all cases.

10. The college experience will help officers communicate and respond to crime and service needs of the public in a competent manner with civility and humanity.

11. The educated officer is more innovative and flexible when dealing with complex policing programs and strategies such as problem-oriented policing, community policing, task force responses, etc.

12. The officer is better equipped to perform tasks and make continual policing decisions with minimal, and sometimes no, supervision.

13. College helps develop better overall community relations skills including the engendering of respect and confidence of the community.

14. More "professional" demeanor and performance is exhibited by college-educated officers.

15. The educated officer is able to cope better with stress and is more likely to seek assistance with personal or stress-related problems thereby making the officer a more stable and reliable employee.

16. The officer can better adapt his/her style of communication and behavior to a wider range of social conditions and "classes."

17. The college experience tends to make the officer less authoritarian and less cynical with respect to the milieu of policing.

18. Organizational change is more readily accepted by and adapted to by the college officer. ■

SOURCE: David Carter, Allen Sapp, and Darrel Stephens, "Higher Education as a Bona fide Occupational Qualification (BFOQ) for Police: A Blueprint," *American Journal of Police* 7 (1988): 16–18.

gaining the public's confidence by helping to dispel the view that police departments are generally bigoted or biased organizations. Furthermore, minority police officers possess special qualities that can improve police performance. For example, Spanish-speaking officers are essential in Hispanic neighborhoods, while Oriental officers are essential for undercover or surveillance work with Asian gangs and drug importers.

Another important reason for recruiting minority police officers may be attributed to the need to comply with the various federal guidelines on employee hiring. A series of legal actions brought by minority representatives have resulted in local, state, and federal courts ordering police departments either to create hiring quotas to increase minority representation or to rewrite entrance exams and requirements in order to increase minority hiring. Court-ordered hiring was deemed necessary because as late as 1940 less than 1 percent of all police officers were minorities, and by 1950 their numbers had increased to only 2 percent.[62]

Examples of hiring plans implemented under court supervision are numerous. For example, the Virginia state police signed a consent decree in federal court in which they agreed to recruitment levels of at least 30 percent black and 25 percent female applicants.[63] Until the agreement was reached, only 4 percent of their force of 1,345 were black and 2 percent were female.

Sometimes the drive to recruit and promote minority officers forces police and city officials to reevaluate the results of normal testing procedures. This occurred in New York when the annual promotion exam was challenged on the basis that it discriminated against black and Hispanic officers. The city decided to promote 1,041 officers of all races who passed the test and the 200 highest-scoring black and Hispanic candidates among the 2,355 officers who failed.[64]

In 1987 in the case of *United States v. Paradise*, the U.S. Supreme Court upheld racial quotas as a means of reversing the effects of past discrimination. Ordering the Alabama Department of Public Safety to promote an equal number of blacks and whites, the Court said, "Discrimination at the entry-level necessarily precluded blacks from competing and resulted in a departmental hierarchy dominated exclusively by nonminorities." The Alabama state patrol had no minority majors, captains, lieutenants, or sergeants and only 4 of 66 corporals were black. The Court justified its ruling on the grounds that only qualified people would be promoted, the restriction was temporary, and it did not require dismissals or layoffs of white officers.[65]

Minority Police Officers

The earliest date that has been found for employment of a minority police officer is 1861 in Washington, D.C.; Chicago hired its first black officer in 1872.[66] By 1890 an estimated 2,000 minority police officers were employed in the United States. At first, black officers suffered a great deal of discrimination. Their work assignments were restricted, as were their chances for promotion. Minority officers were often assigned solely to the patrol of black neighborhoods, and in some cities they were required to call a white officer in order to make an arrest. White officers held highly prejudicial attitudes, and as late as the 1950s, some refused to ride with blacks in patrol cars.[67]

The experience of black police officers has not been an easy one. In his well-known book, *Black in Blue*, Nicholas Alex points out that blacks suffer "double marginality."[68] On the one hand, black officers must deal with the expectation that they will give members of their own race a break. On the other hand, black officers often experience overt racism from their police colleagues. Alex found that black officers' methods of adapting to these pressures ranged from denying that black suspects should be treated differently from whites to treating black offenders more harshly than white offenders to prove their lack of bias. Alex offered a number of reasons for why some black police officers are tougher on black offenders: they desire acceptance from their white colleagues; they are particularly sensitive to any disrespect given them by black teenagers; they view themselves as protectors of the black community.

These attitudes may be changing, however. In a more recent book, *New York Cops Talk Back*, Alex claims to have found a more aggressive and self-assured black police officer, one who is less willing to accept any discriminatory practices by the police department.[69] Similarly, Eva Buzawa found that black officers in Michigan generally were satisfied with their profession and believed they had good chances for advancement.[70] In a study conducted in the aftermath of the Miami riots, Bruce Berg and his associates found that black police officers were actually far less detached and alienated from the local community than white or Hispanic police officers.[71] Thus it appears that black officers are now overcoming the problems of "double marginality."

This is not to say that the black police officer's problems are over. For example, some police officials believe that black police officers have trouble relating to the community because they often identify with their white peers who are limited in terms of understanding existing cultural differences. As one high-ranking police official put it, "many black police officers in this area are insensitive to the people in the community because they don't understand the black community problems any better than non-black police officers."[72]

DISCRIMINATION ON THE JOB. Another significant problem is the difficulty black officers have in attaining command positions. Despite the growing number of minorities in supervisory positions, the percentage of minority officers of senior rank actually lags behind their total representation on police forces. Consequently, minority police organizations have filed lawsuits questioning the promotion practices of some of the nation's largest police departments, including Chicago, Omaha, and Miami. Courts have ordered some departments to promote minorities (and women) so that the racial and sex composition of the supervisory staff reflects the number of minorities (and women) in the department. It should be noted, however, that black chiefs have been appointed in some of the nation's largest cities: Detroit appointed William Hart chief in 1976; Lee Brown was appointed as chief in Houston in 1982; and Benjamin Ward was selected to head the New York City police on 1 January 1984.[73]

Minority police officers have also been victims of intentional and sometimes unintentional departmental discrimination. For example, some departments, in an effort to provide representative coverage to minority areas of the city, assign all their black, Hispanic, or Oriental officers to a single patrol area or beat. In one Florida city, an inner city patrol zone was manned entirely by black officers, and all the department's black officers were assigned to this zone.[74] The U.S. Court of Appeals for the Fifth Circuit labeled this practice discriminatory and ordered a halt to its use. Nevertheless, this practice is not unusual, and minority police officers have resorted to lawsuits to seek relief from what they consider to be discriminatory or demeaning assignments.[75]

Another problem faced by minority officers is resentment from their white colleagues. One of the dangers of court-ordered hiring is that white backlash may occur. As sociologists James Jacobs and Jay Cohen point out, white police officers view affirmative action hiring and promotion programs as a threat to their job security.[76] They note that in Chicago white officers intervened on the side of the city when a black police officer organization filed suit to change promotion criteria.[77] They further cite the case of the Detroit Police Officers' Association, which filed suit to prevent the police department from setting up a quota plan for hiring black police sergeants.[78] In the latter case, the court upheld the white officers' claim and struck down the promotional scheme.[79]

In the 1990s this issue appears unresolved, and many cities around the country are under court order to hire and promote more minority police officers.[80] It is evident that the number of minorities on police forces will continue to increase, especially if the recruitment mechanisms ordered by the courts are followed. Police administrators will face the challenge of maximizing the important contribution minorities can make to effective law enforcement while at the same time easing morale problems posed by court interference in police hiring, promotion, and administration. The Criminal Justice in Review on page 262 discusses the representation of racial and ethnic minorities on the nation's police departments.

Women Police Officers

The first women were admitted to police departments in 1910. For more than half a century, they were subject to separate selection criteria, assigned menial tasks, and denied the opportunity for advancement.[81] Only with the passage of the Civil Rights Act in 1964 and its subsequent amendments did they gain some relief. Court cases have consistently supported the addition of women to police forces by striking down entrance requirements that eliminated almost all female candidates but could not be proven to predict job performance (such as height and upper body strength).[82] Nevertheless, the role of women in police work is still obstructed by social and administrative barriers that have proven difficult to remove. Today, about 7 percent of all sworn officers are women, but they continue to be underrepresented in the senior administrative ranks, and many police women believe they are assigned duties that underutilize their skills and training.[83]

Despite the reluctance of some male officers to accept them as equal partners, policewomen have proven to be highly successful at all phases of police work.

A bias by male police officers towards female officers is certainly not supported by existing research, which indicates that women make highly successful police officers.[84] In an important study of recruits in the Metropolitan Police Department of Washington, D.C., conducted by the Police Foundation, policewomen were found to exhibit extremely satisfactory work performances.[85] When compared to male officers, women were found to respond to similar types of calls, and the arrests they made were as likely to result in conviction. Women were more likely than their male colleagues to receive support from the community and were less likely to be charged with improper conduct. One study by Robert Homant and Daniel Kennedy found that policewomen could be more understanding and sympathetic of the victims of spouse abuse and were more likely than male officers to refer them to shelters.[86]

Traditionally, it was believed that women officers receive somewhat lower supervisory ratings than males and make fewer felony and misdemeanor arrests.[87] More recent research suggests, however, that these factors have diminished. A study of the behavior of 2,293 officers in Texas and Oklahoma, conducted by James David, found that the arrest rates of male and female officers were almost identical.[88] Women police officers have also been described as having lower opinions of their own competency than male officers and more fears regarding the consequences of women being promoted to the superior officer level.[89]

The results of a study of policewomen's performance in New York City were also favorable to women patrol officers. Based on 3,625 hours of observation of patrol, including 2,400 police-civilian encounters, the study found that women police officers were perceived by civilians as being more competent, pleasant,

Employment of Black and Hispanic Police Officers

Samuel Walker, a noted justice historian and scholar, has conducted two national surveys (in 1983 and 1988) of black and Hispanic representation in the police depart-

ments of the nation's 50 largest cities. He found that about half of the departments made significant gains in minority recruitment while the rest reported either no gain or an actual decline in the number of minority officers.

Table A summarizes Walker's findings. It shows the size of the department, the number and percentage of minority officers, and the percentage change in minority representation between the surveys (1983–1988); an asterisk * indicates that the percentage of minority officers is equal to their representation in the general population of the city; an "x" indicates that minority representation is less than half of their representation in the city's population. Walker found that the cities that made the greatest strides in minority recruitment during the survey years include Jacksonville, Florida, Buffalo, Detroit, Tulsa, Birmingham, Philadel-

phia, Indianapolis, and Cincinnati. Walker suggests that financial limitations, institutional racism, and competition from the private sector are all factors that may limit minority recruitment and are problems that should be addressed by future study. ■

SOURCE: Samuel Walker, *Employment of Black and Hispanic Police Officers, 1983–1988: A Follow-up Study* (Omaha, Nebr.: Center for Applied Urban Research, University of Nebraska at Omaha, February 1989).

TABLE A ■ **The Number and Percentage of Minority Police Officers on the Nation's 50 Largest Departments**

| City | Officers | | Percentage Black | Percentage Change (1983-1988) | Hispanic | Percentage Hispanic | Percentage Change (1983-1988) |
	Total	Black					
New York, NY	27,312	2,992	10.9x	7.5	2,850	10.4	44.4
Chicago, IL	12,362	2,805	22.0	7.8	672	5.4x	62.5
Los Angeles, CA	7,305	873	11.9	27.2	1,282	17.5	30.6
Philadelphia, PA	6,519	1,300	19.9	20.4	135	2.0	231.2
Houston, TX	4,323	595	13.7	42.8	479	11.0	28.5
Detroit, MI	4,944	2,806	56.7	83.6	63	1.2	72.4
Dallas, TX	2,381	324	13.6x	64.2	151	6.3	37.8
San Diego, CA	1,704	114	6.6	19.3	174	10.2	30.7
Phoenix, AZ	1,888	69	3.6	29.3	189	10.0	6.3
Baltimore, MD	2,992	701	23.4x	34.3	13	0.4x	33.3
San Antonio, TX	—	—	—	—	—	—	—
Indianapolis, IN	989	139	14.0	6.6	3	0.3x	200.0
San Francisco, CA	1,846	158	8.5	4.6	184	9.9	21.2
Memphis, TN	1,264	371	29.3	34.7	0	0	0
Washington, DC	3,855	1,596	41.4	−16.9	106	2.7	166.6

TABLE A ■ The Number and Percentage of Minority Police Officers on the Nation's 50 Largest Departments—*continued*

City	Officers		Percentage Black	Percentage Change (1983-1988)	Hispanic	Percentage Hispanic	Percentage Change (1983-1988)
	Total	Black					
Milwaukee, WI	1,974	225	11.3x	−2.0	82	4.1	−8.2
San Jose, CA	1,009	35	3.4	60.8	178	17.6*	1.2
Cleveland, OH	—	—	—	—	—	—	—
Columbus, OH	1,370	195	14.2	28.0	0	0	0
Boston, MA	1,943	336	17.2	30.5	63	3.2	51.5
New Orleans, LA	1,347	445	33.0	57.8	20	1.4x	−26.7
Jacksonville, FL	1,031	153	14.8	141.6	10	0.9	31.5
Seattle, WA	1,150	74	6.4	55.8	23	2.0	18.4
Denver, CO	1,343	70	5.2x	−12.2	209	15.5	18.8
Nashville, TN	1,062	122	11.4x	−2.0	5	0.4	31.5
St. Louis, MO	1,529	357	23.3	18.6	0	0x	0
Kansas City, MO	1,165	156	13.3x	25.6	26	2.2	48.8
El Paso, TX	682	13	1.9	−6.3	386	56.4	−1.0
Atlanta, GA	1,365	771	56.4	23.1	20	1.4*	132.5
Pittsburgh, PA	1,062	231	21.7	50.0	0	0x	−100.0
Oklahoma City, OK	682	28	4.1x	3.7	6	0.8x	16.0
Cincinnati, OH	890	130	14.6x	59.2	3	0.3x	192.3
Fort Worth, TX	970	93	9.5x	68.0	73	7.5	15.3
Minneapolis, MN	684	25	3.6x	23.6	15	2.1	90.5
Portland, OR	752	21	2.7x	0	10	1.3	0
Honolulu, HI	—	—	—	—	—	—	—
Long Beach, CA	662	23	3.4x	11.1	58	8.7	58.9
Tulsa, OK	665	52	7.8	83.3	3	0.4x	−17.2
Buffalo, NY	1,002	174	17.3	108.1	55	5.4*	170.2
Toledo, OH	737	115	15.6	−14.2	28	3.7*	2.5
Miami, FL	1,033	180	17.4	0	439	42.4	8.5
Austin, TX	771	80	10.3	47.3	112	14.5	21.8
Oakland, CA	593	147	24.7	8.1	57	9.6*	4.1
Albuquerque, NM	696	18	2.5*	4.1	250	35.9*	9.2
Tucson, AZ	728	21	2.8	−6.1	125	17.1	0
Newark, NJ	1,064	296	27.8x	17.0	71	6.6x	34.6
Charlotte, NC	686	152	22.1	−1.3	0	0	0
Omaha, NE	617	66	10.6	27.5	18	2.9*	38.4
Louisville, KY	640	98	15.3x	50.0	1	0.1	0
Birmingham, AL	660	188	28.4x	70.0	0	0x	0

and respectful; the research team also found that the women's performance seemed to create a better civilian regard for police. The study also found that women officers performed better when serving with other women. Females paired with male companions seemed to be intimidated by their partners and were less likely to be assertive and self-sufficient.[90] Similarly, Sean Grennan's study of patrol teams in New York City found that contrary to popular myth policewomen are less likely to use a firearm in violent confrontations than their

Chapter 8

Issues in Policing

■

male partners, are more emotionally stable, less likely to seriously injure a citizen, and are no more likely to suffer injuries than their male partners.[91] These generally positive results are not dissimilar from findings accumulated in other studies conducted in major American cities.[92]

GENDER CONFLICTS. Despite the overwhelming evidence supporting their performance, policewomen have not always been fully accepted by their male peers or the public. The major bone of contention has been the policewomen's ability to perform in situations involving violence and the consequent need for them to have physical strength and dexterity. For example, in a survey conducted by Kenneth Kerber, Steven Andes, and Michelle Mittler, citizens in Illinois stated that policewomen were well suited for some tasks, such as "settling family disputes" or "dealing with a rape victim," but were inadequate for action-oriented activities, such as "stopping a fist fight."[93] Female officers face the additional problem that a great majority of the people they must control are members of the opposite sex. Sometimes this can be an advantage, however; for example, a normally belligerent suspect may surrender peacefully, rationalizing that he does not want to fight with or hurt a woman.[94]

Another important problem female officers face is that many male police officers believe women are physically incapable of handling the job of patrol officer, a conclusion related to the males' allegiance to a police culture oriented toward "macho" behavior. Female officers who try to adapt to the unwritten subculture are often written off as "bad police material."[95] Women who prove themselves tough enough to gain respect as police officers are then labeled "lesbians" or "bitches" in order to neutralize their threat to male dominance, a process referred to a **defeminization**.[96] Male officers also generally assume that female officers who adopt an aggressive style of policing will be quicker to use deadly force than their male counterparts.[97]

Ironically, these perceptions of female officers are often based on gender stereotypes and consequently are incorrect. In a careful review of the existing literature, Michael Charles found that women can train themselves to achieve a level of strength and fitness well within the normal demands of the police profession.[98] Nevertheless, female officers are often caught in the classic "Catch-22" dilemma: if they are physically weak, male partners view them as a risk in street confrontations; if they are actually more powerful and aggressive than their male partners, the woman is regarded as an affront to the policeman's manhood.

Given the sometimes hostile reception afforded them by their male peers and the general public, policewomen have been forced to perform their jobs under extreme pressure.[99] This condition is bound to affect their performance. Sociologist Susan Martin describes the roles female police officers take as a consequence of this pressure as falling somewhere in a continuum between two idealized professional identities; the *police*woman and police*woman*. The *police*woman gains her peers' acceptance by trying to adhere closely to the norms of behavior governing police in general and exhibits a strong law enforcement orientation.[100] She tries to be more loyal, professional, hardworking, and tough than women are generally expected to be. *Police*women are not afraid to engage in physical action or take punishment. Martin quotes one *police*woman:

> You have to fight the way the people fight out here. . . . You fight to win. . . . You have to be physical. Hit, kick, do what you can . . . and the person who doesn't do

that should be disciplined. Often, it's the women, and they are said not to know any better. But they've been trained; they *do* know better. Generally, the women aren't aggressive enough, but once you've been punched a couple of times, you learn to get the punch in first.[101]

On the other end of the spectrum are police*women*, who behave in a "traditionally feminine manner." They make few arrests, rarely attempt to engage in hazardous physical activity, and put emphasis on "being a lady." Police*women* feel comfortable in a role of secondary importance in a police agency. Martin's interviews with 32 female officers reveal that 7 could be classified as typical police*women* and 8 as *police*women, with the remaining subjects falling in between.

FUTURE GOALS OF WOMEN POLICE OFFICERS. What does the future hold for women police officers? One of the main concerns is the number of female officers in supervisory positions. So far, women, especially black women, have been woefully underrepresented in the police command hierarchy. A number of lawsuits have been filed to reverse this situation. For example, a consent decree required that one-third of all promotions in the Miami police department be given to women (and minorities).[102] Change in this area continues to come slow, however. Some male officers find it difficult to take orders from female supervisors; some female officers may not seek promotion because they fear rejection from their male colleagues.[103]

Another area of future concern is the development of an effective maternity policy. Most departments have not yet developed policies that identify when pregnant officers are "unfit" for patrol or other duties, whether they should be reassigned to lighter duties, and what these should entail. If the number of women on police forces continues to grow, maternity issues will become an important staffing issue for police administrators.[104]

Despite these problems the future of women in policing is becoming progressively brighter. Susan Martin concludes:

> As more women enter the occupation, move slowly into positions of authority, and serve as role models and sponsors for other women there is reason for guarded optimism about the future of women in law enforcement, as well as a large number of questions waiting to be addressed.[105]

■ Problems of Policing

Law enforcement is not an easy job. Role ambiguity, social isolation, and the threat of danger inherent in "working the street" are the police officer's constant companions. What effects do the strains of police work have on the law enforcement community? This section discusses two of the most significant problems: violence and corruption.

Police and Violence

Since their creation, U.S. police departments have wrestled with the charge that they are brutal, physically violent organizations. Early police officers resorted to violence and intimidation to gain the respect that was not freely given by citizens. In the 1920s the Wickersham Commission detailed numerous instances of police brutality, including the use of the "third degree" to extract confessions.

Police violence first became a major topic for discussion in the 1940s, when rioting provoked serious police backlash. Thurgood Marshall, then of the National Association for the Advancement of Colored People (NAACP), referred to the Detroit police as a "gestapo" after a 1943 race riot left 34 people dead.[106] Twenty-five years later, excessive police force was again an issue when television cameras captured police violence against protesters at the Democratic National Convention in Chicago.

Today **police brutality** continues to be a concern. For example, the Los Angeles police stopped using a restraining choke hold that cuts off circulation of blood to the brain after minority citizens complained that it caused permanent damage and may have killed upward of 17 people; in Philadelphia a lawsuit was filed by the Justice Department, charging the city's police with being generally brutal in their operations.[107] It has been suggested that the use of police force is most often directed at blacks and other racial minorities.[108] So strong is the evidence that it has caused one critic to claim:

> The news gets around the community when someone is killed by police. It is part of a history—a very long history of extralegal justice that included whippings and lynching. But let us explore the statistics a bit further. Take the age group where "desperate" criminals are much less likely to be found, the very young, ages 10 to 14, and the very old, those 65 years of age and older. In proportion to population, black youngsters and old men have been killed by the police at a rate 15 to 30 times greater than that of whites of the same age. It is the actual experiences behind statistics like these which suggest that police have one trigger finger for whites and another for blacks.[109]

The use of force against minority citizens was the spark that set off three riots in the city of Miami between 1980 and 1989. The last disturbance, which occurred from 16 January to 18 January 1989, was set off by the shooting of an unarmed black motorcyclist by a Hispanic police officer; 11 citizens were wounded and 13 buildings burned to the ground.[110] The question of police use of force involves two main areas of concern: (1) Are the average police officers generally brutal, violent, and disrespectful to the citizens with whom they come into daily contact? (2) Are the police overzealous and discriminatory in their use of **deadly force** when apprehending suspected felons? Let us examine each of these issues separately.

POLICE BRUTALITY. Police brutality usually involves such actions as the use of abusive language, unnecessary use of force or coercion, threats, prodding with nightsticks, stopping and searching people in order to harass them, and so on. Charges of generalized "police brutality" were common between the 1940s and the 1960s. Surveys undertaken by the President's Commission on Law Enforcement and the Administration of Justice and various other national commissions found that many citizens believed that police discriminated against minorities when they used excessive force in handling suspects, displayed disrespect to innocent bystanders, and so on.[111] However, by 1967, the President's Commission concluded that the police use of physical brutality had somewhat abated:

> The Commission believes that physical abuse is not as serious a problem as it was in the past. The few statistics which do exist suggest small numbers of cases involving excessive use of force. Although the relatively small number of reported complaints cannot be considered an accurate measure of the total problem, most persons, including civil rights leaders, believe that verbal abuse and harassment, not excessive use of force, is the major police-community relations problem today.[112]

Although charges of police brutality continue to be made in many jurisdictions, the evidence suggests that actual instances of physical abuse of citizens by police officers is less frequent than commonly imagined. In a well-known study, Albert Reiss employed 36 college students to observe police-citizen interactions in high-crime areas in Washington, D.C., Chicago, and Boston.[113] Reiss found that although verbal abuse of citizens was quite common, the excessive use of physical force was relatively rare. In only 44 cases out of the 5,360 observations made by Reiss's researchers did police seem to employ excessive or unreasonable force. Moreover, there appeared to be little difference in the way police treated blacks and whites; when force was used, it was against more selective groups—those who showed disrespect or disregard for police authority once they were arrested. A disturbing note, however, was that the police sometimes used force when the suspect was in their control, in a station house or patrol car.

BRUTALITY TODAY. Some experts believe that police officers have reduced their violent interactions with citizens of all races.[114] For example, in a recent research study David Bayley and James Garofalo observed 350 eight-hour tours of duty in three precincts in New York City. They discovered that incidents of violence are relatively rare, even in a large urban area such as New York City. Of 467 potentially violent incidents they encountered, only 78 resulted in some type of actual conflict. Of these, in only 42 encounters was force used by police against citizens or by citizens against police officers. The force used by police consisted almost exclusively of grabbing and restraining; firearms were never used.[115]

Despite such reassuring trends, incidents of police brutality have continued to plague departments around the country. One disturbing incident occurred in January 1989 when Don Jackson, a black police officer from a neighboring town, rode through the streets of Long Beach, California. Jackson, who wanted evidence of the Long Beach police department's harassment of minorities was secretly accompanied by an NBC camera crew. In less than three minutes, his car was pulled over, he was verbally abused by a police officer, and his head was pushed through a plate glass window and then pounded on the trunk of a police car. Soon after, to the embarrassment of law enforcement officials, the tapes were shown to a national television audience. Incidents such as this have been all too common in major cities such as New York, Boston, and Los Angeles.[116]

Police departments around the United States have instituted specialized training programs to reduce the incidence of brutality. In addition, detailed rules of engagement limiting the use of force are now common in major cities. The creation of departmental rules limiting behavior is often haphazard, however, and, as Samuel Walker points out, is usually a reaction to a crisis situation in the department—e.g., a citizen is seriously injured—rather than a systematic effort to improve police-citizen interactions.[117]

Perhaps the single greatest factor for controlling police brutality is the threat of civil judgments against individual officers who use excessive force, police chiefs who ignore or condone violent behavior, and the cities and towns in which they are employed. In December 1988, Chief Daryl Gates was hit with a $170,000 judgment in a case involving Los Angeles police officers who punched and brutalized members of a Hispanic family during a raid on their home. This judgment has put chiefs on notice that they can be held responsible for the illegal behavior of their officers.[118]

DEADLY FORCE. In 1986 the citizens of New York City were shocked to learn that a police officer had shot and killed a 66-year-old woman with a shotgun as she was being evicted from her apartment. Was this case an extreme instance of police brutality? Later, the facts of the case revealed a more complex situation: the woman was mentally unstable; she weighed over 275 pounds; she had attacked the police with a 10-inch knife, and they had tried their best to restrain her with protective shields; the woman was shot twice in order to stop her advances. Were the officers justified in using deadly force? A New York court indicted the officers for involuntary manslaughter, which later resulted in a not guilty verdict.[119]

As commonly used, the term *deadly force* refers to the actions of a police officer who shoots and kills a suspect who is either fleeing from arrest, assaulting a victim, or attacking the police officer.[120] The justification for the use of deadly force can be traced to English common law in which almost every criminal offense merited a felony status and subsequent death penalty. Thus execution while effecting the arrest of a felon was considered expedient in that it saved the state from the burden of a trial (known as the **fleeing felon** rule).[121]

Today, no other issue facing the police is more critical than the use of deadly force. Police violence can be the spark that ignites racial unrest and sets off community uprisings, as was the case of the Miami riot of January 1989.[122]

HOW FREQUENT IS THE USE OF DEADLY FORCE? To determine the frequency of police shootings, researchers generally rely on data provided by the FBI (Supplementary Homicide Reports) and the National Center for Health Statistics ("death by legal intervention of the police") and information volunteered by local police departments. Although these sources provide some indication of patterns and trends, there has been no systematic effort to gather accurate national data on police shootings, and the existing data are at best problematic and susceptible to error.[123] This oversight is particularly vexing considering the seriousness of the problem. In one of the most often cited studies of police use of force, Kenneth Matulia surveyed 57 of the nation's largest cities and found that approximately 260 citizens are killed by police each year, a rate of 2.41 per 1,000 officers and .62 per 100,000 citizen population.[124] Matulia also found indications that the average number of citizens killed by police is steadily decreasing, probably due to both legal and administrative efforts to control police use of force.[125] For example, he estimates that in 1975, 360 people were killed by police whereas by 1983 that number had declined to 229.

Although these data are encouraging, some researchers believe that the actual number of police shootings is far greater and may be hidden or masked by a number of sources. For example, coroners may be intentionally (or accidentally) underreporting police homicides by almost half.[126] In an impressive review of the evidence, James Fyfe estimates that 1,000 citizens are killed by police each year. Though Fyfe recognizes that no accurate measure of fatalities currently exists, he reaches the 1,000 annual death figure by applying the data recorded in the nation's largest jurisdictions to the population as a whole.[127]

FACTORS RELATED TO POLICE SHOOTINGS. Is the police use of deadly force a random occurrence, or are social, legal, and environmental factors associated with its use? The following factors have been related to police shootings:

1. *Variation by jurisdiction.* Research indicates that cities differ markedly in the percentage of police shootings. For example, whereas police in Portland,

Oregon, annually shoot .81 civilians per 1,000 population, New York City police shoot 1.4, Oakland, California, police shoot 5.2, and Jacksonville, Florida, police shoot 7.1.[128] Scholars are still uncertain about the reasons for these differences. Police practices, population characteristics, social trends, and so on may be responsible.

2. *Exposure to violence.* Most police shootings involve suspects who are armed and who either attack the officer or are engaged in violent crimes. Richard Kania and Wade Mackey found that fatal police shootings were closely related to reported violent crime rates and criminal homicide rates.[129]

3. *Police workload.* Violence corresponds to the number of police on the street, the number of calls for service, the number and nature of police dispatches, the number of arrests made in a given jurisdiction, and police exposure to stressful situations.[130]

4. *Firearm availability.* Cities that experience a large number of crimes committed with firearms are also likely to have high police violence rates. For example, Houston, which ranks first in firearm availability, had 21.5 police shootings per 1,000 violent crime arrests, whereas San Francisco, which ranks tenth, had only 1.5 shootings per 1,000 violent arrests.[131] Similarly, in a study of 48 cities, Lawrence Sherman and Robert Langworthy found a strong association between police use of force and "gun density" (the proportion of suicides and murders committed with a gun).[132]

5. *Social variables.* Jurisdictions with large numbers of transients or nonresidents are generally not as heavily populated as the surrounding areas. Research suggests that many individuals shot by police are nonresidents caught at or near the scenes of robberies or burglaries of commercial establishments.[133] David Jacobs and David Britt found that police shootings were most numerous in states where there were great disparities in economic opportunity.[134]

6. *Administrative policies.* The philosophy, policies, and practices of individual police chiefs and departments have a significant influence on the police use of deadly force.[135] Departments that stress restrictive policies on the use of force

The use of force is a key element of the police officer's role.

Chapter 8
Issues in Policing

269

generally have lower shooting rates than those that favor tough law enforcement and encourage officers to shoot when necessary. Poorly written or ambivalent policies encourage shootings because they allow the officer at the scene to decide, often under conditions of undue stress and tension, whether deadly force is warranted.

RACE AND POLICE SHOOTINGS. No issue is as important to the study of the police use of deadly force as the question of racial discrimination. A number of critics have claimed that police are more likely to shoot and kill minority offenders than they are whites. In a famous statement Paul Takagi charged that police have "one trigger finger for whites and another for blacks."[136] Takagi's complaint is supported by a number of research studies showing that a disproportionate number of police killings involve minority citizens—almost 80 percent in some of the cities surveyed.[137]

Do these findings alone indicate that police discriminate in the use of deadly force? Some pioneering research by James Fyfe helps answer this question. In his study of New York City shootings over a five-year period, Fyfe found that police officers are most likely to shoot suspects who are armed and with whom they become involved in violent confrontations. Once such factors as being armed with a weapon, being involved in a violent crime, and attacking an officer were considered, the racial differences in the police use of force became nonsignificant. In fact, Fyfe found that black officers were almost twice as likely as white officers to have shot citizens. Fyfe attributes this finding to the fact that (1) black officers work and live in high-crime, high-violence areas where shootings are more common and (2) black officers hold proportionately more line positions and fewer administrative posts than white officers, which places them more often on the street and less often behind a desk.[138]

SHOOTING INTERACTIONS. Another approach to the study of police shootings is to view them as a product of a social interaction between the police officer and an opponent. William Geller, one of the proponents of this approach, maintains that alternatives to violence can be created if the events leading up to the shooting can be identified and analyzed.[139] Research by Peter Scharf and Arnold Binder indicates that the police use of deadly force is not a simple shoot/don't shoot decision but a consequence of a series of decisions that began to be made minutes or even hours before the shooting incident actually took place.[140] Scharf and Binder identified the following decision phases in a police shooting incident:

1. *Anticipation.* This occurs when the officer first hears of the need for intervention in a potentially dangerous situation and arrives at the scene. Important elements of this phase are the accuracy of the information the officer receives about the situation and the kind of expectations it raises in the officer's mind.
2. *Entry and initial confrontation.* At this stage the officer physically enters the scene of the crime and encounters the potential assailant. At this point various tactical decisions can significantly affect the outcome of the interaction. For example, does the officer seek cover or try for concealment? Is he or she wearing body armor? Has the officer enlisted the aid of people the suspect may trust?
3. *Dialogue and information exchange.* Here the officer assesses the situation and begins oral communication with the suspect. The outcome depends on

whether the suspect obeys such commands as "drop the gun" or makes threatening gestures toward the officer. Does the suspect lead the officer to believe that prolonged negotiation can effect a peaceful outcome?

4. *Final frame decision to shoot or not shoot.* At this stage the officer decides whether to shoot or not.

5. *Aftermath.* This phase includes the activities that follow immediately upon a police shooting incident such as a departmental review board, future contact between the officer and the suspect, and possibly the officer's trial.

SHOOTINGS OF POLICE. Although police officers are often taken to task for being too violent, the public sometimes forgets that police are all too often injured and killed by armed assailants. The situation is not improved by the fact that professional criminals and drug dealers are armed with automatic assault weapons such as Uzi machine guns while police officers carry .38 caliber revolvers. This disparity made national headlines when two FBI agents were killed and 5 seriously wounded when they intercepted two well-armed robbers on 23 April, 1986 in Miami; they were the 28th and 29th agents killed in the agency's 78-year history.[141] As Barbara Raffel Price of John Jay University puts it:

> It would be foolish not to recognize that the violence associated with the drug business puts the police and citizens in greater jeopardy and that it makes the job of policing almost impossible.[142]

Every year about 150 law enforcement and public safety officers are killed in the line of duty; about one-half of these are shooting victims.[143] The most common incident resulting in the death of an officer is an investigation of a traffic violation, followed by a robbery in progress; domestic disturbances also account for a significant number of police deaths, as do situations where police are killed by fellow officers, either by accident or when they are mistaken for perpetrators while undercover.[144]

What factors can be used to predict the shooting of police officers? David Konstantin examined felonious line of duty deaths from 1978–1980 and found that a majority of the incidents were initiated by the officers themselves as opposed to an unexpected attack by a hidden assailant; officers were most at risk when they were attempting to arrest an armed assailant. Black officers had a greater risk of getting killed than white officers and were more likely to be killed by black assailants than by whites. Contrary to popular myth, Konstantin did not find that police were at greatest risk while dealing with domestic disputes.[145] Ecological patterns may also be present when police become the victims of violent crime. In a recent study of the characteristics of cities that have high rates of police officer fatalities, David Lester found they were located in the South and have low population density, high murder rates, and a high proportion of gun ownership.[146]

Research also shows that off-duty police and plainclothes officers are very likely to be shot. One explanation for this is that off-duty officers, who are usually armed, are expected to take appropriate action yet suffer tactical disadvantages such as lack of communication and backup.[147] Plainclothes officers are often mistaken for perpetrators or unwanted intervenors.

Can the shooting of police be prevented? Annesley Schmidt believes that wearing protective equipment can cause a significant reduction in police fatalities. She cites the example of Kevlar body armor, which is believed to have saved the lives of 600 officers and reduced the fatalities from gun shots by almost 30 percent.[148]

CONTROLLING POLICE VIOLENCE. Since police use of deadly force is such a serious problem, an ongoing effort has been made to control its use. Until 1985 the continued use of the fleeing felon rule in a number of state jurisdictions made police shootings difficult to control. In that year, however, in *Tennessee v. Garner*, the U.S. Supreme Court outlawed the indiscriminate use of deadly force; because of the importance of this decision for the criminal justice system, it is examined in detail in the Law in Review on page 273. With *Garner*, the Supreme Court effectively put an end to any local police policy that allowed officers to shoot unarmed or otherwise nondangerous offenders if they resisted arrest or attempted to flee from police custody. However, the Court did not ban police use of deadly force altogether or otherwise enunciate a police shooting policy. Consequently, it is still up to the individual state jurisdictions to establish their own police shooting policies. Some states have now adopted statutory policies that restrict the police use of violence in some fashion.

Another method of controlling police shootings is through internal review and policy making by police administrative review boards. New York's Firearm Discharge Review Board was established over 10 years ago to investigate and adjudicate all police firearm discharges. Among the dispositions available to the board are the following:

1. The discharge was in accordance with law and department policy.
2. The discharge was justifiable, but the officer should be given additional training in the use of firearms or in the law and department policy.
3. The shooting was justifiable under law, but violated department policy and warrants department disciplinary action.
4. The shooting was in apparent violation of law and should be referred to the appropriate prosecutor if criminal charges have not already been filed.
5. The officer involved should be transferred (or offered the opportunity to transfer) to a less sensitive assignment.
6. The officer involved should be the subject of psychological testing or alcoholism counseling.[149]

The review board approach is controversial because it can lead to a department recommending that one of its own officers be turned over for criminal prosecution, an outcome that disturbs some legal scholars.[150] In an analysis of the effect of the Firearm Review Board (and development of a restrictive shooting policy based on the Model Penal Code), James Fyfe found that fleeing felon shootings, warning shots fired, and opponent and officer deaths decreased significantly.[151] Because of the positive results of instituting administrative reform, an increasing number of police departments are turning to administrative guidelines and policy reform, such as those formulated by the Commission for Accreditation for Law Enforcement Agencies, as a means of reducing civilian complaints about violence and the subsequent legal judgments and increases in liability insurance rates that soon follow.[152] Another inducement for police departments to control violence is the growing number of civil lawsuits being filed and won against individual officers and agencies. For example, in December 1988 the City of Boston paid $500,000 to the parents of a teenager shot to death by an officer despite the fact the youth was involved in a high-speed chase with a stolen car.[153] Civil penalties have inspired departments to create specific policies limiting the use of force and to provide in-service training for officers on the proper response to conflict situations.[154] So many suits have been filed that the U.S. Supreme Court, in *Canton v. Harris*, made it more difficult for victims to sue for damages by ruling that to be liable police departments must be "deliberately indifferent" to the

LAW IN REVIEW

Tennessee v. Garner (1985)

This case establishes the rule of law on the police use of deadly force to prevent the escape of a suspected felon.

FACTS

On 3 October, 1974, at about 10:45 P.M., two Memphis police officers were dispatched to answer a prowler call. Upon arriving, they encountered a neighbor who told them she had heard someone breaking into the house next door. While one of the officers radioed for help, the other went behind the house. The pursuing officer saw someone run across the backyard. The fleeing suspect stopped at a chain-link fence at the end of the yard. When the officer shone his flashlight at the suspect, he saw what appeared to him to be a 17- or 18-year-old youth who may have been about 5 feet 7 inches tall. The officer called out, "Police! Halt!" The suspect, however, began to climb the fence. Convinced that the suspect would get away, the police officer shot him; the bullet struck the suspect in the back of the head, and he later died on an operating table.

The dead suspect turned out to be Edward Garner, an eighth grader who was 15 years old and weighed between 100 and 110 pounds. At trial the officer admitted that he knew Garner was unarmed and trying to flee from his pursuit. However, he felt justified in using deadly force because the much younger suspect had a good chance of evading his pursuit and Tennessee Law allowed him to use his weapon under those circumstances. The Tennessee statute read in part, "If after notice of the intention to arrest the defendant, he either flees or forcibly resists, the officer may use all the necessary means to effect the arrest" (section 40–7–108 [1982]).

DECISION

The U.S. Supreme Court ruled that the use of deadly force against apparently unarmed and nondangerous fleeing felons is an illegal seizure of their person under the Fourth Amendment. Deadly force may not be used unless it is necessary to prevent the escape and the officer has probable cause to believe that the suspect poses a significant threat of death or serious injury to the officer or others. The majority opinion stated, "The use of deadly force to prevent the escape of all felony suspects, whatever the circumstances, is constitutionally unreasonable. It is not better that all felony suspects die than they escape. Where the suspect poses no immediate threat to the officer and no threat to others, the harm resulting from failing to ap-

prehend them does not justify the use of deadly force to do so. It is no doubt unfortunate when a suspect who is in sight escapes, but the fact that the police arrive a little late or are a little slower afoot does not always justify killing the suspect. A police officer may not seize an unarmed, nondangerous suspect by shooting him dead."

SIGNIFICANCE OF THE CASE

In deciding *Garner*, the Supreme Court recognized the changes that have occurred in the justice system since the common law fleeing felon doctrine was formulated. No longer are all felonies punished by death nor are law enforcers limited to personal-contact weapons, such as a sword or club. If the fleeing felon rule remained a police policy, future tragedies such as the shooting of Edward Garner would surely occur. The fact that had this nonviolent adolescent been caught he would probably have served a probation sentence was not lost on the Court.

Garner, however, was not a unanimous decision. Three justices argued that police should be able to use whatever force is necessary to capture criminals who commit serious crimes such as burglary. The dissenters espoused a public safety doctrine—the rights of the criminal are less important than the right of honest citizens to be adequately protected by police. Despite such disagreement *Garner* should end use of the fleeing felon rule in the United States. ■

needs of the people with whom police come in contact.[155] Despite this tightening of liability standards, the threat of large civil penalties may prove to be the most effective deterrent yet to the police use of excessive force.

Police Deviance

Since their creation, U.S. police departments have wrestled with the problem of controlling illegal and unprofessional behavior by their officers. Writing of early nineteenth-century police departments, historian Samuel Walker has stated:

> Corruption pervaded the American police. In fact, one could almost say that corruption was their main business. The police systematically ignored laws related to drinking, gambling, and prostitution in return for regular payoffs; they entered into relationships with professional criminals, especially pickpockets, tolerating illicit activity in return for goods or information; they actively supported a system of electoral fraud; and they sold promotions to higher rank within the department.[156]

Since the early nineteenth century, scandals involving police abuse of power have been uncovered in many urban cities, and elaborate methods have been devised to control or eliminate the problem. Though most police officers are probably not corrupt, the few that are dishonest bring discredit to the entire profession.

Police deviance can include a number of different activities. In a general sense, it involves misuse of authority by police officers in a manner designed to produce personal gain for themselves or others.[157] However, there is some debate over whether a desire for personal gain is an essential part of corruption. Some experts argue police misconduct also involves such issues as the unnecessary use of force, unreasonable searches, or an immoral personal life and that these should be considered as serious as corruption devoted to economic gain. Broadening misconduct categories can have unforeseen consequences, however. Although most police departments have regulations governing police officer misconduct (conduct unbecoming an officer), their application can lead to lawsuits, especially when the proscribed conduct involves the officer's personal life. For example, some departments prohibit police officers from engaging in off-duty homosexual conduct or forbid two unmarried officers to live together. The courts have been divided on whether police officers have the same rights of privacy as other citizens.[158]

VARIETIES OF POLICE CORRUPTION. The common image of the corrupt police officer is the greedy cop taking a bribe from a drug dealer, being on the payroll of a racketeer, or shaking down a motorist who should be getting a ticket. But **police corruption** is actually much more complex and takes many different forms, ranging from abuse of power to outright criminality. For example, a Boston police officer was convicted of larceny after he received $88,000 in salary from a fully paid, job-related medical leave at the same time that he was working as a safety and security officer at a local high school.[159]

To understand the forms police corruption can take, a number of scholars have attempted to create typologies categorizing the abuse of police powers. For example, during its investigation of corruption among police officers in New York, the **Knapp Commission** classified abusers into two categories: "**meat eaters**" and "**grass eaters.**"[160] Meat eaters aggressively misuse police power for personal gain by demanding bribes, threatening legal action, or cooperating with criminals. Even today American cities are rocked by scandals in which police officers are accused, indicted, and convicted of "shaking down" club owners and other business people.[161] In contrast, grass eaters accept payoffs when their everyday duties place them in a position to be solicited by the public. Police officers have been investigated for taking bribes in order to look the other way while neighborhood bookmakers ply their trade.[162] The Knapp Commission concluded that the vast majority of police officers "on the take" are grass eaters, although the few meat eaters who are caught capture all the headlines.

Other police experts have attempted to create models that classify police corruption. Michael Johnston divides police corruption into four major categories:[163]

1. *Internal corruption.* Takes place among police officers themselves and involves both the bending of departmental rules and the outright performance of illegal acts. For example, in Chicago, police officers conspired to sell relatively new police cars to other officers at cut-rate prices, forcing the department to purchase new cars unnecessarily. A major scandal hit the Boston police department when a police captain was indicted in an exam-tampering and selling scheme. Numerous officers bought promotion exams from the captain while others paid him to lower the scores of rivals who were competing for the same job.[164]

2. *Selective enforcement or nonenforcement.* Occurs when police abuse or exploit their discretion. An officer who frees a drug dealer in return for valuable information is using discretion legitimately; a police officer who does it for money is abusing police power.

3. *Active criminality.* Involves participation by police in serious criminal behavior. Police may use their positions of trust and power to commit the very crimes they are entrusted with controlling. A police burglary ring in Denver was so large it prompted one commentator to coin the phrase "burglars in blue." During the past 20 years, police burglary rings have been uncovered in Chicago, Reno, Nashville, Cleveland, and Burlington, Vermont, among other cities.[165]

Another disturbing trend has been police use of drugs. Peter Kraska and Victor Kappeler found that more than 20 percent of the officers in a local police department used marijuana and nonprescription drugs while on active duty.[166]

4. *Bribery/extortion.* Refers to practices in which law enforcement roles are exploited specifically to raise money. Bribery is initiated by the citizen, extortion is initiated by the officer. Bribery/extortion can be a one-shot transaction, as when a police officer accepts $20 from a traffic violator to forget about issuing a summons, or the relationship can be an ongoing one in which the officer solicits (or is offered) regular payoffs to ignore criminal activities such as gambling or narcotics. This is known as being **on the pad.**

When Ellwyn Stoddard interviewed a former police officer who had been indicted on charges of robbery and grand larceny, he uncovered additional categories of "blue-coat crime":[167]

5. *Mooching.* Receiving free gifts of coffee, cigarettes, meals, and so on in exchange for possible future acts of favoritism.

6. *Chiseling.* Demanding tickets to entertainment events or price discounts.

7. *Shopping.* Taking small items such as cigarettes from a store whose door was accidentally left unlocked after business hours.

8. *Shakedown.* Appropriating expensive items from a crime scene and blaming the loss on the criminal.

9. *Favoritism.* Giving immunity to friends or relatives for traffic or other violations.

Lawrence Sherman suggests that police departments themselves can be categorized on the basis of the level and type of corruption existing within them.[168] He identifies three different types:

■ *Type I: Rotten apples and rotten pockets.* This type of police department has a few corrupt officers who use their position for personal gain. When these corrupt officers band together, they form a **rotten pocket**. Robert Daley described the activities of such a group in his book *Prince of the City*. Agents of New York City's narcotics control Special Investigations Unit (SIU) kept money they confiscated during narcotics raids and also used illegal drugs to pay off informers. Rotten pockets helped institutionalize corruption because their members expected newcomers to conform to their illegal practices and to a code of secrecy. *Prince of the City* tells the story of New York Detective Frank Leuci, whose testimony against his partners before investigating committees made him an outcast in the police department.

■ *Type II: Pervasive unorganized corruption.* According to Sherman, a Type II department contains a majority of personnel who are corrupt but have little relationship to one another. Though many officers are involved in bribe taking and extortion, they are not cooperating with one another for personal gain.

■ *Type III: Pervasive organized corruption.* In a Type III department almost all members are involved in systematic and organized corruption. The Knapp Commission found this type of relationship in New York City's vice divisions, where payoffs and bribes were an organized and accepted way of police life.

WHAT CAUSES CORRUPTION? CAN IT BE CONTROLLED? No single explanation has satisfactorily accounted for the various forms the abuse of power takes. One view puts the blame on the type of person who becomes a police officer. This position holds that policing tends to attract lower-class individuals who do not have the financial means to maintain a coveted middle-class lifestyle. As they develop the cynical, authoritarian police personality, accepting graft seems an all-too-easy method of achieving financial security.[169]

A second view is that the wide discretion police enjoy, coupled with the low visibility they maintain with the public and their own supervisors, makes them likely candidates for corruption. In addition, the "code of secrecy" maintained by the police subculture helps insulate corrupt officers from the law. Similarly, police managers, most of whom have risen through the ranks, are reluctant to investigate corruption or punish wrongdoers. Thus corruption may also be viewed as a function of police institutions and practices.[170]

A third position holds that corruption is a function of society's ambivalence toward many forms of vice-related criminal behavior that police officers are sworn to control. As Samuel Walker states:

> Unenforceable laws governing moral standards promote corruption because they create large groups with an interest in subverting law enforcement. Interest groups include both consumers and suppliers. The consumers—people who gamble, or wish to drink after the legal closing hour, or patronize a prostitute—do not want to be deprived of their chosen form of recreation. Even though the consumers may not actively corrupt police officers (by offering bribes, for example), their existence creates a climate that tolerates active corruption by others.[171]

Since vice cannot be controlled, and because the public apparently wants it to continue, the police officer may have little resistance to inducements for monetary gain offered by law violators. A good example of this problem can be found in Dade County, Florida. In one case, 11 police officers were arrested on drug-related charges. Two were charged with making off with 150 pounds of cocaine valued at $2 million from a raided boat. Another 4 officers were indicted on murder charges when they hijacked a boatload of cocaine and caused the drug runners to jump into the sea where they drowned.[172]

How can police corruption be controlled? One approach is to strengthen the internal administrative review process within police departments. A strong, well-supported Internal Affairs Division has been linked to lowered corruption rates.[173] Another approach, instituted by New York Commissioner Patrick Murphy in the wake of the Knapp Commission is the **accountability system.** This holds that supervisors at each level are directly accountable for the illegal behaviors of the officers under them. Consequently, commanders can be forced to resign or be demoted if someone in their command is found guilty of corruption.[174]

Close scrutiny by one's own department can lower officer morale and create the suspicion that their own supervisors mistrust them. Another, similar approach is to create outside review boards or special prosecutors, such as the Knapp Commission, to investigate reported incidents of corruption. However, outside investigators and/or special prosecutors are often limited by their lack of intimate knowlege of day-to-day police operations. As a result, they depend on the testimony of a few officers who are willing to cooperate, either to save themselves from prosecution or because they have a compelling moral commitment. Outside evaluators also face the problem of the "blue curtain," which is quickly lowered when police officers feel their department is under scrutiny.

Another approach to controlling police corruption is through court review of police behavior. There has been a trend in the past decade for courts to remove restrictions limiting litigation against the police. Although analyzing the precise effects of legal action on police behavior is difficult, the resulting higher insurance rates caused by large settlements and increased media coverage have almost certainly caused police administrators to take the matter quite seriously.[175]

It is also possible that corruption can be controlled by intensive training and education programs that begin when a police officer first enters a training academy. Thomas Barker has shown that police recruits believe that a certain degree of corruption is present in every department.[176] Therefore, recruits should be made aware of the enticements of police deviance and the steps that can be taken to control it. A more realistic solution to police corruption, albeit a difficult one, might be to change the social context of policing. On the one hand, police operations must be made more visible, and the public must be given freer access to controlling police operations. All too often the public finds out about police problems only when a scandal hits the newspapers.

On the other hand, some of the vice-related crimes the police now deal with might be decriminalized or referred to other agencies. Although decriminalization of vice cannot in itself end the problem, it could lower the pressure placed on individual police officers and help relieve their moral dilemmas.

■ SUMMARY

Police departments today are faced with many critical problems in their own operations and in their relationship with the public.

It has been assumed that police are isolated from the rest of society. Some experts believe police officers have distinct personality characteristics marked by authoritarianism and cynicism. It is also alleged that police maintain a separate culture with distinct rules and loyalties. Police personality traits also influence their working style. Four distinct police styles have been identified, each of which influences police decision making. The complexity and danger of the police role produce an enormous amount of stress that threatens police effectiveness.

A number of social concerns also affect police operations. Today, many police officers are seeking higher education. The jury is still out on whether educated police officers are actually more effective. Women and minority police officers are now being recruited in increasing numbers. Research indicates that, with few exceptions, they perform as well as or even better than other officers. The percentage of minorities on police forces reflects their representation in the general population, but the number of female officers still lags behind. A greater problem at this point is the need to increase the number of women and minorities in supervisory positions.

Police departments have also been concerned about limiting police stress. One critical concern is the police use of deadly force. Research indicates that antishooting policies can limit deaths resulting from police action. Another concern is the need to identify and eliminate police corruption. Though efforts have been made, incidents of corruption still mar the reputations of many police forces.

■ QUESTIONS

1. Should male and female officers have exactly the same duties in a police department?
2. Do you think that working the street will eventually produce a cynical personality and distrust for civilians?
3. How would education help police officers? Can it actually hinder them?
4. Do you think that police work is any more stressful than other professions?

5. Should a police officer who accepts a free meal offered by a restaurant owner be dismissed from the force?
6. A police officer orders an unarmed person running away from a burglary to stop; the suspect keeps running and is shot and killed by the officer. Has the officer committed murder?

■ NOTES

1. Timothy Flanagan and Katherine Jamieson, *Sourcebook of Criminal Justice Statistics, 1987* (Washington, D.C.: Bureau of Justice Statistics, 1988), p. 135.
2. Ibid., p. 179.
3. See, for example, Richard Harris, *The Police Academy: An Inside View* (New York: John Wiley & Sons, 1973); John Van Maanen, "Observations on the Making of a Policeman," in *Order under Law*, R. Culbertson and M. Tezak, eds. (Prospect Heights, Ill.: Waveland Press, 1981), pp. 111–126; Jonathan Rubenstein, *City Police* (New York: Ballantine Books, 1973); John Broderick, *Police in a Time of Change* (Morristown, N.J.: General Learning Press, 1977).
4. M. Steven Meagher and Nancy Yentes, "Choosing a Career in Policing: A Comparison of Male and Female Perceptions," *Journal of Police Science and Administration* 16 (1986): 320–27.
5. Michael K. Brown, *Working the Street* (New York: Russell Sage Foundation, 1981), p. 82.
6. Egon Bittner, *The Functions of Police in Modern Society* (Cambridge, Mass.: Oelgeschlager, Gunn & Hain, 1980), p. 63.
7. Richard Lundman, *Police and Policing* (New York: Holt, Rinehart & Winston, 1980); see also Jerome Skolnick, *Justice without Trial* (New York: John Wiley & Sons, 1966).
8. William Westly, *Violence and the Police: A Sociological Study of Law, Custom, and Morality* (Cambridge, Mass.: M.I.T. Press, 1970).
9. Skolnick, *Justice without Trial*, pp. 42–68.
10. See, for example, Richard Bennett and Theodore Greenstein, "The Police Personality: A Test of the Predispositional Model," *Journal of Police Science and Administration* 3 (1975): 439–45.
11. Milton Rokeach, Martin Miller, and John Snyder, "The Value Gap between Police and Policed," *Journal of Social Issues* 27 (1971): 155–71.
12. Bruce Carpenter and Susan Raza, "Personality Characteristics of Police Applicants: Comparisons across Subgroups and with Other Populations," *Journal of Police Science and Administration* 15 (1987): 10–17; Richard Lawrence, "Police Stress and Personality Factor: A Conceptual Model," *Journal of Criminal Justice* 12 (1984): 247–63; James Teevan and Bernard Dolnick, "The Values of the Police: A Reconsideration and Interpretation," *Journal of Police Science and Administration* 1 (1973): 366–69.
13. Van Maanen, "Observations on the Making of a Policeman," p. 50.
14. Ibid., p. 66.
15. George Kirkham, "A Professor's Street Lessons," in *Order under Law*, R. Culbertson and M. Tezak, eds. (Prospect Heights, Ill.: Waveland Press, 1981), p. 81.
16. Bittner, *Functions of Police in Modern Society*, p. 63.
17. Arthur Niederhoffer, *Behind the Shield: The Police in Urban Society* (Garden City, N.Y.: Doubleday & Co., 1967).
18. Westly, *Violence and the Police*; William Westly, "Violence and the Police," *American Journal of Sociology* 49 (1953): 34–41.
19. Niederhoffer, *Behind the Shield*, pp. 216–20.
20. Robert Regoli and Eric Poole, "Measurement of Police Cynicism: A Factor Scaling Approach," *Journal of Criminal Justice* 7 (1979): 37–52.
21. Ibid., p. 43.
22. Ibid., p. 44.
23. Richard Anson, J. Dale Mann, and Dale Sherman, "Niederhoffer's Cynicism Scale: Reliability and Beyond," *Journal of Criminal Justice* 14 (1986): 295–307.
24. Larry Tifft, "The 'Cop Personality' Reconsidered," *Journal of Police Science and Administration* 2 (1974): 268.
25. David Bayley and Harold Mendelsohn, *Minorities and the Police* (New York: The Free Press, 1969).
26. Robert Balch, "The Police Personality: Fact or Fiction?" *Journal of Criminal law, Criminology, and Police Science* 63 (1972): 117.

27. Carl Klockars, "The Dirty Harry Problem," *Annals* 452 (1980): 33–47.

28. The material in this section was prepared with the assistance of Michael W. O'Neill. See "The Role of the Police: Normative Role Expectation in a Metropolitan Police Department (Ph.D. dissertation, State University of New York at Albany, 1974).

29. Jack Kuykendall and Roy Roberg, "Police Managers' Perceptions of Employee Types: A Conceptual Model," *Journal of Criminal Justice*, 16 (1988): 131–35.

30. William Muir, *Police: Streetcorner Politicians* (Chicago: University of Chicago Press, 1977).

31. Brown, *Working the Street*, pp. 234–35.

32. James Q. Wilson, *Varieties of Police Behavior* (Cambridge, Mass.: Harvard University Press, 1968), chapter 7.

33. Ibid., p. 141.

34. Muir, *Police: Streetcorner Politicians*; Brown, *Working the Street*.

35. Ellen Hochstedler, "Testing Types, a Review and Test of Police Types," *Journal of Criminal Justice* 9 (1981): 451–66.

36. Kathryn Golden, "The Police Role: Perceptions and Preferences," *Journal of Police Science and Administration* 10 (1982): 108–11.

37. Clement Milanovich, "The Blue Pressure Cooker," *Police Chief* 47 (1980): 20.

38. Roy Roberg, David Hayhurst and Harry Allen, "Job Burnout in Law Enforcement Dispatchers: A Comparative Analysis," *Journal of Criminal Justice* 16 (1988): 385–94.

39. Mary Hageman, "Occupational Stress of Law Enforcement Officers and Marital and Familial Relationships," *Journal of Police Science and Administration* 6 (1978): 402–16.

40. William Kroes, Joseph Hurrell, and Bruce Margolis, "Job Stress in Policemen," *Journal of Police Science and Administration* 2 (1974): 145–55

41. Francis Cullen, Terrence Lemming, Bruce Link, and John Wozniak, "The Impact of Social Supports on Police Stress," *Criminology* 23 (1985): 503–22.

42. Ibid.

43. Nancy Norvell, Dale Belles, and Holly Hills, "Perceived Stress Levels and Physical Symptoms in Supervisory Law Enforcement Personnel," *Journal of Police Science and Administration* 16 (1988): 75–79; W. Clinton Terry III, "Police Stress: The Empirical Evidence," *Journal of Police Science and Administration* 9 (1981): 61–75.

44. Cited in John Blackmore, "Police Stress" in *Policing Society*, Clinton Terry, ed. (New York: John Wiley & Sons, 1985), p. 395.

45. Marshall Saper, "Police Wives: The Hidden Pressure," *Police Chief* 47 (1980): 28–29.

46. Ibid.

47. Lynn Lambuth, "An Employee Assistance Program That Works," *Police Chief* 51 (1984): 36–38.

48. Michael Bennett, Ronald Bingham, Swen Nielsen, and Paul Warner, "Intimacy and Satisfaction as a Support System for Coping with Police Officer Stress," *Journal of Police Science and Administration* 14 (1986): 40–44.

49. John Van Maanen, "Observations on the Making of a Policeman," *Human Organization* 32 (1973): 407–18.

50. David Carter and Allen Sapp, *The State of Police Education: Critical Findings* (Washington, D.C.: Police Executive Research Forum, 1988).

51. See Larry Hoover, *Police Educational Characteristics and Curricula* (Washington, D.C.: U.S. Government Printing Office, 1975).

52. Peter P. Lejins, *Introducing a Law Enforcement Curriculum at a State University*, Report of the National Institute of Law. Enforcement and Criminal Justice (Washington, D.C.: U.S. Government Printing Office, 1970), pp. 13–16.

53. Carter and Sapp, *The State of Police Education*, p. 6.

54. Ibid.

55. See, for example, James Erickson and Matthew Neary, "Criminal Justice Education: Is It Criminal?" *Police Chief* 42 (1975): 38.

56. See Lawrence Sherman and Warren Bennis, "Higher Education for Police Officers: The Central Issues," *Police Chief* 44 (1977): 32.

57. Lawrence Sherman et al., *The Quality of Police Education* (San Francisco: Jossey-Bass, 1978).

58. See, for example, B. E. Sanderson, "Police Officers: The Relationship of a College Education to Job Performance," *Police Chief* 44 (1977): 62; James Finnegan, "A Study of Relationships between College Education and Police Performance in Baltimore, Maryland," *Police Chief* 43 (1976): 50; Robert Trojanowicz and Thomas Nicholson, "A Comparison of Behavioral Styles of College Graduate Police Officers vs. Non-College Going Police Officers," *Police Chief* 43 (1976): 57; R. P. Witte, "The Dumb Cop," *Police Chief* 36 (1969): 38.

59. Wayne Cascio, "Formal Education and Police Officer Performance," *Journal of Police Science and Administration* 5 (1977): 89.

60. Lee Bowker, "A Theory of Educational Needs of Law Enforcement Officers," *Journal of Contemporary Criminal Justice* 1 (1980): 17–24.

61. David Carter, Allen Sapp, and Darrel Stephens," Higher Education as a Bona fide Occupational Qualification (BFOQ) for Police: A Blueprint," *American Journal of Police* 7 (1988): 1–29; "Two Cities Take Different Paths in College Education for Recruits," *Police* 6 (January 1983): 35.

62. Jack Kuykendall and David Burns, "The Black Police Officer: An Historical Perspective," *Journal of Contemporary Criminal Justice* 1 (1980): 4–13.

63. "Two Cities Take Different Paths."

64. "The Police Exam That Flunked," *New York Times*, News of the Week in Review, 24 November, 1985, p. 20.

65. *United States v. Paradise*, 107 S.Ct. 1053, 94 L.Ed.2d 203 (1987).

66. Kuykendall and Burns, "The Black Police Officer," p. 4.

67. Ibid.

68. Nicholas Alex, *Black in Blue: A Study of the Negro Policeman* (New York: Appleton-Century-Crofts, 1969).

69. Nicholas Alex, *New York Cops Talk Back* (New York: John Wiley & Sons, 1976).

70. Eva Buzawa, "The Role of Race in Predicting Job Attitudes of Patrol Officers," *Journal of Criminal Justice* 9 (1981): 63–78.

71. Bruce Berg, Edmond True, and Marc Gertz, "Police, Riots, and Alienation," *Journal of Police Science and Administration* 12 (1984): 186–90.

72. Daniel Georges-Abeyie, "Black Police Officers: An Interview with Alfred W. Dean, Director of Public Safety, Harrisburg, Pennsylvania," in *The Criminal Justice System and Blacks*, D. Georges-Abeyie, ed. (Beverly Hills, Calif.: Saye, 1984).

73. "Profiles of Black Police Chiefs of Selected Cities," *Blacks in Criminal Justice* (Spring/Summer 1985): 18–24.

74. *Baker v. City of St. Petersburg*, 400 F.2d 294 (5th Cir. 1968).

75. See, for example, *Allen v. City of Mobile*, 331 F.Supp. 1134 (1971), affirmed 466 F.2d 122 (5th Cir. 1972).

76. James Jacobs and Jay Cohen, "The Impact of Racial Integration on the Police," *Journal of Police Science and Administration* 6 (1978): 182.

77. See *Afro-American Patrolmen's League v. Duck*, 366 F.Supp. 1095 (1973); 503 F.2d 294 (6th Cir. 1974); 538 F.2d 328 (6th Cir. 1976).

78. *Detroit Police Officers Association v. Young*, 46 U.S. Law Week 2463 (E.D. Mich. 1978).

79. Jacobs and Cohen, "Impact of Racial Integration on the Police," p. 183.

80. Steven Marantz, "City review turns up no racial fraud by police, some question finding," *Boston Globe*, 19 October 1988, p. 21.

81. Susan Martin, "Female Officers on the Move? A Status Report on Women in Policing," in Roger Geoffery *Critical Issues in Policing*,

Dunham and Alpert, eds. (Grove Park, Ill.: Waveland Press, 1988) pp. 312–31 at 312.

82. *Le Bouef v. Ramsey*, 26 FEP Cases 884 (9/16/80).

83. Carole Garrison, Nancy Grant, and Kenneth McCormick, "Utilization of Police Women," *Police Chief* 55 (1988): 32–33.

84. Merry Morash and Jack Greene, "Evaluating Women on Patrol: A Critique of Contemporary Wisdom," *Evaluation Review* 10 (1986): 230–55.

85. Peter Bloch and Deborah Anderson, *Policewomen on Patrol: Final Report* (Washington, D.C.: Police Foundation, 1974).

86. Robert Homant and Daniel Kennedy, "Police Perceptions of Spouse Abuse: A Comparison of Male and Female Officers," *Journal of Criminal Justice* 13 (1985): 49–64.

87. Bloch and Anderson, *Policewomen on Patrol*, pp. 1–7.

88. James David, "Perspectives of Policewomen in Texas and Oklahoma," *Journal of Police Science and Administration* 12 (1984): 395–403.

89. Judie Gaffin Wexler and Vicki Quinn, "Considerations in the Training and Development of Women Sergeants," *Journal of Police Science and Administration* 13 (1985): 98–105.

90. Joyce Sichel et al., *Women on Patrol: A Pilot Study of Police Performance in New York City* (Washington, D.C.: National Criminal Justice Reference Service, 1978).

91. Sean Grennan, "Findings on the Role of Officer Gender in Violent Encounters with Citizens," *Journal of Police Science and Administration* 15 (1988): 78–85.

92. See, for example, Jack Molden, "Female Police Officers: Training Implications," *Law and Order* 33 (1985): 62–63.

93. Kenneth Kerber, Steven Andes, and Michelle Mittler, "Citizen Attitudes Regarding the Competence of Female Police Officers," *Journal of Police Science and Administration* 5 (1977): 337–46.

94. Martin, "Female Officers on the Move?", p. 322.

95. Adriane Kinnane, *Policing* (Chicago: Nelson-Hall, 1979), p. 58.

96. Bruce Berg and Kimberly Budnick, "Defeminization of Women in Law Enforcement: A New Twist in the Traditional Police Personality," *Journal of Police Science and Administration* 14 (1986): 314–19.

97. Ibid.

98. Michael Charles, "Women in Policing: The Physical Aspects," *Journal of Police Science and Administration* 10 (1982): 194–205.

99. Daniel Bell, "Policewomen: Myths and Reality," *Journal of Police Science and Administration* 10 (1982): 112–20.

100. Susan Martin, "*Police*women and Police*women*: Occupational Role Dilemmas and Choices of Female Officers," *Journal of Police Science and Administration* 7 (1979): 314.

101. Ibid., pp. 317–18; see also S. Martin, *Breaking and Entering* (Berkeley, Calif.: University of California Press, 1980).

102. Roi Dianne Townsey, "Black Women in American Policing: An Advancement Display," *Journal of Criminal Justice* 10 (1982): 455–68.

103. J. G. Wexler and V. Quinn, "Considerations in the Training and Development of Women Sergeants," *Journal of Police Science and Administration* 13 (1985): 98–105.

104. Susan Martin, "Female Officers on the Move?" pp. 325–26.

105. Ibid.

106. Samuel Walker, *Popular Justice* (New York: Oxford University Press, 1980), p. 197.

107. David Weissler, "When Police Officers Use Deadly Force," *U.S. News and World Report*, 10 January 1983; *United States v. City of Philadelphia*, 482 F.Supp. 1248 (E.D. Pa. 1979). This lawsuit was later dismissed by *United States v. District Court*, which ruled that the Department of Justice did not have standing in the case.

108. See, for example, John Goldkamp, "Minorities as Victims of Police Shootings: Interpretations of Racial Disproportionality and Police Use of Deadly Force," *Justice System Journal* 2 (1976): 169–83.

109. See Paul Takagi, "Death by Police Intervention," in *A Community Concern: Police Use of Deadly Force*, R. N. Brenner and M. Kravitz, eds. National Criminal Justice Research Service (Washington, D.C.: U.S. Government Printing Office, 1979), p. 34.

110. George Hackett, "All of Us Are in Trouble," *Newsweek*, 30 January 1989; Pamela Reynolds, "Legacy of Hostility Pervades Overton," *Boston Globe*, 19 January 1989, p. 1.

111. See, for example, President's Commission on Law Enforcement and the Administration of Justice, *Task Force Report: The Police* (Washington, D.C.: U.S. Government Printing Office, 1967), pp. 181–82; National Advisory Commission on Civil Disorders, *Police and the Community* (Washington, D.C.: U.S. Government Printing Office, 1968), pp. 158–59.

112. President's Commission, *Task Force Report: The Police*, pp. 181–82.

113. Albert Reiss, *The Police and the Public* (New Haven, Conn.: Yale University Press, 1972).

114. Lawrence Sherman, "Causes of Police Behavior: The Current State of Quantitative Research," *Journal of Research in Crime and Delinquency* 17 (1980): 80–81.

115. David Bayley and James Garofalo, "The Management of Violence by Police Patrol Officers," *Criminology* 27 (1989): 1–27.

116. Bill Girdner, "Charges of racism by Calif. police is latest in long line," *Boston Globe*, 19 January 1989, p. 3.

117. Samuel Walker, "The Rule Revolution: Reflections on the Transformation of American Criminal Justice, 1950–1988," Working Papers, Series 3, Institute for Legal Studies, University of Wisconsin Law School, Madison, Wisconsin, December, 1988.

118. Karen Polk, "New York Police: Caught in the Middle and Losing Faith," *Boston Globe*, 28 December 1988, p. 3.

119. *People v. Sullivan*, 116 A.D.2d 101, 500 N.Y.S.2d 518 (1986).

120. Lawrence Sherman and Robert Langworthy, "Measuring Homicide by Police Officers," *Journal of Criminal Law and Criminology* 4 (1979): 546–60.

121. Ibid.

122. "Killing of a Black by Police again Triggers Riots in Miami," *Criminal Justice Newsletter*, 1 February 1989, p. 3.

123. James Fyfe, "Police Use of Deadly Force: Research and Reform," *Justice Quarterly* 5 (1988): 175–76.

124. Kenneth Matulia, *A Balance of Forces*, 2d ed. (Gaithersburg, Md.: International Association of Chiefs of Police, 1985).

125. William Geller, "Deadly Force: What We Know," *Journal of Police Science and Administration* 10 (1982): 151–77.

126. Sherman and Langworthy, "Measuring Homicide by Police Officers."

127. Fyfe, "Police Use of Deadly Force: Research and Reform," 165–205.

128. Ibid., pp. 178–79.

129. Sherman and Langworthy, "Measuring Homicide by Police Officers"; Richard Kania and Wade Mackey, "Police Violence as a Function of Community Characteristics," *Criminology* 15 (1977): 27–48.

130. Ibid.

131. See Steven Brill, *Firearm Abuse: A Research and Policy Report* (Washington, D.C.: Police Foundation, 1977).

132. Sherman and Langworthy, "Measuring Homicide by Police Officers."

133. Ibid.

134. David Jacobs and David Britt, "Inequality and Police Use of Deadly Force: An Empirical Assessment of a Conflict Hypothesis," *Social Problems* 26 (1979): 403–12.

135. Fyfe, "Police Use of Deadly Force: Research and Reform," p. 181.

136. Paul Takagi, "A Garrison State in a 'Democratic' Society," *Crime and Social Justice* 5 (1974): 34–43.

137. Mark Blumberg, "Race and Police Shootings: An Analysis in Two Cities," in *Contemporary Issues in Law Enforcement*, James Fyfe, ed. (Beverly Hills, Calif.: Sage Publications, 1981), pp. 152–66; Catherine Milton et al., *Police Use of Deadly Force* (Washington, D.C.: Police Foundation, 1977).

138. James Fyfe, "Shots Fired" Ph.D. diss., State University of New York, Albany, 1978.

139. William Geller, "Officer Restraint in the Use of Deadly Force: The Next Frontier in Police Shooting Research," *Journal of Police Science and Administration* 13 (1985): 153–71.

140. Peter Scharf and Arnold Binder, *The Badge and the Bullet: Police Use of Deadly Force* (New York: Praeger, 1983).

141. Jacob Lamar, "A Twisted Trail of Blood," *Time*, 28 April 1986, p. 38.

142. Quoted in Karen Polk, "New York Police: Caught in the Middle and Losing Faith," *Boston Globe*, 28 December 1988, p. 3.

143. Annesley Schmidt, "Deaths in the Line of Duty," *NIJ Reports* 4 (1985): 6–8. Data from survey conducted by the National Association of Chiefs of Police.

144. Ibid., p. 8. This table also includes 5 firefighters, 11 correctional officers, and 7 others such as probation and parole officers.

145. David Konstantin, "Law Enforcement Officers Feloniously Killed in the Line of Duty: An Exploratory Study," *Justice Quarterly* 1 (1984): 29–45.

146. David Lester, "The Murder of Police Officers in American Cities," *Criminal Justice and Behavior* 11 (1984): 101–13.

147. "Number of Officers Killed Declined in '81," *Justice Assistance News* 6 (August 1982): 13; see also Geller, "Deadly Force," pp. 166–67.

148. Schmidt, "Deaths in the Line of Duty," p. 8.

149. See James Fyfe, "Administrative Interventions on Police Shooting Discretion: An Empirical Examination," *Journal of Criminal Justice* 7 (1979): 313–25.

150. Ibid., see also Frank Zarb, "Police Liability for Creating the Need to Use Deadly Force in Self-Defense," *Michigan Law Review* 86 (1988): 1982–2009.

151. Ibid. For an opposing finding, see William Waegel, "The Use of Lethal Force by Police: The Effect of Statutory Change," *Crime and Delinquency* 30 (1984): 121–40.

152. "Survey Indicates Accreditation Cuts Liability Insurance Costs," *Criminal Justice Newsletter*, 15 December 1988, p. 3.

153. Sean Murphy, "City Made $500,000 settlement in shooting," *Boston Globe*, 6 December 1988, p. 1.

154. Mark Thompson, "Los Angeles Chief Personally Liable for Officer Misconduct," *Criminal Justice Newsletter*, 17 January 1989, pp. 6–7.

155. *Canton v. Harris*, No. 86–1088, 44 CrL 3157 (1989).

156. Walker, *Popular Justice*, p. 64.

157. Herman Goldstein, *Police Corruption* (Washington, D.C.: Police Foundation, 1975), p. 3.

158. Michael Woronoff, "Public Employees or Private Citizens: The Off-duty Sexual Activities of Police Officers and the Constitutional Right of Privacy," *University of Michigan Journal of Law Reform* 18 (1984): 195–219.

159. John Kennedy, "Officer found guilty of collecting sick pay while on second job," *Boston Globe*, 26 February 1987, p. 61.

160. *Knapp Commission Report on Police Corruption* (New York: George Braziller, 1973), pp. 1–34.

161. Elizabeth Neuffer, "Seven Additional Detectives Linked to Extortion Scheme," *Boston Globe*, 25 October 1988, p. 60.

162. Kevin Cullen, "US Probe Eyes Bookie Protection," *Boston Globe*, 25 October 1988.

163. Michael Johnston, *Political Corruption and Public Policy in America* (Monterey, Calif.: Brooks/ Cole Publishing Co., 1982), p. 75.

164. William Doherty, "Ex-sergeant says he aided bid to sell exam," *Boston Globe*, 26 February 1987, p. 61.

165. Anthony Simpson, *The Literature of Police Corruption*, vol. 1 (New York: John Jay Press, 1977), p. 53.

166. Peter Kraska and Victor Kappeler, "Police On-Duty Drug Use: A Theoretical and Descriptive Examination," *American Journal of Police* 7 (1988): 1–28.

167. Ellwyn Stoddard, "Blue Coat Crime," in *Thinking about Police*, Carl Klockars, ed. (New York: McGraw-Hill, 1983), pp. 338–49.

168. Lawrence Sherman, *Police Corruption: A Sociological Perspective* (Garden City, N.Y.: Doubleday, 1974).

169. Johnston, *Political Corruption and Public Policy in America*, p. 82.

170. Sherman, *Police Corruption*, pp. 40–41.

171. Samuel Walker, *Police in Society* (New York: McGraw-Hill, 1983), p. 181.

172. "Slice of Vice," *Time*, 6 January 1986, p. 72.

173. Ibid., p. 194.

174. Barbara Gelb, *Tarnished Brass: The Decade after Serpico* (New York: Putnam and Sons, 1983).

175. Candace McCoy, "Lawsuits against Police: What Impact Do They Have?" *Criminal Law Bulletin* 20 (1984): 49–56.

176. Thomas Barker, "Rookie Police Officers' Perceptions of Police Occupational Deviance," *Police Studies* 6 (1983): 30–38.

9

Police and the Rule of Law

T he police are charged with both preventing crime before it occurs and identifying and arresting criminals who have already broken the law. To carry out these tasks, police officers want a free hand to search for evidence, to seize contraband such as guns and drugs, to interrogate criminals, and to have witnesses and victims identify suspects. They know their investigation must be thorough. For trial, they will need to provide the prosecutor with sufficient evidence to prove guilt "beyond a reasonable doubt." Therefore, soon after the crime is committed, they must make every effort to gather physical evidence, obtain confessions, and take witness statements that will be adequate to prove the case in court. Police officers also realize that evidence the prosecutor is counting on to prove the case, such as the testimony of a witness or co-conspirator, may evaporate before the trial begins. Then the case outcome may depend on some piece of physical evidence or a suspect's statement taken early during the investigation.

The need for police officers to gather conclusive evidence can conflict with the constitutional rights of citizens. For example, although police want a free hand to search homes and cars for evidence, the Fourth Amendment restricts police activities by requiring that they obtain a warrant before conducting a search. When police wish to vigorously interrogate a suspect, they are bound to honor the Fifth Amendment's prohibition against forcing people to incriminate themselves.

Over the years the confrontation between police and the criminal suspect has been moderated by the courts. Most importantly, the U.S. Supreme Court has used its power of case review and constitutional interpretation to set limits on police operations. At one time the Court did little to curb police and left their authority unchecked. In the 1960s the Warren Court moved vigorously to

At one time the Supreme Court did little to curb the police and left their authority unchecked.

restrict police activities, going so far as to "punish" police by excluding from trial any evidence obtained in violation of the suspect's constitutional rights (the so-called **exclusionary rule**). Some critics charged that Court decisions "handcuffed" the police while giving criminal suspects a free hand to continue their law-violating activities; the rising crime rate in the 1960s and 1970s was blamed on the Warren Court's "submissiveness." Under Chief Justices Burger and Rehnquist the balance seems to be shifting: criminal suspects have received fewer protections; police officers find it easier to obtain search warrants, interrogate suspects, and conduct "lineups."

In sum, police are controlled in their investigatory activities by the rule of law. At some junctures in the nation's history, the Court has "sided" with the police while in others the civil liberties of criminal suspects have been put first. The following sections review these issues and show how the changes in Court rulings have influenced police operations and investigations.

■ Identification of Criminal Behavior

The First Step: Crime Detection

The police are generally the first agency in the criminal system to deal with the commission of a crime. They generally become aware of the crime in one of three ways: through a complaint from a victim, through a reported complaint initiated by a witness, or through personal investigation. Victim-reported crimes include the woman who complains to the police officer on patrol that her purse was stolen, the man who goes to the local police station and claims he is being threatened by a neighbor, or the woman who calls the police to inform them that she was assaulted by her boyfriend. Witness-reported crimes include the neighbor who has observed someone unfamiliar breaking into a home, the passerby who sees a woman molested by a youthful offender, or the woman who observes a teenager stealing a pair of pants from a local clothing shop. When the victim or witness seems to be telling the truth, the police will usually investigate the crime, obtain information about the suspect, and try to apprehend the offender.

In some instances, the police themselves discover the crime. During patrol activities, police often witness crimes and may attempt to arrest a suspect at the scene. For example, a police officer on patrol at night may observe a youth breaking into a gas station; or a traffic officer on the highway may stop a suspicious automobile and discover that its driver is intoxicated. Police also investigate individuals and situations that are linked in some way to criminal activity; for instance, the police chief may ask an officer to talk with a pharmacist about local drug traffic to learn where juveniles are obtaining unauthorized drugs without prescriptions. On a more intensive level, a police department may assign detectives to investigate a vice, gambling, or narcotics ring that is flourishing in the community. This approach to crime detection may often take months, since the police must not only obtain evidence for criminal prosecution, but also must do so within strict legal boundaries. In deciding to proceed with this type of investigation, the police are often influenced by the availability of their own resources, the seriousness of the crime, community attitudes, and societal pressures in that certain types of criminal activities are perceived as being more harmful than others.

In many situations when criminal acts occur, no one is arrested at the scene. For example, the police may be informed that a cab driver has been killed in an attempted robbery and that his body has been found in the cab at a particular location, or that a woman has been raped and her attacker has escaped. These types of criminal cases are often referred to the police agency's detective bureau. The investigating detectives may then question everyone even remotely connected with the crime and examine the crime scene for evidence. People in the general area of the scene will usually be interviewed for information, witnesses will be questioned, skilled crime-scene technicians will gather physical evidence, and other officers will generally search the area for clues to the identification of the offender.

Generally, because these investigative steps are very time-consuming, they are taken in only a few of the criminal acts encountered by police. Obviously, serious crimes such as those mentioned will require many investigative tools; on the other hand, minor offenses, such as the theft of a television set or stereo, do not require a serious police investigative response. Since few formal rules and no uniformity exist regarding procedures used in police investigation, the degree to which a crime is investigated often depends on the overall resources of a given police department. As you may recall, some critics question whether police investigations are actually worthwhile and charge that police investigators rarely "get their man."

Often police are not the only criminal justice agency that initially comes into contact with criminal activity. The district attorney's office, for instance, is frequently involved in special kinds of criminal investigations and in enforcing statutes dealing with such activities as organized crime, white-collar crime, and political corruption.

Range of Police Investigative Techniques

Once a crime has been committed and the purpose of the investigation has been determined, the police may use various means to collect the evidence needed for criminal prosecution. In each crime, police must decide how to proceed with the primary focus of the investigation. Should surveillance techniques be employed to secure information? Is there reasonable suspicion to justify stopping and frisking a suspect? Has the investigation shifted from a general inquiry and begun to focus on a particular suspect so that the police can initiate a legally appropriate interrogation procedure? In certain circumstances, one investigative technique may be more appropriate than another.

The American Bar Association's *Standards Relating to the Urban Police Function* identifies many of the methods currently employed by the police in responding to situations involving both criminal and noncriminal activity:[1]

1. Engaging in surveillance (keeping a situation under observation—overtly or covertly—with the objective of acquiring additional information or evidence, with the objective of discouraging certain forms of activity).
2. Frisking and searching of persons and searching of vehicles and premises (in connection with an arrest or, independent of an arrest, as a means of protecting the officer, acquiring evidence of a crime, acquiring information generally, or simply making the presence of the police known).
3. Confiscating illegal objects (drugs, guns, gambling devices, paraphernalia, or money—either in connection with an arrest or simply as a means of removing such items from use and circulation).

4. Trading immunity from enforcement for information or cooperation (in allowing a narcotics user, a petty gambler, or a prostitute to continue to operate despite evidence of a violation of the law in exchange for their providing information leading to the identity and prosecution of those engaged in more serious forms of behavior).

5. Detaining persons temporarily (the use of arrest and subsequent detention for purposes other than prosecution, such as further investigation, safekeeping, or simply harassment).[2]

Criminal detection, apprehension, and arrest are the primary investigative functions performed by law enforcement officers. Proper police investigations involve collecting facts and information that will lead to the identification, arrest, and conviction of the criminal defendant. Many police operations are informal—such as referring an alcoholic to a hospital or resolving a family dispute—and are based on agency policy or police discretion. In contrast, the primary techniques of investigation—such as stopping and questioning people or interrogating a suspect—are controlled by statute and constitutional case law and are subject to review by the courts.

Police and the Courts

The U.S. Supreme Court has taken an active role in considering the legality of police operations. The Court has reviewed numerous appeals charging that police violated a suspect's rights during the investigation, arrest, and custody stages of the justice process. Of primary concern has been police conduct in obtaining and serving search and arrest warrants, and in conducting postarrest interrogations and lineups. In some instances, the Court has expanded police power, for example, by increasing the occasions when police can search without a warrant. In other cases, the Court has restricted police operations, for example, by ruling that every criminal suspect has a right to an attorney when being interrogated by police. Change in the law often reflects such factors as the justices' legal philosophy, their emphasis on the ability of police to control crime, their views on public safety, and their commitment to the civil liberties of criminal defendants. The issues and cases discussed in the following sections reflect the endless ebb and flow of judicial decision making and its impact on the law enforcement process.

■ Search and Seizure

Evidence collected by the police is governed by the **search and seizure** requirements of the **Fourth Amendment** of the U.S. Constitution.[3] The Fourth Amendment protects the defendant against any unreasonable searches and seizures resulting from unlawful activities. Although there are exceptions, the general rule regarding the application of the Fourth Amendment is that any search or seizure undertaken without a validly obtained **search warrant** is unlawful. Furthermore, the amendment provides that no warrant shall be issued unless there is probable cause to believe that an offense has been or is being committed. A police officer concerned with investigating a crime can undertake a proper search and seizure if a valid search warrant has been obtained from the court or if the officer is functioning under one of the many exceptions to the search warrant requirement.

A search warrant is an order from a court authorizing and directing the police to search a designated place for property stated in the order and to bring that property to court. The order must be based on the sworn testimony of the police officer that the facts on which the request for the search warrant is made are trustworthy. Examples of an application for a search warrant and the search warrant itself appear in Figures 9.1 and 9.2

Search Warrant Requirements

Three critical concepts in the Fourth Amendment are directly related to the search warrant: **unreasonableness, probable cause,** and **particularity.**

"Unreasonableness" in searches and seizures generally refers to whether an officer has exceeded the scope of police authority. Most unreasonable actions are those in which the police officer did not have sufficient information to justify the search. In discussing "probable cause," the Fourth Amendment provides clearly that no warrants shall be issued unless probable cause is supported by oath or affirmation; in other words, a search warrant can be obtained only if the request for it is supported by facts that would convince the court that a crime has been or is being committed.

"Particularity" generally refers to the search warrant itself; the Fourth Amendment requires that a search warrant specify the place to be searched and the reasons for searching it. When the police request a search warrant, the warrant must identify the premises and the personal property to be seized, and it must be signed under oath by the officer requesting it. The essential facts and information justifying the need for the search warrant are set out in an affidavit requesting the warrant. The requirement of particularity was recently addressed in the 1987 U.S. Supreme Court case of *Maryland v. Garrison.*[4] On the basis of information received from an informant, the police obtained a search warrant for the third-floor premises of a building, believing only one apartment existed there; upon arriving, they found that the third floor actually contained two apartments. They proceeded to search the entire floor and seized incriminating evidence that was later used to convict Garrison. Garrison later challenged the search of the entire third floor, claiming that the warrant was imprecise in its description of the premises. The Supreme Court concluded that the factual mistake did not invalidate the warrant even though a complete understanding of the building's floor plan was missing. In other words, when it comes to the essence of *particularity* regarding the place to be searched, the validity of the warrant must be judged on the basis of the information available to the police and disclosed to the issuing magistrate.

In a practical sense, law enforcement officers do not often rely on the use of search warrant for entering a home or searching a person, but in certain kinds of cases—such as organized crime investigations, gambling and drug offenses, and pornography cases—search warrants are particularly useful. They are also often requested during investigations of other offenses when the police can be reasonably sure that the evidence sought cannot be removed from the premises, destroyed, or damaged by the suspect. The police are generally reluctant to seek a warrant, however, because of the stringent evidentiary standards courts require for obtaining the warrant and the availability of search and seizure alternatives.

Use of Informers

The U.S. Supreme Court has played an active role in interpreting the legal requirements of a search warrant. One of the major issues litigated by the

<table>
<tr><td colspan="2">A F F I D A V I T
IN SUPPORT OF APPLICATION FOR SEARCH WARRANT</td><td>TRIAL COURT OF MASSACHUSETTS</td></tr>
</table>

1. I, Robert J. Cronin being duly sworn do depose and say as follows:

2. I am an Andover Police Officer currently assigned to the Lawrence Drug Task Force in the capacity of Police Detective. I have been an Andover Police Officer for the past six and one-half years, being currently attached to the Detective Division. As part of this assignment I have investigated numerous violations of Possession and Sale and Distribution of Class A, B, C, and D Controlled Substances. As a result of these investigations I have personally arrested and/or participated in the arrest of 150 persons. In addition I have been an undercover officer in over 25 operations in which I have purchased Heroin, Cocaine, and Marijuana, in this capacity. I have received training in controlled substance enforcement from the Massachusetts State Police, the Federal Drug Enforcement Administration, and the Lawrence Drug Task Force to which I am currently assigned.

3. During the month of January 1988 this officer was travelling in an undercover capacity in the Merrimac Valley Area. As a result this officer met and had conversation with a female, introduced as Jane. During this conversation Jane, stated to this officer that the best connection for cocaine was Joe Smith. Jane, further stated that Smith had moved to Andover, MA, and was residing at 1 Main Street. Jane, went on to say that if Smith could not be reached at 555-1234 he, Smith would be found at the Pub in Lawrence, MA.

4. During the past three (3) weeks a surveillance was conducted at 1 Main Street. As a result of this surveillance Smith was observed to leave the front unit of 1 Main Street, Andover, and travel directly to the Pub, located in Lawrence, MA. During that time period this officer went to the Pub and tried to locate Smith. Inside the establishment, during conversation with a bartender, it was learned that Smith usually arrived at 8:00 p.m. most evenings.

5. During the last 72 hours this officer met with a confidential reliable informer, hereinafter referred to as CRI. CRI stated that the name Smith was familiar and that the CRI would purchase cocaine from Smith. CRI has provided information in the past that led to the arrest of Steve Jones, Haverhill, MA, for Possession with Intent to Distribute Cocaine a Class B Substance, in December 1984, additionally CRI led to the arrest of Fred Brown, in September 1986, for Major Trafficking in Cocaine which he was convicted and sentenced in Salem Superior Court.

6. Also within the last 72 hours this officer met with CRI and had CRI contact Smith. As a result of the contact it was determined through conversation with Smith that he was expecting a cocaine delivery and that he was out at the moment. A second contact was made by CRI to Smith at his house. Smith stated to meet him at the Pub during the evening. As a result of that conversation a surveillance was conducted and Smith was observed to exit 1 Main Street, front and travel directly to the Pub.

7. After watching Smith enter the Pub, CRI was checked for contraband and given a quantity of U.S. currency. CRI entered the Pub, a short time later CRI exited the Pub and provided this officer with a quantity of powdered substance. The CRI was again checked for contraband with negative results. This powdered substance field tested positive for cocaine, a Class B controlled substance. CRI stated to this officer that Smith sold CRI the substance and that Smith stated that he, Smith, had a lot more cocaine at home and just order up an amount and it would be provided.

8. Based on the above information this officer respectfully requests an order of search and seizure authorizing the search of any and all rooms comprising the apartment at 1 Main Street, Andover, MA, occupied by Smith, also any common areas, cellars, hallways, or porches, to which the occupants of the apartment may have access for Cocaine a Class B Controlled Substance as defined under Chapter 94C Section 31 of the General Laws of Massachusetts and directing that such property or evidence or any part thereof be found that it be seized and brought before the Court.

PRINTED NAME OF AFFIANT	SIGNED UNDER THE PENALTIES OF PERJURY
Robert J. Cronin	x *Robert J. Cronin* Signature of Affiant

SWORN AND SUBSCRIBED TO BEFORE

x *Susan White*
Signature of Justice, Clerk-Magistrate or Assistant Clerk

2-23-88
DATE

PAGE _1_ OF _1_ PAGES OF THIS AFFIDAVIT

FIGURE 9.1 **Affidavit in Support of a Search Warrant**

SEARCH WARRANT

G.L. c. 276, §§ 1-7

TO THE SHERIFFS OF OUR SEVERAL COUNTIES OR THEIR DEPUTIES, ANY STATE POLICE OFFICER, OR ANY CONSTABLE OR POLICE OFFICER OF ANY CITY OR TOWN, WITHIN OUR COMMONWEALTH:

Proof by affidavit, which is hereby incorporated by reference, has been made this day and I find that there is **PROBABLE CAUSE** to believe that the property described below:

☐ has been stolen, embezzled, or obtained by false pretenses.
☐ is intended for use or has been used as the means of committing a crime.
☐ has been concealed to prevent a crime from being discovered.
☒ is unlawfully possessed or concealed for an unlawful purpose.
☐ is evidence of a crime or is evidence of criminal activity.
☐ other *(specify)* _____

YOU ARE THEREFORE COMMANDED within a reasonable time and in no event later than seven days from the issuance of this search warrant to search for the following property:

Cocaine a Class B Controlled Substance as defined under Chapter 94C Section 31 of the General Laws of Massachusetts. Any articles or implements used in the cutting, packaging, bagging, administration, or weighing of the Controlled Substance. Any books, notes, records, written materials, any monies, instruments of money or U.S. currency derived from or relating to the distribution of this Controlled Substance. Any papers pertaining to ownership or occupancy.

☒ at:

Front Unit of 1 Main Street, Andover, a two and one-half story wood frame house, color gray and white trim.

which is occupied by and/or in the possession of: ___ Joe Smith _____

☒ on the person or in the possession of:
Joe Smith

You ☒ are ☐ are not   also authorized to conduct the search at any time of the night.

You ☐ are ☒ are not   also authorized to enter the premises without announcement.

You ☒ are ☐ are not   also commanded to search any person present who may be found to have such property in his or her possession or under his or her control or to whom such property may have been delivered.

YOU ARE FURTHER COMMANDED if you find such property or any part thereof, to bring it, and when appropriate, the persons in whose possession it is found before the
_____ LAWRENCE _____ Division of the _____ DISTRICT _____ Court Department.

DATE ISSUED	SIGNATURE OF JUSTICE, CLERK-MAGISTRATE OR ASSISTANT CLERK
February 26, 1988	X _Susan White_
FIRST OR ADMINISTRATIVE JUSTICE	PRINTED NAME OF JUSTICE, CLERK-MAGISTRATE OR ASSISTANT CLERK
WITNESS: ___ Kevin M. Herlihy ___	Susan White

■ *FIGURE 9.2* **Search Warrant**

Court has been the reliability of the evidence contained in the affidavit. In many instances, the evidence used by the police in requesting a search warrant originates with a police informer rather than with the police officer. Such information is normally referred to as **hearsay evidence.**

The Supreme Court has determined that such evidence must be corroborated to serve as a basis for probable cause and thereby justify the issuance of a warrant. In the case of *Spinelli v. United States* (1969), the Supreme Court held that statements by an informer that he or she had personal knowledge of the facts about the crime and had supplied prior truthful information were sufficient corroboration.[5] In an earlier case, *Aguilar v. Texas* (1964), the court articulated a two-part test for issuing a warrant on the word of an informant: (1) the police had to show why they believed the informant, and (2) the circumstances as to how the informant acquired personal knowledge of the crime had to be explained.[6] Later, in Illinois v. Gates (1983), the Court eased the process of obtaining search warrants by developing a new test (see the Law in Review on page 314).[7] The "two-pronged test" of *Spinelli* and *Aguilar* was replaced with a "totality of the circumstances" test to determine probable cause for the issuance of a search warrant. This means that to obtain a warrant, the police must prove to a judge that, considering the "totality of the circumstances," an informant has relevant and factual knowledge that there exists a fair probability that evidence of a crime will be found in a certain place. Some states have rejected the standard of the "totality of the circumstances." For example in *Commonwealth v. Upton* (1985), a Massachusetts court held that *Gates* was "unacceptably shapeless and permissive" and lacking in precision. It used the old *Aguilar/Spinelli* doctrine in deciding that a police officer's use of an anonymous telephone tip to obtain a warrant was improper.[8]

In sum, to obtain a search warrant, the following procedural requirements must be met: (1) the police officer must request the warrant from the court; (2) the officer must submit an affidavit establishing the proper grounds for the warrant; (3) the affidavit must state the place to be searched and the property to be seized. Whether the affidavit contains sufficient information to justify the issuance of the warrant is the aspect that determines the validity of the warrant once issued.

■ Warrantless Searches

There are some significant exceptions to the search warrant requirement of the Fourth Amendment. Two critical exceptions are: (1) **searches incident to a lawful arrest** and (2) **field interrogations.** Other specialized warrantless searches include automobile searches, consent searches, and drug courier profiles. These exceptions as well as the doctrine of plain view and the law of electric surveillance are discussed in this section.

Searches Incident to a Lawful Arrest

Traditionally, a search without a search warrant is permissible if it is made incident to a lawful arrest. For example, if shortly after the armed robbery of a grocery store, officers arrest a suspect with a briefcase hiding in the basement, a search of the suspect's person and of the briefcase would be a proper search incident to a lawful arrest and without a warrant. The legality of this type of search depends almost entirely on the lawfulness of the arrest. The arrest will be upheld if the police officer observed the crime being committed or had probable cause to believe that the suspect committed the offense. If the arrest is found to have been invalid, then any warrantless search made incident to the arrest would be considered illegal, and the evidence would be excluded from trial.

The police officer who searches a suspect incident to a lawful arrest must generally observe two rules. First, it is important that the police officer search the suspect at the time of or immediately subsequent to the arrest. Second, the police may search only the suspect and the area within the suspect's immediate control; that is, when a police officer searches a person incident to a lawful arrest, such a search may not legally go beyond the area where the person can reach for a weapon or destroy any evidence. The U.S. Supreme Court dealt with the problem of the permissible scope of a search incident to a lawful arrest in the case of *Chimel v. California*, which is summarized in the Law in Review on page 292.[9]

According to the *Chimel* doctrine, the police can search a suspect without a warrant after a lawful arrest in order to protect themselves from danger and to secure evidence. This rule can be interpreted loosely so that the search can be conducted even though the threat of danger is not really imminent. For example, in 1981 in *New York v. Belton* the Court upheld the search of a defendant's jacket pursuant to an arrest for a traffic violation.[10] Belton and three other men had been stopped on a highway for driving at an excessive rate of speed. The police officer discovered that none of the four occupants owned the vehicle. He also smelled marijuana and noticed an envelope marked "Supergold," which he associated with marijuana, on the floor of the car. The officer ordered the men out of the car and stationed them some distance from the vehicle. He then searched the men and the passenger compartment of the car, where Belton's black leather jacket was on the back seat. The officer searched the jacket and found cocaine. The Court concluded that the search of the jacket was a search incident to a lawful arrest and that the jacket was within the area of immediate control within the meaning of the *Chimel*, even though the defendants were not close to the jacket at the time of the search.

ENTERING A PERSON'S HOME. Arresting someone does not give the police the right to invade his or her privacy. Police cannot enter a suspect's home without either a search warrant or an **arrest warrant**.[11] Nor do police have the right to search the homes of friends or relatives of wanted suspects unless they have a warrant authorizing them to do so.[12] However, if police have a legal arrest warrant and believe the suspect is at home, they can enter the premises to take the suspect into custody. The Supreme Court has also ruled that the police can secure the premises while they obtain a search warrant. In *Segura v. United States* in 1984, the police arrested a suspected drug dealer in her apartment and remained there 19 hours until a search warrant could be obtained. On appeal, the Court upheld the legality of Segura's detention.[13]

Field Interrogation: Stop and Frisk

Another important exception to the rule requiring a search warrant is the **threshold inquiry,** or the **stop-and-frisk** procedure. Police examination of a suspect on the street does not always occur during or after arrest; officers frequently stop persons who appear to be behaving in a suspicious manner or

Chimel v. California (1969)

This case illustrates how how the U.S. Supreme Court changed its legal position with regard to the scope of a search incident to a lawful arrest

FACTS

On the afternoon of September 13, 1965, three police officers arrived at the Santa Ana, California, home of Ted Chimel with a warrant authorizing his arrest for the burglary of a coin shop. The officers knocked on the door, identified themselves to Chimel's wife, and asked if they could come inside. She admitted the officers into the house, where they waited 10 or 15 minutes until Chimel returned home from work. When he entered the house, one of the officers handed him the arrest warrant and asked for permission to look around. Chimel objected, but was advised that the officers could conduct a search on the basis of the lawful arrest. No search warrant had been issued.

Accompanied by Chimel's wife, the officers then looked through the entire three-bedroom house. The officers told Chimel's wife to open drawers in the master bedroom and sewing room and "to physically move contents of the drawers from side to side so that [they] might view any items that would have come from [the] burglary." After completing the search, the officers seized numerous items, including some coins. The entire search took between 45 minutes and an hour.

At the defendant's subsequent state trial on two charges of burglary, the coins taken from his house were admitted into evidence against him over his objection that they had been unconstitutionally seized. He was convicted and the judgment was affirmed by the California Supreme Court.

DECISION

The U.S. Supreme Court decided that the search of Chimel's home went far beyond any area where he might conceivably have obtained a weapon or destroyed any evidence, and that no constitutional basis existed for extending the search to all areas of the house. The court concluded that the scope of the search was unreasonable under the Fourth Amendment as applied through the Fourteenth Amendment, and Chimel's conviction was overturned.

SIGNIFICANCE OF THE CASE

The *Chimel* case changed the policy with regard to the scope of a search made by an officer incident to a lawful arrest. In the past, a police officer was permitted to search all areas under the control of the defendant. The Court's ruling in the *Chimel* case allows the officer to search only the defendant and the immediate physical surroundings under the defendant's control, generally interpreted as an arm's length distance around the defendant. No longer can a police officer who arrests a person in that person's home search the entire house with a valid search warrant. ■

about whom complaints are being made. Ordinarily, police are not required to have sufficient evidence for an arrest in order to stop a person for brief questioning. If the only way in which the police could stop a person was by making an arrest, they would be prevented from investigating many potentially criminal situations. For this reason, the courts have given the police the authority to stop a person, ask questions, and search the person in a limited way, such as frisking for a concealed weapon. The courts have concluded that it is unreasonable to expect a police officer to decide immediately whether to arrest a suspect. With a limited power to stop and frisk, the police officer is able to investigate suspicious persons and situations without having to meet the probable cause standard for arrest. If the police officer did not have this authority, many innocent individuals would probably be arrested.

The threshold inquiry, or the stop-and-frisk procedure, applies to an important point of contact between the police officer and the citizen—the street encounter. Stopping a suspect allows for brief questioning of a person, while frisking affords the officer an opportunity to avoid the possibility of attack. For instance, a police officer patrolling a high-crime area observes two young men loitering outside a liquor store after dark. The two men confer several times and stop to talk to a third person who pulls up alongside the curb in an automobile. From this observation the officer may conclude that the men are casing the store for a possible burglary. He can then stop the suspects and ask them for some identification and an explanation of their conduct. If, after questioning the suspects, the officer has further reason to believe that they are planning to engage in criminal activity, and that they are a threat to his safety, the officer can conduct a proper frisk, or a carefully limited search of the suspects' outer clothing.

The Court has given police the right to stop and frisk a suspect for a concealed weapon.

In the case of *Terry v. Ohio* (1968), the Supreme Court upheld the right of the police to conduct brief threshold inquiries of suspicious persons when there is reason to believe that such persons may be armed and dangerous to the police or others.[14] The Court's intention was to allow the officer, who interacts with members of the community many times each day, to conduct proper investigations where necessary, while at the same time keeping invasions of personal rights to a minimum and protecting the officer from harm.[15]

The field interrogation process is based primarily on the ability of the police officer to determine whether there exists suspicious conduct that gives the officer reason to believe a crime is about to be committed. Some jurisdictions have enacted legislation authorizing the stop-and-frisk procedure, thereby codifying the standard established in *Terry v. Ohio*. Courts have ruled that frisking must be limited to instances in which the police officer determines that his or her safety or that of others is at stake. The stop-and-frisk exception cannot be used to harass citizens or conduct exploratory searches.

The Supreme Court has continued to treat the *Terry v. Ohio* ruling as an exception to the general rule requiring probable cause for arrest. In 1979 the Court's decision in *Dunaway v. New York* limited the scope of *Terry v. Ohio* to stop-and-frisk actions.[16] In this case, the police obtained information from an informant that implicated Dunaway in a murder-robbery. He was taken into custody but not placed under arrest. Dunaway then implicated himself during a police interrogation. The Court raised the question of the legality of the custodial questioning on less than probable cause for a full arrest. It concluded that such police action violated the defendant's Fourth and Fourteenth Amendment rights.

Field Detention

Despite the restrictions of *Dunaway*, the police have been given the right to **detain** suspects with less than probable cause. In *Michigan v. Summers* (1981), the Supreme Court held that initial detention of the defendant did not violate his constitutional right to be free from unreasonable search of his person.[17] As the police officers were about to execute a warrant to search a house, they encountered the defendant descending the steps. They requested his assistance to gain entry and detained him while searching the premises. After finding narcotics in the basement, the police searched the defendant and found heroin in his coat pocket. The Court said that because it was lawful to require the suspect to reenter the house until evidence establishing probable cause was found, his subsequent arrest and search did not violate any stop-and-frisk provisions of the Fourth Amendment.

In a different contextual situation, and applying a more traditional approach to field detention and seizure was the Supreme Court's decision in *Michigan v. Chesternut* 1988.[18] While on a routine cruiser patrol, the police observed a car pull up to a curb and an individual exit and approach the defendant. When the defendant saw the cruiser he ran off and was observed to pull several packets from his pocket and discard them. The police examined the discarded packets and concluded that they contained cocaine. Chesternut was arrested and a search revealed other drugs including heroin. The Court rejected both the position that any pursuit is a seizure and the argument that no seizure can occur until the officer apprehends the person. Instead, the Court said that in view of all the circumstances, a reasonable person would not have felt free to leave the scene and therefore Chesternut's detention was not a seizure nor a violation of the Fourth Amendment.

Automobile Searches

The U.S. Supreme Court has also established that certain situations justify the warrantless search of an automobile on a public street or highway. For example, evidence can be seized from an automobile when a suspect is taken into custody subject to a lawful arrest. In *Carroll v. United States*, which was decided in 1925, the Supreme Court ruled that distinctions should be made between searches of automobiles, persons, and homes. The Court also concluded that a warrantless search of an automobile is valid if the police have probable cause to believe that the car contains evidence they are seeking.[19]

The legality of searching automobiles without a warrant has always been a trouble spot for police and the courts. Should the search be limited to the interior of the car, or can the police search the trunk? What about a suitcase contained in the trunk? What about the glove compartment? Does a traffic citation give the police the right to search an automobile? These questions have produced significant litigation over the years. To clear up the matter, the Supreme Court decided the landmark case of *United States v. Ross* in 1982.[20]

In *Ross* the Court held that if probable cause exists to believe that an automobile contains criminal evidence, a warrantless search by the police is

If probable cause exists that a vehicle contains criminal evidence, a warrantless search of that vehicle is legally permissible.

permissible, including a search of closed containers in the vehicle (see the Law in Review on page 296 for a detailed discussion).

An interesting recent case, *California v. Carney* (1985), has held that a mobile home is to be treated as an automobile and does not enjoy the same protection from a police search as a stationary home.[21] In **Colorado v. Bertine** in 1987, the Court addressed the validity of an inventory inspection of the contents of containers found in a van. Inventory searches are conducted by police departments in order to make an accurate tally of an arrestee's possessions so that they may be returned upon his or her release. If police "discover" contraband while making an inventory search, it can be used as evidence in a court of law. In the present case, police arrested Bertine for driving under the influence of alcohol and impounded the van he was driving. During their examination of the van, the police found cannisters of cash and drugs. On appeal, the Supreme Court said that a warrant was not required and, in so doing, further strengthened the Ross holding.[22]

In sum, the most important requirement for a warrantless search of an automobile is that it must be based on the legal standard of probable cause that a crime related to the automobile has been or is being committed. Police who undertake the search of a car must have reason to believe that it contains evidence pertaining to the crime.

ROADBLOCK SEARCHES. Police departments often wish to set up roadblocks to check drivers' licenses or the condition of the driver. Is such a stop an illegal "search and seizure"? In *Delaware v. Prouse* in 1979, the Supreme Court forbade the practice of random stops in the absence of any reasonable suspicion that some traffic or motor vehicle law has been violated.[23] Unless there is at least reasonable belief that a motorist is unlicensed, that an automobile is not registered, or that the occupant is subject to seizure for violation of the law, stopping and detaining a driver to check his or her license violates the Fourth Amendment.

One important purpose of the *Prouse* decision was to eliminate the individual officer's use of discretion to stop cars. However, what has developed from this case is tacit approval for police roadblocks that are set up to stop cars in some systematic fashion. As long as the police can demonstrate that the checkpoints are conducted in a uniform manner and that the operating procedures have been determined by someone other than the officer at the scene, roadblocks can be used to uncover even minor traffic regulation violators.

The new emphasis on roadblocks has come in the area of combatting drunk driving. Courts have ruled that police can stop a predetermined number of cars at a checkpoint and can request the motorist to produce his or her license, registration, and insurance card. While doing so, they can check for outward signs of intoxication. Nevertheless, some state jurisdictions find that such behavior intrudes on citizens' privacy.

Consent Searches

Police officers may also undertake warrantless searches when the person in control of the area or object voluntarily consents to the search. Those who **consent** to a search essentially waive their constitutional rights under the Fourth Amendment. Ordinarily, courts are reluctant to accept such waivers and require the state to prove that the consent was voluntarily given. In

United States v. Ross (1982)

FACTS

Acting on information from an informant that a described individual was selling narcotics kept in the trunk of a certain car parked at a specified location, District of Columbia police officers immediately drove to the location, found the car there, and a short while later stopped the car and arrested the driver, who matched the informant's description. One of the officers opened the car's trunk, found a closed brown paper bag, and, after opening the bag, discovered glassine bags containing white powder (later determined to be heroin). The officer then drove the car to headquarters, where another warrantless search of the trunk revealed a zippered leather pouch containing cash. The defendant was subsequently convicted of possession of heroin with intent to distribute, the heroin and currency found in the searches having been introduced in evidence after a pretrial motion to suppress the evidence had been denied. The court of appeals reversed the decision, holding that while the officers had probable cause to stop and search the car, including the trunk, without a warrant, they should not have opened either the paper bag or the leather pouch found in the trunk without first obtaining a warrant.

DECISION

The U.S. Supreme Court reversed the lower-court ruling, stating, "Police officers who have legitimately stopped an automobile and who have probable cause to believe that contraband is concealed somewhere within it may conduct a warrantless search of the vehicle as thoroughly as a magistrate could authorize by warrant." Furthermore, the rationale justifying the automobile exception does not apply so as to permit a warrantless search of any movable container that is believed to be carrying an illicit substance and that is found in a public place, even when the container is placed in a vehicle not otherwise believed to be carrying contraband. However, where police officers have probable cause to search an entire vehicle, they may conduct a warrantless search of every part of the vehicle and its contents, including all containers and packages, that may conceal the object of the search. The scope of the search is not defined by the nature of the container in which the contraband is secreted. Rather, it is defined by the object of the search and the places in which there is probable cause to believe that it may be found. For example, probable cause to believe that undocu-mented aliens are being transported in a van will not justify a warrantless search of a suitcase.

SIGNIFICANCE OF THE CASE

The U.S. Supreme Court has attempted to clarify the law of warrantless searches of automobiles by applying the singular concept of probable cause to the search of the vehicle and any material, including closed containers, found in the vehicle. The Court emphasized that police officers who have legitimately stopped an automobile and who have probable cause to believe that contraband is concealed somewhere within it may conduct a warrantless search of the vehicle as thoroughly as a magistrate could authorize by warrant. Also, the "automobile exception" to the Fourth Amendment's warrant requirement established in *Carroll v. United States,* (1925) 267 U.S. 132, 45 S.Ct. 280, 69 L.Ed. 543, applies to searches of vehicles that are supported by probable cause to believe that the vehicle contains contraband. In this kind of case, a search is not unreasonable if based on objective facts that would justify the issuance of a warrant, even though a warrant has not actually been obtained.

This decision should result in some order in the area of legal decision making of warrantless automobile searches, but at a loss of privacy to the individual. ■

---

addition, the consent must be given intelligently, and in some jurisdictions consent searches are valid only after the suspect is informed of the option to refuse consent.

The major legal issue in most consent searches is whether the police can prove that consent was given voluntarily. For example, in the case of *Bumper v. North Carolina* (1968), police officers searched the home of an elderly woman after informing her that they possessed a search warrant.[24] At the trial, the prosecutor informed the court that the search was valid because the woman had given her consent. When the government was unable to produce the warrant, the court decided that the search was invalid because the woman's consent was not given voluntarily. In the subsequent appeal, the U.S. Supreme Court upheld the lower court's finding that the consent had been illegally obtained by the false claim of the police that they had a search warrant.

In most consent searches, however, voluntariness is a question of fact to be determined from all the circumstances of the case. Furthermore, the police are usually under no obligation to inform a suspect of the right to refuse consent. Failure to tell a suspect of this right does not make the search illegal, but it may be a factor used by courts to decide if the suspect gave consent voluntarily. The decision whether to inform a defendant of the right of refusal is not equivalent to other enforceable constitutional safeguards. Under the *Miranda* decision, for instance, where the Supreme Court held that a defendant has a right to counsel and a right to be free from self-incrimination, the defendant must be informed of these rights before being able to waive them.

Drug Courier Profiles

A new method of police investigation that can conflict with the law of search and seizure is the use of **drug courier profiles** to spot potential drug violators at transportation centers such as airports.

The profiles are based on physical and psychological descriptions of past offenders. They contain characteristics such as the following: using a number of different airlines, taking a circuitous route, not picking up baggage, being the last one off the plane (in order to look out for agents), and appearing very nervous. A person displaying such traits may come under the suspicion of narcotics agents, but may not have openly broken any law nor provided probable cause sufficient for a search of his or her clothing or carry-on baggage. However, the courts have ruled under the *Terry* doctrine that agents can approach a suspect, ask for identification, and ask him or her to submit to a search.

In *United States v. Mendenhall* (1980), the U.S. Supreme Court upheld the search of a woman detained at an airport after she was identified by a drug courier profile as a suspicious person who might be carrying narcotics.[25] The defendant was not able to explain why she was using a different name on her airline tickets. She subsequently agreed to a voluntary search, which revealed she was in possession of illegal drugs. Since the search of the defendant was not preceded by an impermissible seizure of her person, the Court concluded that the search was legal. As long as the defendant had consented to her search freely and voluntarily, the stop-and-frisk procedure did not violate the law.

In 1983, however, in *Florida v. Royer*, the Court limited the ability of the police to search suspects who fit drug courier profiles.[26] Royer fit the description of a drug courier: he carried heavy luggage, he was young, and he was casually dressed. In addition, Royer had paid for his ticket in cash and had written only a name and destination—not an address and phone number—on his luggage ID tags. The police approached him, requested his driver's license and airline ticket, and then asked him to accompany them to an interrogation room. There Royer was asked to open his luggage, and he voluntarily produced a key. The suitcases contained marijuana. The Court ruled that Royer's detention was a "seizure" because when his ticket and license were taken, the police actually prevented him from leaving voluntarily. Furthermore, the long detention (15 minutes) in the interrogation room was greater than that permitted by the *Terry* doctrine (since Royer was not under arrest).

The Doctrine of Plain View

One final instance in which police can search for and seize evidence without benefit of a warrant is if it is in **plain view.** For example, if a police officer is conducting an investigation and while questioning some individuals notices that one has drugs in her pocket, the officer could seize the evidence and arrest the suspect. Or if the police are conducting a search under a warrant enabling them to look for narcotics in a person's home and they come upon a gun, the police could seize the gun, even though it is not mentioned in the warrant itself. The 1986 case of *New York v. Class* illustrates the plain-sight doctrine.[27] A police officer stopped a car for a traffic violation. Wishing to check the vehicle identification number (VIN) located on the dashboard, he reached into the car to clear away material that was obstructing his view. While clearing the dash, he noticed a gun under the seat—"in plain view." The U.S. Supreme Court upheld the seizure of the gun as evidence because the police officer had the right to check the VIN; therefore, the sighting of the gun was legal.

The doctrine of plain view was applied and further developed in *Arizona v. Hicks* in 1987.[28] Here the Court held that moving a stereo component in plain view a few inches to record the serial number constituted a search under the Fourth Amendment. When a check with police headquarters revealed the item had been stolen, it was seized and offered for evidence at Hick's trial. The Court held that a plain-view search and seizure could only be justified by probable cause, and not reasonable suspicion, and suppressed the evidence against the defendant. In this case, the Court appeared to take a firm stance on protecting Fourth Amendment rights. The *Hicks* decision is uncharacteristic in an era when most decisions have tended to expand the exceptions to the search warrant requirement.

THE CONCEPT OF CURTILAGE. An issue long associated with plain view is whether police can search **open fields,** which are fenced in but are otherwise open to view. In *Oliver v. United States* (1984), the U.S. Supreme Court distinguished between the privacy granted persons in their own home or its adjacent grounds **(curtilage)** and a field. The Court ruled that police can use airplane surveillance to spot marijuana fields and then send in squads to seize the crops, or they can use ground cars to peer into fields for the same purpose.[29]

In *California v. Ciraola* (1986), the Court expanded the police ability to "spy" on the criminal offenders.[29] In this case, the police received a tip that marijuana was growing in the defendant's backyard.[30] The yard was surrounded by fences, one of which was 10-feet high. The officers flew over the yard in a private plane at an altitude of 1,000 feet to ascertain that it contained marijuana plants. On the basis of this information, a search warrant was obtained and executed, and using the evidence, Ciraolo was convicted on drug charges. On appeal, the Supreme Court found that the defendant's privacy had not been violated.

This holding was expanded in 1989 in *Florida v. Riley* when the Court ruled that police do not need a search warrant to conduct even low-altitude helicopter searches of private property.[31] The Court allowed Florida prosecutors to use evidence obtained by a police helicopter that flew 400 feet over a greenhouse in which defendants were growing marijuana plants. The Court said the search was constitutionally permissible because the flight was within airspace legally available to helicopters under federal regulations.

These cases illustrate how the concept of curtilage and open fields seems to be taking on added significance in defining the scope of the Fourth Amendment in terms of the doctrine of plain view.

■ Electronic Surveillance

The use of wiretapping to intercept conversations between parties has significantly affected police investigative procedures. Electronic devices have been created that allow people to listen to and record the private conversations of other people over telephones, through walls and windows, and even over long-distance lines. Using these devices, police are able to intercept communications secretly and obtain information related to criminal activity.

The earliest and most widely used form of electronic surveillance is wiretapping. With approval from the court and upon issuance of a search warrant, law enforcement officers place listening devices on telephones to overhear oral communications of suspects. Such devices are also often placed in homes and automobiles. Admissible evidence is then used in the defendant's trial.

More sophisticated devices have come into use in recent years. A pen register, for instance, is a mechanical device that records the numbers dialed on a telephone. "Trap and tracer" devices ascertain the number from which calls are placed to a particular telephone. Law enforcement agencies also obtain criminal evidence by electronic communication devices, such as electronic mail, video surveillance, and computer data transmissions.

The Law of Electronic Surveillance

Electronic eavesdropping by law enforcement personnel, however, represents an invasion of an individual's right to privacy unless a court gives prior permission to intercept conversations in this manner. Police can obtain criminal evidence by eavesdropping only if such activities are controlled under rigid guidelines established under the Fourth Amendment, and they must normally request a court order based on probable cause before using electronic eavesdropping equipment.

Many citizens believe that electronic eavesdropping through hidden microphones, radio transmitters, and telephone taps and bugs represents a grave threat to personal privacy.[32] Although the application of such devices in the field of criminal justice is a controversial subject, the police are generally convinced of their value in investigating criminal activity. Others, however, believe that these techniques are often used beyond their lawful intent to monitor political figures, harass suspects, or investigate cases involving questionable issues of national security.

In response to concerns about invasions of privacy, the U.S. Supreme Court has increasingly limited the use of electronic eavesdropping in the criminal justice system. *Katz v. United States* (1967) is an example of a case in which the government failed to meet the requirements necessary to justify electronic surveillance.[33] (See the Law in Review on page 304.) The *Katz* doctrine is usually interpreted to mean that the government must obtain a court order if it wishes to listen into conversations in which the parties have a reasonable expectation of privacy, such as in their own homes or on the telephone; public utterances or actions are fair game.

The concept of privacy is still unclear in many instances. For example, in *United States v. Knotts* (1983), the Court upheld the right of police agencies to attach a battery-operated radio transmitter to chemicals related to illegal drug manufacture to aid their surveillance. The Court noted that "nothing in the Fourth Amendment prohibited the police from augmenting the sensory faculties bestowed upon them at birth with such enhancement as science and technology afforded them in this case.[34] In *United States v. Karo* (1984), the Court ruled that although the government can use tracking devices, it cannot monitor them without a court order once they are taken into a home.[35]

If the police conduct warrantless electronic surveillance of conversations, the Supreme Court has ruled that as long as one of the parties consented to the monitoring, the warrantless search does not violate the Fourth Amendment.[36] Law enforcement personnel often rely on this exception when they "wire" or "bug" an informant or undercover agent. It is generally referred to as the "consensual monitoring theory." A number of state courts have not followed the Supreme Court's lead and have ruled instead that single-party consent is insufficient to "bug" a conversation. For example, in the influential state case *Commonwealth v. Blood*, a Massachusetts court held that the evidentiary fruits of a warrantless surveillance of organized crime where police received consent from one party to the conversation, but not from both, was illegal under the Massachusetts State Constitution.[37] The court said conversations in a private home should not be surreptitiously invaded by warrantless electronic transmission in circumstances where the speaker does not intend for the conversation to go beyond known listeners. The importance of the *Blood* case is that the court reached a decision contrary to federal constitutional law. This conflict illustrates how electronic surveillance is an evolving area of the law and one that will be extensively litigated in the future.

Recordings of information obtained through electronic surveillance must be sealed when the court order expires to protect them against tampering and to make certain they are used within the time frame required by the statute. Without a seal, the contents of the interrupted communication may be deemed inadmissible. In the leading case on this issue, *United States v. Mora*, a Circuit Court of Appeals found delays of 21 days and 41 days between expiration of the warrant and sealing of the tape recordings were "not so great" as to require automatic exclusion of the evidence.[38] But the court said the government must present a satisfactory explanation for its failure to have the tape sealed within the stated period.[39]

FEDERAL CONTROLS. As a result of the controversy surrounding the use of electronic eavesdropping over the last 20 years, Congress has passed legislation to provide controls over the interception of oral communications. The Omnibus Crime Control Act (Title III) of 1968 initially prohibited lawful interceptions except by warrant or with consent.[40] It established procedures for judicial approval to be obtained based on "probable cause" and upon application of the attorney general or a designate. Statutory provisions also provide for the suppression of evidence when recordings are obtained in violation of the law.

The federal electronic surveillance law was modified by the Electronic Communications Privacy Act of 1986.[41] In light of technological changes, Title III of the new act was expanded to include not only all forms of wire and oral communications, but virtually all types of nonaural electronic communication. The law added new offenses to the previous list of crimes for which electronic surveillance could be used and liberalized court procedures for permitting and issuing court orders. In addition to this important legislation, the American Bar Association has created standards relating to the use of electronic surveillance in the criminal justice system.[42] These guidelines are helpful to jurisdictions planning statutory changes in electronic surveillance law.

In general, the basic principle of the law of electronic surveillance is that wiretapping and other devices that violate privacy are contrary to the Fourth Amendment. As a result of technological advances, such devices probably pose a greater threat to personal privacy than physical searches. The U.S. Supreme Court has permitted only narrow exceptions, such as court-ordered warrants and consensual monitoring.[43]

■ Arrest

The arrest power of the police involves taking a person into custody in accordance with lawful authority and holding that person to answer for a violation of the criminal law. For all practical purposes, the authority of the police to arrest a suspect is the basis for crime control; without such authority, the police would be powerless to implement the criminal law.

The arrest power is used primarily by law enforcement officers. Generally, law enforcement personnel are employed by public police agencies, derive

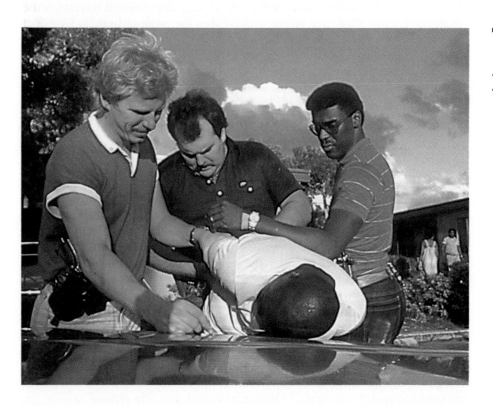

The arrest power of the police involves taking a person into custody and holding that person to answer for a violation of the criminal law.

their authority from statutory laws, and take an oath to uphold the laws of their jurisdiction. Most police officers have complete law enforcement responsibility and unrestricted powers of arrest in their jurisdictions; they carry firearms, and they give evidence in criminal trials. In the United States, private citizens also have the right to make an arrest, generally when a crime is committed in their presence. For the most part, though, private citizens rarely exercise their power of arrest, except when they apprehend offenders who have committed crimes against them.

An **arrest,** the first formal police procedure in the criminal process, occurs when a police officer takes a person into custody or deprives a person of freedom for having allegedly committed a criminal offense. Since the police stop unlimited numbers of people each day for a variety of reasons, the time when an arrest actually occurs may be hard to pinpoint. Some persons are stopped for short periods of questioning, others are informally detained and released, and still others are formally placed under arrest. An actual arrest occurs when the following conditions exist: (1) the police officer believes that sufficient legal evidence exists that a crime is being or has been committed and intends to restrain the suspect; (2) the police officer deprives the individual of freedom; and (3) the suspect believes that he or she is in the custody of the police officer and cannot voluntarily leave. The police officer is not required to use the term *arrest* or some similar word in order to initiate arrest, nor does the officer first have to bring the suspect to the station house. For all practical purposes, a person who has been deprived of liberty is under arrest.

Arrests can be initiated with or without an arrest warrant and must be based on probable cause. The arrest warrant, an order issued by the court, determines that an arrest should be made and directs the police to bring the named person before the court. An arrest warrant must be based on probable cause that the person to be arrested has committed or is attempting to commit a crime. The police will ordinarily go before a judge and obtain a warrant where no danger exists that the suspect will leave the area, where a long-term investigation of organized crime is taking place, or where a probable cause exists to arrest suspects.

Most arrests are made without a warrant. The decision to arrest is often made by the police officer during contact with the suspect. An arrest may be made without a warrant only in the following circumstances:

1. Where the arresting officer is able to establish probable cause that a crime has been committed and that the defendant is the person who committed it.
2. Where the law of a given jurisdiction allows for arrest without a warrant.

In the case of a felony, most jurisdictions provide that a police officer may arrest a suspect without a warrant where probable cause exists, even though the officer was not present when the offense was committed. In the case of a misdemeanor, probable cause and the officer's presence at the time of the offense are required. When there is some question as to the legality of an arrest, it usually involves whether the police officer has probable cause or a reasonable belief based on reliable evidence that the suspect has committed a crime. This issue is reviewed by the judge when the suspect is brought before the court for a hearing.

Police Discretion to Arrest

Chapter 8 discussed the issue of discretion in general terms of how decisions are made in police operations. Discretion is an especially critical issue in the authority of the police to make legal arrests. Although millions of arrests occur annually, police exercise much discretion in deciding whether to invoke their arrest power. The decision to arrest or not is an extremely difficult one because (1) the police are required to enforce numerous laws in a manner that is fair to all citizens; (2) police officials rarely outline through departmental policy when arrest is proper, when it is improper, what criteria should be used for arrest, and what alternatives other than arrest exist; and (3) the probable-cause standard for arrest, although used throughout the United States, is so broad and indefinite that its use often raises questions about the validity of an arrest in a given situation. Richard Donnelly described the plight of the police officer in regard to police discretion:

> The policeman's lot is indeed a difficult one. He is charged with applying or enforcing a multitude of laws or ordinances in a degree or proportion and in a manner that maintains a delicate balance between the liberty of the individual and a high degree of social protection. His task requires a sensitive and wise discretion in deciding whether or not to invoke the criminal process. He must not only know whether certain behavior violates the law but also whether there is probable cause to believe that the law has been violated. He must enforce the law, yet he must determine whether a particular violation should be handled by warning or arrest. . . . He is not expected to arrest every violator. Some laws were never intended by the enactors to be enforced, and others condemn behavior that is not contrary to significant moral values. If he arrested all violators, the courts would find it impossible to do their work, and he would be in court so frequently that he could not perform his other professional duties. Consequently, the policeman must judge and informally settle more cases than he takes to court.[44]

It has long been realized that the patrol officer, the lowest-ranking officer within a police department, is responsible for making some of the most complex and difficult decisions in American society.[45] Kenneth Davis points out the uniqueness of having subordinates make so many policy decisions:

> No other federal, state, or local agency, so far as I know, delegates so much power to subordinates. No other agency, so far as I know, does so little supervising of vital policy determinations which directly involve justice or injustice to individuals.[46]

Whether initiation of criminal prosecution against a citizen should occur is usually a matter of an individual police officer's judgment. Although in theory this judgment is based on the legal definition of each crime, in practice there are many situations in which police do not exercise their arrest authority. As noted earlier, various critics have charged that the police are less likely to take formal action if the suspect is white and middle class and more likely to arrest if the suspect is poor or a minority-group member.[47]

Controlling the Arrest Process

As a general rule, if the police make an illegal arrest, any evidence they recover or statements they take from suspects cannot be used against defendants in a court of law. Beyond this level of control, the police can be held personally liable for civil damages if they willfully or negligently make a false arrest.

The U.S. Supreme Court dealt with this issue in the recent (1986) case of *Malley v. Briggs*.[48] A police officer obtained an arrest warrant on the basis of information obtained through a wiretap. The arrested parties, a prominent family, sued for false arrest after a grand jury failed to indict them. Though the police officer had obtained an arrest warrant from a local magistrate, the Court ruled that the evidence was so sketchy that the officer was negligent in

Katz v. United States (1967)

This case deals with government intrusion by electronic eavesdropping and establishes the important principle that the Fourth Amendment protects people and not places and that searches without prior judicial approval are unlawful, with some exceptions.

FACTS

Katz was convicted of transmitting wagering information by telephone in violation of a federal statue. At his trial, the government was permitted to introduce evidence of Katz's end of the telephone conversations, which had been overheard by FBI agents who had attached an electronic listening and recording device to monitor the outgoing calls. Katz appealed, claiming that the actions of the FBI violated his search and seizure rights under the Fourth Amendment.

DECISION

Justice Potter Stewart of the U.S. Supreme Court, speaking for the majority, reversed the conviction, holding that the interception and recordings of Katz's telephone conversations represented unreasonable searches and seizures of the conversations in violation of the Fourth Amendment. Steward said, "The government agents here ignored 'the procedure of antecedent justification . . . that is central to the Fourth Amendment,' a procedure that we hold to be a constitutional precondition of the kind of electronic surveillance involved in this case. Because surveillance here failed to meet the condition, and because it led to the petitioner's conviction, the judgment must be reversed."

SIGNIFICANCE OF THE CASE

In *Katz* the U.S. Supreme Court declared that the Fourth Amendment was not to apply solely to protected places involving privacy, but that such protections also relate to the privacy of individuals. Thus, the Court abandoned the definition of a search based on property and concluded that a search results whenever police violate a person's privacy.

People in telephone booths, offices, apartments, rooms, and taxicabs, the Court stated, should be able to rely on the safeguards of the Fourth Amendment. The right of privacy protects the person anywhere and is not restricted to certain physical places. ■

requesting that a warrant be issued. The Court ruled that the legal question is whether a reasonably well-trained officer would have known that probable cause had not been established and that a warrant should not have been obtained. If such was the case, the warrant was not reasonable since it created the unnecessary danger of false arrest. Consequently, the police officer in the case was liable to be sued for damages.

■ Custodial Interrogation

A suspect who comes under police custody at the time of arrest—on the street, in a police car, or in the police station—must be warned of the right under the Fifth Amendment to be free from self-incrimination prior to any questioning by the police. In the landmark case of **Miranda v. Arizona** (1966), the U.S. Supreme Court held that the police must give the *Miranda* warning to a person in custody before questioning begins.[49] Suspects in custody must be told that they have the following rights:

1. They have the right to remain silent.
2. If they decide to make a statement, the statement can and will be used against them in a court of law.

3. They have the right to have an attorney present at the time of the interrogation, or they will have an opportunity to consult with an attorney.
4. If they cannot afford an attorney, one will be appointed for them by the state.

Practically speaking, most suspects choose to remain silent, and since oral as well as written statements are admissible in court, police officers often do not elicit any statements without making certain a defense attorney is present. If an accused decides to answer any questions, he or she may also stop at any time and refuse to answer further questions. A suspect's constitutional rights under *Miranda* can be given up (waived) however. Consequently, a suspect should consider the waiver process carefully before abrogating any custodial rights under the *Miranda* warning.

Almost 25 years have passed since this warning was established by the Warren Court. During this time American appellate courts have heard literally thousands of cases involving alleged violations of the *Miranda* standards described above. Legal principles have evolved regarding the waiver of *Miranda* rights, custodial interrogation, right to counsel, and statements made to persons other than the police, among others. Some experts believe guilty felons have been freed because *Miranda* has excluded perfectly reliable confessions. Others claim *Miranda* is the heart of our privilege to be free from self-incrimination. What follows is a detailed analysis of this often litigated and hotly contested legal issue.

Historical Perspective on *Miranda*

Prior to the *Miranda* safeguards, confessions could be obtained from a suspect who had not consulted with an attorney. An early ruling in *Brown v. Mississippi* 1936 held that statements obtained by physical coercion were inadmissible evidence, but limited the use of counsel to aid the accused at this early stage of the criminal process.[50] Not until 1964 in **Escobedo v. Illinois** was the groundwork laid for the landmark *Miranda* decision.[51] In Escobedo, the U.S. Supreme Court finally recognized the critical relationship between the Fifth Amendment privilege against self-incrimination and the Sixth Amendment right to counsel. Danny Escobedo was a convicted murderer who maintained that the police interrogation forced him to make incriminating statements that were regarded as a voluntary confession. In *Escobedo* the Court recognized that he had been denied the assistance of counsel, which was critical during police interrogation. With this decision, the Court made clear its concern that the accused should be permitted certain due process rights during interrogation.

Two years later came the *Miranda* decision, which has had an historic impact on police interrogation practices at the arrest stage of the criminal justice process. Prior to *Miranda*, the police often obtained confessions through questioning methods that violated the constitutional privilege against self-incrimination. The Supreme Court declared in *Miranda* that the police have a duty to warn defendants of their rights. Certain specific procedures (that is, the *Miranda* warning) must be followed or any statements by a defendant will be excluded from evidence. The purpose of the warning is to implement the basic Fifth Amendment right to be free from self-incrimination.

As a result, the interrogation process is protected by the Fifth Amendment and, if the accused is not given the *Miranda* warning, any evidence obtained during interrogation is not admissible to prove the state's case. It is important

Danny Escobedo was convicted of murder in 1960, largely upon the basis of a confession that he made in a preindictment interrogation in which he was denied the assistance of a lawyer. In 1964, the Supreme Court overturned Escobedo's conviction and ruled that the Sixth Amendment, which guarantees the right to counsel, applies to preindictment interrogations when the accused asks to consult with counsel.

Chapter 9

Police and the Rule of Law

■

Miranda v. Arizona (1966)

Miranda v. Arizona is a landmark decision that climaxed a long line of self-incrimination cases in which the police used unlawful methods to obtain confessions from suspects accused of committing a crime.

FACTS

Ernesto Miranda, a 25-year-old mentally retarded man, was arrested in Phoenix, Arizona, and charged with kidnapping and rape. Miranda was taken from his home to a police station, where he was identified by a complaining witness. He was then interrogated and, after about two hours, signed a written confession. Miranda was subsequently convicted and sentenced to 20 to 30 years in prison. His conviction was affirmed by the Arizona Supreme Court, and he appealed to the U.S. Supreme Court, claiming that he had not been warned that any statement he made would be used against him and that he had not been advised of any right to have counsel present at his interrogation.

The *Miranda* case was one of four cases heard simultaneously by the U.S. Supreme Court, which dealt with the legality of confessions obtained by the police from a suspect in custody. In *Vignera v. New York* (1966), the defendant was arrested in connection with a robbery and taken to two different detective headquarters, where he was interrogated and subsequently confessed after eight hours in custody. In *Westover v. United States* (1966), the suspect was arrested by the Kansas City police, placed in a lineup, and booked on a felony charge. He was interrogated by the police during the evening and in the morning, and by the FBI in the afternoon, when he signed two confessions. In *California v. Stewart* the defendant was arrested at his home for being involved in a robbery. He was taken to a police station and placed in a cell, where over a period of five days he was interrogated nine times. The U.S. Supreme Court in *Miranda* described the common characteristics of these four cases:

In each, the defendant was questioned by the police in a room in which he was cut off from the outside world. In none of these cases was the defendant given a full and effective warning of his rights at the outset of the interrogation process. In all the cases, the questioning elicited oral admissions, and in three of them, signed statements as well which were admitted at their trials. They all thus share salient features—incommunicado interrogation of individuals in a police-dominated atmosphere, resulting in self-incriminating statements without full warnings of constitutional rights.

DECISION

The major constitutional issue in *Miranda*, as in the other three cases, was the admissibility of statements ob-

to note, however, that the *Miranda* decision does not deny the police the opportunity to ask a suspect general questions as a witness at the scene of an unsolved crime, as long as the person is not in custody and the questioning is of an investigative and nonaccusatory nature. In addition, a suspect can still offer a voluntary confession after the *Miranda* warning has been issued. The *Miranda* decision is summarized in the Law in Review on this page.

After the *Miranda* decision, many people became concerned that the Supreme Court under Chief Justice Earl Warren had gone too far in providing procedural protections to the defendant. Some nationally prominent persons expressed opinions that made it seem as if the Supreme Court were emptying the prisons of criminals and that law enforcement would never again be effective. Law enforcement officers throughout the nation have generally been disturbed by the *Miranda* decision, believing that it seriously hampers their efforts to obtain confessions and other self-incriminating statements from defendants. Research indicates, however, that the decision has had little or no effect on the number of confessions obtained by the police and that it has not affected the rate of convictions.[52] Since *Miranda*, there has been little empirical evidence that the decision has had a detrimental impact on law

tained from a defendant questioned while in custody or while otherwise deprived of his freedom. The Fifth Amendment provides that no person shall be "compelled" to be a witness against himself. This means that a defendant cannot be required to testify at his trial and that a suspect who is questioned before trial cannot be subjected to any physical or pyschological pressure to confess.

In the opinion of Chief Justice Earl Warren in the *Miranda* case, "the third degree method was still 'sufficiently widespread to be the object of concern.'" Of greater concern, he believed, was the increased use of sophisticated psychological pressures on suspects during interrogation. Thus, in a 5 to 4 decision, Miranda's conviction was overturned, and the Court established specific procedural guidelines for police to follow before eliciting statements from persons in police custody.

The Court's own summary of its decision is:

Our holding will be spelled out with some specificity in the pages which follow but briefly it is this: the prosecution may not use statements, whether exculpatory or inculpatory, stemming from custodial interrogation of the defendant unless it demonstrates the use of procedural safeguards effective to secure the privilege against self-incrimination. By custodial interrogation, we mean questioning initiated by law enforcement officers after a person has been taken into custody or otherwise deprived of his freedom of action in any significant way. As for the procedural safeguards to be employed, unless fully effective means are devised to inform accused persons of their right of silence and to assure a continuous opportunity to exercise it, the following measures are required. Prior to any questioning the person must be warned that he has a right to remain silent, that any statement he does make may be used as evidence against him, and that he has a right to the presence of an attorney, either retained or appointed. The defendant may waive effectuation of these rights, provided the waiver is made voluntarily, knowingly and intelligently. If, however, he indicates in any manner and at any stage of the process that he wishes to consult with an attorney before speaking there can be no questioning. Likewise, if the individual is alone and indicates in any manner that he does not wish to be interrogated, the police may not question him. The mere fact that he may have answered some questions or volunteered some statements on his own does not deprive him of the right to refrain from answering any further inquiries until he has consulted with an attorney and thereafter consents to be questioned.

SIGNIFICANCE OF THE CASE

The *Miranda* decision established that the Fifth Amendment privilege against self-incrimination requires that a criminal suspect in custody or in any other manner deprived of freedom must be informed of his or her rights. If the suspect is not warned, then any evidence given is not admissible by the government to prove its case. ∎

enforcement efforts. Instead, it has become apparent that the police formerly relied too heavily on confessions to prove a defendant's guilt. Other forms of evidence, such as the use of witnesses, physical evidence, and expert testimony, have proved more than adequate to win the prosecution's case. Blaming *Miranda* for increased crime rates is apparently not correct.[53] (See the Criminal Justice in Review on page 308.)

The Legacy of *Miranda*

Despite its apparent clarity, the *Miranda* decision has given rise to a series of litigations. One of the central issues has been the need to define the specific instances in which the *Miranda* warning must be given. Questions here involve, for example, ascertaining what custodial interrogation is, who the interrogator is, and whether damaging statements result from a specific interrogation. Other problems generally raised focus on whether the *Miranda* warning was properly given. Was the warning adequate? Did the defendant waive his or her rights? Was the defendant capable of understanding the

Don't Blame *Miranda*

Two years ago, during the Meese era at the Justice Department, leaders of the American Bar Association became concerned by charges—from inside the federal government as well as elsewhere—that criminals were regularly able to escape justice by invoking their constitutional rights.

The Miranda rule, it was said, the restrictions on search and seizure, and clever defense attorneys paid with public money, were impeding the criminal justice system and working to free thousands of dangerous, and surely guilty, miscreants. A special committee of the ABA was created to investigate whether these perceptions were accurate. . . .

The committee did more than analyze statistical reports and review earlier studies in this area. Hearings were held in three cities; the views of people who work at all stages of the criminal justice system were sought, and a large-scale telephone interview survey was undertaken. More than 800 individual police officers, prosecutors, defense attorneys and judges submitted their views.

The results of the survey are unequivocal: the criminal justice system has many problems, but they are not due to the enforcement of constitutional rights. The police, by and large, are well trained about evidentiary rules and Miranda warnings, and cases are not rejected by prosecutors or thrown out of court because of failure to observe these rules. This is not simply the opinion of those questioned, it is borne out by the facts. Only 0.6 to 2.35 percent of all felony arrests, for example, are lost because of illegal searches. If drug and weapons arrests are excluded, the range is only 0.3 to 0.7 percent. The committee also found that public defenders are severely overburdened and that attorneys in large cities are required to handle hundreds of cases every year, half of which are serious felonies.

What are the real reasons crime seems to be out of control? The drug problem is one answer. Police, prosecutors and judges agree that no significant impact has been made in this area in spite of the fact that enormous resources have been devoted to the arrest, prosecution and trial of drug offenders. These cases have overwhelmed the police, the courts and the corrections system to the point of distortion. And with so many resources devoted to drug-related crimes, there are shortages in other areas.

Less than 3 percent of all public expenditures go to support the civil and criminal justice system, and that is simply not enough. Public dissatisfaction in this area cannot be remedied by repealing the Fourth, Fifth and Sixth Amendments. Police departments, courts and correctional institutions have needs that must be understood by the public and must be addressed. That will be very expensive, but rage and rhetoric about criminals' rights are not a practical alternative. ■

SOURCE: Washington Post, 2 December 1988, p. A26.

meaning of the warning? Did statements made after the initial interrogation require the repetition of the *Miranda* warning? Can persons be questioned without an attorney present after they ask for counsel (or have counsel appointed)?

This latter question was raised in *Brewer v. Williams* (1977), otherwise known as the "Christian burial case."[54] In this case Robert Williams was being transported by the police. Williams's attorney had warned the police not to question him about the killing of a young girl. On the trip the officers asked Williams to tell where her body was buried so that she could get a "Christian burial." Williams remorsefully complied, leading the police to the woods, where he had left the victim's body. The body and his statements were later used against him at trial. Williams was convicted of the sex slaying of the 10-year-old girl and sentenced to life in prison. Though shocked by the gravity of the case, the Supreme Court overturned his conviction on the grounds that the police questioning was improper given the fact that his counsel was not present, that the officers had used psychological coercion, and that they had been warned not to interrogate the suspect without his attorney present. Despite this ruling, there are many cases where psychological coercion by police has been upheld if the Miranda warning has been given.

Not all cases have upheld a strict interpretation of *Miranda*. For example, in *Harris v. New York* (1971), the Court agreed that evidence obtained in violation of the *Miranda* warning could be used by the government to impeach a defendant's testimony during trial.[55] In *Michigan v. Tucker* (1974), the Court allowed the testimony of a witness whose identity was revealed by the suspect, even though a violation of the *Miranda* rule occurred.[56] And in the case of *Michigan v. Mosely* (1975); the Court upheld the renewed questioning of a suspect who had already been given the *Miranda* warning and had refused to answer any questions.[57]

Recent cases stand out as illustrations of the erosion of the protections granted by *Miranda*. *Nix v. Williams* (1984) was the rehearing of the *Brewer v. Williams* case (see above).[58] At Williams' second trial, the court ruled that the body of the young girl located by Williams was admissible as evidence since it would probably have been found anyway by search parties. Although the interrogation of Williams in the patrol car was ruled illegal, the girl's body did not fall under the exclusionary rule because it would have eventually been found in the same condition; this is known as the **inevitable discovery rule**. In the second case, *New York v. Quarles* (1984), police arrested a man who fit the description of an armed rapist.[59] After frisking the suspect and finding an empty holster, the police asked where his gun was. Quarles nodded in the direction of some empty cartons and responded, "The gun is over there." Although the lower courts disallowed the use of the gun at trial on the grounds that Quarles had not been given his *Miranda* warning, the Supreme Court allowed its use on the grounds that the police had the right to protect public safety by immediately asking Quarles to produce the gun (known as the **public safety doctrine**). If the gun had not been quickly found, the Court reasoned, it could have been picked up and discharged accidentally by a passerby.

In *Moran v. Burbine* (1986), a confession by a murder suspect was allowed to be used against him, even though the police failed to let him know that his sister had obtained an attorney for him, and despite the fact that the police had assured the attorney that they would not question the suspect until the following day.[60] The Court ruled that the police do not have to tell suspects that someone else has hired a lawyer for them, nor do they have to be honest with the lawyer; they simply must make sure that suspects know they have the right to remain silent.

The impact of *Miranda* has also been felt in proceedings where the defendant raises the issue of the proper application of the Sixth Amendment right to counsel to interrogation proceedings. For instance, in the recent important case of **Patterson v. Illinois** (1988), the Court reviewed whether the interrogation of the accused after indictment violated the Sixth Amendment right to counsel.[61] The defendant was charged with a street gang murder, after being given his *Miranda* warning and volunteering to answer questions put to him by police. After the indictment, while being transferred to jail, the defendant gave a lengthy statement to police including his involvement in the murder. This statement came subsequent to another *Miranda* warning and waiver, which the defendant initialed and signed for the police officer. The defendant claimed that questioning him about the murder without counsel present violated the Sixth Amendment, and that he had not validly waived his right to have an attorney present during the interview. The Supreme Court decided, however,

In 1977 the Supreme Court overturned the conviction of Robert Williams for the murder of a ten-year-old girl. A police officer who was escorting Williams across the state persuaded him to lead police to the child's body by asking him if the child's parents weren't entitled to give her a "Christian burial," thus violating Williams' privilege against self-incrimination. Williams was later convicted because the state was able to show that searchers would, in all probability, have found the body without Williams' assistance. In 1984, the Supreme Court in Nix v. Williams *ruled that the likelihood that the body would inevitably have been discovered did not justify setting aside the second conviction.*

Chapter 9

Police and the
Rule of Law

During the booking process, the accused may be fingerprinted, photographed, and asked to participate in a lineup.

that (1) the *Miranda* warning given the defendant made him aware of his right to have counsel present at the time of interrogation; and (2) the *Miranda* warning also made the defendant aware of the consequences of his waiver. In other words, as long as the waiver was given "knowingly and intelligently," the confession obtained in the post-indictment questioning was admissible.

Taken in sum, the rulings in these cases indicate that the Supreme Court has somewhat weakened the *Miranda* ruling in recent years. The Court has held that statements made to police can be used in a court of law, even though they seem to have been made at the expense of the defendant's right to remain silent and to be represented by counsel. Overall, it seems that the Burger-Rehnquist Court of the 1970s and 1980s has chipped away at the Warren Court's original decision. Nevertheless, *Miranda* remains an historic and often "symbolic" decision whose progeny continue to affect the philosophical thrust of American criminal jurisprudence.

■ The Pretrial Identification Process

After arrest, the accused is ordinarily brought to the police station, where the police list the possible criminal charges. At the same time they obtain other information, such as a description of the offender and circumstances of the offense, for booking purposes. The booking process is generally a police administrative procedure in which the date and time of the arrest are recorded; arrangements are made for stationhouse bail, detention, or removal to court; and any other information needed for identification purposes is obtained. The defendant may be fingerprinted, photographed, and required to participate in a **lineup.** A lineup is basically a pretrial identification procedure where a suspect is placed in a group for the purpose of being viewed by a witness. In accordance with the U.S. Supreme Court decisions in *United States v. Wade* (1967)[62] and *Kirby v. Illinois* (1972),[63] the accused has the right to have counsel present at what is known as the postindictment lineup or identification procedure.

In the *Wade* case, the Supreme Court held that a defendant has a right to counsel if the lineup takes place after the suspect has been formally charged with a crime. This decision was based on the Court's belief that the postindictment lineup procedure is a critical stage of the criminal justice process. In contrast, the suspect does not have a comparable right to counsel at a pretrial lineup where a complaint or indictment has not been issued. When the right to counsel is violated, the evidence of any pretrial identification must be excluded from the trial.

Suggestive Lineups

One of the most difficult legal issues is this area is determining if the identification procedure is "suggestive'" and consequently in violation of the due process clause of the Fifth and Fourteenth Amendments. In *Simmons vs. United States* (1968), the U.S. Supreme Court said, "The primary evil to be avoided is a very substantial likelihood of irreparable misidentification."[64] In its decision in *Neil v. Biggers* (1972), the Court established the following general criteria to judge the suggestiveness of a pretrial identification procedure: (1) the opportunity of the witness to view the criminal at the time of the crime; (2) the degree of attention by the witness and the accuracy of the prior description by the witness; (3) the level of certainty demonstrated by the witness; and (4) the length of time between the crime and the confrontation.[65]

The offense in the *Biggers* case was a rape. In regard to the witness's opportunity to view the suspect at the time of the crime, the victim spent a considerable period of time with her assailant, up to half an hour. She was with him under adequate artificial light in her house and under a full moon outdoors, and at least twice, once in the house and later in the woods, she faced him directly and intimately. She was no casual observer, but rather the victim of one of the most personally humiliating of all crimes. Her description to the police, which included the assailant's approximate age, height, weight, complexion, skin texture, build, and voice was thorough. She had "no doubt" that he was the person who raped her. In the nature of the crime, there are rarely witnesses to a rape other than the victim, who often has limited opportunity for observation. The victim, a practical nurse by profession, had an unusual opportunity to observe and identify her assailant. She testified at the habeas corpus hearing that there was something about his face "I don't think I could ever forget."

There was a lapse of seven months between the rape and the confrontation. This would be a serious negative factor in most cases, but the testimony was undisputed that the victim had made no previous identification at any of the showups, lineups, or photographic showings. Her record for reliability was thus a good one, as she had previously resisted whatever suggestiveness inheres in a lineup. Weighing all these factors, the Court found no substantial likelihood of misidentification, and the defendant's conviction was upheld. This is the approach the Court takes in analyzing the issue of "suggestiveness" in a lineup identification procedure.

■ The Exclusionary Rule

No review of the legal aspects of policing would be complete without a discussion of the exclusionary rule, the principal means used to restrain police conduct. As previously mentioned, the Fourth Amendment guarantees individuals the right to be secure in their persons, homes, papers, and effects against unreasonable searches and seizures. The exclusionary rule provides that all evidence obtained by illegal searches and seizures is inadmissible in criminal trials. Similarly, it excludes the use of illegal confessions under Fifth Amendment prohibitions.

For many years, evidence obtained by unreasonable searches and seizure which should consequently have been considered illegal, was admitted by state and federal governments in criminal trials. The only criterion for admissibility was whether the evidence was incriminating and whether it would assist the judge or jury in ascertaining the innocence or guilt of the defendant. How evidence was obtained was unimportant; its admissibility was determined by its relevance to the criminal case.

In 1914, however, the rules on the admissibility of evidence underwent a change of direction when the U.S. Supreme Court decided the case of *Weeks v. United States*.[66] The defendant, Freemont Weeks, was accused by federal law enforcement authorities of using the mails for illegal purposes. After his arrest, the home in which Weeks was staying was searched without a valid search warrant. Evidence in the form of letters and other materials was found in his room and admitted at the trial. Weeks was then convicted of the federal offense based on incriminating evidence. On appeal, the Supreme Court held that evidence obtained by unreasonable search and seizure must be excluded in a federal criminal trial. The Court stated:

> If letters and private documents can thus be seized and held and used in evidence against a citizen accused of an offense, the protection of the Fourth Amendment declaring his right to be secure against such searches and seizures is of no value, and, so far as those thus placed are concerned, might as well be stricken from the Constitution. The efforts of the courts and their officials to bring the guilty to punishment, praiseworthy as they are, are not to be aided by the sacrifice of those great principles established by years of endeavor and suffering which have resulted in their embodiment in the fundamental law of the land.[67]

Thus, for the first time the Court held that the Fourth Amendment barred the use in a federal prosecution of evidence obtained through illegal search and seizure. With this ruling, the Court established the exclusionary rule. The rule was based not on legislation but on judicial decision making.

Over the years, subsequent federal and state court decisions have gradually applied the exclusionary rule to state court systems. These decisions have not always been consistent, however. For instance, in 1949 the states received notice that the Supreme Court was considering making the *Weeks* doctrine binding on the state courts in the case of *Wolf v. Colorado*.[68] Wolf was charged in a Colorado state court with conspiring to perform abortions. Evidence in the form of patients' names was secured by a sheriff from a physician's office without a valid search warrant. The patients were subsequently questioned, and the evidence was used at Wolf's trial. The case was appealed, and the Supreme Court was asked to decide the question "Does a conviction by a state for a state offense deny the defendant due process of law because evidence admitted at the trial was obtained under circumstances which would have rendered it inadmissible in a federal trial?[69] In a six-to-three-decision, the Court decided that the evidence was admissible and not in violation of the Fourteenth Amendment. The Court recognized that the Fourth Amendment forbade the admissibility of illegally seized evidence, but did not see fit to impose federal standards of criminal procedure on the states. One important fact the court considered in reaching its decision on *Wolf* was that only 16 states were in agreement with the exclusionary rule, while 31 states had rejected it by 1949.

However, many states changed their positions, and by 1961 approximately half had adopted the exclusionary rule. In that same year, the Supreme Court, despite past decisions, reversed itself and made the exclusionary rule applicable to state courts in the landmark decison of **Mapp v. Ohio** (1961).[70] Because of the importance of the *Mapp* case, it is discussed in the Law in Review on page 313.

Current Status and Controversy

There seems little doubt that a more conservative U.S. Supreme Court has been diminishing the scope of the exclusionary rule. In *Illinois v. Gates* (1983), the Court made it easier for police to search a suspect's home by allowing an anonymous letter to be used as evidence in support of a warrant (see the Law in Review on page 314).[71] In another critical case, *United States v. Leon* (1984), the Court ruled that evidence seized by police relying on a warrant issued by a detached and neutral magistrate can be used in a court proceeding, even if the judge who issued the warrant may have relied on less than sufficient

Mapp v. Ohio (1961)

In this historic case, the U.S. Supreme Court held that all law enforcement agents, federal and state, are affected by the exclusionary rule, which bars the admission of illegally obtained evidence in a criminal trial.

FACTS

On May 23, 1957, three police officers arrived at Dolree Mapp's resident pursuant to information that "a person [was] hiding out in the home, who was wanted for questioning in connection with a recent bombing and that there was a large amount of police paraphernalia being hidden in the home." Mapp and her daughter by a former marriage lived on the top floor of the two-family dwelling. Upon their arrival at the house, the officers knocked on the door and demanded entrance, but Mapp, after telephoning her attorney, refused to admit them without a search warrant.

The officers again sought entrance three hours later when four or more additional officers arrived on the scene. When Mapp did not immediately come to the door, the police forcibly opened one of the doors to the house and gained admittance. Meanwhile, Mapp's attorney arrived, but the officers would not permit him to see Mapp or to enter the house. Mapp was halfway down the stairs from the upper floor to the front door when the officers broke into the hall. She demanded to see the search warrant. A paper, claimed to be a search warrant, was held up by one of the officers. She grabbed the "warrant" and placed it in her bosom. A struggle ensued in which the officers recovered the piece of paper and handcuffed Mapp because she had ostensibly been belligerent.

Mapp was then forcibly taken upstairs to her bedroom, where the officials searched a dresser, a chest of drawers, a closet, and some suitcases. They also looked into a photo album and through personal papers belonging to her. The search spread to the rest of the second floor, including the child's bedroom, the living room, the kitchen, and the dinette. In the course of the search, the police officers found pornographic literature. Mapp was arrested and subsequently convicted in an Ohio court of possessing obscene materials.

DECISION

The question in the *Mapp* case was whether the illegally seized evidence was in violation of the search and seizure provisions of the Fourth Amendment and therefore inadmissible in the state trial, which resulted in an obscenity conviction. The Supreme Court of Ohio found the conviction valid. However, the U.S. Supreme Court overturned it, stating that the Fourth Amendment's prohibition against unreasonable searches and seizures, enforceable against the states through the due process clause, had been violated by the police. Justice Tom Clark, delivering the majority opinion of the Court, made clear the importance of this constitutional right in the administration of criminal justice when he stated:

> There are those who say, as did Justice [then Judge] Cardozo, that under our constitutional exclusionary doctrine "[t]he criminal is to go free because the constable has blundered." In some cases this will undoubtedly be the result. But. . .there is another consideration—the imperative of judicial integrity. . . . The criminal goes free, if he must, but it is the law that sets him free. Nothing can destroy a government more quickly than its failure to observe its own laws, or worse its disregard of the charter of its own existence.

SIGNIFICANCE OF THE CASE

In previous decisions, the U.S. Supreme Court had refused to exclude evidence in state court proceedings based on Fourth Amendment violations of search and seizure. The *Mapp* case overruled such decisions, including that of *Wolf v. Colorado*, and held that evidence gathered in violation of the Fourth Amendment would be inadmissible in a state prosecution. For the first time, the Court imposed federal constitutional standards on state law enforcement personnel. In addition, the Court reemphasized the point that a relationship exists between the Fourth and Fifth Amendments, which forms the constitutional basis for the exclusionary rule. ■

evidence.[72] In this case the Court articulated a **good faith exception** to the exclusionary rule: evidence obtained with less than an adequate search warrant may be admissible in court if the police officers acted in good faith in obtaining court approval for their search. However, deliberately misleading a judge or using a warrant that the police know is unreasonably deficient would be

Chapter 9

Police and the Rule of Law

■

Illinois v. Gates (1983)

Illinois v. Gates significantly altered the way police can obtain search warrants without violating the exclusionary rule.

FACTS

On May 3, 1978, the Bloomington, Illinois, police department received an anonymous handwritten letter that read as follows:

This letter is to inform you that you have a couple in your town who strictly make their living on selling drugs. They are Sue and Lance Gates, they live on Greenway, off Bloomingdale Rd. in the condominiums. Most of their buys are done in Florida. Sue, his wife, drives their car to Florida, where she leaves it to be loaded up with drugs, then Lance flys down and drives it back. Sue flys back after she drops the car off in Florida. May 3 she is driving down there again and Lance will be flying down in a few days to drive it back. At the time Lance drives the car back he has the trunk loaded with over $100,000.00 in drugs. Presently they have over $100,000.00 worth of drugs in their basement.

They brag about the fact they never have to work, and make their entire living on pushers.

I guarantee if you watch them carefully you will make a big catch. They are friends with some big drug dealers, who visit their house often.
Lance & Susan Gates
Greenway
in Condominiums

This letter was referred to a police detective who began an investigation. The investigation corroborated some of the statements in the letter, including the Gates's home address and the fact that they were on a trip to Florida. Using the letter and follow-up information, the police were able to obtain a search warrant for the Gates's car and home. When the Gateses returned, the police were waiting for them. A search of their car and home yielded marijuana, weapons, and other contraband.

DECISION

The U.S. Supreme Court was asked to decide whether an anonymous letter could be used to obtain a legal search warrant. Prior to this case the police had been forced to use what is known as the two-pronged test in obtaining a warrant upon the testimony of an informer. First, the police had to show that the informer was reliable; second, they had to indicate how the informer had knowledge of the alleged crime. In *Illinois v. Gates* the Court ruled that the standard to obtain a warrant was the totality of the circumstances surrounding the information. If police can show that they have reliable and relevant information on a crime, they can use it to obtain a warrant regardless of its source. In this case the letter was not enough. However, the subsequent police corroboration of details of the case was sufficient for the judge to grant a legal search warrant.

SIGNIFICANCE OF THE CASE

Illinois v. Gates made it easier for police to obtain warrants in criminal cases. It has been hailed as a significant erosion of the exclusionary rule. Further questions raised by this case are, Can the police obtain a warrant from information received by an anonymous phone tip? How can the public be sure that the police themselves are not sending anonymous letters to themselves in order to obtain warrants? ■

grounds to invoke the exclusionary rule. A 1988 empirical study of the effects of *United States v. Leon* on police search warrant practices found the impact on judicial suppression of evidence was virtually nonexistent.[73] Although prosecutors initially applauded the decision and defense lawyers feared that the police would be inclined to secure warrants from sympathetic judges, both groups agree that *Leon* has had little practical impact on the processing of criminal cases.

It appears that the Supreme Court has expanded the good faith exception to the exclusionary rule in its decision in ***Illinois v. Krull*** (1987).[74] A Chicago police officer engaged in a warrantless search of a junkyard relying on a state statue allowing such inspections. The Court held the evidence was admissible even though the statute allowing the search was subsequently found to be unconstitutional. In this case, the Court felt the police officer could not be responsible for an illegal search when the legislature had passed the law and the officer relied in "good faith" on that law.

The Court has also ruled that evidence can be used at trial even if its discovery was in violation of the exclusionary rule, if it would have been found within a short time by independent means. This is known as the "inevitable discovery rule." Thus, if police seize evidence in violation of the exclusionary rule, it may still be used at trial if a judge rules that it would most likely have been found anyway (for example, it was in an open field and people were already looking for it).[75]

Finally, the Supreme Court continued this conservative trend by ruling in a 1988 case *(Arizona v. Youngblood)* that a criminal defendant's rights are not violated when police lose or destroy evidence that might prove the person's innocence, unless the police acted maliciously.[76] In *Youngblood* the Court ruled that police failure to preserve important evidence properly simply because of incompetence or mistake is not sufficient reason to reverse a conviction. According to conservative Chief Justice William Rehnquist, "unless a defendant can show bad faith on the part of the police, failure to preserve potentially useful evidence does not constitute a denial of due process of law".

In these and other cases, the Court seems to be making it easier for the police to conduct searches of criminal suspects and their possessions and then use the seized evidence in court proceedings. The Court has indicated that as a general rule the protection afforded the individual by the Fourth Amendment may take a back seat to concerns about public safety if criminal actions pose a clear threat to society.[77]

The Future of the Exclusionary Rule

The exclusionary rule has long been a controversial subject in the administration of criminal justice. It was originally conceived to control illegitimate police practices, and that remains its primary purpose today. It is justified on the basis that it is a deterrent to illegal searches and seizures. Yet most experts believe that no impartial data exist to prove that the rule has a direct impact on police behavior. This is by far the most significant criticism of the rule. By excluding evidence, the rule has a more direct effect on the criminal trial than on the police officer on the street. Furthermore, the rule is powerless when the police have no interest in prosecuting the accused or in obtaining a conviction. In addition, it does not control the wholesale harassment of individuals by law enforcement officials bent on disregarding constitutional rights.

The most popular criticism of the exclusionary rule, however, is that it allows guilty defendants to go free. Because courts frequently decide in many types of cases (particularly those involving victimless offenses such as gambling and drug use) that certain evidence should be excluded, the rule is believed to result in excessive court delays and to have a negative effect on plea-bargaining negotiations.[78] However, there is indication that the rule results in relatively few case dismissals.

Because the exclusionary rule may not deter illegal police action, and because its use may result in some offenders escaping conviction, proposals for modifying the rule have been suggested. The American Law Institute's *Model Code of Pre-Arraignment Procedure* limits use of the exclusionary rule to substantial violations by law enforcement officials. This means that evidence should be suppressed only if the court finds that the constitutional violations are substantial. The code does not precisely define the term *substantial*, but it enumerates six criteria for determining substantial violations:

1. (The) extent of deviation from lawful conduct
2. (The) extent to which (the) violation was willful
3. (The) extent to which privacy was invaded
4. (The) extent to which exclusion will tend to prevent violations of this Code
5. (W)hether, but for the violation, the things seized would have been discovered
6. (The) extent to which the violation prejudiced the moving party's ability to support his motion, or to defend himself in the proceedings in which the things seized are sought to be offered in evidence against him.[79]

Although the code is only a proposed model, its modification of the exclusionary rule would seem to offer some relief from the problem of having to free criminals due to minor Fourth Amendment violations by police officials. On the other hand, modification of the rule could lead police to become sloppy in their application of constitutional rights and cause them to care more about developing excuses for their actions, such as "we acted in good faith" or "the evidence would have been discovered anyway," than they do about individuals' rights.[80]

Another approach has been to legislate the exclusionary rule out of existence. Voters in California attempted to do this when they passed Proposition 8 in the early 1980s. The proposition stated: That relevant evidence should not be excluded in any criminal proceeding. In 1988, the U.S. Supreme Court had the opportunity to litigate this issue in the case of *California v. Greenwood*.[81] Concerned that the defendant Greenwood might be involved in selling drugs, the police collected Greenwood's trash bags from the curb of his home, searched them without a warrant and found items indicating the defendant used drugs. A subsequent search of Greenwood's home with a warrant disclosed additional drugs. The California Supreme Court held that the police officers' conduct was an impermissible and illegal search. The U.S. Supreme Court, however, took cognizance of the 1982 amendment to the California State Constitution that provided that evidence was not to be excluded in criminal trials on this basis. Greenwood argued that since state law prohibited the police from examining the trash, this gave him a right of privacy protected by the Fourth Amendment. But the Supreme Court rejected Greenwood's argument, holding that the state could establish the scope of its exclusionary rule and weigh the benefits of controlling police misconduct against the price of excluding reliable evidence. The *Greenwood* case certainly suggests that the exclusionary rule could be legislated out of existence.

At the same time, we should note that although Proposition 8 has been touted as a boon to crime victims, it could also result in evidence involving the personal lives of police officers, victims, and witnesses being made public on the grounds that it is "relevant" evidence for the trial's outcome.[82]

Other suggested approaches to dealing with violations of the exclusionary rule include (1) criminal prosecution of police officers who violate constitutional rights; (2) internal police control; (3) civil lawsuits against state or municipal police officers; and (4) federal lawsuits against the government under the Federal Tort Claims Act. An individual using any of these alternatives, however, would be faced with obstacles such as the cost of bringing a lawsuit, the difficulty of proving damages, and the problems of dealing with a bureaucratic law enforcement system.

In the end, of all the civilized countries in the world, only the United States applies an exclusionary rule to illegal searches and seizures of material evidence.[83] Whether the Supreme Court or legislative bodies adopt any more significant changes to the rule will depend largely on efforts by police to discipline themselves. It will also depend on the existence of a tough civil tort remedy, which allows lawsuits and claims for damages against offending police officers.

The fate of the exclusionary rule will remain difficult to predict. Although it is a simple rule of evidence, it masks complex issues involving fairness, justice, and crime control that plague the criminal justice system.[84]

■ SUMMARY

Law enforcement officers use many different investigatory techniques to detect and apprehend criminal offenders. These include searches, electronic eavesdropping, interrogation, the use of informants, surveillance, and witness identification procedures. Over the past three decades, in particular through U.S. Supreme Court decisions, serious constitutional limitations have been placed on the pretrial process. In the area of the Fourth Amendment, for example, police are required to use search warrants or conduct searches only under clearly defined exceptions to this rule. The exceptions to the search warrant rule include searches of automobiles used in a crime, stop and frisks, searches incident to an arrest, searches of material in plain view and some instances of electronic eavesdropping.

Police interrogation procedures have also been reviewed extensively. Through the *Miranda* rule, the Supreme Court established an affirmative procedure as a requirement for all custodial interrogations. Many issues concerning *Miranda* continue to be litigated. Lineups and other police practices, have also been subject to court review. The degree to which a defendant's rights should be protected at the pretrial stage while maintaining the government's interest in crime control remains a source of constant debate in the present criminal justice system.

Lastly, the exclusionary rule remains one of the most controversial issues in the criminal justice system. Even though the courts have curtailed its application in recent years, it still generally prohibits the admission of evidence that violates the defendant's constitutional rights. The exclusionary rule is an example of a federal rule being made binding on the states.

■ QUESTIONS

1. Should obviously guilty persons go free because police originally arrested them with less than probable cause?

2. Should illegally seized evidence be excluded from trial even though it is conclusive proof of a person's criminal acts?

3. Should police be personally liable if they violate a person's constitutional rights? How might this influence their investigations?

4. Should a person be put in a lineup without the benefit of counsel?

5. Have criminals been given too many rights? Should courts be more concerned with the rights of victims or the rights of offenders?

6. Does the exclusionary rule effectively deter police misconduct?

7. Can a search and seizure be "reasonable" if it is not authorized by a warrant?

■ NOTES

1. See, generally, American Bar Association, *Standards Relating to the Urban Police Function* (New York: Institute of Judicial Administration, 1973); see also Herman Goldstein, *Policing a Free Society* (Cambridge, Mass.: Ballinger, 1977).

2. Ibid., pp. 91–93. Reprinted with the permission of the American Bar Association, which authored these standards and which holds the copyright.

3. See Wayne R. LaFave, *Arrest: The Decision to Take a Suspect into Custody* (Boston: Little, Brown & Co., 1965); see also Lawrence P. Tiffany, Donald McIntyre, and Daniel Rotenberg, *Detection of Crime: Stopping and Questioning, Search and Seizure* (Boston: Little, Brown & Co., 1967).

4. 480 U.S. 79, 107 S.Ct. 1013, 94 L.Ed.2d 72 (1987).

5. 393 U.S. 410, 89 S.Ct. 584, 21 L.Ed. 2d 637 (1969).

6. 378 U.S. 108, 84 S.Ct. 1509, 12 L.Ed.2d 723 (1964).

7. 462 U.S. 213 103 S.Ct. 2317, 76 L.Ed.2d 527 (1983).

8. 476 N.E.2d 548 (1985).

9. 395 U.S. 752, 89 S.Ct. 2034, 23 L.Ed.2d 685 (1969).

10. 453 U.S. 454, 101 S.Ct. 2860, 69 L.Ed.2d 768 (1981).

11. *Payton v. New York*, 445 U.S. 573 100 S.Ct. 1371, 63 L.Ed.2d 639 (1980).

12. *Steagald v. United States, 451 U.S. 204 101 S.Ct. 1642, 68 L.Ed.2d 38 (1981).*

13. 468 U.S. 796, 104 S.Ct. 3380, 82 L.Ed.2d 599 (1984).

14. 392 U.S. 1, 88 S.Ct. 1868, 20 L.Ed.2d 889 (1968).

15. Ibid at 20–27.

16. 442 U.S. 200, 99 S.Ct. 2248, 60 L.Ed.2d 824 (1979).

17. 452 U.S. 692, 101 S.Ct. 2587, 69 L.Ed.2d 340 (1981).

18. *Michigan v. Chesternut* 108 S.Ct. 1975, 100 L.Ed.2d 566 (1988).

19. 267 U.S. 132, 45 S.Ct. 280, 69 L.Ed. 543 (1925).

20. 456 U.S. 798, 102 S.Ct. 2147, 72 L.Ed.2d 572 (1982); see also Barry Latzer, "Searching Cars and Their Contents: *U.S. v. Ross,*" *Criminal Law Bulletin* (1982); Joseph Grano, "Rethinking the Fourth Amendment Warrant Requirement," *Criminal Law Review* 19 (1982): 603.

21. 471 U.S. 386, 105 S.Ct. 2066, 85 L.Ed.2d 406 (1985).

22. 479 U.S. 367, 107 S.Ct. 738, 93 L.Ed.2d 739 (1987).

23. 440 U.S. 213 59 L.Ed.2d 660, 99 S.Ct. 1391 (1979); see also Lance Rogers, "The Drunk-Driving Roadblock: Random Seizure or Minimal Intrusion?" *Criminal Law Bulletin* 21 (1985): 197–217.

24. 391 U.S. 543, 88 S.Ct. 1788, 20 L.Ed.2d 797 (1968).

25. 446 U.S. 544, 100 S.Ct. 1870, 64 L.Ed.2d 497 (1980).

26. 460 U.S. 491 103 U.S. 1319, 75 L.Ed.2d. 229 (1983).

27. 475 U.S. 106, 106 S.Ct. 960, 89 L.Ed.2d 81 (1986).

28. 480 U.S. 321 107 S.Ct. 1149, 94 L.Ed.2d 347 (1987); see also Note, "Fourth Amendment Requires Probable Cause for Search and Seizure under Plain View Doctrine," *The Journal of Criminal Law and Criminology* 78 (1988): 763.

29. 466 U.S. 170, 104 S.Ct. 1735 80 L.Ed.2d 214 (1984).

30. 476 U.S. 207, 106 S.Ct. 1807, 90 L.Ed.2d 210 (1986).

31. *Florida v. Riley*, 109 S.Ct. 693, 44 CrL. 3079 (January 23, 1989).

32. See, generally, P. Allan Dionesopoulos and Craig R. Ducat, *The Right to Privacy: Essays and Cases* (St. Paul, Minn.: West Publishing Company, 1976).

33. 389 U.S. 347, 88 S.Ct. 507, 19 L.Ed.2d 576 (1967).

34. 460 U.S. 276 103 St.Ct. 1081, 75 L.Ed.2d. 55, (1983).

35. 468 U.S. 705, 104 S.Ct. 3296, 82 L.Ed.2d 530 (1984).

36. See *United States v. White*, 401 U.S. 745, 91 S.Ct. 1122, 28 L.Ed.2d 453 (1971).

37. 400 Mass. 61 (1987).

38. 821 F.2d 860 (1st Cir. 1987).

39. For an important state case, see *Commonwealth v. Vitello*, 367 Mass 224 (1975).

40. Omnibus Crime Control Act, Title III, 90th Congress 1968; 18 U.S.C. § § 2511—2520.

41. Electronic Communications and Privacy Act of 1986, Public Law No. 99—508, Title 18 USC § 2510.

42. American Bar Association, *Standards Relating to Electronic Surveillance, 2d ed.* (New York: Institute of Judicial Administration, 1980).

43. See Michael Goldsmith, "The Supreme Court and Title III Rewriting the Law of Electronic Surveillance," *The Journal of Criminal Law and Criminology* 74 (1983): 76–85.

44. Richard C. Donnelly, "Police Authority and Practices," *Annals of the American Academy of Political and Social Sciences* 339 (January 1962): 91–92.

45. President's Commission on Law Enforcement and Administration of Justice, *The Challenge of Crime in a Free Society* (Washington, D.C.: U.S. Government Printing Office, 1967), p. 103.

46. Kenneth C. Davis, *Discretionary Justice—A Preliminary Inquiry* (Baton Rouge: Louisiana State University Press, (1964), p. 4.

47. American Bar Association *Standards Relating to the Urban Police Function*; see also National Advisory Commission on Criminal Justice Standards and Goals, *Police* (Washington, D.C.: U.S. Government Printing Office, 1973).

48. 471 U.S. 1124, 105 S.Ct. 1092, 86 L.Ed. 271 (1986).

49. 384 U.S. 436, 86 S.Ct. 1602, L.Ed.2d 694 (1966).

50. 297 U.S. 278, 56 S.Ct. 461. 80 L.Ed. 682 (1936).

51. 378 U.S. 478, 84 S.Ct. 1758, 12 L.Ed.2d 977 (1964).

52. Michael Wald et al., "Interrogations in New Haven: The Impact of Miranda," *Yale Law Journal* 76 (1967): 1519.

53. "Don't Blame Miranda," *Washington Post*, 2 December 1988, p. A26.

54. 430 U.S. 387, 97 S.Ct. 1232, 51 L.Ed.2d 424 (1977).

55. 401 U.S. 222, 91 S.Ct. 644, 28 L.Ed.2d 420 (1971).

56. 417 U.S. 433, 94 S.Ct. 2357, 41 L.Ed.2d 182 (1974).

57. 423 U.S. 96, 46 S.Ct. 321, 46 L.Ed.2d 313 (1975).

58. 104 S.Ct. 2501, 467 U.S. 431, 81 L.Ed.2d 377 (1984).

59. 104 S.Ct. 2626, 467 U.S. 649, 81 L.Ed.2d 550 (1984).

60. 475 U.S. 412, 106 S.Ct. 1135, 89 L.Ed.2d 410 (1986); see also Walter Lippman, "Miranda v. Arizona—Twenty Years Later," *Criminal Justice Journal* 9 (1987): 241; Stephen J. Scholhofer "Reconsidering Miranda," *University of Chicago Law Review* 54 (1987): 435–61.

61. U.S. 108 S.Ct. 2389, L.Ed.2d (1988).

62. 388 U.S. 218, 87 S.Ct. 1926, 18 L.Ed.2d 1149 (1967).

63. 306 U.S. 682, 92 S.Ct. 1877, 32 L.Ed.2d 411 (1972).

64. 390 U.S. 377, 88 S.Ct. 967, 19 L.Ed.2d 1247 (1968).

65. 409 U.S. 188, 93 S.Ct. 375, 34 L.Ed.2d 401 (1972).

66. 232 U.S. 383, 334 S.Ct. 341, 58 L.Ed. 652 (1914).

67. Ibid., at 393.

68. 338 U.S. 25, 69 S.Ct. 1359, 93 L.Ed. 1782 (1949).

69. Ibid., at 25, 26.

70. 367 U.S. 643, 81 S.Ct. 1684, 6 L.Ed.2d 1081 (1961).

71. 462 U.S. 213, 103 S.Ct. 2317, 76 L.Ed.2d. 527 (1983).

72. 468 U.S. 897, 104 S.Ct. 3405, 82 L.Ed.2d 677 (1984).

73. Craig V. Chida et al., *The Effects of U.S. v. Leon on Police Search Warrant Practices*, National Institute of Justice, U.S. Department of Justice (Washington, D.C.: U.S. Government Printing Office, 1988).

74. 480 U.S. 340, 107 S.Ct. 1160, 94 L.Ed.2d 364 (1987).

75. *Nix v. Williams* 467 U.S. 431, 104 S.Ct. 2501, 81 L.Ed.2d 377 (1984).

76. 109 S.Ct. 333 (1988).

77. *New Jersey v. T.L.O.*, 469 U.S. 325, 105 S.Ct. 733, 83 L.Ed.2d 720 (1985).

78. See, generally, Arnold Enker, "Prospectives on Plea Bargaining" in President's Commission on Law Enforcement and Administration of Justice, *Task Force Report: The Courts* (Washington, D.C.: U.S. Government Printing Office, (1967), pp. 109–19.

79. American Law Institute, *A Model Code of Pre-Arraignment Procedure* (Washington, D.C.: American Law Institute, (1975), Articles 290 and 290.2(4).

80. See, generally, James Fyfe, "In Search of the 'Bad Faith' Search," *Criminal Law Bulletin* 18 (1982): 260–64.

81. 108 S.Ct. 1625, 100 L.Ed.2d 30 (1988).

82. Samuel Walker, *Sense and Nonsense about Crime* (Monterey, Calif.: Brooks/Cole, 1985), pp. 97–98.

83. See "The Exclusionary Rule," *American Bar Association Journal* 19 (February 1983): 3; "Rule Prohibiting Illegal Evidence Faces Limitation," *Wall Street Journal*, 30 November 1982.

84. See Bradford Wilson, *Exclusionary Rule*, National Institute of Justice, U.S. Department of Justice (Washington, D.C.: U.S. Government Printing Office, 1986).

Chapter 9

**Police and the
Rule of Law**

■

PART THREE

Courts and Adjudication

10
Courts and the Judiciary

11
The Prosecution and the Defense

12
Pretrial Procedures

13
The Criminal Trial

14
Punishment and Sentencing

10

Courts and the Judiciary

*I*n previous chapters we discussed how the accused is processed through the early stages of the criminal justice system. Now attention is focused on the central stage—the **criminal court,** the personnel who operate it, and the processes that fall under its jurisdiction.

The criminal court is the arena in which many of the most important decisions in the criminal justice system are made: the setting of bail, trial, plea negotiation, and sentencing all involve court-made decisions. Within the confines of the court, those accused of crime (**defendants**) call on the tools of the legal system to prove that they are "not guilty" as charged; their victims ask the government to provide them with "justice" for the wrongs and the injuries they have suffered; agents of the criminal justice system attempt to find solutions that benefit the victim, the defendant, and society in general. The court process is designed to provide an open, impartial forum for determining the truth of the matter and reaching a solution, which, though punitive, is fairly arrived at and satisfies the rule of law.

Regardless of the issues or parties involved, the court process should guarantee that they will receive a hearing conducted under fair, equitable, and regulated rules of procedure, that the outcome of the hearing will be clear, and that the hearing will take place in an atmosphere of legal competence and objectivity. If either party, defense or prosecution, believes that these ground rules have been violated, they may take the case to an **appellate,** or higher, court, where the procedures of the original trial will be examined. If, on reexamination, the appellate court finds that a violation of criminal procedure has occurred, it may deem the findings of the original trial improper and either order a new hearing or hold that some other measure must be carried out—for example, the court may dismiss the charge outright.

As you already know, in today's crowded court system such abstract goals are often impossible to achieve. In reality the U.S. court system often provides a setting for accommodation and "working things out" rather than an arena for a vigorous criminal defense. Consequently, plea negotiations and other nonjudicial alternatives such as diversion far outnumber formal trials.

In this and the following four chapters, the structure and function of the court system will be closely examined. Here we set out the structure of the American court system and its guiding hand, the judge. The following chapters cover the prosecutor and defense attorney, the pretrial process, the trial, and, finally, sentencing and punishment.

■   ■   ■

KEY TERMS

Criminal court
Defendants
Appellate courts
Assembly-line justice
Courts of limited jurisdiction
Lower courts
Courts of general jurisdiction
Felony courts
Trial *de novo*
Court of last resort
Intermediate appellate courts
U.S. District Courts
U.S. circuit courts
U.S. Supreme Court
Writ of certiorari
Landmark decision
Judge
Jury trial
Sentencing
Missouri Plan
Dispute resolution
Referees
Magistrates
Part-time judges
Court administration
Clerk of court
Court administrator

■ Criminal Court Process

The court is a complex social agency with many independent but interrelated subsystems: the prosecution, criminal defense agencies, the judiciary, court administration, and the probation department. It is also the scene of many important criminal justice decisions relating to bail, detention, charging, jury selection, trial, and sentencing. As you may recall, the criminal court process can be viewed in two ways. In the traditional model, the court is viewed as a setting for an adversarial procedure that pits defendant against the state, defense counsel against prosecutor. Procedures are fair and formalized, controlled by the laws of criminal procedure and the rules of evidence.

In the second model, the court is viewed as a system that encourages settling matters in the simplest, quickest, and most efficient manner possible. Rather than adversaries, prosecutors and defense attorneys along with the judge and

**Chapter 10
Courts and the Judiciary**

■

The county courthouse is a symbol of justice and represents the right of citizens to receive a fair tribunal.

other court personnel form a "work group" that tries to handle the situation with as little fuss as possible. This usually involves dropping the case if the defendant agrees to make restitution or enter a treatment or diversion program, plea bargaining, or some other "quick fix." In Malcolm Feeley's study of a lower court in Connecticut, not one defendant out of 1,640 cases analyzed insisted on a jury trial, and only half made use of legal counsel. Because cases dragged on endlessly, people were encouraged to plea bargain. Furthermore, the haphazard nature of the process produced a situation in which a defendant's prior criminal record and the seriousness of the current charge had little influence on the outcome of the case. Felons with prior records fared as well as first-time misdemeanants.[1]

The U.S. court system, which has evolved over the years into an intricately balanced legal process, has recently come under siege because of the sheer number of cases it must consider and the ways in which it is forced to handle such overcrowding. Overloaded court dockets have given rise to charges of **"assembly-line justice"** in which a majority of defendants are induced to plead guilty, jury trials are rare, and the speedy trial is a highly desired but unattainable concept.

Because of overcrowding, the poor languish in detention while the wealthier go free on bail, and an innocent person may be frightened into pleading guilty and conversely a guilty person may be released because a trial has been so long delayed.[2] Whether providing for more judges or establishing new or enlarged courts will solve the problem of overcrowding remains to be seen. Meanwhile, diversion programs, decriminalization of certain offenses, and bail reform provide other avenues of possible relief. More efficient court management and administration in the future may also ease the congestion of the courts. Finding a solution to this problem is extremely important if defendants are ever to view their experience as a fair one in which they were able to present their side of the case and influence its outcome. Ironically, there is evidence that the informal justice system, which is often deplored by experts, may provide criminal suspects a greater degree of control and satisfaction than the more formal criminal trial.[3]

To carry out this rather complex process, each state, and the federal government, maintains its own court organization and structure. Usually three (or more) separate court systems exist within each jurisdiction. These are described in the next sections.

■ Courts of Limited Jurisdiction

There are approximately 13,000 **courts of limited jurisdiction** in the United States. Most (87 percent) are organized along town, municipal, and county lines of government; about 700 are controlled by state governments.[4]

Courts of limited jurisdiction (sometimes called municipal courts, or **lower courts**) are restricted in the types of cases they may hear. Usually, they will handle misdemeanor criminal infractions, violations of municipal ordinances, traffic violations, and civil suits where the damages involve less than a certain amount of money (usually $10,000). Limited courts also conduct preliminary hearings for felony criminal cases.

The lower criminal courts are restricted in the criminal penalties they can impose. Most can levy a fine of $1,000 or less and incarcerate a person for 12 months or less in the local jail.

Included within the category of courts of limited jurisdictions are special courts such as juvenile and family courts and probate (divorce, estate issues, and custody) courts.

Process and Punishment in Lower Courts

The nation's lower courts are those most often accused of providing assembly-line justice. Since the matters they decide involve minor personal confrontations and conflicts—family disputes, divorces, landlord-tenant conflicts, barroom brawls—the rule of the day is "handling the situation" and dispute resolution. Social commentator Charles Silberman describes his experience in such a criminal court:

> My first visit to a criminal court, in fact, reminded me of nothing quite so much as a long evening spent in the emergency room of a large city hospital, trying to get medical care for an elderly relative who had been knocked down by an automobile. In the courtroom, defendants, witnesses, and complainants, along with their families, sat in hard-backed chairs, waiting with the same air of resignation that patients and their families had displayed in the hospital emergency room; waiting sometimes seems to be a principal occupation of the poor.[5]

In his well-received book, *The Process Is the Punishment*, Malcolm Feeley describes the lower courts as a "world apart . . . their facilities are terrible." Courtrooms are crowded, chambers are dingy, and libraries are virtually nonexistent. Even the newer courtrooms age quickly, worn down by hard use and constant abuse.[6] According to Feeley, lower courts are basically informal institutions in which all parties work together to settle the situation in an equitable fashion. In this respect the criminal process resembles the civil justice system. According to Feeley, the "process is the punishment" in the lower courts. By this he means that nothing much happens by way of formal

Crowded lower courts have resulted in a condition where the "process is the punishment".

punishment in the lower courts. Just having to appear at hearings, retain counsel, miss work and so on is the real punishment for offenders. The reason so many cases are plea bargained is that the defendant is trying to avoid the pains of the court process, not the pains of imprisonment. In this goal, the defendant is aided by the court personnel who practice accommodative rather than adversarial justice.

■ Courts of General Jurisdiction

There are approximately 3,235 **courts of general jurisdiction,** or **felony courts,** in the United States, which process about 1.5 million criminal cases each year.[7] About 90 percent are state administered, and the remainder are controlled by local counties or municipalities. The overwhelming majority (95 percent) of general courts hear both serious civil and criminal matters (felonies).

About three-fourths of the courts of general jurisdiction also have the responsibility of reviewing cases on appeal from courts of limited jurisdiction. In some instances, they will issue a decision based on their review of the transcript of the case, whereas in others they will actually grant a new trial; this latter procedure is known as the **trial** *de novo* process.

In summary, courts of general jurisdiction handle the more serious felony cases (e.g., murder, rape, robbery), while courts of limited jurisdiction handle misdemeanors (e.g., simple assault, shoplifting, bad checks).

■ Appellate Courts

Defendants who believe that the procedures used in their case were in violation of their constitutional rights may appeal the outcome of the case. An appeal can be filed if the defendants believe the law they were tried under violates constitutional standards (e.g., it was too vague) or if the procedures used in the case contravened principles of due process and equal protection or were in direct opposition to a constitutional guarantee (e.g., the defendants were denied the right to have legal representation). Appellate courts do not try cases; they review the procedures of the case in order to determine whether an error was made by judicial authorities. Judicial error can include admitting into evidence illegally seized material, improper charging of a jury, allowing a prosecutor to ask witnesses improper questions, and so on. The appellate court can either order a new trial, allow the defendant to go free, or uphold the original verdict.

The federal government has two levels of appeal: the Circuit Court of Appeals and the U.S. Supreme Court. Each state has at least one appellate **court of last resort,** usually called a state supreme court, which reviews issues of law and fact appealed from the trial courts; two states, Texas and Oklahoma, have two supreme courts, one that hears civil appeals and another for criminal cases. In addition, 36 states have established **intermediate appellate courts** to review decisions by trial courts and administrative agencies before they reach the supreme court stage. Five states including New York, Pennsylvania, and Indiana have established more than one intermediate appellate court. In Hawaii, Idaho, Iowa, Oklahoma, and South Carolina, intermediate courts do not have original jurisdiction over appeals but are assigned cases when the supreme court's caseload is "overflowing."

Appellate Overflow?

Many people believe that criminal appeals clog the nation's court system because so many convicted criminals try to "beat the rap" on a technicality. Actually, criminal appeals represent a small percentage of the total number of cases processed by the nation's appellate courts. Only 17 percent of the appeals in federal courts are criminal matters, and the number of criminal appeals has been relatively stable (about 5,000 per year).[8]

State courts have witnessed an increase of about 9 percent per year in the number of appellate cases; in the meantime the number of judges has increased at one-sixth that rate.[9] Some states such as New York and Florida process upwards of 9,000 appeals each year.[10] The resulting imbalance has been dealt with by increasingly using the intermediate courts to screen cases.

Although criminal cases do in fact make up only a small percentage of appellate cases, they are still of concern to the judiciary. Steps have been taken to make it more difficult to appeal. For example, the U.S. Supreme Court has tried to limit access to federal courts by prisoners being held in state prisons who have complaints arising out of the conditions of their captivity. Prisoner complaints have more than doubled since the 1970s.

■ The State Court Structure

Figure 10.1 depicts a model state court structure showing the interrelationship of appellate and trial courts. Of course, each state's court organization varies from this standard pattern. Each state has a tiered court organization (lower, upper, and appellate courts), but state jurisdictions vary somewhat in the way they have delegated responsibility to a particular court system. The court organizations of the states of Texas and New York are illustrated in Figures 10.2 and 10.3. Note the complexity of their structures in comparison to the "typical" model court structure. Texas separates its appellate divisions into civil and criminal courts. The Texas Supreme Court hears civil, administrative, and juvenile cases, while an independent Court of Criminal Appeals has final say on criminal matters. Note also that the general jurisdiction District Court is divided into two branches—one handles general civil and administrative matters, while the other is restricted to criminal matters. New York's unique structure features two separate intermediate appellate courts with different geographic jurisdictions, and an independent family court that handles domestic relations (such as guardianship and custody), neglect and abuse, and juvenile delinquency. In contradistinction to New York, which has 10 independent courts, six states (Idaho, Illinois, Iowa, Massachusetts, Minnesota, and South Dakota) have unified their trial courts into a single system.

■ The Federal Courts

The legal basis for the federal court system is contained in Article 3, Section 1 of the U.S. Constitution, which provides that "the judicial power of the United States shall be vested in one Supreme Court, and in such inferior courts as Congress may from time to time ordain and establish." The important clauses in Article 3 indicate that the federal courts have jurisdiction over the laws of the

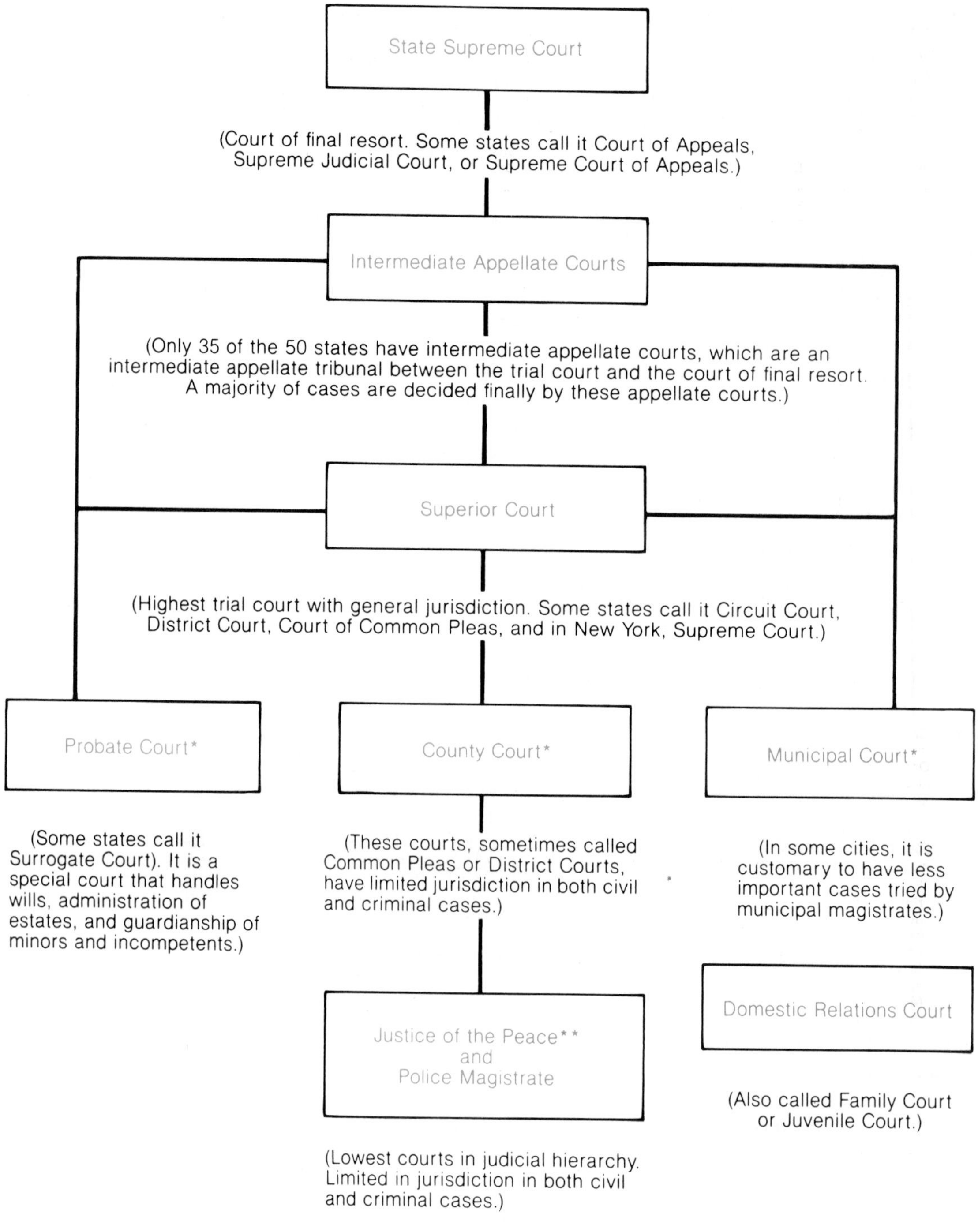

```
                    ┌─────────────────────────┐
                    │   State Supreme Court    │
                    └─────────────────────────┘
                                 │
          (Court of final resort. Some states call it Court of Appeals,
            Supreme Judicial Court, or Supreme Court of Appeals.)

                    ┌─────────────────────────┐
                    │ Intermediate Appellate Courts │
                    └─────────────────────────┘

          (Only 35 of the 50 states have intermediate appellate courts, which are an
        intermediate appellate tribunal between the trial court and the court of final resort.
              A majority of cases are decided finally by these appellate courts.)

                    ┌─────────────────────────┐
                    │     Superior Court       │
                    └─────────────────────────┘

          (Highest trial court with general jurisdiction. Some states call it Circuit Court,
            District Court, Court of Common Pleas, and in New York, Supreme Court.)
```

Probate Court*	County Court*	Municipal Court*
(Some states call it Surrogate Court). It is a special court that handles wills, administration of estates, and guardianship of minors and incompetents.)	(These courts, sometimes called Common Pleas or District Courts, have limited jurisdiction in both civil and criminal cases.)	(In some cities, it is customary to have less important cases tried by municipal magistrates.)

```
                          ┌─────────────────────────┐      ┌─────────────────────────┐
                          │  Justice of the Peace**  │      │ Domestic Relations Court │
                          │          and             │      └─────────────────────────┘
                          │     Police Magistrate    │
                          └─────────────────────────┘       (Also called Family Court
                                                                or Juvenile Court.)
           (Lowest courts in judicial hierarchy.
             Limited in jurisdiction in both civil
             and criminal cases.)
```

■ *FIGURE 10.1* **State Judicial System**

*Courts of special jurisdiction, such as probate, family, or juvenile courts, and the so-called inferior courts, such as common pleas or municipal courts, may be separate courts or part of the trial court of general jurisdiction.
**Justices of the peace do not exist in all states. Where they do exist, their jurisdictions vary greatly from state to state.

SOURCE: American Bar Association, *Law and the Courts* (Chicago: American Bar Association, 1974), p. 20. Updated information provided by West Publishing Company, St. Paul, Minnesota.

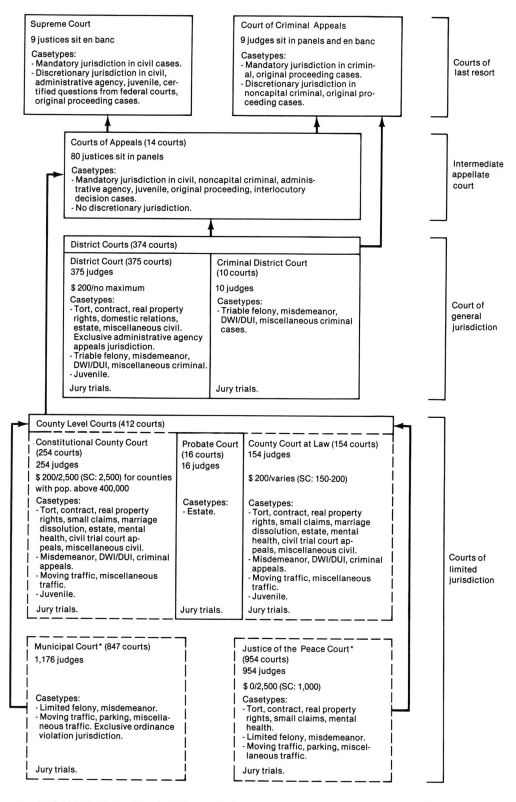

■ *FIGURE 10.2* **Texas Court Structure**

*Some Municipal and Justice of the Peace Courts may appeal to the District Court.

SOURCE: Conference of State Court Administrators and National Center for State Courts, *State Court Organization, 1987*, (Williamsburg, Va.: National Center for State Courts, 1988), p. 64.

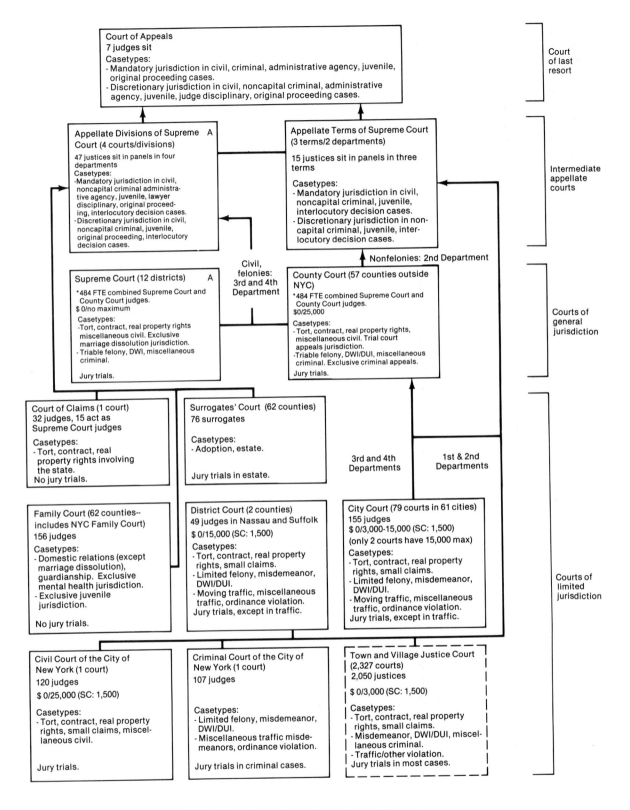

Court of Appeals
7 judges sit
Casetypes:
- Mandatory jurisdiction in civil, criminal, administrative agency, juvenile, original proceeding cases.
- Discretionary jurisdiction in civil, noncapital criminal, administrative agency, juvenile, judge disciplinary, original proceeding cases.

Court of last resort

Appellate Divisions of Supreme Court (4 courts/divisions) A
47 justices sit in panels in four departments
Casetypes:
- Mandatory jurisdiction in civil, noncapital criminal administrative agency, juvenile, lawyer disciplinary, original proceeding, interlocutory decision cases.
- Discretionary jurisdiction in civil, noncapital criminal, juvenile, original proceeding, interlocutory decision cases.

Appellate Terms of Supreme Court (3 terms/2 departments)
15 justices sit in panels in three terms
Casetypes:
- Mandatory jurisdiction in civil, noncapital criminal, juvenile, interlocutory decision cases.
- Discretionary jurisdiction in noncapital criminal, juvenile, interlocutory decision cases.

Intermediate appellate courts

Civil, felonies: 3rd and 4th Department

Nonfelonies: 2nd Department

Supreme Court (12 districts) A
*484 FTE combined Supreme Court and County Court judges.
$ 0/no maximum
Casetypes:
- Tort, contract, real property rights miscellaneous civil. Exclusive marriage dissolution jurisdiction.
- Triable felony, DWI, miscellaneous criminal.
Jury trials.

County Court (57 counties outside NYC)
*484 FTE combined Supreme Court and County Court judges.
$0/25,000
Casetypes:
- Tort, contract, real property rights, miscellaneous civil. Trial court appeals jurisdiction.
- Triable felony, DWI/DUI, miscellaneous criminal. Exclusive criminal appeals.
Jury trials.

Courts of general jurisdiction

Court of Claims (1 court)
32 judges, 15 act as Supreme Court judges
Casetypes:
- Tort, contract, real property rights involving the state.
No jury trials.

Surrogates' Court (62 counties)
76 surrogates
Casetypes:
- Adoption, estate.
Jury trials in estate.

3rd and 4th Departments

1st & 2nd Departments

Family Court (62 counties-- includes NYC Family Court)
156 judges
Casetypes:
- Domestic relations (except marriage dissolution), guardianship. Exclusive mental health jurisdiction.
- Exclusive juvenile jurisdiction.
No jury trials.

District Court (2 counties)
49 judges in Nassau and Suffolk
$ 0/15,000 (SC: 1,500)
Casetypes:
- Tort, contract, real property rights, small claims.
- Limited felony, misdemeanor, DWI/DUI.
- Moving traffic, miscellaneous traffic, ordinance violation.
Jury trials, except in traffic.

City Court (79 courts in 61 cities)
155 judges
$ 0/3,000-15,000 (SC: 1,500)
(only 2 courts have 15,000 max)
Casetypes:
- Tort, contract, real property rights, small claims.
- Limited felony, misdemeanor, DWI/DUI.
- Moving traffic, miscellaneous traffic, ordinance violation.
Jury trials, except in traffic.

Courts of limited jurisdiction

Civil Court of the City of New York (1 court)
120 judges
$ 0/25,000 (SC: 1,500)
Casetypes:
- Tort, contract, real property rights, small claims, miscellaneous civil.
Jury trials.

Criminal Court of the City of New York (1 court)
107 judges
Casetypes:
- Limited felony, misdemeanor, DWI/DUI.
- Miscellaneous traffic misdemeanors, ordinance violation.
Jury trials in criminal cases.

Town and Village Justice Court (2,327 courts)
2,050 justices
$ 0/3,000 (SC: 1,500)
Casetypes:
- Tort, contract, real property rights, small claims.
- Misdemeanor, DWI/DUI, miscellaneous criminal.
- Traffic/other violation.
Jury trials in most cases.

■ *FIGURE 10.3* **New York Court Structure**

NOTE: FTE stands for Full Time Equivalent.

SOURCE: Conference of State Court Administrators and National Center for State Courts, *State Court Organization, 1987*, (Williamsburg, Va.: National Center for State Courts, 1988), p. 52.

United States and treaties, cases involving admiralty and maritime jurisdiction, and controversies between two or more states and citizens of different states.[11] This complex language generally means that state courts have jurisdiction over all legal matters, *unless* they involve the violation of a federal criminal statute or a civil suit between citizens of different states or between a citizen and an agency of the federal government.

Within this authority, the federal government has established a three-tiered hierarchy of court jurisdiction; in order of ascendancy, this consists of the (1) U.S. District Courts, (2) the U.S. Courts of Appeals (circuit courts), and (3) the U.S. Supreme Court (see Figure 10.4).

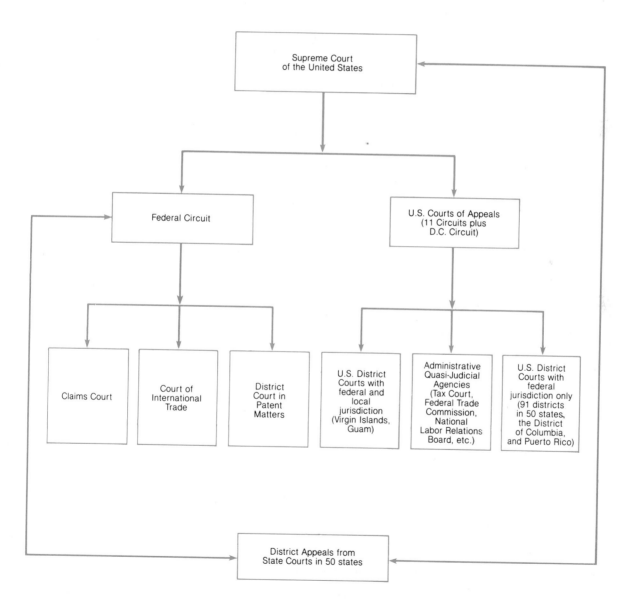

■ *FIGURE 10.4* **Federal Judicial System**

SOURCE: American Bar Association, *Law and the Courts* (Chicago: American Bar Association, 1974), p. 21. Updated information provided by the Federal Courts Improvement Act of 1982 and West Publishing Company, St. Paul, Minnesota.

District Courts

U.S. District Courts are the trial courts of the federal system. They have jurisdiction over cases involving violations of federal laws, including civil rights abuses; interstate transportation of stolen vehicles; and kidnappings. They may also hear cases on questions involving citizenship and the rights of aliens. The jurisdiction of the U.S. District Courts will occasionally overlap with that of state courts. For example, citizens who reside in separate states and are involved in litigation of an amount in excess of $10,000 may choose to have their cases heard in either of the states or in the federal court. Finally, federal district courts hear cases in which one state sues a resident (or firm) in another state, where one state sues another, or where the federal government is a party in a suit.

Congress established the federal district courts in the Judiciary Act of 1789, and 94 independent courts are currently in operation. Originally, each state was allowed one court; as the population climbed, however, so did the need for courts. Now each state has from one to four district courts, and the District of Columbia maintains one for itself.

In most cases, a single judge presides over trials; a defendant may request that a jury also be present. In complex civil matters, a three-judge panel may be convened.

Federal Appeals Courts

Appeals from the district courts are heard in one of the 12 federal courts of appeals, sometimes referred to as **U.S. circuit courts.** This name is derived from the historical practice of having judges ride the circuit and regularly hear cases in the county seats of their various jurisdictions. Today appellate judges are not required to travel by horseback though some may sit in more than one court. Each federal appellate court jurisdiction contains a number of associate justices who share the caseload. Circuit court offices are usually located in major cities such as San Francisco or New York, and cases must be brought to these locations by attorneys in order to be heard.

Circuit courts are empowered to review federal and state appellate court cases on substantive and procedural issues involving rights guaranteed by the U.S. Constitution. Circuit courts do not actually retry cases, nor do they determine whether the facts brought out during trial support conviction or dismissal. Instead they analyze judicial interpretations of the law, such as the charge (or instructions) to the jury, and assess the constitutional issues involved in each case they hear.

Federal appellate courts also enforce orders of federal administrative agencies, such as the Food and Drug Administration and the Securities and Exchange Commission. Federal appellate decisions in these matters are final, except when reviewed by the U.S. Supreme Court. Any dissatisfied litigant in a federal district court has the right to appeal the case to a circuit court.

The U.S. Supreme Court

The **U.S. Supreme Court** is the nation's highest appellate body and the court of last resort for all cases tried in the various federal and state courts. In addition, in certain rare instances, the Supreme Court can actually sit as a trial court—for example, in cases involving ambassadors or in suits between states.

The Supreme Court is composed of nine members appointed for lifetime terms by the president with the approval of Congress. The Court has discretion over most of the cases it will consider and may choose to hear only those it deems important, appropriate, and worthy of its attention. When the Court decides to hear a case, it grants a **writ of certiorari,** requesting a transcript of the proceedings of the case for review. However, the Supreme Court must grant jurisdiction in all cases in which any of the following has occurred:

1. A federal court holds an act of Congress to be unconstitutional.
2. A U.S. Court of Appeals finds a state statute unconstitutional.
3. A state's highest court holds a federal law to be invalid.
4. A state supreme court upholds an individual's challenge to a state statute on constitutional grounds.

The United States Supreme Court is the "court of last resort" for all legal matters.

When the Supreme Court rules on a case, usually by majority decision (at least five votes), its holding becomes a precedent that must be honored by all lower courts. For example, if the Court grants a particular litigant the right to counsel at a police lineup, then all similarly situated clients must be given the same right. Such a ruling is known as a **landmark decision.** The use of precedent in the legal system gives the Supreme Court power to influence and mold the everyday operating procedures of the police, trial courts, and corrections. In the past, this influence was not nearly as pronounced as it became during the tenure of the two previous chief justices, Earl Warren and Warren Burger, who greatly amplified and extended the power of the Court to influence criminal justice policies. Under Chief Justice William Rehnquist, the Court has continued to influence criminal justice matters, ranging from the investigation of crimes to the execution of criminals. There is little question that the personal legal philosophy of the justices and their orientation toward the civil and personal rights of victims and criminals have a significant impact on the daily operations of the justice system.

HOW A CASE GETS TO THE SUPREME COURT. The U.S. Supreme Court is unique in several respects. First of all, it is the only court established by constitutional mandate. Second, it decides basic social and political issues of grave consequence to the nation. Third, the Court's nine justices shape the future meaning of the U.S. Constitution. Their decisions identify the rights and liberties of individuals throughout the United States.

When our nation was first established, the Supreme Court did not review state court decisions involving issues of federal law. Even though Congress had given the Supreme Court jurisdiction to review state decisions, the relationship between the states and the federal government was somewhat controversial. However, in a famous decision in *Martin v. Hunter's Lessee* (1816), the Supreme Court reaffirmed the legitimacy of the Court's jurisdiction over state court decisions when such courts handle issues of federal or constitutional law.[12] This decision allowed the Court to actively review actions by states and their courts and reinforced its power to make the supreme law of the land. Since that time, a defendant who maintains that governmental action—whether state or federal—has violated the Constitution is in a position to have the Supreme Court review the case.

In order for the Court to carry out its responsibilities, it had to develop a method of dealing with the large volume of cases coming from the state and federal courts for final review. In the early years of its history, the Court sought to review every case brought on appeal. Since the middle of the twentieth century, however, the Court has used a technical device known as a writ of certiorari to decide what cases it should hear. *Certiorari* is an old Latin term that means "to bring the record of a case from a lower court up to a higher court for immediate review." When applied, it means that an accused in a criminal case is requesting the Supreme Court to hear the case. The other method by which a case reaches the Supreme Court is through an absolute right to appeal.

More than 90 percent of the cases heard by the Supreme Court are brought by petition for a writ of certiorari. Under this procedure, the Court and its justices have discretion to select cases that they will review for a decision. Of the thousands of cases filed before the Court every year, only 150 receive a full opinion. for a case to be selected for review, four of the nine justices sitting on the Supreme Court must vote to hear a case brought by a writ of certiorari. Generally, these votes are cast in a secret meeting attended only by the justices.

After the Supreme Court has decided to hear a case, both parties provide written materials known as legal briefs for review by the Court and present oral arguments before the justices, normally at the U.S. Supreme Court Building in Washington, D.C.

After reviewing the legal briefs and hearing the oral arguments, the justices of the Court normally meet in what is known as a "case conference," where they discuss the case and vote to reach a decision. The cases decided by the Court generally come from the judicial systems of the various states, or from the U.S. Courts of Appeals, and represent the entire spectrum of law. Figure 10.5 depicts the steps involved when a case is appealed to the Supreme Court.

In reaching a decision, the U.S. Supreme Court reevaluates and reinterprets state statutes, the U.S. Constitution, and previous case decisions. On the basis of a review of the case, the decision of the lower court is either affirmed or reversed. When the justices reach a decision, if the chief justice has voted with the majority, he assigns someone in the majority group to write the opinion; if the chief justice has voted with the minority, the ranking justice (in terms of years on the Court) in the majority group assigns the opinion. In addition, one or more justices in the minority usually write a dissenting or minority opinion. In the final analysis, the justices join with either the majority opinion or the dissenting opinion. When the decision is finished, it is submitted to the public and becomes the law of the land. The decision is a legal precedent that adds to the existing body of law on a given subject, changes it, and guides its future development.

■ Court Caseloads

The nation's courts handle millions of cases each year, resulting in backlogs, delays, and what is sometimes called "assembly-line justice." Each year state court systems process approximately 80 million civil, criminal, and traffic cases.[13] Of these, approximately 13 percent, or 10.5 million, involve criminal matters. In addition, the federal district courts hear approximately 50,000 criminal and 200,000 civil cases a year.[14]

Overwhelming as these figures seem, even more disturbing is the fact that both civil and criminal litigation have increased sharply in the past few years. For example, in 1980, federal district courts disposed of 36,000 criminal cases; by 1986 the number of case dispositions had increased to 50,000. The number of appeals in many state jurisdictions has increased more than 50 percent

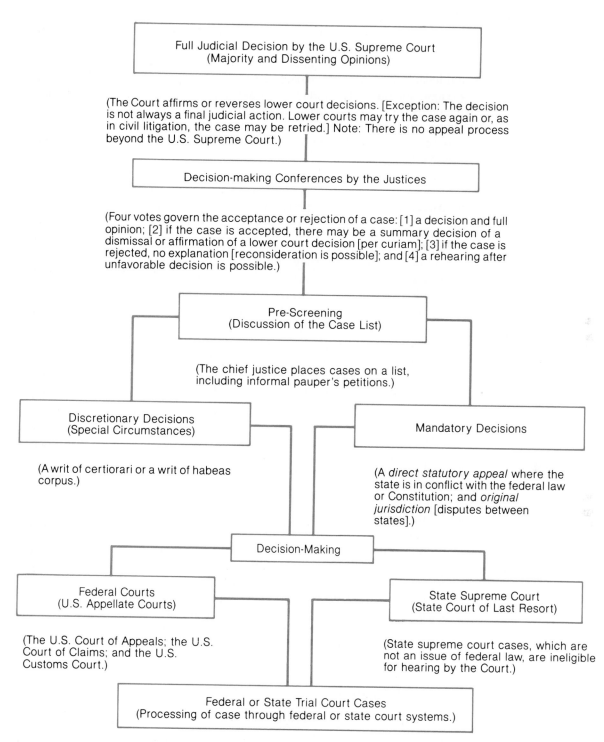

■ FIGURE 10.5
Tracing the Course of a Case to the U.S. Supreme Court

during the past five years. In 1973, about 13,000 appeals were filed in federal circuit courts; by 1986, the number of appeals approached 30,000.[15]

The significant increase in both criminal and civil litigation has forced state and local governments to allocate ever greater resources to the courts. Court services, including the judiciary, prosecution, legal services such as public defenders, and other court-related matters (jury fees, stenographers, clerks, bailiffs, maintenance fees), today cost over $10 billion per year.[16] Despite such resource allocation, there is no guarantee that services will significantly improve.[17]

Reducing Court Congestion

What causes court caseloads to overflow? Two factors that stood out in a survey of judges and trial court administrators were the excessive number of continuances demanded by attorneys and the increasing number of pretrial motions on evidence and procedural issues.[18] The more complicated the law becomes, involving such issues as electronic monitoring and computer crimes, the more complex the court process must be. Ironically, efforts to reform the criminal law may also be increasing the overload. For example, the increase in mandatory prison sentences for some crimes may reduce the extent of plea bargaining and increase the number of jury trials because defendants fear that a conviction will lead to an incarceration sentence and wish to avoid a conviction at all costs. Second, since most courts handle both criminal and civil matters, the recent explosion in civil litigation has helped increase the backlog.

If aid is forthcoming, it will probably be in the form of administrative and management techniques that improve the use of existing resources. For example, legal jurisdictions may reduce trial delays by establishing policies mandating speedy trials. An analysis of two policy initiatives designed to facilitate the processing of federal cases, the Federal Speedy Trial Act of 1974 and Rule 50 (b) of the Federal Rules of Criminal Procedure, shows that these initiatives significantly reduced the processing time of federal criminal cases.[19]

Another possibility is to create a more efficient court system by unifying existing state courts into a single administrative structure employing modern management principles. Massachusetts, Illinois, Iowa, Minnesota, North Dakota, and Idaho have implemented unified court systems.

Regardless of its source, immediate relief is needed: about 39 percent of the judges replying to a recent national survey said that workloads were so heavy that they needed stress management training to reduce job-related tension.[20]

■ The Judiciary

The **judge** is the senior officer in a court of criminal law. His or her duties are quite varied and far more extensive than the average citizen might expect. During trials, the judge rules on the appropriateness of conduct, settles questions of evidence and procedure, and guides the questioning of witnesses. When a jury trial occurs, the judge must instruct its members on which evidence may properly be examined and which should be ignored. The judge also formally charges the jury by instructing its members on what points of law and evidence they must consider in order to reach a decision on the guilt or innocence of the defendant. When a **jury trial** is waived, the judge must decide

whether to hold for the complainant or the defendant. Finally, in the event that a defendant is found guilty, the judge has the authority to determine the sentence. This duty includes choosing the type of sentence, its length, and (in the case of probation) the conditions under which it may be revoked. Judicial background may influence these decisions as the Criminal Justice in Review on page 337 explains.

Beyond these stated duties, the trial judge has extensive control and influence over the other service agencies of the court: probation, the court clerk, the police, and the district attorney's office. Probation and the clerk may be under the judge's explicit control. In some courts, the operations, philosophy, and procedures of these agencies are within the magistrate's administrative domain. In others, such as those where a state agency controls the probation department, the attitudes of the county or district court judge still have a great deal of influence on the way the probation department is run and how its decisions are made.

Police and prosecutors are also directly influenced by the judge, whose **sentencing** discretion influences the arrest and charging processes. For example, if a judge usually imposes minimal sentences—such as a fine for a particular offense—the police may be reluctant to arrest offenders for that crime because they believe that sending an offender through the criminal justice process for that offense will basically be a waste of their time. Similarly, if a judge is known to look favorably on police discretion, the local department may be more inclined to engage in practices that border on entrapment or to become involved in cases requiring the use of easily obtained wiretaps. In contrast, a magistrate oriented toward strict use of due process guarantees would stifle such activities by dismissing all cases involving apparent police abuses of personal freedoms. The district attorney's office may also be sensitive to judicial attitudes. The district attorney might forgo indictments in cases the presiding magistrate considers trivial or quasi-criminal and worthy of only token action, such as the prosecution of pornographers.

Chapter 10

Courts and the Judiciary

■

337

Judicial Background and Sentencing

Does a judge's personal background influence his or her treatment of criminal defendants? To answer this critical question, sociologist Martha Myers compared various characteristics of Superior Court judges in Georgia with their sentencing decisions. Myers found that although, in general, judicial background has little direct bearing on sentencing outcomes, some subtle differences that were associated with judicial characteristics could be detected.

Myers found that judges who were once prosecutors were more likely to be "tougher" on female and violent offenders, while giving males who committed property crimes and/or drug offenses greater consideration. Although sentences imposed by former prosecutors could not be distinguished on the basis of the offender's age or race, such judges were more likely to take the offense into account than other judges.

Religion also played a role in judicial sentencing decisions. Baptist and fundamentalist judges were more likely to show leniency to married and younger offenders and to be considerably tougher than their colleagues when dealing with older, single criminals. Interestingly, Myers found that fundamentalist judges were more likely to incarcerate minorities than their more secular colleagues; however, fundamentalist judges gave black offenders shorter prison sentences than white offenders.

Myers found a number of other associations between the judges' background and their sentencing decisions. For example, judges who had grown up in the jurisdiction they presided over were more likely to incarcerate offenders than nonlocal judges; however, locals usually gave shorter prison terms. Local judges seemed to be tougher on white, older, and employed criminals and more lenient toward black, younger, and unemployed offenders. Locals were especially tough on drug offenders, sentencing them to much longer prison terms than nonlocal judges.

Myers also found that older judges were more punitive than younger judges, especially when dealing with drug violators, robbers, property offenders, and those with prior arrests.

In sum, although Myers did not find overwhelming support for the hypothesis that judicial background controls sentencing decision making, there was evidence that the social background of judges interacts with offender characteristics to influence sentencing outcomes. The practice of "judge shopping" in criminal court might therefore pay dividends for the criminal defendant (or defense lawyer) who is savvy enough to know how particular kinds of judges view criminal offenses. ■

SOURCE: Martha Myers, "Social Background and the Sentencing Behavior of Judges," *Criminology* 26 (1988): 649–75.

Finally, the judge considers requests by police and prosecutors for leniency (or severity) in sentencing. The judge's reaction to these requests is important if police and/or the district attorney are to honor the bargains they may have made with defendants in order to secure information, cooperation, or guilty pleas. For example, when police tell informers that they will try to convince the judge to go easy on them in exchange for certain information, the police department and representatives of the court often negotiate about the terms of the promised leniency. If a judge chooses to ignore police requests, the department's bargaining power is severely diminished, and communication within the criminal justice system is impeded. Efforts to curb the power of the judiciary and harness judicial discretion have not met with unqualified success.

Judicial Qualifications

The qualifications for appointment to one of the existing 26,000 judgeships vary from state to state and court to court. Typically, the potential judge must be a resident of the state, licensed to practice law, a member of the state bar association, and at least 25 and less than 70 years of age.[21] The basic qualifications vary significantly, however, depending on the level of court jurisdiction. Although almost every state requires judges on appellate courts or courts of general jurisdiction to have a law degree, it is not uncommon for municipal or town court judges to lack a legal background, even though they have the power to incarcerate criminal defendants. Surprising as it may seem, about 43 percent of lower court judges are not trained attorneys. For example, as of 1987 of the 1,176 municipal judges in Texas, 706 were not legally trained; and of the 2,050 town and village judges in New York, 1,585 were not attorneys. Yet, as Figures 10.2 and 10.3 indicate, municipal courts in Texas and town and village courts in New York routinely handle criminal matters.[22] In contrast, 14 states, including California, Florida, Nebraska, and New Jersey, require all candidates for judicial appointments to have a law degree or be "learned in the law."[23]

Judicial Selection

Despite the need for well-qualified judges, it is often difficult to fill vacancies with desirable candidates. Although top appellate court judges can make from $40,000 to $115,000 a year, depending on the jurisdiction (the top figure is for U.S. Supreme Court justices), this is actually limited compensation considering the financial reward individuals with their qualifications would receive from a prestigious private law firm where first-year associates begin at salaries approaching $100,000.[24] It has been alleged that some federal judgeships have been offered to as many as 10 candidates before one was willing to sacrifice and accept the position.[25] Thus, the process of selecting judges is quite important if courts are to function efficiently.

Many different methods are used to select judges depending on the level of court jurisdiction.[26] In some jurisdictions, the governor simply appoints judges. In others, judicial recommendations must be confirmed by either (1) the state senate, (2) the governor's council, (3) a special confirmation commit-

Judge Roy Bean dispensed eccentric frontier justice and cold beer from his store in west Texas.

tee, (4) an executive council elected by the state assembly, or (5) an elected review board. Some states employ a judicial nominating commission that submits names to the governor for approval.

Another form of judicial selection is popular election. In some jurisdictions judges run as members of the Republican, Democratic, or other parties, while in others they run without party affiliation. About 13 states use partisan elections for selecting judges in courts of general jurisdiction, and 17 states use a nonpartisan election.

About 16 states have adopted some form of what is known as the **Missouri Plan** to select appellate court judges, and 6 states also use this method to select trial court judges. This three-part approach consists of: (1) a judicial nominating commission that nominates candidates for the bench, (2) an elected official (usually from the executive branch) who makes appointments from the list submitted by the commission, and (3) subsequent nonpartisan and noncompetitive elections in which incumbent judges run on their records.[27]

It should be noted that some states use a variety of methods for selecting judges. For example, New York and Texas use different methods to select judges on the appellate and trial court levels. New York appellate court judges are appointed by the governor from a judicial nominating commission with the consent of the Senate; judges in courts of general jurisdiction, limited jurisdiction, and family courts are selected in partisan elections; and criminal court and family court judges in New York City are appointed by the mayor.

PROBLEMS OF JUDICIAL SELECTION. The quality of the judiciary has aroused some concern. Although merit plans, screening committees, and popular elections are designed to ensure a competent judiciary, it has often been charged that many judges are selected to pay off political debts or to reward cronies and loyal friends. It is also not uncommon to hear charges that those desiring to be nominated for judgeships are required to make significant political contributions.

Another problem is the limited requirements for judicial appointments. As you may recall, a majority of the states still do not require lower court judges to be attorneys or members of the bar or to have any legal experience at all.

The qualifications of many judges have also been questioned. In most states, people appointed to the bench have had little or no training in the judicial role. Others may have held administrative posts and may not have appeared before a court in years.

A number of agencies have been created to improve the quality of the judiciary. The National Conference of State Court Judges and the National College of Juvenile Justice both operate judicial training seminars and publish manuals and guides on state-of-the-art judicial technologies.

Judicial Alternatives

The increased caseloads confronted by the judicial system have prompted the use of alternatives to the traditional judge. To expedite matters in civil cases, it has become common for both parties to agree to hire a retired judge and abide by his or her decision. Another method is for jurisdictions to set up **dispute resolution** systems that settle minor complaints informally upon agreement of both parties. An estimated 700 dispute resolution programs are now in operation, handling domestic conflicts, landlord/tenant cases, misdemeanors, consumer/merchant disputes, and so on.[28]

Other jurisdictions have created new quasi-judicial officers such as **referees** or **magistrates** to relieve the traditional judge of time-consuming responsibilities.[29] The Federal Magistrate Act of 1968 created a new type of judicial officer in the federal district court system who handles pretrial motions and civil trials if both parties agree to the arrangement.[30]

Other jurisdictions make use of **part-time judges.** Many of these are attorneys who carry out their duties pro bono—for little or no compensation. These "judicial adjuncts" assist the courts on a temporary basis while maintaining an active law practice. The roles they carry out can be grouped into the following six categories:[31]

1. *Alternative dispute resolution mechanisms.* Judicial adjuncts may serve in court-annexed arbitration or mediation programs. In most courts, parties in civil cases involving less than a defined dollar amount must participate in an arbitration or mediation hearing presided over by a lawyer before they may proceed to trial before a judge or jury. Most of these cases accept the arbitrator's award or the mediated result, and plaintiffs do not insist on a trial before a judge or jury.

2. *Settlement conferences.* Typically, settlement conferences are mandated by the court for some or all civil cases and are conducted before a lawyer, a team of lawyers, or two lawyers and a judge. The lawyers usually have expertise in the general subject areas of the lawsuit in question. The settlement conferences are used to provide the parties and their counsel with an assessment by a disinterested third party of how much the case is "worth" for settlement purposes (not always the same as how much a judge or jury would award if there were a trial). The hope is that these conferences will encourage parties to settle their dispute without going to trial.

3. *Quasi judges.* Although the terminology can differ, these are usually known as referees, factfinders, or masters. The majority are granted power to compel testimony, hold hearings, and make recommended findings of fact and law to the supervising judge, who then enters a formal order or a final judgment, as appropriate.

4. *Commissioners or magistrates.* They are empowered to perform limited judicial duties, such as signing warrants and subpoenas, setting bail, hearing arraignments, and presiding over preliminary hearings, nonjury misdemeanor cases, traffic infractions, and small claims cases. Typically, they serve part-time for an indefinite term.

5. Pro tempore *trial judges.* These judicial adjuncts are given full judicial powers on a temporary basis. They may hear and decide any case, although usually in courts of general jurisdiction they sit only in civil cases. Their rulings are as appealable as those of any other judge of the court. This classification includes lawyers who serve as substitute judges while a regular judge is absent and those who routinely supplement existing judicial resources in an effort to reduce a backlog. Their tenure is more limited than that of commissioners or magistrates. In most jurisdictions, their term of service is limited either to the time a regular judge is sick or unavailable or to a specified number of months.

6. Pro tem *judges on the appellate bench.* They serve as full-fledged members of the appellate court for hearing and deciding one or more cases and draft their share of opinions for the court. Currently, only Arizona authorizes the general use of *pro tem* judges on an intermediate appellate court, but several other states allow temporary appointments by the governor when an appellate judge is disqualified.

The use of alternative court mechanisms should continue to grow as court congestion increases.

■ Court Administration

Former Chief Justice Warren Burger has stated, "The days are . . . past when a chief judge, with the help of a secretary and the clerk of the court, can manage the increasingly complex tasks required of them to keep courts functioning effectively. We must be constantly alert to new ideas, new methods, new ways of looking at the judiciary."[32]

The need for efficient management techniques in an ever-expanding criminal court system has led to the recognition that improved **court administration** may help relieve court congestion. Management goals include improving organization and scheduling of cases, devising methods to allocate court records efficiently, administering fines and monies due the court, preparing budgets, and overseeing personnel.

The federal courts have led the way in creating and organizing court administration. In 1939, Congress passed the Administrative Office Act, which established the Administrative Office of the United States Courts. Its director was charged with gathering statistics on the work of the federal courts and also with preparing the judicial budget for approval by the Conference of Senior Circuit Judges. One clause of the act created a judicial council with general supervisory responsibilities for the district and circuit courts.

Unlike the federal government, the states have experienced a slow and uneven growth in the development and application of court management principles. The first state to establish an administrative office was North Dakota in 1927. Today all states except New Hampshire employ some form of central administration. In New Hampshire the secretary of the Judicial Council serves in an administrative capacity.

The federal government has influenced the development of state court management by making funding available to state court systems. In addition, the federal judiciary has provided the philosophical impetus for better and more effective court management. A court system is an extremely complex organization that is far more difficult to manage than the typical business enterprise or government agency for several reasons:

1. The key people are accustomed to working as individuals and do not take kindly to regimentation.
2. A very high value is placed on judicial independence, and this severely limits the pressures that can be brought to bear to produce desired administrative results.
3. Persons involved in the judicial process—attorneys, jurors, witnesses, litigants—are not employed by the judiciary.
4. Participants in the judicial process often have conflicting goals.[33]

Another obstacle facing court administration is the generally low profile of the courts themselves. Except in times of unusual stress, judicial performance is hidden from public view, and the taxpaying public is rarely aware of mismanagement. Despite increased efforts to manage courts efficiently, successes have been few and far between. For example, a survey of the nation's state and local courts revealed that many have fragmented and overlapping jurisdictions, lack sufficiently trained personnel, and have no consistent pattern for handling various types of proceedings. The study concluded:

> Each court in each county in each state is different. Each has its own set of challenges. These are closely tied to the experience and temperament of the judge, the size and quality of the bar, the people who live in the area and the kind of justice they demand.[34]

Despite the multitude of problems facing those who believe in reforming court management, some progress is being made. By order of its state supreme court, effective February 1, 1973, Florida became the first state to implement most of the American Bar Association Standards by formal court rule. Under the state constitution, the Florida Supreme Court exercised the power to prescribe rules of practice and procedures for all courts in the state. By 1974, some 85 percent of the principles in the standards needing statutory implementation had been adopted in Florida.

Today, centralized court administrative services perform numerous functions that free the judiciary to fulfill their roles as arbiters of justice. Table 10.1 lists some of the various activities of centralized court administration.

The Court Administrator

Traditionally, a jurisdiction's legal process was controlled by the **clerk of court,** who was appointed by a presiding magistrate or chosen in a regional election. Typically, a clerk of court was responsible for docketing cases, collecting fees and costs, overseeing jury selection, and maintaining court records.[35] In recent years the role of the clerk has been supplemented by **court administrators** hired to take charge of the difficult task of efficient court management. By 1988, all states except Montana, New York, South Carolina, and Wyoming had professional trial court managers appointed at either the state or county level or both.[36] However, relatively few states, among them California, Michigan, New Jersey, and Washington, deployed court administrators throughout the entire system; most other states employ administrators in courts of general but not limited jurisdiction, though a few including Colorado, Florida and Minnesota give the court administrator jurisdictions over both systems.

The court administrator's job description would include the following: personnel, financial, and records administrator (subject to the standards of the central administrative office); governmental secretary for meetings of the judges of the court that he or she serves; liaison with the local government, bar, news media, and general public; and manager of physical facilities and equipment and purchaser of outside services.

The job of the court administrator is not to usurp the judge's authority but to develop the court's organizational structure so that it may be more effective. The judge remains policymaker for the court and relies on the administrator to assist in that role to whatever degree the judge finds comfortable. The administrator's job is to recommend and implement innovative ways of executing policy and help direct the court along whatever avenues seem appropriate to improving the administration of justice.

For example, in New Jersey, a state that has employed state court administrators for over 25 years, the administrator's role includes keeping court records

TABLE 10.1 ■ Activities of State Court Central Administration

Activities and Services

Management activities

Appears before legislative committees dealing with court-related legislation

Obtains sponsors for legislation relating to work

Represents judiciary before agencies of the executive branch

Recommends to court of last resort the creation or dissolution of judgeships

Recommends to court of last resort the assignment of judges

Nominates trial court administrators for selection by trial courts

Information systems activities

Responsible for records management systems

Responsible for managing data processing

Responsible for forms design

Responsible for managing information systems

Establishes records for automated administrative systems

Responsible for budgeting financial requirements of state information system

Responsible for statewide inventory control of facilities/equipment

Court support services

Provides secretarial services to boards and committees

Researches court organization and function

Supplies reports and documents to the legislature as required

Provides technical assistance to court jurisdiction

Manages physical facilities for courts

Supervises probation services

Supervises court reporter services

Responsible for managing indigent defense

Assists court in exercise of its rule-making function

Finance and budget activities

Prepares budget for submission to the court of last resort

Conducts audit of judicial expenditures

Requires accounting and budget report from the courts

Approves requisitions for capital equipment/construction

Determines compensation for nonjudicial court personnel

Personnel services

Establishes qualifications for nonjudicial court personnel

Education and training activities

Responsible for judicial training programs and seminars

Responsible for nonjudicial training programs and seminars

Responsible for managing state law libraries

Public information and liaison activities

Disseminates information on court operations to the media and public

Disseminates information on court decisions to the media and public

Planning and research activities

Responsible for court planning and grant management

Collects/analyzes/publishes court caseload statistics

Requires caseload reports from the courts

Collects statistics on expenditures of state

SOURCE: Bureau of Justice Statistics, *State Court Organization, 1980* (Washington, D.C.: U.S. Government Printing Office, 1982), p. 96.

in order, assigning trial schedules, reviewing judge's time sheets, keeping track of overly prolonged cases, employing modern budgeting procedures, and coordinating computerized information.

Despite the apparent logic in employing court administrators as overall court managers, some courts do not respond well to centralized administrative authority. Many incentives that influence employees to respond to central executive authority in business organizations—such as increased compensation or promotion as rewards for performance, or the termination of employment as a penalty for failure—generally do not exist in the judicial system. As a result, courts have failed to make full use of business management methods and machinery.

However, former Chief Justice Warren Burger's concern has done much to focus attention on the need to develop qualified court managers. With help of such qualified personnel, modern technology and business systems can be applied to daily court operations.

Technology and Court Management

Computers are becoming an important aid in the administration and management of courts. Rapid retrieval and organization of data can be used for such functions as the following:

1. Maintaining case histories and statistical reporting.
2. Monitoring and scheduling of cases.
3. Document preparation.
4. Case indexing.
5. Issuing summonses
6. Notifying, witnesses, attorneys, and others of required appearances.
7. Circuit-wide selection and notification of jurors.
8. Budgets and payrolls.[37]

The federal government has encouraged the states to experiment with computerized information systems. Federal funds were used to begin a 50-state consortium for the purpose of establishing a standardized crime-reporting system called SEARCH (Systems for the Electronic Analysis and Retrieval of Criminal Histories).

Other projects apply modern technology in such areas as videotaped testimonies, the development of new court reporting devices, the installation of computer-based information systems, and the use of data-processing systems to handle functions such as court docketing and jury management. In 1968 only 10 states had state-level automated information systems; today all states employ such systems for a mix of tasks an duties. A recent survey of Georgia courts found that 84 percent used computers for three or more court administration applications.[38]

Another modern use of technology for court administration is the employment of facsimile machines (fax) to improve efficiency and speed. In Minnesota, fax machines allow the courts to relay criminal arrest or search warrants, juvenile warrants, and temporary restraining orders instantly to police officers. The Minnesota Supreme Court even allows fax documents to be filed as permanent court documents.[39]

It has also become common for court jurisdictions to cooperate with police departments in the installation of communications equipment that allows defendants to be arraigned via closed-circuit television while they are in police custody. Closed-circuit television has been used for judicial conferences and scheduling meetings. Courts in Kentucky, Michigan, North Carolina, and Washington are using voice-activated cameras to record all testimony during trials; these are the sole means of keeping trial records. Four videos are made: one each for the prosecution and defense and two for the court records.[40]

The American Bar Association Standards have classified the uses of computerized information retrieval into the following three categories:[41]

1. Judicial and administrative decision making

a. Rules on motions
b. Assigning cases for trial

2. Information handling

a. Making entries into official records
b. Sending out notices
c. Computerizing financial accounts

3. Monitoring and planning in court administration

a. Analyzing case flow
b. Preparing budgets
c. Projecting future needs

The Standards stress that many essential procedures and vital decisions in a court system are made outside the direct supervision of the judge. The computer cannot replace the judge, but it can be used as an ally to help speed the trial process by identifying backlogs and bottlenecks that can be eradicated if intelligent managerial techniques are applied. Just as an industrialist must know the type and quantity of goods on hand in a warehouse, so an administrative judge must have available information concerning those entering the judge's domain, what happened to them once they were in it, and how they have fared since judgment has been rendered.

■ SUMMARY

The U.S. court system is a complex social institution. There is no set pattern of court organization, and court structures vary considerably among the various state jurisdictions.

Courts are organized on the federal, state, county, and local levels of government. Ordinarily, states process felony and misdemeanant cases separately and operate independent trial and appellate courts. This structure is repeated on the federal level of jurisdiction. However, federal appellate courts also rule on state cases, and the U.S. Supreme Court is the court of last resort for all cases involving constitutional issues decided in the United States.

Directly supervising our nation's courts is the judiciary. Judges come from a variety of backgrounds and possess individual skills and qualifications. Their functions vary according to the courts in which they sit; some rule at the trial level, others concern themselves with appellate cases. In addition to these tasks, judges administer probation departments and work with district attorneys and police. Some judges are appointed by the state's chief executive, the governor, while others are elected to office by popular vote.

A recent trend in the court process has been the creation of administrative bodies to oversee court operations. Within this operational sphere are court administrators, who use sophisticated computer operations to ease the flow of cases and improve court efficiency.

■ QUESTIONS

1. What qualities should a judge have? Should the judgeship be a lifetime appointment, or should judges be reviewed periodically?
2. Do the pomp and formality of a courtroom impede justice by setting it apart from the common person?
3. What is meant when we say that the Supreme Court is "the court of last resort"?

4. Should all judges be lawyers? When can people with no legal training be of benefit to the court system?
5. What are the benefits and drawbacks of holding judicial elections?

■ NOTES

1. Malcolm Feeley, *The Process Is the Punishment* (New York: Russell Sage, 1979), pp. 9–11.

2. Thomas Henderson, *The Significance of Judicial Structure: The Effect of Unification on Trial Court Operations* (Washington, D.C.: National Institute of Justice, 1984).

3. Jonathan Casper, Tom Tyler, and Bonnie Fisher, "Procedural Justice in Felony Cases," *Law and Society Review* 22 (1988): 497–505.

4. This section relies heavily on Conference of State Court Administrators and National Center for State Courts, *State Court Organization, 1987* (Williamsburg, Va.: National Center for State Courts, 1988). Herein cited as *State Court Organization, 1987.*

5. Charles Silberman, *Criminal Violence/Criminal Justice* (New York: Vintage Books, 1980), p. 347.

6. Feeley, *The Process Is the Punishment*, p. 3.

7. Patrick Langan, *State Felony Courts and Felony Laws* (Washington, D.C.: Bureau of Justice Statistics, 1987).

8. Timothy Flanagan and Katherine Jamieson, *Sourcebook of Criminal Justice Statistics* (Washington, D.C.: U.S. Government Printing Office, 1988), p. 450.

9. Bureau of Justice Statistics, *Report to the Nation on Crime and Justice* (Washington, D.C.: Bureau of Justice Statistics, 1988), p. 88.

10. Ibid.

11. United States Constitution, Article 3, secs. 1 and 2 (1789).

12. 1 Wharton 304, 4 L.Ed. 97 (1816).

13. Bureau of Justice Statistics, *State Court Caseload Statistics* (Washington, D.C.: U.S. Government Printing Office, 1983).

14. Administrative Office of U.S. Courts, *1987 Annual Report of the Director* (Washington, D.C.: Administrative Office of the United States Courts, 1987).

15. Flanagan and Jamieson, *Sourcebook of Criminal Justice Statistics.*

16. Ibid., p. 2.

17. H. Jacobs with D. Swank, J. Beecher, and M. Rich, "Keeping Pace: Court Resources and Crime in Ten U.S. Cities," *Judicature* 66 (1982): 73–83.

18. "Too Many Continuances #1 Factor in Court Delays, Survey Finds," *Criminal Justice Newsletter*, 15 November 1988, p. 7.

19. Joel Garner, "Delay Reduction in the Federal Courts: Rule 50(b) and the Federal Speedy Trial Act of 1974," *Journal of quantitative Criminology* 3 (1987): 229–50.

20. "Too Many Continuances #1 Factor in Court Delays," p. 7.

21. *State Court Organization, 1987.*

22. Ibid., pp. 204–7.

23. Ibid., p. 10.

24. Bureau of Justice Statistics, *State Court Organization, 1980,* (Washington, D.C.: U.S. Government Printing Office, 1981), p. 7.

25. "Judging the Judges," *Time*, 20 August 1979, p. 38.

26. *State Court Organization, 1987*, pp. 5–10; Bureau of Justice Statistics, *State Court Organization, 1980*, pp. 34, 40.

27. Sari Escovitz with Fred Kurland and Nan Gold, *Judicial Selection and Tenure* (Chicago: American Judicature Society, 1974), pp. 3–16.

28. "State Adoption of Alternative Dispute Resolution," *State Court Journal* 12 (1988): 11–15.

29. Public Law 90–578, tit. I sec. 101, 82 Stat. 1113 (1968); amended Public Law 94–577, sec. 1, Stat. 2729 (1976); Public Law 96–82 sec. 2, 93 Stat. 643 (1979).

30. See, generally, Carroll Seron, "The Professional Project of Parajudges: The Case of U.S. Magistrates," *Law and Society Review* 22 (1988): 557–75.

31. Alex Aikman, "Volunteer lawyer-judges bolster court resources," U.S. Department of Justice, *NIJ Reports* (January 1986): 2–6.

32. Warren Burger, "Rx for Justice: Modernize the Courts," *Nation's Business* (September 1974): 62.

33. Cited in National Advisory Commission on Criminal Justice Standards and Goals, *Courts* (Washington, D.C.: U.S. Government Printing Office, 1973), p. 171.

34. Edward McConnell in Swindler, *Justice in the States.*

35. *State Court Organization, 1987*, p. 13.

36. Ibid.

37. National Center for State Courts, *Report on Trends in the State Courts* (Williamsburg, Va.: National Center for State Courts, 1988).

38. Ibid.

39. Ibid.

40. Ibid.

41. See, generally, American Bar Association, *Standards Relating to Court Organization* (New York: Institute for Judicial Administration, 1973).

11

The Prosecution and the Defense

A fter a criminal defendant has been processed by police agencies and relevant evidence has been gathered in the case, the focus of justice shifts from the law enforcement to the criminal court system.

In the preceding chapter, we discussed the organization of the court system and the manner in which the criminal court as a complex social agency deals with different types of cases. Issues involving court administration, judicial selection, and court reform were analyzed.

This chapter explores the role of the prosecutor and the defense attorney in the criminal process. The prosecutor, to a great extent, is the person who single-handedly controls the "charging" decision. To charge or not, and for what offense, is the prosecutor's great discretionary authority. The defense attorney acts in a different capacity. Although defendants have a right to defend themselves, most are represented by a lawyer who is knowledgeable about the criminal law. The criminal lawyer has a legal obligation to utilize every effort to provide a competent and adequate defense.

Although the formal criminal trial that both service is an important aspect of our justice system, it is actually used in a small minority of cases. The greater majority of criminal cases are decided rather informally due to negotiations and actions by the attorneys in the case: the prosecutor who represents the state and the defense counsel representing the accused. Whether they are acting formally in a trial or informally through negotiated settlements, questions about the critical roles of the prosecutor and defense attorney pervade the system.

■ The Prosecutor

Depending on the level of government and jurisdiction in which he or she functions, the **prosecutor** may be known as a **district attorney,** a county attorney, a state's attorney, or a **U.S. attorney.** Whatever the title, the prosecutor is ordinarily a member of the practicing bar who has become a public prosecutor via political appointment or popular election.

Although the prosecutor participates with the judge and defense attorney in the adversary process, it is the prosecutor's responsibility to bring the state's case against the accused. The prosecutor focuses the power of the state on those who disobey the law by charging a person with a crime, releasing the individual from prosecution, or eventually bringing the accused to trial.

Although the prosecutor's primary duty is to enforce the criminal law, his or her fundamental obligation as an attorney is to seek justice as well as to convict those who are guilty. For example, if the prosecutor discovers facts suggesting that the accused is innocent, this information must be brought to the attention of the court. The American Bar Association's Code of Professional Responsibility, Canon 7-103, deals with the ethical duties of the attorney as a public prosecutor:

Dr 7-103 Performing the Duty of Public Prosecutor or Other Government Lawyer

A. A public prosecutor or other government lawyer shall not institute or cause to be instituted criminal charges when he knows or it is obvious that the charges are not supported by probable cause.

B. A public prosecutor or other government lawyer in criminal litigation shall make timely disclosure to counsel for the defendant, or to the defendant, if he has no counsel, of the existence of evidence, known to the prosecutor or other government lawyer, that tends to negate the guilt of the accused, mitigate the degree of the offense, or reduce the punishment.[1]

Chapter 11

The Prosecution and the Defense

■

The senior prosecutor must make policy decisions to exercise prosecutorial enforcement powers in a wide range of cases in criminal law, consumer protection, housing, and other areas. In so doing, the prosecutor determines and ultimately shapes the manner in which justice is exercised in society. In *Berger v. United States* (1935), Justice George Sutherland described the role of the prosecutor:

> The United States Attorney is the representative not of an ordinary part of a controversy, but of a sovereignty whose obligation to govern impartially is as compelling as its obligation to govern at all; and whose interest, therefore, in a criminal prosecution is not that it shall win a case, but that justice shall be done. As such, he is in a peculiar and very definite sense the servant of the law, the twofold aim of which is that the guilty shall not escape or innocence suffer. He may prosecute with earnestness and vigor—indeed, he should do so. But while he may strike hard blows, he is not at liberty to strike foul ones. It is as much his duty to refrain from improper methods calculated to produce a wrongful conviction as it is to use very legitimate means to bring about a just one.[2]

Many individual prosecutors are often caught between being compelled by their supervisors to do everything possible to obtain a guilty verdict and acting as a concerned public official to ensure that justice is done. Sometimes this can lead to prosecutorial misconduct. According to some legal authorities, unethical prosecutorial behavior is often motivated by the desire to obtain a conviction and by the fact that prosecutorial misbehavior is rarely punished by the courts.[3] Some prosecutors may conceal evidence or misrepresent it, or influence juries by impugning the character of opposing witnesses. Even where a court may instruct a jury to ignore certain evidence, a prosecutor may attempt to sway the jury or judge by simply mentioning the tainted evidence. Since appellate courts generally uphold convictions where misconduct is not considered serious (the harmless error doctrine), prosecutors are not penalized for their misbehavior; nor are they personally liable for their conduct. Overzealous, excessive, and even cruel prosecutors, motivated by political gain or notoriety, produce wrongful convictions, thereby abusing their office and the public trust.[4] According to legal expert Stanley Fisher, prosecutorial excesses appear when the government (1) always seeks the highest charges; (2) interprets the criminal law expansively; (3) wins as many convictions as possible; and (4) obtains the most severe penalties.[5]

In recent years, prosecutors have received a great deal of attention in the media. Much of this publicity resulted from the Watergate scandal and other famous criminal trials of recent decades, including the cases involving Charles Manson, Theodore Bundy, John Hinckley, Oliver North, and Joel Steinberg. Some prosecutors have even sought higher political office based on the publicity they received while participating in nationally publicized trials. Earl Warren, Thomas Dewey, Robert Kennedy, James Thompson, Eliot Richardson, and Paul Tsongas are examples of national political leaders who at one time were prosecuting attorneys.[6]

Politics and Prosecutors

The prosecutor is either elected or appointed and is, consequently, a political figure in the criminal justice system. The prosecutor normally has a party affiliation, a constituency of voters and supporters, and a need to respond to community pressures and interest groups. In this regard, the American Bar

Association's *Standards Relating to the Prosecution Function and Defense Function* states:

> The political process has played a significant part in the shaping of the role of the American prosecutor. Experience as a prosecutor is a familiar stepping stone to higher political office. The "DA" has long been glamorized in fiction, films, radio, television, and other media. Many of our political leaders had their first exposure to public notice and political life in this office. A substantial number of executive and legislative officials as well as judges have served as prosecuting attorneys at some point in their careers. The political involvement of a prosecutor varies. In most jurisdictions he is required to run with a party designation. In some places prosecutors are elected on a nonpartisan basis. The powers of a prosecutor are formidable and he is an important personage in his community. If he is not truly independent and professional, his powers can be misused for political or other improper purposes. Perhaps even more than other American public officials, the prosecutor's activity is in large part open to public gaze—as it should be—and spotlighted by the press. The importance of his function is such that his least mistake is likely to be magnified, as are many of his successful exploits.[7]

The political nature of the prosecutor's office can weigh heavily on decision making. When deciding if, when, and how to handle a case, the prosecutor cannot forget that he or she may be up for election soon and have to answer to an electorate who will scrutinize his or her actions. In for example, a murder trial involving a highly charged issue, such as child killing, the prosecutor's decision to ask for the death penalty may hinge on his or her perception of the public's will. The role of politics in the prosecutor's office is discussed in great detail in the Criminal Justice in Review on page 352.

The Duties of the Prosecutor

The prosecutor is also the chief law enforcement officer of a particular jurisdiction. His or her participation spans the entire gamut of the justice system, from the time search and arrest warrants are issued, or a grand jury empaneled, to the final sentencing decision and appeal. General duties of a prosecutor include (1) enforcing the law, (2) representing the government, (3) maintaining proper standards of conduct as an attorney and court officer, (4) developing programs and legislation for law and criminal justice reform, and (5) being a public spokesperson for the field of law. Of these, representing the government while presenting the state's case to the court is the prosecutor's most frequent task. In this regard, the prosecutor does many of the following:

1. Investigates possible violations of the law
2. Cooperates with police in investigating a crime
3. Determines what the charge will be
4. Interviews witnesses in criminal cases
5. Reviews applications for arrest and search warrants
6. Subpoenas witnesses
7. Represents the government in pretrial hearings and in motion procedures
8. Enters into plea-bargaining negotiations
9. Tries criminal cases
10. Recommends sentences to courts upon convictions
11. Represents the government in appeals

CRIMINAL JUSTICE IN REVIEW

The Role of Politics and Partisanship in Law Enforcement

The following article describes the relationship between politics and criminal prosecution.

Politics, properly understood, is the essence of democracy. It is the way a free and vigorous people seek to determine and then change public policy. Federal law enforcement is, in this sense, political. As we have recently observed, criminal justice issues such as drug enforcement are often important to citizens, and presidential candidates regularly address them in their campaigns.

When a president is elected, he is entitled to be served by an attorney general and others, including the 94 U.S. attorneys, who share his law enforcement priorities and—where the law is uncertain—who share the interpretation of the law the president prefers. It is natural that a president who believes in his law enforcement program and will be held accountable for it at the next election will likely seek members of his own party to implement that program.

Once appointed, however, an attorney general or U.S. attorney must recognize that politics is limited to the development of policies. There can be no political favoritism or partisan bias in the enforcement of those policies.

In law enforcement, there simply can be no friends or enemies. The law must treat important and anonymous interests alike. To achieve this, neutral standards and procedures for initiating investigations and authorizing prosecutions must be established and then applied without fear or favor.

A corollary of this is that an attorney general or U.S. attorney should be a person who has earned a reputation as trustworthy and professional, rather than partisan, because often he cannot properly explain what his office is doing, or why it has failed to act. For example, a prosecutor usually has a responsibility not to confirm or deny the existence of an investigation. This is a matter of fairness to the subjects of investigations and of self-interest to the government, because public disclosure of the details of an investigation may facilitate its frustration. Similarly, a prosecutor can rarely properly explain why an indictment was not sought in a matter known to have been investigated.

Thus, it is essential that the public trust the integrity and ability of an attorney general or U.S. attorney. Immediately after Watergate, it was widely recognized that it would be inappropriate to continue the tradition of appointing attorney general someone such as the president's campaign manager—be he Robert Kennedy or John Mitchell—because it would be difficult for the person to cease making partisan decisions and virtually impossible for the public to believe he had done so. Although this lesson of Watergate has not always been faithfully followed, the deviations may, perhaps, remind us of its continuing validity.

It should also be recognized, however, that neither an attorney general nor a U.S. attorney is solely responsible for federal law enforcement. Rather, he or she is the captain—but not necessarily the star—of a team of prosecutors, usually attracted by the highest tradition of public service, who tend to endure from administration to administration. They work with dedicated professionals in the federal investigative agencies. As Edward Levi said when President Ford appointed him attorney general in the aftermath of Watergate, the nation has been fortunate because the Department of Justice has historically been staffed by people who understand that "if we are to have a government of laws and not men, then it particularly takes dedicated men and women to accomplish this through their zeal and determination, and also their concern for fairness and impartiality."

Indeed, this may be an appropriate time to recall an exemplar of that tradition. Emory Buckner was an assistant U.S. attorney in New York when Felix Frankfurter served as Henry Stimson's deputy in that office. Buckner went on to become the US attorney in New York when Felix Frankfurter served as Henry Stimson's deputy in that office. Buckner went on to become the U.S. attorney and also a special prosecutor of public corruption. When Buckner died in 1941, Frankfurter described Buckner's "uncompromising conception of the functions and standards of a prosecutor."

"He was," Frankfurter said, "an instinctive ethical nature, but one whose comic spirit precluded the taint of self-righteousness and the dullness of moralizing. . . . Buckner displayed uncommon energy and skill in the successful prosecution of subtle and complicated crimes, against powerful opposition."

"But what is much more important is that . . . Buckner realized that he who wields the instruments of criminal justice wields the most terrible instruments of government. In order to assure their just and compassionate use, a prosecutor must have an almost priest-like attitude toward his duties. Buckner practiced this attitude without deviation." ■

SOURCE: Mark Wolf, "U.S. Federal Court Judge," *Boston Globe*, 3 February, 1989.

In addition, many jurisdictions have established special prosecution programs aimed at seeking indictments and convictions of those committing major felonies, violent offenses, rapes, and white-collar crimes.

Types of Prosecutors

In the federal system, prosecutors are known as U.S. attorneys and are appointed by the president. They are responsible for representing the government in federal district courts. The chief prosecutor is usually an administrator, while assistants normally handle the actual preparation and trial work. Federal prosecutors are professional civil service employees with reasonable salaries and job security.

On a state or county level, the **attorney general** and district attorney, respectively, are the chief prosecutorial officers. Again, the bulk of criminal prosecution and staff work is performed by scores of full-time and part-time attorneys, police investigators, and clerical personnel. Most attorneys who work for prosecutors on state and county levels are political appointees who earn low salaries, handle many cases, and in some jurisdictions maintain private law practices. Many young lawyers serve in this capacity in order to gain trial experience and leave when they obtain better-paying positions. In most state, county, and municipal jurisdictions, however, the office of the prosecutor can be described as having the highest standards of professional skill, personal integrity, and work conditions.

In urban settings the structure of the district attorney's office is often specialized, having separate divisions for felonies, misdemeanors, and trial and appeal assignments. In rural offices, chief prosecutors will handle many of the criminal cases themselves. Where assistant prosecutors are employed, they often work part-time, have limited professional opportunities, and are dependent on the political patronage of chief prosecutors for their positions.

Chapter 11

The Prosecution and the Defense

■

Many prosecutors receive national fame for their exploits. Rudolph Guiliani, who successfully prosecuted the Boesky case and also put many leading organized crime bosses in prison, has become a prominent national political figure.

Today the personnel practices, organizational structures, and political atmospheres of many prosecutor's offices restrict the effectiveness of individual prosecutors in investigating and prosecuting criminal offenses. For many years, prosecutors have been criticized for bargaining justice away, for using their positions as a stepping stone to higher political office, and often for failing to investigate or simply dismissing criminal cases. Of late, however, the prosecutor's public image has improved. Violations of federal laws, such as white-collar crime, drug peddling, and corruption, are being more aggressively investigated by the 94 U.S. attorneys and the nearly 2,000 assistant U.S. attorneys.

Aggressive federal prosecutors in New York, for instance, have made extraordinary progress in the war against insider trading and security fraud on Wall Street, with the use of informants, wiretaps, and the federal racketeering law. Using RICO (Racketeer Influenced and Corrupt Organization Law), the government successfully obtained convictions of important Mafia gangsters.[8] In Boston, prosecutors were credited with the recent dramatic and hard-won conviction of Gennaro (Jerry) Angiulo and the collapse of his Mafia family.[9]

State crimes ranging from murder to larceny are prosecuted in state courts by district attorneys who are stepping up their efforts against career criminals, shortening the time it takes to bring serious cases to trial, and addressing the long-neglected problems of victims and witnesses. With such actions, the prosecutor will continue to be one of the most powerful and visible professionals in the justice system.

The Law Enforcement Role of Prosecutors

One of the most important of the prosecutor's many functions involves the relationship between the prosecutor and the police officer. The prosecutor has broad discretion in decisions to charge the suspect with a crime and is generally the chief law enforcement official of the jurisdiction. When it comes to processing everyday offenses and minor fines, the prosecutor often relies on law enforcement officers to provide and initiate the formal complaint. In the area of more serious offenses, such as felonies, the prosecutor is involved in investigating criminal violations. Some offices of the district attorney are involved in special investigations concerning organized crime, corruption of public officials, and corporate and white-collar crime, as well as vice and drug investigations. Much of the staff and investigative work in such offices is handled by police personnel.

Police and prosecutorial relationships vary from one jurisdiction to another and often depend on whether the police agency is supplying the charge or the district attorney is investigating the matter. In either case, the prosecutor is required to maintain regular liaison with the police department in order to develop the criminal prosecution properly. Some of the areas where the police officer and prosecutor work together include the following:

1. *Police investigation report.* This report is one of the most important documents in the prosecutor's case file. It is basically a statement of the details of the crime including all the evidence needed to support each element of the offense. Such a report is a critical first step in developing the government's case against a suspect.

2. *Providing legal advice.* Often the prosecutor advises the police officer about the legal issues in a given case. The prosecutor may also assist the officer in

limiting unnecessary court appearances, informing police officers of the disposition of cases, and helping to prepare the police officer for pretrial appearances.

3. *Prosecutorial training of police personnel.* In many jurisdictions, prosecutors assist police departments in training police officers. Through such training programs, police officers are made more aware of what is involved in securing a warrant, making a legal arrest, interrogating a person in custody, and conducting legal lineups for the purposes of identification. Some police departments have police legal advisers who cooperate with the prosecutor in providing legal training for new and experienced police personnel.[10]

POLICE-PROSECUTOR CONFLICTS. Although police and prosecutor work together in many areas and maximize coordination within the criminal justice system, in other situations they function with minimal cooperation and even mistrust because of their different roles. Police and prosecutor often compete with each other in seeking credit for the successful arrest, prosecution, and conviction of a particular defendant. In some cases, the prosecutor is insensitive to the problem of unnecessary court appearances by police officers. And in some jurisdictions outright antagonism between police and prosecutor may exist if there is little or no exchange of information about a particular case. Furthermore, the police department may be unwilling to understand the prosecutor's decision not to charge a suspect with a crime after much police work has gone into an investigation. The police may not agree with alternative procedures developed by the prosecutor and would prefer to press for full enforcement in the charging decision. In some cases, the prosecutor may not handle the witnesses or informants properly, which may place the police officer in an embarrassing position. On the other hand, the prosecutor may believe the police have legally bungled and mishandled evidence in a criminal investigation. Such problems exist between prosecutors and police officers in varying degree from one court to another.

At the same time, the prosecutor, as the chief law enforcement official of a given jurisdiction, ordinarily is dependent on police and other investigative agencies for information regarding criminal violations. A large part of the prosecutor's work comes from complaints made by citizens or arrests made directly by police agencies. Consequently, the prosecutor needs the cooperation of the police in processing the case. Even in those cases in which the prosecutor initiates investigation of suspected criminal acts, the investigations are generally conducted by police personnel. Most professional prosecutors willingly cooperate with law enforcement personnel so as to have a greater impact on the investigation and a higher probability of successfully prosecuting their cases.

■ Prosecutorial Discretion

After the police arrest and bring a suspect to court, it might be expected that the entire criminal court process would be mobilized. This is often not the case. For a variety of reasons a substantial percentage of defendants are never brought to trial. It is the prosecutor's decision to bring a case to trial or dismiss it outright. Even if the prosecutor decides to pursue a case, the charges may later be dropped if conditions are not favorable for a conviction in a process called *nolle prosequi.*

Even in felony cases, the prosecutor ordinarily exercises much discretion in deciding whether to charge the accused with a crime.[11] After a police investigation, the prosecutor may be asked to review the sufficiency of the evidence to determine if a criminal complaint should be filed. In some jurisdictions, this may involve presentation of the evidence at a preliminary hearing. In other cases, the prosecutor's recommendation may involve seeking a criminal complaint through the grand jury or other information procedure. These procedures, representing the formal methods of charging the accused with a felony offense, are discussed in Chapter 12.

There is little question that prosecutors exercise a great deal of discretion in even the most serious cases. Figure 11.1 illustrates the flow of felony cases through four jurisdictions in the United States: Golden, Colorado; Manhattan, New York; Salt Lake City, Utah; and Washington, D.C. Barbara Boland collected the data for a study of the differences in how prosecutors handle felony arrests.[12] Note that although procedures were different in the four districts, prosecutors used their discretion to dismiss a high percentage of the cases prior to trial. Also note that when the cases were forwarded for trial, very few defendants were actually acquitted, indicating that the prosecutorial discretion was exercised to screen out the weakest cases. In addition, of those accepted for prosecution, a high percentage pleaded guilty. All the evidence here points to the conclusion that prosecutorial discretion is used to reduce potential trial cases to a minimum.

The reasons why some cases are rejected or dismissed are analyzed in the Criminal Justice in Review on page 358.

The prosecutor may also play a limited role in exercising discretion in minor offenses. This may consist of simply consulting with the police after their investigation results in a complaint being filed against the accused. In these instances, the decision to charge a person with a crime may be left primarily to the discretion of the law enforcement agency. The prosecutor may decide to enter this type of case after an arrest has been made and a complaint has been filed with the court and subsequently determine whether to adjust the matter or proceed to trial. In some minor crimes, the prosecutor may not even appear until the trial stage of the process (or not at all); in some jurisdictions, the police officer handles the entire case, including its prosecution.

Extent of Discretion

The power to institute formal charges against the defendant is the key to the prosecutorial function. The ability to initiate or discontinue charges against a defendant represents the control and power the prosecutor has over an individual's liberty. The prosecutor has broad discretion in the exercise of his or her duties. It is the prosecutor's primary responsibility to institute criminal proceedings against the defendant; this discretionary decision is subject to few limitations and often puts the prosecutor in the position of making difficult decisions without appropriate policies and guidelines. Over 50 years ago, Newman Baker commented on the problems of prosecutorial decision making:

"To prosecute or not to prosecute?" is a question which comes to the mind of this official scores of times each day. A law has been contravened and the statute says he is bound to commence proceedings. His legal duty is clear. But what will be the result? Will it be a waste of time? Will it be expensive to the state? Will it be unfair to the defendant (the prosecutor applying his own ideas of justice)? Will it serve any good purpose to society in general? Will it have good publicity value? Will it cause a

FIGURE 11.1 Differences in How Prosecutors Handle Felony Cases Can Be Seen in Four Jurisdictions

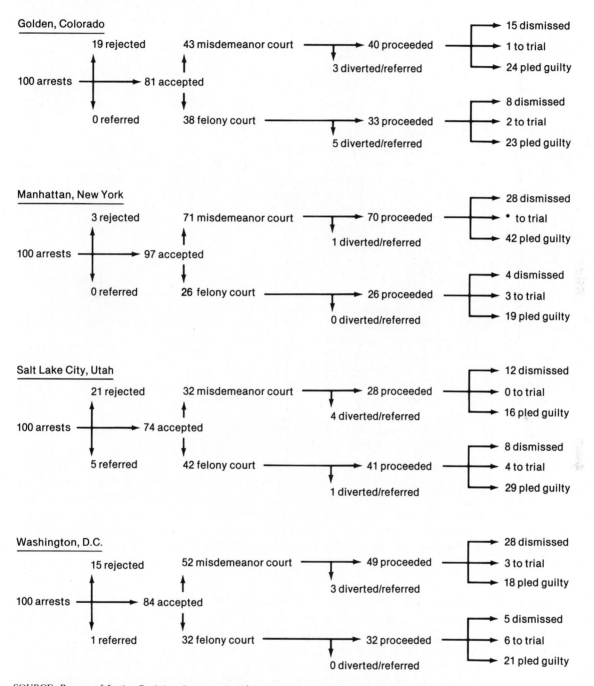

Golden, Colorado

	19 rejected	43 misdemeanor court → 40 proceeded	→ 15 dismissed
			→ 1 to trial
100 arrests → 81 accepted		3 diverted/referred	→ 24 pled guilty
	0 referred	38 felony court → 33 proceeded	→ 8 dismissed
			→ 2 to trial
		5 diverted/referred	→ 23 pled guilty

Manhattan, New York

	3 rejected	71 misdemeanor court → 70 proceeded	→ 28 dismissed
			→ • to trial
100 arrests → 97 accepted		1 diverted/referred	→ 42 pled guilty
	0 referred	26 felony court → 26 proceeded	→ 4 dismissed
			→ 3 to trial
		0 diverted/referred	→ 19 pled guilty

Salt Lake City, Utah

	21 rejected	32 misdemeanor court → 28 proceeded	→ 12 dismissed
			→ 0 to trial
100 arrests → 74 accepted		4 diverted/referred	→ 16 pled guilty
	5 referred	42 felony court → 41 proceeded	→ 8 dismissed
			→ 4 to trial
		1 diverted/referred	→ 29 pled guilty

Washington, D.C.

	15 rejected	52 misdemeanor court → 49 proceeded	→ 28 dismissed
			→ 3 to trial
100 arrests → 84 accepted		3 diverted/referred	→ 18 pled guilty
	1 referred	32 felony court → 32 proceeded	→ 5 dismissed
			→ 6 to trial
		0 diverted/referred	→ 21 pled guilty

SOURCE: Bureau of Justice Statistics, *Report to the Nation on Crime and Justice* (Washington, D.C.: U.S. Government Printing Office, 1988), p. 71 adapted from Barbara Boland, INSLAW, Inc., *The Prosecution of Felony Arrests* (Washington, D.C.: U.S. Government Printing Office, 1983).

political squabble? Will it prevent the prosecutor from carrying the offender's home precinct when he, the prosecutor, runs for Congress after his term as prosecutor? Was the law violated a foolish piece of legislation? If the offender is a friend, is it the square thing to do to reward friendship by initiating criminal proceedings? These and many

Chapter 11

The Prosecution and the Defense

■

What Are the Most Common Reasons for Rejection or Dismissal of a Criminal Case?

Many criminal cases are rejected or dismissed because of—

■ *Insufficient evidence* that results from a failure to find sufficient physical evidence that links the defendant to the offense

■ *Witness problems* that arise, for example, when a witness fails to appear, gives unclear or inconsistent statements, is reluctant to testify, is unsure of the identity of the offender or where a prior relationship may exist between the victim/witness and offender

■ *The interests of justice*, wherein the prosecutor decides not to prosecute certain types of offenses, particularly those that violate the letter but not the spirit of the law (for example, offenses involving insignificant amounts of property damage)

■ *Due process problems* that involve violations of the constitutional requirements for seizing evidence and for questioning the accused

■ A *plea on another case*, for example, when the accused is charged in several cases and the prosecutor agrees to drop one or more of the cases in exchange for a plea of guilty on another case

■ *Pretrial diversion* that occurs when the prosecutor and the court agree to drop charges when the accused successfully meets the conditions for diversion, such as completion of a treatment program

■ *Referral for other prosecution*, such as when there are other offenses, perhaps of a more serious nature, in a different jurisdiction, or deferral to federal prosecution.

Table A and B present data taken from a study of prosecutorial practices in a number of jurisdictions around the U.S. As Table A shows, evidence problems are the most common reasons for prosecutors to reject cases. Table B indicates that many cases are dropped because defendants plead guilty to lesser charges. ■

---

similar considerations are bound to come to the mind of the man responsible for setting the wheels of criminal justice in motion.[13]

Once involved in a case, the prosecutor must also determine the formal charge. The decision to charge or not to charge a person with a crime is often not an easy one. Should a 17-year-old boy be charged with burglary or handled as a juvenile offender in the juvenile court? Would it be more appropriate to reduce a drug charge from sale of marijuana to mere possession? What if the offense could be considered mayhem, battery, or simple assault? What then are the factors that influence prosecutorial decision making?

SYSTEM FACTORS. In determining what course of action to take, the prosecutor has a significant effect on the criminal justice system. Initiating formal charges against all defendants arrested by the police would clog the courts with numerous petty crimes and cases in which little chance of conviction exists. The prosecutor will waste time on minor cases that could have been better spent on the investigation and prosecution of more serious crimes. Effective screening by prosecutors can eliminate many cases from the judicial system in which convictions cannot reasonably be obtained or which may be inappropriate for criminal action, such as petty thefts, minor crimes by first offenders, and criminal acts involving offenders in need of special services (for example, emotionally disturbed or mentally retarded offenders). The prosecutor can then concentrate on bringing to trial offenders who commit serious personal and property crimes such as homicide, burglary, rape, and robbery.[14]

TABLE A ■ Evidence Problems Are the Most Common Reason for Prosecutors to Reject Cases

Jurisdiction	Declined Cases*	Percentage of Felony Arrests Declined for Prosecution because of							
		Insufficient Evidence	Witness Problems	Due Process Problems	Interest of Justice	Plea on Another Case	Referral to Diversion	Referral for Other Prosecution	Other
Golden, Colo.	41	59%	27%	2%	5%	2%	2%	2%	0%
Greeley, Colo.	235	52	7	0	38	0	1	2	0
Manhattan, N.Y.	995	61	23	5	4	0	—	3	4
New Orleans, La.	4,114	38	30	12	8	0	7	4	—
Salt Lake City, Utah	973	58	12	1	8	1	2	19	—
San Diego, Calif.	4,940	54	15	6	9	1	0	9	7
Washington, D.C.	1,535	30	24	—	13	0	—	3	29

*Excludes cases for which reasons are unknown. —Insufficient data to calculate.

SOURCE: Barbara Boland with Ronald Sones, INSLAW, Inc., *The Prosecution of Felony Arrests* (Washington, D.C.: U.S. Government Printing Office, 1983); 1981, BJS, 1986).

TABLE B ■ Guilty Pleas on Other Charges Are a Major Cause of Dismissals

Jurisdiction	Dismissed Cases*	Percentage of Cases Dismissed because of							
		Insufficient Evidence	Witness Problems	Due Process Problems	Interest of Justice	Plea on Another Case	Referral to Diversion	Referral for Other Prosecution	Other
Brighton, Colo.	443	16%	7%	1%	10%	43%	21%	2%	0%
Colorado Springs, Colo.	675	13	11	2	3	40	16	14	0
Fort Collins, Colo.	257	4	5	1	5	41	27	15	0
Golden, Colo.	709	14	14	1	7	38	17	9	0
Greeley, Colo.	207	12	25	1	4	18	20	20	0
Indianapolis, Ind.	639	27	15	1	33	21	—	1	1
Los Angeles, Calif.	8,351	29	16	2	17	2	10	10	14
Louisville, Ky.	272	11	10	3	28	5	15	3	24
Manhattan, N.Y.	10,233	26	24	1	17	4	0	1	26
New Orleans, La.	429	22	16	20	15	6	7	1	14
Portland, Ore.	906	15	22	—	6	23	7	13	13
Pueblo, Colo.	146	16	11	2	7	43	14	6	0
St. Louis, Mo.	1,097	22	20	9	4	10	—	1	32
Salt Lake City, Utah	917	16	17	1	2	27	9	9	19
San Diego, Calif.	2,630	25	11	3	7	18	10	6	20
Washington, D.C.	3,656	21	16	1	4	9	7	1	41

NOTE: Dismissed cases in this table include diversions.
*Excludes cases for which reasons are unknown. —Insufficient data to calculate.

SOURCE:Bureau of Justice Statistics, *Report to the Nation on Crime and Justice* (Washington, D.C.: U.S. Government Printing Office, 1988); Barbara Boland, *The Prosecution of Felony Arrests* (Washington, D.C.: U.S. Government Printing Office, 1983).

CASE FACTORS. As the person ultimately responsible for deciding whether to prosecute, prosecutors must be aware of the wide variety of circumstances that affect their decisions. Frank Miller has identified a list of factors that affect discretion and the charging decision. Some of these include (1) the attitude of the victim, (2) the cost of prosecution to the criminal justice system, (3) the avoidance of undue harm to the suspect, (4) the availability of alternative procedures, (5) the use of civil sanctions, and (6) the willingness of the suspect to cooperate with law enforcement authorities.[15]

Recent evidence indicates that the relationship between the victim and criminal may have a great deal of influence on whether a prosecutor wishes to pursue a case. Barbara Boland found that conviction rates were much lower in cases involving friends (30 percent) or relatives (19 percent) than they were in cases involving strangers (48 percent).[16] Prosecutors who are aware of the drop-off in conviction probability in friend-relative cases may be reluctant to pursue them unless they are of the most serious kind.

DISPOSITION ALTERNATIVES. While determining which cases should be eliminated from the criminal process or brought to trial, the prosecutor has the opportunity to select more appropriate alternative actions. There are many situations in which the prosecutor must decide if noncriminal alternatives are more appropriate. For example, offenders may be alcoholics or narcotics addicts; they may be mentally ill; they may have been led to crime by their family situation or by their inability to get a job. If they are not helped, they may well return to crime. In many cases only minimal intrusions on defendants' liberty seem necessary. Often it will be enough simply to refer offenders to the appropriate agency in the community, and hope that they will take advantage of the help offered. The prosecutor might, for example, be willing to drop charges if a man goes to an employment agency and makes a bona fide effort to get a job, or if he consults a family service agency, or if he resumes his education. The prosecutor retains legal power to file a charge until the period of limitations has expired, but as a practical matter, unless the offense is repeated, it would be unusual for the initial charge to be reviewed.[17]

Today, particularly in those jurisdictions where alternative programs exist, prosecutors are identifying and diverting offenders to community agencies in cases where the full criminal process does not appear necessary. This may occur in certain juvenile cases, with alcoholic and drug offenders, and in nonsupport paternity, prostitution, and gambling offenses. The American Bar Association recommends the utilization of social service programs as appropriate alternatives to prosecution.[18]

The opportunity to deal with the accused in a noncriminal fashion represents what has come to be known as pretrial diversion, in which the prosecutor postpones or eliminates criminal prosecution in exchange for the alleged offender's participation in a rehabilitation program.[19] In recent years, the reduced cost and general utility of such programs has made them an important factor in prosecutorial discretion and a major part of the criminal justice system. A more detailed discussion of pretrial diversion is found in Chapter 12.

The Role of Prosecutorial Discretion

Regardless of its source, the proper exercise of prosecutorial discretion can improve the criminal justice process. For example, its use can prevent unnecessarily rigid implementation of the criminal law. Discretion allows the prosecutor to consider alternative decisions and humanize the operation of the criminal justice system. If prosecutors had little or no discretion, they would be forced to prosecute all cases brought to their attention. Judge Charles Breitel has stated, "If every policeman, every prosecutor, every court, and every post sentence agency performed his or its responsibility in strict accordance with rules of law, precisely and narrowly laid down, the criminal law would be ordered but intolerable."[20]

On the other hand, too much discretion can lead to abuses that result in the abandonment of the law. One of America's most eminent legal scholars, Roscoe Pound, has defined discretion as

> an authority conferred by law to act in certain conditions or situations in accordance with an official's or an official agency's considered judgment and conscience. It is an idea of morals, belonging to the twilight between law and morals.[21]

In terms of prosecutorial practices, this definition of discretion implies the need to select and choose among alternative decisions—to remove cases from the criminal process, to modify criminal charges, or to prosecute to the fullest intent of legal authority. Because there is no easy way to make these decisions, it has been recommended that the prosecutor establish standards for evaluating whether criminal proceedings should be brought against an accused. The American Bar Association's *Standards Relating to the Prosecution Function and Defense Function* provides the following guidelines for prosecutorial discretion in the charging decision:

A. In addressing himself to the decision whether to charge, the prosecutor should first determine whether there is evidence which would support a conviction.
B. The prosecutor is not obliged to present all charges which the evidence might support. The prosecutor may in some circumstances and for good cause consistent with the public interest decline to prosecute, notwithstanding that evidence exists which would support a conviction. Illustrative of the factors which the prosecutor may properly consider in exercising his discretion are:
   1. The prosecutor's reasonable doubt that the accused is in fact guilty
   2. The extent of the harm caused by the offense
   3. The disproportion of the authorized punishment in relation to the particular offense or the offender
   4. Possible improper motives of a complainant
   5. Prolonged nonenforcement of a statute, with community acquiescence
   6. Reluctance of the victim to testify
   7. Cooperation of the accused in the apprehension or conviction of others
   8. Availability and likelihood of prosecution by another jurisdiction
C. In making the decision to prosecute, the prosecutor should give no weight to the personal or political advantages or disadvantages which might be involved or to a desire to enhance his record of convictions.
D. In cases which involve a serious threat to the community, the prosecutor should not be deterred from prosecution by the fact that in his jurisdiction juries have tended to acquit persons accused of the particular kind of criminal act in question.
E. The prosecutor should not bring or seek charges greater in number or degree than he can reasonably support with evidence at trial.[22]

These standards are aimed at controlling and improving prosecutorial decisions regarding what cases should be prosecuted in the criminal process. Other methods of controlling prosecutorial decision making include (1) identification of the reasons for charging decisions, (2) publication of office policies, (3) review by nonprosecutorial groups, (4) charging conferences, and

(5) evaluation of charging policies and decisions and development of screening, diversion, and plea negotiations procedures.[23]

Controlling Prosecutorial Discretion

The prosecutor's charging discretion has also been given consideration by the U.S. Supreme Court. For example, in **Town of Newton v. Rumery** (1987), a defendant entered into an agreement with a prosecutor under which the criminal charges against him would be dropped in exchange for his agreeing not to file a civil suit against the town police. The defendant later filed the suit anyway, maintaining that the original agreement was coercive and interfered with his right to legal process. He lost the case when the trial court ruled that his earlier agreement not to file suit against the town was binding. On appeal the Supreme Court found for the town of Newton. It upheld the legality of the prosecutor's actions because the idea for the bargain had originated with the defense and therefore was not inherently "coercive." *Rumery* illustrates that prosecutors maintain significant discretion to work out bargains and deals as long as they do not deprive defendants of their legal rights.[24]

PROSECUTORIAL VINDICTIVENESS. Courts have been more concerned about prosecutors who use their discretion in a vindictive manner to punish defendants who exercise their legal rights. For example, in *North Carolina v. Pearce* (1969), the U.S. Supreme Court held that a judge in a retrial cannot impose a sentence more severe than that originally imposed. In other words, a prosecutor cannot seek a stricter sentence for a defendant who succeeds in setting aside his or her first conviction.[25] In *Blackledge v. Perry* (1974), the Court dealt with the issue of vindictiveness on the part of the prosecutor. Imposing a penalty on a defendant for having successfully pursued a statutory right of appeal is a violation of due process of law.[26] But in *Bordenkircher v. Hayes* (1978), the Court allowed the prosecutor to carry out threats of increased charges made during plea negotiations when the defendant refused to plead guilty to the original charge.[27] This case is highlighted in Chapter 12.

In 1982 the Supreme Court dealt with prosecutorial discretion in **United States v. Goodwin**. In *Goodwin* the Court held that no realistic likelihood of vindictiveness exists where the prosecutor increases charges after plea negotiations fail and the defendant asserts his or her right to a trial by jury.[28] The defendant, Goodwin, was stopped for speeding. After Goodwin stepped out of his car, the officer noticed a clear plastic bag under the armrest and instructed Goodwin to return to the car. Goodwin placed the car in gear and accelerated, knocking the officer aside. A complaint was filed, charging Goodwin with various misdemeanor offenses. When Goodwin chose to plead not guilty, the U.S. attorney's office obtained an indictment that, unlike the original charges, included a felony of assaulting an officer. The defendant was convicted, and he appealed on the basis that the case presented a genuine effort at retaliation by the prosecutor. Although the federal circuit court set aside the conviction, the U.S. Supreme Court held that the increased charges did not present a likelihood of vindictiveness on the prosecutor's part. First, the Court reasoned that in preparing a case the prosecutor may uncover additional relevant information, thus justifying increased charges. Second, the Court felt there was a greater likelihood that posttrial actions were more vindictively motivated than pretrial changes in criminal charges.

These decisions provide the framework for the "prosecutorial vindictiveness" doctrine. Due process of law may be violated if the prosecutor retaliates against a defendant and there is proof of actual vindictiveness. The prosecutor's legitimate exercise of discretion must be balanced against the defendant's legal rights.

■ The Defense Attorney

The **defense attorney** is the counterpart of the prosecuting attorney in the criminal process. The accused has a constitutional right to counsel, and, when the defendant cannot afford one, the state must provide the cost of a legal defense. The accused may obtain counsel from the private bar if he or she is in a financial position to do so; in the case of the indigent defendant, private counsel or a **public defender** may be assigned by the court. (See the discussion on defense of the indigent later in this chapter.)

For many years, much of the legal community looked down the role of the criminal defense attorney and the practice of criminal law. This attitude stemmed from the kinds of legal work a defense attorney was forced to do—working with shady characters, negotiating for the release of known thugs and hoods, and often overzealously defending alleged criminals in the criminal trial. Lawyers have been reluctant to specialize in criminal law because the pay is relatively low, and criminal lawyers often provide services without receiving any compensation. In addition, law schools in the past seldom developed courses in the criminal law and trial practices beyond the one or two courses traditionally in their curricula.

In recent years, however, with the advent of constitutional requirements regarding the assistance of counsel, interest in the area of criminal law has grown. Almost all law schools today have clinical programs that employ students as voluntary defense attorneys. They also offer courses in trial tactics, brief writing, and appellate procedures. In addition, legal organizations such as the American Bar Association, the National Legal Aid and Defenders Association, and the National Association of Criminal Defense Lawyers have assisted in recruiting able lawyers to participate in criminal defense work. As the American Bar Association has noted, "An almost indispensable condition to fundamental improvement of American criminal justice is the active and knowledgeable support of the bar as a whole."[29]

The Role of the Criminal Defense Attorney

The defense counsel is an attorney as well as an officer of the court. As an attorney, the defense counsel is obligated to uphold the integrity of the legal profession and to observe the requirements of the Code of Professional Responsibility in the defense of a client. According to the code, the duties of the lawyer to the adversary system of justice are as follows:

> Our legal system provides for the adjudication of disputes governed by the rules of substantive, evidentiary, and procedural law. An adversary presentation counters the natural human tendency to judge too swiftly in terms of the familiar that which is not yet fully known; the advocate, by his zealous preparation of facts and law, enables the tribunal to come to the hearing with an open and neutral mind and to render impartial judgements. The duty of a lawyer to his client and his duty to the legal system are the same: To represent his client zealously within the boundaries of the law.[30]

As an officer of the court, along with the judge, prosecutors, and other trial participants, the defense attorney participates in a process of seeking to uncover the basic facts and elements of the criminal act. In this dual capacity of being both a defensive advocate and an officer of the court, the attorney is often confronted with conflicting obligations to his or her client and profession. Monroe Freedman identifies three of the most difficult problems involving the professional responsibility of the criminal defense lawyer:

1. Is it proper to cross-examine for the purpose of discrediting the reliability or credibility of an adverse witness whom you know to be telling the truth?
2. Is it proper to put a witness on the stand when you know he will commit perjury?
3. Is it proper to give your client legal advice when you have reason to believe that the knowledge you give him will tempt him to commit perjury?[31]

These questions and others reveal serious difficulties with respect to a lawyer's ethical responsibilities.

There are other equally important issues. Suppose, for example, a client confides that he is planning to commit a crime. What are the defense attorney's ethical responsibilities in this case? Obviously, the lawyer would have to counsel the client to obey the law; if the lawyer assisted the client in engaging in illegal behavior, the lawyer would be subject to charges of unprofessional conduct and even criminal liability. In another area, suppose the defense attorney is aware that the police made a procedural error and that the guilty client could be let off on a technicality. What are the attorney's ethical responsibilities in this case? The criminal lawyer needs to be aware of these troublesome situations in order to properly balance the duties of being an attorney with those of being an officer of the court.

The defense counsel performs many functions while representing the accused in the criminal process. These include, but are not limited to, (1) investigating the incident; (2) interviewing the client, police, and other witnesses; (3) discussing the matter with the prosecutor; (4) representing the defendant at the various pre-judicial procedures, such as arrest, interrogation, lineup, and arraignment; (5) entering into plea negotiations; (6) preparing the case for trial, including developing tactics and strategy to be used; (7) filing and arguing legal motions with the court; (8) representing the defendant at trial; (9) providing assistance at sentencing; and (10) determining the appropriate basis for appeal. These are some of the major duties of any defense attorney, whether privately employed by the accused, appointed by the court, or serving as a public defender.

■ The Right to Counsel

Over the past decade, the rules and procedures of criminal justice administration have become extremely complex. Specialized knowledge has become essential for the adversary system to operate effectively. Preparation of a case for court involves detailed investigation of a crime, knowledge of court procedures, use of rules of evidence, and skills in criminal advocacy. Both the state and the defense must have this expertise, particularly when an individual's freedom is at stake. Consequently, the right to the assistance of counsel in the criminal justice system is essential if the defendant is to have a fair chance of presenting a case in the adversary process.

One of the most critical issues in the criminal justice system has been whether an **indigent** defendant has the right to counsel. Can the accused who is poor and cannot afford an attorney have a fair trial without the assistance of counsel? Is counsel required at preliminary hearings? Should the convicted indigent offender be given counsel at state expense in appeals of the case? Questions such as these have arisen constantly in recent years. The federal court system has long provided counsel to the indigent defendant on the basis of the **Sixth Amendment** to the U.S. Constitution, unless he or she desired to waive this right.[32] This constitutional mandate clearly applies to the federal courts, but its application to state criminal proceedings has been less certain.

In the landmark case of *Gideon v. Wainwright* in 1963, the U.S. Supreme Court took the first major step on the issue of right to counsel by holding that state courts must provide counsel to the indigent defendant in felony prosecutions.[33] Some 10 years later, in the case of *Argersinger v. Hamlin* in 1972, the Court extended the obligation to provide counsel to all criminal cases where the penalty includes imprisonment—regardless of whether the offense is a felony or misdemeanor.[34] These two major decisions relate to the Sixth Amendment right to counsel as it applies to the presentation of a defense at the trial stage of the criminal justice system.

In numerous Supreme Court decisions since *Gideon v. Wainwright*, the states have been required to provide counsel for indigent defendants at virtually all other stages of the criminal process, beginning with arrest and concluding with the defendant's release from the system.

Today, the Sixth Amendment right to counsel and the Fourteenth Amendment guarantee of due process of law have been judicially interpreted together to provide the defendant with counsel by the state in all types of criminal proceedings. The right to counsel attaches at the earliest stages of the justice system, usually when a criminal suspect is interrogated while in the custody of the police: *Miranda v. Arizona* (see Chapter 9) held that any statements made by the accused when in custody are inadmissible at trial unless the accused is informed of the right to counsel and to have an attorney appointed by the state if indigent.[35]

In addition to guaranteeing the right of counsel at the earliest stages of the justice system, as well as at trials, the Supreme Court has moved to extend the right to counsel to postconviction and other collateral proceedings, such as probation and parole revocation and appeal. When, for example, the court intends to revoke a defendant's probation and impose a sentence, the probationer has a right to counsel at the deferred sentence hearing.[36] Where the state provides for an appellate review of the criminal conviction, the defendant is entitled to the assistance of counsel for this initial appeal.[37] The defendant does not have the right to counsel for an appellate review beyond the original appeal or for a discretionary review to the U.S. Supreme Court. The Supreme Court has also required the states to provide counsel in other proceedings that involve the loss of personal liberty such as juvenile delinquency hearings[38] and mental health commitment proceedings.[39]

Areas still remain in the criminal justice system where the courts by judicial decree have not required assistance of counsel for the accused. These include (1) preindictment lineups, (2) booking procedures including the taking of fingerprints and other forms of identification, (3) grand jury investigations, (4) appeals beyond the first review, and (5) disciplinary proceedings in correctional institutions. Nevertheless, the general rule of thumb is that no person can be deprived of freedom or lose a "liberty interest" without representation of counsel.

The right to counsel can also be spelled out in particular federal or state statutes. For example, beyond abiding by present constitutional requirements, a state may provide counsel by statute at all stages of juvenile proceedings, or when dealing with inmate prison infractions or pretrial release hearings, or when considering temporary confinement of drug or sex offenders for psychiatric examination.

Today the scope of representation for the indigent defendant is believed to cover virtually all areas of the criminal process, and most certainly those critical points at which a person's liberty is at stake. Table 11.1 summarizes the major U.S. Supreme Court decisions granting defendants counsel throughout the criminal justice system.

The Private Bar

Today, the lawyer whose practice involves a substantial proportion of criminal cases is often considered a specialist in the field. Since most lawyers are not prepared in law school for criminal work, their skill often results from their experience in the trial courts. Lawyers like F. Lee Bailey, Alan Dershowitz, Melvin Belli, William Kunstler, James St. Clair, and Gerry Spence are the elite of the private criminal bar; they are nationally known criminal defense attorneys who often represent defendants for large fees in celebrated and widely publicized cases. Attorneys like these are relatively few in number and do not regularly defend the ordinary criminal defendant.

In addition to this limited group of well-known criminal lawyers, some lawyers and law firms serve as house counsel for such professional criminals as narcotics dealers, gamblers, prostitutes, and even big-time burglars. Because of

TABLE 11.1 ■ **Major U.S. Supreme Court Cases Granting Right to Counsel throughout the Pretrial, Trial, and Posttrial Stages of Criminal Justice Process**

Case	Stage and Ruling
Escobedo v. Illinois 378 U.S. 478 (1964)	The defendant has the right to counsel during the course of any police interrogation.
Miranda v. Arizona 384 U.S. 694 (1966)	Procedural safeguards, including the right to counsel, must be followed at custodial interrogation to secure the privilege against self-incrimination.
Brewer v. Williams 430 U.S. 387 (1977) (see also *Massiah v. United States* 377 U.S. 201 [1961])	Once adversary proceedings have begun against the defendant, he or she has a right to the assistance of counsel.
Hamilton v. Alabama 368 U.S. 52 (1961)	The "arraignment" is a critical stage in the criminal process, so that denial of the right to counsel is a violation of due process of law.
Coleman v. Alabama 399 U.S. 1 (1970)	The preliminary hearing is a critical stage in a criminal prosecution requiring the state to provide the indigent defendant with counsel.

TABLE 11.1 ■ Major U.S. Supreme Court Cases Granting Right to Counsel throughout the Pretrial, Trial, and Posttrial Stages of Criminal Justice Process—*continued*

Case	Stage and Ruling
Moore v. Illinois 434 U.S. 220 (1977)	An in-court identification at a preliminary hearing after a criminal complaint has been initiated requires counsel to protect the defendant's interests.
United States v. Wade 388 U.S. 218 (1967)	A defendant in a pretrial postindictment lineup for identification purposes has the right to assistance of counsel.
Moore v. Michigan 355 U.S. 155 (1957)	The defendant has the right to counsel when submitting a guilty plea to the court.
Powell v. Alabama 287 U.S. 45 (1932)	Defendants have the right to counsel at their trial in a state capital case.
Gideon v. Wainwright 372 U.S. 335 (1963)	An indigent defendant charged in a state court with a noncapital felony has the right to the assistance of counsel at trial under the due process clause of the Fourteenth Amendment.
Argersinger v. Hamlin 407 U.S. 25 (1972)	A defendant has the right to counsel at trial whenever he or she may be imprisoned for any offense, even for one day, whether classified as a misdemeanor or felony.
Scott v. Illinois 440 U.S. 367 (1979)	A criminal defendant charged with a statutory offense for which imprisonment on conviction is authorized but not imposed does not have the right to appointed counsel.
In re Gault 387 U.S. 1 (1967)	Procedural due process, including the right to counsel, applies to juvenile delinquency adjudication that may lead to a child's commitment to a state institution.
Faretta v. California 422 U.S. 806 (1975)	A defendant in a state criminal trial has a constitutional right to proceed without counsel when he or she voluntarily and intelligently elects to do so.
Townsend v. Burke 334 U.S. 736 (1948)	A convicted offender has a right to counsel at the time of sentencing.
Douglas v. California 372 U.S. 353 (1963)	An indigent defendant granted a first appeal from a criminal conviction has the right to be represented by counsel on appeal.
Mempa v. Rhay 389 U.S. 128 (1967)	A convicted offender has the right to assistance of counsel at probation revocation hearings where the sentence has been deferred.
Gagnon v. Scarpelli 411 U.S. 778 (1973)	Probationers and parolees have a constitutionally limited right to counsel on a case-by-case basis at revocation hearings.

Criminal cases which receive widespread media coverage often receive top flight legal representation. Here attorney Brendan Sullivan represents his client Oliver North.

their expertise in criminal law, these lawyers are often involved in representing organized crime and syndicate members on a continuing basis. Well-known lawyers and proficient house counsel criminal lawyers, however, constitute a very small percentage of the private criminal bar.

A larger number of criminal defendants are represented by lawyers who often accept many cases for small fees and are frequent participants in the criminal court process. They may belong to small law firms or work alone, but a sizable portion of their practice involves representing those accused of crime. There are also private practitioners who occasionally take on criminal matters as part of their general practice. Criminal lawyers often work on the fringe of the legal business, and they do not receive the professional respect of their colleagues or the community as a whole. As one prominent authority put it:

> All but the most eminent criminal lawyers are bound to spend much of their working lives in overcrowded, physically unpleasant courts, dealing with people who have committed questionable acts, and attempting to put the best possible construction on those acts. It is not the sort of working environment that most people choose. Finally, the professional status of the criminal lawyer tends to be low. To some extent the criminal lawyer is identified unjustifiably in the public eye with the client he represents. Indeed some criminal lawyers are in fact house counsel for criminal groups engaged in gambling, prostitution, and narcotics. The reprehensible conduct of the few sometimes leads the public to see honest, competent practitioners as "mouthpieces" also. Furthermore, in nearly every large city a private defense bar of low legal and dubious ethical quality can be found. Few in number, these lawyers typically carry large caseloads and in many cities dominate the practice in routine cases. They frequent courthouse corridors, bondsmen's offices, and police stations for clients, and rely not on legal knowledge but on their capacity to manipulate the system. Their low repute often accurately reflects the quality of the services they render. This public image of the criminal lawyer is a serious obstacle to the attraction of able young lawyers, and reputable and seasoned practitioners as well, to the criminal law.[40]

Another problem associated with the private practice of criminal law is the fact that the fee system can create a conflict of interest. Since private attorneys are usually paid in advance and do not expect additional funds if their client is convicted, and since many are aware of the guilt of their client before the trial begins, their profit is maximized if they get the case settled as quickly as possible. This usually means bargaining with the prosecutor rather than going to trial. Even if attorneys win the case at trial, they may lose personally since the time expended will not be compensated by more than the gratitude of their client. And, of course, many criminal defendants cannot afford even a modest legal fee and therefore cannot avail themselves of the services of a private attorney. If they could afford the fee why commit crime in the first place? For these reasons an elaborate, publicly funded legal system has developed.

■ Legal Services for the Indigent

To satisfy the constitutional requirements that indigent defendants be provided with the assistance of counsel at various stages of the criminal process, the federal government and the states have had to evaluate and expand existing criminal defense services. Prior to the mandate of *Gideon v. Wainwright*, public defender services were provided mainly by local private attorneys appointed and paid for by the court, called assigned counsels, or by limited public defender programs. In 1961, for example, public defender services existed in only 3 percent of the counties in the United States, serving only about a quarter of the country's population.[41] The traditional reasons for the general lack of defense services for indigents have included the following: (1) until fairly recently, the laws of most jurisdictions did not require the assistance of counsel for felony offenders and others; (2) only a few attorneys were interested in criminal law practice; (3) the organized legal bar was generally indifferent to the need for criminal defense assistance; and (4) the caseloads of lawyers working in public defender agencies were staggering.

However, beginning with the *Gideon* case in 1963 and continuing through the *Argersinger* decision in 1972, the criminal justice system has been forced to increase public defender services. Today, about 3,000 state and local agencies are providing indigent legal services in the United States.

More than a thousand legal aid and public defender offices are operating around the United States.

Types of Indigent Defender Systems

Providing legal services for the indigent offender is a huge undertaking. Over 4.4 million offenders are given free legal services. And, although most states have a formal set of rules to signify who is an indigent and 75 percent require indigents to repay the state for at least part of their legal services (known as **recoupment**), indigent legal services in 1986 still cost over one billion dollars annually. This is an increase of over 60 percent from the $600 million spent to provide legal representation to the poor in 1982.

Programs providing assistance of counsel to indigent defendants can be divided into three major categories: public defender systems, assigned counsel systems, and contract systems. In addition, other approaches to the delivery of legal services include the use of mixed systems, such as representation by both the public defender and the private bar, law school clinical programs, and prepaid legal services. The major forms of legal aid are discussed individually below. Of the three major approaches, assigned counsel systems dominate defender programs, with about 60 percent of U.S. courts using this method. Thirty-four percent use public defenders, and 6 percent employ contract attorneys (see Figure 11.2).[42]

PUBLIC DEFENDERS. Approximately 1,100 public defender offices are located in about 37 percent of the total number of counties in the United States.[43] However, public defender services are housed in 43 of the 50 largest American counties so they serve a majority (68 percent) of the population; all but two states (Maine and North Dakota) have some form of public defender services.

Most public defender offices can be thought of as law firms whose only clients are criminal offenders. However, there is a major division in the administration of public defender services. About 20 states, including Connecticut, Colorado, and Wyoming, have a statewide public defender's office headed by a chief public defender who administers the operation. In some states the chief defender establishes offices in all counties around the state, while in others the chief defender relies on part-time private attorneys to provide indigent legal services in rural counties. Statewide public defenders are organized as either part of the judicial branch, as part of the executive branch, as an independent state agency, or even as a private, nonprofit organization.

In the remaining 32 states, the public defender's office is organized on the county level of government, and each office is autonomous. For example, in

**Indigent Criminal Defense
Systems in the United States**

SOURCE: Carla Gaskins, *Criminal Defense for
the Poor—1986* (Washington, D.C.: Bureau of
Justice Statistics, September 1988).

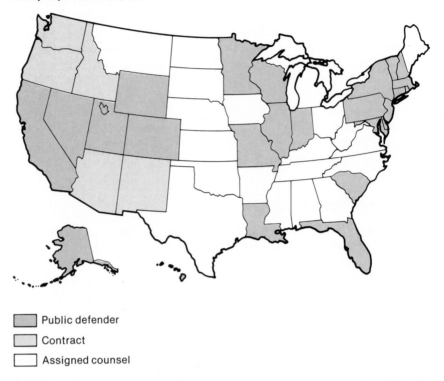

State defense systems, by type
In majority of counties, 1986

■ Public defender
▨ Contract
□ Assigned counsel

Florida elected public defenders operate separately in each of the 20 judicial
circuits in the state. In Pennsylvania a local public defender is legislatively
mandated in each of the state's 67 counties. In Illinois, each county with a
population over 30,000 has a legislatively mandated public defender's office.

Major changes have recently occurred in indigent services in such states as
Massachusetts, Minnesota, and New Hampshire where state-funded public
defender programs were made available to all counties in each state. And in
South Carolina, each county is represented by an independent public defender
program.[44] Table 11.2 presents the characteristics of public defender's offices in
each state by county.

ASSIGNED COUNSEL SYSTEM. In contrast to the public defender
system, the assigned counsel system involves the use of private attorneys
appointed by the court to represent indigent defendants. The private attorney
is selected from a list of attorneys established by the court and is reimbursed by
the state for any legal services rendered to the client. Today, about 60 percent
of all counties, containing 27 percent of the U.S. population, use an assigned
counsel system. Assigned counsels are usually used in rural areas, which do not
have sufficient criminal caseloads to justify a full-time public defender staff.
Only two states, Maine and North Dakota, use predominantly assigned
counsel in all jurisdictions.

There are two main types of assigned counsel systems. In the first, which
makes up about 75 percent of all assigned counsel systems, the presiding judge
appoints attorneys on a case-by-case basis; this is referred to as an **ad hoc
assigned counsel system**. In a **coordinated assigned counsel system**, an
administrator oversees the appointment of counsel and sets up guidelines for

TABLE 11.2 ■ Type of Indigent Criminal Defense Programs in Counties, by State

| State | Total counties in 1986 | Number of Counties Using Each Type of Indigent Defense Program | | | | | |
| | | Public defender | | Assigned counsel | | Contract | |
		1982	1986	1982	1986	1982	1986
Total	3,083	1,048	1,144	1,833	1,609	201	330
Alabama	67	6	9	61	58	0	0
Alaska	4	4	4	0	0	0	0
Arizona	15	2	5	5	4	7	6
Arkansas	75	18	9	57	66	0	0
California	58	49	49	0	0	9	9
Colorado	63	63	63	0	0	0	0
Connecticut	8	8	8	0	0	0	0
Delaware	3	3	3	0	0	0	0
District of Columbia	1	1	1	0	0	0	0
Florida	67	67	67	0	0	0	0
Georgia	159	19	19	127	127	13	13
Hawaii	4	4	4	0	0	0	0
Idaho	44	14	14	1	1	29	29
Illinois	102	74	74	28	28	0	0
Indiana	92	44	61	44	31	4	0
Iowa	99	15	15	84	84	0	0
Kansas	105	6	11	99	94	0	0
Kentucky	120	55	41	28	0	37	79
Louisiana	64	49	49	15	15	0	0
Maine	16	0	0	16	16	0	0
Maryland	23	23	23	0	0	0	0
Massachusetts	14	12	12	2	0	0	2
Michigan	83	5	8	41	46	37	29
Minnesota	87	42	66	45	21	0	0
Mississippi	82	20	20	62	62	0	0
Missouri	114	20	59	94	0	0	55
Montana	56	4	4	37	30	15	22
Nebraska	93	26	16	62	75	5	2
Nevada	17	15	16	0	0	2	1
New Hampshire	10	4	10	6	0	0	0
New Jersey	21	21	21	0	0	0	0
New Mexico	32	16	8	16	0	0	24
New York	62	55	40	7	22	0	0
North Carolina	100	14	10	86	90	0	0
North Dakota	53	0	0	50	49	3	4
Ohio	88	30	30	58	58	0	0
Oklahoma	77	2	2	66	72	9	3
Oregon	36	13	11	20	11	3	14
Pennsylvania	67	67	67	0	0	0	0
Rhode Island	5	5	5	0	0	0	0
South Carolina	46	39	46	7	0	0	0
South Dakota	66	2	4	64	62	0	0
Tennessee	95	4	8	83	87	8	0
Texas	254	2	6	252	248	0	0
Utah	29	17	17	0	0	12	12
Vermont	14	8	8	0	0	6	6
Virginia	104	5	13	99	91	0	0
Washington	39	6	4	31	15	2	20
West Virginia	55	0	9	55	46	0	0
Wisconsin	72	47	72	25	0	0	0
Wyoming	23	23	23	0	0	0	0

SOURCE: Carla Gaskins, *Criminal Defense for the Poor—1986* (Washington, D.C.: Bureau of Justice Statistics, September 1988).

the administration of indigent legal services. The fees awarded assigned counsels can vary widely, ranging from a low of $10 per hour for handling a misdemeanor out of court to a high of $65 per hour for in-court felony work. Some jurisdictions may establish a maximum allowance per case of $750 for a misdemeanor and $1,500 for a felony.

The assigned counsel system, unless organized properly, suffers from problems such as unequal assignments, inadequate legal fees, and the lack of supportive or supervisory services. Other disadvantages are the frequent use of inexperienced attorneys and the tendency to use the guilty plea too quickly. However, the assigned counsel system is simple to operate.[45] It also offers the private bar an important role in providing indigent legal services, since most public defender systems are not in a position to represent all needy criminal defendants. Thus, the appointed counsel system gives attorneys the opportunity to participate in criminal defense work.

CONTRACT SYSTEM. The **contract system** is a relative newcomer to providing legal services to the indigent; it is currently being used in 11 percent (330) of the counties around the United States. In this system a block grant is given to a lawyer or law firm to handle indigent defense cases. In some instances, the attorney is given a set amount of money and is required to handle all cases assigned. In other jurisdictions, contract lawyers agree to provide legal representation for a set number of cases at a fixed fee. A third system involves representation at an estimated cost per case until the dollar amount of the contract is reached. At that point the contract may be renegotiated, but the lawyers are not obligated to take new cases. The contract program payment method has recently come under attack by state courts, claiming that assigning indigent defense services to the lowest bidder violates the Fifth and Sixth Amendments of the U.S. Constitution.[46]

The contract system is used quite often in counties that also have public defenders. Such counties have a need for independent counsel when a conflict

TABLE 11.3 ■ States with the Highest and Lowest Average Cost per Indigent Defense Case, 1982 and 1986

1982		1986	
State	Cost per Case	State	Cost per Case
Hawaii	$567	New Jersey	$540
District of Columbia	434	Alaska	468
New Jersey	362	Wyoming	431
Alaska	338	Montana	413
Wyoming	332	New Hampshire	402
New Hampshire	319	South Dakota	367
Iowa	283	District of Columbia	334
Oregon	282	Michigan	316
Montana	266	Nevada	291
Rhode Island	259	California	284

NOTE: Sampling error may affect the precision of the order of states in this table.

1982		1986	
State	Cost per Case	State	Cost per Case
Oklahoma	$ 85	Arkansas	$ 63
Connecticut	105	Oklahoma	102
Louisiana	111	Mississippi	107
Virginia	111	Virginia	116
Maine	112	Kentucky	118
Arkansas	115	Illinois	130
Nebraska	117	Connecticut	138
Idaho	121	Georgia	138
Mississippi	123	Massachusetts	143
Illinois	130	Nebraska	152

SOURCE: Carla Gaskins, *Criminal Defense for the Poor—1986* (Washington, D.C.: Bureau of Justice Statistics, 1988), p. 6.

of interest arises or when there is a constant overflow of cases. Pauline Houlden and Steven Balkin recently found that contract attorneys were at least as effective as assigned counsel and were more cost-effective.[47] The per case cost in any jurisdiction for indigent defense services is determined largely by the type of program offered. In most public defender programs, funds are obtained through annual appropriations; assigned counsel costs relate to legal charges for appointed counsel, and contract programs negotiate a fee for the entire service. No research currently available indicates which method is the most effective way to represent the indigent on a cost per case basis. Table 11.3 identifies the jurisdictions with the highest and lowest average cost per case.

MIXED SYSTEMS. A mixed system uses both public defenders and private attorneys in an attempt to draw on the strengths of both. In this approach, the public defender system operates simultaneously with the assigned counsel system or contract system to offer total coverage to the indigent defendant. This need occurs when there is a significant increase in caseload, and the existing public defender's office is not equipped to handle the overload. In addition, many counties (34 percent) supply independent counsel to all co-defendants in a single case to prevent a conflict of interest. In most others, separate counsel will be provided if a co-defendant requests it, or if the judge or public defender perceives a conflict of interest. Since all lawyers in a public defender's office are considered to be working for the same firm, outside counsel is required if co-defendants are in conflict with one another. It is estimated that 60 percent of all counties having public defenders also have a program to assign counsel in overflow and conflict-of-interest cases; the cost of this program amounts to 12 percent of the total budget for indigent defense.

Other methods of providing counsel to the indigent include the use of law school students and the development of prepaid legal service programs (similar to comprehensive medical insurance). Most jurisdictions have a student practice rule of procedure; third-year law school students in clinical programs provide supervised counsel to defendants in nonserious offenses. In *Argersinger v. Hamlin*, Justice William Brennan suggested that law students are an important resource in fulfilling constitutional defense requirements.[48]

In the future, prepaid legal service programs may offer criminal defense services to the indigent as well as legal aid in civil matters. Federal or state governments may even legislate to support the development of prepaid defense services for persons unable to afford their own attorneys. But for the present, since the Sixth Amendment to the U.S. Constitution provides the accused the right to be assisted by counsel, each state is required to adopt its own approach to indigent defense services. And among the states, traditional public defender programs, ad hoc assigned counsel systems, and relatively new contract services are the accepted methods today.

■ The Defense Lawyer as a Professional Advocate

An estimated 600,000 lawyers practice law in America. Many work for the government, but the largest number are in private practice. The legal profession has seen a significant increase in membership in the last 10 years. Since the right to counsel has been accomplished nationwide for the most part, and at virtually all stages of criminal proceedings, more lawyers than ever are involved in criminal prosecution or defense work. In light of this rapid growth, the role of the lawyer as an advocate for the state or for the defendant requires constant review. Fees, ethics, disciplinary procedures, relationships with clients, competency, and training are controversial issues. However, one fact remains clear: the present legal system cannot survive unless accused persons are represented by attorneys who act as their champion.[49] The professional criminal attorney must be an equalizer between the power and resources of the state and the vulnerable position of clients.

In the adversary system attorneys for the defense must use all their accumulated skills to obtain a fair and just trial for their clients. This is often complicated by the fact that their clients are despised persons whose actions may have offended the community's common morality. Such clients rely on their attorneys as a buffer between the community and themselves, and they must be assured that their interests will be protected to the fullest extent of the law.

Defense attorneys are also an intermediary between their clients and the justice system. They must be free to bring to bear the skill, experience, and judgment that their clients probably lack. Professional attorneys must insist on

Professional attorneys must bring skill, experience and judgment to bear in the defense of their clients.

absolute honesty from their clients and be able to conduct their defense free from interference. Sometimes interface with the justice system involves negotiating what is in their clients' best interest. For example, the defense counsel must convince the prosecutor that the most serious charges are the hardest to prove and that it would be in the state's interest to drop them. If a conviction cannot be avoided, competent attorneys will be able to convince the prosecution and court that their clients are deserving of a second chance or will respond better to rehabilitation efforts than to a prison sentence.

Professional attorneys must also act as a "learned friend" to their clients, someone they can turn to for advice. The defendant may have information beneficial to his or her case, but the information incriminates a friend. What should the defendant do? The defense lawyer may be the only person to whom the defendant can turn in total confidence to explain his or her position and seek expert advice.

Criminal lawyers constantly find themselves caught in the conflict between their role as an advocate for their clients and their role as an officer of the court. Should they be cooperative when the judge offers a settlement that seems beneficial to both prosecution and defense? How should they react to the prosecutor's offer to advocate placing the defendant in a treatment program in exchange for a guilty plea? Or should every offer of cooperation be viewed as interfering with the client's right to the strongest possible advocacy?

Professional advocates who have the requisite skill must be prepared to deal with such conflicts in the many cases they handle during their career. Yet the problems of criminal defense often seem overwhelming to its practitioners.

Chapter 11

The Prosecution and the Defense

Conflicts of Defense

The problems of the criminal bar are numerous. Private attorneys are accused of sacrificing their clients' interests for the pursuit of profit. Many have a bad reputation in the legal community because of their unsavory clientele and reputation as "shysters" who hang out in court hoping for referrals. Attorneys who specialize in criminal work base their reputation on their power and influence. A good reputation is based on the ability to get obviously guilty offenders off on legal technicalities, to arrange the best "deal" for clients who cannot hope to evade punishment, and to protect criminals whose illegal activities are shocking to middle-class citizens. Consequently, the private criminal attorney is not often held in high esteem by his or her colleagues.

Public defenders are in the unenviable position of being paid by the government, yet acting in the role of the government's adversary. They may be considered at the bottom of the legal profession's hierarchy because they represent clients without social prestige for limited wages.[50] Public defenders are often young attorneys who are seeking trial practice before they go on to high-paying jobs in established law firms. Today the top-rated firms pay partners around $500,000 per year, and some New York firms start associates at a salary of $65,000, far outstripping any income state-compensated attorneys can hope for. In addition, public defenders are forced to work under bureaucratic conditions, which can lead to routine processing of cases. Their large caseloads prevent them from establishing more than a perfunctory relationship with their clients. To keep their caseload under control, they may push for the quickest and easiest solution to a case—plea bargaining.

Assigned counsel and contract attorneys may also be young lawyers just starting out and hoping to build their practice by taking on indigent cases. Since their livelihood depends on getting referrals from the court, public defender, or other governmental body, they risk the problem of conflict of interest. If they pursue too rigorous a defense or handle cases in a way not approved by the presiding judge or other authorities, might they not risk being removed from the assigned counsel lists? And, though the fees of an assigned counsel are not as high as those paid the private bar, billings at $50 per hour can mount up significantly in a long felony trial. In a recent Nebraska murder case, the assigned counsels billed a total of $145,000.[51]

Very often large firms will contribute the services of their newest members for legal aid to indigents, referred to as *pro bono* work. Although such efforts may be made in good spirit, it means that inexperienced lawyers are handling legal cases in which a person's life may be at stake.

What has emerged is a system in which **plea bargaining** predominates because little time and insufficient recourses are available to give criminal defendants a full-scale defense. Moreover, because prosecutors are under pressure to win their cases, they are often more willing to work out "a deal" than pursue a case to trial. After all, half a loaf is better than none. Defense attorneys, too, often find it easier to encourage their clients to plead guilty and secure a reduced sentence or probation rather than seek an acquittal and risk a long prison term.

The Adversary System Reconsidered

These conflicts have helped erode the formal justice process. As you may recall, the formal justice system is based on the adversary system: prosecutors and defense attorneys meet in the arena of the courtroom to do battle over the merits of the case. Through the give and take of the trial process, the truth of the matter becomes known. Guilty defendants are punished and the innocent go free. Yet the American legal system seldom works that way. Because of the pressures faced by defense attorneys and prosecutors, more frequently today the prosecution and defense work together in a spirit of cooperation to get the case over with rather than to "fight it out," wasting each other's time and risking an outright loss. In the process of this working relationship, the personnel in the courtroom—judge, prosecutor, defense attorney—form working groups that leave the defendant on the "outside." Criminal defendants may find that everyone they encounter in the courthouse seems to be saying "plead guilty," "take the deal," "let's get it over with."

The informal justice system revolves around the common interest of its members to move the case along and settle matters. In today's criminal justice system defense attorneys share a common history, goals, values, and beliefs with their colleagues in the prosecution. They are alienated by class and social background from the clients they defend. Considering the social reality of who commits crime, who are its victims, and who defends, prosecutes, and tries the case, it should not be surprising that the adversary system has suffered.

■ The Competence of Defense Lawyers

The presence of competent and effective counsel has long been a basic principle of the adversary system. With the Sixth Amendment's guarantee of counsel for virtually all defendants, the performance of today's attorneys has come into question.

Inadequacy of counsel may occur in a variety of instances. The attorney may refuse to meet regularly with his or her client, fail to cross-examine key government witnesses, or fail to investigate the case properly. A defendant's plea of guilty may be based on poor advice, where the attorney may misjudge the admissibility of evidence. When co-defendants have separate counsel, conflicts of interest between the defense attorneys may arise. On an appellate level, the lawyer may decline to file a brief, instead relying on a brief submitted for one of the co-appellants. Such problems as these are being raised with increasing frequency.

The U.S. Supreme Court dealt with the issue of conflict of interest between defense lawyers in **Burger v. Kemp** (1987).[52] Two defendants charged with murder were represented by law partners. Each defendant was tried separately, but the attorneys conferred and assisted each other in the trial process. One defendant, who was found guilty and sentenced to death, claimed ineffective legal representation because he believed his attorney failed to present mitigating circumstances to show that he was less culpable than the co-defendant. But the Supreme Court said this view was unfounded because the defendant claiming the conflict of interest actually perpetrated the crime. The Court also said it is not "per se" a violation of constitutional guarantees of effective assistance of counsel when a single attorney represents two defendants, or when two partners supplement one another in the trial defense.

Even a legally competent attorney sometimes makes mistakes that can prejudice a case against his or her client. For example, in *Taylor v. Illinois* (1988) a lawyer sprung a "surprise witness" against the prosecution. The judge ruled the witness out of order (invoking the **surprise witness rule**), thereby depriving the defendant of valuable testimony and evidence.[53] The Supreme Court affirmed the conviction despite the defense attorney's error in judgment because the judge had correctly ruled that "surprising" the prosecutor was not legally defensible.

The key issue is the level of competence that should be required of defense counsel in criminal cases. This question concerns appointed counsel, as well as counsel chosen by the accused. Some appellate court decisions have overturned lower court convictions when it was judged that the performance of counsel had reduced the trial to a farce or a mockery. Other appellate courts have held that there was ineffective counsel where gross incompetence had the effect of eliminating the basis for a substantial defense.

In recent years the courts have adopted a **reasonable competence standard,** but there are differences on the formulation and application of this standard. For example, is it necessary for defense counsel to answer on appeal every nonfrivolous issue requested by his or her convicted client? What if counsel does not provide the court with all the information at the sentencing stage and the defendant feels counsel's performance is inadequate? Whether any of these instances is an appropriate situation for stating that counsel is incompetent requires court review. In other words, although there may be general agreement regarding the use of the "reasonable competence" standard, a defendant must demonstrate that counsel has substantially departed from the standard governing his or her performance. In addition, it may also be necessary to prove prejudice to the defendant.

Defining Attorney Competence

The concept of attorney competence was defined by the U.S. Supreme Court in the case of **Strickland v. Washington** in 1984.[54] Strickland had been arrested for committing a string of extremely serious crimes including murder, torture, and kidnapping. Against his lawyer's advice, Strickland pleaded guilty and threw himself on the mercy of the trial judge at a capital sentencing hearing. He also ignored his attorney's recommendation that he exercise his right to have an advisory jury at his sentencing hearing.

In preparing for the hearing, the lawyer spoke with Strickland's wife and mother, but did not otherwise seek character witnesses. Nor was a psychiatric examination requested since, in the attorney's opinion, defendant Strickland did not have psychological problems. The attorney also did not ask for a presentence investigation because he felt such a report would contain information damaging to his client.

Though the presiding judge had a reputation for leniency in cases where the defendant had confessed, Strickland was sentenced to death. He appealed on the grounds that his attorney had rendered ineffective counsel, citing his failure to seek psychiatric testimony and present character witnesses.

The case eventually went to the Supreme Court where Strickland's sentence was upheld. The justices found that a defendant's claim of attorney incompetence must have two components. First, the defendant must show that the counsel's performance was deficient and that such serious errors were made as to eliminate the presence of "counsel" guaranteed by the Sixth Amendment. Second, the defendant must also show that the deficient performance prejudiced the case to an extent that the defendant was deprived of a fair trial (that is, a trial with reliable results). In the case at hand, the Court found insufficient evidence that the attorney had acted beyond the boundaries of professional competence. Though the strategy he had adopted might not have been the best one possible, it certainly was not unreasonable considering minimum standards of professional competence.

The court recognized the defense attorney's traditional role as an advocate of the defendant's cause, which includes such duties as consulting on important decisions, keeping the client informed of important developments, bringing knowledge and skill to the trial proceeding, and making the trial a reliable adversary proceeding. Yet the Court found that a mechanical set of rules that define competency would be unworkable.

Developing a workable standard, however, is solving only half the problems. According to Judge Irving Kaufman of the U.S. Court of Appeals, an influential spokesman on judicial issues, competency of counsel at all stages of the criminal process, particularly at trial, is an elusive concept, and remedies must be adopted to reduce the claims of inadequate representation.[55]

Postconviction review by the appellate courts is one approach, but this has limitations because the appellate judge cannot get a full picture of trial counsel's performance from the record. Counsel's knowledge of the law, ability to handle legal issues, and capacity to conduct effective examination of witnesses cannot be personally observed by the appellate judge. What is needed, according to Judge Kaufman, is more penetrating supervision by the trial judge, a reduction in caseloads, and a review of traditional methods of legal education in criminal law, so that advocacy skills and trial techniques can be developed.[56] Through such efforts, competent counsel in prosecutorial and defense work will help the adversary system arrive at the truth and produce fairer trials.[57]

Competency and Cooperation

In the final analysis, the competency of the prosecutor and defense attorney depends on their willingness to work together in the interest of the client, the criminal justice system, and the rest of society. Recent years have seen serious adversarial conflicts between both groups. The prosecutor, for instance, should exercise discretion in seeking to subpoena other lawyers to testify about any relationship with their clients. Although not all communication between a lawyer and client is privileged, confidential information entrusted to a lawyer is ordinarily not available for prosecutorial investigation. Often, however, overzealous prosecutors try to use their subpoena power against lawyers whose clients are involved in drug or organized crime cases in order to obtain as much evidence as possible. As a result, prosecutors interested in confidential information about defendants have subpoenaed lawyers to testify against them. Court approval should be needed before forcing a lawyer to give information about a client. Otherwise, the defendant is really not receiving his or her right to effective legal counsel under the Sixth Amendment.

By the same token, some criminal lawyers ignore situations where a client informs them of his or her intention to commit perjury. The real purpose of the defense attorney's investigation is to learn the truth from the client. It is also the defense attorney's professional responsibility to persuade the defendant not to commit perjury, which is a crime.

■ Other Courtroom Personnel

In addition to the judge, prosecutor, and defense attorney, the rest of the courtroom team, clerk, bailiff, and court reporter also have an impact on the quality of justice in our federal and state judicial systems. Some experts may discount the importance of this group, but they exercise considerable control over various aspects of the courtroom environment.

Court Clerks and Bailiffs

The clerk of court position is a traditional one in both state and federal court systems.[58] The clerks have the responsibility for calendar development, maintaining files, and overall management of the court docket. They also often collect court fees and costs and oversee jury selection procedures. Some even have statutory responsibility to process minor criminal offenses, such as traffic violations and petty misdemeanors. Over the last two decades, the clerk's role has been greatly influenced by the establishment of unified court systems and more efficient administration programs, which were described in Chapter 10.

Court clerks have varying degrees of skill and education. In many court systems, they are political appointees with routine and limited administrative responsibilities, and no formal training. Others occupy key positions, particularly in large urban court systems, and even have legal backgrounds. Appellate court clerks, for instance, as distinguished from trial court personnel, are specifically requested by statute to have a law degree in 12 states.[59]

Appointed clerks often serve at the pleasure of the presiding justice. Some may have civil service stature. Elected clerks generally serve a fixed term. Salaries for these positions are ordinarily derived from local funds in the majority of jurisdictions.

Bailiffs as we know them today, are uniformed personnel who sit in courtrooms, both criminal and civil, to maintain order. Oftentimes they run errands for court personnel and judges and maintain the flow of courtroom activity and security. Their presence in criminal court is particularly useful. Criminal defendants charged with violent crimes, drug trafficking, and terrorism present serious security risks in the courtroom. So do those with unstable personalities, where violent behavior might be triggered by some unusual statement or event. Today's bailiff has become a security officer, although this role is less important in civil proceedings, where matters are not as acute.

Court Reporters

The judicial system requires accurate case recording. Judges are concerned about higher courts reversing their decisions. Lawyers, whether prosecutors or defense attorneys who appeal, know how critical it is to have an accurate, documented record of trial court proceedings.

Traditionally, shorthand reporters, often referred to as "court stenographers," have handled the transcription workload in the judicial system.[60] In recent years, electronic recording systems have been installed in many courts to retain the needed information for appellate proceedings. Early efforts to record court proceedings electronically often met with resistance or failure because of poor equipment or high cost. Judges and lawyers objected to undecipherable courtroom noises. Today, however, court reporters are used sparingly for the most part. Electronic transcription equipment and computer programs have become a way of life in most urban courts. Some state courts, Kentucky, Michigan, and North Carolina to name a few, are even experimenting with highly sophisticated audiovisual recording systems that replace the court reporter. One system, called the Automatic Court Documentation Program, allows witnesses to put their testimony on videotape.[61] The judge watches the tape at a later date, rules on objections, edits inadmissible evidence, and renders an opinion. For defendants and lawyers, the system allows instant access to the transcript at lower cost. But no system is perfect.

How official the videotape is remains a legal problem. In addition, most appellate courts dealing with criminal matters still prefer to deal with written documents. Serious judicial experimentation has begun in this field, however, and will undoubtedly continue in the next decade. In addition, since little attention has been given to researching the role of clerks, bailiffs, and court reporters, more professional information needs to be developed about this group.

■ SUMMARY

The judge, prosecutor, and defense attorney are the major officers of justice in the judicial system. The judge approves plea bargains, tries cases, and determines the sentence given the offender. The prosecutor, who is the people's attorney, has discretion to decide the criminal charge and disposition. The prosecutor's daily decisions have a significant impact on police and court operations.

The role of the defense attorney in the criminal justice system has grown dramatically during the past 30 years. Today, providing defense services to the indigent criminal defendant is an everyday practice. Under landmark decisions of the U.S. Supreme Court, particularly *Gideon v. Wainwright* and *Argersinger v. Hamlin*, all defendants who may be imprisoned for any offense must be afforded counsel at trial. Methods of providing

counsel include systems for assigned counsel, where an attorney is selected by the court to represent the accused, and defender programs, where public employees provide legal services. Lawyers doing criminal defense work have discovered an increasing need for their services, not only at trial, but also at the pre- and postjudicial stages of the criminal justice system. Consequently, the issue of their competency has become an important one for judicial authorities. The prosecutor and the defense attorney are the principal adversaries in the courtroom workplace because they represent the public and the accused. How they fulfill their respective roles, responsibilities, and decision making all too often reflect society's fundamental ability to control crime and the public's perception of the justice system.

■ QUESTIONS

1. Should attorneys disclose information given them by their clients concerning participation in an earlier unsolved criminal act?
2. Should defense attorneys cooperate with a prosecutor if it means that their clients will go to jail?
3. Should a prosecutor have absolute discretion over which cases to proceed on and which to drop?
4. Should a client be made aware of an attorney's track record in court?

5. Does the assigned counsel system present an inherent conflict of interest since attorneys are hired and paid by the institution they are to oppose?
6. Do you believe prosecutors have a great deal of discretion? Why?
7. Discuss the role of court support personnel in the justice system.

■ NOTES

1. American Bar Association, Special Committee on Evaluation of Ethical Standards, *Code of Professional Responsibility* (Chicago: American Bar Association, 1970), p. 87; see also John Jay Douglas, *Ethical Issues in Prosecution* (University of Houston Law Center: National College of District Attorneys, 1988).
2. 295 U.S. 78, at 88, 55 S.Ct. 629, 79 L.Ed. 1314 (1935).
3. See Bennett Gershman, "Why Prosecutors Misbehave," *Criminal Law Bulletin* 22 (1986): 131–43.
4. American Bar Association, *Model Rules of Professional Conduct* (Chicago: American Bar Association, 1981), Rule 3.8; see also Stanley

Fisher, "In Search of the Virtuous Prosecutor: A Conceptual Framework," *American Journal of Criminal Law* 15 (1988): 197.
5. Stanley Fisher, "Zealousness and Overzealousness: Making Sense of the Prosecutor's Duty to Seek Justice," *The Prosecutor* 22 (1989): 9; see also Bruce Green, "The Ethical Prosecutor and the Adversary System," *Criminal Law Bulletin* 24 (1988): 126–45.
6. See Alan Alschuler, "Prosecutor's Role in Plea Bargaining," *University of Chicago Law Review* 50 (1968).
7. American Bar Association, *Standards Relating to the Prosecution Function and Defense Function* (New York: Institute of Judicial Admin-

istration, 1971), pp. 18–19. Reprinted with the permission of the American Bar Association, which authored these standards and holds the copyright.

8. "Litigator's Legacy," *Wall Street Journal*, 11 January 1989, p. 1.

9. See, generally, Gerard O'Neill and Dick Lehr, *The Underboss—The Rise and Fall of a Mafia Family* (New York: St. Martin's Press, 1989).

10. National Advisory Commission on Criminal Justice Standards and Goals, *Courts* (Washington, D.C.: U.S. Government Printing Office, 1973), p. 439.

11. Kenneth C. Davis, *Discretionary Justice* (Baton Rouge: Louisiana State University Press, 1969), p. 180; see also James B. Stewart, *The Prosecutor* (New York: Simon and Schuster, 1987).

12. Barbara Boland, *The Prosecution of Felony Arrests* (Washington, D.C.: U.S. Government Printing Office, 1983).

13. Newman Baker, "The Prosecutor—Initiation of Prosecution," *Journal of Criminal Law, Criminology, and Police Science* 23 (1933), pp. 770–71; see also Joan Jacoby, *The American Prosecutor: A Search for Identity* (Lexington, Mass.: Lexington Books, 1980).

14. See, generally, W. Jay Merrill, Marie N. Malks, and Mark Sendrow, *Case Screening and Selected Case Processing in Prosecutor's Offices* (Washington, D.C.: U.S. Department of Justice, Law Enforcement Assistance Administration, National Institute of Law Enforcement and Criminal Justice, March 1973).

15. Frank W. Miller, *Prosecution: The Decision to Charge a Suspect with a Crime* (Boston: Little, Brown & Co., 1970).

16. Boland, *Prosecution of Felony Arrests*.

17. President's Commission on Law Enforcement and Administration of Justice, *The Courts* (Washington, D.C.: U.S. Government Printing Office, 1967), pp. 8–9.

18. American Bar Association, *Standards Relating to the Prosecution Function and Defense Function*, Standard 3.8, 33.

19. See, generally, "Pretrial Diversion from the Criminal Process," *Yale Law Journal* 83 (1974): 827.

20. Charles D. Breitel, "Controls in Criminal Law Enforcement," *University of Chicago Law Review* 27 (1960): 427.

21. Roscoe Pound, "Discretion, Dispensation, and Mitigation: The Problem of the Individual Special Case," *New York University Law Review* 35 (1960): 925; "Unleashing the Prosecutor's Discretion: *United States v. Goodwin*," *American Criminal Law Review* 20 (1983): 507.

22. American Bar Association, *Standards Relating to the Prosecution Function and Defense Function*, Standard 3.8. Reprinted with the permission of the American Bar Association, which authored these standards and holds the copyright.

23. See, generally, "A Symposium of Prosecutorial Discretion," *American Criminal Law Review* 13 (1976): 379; "Prosecutorial Vindictiveness: Divergent Lower Court Applications of the Due Process Prohibition," *George Washington Law Review* 50 (1982): 331; F. Smaltz, "Due Process Limitations on Prosecutorial Discretion: Pearce to Blackledge to Bordenkircher," *Washington and Lee Law Review* 36 (1979): 347.

24. *Town of Newton v. Rumery*, 107 S.Ct. 1187, 94 L.Ed.2d 405 (1987).

25. 395 U.S. 711, 89 S.Ct. 2072, 23 L.Ed.2d 768 (1969).

26. 417 U.S. 21, 94 S.Ct. 2098, 40 L.Ed.2d 628 (1974).

27. 434 U.S. 357, 98 S.Ct. 663, 54 L.Ed.2d 604 (1978).

28. 457 U.S. 368, 102 S.Ct. 2485, 73 L.Ed.2d 74 (1982).

29. President's Commission on Law Enforcement and Administration of Justice, *The Challenge of Crime in a Free Society* (Washington, D.C.: U.S. Government Printing Office, 1968), p. 150.

30. See American Bar Association, Special Committee, *Code of Professional Responsibility*, p. 81.

31. Monroe H. Freedman, "Professional Responsibility of the Criminal Defense Lawyer: The Three Hardest Questions," *Michigan Law Review* 64 (1966): 1468.

32. The Sixth Amendment provides: "In all criminal prosecutions, the accused shall enjoy the right . . . to have the assistance of counsel for his defense."

33. 372 U.S. 335, 83 S.Ct. 792, 9 L.Ed.2d 799 (1963).

34. 407 U.S. 25, 92 S.Ct. 2006, 32 L.Ed.2d 530 (1972).

35. 384 U.S. 436, 86 S.Ct. 1602, 16 L.Ed.2d 694 (1966).

36. *Mempa v. Rhay*, 389 U.S. 128, 88 S.Ct. 254, 19 L.Ed.2d 336 (1967).

37. *Douglas v. California*, 372 U.S. 353, 83 S.Ct. 814, 9 L.Ed.2d 811 (1963).

38. *In re Gault*, 387 U.S. 1, 875 S.Ct. 1428, 18 L.Ed.2d 527 (1967).

39. *Specht v. Patterson*, 386 U.S. 605, 87 S.Ct. 1209, 18 L.Ed.2d 326 (1967).

40. President's Commission on Law Enforcement and Administration of Justice, *The Challenge of Crime in a Free Society*, p. 152.

41. See F. Brownell, *Legal Aid in the United States* (Chicago: National Legal Aid and Defender Association, 1961); for an interesting study of Cook County, Illinois Office of Public Defenders, see Lisa McIntyre, *Public Defenders—Practice of Law in Shadows of Dispute* (Chicago: University of Chicago Press, 1987).

42. Carla Gaskins, *Criminal Defense for the Poor—1986* (Washington, D.C.: Bureau of Justice Statistics, September 1988), p. 2.

43. Ibid., pp. 1–8.

44. Ibid., p. 7.

45. Note "Providing Counsel for the Indigent Accused: The Criminal Justice Act," *American Criminal Law Review* 12 (1975): 794.

46. See *Smith v. Smith*, 140 Arizona 355 (1984).

47. Pauline Houlden and Steven Balkin, "Quality and Cost Comparisons of Private Bar Indigent Defense Systems: Contract vs. Ordered Assigned Counsel," *Journal of Criminal Law and Criminology* 76 (1985): 176–200.

48. 407 U.S. 25, 92 S.Ct. 2006, 32 L.Ed.2d 530 (1972).

49. Adapted from the American Bar Association, *Standards Relating to the Prosecution Function and Defense Function*.

50. J. P. Heinz and E. O. Laumann, *Chicago Lawyers: The Social Structure of the Bar* (New York: Russell Sage Foundation, 1983).

51. "Judge, 8 Attorneys in Rulo Case Dispute Review of Fee Payment," *Omaha World Herald*, May 19, 1986.

52. *Burger v. Kemp*, 473 U.S. 629, 107 S.Ct. 3114, 97 L.Ed.2d 638 (1987).

53. *Taylor v. Illinois*, 108 S.Ct. 646, 98 L.Ed.2d 798 (1988).

54. *Strickland v. Washington*, 104 S.Ct. 2052 (1984). 466 U.S. 668, 80 L.Ed.2d 674.

55. Irving Kaufman, "Attorney Incompetence: A Plea for Reform," *American Bar Association Journal* 69 (1983), 308.

56. Ibid., at 311.

57. See *Culver v. Sullivan*, 446 U.S. 335, 100 S.Ct. 1708, 64 L.Ed.2d 333 (1980), where a state prisoner sought habeas corpus relief by showing that counsel represented a potential conflicting interest, but he did not prevail.

58. Conference of State Court Administrators, State Court Organization—1987 (Williamsburg, Virginia: National Center for State Courts, 1988), 12. See Howard James, *Crisis in the Courts* (New York: David McKay Company, 1967), 106–108.

59. Ibid., at 7.

60. News note, "Court Reporters on Way Out," *American Bar Association Journal*, February 1989, 28.

61. Ibid, at 29.

12

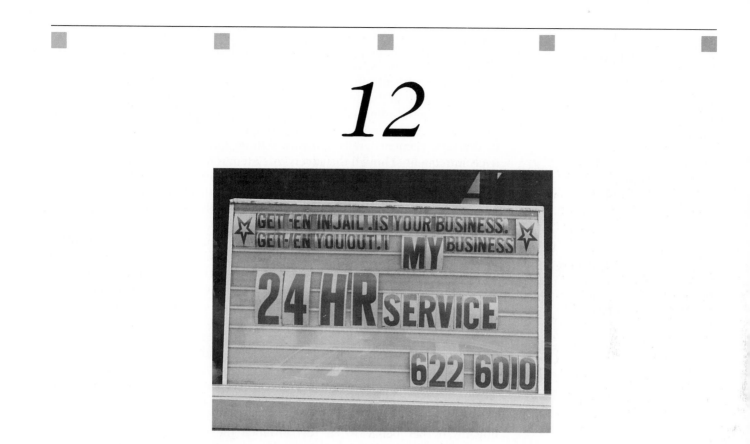

Pretrial Procedures

Between arrest and trial occurs a series of events that are critical links in the chain of justice. These include arraignments, grand jury investigations, bail hearings, plea bargaining negotiations, and predisposition treatment efforts. These **pretrial procedures** are critically important components of the justice process because the *great majority* of all criminal cases are resolved informally at this stage and never come before the courts. Although television and the media like to focus on the elaborate jury trial with its dramatic elements and impressive setting, formal criminal trials are relatively infrequent. Though the adversary system is not a myth, the social reality of justice in the United States is that it is more often "handled" than fought over. Consequently, understanding the events that take place during the pretrial period is essential if the student is to grasp the reality of criminal justice policy.

Cases are settled during the pretrial stage in a number of ways. Prosecutors can use their discretion to drop cases before formal charges are filed because of insufficient evidence, office policy, witness conflicts, or similar problems. Even if charges are filed, the prosecutor can decide to *nolle prosequi* because of a change in the circumstances of the case.

In addition, the prosecution and defense almost always meet to try to arrange a nonjudicial settlement for the case. Plea bargaining, in which the defendant exchanges a guilty plea for some consideration such as a reduced sentence, is commonly used to terminate the formal processing of the case. The prosecution and/or defense may believe that a trial is not in the best interests of the victim, defendant, or society because the defendant is physically or emotionally incapable of understanding the charges or controlling his or her behavior. In this instance the defendant may undergo a competency hearing before a judge and be placed in a secure treatment facility until ready to stand trial. Or the prosecutor may waive further action so that the defendant can be placed in a special treatment program such as a detox unit at a local hospital instead of utilizing the formal justice system to handle the case.

Students must be aware of the pretrial stage of justice not only because so many cases are dealt with at this time, but also because the procedures used are often insulated from external scrutiny. That is, deals are made and decisions are reached in secret, often with little regard for the public's will or the defendant's rights.

■ Procedures Following Arrest

After arrest, the accused is ordinarily taken to the police station, where the police list the possible criminal charges against him or her and obtain other information for **booking** purposes. This may include a description of the offender and the circumstances of the offense. The offender may then be fingerprinted, photographed, and required to participate in a lineup. During this stage the police will compile additional information on the suspect that can have little to do with the charge for which he or she was arrested. For example, a person picked up in a break-in may admit to committing other burglaries, or witnesses brought in to view suspects may implicate them in additional crimes. All this information is then turned over to the prosecutor who has jurisdiction in the case for possible legal action.

Misdemeanor Procedures

Individuals arrested on a misdemeanor charge are ordinarily released from the police station on their own recognizance to answer the criminal charge before the court at a later date. They are usually detained by the police until it is decided whether a criminal complaint will be filed. The **complaint** is the formal written document identifying the criminal charge, the date and place where the crime occurred, and the circumstances of the arrest. The complaint is sworn to and signed under oath by the complainant, usually a police officer. The complaint will request that the defendant be present at an **initial hearing** held soon after the arrest was made; in some jurisdictions this may be referred to by other names such as "arraignment." The defendant may plead guilty at the initial hearing, and the case may be disposed of immediately. Defendants who plead not guilty to a minor offense are informed of the formal charge, provided with counsel if they are unable to afford a private attorney, and are asked to plead guilty or not guilty as charged. A date some time in the near future is set for trial, and the defendants are generally released on bail or on their own recognizance to await trial.

Felony Procedures

Where a felony or more serious crime is involved, the U.S. Constitution requires that an intermediate step take place before a person can be tried. This involves proving to an objective body that there is probable cause to believe that a crime has taken place and that the accused should be tried on the matter. The formal charging process is ordinarily an **indictment** from a **grand jury** or an *information* issued by a lower court. An indictment is a written accusation charging a person with a crime that is drawn up by a prosecutor and submitted to a grand jury. The grand jury, after considering the evidence presented by the prosecutor, votes to endorse or deny the indictment. An information is a charging document drawn up by a prosecutor in jurisdictions that do not employ the grand jury system. The information is brought before a lower court judge in a **preliminary hearing** (sometimes called a **probable cause hearing**). The purpose of this hearing is to require the prosecutor to present the case so that the judge can determine whether the defendant should be held to answer for the charge in a felony court.

After an indictment or information in a felony offense is filed, the accused is brought before the trial court for arraignment, during which the judge informs the defendant of the charge, ensures that the accused is properly represented by counsel, and determines whether he or she should be released on bail or some other form of release pending a hearing or trial.

The defendant who is arraigned on an indictment or information can ordinarily plead guilty, not guilty, or **nolo contendere,** which is equivalent to a guilty plea but cannot be used as evidence against the defendant in a civil case on the same matter. For example, a plea of *nolo* in a rape case could not be used as an admission of guilt if the offender was later sued for damages by his victim.

Where a guilty plea is entered, the defendant admits to all the elements of the crime, and the court begins a review of the person's background for sentencing purposes. A plea of not guilty sets the stage for a trial on the merits or for negotiations between the prosecutor and defense attorney known as plea bargaining.

A bail bond issued to William Greenwood of Leicester Fields, Middlesex, England, in the late seventeenth or early eighteenth century. This document is written in Latin and is from the records of the King's Bench.

Before discussing these issues, it is important to address the question of bail, or pretrial release, which may occur at the police station, at the initial court appearance in a misdemeanor, or at the arraignment in most felony cases.

■ Bail

Bail is money or some other security provided to the court to ensure the appearance of the defendant at every subsequent stage of the criminal justice process. Its purpose is to obtain the release from custody of a person charged with a crime. Once the amount of bail is set by the court, the defendant is required to deposit all or a percentage of the entire amount in cash or security (or to pay a professional bail bondsman to submit a bond). If the defendant is released on bail but fails to appear in court at the stipulated time, the bail deposit is forfeited. A defendant who fails to make bail is confined in jail until the court appearance. The various stages of the justice process in which bail may be posted are listed in Table 12.1.

Right to Bail

The Eighth Amendment to the U.S. Constitution does not guarantee a constitutional right to bail but rather prohibits "excessive bail." Since many state statutes place no precise limit on the amount of bail a judge may impose, many defendants who cannot make bail are often placed in detention while awaiting trial. It has become apparent over the years that the bail system is discriminatory because defendants who are financially well-off are able to make bail while indigent defendants languish in pretrial detention in the county jail. In addition, keeping a person in jail imposes serious financial burdens on local and state governments—and, in turn, taxpayers—who must pay for the cost of confinement. These factors have given rise to bail reform programs that depend on the defendant's personal promise to appear in court for trial (recognizance) rather than on the financial ability to meet bail. Despite these reforms, which have enabled many deserving but indigent offenders to go free, another trend has been to deny people bail on the grounds that they are a danger to themselves or others in the community.

The Eighth Amendment restriction on excessive bail may also be interpreted to mean that the sole purpose of bail is to ensure that the defendant return for trial; bail may not be used as a form of punishment, nor may it be used to coerce or threaten a defendant. In most cases, a defendant has the right to be released on reasonable bail. Many jurisdictions also require a bail review hearing by a higher court in cases in which the initial judge set what might be considered excessive bail.

The U.S. Supreme Court's interpretation of the Eighth Amendment's provisions on bail was set out in the case of *Stack v. Boyle* (1951).[1] Here the Supreme Court found bail to be a traditional right to freedom before trial that permits unhampered preparation of a defense and prevents the criminal defendant from being punished prior to conviction. The Court held that bail is excessive when it exceeds an amount reasonably calculated to ensure that the defendant will return for trial. The Court indicated that bail should be in the amount that is generally set for similar offenses. Higher bail can be imposed when evidence supporting the increase is presented at a hearing at which the defendant's constitutional rights can be protected. Although *Stack*

TABLE 12.1 ■ Bail Release Mechanisms

Field citation release Under this form of release, an arresting officer releases the arrestee on a written promise to appear in court, at or near the actual time and location of the arrest. This procedure is commonly used for misdemeanor charges and is similar to issuing a traffic ticket. The criteria used by the arresting officer are those established by the local police department in conformity with the provisions of state statutes. At a minimum, these criteria require that the arrestee be properly identified and have no outstanding warrants. A field citation release is the least formal nonfinancial technique available to assure court appearance of an arrestee.

Station house citation release Under this form of release, the determination of an arrestee's eligibility and suitability for release and the actual release of the arrestee are deferred until after he or she has been removed from the scene of an arrest and brought to the department's station house or headquarters. Station house release allows the police officer or pretrial services officer to verify the information provided by the arrestee prior to the issuance of a citation and permits the release of an arrestee without booking. Station house release may save the police officer some traveling time in that it eliminates transporting the arrestee to jail where final booking takes place.

Jail citation release Under this form of release, the determination of an arrestee's eligibility and suitability for citation release and the actual release of the arrestee is deferred until after he or she has been delivered by the arresting department to a jail or other pretrial detention facility for screening, booking, and/or admission. This form of release is used extensively in California. In some counties in California, the booking sergeant or watch commander in the jail is assisted in the selection of persons for citation release by pretrial program staff.

Direct release authority by pretrial program To streamline release processes and reduce length of stay, courts may authorize pretrial programs to release defendants without direct judicial involvement. Where court rule delegates such authority, the practice is generally limited to misdemeanor charges, but felony release authority has been granted in some jurisdictions.

Bail schedule Under this form of release, an arrestee can post bail at the station house or jail according to amounts specified in a bail schedule. The schedule is a list of all bailable charges and a corresponding dollar amount for each. Schedules may vary widely from jurisdiction to jurisdiction. An arrestee may effect release by posting the full amount of bail required or by engaging a bondsman who will post the bail amount for a fee (usually 10 percent of the total bail).

Judicial release Arrestees who have not been released either by the police or jailer and who have not posted bail appear at the hearing before a judge, magistrate, or bail commissioner within a set period of time. In jurisdictions with pretrial release programs, program staff often interview arrestees detained at the jail prior to the first hearing, verify the background information, and present recommendations to the court at arraignment. At the arraignment hearing, the judicial officer can authorize a variety of nonfinancial and financial release options. There are two types of nonfinancial release options: release on recognizance and conditional release.

SOURCE: Andy Hall, *Pretrial Release Program Options* (Washington, D.C.: National Institute of Justice, 1984), pp. 30–31.

did not mandate an absolute right to bail, it did set guidelines for state courts to follow: if a crime is bailable, the amount set should not be frivolous, unusual, or beyond a person's ability to pay under similar circumstances.

Receiving Bail

Whether a defendant can be expected to appear at the next stage of the criminal proceedings is a key issue in determining bail. Bail cannot be used to punish an accused, nor can it be denied or revoked at the indulgence of the court. Many experts believe that money bail is one of the most unacceptable aspects of the criminal justice system: it is discriminatory because it works against the poor; it is costly because the government must pay to detain those offenders who are unable to make bail and who would otherwise be in the community; it is unfair because a higher proportion of detainees receive longer sentences than people released on bail; and it is dehumanizing because innocent people who cannot make bail suffer in the nation's deteriorated jail system.

Another question is whether discrimination occurs in setting the amount of bail. Are minorities asked to pay larger dollar amounts of bail, increasing the probability they will be detained in jail and receive longer prison sentences upon conviction?

A survey of bail practices in federal courts conducted by William Rhodes sheds some light on this issue.[2] The study found that, contrary to the fears of some critics, there was little actual relationship between the amount of bail and a person's race, age, economic status, and/or other social variables. Instead, Rhodes found that the amount of bail requested by judges was more closely associated with the seriousness of the offense and the offender's prior record, two factors that by most legal standards should legitimately influence the bail decision. Rhodes also found significant differences in bail practices within and between legal jurisdictions. This indicates that the probability of making bail is often a function of which judge hears the case and the jurisdiction in which the case is brought to justice. Rhodes' data are important because they show that extralegal factors such as race and social class do not play as important a role in determining bail amounts as some critics have feared.

Success of Bail

How successful is bail? That depends on your perspective. Mary Toborg evaluated bail procedures in eight urban jurisdictions (including Baltimore, Washington, D.C., Miami, Tucson, Louisville, and San Jose, California) and found that about 85 percent of all defendants received bail prior to trial. Of these, about 15 percent did not return for trial because they absconded. An additional 15 percent were rearrested for another crime prior to their trial date. Thus about 30 percent of those released on bail could be considered failures for one reason or another.[3]

A more recent study found that about 10 percent of the defendants released by federal trial courts were unsuccessful on bail; the failures included rearrest, failure to appear, or violation of the conditions of bail.[4] Those rearrested tended to (1) be on bail longer (nine months or more); (2) have a serious prior record; (3) be drug abusers; (4) have a poor work record; and (5) be disproportionately young, male, and nonwhite.

The differences between the state and federal studies may be attributed to the type of offenders who pass through their jurisdictions. The federal courts probably see more white-collar offenders and fewer violent offenders. Thus, although the state statistics are less than encouraging, the 10 percent failure rate recorded by the federal government indicates that pretrial release has been quite successful in some jurisdictions.

Bail Bondsmen

One of the collateral occurrences that has developed with the bail system is the practice of **bail bonding.** For a fee bondsmen lend money to people who cannot make bail on their own. Powerful ties often exist between bondsmen and the court with the result that defendants are steered toward particular operations. Charges of kickbacks and cooperation accompany such arrangements. Consequently, five states—Nebraska, Wisconsin, Kentucky, Oregon, and Illinois—have abolished bondsmen at the time of this writing. They have replaced them with bail systems in which the state itself acts as a bonding agency. Defendants put up 10 percent of the total bail but are responsible for paying the entire amount if they abscond, referred to as the "10 percent cash match," or **deposit bail,** system. Nevertheless, an estimated 5,000 professional bail bondsmen are operating in the United States today.[5] The potential for abuse inherent in the system has led many critics to suggest that in many instances the traditional bail system is an unsatisfactory pretrial release procedure.[6]

Bail Reform

Efforts have been made to reform and even eliminate money bail and reduce the importance of bail bondsmen. Many states now allow defendants to be released on their own recognizance without any money bail. **Release on recognizance (ROR)** was pioneered by the Vera Institute of Justice in an experiment called the **Manhattan Bail Project,** which began in 1961 with the cooperation of the New York City criminal courts and local law students.[7] This project found that if the court had sufficient background information about the defendant, it could make a reasonably good judgment as to whether the accused would return to court. When release decisions were based on such information as the nature of the offense, family ties, and employment record, most defendants returned to court when placed in the community on their own recognizance. The results of the Vera Institute's initial operation show that from October 16, 1961, through April 8, 1964, out of a total of 13,000 defendants,

3,000 fell into the excluded offense category, 10,000 were interviewed, 4,000 were recommended, and 2,195 were given ROR. Only 15 of these failed to show up in court, a default rate of less than seven-tenths of 1 percent. The bail project's experience suggested that releasing a person on the basis of verified information more effectively guaranteed appearance in court than did money bail. Highly successful ROR projects were set up in major cities around the country including Philadelphia and San Francisco.

By 1980 more than 120 formal programs were in operation, and today they exist in almost every major jurisdiction.[8] Current programs are organized as part of the court structure itself, as part of the probation department, or under some other public agency such as the sheriff's department, district attorney, or county board of supervisors. In some jurisdictions pretrial programs are administered by private nonprofit organizations on a voluntary or contractual basis.

The success of ROR programs resulted in further bail reforms that culminated with the enactment of the federal **Bail Reform Act of 1966,** the first change in federal bail laws since 1789.[9] This legislation sought to ensure that release would be granted in all noncapital cases where there was sufficient reason to believe that the defendant would return to court. The law clearly established the presumption of ROR that must be overcome before money bail is required.

The more recent federal **Bail Reform Act of 1984** mandates that no defendants shall be kept in pretrial detention simply because they cannot afford money bail and establishes the presumption for ROR in all cases in which a person is bailable (though some provisions of this act are restrictive, as explained later in this chapter).[10] A number of innovative programs in use today are discussed in Table 12.2.

CRITIQUE OF BAIL REFORM. Bail reform is considered one of the most successful programs in the recent history of the criminal justice system. Yet it is not without critics, who suggest that emphasis should be put on controlling the behavior of serious criminals rather than on making sure that nondangerous offenders are released prior to their trials. In addition, research conducted by John Goldkamp has uncovered evidence that race and other social variables may play an important role in the decision to grant ROR.[11] This is particularly troubling since suspicion of social bias in granting bail was among the most important reasons for bail reform in the first place. Because of these considerations, recent efforts have concentrated on toughening the standards for bail rather than easing its application.

Bail Guidelines

One way to eliminate disparity in the delivery of bail is to set up guidelines for bail decision makers. This approach has been tried in Philadelphia and other cities under the guidance of researchers Michael Gottfredson and John Goldkamp.[12] Their approach is designed to provide judges with a tool that uniformly defines the criteria for bail decision making while at the same time is flexible enough to deal with individual differences. Gottfredson and Goldkamp created a two-dimensional grid that can be used to define an offenders' bail risk. One dimension lists 15 categories relating to the severity of the

TABLE 12.2 ■ Alternative Bail Systems

Release on recognizance Under this form of release, the defendant is released on a promise to appear, without any requirement of money bond. This form of release is unconditional; that is, without imposition of special conditions, supervision, or specially provided services. The defendant must simply appear in court for all scheduled hearings.

Conditional release Under this form of release, the defendant is released on a promise to fulfill some stated requirements that go beyond those associated with release on recognizance. Four types of conditions are placed on defendants, all of which share the common aims of increasing the defendant's likelihood of returning to court, and/or maintaining community safety: (1) status quo conditions, such as requiring that the defendant maintain residence or employment status; (2) restrictive conditions, such as requiring that the defendant remain in the jurisdiction, stay away from the complainant, or maintain a curfew; (3) contact conditions, such as requiring that the defendant report by telephone or in person to the release program or a third party at various intervals; and (4) problem-oriented conditions, such as requiring that the defendant participate in drug or alcohol treatment programs. While some defendants are released on conditions without supervision, the effectiveness of conditional release is enhanced when the conditions are supervised. When the defendant's release conditions are supervised, either by a release agency or a third-party individual or agency, the supervising entity agrees to monitor the defendant's activities regularly and notify the court of any violation of the conditions set.

In addition to these nonfinancial release options, there are six types of financial release conditions that the court may impose: unsecured bail, privately secured bail, property bail, deposit bail, surety bail, and cash bail.

Unsecured bail This type of bail permits the release of the defendant with no immediate requirement of payment. However, if the defendant fails to appear, he or she is liable for the full amount.

Privately secured bail With this type of bail, a private organization or individual posts the bail amount, which is returned when the defendant appears in court. In effect, the organization provides services akin to those of a professional bonding agent, but without cost to the defendant.

Property bail With this type of bail the defendant may post evidence of real property in lieu of money.

Deposit bail With this type of bail, the defendant deposits a percentage of the bail amount, typically 10 percent, with the court. When the defendant appears in court, the deposit is returned, sometimes minus an administrative fee. If the defendant fails to appear, he or she is liable for the full amount of the bail.

Surety bail With this type of bail the defendant pays a percentage of the bond, usually 10 percent, to a bonding agent who posts the full bail. The fee paid to the bonding agent is not returned to the defendant if he or she appears in court. The bonding agent is liable for the full amount of the bond should the defendant fail to appear. Bonding agents often require posting of collateral to cover the full bail amount.

Cash bail With this type of bail, the defendant pays the entire amount of bail set by the judge in order to secure release. The bail is returned to the defendant when he or she appears in court.

SOURCE: Andy Hall, *Pretrial Release Program Options* (Washington, D.C.: National Institute of Justice, 1984), pp. 32–33.

current offense, while the other dimension is a five-point scale associated with the offenders' personal characteristics such as demeanor, probability of conviction, and probability they will interfere with witnesses (see Figure 12.1). The resulting information can then be used to determine whether the defendant receives ROR or a particular amount of cash bail.

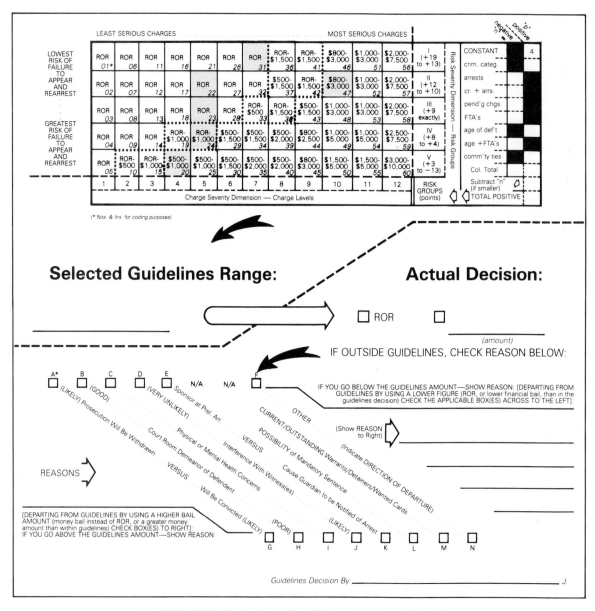

FIGURE 12.1 Bail Guidelines Judicial Worksheet

SOURCE: John Goldkamp and Michael Gottfredson, *Judicial Decision Guidelines for Bail: The Philadelphia Experiment* (Washington, D.C.: National Institute of Justice, 1983).

Evaluation of the use of guidelines in the Philadelphia court indicated that disparity among judges using the guidelines was significantly reduced. The guidelines did not change the number of people receiving ROR, cash bail, or detention. In addition, although equity was increased, failure-to-appear rates and pretrial arrest rates did not decline.

Preventive Detention

Those who promote bail reform point to the Eighth Amendment of the Constitution as evidence that bail should be made available to almost all people accused of crime. The presumption of bail is challenged by those who believe that releasing dangerous criminals before trial poses a threat to public safety. They point to the evidence showing that many people released on bail commit further crimes while at large and often fail to appear for trial. One response to the alleged failure of the bail system to protect citizens is the adoption of preventive detention statutes. These require that certain dangerous offenders be confined prior to trial for their own protection and that of the community. Preventive detention is an important manifestation of the crime control perspective on justice, since it favors the use of incapacitation to control the future behavior of suspected criminals.

The most striking use of preventive detention can be found in the federal Bail Reform Act of 1984, which contrasts sharply with previous law.[13] Table 12.3 describes the key provisions of the act. Although the act does contain provisions for ROR, it also allows judges to order preventive detention if they determined "that no condition or combination of conditions will reasonably assure the appearance of the person as required and the safety of any other person and the community . . . ." The decision to detain is evaluated at a hearing where the accused has the right to counsel, to testify, and to confront and cross-examine witnesses, and the government must present clear and convincing evidence of dangerousness. In addition, the act creates a presumption against release while the case is being appealed. This means that the judicial officer must find that

---

TABLE 12.3 ▪ **The Bail Reform Act of 1984**

Persons charged with Federal offenses may be released or detained prior to trial. The determination is typically made by a judge or magistrate at a hearing shortly after arrest. Specifically, the defendant may be:

▪ released on nonfinancial conditions (generally, personal recognizance, unsecured bond, or compliance with other conditions relating to travel, custody, or treatment);

▪ released on condition that the individual meet financial bail conditions (deposit, surety, or collateral bond), possibly in conjunction with other nonfinancial conditions;

▪ detained for failure to meet bail conditions; or

▪ detained without bail (pretrial detention).

Under the Bail Reform Act of 1966, the judicial officer was generally required to impose the minimal conditions of release necessary to assure only that the defendant appear in court. Further, while an individual might be held for failure to post bail, detention without bail was permitted only in cases involving capital crimes.

The Bail Reform Act of 1984 materially changed these provisions. In particular, the act provides that, in reaching decisions on bail and release, the court shall give consideration not only to ensuring the defendant's appearance in court but also to protecting the safety of individuals and the community.

The pretrial detention provisions of the act make special reference to particular categories of offenses and offenders. The act authorizes pretrial detention for defendants charged with crimes of violence, offenses with possible life (or death) penalties, major drug offenses, and felonies where the defendant has a specified serious criminal record.

Additionally, the act creates a rebuttable presumption that no conditions of release will assure the appearance of the defendant and the safety of the community under the following circumstances: the defendant committed a drug felony with a 10-year maximum sentence; the defendant used a firearm during the commission of a violent or drug trafficking offense; or the defendant was convicted of specified serious crimes within the preceding 5 years while on pretrial release.

The act does not require that prosecutors request pretrial detention for all defendants in these groups.

The act also provides for temporary detention (up to 10 working days) of illegal aliens or persons under pre- or posttrial release, probation, or parole at the time of the current offense. This provision was added for the purpose of allowing time for other law enforcement or immigration officials to take appropriate action.

SOURCE: Stephen Kennedy and Kenneth Carlson, *Pretrial Release and Detention*, p. 2.

TABLE 12.4 ■ **Legislative Provisions to Assure Community Safety**

Type of Provision	States That Have Enacted the Provision
Exclusion of certain crimes from automatic bail eligibility	Colorado, District of Columbia, Florida, Georgia, Michigan, Nebraska, Wisconsin
Definition of the purpose of bail to ensure appearance and safety	Alaska, Arizona, California, Delaware, District of Columbia, Florida, Hawaii, Minnesota, South Carolina, South Dakota, Vermont, Virginia, Wisconsin
Inclusion of crime control factors in the release decision	Alabama, California, Florida, Georgia, Minnesota, South Dakota, Wisconsin
Inclusion of release conditions related to crime control	Alaska, Arkansas, Delaware, District of Columbia, Florida, Hawaii, Illinois, Minnesota, New Mexico, North Carolina, South Carolina, Vermont, Virginia, Washington, Wisconsin
Limitations on the right to bail for those previously convicted	Colorado, District of Columbia, Florida, Georgia, Hawaii, Michigan, New Mexico, Texas, Wisconsin
Revocation of pretrial release when there is evidence that the accused committed a new crime	Arkansas, Colorado, Illinois, Indiana, Massachusetts, Nevada, New York, Rhode Island, Virginia, Wisconsin
Limitations on the right to bail for crimes alleged to have been committed while on release	Colorado, District of Columbia, Florida, Maryland, Michigan, Nevada, Tennessee, Texas, Utah
Provisions for pretrial detention to ensure safety	Arizona, California, District of Columbia, Florida, Georgia, Hawaii, Michigan, Wisconsin

SOURCE: *Report to the Nation on Crime and Justice* (Washington, D.C.: Bureau of Justice Statistics, 1988), p. 59.

there is clear and convincing evidence that the convicted offender is not dangerous and that the appeal is not frivolous. Finally, the act orders judges to detain bail violators for up to 10 days after their arrest.[14] The Criminal Justice in Review on page 395 discusses the effects of this statute.

In addition to the federal act, a number of state jurisdictions have incorporated elements of preventive detention into their bail systems. Table 12.4 lists the various restrictions now being placed on the granting of bail. Although most of them are not outright preventive detention, they serve to narrow the scope of bail eligibility.

THE LEGALITY OF PREVENTIVE DETENTION. Preventive detention has been a source of concern for civil libertarians who believe it violates the due process clause of the U.S. Constitution since it means that a person will be held in custody before guilt has been proven. In two recent cases the U.S. Supreme Court disagreed with this analysis. In *Schall v. Martin*, the Court upheld the application of preventive detention statutes to juvenile offenders on the grounds that such detention is useful to protect the welfare of the minor and society as a whole.[15] In *United States v. Salerno*, the Court upheld the Bail Reform Act's provision on preventive detention. Because of the importance of this case, it is analyzed in the Law in Review on page 397.[16]

The Effects
of Preventive
Detention

Despite its potential drawbacks in terms of costs, jail overcrowding, and loss of freedom, it appears that preventive detention statutes may become more common in the years ahead. How is this likely to affect the criminal defendant and the justice system?

In order to better understand the effects of preventive detention, Stephen Kennedy and Kenneth Carlson compared the pretrial experiences of people released in 1983 before the federal Bail Reform Act went into effect with cases from 1985 that were handled under the new law. Kennedy and Carlson found that although the Bail Reform Act's preventive detention provisions did have a significant effect on federal pretrial release and detention practices, the number of defendants released before trial remained relatively stable (76 percent in 1983 and 71 percent in 1985). About 54 percent of all defendants received ROR in both 1983 and 1985.

At the same time, the passage of the preventive detention statute did result in a number of changes. Although about 2 percent of defendants were denied bail outright in 1983, by 1985 the number held without bail rose to 19 percent. The number of defendants making bail remained stable because a higher percentage of defendants in 1985 who were eligible for bail were able to put up the required funds. It is evidence that before the Bail Reform Act took effect, judges detained the most dangerous offenders by requiring bail amounts they simply could not afford; after 1985 judges relied more heavily on the Bail Reform Act's pretrial detention provisions.

Who received preventive detention? Most (40 percent) were charged with drug violations, immigration offenses, and violent offenses. However, as Table A indicates, defendants classified as dangerous by the Federal Pretrial Services Agency and those who were accused of using firearms were the most likely to be denied bail. There was little relationship between social variables such as race and economic status and the probability of preventive detention.

These data indicate that judges will use preventive detention, but that its actual effect on the total number of people detained before trial may be marginal. Those offenders who are now subject to preventive detention would in the past have been assigned high bail amounts designed to keep them incarcerated before trial. Rather than being a new "get tough" approach, preventive detention continues the judiciary's long-term practice of detaining offenders they view as dangerous and releasing those who meet their standards of behavior. ■

TABLE A ■ **Detention Rate of Federal Defendants, by Public Safety Considerations, 1983 and 1985**

Public safety considerations	Percentage of all Defendants with Characteristics Who Were Held until Trial			
	Total		Pretrial detention only	
	1983	1985	1983	1985
Firearms	40.8%	50.1%	3.3%	39.2%
Used firearms				
Did not use firearms	22.7	27.6	1.6	17.6
Injury	30.2%	49.3%	3.0%	37.9%
Injury reported				
No injury reported	23.7	28.3	1.7	18.4
Danger classification*	40.2%	47.0%	2.6%	35.5%
Considered dangerous				
Not considered dangerous	21.8	25.0	1.6	15.2

*Classification made by Pretrial Services Agency interviewer and included in defendant's record.

SOURCE: Stephen Kennedy and Kenneth Carlson, *Pretrial Release and Detention: The Bail Reform Act of 1984* (Washington, D.C.: Bureau of Justice Statistics, 1988).

■ Detention

The criminal defendant who is not eligible for bail or ROR is subject to **pretrial detention** in the local county jail. The jail has long been a trouble spot for the criminal justice system. Conditions tend to be poor and rehabilitation nonexistent.

In terms of the number of persons affected per year, pretrial custody accounts for more incarceration in the United States than does imprisonment after sentencing.[17]

On any given day in the United States, more than 290,000 people are held in more than 3,500 local jails. Over the course of a year, many times that number pass through these local places of confinement. More than 50 percent of those held in local jails have been accused of crimes but not convicted. They are **pretrial detainees.** In the United States people are detained at a rate twice that of neighboring Canada and three times that of Great Britain. Hundreds of jails are overcrowded, and many are under court orders to reduce their populations and improve conditions.

Jails are often considered the weakest link in the criminal justice process—they are frequently dangerous, harmful, decrepit, and filled by the poor and friendless. Costs of holding a person in jail range up to more than $30,000 per year.[18] In addition, detainees are often confined with those convicted of crimes and those who have been transferred from other institutions because of overcrowding. Many felons are transferred to jails from state prisons to ease crowding. It is possible to have in close quarters a convicted rapist, a father jailed for nonpayment of child support, and a person awaiting trial for an act that he did not actually commit. Thus jails contain a mix of inmates that can lead to violence, brutality, and suicide.

Over the past 25 years, numerous organizations and publications have recommended reduced reliance on bail and advocated more extensive use of alternative release procedures. These include the President's Commission on Law Enforcement and Administration of Justice (1967), the National Advisory Commission on Criminal Justice Standards and Goals (1974), the Uniform Rules of Criminal Procedure of the National Conference of Commissioners on Uniform State Laws (1974), the National District Attorneys Association's Standards and Goals (1977), and the American Bar Association Standards on Pretrial Release (1979).[19] The National Coalition for Jail Reform recommends that all jurisdictions recognize a presumption favoring pretrial liberty and eliminate unnecessary pretrial detention.[20] Even the Bail Reform Act of 1984, which authorized preventive detention, provides for a presumption of ROR for defendants entitled to pretrial release. These national efforts have generally supported a public policy involving a presumption in favor of pretrial release, abolition of bail bondsmen, and consideration that the release decision be based on assuring the appearance of the defendant in court.

The Consequences of Detention

What happens to people who do not get bail or who cannot afford to put up bail money? Traditionally, one result has been longer prison sentences. In other words, people who do not qualify for bail also find themselves getting a long prison sentence if they are convicted at trial.[21] Data on cases processed through the federal court system indicate that detainees received significantly longer sentences than those who had been released on bail; for some crime categories the detainees' sentences were double that of bailees.[22]

United States v. Salerno (1987)

In this case, the U.S. Supreme Court held that the use of preventive detention is constitutionally permissible.

FACTS

On March 21, 1986, Anthony Salerno and co-defendant Vincent Cafaro were charged in a 29-count indictment alleging various racketeering (RICO) violations including gambling, wire fraud, extortion, and conspiracy to commit murder. At their arraignment the government moved to have them detained on the grounds that no condition of release could assure community safety. At a detention hearing, the prosecution presented evidence that Salerno was the "boss" of the Genovese crime family and that Cafaro was a "captain." Wiretap evidence indicated that the two men had participated in criminal conspiracies including murder. The court heard testimony from two witnesses who had personally participated in the murder conspiracies. In rebuttal, Salerno pro-

vided character statements, presented evidence that he had a heart condition, and challenged the veracity of the government's witnesses. Cafaro claimed the wiretaps had merely recorded "tough talk." The trial court allowed the detention on the grounds that the defendants wanted to use their pretrial freedom to continue their "family" business and "when business as usual involves threats, beatings, and murder, the present danger such people pose to the community is self-evident."

On appeal, the U.S. Court of Appeals for the Second Circuit agreed with the defendants' claim that the government could not detain suspects simply because they were thought to represent a danger to the community. The circuit court found that the criminal law system holds people accountable for their past deeds, not their anticipated future actions. The government then reappealed the case to the Supreme Court.

DECISION

The Supreme Court held that the preventive detention act had a legitimate and compelling regulatory purpose and did not violate the due process clause. Preventive detention was not designed to punish dangerous individuals but to find a solution for the social problem of people committing crimes while on bail; preventing danger to the

community is a legitimate societal goal.

The Court also stated that society's need for protection can outweigh an individual's liberty interest: under some circumstances individuals can be held without bail. The act provides that only the most serious criminals can be held and mandates careful procedures to ensure that the judgment of future dangerousness is made after careful deliberation. Finally, the Court found that the Eighth Amendment does not limit the setting (or denial) of bail simply to prohibit defendants' flight to avoid trial and held that considerations of dangerousness are a valid reason to deny pretrial release.

SIGNIFICANCE OF THE CASE

Salerno legitimizes the use of preventive detention as a crime control method. It permits the limitations on bail already in place in many state jurisdictions to continue. *Salerno* further illustrates the concern for community protection that has developed in the past decade. It is a good example of the recent efforts by the Court to give the justice system greater control over criminal defendants. At this time it is still unclear how often judges will rely on preventive detention statutes that require a hearing on the facts or whether they will simply continue to set extremely high bail for defendants they wish to remain in pretrial custody. ■

Although this evidence indicates that failure to receive bail is associated with longer prison sentences, the bail-conviction relationship is less clear. John Goldkamp's well-known study of bail in Philadelphia found no relationship between defendants' custody status before trial and the probability they would be convicted at trial. Goldkamp also found, however, that convicted offenders who did not receive bail were much more likely to receive prison terms than those who were not detained.[23]

How can these relationships be explained? It is possible that people who do not make bail are the more violent chronic offenders who, upon conviction, are punished more severely by sentencing judges. However, this explanation would not apply to individuals involved in white-collar crimes such as fraud

Crowded and dangerous detention facilities make bail reform essential.

and forgery, for it is unlikely that detainees for those crimes are more "dangerous" than those receiving bail; research indicates, however, that even for white-collar crimes detainees are punished far more severely than those making bail.[24] It is also likely that judges are reluctant to give probation or even a relatively short prison sentence to people who have already been detained in jail. The justice system would look foolish if a person who has already spent a considerable period behind bars did not receive a prison sentence that at least matched the jail time.

It is also likely that judges' decision making is influenced by the pretrial behavior of bailees. People who make bail have a chance to demonstrate they can adjust to society and make use of community social services; detainees are not afforded this opportunity to prove themselves. While bailees can demonstrate that they have refrained from any further criminal activity, detainees are not afforded the opportunity to show their trustworthiness. Consequently, detainees may receive a greater period of secure confinement while bailees are considered better risks.

In sum, the evidence suggests that, if convicted, people who do not receive bail are much more likely to be sent to prison and to do more time than people who avoid pretrial detention.

■ The Grand Jury

The grand jury was an early development of the English common law. According to the Magna Carta (1215), no freeman could be seized and imprisoned unless he had been judged by his peers. In order to determine fairly who was eligible to be tried, a group of freemen from the district where the crime was committed would be brought together to examine the facts of the case and determine whether the charges had merit. Thus the grand jury was created as a check against arbitrary prosecution by a judge who might be functioning as a puppet of the government.

The concept of the grand jury was brought to the United States by early settlers and later incorporated into the Fifth Amendment of the U.S. Constitution, which states that "no person shall be held to answer for a capital, or otherwise infamous crime, unless on presentment or indictment of a grand jury."

Today use of the grand jury is diminishing. In 1961 33 states required grand jury indictments (8 for all prosecutions, 22 for all felonies, and 3 for offenses leading to capital punishment or prison). Currently, 14 states require a grand jury indictment to begin all felony proceedings, and 2 others (Florida and Rhode Island) use it for capital cases.[25] About 25 states still allow a grand jury to be called at the option of the prosecutor. The federal government employs both the grand jury and the preliminary hearing system.

What is the role of the grand jury today? First, the grand jury has the power to act as an independent investigating body. In this role, it examines the possibility of criminal activity within its jurisdiction. These investigative efforts are directed toward general rather than individual criminal conduct. After an investigation is completed, a report called a **presentment** is issued. The presentment contains not only information concerning the findings of the grand jury but also usually a recommendation of indictment.

The grand jury's second and better known role is accusatory in nature. In this capacity, the grand jury acts as the community's conscience in determining whether the accusation of the state (the prosecution) justifies a trial. The grand jury relies on the testimony of witnesses called by the prosecution through its **subpoena** power. After examining the evidence and testimony of witnesses, the grand jury decides whether probable cause exists for prosecution. If it does, an indictment, or **true bill,** is affirmed. If the grand jury fails to find probable cause, a **no bill** (meaning that the indictment is ignored) is passed. In some states a prosecutor can present evidence to a different grand jury if a no bill is returned; in other states this action is prohibited by statute.

A grand jury is ordinarily comprised of from 16 to 23 individuals, depending on the requirements of the jurisdiction. This group theoretically represents a county. Selection of members varies from state to state, but for the most part they are chosen at random (e.g., from voting lists). To qualify to serve on a grand jury, an individual must be at least 18 years of age, a U.S. citizen, a resident of the jurisdiction for one year or more, and possess sufficient English-speaking skills for communication.

The grand jury usually meets at the request of the prosecution. Hearings are closed and secret. The prosecuting attorney presents the charges and calls witnesses who testify under oath to support the indictment. Usually, the accused individuals are not allowed to attend the hearing unless they are asked to testify by the prosecutor or grand jury.

The effectiveness and efficiency of the grand jury procedure have been questioned for a number of reasons. One standard complaint is that the grand jury is costly in terms of space, manpower, and money. The members must be selected, notified, sworn, housed, fed, and granted other considerations. More importantly, the grand jury has been criticized as being a "rubber stamp" for the prosecution. The presentation of evidence is under prosecutorial control, and the grand jury merely assents to the actions of the prosecutor.[26]

The grand jury, which accuses but does not decide guilt or innocence, can be traced to procedures instituted in twelfth-century England by King Henry II. Henry required local men to report to the county court the names of persons whom they suspected for having committed crimes in their neighborhood.

Studies of grand jury effectiveness have noted that it indicts almost all cases presented to it and has a negligible effect—other than delay—on the criminal process. The general view is that the grand jury should be avoided except in cases where a community voice is needed in a troublesome or notorious case.[27]

It is generally agreed, however, that the investigative role of the grand jury is a valuable and necessary function that should not only be maintained but expanded. Because the grand jury is often controlled solely by the state prosecutor, however, some legal experts believe that the system should provide the defendant with more due process protection. The American Bar Association's Grand Jury Policy and Model Act suggests the following changes in state grand jury statutes: (1) Witnesses should have their own attorneys when they give testimony; (2) prosecutors should be required to present evidence that might show that a suspect is innocent; (3) witnesses should be granted constitutional privileges against self-incrimination; and (4) grand jurors should be informed of all the elements of the crimes being presented against the suspect.[28] Such changes would permit the grand jury to perform its complex investigative tasks, while avoiding any serious abuses of its powers. A federally sponsored study of the implementation of these reforms in various sites across the country found that they are being complied with in varying degrees. The study concluded that each jurisdiction must determine the alternatives to the traditional grand jury that meet its particular needs.[29]

■ The Preliminary Hearing

The preliminary hearing is employed in about half the states as an alternative to the grand jury. Although the purpose of preliminary and grand jury hearings is the same—to establish whether probable cause is sufficient to merit a trial—the procedures differ significantly.

The preliminary hearing is conducted before a magistrate or inferior court judge, and, unlike the grand jury hearing, the proceedings are open to the public unless the defendant requests otherwise. Also present at the preliminary hearing are the prosecuting attorney, the defendant, and defendant's counsel if already retained. The prosecution presents its evidence and witnesses to the judge. The defendant or the defense counsel then has the right to cross-examine witnesses and may also challenge the prosecutor's evidence.

After hearing the evidence, the judge decides whether there is sufficient probable cause to believe that the defendant committed the alleged crime. If the answer is in the affirmative, the defendant is bound over for trial, and the prosecuting attorney's information (same as an indictment) is filed with the superior court, usually within 15 days. When the judge does not find sufficient probable cause, the charges are dismissed, and the defendant is released from custody.

A unique aspect of the preliminary hearing is the defendant's right to waive the proceeding. In most states, the prosecutor and the judge must agree to this **waiver.** A waiver has advantages and disadvantages for both the prosecutor and the defendant. In most situations, a prosecutor will agree to a waiver because it avoids revealing evidence to the defense before trial. However, if the state believes it is necessary to obtain a record of witness testimony because of the possibility that a witness or witnesses may be unavailable for the trial or unable to remember the facts clearly, the prosecutor might override the waiver. In this situation, the record of the preliminary hearing can be used at the trial.

At an arraignment, defendants are informed of the charges against them and asked to make an initial plea. This photo shows the arraignment of the suspects in a widely publicized case which alleged that children had been sexually abused by employees in a California day care center.

The defense will most likely waive the preliminary hearing for one of three reasons: (1) it has already decided to plead guilty; (2) it wants to speed up the criminal process; or (3) it hopes to avoid the negative publicity that might result from the hearing. On the other hand, the preliminary hearing is of obvious advantage to the defendant who believes that the hearing will result in a dismissal of the charges. In addition, the preliminary hearing gives the defense the opportunity to learn what evidence the prosecution has in its possession.

■ Arraignment

An arraignment takes place after an indictment or information is filed following a grand jury or preliminary hearing. At the arraignment, the judge informs the defendant of the charges against him or her and appoints counsel if it has not yet been retained. According to the Sixth Amendment of the U.S. Constitution, the accused has the right to be informed of the nature and cause of the accusation; thus the judge at the arraignment must make sure that the defendant clearly understands the charges.

After the charges are read and explained, the defendant is asked to enter a plea. If a plea of not guilty or not guilty by reason of insanity is entered, a trial date is set. When the defendant pleads guilty or *nolo contendere*, a date for sentencing is arranged. The magistrate then either sets bail or releases the defendant on personal recognizance.

■ The Plea

Ordinarily, a defendant in a criminal trial will enter one of the following pleas:

■ *Guilty.* More than 90 percent of defendants appearing before the courts plead guilty prior to the trial stage. A guilty plea has several consequences:

Such a plea functions not only as an admission of guilt but also as a surrender of the entire array of constitutional rights designed to protect a criminal defendant against unjustified conviction, including the right to remain silent, the right to confront witnesses against him, the right to a trial by jury, and the right to be proven guilty by proof beyond a reasonable doubt.[30]

As a result, a judge must take certain precautions when accepting a plea of guilty. First, the judge must clearly state to the defendant the constitutional guarantees automatically waived by this plea. Second, the judge must believe that the facts of the case establish a basis for the plea and that the plea is made voluntarily. Third, the defendant must be informed of the right to counsel during the pleading process. In many felony cases the judge will insist on the presence of counsel. Finally, the judge must inform the defendant of the possible sentencing outcomes, including the maximum sentence that can be imposed.

After a guilty plea has been entered, a sentencing date is arranged. In a majority of states, a guilty plea may be withdrawn and replaced with a not guilty plea at any time prior to sentencing if good cause is shown.

■ *Not guilty.* At the arraignment or prior to the trial, a not guilty plea is entered in two ways: (1) it is verbally stated by the defendant or the defense counsel; or (2) it is entered for the defendant by the court when the defendant stands mute before the bench.

Once a plea of not guilty is recorded, a trial date is set. In misdemeanor cases, trials take place in the interior court system, whereas felony cases are normally transferred to the superior court. At this time, a continuance or issuance of bail is once again considered.

■ *Nolo contendere.* The plea *nolo contendere*, which means "no contest," is essentially a plea of guilty. This plea has the same consequences as a guilty plea, with one exception: it may not be held against the defendant as proof in a subsequent civil matter because technically there has been no admission of guilt.

The *nolo contendere* plea is utilized in those situations where the defendant is also subject to a civil suit for damages (e.g., extortion of corporate funds). This plea is acceptable in federal court cases and in about half the states. It may be entered only at the discretion of the judge and the prosecutor, however.

■ Plea Bargaining

One of the most common practices in the criminal justice system today, and a cornerstone of the "informal justice" system, is the process of plea bargaining. It has been estimated that more than 90 percent of criminal convictions result from negotiated pleas of guilty. Even in serious felony cases some jurisdictions will experience about four bargains for every trial.

Plea bargaining has been defined concisely as the exchange of prosecutorial and judicial concessions for pleas of guilty.[31] There are normally four ways in which a bargain can be made between the prosecutor and the defense attorney. (1) The initial charges may be reduced to those of a lesser offense, thus automatically reducing the sentence imposed; (2) in cases where many counts are charged, the prosecutor may reduce the number of counts; (3) the prosecutor may promise to recommend a lenient sentence, such as probation; and (4) when the charge imposed has a negative label attached (e.g., child molester), the prosecutor may alter the charge to a more "socially acceptable" one (e.g., assault) in exchange for a plea of guilty. In a jurisdiction where it is common knowledge that sentencing disparity between judges exists, the prosecutor may even agree to arrange for the defendant to appear before a lenient judge in exchange for a plea; this practice is known as "judge shopping."

Because of overcrowded criminal court caseloads and the personal and professional needs of the prosecution and defense (to get the case over with in the shortest amount of time), plea bargaining has become an essential yet controversial part of the administration of justice. Proponents contend that plea bargaining actually benefits both the state and the defendant in the following ways: (1) the overall financial costs of the criminal prosecution are reduced; (2) the administrative efficiency of the courts is greatly improved; (3) the prosecution is able to devote more time to more serious cases; and (4) the defendant avoids possible detention and an extended trial and may receive a reduced sentence.[32] Those in favor of plea bargaining believe it is appropriate to enter into plea discussions where the interests of the state in the effective administration of justice will be served.

Opponents of the plea-bargaining process believe that the negotiated plea should be eliminated. In 1973, the National Advisory Commission on Criminal Justice Standards and Goals stated:

> As soon as possible, but in no event later than 1978, regulations between prosecutors and defendants—either personally or through their attorneys—concerning concessions to be made in return for guilty pleas should be prohibited.[33]

This has never been accomplished.

It has been argued that plea bargaining is objectionable because it encourages defendants to waive their constitutional right to a trial. In addition, some experts suggest that sentences tend to be less severe when a defendant enters a guilty plea than in actual trials and that plea bargains result in even greater sentencing disparity. Particularly in the eyes of the general public, this allows the defendant to beat the system and further tarnishes the criminal process. Plea bargaining also raises the danger that an innocent person will be convicted of a crime if he or she is convinced that the lighter treatment from a guilty plea is preferable to the risk of a harsher sentence following a formal trial.

It is unlikely that plea negotiations will be eliminated or severely curtailed in the near future. Those who support total abolition of plea bargaining are in the minority. As a result of abuses, however, efforts are being made to improve plea-bargaining operations. Such reforms include (1) the development of uniform plea practices, (2) the representation of counsel during plea negotiations, and (3) the establishment of time limits on plea negotiations.

Legal Issues in Plea Bargaining

The U.S. Supreme Court has reviewed the propriety of plea bargaining in several court decisions, particularly in regard to the voluntariness of guilty pleas. Defendants are entitled to the effective assistance of counsel to protect them from pressure and influence. The Court ruled in *Hill v. Lockhart* (1985) that to prove ineffectiveness the defendant must show a "reasonable probability that, but for counsel's errors, he would not have pleaded guilty and would have insisted on going to trial."[34]

In *Boykin v. Alabama* (1969), the Court held that an affirmative action (such as a verbal statement) that the plea was made voluntarily must exist on the record before a trial judge may accept a guilty plea.[35] This is essential because a guilty plea essentially constitutes a waiver of the defendant's Fifth Amendment privilege against self-incrimination and Sixth Amendment right to a jury trial. Subsequent to *Boykin*, the Court ruled in *Brady v. United States* (1970) that a guilty plea is not invalid merely because it is entered to avoid the possibility of the death penalty.[36]

In *Santobello v. New York* (1971), the Court held that the promise of the prosecutor must be kept and that the breaking of a plea-bargaining agreement by the prosecutor required a reversal for the defendant.[37] In *Ricketts v. Adamson* (1987), the Court ruled that defendants must also keep their side of a bargain in order to receive the promised offer of leniency. In this case the defendant was charged with first-degree murder but was allowed to plead guilty to second-degree murder in exchange for testifying against his accomplices. The testimony was given, but the co-defendants' conviction was later reversed on appeal. Ricketts refused to testify a second time, and the prosecutor withdrew the offer of leniency in favor of the first-degree murder charge. On appeal, the Supreme Court allowed the recharging and held that Ricketts had to suffer the consequences of his voluntary choice not to retestify.[38]

How far can prosecutors go to convince a defendant to plead guilty? The Supreme Court ruled in the 1978 case of *Bordenkircher v. Hayes* that a defendant's due process rights are not violated when a prosecutor threatens to reindict the accused on more serious charges if he or she does not plead guilty to the original offense.

Plea-Bargaining Decision Making

Because the plea-bargaining process is largely informal, lacking in guidelines, and discretionary in nature, some effort has been made to determine what kinds of information and how much information is used by the prosecutor to make plea-bargaining decisions. A study conducted by Stephen Lagoy, Joseph Senna, and Larry Siegel found that certain information weighed heavily in the prosecutorial decision to accept a plea negotiation.[39] Such factors as the offense, the defendant's prior record and age, and the type, strength, and admissibility of evidence were considered important in the plea-bargaining decision. It was also discovered that the attitude of the complainant was an important factor in the decision-making process; for example, in victimless cases such as heroin possession the police attitude was most often considered, whereas in victim-related crimes such as rape the attitude of the victim was a primary concern. The study also revealed that prosecutors in low-population or rural settings not only employ more information while making their decisions but also seem more likely than their urban counterparts to accept bargains. It was suggested that "this finding tends to dispute the notion that plea bargaining is a response to overcrowding in large urban courts."[40] It appears that where caseload pressures are less, there is actually a greater probability of the acceptance of a plea bargain.

Similar conclusions were reached by William McDonald in a study of plea bargaining in six court jurisdictions. McDonald found that plea negotiations were not conducted in a haphazard manner nor were they used by prosecutors to engage in frauds or other deceptive practices. For example, prosecutors did not overcharge suspects with the idea of forcing them to plea to a more reasonable charge.[41]

The Nature of Plea Bargaining

A federal study of plea negotiations sheds some light on the plea-bargaining process. The study by Barbara Boland and Brian Forst looked at 14 jurisdictions around the country.[42] Boland and Forst found a wide discrepancy in the use of pleas. Although the overall average was 1 trial for 11 plea bargains, the range was between 37:1 in Geneva, Illinois, and 4:1 in Portland, Oregon. Interestingly, the high plea bargain jurisdictions were not located exclusively in high-crime areas where case pressure was a factor. Correspondingly, some of the jurisdictions that hold a large number of trials, such as Washington, D.C., St. Louis, and New Orleans, are big cities with high caseloads. Thus case pressure does not seem to play as an important a role in plea negotiations as might have been thought. The study also found that jurisdictions that hold a great many trials tend to be more selective in the cases they process and are more likely to screen out weak cases before trial.

CASE OUTCOME. What is the effect of plea bargaining on the outcome of a case? Many people believe that "copping a plea" lets a criminal "get away with murder." This charge is supported by research conducted by Mark Cuniff in 28 large legal jurisdictions. As Table 12.5 shows, Cuniff found that people convicted after a plea bargain were much less likely to be sent to prison than those convicted after a jury trial. Interestingly, those convicted after a bench trial (before a judge alone) had the same probability of being sent to prison as defendants who plea bargained.[43] Table 12.5 also indicates that those who plea bargain receive lower average prison terms than those who go to trial, which supports the argument that plea bargaining helps the defendant avoid punishment.

Other research, however, indicates that plea bargains may not be that helpful to criminal defendants. Douglas Smith's study of 3,397 felony cases in six separate legal jurisdictions found that the probability of receiving an incarceration sentence was roughly equal for those who pleaded guilty and for those who actually went to trial.[44] Those defendants who seemed to benefit the

---

TABLE 12.5 ■ **The Effect of Plea Bargaining on Prison Sentences and Prison Terms**

Conviction Offense	Percentage of Prison Sentences by Type of Conviction					Average Prison Term by Type of Conviction			
	Jury Trial	Bench Trial	Trial, but Type not Known	Guilty Plea	Total	Jury Trial	Bench Trial	Trial, but Type not Known	Guilty Plea
Overall average	82%	42%	76%	43%	46%	194 months	98 months	133 months	13 months
Homicide	93	88	96	79	84	272	168	125	162
Rape	90	63	83	60	65	247	146	274	132
Robbery	89	50	82	66	67	210	113	142	89
Aggravated assault	73	37	50	39	42	139	115	100	66
Burglary	79	31	81	49	49	152	57	114	61
Larceny	54	29	50	32	32	152	42	46	43
Drug trafficking	69	36	68	26	27	121	34	96	51

SOURCE: Mark Cuniff, *Sentencing Outcomes in 28 Felony Courts 1985* (Washington, D.C.: Bureau of Justice Statistics, 1987), pp. 26–28.

most from plea bargaining committed the least serious offenses and had the best prior records.

Another project conducted by the federal government found that about 60 percent of the defendants pleaded guilty to the top charge filed against them.[45] A plea to the top charge did not necessarily mean the absence of negotiation or concession. The study found that bargaining often included judicial agreement to give a more lenient sentence than might be expected if the defendant went to trial. In other cases the negotiation involved the dropping of other charges or pending cases. Sometimes the lesser charges involved acts that required add-ons to a sentence such as possession of a handgun; in that case dropping the lesser offense automatically shortened the defendant's prison term. People who pleaded guilty were also less likely to do their time in a state prison and more likely to be sent to a less restrictive correctional facility such as a county jail. This conclusion is supported by McDonald's study of plea bargaining in six court jurisdictions. He found that in five of the six jurisdictions, people who did not plead guilty increased their chances of receiving a prison sentence and also received significantly longer prison terms.[46]

In sum, although punishment is a certainty when defendants decide to plead guilty, it is likely to be somewhat less severe than if they were found guilty after a trial. The plea-bargaining process reflects the "wedding cake" model of justice: pleas are a quick and efficient way of disposing of cases that fall into the "bottom layers." Plea bargains also reduce the time the defendant is involved with the justice system: cases that go to trial take significantly longer than those that are bargained. So defendants, especially those placed in pretrial detention, have the extra burden of remaining within the justice system if they refuse to plea bargain, a burden few wish to bear.

The Role of the Prosecutor in Plea Bargaining

The prosecutor in the American system of criminal justice has broad discretion in the exercise of his or her responsibilities. Such discretion includes whether to initiate a criminal prosecution, the nature of the criminal charge, the number of criminal charges, and whether to plea bargain a case and under what conditions. Plea bargaining is one of the major tools the prosecutor uses to control and influence the criminal justice system (the other two are the decision to initiate a charge and the ability to take the case to trial). Few states have placed limits on the discretion of prosecutors in plea-bargaining situations. Instead, in making a plea-bargaining decision, the prosecutor is generally free to weigh competing alternatives and factors, such as the seriousness of the crime, the attitude of the victim, the police report regarding the incident, and applicable sentencing provisions. Plea bargaining frequently occurs in cases where the government believes the evidence is weak, for example, where a key witness seems unreliable or unwilling to testify. Bargaining permits a compromise settlement in a weak case where the criminal trial outcome is in doubt.

On a case-by-case basis, the prosecutor determines the concessions to be offered in the plea bargain and seeks to dispose of each case quickly and efficiently. On the broader scale, however, the role of the chief prosecutor as an administrator also has an impact on plea bargaining. While the assistant prosecutor evaluates and moves individual cases, the chief prosecutor must establish plea-bargaining guidelines for the entire office. In this regard the prosecutor may be acting as an administrator.[47] In the Manhattan district attorney's office in New York City, for example, guidelines include such requirements as avoiding overindictment, control over nonprovable indictments, reduction of felonies to misdemeanors, and control over bargaining with defendants.

Some jurisdictions have established guidelines to provide consistency in plea-bargaining cases. For instance, a given office may be required to define the kinds and types of cases and offenders that may be given a plea bargain. In other jurisdictions, approval to plea bargain may be required. Other controls might include procedures for internal review of decisions by the chief prosecutor and the use of written memorandums to document the need and acceptability for a plea bargain in a given case. For example, in New Orleans pleas are offered on a "take it or leave it" basis. In each case a special prosecutor, whose job it is to screen cases, sets the bargaining terms. If the defense counsel cannot abide by the agreement, there is no negotiation, and the case must go to trial. Only if complications arise in the case, such as witnesses changing their testimony, can negotiations be reopened.[48]

The prosecutor's role in plea bargaining is also important on a statewide or systemwide basis because it involves leadership in the criminal justice system. The most extreme example of a chief prosecutor influencing the plea negotiation process has occurred where efforts have been made to eliminate plea bargaining from the system. In Alaska, efforts to eliminate plea bargaining met with resistance from assistant prosecutors and others in the system, namely, judges and defense attorneys.[49] The more moderate approach by prosecutors in providing leadership in plea bargaining generally involves the establishment of guidelines for the plea-bargaining process as discussed above.

Thus the prosecutor plays a role in plea bargaining on an overall policy basis as well as on a case-by-case basis. In evaluating cases for plea bargaining, the strength or weakness of the government's case is generally the most important factor in the decision to bargain or establish a plea agreement. When evaluating the role of the prosecutor on a policy level, efforts have been made to provide on-line assistant prosecutors with formulas or guidelines to help them properly evaluate cases for discretionary decision making in plea bargaining.

The Role of Defense Counsel in Plea Bargaining

Both the U.S. Supreme Court and such organizations as the American Bar Association in its *Standards Relating to Pleas of Guilty* have established guidelines for the court receiving a guilty plea and for the defense counsel representing the accused in plea negotiations.[50] No court should accept a guilty plea unless the defendant has been properly advised by counsel and the court has determined that the plea is voluntary and has a factual basis; the court has the discretion to reject a plea if it is inappropriately offered. The defense attorney—a public defender or a private attorney—is required to act in an advisory role in plea negotiations. The defendant's counsel is expected to be aware of the facts of the case and of the law and to advise the defendant of the alternatives available. It is basically the responsibility of the defense attorney to make certain that the accused understands the nature of the plea-bargaining process and the guilty plea. This means that the defense counsel should explain to the defendant that by pleading guilty he or she is waiving certain rights that would be available on going to trial. In addition, the defense attorney has the duty to keep the defendant informed of developments and discussions with the prosecutor regarding plea bargaining. While doing so, the attorney for the accused cannot misrepresent evidence or mislead the client into making a detrimental agreement.

In reality, most plea negotiations occur in the chambers of the judge, in the prosecutor's office, or in the courthouse hallway. Under these conditions, it is often difficult to assess the actual roles played by the prosecutor and the defense attorney. Even under these conditions, however, it is fundamental that a defendant should not be required to plead guilty until advised by counsel, and that a guilty plea should not be made unless it is given with the consent of the accused.

The Judge's Role in Plea Bargaining

One of the most confusing problems in the plea-bargaining process has been the proper role of the judge. Should the judge act only in a supervisory capacity or actually enter into the negotiation process? The leading national legal organizations, such as the American Bar Association, are opposed to judicial participation in plea negotiations.[51] The American Bar Association sets out its position on the role of the judge in the plea-bargaining process as follows:

Standard 3.3: Responsibilities of the Trial Judge:
A. The trial judge should not participate in plea discussions.
B. If a tentative plea agreement has been reached which contemplates entry of a plea of guilty in the expectation that other charges before that court will be dismissed, or that sentence concessions will be granted, upon request of the parties, the trial judge may permit the disclosure to him of the agreement and the reasons therefore in advance of the time for tender of the plea. He may then indicate to the prosecuting attorney and defense counsel whether he will concur in the proposed disposition, if the information in the pre-sentence report is consistent with the representations made to him. That the trial judge concurs but the final disposition does not include the charge or sentence concessions contemplated in the plea agreement, he shall state for the record what information in the pre-sentence report contributed to his decision not to grant these concessions.[52]

In addition, the Federal Rules of Criminal Procedure prohibit federal judges from participating in plea negotiations.[53] A few states disallow any form of judicial involvement in plea bargaining, but others permit the judge to participate.

The American Bar Association objects in general to the judge participating in plea negotiations because of his or her position as chief judicial officer. A judge should not be a party to arrangements for the determination of a sentence, whether as a result of a guilty plea or a finding of guilty based on proof. Furthermore, judicial participation in plea negotiations (1) creates the impression in the mind of the defendant that he or she could not receive a fair trial; (2) lessens the ability of the judge to make an objective determination of the voluntariness of the plea; (3) is inconsistent with the theory behind the use of presentence investigation reports; and (4) may induce an innocent defendant to plead guilty because he or she is afraid to reject the disposition desired by the judge.[54]

On the other hand, those who suggest that the judge should participate directly in plea bargaining argue that such an approach would make sentencing more uniform and ensure that the plea-bargaining process would be fairer and more efficient.

It appears that judges play an active role in the negotiation process in most jurisdictions in the United States. Where judges simply supervise plea bargaining, they oversee the taking of the guilty plea, determine a factual basis for the plea, inform the defendant of the sentencing consequences, and control the withdrawal of the plea. McDonald found that this type of judicial involvement can have a beneficial effect but that judges usually play an extremely neutral role and do not look into how a plea was arrived at nor examine the strength of the state's case.[55]

When judges participate more actively in plea bargaining, their role may include influencing the kind and type of agreement that is reached, encouraging prosecutors and defense attorneys to arrive at an agreement, expediting cases, and contributing to the efficient management of the court.

Plea-Bargaining Reform

Plea bargaining is so widespread that it is recognized as one of the major elements of the criminal justice system. Despite its prevalence, its merits are hotly debated. Those opposed to the widespread use of plea bargaining assert that it is coercive in its inducement of guilty pleas, that it encourages the unequal exercise of prosecutorial discretion, and that it complicates sentencing as well as the job of correctional authorities. Others argue that it is unconstitutional and that it results in cynicism and disrespect for the entire system.

On the other hand, its proponents contend that the practice ensures the flow of guilty pleas essential to administrative efficiency. It allows the system the flexibility to individualize justice and inspires respect for the system because it is associated with certain and prompt punishment.[56]

In recent years, efforts have been made to convert the practice of plea bargaining into a more visible, understandable, and fair dispositional process. Many jurisdictions have developed safeguards and guidelines to prevent violations of due process and to ensure that innocent defendants do not plead guilty under coercion. Such safeguards include the following: (1) the judge questions the defendant about the facts of the guilty plea before accepting the plea; (2) the defense counsel is present and able to advise the defendant of his or her rights; (3) the prosecutor and the defense attorney openly discuss the plea; and (4) full and frank information about the offender and the offense are made available at this stage of the process. In addition, judicial supervision ensures that plea bargaining is conducted in a fair manner.

Another reform involves the development of specific guidelines by the office of the chief prosecutor. Some jurisdictions have also adopted pre-pleading investigations, which provide summaries of the case before a plea rather than after the plea is given to the court. The pre-pleading report provides information to all participants in the negotiations. The pretrial settlement conference also improves the visibility and fairness of plea bargaining. The participants in such a conference include the judge, the victim, the defendant, and members of the police as well as the prosecutor and the defense attorney. Generally, the parties assume that the defendant is guilty as charged and negotiate from there to settle the case. If a settlement is reached and approved by the judge, the defendant enters a plea in open court.

BANNING PLEA NEGOTIATIONS. What would happen if plea bargaining were banned outright as its critics advocate? Numerous jurisdictions throughout the United States have experimented with bans on plea bargaining. In 1975 the state of Alaska eliminated the practice. Honolulu, Hawaii made efforts to abolish plea bargaining. Jurisdictions in other states, including Iowa, Arizona, Delaware, and the District of Columbia, also sought to limit the use of plea bargaining.[57] The U.S. Coast Guard banned plea bargaining in service-related crimes.[58] In theory, eliminating plea bargains means that prosecutors in these jurisdictions give no consideration or concessions to a defendant in exchange for a guilty plea.

In reality, however, in these and most jurisdictions sentence-related concessions, charge-reduction concessions, and alternative methods for prosecution continue to occur in one fashion or another.[59] In areas where plea bargaining is limited or abolished, the number of trials may increase, the sentence severity may change, and more questions regarding the right to a speedy trial may arise. Discretion may also be shifted further up the system. Instead of spending countless hours preparing and conducting a trial, prosecutors may dismiss more cases outright or *nolle prosequi* them after initial action has been taken.

These predictions have been supported by experience. An evaluation of the Alaska experiment found that the ban on plea bargaining had the effect of increasing sentence severity in minor cases that would ordinarily have been dealt with informally; at the same time it had no effect on serious cases (robberies, murders, and rapes), probably because these were the cases that were going to trial before the ban was put into effect.[60] California's attempt to reduce plea negotiations in drunk driving cases also did not meet prereform expectations: although some forms of plea bargaining were initially reduced, they soon rose back to their early levels; trial rates increased; rates of conviction at trial decreased; court congestion became a problem; and sentence disparity increased.[61]

Studies have also shown that a ban on plea bargaining will push discretion further up the line. For example, when New York's narcotics control law banned plea bargaining in serious drug-related cases in 1973, it was hailed as a "get tough" measure that would certainly help control the drug trade. An evaluation conducted three years later found that the law's effect was somewhat less than expected.[62] The same percentage (11 percent) of people arrested for heroin sale or possession were incarcerated both before and after the law went into effect. One reason was that prosecutors began to process fewer cases, indicting 25 percent of arrested drug traffickers after the law went into effect as opposed to about 40 percent before. Although the conviction rate remained high, it declined about 6 percent. Though the length of prison sentences increased, the drug trade was virtually unaffected. The law was amended three years later. These results suggest that, despite the intentions of policymakers who attempt to abolish plea bargaining, the system will not easily change its ways.

In view of the problems associated both with plea bargaining and with its reform, there appears to be no ideal system of adjudication and disposition in the criminal justice process. Current trends include the development of guidelines and safeguards as well as the experimental banning of plea bargaining in some jurisdictions. Efforts are also being made to examine prosecutorial discretion and to make plea bargaining a more visible and structured process. Despite all the efforts to reform, control, or even ban plea bargaining, it remains one of the key elements of the informal justice process.

■ Pretrial Diversion

Another important feature in the early court process is the placing of offenders into noncriminal **diversion** programs prior to their formal trial or conviction. Pretrial diversion programs were first established in the late 1960s when it became apparent that a viable alternative to the highly stigmatized judicial sentences was needed. In diversion programs formal criminal proceedings against an accused are suspended while that person participates in a community treatment program under court supervision. Diversion helps the offender avoid the stigma of a criminal conviction and also enables the justice system to reduce costs and alleviate overcrowding.

Many diversion programs exist throughout the United States. These programs vary in size and emphasis but generally pursue the same goal: to constructively bypass criminal prosecution by providing a reasonable alternative in the form of treatment, counseling, or employment programs.

Diversion programs can take many forms. Some are separate, independent agencies that were originally set up with federal funds but are now being continued with county or state assistance. Others are organized as part of a police, prosecutors, or probation department's internal structure. Still others are a joint venture between the county government and a private nonprofit organization that actually carries out the treatment process.

The Diversion Process

Many pretrial diversion programs have similar operating processes and procedures, yet each maintains its own unique characteristics.[63] Figure 12.2 is a typical model showing how diversion cases are processed through the criminal justice system.

All existing diversion programs have admission criteria that control the selection of clients. Diversion priority is given to first-offender misdemeanors. The age, residency, and employment status of diversion candidates are also taken into consideration.

The diversion is considered after the arrest and arraignment of the individual but before the trial. The defendant chosen for a diversion program is released on a **continuance**—that is, the trial is postponed—if the relevant court personnel (judge, probation officer, assistant district attorney, arresting officer) and the program representative agree on the potential of the accused for the program. During this initial period, the program's staff teams with the potential client to assess the individual's suitability for the program. Acceptance may begin with a long continuance (the time limit varies from program to program) without entry of a plea, and on the written waiver by the defendant of the right to a speedy trial.

During the evaluation, one of three things may occur:

1. Charges may be dismissed upon successful completion of the program.
2. The continuance may be extended if project members are unsure of the client's progress.
3. The client's participation in the program may be terminated because of his or her failure to comply with program guidelines and structures; in this case the normal court process of trial and disposition takes place.

Some of the most important goals and purposes of the typical diversion program include the following:

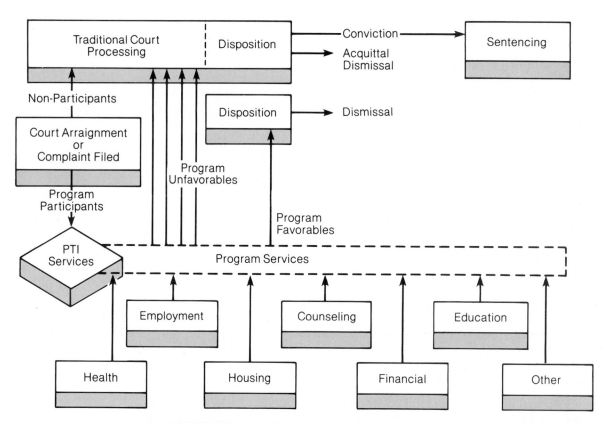

■ *FIGURE 12.2* **Flow of Pretrial Intervention (PTI) Cases through the Criminal Court**

SOURCE: Roberta Rovner Pieczenik, *Pretrial Intervention Strategies: An Evaluation of Policy-related Research and Policymaker Perceptions* (American Bar Association National Pretrial Intervention Center, November 1974), Fig. 1.

1. To divert selected individuals from trial to fruitful training, employment, and counseling experiences.
2. To provide the court and legal systems with much-needed resources.
3. To help the court system become more aware of its rehabilitative role.
4. To help break a beginning pattern of crime and failure.
5. To sensitize employers to offenders' needs and to help alter restrictive hiring practices.
6. To create effective resources where none exist.
7. To assist in the reintegration of potential offenders into the community.
8. To help establish pretrial diversion as a permanent part of the state's criminal justice system.

Critique of Diversion

First viewed as a panacea that could reduce court congestion and help treat minor offenders, diversion programs have come under fire for their alleged failures. Some national evaluations have concluded that diversion programs are no more successful at avoiding stigma and reducing recidivism than traditional justice processing.[64] The most prominent criticism is that they help *widen the net* of the justice system. By this, critics mean that the people put in diversion programs are the ones most likely to have been dismissed after a brief hearing with a warning or small fine.[65] Those who would have ordinarily received a more serious sentence are not eligible for diversion anyway. Thus, rather than limiting interface with the system, the diversion programs actually increase it. Of course, not all justice experts agree with this critique, and some such as Arnold Binder and Gilbert Geis have championed diversion as a worthwhile exercise of the criminal justice system's rehabilitation perspective.[66] As supporters such as Binder and Geis point out, though diversion may not be a "cure all" for criminal behavior, it is an important effort that continues to be made in most jurisdictions across the United States.

■ SUMMARY

Many important decisions about what happens to a defendant occur prior to trial. Hearings such as the grand jury and preliminary hearing are held to determine if probable cause exists to charge the accused with a crime. If so, the defendant is arraigned, enters a plea, is informed of his or her constitutional rights, particularly the right to the assistance of counsel, and is considered for pretrial defense. The use of money bail and other alternatives, such as release on recognizance statutes, allow most defendants to be free pending their return for trial. Bail provisions are beginning to be toughened, resulting in the preventive detention of people awaiting trial. Preventive detention has been implemented because many believe that significant numbers of criminals violate their bail and commit further crimes while on pretrial release.

The issue of discretion plays a major role at this stage of the criminal process. Since only a small percentage of criminal cases eventually go to trial, many defendants agree to plea bargains or are placed in diversion programs. Not enough judges, prosecutors, defense attorneys, and courts exist to enable the criminal justice system to try every defendant accused of a crime. As a result, subsystems such as plea bargaining and diversion are essential elements in the administration of our justice system. Research indicates that most cases never go to trial but are bargained out of the system. Though plea bargaining has been criticized, efforts to control it have not met with success. Similarly, diversion programs have not been overly successful yet they continue to be used throughout the United States.

■ QUESTIONS

1. Should criminal defendants be allowed to bargain for a reduced sentence in exchange for a guilty plea?
2. Should those accused of violent acts be subjected to preventive detention instead of bail even though they have not been convicted of a crime?
3. What purpose does a grand jury or preliminary hearing serve in felony offenses?

4. Should a judge participate in plea bargaining? Is this a conflict of interest?
5. Do rehabilitation-oriented programs, such as pretrial diversion, create a whole new set of problems for people, such as net widening, or are they essentially beneficial?

■ NOTES

1. 342 U.S. 1, 72 S.Ct. 1, 96 L.Ed. 3 (1951).
2. William Rhodes, *Pretrial Release and Misconduct* (Washington, D.C.: Bureau of Justice Statistics, 1985).
3. Mary Toborg, *Pretrial Release: A National Evaluation of Practices and Outcomes* (Washington, D.C.: National Institute of Justice, 1982).
4. Rhodes, *Pretrial Release and Misconduct*.
5. Andy Hall, *Pretrial Release Program Options* (Washington, D.C.: National Institute of Justice, 1984).
6. President's Commission on Law Enforcement and Administration of Justice, *Task Force Report: The Courts* (Washington, D.C.: U.S. Government Printing Office, 1967), p. 38.

7. Vera Institute of Justice, *1961–1971: Programs in Criminal Justice* (New York: Vera Institute of Justice, 1972).
8. Chris Eskridge, *Pretrial Release Programming* (New York: Clark Boardman, 1983), p. 27.
9. 4 Public Law 89–465, 18 U.S.C. 3146 (1966).
10. 18 U.S.C. 3142 (1984).
11. John Goldkamp, "Judicial Reform of Bail Practices: The Philadelphia Experiment," *Court Management Journal* 17 (1983): 16–20.
12. John Goldkamp and Michael Gottfredson, *Judicial Decision Guidelines for Bail: The Philadelphia Experiment* (Washington, D.C.: National Institute of Justice, 1983).

13. 18 U.S.C. 3142 (1984).

14. See, generally, Fred Cohen, "The New Federal Crime Control Act," *Criminal Law Bulletin* 21 (1985): 330–37.

15. 467 U.S. 253; 104 S.Ct. 2403 81 L.Ed.2d 207 (1984).

16. 481 U.S. 739; 107 S.Ct. 2095, 95 L.Ed.2d. 697 (1987).

17. Susan Kline, *Jail Inmates, 1987* (Washington, D.C.: Bureau of Justice Statistics, 1988).

18. National Coalition for Jail Reform, "Position Paper on Pre-trial Release," *Prison Journal* 61 (1981): 28–41.

19. See President's Commission on Law Enforcement and Administration of Justice, *Task Force Reports: Corrections* (Washington, D.C.: U.S. Government Printing Office, 1967); National Advisory Commission on Criminal Justice Standards and Goals, *Task Force Report on Courts* (Washington, D.C.: U.S. Government Printing Office, 1973); American Bar Association, *Standards on Pretrial Release* (New York: Institute of Judicial Administration, 1979); *Uniform Rules of Criminal Procedure of National Conference of Commissions on Uniform State Laws* (Philadelphia: 1974); National District Attorney's Association, *Standards on Pretrial Release* (New York: 1977).

20. National Coalition for Jail Reform, "Position Paper on Pre-trial Release," pp. 30–35.

21. Two excellent studies are Caleb Foote, "Compelling Appearance in Court: Administration of Bail in Philadelphia," *University of Pennsylvania Law Review* 102 (1956): 1056 and "A Study of Administration of Bail in New York City," *University of Pennsylvania Law Review* 106 (1960): 693–730.

22. Rhodes, *Pretrial Release and Misconduct*; see also Foote, "A Study of Administration of Bail in New York."

23. John Goldkamp, *Two Classes of Accused* (Cambridge, Mass.: Ballinger, 1979).

24. Rhodes, *Pretrial Release and Misconduct*, p. 2.

25. Conference of State Court Administrators and National Center for State Courts, *State Court Organization, 1987* (Williamsburg, Va.: National Center for State Courts, 1988), p. 12.

26. National Advisory Commission on Criminal Justice Standards and Goals, *Task Force Report on Courts*, p. 74.

27. Ibid.

28. American Bar Association, *Grand Jury Policy and Model Act* (Chicago: American Bar Association, 1982).

29. Deborah Day Emerson, *Grand Jury Reform: A Review of Key Issues* (Washington, D.C.: National Institute of Justice, 1983).

30. National Advisory Commission on Criminal Justice Standards and Goals, *Task Force Report on Courts*, p. 42.

31. Alan Alschuler, "The Prosecutor's Role in Plea Bargaining," *University of Chicago Law Review* (1968): 36–50.

32. For arguments favoring plea bargaining, see John Wheatley, "Plea Bargaining—A Case for Its Continuance," *Massachusetts Law Quarterly* 59 (1974): 31.

33. National Advisory Commission on Criminal Justice Standards and Goals, *Task Force Report on Courts*, p. 46.

34. 474 U.S. 52, 106 S.Ct. 366, 88 L.Ed.2d 203 (1985).

35. 395 U.S. 238, 89 S.Ct. 1709, 23 L.Ed.2d 274 (1969).

36. 397 U.S. 742, 90 S.Ct. 1463, 25 L.Ed.2d 747 (1970).

37. 404 U.S. 257, 92 S.Ct. 495, 30 L.Ed.2d 427 (1971).

38. 481 U.S. 1, 107 S.Ct. 2680, 97 L.Ed.2d 1 (1987).

39. Stephen P. Lagoy, Joseph J. Senna, and Larry J. Siegel, "An Empirical Study on Information Usage for Prosecutorial Decision Making in Plea Negotiations," *American Criminal Law Review* 13 (1976): 435–71.

40. Ibid., p. 462.

41. William McDonald, *Plea Bargaining: Critical Issues and Common Practices* (Washington, D.C.: U.S. Government Printing Office, 1985).

42. Barbara Boland and Brian Forst, *The Prevalence of Guilty Pleas* (Washington, D.C.: Bureau of Justice Statistics, 1984).

43. Mark Cuniff, *Sentencing Outcomes in 28 Felony Courts 1985* (Washington, D.C.: Bureau of Justice Statistics, 1987), p. 25.

44. Douglas Smith, "The Plea Bargaining Controversy," *Journal of Criminal Law and Criminology* 77 (1986): 949–67.

45. Boland and Forst, *The Prevalence of Guilty Pleas*.

46. McDonald, *Plea Bargaining: Critical Issues and Common Practices*, p. 97.

47. Alschuler, "The Prosecutor's Role in Plea Bargaining."

48. Boland and Forst, *The Prevalence of Guilty Pleas*, p. 3.

49. National Institute of Law Enforcement and Criminal Justice, *Plea Bargaining in the United States* (Washington, D.C.: Georgetown University, 1978), p. 8.

50. See American Bar Association, *Standards Relating to Pleas of Guilty* (New York: Institute of Judicial Administration, 1968): see also *North Carolina v. Alford*, 400 U.S. 25, 91 S.Ct. 160; 27 L.Ed.2d 162 (1970).

51. American Bar Association, *Standards Relating to Pleas of Guilty*, standard 3.3; National Advisory Commission on Criminal Justice Standards and Goals, *Task Force Report on Courts*, p. 42.

52. American Bar Association, *Standards Relating to Pleas of Guilty*, standard 3.3, p. 71.

53. *Federal Rules of Criminal Procedure*, rule 11.

54. American Bar Association, *Standards Relating to Pleas of Guilty*, p. 73; see also Alan Alschuler, "The Trial Judge's Role in Plea Bargaining," *Columbia Law Review* 76 (1976): 1059.

55. McDonald, *Plea Bargaining: Critical Issues and Common Practices*, pp. 109–24.

56. *Santobello v. New York*, 404 U.S. 257, 92 S.Ct. 495, 30 L.Ed.2d 427 (1971).

57. National Institute of Law Enforcement and Criminal Justice, *Plea Bargaining in the United States*, pp. 37–40.

58. Jack Call, David England, and Susette Talarico, "Abolition of Plea Bargaining in the Coast Guard," *Journal of Criminal Justice* 11 (1983): 351–58.

59. For a discussion of this issue, see Michael Tonry, "Plea Bargaining Bans and Rules," *Sentencing Reform Impacts* (Washington, D.C.: U.S. Government Printing Office, 1987).

60. Michael Rubenstein, Steven Clarke, and Theresa White, *Alaska Bans Plea Bargaining* (Washington, D.C.: U.S. Government Printing Office, 1980).

61. Rodney Kingsworth and Michael Jungsten, "Driving Under the Influence: The Impact of Legislative Reform on Court Sentencing Practices," *Crime and Delinquency* 34 (1988): 3–28.

62. U.S. Department of Justice, *The Nation's Toughest Drug Law: Evaluating the New York Experience* (Washington, D.C.: U.S. Government Printing Office, 1978).

63. The information in this and the following section was adapted from the Court Resource Program, *A Program Manual Describing the Purpose, History, and Implementation of Pre-trial Diversion in Boston* (Boston: Justice Resource Institute, 1974); see also Roberta Rovner-Pieczenik, *Pretrial Intervention Strategies: An Evaluation of Policy-related Research and Policymaker Perceptions* (Chicago: American Bar Association, 1974).

64. Franklyn Dunford, D. Wayne Osgood, and Hart Weichselbaum, *National Evaluation of Diversion Programs* (Washington, D.C.: U.S. Government Printing Office, 1982).

65. Sharla Rausch and Charles Logan, "Diversion from Juvenile Court, Panacea or Pandora's Box?" in *Evaluating Juvenile Justice*, James Kleugel, ed. (Beverly Hills, Calif.: Sage Publications, 1983), pp. 19–30.

66. Arnold Binder and Gilbert Geis, "Ad Populum Argumentation in Criminology: Juvenile Diversion as Rhetoric," *Criminology* 30 (1984): 309–33.

13

The Criminal Trial

T he **adjudication** stage of the criminal justice process begins with a hearing that seeks to determine the truth of the facts of a case before the courts. This process is usually referred to as the criminal trial.

As mentioned previously, the classic jury trial of a criminal case is an uncommon occurrence. The greatest proportion of individuals charged with crimes plead guilty. Others have their cases dismissed by the judge for a variety of reasons: The government may decide not to prosecute (*nolle prosequi*), the accused may be found emotionally disturbed and unable to stand trial, the court may be unwilling to attach the stigma of a criminal record to a particular defendant.

Still other defendants waive their constitutional right to a jury trial. In this situation, which occurs daily in the lower criminal courts, the judge may initiate a number of formal or informal dispositions, including dismissing the case, finding the defendant not guilty or guilty and imposing a sentence, or even continuing the case indefinitely. The type of decision the judge makes often depends on the seriousness of the offense, the background and previous record of the defendant, and the judgment of the court as to whether the case can be properly dealt with in the criminal process.

In a minor case in some jurisdictions, for example, the continuance is a frequently used disposition. In this instance, the court holds a case in abeyance without a finding of guilt in order to induce the accused to improve his or her behavior in the community; if the defendant's behavior does improve, the case is ordinarily closed within a specific amount of time.

Thus, the number of actual criminal jury trials is small in comparison to all the cases processed through the criminal justice system. Since upward of 90 percent of all defendants plead guilty and about 5 percent are dealt with by other methods, it appears that fewer than 5 percent ever reach the trial stage. Those cases that are actually tried before a jury often involve serious crimes. Such crimes require a formal inquiry into the facts to determine the guilt or innocence of the accused. (See the Criminal Justice in Review on page 417.)

Even though proportionately few cases are actually tried by juries, the trial process remains a focal point in the criminal justice system. It symbolizes the American system of jurisprudence, in which an accused person can choose to present a defense against the government's charges. The fact that the defendant has the option of going to trial significantly affects the operation of the criminal justice system. A federal government commission has stated:

> Although most criminal prosecutions do not involve the adversary determination of guilt or innocence that occurs at the formal trial of a criminal case, the trial process remains a matter of vital importance to the criminal justice system. Whether or not a defendant chooses to invoke his right to trial, he has an interest in the trial process because in many cases it represents to him a legal option guaranteed by the Constitution of the United States. The opportunity to go to trial provides a valuable safeguard against abuse of informal processing and a basis for encouraging faith in the system on the part of those who acknowledge that their situation does not present any contestable issues.
>
> Since informal disposition of a case often occurs only after the case proceeds along the formal route towards trial, procedures for formal processing at the earlier court stages may be used for a much greater number of cases than actually comes to trial. Because all other means of processing cases must be evaluated as alternatives to formal trial, the attractiveness of trial is a major consideration in both prosecution and defense willingness to process a case administratively.[1]

Processing Criminal Cases

Which cases get processed through court the quickest? Which move slowly forward to a conclusion? To answer these questions, Marjorie Zatz and Alan Lizotte analyzed data on case processing in California over a three-year period. They found that cases involving first-time offenders are allowed to move quickly through the system under four general conditions. First, the offenses must not have been committed by hardened criminals (justice moves especially fast for women and younger males). Second, the cases must be seen as "normal" crimes that can be processed in a routine way. Third, less serious cases are dealt with sooner. And, finally, cases tend to get speedy resolutions when there is irrefutable hard evidence, such as possession of a gun or narcotics.

Conversely, serious cases (for example, a homicide or narcotics case) move slowly, especially when a first-time offender's rights or society's well-being is at stake. Justice is much slower for repeaters, especially those who specialize in one type of crime such as robbery or burglary. One reason is that prosecutors may feel society must be protected from repeat offenders. Another reason is that these particular offenders face serious consequences and their rights have to be carefully protected.

In a more recent analysis of felony case processing in 12 major jurisdictions, Barbara Boland also found that serious crimes such as homicide and sexual assault take longer to deal with than more minor charges such as larceny. Whereas the average time from arrest to disposition for a homicide case was 7.1 months, and a serious assault 6.0 months, larcenies were dealt with within 4.7 months, and burglaries took 4.1 months. Boland concludes that most serious crimes take longer to dispose of because a higher percentage of them go to trial rather than being settled through plea negotiations. Nevertheless, her findings show that homicides usually take longer to dispose of than do other crimes whether through dismissals, guilty pleas, or trials.

It appears, therefore, that the most serious cases do take longer to get through the court system, while minor, average cases are dealt with more quickly. ■

SOURCE: Marjorie Zatz and Alan Lizotte, "The Timing of Court Processing: Towards Linking Theory and Method," *Criminology* 23 (1985): 313–35. Barbara Boland, *Felony Case Processing Time* (Washington, D.C.: Bureau of Justice Statistics, 1986).

■ Legal Rights during Trial

Underlying every trial are constitutional principles, complex legal procedures, rules of court, and interpretations of statutes, all designed to ensure that the accused will receive a fair trial. This section discusses the most important constitutional rights of the accused at the trial stage of the criminal justice system and reviews the legal nature of the trial process. The major legal decisions and statutes involving the right to jury trial, counsel, self-representation, and speedy and public trial are examined in the following sections.

The Right to Jury Trial

The defendant has the right to choose whether the trial will be before a judge or a jury. Although the Sixth Amendment to the U.S. Constitution guarantees to the defendant the right to a jury trial, the defendant can and often does waive this right. In fact, a substantial proportion of defendants, particularly those charged with misdemeanors, are tried before the court without a jury.

The major legal issue surrounding jury trial has been the question of whether all offenders, both misdemeanants and felons, have an absolute right to a jury trial. Because the U.S. Constitution is silent on this point, the U.S.

Chapter 13
The Criminal Trial

■

417

Accused and accuser fight a judicial duel in a miniature from a fifteenth-century French manuscript. Such trials, which were also known as wagers of battel, were used on some occasions in the Middle Ages in the belief that God would give victory to the party who was in the right.

Supreme Court has ruled that all defendants in felony cases have this right. In *Duncan v. Louisiana* (1968), the Court held that the Sixth Amendment right to a jury trial is applicable to the states as well as to the federal government, and that it can be interpreted to apply to all defendants accused of serious crimes.[2] The Court in *Duncan* based its holding on the premise

> that in the American States, as in the federal judicial system, a general grant of jury trial for serious offenses is a fundamental right, essential for preventing miscarriages of justice and for assuring that fair trials are provided for all defendants.[3]

The *Duncan* decision did not settle whether all defendants charged with crimes in state courts are constitutionally entitled to jury trials. It seemed to draw the line at serious offenses only, leaving the question of whether to grant jury trials to defendants in minor cases to the discretion of the individual states.

In 1970, in the case of *Baldwin v. New York*, the Supreme Court departed from the distinction of serious versus minor offenses and decided that a defendant has a constitutional right to a jury trial when facing a prison sentence of six months or more, regardless of whether the crime committed was a felony or a misdemeanor.[4] Where the possible sentence is six months or less, the accused is not entitled to a jury trial unless it is authorized by state statute.

Most, if not all, jurisdictions place some limitations on the right to jury trial in criminal cases. Some states provide for a jury trial in all criminal cases; others provide this right to all but defendants in cases involving petty offenses such as minor gambling, traffic violations, and disorderly conduct; still others limit jury trials in accordance with the constitutional role of *Baldwin v. New York*.

The latest U.S. Supreme Court decision on jury trials occurred in 1989 in the case of *Blanton v. North Las Vegas*.[5] Here, the Court ruled unanimously that when a state defines the crime of drunk driving as a petty offense, the U.S. Constitution does not require that the defendant receive a jury trial. If however, a state treats drunk driving (driving under the influence) as a serious crime, a jury trial would be required. This decision upheld a Nevada law classifying drunk driving as a petty offense and similar procedures in at least five other jurisdictions in the United States.

JURY SIZE. Other important issues related to the defendant's rights in a criminal jury trial include the right to a jury consisting of 12 people or less and the right to a unanimous verdict.

The actual size of the jury has been a matter of great concern. Can a defendant be tried and convicted of a crime by a jury of fewer than 12 persons? Traditionally, 12 jurors have deliberated as the triers of fact in criminal cases involving misdemeanors or felonies. However, the U.S. Constitution does not specifically require a jury of 12 persons. As a result, in *Williams v. Florida* in 1970, the U.S. Supreme Court held that a **6-person jury** in a criminal trial does not deprive a defendant of the constitutional right to a jury trial.[6] The Court made clear that the 12-person panel is not a necessary ingredient of a trial by jury and upheld a Florida statute permitting the use of a 6-person jury in a robbery trial. The majority opinion in the *Williams* case traced the Court's rationale for its decision:

> We conclude, in short, as we began: the fact that a jury at common law was composed of precisely twelve is a historical accident, unnecessary to effect the purposes of the jury system and wholly without significance "except to mystics."[7]

Justice Byron White, writing further for the majority, said "In short, while sometime in the 14th century the size of the jury came to be fixed generally at 12, that particular feature of the jury system appears to have been a historical accident, unrelated to the great purpose which gave rise to the jury in the first place."[8]

On the basis of this decision, many states are using six-person juries in misdemeanor cases, and some states, such as Florida, Louisiana, and Utah, even use them in felony cases (except in capital offenses). In the *Williams* decision, Justice White emphasized, "We have occasion to determine what minimum number can still constitute a jury, but do not doubt that six is above that minimum."[9] The six-person jury can play an important role in the criminal justice system because it promotes court efficiency and also helps implement the defendant's rights to a speedy trial. It should be noted, however, that the Supreme Court has ruled that a less than six-person jury is unconstitutional[10] and that if a six-person jury is used in serious crimes, its verdict must be unanimous.[11]

In addition to the convention of 12-person juries in criminal trials, tradition held that the jurors' decision must be unanimous. In the case of *Apodica v. Oregon* (1972), the Supreme Court held that the Sixth and Fourteenth Amendments do not prohibit criminal convictions by less than unanimous jury verdicts in noncapital cases.[12] In the *Apodica* case, the Court upheld an Oregon statute requiring only 10 of 12 jurors to convict the defendant of assault with a deadly weapon, burglary, and grand larceny. It is not unusual to have such verdicts in civil matters, but much controversy remains regarding their use in the criminal process. Those in favor of less than unanimous verdicts argue, as the Court stated in *Apodica*, that unanimity does not materially contribute to the exercise of commonsense judgment. On the other hand, some persons believe that it would be easier for the prosecutor to obtain a guilty verdict if the law required only a substantial majority to convict the defendant. Today, the unanimous verdict remains the rule in most state jurisdictions and in the federal system.

The Right to Counsel at Trial

Mention has already been made in previous chapters of the defendant's right to counsel at numerous points in the criminal justice system. Through a series of leading U.S. Supreme Court decisions (*Powell v. Alabama* in 1932,[13] *Gideon v. Wainwright* in 1963,[14] and *Argersinger v. Hamlin* in 1972[15]), the right of a criminal defendant to have counsel in state trials has become a fundamental right in the American criminal justice system. Today, state courts must provide counsel at trial to indigent defendants who face the possibility of incarceration.

It is interesting to note the historical development of the law regarding right to counsel, for it shows the gradual process of decision making in the Supreme Court, as well as reiterates the relationship between the Bill of Rights and the **Fourteenth Amendment.** The Bill of Rights protects citizens against federal encroachment, while the Fourteenth Amendment provides that no state shall deprive any person of life, liberty, or property without due process of law. A difficult constitutional question has been whether the Fourteenth Amendment incorporates the Bill of Rights and makes its provisions binding on individual states. In *Powell v. Alabama* (also known as the *Scottsboro Boys* case), for example, nine young black men were charged in an Alabama court with raping

Defense attorneys Samuel Leibowitz, left, and George W. Chamlee, right, sit with their client Haywood Patterson, center, as the second trial of the Scottsboro nine begins in Decatur, Alabama, in 1933. Patterson holds a horseshoe and a rabbit foot for good luck.

two young white women. They were tried and convicted without the benefit of counsel. The U.S. Supreme Court concluded that the presence of a defense attorney is so vital to a fair trial that the failure of the Alabama trial court to appoint counsel was a denial of due process of law under the Fourteenth Amendment of the U.S. Constitution. In this instance, due process meant the right to counsel for defendants accused of committing a capital offense. The *Powell* decision is discussed in detail in the Law in Review on page 421.

Then, in the case of *Gideon v. Wainwright* some 30 years later, the Supreme Court in a unanimous and historic decision stated that while the Sixth Amendment does not explicitly lay down a rule binding on the states, right to counsel is so fundamental and ethical to a fair trial that states are obligated to abide by it under the Fourteenth Amendment's due process clause. Thus the Sixth Amendment requirement regarding right to counsel in the federal court system is also binding on the state criminal justice system. The Law in Review on page 422 examines the *Gideon* case.

The *Gideon* decision made it clear that a person charged with a felony in a state court has an absolute constitutional right to counsel. But, while some states applied the *Gideon* ruling to all criminal trials, others did not provide a defendant with an attorney in misdemeanor cases. Then, in 1972 in the momentous decision of *Argersinger v. Hamlin*, the Supreme Court held that no person can be imprisoned for any offense—whether classified as a petty offense, a misdemeanor, or a felony—unless he or she is offered representation by counsel at trial. (See the Law in Review on page 424.) The decision extended this right to virtually all defendants in state criminal prosecutions.

Closely related to the right to counsel is the right to free psychiatric services, which was at issue in the case of *Ake v. Oklahoma* (1985).[16] Here, a death row inmate appealed his conviction for murder on the ground that he had been found competent to stand trial even though he was mentally ill at the time and was unable to afford psychiatric services. The Supreme Court held it was an error to deny a visibly psychotic defendant the assistance of a psychiatrist. Although defense attorneys initially applauded the decision, they recognized

Powell v. Alabama (1932)

FACTS

 The defendants, nine black youths, were charged with the crime of raping two white women. While they were riding on a freight train through Alabama with two white girls as passengers, a fight broke out, and all the white male participants were thrown off the train. After the fight was reported, a sheriff's posse seized the defendants. All the black youths were taken to Scottsboro, Alabama, the county seat, where the two women claimed they were raped on the train. In an atmosphere of hostility in which the militia was called out to safeguard the prisoners, the "Scottsboro Boys" were indicted, arraigned, and held for trial. The pre-trial proceedings began when a lawyer expressed an interest in assisting the court as counsel for the defense. Separate trials were held for groups of the defendants, and in spite of the evidence to the contrary, eight were convicted and sentenced to death. The record of the trial indicated that the exact ages of the youths were unknown, that all were illiterate, and that they had been arrested, charged, convicted, and sentenced in an atmosphere of public hostility under close surveillance by the militia. They were not allowed to contact family or friends, and the court failed to give them reasonable time and the opportunity to secure legal counsel to represent them. It was also alleged that the two women were known to be prostitutes.

DECISION

The trial began six days after the indictment. The court did not ask the defendants whether they were able to obtain counsel, but simply appointed "all members of the bar" as counsel for the limited purpose of representing the defendants at the initial arraignment. One attorney assisted at the trial and represented the Scottsboro Boys in only a perfunctory, haphazard, and *pro forma* manner. The defendants were convicted of rape, a capital offense, and appealed their conviction on the ground that they had not been accorded the right to counsel in a trial involving a capital offense. The Supreme Court of Alabama upheld the convictions of seven of the eight defendants, and the case was eventually appealed to the U.S. Supreme Court on the ground that the defendants had been denied their due process rights under the Fourteenth Amendment. In a limited and narrow opinion, the Court agreed that the defendants had been denied their rights to counsel because they were not afforded a reasonable time to secure counsel to defend themselves against very serious charges. Accordingly, the Court held that because it was a capital case, the defendants' Fourteenth Amendment rights to due process had been violated, and reversed the judgments of the Alabama state courts.

SIGNIFICANCE OF THE CASE

The *Scottsboro Boys* case began in 1931, and appeals lasted until the 1940s. The case marked the beginning of a long line of cases that eventually would guarantee every criminal defendant in the criminal justice system the right to counsel. It also reveals the legal struggle and life and death ordeal of a group of black youths falsely accused of raping two white girls, who fought for almost a decade to secure their freedom. ■

---

that the right was limited because the defendant was unable to select a psychiatrist of his choice. The *Ake* decision guaranteed, however, that the most serious ill indigent defendants must be given psychiatric services to support their insanity defense. It was a first step in extending fundamental rights under *Gideon v. Wainwright* to the mentally ill in the criminal justice system.

The Right to Self-Representation

Another important question regarding the right to counsel is whether criminal defendants are guaranteed the right to represent themselves, that is, to act as their own lawyers. Prior to the U.S. Supreme Court decision in *Faretta v. California* in 1975,[17] defendants in most state courts and in the federal system

Gideon v. Wainwright (1963)

FACTS

Clarence Gideon was charged in a Florida state court with having broken and entered a poolroom with intent to commit a misdemeanor. This offense is a felony under Florida law. Appearing in court without funds and without a lawyer, the petitioner asked the court to appoint him counsel. The court replied that it could not appoint counsel because under Florida law the only time the court can appoint counsel for a defendant is when that person is charged with a capital offense.

Put to a trial before a jury, Gideon conducted his defense about as well as could be expected from a layman. He made an opening statement to the jury, cross-examined the state's witnesses, presented witnesses in his own defense, declined to testify himself, and made a short argument emphasizing his innocence of the charge contained in the information filed in the case. The jury returned a verdict of guilty, and Gideon was sentenced to serve five years in the Florida state prison.

Gideon filed a habeas corpus petition in the Florida Supreme Court attacking his conviction and sentence on the ground that the trial court's refusal to appoint counsel for him denied him rights guaranteed by the Constitution and the Bill of Rights. Relief was denied.

Gideon then filed an *in forma pauperis* appeal to the U.S. Supreme Court, which granted certiorori and appointed counsel to represent him. The Supreme Court took on this case to review its earlier decision in *Betts v. Brady* (1942), which held that the refusal to appoint counsel is not so "offensive to the common and fundamental ideas of fairness" as to amount to a denial of due process.

The issues faced by the Supreme Court were simple but of gigantic importance: (1) Is an indigent defendant charged in a state court with a noncapital felony entitled to the assistance of a lawyer under the due process clause of the Fourteenth Amendment? (2) Should *Betts v. Brady* be overruled?

DECISION

Justice Hugo Black delivered the opinion of the Court. "We accept *Betts v. Brady's* assumption, based as it was on our prior cases, that a provision of the Bill of Rights which is fundamental and essential to a fair trial is made obligatory upon the States by the Fourteenth Amendment. We think the Court in *Betts v. Brady* was wrong, however, in concluding that the Sixth Amendment's guarantee is not one of the fundamental rights. In our adversary system of criminal justice, any person brought into court, who is too poor to hire a lawyer, cannot be assured a fair trial unless counsel is provided for him. That government hires lawyers to prosecute and defendants who have the money to hire lawyers to defend, are the strongest indications of the widespread belief that lawyers in criminal court are necessities, not luxuries. The right of one charged with crime to counsel may not be deemed essential to fair trial in some countries, but it is in ours."

SIGNIFICANCE OF THE CASE

The U.S. Supreme Court unanimously overruled its earlier decision in *Betts v. Brady* and explicitly held that the right to counsel in criminal cases is fundamental and essential to a fair trial and as such applicable to the states by way of the Fourteenth Amendment. The *Gideon* decision thus guarantees the right to counsel in criminal cases in both federal and state proceedings. The refusal to appoint counsel for indigent defendants consequently violates the due process clause of the Fourteenth Amendment and the right to counsel of the Sixth Amendment. ∎

claimed the right to proceed **pro se,** or for themselves, by reason of federal and state statutes and on state constitutional grounds. This permitted defendants to choose between hiring counsel or conducting their own defense. Whether a constitutional right to represent oneself in a criminal prosecution existed remained an open question until the *Faretta* decision.

The defendant, Anthony Faretta, was charged with grand theft in Los Angeles County, California. Before the date of his trial, he requested that he be permitted to represent himself. The judge told Faretta that he believed this would be a mistake, but accepted his waiver of counsel. The judge then held a hearing to inquire into Faretta's ability to conduct his own defense and subsequently ruled that Faretta had not made an intelligent and knowing waiver of his right to the assistance of counsel. As a result, the judge appointed a public defender to represent Faretta, who was brought to trial, found guilty, and sentenced to prison. He appealed, claiming that he had a constitutional right to self-representation.

Upon review, the U.S. Supreme Court recognized Faretta's *pro se* right on a constitutional basis, while making it conditional on a showing that the defendant could competently, knowingly, and intelligently waive his right to counsel. The Court's decision was based on the belief that the right of self-representation finds support in the structure of the Sixth Amendment, as well as in English and colonial jurisprudence from which the amendment emerged.[18] Thus, in forcing Faretta to accept counsel against his will, the California trial court deprived him of his constitutional right to conduct his own defense.

It is important to recognize that the *Faretta* case dealt only with the constitutional right to self-representation. It did not provide guidelines for administering the right during the criminal process.[19]

Today, a defendant in a criminal trial is able to waive the right to the assistance of counsel. Generally, however, the courts have encouraged defendants to accept counsel so that criminal trials may proceed in an orderly and fair manner. Where defendants ask to be permitted to represent themselves and are found competent to do so, the court normally approves their requests. The defendants in these cases are almost always cautioned by the courts against self-representation. When *pro se* defendants' actions are disorderly and disruptive, the court can terminate their right to represent themselves.

Joint representation by counsel and defendant, in which the attorney would be retained on a standby basis, has been suggested as an alternative to the exclusive use of either representation by counsel or self-representation.[20] However, under current federal and state law, the defendant who has waived the right to counsel and is proceeding with the trial *pro se* is not entitled to standby counsel.

The Right to Speedy Trial

The requirement of the right to counsel at trial in virtually all criminal cases often causes delays in the formal processing of defendants through the court system. Counsel usually seeks to safeguard the interests of the accused, and in so doing may employ a variety of legal devices—pretrial motions, plea negotiations, trial procedures, and appeals—that require time and extend the decision-making period in a particular case. The involvement of counsel, along with inefficiencies in the court process—such as the frequent granting of continuances, poor scheduling procedures, and the abuse of time by court personnel—has made the problem of delay in criminal cases a serious practice and constitutional issue. As the American Bar Association's *Standards Relating to Speedy Trial* state, "Congestion in the trial courts of this country, particularly in urban centers, is currently one of the major problems of judicial administration."[21]

The Sixth Amendment guarantees a criminal defendant the right to a speedy trial in federal prosecutions. This right has been made applicable to the states by the decision in *Klopfer v. North Carolina* (1967).[22] In this case, the defendant Klopfer was charged with criminal trespass. His original trial ended in a

Argersinger v. Hamlin (1972)

FACTS

The indigent defendant was charged in a Florida state court with carrying a concealed weapon, an offense for which a maximum sentence of six months imprisonment, a fine of $1,000, or both could be imposed. At his trial the defendant was not represented by counsel. He was convicted and sentenced by the judge to 90 days in jail. The defendant brought a habeas corpus petition to the Florida Supreme Court, arguing that he was not appointed counsel as an indigent defendant and consequently could not present his defense to the charges against him. The defendant's claim was rejected by the Florida Supreme Court in a 4 to 3 vote, holding that the right to court-appointed counsel extended only to trials for nonpetty offenses punishable by more than six months imprisonment.

The U.S. Supreme Court granted certiorari. It was faced with the question of whether the Sixth Amendment's right to counsel, applicable to the states by way of the Fourteenth Amendment (see *Gideon v. Wainwright* [1963]), extended to include the right to counsel in misdemeanors.

DECISION

The U.S. Supreme Court held that the indigent defendant has a right to counsel in all criminal cases for which he could be jailed. The Court stated that because prosecution for crimes punishable by imprisonment for less than six months may be tried without a jury, this does not mean that they may be tried without a lawyer. Assistance of counsel is often requisite to the very existence of a fair trial. In a misdemeanor case, the Court emphasized, the questions that can lead to imprisonment even for a brief period can be as complex as those leading to a sentence for a felony.

SIGNIFICANCE OF THE CASE

The U.S. Supreme Court was asked to decide how far the right to have court-appointed counsel for indigent defendants would extend. In other words, did the *Gideon* decision include the right to counsel in all criminal cases? The Court specifically held that this right to counsel should extend to all criminal cases in which the defendant could face imprisonment. It was not a matter of petty offenses versus felonies, but a matter of whether imprisonment could be imposed for the crime charged. ■

mistrial, and the defendant sought to determine if and when the government intended to retry him. The prosecutor asked the court to take a *"nolle prosequi with leave,"* a legal device discharging the defendant but allowing the government to prosecute him in the future. The U.S. Supreme Court held that the effort by the government to postpone Klopfer's trial indefinitely without reason denied him the right to a speedy trial guaranteed by the Sixth and Fourteenth Amendments.

In *Klopfer* the Supreme Court emphasized the importance of the speedy trial in the criminal process by stating that this right was "as fundamental as any of the rights secured by the Sixth Amendment."[23] Its primary purposes are

1. To improve the credibility of the trial by seeking to have witnesses available for testimony as early as possible
2. To reduce the anxiety for the defendant in awaiting trial as well as avoid pretrial detention
3. To avoid extensive pretrial publicity and questionable conduct of public officials that would influence the defendant's right to a fair trial
4. To avoid any delay that can affect the defendant's ability to defend himself or herself

What is meant by the term **speedy trial** has been the subject of much litigation. First of all, the speedy trial guarantee is not initiated when the defendant is first accused of a crime. In *United States v. Marion* (1971), the Supreme Court held that the speedy trial guarantee takes effect only on "either a formal indictment or information or else when the actual restraints [are] imposed by arrest and holding to answer a criminal charge.[24] In other words, the time period that determines whether the defendant receives a speedy trial begins only after the defendant has been arrested or when formal charges have been made. There are, for example, no time provisions in the speedy trial guarantee covering the period during which the police must discover, investigate, or apprehend persons accused of a crime.[25] Law enforcement officials are therefore not required to curtail criminal investigations, even though they may have sufficient evidence to bring charges against the accused.

A second question regarding the speedy trial is how to determine whether a delay violates the constitutional requirements of the Sixth Amendment. In *Barker v. Wingo* (1972), the Supreme Court identified certain factors to be considered when determining if the speedy trial requirements have been met.[26] These are (1) the length of the delay, (2) the reason for the delay, (3) the defendant's claim of the right to a speedy trial, and (4) prejudice toward the defendant. In *Barker*, the defendant's trial was delayed for over five years after his arrest while the government sought numerous continuances. When Willie Barker was eventually brought to trial, he was convicted and given a life sentence. The defendant did not ask for a speedy trial and did not assert that his right to a speedy trial had been violated until three years after his arrest. Based on an evaluation of these factors in relation to his case, the Court held that Barker had not been deprived of his due process right to a speedy trial.

Barker is a significant case because it constitutionally rejects (1) the *fixed time rule* and (2) the *demand waiver rule* as methods of measuring a speedy trial. The **fixed time rule** requires that a defendant be offered a trial within a specific period of time, while the **demand waiver rule** restricts consideration of the issue to those cases in which the defendant has demanded a speedy trial. Instead, the Supreme Court took the approach that the speedy trial right can be determined by a test balancing the actions of the government and the accused on a case-by-case basis.

DEFINITION OF SPEEDY TRIAL. Because the number of persons accused of crimes continues to be great, while the number of courtrooms and judges is limited, the government has been forced to deal with the problem of how to meet the constitutional requirement of a speedy trial. In 1967, the President's Commission on Law Enforcement and the Administration of Justice suggested that nine months would be a reasonable period of time in which to litigate the typical criminal felony case through appeal. The process from arrest through trial would involve four months, and the decision of an appeals court an additional five months.[27] Then in 1973 the National Advisory Commission on Criminal Justice Standards and Goals recommended that the period from the arrest of the defendant in a felony prosecution to the beginning of the trial generally should not be longer than 60 days and that the period from arrest to trial in a misdemeanor prosecution should be 30 days or less.[28] Figure 13.1 summarizes the time frame suggested by the National Advisory Commission for the prompt processing of criminal cases. This time frame is the standard in many jurisdictions today.

Today, most states and the federal government have statutes fixing the period of time during which an accused must be brought to trial. These ensure that a person's trial cannot be unduly delayed and that the suspect cannot be held

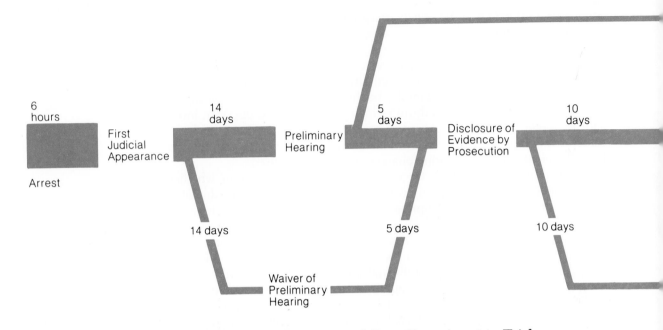

6 hours

Arrest

First Judicial Appearance

14 days

14 days

Waiver of Preliminary Hearing

Preliminary Hearing

5 days

5 days

Disclosure of Evidence by Prosecution

10 days

10 days

■ *FIGURE 13.1* **The Litigated Case: From Arrest to Trial**

SOURCE: National Advisory Commission on Criminal Justice Standards and Goals, *Courts* (Washington, D.C.: U.S. Government Printing Office, 1973), pp. xx–xxi.

in custody indefinitely. Congress enacted the **Speedy Trial Act** of 1974 to guarantee the accused the right to a speedy trial by establishing the following time limits: (1) an information or indictment charging a person with a crime must be filed within 30 days from the time of arrest; (2) the arraignment must be held within 10 days from the time of the information or indictment; and (3) the trial must be held within 60 days after the arraignment.[29] This means that the accused must be brought to trial in the federal system within 100 days. Other special provisions of the Speedy Trial Act include the gradual phasing in of time standards, the use of fines against defense counsels for causing delays, and the allocation of funds with which to plan speedy trial programs in the federal judicial districts. The Speedy Trial Act was amended in 1979 to give further precision to the guarantee of a speedy trial and to encourage state jurisdictions to adopt similar procedures. Many state speedy trial statutes provide even shorter time limits for cases when a defendant is detained in jail.

In addition, many jurisdictions give trial preference to criminal matters and to cases where the defendant is in custody. This practice is one of the major recommendations of the American Bar Association's *Standards Relating to Speedy Trial*:

> *Priorities in scheduling criminal cases.* To effectuate the right of the accused to a speedy trial and the interest of the public in prompt disposition of criminal cases, insofar as is practicable; (a) the trial of criminal cases should be given preference over civil cases; and (b) the trial of defendants in custody and defendants whose pretrial liberty is reasonably believed to present unusual risks should be given preference over other criminal cases.[30]

Although entitled to a speedy trial, the accused can waive this right either by pleading guilty or by failing to demand a prompt trial. However, if the accused

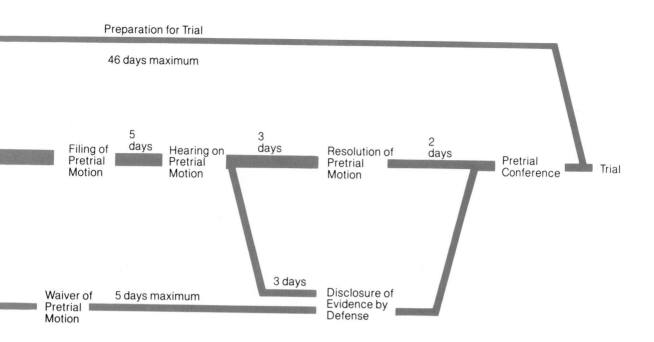

Preparation for Trial

46 days maximum

Filing of Pretrial Motion — 5 days — Hearing on Pretrial Motion — 3 days — Resolution of Pretrial Motion — 2 days — Pretrial Conference — Trial

Waiver of Pretrial Motion — 5 days maximum — 3 days — Disclosure of Evidence by Defense

makes a claim under the Sixth Amendment and it is upheld, the consequences of denying a speedy trial may involve the complete dismissal of the charges against the defendant. Although this might seem extreme, the U.S. Supreme Court in *Strunk v. United States* (1973) held that the restraint on the defendant's liberty, as well as his uncertainty and anxiety over his guilt or innocence, made dismissal of the charges appropriate.[31]

In a very important recent case involving the federal Speedy Trial Act, *United States v. Taylor* (1988), the Supreme Court considered the legality of a U.S. District Court's discretion to dismiss charges against a defendant who failed to appear for trial, rather than permit reprosecution.[32] The District Court found that the government had exhibited "lackadaisical" behavior and slow processing in returning the defendant for trial. According to the District Court, 15 nonexcludable days in the speedy trial time clock had passed since the defendant's failure to appear for his trial, and therefore dismissal of the original indictment was mandated. But the Supreme Court found that the District Court had ignored other relevant facts, such as the brevity of the delay, lack of prejudice to the defendant, and the defendant's own illegal contribution to the delay. Thus, according to the Supreme Court, barring reprosecution as a remedy was an abuse of the District Court's discretion.

■ Fair Trial v. Free Press

Every person charged with a crime also has a fundamental right to a fair trial. What does it mean to have a fair trial in the criminal justice system? A fair trial is one before an impartial judge and jury, in an environment of judicial restraint, orderliness, and fair decision making. Although it is not expressly stated in the U.S. Constitution, the right of the accused to a fair trial is guaranteed by the due process clauses of the Fifth and Fourteenth Amendments. This fair trial right may be violated in a number of ways. Such actions as a hostile courtroom crowd, improper pressure on witnesses, or any behavior that produces prejudice toward the accused can preclude a fair trial. When, for example, a defendant was required to go to trial in prison clothing, the U.S. Supreme Court found a violation of the due process clause of the Fourteenth Amendment.[33] Adverse pretrial publicity can also deny a defendant a fair trial. The release of premature evidence by the prosecutor, extensive and critical reporting by the news media, and vivid and uncalled for details in "talking indictments" all can prejudice a defendant's case.

Recently, one of the controversial issues involving the conduct of a trial has been the apparent conflict between the constitutional guarantees of fair trial and freedom of the press. When there is wide pretrial publicity, as in the Jean Harris murder case, the John Delorean case, the Atlanta child killings, and other cases, whether an accused can have a fair trial as guaranteed by the Fifth, Sixth, and Fourteenth Amendments has been a matter of great concern.

The murder conviction of Dr. Sam Shepard over 20 years ago was reversed by the U.S. Supreme Court because negative publicity generated by the government denied Shepard a fair trial.[34] More recently, in one of the most highly publicized trials in American history, Claus von Bulow was acquitted of attempted murder after two trials.[35] Both the prosecution and the defense used the media to reflect their side. Press conferences, leaked news stories, daily television and radio coverage all contributed to a media sideshow. Even jury sequestration was not successful since many of the jurors had prior knowledge of the case. In the end, the media played a critical role in both the conviction and the acquittal of the defendant.

Judges involved in newsworthy criminal cases have attempted to place restraints on press coverage to preserve the defendant's right to a fair trial; at the same time, it is generally believed that the press has a constitutional right to provide news coverage. In the politically significant and highly publicized trial of Oliver North, U.S. District Court Judge Gerhard Gesell struggled with the fair trial/free press issue. North's lawyers argued that the defendant's constitutional right to a fair trial and complete defense required the disclosure of classified information. The U.S. Justice Department showed that national security concerns prevented certain material from becoming public, and the court was forced to dismiss conspiracy and theft charges against North, although he was subsequently convicted on other criminal matters. In light of such problems, the U.S. Supreme Court approved an agreement designed to protect classified data so that North's trial in regard to the Iran-Contra affair could proceed.

Some critics of the media have even suggested that the press should be prohibited from reporting about ongoing criminal trials. Such an approach, however, would inhibit the role of the press in monitoring the criminal justice system and violate the constitutional right to a free press under the First Amendment. Public information about criminal trials, the judicial system, and other areas of government is an essential and indispensable characteristic of a free society. At the same time, trial by the media violates a defendant's right to a fair trial.

The Law of Fair Trial

The U.S. Supreme Court dealt with the fair trial/free press issue in the case of *Nebraska Press Association v. Stuart* (1976).[36] The Court ruled unconstitutional a trial judge's order prohibiting the press from reporting the confessions implicating the defendant in the crime. The Court's decision was based primarily on the fact that "prior restraints on speech and publication are the most serious and least tolerable infringement on First Amendment rights."[37]

In *Gannett Co. v. DePasquale* (1979), the Court was asked to decide if the public had an independent constitutional right of access to a pretrial judicial hearing even though all the parties agreed to closure to guarantee a fair trial.[38] Justice Potter Stewart, writing for the Court, said that the trial court was correct in finding that the press had a right of access of constitutional dimensions, but that this right was outweighed by the defendant's right to a fair trial.[39] In other words, the Court balanced competing social interests and found that denial of access by the public did not violate the First, Sixth, or Fourteenth Amendment rights of the defendant. The interest of justice requires that the defendant's case should not be jeopardized, and the desire for a fair trial far outweighed the public's right of access to a pretrial suppression hearing. The *Gannett* decision is not ordinarily cited as precedent to determine whether a right of access to trials is constitutionally guaranteed, since the Court believes that motion hearings are not trials.

The question of the **First Amendment** right of access to preliminary hearings was raised again in the case of *Press-Enterprise Co. v. Superior Court* (1986).[40] The defendant, charged with murder, agreed to have the preliminary hearing closed to the press and the public. But the Supreme Court said that closure is permissible under the First Amendment only if there is a substantial probability that the defendant's right to a fair trial would be prejudiced by publicity that closed proceedings would prevent. According to the Court, preliminary hearings have traditionally been open to the public and should remain so.

Right to Public Trial

The U.S. Supreme Court has also interpreted the First Amendment to mean that members of the press (and the public) have a right to attend trials. The most important case on this issue is *Richmond Newspapers Inc. v. Virginia* (1980).[41] Here the Supreme Court clearly established that criminal trials must remain public. Because of its significance, the case is summarized in the Law in Review on page 430. Following the *Richmond Newspapers* case, the Supreme Court extended the right of the press to attend trials involving even highly sensitive, sexually related matters in which the victim was under 18 years of age.[42] The right was further extended to the selection and questioning of potential jurors[43] and to the hearing on pretrial motions.[44]

Although the Court has ruled that criminal trials are open to the press, the right to a public trial is basically for the benefit of the accused.[45] The familiar language of the Sixth Amendment clearly states that "the accused shall enjoy the right to a speedy and public trial." Underlying this provision is the belief that a trial in the criminal justice system must be a public activity. The amendment is rooted in the principle that justice cannot survive behind walls of silence.[46] It was enacted because the Framers of the Constitution distrusted secret trials and arbitrary proceedings. In the 1948 case of *In re Oliver*, for instance, the Supreme Court held that the secrecy of a criminal contempt trial violated the right of the defendant to a public trial under the Fourteenth Amendment.[47] In *Oliver* the Court recognized the constitutional guarantee of a public trial for the defendant in state and federal courts. Three decades later

Richmond Newspapers Inc. v. Virginia (1980)

FACTS

Defendant Stevenson was indicted and convicted for the murder of a hotel manager in 1975. The Virginia Supreme Court reversed the conviction in 1977, holding that a bloodstained shirt was improperly admitted into evidence. Stevenson was retried a second and third time when prospective jurors read about his previous trials in the newspaper.

When Stevenson was tried a fourth time in 1978, his counsel moved that the trial be closed to the public. He felt there was a problem with information passing between the jurors and that the media might publish inaccurate news reports.

When the judge ordered the trial closed to the public, two reporters with Richmond Newspapers Inc. were present in the courtroom. When a hearing was held on a motion to vacate the closure order and this hearing was treated as part of the trial, the reporters were ordered to leave the courtroom. They complied.

The court subsequently denied the motion to vacate and ordered the trial to continue with the press and public excluded. At the close of the Commonwealth of Virginia's evidence, the court ordered a directed verdict of not guilty of murder. Appellants (Richmond Newspapers) petitioned the Virginia Supreme Court (for a writ of mandamus) and filed an appeal from the trial court's closure order, but the court denied the petition for appeal. Appellants then filed a petition with the U.S. Supreme Court.

DECISION

The U.S. Supreme Court was presented with the question of whether the right of the public and press to attend criminal trials is guaranteed under the U.S. Constitution. The Court said:

The origins of the proceeding which has become the modern criminal trial in Anglo-American justice can be traced back beyond reliable historical records. We need not here review all details of its development, but a summary of that history is instructive. What is significant for present purposes is that throughout its evolution, the trial has been open to all who cared to observe.

In the days before the Norman Conquest, cases in England were generally brought before moots, such as the local court of the hundred or the county court, which were attended by the freemen of the community. . . . Somewhat like modern jury duty, attendance at these early meetings was compulsory on the part of the freemen, who were called upon to render judgment. . . .

With the gradual evolution of the jury system in the years after the Norman Conquest . . . the duty of all freemen to attend trials to render judgment was relaxed, but there is no indication that criminal trials did not remain public. From these early times, although great changes in courts took place one thing remained constant: the public character of the trial at which guilt or innocence was decided. One of the most conspicuous features of English justice, that all judicial trials are held in open court, appears to have been the rule in England from time immemorial. And all contemporary writings in America confirm the recognition of the openness of those who wish to attend such a trial. From this history, the Court believed a presumption of openness exists in the very nature of the criminal trial itself.

The Court also said that the First Amendment prohibits governments from abridging freedom of the press. This means that government cannot summarily close courtroom doors that had been open to the public since that amendment was adopted. The explicit guarantees of the right to speak and publish concerning what takes place at a trial would lose meaning if access to observe the trial were cut off arbitrarily.

Consequently, the Court said that the right to attend criminal trials is implicit in the guarantees of the First Amendment, and it reversed the judgment of the state supreme court.

SIGNIFICANCE OF THE CASE

The *Richmond Newspapers'* decision established that the First Amendment requires that the public be allowed the freedom to attend criminal trials. Although there may be an occasion where all or part of a criminal trial may be closed to the public, this requires an overriding interest articulated in the findings of the trial court. The Court's decision does not mean that the First Amendment rights of the public are absolute. Just as a government may impose reasonable restrictions, so may a trial judge, in the interest of the fair administration of justice. ■

the *Richmond Newspapers* decision clearly affirmed the right of the public and the press to attend criminal trials.

Other fair trial/free press issues remain, however. Whether jury trials should be televised, for instance, is a controversial question in the criminal justice system today. Many state courts permit such coverage, but the use of television cameras, video recorders, and still photography is banned in the federal court system.[48] In addition, William Rehnquist, the chief justice of the United States, opposes televising Supreme Court proceedings. Yet, the truth is that televising criminal proceedings has significant advantages. Judges would be better prepared; the public would be informed about important legal issues; and the proceedings would provide an educational function that would offset the simplistic views offered by popular movies and television programs such as "The People's Court," "Miller's Court," and "L.A. Law."

The extent to which judges, witnesses, and the accused would be influenced by the use of modern technology in the courtroom remains unknown, however, and is the major argument against adopting complete and total media coverage. In extreme cases, the judge might clear the courtroom where violence is threatened, or where the rights of the accused and the state are at risk. Also, under the statutes of different jurisdictions, spectators and the press, for example, might be excluded from the trial of juvenile cases, certain sordid sex crimes, or national security offenses. Regardless of the kind of crime committed, a defendant is always permitted to have family, close associates, and legal counsel at his or her trial. In the final analysis, the Supreme Court has held, in *Chandler v. Florida* (1981), that, subject to certain safeguards, a state may allow electronic media coverage by television stations and still photography of public criminal proceedings over the objection of the defendant in a criminal trial.[49] Although the Supreme Court did not maintain in *Chandler* that the press had a constitutional right to televise trials, it left it up to state courts to decide whether they wished trials televised in their jurisdictions.

A state may allow the news media to televise a trial unless there are specific reasons why coverage would be improper or inappropriate.

The controversy surrounding the issue of televising trials has prompted bar and press groups to develop standards in an attempt to find an acceptable middle ground between the First and Sixth Amendment rights concerning public trials. To be sure, the defendant has a constitutional right to a public trial, but it is equally imperative that the media exercise its First Amendment rights. And, above all, the court must seek to protect the rights of the accused to a fair trial by an unbiased jury.

■ The Trial Process

The trial of a criminal case is a formal process conducted in a specific and orderly fashion in accordance with rules of criminal law, procedure, and evidence. Unlike what transpires in popular television programs involving lawyers—where witnesses are often asked leading and prejudicial questions and where judges go far beyond their supervisory role—the modern criminal trial is a complicated and often time-consuming technical affair. It is a structured **adversary proceeding** in which both the prosecution and defense follow specific procedures and argue the merits of their cases before the judge and jury. Each side seeks to present its case in the most favorable light. When possible, the prosecutor and the defense attorney will object to evidence they consider damaging to their individual points of view. The prosecutor will use direct testimony, physical evidence, and a confession, if available, to convince the jury that the accused is guilty beyond a reasonable doubt. On the other hand, the defense attorney will rebut the government's case with his or her own evidence, make certain that the rights of the criminal defendant under the federal and state constitutions are considered during all phases of the trial, and determine whether an appeal is appropriate if the client is found guilty. The defense attorney will use his or her skill at cross-examination to discredit government witnesses: perhaps they have changed their statements from the time they gave them to the police; perhaps their memory is faulty; perhaps their background is unsavory, and so on. From the beginning of the process to its completion, the judge promotes an orderly and fair administration of the criminal trial.

Although each jurisdiction in the United States has its own trial procedures, all jurisdictions conduct criminal trials in a generally similar fashion. The basic steps of the criminal trial, which proceed in an established order, are described in this section.

Jury Selection

Jurors are selected randomly in both civil and criminal cases from tax assessment or voter registration lists within each court's jurisdiction.

Few states impose qualifications on those called for jury service. Over 30 states mandate a residency requirement.[50] There is also little uniformity in the amount of time served by jurors, with jurors serving anywhere from one day to months, depending on the nature of the trial. In addition, most jurisdictions also prohibit convicted felons from jury service, as well as others exempted by statute, such as public officials, medical doctors, and attorneys. The initial list of persons chosen, which is called **venire,** or jury array, provides the state with a group of potentially capable citizens able to serve on a jury. Many states, by rule of law, review the venire to eliminate unqualified persons and to exempt those who by reason of their professions are not allowed to be jurors; this latter group may include (but is not limited to) physicians, clergy, and government officials. The actual jury selection process begins with those remaining on the list.

The court clerk, who handles the administrative affairs of the trial— including the processing of the complaint, evidence, and other documents— randomly selects enough names (sometimes from a box) to fill the required number of places on the jury. In most cases, the jury in a criminal trial consists of 12 persons, with two alternate jurors standing by to serve should one of the regular jurors be unable to complete the trial.

Once the prospective jurors are chosen, the process of **voir dire** is begun, in which all persons selected are questioned by both the prosecution and the defense to determine their appropriateness to sit on the trial. They are examined under oath by the government, the defense, and sometimes the judge about their backgrounds, occupations, residences, and possible knowledge or interest in the case. A juror who acknowledges any bias for or prejudice against the defendant—if the defendant is a friend or relative, for example, or if the juror has already formed an opinion about the case—is removed for "cause" and replaced with another. Thus any prospective juror who declares he or she is unable to be impartial and render a verdict solely on the evidence to be presented at the trial may be removed by attorneys for either the prosecution or the defense. Because normally no limit is placed on the number of **challenges for cause** that can be exercised, it often takes considerable time to select a jury for controversial and highly publicized criminal cases.

Jury selection in the famous 1989 Iran-Contra trial of Oliver North lasted for over three months, and hundreds of prospective jurors were examined. The *voir dire* process was made especially difficult because the trial judge insisted on disqualifying all jurors who had heard or read anything about the defendant's public testimony before congressional committees. According to some experts, this is an example of an extreme application of the impartiality requirement (no knowledge of the case) as opposed to simply determining that a juror lacks any prejudice toward the accused.[51]

PEREMPTORY CHALLENGES. In addition to challenges for cause, both the prosecution and the defense are allowed **peremptory challenges,** which enable the attorneys to excuse jurors for no particular reason or for reasons that remain undisclosed. For example, a prosecutor might not want a bartender as a juror in a drunk driving case, believing that a person with that occupation would be sympathetic to the accused. Or the defense attorney might excuse a prospective male juror because the attorney prefers to have a predominantly female jury. The number of peremptory challenges permitted is limited by state statute and often varies by case and jurisdiction.

The peremptory challenge has been criticized by legal experts who question the fairness and propriety with which it has been employed.[52] The most significant criticism is that it has been used to exclude blacks from hearing cases in which the defendant is also black. In *Swain v. Alabama* (1964), the U.S. Supreme Court upheld the use of peremptory challenges in isolated cases to exclude jurors by reason of racial or other group affiliations.[53] This policy was extremely troublesome because it allowed what seemed to be legally condoned discrimination against minority group members. Consequently, in 1986 the

Jurors take criminal trials seriously and reach decisions not too different from those of legal professionals.

Court struck down the *Swain* doctrine in *Batson v. Kentucky*.[54] Because of the importance of this case, it is set out in the Law in Review on page 435. James Archer, in a recent analysis of the peremptory challenge since the *Batson* decision, suggested that this legal procedure can still be used fairly with improved systematic jury selection, appropriate judicial discretion, and the identification of *prima facia* constitutional violations in the jury process.[55] Other authors believe that if the *Batson* standard is to work and maximize equal protection under the law, its success depends primarily on the discretion of the trial judge.[56]

IMPARTIAL JURIES. The Sixth Amendment provides for the right to a speedy and public trial by an impartial jury. This concept of an impartial jury has always been controversial. For one thing, research indicates that jury members often have little in common with their criminal "peers." Moreover, studies of jury deliberations indicate that the dynamics of decision making often involve pressure to get the case over with and convince recalcitrant jurors to join the majority. Nevertheless, jurors also appear to take cases seriously and reach decisions not too different from those made by legal professionals.[57] Judges, for instance, often agree with jury decisions. However, jurors often have problems understanding judicial instructions and legal rule-making in criminal trials.

The U.S. Supreme Court has sought to ensure compliance with this constitutional mandate of impartiality by decisions eliminating racial discrimination in jury selection. For instance, in *Ham v. South Carolina* in 1973, the Court held that the defense counsel of a black civil rights leader was entitled to question each juror on the issue of racial prejudice.[58] In *Taylor v. Louisiana* in 1975, the Court overturned the conviction of a man by an all-male jury because a Louisiana statute allowed women but not men to exempt themselves from jury duty.[59]

The issue of the racial composition of the jury is particularly acute in cases involving the death penalty. In 1986 the Court ruled in *Turner v. Murray* that a defendant accused of an interracial crime in which the death penalty is an option can insist that prospective jurors be informed of the victim's race and be questioned on the issue of their racial bias. A trial judge who refuses this line of questioning during *voir dire* risks having the death penalty vacated but not the reversal of the conviction.[60] These and other similar decisions have had the effect of providing safeguards against jury bias.

Jury selection can be made even more difficult in capital punishment cases where jurors are asked their views about the death penalty. In *Lockhart v. McCree* (1986), the Supreme Court decided that jurors who strongly oppose capital punishment may be disqualified from determining a defendant's guilt or innocence in capital cases.[61]

The *Lockhart* decision raises certain questions, however. Juries are not supposed to represent only one position or another. An impartial jury of one's peers is rooted in the idea that the defendant should be judged by a cross section of members of the local community. Their views should not be disproportionate on any one issue. Consequently, a ruling such as *Lockhart* could theoretically result in higher conviction rates in murder cases.

Defendants often appeal their convictions, alleging jury bias, but are ordinarily unsuccessful with this approach. But a recent federal appeals court decision held that if a juror deliberately lies during the jury selection process, the defendant's conviction can be vacated.[62] What about the opinions of jurors

Batson v. Kentucky (1986)

FACTS

During the criminal trial of a black defendant in Kentucky, the prosecutor used his peremptory challenges to remove four blacks from the venire. Consequently, an all-white jury was selected. Although defense counsel protested that this deprived Batson, his client, of a fair jury representing a cross section of the community, the trial judge denied the motion. Batson was ultimately convicted. The Kentucky Supreme Court relied on the *Swain* doctrine in upholding the case, arguing that the defense did not demonstrate systematic exclusion of black jurors in other cases.

DECISION

The U.S. Supreme Court held that defendants have no right to a jury composed of members in whole or in part of their own race. However, the Fourteenth Amendment's Equal Protection Clause guarantees that the state will not exclude jury members on account of race or under the false assumption that members of the defendant's own race cannot render a fair verdict. This would also discriminate against the jury members and undermine public confidence in the jury system. Thus, the state is forbidden to preempt jurors solely on the basis of their race.

In addition, if defendants wish to show racism in the use of the peremptory challenge, they no longer must show a pattern of discrimination as the *Swain* doctrine indicated. Defendants may show purposeful racial discrimination in selection of the venire by relying solely on the facts of their own case. They must show that they are members of a particular race and that the prosecutor has exercised his or her peremptory challenges to remove

members of that racial group from the jury. They may rely on the fact that such practices permit "those to discriminate who have a mind to discriminate." The burden is then on the prosecutor to come forward with a neutral explanation for challenging the jurors.

Finally, the Court argued that the peremptory challenge can still play an important role in the adversarial process. It can be used in most criminal cases as long as it is not employed in a racially biased manner.

SIGNIFICANCE

Batson strikes down a legal procedure that was out of synch with modern ideas of justice and fairness. It prevents an element of racial discrimination from entering into the trial stage of justice, which is one of the cornerstones of American freedom. Yet it preserves, under controlled circumstances, the use of the peremptory challenge, which is an integral part of the jury selection process. ■

---

in capital cases? Or asking jurors about racial bias? And what are the implications where jurors fail to disclose personal relationships? The Supreme Court has not yet answered fully all of the important questions regarding the role and qualifications of jurors in criminal cases regarding impartiality.

Opening Statements

Once the jury has been selected and the criminal complaint has been read to the jurors by the court clerk, the prosecutor and the defense attorney may each make an opening statement about the case to the jury. The purpose of the prosecutor's statement is to introduce the judge and the jury to the particular criminal charges, to outline the facts, and to describe how the government will prove the defendant guilty beyond a reasonable doubt. The defense attorney reviews the case and indicates how the defense intends to show that the accused is innocent of the charge.

Usually, the defense attorney makes an opening statement after the government reads its case. In some jurisdictions, the court in its discretion can permit the defense to make opening remarks before any evidence is introduced. But,

The presentation of evidence is made through the cross-examination of witnesses.

for the most part, present rules dictate that the prosecutor is entitled to offer an opening statement first.

The opening statement gives the jury a concise overview of the evidence that is to follow. In the opening statement neither attorney is allowed to make prejudicial remarks or inflammatory statements or mention irrelevant facts. Both are free, however, to identify what they will eventually prove by way of evidence, which includes witnesses, physical evidence, and the use of expert testimony. The actual content of the statement is left to the sound discretion of the trial judge. As a general rule, the opening statements used in jury trials are important because they provide the finders of fact (the jury) with an initial summary of the case. They are infrequently used and less effective in **bench trials,** however, where juries are not employed. Most lower court judges have handled hundreds of similar cases and do not need the benefit of an opening statement.

Presentation of the Prosecutor's Evidence

Following the opening statements, the government begins its case by presenting evidence to the court through its witnesses. Those called as witnesses—such as police officers, victims, or expert witnesses—provide testimony via **direct examination.** During direct examination the prosecutor questions the witness to reveal the facts believed pertinent to the government case. Testimony involves what the witness actually saw, heard, or touched and does not include opinions. However, a witness' opinion can be given in certain situations, such as when describing the motion of a vehicle or indicating whether a defendant appeared to act intoxicated or insane. Witnesses may also qualify because of their professions as experts on a particular subject relevant to the case; for example, a psychiatrist may testify as to a defendant's mental capacity at the time of the crime.

After the prosecutor finishes questioning a witness, the defense cross-examines the same witness by asking questions in an attempt to clarify the defendant's role in the crime. The right to cross-examine witnesses is an essential part of a trial, and unless extremely unusual circumstances exist (such as a person's being hospitalized), statements will not be considered unless they are made in court and open for question. For example, in a recent case, *Lee v. Illinois* (1986), the U.S. Supreme Court ruled that a confession made to police by a co-defendant in a criminal trial cannot be used in court unless the person making the confession is available for **cross-examination.**[63] If desired, the prosecutor may seek a second direct examination after the defense attorney has completed cross-examination; this allows the prosecutor to ask additional questions about information brought out during cross-examination. Finally, the defense attorney may then question or cross-examine the witness once again. All witnesses for the trial will be sworn in and questioned in the same basic manner.

Types of Evidence at a Criminal Trial

In addition to testimonial evidence given by police officers, citizens, and experts, the court also acts on **real,** or nonverbal, **evidence.**[64] Real evidence often consists of the exhibits taken into the jury room for review by the jury. A revolver that may have been in the defendant's control at the time of a murder, tools in the possession of a suspect charged with a burglary, and a bottle allegedly holding narcotics are all examples of real or physical evidence. Photographs, maps, diagrams, and crime scene displays are further types of real evidence. The criminal court judge will also review documentary evidence, such as writings, government reports, public records, and business or hospital records.

In general, the primary test for the admissibility of evidence in either a criminal or civil proceeding is its relevance.[65] In other words, the court must ask itself whether the gun, shirt, or photograph, for instance, has relevant evidentiary value in determining the issues in the case. Ordinarily, evidence that establishes an element of the crime is acceptable to the court. For example, in a prosecution for possession of drugs, evidence that shows the defendant to be a known drug user might be relevant. In a prosecution for bribery, monies received in the form of a cancelled check identified as the amount received would clearly be found relevant to the case.

The term "circumstantial," or indirect, evidence is also often used in trial proceedings. Such evidence is often inferred or indirectly used to prove a fact in question. On the issue of malice in a criminal murder trial, for instance, it would be appropriate to use circumstantial evidence to prove the defendant's state of mind. Such evidence has often been the controversial issue in many celebrated criminal cases. The Dr. George Parkman case, more than a century ago, attracted national attention when his colleague at Harvard, Dr. Webster, was convicted of murder after Parkman's disappearance.[66] Because there was no "corpus delecti", Webster's conviction was based on circumstantial evidence.

And in the famous Sacco-Vanzetti trial in the 1920s, two men were tried and convicted of murder and finally executed seven years later, possibly because they were Italian anarchists.[67] Circumstantial evidence, bearing on or establishing the facts in a crime is ordinarily admissible, but evidence that is prejudicial, remote, or unrelated to the crime should be excluded by the court. In general, however, the admissibility of such evidence remains governed by the laws recognizing the constitutional rights of the accused, such as the right to be free from unreasonable search and seizure, the privilege against self-incrimination, and the right to counsel.

Motion for a Directed Verdict

Once the prosecution has provided all the government's evidence against a defendant, it will inform the court that it rests the people's case. The defense attorney at this point may enter a motion for a **directed verdict.** This is a procedural device by means of which the defense attorney asks the judge to order the jury to return a verdict of not guilty. The judge must rule on the motion and will either sustain it or overrule it, depending on whether he or she believes that the prosecution proved all the elements of the alleged crime. In essence, the defense attorney argues in the directed verdict that the prosecutor's case against the defendant is insufficient to prove the defendant guilty beyond a reasonable doubt. If the motion is sustained, the trial is terminated. If it is rejected by the court, the case continues with the defense portion of the trial.

Basically, the defense usually makes a motion for a directed verdict so that a finding of guilt can later be appealed to a higher court. If the judge refuses to grant the motion, this decision can be the focus of an appeal charging that the judge did not use proper procedural care in making his or her decision. In some cases, the judge may reserve decision on the motion, submit the case to the jury, and consider a decision on the motion before a jury verdict or order a verdict of guilty.

Presentation of Evidence by the Defense Attorney

The defense attorney has the option of presenting many, some, or no witnesses on behalf of the defendant. In addition, the defense attorney must decide if the client should take the stand and testify in his or her own behalf. In a criminal trial, the defendant is protected by the Fifth Amendment right to be free from self-incrimination, which means that a person cannot be forced by the state to testify against him- or herself in a criminal trial. However, defendants who choose voluntarily to tell their side of the story can be subject to cross-examination by the prosecutor.

After the defense concludes its case, the government may then present **rebuttal evidence.** This normally involves bringing evidence forward that was not used when the prosecution initially presented its case. The defense may examine the rebuttal witnesses and introduce new witnesses in a process called a **surrebuttal.** After all the evidence has been presented to the court, the defense attorney may again submit a motion for a directed verdict. If the motion is denied, both the prosecution and the defense prepare to make closing arguments, and the case on the evidence is ready for consideration by the jury.

Closing Arguments

Closing arguments are used by the attorneys to review the facts and evidence of the case in a manner favorable to each of their positions. At this stage of the trial, both prosecution and defense are permitted to draw reasonable inferences and to show how the facts prove or refute the defendant's guilt. Often both attorneys have a free hand in arguing about the facts, issues, and evidence, including the applicable law. They cannot comment on matters not in evidence, however, or on the defendant's failure to testify in a criminal case. Normally, the defense attorney will make a closing statement first, followed by the prosecutor. Either party can elect to forgo the right to make a final summation to the jury.

Instructions to the Jury

In a criminal trial, the judge will instruct, or **charge,** the jury members on the principles of law that ought to guide and control their decision on the defendant's innocence or guilt. Included in the charge will be information about the elements of the alleged offense, the type of evidence needed to prove each element, and the burden of proof required to obtain a guilty verdict. Although the judge commonly provides the instruction, he or she may ask the prosecutor and the defense attorney to submit instructions for consideration; the judge will then use discretion in determining whether to use any of their instructions. The instructions that cover the law applicable to the case are extremely important because they may serve as the basis for a subsequent criminal appeal. Procedurally, in highly publicized and celebrated cases, the judge may have sequestered the jury to prevent it from contacts with the outside world. This process, called **sequestration,** is discretionary with the trial judge, and most courts believe "locking a jury up" is needed only in sensational cases.

The Verdict

Once the charge is given to the jury members, they retire to deliberate on a verdict. As previously mentioned, the **verdict** in a criminal case—regardless of whether the trial involves a 6-person or a 12-person jury—is usually required to be unanimous. A review of the case by the jury may take hours or even days. The jurors are always sequestered during their deliberations, and in certain lengthy and highly publicized cases they are kept overnight in a hotel until the verdict is reached. In less sensational cases, the jurors may be allowed to go home, but they are cautioned not to discuss the case with anyone.

If a verdict cannot be reached, the trial may result in a **hung jury,** after which the prosecutor must bring the defendant to trial again if the prosecution desires a conviction. If found not guilty, the defendant is released from the criminal process. On the other hand, if the defendant is convicted, the judge will normally order a presentence investigation by the probation department preparatory to imposing a sentence. Prior to sentencing, the defense attorney will probably submit a motion for a new trial, alleging that legal errors occurred in the trial proceedings. The judge may deny the motion and impose a sentence immediately, a practice quite familiar in most misdemeanor offenses. In felony cases, however, the judge will set a date for sentencing, and the defendant will either be placed on bail or held in custody until that time.

The Sentence

The imposition of the criminal **sentence** is normally the responsibility of the trial judge. In some jurisdictions, the jury may determine the sentence or be called on to make recommendations involving leniency for certain offenses. Often, the sentencing decision is based on information and recommendations given to the court by the probation department after a presentence investigation of the defendant. The sentence itself is determined by the statutory requirements for the particular crime as established by the legislature; in addition, the judge ordinarily has a great deal of discretion in reaching a sentencing decision. The different criminal sanctions available include fines, probation, imprisonment, and even commitment to a state hospital. The sentence actually imposed is a result of a combination of all these factors. Sentencing is discussed in detail in the following chapter.

The Appeal

Defendants have as many as three possible avenues of appeal: the direct appeal, postconviction remedy, and federal court review.[68] Both the direct appeal and federal court review provide the convicted person with the opportunity to appeal to a higher state or federal court on the basis of an error that affected the conviction in the trial court. Extraordinary trial court errors, such as the denial of the right to counsel or inability to provide a fair trial, are subject to the "plain error" rule of the federal courts.[69] "Harmless errors" such as the use of innocuous identification procedures, or the denial of counsel at a noncritical stage of the proceeding would not necessarily result the overturn of a criminal conviction. A postconviction appeal, on the other hand, or what is often referred to as "collateral attack" takes the form of a legal petition, such as **habeas corpus,** and is the primary means by which state prisoners have their convictions or sentence reviewed in the federal court. A writ of habeas corpus (meaning you take the body) seeks to determine the validity of a detention by asking the court to release the person or give legal reasons for the incarceration.

In most jurisdictions, direct criminal appeal to an appellate court exists as a matter of right. This means that the defendant has an automatic right to appeal a conviction based on errors that may have occurred during the trial proceedings. A substantial number of criminal appeals are the result of disputes over points of law, such as the introduction at the trial of illegal evidence detrimental to the defendant, or statements made during the trial that were prejudicial to the defendant. Through objections made at the pretrial and trial stages of the criminal process, the defense counsel will reserve specific legal issues on the record as the basis for appeal. A copy of the transcript of these proceedings will serve as the basis on which the appellate court will review any errors that may have occurred during the lower court proceedings.

Because an appeal is an expensive, time-consuming, and technical process involving a review of the lower court record, the research and drafting of briefs, and the presentation of oral arguments to the appellate court, the defendant has been granted the right to counsel at this stage of the criminal process. In the U.S. Supreme Court case of *Douglas v. California* (1963), the Court held that an indigent defendant has a constitutional right to the assistance of counsel on a direct first appeal.[70] If the defendant appeals to a higher court, the defendant must have private counsel or apply for permission to proceed *in forma pauperis,* meaning that the defendant may be granted counsel at public expense if the court believes the appeal has merit.

The right of appeal normally does not extend to the prosecution in a criminal case. In the United States, according to the American Bar Association, considerable differences among the states and the federal government exist as to the appropriate scope of prosecution appeals.[71] At one extreme are states that grant no right of appeal to the prosecution in criminal cases. On the other hand, some jurisdictions permit the prosecution to appeal in those instances that involve the unconstitutionality of a statute, or from pretrial orders that terminate the government's case. However, the prosecutor cannot bring the defendant to trial again on the same charge after an acquittal or a conviction; this would violate the defendant's right to be free from double jeopardy under the Fifth Amendment. As discussed in Chapter 4, the purpose of the double jeopardy guarantee is to protect the defendant from a second prosecution for the same offense.

After an appeal has been fully heard, the appeals court renders an opinion on the procedures used in the case. If an error of law is found—such as an improper introduction of evidence, or an improper statement by the prosecutor that was prejudicial to the defendant—the appeals court may reverse the decision of the trial court and order a new trial. If the lower court is upheld, the case is finished, unless the defendant seeks a discretionary appeal to a higher state or federal court.

Over the last decade, criminal appeals have increased significantly in almost every state and the federal courts. Criminal case appeals make up close to 50 percent of the state appellate caseload and over 35 percent of the total caseload in federal cases, which include prisoner petitions and ordinary criminal appeals.[72]

Although the steps in the criminal trial might seem totally mechanical and inflexible, informal procedures and subjective judgments affect how judicial decisions are made. Questions such as how the judge relates to the prosecutor and the defense attorney, the attitude of the jury toward the defendant, or the credibility and competency of certain witnesses all bring a human element to play in the trial process.

■ Evidentiary Standards

Proof beyond a **reasonable doubt** is the standard required to convict a defendant charged with a crime at the adjudicatory stage of the criminal process. This requirement dates back to early American history and over the years has become the accepted measure of persuasion needed by the prosecutor to convince the judge or jury of the defendant's guilt. Many twentieth-century U.S. Supreme Court decisions have reinforced the history of this standard by making "beyond a reasonable doubt a due process and constitutional requirement."[73] In *Brinegar v. United States* (1948), for instance, the Supreme Court stated:

> Guilt in a criminal case must be proved beyond a reasonable doubt and by evidence confined to that which long experience in the common-law tradition, to some extent embodied in the Constitution, has crystallized into rules of evidence consistent with that standard. These rules are historically grounded rights of our system, developed to safeguard men from dubious and unjust convictions with resulting forfeitures of life, liberty, and property.[74]

And in the earlier case of *Davis v. United States* (1895), where a murder conviction was reversed because the judge had instructed the jury to convict when the evidence was equally balanced regarding the sanity of the accused, the Supreme Court held that the defendant is entitled to an acquittal where there is reasonable doubt of the capability in law of committing a crime.[75] The Court further stated, "No man should be deprived of his life under the forms of law unless the jurors who try him are able, upon their consciences, to say that the evidence before them . . . is sufficient to show beyond a reasonable doubt the existence of every fact necessary to constitute the crime charged."[76]

The reasonable doubt standard is an essential ingredient of the criminal justice process. It is the prime instrument for reducing the risk of convictions based on factual errors.[77] The underlying premise of this standard is that it is better to release a guilty person than to convict someone who is innocent. Since the defendant is presumed innocent until proven guilty, this standard forces the prosecution to overcome this presumption with the highest standard of proof. Unlike the civil law, where a mere **preponderance of the evidence** is the standard, the criminal process requires proof beyond a reasonable doubt for each element of the offense. As the Supreme Court pointed out in *In re Winship* (1970), where the reasonable doubt standard was applied to juvenile trials, "[i]f the standard of proof for a criminal trial were a preponderance of the evidence rather than proof beyond a reasonable doubt, there would be a

TABLE 13.1 ■ Evidentiary Standards of Proof—Degrees of Certainty

Standard	Definition	Where Used
Absolute certainty	No possibility of error; one hundred percent certainty.	Not used in civil or criminal law.
Beyond reasonable doubt; moral certainty	Conclusive and complete proof, while leaving any reasonable doubt as to the innocence or guilt of the defendant; allowing the defendant the benefit of any possibility of innocence.	Criminal trial.
Clear and convincing evidence	Prevailing and persuasive to the trier of fact.	Civil commitments, insanity defense.
Preponderance of evidence	Greater weight of evidence in terms of credibility; more convincing than an opposite point of view.	Civil trial.
Probable cause	U.S. constitutional standard for arrest and search warrants, requiring existence of facts sufficient to warrant that a crime has been committed.	Arrest, preliminary hearing, motions.
Sufficient evidence	Adequate evidence to reverse a trial court.	Appellate review.
Reasonable suspicion	Rational, reasonable belief that facts warrant investigation of a crime on less than probable cause.	Police investigations.
Less than probable cause	Mere suspicion. Less than reasonable to conclude criminal activity exists.	Prudent police investigation where safety of an officer or others is endangered.

smaller risk of factual errors that result in freeing guilty persons, but a far greater risk of factual errors that result in convicting the innocent."[78] According to Oliver Wendell Holmes, one of the best known Supreme Court justices of the twentieth century, "We have to choose, and for my part I think it a less evil that some criminals should escape than that the government should play an ignoble part."[79] The various evidentiary standards of proof are analyzed and compared in Table 13.1.

■ SUMMARY

The number of cases disposed of by trials is relatively small in comparison to the total number of cases that enter the criminal justice system. Nevertheless, the criminal trial provides the defendant with a very important opinion. Unlike other steps in the system, the American criminal trial allows the accused to assert the right to a day in court. The defendant may choose between a trial before a judge alone or a trial by jury. In either case, the purpose of the trial is to adjudicate the facts, ascertain truth, and determine the guilt or innocence of the accused.

Criminal trials represent the adversary system at work. The state uses its authority to seek a conviction, and the defendant is protected by constitutional rights, particularly those under the Fifth and Sixth Amendments. When they involve serious crimes, criminal trials are complex legal affairs. Each jurisdiction relies on rules and procedures that have developed over many years to resolve legal issues. As the U.S. Supreme Court has extended the rights of the accused, as described in this chapter, the procedures have undoubtedly contributed to the complexities and delays within the system. Some solutions have included smaller juries, more efficient control of police misconduct, and reducing time delays between arrest, indictment, and trial.

An established order of steps is followed throughout a criminal trial, beginning with the reading of the complaint, proceeding through the introduction of evidence, and concluding with closing arguments and a verdict. Overall, the criminal trial is an established institution in the criminal justice system. It serves both a symbolic and pragmatic function for defendants who require a forum of last resort to adjudicate their differences with the state.

■ QUESTIONS

1. Identify the steps involved in the criminal trial. Consider the pros and cons of a jury trial versus a bench trial.
2. What are the legal rights of the defendant in the trial process? Trace the historical development of the right to counsel at the trial stage of the criminal justice system.
3. Discuss the significance of the Supreme Court decisions in *Gideon v. Wainwright* and *Argersinger v. Hamlin*.
4. The burden of proof in a criminal trial to show that the defendant is guilty beyond a reasonable doubt is on the government in the adversary system of criminal justice. Explain the meaning of this statement in terms of other legal standards of proof.
5. If a 17-year-old is tried by a jury, should the jurors also be under 21 years of age to maintain fairness?
6. Devise a charge to the jury for a first-degree murder case.
7. What is the meaning of "prior restraint"?
8. What factors support televising criminal trials?

■ NOTES

1. National Advisory Commission on Criminal Justice Standards and Goals, *Courts* (Washington, D.C.: U.S. Government Printing Office, 1973), p. 66; see also Donald Newman, *Conviction: The Determination of Guilt or Innocence without Trial* (Boston: Little, Brown, & Co., 1966).
2. 391 U.S. 145, 88 S.Ct. 144, 20 L.Ed.2d 491 (1968).
3. Ibid., at 157–158.
4. 399 U.S. 66, 90 S.Ct. 1914, 26 L.Ed.2d 437 (1970).
5. U.S., 109 S.Ct. 1289, 44 CrL 3171 (March 6, 1989).
6. 399 U.S. 78, 90 S.Ct. 1893, 26 L.Ed.2d 446 (1970).
7. Ibid., at 102–3.
8. Ibid., at 101.
9. Ibid., at 102.
10. *Ballew v. Georgia*, 435 U.S. 223, 98 S.Ct. 1029, 55 L.Ed.2d 234 (1978).
11. *Burch v. Louisiana*, 441 U.S. 130 99 S.Ct. 1623, 60 L.Ed.2d 96, (1979).
12. 406 U.S. 404, 92 S.Ct. 1628, 32 L.Ed.2d 184 (1972).
13. 287 U.S. 45, 53 S.Ct. 55, 77 L.Ed. 158 (1932).
14. 372 U.S. 335, 83 S.Ct. 792, 9 L.Ed.2d 799 (1963).
15. 407 U.S. 25, 92 S.Ct. 2006, 32 L.Ed.2d 530 (1972).
16. 470 U.S. 68, 105 U.S. 1087, 84 L.Ed.2d 53 (1985).
17. 422 U.S. 806, 95 S.Ct. 2525, 45 L.Ed.2d 562 (1975).
18. Ibid.
19. Ibid., at 592.
20. See "Criminal Defendants at the Bar of Their Own Defense—*Faretta v. California*," *American Criminal Law Review* 60 (1975): 335.
21. See American Bar Association, *Standards Relating to Speedy Trial* (New York: Institute of Judicial Administration, 1968), p. 1.
22. 386 U.S. 213, 87 S.Ct. 988, 18 L.Ed.2d 1 (1967).
23. Ibid., at 230.
24. 404 U.S. 307, 92 S.Ct. 455, 30 L.Ed.2d 468 (1971).
25. Ibid., at 321.
26. 407 U.S. 514, 92 S.Ct. 2182, 33 L.Ed.2d 101 (1972).
27. President's Commission on Law Enforcement and Administration of Justice, *The Courts* (Washington, D.C.: U.S. Government Printing Office, 1967), pp. 86–87; see also B. Mahoney, et al., *Implementing Delay Reduction and Delay Prevention: Programs in Urban Trial Courts* (Williamsburg, Va.: National Center for State Courts, 1985).
28. National Advisory Commission, *Courts*, pp. xx–xxi; see also Gregory S. Kennedy, "Speedy Trial," *Georgetown Law Journal* 75 (1987): 953–64.
29. 18 U.S.C.A. § 3161 (Supp. 1975). For a good review of this legislation, see Marc I. Steinberg, "Right to Speedy Trial: The Constitutional Right and Its Applicability to the Speedy Trial Act of 1974," *Journal of Criminal Law and Criminology* 66 (1975): 229.
30. American Bar Association, *Standards Relating to Speedy Trial*, Standard 1.1. Reprinted with the permission of the American Bar Association, which authored these standards and which holds the copyright. See also Paul B. Wice, "The Speedy Trial Dilemma: A Handbook on Reform," *Criminal Law Bulletin* 23 (1987): 323–38.
31. 412 U.S. 434, 93 S.Ct. 2260, 27 L.Ed.2d 56 (1973).
32. U.S., 108 S.Ct. 2413, 101 L.Ed.2d 297 (1988).
33. 425 U.S. 501, 96 S.Ct. 1691, 48 L.Ed.2d 126 (1976). Estelle V. Williams.
34. 384 U.S. 333, 86 S.Ct. 1507, 16 L.Ed.2d 600 (1966).
35. See *State v. von Bulow*, 475 A.2d 995 (1984); see also Alan Dershowitz, *Reversal of Fortune: The von Bulow Affair* (New York: Random House, 1986).
36. 427 U.S. 539, 96 S.Ct. 2791, 49 L.Ed.2d 683 (1976).
37. Ibid., at 547.
38. 443 U.S. 368, 99 S.Ct. 2898, 61 L.Ed.2d 608 (1979).
39. Ibid., at 370.
40. 478 U.S. 1, 106 S.Ct. 2735, 92 L.Ed.2d 1 (1986).
41. 448 U.S. 555, 100 S.Ct. 2814, 65 L.Ed.2d 973 (1980).
42. 457 U.S. 596, 102 S.Ct. 2613 (1982). Globe Newspaper Co. v. Superior Court for County of Norfolk.

43. 464 U.S. 501, 104 S.Ct. 819, 78 L.Ed.2d 629 (1984). Press-Enterprise Co. v. Superior Ct. of California, Riverside County.

44. 467 U.S. 37, 104 S.Ct. 2210, 81 L.Ed.2d 31 (1984). Waller v. Georgia.

45. Nicholas A. Pellegrini, "Extension of Criminal Defendant's Right to Public Trial," St. Johns University Law Review 611 (1987), 277–289.

46. 333 U.S. 257 at 270.

47. 333 U.S. 257, 68 S.Ct. 499, 92 L.Ed. 682 (1948).

48. T. Dyk and B. Donald, "Cameras in the Supreme Court," American Bar Association Journal, January 1989, 34.

49. 449 U.S. 560, 101 S.Ct. 802, 66 L.Ed.2d 740 (1981).

50. Conference of State Court Administrators, *State Court Organization, 1987* (Williamsburg, Va.: National Center for State Courts, 1988), p. 10.

51. See Richard Moran and Peter D'Errico, "The Law—An Impartial Jury or An Ignorant One," *Boston Globe*, 12 February, 1989, p. A18.

52. George Hayden, Joseph Senna, and Larry Siegel, "Prosecutorial Discretion in Peremptory Challenges: An Empirical Investigation of Information Use in the Massachusetts Jury Selection Process," *New England Law Review* 13 (1978): 768.

53. 380 U.S. 202, 85 S.Ct. 824, 13 L.Ed.2d 759 (1964).

54. 476 U.S. 79, 106 S.Ct. 1712, 90 L.Ed.2d 69 (1986).

55. James Archer, "Exercising Peremptory Challenges After Batson," *Criminal Law Bulletin* 24 (1988): 187–211.

56. Brian Sern and Mark Maney, "Racism, Peremptory Challenges and the Democratic Jury—The Jurisprudence of Delicate Balance," *The Journal of Criminal Law and Criminology* 79 (1988): 65.

57. For a review of jury decision making, see John Baldwin and Michael McConville, "Criminal Juries," in *Crime and Justice*, vol. 2, Norval Morris and Michael Tonry, eds. (Chicago: University of Chicago Press, 1980), pp. 269–320.

58. 409 U.S. 524, 92 S.Ct. 848, 35 L.Ed.2d 46 (1973).

59. 419 U.S. 522, 95 S.Ct. 692, 42 L.Ed.2d 690 (1975).

60. *Turner v. Murray*, 476 U.S. 28, 106 S.Ct. 1683, 90 L.Ed.2d 27 (1986). See James Gobert, "In Search of an Impartial Jury," *Journal of Criminal Law and Criminology* 79 (1988): 269; see also Martin Levin, "The Jury in a Criminal Case—Obstacles to Impartiality," *Criminal Law Bulletin* 24 (1988): 321.

61. *Lockhart v. McCree*, 476 U.S. 162, 106 S.Ct. 1758, 90 L.Ed.2d 137 (1986).

62. See *U.S.A. v. Klan*, decided February 23, 1989, U.S. Court of Appeals, 2nd Circuit #881266 (1989).

63. *Lee v. Illinois*, 460 U.S. 530, 106 S.Ct. 2056, 90 L.Ed.2d 514 (1986).

64. See Charles McCormick, Frank Elliott & John Sutton, Jr., Evidence-Cases & Materials (St. Paul, Minn.: West, 1981), Chapter I.

65. I.B.D.

66. See the fascinating case study of states case v. Dr. Webster in Helen Thomson, *Murder At Harvard* (Boston: Houghton-Mifflin, 1971).

67. See Francis Russell, *Sacco and Vanzetti—The Case Resolved*, (New York: Harper & Row, 1986).

68. U.S. Department of Justice, *Report to the Nation on Crime and Justice*, 2d ed. (Washington, D.C.: Bureau of Justice Statistics, 1988), p. 88.

69. *Chapman v. California*, 386 U.S. 18, 87 S.Ct. 824, 17 L.Ed.2d 705 (1967).

70. 372 U.S. 353, 83 S.Ct. 814, 9 L.Ed.2d 811 (1963).

71. American Bar Association, *Standards Relating to Criminal Appeals* (New York: Institute of Judicial Administration, 1970), p. 34.

72. U.S. Department of Justice, *Report to the Nation on Crime and Justice*, p. 88.

73. See *Brinegar v. United States*, 338 U.S. 160, 69 S.Ct. 1302, 93 L.Ed. 1879 (1949); *Speiser v. Randall*, 357 U.S. 513, 78 S.Ct. 1332, 2 L.Ed.2d 1460 (1958); *In re Winship*, 397 U.S. 358, 90 S.Ct. 1068, 25 L.Ed.2d 368 (1970).

74. 338 U.S. 160, at 174, 69 S.Ct. 1302, 93 L.Ed. 1879 (1949).

75. 160 U.S. 469 (1895).

76. Ibid., at 493.

77. See *In re Winship*, 397 U.S. 358, 90 S.Ct. 1068, 25 L.Ed.2d 368 (1970).

78. Ibid., at 371.

79. See *Olmstead v. United States*, 277 U.S. 438, 48 S.Ct. 564, 72 L.Ed. 944 (1928).

14

Punishment and Sentencing

After defendants have been found guilty of a crime, either because of a jury's verdict, a judge's decision, or their own admission of guilt, the state has the right to impose a criminal **sanction** or **punishment** upon them. In the modern criminal justice system, the procedure in which the nature and extent of punishment are determined is known as the **sentencing process.**

Historically, criminal defendants were subject to a full range of punishments, including physical torture, branding, whipping, and, for most felony offenses, death. The philosophical reasoning behind such punishments was that the body must be tormented for the sins of the soul.[1] People who violated the laws were considered morally reprehensible and in need of strong discipline. If punishment was harsh enough, it was assumed that they would never repeat their mistakes, a concept referred to as **specific deterrence.** Punishment was also viewed as an opportunity to teach a moral lesson to the public. The more gruesome and public the sentence, the greater the impact it would have on the local populace.[2] And, of course, harsh physical punishments would discourage any thoughts of rebellion and dissent against the central government and those who held political and economic power.

In modern American society, the four most common forms of criminal punishment are the following.

1. *Fines.* Monetary payments made to the court reflecting the costs to society of the criminal act.
2. *Community sentences.* A period under supervision in the community during which the defendant is required to obey predetermined rules of behavior and may be asked to perform such tasks as paying restitution to the victim.
3. *Incarceration.* A period of confinement in a state or federal prison, jail, or community-based treatment facility.
4. *Capital punishment.* A sentence to death in the electric chair, gas chamber, firing squad, and the like.

The punishment of criminal offenders continues to be one of the most complex and controversial issues in the criminal justice system. Its complexity stems from the wide variety of sentences available and the discretion judges have in deciding the outcome of criminal cases. The proper sanction for a particular criminal defendant is often difficult to determine, and there is little coordination in judicial decision making. The controversy over punishment involves both its nature and its extent. Is there sentencing disparity? Do judges have too much or too little discretion in handing down sentences? Is sentencing discriminatory by race, sex, or class?[3] These are but a few of the most significant issues in the criminal sentencing process.

This chapter examines the history of punishment and focuses on incarceration and capital punishment, the two most "traditional" and punitive forms of criminal sanctions imposed today. The following chapter examines sentences that have been developed to reduce the strain on the overburdened correctional system; these provide for "intermediate sanctions," which are designed to control people whose behavior and personality makes an incarceration sentence unnecessary.

■ History of Punishment

The methods that a society uses to punish and correct criminals tend to reflect its customs, economic conditions, and religious and political ideals; consequently, these methods have undergone considerable change through the ages.[4]

In the early Greek and Roman civilizations, the most common state-administered punishment was banishment or exile. Only slaves were commonly subjected to harsh physical punishment for their misdeeds. In the earliest period of Roman history, for example, the only crime for which capital punishment could be administered was *furtum manifestum* (open theft)—a thief caught in the act was executed on the spot. More common were economic sanctions and fines, which were levied for such crimes as assault on a slave, arson, or housebreaking.

In both ancient Greece and ancient Rome (prior to 400 B.C.), interpersonal violence, even that which resulted in death, was viewed as a private matter. The state laws of Greece and Rome (until quite late in their histories) did not provide for punishment of a violent crime. Execution of an offender was viewed as the prerogative of the deceased's family.

During the early Middle Ages (fifth to eleventh century A.D.), there was little law or governmental control. Offenses were often settled by feuds carried out by the families of the injured parties. When possible, the Roman custom of settling disputes by fine or an exchange of property was adopted as a means of resolving interpersonal conflicts with a minimum of bloodshed.

After the eleventh century, during the feudal period, forfeiture of land and property was a common punishment for persons who violated law and custom or failed in their feudal obligations to their lord. The word *felony* actually comes from the twelfth century, when the term *felonia* referred to a breach of faith with one's feudal lord.

During this period, the main emphasis of criminal law and punishment was on maintaining public order.[5] If in the heat of passion or in a state of intoxication one person severely injured or killed his neighbor, free men in the area would gather to pronounce a judgment and make the culprit do penance or pay compensation called **wergild**. Wergild contained two elements: the **wite**, which went to the local lord as a fine for disturbing the peace; and the **bot**, which was compensation to the victim or his or her family. The purpose of the wergild was to assuage the vengeance of the injured party and ensure that the conflict would not develop into a blood feud and anarchy. The inability of the peasantry to pay monetary compensation led to the development of corporal punishment such as whipping or branding as a substitute penalty.

The development of the common law in the eleventh through the thirteenth centuries brought some standardization to penal practices. However, corrections remained an amalgam of fines and brutal physical punishments. By the fifteenth century, changing social conditions had begun to influence the relationship between crime and punishment. First, the population of England and Europe began to increase after a century of decimation by constant warfare and plague. At the same time, the developing commercial system caused large tracts of agricultural fields to be converted to grazing lands. Soon unemployed peasants and landless gentry began flocking to newly developing urban centers, such as London and Paris, or taking to the roads as highwaymen, beggars, or vagabonds.

The later Middle Ages also saw the rise of strong monarchs such as Henry VIII and Elizabeth I of England, who were determined to keep a powerful grip on their realm. The administration of the "King's Peace" under the shire reeve and constable was strengthened.

These developments led to the increased use of **capital** and **corporal punishment** to control the criminal poor. While the wealthy could buy their way out of punishment and into exile, the poor were executed and mutilated at ever-increasing rates. It is estimated that 72,000 thieves were hanged during the reign of Henry VIII alone.[6] Execution, banishment, mutilation, branding, and flogging were inflicted on a whole range of offenders, from murderers and robbers to vagrants and gypsies. Punishments became unmatched in their cruelty, featuring a gruesome variety of physical tortures. Also during this period, punishment became a public spectacle, presumably so that the sadistic sanctions would act as a deterrent. But the variety and imagination of the tortures inflicted on even minor criminals before their death suggests that retribution, sadism, and spectacle were more important than any presumed deterrent effect.

Public Work and Transportation

By the end of the sixteenth century, the rise of the cities and overseas colonization provided tremendous markets for manufactured goods. In England and France, population growth was checked by constant warfare and internal disturbances. Labor was scarce in many manufacturing areas of England, Germany, and Holland. The Thirty Years' War in Germany and the constant warfare among England, France, and Spain helped drain the population.

Punishment of criminals changed to meet the demands created by these social conditions. Instead of the wholesale use of capital and corporal punishment, many offenders were sentenced to hard labor for their crimes. **Poor laws** enacted at the end of the sixteenth century required that the poor, vagrants, and vagabonds be put to work in public or private enterprises. Houses of correction were developed to make it convenient for petty law violators to be assigned to work details. In London a workhouse was developed at Brideswell in 1557, and its use became so popular that by 1576 Parliament ordered a "brideswell" type workhouse to be built in every county in England. Many convicted offenders were pressed into sea duty as galley slaves, a fate considered so loathsome that many convicts practiced self-mutilation rather than submit to it.

The constant shortage of labor in the colonies also prompted the authorities to transport convicts overseas. In England, the Vagrancy Act of 1597 legalized deportation for the first time. Similarly, an Order in Council of 1617 granted a reprieve and stay of execution to people convicted of robbery and other felonies who were strong enough to be employed overseas. Similar measures were employed in France and Italy to recruit galley slaves and workers.

Transportation to the colonies became popular; it supplied labor, cost little, and was actually profitable for the government, since manufacturers and plantation owners paid for the convicts' services. The Old Bailey Court in London supplied at least 10,000 convicts between 1717 and 1775.[7] Convicts would serve a period as workers and then become free again.

Transportation to the colonies waned as a method of punishment with the increase in colonial populations, the further development of the land, and the increasing importation of African slaves in the eighteenth century. The American Revolution ended the transportation of felons to North America, but convicts were still sent to Australia and New Zealand. Between 1787 and 1875, when the practice was abandoned, over 135,000 felons were transported to Australia.

Although transportation in lieu of a death sentence may at first glance seem advantageous, transported prisoners endured enormous hardships. Those who were sent to Australia suffered incredible physical abuse including severe whippings and mutilation. Many of the British prison officials in charge of the Australian penal colonies could best be described as sociopaths or sadists. The popular book, *The Fatal Shore*, described in gory detail the almost inhuman treatment of both male and female prisoners transported to Australian penal colonies and the harsh discipline that often resulted in disfigurement or death. Women were forced to dispense sexual favors and suffered physical and psychological abuse. Conditions were so brutal that some inmates mutilated themselves in order to be sent to a hospital, while others volunteered to be killed by their fellow inmates so that their attackers would have a few good meals while awaiting execution.[8]

The Rise of the Prison

Between the beginning of the American Revolution in 1776 and the first decades of the nineteenth century, the populations of Europe and America increased rapidly. Transportation to the American colonies was no longer an option. The increased use of machinery made industry capital- and not labor-intensive. As a result, there was less need for unskilled laborers, and many workers could not find suitable employment.

The gulf between poor workers and wealthy landowners and merchants widened. The crime rate rose significantly, prompting a return to physical punishment and increased use of the death penalty. During the latter part of the eighteenth century, 350 types of crime in England were punishable by death.[9] Although many people sentenced to death for trivial offenses were spared the gallows, there is little question that the use of capital punishment was extremely common in England during the mid-eighteenth century.[10]

Prompted by these excesses, legal philosophers such as Jeremy Bentham and Cesare Beccaria argued that physical punishment should be replaced by periods of confinement and incapacitation. The use of gaols and workhouses to hold petty offenders, vagabonds, the homeless, and debtors had become common practice, but these institutions were not intended for hard-core criminals. One solution to the growing crime problems was to use abandoned ships or **hulks** anchored in rivers and harbors throughout England. The degradation under which prisoners lived in these ships inspired John Howard, the sheriff of Bedfordshire, to write the *State of the Prisons* in 1777. The influence of the book led Parliament to pass the Penitentiary Act in 1779, mandating the construction of secure and sanitary structures to house prisoners.

By 1820 long periods of incarceration in walled institutions called reformatories or **penitentiaries** began to replace physical punishment in England and the United States. These institutions were considered liberal reforms during a time when harsh physical punishment and/or incarceration in filthy holding facilities was the norm. The history of the prison will be explored more fully in Chapter 16.

Incarceration has remained the primary mode of punishment for serious offenses in the United States since it was introduced early in the nineteenth century. It is ironic that in our "high tech" society some of the institutions constructed soon after the Revolutionary War are still in use today. In recent

The deterrence goal of sentencing mandates that punishment be sufficient to dissuade people from committing crime.

times prison has been the punishment reserved for those considered to be the most serious, hardened, and dangerous criminals.

■ The Goals of Criminal Punishment

When we hear that a notorious criminal, such as Ted Bundy, has received a long prison sentence or even the death penalty for a particularly heinous crime, each of us has a distinct reaction: some of us are gratified that a truly evil person "got just what he deserved"; many people feel safer because a dangerous person is "where he can't harm any other innocent victims"; others hope the punishment serves as a warning to potential criminals, helping them realize that "everyone gets caught in the end"; some of us feel sorry for the defendant because "he got a raw deal, he needs help not punishment"; still others hope that "when he gets out he'll have learned his lesson."

Experts believe that all of these common reactions and sentiments are present when criminal sentences are handed down. After all, sentences are devised and implemented by people who represent the general public and share many of its sentiments and fears. The five goals that are generally recognized as the motives behind the imposition of a criminal sentence are discussed in this section.

General Deterrence

It has long been assumed that the punishments associated with the criminal law should deter potential law violators from criminal behavior. It follows that by punishing a known offender severely, the state can demonstrate to the general public its determination to control crime, and therefore deter other potential offenders. Consequently, when an offender is sentenced, one consideration is the impact the sentence will have on the community. Too lenient a sentence might encourage criminal conduct, too severe a sentence might destroy society's faith in the fairness of the system of justice. Finding a sentence that has a deterrent capability but is still fair and just has been an ongoing quest in the justice system.

A sentence based on general deterrence reflects the assumed future impact individual punishment has on the rest of society. Sentencing a student to a month in jail for drunk driving should inhibit her dormmates from driving after they've had a few drinks at the pub.[11] Sentencing a traitor to death for espionage serves as a warning to those who might consider betraying their country to a foreign power. The death sentence in this case serves no practical purpose beyond deterrence: the damage has already been done, and even if the spy were released, he would present no future danger to society since he would never again be given access to any sensitive material.

Sentencing an offender to serve as an "example" for others raises questions of justice and propriety. To some it seems unjust to punish offenders solely because we believe others will be frightened by their fate. In other words, is it just to "take a life to save a life"?

Sentencing for the purpose of deterrence is also questioned because there is little clear-cut evidence that perceptions of severe punishment influence criminal behavior.[12] Though research efforts do show that people who commit crime also believe they will not be caught and punished, it is difficult to determine whether their attitudes were formed before or after their law violations took place. Put another way, it is possible that people who successfully commit crime later come to believe that the criminal justice system is not very effective.[13] Rather than committing crime because they do not fear punishment, successful criminals may simply learn from experience that they have little to fear from the law.

Other deterrence experts find that it may be impossible to accurately determine if the fear of criminal punishment influences behavior.[14] Evidence suggests that apprehension about being rejected by parents, friends, and other social relations is a greater crime deterrent than the fear of legal sanctions.[15] For example, Kirk Williams and Richard Hawkins found that fear of getting arrested can deter spouse abuse, but that potential abusers were more afraid of personal humiliation and social costs such as the loss of friends and family disapproval than they were of legal punishments such as going to jail.[16]

Incapacitation

An issue that must be addressed in the sentencing decision is whether the offender is a risk to society and therefore requires a period of supervision and/or confinement. It is assumed that for at least the period offenders are under state control they will not be able to repeat their criminal acts. For some, this means a period in a high-security state prison where their behavior will be strictly controlled. Fixing sentence length often involves a determination of how long a particular offender needs to be incarcerated in order to ensure that society is protected.

The incapacitation element of sentencing also relies on prediction of future behavior: offenders are confined not so much for what they have done but for what it is feared they will do in the future. However, there is little evidence that future behavior can be accurately predicted. Most research indicates that incapacitating criminals has little effect on their future behavior.[17] In addition, there seems to be little relationship between the number of criminals behind bars and the crime rate: though more convicted criminals have been sentenced to prison than ever before, the crime rate has been steadily increasing.[18] The "get tough" sentencing approaches now in vogue have led to an American jail and prison inmate population totaling *1 million people.*[19]

Specific Deterrence

Specific deterrence refers to the ability of criminal sentences to deter an offender's future law-violating behavior: experiencing punishment should be sufficient to convince even the most hardened criminals that **recidivism** would not be in their best interests.

Judges have had difficulty formulating sentences that are of sufficient length and severity to act as a specific deterrent yet do not preclude or interfere with the offender's return to conventional society.[20] High recidivism rates indicate that the specific deterrent function of sentencing has not been achieved. A few research efforts, such as the one conducted by Douglas Smith and Patrick Gartin, have found a significant specific deterrent effect of punishment, but such efforts have been in the minority.[21] Others show that specific deterrence may depend less on the severity of punishment and more on perceptions of its likelihood.[22] It therefore is possible that the failure of criminal punishment to restrict repeat offending is a function of the justice system's preoccupation with sentencing *severity* and not sentencing *certainty*.

Retribution/Desert

Offenders are also punished because they have harmed others and are therefore deserving of retribution for what they have done; as the old saying goes, "let the punishment fit the crime."[23]

The influence of the retributive or **just desert** philosophy of sentencing can be traced to the publication of Andrew von Hirsch's influential work, *Doing Justice*, in 1976.[24] In essence, von Hirsch found that sentences should be proportional to the seriousness of the criminal act. He forcefully argued that offenders should be punished for what they have already done and not for what they may do in the future or for what others may do unless they are made to suffer. We can observe this philosophy at work in the extremely large fines and assessments some in excess of $100 million, handed down to investment bankers who profited from illegal stock market practices such as insider trading.

Desert is based on **equity:** the criminals profited from their misdeeds, now they must repay society to restore the social balance. Desert-based sentencing considers the gravity of the criminal act, not the needs of the offender or the community. It demands that punishments be equally and fairly distributed to all people who commit similar illegal acts. This leads to one of the critical issues in sentencing today: how do we gauge desert? Should punishment reflect the values of professional jurists? The general public? Crime victims? Determining just punishment can be a difficult problem because there is generally little consensus on the appropriate punitive response to criminal acts.[25]

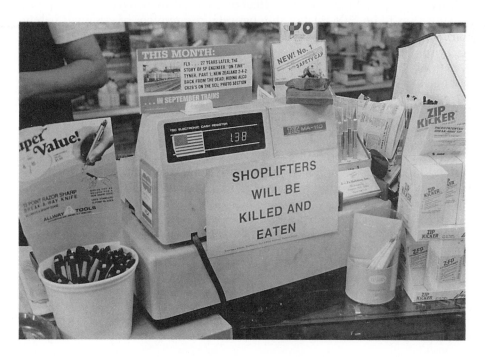

Offenders are penalized because they have harmed others and are deserving of punishment for their misdeeds. This sign in a Kingston, New York store promises a rather severe form of retribution.

Rehabilitation

Another factor that enters into the sentencing decision is whether offenders can be effectively treated so that they can eventually readjust to society. In some cases this means using the resources of the community when the offenders are placed on probation. While on probation the offenders might enter an outpatient substance abuse clinic or make restitution to the victim of their crime. Community supervision is used to teach them commitment, conformity, responsibility, and so on. Even serious criminals, including armed robbers and rapists, are often given probationary sentences because they are considered amenable to nonsecure treatment.[26]

If the crime is serious, and the offender unstable, the situation demands that rehabilitation take place in a secure environment under the auspices of state correctional authorities. In this instance the magistrate will require that the convicted offender remain in secure confinement such as a prison or jail while undergoing a period of correctional treatment.

The rehabilitation aspect of sentencing is based on a prediction of the future needs of the offender as well as on the gravity of the current offense. For example, a judge who sentences a person convicted of a felony to a period of community supervision believes that the defendant can be successfully treated and presents no further threat to society.

Recently, the rehabilitation aspect of sentencing has come under increased criticism from those advocating desert- or deterrence-based sentences, yet surveys indicate that the general public still supports treatment efforts.[27]

■ Choosing the Sentence: Presentence Investigations

When choosing among sentence possibilities, the judge must consider all the factors discussed in the preceding section in order to assess the offender's need for treatment or confinement, society's need for protection and retribution, the victim's desire for justice and equity, and the justice system's need for fairness and efficiency. Judges will also consider such issues as the following:

Proportionality. Is the punishment commensurate with the seriousness of the crime?
Equivalency. Is the offender being treated as similar criminals have been treated?
Social debt. Does the severity of punishment take into account the offender's prior criminal behavior?[28]

In choosing a sentence that satisfies the needs of all parties involved, a judge will rely heavily on a **presentence investigation** report prepared by the local probation department. Depending on the case, the probation staff will conduct a thorough background investigation of the defendant, including education, family, employment, offense, and psychological histories. These reports are used by the court in deciding whether to grant probation, incarcerate, or use other forms of treatment. In juvenile probation services, the presentence investigation can recommend outright release, continuance of a case with no finding, probation, or placement in a youth center.

The presentence investigation serves a number of purposes:

1. The report aids the court in determining an appropriate sentence. The information in the report helps the court decide whether there is reason to maintain the offender in the community or whether institutionalization is required.

2. It aids the probation officer in developing a treatment program in the event that the offender is placed on probation. The social and psychological strengths and weaknesses of the offender as revealed in the report may be taken into account in planning treatment strategy.

3. It develops a body of personal knowledge of the offender that can aid prison or other institutional officials in the classifying, treating, and releasing functions.

4. It furnishes the parole board with information that may help them plan a proper parole program if and when the imprisoned offender is released.

5. It serves as a source of information for systematic research in criminal justice; for example, researchers using these reports can determine the characteristics that correlate with or predict probation success or failure.[29]

Despite their importance, use of these reports is not uniform throughout the nation. Some states require reports for certain classes of offenses, such as felonies; others make the report discretionary and prepare them on a request from the court; and still others make the presentence report mandatory for certain types of crimes and dispositions and discretionary for others.[30] Thus, many offenders are sentenced by courts that lack information necessary for making the sentencing decision.

It has also been charged that presentence investigations are superfluous because probation officers ignore social and behavioral factors and base their recommendations on the offense and the offender's prior record. According to John Rosencrance, weighting the offender's prior criminal record heavily is an effort to meet judicial expectations of what a sentence should really be based on: the offender's criminal behavior and not the need for treatment in the community.[31]

In sum, when choosing a sentence, criminal court judges are influenced by their personal sentencing approach and convictions about the purpose of criminal sentences as well as by the information contained in a presentence investigation prepared by the probation department.

■ Incarceration Sentences

The possible penalties that a court may impose on a convicted offender who is to be sentenced to prison are determined by the statutes of the jurisdiction. Over the years, the states have adopted a variety of sentencing approaches; these are usually defined by the legislature, which has the power to determine the content of the criminal law. Although there is no single format for criminal sentencing, most state codes can be categorized as falling into one of three groupings: the legislative, judicial, and administrative models.[32]

In the legislatively fixed model, the state legislature determines the penalty for specific crimes, such as five years for a robbery, and all people convicted of that crime receive that sentence. Judicial and/or administrative discretion is severely reduced. The system retains some flexibility and discretion, however, because police can still decide which cases and what charges to proceed on, and prosecutors can still arrange plea negotiations.

In the judicially fixed model, the legislature establishes a general range of prison sentences for a given crime, and the sentencing judge chooses a sentence within that range. For example, if the legislature established a sentence of not less than 3 years nor more than 10 years for a robbery, the judge would impose a sentence between these ranges in each case, for example, 5 years for one robber, 7 for another. The sentence cannot be increased or reduced by any other state authority. Discretion is vested with the sentencing judge within the range of imprisonment authorized by the legislature.

In the administrative model, the legislature creates an extremely wide range of imprisonment for a particular crime, for example, from 3 to 50 years for robbery. The actual duration of the sentence is controlled by an administrative agency who monitors the offender while he or she serves the prison sentence. For example, a judge sentences a robber to a prison term of not less than 3 years nor more than 25 years; after serving 5 years, the person is released on parole. In this model, control over criminal punishment is for all practical purposes in the hands of correctional administrative authorities, the parole board.

Regardless of which model is used, most sentencing schemes give the presiding judge discretion to impose a particular type of sentence. Based on his or her discretion, the judge can order a first-time nonviolent offender to serve a relatively long prison sentence or to probation only. In addition, when an offender is convicted on two or more charges, the judge may decide how the sentences are to run. If the convicted offender is given a **concurrent sentence,** the sentence is completed after the longest term has been served. For example, if a defendant is convicted of rape and two counts each of assault and robbery and is sentenced to 10 years for the rape, 8 years on each of the robbery charges, and 5 on each of the assault charges, to run concurrently, he would be released after 10 years (the term of the single most serious offense). If, however, the sentences were imposed consecutively, the defendant would begin serving time for the second charge at the completion of the first term. If he were serving a **consecutive sentence,** the aforementioned criminal would serve 36 years instead of 10. In most instances, sentences are served concurrently, with consecutive sentences being reserved for the most serious, unrepentant, and uncooperative defendants.

Thus, there are a variety of sentencing structures in operation today. Some rely on judicial discretion, whereas others adhere to legislatively fixed or administrative models. In the sections below, the four most common types of sentencing models are discussed in some detail.

Indeterminate Sentences

In the 1870s, prison reformers such as Enoch Wines and Zebulon Brockway called for the creation of **indeterminate sentences.** They believed that prison sentences should be tailored to fit individual needs and that offenders should be placed in confinement only until they were rehabilitated. Indeterminate sentencing was influenced by positivist criminology and the belief that criminals were "sick" people who could be treated in prison. The wisdom of putting an offender away for a fixed period of time was disputed. Rather than the "punishment fitting the crime," reformers believed the "treatment should fit the offender." The indeterminate sentence becomes the most widely used type of sentence in the United States.

This concept (sometimes called **indefinite sentences**), which is still used in the majority of states, gives convicted offenders who are not eligible for community supervision a light minimum sentence that must be served and a lengthy maximum sentence that is the outer boundary of the time that can be served. For example, the legislature might set a sentence of a minimum of 1 year and a maximum of 20 years for burglary.

Under this scheme, the actual length of time served by the inmate is controlled by the corrections agency. The inmate can be paroled from confinement after serving the minimum sentence whenever the institution and parole personnel believe that he or she is ready to live in the community. The basic purpose of the indeterminate sentencing approach is to individualize each sentence in the interests of rehabilitating the offender. This type of sentencing allows for flexibility not only in the type of sentence to be imposed but also in the length of time to be served.

The indeterminate sentencing approach has a number of possible variations. In the most common, the judge sets both the maximum and minimum sentence within guidelines established by legislature. For example, the minimum and maximum sentence for burglary is 1 to 20 years. Offender A gets 1 to 20 years; offender B, 4 to 10; offender C, 3 to 6. The maximum sentence the judge imposes cannot exceed 20 years; the minimum cannot be less than 1 year. Another variation on this model is to have the judge set the maximum within an upper limit, with the minimum determined by the legislature. For example, all sentenced burglars do at least 1 year in prison but no more than 20. Offender A receives 1 to 10; offender B, 1 to 20; offender C, 1 to 5.

Today about 40 states still use indeterminate sentencing. Most have statutes that specify minimum and maximum terms but allow the judge discretion to fix the actual sentence within those limits. The typical minimum sentence in all states is at least 1 year although a few require more than a 2-year minimum sentence for felons.[33]

The indeterminate sentence is the predominant form of sentence used in the criminal process. It is the heart of the rehabilitation model of justice, because offenders may be released after a relatively short prison stay if they convince correctional authorities that they can forgo a criminal career. Yet because many policymakers believe that the rehabilitation of offenders has generally failed, alternative sentencing schemes are being given more consideration.

Determinate Sentences

In past years, the process of sentencing and the correctional course to be taken by the defendant were largely determined by the presiding justice. The judge imposed a sentence based on limits set by statute as well as on personal and professional inclinations. Sentencing statutes were generally quite broad, giving judges the right to place one defendant on probation while giving another a 20-year prison sentence for the same crime. Such unbridled discretion left the door open to **disparity** and unfairness in the sentencing process.

In 1969 Kenneth Culp Davis published *Discretionary Justice*, which was followed in 1972 by Judge Marvin Frankel's landmark study *Criminal Sentences: Law without Order.*[34] These works exposed the disparity that existed in the justice process and called for reform of the criminal law. As Frankel stated, "The almost wholly unchecked and sweeping powers we give to judges in the fashioning of sentences are terrifying and intolerable for a society that professes devotion to the rule of law."[35]

The focus of concern was the degree to which disparity exists in the sentencing process. Disparity in sentencing is particularly acute when offenders with similar backgrounds who are convicted of similar offenses receive different sentences.

In a response to this concern, a number of states have attempted to create new sentencing models that limit judicial discretion and attempt to reduce disparity. One of the most important efforts has been the creation of **determinate sentencing** structures.

Determinate sentences were the first kind used in the United States and are employed in about 10 states today.[36] With determinate sentencing, parole has been abolished, and the duration of the offender's prison stay can be determined at the time of sentencing (unless the offender gets into further difficulty while in prison). Determinate sentences are thus designed to take sentencing discretion away from correctional administrators and return it to judges and prosecutors. Determinate sentences stress the concepts of just desert, deterrence, and equality at the expense of treatment and rehabilitation.[37]

A variety of determinate sentencing structures are in use today. In one approach the legislature sets a fixed term of years for all people convicted of a crime who are not eligible for community supervision. If the judge decides to impose a prison sentence, it must be for the legislated sentence, and it must be served in its entirety without parole. This approach is known as **definite, flat, or fixed sentencing.** Maine is an example of a state that has adopted fixed sentencing.

In another variation of the determinate sentence, the legislature sets the minimum and maximum terms a person may serve for a crime but allows the judge discretion within these limits. For example, the minimum sentence for robbery may be 3 years and the maximum sentence 10 years, and judges have the discretion of choosing a single sentence of between 3 and 10 years. The resulting sentence must be served in its entirety (less time off for good behavior).[38]

PRESUMPTIVE SENTENCING. Determinate sentencing in its various forms is viewed as a way to increase fairness in sentencing and reduce sentencing disparity. But such an approach does not work in every case. Often similar offenses are committed in different ways, and each offender has unique characteristics. In addition, a number of determinate sentencing states give judges a wide latitude in choosing the proper sentence, which creates a disparity problem. Consequently, a number of states including Illinois, Indiana, and North Carolina have instituted a form of determinancy called **presumptive sentencing.** In this approach, the legislature sets minimum and maximum terms for a particular crime, with the judge setting a fixed or determinate sentence within this range. In this situation, the legislature retains the authority to exercise policy decisions, and the judge maintains some degree of sentencing discretion. Offenders convicted under this scheme are given a specific sentence unless there are mitigating or aggravating circumstances in the commission of the offense or in the offender's personal background. In other words, a judge is permitted to sentence below or above the prescribed sentence but must write an opinion justifying such action. For example, the legislature might set a range of 5 to 10 years for the crime of armed robbery in the first degree, with the presumptive, or expected, sentence being 7 years. Here the "average" robber should expect a prison sentence of at least 7 years. However, the sentencing judge can raise the sentence up to 10 years in a particularly serious case or lower it to 5 years if there are unusual mitigating circumstances. Table 14.1 lists the aggravating and mitigating circumstances that affect sentencing in Illinois.

Presumptive sentencing offers the advantage of retaining flexibility in sentencing while providing a substantial degree of certainty about the imposition of the sentence for the offender and the general public. It also seeks to eliminate the problem of widely disparate sentences for similar crimes imposed by judges with different sentencing philosophies.

Thus the important objectives of presumptive sentencing are (1) to reduce sentencing disparity, (2) to limit judicial discretion without completely eliminating it, and (3) to impose a sentence that the offender is required to serve. Marvin Zalman points out that presumptive sentencing proposals have grown out of a climate of distrust of judicial and parole board discretion.[39] In order to restrict such discretion, legislatures are expanding their role in the sentencing process.

TABLE 14.1 ■ **Factors in Sentence Mitigation and Aggravation, Illinois**

§ 1005–5–3.1 Factors in mitigation
(a) The following grounds shall be accorded weight in favor of withholding or minimizing a sentence of imprisonment:
 (1) the defendant's criminal conduct neither caused nor threatened serious physical harm to another;
 (2) the defendant did not contemplate that his criminal conduct would cause or threaten serious physical harm to another;
 (3) the defendant acted under a strong provocation;
 (4) there were substantial grounds tending to excuse or justify the defendant's criminal conduct, though failing to establish a defense;
 (5) the defendant's criminal conduct was induced or facilitated by someone other than the defendant;
 (6) the defendant has compensated or will compensate the victim of his criminal conduct for the damage or injury that he sustained;
 (7) the defendant has no history of prior delinquency or criminal activity or has led a law-abiding life for a substantial period of time before the commission of the present crime;
 (8) the defendant's criminal conduct was the result of circumstances unlikely to recur;
 (9) the character and attitudes of the defendant indicate that he is unlikely to commit another crime;
 (10) the defendant is particularly likely to comply with the terms of a period of probation;
 (11) the imprisonment of the defendant would entail excessive hardship to his dependents;
 (12) the imprisonment of the defendant would endanger his or her medical condition.

§ 1005–5–3.2 Factors in aggravation
(a) The following factors shall be accorded weight in favor of imposing a term of imprisonment or may be considered by the court as reasons to impose a more severe sentence under Section 5–8–1:
 (1) the defendant's conduct caused or threatened serious harm;
 (2) the defendant received compensation for committing the offense;
 (3) the defendant has a history of prior delinquency or criminal activity;
 (4) the defendant, by the duties of his office or by his position, was obliged to prevent the particular offense committed or to bring the offenders committing it to justice;
 (5) the defendant held public office at the time of the offense, and the offense related to the conduct of that office;
 (6) the defendant utilized his professional reputation or position in the community to commit the offense, or to afford him an easier means of committing it;
 (7) the sentence is necessary to deter others from committing the same crime.

SOURCE: Illinois Criminal Code, sections 1005–5–3.1; 1005–5–3.2.

STRUCTURED SENTENCING. For the past decade advocates of determinate sentencing, the "justice model" of criminal justice and the philosophy of just desert have argued that sentencing decisions must be fair, equal, and based primarily on the seriousness of the current offense; deterring future criminality or rehabilitating offenders should be of secondary importance in the sentencing decision.[40] An offshoot of this call for rational sentencing has been the development of **sentencing guidelines** to control and structure the determinate sentencing process. Guidelines are usually based on the seriousness of the crime and the background of the offender: the more serious the crime and the more extensive the offender's prior criminal record, the longer the prison term recommended by the guidelines.

Sentencing guidelines, which are currently used in such states as Michigan, Washington, Pennsylvania, and Minnesota, and by judges in U.S. District Courts, are usually devised by analyzing how similar offenders were treated in the past and determining what the ideal sentence should be for a particular crime and offender. For example, guidelines might suggest that all people convicted of robbery who have no prior offense record and who did not use excessive force or violence be given an average sentence of five years. Though judges are required by law to follow the guidelines in relatively few jurisdictions (Minnesota legally requires compliance by judges), states that have developed guidelines have heavily promoted judicial cooperation.

Sentencing guidelines can be computed for a variety of offense and offender types, and these models are usually quite complex. Figure 14.1 illustrates the guidelines used in Minnesota. Analysis of Minnesota's experiment with guidelines has yielded mixed results. One study found that Minnesota's judges closely followed the guidelines' recommended sentences during the first year they were in effect (1980), but began to deviate from them after two years. Some racial disparity was found the first year after the guidelines were adopted, but it diminished over time. Most importantly, there was a 73 percent increase in incarceration rates for serious offenders and a 72 percent reduction for petty offenders.[41] Further research by Terance Miethe and Charles Moore found that the guidelines were largely successful in controlling sentencing disparity.[42]

THE FUTURE OF SENTENCING GUIDELINES. Despite their drawbacks, there seems little question that guidelines will continue to be used in the future now that the federal government has adopted them and the U.S. Supreme Court has upheld the manner in which they have been implemented.[43] States such as Louisiana, Oregon, and Tennessee are developing guidelines, and Vermont and New Mexico are considering them.[44]

Despite the widespread acceptance of guidelines, some nagging problems remain. For example, though the study by Miethe and Moore of the Minnesota guidelines found that the effects of race and economic status were reduced in post-guideline decision making, the influence of race and social indicators continued to be felt indirectly. Black offenders were more likely to be charged with weapons violations and therefore more likely to go to prison.[45] Joan Petersilia and Susan Turner duplicated these results in their national evaluation of sentencing guidelines.[46] They found that although extralegal social variables such as race, income, and sex were absent from the sentencing guidelines used in most jurisdictions, many of the criteria that were used resulted in racial disparity, if not racial discrimination. This occurred because some of the criteria used in the guidelines correlated with the offender's race; these criteria included prior juvenile convictions, current crime being violent,

FIGURE 14.1
Minnesota Sentencing Guidelines Grid

Severity Levels of Conviction Offense		Criminal History (# of Prior Offenses) (presumptive sentence lengths in months)						
		0	1	2	3	4	5	6 or more
Unauthorized use of motor vehicle Possession of marijuana	I	12*	12*	12*	15	18	21 24 23–25	
Theft-related crimes ($150–$2,500) Sale of marijuana	II	12*	12*	14	17	20	23	27 25–29
Theft crimes ($150–$2,500)	III	12*	13	16	19	22 21–23	27 25–29	32 30–34
Burglary—Felony intent Receiving stolen goods ($150–$2,500)	IV	12*	15	18	21	25 24–26	32 30–34	41 37–45
Simple robbery	V	18	23	27	30 29–31	38 36–40	46 43–49	54 50–58
Assault, 2nd degree	VI	21	26	30	34 33–35	44 42–46	54 50–58	65 60–70
Aggravated robbery	VII	24 23–25	32 30–34	41 38–44	49 42–53	65 60–70	81 75–87	97 90–104
Assault, 1st degree Criminal sexual conduct, 1st degree	VIII	43 41–45	54 50–58	65 60–70	76 71–81	95 89–101	113 106–120	132 124–140
Murder, 3rd degree	IX	97 94–100	119 116–122	127 124–130	149 143–155	176 168–184	205 192–215	230 218–242
Murder, 2nd degree	X	116 111–121	140 133–147	162 153–171	203 192–214	243 231–255	284 270–298	324 309–339

Italicized numbers within the grid denote the range within which a judge may sentence without the sentence being deemed a departure.

1st-degree murder is excluded from the guidelines by law and continues to have a mandatory life sentence.

Cells below heavy line receive a presumptive prison sentence.

Cells above line receive a presumptive nonprison sentence.

The numbers in these cells refer to durations of confinement if probation is evoked.

*One year and one day.

SOURCE: Minnesota Sentencing Guidelines Commission, 1981.

victim injured, weapon involved, having vulnerable victims, and being on juvenile probation or parole at arrest. Though some research efforts have found that the use of guidelines decreases racial disparity in sentencing, the fact remains that if black offenders are convicted of more serious crimes and have more prior convictions, use of the guidelines could well increase racial disproportion in sentencing.

Research also indicates that judges deviate from the sentences suggested by their state's guidelines. David Griswold found that such factors as whether the case was settled by plea or trial, whether the offender was a probation violator, and the defendant's gender all influenced sentencing disparity in Florida, a state that uses guidelines.[47]

Some defense attorneys oppose the use of guidelines because they result in longer prison terms, prevent judges from considering mitigating circumstances in a case, and reduce the use of probation. Some pending cases challenge the federal guidelines on the grounds that they unconstitutionally interfere with the defendant's right to have an individualized sentence and thereby deprive him or her of due process of law.[48] The following Criminal Justice in Review discusses the impact of federal sentencing guidelines. Some federal jurisdictions have ruled the guidelines unconstitutional on these grounds, and judges in some federal trial courts, such as the Eastern District of Arkansas, are sentencing defendants under the old discretionary methods pending further review by the Supreme Court.[49] Thus the case against sentencing guidelines has not been completed. As Chris Eskridge warns:

> . . . sentencing guidelines as implemented to date have not had the impacts anticipated by guideline proponents. There is some evidence, in fact, that sentencing guidelines may only be making the problem worse. In other words, the cure may be worse than the ailment. Presumptive sentencing guidelines, therefore, should not be adopted.[50]

Mandatory Sentences

Another effort to limit judicial discretion has been the development of mandatory sentences that require the incarceration of all offenders convicted of specific crimes.

Some states, for example, exclude offenders convicted of certain offenses from being placed on probation; others exclude recidivists; still others bar certain offenders from being considered for parole. Mandatory sentencing legislation may impose minimum-maximum terms or fixed prison sentences. Crimes that often call for mandatory prison sentences include murder and multiple convictions for crimes such as rape, drug violations, and robbery. Mandatory sentencing generally limits the judge's discretionary power to impose any disposition but that authorized by the legislature; as a result, it destroys the idea of the individualized sentence and often impedes rehabilitation efforts by the courts. On the other hand, mandatory sentencing provides equal treatment for all offenders who commit the same crime regardless of age, sex, or other individual characteristics.

Well-known mandatory sentencing laws include New York State's efforts to control narcotics through passage of a series of laws prescribing mandatory sentences for narcotics offenses; Massachusetts's firearms control law, which gives offenders a one-year prison sentence that cannot be suspended by the court; and the Michigan Felony Firearm Statute, which provides a two-year add-on sentence for possessing a handgun during the commission of a felony.[51]

Federal Sentencing Guidelines

One of the most important developments in the criminal justice system has been the adoption of sentencing guidelines by the federal judicial system. Consequently, when a defendant appears in federal court for sentencing, his or her fate will not be solely in the hands of the judge, but will be determined by a very complex set of rules set down by the seven-member United States Sentencing Guideline Commission, which also abolished the federal parole system.

The guidelines themselves are quite extensive and detailed. To determine the actual sentence, a magistrate must first determine the **base penalty** that a particular charge is given in the guidelines and then add to or subtract from that sentence because of mitigating factors particular to the case. Table A gives the base score and mitigation factors for robbery. Robbery has a Base Offense Level of 18 points. The base level can be adjusted upward if the case was particularly serious or violent. For example, 5 points can be added to the robbery base if a firearm was discharged during the crime; 4 points if a gun was "otherwise used," and 3 points if a weapon was merely "brandished." Similarly, points can be added to a robbery if a large amount of money was taken, if a victim was injured, a person was abducted or restrained in order to facilitate an escape,

TABLE A ■ Base Score and Mitigation Factors for Robbery

§ 2B3.1. *Robbery*

(a) Base Offense Level: 18

(b) Specific Offense Characteristics

(1) If the value of the property taken or destroyed exceeded $2,500, increase the offense level as follows:

	Loss	Increase in Level
(A)	$2,500 or less	no increase
(B)	$2,501–$10,000	add 1
(C)	$10,001–$50,000	add 2
(D)	$50,001–$250,000	add 3
(E)	$250,001–$1,000,000	add 4
(F)	$1,000,001–$5,000,000	add 5
(G)	more than $5,000,000	add 6

Treat the loss for a financial institution or post office as at least $5,000.

(2) (A) If a firearm was discharged increase by 5 levels; (B) if a firearm or a dangerous weapon was otherwise used, increase by 4 levels; (C) if a firearm or other dangerous weapon was brandished, displayed or possessed, increase by 3 levels.

(3) If any victim sustained bodily injury, increase the offense level according to the seriousness of the injury:

	Degree of Bodily Injury	Increase in Level
(A)	Bodily Injury	add 2
(B)	Serious Bodily Injury	add 4
(C)	Permanent or Life-Threatening Bodily Injury	add 6

Provided, however, that the cumulative adjustments from (2) and (3) shall not exceed 9 levels.

(4) (A) If any person was abducted to facilitate commission of the offense or to facilitate escape, increase by 4 levels; or (B) if any person was physically restrained to facilitate commission of the offense or to facilitate escape, increase by 2 levels.

(5) If obtaining a firearm, destructive device, or controlled substance was the object of the offense, increase by 1 level.

or if the object of the robbery was to steal weapons or drugs. Upward adjustments can also be made if the defendant was a ringleader in the crime, obstructed justice, or used a professional skill or position of trust (such as doctor, lawyer, or politician) to commit crime. Offenders designated as "career criminals" by a court can likewise receive longer sentences. The final sentence is derived by looking up the final score in a sentencing table. According to the guidelines, a "Simple" Robbery (18 points) is punished by *27–33 months* in prison. A robbery by a fourth-time offender, of more than $1 million, in which a firearm was used, and a victim permanently injured, and another kidnapped in order to make an escape (31

points) would carry a sentence of *135–168 months.*

The guidelines still leave some "gray areas." Some offenses, especially petty misdemeanors, are not covered; other offenses fall into more than one category. It is also difficult to determine the exact sentence when there are multiple counts of a single offense, for example, importing narcotics on four different occasions. According to the guidelines, importing 40 kilograms of cocaine four times would be treated as if the offender imported 160 kilograms once; however, committing two different burglaries would be treated separately. If there are multiple counts of multiple offenses, the calculation becomes more complex.

It is difficult to assess the impact of the guidelines. The use of probation will probably decrease, and the size of the federal prison population will most likely increase. Plea bargaining may diminish because once offenders are convicted, their sentences are predetermined and the chances for leniency are reduced. Ultimately, sentencing should become more rational and disparity should be reduced. ■

SOURCE: Sentencing Reform Act of 1984 (18 U.S.C. 3551 et. seq.); *Federal Sentencing Guideline Manual* (Saint Paul, Minn.: West Publishing Company, 1987); Stefan Cassella, "A Step-by-Step Guide to the New Federal Sentencing Guidelines," *The Practical Lawyer* 34 (1988): 13–23.

Although mandatory sentences have not traditionally been common in the penal laws of the United States, they seem to be receiving considerable attention today. State parole boards exclude certain offenders from parole; and many state legislatures are currently studying mandatory sentences for serious drug offenses, auto theft, and the illegal possession of firearms. More than 30 states have already replaced discretionary sentencing with fixed-term mandatory sentences for such offenses as the sale of hard drugs, kidnapping, and arson.[52] The primary purpose behind such laws is to impose swift and certain punishment on the offender. It is difficult to say if depriving the judiciary of discretion and placing all sentencing power in the hands of the legislature will have a deterrent effect on the commission of these offenses.[53] Grouping all offenders who commit a particular crime into one category can result in hardships for defendants with particular personal characteristics. In addition, the use of mandatory sentences for some crimes can lead to an increase in plea bargaining as offenders seek avenues to escape harsh sentences, and prosecutors use the threat of mandatory sentences to force guilty pleas to lesser offenses. A critique of mandatory sentencing by the Twentieth Century Fund found that it may lead to court delays, arbitrary judicial decision making, and an increase in prosecutorial discretion and overcrowded prisons.[54] Similarly, Michael Tonry makes these claims after reviewing the literature on mandatory sentencing:

1. lawyers and judges will take steps to avoid application of laws they consider unduly harsh;
2. dismissal rates typically increase at early stages of criminal justice process after implementation of mandatory laws as practitioners attempt to shield some defendants from the law's reach;
3. defendants whose case is not dismissed or diverted make more vigorous efforts to avoid conviction and delay sentencing;

Chapter 14
Punishment and Sentencing

■

4. defendants who are convicted of the target offense are often sentenced more severely than they would be in the absence of the mandatory law;

5. because declines in conviction rates for those arrested tend to offset increases in imprisonment rates for those convicted, the overall probability that defendants will be incarcerated remains about the same after enactment of a mandatory sentencing law.[55]

Thus, although some of the desired effects of mandatory sentencing have been achieved (serious criminals do get longer sentences), they are counterbalanced by the efforts of justice system personnel to shield some offenders from the more punitive aspects of mandatory sentencing.

Habitual Criminal Statutes

A final sentencing approach worth noting is the use of habitual criminal statutes. Used today in 14 states, these laws mandate that people who have been convicted and served time for multiple felony offenses become eligible for a mandatory life term without hope of parole if they commit any subsequent offense.[56]

Though chronic offender statutes have been upheld by the U.S. Supreme Court, it is likely that the "use of this sanction indiscriminately for habitual offenders will not be tolerated."[57] In *Rummel v. Estelle* the Supreme Court upheld the use of these statutes if a chance of release through commutation or other means existed.[58] In *Solem v. Helm* the Court ruled that such a sentence was inappropriate for a relatively minor crime (Helm had passed a $100 bad check) when there was no hope of parole.[59] In *Helm* the Court held that a sentence of imprisonment can be cruel and unusual if it is disproportionate to the crime committed.

■ Sentencing Practices

What kind of prison sentence can a criminal defendant expect if he or she is found guilty as charged? To answer this question, the federal government's Bureau of Justice Statistics has conducted a number of national surveys that track sentencing practices around the United States. In 1989 the bureau presented evidence from the first national survey of sentencing in state felony courts ever conducted, the National Judicial Reporting Program (NJRP). This elaborate project provides data on sentencing practices in the nation as a whole and, separately, for the 75 most populous counties.[60] The major findings from this study are presented in Table 14.2.

This national survey makes an important contribution to the understanding of sentencing dynamics. First, as Table 14.2 indicates, of the 583,000 people convicted on felony charges in the United States in 1986, those who committed the most serious crimes had the greatest likelihood of receiving an incarceration sentence. However, a surprising number of convicted felons received a sentence of probation or community supervision only: 5 percent of convicted murderers, 12 percent of rapists, 26 percent of burglars, and 36 percent of those convicted on drug trafficking charges did not receive incarceration. These findings are not dissimilar from other federally sponsored sentencing surveys.[61]

The NJRP also tells us something about the average (mean) and middle-range (median) sentence received for typical felony offenses (the mean is usually greater because it can be influenced by a few extreme cases). As the

TABLE 14.2 ■ **Types and Length of Sentences Imposed for Felony Offenses in the United States and the 75 Largest Counties**

United States

Most serious conviction offense	Total	Percentage of Felons Sentenced to:					
		Incarceration			Nonincarceration		
		Total	Prison	Jail	Total	Probation	Others
All	100%	67%	46%	21%	33%	31%	2%
Murder	100	95	92	3	5	4	1
Rape	100	88	75	13	12	10	2
Robbery	100	87	76	11	13	12	1
Aggravated assault	100	71	45	26	29	26	3
Burglary	100	74	53	21	26	24	2
Larceny	100	64	40	24	36	34	2
Drug trafficking	100	64	37	27	36	35	1
Other felonies	100	58	36	22	42	39	3

75 Largest Counties

Most serious conviction offense	Total	Percentage of Felons Sentenced to:					
		Incarceration			Nonincarceration		
		Total	Prison	Jail	Total	Probation	Other
All	100%	71%	41%	30%	29%	27%	2%
Murder	100	95	91	4	5	4	1
Rape	100	86	68	18	14	13	1
Robbery	100	87	71	16	13	12	1
Aggravated assault	100	74	43	31	26	23	3
Burglary	100	75	50	25	25	23	2
Larceny	100	65	36	29	35	33	2
Drug trafficking	100	75	35	40	25	23	2
Other felonies	100	60	27	33	40	36	4

Most serious conviction offense	United States				75 Largest Counties			
	Average Maximum Sentence Length for Felons Sentenced to:				Average Maximum Sentence Length for Felons Sentenced to:			
	Incarceration				Incarceration			
	Total	Prison	Jail	Probation	Total	Prison	Jail	Probation
All	58 mos.	81 mos.	9 mos.	46 mos.	47 mos.	75 mos.	8 mos.	41 mos.
Murder	213	221	20	81	210	222	17	56
Rape	129	151	11	54	132	164	10	58
Robbery	124	139	10	49	91	109	10	52
Aggravated assault	66	97	10	57	51	80	10	41
Burglary	57	75	10	54	43	60	10	45
Larceny	31	46	7	42	26	40	7	41
Drug trafficking	42	69	9	53	33	62	7	42
Other felonies	38	56	8	41	26	50	7	38

SOURCE: Langan, Felony Sentences in State Courts, 1986, pp. 2–3.

data in Table 14.2 indicate, the national average for a sentence to a state prison was about seven years (the median term was five years). It appears that sentence length for the nation as a whole was somewhat greater than that experienced in the 75 largest counties, perhaps because serious crimes are more commonplace in these populous urban areas and judges treat them more routinely. As might be expected, offenders committing the most serious crimes—rape, murder, and robbery—received the longest maximum sentences. About 24 percent of all those convicted on murder charges received a life sentence, and 2 percent received the death penalty.

These data show the surprising amount of flexibility and disparity built into the adjudicatory system. Not all criminals convicted of the most serious crimes actually go to prison or jail, and those who do can receive significantly different sentences. Why such disparities exist is a very critical issue and an impetus for calls for reform of the sentencing process.

■ Extralegal Factors in Sentencing

One suspected cause of sentencing disparity is that race, sex, and economic factors affect sentencing decisions even though consideration of such variables would be a direct violation of the constitutional guarantees of due process and equal protection as well as federal statutes such as the Civil Rights Act.

Do these extralegal factors actually play a role in criminal sentencing? So far research has not provided any definitive answers. For example, although it seems logical that the poor might be more likely to be punished more harshly than the wealthy, the evidence in support of this contention is at best inconclusive. There is some indication that economic status is directly related to sentence length, but this factor is hard to establish since indigency is also strongly related to such factors as quality of legal representation, ability to make bail, and reluctance to plea bargain, all of which influence the sentencing outcome.[62]

Of similar concern is whether minority defendants receive disproportionately longer and harsher punishments than white defendants who are convicted of similar crimes. Attention to this problem has been prompted by the disproportionate number of black inmates in state prisons and on death row.[63]

Over the years research on racial disparity in sentencing has failed to show a definitive pattern of discrimination. Although some of the most important research efforts do show that defendants' race does impact on sentencing outcomes, research findings have been generally inconsistent and less clear-cut than anticipated. For example, Joan Petersilia's analysis of racial disparity concluded that black defendants do receive longer sentences than whites, but that the difference could be measured in months, not years. Petersilia attributes these differences to legal factors correlated with race, such as the fact that white defendants more frequently plea bargain and people who plead guilty as charged are more likely to receive shorter sentences.[64]

In another oft-cited research effort, Alfred Blumstein approached this issue by focusing on the racial disparity in the nation's prison system.[65] Although almost half of all prison inmates are black, racial minorities account for only 12 percent of the total U.S. population. Blumstein concludes that most of this discrepancy can be explained by arrest rate differentials: minorities account for a percentage of the arrest rate that is similar to the percentage of black inmates in the prison population. However, the percentages are not identical; Blumstein concluded that *at least 20 percent* of the racial differences in the prison population could not be explained away by arrest statistics or any other legal factor. This finding led him to speculate that racial disparity in the sentencing process might help explain *at least part* of the overrepresentation of minorities in the prison system.

One reason that the relationship between race and sentencing is so complex and difficult to establish is that the association may not be linear: although black defendants may be punished more severely for some crimes, they are treated more leniently for others.[66] As sociologist Darnell Hawkins explains:

> Certain crime types are considered less "appropriate" for blacks than for whites. Blacks who are charged with committing these offenses will be treated more severely than blacks who commit crimes that are considered more "appropriate." Included in the former category are various white collar offenses and crimes against political and social structures of authority. The latter groups of offenses would include various forms of victimless crimes associated with lower social status (e.g., prostitution, minor drug use or drunkenness). This may also include various crimes against the person, especially those involving black victims.[67]

Accurately assessing the reasons for this pattern is difficult. One explanation is that racial bias is distributed between and within legal jurisdictions: some judges operate in a racially biased manner while others do not; some judges favor black defendants while others give preferential treatment to white defendants.[68] This pattern would mask the true extent of racial bias in sentencing.

Another view is that racial bias occurs in relatively few cases but that its presence is linked to the characteristics of the victim-criminal relationship. For example, black defendants have been shown to receive more severe punishment if they victimize whites than if their target is another minority group member.[69] Judges may be basing their sentencing decisions on the race of the victim, not the race of the defendant.

There is also evidence that women are less likely to receive incarceration sentences than men. Most research indicates that women receive more favorable outcomes the further they go up the criminal justice system: they are more likely to receive preferential treatment from a judge at sentencing than they are from the police officer making an arrest or the prosecutor seeking an indictment.[70]

Another extralegal factor that may play a role in sentencing is age. Recent research by Dean Champion found that judges are generally more lenient toward elderly defendants and more punitive toward younger ones.[71] Although sentencing leniency may be a result of the judges' perception that the elderly pose little risk to society, Champion views such practices as a violation of the civil rights of the younger defendant.[72]

In sum, although there is some evidence that judges let extralegal factors influence their sentencing decisions, it would be unfair to say that the court system practices systematic discrimination. Nevertheless, race, class, gender, and age may be *associated* with factors that influence sentencing outcomes (such as making bail, plea bargaining, and appearing "nondangerous") and therefore may create the *appearance* of racism, classism, sexism, and ageism in the sentencing process. Outcomes that favor one group over another, regardless of their cause, cannot be tolerated in a democratic society.

Chapter 14

Punishment and Sentencing

■ Sentencing Reform

During the past two decades almost every state and the federal government have been examining their penal codes in an effort to simplify the classification of offenses and create a more rational approach to sentencing. In some instances, sentencing reform has been motivated by a growing fear of violent crime and can be considered a response to the public's demand for "law and order." Some critics view sentencing reform efforts with suspicion, charging that they are veiled efforts to control rebellious lower-class populations of young and minority group members.[73]

In either event, both the states and the federal government have set up sentencing review commissions to revise and restructure their codes. The efforts to create mandatory, presumptive, and (guideline) structured sentences have already been mentioned. In addition, national law reform groups have attempted to create model sentencing standards that can be accepted in full or in part by state jurisdictions. These model codes include the American Law Institute's Model Penal Code;[74] the Model Sentencing Act of the National Council on Crime and Delinquency;[75] and the American Bar Association's *Standards Relating to Sentencing Alternatives and Procedures*. These standards include recommendations regarding the sentence authority, statutory structure, judicial discretion, an information base for sentencing, and the development of sentencing criteria. They have been used as guidelines to help jurisdictions amend their sentencing codes to conform more closely to the needs of a modern criminal justice system.

Other efforts to promote greater efficiency and fairness in the sentencing decision include (1) sentencing institutes, (2) sentencing councils, and (3) appellate reviews of sentences.

Groups of judges meet at sentencing institutes for the purpose of discussing problems relating to sentencing. These institutes came into being through federal legislation passed by Congress in 1958 and have existed in the federal judicial system since that time. Some states, such as New York, California, and Massachusetts, have also been successful in developing sentencing institutes. The goals of proceedings such as these, as stated in the American Bar Association's *Standards Relating to Sentencing Alternatives and Procedures*, are "to develop criteria for the imposition of sentences, to provide a forum in which newer judges can be exposed to more experienced judges, and to expose all sentencing judges to new developments and techniques."[76]

Sentencing councils are meetings of judges who sit regularly in a particular court. During a sentencing council, the judges discuss appropriate dispositions of defendants who are awaiting sentencing. The sentencing judge retains the ultimate responsibility for selecting and imposing the sentence, while the other judges act in an advisory capacity. Normally, the judges meet in groups of three to consider the sentencing alternatives in pending cases. The sentencing council has the following advantages: (1) it makes judges aware of the differences in their sentencing philosophies; (2) it provides an opportunity for judges to debate their differences; and (3) it provides a forum for periodic evaluation of a court's sentencing practices.

Ordinarily, the sentencing decision for a particular case is in the hands of a single judge. Although sentencing councils provide a departure from this individual approach, they are particularly useful in that they serve to lessen the amount of disparity in sentencing practices. One major difficulty of the sentencing council is that information gathered from other judges may impair the ability of the sentencing judge to give open-minded consideration to all arguments at the dispositional hearing. The U.S. District Court for the Eastern District of Michigan originally developed the idea for the sentencing council, and such councils have since been implemented in other federal as well as state court systems.

Another effort at sentencing reform provides the convicted offender with an **appellate review** of the sentence in an attempt to prevent the excessive and arbitrary use of judicial discretion, which often results in widely disparate sentences for the same offense. This device, which was established through statutory authority, allows a person sentenced to a prison term to appeal for a review of the sentence and not for a retrial of the case. An appellate court, often sitting with three judges, reviews the petition for the change in sentence and is empowered to reduce or increase the original sentence of the trial court.

In the past, few states allowed appellate review of sentences. Review is still unavailable in some jurisdictions because (1) there are fears that it might greatly increase litigation, (2) appellate judges are less able to determine appropriate sentences because they do not observe the defendants, and (3) sentencing is generally a matter of judicial discretion and not a matter of law.[77] It is still evident that improved state court procedures that ensure informed decision making and limit the need for post-conviction review are needed.[78]

Results of Reform

How have these reform efforts influenced the justice system? The manner in which inmates are released from the nation's prisons provides an answer. In 1977 about 72 percent of all inmates were released on parole granted at the administrative discretion of correctional authorities, and about 6 percent were subject to mandatory release after serving their sentences. Today the number of parolees has declined to 40 percent and the mandatory releasees have risen to about 31 percent.

This shift indicates that a dramatic change has occurred in the nation's sentencing policy. Control over the length of sentences has shifted in some large jurisdictions from the judicial and administrative branches to the legislative branch of government. More than half the states now employ sentencing schemes, such as guideline-based or other forms of determinate sentencing or mandatory sentences, which are legislatively determined and insulated from judicial or administrative discretion.

Of course, such changes do not always work the way policymakers envisioned. Judges rebel against sentencing policies that handcuff their discretion and often ignore guideline suggestions or work around them. In addition, changing the way sentences are handed down can move discretion further up or further down the system. For example, when California restricted plea bargaining for sentence reductions in felony cases, prosecutors began bringing the cases to the lower courts where bargaining was permissible.[80]

Where reform has occurred, it has moved criminal sentences toward a model that stresses the equitable but firm distribution of sentences. A greater proportion of people are going to prison than ever before, but the sentences they receive for similar crimes are less likely to vary widely than in previous years. By reducing the discretion in sentencing, state and federal legislative bodies hope to eliminate disparity.[81]

■ Capital Punishment

The most severe sentence imposed in our nation is capital punishment, or execution. Applied extensively throughout American history, capital punishment was usually reserved for the two most serious criminal offenses: murder and rape. However, federal, state, and military courts have handed down this sentence for other crimes, such as kidnapping, treason (offenses against the federal government), espionage (spying for a foreign government), and desertion. The U.S. Supreme Court has generally limited the death penalty to first-degree murder in which aggravating circumstances such as profit or extreme cruelty were present.[82] However, federal statutes still allow the death penalty for espionage by a member of the armed forces and for treason.[83] Some states such as Mississippi have recently sentenced criminals to death for child rape.

Between 1930 and 1967, some 3,859 alleged criminals were executed in the United States: 86.4 percent for murder, 11.8 percent for rape, and 1.8 percent for other offenses. Of those executed, 53.5 percent were black and 45.4 percent were white.[84] A moratorium was put on capital punishment in 1967 while legal problems were worked out. Executions were resumed in 1976, and over 100 people have been executed since then; 11 people were executed in 1988.

Currently, about 2,100 people are on death row. Of these the majority are white (58 percent) males (99 percent) about 33 years old, who have completed the tenth grade, and are not married (71 percent).[85] One of the most controversial issues surrounding the death penalty is the fact that a disproportionate number of those sentenced to death are black: about 40 percent of the inmates currently on death row are black and about 1 percent are from other minority groups (see Table 14.3).

Arguments for the Death Penalty

A number of arguments are given for the retention of the death penalty as the most severe form of punishment. Some supporters argue that death is the "ultimate incapacitation" and the only one that can ensure that convicted killers will never be pardoned, paroled, or escape. Most states that do not have capital punishment provide for the sentence of "life in prison without the chance of parole." In 48 states, however, the chief executive has the right to grant clemency and commute a life sentence and in many states "lifers" are eligible for various furlough and release programs.[86] The potential for recidivism is a serious enough threat to require that murderers be denied further access to the public. In one research study, Stephen Markham and Paul Cassell found that of the 52,000 state prison inmates serving time for murder in 1984, 810 had previously been convicted of murder and had killed 821 people following their convictions.[87] In 1988 about 8% percent of all inmates on death row had prior convictions for homicide.[88] If all these people had been executed, many innocent lives would have been saved.

Proponents of capital punishment argue that executions serve as a strong deterrent for serious crimes. Although capital punishment probably cannot deter the mentally unstable, it could have an effect on the cold, calculating murderer, for example, the hired killer or one who kills for profit. As evidence that potential killers are swayed by the threat of capital punishment, its advocates point to studies that indicate that the murder rate declines substantially for every individual executed.[89]

TABLE 14.3 ■ **Demographic Profile of Prisoners under Sentence of Death**

	Year-end 1988	1988 Admissions	1988 Removals
Total number under sentence of death	2,124	296	139
Sex			
Male	98.9%	98.3%	97.8%
Female	1.1	1.7	2.2
Race			
White	58.3%	66.2%	61.9%
Black	40.2	30.7	36.7
Other	1.6	3.0	1.4
Ethnicity			
Hispanic	6.7%	10.1%	2.9%
Non-Hispanic	93.3	89.9	97.1
Age			
Less than 20 years	.5%	3.0%	0%
20–24	9.2	20.3	13.7
25–29	24.4	24.3	17.3
30–34	25.0	20.9	23.7
35–39	17.0	11.5	19.4
40–54	21.8	17.2	23.7
55 +	2.2	2.7	2.2
Median age	32.6 years	30.5 years	33.3 years
Education			
7th grade or less	9.5%	6.4%	8.8%
8th	9.7	8.4	14.4
9th–11th	36.6	35.3	40.0
12th	34.7	41.0	28.0
Any college	9.5	8.8	8.8
Median education	10.7 years	11.0 years	10.4 years
Marital status			
Married	29.7%	26.9%	31.5%
Divorced/separated	23.3	27.3	18.5
Widowed	2.1	3.5	4.6
Never married	44.9	42.3	45.4

SOURCE: Lawrence Greenfield, *Capital Punishment, 1988* (Washington, D.C.: Bureau of Justice Statistics, 1989).

Advocates of capital punishment justify it morally on the grounds that it is mentioned in the Bible and is part of the Judeo-Christian heritage. Although the U.S. Constitution forbids "cruel and unusual punishments," this prohibition could not be aimed at the death penalty since capital punishment was in use at the time the Constitution was drafted; the "original intent" of the Founding Fathers was to allow the states to impose the death penalty; capital punishment may be "cruel," but it is not "unusual."

Putting dangerous criminals to death also conforms to the requirement that punishment should be proportional to the seriousness of the crime. Since we currently use a system of escalating punishments, it follows that the most serious punishment should be employed to sanction the most serious crime. In addition, before the brutality of the death penalty is considered, the brutality that the offender showed the victim must not be forgotten.

Chapter 14

Punishment and Sentencing

■

Those who favor capital punishment maintain that a majority of the public believes that criminals who kill innocent victims should forfeit their own lives. Recent public opinion polls show that more than 70 percent of Americans favor the death penalty, almost double the percentage of 20 years ago.[90] Public approval was an important factor in the U.S. Supreme Court's decision to uphold the use of the death penalty in *Gregg v. Georgia*:

> Indeed, the decision that capital punishment may be the appropriate sanction in extreme cases is an expression of the community's belief that certain crimes are themselves so grievous an affront to humanity that the only adequate response may be the penalty of death.[91]

Finally, proponents of capital punishment insist that the many legal controls and appeals currently in use make it almost impossible for an innocent person to be executed or for the death penalty to be used in a racist or capricious manner. Although some unfortunate mistakes may have been made in the past, the current system makes it virtually impossible to execute an "innocent" person.

In sum, those who favor the death penalty view it as a traditional punishment for serious criminals, which can help prevent further criminality and is in keeping with the traditional moral values of fairness and equity.

Arguments against the Death Penalty

Critics of the death penalty regard it as a barbaric custom that has no place in a mature democratic society.[92] As important reasons for abolishing capital punishment, they point to its finality and brutality and the possibility that innocent persons will mistakenly be executed. Randall Adams spent many years on death row in Texas before being released in 1989 after the movie *The Thin Blue Line* drew attention to his case. According to Michael Radelet and Hugo Bedeau, in this century about 350 wrongful convictions for crimes which carry the death penalty have occurred, of which 23 led to executions. They estimate that approximately 3 death sentences are returned every two years in cases where the defendant has been falsely accused. More than half the errors stem from perjured testimony, false identifications, coerced confessions, and suppression of evidence. In addition to the 23 who were executed, 128 of the falsely convicted served more than 6 years in prison; 39 served more than 16 years in confinement, and 8 died while serving their sentence![93] From this Bedeau and Radelet conclude that although the system attempts to be especially cautious in capital cases, it is evident that unacceptable mistakes can occur. Bedeau and Radelet's disturbing conclusion has been challenged on the grounds that they used faulty methodology and overstate their case. Although their critics argue that miscarriages of justice in the use of the death penalty have become increasingly rare, Bedeau and Radelet have made an eloquent defense of their research.[94]

The question remains: Is the execution of even one innocent person too great a burden for our modern ("kinder and gentler") society to bear? This question must be answered carefully. As the number of people on death row increases, there will be renewed pressure on the justice system to process and review death penalty decisions. The backlog has prompted Chief Justice William Rehnquist to call for a speedup of the death penalty appeal process by such devices as consolidating all federal-level appeals into one petition that must be filed in a "reasonable time."[95] Limiting the appellate process may result in the type of error that Bedeau and Radelet have warned against.

Critics also frown upon the tremendous discretion used in seeking the death penalty and the arbitrary manner in which it is imposed.[96] Of the 17,000–20,000 persons arrested each year on homicide charges, only 250–300 are sentenced to death.[97] Although it is true that many of the arrested murderers are not eligible for execution because they did not commit first-degree murder, it is also likely that many serious criminals are not sentenced to death because of prosecutorial discretion. Individuals who have committed particularly serious crimes and know full well they will receive the death penalty if convicted may be moved to plea bargain to avoid capital punishment. In contrast, those who protest their innocence and demand a trial will be the ones most likely to receive the death penalty. When serial killer Theodore Bundy was executed in January 1989, he was one of the few notorious murderers actually put to death in modern times. Thus, the criminals who commit the most gruesome crimes may be the least likely to receive capital punishment.

Critics of the death penalty acknowledge it is approved by the general public, but they maintain that prevailing attitudes reflect a primitive desire for revenge and not "just desert." Therefore the U.S. Supreme Court's justification of that death penalty on the basis that it reflects public opinion should be reassessed.[98]

Those opposed to the death penalty also find little merit in the argument the capital punishment is a deterrent to crime. They charge that there is insufficient evidence that the threat of a death sentence can convince potential murderers to forgo their criminal activity. Most murders involve people who knew each other, very often friends and family members. Since murderers are often under the influence of alcohol and drugs or are suffering severe

Though advocates of capital punishment feel the sentence is necessary to remove dangerous criminals from society, most people who have been executed are not mass murderers like Ted Bundy. However, Bundy was executed in January, 1989.

psychological turmoil, it is unlikely that any penalty can have a deterrent impact. There is little current research that concludes that the death penalty is an effective deterrent.

The death sentence also rules out any hope of offender rehabilitation, no matter how old they were when convicted. Some evidence indicates that convicted killers actually can make good parole risks. James Marquart and Jonathan Sorensen followed the careers of murderers originally sentenced to death but given a reprieve when the Supreme Court changed the legal basis of the death penalty statutes in their states. Marquart and Sorensen found that convicted murderers were actually model inmates while in prison and once released committed fewer crimes than the typical releasee. They conclude that the execution of these inmates would not have greatly protected society.[99]

Critics also argue that the system of capital punishment is carried out in a racially biased manner. These charges are supported by the disproportionate numbers of blacks who have received the death sentence, are currently on death row, and have been executed (53.5 percent of all executions). We turn now to a more detailed discussion of this very important issue.

Racial Bias in the Death Penalty

One of the most compelling arguments against the use of the death penalty is that it is employed in a racially discriminatory fashion. About 41 percent of the inmates on death row are black, and this number is disproportionate to their representation in the population. Numbers alone are not sufficient evidence to prove discrimination, however. One way to evaluate the use of the death penalty is to compare the number of blacks on death row with the percentage of black citizens arrested for murder. Research by the federal government has shown that white criminals arrested for homicide actually have a slightly greater chance of getting the death penalty than blacks arrested for murder.[100] Similarly, the majority of murderers executed since 1980 have been white. Government researchers Lawrence Greenfield and David Hinners also found that whereas 11.6 percent of blacks arrested for homicide are sentenced to death, more than 15 percent of whites arrested for homicide received the death penalty. In addition, a higher proportion of white inmates were under a death sentence than were blacks.

Do these data prove that discrimination in the use of the death penalty does not exist? The answer to this question may lie outside simple calculation of the relative proportion of people sentenced to death. A number of researchers including Raymond Paternoster, David Baldus, and Gennaro Vito and Thomas Keil have found that the probability of receiving the death penalty is dependent more on the race of the *victim* than the race of the *offender*.[101] Regardless of whether they themselves are white or black, people who kill whites are much more likely to receive the death penalty than those who kill blacks. Prosecutors are significantly more likely to ask for the death penalty in a case involving a black offender and a white victim than they are in a case where both victim and criminal are black. Most murders are intraracial so it is not surprising that more whites get the death penalty than blacks, since in all likelihood they are being tried for killing a white victim.

It is possible that prosecutors are more likely to ask for the death penalty when a black offender kills a white victim because they believe it will be easier to obtain a conviction or because they are under public pressure to take a "hard line" in such cases. Though the prosecutors themselves may not personally hold racist attitudes, the fact remains that racial discrimination is present in the capital sentencing process.[102]

The Legality of Capital Punishment

In recent years, the constitutionality of the death penalty has been a major concern for both the nation's courts and its concerned social scientists. In 1972, in *Furman v. Georgia* the U.S. Supreme Court ruled that the discretionary imposition of the death penalty was **cruel and unusual punishment** that violated the Eighth and Fourteenth Amendments of the U.S. Constitution.[103] This case not only raised the question of whether capital punishment is a more effective deterrent than life imprisonment, but also challenged the very existence of the death penalty on the grounds of its brutality and finality. The Court, however, did not rule out the use of capital punishment as a penalty; rather, it objected to the arbitrary and capricious manner in which the death penalty was imposed. After *Furman*, many states revised their statutes that had allowed the death penalty to be imposed by jury discretion. Some states accomplished this by enacting statutory guidelines for jury decisions; others made the death penalty mandatory only for certain crimes. Despite these changes in statutory law, no further executions were carried out while the Supreme Court considered additional cases concerning the death penalty.

Then, in July 1976, the Supreme Court ruled on the constitutionality of five state death penalty statutes. In the first case, *Gregg v. Georgia*, the Court upheld a Georgia statute that required a jury to find at least one "aggravating circumstance" out of 10 in pronouncing the death penalty in murder cases.[104] In the *Gregg* case, for example, the jury imposed the death penalty after finding beyond a reasonable doubt two aggravating circumstances: (1) the offender was engaged in the commission of two other capital felonies; and (2) the offender committed the offense of murder for the purpose of receiving money and other financial gains (e.g., an automobile). In delivering the opinion of the court, Justice Potter Stewart stated:

> The basic concern of *Furman* centered on those defendants who were being condemned to death capriciously and arbitrarily. Under the procedures before the Court in that case, sentencing authorities were not directed to give attention to the nature or circumstance of the crime committed or to the character or record of the defendant. Left unguided, juries imposed the death sentence in a way that could only be called freakish. The new Georgia sentencing procedures, by contrast, focus the jury's attention on the particularized nature of the crime and the particularized characteristics of the individual defendant. While the jury is permitted to consider any aggravating or mitigating circumstances, it must find and identify at least one statutory aggravating factor before it may impose a penalty of death. In this way the jury's discretion is channeled. No longer can a jury wantonly and freakishly impose the death sentence; it is always circumscribed by the legislative guidelines. In addition, the review function of the Supreme Court of Georgia affords additional assurance that the concerns that prompted our decision in *Furman* are not present to any significant degree in the Georgia procedure applied here.
>
> For the reasons expressed in this opinion, we hold that the statutory system under which Gregg was sentenced to death does not violate the Constitution. Accordingly, the judgment of the Georgia Supreme Court is affirmed.[105]

The Court also upheld the constitutionality of a Texas statute on capital punishment in *Jurek v. Texas*,[106] and of a Florida statute in *Proffitt v. Florida*.[107]

The statutes of these states are similar to the Georgia statute in that they limit sentencing discretion not only by specifying the crimes for which capital punishment can be imposed, but also by stipulating criteria concerning the circumstances surrounding the crimes. For example, the Texas statute allowed the death sentence to be imposed only if the jury in a proceeding following the verdict responded in the affirmative to two and sometimes three of the following questions:

1. Whether the conduct of the defendant that caused the death of the deceased was committed deliberately and with the reasonable expectation that the death of the deceased or another would result.
2. Whether there is a probability that the defendant would commit criminal acts of violence that would constitute a continuing threat to society.
3. If raised by the evidence, whether the conduct of the defendant in killing the deceased was unreasonable in response to the provocation, if any, by the deceased.[108]

The Supreme Court, however, overruled the death penalty statutes of Louisiana, in *Roberts v. Louisiana*,[109] and North Carolina, in *Woodson v. North Carolina*.[110] Both these statutes provided for a mandatory death penalty in all first-degree murder cases. The Court's reasoning on the unconstitutionality of the statutes was expressed in *Woodson*:

> The history of mandatory death penalty statutes in the United States thus reveals that the practice of sentencing to death all persons convicted of a particular offense has been rejected as unduly harsh and unworkably rigid. . . . While the prevailing practice of individualizing sentencing determinations generally reflects simply enlightened policy rather than a constitutional imperative, we believe that in capital cases, the fundamental respect of humanity underlying the Eighth Amendment requires consideration of the character and record of the individual offender and the circumstances of the particular offense as a constitutionally indispensable part of the process of inflicting the penalty of death.[111]

The Supreme Court continued to deal with the death penalty and the "cruel and unusual punishment" question in the major cases *Coker v. Georgia, Gardner v. Florida*, and *Lockett v. Ohio*. In *Coker*, the Court ruled unconstitutional a death penalty sentence in Georgia for the crime of rape, but left unanswered the question of whether the death penalty can be imposed to prevent and deter other types of crime.[112] The Court overruled a death sentence penalty in *Gardner* because information contained in the presentence report was not disclosed to the defense attorney.[113] In *Lockett v. Ohio* the Court declared that the imposition of a capital punishment sentence must be based on reason and not on emotion. Limiting a judge's sentencing discretion to the narrow circumstances of the crime and the record of the offender makes it impossible to consider the individualized decision essential in capital cases.[114] In other cases the Supreme Court has upheld the right of a trial judge to disregard a jury's recommendation for leniency in a capital case and has ruled that it is not necessary for an appellate court to determine whether the sentence in a particular case was proportional to those given to others in that state, though most states hold proportionality hearings anyway.[115] However, the Court has limited the use of the death penalty by insisting that mitigating circumstances be considered before a capital sentence is handed down *(Eddings v. Oklahoma)* and has refused to allow minors under the age of 16 to be executed *(Thompson v. Oklahoma)* though upholding the execution of 16 and 17 year old defendants in *Wilkins v. Missouri* and *Stanford v. Kentucky* in 1989.[116]

In the most important death penalty case of the past few years, *McLesky v. Kemp*, the Court upheld the conviction of a black defendant in Georgia despite social science evidence that black criminals who kill white victims have a significantly greater chance of receiving the death penalty than white offenders who kill black victims. The Court ruled that the evidence of racial patterns in capital sentencing was not persuasive absent a finding of racial bias in the immediate case.[117] Many observers believe that *McLesky* presented the last significant legal obstacle that death penalty advocates had to overcome and that capital punishment will be used as a sentence in the United States for years to come.

Death-Qualified Juries

Another legal issue that has troubled opponents of capital punishment has been the removal of jurors who are opposed to the death penalty. In 1968 the Supreme Court upheld this practice in *Witherspoon v. Illinois*.[118] In addition, the Court has made it easier to convict people in death penalty cases by ruling that any jurors can be excused if the trial judge deems that their views on capital punishment will "prevent or substantially impair the performance of their duties."[119] In *Lockhart v. McCree* in 1986, the Court ruled that jurors can be removed because of their opposition to the death penalty at the guilt phase of a trial even though they would not have to consider the issue of capital punishment until a separate sentencing hearing. In this case the Court also ruled that removing anti–capital punishment jurors does not violate the Sixth Amendment's requirement that juries represent a fair cross section of the community nor does it unfairly tip the scale toward jurors who are prone to convict people in capital cases.[120] Thus it appears that for the present prosecutors will be able to excuse persons from serving on a jury who feel that the death penalty is wrong or immoral.

Research on the Death Penalty

Considerable empirical research has been carried out on the effectiveness of capital punishment as a deterrent. In particular, studies have tried to discover whether the mandatory death sentence serves as a more effective deterrent than life imprisonment for capital crimes such as homicide. One of the first noteworthy studies was conducted in Philadelphia in 1935 by Robert Dann.[121] He chose five highly publicized executions of convicted murderers in different years and determined the number of homicides in the 60-day period prior to and after each execution. Each 120-day period had approximately the same number of homicides, as well as the same number of days on which homicides occurred. Dann reasoned that if capital punishment does deter crime, this deterrent effect should cause a drop in the number of homicides in the days immediately following an execution. His study revealed, however, that more homicides occurred during the 60 days following an execution than prior to it, suggesting that the overall impact of executions might actually be to increase the incidence of homicide. Dann concluded that no deterrent effect was demonstrated. Dann's conclusion that capital punishment has little short-term effect has been supported by more recent research by David Phillips[122] and Sam McFarland.[123]

The view that capital punishment has no deterrent effect on crime was also confirmed by Karl Schuessler in 1952 after his analysis of 11 states during the years 1930 to 1949.[124] Schuessler examined annual data for homicide rates and execution risks (the number of executions for murder per 1,000 homicides per year) and concluded that homicide rates and execution rates move independently of each other. Extending this analysis to include an examination of European countries before and after the abolition of the death penalty, Schuessler found nothing in the data to suggest that homicide trends were influenced by the abolition of capital punishment. More recent research by Dane Archer, Rosemary Gartner, and Marc Beittel comparing homicide rates in 14 nations around the world found evidence to support Schuessler's earlier work. In fact, Archer, Gartner, and Beittel found that homicide rates declined in more than half the countries studied after capital punishment was abolished, a direct contradiction of its supposed deterrent effect.[125]

One of the most noted capital punishment studies was conducted by Thorsten Sellin in 1959.[126] Contiguous states were grouped in threes wherever at least one of the group differed from the others in maximum penalties for homicide; in each set, at least one state did not provide the death penalty for the research period in question, while the other two did. Within these clusters of similar jurisdictions, the homicide rates in states with capital punishment were compared with the homicide rates in states without a mandatory death penalty. Since the homicide trends in all states studied were found to be similar regardless of whether the death penalty was provided, Sellin concluded that capital punishment did not appear to have any influence on the reported rate of homicide. A recent update of the Sellin research by Richard Lempert was consistent in showing that there is no reason to believe that executions deter homicide.[127]

Another contiguous-state analysis was carried out in 1969 by Walter Reckless, who compared nine states in which the death penalty had been abolished with nine states in which it was still applied.[128] Using data from the 1967 Uniform Crime Reports, Reckless compared rates of murder, aggravated assault, and combined violent crimes. He found that five out of seven abolition states had lower crime rates than their contiguous death penalty states, while the remaining two states tied. He concluded that the death penalty is not an effective deterrent in such capital crimes.

Only a few studies have found that capital punishment may actually reduce the murder rate. The most oft-cited study was conducted in 1975 by Isaac Ehrlich of the University of Chicago.[129] Using highly advanced, complex statistical techniques, Ehrlich found evidence that murder is committed as a result of the hatred produced by interpersonal conflicts, and that the likelihood of a person's committing a crime is influenced by that person's perception of what can be gained by the criminal act. Thus, according to Ehrlich, the perception of execution risk (the number of people executed on being convicted of murder) is an important determinant of whether one individual will murder another. As a result of his analysis, Ehrlich concluded that each additional execution per year in the United States would save seven or eight people from being victims of murder. Additional research by Stephen Layson indicates that each execution can potentially save 18 lives.[130]

These few research efforts have been widely cited by death penalty advocates as empirical proof of the deterrent effect of capital punishment. Most notably, Ehrlich's results were used in the solicitor general's brief in the case of *Gregg v. Georgia* as new proof of the effectiveness of the death penalty. Subsequent analysis has questioned the methodology used in these studies, however, and indicates that the deterrent effects they uncovered resulted from errors in the statistical techniques used in the research.[131] In fact, reanalysis of the Ehrlich research by William Bowers and Glenn Pierce also turned up what is known as the **brutalization effect.**[132] This refers to the belief that executions actually increase murder rates because they raise the general violence level in society and because violence-prone people identify with the executioner and not the target of the death penalty. Consequently, when someone gets into a conflict with them or challenges their authority, they execute him or her in the same manner the state executes people who violate its rules.[133] The brutalization effect has been substantiated by other researchers including William Bailey in his study of the effect of executions in Chicago.[134]

In sum, studies that have attempted to show the actual impact of capital punishment on the murder rate indicate that the execution of convicted criminals has relatively little effect as a deterrent measure. Nevertheless, many people still hold to the efficacy of the death penalty as a crime deterrent, and recent Supreme Court decisions seem to herald a resumption of its use. And, of course, even if executions were no greater deterrent than a life sentence, people would still advocate their use on the grounds of desert and incapacitation.

Capital Punishment Today

When the state of Utah executed Gary Gilmore, a convicted murderer, by firing squad on January 17, 1977, it was the first execution in the United States in over a decade; since then there have been more than 100 executions. Opinion polls show that a majority of people believe that murderers ought to be given the death penalty and that public support for the death penalty has increased markedly in recent years. For example, in 1972 only 53 percent of those surveyed approved of the use of capital punishment whereas today the figure is about 70 percent. Furthermore, this approval cuts across racial, religious, and economic lines.[135] At least 38 states and the federal government have adopted new laws allowing capital punishment for murder and other serious crimes (see Table 14.4).[136] New laws allowing the death penalty are

The imposition of capital punishment, whether by electric chair or other means, has become increasingly controversial. Some persons have argued that the death penalty constitutes cruel and unusual punishment, but the Supreme Court has never held that capital punishment itself violates the Eighth Amendment. The Court has ruled, however, that the death penalty may not be imposed in an arbitrary or discriminatory manner.

TABLE 14.4 ■ **Method of Execution, by State**

Lethal injection	Electrocution	Lethal gas	Hanging	Firing squad
Arkansas	Alabama	Arizona	Montana	Idaho
Delaware	Connecticut	California	Washington	Utah
Idaho	Florida	Colorado		
Illinois	Georgia	Maryland		
Mississippi	Indiana	Mississippi		
Montana	Kentucky	Missouri		
Nevada	Louisiana	North Carolina		
New Hampshire	Nebraska			
New Jersey	Ohio			
New Mexico	Pennsylvania			
North Carolina	South Carolina			
Oklahoma	Tennessee			
Oregon	Vermont			
South Dakota	Virginia			
Texas				
Utah				
Washington				
Wyoming				

Chapter 14
Punishment and Sentencing

■

SOURCE: Lawrence Greenfield, *Capital Punishment, 1987* (Washington, D.C.: Bureau of Justice, 1988).

being seriously considered in some of the remaining jurisdictions.[137] Executions are carried out by a variety of methods including hanging, electrocution, gas, and, the most recent method, death by an injection of lethal drugs (see Table 14.4).

Since the *Furman* decision, the number of persons sentenced to death each year by state courts has increased markedly. As a result of recent court decisions, the go-ahead by the U.S. Supreme Court, and the implementation of death penalty statutes, many other states where offenders are on death row may contemplate carrying out the death sentence in the near future. Capital punishment will continue to be a viable and controversial issue in the American justice system in the 1990s.

■ SUMMARY

Punishment and sentencing have undergone many changes throughout the history of Western civilization. Initially, sentencing was characterized by the concepts of retribution, punishment, and the desire to fix sentences for convicted offenders. Throughout the middle years of the twentieth century, individualized sentencing was widely accepted, and the concept of rehabilitation was utilized in sentencing and penal codes. During the 1960s, however, experts began to become disenchanted with rehabilitation and other concepts that focused on treating the individual offender. Emphasis on treatment declined while emphasis on the individual legal rights of offenders increased. Entering the 1980s, many states returned to the concept of punishment in terms of mandatory and fixed sentences.

This development has led theorists to suggest that the philosophy of sentencing has changed from a model of rehabilitation to a model of "retributive justice," where the focus is on the offense and on a sentence likely to achieve equality of punishment and justice under the law.

The practice of sentencing can be traced back to ancient history, when retaliation and physical abuse were used to punish offenders for wrongdoing. Modern sentencing in the American criminal justice system is based on deterrence, incapacitation, and rehabilitation. Traditional dispositions include fines, probation, and incarceration, with probation being the most common choice. One of the most significant features of the sentencing process is its tripartite structure involving the legislature, the judge, and the correctional agency. Actions of each of these agencies affect the type of sentence, the length of sentence, and the release time imposed on the offender.

Although the courts today seek to fit the sentence to the individual and not to the crime, this philosophy often results in sentencing disparity. A number of states have developed determinate sentences that eliminate parole and attempt to restrict judicial discretion. Methods for making dispositions more uniform include appellate reviews of sentences and the use of sentencing guidelines, councils, and institutes.

The death penalty continues to be the most controversial sentence, with over half the states reinstituting capital punishment laws since the *Furman v. Georgia* decision of 1972. There is little evidence that the death penalty deters murder, but supporters view it as necessary in terms of incapacitation and retribution. Opponents point out that mistakes can be made, that capital sentences are apportioned in a racially biased manner, and that the practice is cruel and barbaric. Nevertheless, the courts have generally upheld the legality of capital punishment, and it has been used more frequently in recent years.

■ QUESTIONS

1. Discuss the sentencing dispositions in your jurisdiction. What are the pros and cons of each?

2. Compare the different types of incarceration sentences. What are the similarities and differences? Why are many jurisdictions considering the passage of mandatory sentencing laws?

3. Discuss the issue of capital punishment. In your opinion, does it serve as a deterrent? What new rulings has the U.S. Supreme Court made on the legality of the death penalty?

4. Why does the problem of sentencing disparity exist? Do programs exist that can reduce disparate sentences? If so, what are they?

5. Should all people who commit the same crime receive the same sentence?

6. Should convicted criminals be released from prison when correctional authorities are convinced they are rehabilitated?

■ NOTES

1. Michel Foucault, *Discipline and Punish* (New York: Vintage Books, 1978).

2. Graeme Newman, *The Punishment Response* (Philadelphia: J. B. Lippincott Co., 1978), p. 13.

3. Kathleen Daly, "Neither Conflict Nor Labeling Nor Paternalism Will Suffice: Intersections of Race, Ethnicity, Gender, and Family in Criminal Court Decisions," *Crime and Delinquency* 35 (1989): 136–68.

4. Among the most helpful sources for this section are Benedict Alper, *Prisons Inside-Out* (Cambridge, Mass.: Ballinger Publishing Co., 1974); Gustave de Beaumont and Alexis de Tocqueville, *On the Penitentiary System in the United States and Its Applications in France* (Carbondale, Ill.: Southern Illinois University Press, 1964); Orlando Lewis, *The Development of American Prisons and Prison Customs, 1776–1845* (Montclair, N.J.: Patterson-Smith, 1967); Leonard Orland, ed., *Justice, Punishment, and Treatment* (New York: Free Press, 1973); Julius Goebel, *Felony and Misdemeanor* (Philadelphia: University of Pennsylvania Press, 1976); Georg Rusche and Otto Kircheimer, *Punishment and Social Structure* (New York: Russell & Russell, 1939); Samuel Walker, *Popular Justice* (New York: Oxford University Press, 1980); Newman, *The Punishment Response*; David Rothman, *Conscience and Convenience* (Boston: Little, Brown & Co., 1980).

5. Rusche and Kircheimer, *Punishment and Social Structure*, p. 9.

6. Ibid., p. 19.

7. George Ives, *A History of Penal Methods* (Montclair, N.J.: Patterson-Smith, 1970).

8. Robert Hughes, *The Fatal Shore* (New York: Alfred A. Knopf, 1987).

9. Leon Radzinowicz, *A History of English Criminal Law*, vol. 1 (London: Stevens, 1943), p. 5.

10. Newman, *The Punishment Response*, p. 139.

11. Lonn Lanza-Kaduce, "Perceptual Deterrence and Drinking and Driving among College Students," *Criminology* 26 (1988): 321–41.

12. Ibid.

13. Raymond Paternoster, "The Deterrent Effect of the Perceived Certainty and Severity of Punishment," *Justice Quarterly* 4 (1987): 173–217.

14. Raymond Paternoster, "Examining Three-Wave Deterrence Models: A Question of Temporal Order and Specification," *Journal of Criminal Law and Criminology* 79 (1988): 135–79.

15. Charles Tittle, "Sanction Fear and the Maintenance of the Social Order," *Social Forces* 55 (1977): 579–96.

16. Kirk Williams and Richard Hawkins, "The Meaning of Arrest for Wife Assault," *Criminology* 27 (1989): 163–81; see also Donald Dutton, *The Domestic Assault of Women: Psychological and Criminal Justice Perspectives* (Boston: Allyn and Bacon, 1988).

17. Allen Beck and Bernard Shipley, *Recidivism of Young Parolees* (Washington, D.C.: Bureau of Justice Statistics, 1987).

18. Bureau of Justice Statistics, *Report to the Nation on Crime and Justice* (Washington, D.C.: Bureau of Justice Statistics, 1988). p. 105.

19. "Inmate Population Predicted to Surpass 1 Million This Year," *Criminal Justice Newsletter*, 15 February 1989, p. 5.

20. Gerald Wheeler and Rodney Hissong, "Effects of Sanctions on Drunk Drivers: Beyond Incarceration," *Crime and Delinquency* 34 (1988): 29–42.

21. Douglas Smith and Patrick Gartin, "Specifying Specific Deterrence: The Influence of Arrest in Future Criminal Activity," *American Sociological Review* 54 (1989): 94–105.

22. Jeffrey Fagan, "Cessation of Family Violence: Deterrence and Dissuasion," in *Crime and Justice: An Annual Review of Research*, vol. 11, Lloyd Ohlin and Michael Tonry, eds. (Chicago: University of Chicago Press, 1989), pp. 100–151.

23. Alexis Durham, "The Justice Model in Historical Context: Early Law, the Emergence of Science, and the Rise of Incarceration," *Journal of Criminal Justice* 16 (1988): 331–46.

24. Andrew von Hirsch, *Doing Justice: The Choice of Punishments* (New York: Hill and Wang, 1976).

25. Alexis Durham, "Crime Seriousness and Punitive Severity: An Assessment of Social Attitudes," *Justice Quarterly* 5 (1988): 131–53.

26. Joan Petersilia, Susan Turner, James Kahan, and Joyce Peterson, *Granting Felons Probation: Public Risks and Alternatives* (Santa Monica, Calif.: Rand Corporation, 1986).

27. Francis Cullen, John Cullen, John Wozniak, "Is Rehabilitation Dead? The Myth of the Punitive Public," *Journal of Criminal Justice* 16 (1988): 303–16.

28. Bureau of Justice Statistics, *Report to the Nation on Crime and Justice*, vol. 2, p. 90.

29. Division of Probation, "The Selective Presentence Investigation Report," *Federal Probation* 38 (December 1974): 48.

30. See American Bar Association, *Standards Relating to Sentencing Alternatives and Procedures* (New York: Institute of Judicial Administration, 1968), sec, 4.1, pp. 202–3.

31. John Rosencrance, "Maintaining the Myth of Individualized Justice: Probation Presentence Reports," *Justice Quarterly* 5 (1988): 236–56.

32. Adapted from Alan Dershowitz, *Fair and Certain Punishment: Report of the Twentieth Century Task Force on Criminal Sentencing* (New York: Twentieth Century Fund, 1976).

33. Patrick Langan, *State Felony Courts and Felony Laws* (Washington, D.C.: Bureau of Justice Statistics, 1987), p. 6.

34. Kenneth Culp Davis, *Discretionary Justice: A Preliminary Inquiry* (Baton Rouge: Louisiana State University Press, 1969); Marvin Frankel, *Criminal Sentences: Law without Order* (New York: Hill and Wang, 1972).

35. See Frankel, *Criminal Sentences: Law without Order*, Bureau of Justice Statistics, p. 5.

36. *Report to the Nation on Crime and Justice*, vol. 2, p. 91.

37. Kay Knapp, "Structured sentencing: building on experience," *Judicature* 72 (1988): 47–52.

38. Ibid., p. 7.

39. Marvin Zalman, "The Rise and Fall of the Indeterminate Sentence," *Wayne Law Review* 24 (1978): 857–88, at 877.

40. Andrew von Hirsch, *Past or Future Crimes* (New Brunswick, N.J.: Rutgers University Press, 1985).

41. Minnesota Sentencing Guidelines Commission, *The Impact of the Minnesota Sentencing Guidelines: Three Year Evaluation* (St. Paul, Minn.: 1984), p. 162.

42. Terance Miethe and Charles Moore, "Socioeconomic Disparities under Determinate Sentencing Systems: A Comparison of Preguideline and Postguideline Practices in Minnesota," *Criminology* 23 (1985): 337–63.

43. *Mistretta v. United States*, 44 CrL 3061 (January 15, 1989).

44. Knapp, "Structured sentencing: building on experience."

45. Miethe and Moore, "Socioeconomic Disparities under Determinate Sentencing Systems."

46. Joan Petersilia and Susan Turner, *Guideline-Based Justice: The Implications for Racial Minorities* (Santa Monica, Calif.: Rand Corporation, 1985).

47. David Griswold, "Deviation from Sentencing Guidelines: The Issue of Unwarranted Disparity," *Journal of Criminal Justice* 16 (1988): 317–29.

48. "Defense Lawyers Will Continue to Fight Sentencing Guidelines," *Criminal Justice Newsletter*, 15 February 1989, p. 1–2.

49. Ibid., p. 2.

50. Chris Eskridge, "Sentencing Guidelines: To Be or Not to Be," *Federal Probation* 50 (1986): 70–76.

51. Timothy Bynum, "Prosecutorial Discretion and the Implementation of a Legislative Mandate," in *Implementing Criminal Justice Policies*, Merry Morash, ed. (Beverly Hills, Calif.: Sage Publications, 1982); Massachusetts General Laws, chap. 269, 10, chap. 649, Acts of 1974; see also Kenneth Carlson, *Mandatory Sentencing: The Experiences of Two States* (Washington, D.C.: U.S. Government Printing Office, 1982).

52. Timothy Schellhardt, "Law and Order," *Wall Street Journal*, 24 June 1976.

53. See, generally, "A Symposium on Sentencing, Parts I & II," *Hofstra Law Review* 7 (1979): 1.

54. Alan Dershowitz, *Fair and Certain Punishment: Report of the Twentieth Century Task Force on Criminal Sentencing* (New York: Twentieth Century Fund, 1976).

55. Michael Tonry, *Sentencing Reform Impacts* (Washington, D.C.: U.S. Government Printing Office, 1987), pp. 26–27.

56. Derral Cheatwood, "The Life-Without-Parole Sanction: Its Current Status and a Research Agenda," *Crime and Delinquency* 34 (1988): 43–59.

57. Ibid., p. 48.

58. 445 U.S. 263, 100 S.Ct. 1133, 63 L.Ed.2d 382 (1980).

59. 463 U.S. 277; 103 S.Ct. 3001, 77 L.Ed.2d 637 (1983).

60. Patrick Langan, *Felony Sentences in State Courts, 1986* (Washington, D.C.: Bureau of Justice Statistics, 1989).

61. Edward Lisefski and Donald Manson, *Tracking Offenders, 1984* (Washington, D.C.: Bureau of Justice Statistics, 1988).

62. For a general look at the factors that affect sentencing, see Susan Welch, Cassia Spohn, and John Gruhl, "Convicting and Sentencing Differences among Black, Hispanic, and White Males in Six Localities," *Justice Quarterly* 2 (1985): 67–80.

63. Alfred Blumstein, "On the Racial Disproportionality of the United States Prison Population," *The Journal of Criminal Law and Criminology* 73 (1982): 1259–81.

64. Joan Petersilia, *Racial Disparities in the Criminal Justice System* (Santa Monica, Calif.: Rand Corporation, 1983).

65. Blumstein, "On the Racial Disproportionality of the United States Prison Population."

66. Darnell Hawkins, "Race, Crime Type and Imprisonment," *Justice Quarterly* 3 (1986): 251–69; James Unnever and Larry Hembroff,

"The Prediction of Racial/Ethnic Sentencing Disparities: An Expectation States Approach," *Journal of Research in Crime and Delinquency* 25 (1988): 53–82.

67. Hawkins, "Race, Crime Type and Imprisonment," p. 267.

68. George Bridges, Robert Crutchfield and Edith Simpson, "Crime, Social Structure and Criminal Punishment: White and Nonwhite Rates of Imprisonment," *Social Problems* 34 (1987): 345–61; Terance Miethe and Charles Moore, "Racial Differences in Criminal Processing: The Consequences of Model Selection on Conclusions about Differential Treatment," *Sociological Quarterly* 27 (1987): 217–37.

69. See, generally, Martha Myers, "Offended Parties and Official Reactions: Victims and the Sentencing of Criminal Defendants," *Sociological Quarterly* 20 (1979): 529–40.

70. See, generally, Janet Johnston, Thomas Kennedy, and I. Gayle Shuman, "Gender Differences in the Sentencing of Felony Offenders," *Federal Probation* 87 (1987): 49–56; Cassia Spohn and Susan Welch, "The Effect of Prior Record in Sentencing Research: An Examination of the Assumption That Any Measure Is Adequate," *Justice Quarterly* 4 (1987): 286–302; Candace Kruttschnitt, "Sex and Criminal Court Dispositions," *Journal of Research in Crime and Delinquency* 21 (1984): 213–32; Cynthia Kempinen, "Changes in the Sentencing Patterns of Male and Female Defendants," *Prison Journal* 63 (1983): 3–11; David Willison, "The Effects of Counsel on the Severity of Criminal Sentences: A Statistical Assessment," *Justice System Journal* 9 (1984): 87–101.

71. Dean Champion, "Elderly Felons and Sentencing Severity: Interregional Variations in Leniency and Sentencing Trends," *Criminal Justice Review* 12 (1987): 7–15.

72. Ibid., p. 13.

73. Christopher Link and Neal Shover, "The Origins of Sentencing Reforms," *Justice Quarterly* 3 (1986): 329–41.

74. American Law Institute, *Model Penal Code*, Proposed Official Draft, 1962.

75. National Council on Crime and Delinquency, *Model Sentencing Act*, 1963 and 1972.

76. American Bar Association, *Standards Relating to Sentencing Alternatives and Procedures*, standard 7.2 and commentary, p. 299.

77. See, generally, American Bar Association, *Standards Relating to Appellate Review of Sentences* (New York: Institute of Judicial Administration, 1968).

78. Frank Remington, "Post-conviction review—what state trial courts can do to reduce problems," *Judicature* 72 (1988): 53–58.

79. Thomas Hester, *Probation and Parole, 1987* (Washington, D.C.: Bureau of Justice Statistics, 1988), p. 4.

80. Scott Paltrow, "New Anti-Crime Law in California Is Helping Some Accused Felons," *Wall Street Journal*, 26 November 1982.

81. Susan D. Krup, "A Retributive-Justice Model of Sentencing," *Federal Probation* (December 1981): 24–29; von Hirsch, *Doing Justice: The Choice of Punishments*, chaps. 8, 9, 10; Raymond Paternoster and Tim Byrum, "The Justice Model as Ideology: A Critical Look at Sentencing Reform," *Contemporary Crisis* 6 (1982): 7–24.

82. *Coker v. Georgia*, 433 U.S. 584, 97 S.Ct. 2861, 53 L.Ed.2d 982 (1977).

83. Espionage (10 U.S.C. 906[a]); treason (18 U.S.C. 2381).

84. William Bowers, *Executions in America* (Lexington, Mass.: D.C. Heath Co., 1974).

85. Lawrence Greenfield, *Capital Punishment, 1988*, (Washington, D.C.: Bureau of Justice Statistics, 1989), p. 7.

86. Cheatwood, "The Life-Without-Parole Sanction: Its Current Status and a Research Agenda," p. 49.

87. Stephen Markman and Paul Cassell, "Protecting the Innocent: A Response to the Bedau-Radelet Study," *Stanford Law Review* 41 (1988): 121–70, at 153.

88. Greenfield, *Capital Punishment, 1988*, p. 8.

89. Stephen Layson, "United States Time-Series Homicide Regressions with Adaptive Expectations," *Bulletin of the New York Academy of Medicine* 62 (1986): 589–619.

90. Timothy Flanagan and Katherine Jamieson, *Sourcebook of Criminal Justice Statistics* (Washington, D.C.: Bureau of Justice Statistics, 1988), p. 161; see also James Finckenauer, "Public Support for the Death Penalty Retribution as Just Deserts or Retribution as Revenge?" *Justice Quarterly* 5 (1988): 83.

91. 428 U.S. 153, 96 S.Ct. 2909, 49 L.Ed.2d 859 (1976).

92. See, generally, Hugo Bedau, *Death Is Different: Studies in the Morality, Law, and Politics of Capital Punishment* (Boston: Northeastern University Press, 1987); Keith Otterbein, *The Ultimate Coercive Sanction* (New Haven, Conn.: HRAF Press, 1986).

93. Michael Radelet and Hugo Bedau, "Miscarriages of Justice in Potentially Capital Cases," *Stanford Law Review* 40 (1987): 21–181.

94. Markman and Cassell, "Protecting the Innocent: A Response to the Bedau-Radelet Study"; Hugo Adam Bedau and Michael Radelet, "The Myth of Infallibility: A reply to Markman and Cassell," *Stanford Law Review* 42 (1989): 161–70.

95. Associated Press, "Rehnquist calls for more speed in carrying out death sentences," *Boston Globe*, 7 February 1989, p. 10.

96. Barry Nakell and Kenneth Hardy, *The Arbitrariness of the Death Penalty* (Philadelphia: Temple University Press, 1987).

97. Lawrence Greenfield and David Hinners, *Capital Punishment 1984* (Washington, D.C.: Bureau of Justice Statistics, 1985), p. 5.

98. Finckenauer, "Public Support for the Death Penalty," pp. 81–100.

99. James Marquart and Jonathan Sorensen, "Institutional and Postrelease Behavior of Furman-Commuted Inmates in Texas," *Criminology* 26 (1988): 677–93.

100. Greenfield and Hinners, *Capital Punishment 1984*.

101. Gennaro Vito and Thomas Keil, "Capital Sentencing in Kentucky: An Analysis of the Factors Influencing Decision Making in the Post-Gregg Period," *The Journal of Criminal Law and Criminology* 79 (1988): 483–503; David Baldus, C. Pulaski, and G. Woodworth, "Comparative Review of Death Sentences: An Empirical Study of the Georgia Experience," *The Journal of Criminal Law and Criminology* 74 (1983): 661–85; Raymond Paternoster, "Race of the Victim and Location of Crime: The Decision to Seek the Death Penalty in South Carolina," *The Journal of Criminal Law and Criminology* 74 (1983): 754–85.

102. Vito and Keil, "Capital Sentencing in Kentucky," pp. 502–3.

103. 408 U.S. 238, 92 S.Ct. 2726, 33 L.Ed.2d 346 (1972).

104. 428 U.S. 153, 96 S.Ct. 2909, 49 L.Ed.2d 859 (1976).

105. Ibid., 96 S.Ct. at 2940–2941.

106. 428 U.S. 262, 96 S.Ct. 2950, 49 L.Ed.2d 929 (1976).

107. 428 U.S. 242, 96 S.Ct. 2960, 49 L.Ed.2d 913 (1976).

108. *Jurek v. Texas*, 96 S.Ct. at 2955.

109. 428 U.S. 325, 96 S.Ct. 3001, 49 L.Ed.2d 974 (1976).

110. 428 U.S. 280, 96 S.Ct. 2978, 49 L.Ed.2d 944 (1976).

111. Ibid., 96 S.Ct. at 2986, 2991.

112. 438 U.S. 584, 97 S.Ct. 2861, 53 L.Ed.2d 982 (1977).

113. 430 U.S. 349, 97 S.Ct. 1197, 51 L.Ed.2d 393 (1977).

114. 438 U.S. 801, 98 S.Ct. 2981, 57 L.Ed.2d 973 (1978).

115. *Spaziano v. Florida*, 468 U.S. 447, 104 S.Ct. 3154, 82 L.Ed.2d 340 (1984); *Pulley v. Harris*, 465 U.S. 37; 104 S.Ct. 871; 79 L.Ed.2d 29 (1984).

116. *Eddings v. Oklahoma*, 455 U.S. 104, 102 S.Ct. 869, 71 L.Ed.2d 1 (1982); *Thompson v. Oklahoma*; *Wilkins v. Missouri* and *Stanford v. Kentucky* 1989.

117. 478 U.S. 1019, 106 S.Ct. 3331, 92 L.Ed.2d 737 (1986).

118. 391 U.S. 510, 88 S.Ct. 1770, 20 L.Ed.2d 776 (1968).

119. *Wainwright v. Witt*, 469 U.S. 412, 105 S.Ct. 844, 83 L.Ed.2d 841 83 L.Ed. 841 (1985).

120. 176 U.S. 162, 106 S.Ct. 1758, 90 L.Ed.2d 137 (1986).

121. Robert H. Dann, "The Deterrent Effect of Capital Punishment," *Friends Social Service Series* 29 (1935): 1.

122. David Phillips, "The Deterrent Effect of Capital Punishment," *American Journal of Sociology* 86 (1980): 139–48.

123. Sam McFarland, "Is Capital Punishment a Short-term Deterrent to Homicide? A Study of the Effects of Four Recent American Executions," *The Journal of Criminal Law and Criminology* 74 (1984): 1014–32.

124. Karl F. Schuessler, "The Deterrent Influence of the Death Penalty," *Annals* 284 (1952): 54.

125. Dane Archer, Rosemary Gartner and Marc Beittel, "Homicide and the Death Penalty: A Cross-National Test of a Deterrence Hypothesis," *The Journal of Criminal Law and Criminology* 74 (1983): 991–1014.

126. Thorsten Sellin, "Effect of Repeal and Reintroduction of the Death Penalty on Homicide Rates," in *The Death Penalty*, Thorsten Sellin, ed. (Philadelphia: American Law Institute, 1959).

127. Richard Lempert, "The Effect of Executions on Homicides: A New Look in an Old Light," *Crime and Delinquency* 29 (1983): 88–115.

128. Walter C. Reckless, "Use of the Death Penalty," *Crime and Delinquency* 15 (1969): 43.

129. Isaac Ehrlich, "The Deterrent Effect of Capital Punishment: A Question of Life or Death," *American Economic Review* 65 (1975): 397.

130. Layson, "United States Time-Series Homicide Regressions with Adaptive Expectations."

131. William J. Bowers and Glenn L. Pierce, "The Illusion of Deterrence in Isaac Ehrlich's Research on Capital Punishment," *Yale Law Journal* 85 (1975): 187–208.

132. William Bowers and Glenn Pierce, "Deterrence or Brutalization: What Is the Effect of Executions?" *Crime and Delinquency* 26 (1980): 453–84.

133. Ibid., p. 480.

134. William Bailey, "Disaggregation in Deterrence and Death Penalty Research: The Case of Murder in Chicago," *The Journal of Criminal Law and Criminology* 74 (1986): 827–59.

135. Flanagan and Jamieson, *Sourcebook of Criminal Justice Statistics*, 1987, p. 162.

136. "Capital Punishment in the United States," *Crime and Delinquency Journal* 26 (1980): 441.

137. Karen Polk, "New York assembly votes 97–48 to restore death penalty," *Boston Globe*, 8 March 1989, p. 71.

Chapter 14

Punishment and Sentencing

■

PART FOUR

Corrections

15

Probation and Intermediate Sanctions

The general public usually equates being sentenced for a serious crime with a stay in a prison or jail. And though many Americans would like to see dangerous offenders "do hard time," incarcerating every convicted criminal is both expensive and unworkable. The existing prison system is overcrowded to the breaking point, and building new institutions is a costly, long-term proposition. Furthermore there is little evidence that a prison stay rehabilitates many inmates; recidivism rates are disturbingly high. This failure of traditional correctional models has prompted criminal justice policymakers to create **alternatives to incarceration** that are both effective and economical. The most customary of these, probation, involves maintaining an offender in the community under a set of behavioral rules created and administered by judicial authority. Considering the potential benefits and cost-effectiveness of a probation sentence, it is not surprising that the number of probationers is at an all-time high—more than 2 million.

The need to create effective, efficient methods of controlling offenders in the community has also prompted correctional policymakers to develop new forms of community-based **intermediate sanctions: pre-trial programs, fines** and **forfeiture, restitution, shock probation/split sentencing, house arrest, electronic monitoring, intensive probation supervision,** and **residential community corrections.** These are designed to provide greater control over an offender and increase the level of state sanctions without resorting to a prison sentence.

Both traditional probation and the newer intermediate sanctions have the potential to become reasonable answers to many of the economic and social problems faced by correctional administrators: they are less costly than jail or prison sentences; they help the offender maintain family and community ties; they can be structured to maximize security and maintain public safety; and they can be scaled in severity to correspond to the seriousness of the crime. No area of the criminal justice system is currently undergoing more change and greater expansion than probation and intermediate sanctions.

This chapter reviews this emerging area of criminal sanctions. It begins with a brief history of probation and examines probation as an organization, sentence, and correctional practice. Then attention is focused on such alternative sanctions as intensive supervision, house arrest, and electronic monitoring.

■ History of Probation

The roots of probation can be traced back to the traditions of the English common law.[1] During the Middle Ages, judges wishing to spare deserving offenders from the pains of the then-common punishments of torture, mutilation, and death used their power to grant clemency and stays of execution. The common law practice of **judicial reprieve** allowed judges to suspend punishment so that convicted offenders could seek a pardon, gather new evidence, or demonstrate that they had reformed their behavior. Similarly, the practice of **recognizance** enabled convicted offenders to remain free if they agreed to enter into a debt obligation with the state. The debt would have to be paid only if the offender was caught engaging in further criminal behavior.[2] Sometimes **sureties** were required. These were people who made themselves responsible for the behavior of the offenders after they were released.

Although early American courts continued the practice of indefinitely suspending sentences of offenders who seemed deserving of a second chance,

KEY TERMS

Alternatives to incarceration
Intermediate sanctions
Pretrial programs
Fines
Forfeiture
Restitution
Shock probation
Split sentencing
House arrest
Electronic monitoring
Intensive probation supervision (IPS)
Residential community corrections
Judicial reprieve
Recognizance
Sureties
John Augustus
Revoked
Suspended sentence
Model Penal Code
Standard rules
Chief probation officer
Intake
Volunteers
Diagnosis
Risk classification
Day fees
Day fines
Racketeer Influenced and Corrupt
    Organizations Act (RICO)
Continuing Criminal Enterprises Act
    (CCE)
Zero tolerance
Monetary restitution
Community service restitution
James Byrne
Surveillance officers

Chapter 15
Probation and Intermediate Sanctions

■

John Augustus of Boston is usually credited with originating the modern concept of probation. Though only a private citizen, in 1841 Augustus began to supervise offenders released to his custody by a Boston judge. Over an 18-year period, Augustus supervised close to 2,000 probationers and helped them find jobs and establish themselves in the community. He had an amazingly high success rate, and few of his charges became involved in crime again.

In 1878, Augustus' work inspired the Massachusetts state legislature to pass a statute authorizing the appointment of a paid probation officer for the city of Boston. In 1880 probation was extended to other jurisdictions in Massachusetts, and by 1898 the probation movement had spread to the superior (felony) courts.[3] The Massachusetts experience was copied by Missouri (1887), Vermont (1898), and soon after by most other states. In 1925 the federal government established a probation system for the U.S. District Courts. Although some critics, such as historian David Rothman, view these early efforts as ineffectual measures that merely expanded society's control over the poor, the probation concept soon became the most widely used correctional mechanism in the United States.[4]

■ The Concept of Probation

Probation is a criminal sentence that mandates that a convicted offender be placed and maintained in the community under the supervision of a duly authorized agent of the court. Once on probation, the offender is subject to certain rules and conditions that must be followed in order for that person to remain in the community. The probation sentence is managed by a probation department that supervises offenders' behavior and treatment and carries out other tasks for the court. Although the term has many meanings, probation usually refers to a nonpunitive form of sentencing for convicted criminal offenders and delinquent youth, which emphasizes maintenance in the community and treatment without institutionalization or other forms of punishment.[5]

The philosophy behind probation is that the average offender is not actually a dangerous criminal or a menace to society. When offenders are institutionalized instead of being granted community release, however, the prison community becomes their new reference point, they are forced to interact with hardened criminals, and the "ex-con" label prevents them from making successful adjustments to society. Probation provides offenders with the opportunity to prove themselves, gives them a second chance, and allows them to be closely supervised by trained personnel who can help them reestablish proper forms of behavior in the community.

In practice, probation usually involves suspension of the offender's prison sentence in return for the promise of good behavior in the community under the supervision of the probation department. As practiced in all 50 states and by the federal government, probation implies a contract between the court and the offender in which the former promises to hold a prison term in abeyance while the latter promises to adhere to a set of rules or conditions mandated by the court. If the rules are violated, and especially if the probationer commits another criminal offense, probation may be **revoked;** in this case the contract is terminated, and the original sentence is enforced. If an offender on probation commits a second offense that is more serious than the first, he or she may also be indicted, tried, and sentenced on that second offense. However, probation may be revoked simply because the offender has failed to comply with the rules and conditions of probation; it is not necessary for an offender to commit further crime.

Each probationary sentence is for a fixed period of time, depending on the seriousness of the offense and the statutory law of the jurisdiction. Probation is considered served when the offender fulfills the conditions set by the court for that period of time; he or she can then live without state supervision.

■ Awarding Probation

Probationary sentences may be granted by state and federal district courts and state superior (felony) courts. Probation has become an accepted and widely used sentence for adult felons and misdemeanors and for juvenile delinquents.

In some states, juries may recommend probation as part of their sentencing power, or they may make recommendations to judges, which they will usually follow if the case meets certain legally established criteria (e.g., if it falls within a certain class of offenses as determined by statute).[6] Although juries can recommend probation, the judge has the final say in the matter and may grant probation at his or her discretion. In nonjury trials probation is granted solely by judicial mandate.

In most jurisdictions, all juvenile offenders are eligible for probation, as are most adults. Some state statutes prohibit probation for certain types of adult offenders, usually those who have engaged in repeated and serious violent crimes such as murder or rape, or those who commit crimes for which mandatory prison sentences have been legislated.

The most common manner in which a probationary sentence is imposed is for the judge to formulate a prison sentence and then suspend it if the offender agrees to obey the rules of probation while living in the community (**suspended sentence**). An estimated 52 percent of all probationary sentences are distributed in this manner.[7] The term of a probationary sentence may extend to the limit of the suspended prison term, or the court may set a shorter time limit. For misdemeanors, probation usually extends for the entire period of the jail sentence, while felonies are more likely to warrant probationary periods that are actually shorter than their prison sentences would have been. The Federal Criminal Code allows probationary sentences to last up to five years. Juveniles are typically placed on probation for periods ranging from 6 to 24 months.

Probation may also be granted to an offender whose sentence is deferred pending successful completion of his or her probationary period (about 6 percent of all cases).[8] This step is usually taken to encourage the defendant to pursue a specific treatment program, for example, alcohol rehabilitation. If the program is successfully completed, usually no further legal action is taken. Probation can also be a sole sentence (42 percent) in which no prison sentence is imposed or contemplated, but if the probationer violates the rules, he or she can be returned to court for resentencing.

■ The Extent of Probation

There are approximately 1,920 adult probation agencies in the United States.[9] Most (56 percent) are associated with a state-level agency, while the remainder

Woodrow Wilson Collums pleaded guilty in 1982 to the "mercy killing" shooting of his brother who suffered from Alzheimer's disease. Taking the extenuating circumstances into account, the judge sentenced Collums to spend ten years on probation and to work ten hours per week in a home for older citizens.

are organized at the county or municipal level of government. About 30 states combine probation and parole supervision into a single agency.

A recent federal survey found that approximately 2,242,053 adults, or about 65 percent of all adults under some form of correctional supervision, were on probation at the beginning of 1988.[10] The survey also found that the probation population had increased 6 percent from the previous year, which indicates that U.S. judges were enthusiastic about using probation as an alternative to a prison or jail term. In fact, the ratio of the probation population to the prison population has actually increased in recent years indicating that, if anything, the probation population is increasing at a faster rate than the prison population. As of 1988, about 1.4 million adult offenders were being put on probation and about 1.2 million were completing their probationary sentences each year.

Probation is used more frequently in some states than others. In 18 states, led by Georgia and the District of Columbia, more than 1 percent of the adult residents were on probation. Overall, about 1.2 of every hundred adults were on probation at the beginning of 1988. The extensive use of probation is probably a reflection of its low cost and its importance to the efficient operation of the justice system. A study by the Texas Adult Probation Commission found that it costs about 12 times as much to incarcerate an offender as it does to supervise an individual on probation.[11] Without probation the correctional system would be rapidly overcrowded and undoubtedly in serious financial distress.

■ Eligibility for Probation

Whether an offender will be granted probation depends on several factors. Some states limit the use of probation in serious felony cases and for specific crimes whose penalties are controlled by mandatory sentencing laws. The granting of probation to serious felons is not unknown, however.

In most states, the criminal code lists the factors that a judge should take into account when deciding whether to grant probation. Despite these statutory efforts, the probation decision is often a discretionary one based on the beliefs and attitudes of the presiding judge and probation staff. Many states have attempted to control judicial discretion by creating probation guidelines. The American Law Institute's **Model Penal Code** standard (see Table 15.1) has been adopted by a number of states seeking more uniform probation criteria.[12]

Although judges often follow these suggested criteria, probation decision making is still far from uniform, and an individual offender who is granted probation in one jurisdiction might not receive it in another.

Felony Probation

Many people believe that probation is given to minor or first offenders who are deserving of "a break," but this is not actually the case. Many serious criminal offenders are granted probation sentences. One study of sentencing procedures in 28 large legal jurisdictions found that about 25 percent of all convicted felons are granted probation including people convicted of homicide (8 percent), rape (16 percent), robbery (13 percent), and burglary (25 percent).[13]

An oft-cited study conducted by Joan Petersilia and her colleagues at the Rand Corporation tracked 1,672 men convicted of felonies and granted

TABLE 15.1 ■ Suggested Criteria for Granting Probation

1. The court shall deal with a person who has been convicted of a crime without imposing sentence of imprisonment unless, having regard to the nature and circumstances of the crime and the history, character and condition of the defendant, it is of the opinion that his imprisonment is necessary for protection of the public because:
   a. there is undue risk that during the period of a suspended sentence or probation the defendant will commit another crime; or
   b. the defendant is in need of correctional treatment that can be provided most effectively by his commitment to an institution; or
   c. a lesser sentence will depreciate the seriousness of the defendant's crime.
2. The following grounds, while not controlling the direction of the court, shall be accorded weight in favor of withholding sentence of imprisonment:
   a. the defendant's criminal conduct neither caused nor threatened serious harm;
   b. the defendant did not contemplate that his criminal conduct would cause or threaten serious harm;
   c. the defendant acted under a strong provocation;
   d. there were substantial grounds tending to excuse or justify the defendant's criminal conduct, though failing to establish a defense;
   e. the victim of the defendant's criminal conduct induced or facilitated its commission;
   f. the defendant has compensated or will compensate the victim of his criminal conduct for the damage or injury that he sustained;
   g. the defendant has no history of prior delinquency or criminal activity or has led a law-abiding life for a substantial period of time before the commission of the present crime;
   h. the defendant's criminal conduct was the result of circumstances unlikely to recur;
   i. the character and attitudes of the defendant indicate that he is unlikely to commit another crime;
   j. the defendant is particularly likely to respond affirmatively to probationary treatment;
   k. the imprisonment of the defendant would entail excessive hardship to himself or his dependents.
3. When a person has been convicted of a crime and is not sentenced to imprisonment, the court shall place him on probation if he is in need of the supervision, guidance, assistance or direction that the probation service can provide.

SOURCE: American Law Institute, *Model Penal Code* § 7.01. Copyright 1962 by the American Law Institute. Reprinted with the permission of the American Law Institute.

probation in Los Angeles and Alameda counties in California.[14] They found that of that total, 1,087 (65 percent) were rearrested, 853 (51 percent) were convicted, and 568 (34 percent) ended up in jail or prison. Of the new charges filed against the probationers, 75 percent were for burglary, theft, robbery, and other predatory-type crimes. Eighteen percent were convicted of serious, violent-type crimes.

The Rand researchers found that probation is by far the most common sentencing alternative to prison and is used in about 60 to 80 percent of all criminal convictions. What is disturbing, however, is that the crimes and criminal records of about 25 percent of all probationers are indistinguishable from those of offenders who go to prison.

The picture painted by the Petersilia research effort is not an encouraging one. At the same time the prison alternative is neither economically feasible nor more efficient or effective. Petersilia and her colleagues argue instead for more intensive probation with more stringent rules, such as curfews, and closer supervision. Even though such measures would dramatically increase the cost of client maintenance, probation would still be far less expensive than a term of incarceration.

■ Conditions of Probation

A probation sentence is usually viewed as an act of clemency on the part of the court and is reflective of the rehabilitative aspects of the criminal justice system. Yet the probationary contract drawn up between the offender and the court has two distinct sides. One side involves the treatment and rehabilitation of the offender through regular meetings with trained probation staff or other treatment personnel; the other side reflects the supervision and enforcement aspects of probation. Probation as practiced today often saddles the probationer with rules and conditions that may impede achievement of the stated treatment goals of the probation department by emphasizing the punitive aspects of criminal justice.

When probation is imposed as a sentence, the court sets down certain rules as conditions for qualifying for community treatment. In many jurisdictions, statutory law mandates that certain conditions be applied in every probation case; usually the sentencing judge maintains broad discretion to add to or lesson these standard conditions on a case-by-case basis. A presiding judge may not, of course, impose capricious or cruel conditions, such as requiring an offender to make restitution out of proportion to the seriousness of his or her criminal act. In the case of *Higdon v. United States* (1980), a federal court rejected a probation order requiring the offender to do 6,200 hours of volunteer time over a three-year period.[15] The court used the following test to determine whether probation rules are reasonable:

> First we consider the purposes for which the judge imposed the conditions. If the purposes are permissible, the second step is to determine whether the conditions are reasonably related to the purposes. In conducting the latter inquiry the court examines the impact which the conditions have on the probationer's rights. If the impact is substantially greater than is necessary to carry out the purposes, the conditions are impermissible.[16]

Table 15.2 illustrates the rules of probation employed by the federal government.

SPECIAL RULES. In addition to **standard rules,** judges may legally impose on a probationer restrictions tailored both to fit his or her individual needs and to protect society from additional harm.[17] A judge may limit the interpersonal relationships a probationer may have if they pose potential threats to society; a child molester can be forbidden to associate with minor children.[18] For example, in *U.S. v. Cothran* (1988), the U.S. Court of Appeals for the Eleventh Circuit upheld a judge's decision to order a probationer banished from the county in which he lived on the grounds that he was a popular figure among drug-using adolescents to whom he sold cocaine; barring him from his residence also gave him an opportunity for a fresh start.[19]

Probationers can be ordered to abstain from using alcohol and illegal drugs and can be required to submit to chemical tests at the request of their probation officer to determine if they have recently used controlled substances.[20] Some courts have permitted probation officers to demand drug tests even though such testing was not part of the original conditions of probation.[21] Probationers can be required to cooperate with legal authorities; for instance, they may be required to testify against others in grand jury hearings.[22] Similarly, probation rules can require periodic reporting of personal practices; for example, tax violators can be required to submit their tax returns.[23] A common procedure today is to require that probationers make restitution to the victim of their crimes (restitution will be covered later in this chapter). An Illinois appeals court, however, recently ruled that requiring a probationer to make a public apology in the local newspaper for drunk driving was too punitive and a more drastic penalty than the state's probation laws authorized.[24]

TABLE 15.2 ■ Conditions of Federal Probation

(a) Mandatory conditions.—The court shall provide, as an explicit condition of a sentence of probation—

(1) for a felony, a misdemeanor, or an infraction, that the defendant not commit another Federal, State, or local crime during the term of probation; and

(2) for a felony, that the defendant also abide by at least one condition set forth in subsection (b)(2), (b)(3), or (b)(13). If the court has imposed and ordered execution of a fine and placed the defendant on probation, payment of the fine or adherence to the court-established installment schedule shall be a condition of the probation.

(b) Discretionary conditions.—The court may provide, as further conditions of a sentence of probation, to the extent that such conditions are reasonably related to the factors set forth in section 3553(a)(1) and (a)(2) and to the extent that such conditions involve only such deprivations of liberty or property as are reasonably necessary for the purposes indicated in section 3553(a)(2), that the defendant—

(1) support his dependents and meet other family responsibilities;

(2) pay a fine imposed pursuant to the provisions of subchapter C;

(3) make restitution to a victim of the offense pursuant to the provisions of section 3556;

(4) give to the victims of the offense the notice ordered pursuant to the provisions of section 3555;

(5) work conscientiously at suitable employment or pursue conscientiously a course of study or vocational training that will equip him for suitable employment;

(6) refrain, in the case of an individual, from engaging in a specified occupation, business, or profession bearing a reasonably direct relationship to the conduct constituting the offense, c. engage in such a specified occupation, business, or profession only to a stated degree or under stated circumstances;

(7) refrain from frequenting specified kinds of places or from associating unnecessarily with specified persons;

(8) refrain from excessive use of alcohol, or any use of a narcotic drug or other controlled substance, as defined in section 102 of the Controlled Substances Act (21 U.S.C. 802), without a prescription by a licensed medical practitioner;

(9) refrain from possessing a firearm, destructive device, or other dangerous weapon;

(10) undergo available medical, psychiatric, or psychological treatment, including treatment for drug or alcohol dependency, as specified by the court, and remain in a specified institution if required for that purpose;

(11) remain in the custody of the Bureau of Prisons during nights, weekends, or other intervals of time, totaling no more than the lesser of one year or the term of imprisonment authorized for the offense during the first year of the term of probation;

(12) reside at, or participate in the program of, a community corrections facility for all or part of the term of probation;

(13) work in community service as directed by the court;

(14) reside in a specified place or area, or refrain from residing in a specified place or area;

(15) remain within the jurisdiction of the court, unless granted permission to leave by the court or a probation officer;

(16) report to a probation officer as directed by the court or the probation officer;

(17) permit a probation officer to visit him at his home or elsewhere as specified by the court;

(18) answer inquiries by a probation officer and notify the probation officer promptly of any change in address or employment;

(19) notify the probation officer promptly if arrested or questioned by a law enforcement officer; or

(20) satisfy such other conditions as the court may impose.

(c) Modifications of conditions.—The court may modify, reduce, or enlarge the conditions of a sentence of probation at any time prior to the expiration or termination of the term of probation, pursuant to the provisions of the Federal Rules of Criminal Procedure relating to the revocation or modification of probation.

(d) Written statement of conditions.—The court shall direct that the probation officer provide the defendant with a written statement that sets forth all the conditions to which the sentence is subject, and that is sufficiently clear and specific to serve as a guide for the defendant's conduct and for such supervision as is required.

SOURCE: 8 U.S.C. § 3563 (subchapter B) (1984).

In sum, probation conditions have been allowed as long as they are reasonably related to the purposes of probation and are not capricious or cruel, even though they infringe on some constitutional rights.[25]

■ Administration of Probation Services

Probation services are organized in a variety of different ways, depending on the state and the jurisdiction in which they are located.[26] In some states a statewide probation service exists, but actual control over departments is localized within each court jurisdiction. Other states maintain a strong statewide authority with centralized control and administration. Thirty states combine probation and parole services in a single unit; some combine juvenile and adult probation departments, whereas others maintain these departments separately.

The typical probation department is situated in a single court district, such as a juvenile, superior, district, or municipal court. The relationship between the department and court personnel (especially the judge) is extremely close.

In the typical department, the **chief probation officer** (CPO) sets policy, supervises hiring, determines what training should be emphasized, and may personally discuss with or recommend sentencing to the judge. In state-controlled departments, some of the CPO's duties are mandated by the central office; training guidelines, for example, may be determined at the state level. If, on the other hand, the department is locally controlled, the CPO is invested with great discretion in the management of the department.

Most large probation departments also include one or more assistant chiefs. Sometimes, in departments of moderate size, each of these middle managers will be responsible for a particular aspect of probation services: one assistant chief will oversee training; another will supervise treatment and counseling services; another will act as a liaison with police or other agencies. In smaller departments, the CPO and the executive officers may also maintain a caseload or investigate cases for the court. For example, the chief may handle a few of the most difficult cases personally and concentrate on these. In larger municipal departments, however, the probation chief is a purely administrative figure.

The line staff, or the probation officers (POs), may be in direct, personal contact with the entire supervisory staff, or they may be independent from the chief and answer mainly to the assistant chiefs. Line staff perform the following major functions: (1) they supervise or monitor cases assigned to them to ensure that the rules of probation are maintained; (2) they attempt to rehabilitate their cases through specialized treatment techniques; (3) they investigate the lives of convicted offenders to enable the court to make intelligent sentencing decisions; (4) occasionally, they collect fines due the court or oversee the collection of delinquent payments, such as child support; and (5) they interview complainants and defendants to judge whether criminal action should be taken, whether cases can be decided informally, or whether a diversion should be advocated, and so on. This last procedure, called **intake,** is common in juvenile probation.

In some major cities the probation department is quite complex, controlling detention facilities, treatment programs, research operations, and evaluation staffs. In such a setting the CPO's role is similar to that of a director of a multiservice public facility. This CPO rarely comes into direct contact with clients, and behavior, attitudes, and values are quite different from the rural CPO who maintains a full caseload.

Volunteers

Since probation services are so widely used, the burden on individual probation officers is tremendous. It is not unusual for probation officers to maintain over a hundred clients. To meet this challenge, it has become commonplace for probation departments to employ paraprofessionals and **volunteers** in what might be considered regular-line positions. Volunteers make up a significant portion of probation department staffs.

This practice is not without controversy. Although volunteers and paraprofessionals can certainly make an important contribution, their employment has not always been welcomed enthusiastically by regular probation staff. They are sometimes viewed as a threat to job security and as an excuse for legislatures to deny budgetary increases for probation services. Despite such concerns, it has been estimated that between 300,000 and 500,000 volunteers now serve in more than 2,000 probation jurisdictions and contribute in excess of 20 million hours of service per year.[27] Volunteers make it possible for probation departments to provide greater service to their clients. In some instances, volunteers provide direct service, while in others they are given administrative, clerical, or management tasks.[28]

Volunteers can have a significant impact on successful completion of a probationary sentence. For example, the Macomb County court in Mount Clemens, Michigan, reported that the recidivism rates of probationers assigned to volunteers was 6 percent, while the regular probationers recidivated at an 18 percent rate.[29] A similar program in Lancaster County, Pennsylvania, found that the greater client contact provided by volunteers produced recidivism rates half those of regularly managed probationers.[30] The Volunteer Probation Counselor Program of Lincoln, Nebraska, matched volunteers on a one-to-one basis with a group of probationers identified as "high risk." An in-house evaluation indicated that clients assigned to volunteers committed fewer additional offenses than those assigned to regular staff. The recidivism rate for those assigned to volunteers was 15 percent, while regular probationers recidivated at a 24 percent rate.[31]

Despite these successes, national evaluations of volunteer programs indicate that they are about as successful as traditional approaches. There is also concern that volunteers may lower staff morale and be rewarded with less than adequate staff support.[32]

Duties of Probation Officers

Staff officers in probation departments are usually charged with four primary tasks: investigation, intake, diagnosis, and treatment supervision.[33]

In the investigative stage, the officer conducts an inquiry within the community in an effort to discover the factors related to the criminality of the offender. The presentence investigation is conducted primarily to gain information for judicial sentences, but in the event the offender is placed on probation the investigation can become a useful basis for treatment and supervision.

Intake is a process in which probation officers interview offenders who have been summoned to the court for initial appearances. Intake is most common in the juvenile justice process but may also be employed in adult misdemeanant cases. During juvenile court intake, the petitioner (e.g., the juvenile) and the complainant (e.g., the private citizen or the police officer) may work with the probation officer to determine an equitable solution to the case. The probation officer may settle the case without further court action, recommend restitution or other compensation, initiate actions that result in a court hearing, or recommend unofficial or informal probation.

Diagnosis is the analysis of the probationer's personality and the subsequent development of a personality profile that may be helpful in treating the offender. Diagnosis involves the evaluation of the probationer, using information from an initial interview (intake) or the presentence investigation, for the purpose of planning a proper treatment schedule. The diagnosis should not merely reflect the desire or purpose of labeling the offender as neurotic or psychopathic, for example, but should "codify all that has been learned about the individual, organized in such a way as to provide a means for the establishment of future treatment goals."[34]

Treatment Supervision

Based on knowledge of psychology, social work, or counseling and the diagnosis of the offender, the probation officer plans a treatment schedule that will hopefully allow the probationer to fulfill the probation contract and make a reasonable adjustment to the community.

In years past the probation staff had primary responsibility over supervision and treatment, but it is now more common for probation officers to use the resources of the community to carry out the treatment function while they serve as supervision coordinators. In fact, some experts, such as John Rosecrance have called for the elimination of the personal involvement of probation officers in the treatment-supervision function.[35] With the increasing number of narcotics abusers in probation caseloads and the lack of effective community-based programs that deal with substance abuse problems, however, probation officers have been forced to rely on their own skills to provide treatment services. A recent survey of 231 probation departments found that more than half continue to provide hands-on counseling and behavior modification techniques with drug abusers.[36]

The treatment function is a product of both the investigative and the diagnostic aspects of probation. It is based on the probation officer's perceptions of the probationer, including family problems, peer relationships, and

Probation counseling is an important part of probation services. Probation officers often maintain large caseloads and have little time for individual cases.

employment background. Treatment may also involve the use of community resources. A probation officer who discovers that a client has a drinking problem may help to find a detoxification center willing to accept the case, while a chronically underemployed offender may be given job counseling or training, and a person undergoing severe psychological stress may be placed in a more therapeutic treatment program.[37] Or, in the case of juvenile delinquency a probation officer may work with teachers and other school officials to help a young offender stay in school. Of course, most cases do not (or cannot) receive such individualized treatment; some treatment mechanisms merely involve a weekly or biweekly telephone call to determine whether a job is being maintained or school attendance is satisfactory.

The proper diagnostic, treatment, and investigative skills needed for effective probation work are difficult to find in a single individual. Probation officers are often recruited from social work backgrounds, and the master's degree may be a prerequisite to advancement to senior levels in large departments. Today most jurisdictions require officers to have a background in the social sciences and to hold at least a bachelor's degree.

Presentence Investigations

Another important task of probation officers is the investigation and evaluation of defendants coming before the court for sentencing. As you may recall, presentence investigations are reports used by the court in making decisions whether to grant probation, incarcerate, or use other forms of treatment.

The style and content of presentence investigations may vary among jurisdictions and also among individual probation officers within the same jurisdiction. On the one hand, some departments require voluminous reports covering every aspect of the defendant's life; other departments, which may be rule oriented, require that officers stick to the basic facts, such as the defendant's age, race, sex, and previous offense record. These disparities are heightened by the fact that each department has its own standards for presentence investigations. A number of national committees and organizations have attempted to design a standard form for the presentence investigation that embodies the most important sentencing information in a concise format.

At the conclusion of most presentence investigation, the department makes a recommendation to the presiding judge that reflects its sentencing posture on the case at hand. This is a crucial aspect of the report because it has been estimated that the probation department's recommendation is followed in about 95 percent of all cases.[38] Thus in conducting presentence investigations and making a sentencing recommendation, the probation officer is exercising discretion similar to that of a judge making sentencing decisions.[39] Federal courts have prohibited defendants from suing probation officers who have made errors in their presentence investigations on the grounds that liability "would seriously erode the officers' independent fact finding function and would as a result impair the sentencing judge's ability to carry out his judicial duties."[40]

The following personal characteristics of offenders are also believed to have a significant effect on the probation officer's recommendations: attitude, family data, prior record, present offense, impression made on the probation officer at the interview, education, psychological profile, interests and activities, and religious data.[41] In a study comparing male and female probation officers, Anthony Walsh found that the probation officer's gender influences his or her

TABLE 15.3 ■ **Risk Prediction Scale**

Automatic Component: Automatically places an individual in low-activity supervision if two conditions are satisfied.
  A. Offender has a 12th-grade education or better; and
  B. The individual has a history free of opiate usage
If the two conditions are not met, the remaining items are scored.
  C. Twenty-eight years of age, or older, at time of offense (7 points) If not, score as 0.
  D. Arrest-free period of five or more consecutive years (4 points) If not, score as 0.
  E. Few prior arrests (none, one, or two = 10 points) If not, score as 0.
  F. History free of opiate usage (9 points) If not, score as 0.
  G. At least four months of steady employment immediately prior to arraignment for present offense (3 points)
     If not, score as 0.

Risk score	Supervisor level	Minimum personal contacts	Maximum personal contacts	Collateral contacts
Automatic Assignment or 20–33	Low activity	1 per quarter	1 per quarter	Unlimited
0–19	High activity	1 per month	No maximum	Unlimited

SOURCE: Adopted from the Classification and Supervision Planning System, Probation Division, Administrative Office, U.S. Courts, January 1981.

decision making: male officers were actually more punitive with sexual offenders than female officers, primarily because the latter regarded rape as a victim-precipitated crime.[42] It is generally believed, however, that the two most important factors influencing the probation officer's investigation report are the nature of the current offense and the offender's criminal history.[43]

Risk Classification

A presupervision task related to both the investigation and the management function is **risk classification.** This involves classifying cases chosen for probation on the basis of their particular needs and then assigning the cases to a level and type of probation based on the clients' perceived needs and the risks they present to the community. For example, some cases may receive frequent (intensive) supervision while others receive minimal probation officer monitoring. The risk prediction scale used by the federal probation authorities is illustrated in Table 15.3. Note how the offender's score determines the level of treatment and personal contacts with a probation officer.

Does classification make a dramatic difference in the success of probation? Peter Kratcoski evaluated existing programs and found that although classification did not have a substantial impact on reducing recidivism, it may be a useful tool in case management and treatment delivery.[44] Moreover, as Todd Clear and Vincent O'Leary suggest, the classification of offenders promotes the important feature of supervision: reducing the risk the probationer presents to the community. In addition, Clear and O'Leary find that classification schemes are in synch with desert-based sentencing models, e.g., more serious cases get the most intensive supervision.[45]

■ The Success of Probation

Probation is the most commonly used alternative sentence for a number of reasons: it is humane; it helps offenders maintain community and family ties;

it is cost-effective. But is probation truly "successful"? A federal survey of probation practices in 37 states found that about 81 percent of the people who complete their probation terms could be classified as "successful." Of the 19 percent classified as "failures," about 11 percent were incarcerated for a new offense while the remaining 8 percent either absconded, were discharged to another jurisdiction, or released because they had a warrant issued against them. Of the 37 reporting districts, 4 reported success rates of 90 percent or better, led by New Hampshire, which had a 99 percent rate. Florida reported the lowest success rate, 68.5 percent.[46]

Probation's success rate and its cost-effectiveness have led to its increased use in the United States. Despite the trend toward mandatory sentences and a "get tough" policy, the number of people on probation is higher than ever. Even more importantly, the ratio of probationers to prisoners has increased in recent years, from 3.60: 1 in 1979 to 4: 1 in 1987. Thus, while the prison population has increased in recent years, the probation population has more than kept pace.

A careful review of probation effectiveness prepared for the federal government by Harry Allen, Eric Carlson, and Evalyn Parks outlined the available information on various probation practices and programs.[47] The researchers reached the following conclusions:

1. Probation appears to be effective for first offenders.
2. Probation is less costly than incarceration, especially when the benefits of the offender's community ties are considered.
3. Employment is closely related to successful completion of probation.
4. Unsupervised probation may be just as effective (for misdemeanants) as supervised probation.
5. Paraprofessionals are at least as effective as professional probation officers.
6. Immersed in paperwork, probation officers are unable to devote much time to actually supervising or assisting offenders.
7. Sentencing decisions correspond closely to probation officers' recommendations in presentence reports.
8. Caseload reduction does not appear to be the answer to more effective probation supervision. Rather, offender types and treatment needs should be matched more carefully with officers.
9. Even if probation did not have a better rate of success than incarceration, it is certainly no worse and is therefore at least as effective.
10. Some evidence suggests that the success or failure of the client does not depend on the amount of attention he or she receives from the probation officer.

■ Legal Rights of Probationers

Probation raises a number of important legal issues, in particular the civil rights of probationers and the rights of probationers during the revocation process.

Civil Rights

The U.S. Supreme Court has ruled that probationers hold a unique status and are therefore entitled to fewer constitutional protections than other individuals. One area that has been circumscribed is the Fifth Amendment right of freedom from self-incrimination. The Court dealt with this issue in its decision in *Minnesota v. Murphy* (1984).[48] In this case Murphy was ordered to seek psychological counseling. During his therapy session he admitted to his counselor that he had engaged in a rape/murder. Murphy's counselor reported his admission to his probation officer. Though Murphy had earlier been suspected of the crime, there was insufficient evidence to try him on this charge, and he had been convicted on a lesser offense. The probation officer confronted Murphy, who admitted that he had committed murder. The probation officer informed the police who now had sufficient evidence to bring the case to the prosecutor.

Murphy contested his subsequent conviction on rape/murder on the grounds that he had given the information to the probation officer during an in-custody interrogation and that he should therefore have been given the *Miranda* warning. The Supreme Court disagreed, however, and held that the interrogation was noncustodial and that a probation officer has every right to turn information over to the police. Just because a probation officer can require a probationer to appear for an interview does not make it a police arrest, and therefore the client does not have to be protected from making incriminating statements.

According to the ruling in this case, the probation officer–client relationship is not protected by the right of confidentiality that applies to doctor-patient or attorney-client relationships. Furthermore, in *Murphy* the Court held that a probation officer could even use trickery or psychological pressure to obtain information and to be turned over to police.

In *Griffin v. Wisconsin*, the Supreme Court held that a probationer's home may be searched without a warrant on the grounds that probation departments "have in mind the welfare of the probationer" and must "respond quickly to evidence of misconduct." The usual legal standards were deemed inapplicable to probation because they "would reduce the deterrent effect of the supervisory arrangement" and "the probation agency must be able to act based upon a lesser degree of certainty than the Fourth Amendment would otherwise require in order to intervene before a probationer does damage to himself or society."[49]

Revocation Rights

During the course of a probationary term, a violation of the rules of probation or commitment of a new crime can result in probation being revoked, at which time the offender may be placed in an institution. Revocation is often not an easy decision, since it conflicts with the treatment philosophy of most probation departments.

Once a department has decided on revocation, the offender is given notice of the pending revocation procedure, and a formal hearing is scheduled. If the charges against the probationer are upheld, he or she can then be placed in an institution to serve the remainder of the sentence. Most departments will not revoke probation unless the offender commits another crime or seriously violates the rules of probation.

Because placing a person on probation implies that probation will continue unless the probationer commits some major violation, the defendant has been given certain procedural due process rights at this stage of the criminal process. In three significant decisions, the U.S. Supreme Court provided procedural safeguards to apply at revocation of probation (and parole) proceedings.

In *Mempa v. Rhay* in 1967, the Court unanimously held that a probationer was constitutionally entitled to counsel in a revocation of probation proceeding in cases where a sentence had been suspended.[50] Questions still remained after the *Mempa* decision, however, such as whether the right to counsel applied only to revocation proceedings involving deferred sentences or also to proceedings where the probationer had been sentenced at the time of the trial. A second important question left answered was whether indigent probationers must be provided with counsel.

A few years later, in 1972, in *Morrissey v. Brewer*, the Supreme Court issued an important decision detailing the procedural safeguards required for parole revocation.[51] Because the revocation of probation and parole are similar in nature, the standards in the *Morrissey* case affected the probation process as well. In *Morrissey*, the Court required an informal inquiry to determine if there was probable cause to believe the arrested parolee had violated the conditions of parole, as well as a formal revocation hearing with minimum due process requirements. The Court did not deal with the issue of the right to counsel, however. (See Chapter 18 for the full details of the *Morrissey* decision.)

The question of the right to counsel in revocation proceedings did come up again in 1973 in *Gagnon v. Scarpelli*.[52] In that decision, which involved a probationer, the Supreme Court held that both probationers and parolees have a constitutionally limited right to counsel in revocation proceedings. The Court held:

1. That due process requires that preliminary and final revocation hearings in the case of a probationer be similar to conditions for a parolee.
2. That the body conducting the hearings should decide in each individual case whether due process requires that an indigent probationer or parolee be represented by counsel. Though the state is not constitutionally obliged to provide counsel in all cases, it should do so where the indigent probationer or parolee may have difficulty presenting his or her version of disputed facts without the examination or cross-examination of witnesses or the presentation of complicated documentary evidence. "Presumptively, counsel should be provided where, after being informed of his right, the probationer or parolee requests counsel, based on timely and colorable claim that he has not committed the alleged violation or, if the violation is a matter of public record or uncontested, there are substantial reasons in justification or mitigation that make revocation inappropriate."
3. That any case where a request for counsel is refused the grounds for refusal should be stated in the record.
4. That in the present case because Scarpelli made an admission he claims was taken under duress, he should have been given counsel and the case should be reconsidered in light of the new guidelines.

One of the most important features of the *Gagnon* case was that it equated probation revocation with parole revocation. In so doing, it concluded that a hearing was to be held as outlined in the *Morrissey* case (see Chapter 18) and that the need for counsel was to be decided on a case-by-case basis. *Gagnon* also apparently answered the question left undecided in *Morrissey* regarding right to counsel at parole revocation hearings. Finally, the decision in *Gagnon* was a firm denial that the U.S. Constitution requires counsel to be present at the probation and parole revocation hearings.

The *Gagnon* case can be viewed as a step forward in the constitutional application of procedural safeguards to the correctional process. It provides some control over the unlimited discretion exercised in the past by probation and parole personnel in revocation proceedings. In practice, almost all states today automatically provide counsel to indigent defendants at probation revocation hearings, while fewer states provide counsel at parole proceedings.[53]

With the development of innovative probation programs, courts have had to review the legality of changing probation rules and their effect on revocation. In general, courts have upheld the demand that restitution be made to the victim of a crime. For example, in *United States v. Carson* (1982), the U.S. Court of Appeals for the Fifth Circuit required a probationer to repay the victim for his crime even though the debt had been discharged in a civil bankruptcy hearing.[54] Since restitution is designed to punish and reform the offender rather than simply repay the victim, the court ruled that the probationer was still responsible for paying restitution despite his bankrupt status. Similarly, in *United States v. Stine* (1982), a federal court ruled that a probationer could be required to receive psychological counseling unless it forced him to undergo drug therapy or to be placed in seclusion.[55]

United States v. Davis (1987) raised an interesting question about probation revocation: can a person's probation be revoked for violations of conditions that occur *prior* to starting his or her probationary period? In *Davis* a federal court ruled that probation was a "favor" and could be revoked at any time a court authority realized it was improvidently granted, even if the person was in a penal institution awaiting release so that the probation sentence could begin.[56]

■ The Future of Probation

It seems evident that probation will continue to be the most popular alternative sentence used by American courts, and, if anything, its use as a community-based correction will continue to grow in the 1990s.[57] Part of probation's appeal stems from its flexibility, which allows it to be coupled with a wide variety of treatment programs including residential care. As prison overcrowding continues to be a major problem, more than half the states have taken some measures to change their probation guidelines to help reduce the prison population.[58] Not inconsequential is the great saving in cost offered by probation at a time when many state budgets are undergoing reductions; a probationary sentence is far cheaper than a prison stay. In addition, at least 25 states now impose some form of fee on probationers in order to defray the cost of corrections. Massachusetts has instituted **day fees,** which are geared to the probationer's wages (the usual "fee" is between one and three days' wages each month).[59] A recent analysis of the probation fee system found that it may actually improve the quality of services afforded clients.[60]

How will probation hold up in a society that is growing increasingly conservative and in which the prison population is growing at an alarming rate? One view is that probation should fall more in line with the "justice model's" call for equality under the law and proportionate sentencing.[61] Patrick McAnany suggests that probation should be used more frequently as the sentence of choice and not merely as a substitute for the "real one." Probation should be part of a graduated range of sentences and be available to all offenders except the most serious felons. In order to adhere to the justice model, McAnany argues, the terms of probation should be proportional to the seriousness of the crime. Consequently, the length of the probationary period and the conditions of probation should reflect the original charge. For example, the most serious felonies might have conditions of restitution and community service attached to them.[62] In a similar vein, he suggests that in coming years the mission of probation should be reviewed with the goal of changing its focus from the needs of the offender to the concerns of the victims of crime and the need to be objective and fair. Not all probationers need or require treatment, and they should only receive it on a voluntary basis. For many offenders the primary purpose of their probation stint should be maintenance in the community, and the probation department's role should be purely one of surveillance.[63] In contrast, John Conrad suggests that the proper role of probation is providing rehabilitative services; he argues that the surveillance of offenders should be taken over by the police while presentence investigation should be left to the courts.[64] These suggestions indicate that the future model of probation is still uncertain. A number of important questions remain unanswered: Should felons be granted probation despite their spotty success record? Should probation sentences more closely reflect the criminal charge? Should probation officers continue to perform the multitude of tasks they are currently assigned?

Although the answers to these questions remain elusive, there is little doubt that probation services are undergoing dramatic expansion. Widening the scope of probation has created a new set of penalties that fall between traditional community supervision and confinement in jail or prison; these are known as *intermediate sanctions*. This new breed of correctional services will be discussed in detail in the next section.

■ Intermediate Sanctions

Around the country intermediate sanctions have been gaining recognition and popularity. Today, many programs operated by probation departments involve intermediate sanctions such as intensive probation supervision, house arrest, electronic monitoring, restitution orders, shock probation/split sentences, and residential community corrections. Intermediate sanctions also involve sentences that may operate independently of probation staffs: fines and forfeiture; pretrial programs; and residential programs. Thus they range from the least intrusive sentence, such as a small fine, to the highly restrictive, such as house arrest accompanied by electronic monitoring and a stay in a community correctional center.

What are the advantages of intermediate sanctions? A primary advantage is that they provide alternatives to prison sentences, which have often proved to be both ineffective and injurious. Research indicates that about half of all prison inmates are likely to be rearrested and returned to prison, many within a short period after their release from an institution.[65] There is little evidence that incapacitation is either a deterrent to crime or a specific deterrent against future criminality.

Intermediate sanctions also aid in developing sentences that are fair, equitable, and proportional even for people not bound for prison. In other words, it seems unfair that a rapist and a shoplifter should receive the same type of community sentence, given the differences in their criminal acts. Intermediate sanctions can provide the successive steps of a meaningful "ladder" of scaled punishments outside prison, thereby restoring fairness and equity to nonincarceration sentences.[66] For example, forgers may be ordered

■ *FIGURE 15.1*
The Punishment Ladder

The ladder (from top to bottom) reads:

Death Penalty

Prison

Shock Probation

Residential Community Center

Electronic Monitoring

House Arrest

Intensive Probation

Restitution

Probation

Forfeiture

Fines

Pretrial Release

to make restitution to their victims, whereas rapists can be ordered to reside in a community correctional center while they receive counseling at a local psychiatric care institute. This feature of intermediate sanctions allows judges to fit the punishment to the crime without resorting to a prison sentence. Intermediate sanctions can be designed to increase punishment for people whose serious and/or repeat crimes make a straight probation sentence inappropriate yet for whom a prison sentence would be unduly harsh and/or dysfunctional.[67]

Target Populations

In the broadest sense, intermediate sanctions can serve the needs of a number of different offender groups. The most likely candidates are convicted criminals who would normally be sent to prison but pose either a low risk of recidivism or little threat to society (such as nonviolent property offenders). Used in this way, intermediate sanctions are a viable solution to the critical problem of prison overcrowding.

Intermediate sanctions can also be used to reduce the equally overcrowded jail population both by providing alternatives to incarceration for misdemeanants and also by reducing the number of pretrial detainees who currently make up about 40 percent of the jail population. As you may recall, some new forms of bail already require conditions, such as supervision by court officers and periods of home confinement (conditional bail), that are similar to intermediate sanctions.

Intermediate sanctions also have potential as "halfway back" strategies for probation and parole violators. Probationers who violate the conditions of their community release could be placed under increasingly more intensive supervision before actual incarceration is required. Parolees who pose the greatest risk of recidivism might receive conditions that require close monitoring or home confinement. Parole violators could be returned to a community correctional center rather than a walled institution.

In the following sections, the forms of intermediate sanctions currently in use will be more thoroughly discussed.

Pretrial Programs

As you may recall from Chapter 12, pretrial diversion programs are designed to minimize the interface between offenders and agents of the law while requiring offenders to conform to a set of restrictive rules or conditions. These include release on recognizance programs (ROR), which allow suspects who lack bail money to avoid pretrial detention in jails, and diversion programs, which provide noncriminal alternatives for first-time or minor criminal offenders. The goal of pretrial programs is to provide a degree of control and custody while insulating the offender from the stigma and labeling effects of the formal justice process.

An example of one of the more successful pretrial diversion programs is Operation De Novo in Hennepin County, Minnesota. Originally developed by the Urban Coalition of Minneapolis and sponsored by the Law Enforcement Assistance Administration, the program has been operated by the Hennepin County Probation Department since 1975.[68]

Operation De Novo now works with juvenile and adult offenders of both sexes, excluding only those accused of crimes of violence.[69] The staff is composed of both professionals and paraprofessionals, with substantial minority representation. Some of those hired would not meet prevailing civil service requirements. The program directors believe this greater flexibility in choice of staff contributes to the program's effectiveness.

In addition to individual counseling, clients participate in group sessions that address survival skills, personal growth, and problems related to juveniles, parents, drug dependency, and the family. Program staff members work with clients to meet emergency needs, explore vocational options and set career goals, find suitable training or educational programs, and work out an acceptable restitution payment plan. In-house resources are supplemented by those available from community service agencies.

Fines

Fines are monetary payments imposed on offenders as an intermediate punishment for their criminal acts. They are a direct offshoot of the early common law practice requiring that compensation be paid to the victim and the King (wergild) for criminal acts.

Although fines are most commonly used in misdemeanors, they are also frequently used in felonies where the offender benefited financially. Investor Ivan Boesky paid over $100 million in fines for violating insider stock trading rules; the firm of Drexel, Burnham Lambert paid a fine of $650 million in 1988 for securities violations.[70]

Fines may be used as a sole sanction or combined with other punishments such as probation or confinement. Quite commonly, judges levy other monetary sanctions along with fines, such as court costs, public defender fees, probation and treatment fees, and victim restitution, in order to increase the force of the financial punishment.[71] Some jurisdictions like New York City are experimenting with **day fines,** a concept that originated in Europe, which gears the fines to an offender's net daily income in an effort to make them more equitable.[72]

The statutes on criminal fines are inconsistent and chaotic and give little guidance to the sentencing judge regarding the appropriate amount of a fine. Because judges often have inadequate information on the offender's ability to pay, defaults and contempt charges are common. Since the standard sanction for nonpayment is incarceration, many offenders held in local jails are confined for nonpayment of criminal fines. Though the U.S. Supreme Court in *Tate v. Short* (1971) recognized that incarcerating a person who is financially unable to pay a fine discriminates against the poor, many judges continue to incarcerate offenders for noncompliance with financial orders.[73]

Thus, although it is far from certain that fines are an effective sanction, either alone or in combination with other penalties, they remain one of the most commonly used criminal penalties. A recent research study sponsored by the federal government found that lower court judges impose fines alone or in tandem with other penalties in 86 percent of their cases; superior court judges impose fines in 42 percent of their cases.[74]

Forfeiture

Another alternative sanction, which has a financial basis and is therefore similar to a fine, is criminal (*in personam*) and civil (*in rem*) forfeiture. Both involve the seizure of goods and instrumentalities related to the commission or

Federal authorities have used the RICO and other statutes to seize the property of drug users and dealers. Here the yacht "Monkey Business", which first found fame when Senator Gary Hart used it to entertain Donna Rice, is shown being seized after Coast Guard officers found marijuana aboard.

outcome of a criminal act. For example, federal law provides that after arresting a drug trafficker, the government may seize the boat used to import the narcotics, the car used to carry the drugs overland, the warehouse in which the drugs were stored, and the home paid for with drug money; upon conviction the drug dealer loses permanent ownership of these "instrumentalities" of crime.

Forfeiture is not a new sanction. During the Middle Ages, "forfeiture of estate" was a mandatory result of most felony convictions. The crown could seize all of a felon's real and personal property. Forfeiture derived from the common law concept of "corruption of blood" or "attaint," which prohibited a felon's family from inheriting or receiving his or her property or estate. The common law mandated that descendants could not inherit property from a relative who might have attained the property illegally: "[T]he Corruption of Blood stops the Course of Regular Descent, as to Estates, over which the Criminal could have no Power, because he never enjoyed them."[75]

The use of forfeiture has been reintroduced to American law with the passage of the **Racketeer Influenced and Corrupt Organizations Act (RICO)** and the **Continuing Criminal Enterprises Act (CCE),** both of which are designed to allow the seizure of any property derived from illegal enterprises or conspiracies. Although these statutes were designed to apply to ongoing criminal conspiracies such as drug or pornography rings, they are now being applied to a far-ranging series of criminal acts including white-collar crimes. Though law enforcement officials at first applauded the use of forfeiture as a hard-hitting way of seizing the illegal profits of drug law violators, the practice has been criticized because the government has often been overzealous in its application. For example, million dollar yachts have been seized because someone aboard possessed a small amount of marijuana; this confiscatory practice is known as **zero tolerance.**

David Freid has criticized zero tolerance on the grounds that it is often used capriciously, that the penalty is sometimes disproportionate to the crime involved, and that it makes the government "a . . . partner in crime."[76] Freid maintains that the originators of modern criminal forfeiture law viewed it as a way of preventing organized crime figures from invading legitimate businesses, not as a way for the state to increase punishments unfairly and create a new class of "crime victim." He concludes that forfeiture "leads to capricious and disproportionate punishments and is capable of dangerously discriminatory application."[77] Despite these drawbacks forfeiture is likely to continue to be used as an alternative sanction against selective targets such as drug dealers and white-collar criminals.

Restitution

Another popular intermediate sanction is restitution, in which convicted defendants are required either to pay back the victims of their crime (**monetary restitution**) or to serve the community to compensate for their criminal acts (**community service restitution**).[78] Restitution programs got their start in federally funded programs that attempted to provide alternatives to incarceration while sparing convicted offenders the burdens of a criminal label. When federal seed money was terminated in the 1980s, however, many ongoing programs were incorporated into existing court structures such as probation departments.

Ordinarily, restitution programs require offenders to recompense victims of crime (or serve the community) as a condition of probation. The process thus offers the convicted offender a chance to avoid a jail or prison sentence or a more lengthy probationary period. Restitution may also be used as a diversionary device that offers some offenders the chance to avoid a criminal record altogether. In this instance, a judge will continue the case "without a finding" while the defendant completes the restitution order; after the probation department determines that restitution has been made, the case is dismissed.[79]

Because it appears to have benefits for the victim of crime, the offender, the criminal justice system, and society as a whole, there has been tremendous national interest in the restitution concept. Restitution is inexpensive, avoids stigma, and helps compensate victims of crime. Clients doing community service work have been placed in schools, hospitals, and nursing homes. Helping them avoid a jail sentence can mean saving the public thousands of dollars that would have gone to maintaining them in a secure institution, frees up needed resources, and gives the community the sense that equity has been returned to the justice system.

Does restitution work? Most reviews give it a qualified success rating. A national survey of juvenile restitution programs found that in a single year some 17,000 referrals were made, ordering $2.6 million in monetary restitution, 340,000 hours of community service, and 5,300 hours of direct service work.[80] It is estimated that almost 90 percent of the eligible clients successfully completed their restitution orders and that 86 percent had no subsequent contact with the justice system.[81] Other research indicates that those receiving restitution sentences have equal or lower recidivism rates than control groups of various kinds.[82]

Although many restitution programs have lost their federal funding, a number have been continued by local probation offices. One of the most successful programs was developed by Judge Albert Kramer of the Quincy,

Massachusetts, district court. The Alternative Work Sentencing Program (EARN-IT) services juveniles referred by the court, the county probation department, and the district attorney's office. This program seeks to bring the youth together with the victim of the crime in order to arrive at an equitable work program. The program staff members also help determine the extent of the loss the victim incurred and help place the offender in a paying job so that he or she can earn the required restitution. Some jobs are in reality nonpaying community service placements in which youths work off court orders such as court costs, fines, and program costs. All indications suggest that EARN-IT has been a tremendous success. In 1975, during the first year of its operation, the program returned $36,000 in restitution payments; since 1978 over $100,000 has been collected annually to be returned to victims, the court, and the community. The success of EARN-IT has encouraged programs of a similar nature in many other areas around the nation.[83]

The original enthusiasm for the restitution concept has been dampened somewhat by concern that it has not lived up to its promise of being an alternative to incarceration. Critics charge that restitution merely serves to "widen the net" and increase the proportion of persons whose behavior is regulated and controlled by the state.[84] Thus, rather than replacing a prison sentence, restitution is believed to add to the burden of people who would ordinarily have been given a relatively lenient probation sentence.[85]

Evidence for this charge is provided by an evaluation of the PACT (Prisoner and Community Together) program in Indiana.[86] In a single year, PACT clients contributed 15,000 hours of community service work to 56 local agencies and eliminated an estimated 3,100 days in jail, for a total savings of $106,000. An evaluation of the program concluded, however, that only 50 percent of the clients would have spent time in jail and that the remainder had actually received a greater sentence than they would normally have received had the program not been in operation.

Restitution remains a popular intermediate sanction. As Burt Galaway, a leading restitution expert, claims:

> The promise of restitution as a lower-cost penalty . . . and as a penalty which addresses victim interest will be achieved as restitution is used to reduce reliance on prisons and jails which do nothing for victims, burden taxpayers, and return offenders to society less competent to live law-abiding lives and probably more dangerous than when they were admitted.[87]

Shock Probation and Split Sentencing

Split sentences and shock probation are alternative sanctions designed to allow judges to grant offenders community release only after they have sampled prison life. These sanctions are based on the premise that if offenders are given a taste of incarceration sufficient to "shock" them into law-abiding behavior, they will be reluctant to violate the rules of probation or commit another criminal act.

In a number of states and in the Federal Criminal Code, a jail term can actually be a condition of probation, under an approach known as split sentencing. Under current federal practices, about 15 percent of all convicted federal offenders receive some form of split sentence that includes both prison and jail as a condition of probation; this number is expected to rise to 25 percent as tougher sentencing laws take effect.[88]

Another approach, known as shock probation, involves the resentencing of an offender after a short prison stay. The "shock" becomes because the offender originally receives a long maximum sentence but is then eligible for release to community supervision at the discretion of the judge (usually within 90 days of incarceration). About one-third of all probationers in the 14 states that use the program, including Ohio, Kentucky, Idaho, New Jersey, Tennessee, Utah, and Vermont, receive a period of confinement.[89] Evaluations of shock probation have indicated that it is between 78 percent and 91 percent effective.[90]

Some states have linked the short prison stay with a boot camp experience, called shock incarceration, in which young inmates undergo a brief but intense period of military-like training and hard labor designed to impress them with the rigors of prison life.[91] (Shock incarceration will be discussed further in Chapter 16.)

Shock probation has been praised as a program that limits prison time, provides a chance for the offender to be quickly integrated into the community, offers a mechanism that can maintain family ties, and provides a way of reducing prison populations and the costs of corrections.[92] Nevertheless, the granting of probation after a jail sentence is frowned on by some experts who believe that even a brief period of incarceration can mitigate the purpose of probation, which is to provide the offender with nonstigmatized community-based treatment:

> With this goal in mind the practice of commitment to an institution for the initial period of probation (variously known as shock probation, split sentence, etc.), as the Federal and some State statutes permit, should be discontinued. This type of sentence defeats the purpose of probation, which is the earliest possible reintegration of the offender into the community. Short-term commitment subjects the probationer to the destructive effects of institutionalization, disrupts his life in the community, and stigmatizes him for having been in jail. Further, it may add to his confusion as to his status.[93]

Some states have enacted statutes disallowing the practice of combining probation with jail sentences. Those who disagree with this view, however, argue that an initial jail sentence probably makes the offender more receptive to the conditions of probation, since it amply illustrates the problems the offender will face if probation is violated.

In a study of federal probationers, Nicolette Parisi found that about one-third of the offenders who received split sentences had previously been incarcerated, thereby negating any shock value associated with a short prison stay.[94] Parisi found little evidence that those receiving split sentences were more successful on probation than those who were maintained in regular probation caseloads.[95]

Intensive Probation Supervision

Intensive probation supervision (IPS) programs, which have been implemented in some form in about 45 states, make use of small caseloads of 15–40 clients who are kept under close watch by probation officers.[96] The primary goal of IPS is *diversion:* without intensive supervision, clients would normally have been sent to already overcrowded prisons or jails.[97] The second goal is *control:* high-risk offenders can be maintained in the community under much closer security than traditional probation efforts can provide. A third goal is *reintegration:* offenders can maintain community ties and be reoriented toward a more productive life while avoiding the pains of imprisonment.

In general, IPS programs rely on a greater degree of client contact to achieve the goals of diversion, control, and reintegration. This level of supervision has been described as having six unique dimensions:[98]

- Supervision is *extensive.* Probation officers have multiple, weekly face-to-face contacts with offenders, which are coupled with collateral contacts with employers and family members and with frequent arrest checks.
- Supervision is *focused.* Monitoring activities concentrate on specific behavioral regulations governing curfews, drug use, travel, employment, and community service.
- Supervision is *ubiquitous.* Offenders are frequently subjected to randomized drug tests and unannounced curfew checks.
- Supervision is *graduated.* Offenders commonly proceed through IPS programs in a series of progressive phases—each of which represents a gradual tempering of the proscriptions and requirements of IPS—until they are committed to regular supervision as the final leg of their statutory time on probation.
- Supervision is strictly *enforced.* Violations are often swift and penalties are severe in response to new arrests and noncompliance with program conditions.
- Supervision is *coordinated.* IPS offenders are usually monitored by specially selected and trained officers who are part of a larger specialized and autonomous unit.

ELIGIBILITY FOR INTENSIVE SUPERVISION. Who is eligible for IPS? Most programs have set up admissions criteria based on the nature of the offense and the offender's criminal background. Some programs such as New Jersey's exclude violent offenders; others will not consider substance abusers. In contrast some jurisdictions, such as Massachusetts do not exclude offenders based on their prior criminal history. About 60 percent of existing programs exclude offenders who have already violated probation orders or otherwise failed on probation.

Entry into IPS programs also takes a number of different forms. In some states IPS is a direct sentence imposed by a judge; in others it is a postsentencing alternative used as a method of diverting offenders from the correctional system; a third practice is to use IPS as a case management tool that gives the local probation staff flexibility in dealing with clients. Other jurisdictions such as Georgia utilize all three methods of IPS entry and also assign probation violators to the programs; in the latter case intensive supervision is intended to bring the violators "halfway" back into the community without resorting to a prison term.

PROGRAM ISSUES. There is also a great deal of variation in the form and structure of IPS programs. The typical model requires clients to meet with their supervisors almost every day. However, a national survey conducted by **James Byrne,** a leading authority on IPS, discovered significant variations between programs.[99] While 16 percent demanded almost daily contacts, 13 percent required only one to four contacts with clients per month. Other variations uncovered by Byrne involve the length and types of contacts. For example, most IPS programs are divided into treatment phases with the number of contacts diminishing as the client progresses between program stages. In some programs the most intensive stage in which clients are seen daily lasts almost six months, whereas in others daily contact is terminated in 90 days.

Another program variation occurs in the manner in which clients are visited. Some demand face-to-face contacts at home, work, or in the office, whereas others rely on telephone contacts, curfew checks, or collateral contacts (with family, friends, or employers).

Beyond these differences, Byrne found that programs in the 31 states he contacted tacked on a variety of other features to their IPS models. Some required that each client have a curfew that was rigorously enforced; others required a period of confinement in the home, or "house arrest." Other additions include drug and alcohol testing, community service, electronic monitoring, fines, and counseling.

IPS PROGRAMS TODAY. Numerous IPS programs are in operation around the United States today. The most well-known is Georgia's, which serves as a model for many other state efforts. Georgia's program include such measures as the following:

- Five face-to-face contacts per week
- 132 hours of mandatory community service
- Mandatory curfew
- Mandatory employment
- Weekly check of local arrest records
- Automatic notification of arrest via the State Crime Information Network listing
- Routine and unannounced drug and alcohol testing[100]

An evaluation of the Georgia program by Billie Erwin and Lawrence Bennett gave it generally high marks: it reached its target audience and resulted in a 10 percent reduction in the percentage of felons who were incarcerated without a significant increase in the recidivism rate.[101] Although IPS is more expensive than a straight probation sentence, it is far less costly than prison.

New Jersey's IPS has an active caseload of approximately 400 nonviolent offenders.[102] It requires that clients be employed and uses a high number of field contacts, including random drug testing, to ensure compliance with rules. It also requires that participants spend a few months in an institution, perform community service, and obey curfews. An evaluation of the New Jersey program by Frank Pearson shows that IPS works fairly well with felons who are neither dangerous nor habitual criminals. The program saves prison space, is cost-effective, and participants have slightly lower recidivism rates than would be expected if they had been placed in the general prison population.

The New Jersey and Georgia programs are models for IPS programs around the United States. Evaluations indicate they are successful, deliver more services than would normally be received by probationers, are cost-effective, and produce recidivism rates that improve or equal probation or confinement.[103] However, program evaluations have so far not been definitive, in that they often ignore such issues as whether the program met its stated goals, whether IPS is more attractive than other alternative sanctions, and which types of offenders are particularly suited for IPS. For example, in an evaluation of the Massachusetts IPS program, James Byrne and Linda Kelly found that the original program model was not fully implemented in some courts, and that full implementation was related to program success. The researchers found that offenders who improved their employment status while on intensive supervision were less likely to recidivate than those who did not improve, indicating that program success may vary between offender types and groups.[104] These findings suggest that although there is insufficient evidence that IPS can significantly reduce offending, it is an attractive alternative to the traditional correctional system.

House Arrest

A number of states including Florida, Oklahoma, Oregon, Kentucky, and California have developed house arrest programs as an intermediate sanction. The house arrest concept requires convicted offenders to spend extended periods of time in their own homes as an alternative to an incarceration sentence. For example, an individual convicted on a drunk driving charge might be sentenced to spend the period between 6 P.M. Friday and 8 A.M. Monday and every weekday after 5:30 P.M. in his or her home for the next six months. Current estimates indicate that as many as 10,000 people are placed under house arrest each year.[105]

Like IPS programs, house arrest initiatives vary considerably: some are administered by probation departments, while others are simply judicial sentences monitored by **surveillance officers;** some check clients 10 or more times a month, while others make only a few curfew checks; some use 24-hour confinement, while others allow offenders to attend work or school. Regardless of the model used, house arrest programs are designed to be more punitive than IPS or any other community supervision model and are considered a "last chance" before prison.[106]

As of yet, there are no definitive data indicating whether house arrest is an effective crime deterrent, nor is there sufficient evidence to conclude that it has utility in lowering the recidivism rate. Nevertheless, considering its advantages in cost and the overcrowding conditions in prisons and jails, it is evident that house arrest will continue to grow in the 1990s.

Electronic Monitoring

In order for house arrest to work, sentencing authorities must be assured that arrestees are actually at home during their assigned times. Random calls and visits are one way to check on compliance with house arrest orders. One of the more interesting developments in the criminal justice system, however, has been the introduction of electronic monitoring devices to manage offender obedience to home confinement orders. As Figure 15.2 shows, electronic monitoring can be used with offenders at a variety of points in the criminal justice system.

Electronically monitored offenders wear devices attached to their ankles or wrists or around their necks, which send signals back to a control office. Two basic types of systems are in use: active and passive. Active systems constantly monitor the offender by continuously sending a signal back to the central office. If the offender leaves his or her home at an unauthorized time, the signal is broken and the "failure" recorded. In some cases the control officer is automatically notified electronically through a "beeper."

In contrast, passive systems usually involve random phone calls generated by computers to which the offender must respond within a particular time frame (e.g., 30 seconds). Some passive systems require the offender to place his or her monitoring device into a verifier box, which then sends a signal back to the

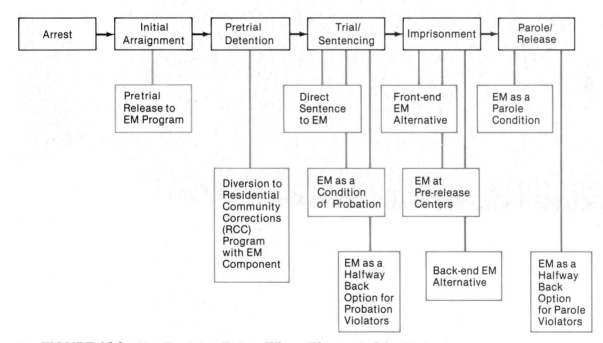

■ *FIGURE 15.2* **Key Decision Points Where Electronic Monitoring Programs Are Being Used**

SOURCE: James Byrne, Arthur Lurigio, and Christopher Baird, *The Effectiveness of the New Intensive Supervision Programs*, Research in Corrections Series, vol. 2, no. 2 (preliminary unpublished draft; Washington, D.C.: National Institute of Corrections, 1989).

control computer; another approach is to have the offender repeat words that are analyzed by a voice verifier. Although most electronic surveillance systems use telephone lines, others employ radio transmitters, which receive a signal from a device worn by the offender and relay it back to the local area computer monitoring system.

Though a recent development, electronic monitoring combined with house arrest is being hailed as one of the most important developments in correctional policy.[107] It has the benefits of relatively low cost and high security, while at the same time it helps offenders avoid the pains of imprisonment in overcrowded, dangerous state facilities. Electronic monitoring is capital rather than labor intensive. Since offenders are monitored by computers, an initial investment in hardware eliminates the need to hire many more supervisory officers to handle large numbers of clients. The Criminal Justice in Review on page 516 discusses a recent survey of electronic monitoring.

THE LIMITS OF ELECTRONIC MONITORING. Electronic monitoring holds the promise of becoming a widely used intermediate sanction in the 1990s. Nevertheless, the concept contains drawbacks that can counterbalance the advantages gained from its provision of low-cost confinement.[108] First, current technology is limited. Existing systems can be affected by faulty telephone equipment, radio beacons from powerful transmitters such as those located at airports or radio stations, storms and weather disturbances, and even large concentrations of iron and steel, which can block signals or cause an electromagnetic effect. It is difficult to assess what the proper response should be when tracking equipment reveals a breach of home confinement: can we incarcerate someone for what might be an equipment failure?

It may also be inaccurate to assume that electronic monitoring can provide secure confinement at a relatively low cost. In addition to the initial outlay for the cost of equipment, other expenses involved with electronic monitoring include overtime pay for control officers who are on duty at night or weekends, the cost of training personnel in the use of sophisticated new equipment, and the expense of educating judges in the legality of home confinement. Joan Petersilia estimates the cost of home confinement with electronic monitoring to be four times greater than traditional probation.[109] In addition, electronic monitoring/house arrest does not provide for rehabilitation services since its focus is on guaranteeing the secure incapacitation of offenders and not their treatment. Ultimately, it may lack the deterrent power of a prison sentence while containing little of the rehabilitative effects of traditional probation.

Finally, electronic monitoring seems out of step with traditional American values of privacy and liberty. It smacks of the ever-vigilant "big brother" centralized state authority that we deplore in totalitarian societies such as Iran and East Germany. Do we really want U.S. citizens to be watched over by a computer? What are the limits of electronic monitoring? Can it be used with mental patients, HIV virus carriers, suicidal teenagers, or those considered high-risk future offenders? Our democratic principles make us recoil at the prospect of having our behavior monitored by an all-powerful central government computer.

Residential Community Corrections

The most secure intermediate sanction is a sentence to a residential community corrections (RCC) facility, which has been defined as:

a freestanding nonsecure building that is not part of a prison or jail and houses pre-trial and adjudicated adults. The residents regularly depart to work, to attend school, and/or participate in community corrections activities and programs.[110]

The traditional community corrections facility is the nonsecure "halfway house," designed to reintegrate soon-to-be-paroled prison inmates back into the community. Inmates spend the last few months in the halfway house acquiring suitable employment, building up cash reserves, obtaining an apartment, and developing a job-related wardrobe. These facilities often look like residential homes since in many instances they were originally designed as private residences. In urban centers, small apartment buildings have been used to house clients. Usually, these facilities specialize in a particular kind of treatment, such as group therapy or reality therapy, which is used to rehabilitate and reintegrate clients. Another popular approach in community-based corrections is the use of ex-offenders as staff members. These individuals have experienced the transition between closed institutions and society and can be invaluable in helping residents overcome the many hurdles they face in proper readjustment. Clients learn how to reestablish family and friendship ties, and the shock of sudden reentry into society is considerably reduced.

The traditional concept of community corrections has undergone a recent expansion. Today the community correctional facility serves as a vehicle to provide intermediate sanctions as well as a pre-release center for those about to be paroled from the prison system. For example, RCC has been used as a direct sentencing option by judges who believe particular offenders need a correctional alternative "halfway" between traditional probation and a stay in prison. Placement in an RCC center can be used as a condition of probation for special needs offenders who need a nonsecure community facility that provides a more structured treatment environment than traditional probation.

Probation departments and other correctional authorities run RCC centers that serve as a pre-prison sentencing alternative. In addition, some RCC facilities are operated by private nonprofit groups who receive referrals from the county or district courts. For example, Portland House, a private residential center in Minneapolis, operates as an alternative to incarceration in county jail for young adult felony offenders. Residents receive group therapy and financial, employment, education, family, and personal counseling on a regular basis. With funds withheld from their earnings at work-release employment, residents pay room and board, family and self-support, and income taxes. Portland House appears to be successful. It is significantly cheaper to run than a state institution, and the recidivism rate of clients is much lower than for those who have gone through traditional correctional programs.[111]

Nexus, in Minnetonka, Minnesota, accepts males aged 15 to 28 who have a more intensive history of involvement in the criminal justice system. The Nexus program provides primary treatment for chemical dependency as well as educational, financial, and vocational counseling. Residents are often asked to make restitution to the victims of their crime.[112]

In addition to being used as sentencing alternatives and as halfway houses, RCC programs have also been used as residential pretrial release centers for offenders who are in immediate need of social services before their trial and as halfway back alternatives for both parole and probation violators who might otherwise have to be imprisoned. In this capacity, RCC programs serve as a base from which offenders can be placed in outpatient psychiatric facilities, drug or alcohol treatment programs, job training, and so on.

More than 200 state-run community-based facilities are in use today holding in excess of 14,000 clients. In addition, there may be up to 2,500 private

Residential community treatment programs are the most secure form of intermediate sanctions.

Electronic Monitoring

Officials in 33 states were using electronic monitoring devices to supervise nearly 2,300 offenders in 1988—about three times the number using this new approach a year earlier, according to a National Institute of Justice survey.

In 1988, most of those monitored were sentenced offenders on probation or parole, participating in a program of intensive supervision in the community. A small portion of those being monitored had been released either pretrial or while their cases were on appeal.

WHERE ARE THE PROGRAMS?

As shown in Figure A, 33 states in all regions had monitoring programs, a substantial increase over the 21 states with programs in 1987.

The level of monitoring activities varies widely. Florida and Michigan, with 667 and 461 electronically monitored offenders, respectively, account for a large proportion of the offenders—49.5 percent.

Many monitoring programs involve limited numbers of offenders. Responses were received from more than one locality in almost every state with such programs. Yet as Figure A shows, 7 states were monitoring between 25 and 49 offenders, and 12 were monitoring fewer than 25. Two states had established programs but were not monitoring any offenders on the date information was gathered. One state's program had not quite begun by February 14, 1988.

Monitoring programs have been developed by a broad range of state and local criminal justice agencies, from departments of corrections, probation, and parole, to court systems, sheriff's offices, and police departments. Some began a few days or weeks before the survey response date. About a quarter of the programs had been operating 4 months or less. Others, like the one in Palm Beach County, were more than 3 years old. Regardless of the length of time in operation, most programs were monitoring fewer than 30 offenders.

The two states with the largest number of electronically monitored offenders structure their programs differently. In Michigan, the State Department of Corrections monitors most offenders, and local courts, sheriffs, or private agencies monitor the rest.

In contrast, the Florida Department of Corrections monitors only a little over half the participating offenders. Another quarter are monitored by city or county agencies, including sheriff's offices, local departments of corrections, and police departments. Most of the rest are monitored by one of several private agencies that offer monitoring services, and a very small num-

FIGURE A

Number of Offenders Being Electronically Monitored on February 14, 1988

*Programs exist, but no offenders were being monitored on this date.
**No response.

NOTE: There are no programs in Alaska.

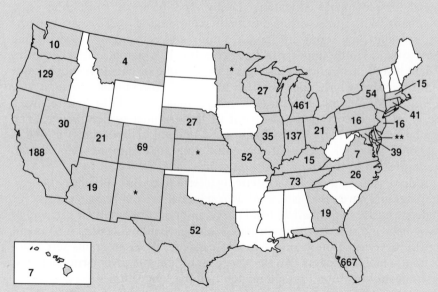

ber are monitored by a federal demonstration project.

Florida is a microcosm of the country as a whole in that monitoring activities take place in all areas—large metropolitan areas, medium-sized cities, small towns, and rural areas—by all levels of government. The government may provide the service with its own staff or contract for it. These public agencies represent all elements of the criminal justice system, including police departments, sheriffs, courts, correctional systems, and probation and parole agencies.

WHO ARE BEING MONITORED AND WHAT KINDS OF OFFENSES DID THEY COMMIT?

The characteristics of the 2,277 offenders monitored in 1988 do not differ much from those of the 826 who were monitored in 1987. Both years,

the programs monitored mostly men, with women constituting 12.7 percent of monitored offenders in 1988 and only 10.2 percent in 1987.

Survey results show that offenders monitored in 1988 were convicted of a wide range of criminal violations (see Figure B).

A quarter (25.6 percent) of offenders were charged with major traffic offenses. Most of the offenders in this group (71 percent) were charged with driving under the influence or while intoxicated. The other offenses in this category reflect primarily current or previous drunk driving convictions such as driving on a revoked or suspended permit.

In 1988, however, a smaller proportion of major traffic offenders were monitored than in 1987. This change reflects the expanding number of programs run by state departments of corrections, such as Michigan and Florida. Offenders monitored by these

two states generally had committed more serious offenses. These state programs included prison-bound offenders or parolees and releasees from state institutions.

Property offenders were strongly represented. They committed a few closely related offenses—burglary (28 percent), thefts or larcenies (39.6 percent), and breaking and entering (16.6 percent).

Drug law violators constituted 15.3 percent of monitored offenders, with slightly over half of these charged with possession of drugs and the rest charged with distribution.

HOW ARE THE OFFENDERS MONITORED?

The monitoring equipment used can be roughly divided into two kinds: continuously signaling devices that constantly monitor the presence of an

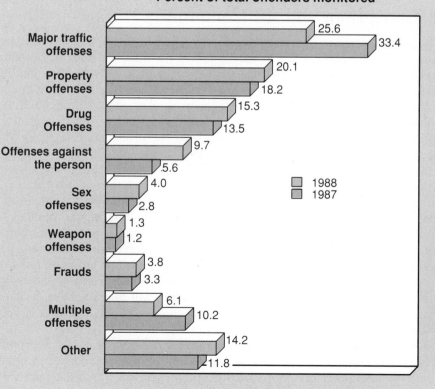

Percent of total offenders monitored

Major traffic offenses: 25.6 (1988), 33.4 (1987)
Property offenses: 20.1 (1988), 18.2 (1987)
Drug Offenses: 15.3 (1988), 13.5 (1987)
Offenses against the person: 9.7 (1988), 5.6 (1987)
Sex offenses: 4.0 (1988), 2.8 (1987)
Weapon offenses: 1.3 (1988), 1.2 (1987)
Frauds: 3.8 (1988), 3.3 (1987)
Multiple offenses: 6.1 (1988), 10.2 (1987)
Other: 14.2 (1988), 11.8 (1987)

1988
1987

■ *FIGURE B*

Electronically Monitored Offenders Categorized by Offense

offender at a particular location, and programmed contact devices that contact the offender periodically to verify his or her presence.

Survey results show that the continuously signaling equipment was used for 56 percent of offenders nationwide. Another 42 percent were monitored by programmed contact devises that mechanically verified that the telephone was being answered by the offender, and 2 percent were monitored by programmed contact devices without mechanical verification. Continuously signaling devices were used with roughly the same proportion of offenders in 1988 as 1987.

In 1988, however, many offenders had been monitored only a short time—54.1 percent for 6 weeks or less. Only 4.1 percent had been monitored for between 6 months and a year and 1.4 percent for more than a year.

Offenders belonged to all age groups, in proportions roughly corresponding to the general population. In 1988 they ranged in age from 10 to 79, with 54.9 percent under age 30. ∎

SOURCE: Annesley Schmidt, *Electronic Monitoring of Offenders Increases* (Washington, D.C.: National Institute of Justice, 1989).

nonprofit RCC programs operating in the United States. About half of these are traditional halfway houses, and the remainder, including about 400 federally sponsored programs, are "true" intermediate sanctions.[113]

Despite the thousands of traditional and innovative RCC programs in operation around the United States, there have been relatively few efforts to evaluate their effectiveness. One reason is that programs differ considerably with respect to target population, treatment alternatives, and goals. Some are rehabilitation oriented and operate under loose security, whereas others are control oriented and utilize such security measures as random drug and alcohol testing.

∎ Corrections and the Community

The rapid increase in the use of community corrections and the new variety of correctional alternatives now available reflect the dual concerns of economy and control. On the one hand, the public is concerned because the criminal justice system is so expensive. Existing facilities are overcrowded and budget cutbacks in many states promise little chance of relief. On the other hand, the public wants to feel safe at home and protected from predatory criminals. Alternative, community-based sanctions hold the promise of satisfying both needs by being cost-effective crime control strategies.

Before intermediate sanctions can be fully embraced, there must be some recognition of their impact on the community in which they are to operate. As criminologist James Byrne warns, there are four elements of every community that can impact on program success and must be carefully considered by policymakers.[114] First, what are the *community attitudes* toward alternative sanctions? If people are opposed to programs in which offenders are returned home without being incarcerated, they will form opposition groups to pressure local politicians to terminate the policy. Similarly, *community tolerance* for misbehavior must be gauged: some communities will tolerate more deviance than others; offenders in low-tolerance areas must be supervised more closely, or their program participation will be quickly terminated.

Byrne also argues that each area maintains different levels of *community support* and resources it can offer program planners and participants. Support is usually unavailable in deteriorated neighborhoods in which the *community structure* is too disorganized to provide much help to a correctional client; instead it produces inducements toward deviance such as the easy availability of drugs.

According to Byrne, correctional policymakers have not considered these community issues as they rush to embrace alternative sanctions. He argues that if these community issues are not addressed, the long-term effect will be increased failure rates among the alternative corrections population, leading to increased costs and a higher concentration of "ex-offenders" who have substance abuse, employment, and family problems as well as a recent incarceration experience. In sum, properly assessing the *community* aspect of community corrections is an important issue.

■ SUMMARY

Probation can be traced to the common law practice of granting clemency to deserving offenders. The "modern" probation concept was developed by John Augustus of Boston, who personally sponsored 2,000 convicted inmates over an 18-year period.

Today, probation is the community supervision of convicted offenders by order of the court. It is a sentence reserved for defendants whom the magistrate views as having potential for rehabilitation without serving prison or jail terms. Probation is practiced in every state and by the federal government and includes both adult and juvenile offenders.

In the decision to grant probation, most judges are influenced by their own personal views and the presentence reports of the probation staff. Once on probation, the offender must follow a set of rules or conditions, the violation of which may lead to revocation of probation and reinstatement of a prison sentence. These rules vary from state to state, but usually involve such demands as refraining from the use of alcohol, curfew maintenance, and termination of past criminal associations.

Probation officers are usually organized into county-wide departments, although some agencies are state-wide and others are combined parole-probation departments. Probation departments have instituted a number of innovative programs designed to bring better services to their clients. These include restitution and diversionary programs, the use of volunteers in probation, intensive probation, and residential probation.

In recent years, the U.S. Supreme Court has granted the probationer greater due process rights; today, when the state wishes to revoke probation, it must conduct a full hearing on the matter and provide the probationer with an attorney when that assistance is warranted.

To supplement probation, a whole new array of alternative sanctions has been developed. These range from pretrial diversion to residential community corrections. Other widely used alternative sanctions include fines and forfeiture, electronic monitoring by computers, house arrest, and intensive probation supervision. Although it is too soon to determine whether these programs will be successful, they offer the possibility of being low-cost, high-security alternatives to traditional corrections.

■ QUESTIONS

1. What is the purpose of probation? Identify some conditions of probation, and discuss the responsibilities of the probation officer.
2. Discuss the procedures involved in probation revocation. What are the rights of the probationer?
3. Should probation be a privilege and not a right?

4. Should a convicted criminal make restitution to the victim? When is restitution inappropriate?
5. What are the pros and cons of electronic monitoring?
6. Does house arrest involve a violation of personal freedom?

■ NOTES

1. This section relies heavily on Harry Allen, Eric Carlson, and Evalyn Parks. *Critical Issues in Adult Probation* (Washington, D.C.: U.S. Government Printing Office, 1979); Samuel Walker, *Popular Justice* (New York: Oxford University Press, 1980).

2. Allen, Carlson, and Parks, *Critical Issues in Adult Probation*, pp. 15–16.

3. Ibid., p. 20.

4. David Rothman, *Conscience and Convenience* (Boston: Little, Brown & Co., 1980), pp. 82–117.

5. See, generally, Todd Clear and Vincent O'Leary, *Controlling the Offender in the Community* (Lexington, Mass.: Lexington Books, 1983).

6. George Killinger, *Probation and Parole in the Criminal Justice System* (St. Paul, Minn.: West Publishing Company, 1976), p. 35.

7. Lawrence Greenfeld, *Probation and Parole, 1987* (Washington, D.C.: Bureau of Justice Statistics, 1988), p. 2.

8. Ibid.

9. Data in this section come from Greenfeld, *Probation and Parole, 1987*.

10. Ibid.

11. "Incarceration vs. Probation: A Look at the Numbers," *Criminal Justice Newsletter*, 14 March 1983, p. 5.

12. American Law Institute, *Model Penal Code*, Proposed Official Draft, § 7.01.

13. Mark Cuniff, *Sentencing Outcomes in 28 Felony Courts, 1985* (Washington, D.C.: National Institute of Justice, 1987), p. 5.

14. Joan Petersilia, Susan Turner, James Kahan, and Joyce Peterson, *Granting Felons Probation: Public Risks and Alternatives* (Santa Monica, Calif.: Rand Corporation, 1985).

15. 627 F.2d 893 (9th Cir. 1980).

16. Ibid., p. 897.

17. Jerome Weissman, "Constitutional Primer on Modern Probation Conditions," *New England Journal on Prison Law* 8 (1982): 367–93.

18. *Ramaker v. State*, 73 Wis.2d. 563, 243 N.W.2d 534 (1976).

19. 855 F.2d. 749 (11th Cir. 1988).

20. *State v. McCoy*, 45 N.C.App. 686, 263 S.E.2d 801 (1980).

21. *United States v. Duff*, 831 F.2d. 176 (9th Cir. 1987).

22. *United States v. Pierce*, 561 F.2d 735 (9th Cir.) *cert. denied*, 435 U.S. 923 (1977).

23. *United States v. Kahl*, 583 F.2d 1351 (5th Cir. 1978); see also Harvey Jaffe, "Probation with a Flair: A Look at Some Out-of-the-Ordinary Conditions," *Federal Probation* 33 (1979): 29.

24. *People v. Johnson*, 44 CrL 2015 (Ill.App.Ct. 1988).

25. *United States v. Williams*, 787 F.2d. 1182 (7th Cir. 1986).

26. For an in-depth look at probation administration, see Eric Carlson and Evalyn Parks, *Critical Issues in Adult Probation: Issues in Probation Management* (Washington, D.C.: U.S. Government Printing Office, 1979).

27. Chris Eskridge and Eric Carlson, "The Use of Volunteers in Probation," *Journal of Offender Counseling Services and Rehabilitation* 4 (1975): 175–89.

28. Edward Latessa, Eric Carlson, and Harry Allen, "Paraprofessionals in Probation: A Synthesis of Management Issues and Outcome Studies," *Journal of Offender Counseling Services and Rehabilitation* 4 (1979): 163–73.

29. Cited in Carlson and Parks, *Critical Issues in Adult Probation*, pp. 255–62.

30. E. Kim Nelson, Howard Ohmart, and Nora Harlow, *Promising Strategies in Probation and Parole* (Washington, D.C.: U.S. Government Printing Office, 1978), p. 29.

31. Frank Scioli and Thomas Cook, "How Effective Are Volunteers," *Crime and Delinquency* 22 (1976): 192–200.

32. Eskridge and Carlson, "The Use of Volunteers in Probation."

33. Charles Newman, "Concepts of Treatment in Probation and Parole Supervision," *Federal Probation* 25 (March 1961): 11.

34. Ibid.

35. John Rosecrance, "Probation Supervision: Mission Impossible," *Federal Probation* 50 (1986): 25–31.

36. "Drug Treatment Role Increasing for Probation, Parole Agencies," *Criminal Justice Newsletter*, 9 September 1988, p. 6.

37. For example, see John Vandeusen, Joseph Yarbrough, and David Cornelson, "Short-Term System-Therapy with Adult Probation Clients and Their Families," *Federal Probation* 49 (1985): 21–26.

38. Robert Carter, "It Is Respectfully Recommended," *Federal Probation* 30 (1966): 38–40.

39. *Turner v. Barry*, 856 F.2d 1539 (D.C. Cir. 1988).

40. Ibid. at 1538.

41. Seymour Gross, "The Prehearing Juvenile Report, Probation Officer's Conceptions," in *Probation and Parole*, Robert Carter and Leslie Wilkins, eds. (New York: John Wiley & Sons, 1970), p. 109.

42. Anthony Walsh, "Gender-Based Differences," *Criminology* 22 (1984): 371–88.

43. John Hagan, "The Social and Legal Construction of Criminal Justice: A Study of the Pre-sentencing Process," *Social Problems* 22 (1975): 88–90.

44. Peter Kratcoski, "The Functions of Classification Models in Probation and Parole: Control or Treatment-Rehabilitation?" *Federal Probation* 49 (1985): 49–56.

45. Clear and O'Leary, *Controlling the Offender in the Community*, pp. 11–29, 77–100.

46. Greenfield, *Probation and Parole, 1987*.

47. Allen, Carlson, and Parks, *Critical Issues in Adult Probation*.

48. 465 U.S. 420, 104 S.Ct. 1136, 79 L.Ed.2d 409 (1984).

49. 483 U.S. 868, 107 S.Ct. 3164, 97 L.Ed.2d 709 (1987).

50. 389 U.S. 128, 88 S.Ct. 254, 19 L.Ed.2d 336 (1967); Fred Cohen, "Sentencing, Probation, and the Rehabilitation Ideal: The View from *Mempa v. Rhay*," *Texas Law Review* 47 (1968): 1.

51. 408 U.S. 471, 92 S.Ct. 2593, 33 L.Ed.2d 484 (1972).

52. 411 U.S. 778, 93 S.Ct. 1756, 36 L.Ed.2d 655 (1973).

53. Joseph J. Senna, "Right to Counsel at Adult Probation Revocation Hearings—A Survey and Analysis of Current Law: A Commitment," *Criminal Law Bulletin* 10 (1974): 228.

54. 669 F.2d 216 (5th Cir. 1982).

55. 31 Cr.L.Rptr. 2081 (1982).

56. 828 F.2d 968 (3rd. Cir. 1987) at 828; see also *United States v. Camarata*, 828 F.2d 974 (3rd Cir. 1987); *United States v. Yancey*, 827 F.2d. 83 (1987).

57. Vincent O'Leary, "Probation: A System in Change," *Federal Probation* 51 (1987): 8–11.

58. Peter Finn, "Prison Crowding: The Response of Probation and Parole," *Crime and Delinquency* 30 (1984): 141–53.

59. "Law in Massachusetts Requires Probationers to Pay 'Day Fees,'" *Criminal Justice Newsletter*, 15 September 1988.

60. Gerald Wheeler, Therese Macan, Rodeny Hissong, and Morgan Slusher, "The Effects of Probation Service Fees on Case Management Strategy and Sanctions," *Journal of Criminal Justice* 17 (1989): 15–24.

61. Patrick McAnany, Douglas Thomson, and David Fogel, *Probation and Justice: Reconsideration of Mission* (Cambridge, Mass.: Oelgeschlager Gunn and Hain, 1984).

62. Patrick McAnany, "Mission and Justice: Clarifying Probation's Legal Context," in McAnany, Thomson, and Fogel, *Probation and Justice: Reconsideration of Mission*, pp. 39–63.

63. David Fogel, "The Emergence of Probation as a Profession in the Service of Public Safety: The Next Ten Years," in McAnany, Thomson, and Fogel, *Probation and Justice: Reconsideration of Mission*, pp. 65–99.

64. John Conrad, "The Redefinition of Probation: Drastic Proposals to Solve an Urgent Problem," in McAnany, Thomson, and Fogel, *Probation and Justice: Reconsideration of Mission*, pp. 251–73.

65. Allen Beck, *Recidivism of Prisoners Released in 1983* (Washington, D.C.: Bureau of Justice Statistics, 1989).

66. Michael Tonry and Richard Will, *Intermediate Sanctions*, Preliminary Report to the National Institute of Justice, (1988), p. 6.

67. Ibid., p. 8.

68. Information provided by Project De Novo Staff members, 7 April 1989.

69. For more information contact James Brown, Operation De Novo, 251 Portland Avenue South Minneapolis, Minn. 55415.

70. David Pauly and Carolyn Friday, "Drexel's Crumbling Defense," *Newsweek*, 19 December 1988, p. 44.

71. George Cole, Barry Mahoney, Marlene Thorton, and Roger Hanson, *The Practices and Attitudes of Trial Court Judges Regarding Fines as a Criminal Sanction* (Washington, D.C.: U.S. Government Printing Office, 1987).

72. "Day Fines' Being Tested in a New York City Court," *Criminal Justice Newsletter*, 1 September 1988, pp. 4–5.

73. 401 U.S. 395, 91 S.Ct. 668, 28 L.Ed.2d 130 (1971).

74. Cole, Mahoney, Thorton, and Hanson, *The Practices and Attitudes of Trial Court Judges Regarding Fines as a Criminal Sanction*.

75. C. Yorke, *Some Consideration on the Law of Forfeiture for High Treason*, 2d ed. (1746), p. 26; cited in David Fried, "Rationalizing Criminal Forfeiture," *The Journal of Criminal Law and Criminology* 79 (1988): 328–436, at 329.

76. Fried, "Rationalizing Criminal Forfeiture," p. 436.

77. Ibid., p. 436.

78. For a general review, see Robert Carter, Jay Cocks, and Daniel Glazer, "Community Service: A Review of the Basic Issues," *Federal Probation* 51 (1987): 4–11.

79. For a further analysis of restitution, see Larry Siegel, "Court Ordered Victim-Restitution: An Overview of Theory and Action," *New England Journal of Prison Law* 5 (1979): 135–50.

80. Peter Schneider, Anne Schneider, and William Griffith, *Monthly Report of the National Juvenile Restitution Evaluation Project* V (Eugene, Ore.: Institute for Policy Analysis, 1981).

81. Peter Schneider, Anne Schneider, and William Griffith, *Two-Year Report on the National Evaluation of the Juvenile Restitution Initiative: An Overview of Program Performance* (Eugene, Ore.: Institute of Policy Analysis, 1982).

82. Anne Schneider "Restitution and Recidivism Rates of Juvenile Offenders: Four Experimental Studies," *Criminology* 24 (1986): 533–52.

83. Descriptive materials may be obtained from the EARN-IT Program, District Court of East Norfolk, 50 Chestnut Street, Quincy, Mass. 02169.

84. James Austin and Barry Krisberg, "The Unmet Promise of Alternatives to Incarceration," *Crime and Delinquency* 28 (1982): 374–409.

85. Alan Harland, "Court-ordered Community Service in Criminal Law: The Continuing Tyranny of Benevolence," *Buffalo Law Review* (Summer 1980): 425–86.

86. Mark Umbreit, "Community Service Sentencing: Jail Alternative or Added Sanction," *Federal Probation* 45 (1981): 3–14.

87. Burt Galaway, "Restitution as Innovation or Unfilled Promise?" *Federal Probation* 52 (1988): 3–15.

88. Michael Block and William Rhodes, *The Impact of Federal Sentencing Guidelines* (Washington, D.C.: National Institute of Justice, 1987).

89. Greenfeld, *Probation and Parole, 1987*, p. 2.

90. Harry Allen, Chris Eskridge, Edward Latessa, and Gennaro Vito, *Probation and Parole in America* (New York: Free Press, 1985), p. 88.

91. Joan Petersilia, *The Influence of Criminal Justice Research* (Santa Monica, Calif.: Rand Corporation, 1987).

92. Ibid.

93. National Advisory Commission on Criminal Justice Standards and Goals, *Corrections* (Washington, D.C.: U.S. Government Printing Office, 1974), p. 321.

94. Nicolette Parisi, "A Taste of the Bars," *The Journal of Criminal Law and Criminology* 72 (1981): 1109–1123.

95. Ibid.

96. James Byrne, Arthur Lurigio, and Christopher Baird, *The Effectiveness of the New Intensive Supervision Programs*, Research in Corrections Series, vol. 2, no. 2 (Washington, D.C.: National Institute of Corrections, 1989), p. 16 (preliminary unpublished draft).

97. Stephen Gettinger, "Intensive Supervision, Can It Rehabilitate Probation?" *Corrections Magazine* 9 (April 1983): 7–18.

98. Byrne, Lurigio, and Baird, *The Effectiveness of the New Intensive Supervision Programs*, p. 16.

99. James Byrne, "The Control Controversy: A Preliminary Examination of Intensive Probation Supervision Programs in the United States," *Federal Probation* 50 (1986): 4–16.

100. Billie Erwin and Lawrence Bennett, *New Dimensions in Probation: Georgia's Experience with Intensive Probation Supervision (IPS)* (Washington, D.C.: National Institute of Justice, 1987).

101. Ibid.

102. Frank Pearson, "Evaluation of New Jersey's Intensive Supervision Program," *Crime and Delinquency* 34 (1988): 437–48.

103. Edward Latessa and Gennaro Vito, "The Effects of Intensive Supervision on Shock Probationers," *Journal of Criminal Justice* (1988): 319–30.

104. James Byrne and Linda Kelly, *Restructuring Probation as an Intermediate Sanction: An Evaluation of the Massachusetts Intensive Probation Supervision Program* (Final Report to the National Institute of Justice, Research Program on the Punishment and Control of Offenders, 1989).

105. Ibid., p. 28.

106. Joan Petersilia, *Expanding Options For Criminal Sentencing* (Santa Monica, Calif.: Rand Corporation, 1987), p. 32.

107. Kenneth Moran and Charles Lindner, "Probation and the Hi-Technology Revolution: Is Reconceptualization of the Traditional Probation Officer Role Model Inevitable?" *Criminal Justice Review* 3 (1987): 25–32.

108. This section leans heavily on James Byrne, Linda Kelly, and Susan Guarino-Ghezzi, "An Examination of the Use of Electronic Monitoring in the Criminal Justice System," *Perspectives* (Spring 1988): 30–37.

109. Joan Petersilia, "Exploring the Option of House Arrest," *Federal Probation* (1986): 50–55.

110. Byrne and Kelly, *Restructuring Probation as an Intermediate Sanction*, p. 33.

111. Updated with personal correspondence with Jan Cartalucca, administrative assistant, February 1989.

112. Personal correspondence, February 1989; Nexus may be contacted at 5915 Eden Prairie Road, Minnetonka, Minn. 55343.

113. Byrne and Kelly, *Restructuring Probation as an Intermediate Sanction*.

114. James Byrne, "Reintegrating the Concept of *Community* into Community-Based Corrections," (Unpublished paper, University of Lowell, Criminal Justice Research Center, 1989).

16

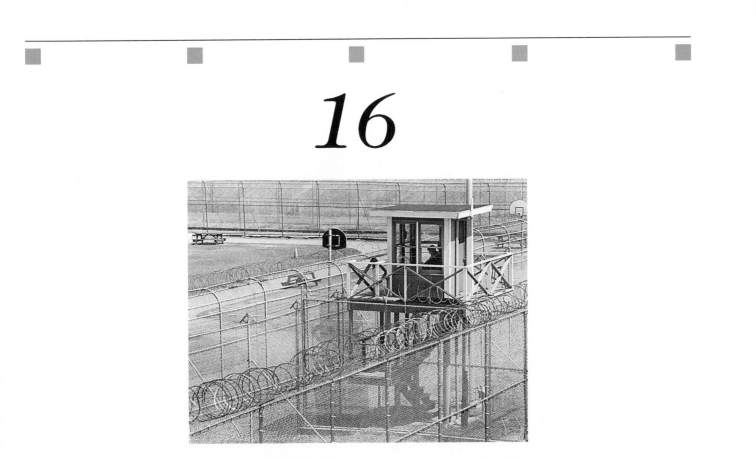

Correctional History and Institutions

When a person is convicted for a criminal offense, state and federal governments through their sentencing authority reserve the right to confine the offender in an institution for an extended period of time. The system of **secure corrections** comprises the entire range of treatment and/or punishment options available to the government, including community residential centers, jails, **reformatories,** and penal institutions (**prisons**).

Correctional treatment is currently practiced on federal, state, and local county levels of government. Felons may be placed in state or federal penitentiaries (prisons), which are usually isolated, fortress-like structures; misdemeanants are housed in county jails, sometimes called reformatories or houses of correction; and juvenile offenders have their own institutions, sometimes euphemistically called schools, camps, ranches, or homes. Typically, the latter are nonsecure facilities, often located in rural areas, which provide both confinement and rehabilitative services for young offenders.

Other types of correctional institutions currently employed are ranches and farms for adult offenders and community correctional settings such as halfway houses for inmates who are about to return to society. Today's correctional facilities cover a wide range of institutions, ranging from maximum security institutions such as Statesville Prison in Joliet, Illinois, to low security camps that house white-collar criminals who are convicted of such crimes as insider trading and mail fraud.

One of the great tragedies of our time is that correctional institutions, whatever form they may take, do not seem to correct. They are in most instances overcrowded, understaffed, outdated warehouses for the human outcasts of our society. Prisons are more suited to control, punishment, and security than to rehabilitation and treatment. It is a sad but unfortunately accurate assessment that today's correctional institution has become a revolving door and that all too many of its residents return time and again. Although no completely accurate figures on the *recidivism* rate are available, it is estimated that about half of all inmates will be back in prison within six years of their release (see the Criminal Justice in Review on page 524).[1]

Despite the apparent lack of success experienced by penal institutions, great debate still ranges over the direction of their future operations. Some penal experts maintain that prisons and jails are not really places for rehabilitation and treatment but should be used to keep dangerous offenders apart from society and give them the "just deserts" for their crimes.[2] In this sense, prison success would be measured by such factors as physical security, length of incapacitation, relationship between the crime rate and the number of incarcerated felons, and inmate perceptions that their treatment was fair and proportionate. The dominance of this correctional philosophy is illustrated by the facts that (1) presumptive and mandatory sentencing structures are now used in such traditionally progressive states as California, Massachusetts, and Illinois; (2) the number of people under lock and key has risen rapidly in the past few years; (3) political candidates who are portrayed by their opponents as advocates of inmate rehabilitation, such as Michael Dukakis was in the 1988 presidential election, soon find themselves on the defensive with a majority of voters; (4) the percentage of convicted defendants sentenced to prison has increased.

Despite the conservative trend in corrections, many correctional experts still maintain that prisons can be useful places for offender rehabilitation, that beneficial programs can be devised, and that offenders should be granted furloughs and/or paroled once prison authorities decide they have made

KEY TERMS

Secure corrections
Reformatories
Prisons
John Howard
Society for Alleviating the Miseries of Public Prisons
Walnut Street Jail
Penitentiary house
Auburn system
Convict-lease system
Z. R. Brockway
Mutual Welfare League
Prisoners' rights movement
Lockups
House of corrections
Custodial convenience
Maximum security
Medium security
Minimum security
Shock incarceration
Community corrections
Halfway houses

Chapter 16

Correctional History and Institutions

CRITICAL JUSTICE
IN REVIEW

The Recidivism Factor

The effectiveness of correctional policy can be evaluated on the basis of whether former inmates return to a life of crime. To assess the extent of recidivism in the prison system, Lawrence Greenfeld of the Bureau of Justice Statistics analyzed data from a national survey of prison inmates. Greenfeld found that an estimated 61 percent of those admitted to prison had previously served a sentence of incarceration as a juvenile, an adult, or both. Of the 39 percent entering prison who had no prior incarceration record, nearly 60 percent had convictions that resulted in probation, and 27 percent were on probation at the time of their offense. In all, about 85 percent of entering inmates had prior convictions that had resulted in correctional treatment.

Another disturbing fact uncovered by Greenfeld was that 46 percent of the recidivists would still have been in prison had they been forced to serve the entire term of the sentence given them at their previous trial. This group, known as "avertable recidivists," constituted 28 percent of all people entering prison. Their criminal behavior could be termed avoidable if prison sentences did not hold the hope of time off for good behavior or early release via parole.

The research also found that recidivists accounted for a two-thirds majority of property-type offenses such as burglary or auto theft, although they were no more violent than first-time offenders. However, "avertable recidivists" accounted for 20 percent of the violent crime, 28 percent of the burglaries and auto thefts, and 30 percent of the forgery/fraud/embezzlement reported by the surveyed inmates.

The table illustrates the prior conviction history for first-timers (those who were serving a prison sentence for the first time), avertable recidivists, and nonavertable recidivists (those who were released after serving their entire sentence). As the table shows, many offenders had long criminal records before they committed the offense that gained them their current sentence—the average being almost three convictions per person. About 60 percent of the first-timers had prior convictions.

In sum, this research reveals that, in fact, most inmates had prior criminal records. It also suggests that current correctional policy is not sufficient to deter offenders from repeating their law-violating behavior. The multiple offender or career criminal has become one of the great criminal justice concerns of the 1980s. ■

SOURCE: Lawrence Greenfeld, Bureau of Justice Statistics, *Examining Recidivism* (Washington, D.C.: U.S. Government Printing Office, 1985).

TABLE A ■ Prior Conviction History at Time of Entry to State Prison

	Admission Types			
	Nonavertable Recidivists	Avertable Recidivists	First-Timers	Total
Number of admissions	50,899	43,235	59,331	153,465
Percent of each admission type with prior convictions	100.0%	100.0%	100.0%	100.0%
No prior convictions	0.0	0.0	40.6	16.1
1 prior conviction	10.1	14.2	30.3	19.2
2	19.1	16.0	15.3	16.8
3	17.0	13.1	5.3	11.3
4	13.6	10.9	2.7	8.6
5	8.5	8.6	2.1	6.0
6–10	22.2	23.4	2.6	14.7
11–20	7.7	11.1	0.8	5.9
21+	1.8	2.7	0.3	1.4
Median number of convictions per offender	4.3	4.6	1.3	2.9

NOTE: Prior conviction history is defined as the sum of all prior juvenile or adult sentences to probation, jail, prison, or juvenile facilities.

satisfactory progress.[3] Many examples of the treatment philosophy still flourish in prison: educational programs range up to the college level; vocational training has become more sophisticated; counseling and substance abuse programs are almost universal; every state maintains some type of early release programs and community corrections models.

In this chapter, we will explore the correctional system, beginning with the history and nature of correctional institutions. Next in Chapter 17 institutional life will be examined in some detail. Chapter 18 discusses how inmates leave the correctional system and the problems they face when they return to society.

■ History of Correctional Institutions

As you may recall, the original legal punishments were banishment or slavery, restitution (wergild), corporal punishment, and execution. The idea of incarcerating convicted offenders for long periods of time as a punishment for their misdeeds did not become popular until the nineteenth century.[4] Consequently, the first penal institutions were not places of punishment but municipal and county jails constructed in England during the tenth century to house individuals before their trials and while they awaited for their sentences to be carried out.[5] During the twelfth century, King Henry II of England rapidly expanded the construction of county jails to provide for the incarceration of thieves and vagrants prior to their actual punishment. In 1557 a workhouse was built in Bridewell, England, to hold people convicted of relatively minor offenses who would work to pay off their debt to society.

These first penal institutions were foul places devoid of proper care, food, or medical treatment. The jailer, usually a shire reeve (sheriff)—the chief law enforcement official of a county appointed by the king or a major landholder—ran the jail under the "fee system." This required inmates to pay for their own food and services. Those who could not pay were fed scraps until they literally starved to death:

> In 1748 the admission to Southwark prison was eleven shillings and four pence. Having got in, the prisoner had to pay for having himself put in irons, for his bed, of whatever sort, for his room if he was able to afford a separate room. He had to pay for his food, and when he had paid his debts and was ready to go out, he had to pay for having his irons struck off, and a discharge fee. . . . The gaolers [jailers] were usually "low bred, mercenary and oppressive, barbarous fellows, who think of nothing but enriching themselves by the most cruel extortion, and have less regard for the life of a poor prisoner than for the life of a brute."[6]

Jail conditions were deplorable because jailers ran them for personal gain; the fewer the services provided, the greater their profit. Early jails became catchalls, holding not only criminal offenders awaiting trial but vagabonds, debtors, the mentally ill, and assorted others.

From 1776 to 1785 a growing inmate population cut off from transportation to the United States by the American Revolution forced the English to house prisoners on *hulks*, abandoned ships anchored in harbors. The hulks became infamous for their degrading conditions and brutal punishments but were not totally abandoned until 1858.

Not until the end of the eighteenth century did conditions begin to improve. Due in large part to the efforts of **John Howard,** the reform-oriented sheriff of Bedfordshire, whose famous book *The State of Prisons*, was published in 1777,[7]

Parliament passed the Penitentiary Act. This Act established a more orderly penal system, with periodic inspections, elimination of the fee system, and greater consideration for inmates.

American Developments

Though Europe contained jails and a variety of other penal facilities, it was in the United States that correctional reform was first instituted. The first American jail was built in James City in the Virginia colonies in the early seventeenth century. However, the "modern" American correctional system had its origin in Pennsylvania under the leadership of William Penn.

At the end of the seventeenth century, Penn revised Pennsylvania's criminal code to forbid torture and the capricious use of mutilation and physical punishment. Such punishments were replaced by imprisonment at hard labor, moderate flogging, fines, and forfeiture of property. All lands and goods belonging to felons were to be used to make restitution to the victims of crimes, with restitution being limited to twice the value of the damages. Felons who owned no property were required by law to work in the prison workhouse until the victim was compensated.

Penn ordered that a new type of institution be built to replace the widely used public forms of punishment—stocks, pillories, the gallows, and the branding iron. Each county was instructed to build a house of corrections similar to today's jails. County trustees or commissioners were responsible for raising money to build the jails and providing for their maintenance although they were operated on a day-to-day level by the local sheriff.

Penn's reforms remained in effect until his death in 1718, when the criminal penal code reverted to its earlier format of public punishment and harsh brutality.

In 1776, postrevolutionary Pennsylvania again adopted William Penn's code, and in 1787 a group of Quakers led by Dr. Benjamin Rush formed the Philadelphia **Society for Alleviating the Miseries of Public Prisons.** The aim of the society was to bring some degree of humane and orderly treatment to the growing penal system. Due to the Quakers' influence, the legislature limited the death penalty to cases involving treason, murder, rape, and arson. Their next goal was to reform the existing institutional system so that the prison could serve as a suitable alternative to physical punishment.

The only models of custodial institutions at that time were the local county jails that Penn had established. These facilities were designed to detain offenders, to incarcerate convicts awaiting other punishment, or to hold offenders who were working off their crimes. The Pennsylvania jails placed men, women, and children of all ages indiscriminately in one room. Liquor was often freely sold.

Under pressure from the Quakers to improve these conditions, the Pennsylvania state legislature in 1790 called for the renovation of the prison system. The ultimate result was the creation of a separate wing of Philadelphia's **Walnut Street Jail** to house convicted felons (except those sentenced to death). Prisoners were placed in separate cells, where they remained in isolation and solitude and did not have the right to work.[8] The wing that contained the solitary or separate cells was called the **penitentiary house,** as was already the custom in England.

The new Pennsylvania prison system took credit for a rapid decrease in the crime rate—from 131 convictions in 1789 to 45 in 1793.[9] The prison became

On March 9, 1787, Dr. Benjamin Rush, a professor of chemistry at the University of Pennsylvania and a signer of the Declaration of Independence, spoke to a gathering about the effects of public punishment on criminals and society. Rush argued that, rather than preventing crime, punishments such as whipping in public actually increased crime because persons who endured cruel punishments in public were likely to seek revenge on the community after their release.

known as a school for reform and a place for public labor. The Walnut Street Jail's equitable conditions were credited for reducing escapes to none in the first four years of its existence (except for 14 on opening day).

The Walnut Street Jail was not a total success, however. Overcrowding undermined the goal of solitary confinement of serious offenders, and soon many cells contained more than one inmate. Inmates who did remain in isolation found it a terrible psychological ordeal, made worse by the fact that they had no work to occupy their time; eventually, inmates were given in-cell piecework to work on up to eight hours a day. Despite these difficulties, similar institutions were erected in New York (Newgate in 1791), New Jersey (Trenton in 1798), Virginia (1800), and Kentucky (1800).

The Auburn System

In the early 1800s both the Pennsylvania and the New York prison systems were experiencing difficulties maintaining the ever-increasing numbers of convicted criminals. Initially, administrators dealt with the problem by issuing more pardons, relaxing prison discipline, and limiting supervision.

In 1816 the state of New York built a new prison at Auburn, which it hoped would alleviate some of the overcrowding at Newgate. The Auburn Prison design became known as the *tier system* because cells were built vertically on five floors of the structure. It was sometimes also referred to as the *congregate system* since most prisoners ate and worked in groups. Later, in 1819, construction was started on a wing of solitary cells to house unruly prisoners. The prisoners were then divided into three classes: one group remained continually in solitary confinement as a result of breaches of prison discipline; the second group was allowed to work as an occasional form of recreation; and the third and largest class worked and ate together during the day and went into seclusion only at night.

The philosophy of the **Auburn system** was crime prevention through fear of punishment and silent confinement. The worst felons were to be cut off from all contact with other prisoners, and although they were treated and fed relatively well, they had no hope of pardon to relieve their solitude or isolation. For a time, some of the worst convicts were forced to remain totally alone and silent during the entire day; this practice caused many prisoners to have mental breakdowns, resulting in a number of suicides and self-mutilations. Consequently, the practice was abolished in 1823.

Nevertheless, the combination of silence and solitude as a method of punishment was not abandoned easily. Prison officials looked for a way to overcome the side effects of total isolation while maintaining the penitentiary system. The solution Auburn adopted was to keep convicts in separate cells at night but allow them to work together during the day under enforced silence. Hard work and silence became the foundation of the Auburn system wherever it was adopted. Silence was the key to prison discipline; it prohibited the formulation of escape plans, it averted plots and riots, and it allowed prisoners to contemplate their infractions.

The concept of using harsh discipline and control to "retrain" the heart and soul of offenders has been the subject of an important book on penal philosophy, *Discipline and Punishment*, by French sociologist Michel Foucault.[10] Foucault's thesis is that as societies evolve and become more complex, they create increasingly more elaborate mechanisms to discipline their recalcitrant members and make them docile enough to obey social rules.

In the seventeenth and eighteenth centuries, discipline was directed toward the human body itself, through torture. In the nineteenth-century prisons, the object was to discipline the offender psychologically; "the expiation that once rained down on the body must be replaced by a punishment that acts in the depths of the heart."[11] We can still see the remnants of that philosophy in today's prisons.

According to one historian, David Rothman, regimentation became the standard mode of prison life. Convicts did not simply walk from place to place; they went in close order and single file, each looking over the shoulder of the preceding person, faces inclined to the right, feet moving in unison. The lockstep prison shuffle was developed at Auburn and is still employed in some institutions today.[12]

When discipline was breached in the Auburn system, punishment was applied in the form of a rawhide whip on the inmate's back. Immediate and effective, Auburn discipline was so successful that when a hundred inmates were chosen to build the famous Sing Sing Prison in 1825, not one dared escape, although they were housed in an open field with only minimal supervision.[13]

The Pennsylvania System

In 1818, the state of Pennsylvania took the radical step of establishing a prison that placed each inmate in a single cell for the duration of his sentence. Classifications of prisoners were abolished, because each cell was intended as a miniature prison that would prevent the inmates from contaminating one another.

The new Pennsylvania state prison, called the Western Penitentiary, had an unusual architectural design. It was built in a semicircle, with the cells positioned along its circumference. Built back-to-back, some cells faced the boundary wall while others faced the internal area of the circle. Inmates were kept in almost constant solitary confinement except for about an hour a day for exercise. In 1820 a second, similar penitentiary using the isolate system was built in Philadelphia and called the Eastern Penitentiary.

The Pennsylvania system reflected the influence of religion and religious philosophy on corrections. Its supporters believed that the penitentiary was truly a place to do penance. Accordingly, they advocated totally removing sinners from society and allowing them a period of isolation in which to reflect alone on the evils of crime. Advocates of the system believed that solitary confinement (with in-cell labor) would eventually make working so attractive that on release the inmate would be well suited to resume a productive existence in society.

The Pennsylvania system eliminated the need for large numbers of guards or disciplinary measures. Isolated from one another, inmates could not plan escapes or collectively break rules. When discipline was a problem, however, the whip and the iron gag were used.

Many fiery debates occurred between advocates of the Pennsylvania system and the Auburn system. Those supporting the latter position boasted of its supposed advantages: their system was the cheapest and most productive way to reform prisoners. They criticized the Pennsylvania system as cruel and inhumane, suggesting that solitary confinement was both physically and mentally damaging. In response, the Pennsylvania system's devotees argued that their system was quiet, efficient, humane, well ordered, and provided the ultimate correctional facility.[14] They chided the Auburn system for tempting inmates to talk by putting them together for meals and work and then punishing them when they did talk. Finally, they accused the Auburn system of becoming a breeding place for criminal associations by allowing inmates to get to know one another.

The Auburn system eventually prevailed and spread throughout the United States; many of its features are still used today. Its innovations included congregate working conditions, the use of solitary confinement to punish unruly inmates, military regimentation, and discipline. In Auburn-like institutions, prisoners were marched from place to place; their time was regulated by bells telling them to wake up, sleep, and work. The system was so like the military that many of its early administrators were recruited from the armed services.

Although the prison was viewed as an improvement over capital and corporal punishment, it quickly became the scene of depressed conditions; inmates were treated harshly and routinely whipped and tortured. As one historian, Samuel Walker, notes:

> Prison brutality flourished. It was ironic that the prison had been devised as a more humane alternative to corporal and capital punishment. Instead, it simply moved corporal punishment indoors where, hidden from public view, it became even more savage.[15]

The Civil War Era

The prison of the late nineteenth century was remarkably similar to that of today. The congregate system was adopted in all states except Pennsylvania. Prisons experienced overcrowding, and the single-cell principle was often ignored. The prison, like the police department, became the scene of political intrigue and efforts by political administrators to control the hiring of personnel and dispensing of patronage.

Prison industry developed and became the predominant theme around which institutions were organized. Some prisons used the contract system, in which officials sold the labor of inmates to private businesses. Sometimes the contractor supervised the inmates inside the prison itself. Under the **convict-lease system,** the state leased its prisoners to a business for a fixed annual fee and gave up supervision and control. Other prisons used the state account system in which prisoners produced goods in prison for state use.[16]

The development of prison industry quickly led to abuse of inmates, who were forced to work for almost no wages, and to profiteering by dishonest administrators and businesses. During the Civil War era, prisons were major manufacturers of clothes, shoes, boots, furniture, and the like. Beginning in the 1870s, opposition by trade unions sparked restrictions on interstate commerce in prison goods.

The 1870s also produced some reforms in prison operations. The National Congress of Penitentiary and Reformatory Discipline, held in Cincinnati in 1870, heralded a new era of prison reform. Organized by penologists Enoch Wines and Theodore Dwight, the congress provided a forum for corrections experts from around the nation to call for the treatment, education, and training of inmates.

One of the most famous participants at the congress, **Z. R. Brockway,** warden at the Elmira Reformatory in New York, advocated individualized treatment, the indeterminate sentence, and parole. The reformatory program initiated by Brockway included elementary education for illiterates, designated library hours, lectures by faculty members of the local Elmira College, and a group of vocational training shops. From 1888 to 1920, Elmira used quasi-military training to discipline the inmates and organize the institution. The military organization could be seen in every aspect of the institution: schooling, manual training, sports, supervision of inmates, and even the parole decision.[17] The cost to the state of the institution's operations was to be held to a minimum. Although Brockway proclaimed Elmira an ideal reformatory, his actual achievements were limited. The greatest significance of his contribution was the injection of a degree of humanitarianism into the industrial prisons of that day (though there were accusations that excessive corporal punishment was used and that Brockway personally administered whippings).[18] Although many institutions were constructed across the nation and labeled reformatories as a result of the Elmira model, most of them continued to be industrially oriented.[19]

Reform Movements

The early twentieth century was a time of contrasts in the prison system of the United States.[20] At one extreme were those who advocated reform, such as the **Mutual Welfare League** led by Thomas Mott Osborne. Prison reform groups proposed better treatment for inmates, an end to harsh corporal punishment, the creation of meaningful prison industries, and educational programs. Reformers argued that prisoners should not be isolated from society, but that the best elements of society—education, religion, meaningful work, self-governance—should be brought to the prison. Osborne went so far as to spend one week in New York's notorious Sing Sing Prison in order to learn about its conditions firsthand.

Opposed to the reformers were conservative prison administrators and state officials who believed that stern disciplinary measures were needed to control dangerous prison inmates. They continued the time-honored system of regimentation and discipline. Although the whip and the lash were eventually abolished, solitary confinement in dark, bare cells became a common penal practice.

In time, some of the more rigid prison rules gave way to liberal reform. By the mid-1930s, few prisons required inmates to wear the red-and-white-striped convict suit and substituted nondescript gray uniforms. The code of silence ended, as did the lockstep shuffle. Prisoners were allowed "the freedom of the yard" to mingle and exercise an hour or two each day.[21] Movies and radio appeared in the 1930s. Visiting policies and mail privileges were liberalized.

A more important trend was the development of specialized prisons designed to treat particular types of offenders. For example, in New York the prisons at Clinton and Auburn were viewed as industrial facilities for hard-core inmates, Great Meadow as an agricultural center to house nondangerous offenders, and Dannemora as a facility for the criminally insane. In California, San Quentin housed inmates considered salvageable by correctional authorities, while Folsom was reserved for the hard-core offender.[22]

Prison industry also evolved. Opposition by organized labor helped put an end to the convict-lease system and forced inmate labor. By 1900 a number of states had restricted the sale of prisoner-made goods on the open market. The world-wide depression that began in 1929 prompted industry and union leaders to put further pressure on state legislators to reduce the competition prison industries presented to outside employers. A series of ever-more restrictive federal measures led to the Sumners-Ashurst Act (1940), which made it a federal offense to transport in interstate commerce goods made in prison for private use, regardless of the laws of the state receiving the goods.[23] The restrictions imposed by the federal government helped severely curtail prison industry for 40 years. Private entrepreneurs shunned prison investments because they were no longer profitable, which led in turn to inmate idleness and make-work jobs.[24]

Despite these changes and reforms, the prison in the mid-twentieth century remained on the whole a destructive institution. Although some aspects of inmate life improved, severe discipline, harsh rules, and solitary confinement were still the way of life.

The Modern Era

The modern era has been a period of change and turmoil in the nation's correctional system. Three trends stand out. First, between 1960 and 1980 occurred what is referred to as the **prisoners' rights movement.** After many years of indifference, state and federal courts ruled in case after case that institutionalized inmates had rights to freedom of religion and speech, medical care, procedural due process, and proper living conditions. Inmates won rights unheard of in nineteenth- and early twentieth-century prisons. Since 1980, however, an increasingly conservative judiciary has curtailed the growth of inmate rights.

Second, violence within the correctional system became a national concern. Well-publicized riots at New York's Attica Prison and the New Mexico State Penitentiary drew attention to the potential for death and destruction that lurks in every prison. One reaction has been to try to improve conditions and provide innovative programs that give inmates a voice in running the institution. Another reaction has been to tighten discipline and call for the building of new maximum security prisons to control dangerous offenders.

Third, the sense that traditional correctional rehabilitation efforts have failed has prompted many penologists to reconsider the purpose of incapaci-

Until the late 1960s, prison officials usually determined the rights and treatment of prisoners. Here inmates of a North Carolina chain gang in 1910 live in wagons equipped with bunks, which transport the prisoners from one job to the next. Armed guards and bloodhounds deter attempts to escape.

Chapter 16

Correctional History and Institutions

tating criminals. Between 1960 and 1980, correctional administrators liked to characterize their efforts as a *"medical model"* that would help rehabilitate people who were suffering from some social malady that prevented them from adjusting to society. In the 1970s effort were also made to help offenders become reintegrated into society by providing them with new career opportunities and work release and furlough programs. During the past decade, however, prisons have more frequently been viewed as places for control, incapacitation, and punishment than as sites for rehabilitation and reform. Nevertheless, efforts to use correctional institutions as treatment facilities have not ended, and such innovations as the introduction of private industries onto prison grounds have kept the rehabilitative ideal alive.

The alleged failure of correctional treatment, coupled with constantly increasing correctional costs, has prompted the development of alternatives to incarceration such as intensive probation supervision, house arrest, and electronic monitoring. What has developed is a bifurcated correctional policy: as many nonviolent offenders as possible are kept out of the correctional system by means of community-based programs, while dangerous, violent offenders are incarcerated for long periods of time.[25] These efforts have been compromised by a growing "get tough" stance in judicial and legislative sentencing policy so that, despite the development of alternatives to incarceration, the number of people under lock and key has skyrocketed.

The following sections review the most prominent types of correctional facilities in use today.

■ Jails

The nation's jails are institutional facilities with five primary purposes: (1) they detain accused offenders who cannot make or are not eligible for bail prior to trial; (2) they hold convicted offenders awaiting sentence; (3) they serve as the principal institution of secure confinement for offenders convicted of misdemeanors; (4) they hold probationers and parolees picked up for violations who are awaiting a hearing; and (5) they house felons when state prisons are overcrowded.

A number of different formats are used to jail offenders. About 15,000 local jurisdictions maintain short-term police or municipal **lockups** that house offenders for no more than 48 hours before a bail hearing can be held; thereafter detainees are kept in county jail. In some jurisdictions, such as New Hampshire and Massachusetts, a **house of corrections** holds convicted misdemeanants, while a county jail is used for pretrial detainees.

According to the most recent statistics, about 52 percent of jail inmates are unconvicted, awaiting formal charges (arraignment), bail, or trial. The remaining 48 percent are convicted offenders, serving time, awaiting parole or probation revocation hearings, or were transferred from a state prison due to overcrowding (about 4 percent of the population or 7,000 jail inmates).[26]

Unfortunately, jails are low-priority items in the criminal justice system. Since they are almost always administered on a county level, jail services have not been sufficiently regulated, nor has a unified national policy been developed to mandate adequate jail conditions. Many jails have consequently developed into squalid, crumbling holding pens. In addition, jails are considered holding pens for the county's undersirables rather than correctional institutions that provide meaningful treatment. They may house indigents looking for a respite from the winter's cold by committing a minor offense, the mentally ill who will eventually be hospitalized after a civil commitment hearing, and substance abusers who are suffering the first shocks of confinement. In his study of the county jail in San Francisco, John Irwin found that the jail does not confine real "criminals," most of whom are able to make bail.[27] Instead, the jail holds the people considered detached and disreputable in local society, who are frequently arrested because they are considered "offensive" by the local police. The purpose of the jail is to "manage" these persons and keep them separate from the rest of society. By intruding into their lives, the jail actually increases their involvement with the law.

Jail Population

There are about 3,400 jails in the United States—2,900 county facilities run by sheriffs and 600 municipal jails run by local corrections departments.[28]

At mid-year 1987 it was estimated that about 8.6 million people enter jails annually; the average daily population in the nation's jails was 295,873 people, a majority of whom were white (57 percent) males (92 percent). The daily population had increased 8 percent during the preceding 12 months with a total increase of 28 percent between 1983 and 1987.[29] Thus, despite the growth in release on own recognizance and other pretrial release programs, jail populations have increased significantly in the past decade, creating a crisis-like atmosphere in many American jurisdictions. Although many jail inmates are repeat offenders who are incarcerated many times each year, it is likely that a significant percentage of the total U.S. population is jailed each year.

Another troubling practice is the housing of juvenile offenders within adult jails. Despite ongoing efforts to remove juveniles from adult jails, it is likely that more than 250,000 youths under 18 are incarcerated in adult facilities during a given 12-month period. In some jurisdictions, juveniles are held with adults because no other facilities are available; in others, such as New York, the legal definition of "adult" includes anyone over 16 years of age.

Jail Conditions

Jails are the oldest and most deteriorated institutions in the criminal justice system. Since they are usually run by the county government (and controlled by a sheriff), it is difficult to encourage taxpayers to appropriate money for improved facilities. In fact, jails are usually administered under the concept of **custodial convenience**, which involves giving inmates minimum standards of treatment and benefits while controlling the cost of jail operations. Jail employees are often underpaid, ill-trained, and totally lacking in professional experience.

Some jails are practically run by violent inmate cliques who terrorize other prisoners; one former IBM executive, who served time in jail for writing bad checks, relates this story:

> I've seen people raped, especially young kids. You can get a kid as young as . . . 16. These young boys would come in and if they were fresh and young, the guys who run the tank and lived in the first cell, they would take the kid, forcibly hold him and someone would rape him. . . . Some of them go to pieces just right there and then, kids who can't hack it and are torn apart.[30]

Well aware of these problems, some judges are reluctant to sentence offenders to a jail term. In one case a New York judge refused to sentence a slightly built man even though he "deserved it." The judge stated in court: "He would be immediately subject to homosexual rape . . . and to brutalities from fellow prisoners such as make the imagination recoil in horror."[31]

Jails are also scenes of serious fires and other neglect-related tragedies. For example, in November 1982, some 27 people were killed and 53 seriously injured in a fire at the Harrison County Jail in Biloxi, Mississippi.[32] Similarly, lack of screening and control procedures results in hundreds of in-jail suicides every year. At last tally, about 400 people (mostly white male detainees arrested on alcohol- or drug-related charges) kill themselves, usually by hanging, each year.[33]

Jail Overcrowding and Its Alternatives

One of the most critical problems of jails is overcrowding.[34] The 100 largest jails—including the Los Angeles County Central Jail, Chicago's Cook County Jail, and New York's Correctional Institute for Men—hold about 40 percent of the total jail population in the United States. As Table 16.1 indicates, Los Angeles County averages over 17,000 inmates on any given day, and New York City jails hold nearly 11,000. A 1987 survey found that overall occupancy

TABLE 16.1 ■ **The Nation's Largest Jail Populations**

Jurisdiction	Average Daily Population, 1987	One-Day Count, June 30, 1987
Los Angeles County, Calif.	17,115	18,593
New York City, N.Y.	10,792	11,083
Cook County, Ill.	5,655	5,745
Harris County, Tex.	4,498	4,549
Philadelphia County, Penn.	4,185	3,936
Dade County, Fla.	3,491	3,753
San Diego County, Calif.	3,452	3,535
Orange County, Calif.	3,250	3,471
Maricopa County, Ariz.	3,226	3,168
Santa Clara County, Calif.	3,066	3,094
Dallas County, Tex.	2,887	2,785
Alameda County, Calif.	2,729	2,779
Orleans Parish, La.	2,652	2,855
Shelby County, Tenn.	2,536	2,562
Kern County, Calif.	2,178	2,180
Baltimore City, Md.	2,177	2,296
Sacramento County, Calif.	1,996	2,071
Orange County, Fla.	1,951	1,980
Broward County, Fla.	1,893	2,042
San Bernardino County, Calif.	1,850	1,907
Washington, D.C.	1,682	1,691
Tarrant County, Tex.	1,673	1,798
Fulton County, Ga.	1,663	1,755
San Francisco County/City, Calif.	1,651	1,542
Wayne County, Mich.	1,597	1,673

SOURCE: Susan Kline *Jail Inmates, 1987* (Washington, D.C.: Bureau of Justice Statistics, 1988), p. 3.

nationwide was 111 percent of stated capacity. Due to overcrowding, 44 percent of the largest jurisdictions reported that they had to hold inmates for other jurisdictions; prison inmates transferred to county jails because of overcrowded conditions in the correctional system made up 12 percent of the total jail population.

Considering these conditions, it is not surprising that 28 percent of the jurisdictions with large jail populations had at least one jail under court order to reduce the number of inmates. As Table 16.2 shows, among the reasons for judicial concern were crowded living conditions, inadequate medical and recreational facilities, visitation policies, and inadequate food services.

Some jails are so overcrowded that there is simply no room to put people. The Washington, D.C., jail system seems to be in a constant state of crisis. Officials have resorted to putting inmates on school buses for as long as 10 hours because there was no room in a correctional facility.[35] In Philadelphia the jails have been so overcrowded that a moratorium has been placed on new admissions, and the city has actually been forced to pay the bail for hundreds of detainees in order to free cells; many new arrestees charged with relatively minor offenses were released on their own recognizance without having to put up bail money.[36] In New York, overcrowding has prompted the city to purchase barges to house the jail overflow.

THE DWI PROBLEM. One factor that has helped to fuel jail overcrowding is the concerted effort being made to reduce the incidence of driving while

TABLE 16.2 ■ **Jurisdictions with Large Jail Populations: Number of Jurisdictions under Court Order to Reduce Population or to Improve Conditions of Confinement, 1987**

	Number of Jurisdictions with Large Jail Populations		
	Total	Ordered to Limit Population	Not Ordered to Limit Population
Total	358	102	256
Jurisdictions under court order citing specific conditions of confinement	118	94	24
Subject of court order			
Crowded living units	99	87	12
Recreational facilities	66	51	15
Medical facilities or services	61	46	15
Visitation practices or policies	51	39	12
Disciplinary procedures or policies	50	38	12
Food service (quantity or quality)	38	28	10
Administrative segregation procedures or policies	34	29	5
Staffing patterns	53	40	13
Grievance procedures or policies	48	37	11
Education or training programs	40	27	13
Fire hazards	30	26	4
Counseling programs	33	24	9
Other	21	17	4

SOURCE: Susan Kline, *Jail Inmates, 1987* (Washington, D.C.: Bureau of Justice Statistics, 1988), p. 4.

intoxicated (DWI) through the deterrent effect of punishment. To achieve this goal many state jurisdictions have passed legislation creating mandatory jail sentences for people convicted of drunk driving.

An evaluation of the mandatory jailing of drunk drivers in four cities (Seattle, Memphis, Cincinnati, and Minneapolis) found that such legislation can have a devastating effect on the justice system.[37] After a well-publicized campaign to alert the public about mandatory jail terms, arrests of drunk drivers began to increase, indicating that police departments were devoting greater resources and effort to controlling the DWI problem. Court caseloads also increased because more of the arrested violators contested their case rather than face a jail term.

The greatest effect the new legislation had was on the local correctional systems. The number of drunk drivers sent to jail increased dramatically. Whereas before the legislation only 9 percent of convicted offenders went to jail in the four jurisdictions, the number climbed to 97 percent after the DWI laws took effect; in Memphis, the incarceration rate jumped from 29 percent to 100 percent. Jailing DWI violators puts a tremendous strain on the correctional system. Since many drunk drivers did not have criminal histories, they were confined separately from the general jail population; many were entitled by law to special treatment and reform programs, which created additional costs and system overload. In Cincinnati offenders have to wait 6 to 7 months before serving their sentences due to overcrowding, and Seattle had to construct a new facility less than 18 months after the legislation was passed (Minneapolis avoided some of these problems by mandating that sentences be carried out within 48 hours of conviction, thereby avoiding the weekend overcrowding experienced in other jurisdictions).

In sum, the mandatory jailing of drunk drivers can place an enormous strain on the local correctional systems, causing program overcrowding and the need to expend additional resources. Is it worth it? Although it is impossible to show a direct relationship, the fatality rate linked to drunk driving accidents declined in the four test sites at a greater rate than in the nation as a whole, indicating that despite the costs a "get tough" policy can have some significant benefits.

The Future of Jails

Despite all these problems and handicaps, there is still hope for the future. A number of methods have been suggested to help alleviate jail overcrowding. With a price tag of $100,000 per cell and $25,000+ per year for upkeep, simply building new facilities is intolerably expensive. Moreover, most communities are reluctant to be the site for the new county jail (the "not in my backyard" phenomenon). A more realistic approach is to reduce overcrowded conditions by relying on more responsive pretrial release programs such as bail reform and speedy trial provisions to shorten court delays and reduce the number of detainees.

A number of jurisdictions are attacking jail problems by reducing the number of sentenced jail inmates. As you may recall, this can include turning to such community-based alternatives as diversion, restitution, intensive probation supervision, and house arrest.[38]

Ongoing efforts are also being made to improve conditions in existing jails. The federal government and the American Correctional Association have cooperated to form the Commission on Accreditation for Corrections. This body has set up standards on health care, food service, treatment, and visitation, which are contained in a *Manual of Standards for Local Detention Facilities*.

Individual states have also taken steps to improve their facilities. Washington passed a minimum Physical Plant and Custodial Standards Act of 1979, which mandates an improvement in jail conditions. Funds were made available for areas that could not comply with conditions due to funding problems. A similar program was begun in New York State in October 1979 to ensure tighter admissions, food, and sanitation standards, and improved medical care.[39]

In an effort to improve the quality of jail personnel—who are often the lowest paid and most poorly trained in the criminal justice system—the National Institute of Corrections has established a National Jail Center in Boulder, Colorado. The center is equipped to develop training materials and hold workshops for jail employees.

There have also been efforts to improve the management and administration of jails. Some jurisdictions now use the "direct supervision" approach in which the staff is stationed inside a housing unit of approximately 50 cells.[40] Instead of isolating the staff from the inmates for security purposes, the direct supervision concept encourages interaction between staff and inmates to prevent negative inmate behavior. Those jurisdictions that have experimented with direct supervision report that the method seems to improve overall custodial operations.

Whether new construction or improvement of existing jails should be encouraged is also a question for debate. New or improved facilities may mean increased reliance on an institution that by its very nature cannot function as it should. Furthermore, jail administrators, most often local county sheriffs, resist changing their policies. Evaluations of the Washington State and New York jail reform efforts indicate that little has actually been done to improve facilities. Increasing costs, overcrowding, conservative administrators, and the absence of public concern make improving jails a difficult task.[41]

Finally, if nothing else, the integration of sentenced offenders, detainees, and juvenile offenders in the same facilities must be ended. Although some county jails maintain separate juvenile wings, these are often in close proximity to the adult sections and are physically their equivalent. It is difficult to maintain a separate juvenile justice system when in practice children and adults are housed in identical quarters.

■ Prisons

The Federal Bureau of Prisons and every state government maintain closed correctional facilities, also called prisons, penitentiaries, or reformatories. Usually, prisons are organized or classified on three levels—maximum, medium, and minimum security—each of which has distinct characteristics.

1. Maximum security prisons are probably the correctional institution most familiar to the public, since they house the most famous criminals and are often the subject of films and stories. Famous "max prisons" have included Sing Sing, Joliet, Attica, Walpole, and the most fearsome of all, the now-closed federal facility on Alcatraz Island known as The Rock.

A typical maximum facility is fortress-like, surrounded by stone walls as high as 25 feet with guard towers at strategic places. Sometimes inner and outer walls divide the prison into courtyards. Barbed wire or electrified fences are designed to discourage escape. High security, armed guards, and stone walls

Maximum security prisons hold the most dangerous repeat criminal offenders.

give the inmate the sense that the facility is impregnable and reassure the citizen outside that convicts will be completely incapacitated.

Inmates live in interior, metal-barred cells that contain their own plumbing and sanitary facilities and are locked securely either by key or by electronic device. Cells are organized in sections called blocks; in large prisons a number of cell blocks comprise a wing. During the evening period, each cell block is sealed off from the others, as is each wing. Thus, an inmate may be officially located in, for example, Block 3 of E Wing.

Every inmate is assigned a number and a uniform on entering the prison system. Unlike the striped, easily identifiable uniforms of old, the max-inmate today wears khaki attire not unlike military fatigues. Some institutions strictly enforce dress codes, but the closely cropped scalp and other such features are vestiges of the past.

During the day, the inmates engage in closely controlled activities: meals, workshops, education, and so on. Rule violators may be confined to their cells, and working and shared recreational activities are viewed as privileges.

The byword of the maximum security prison is security. Guards and other correctional workers are made aware that each inmate may be a dangerous or violent criminal, and as a result the utmost in security must be maintained. In keeping with this philosophy, maximum security prisons are designed to eliminate hidden corners where people can congregate, and passages are constructed so that they can be easily blocked off to quell disturbances.

2. Medium security prisons may be similar in appearance to maximum security prisons; however, security and the general atmosphere are neither so tense nor so vigilant. Medium security prisons are also surrounded by walls, but may not have as many guard towers or other security precautions. For example, visitor privileges may be more extensive and personal contact may be allowed; in a max-prison, visitors may be separated from inmates by plexiglass or other barriers (to prohibit the passing of contraband). Although most prisoners are housed in cells, individual honor rooms in medium security prisons are used to reward those who make exemplary rehabilitation efforts.

Prison farms and ranches are still used in the South and West. The agricultural products they produce are used in the correctional system and other state institutions.

Finally, medium security prisons promote greater treatment efforts, and the relaxed atmosphere allows freedom of movement for rehabilitation workers and other therapeutic personnel.

3. Minimum security prisons operate without armed guards or walls; usually, they are constructed in compounds surrounded by a cyclone-type fence. Minimum security prisons usually house the most trustworthy and least violent offenders; white-collar criminals may be their most numerous occupants. Inmates are allowed considerable personal freedom. Instead of being marched to activities by guards, they are summoned by bells or loudspeaker announcements and assemble on their own. Work furloughs and educational releases are encouraged, and vocational training is of the highest level. Dress codes are lax, and inmates are allowed to grow beards or mustaches or demonstrate other individual characteristics.

Minimum facilities may employ dormitory living or have small private rooms for inmates. Prisoners are allowed quite a bit of discretion in acquiring or owning personal possessions, such as radios, that might be deemed dangerous in a max-prison.

Minimum security prisons have been scoffed at for being too much like country clubs; some federal facilities catering to white-collar criminals even have tennis courts and pools. Yet they remain prisons, and the isolation and loneliness of prison life deeply affects the inmates at these facilities.

■ Farms and Camps

In addition to closed institutions, prison farms and camps are used to detain offenders. Such facilities are found primarily in the South and the West. Today, about 40 farms, 40 forest camps, 80 road camps, and 67 similar facilities (vocational training centers, ranches, and the like) are in use throughout the nation. Prisoners on farms produce dairy products and grain and vegetable crops that are used in the state correctional system and other government facilities such as hospitals and schools. Forestry camp inmates maintain state parks, fight forest fires, and aid in reforestation. Ranches, primarily a western phenomenon, employ inmates in cattle raising and horse breeding, among other activities. Road gangs repair roads and state highways.

■ Shock Incarceration

A recent approach to correctional care that is gaining popularity around the United States is **shock incarceration (SI)**. These new facilities are designed for youthful, first-time offenders and feature military discipline and physical training. The concept is that short periods (90 to 180 days) of high-intensity exercise and work will "shock" the inmate into going straight. Most state programs also include educational and training components, counseling sessions, and treatment for special needs populations. Examples of shock incarceration programs include the Regimented Inmate Discipline Programs in Mississippi, the About Face Program in Louisiana, and the Special Alternative Incarceration (SAI) program in Georgia. The U.S. Army has created a shock program, Specialized Treatment and Rehabilitation in Army Corrections (STRAC) at its prison in Fort Riley, Kansas.

A recent review of shock incarceration by Dale Parent found existing programs to be multi-purpose.

These inmates at Sumter Correctional Institution in Bushnell, Florida are undergoing a high intensity boot camp experience.

Most SI programs operate within a conventional state prison, but with SI participants separated throughout their confinement from regular inmates. Supposedly, this will deter participants from future crime by giving them a close and sobering exposure to the realities of prison life, but without subjecting them to abuse, exploitation, or corruption by hardened criminals. However, some SI programs reject deterrence as a purpose, and operate in a separate institution (like a forestry camp) that does not contain regular inmates.

SI has a rehabilitation goal as well. Officials note that the disciplined regimen, as well as traditional treatment services, may enhance participants' impulse control and diminish problems that hinder lawful living, thereby making them better able to avoid criminal behavior in the future. Often SI is intended to reduce prison populations, by shortening the length of confinement for offenders who would be in prison anyway.[42]

The Criminal Justice in Review on page 542 describes two well known SI programs.

To date there has been no definitive evaluation of the shock incarceration approach. It has the advantage of being a lower cost alternative to overcrowded prisons since programs are held in nonsecure facilities and are of short duration. Some states, such as New Hampshire, are constructing shock incarceration components within their already existing facilities.

■ Community Facilities

One of the goals of correctional treatment is to help reintegrate the offender back into society. An offender placed in a prison, however, is more likely to become acculturated into an inmate lifestyle than to reassimilate conventional social norms. With this goal in mind, the **community corrections** concept began to gain popularity in the 1960s. State and federal correctional systems created community-based correctional models as an alternative to closed institutions. Today, hundreds of community-based facilities are holding an estimated 12,000 residents.[43] Many are **halfway houses** to which inmates are transferred just prior to their release into the community. Such facilities, which may offer specialized treatment, are designed to bridge the gap between institutional living and the community.

As you may recall, commitment to a community correctional center may also be used as an intermediate sanction and sole mode of treatment. An offender may be assigned to a community treatment center that is operated by the state department of corrections or probation. Alternatively, the department of corrections may contract with a private community center and use it as the sole means of incarceration. This practice is common in the treatment of drug addicts and other nonviolent offenders whose special needs can be met in a self-contained community setting that specializes in certain types of treatment.

Despite the encouraging philosophical concept presented by the halfway house, evaluation of specific programs has not led to a definite endorsement.[44] One significant problem has been a lack of support from community residents, who fear the establishment or an institution housing "dangerous offenders" in their neighborhood. Court actions have been brought and zoning restrictions have been imposed in some areas to foil efforts to create halfway houses.[45] As a result, many halfway houses are located in decrepit neighborhoods, in the worst area of town—certainly, a condition that must influence the attitudes and behavior of inmates. Furthermore, the average inmate may find little to distinguish the climate of control exercised in most halfway houses, where rule violation can be met with a quick return to the institution, from that of his or her former high-security penal institution. Conflict theorist Andrew Scull suggests that community-based corrections are simply a way of managing offenders at a lower cost than prison.[46] And John Hylton argues that they help "widen the net": "Persons who were not subjected to control previously," he charges, "may not be controlled under the guise of community treatment."[47]

Despite these problems, the promise held by community correctional centers, coupled with their low cost of operations, has led to their continued use through the 1980s and into the 1990s. In addition, some recent research efforts indicate that offenders from community correctional centers may have lower recidivism rates than the general prison population.[48]

■ Private Institutions

One of the newest developments in corrections is the use of facilities run by private firms who operate secure care institutions as a business enterprise.

The federal government has used private companies to run detention centers for illegal aliens who are being held for trial and/or deportation.[49] One private firm, the Corrections Corporation of America, runs a federal halfway house, two detention centers, and a 370-bed jail in Bay County, Florida. On January 6, 1986, the U.S. Corrections Corporation opened the first private state prison in Marion, Kentucky, a 300-bed minimum security facility for inmates who are within three years of parole. Today, more than 20 companies are trying to enter the private prison market while 3 states have passed enabling legislation and more than 10 others are actively considering doing so.

Though privately run institutions have been around for a few years, their increased use may present a number of problems. For example, will private providers be able to evaluate programs effectively, knowing that a negative evaluation might cause them to lose their contract? Will they skimp on services and programs in order to reduce costs? Might they not skim off the "easy" cases and leave the hard-core inmates for state care? Will the need to keep business booming require "widening the net" to fill empty cells? Must private providers maintain state-mandated liability insurance to cover inmate claims?[50]

Shock Incarceration Programs

GEORGIA'S SPECIAL ALTERNATIVE INCARCERATION (SAI) PROGRAMS

The Georgia Department of Corrections operates two Special Alternative Incarceration (SAI) programs for male offenders. Their basic structure and design are the same, although they differ in minor respects. Judges control SAI selection and impose SAI as a condition of probation sentence. If offenders complete SAI successfully, there is no need to resentence them to probation.

The first SAI program opened in December 1983 at the Dodge Correctional Institution in Southcentral Georgia, near Chester. The DOC opened a second program in March 1985 at Burruss Correctional Institution near Forsyth to reduce the backlog of cases waiting for an available SAI slot. Both are relatively new medium security institutions. In both SAI inmates are completely segregated from general population inmates who also reside at the institutions.

Burruss takes cases from northern Georgia, including metropolitan Atlanta. Dodge takes cases from more rural southern Georgia.

Georgia's 90 day SAI programs involve physical training, drill, and hard work. There are two exercise and drill periods each day, with eight hours of hard labor in between. At Dodge, SAI inmates often are transported to other state facilities or prisons to perform labor-intensive tasks. Sometimes they perform community service for nearby municipalities and school districts. At Burruss SAI inmates work on the grounds of the Georgia Public Safety Training Academy, adjacent to the prison. Except when they are doing community service, SAI inmates work under supervision of armed guards.

There is little emphasis on counselling or treatment. Programs are offered on drug abuse education and sexually transmitted diseases. A parole officer assigned to each program coordinates reentry planning. When SAI graduates are released, they go on regular probation supervision.

At Dodge CI, 100 inmates are double-bunked in two 25-cell units connected by a central control room. At Burruss, 100 inmates are single-bunked in four 25-cell units, each two of which share a central control room. Because it takes more staff to cover four units than two, the Burruss SAI program has 20 staff positions, compared with 12 for Dodge. The annual operating budget for Burruss' SAI program is $468,734, compared to $320,729 for Dodge. Georgia officials

In addition to these problems, private corrections may encounter opposition from existing state correctional staff and management who fear the loss of jobs and autonomy. Moreover, the public may be skeptical about untested private firms' ability to provide security and protection.

Private corrections also poses administrative problems. How will program quality be controlled? In order to compete on price, a private facility may have to cut corners to beat out the competition. Determining accountability for problems and mishaps may be difficult when dealing with a corporation, which is a legal fiction whose officers are shielded from personal responsibility for their actions. Furthermore, legal problems may soon arise: can privately employed guards patrol the perimeter and use deadly force to stop escape attempts?

The very fact that individuals can profit from running a prison may also prove unpalatable to large segments of the population. Should profit be made from human tragedy and suffering? At the same time, is private corrections really much different from a private hospital or mental health clinic that provides services to the public in competition with state-run institutions? This suggests that the future of private corrections may be determined on the basis of efficiency and cost-effectiveness, not fairness and morality.

Although a private correctional enterprise may be an attractive alternative to a costly correctional system, these legal, administrative, and cost issues must

maintain that it costs no more to operate SAI at Dodge and Burruss than to run other living units at those prisons.

OKLAHOMA'S REGIMENTED INMATE DISCIPLINE (RID) PROGRAM

Oklahoma's Regimented Inmate Discipline (RID) program is located in a 145 bed quadrangle at the Lexington Assessment and Reception Center, about 60 miles south of Oklahoma City. It was the first SI program, established in November, 1983. Lexington is Oklahoma's main reception center and also houses about 600 long term general population inmates. The RID living unit is classified as medium security.

The DOC screens offenders received at Lexington for placement in RID. Those who meet statutory criteria may volunteer for RID. Inmates live in single or double-bunked cells.

As in other SI programs, RID emphasizes strict discipline, physical training and drill. However, other than housekeeping and institutional maintenance, there is no formal hard labor component. Rather, inmates spend three to six hours each day in educational and vocational programs. Drug abuse education programs, and individual and group counseling also are provided. Oklahoma gives greater emphasis to education and vocational training than any other existing SI program. RID participants are separated from general population inmates except during vocational training and education programs.

The DOC prepares a resentencing plan for each inmate. When inmates complete the 120 day SI program, the DOC recommends that the judge resentence them to probation, under supervision requirements outlined in the resentencing plan. If the judge refuses to resentence, the DOC can transfer the offender to "community custody", where he will serve the balance of his prison term in a tightly structured community setting, supervised by a correctional officer and will comply with the supervision requirements established in the resentencing plan. The offender may begin community custody with a six-month stay at a halfway house, followed by home detention and intensive supervision.

Oklahoma officials acknowledge that their RID program costs more than similar living units at Lexington. The RID unit has 17 staff positions, including 9 custody and 6 program staff—about 6 more total positions than a comparable non-Rid unit. It costs about $349,500 to operate RID each year, or about $129,500 more than a comparable living unit at Lexington.

In late 1987 Oklahoma opened a RID program for females at the Mabel Bassett Correctional Facility in Oklahoma City. ■

SOURCE: Dale Parent, Shock Incarceration: An Overview of Existing Programs, (Washington, D.C.: National Institute of Justice, 1989), pp. 7, 9.

be solved before private prisons can become widespread.[51] A balance must be reached between the need for a private business to make a profit and the integrity of a prison administration that must be concerned with such complex issues as security, rehabilitation, and the maintenance of highly dangerous people in a closed environment.[52] The Criminal Justice in Review on page 544 further examines the issues presented by the creation and maintenance of privately run prisons.

■ Correctional Population Trends

The precise number of people under correctional care in the United States is always difficult to calculate since there are hundreds of correctional facilities and their population changes daily. Nevertheless, a major concern of criminal justice policymakers has been the rapid increase in the nation's prison population. As Figure 16.1 shows, the number of inmates in state and federal prisons reached 627,000 in 1988, an increase of 6.7 percent during the preceding 12 months; the prison population has increased 76 percent since 1980 when 329,821 inmates were in state and federal prisons.[53]

Private Prisons

By the beginning of 1987, three states had enacted laws authorizing privately operated state correctional facilities, while more than a dozen were actively considering the option. In 1985, Corrections Corporation of America (CCA), a leader among the 20 or so firms that have entered the "prison market," made a bid to take over the entire Tennessee prison system. Though this bid was unsuccessful, CCA now operates several correctional facilities, among them a Federal Bureau of Prisons halfway house, two Immigration and Naturalization Service facilities for the detention of illegal aliens, and a 370-bed maximum security jail in Bay County, Florida. On January 6, 1986, U.S. Corrections Corporation opened what is currently the nation's only private state prison, a 300-bed minimum security facility in Marion, Kentucky, for inmates who are within 3 years of meeting the parole board.

More than three dozen states now contract with private firms for at least one correctional service or program. The most frequent contracts involve medical and mental health services, community treatment centers, construction, remedial education, drug treatment, college courses, staff training, vocational training, and counseling.

The paramount question in the debate over the privatization of corrections is not whether private firms can succeed where public agencies have ostensibly faltered, but whether the privatization movement can last.

Many observers believe that the movement, though only 6 or 7 years old, is already running out of steam. They point to such things as the failure of CCA to win control of the Tennessee system, Pennsylvania's 1-year statutory moratorium on privatization initiatives, enacted in 1986, and the fact that private prison operations have not advanced much beyond the proposal stage in most jurisdictions.

The history of private-sector involvement in corrections is unrelievedly bleak, a well-documented tale of inmate abuse and political corruption. In many instances, private contractors worked inmates to death, beat or killed them for minor rule infractions, or failed to provide them with the quantity and quality of life's necessities (food, clothing, shelter) specified in often meticulously drafted contracts.

Is this history bound to repeat itself? Could such abuses occur today beneath the eyes of a watchful, activist judiciary and vigilant media? Has the corrections profession itself grown beyond the days when such situations were tolerated? To date, no private corrections firm has been found guilty of mistreating inmates or bribing officials, and most private facilities are accredited. What, if any, institutional "checks and balances" exist to ensure that this does not change as the industry matures and becomes more powerful politically?

POLITICS

Much of domestic politics in this country involves competition and struggle among two or more groups which seek to influence public policy. Correctional policy, however, is often made in the context of what political scientists like to call "subgovernments"—small groups of elected officials and other individuals who make most of the decisions in a given policy area. As the late penologist and correctional practitioner Richard A. Mc-

The nation's prison population has undergone a number of cycles of growth and decline.[54] Between 1925 and 1939, it increased at about 5 percent per year, a reflection of the nation's concern for the lawlessness of that time period. The incarceration rate reached a high of 137 per 100,000 U.S. population in 1939. Then during World War II the prison population declined by 50,000 as potential offenders were drafted into the armed services. By 1956 the incarceration rate dropped to 99 per 100,000 U.S. population.

The postwar era saw a steady increase in the prison population until 1961, when 220,000 people were in custody, a rate of 119 per 100,000. During the Vietnam era (1961–1968), the prison population declined by 30,000. The incarceration rate remained rather stable until 1974, when the current dramatic rise began. By 1988 the incarceration rate reached 228 per 100,000 population, the highest in history.

Gee observed, since the 1960s correctional policy has been affected by a larger than ever contingent of "coaches, customers, and critics," among them federal judges. Still, the coaches are relatively few, the customers are virtually powerless, the critics are divided (liberals versus conservatives), and the institutions are normally hidden from public view (except in the immediate aftermath of a major disorder or scandal).

Will privatization perpetuate correctional subgovernments, or will it serve to break them up? If the former, is there a danger that private executives will enter into relationships with public officials that undermine the whole array of regulatory mechanisms, perhaps fostering a correctional version of the military-industrial complex? If the latter, will the quality of correctional activities necessarily improve (and the costs of these activities decrease) as a result?

ADMINISTRATION

The practices and performance of public correctional agencies vary widely. In administering prisons, some jurisdictions have relied on paramilitary structures while others have employed more complex management systems. Some field services units have adopted computer technologies; others have not.

Some prisons are orderly; others are riotous. Some jails are clean; others are filthy. Some agencies offer a rich menu of work and educational opportunities; others offer few or offer them only on paper. And some departments spend much money per prisoner and perform badly while others spend less and seem to do much better.

Whatever else it may suggest, the existence of such concrete differences in correctional practices and outcomes makes it impossible to accept that public correctional bureaucracies have failed. What are the administrative and related factors associated with better public correctional facilities and programs? Only after we have studied the enormous variation in the public sector experience does it make good sense to ask whether private firms can do better (and more consistently) than government bureaucracies. From an administrative perspective, the issue is not public versus private management, but under what conditions competent, cost-effective management can be institutionalized. On this and related questions about privatization, the jury is still out.

PHILOSOPHY

In weighing the morality of private prisons, the profit motive of the privatizers may be less important than is commonly supposed. The real issue may be instead whether the authority to deprive fellow citizens of their liberty, and to coerce (even kill) them in the course of this legally mandated deprivation, ought to be delegated to private, nongovernmental entities. Inescapably, corrections involves the discretionary exercise of coercive authority.

Even if the corporations were to offer their correctional services for free (as do a small number of foundations and other groups), and even if it were a certainty that the firms could reduce costs and improve services without realizing a single fear of their opponents, would privatization be justifiable? What is the proper scope of the government's authority? Where does its responsibility begin? Where does it end? Should the government's responsibility to govern end at the prison gates, or are not imprisonment (and other forms of correctional supervision) the most significant powers that the government must exercise, on a regular basis, over a large body of citizens? ∎

SOURCE: John DiIulio, *Private Prisons* (Washington, D.C.: National Institute of Justice, 1988).

∎ The Problems of Overcrowding

How can this significant rise in the prison population be explained? First, the tremendous public concern about crime has been translated by state lawmakers into mandatory and fixed sentencing laws, which increase the number of people eligible for incarceration and limit the offender's chances for early release on parole. Similarly, concern over such criminal offenses as drug trafficking and violence has spurred state lawmakers to toughen penalties in these areas. These policies may have increased the probability that a criminal will be incarcerated: in 1960 there were 62 prison commitments for every 1,000 reported index crimes. This number declined steadily until 1970 when only 23 were incarcerated and then began a steady rise throughout the 1980s; by 1988, it had reached about 48 per 1,000 crimes, an increase of 72 percent. Similarly,

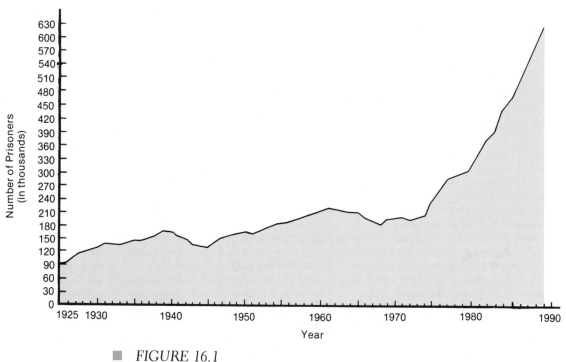

FIGURE 16.1

Number of Sentenced State and Federal Prisoners, Year-End, 1925–1990

SOURCE: Bureau of Justice Statistics, *Prisoners 1925–1981*. (Washington, D.C.: U.S. Government Printing Office, 1982), updated.

whereas 196 people were incarcerated for every 1,000 felony arrests in 1980, the rate rose to 301 per 1,000 arrests by 1988. These data once again illustrate the dominance of the crime control model in the 1980s. Table 16.3 lists some of the factors that have led to overcrowding in the entire correctional system.

As a result of such factors, prisons are desperately overcrowded. A recent national survey indicates that 37 states, plus the District of Columbia, Puerto

Overcrowding has created a volatile atmosphere in many state prisons.

TABLE 16.3 ■ An Overview of the Extent and Likely Causes of the Correctional Crowding Problem

Problem(s)	Primary Cause(s)
Prison crowding Prison population has doubled in the past decade. The rate of incarceration has doubled since 1970. The rate of commitments per 100 serious crimes increased by 50% between 1980 and 1984. The rate of commitments per 100 adult arrests for serious crimes increased by 25% between 1984 and 1985. The nation's federal and state prisons are between 10% and 20% over capacity. At last count, 37 states were under some type of court order related to crowding.	Changes in both *sentencing statutes* and *sentencing practices* have resulted in (1) longer sentences for many offenders, and (2) the increased use of *short-term* confinement before probation supervision (i.e., split sentencing). Changes in the *age composition* of U.S. population have an impact on prison populations; specifically, the number of people in the "prison prone" ages (mid-20s) has increased steadily since 1960. Changes in *return to prison rates* have occurred, resulting in a greater proportion of new admissions who have failed under community supervision. Interstate variations in imprisonment rates can be linked to variations in crime rates and arrest rates in these states.
Jail crowding The U.S. jail population has increased dramatically over the past several years. Between 1983 and 1985, jail population increased by 14.6%. Prison crowding has resulted in jail crowding in many states due to (1) the practice of housing state inmates in local jails, (2) delays in transferring state-bound convicted offenders, and (3) the need to hold offenders in jail who would normally be returned to prison as probation or parole violators. Increases in jail population have occurred in both the convicted *and* pretrial jail population. Many jails are overcrowded and under federal court orders limiting their capacity.	There have been changes in local sentencing policies for specific offender groups (e.g., drunk drivers, repeat minor offenders), including short jail terms and split sentences. Pretrial detention policies have been "toughened" to reflect public safety concerns. Age composition shifts are related to changes in the jail population for both pretrial detainees and sentenced offenders.
Probation crowding Almost ⅔ of all convicted adult offenders are placed on probation, yet probation receives less than ⅓ of the correctional resource pie. The probation population *doubled* in the past decade. Probation populations are increasing at a slightly higher rate than prison, jail, and parole populations. For example, the adult imprisoned population increased by 47.7% between 1979 and 1984 while the adult probation population increased by 57.75%. Nationwide, approximately 15% of all new probationers are committed to prison within *one* year due to either a technical violation, rearrest, or reconviction. However, there is considerable interstate variation in the rate of subsequent imprisonment for probationers. A subgroup of high risk probationers can be identified who fail at very high rates (over 60% rearrested in the first year on probation). The increased use of split sentencing is transforming probation into a *parole* agency.	Changes in *sentencing statutes* have directly and indirectly affected probation via (1) the increased rate of probation (i.e., net widening), (2) the use of split sentences, and (3) the need to utilize probation as an alternative to prison. Changes in *age composition* have placed more offenders "at risk" for probation. In general, states with *higher reported crime rates and higher arrest rates* also have higher rates of all forms of correctional control, including probation. Prison crowding results in the use of *back-door* early release strategies. When these offenders fail (i.e., they are reconvicted) they are placed on probation as a *front-door* diversionary strategy. The cycle continues unabated as prison failures become probation failures who get returned to prison.
Parole crowding Despite changes in parole *release* decision making (including the abolition of parole boards in eight states), the number of offenders under parole *supervision* has been rising steadily in recent years. Between 1979 and 1984, the adult parole population increased by 22.7%. An increasing percentage of new prison admissions are parolees who have failed while under supervision. Almost half of all parolees can be expected to return to prison within six years after initial release. Many (approximately 60%) will return within the first three years after release. A subgroup of parolees (10–15%) can be identified with very high predicted return to prison rates.	Pressures to relieve prison and jail crowding have resulted in back-door early release programs which usually include parole supervision. Higher parole "failure" rates can be linked to two factors: (1) a tougher administrative response to technical violators, and (2) a tougher sentencing policy toward repeat offenders, resulting in longer prison terms. *Age composition* changes are related to increases in prison population and by extension, the subsequent increases in the parole population. Since younger releases have noticeably higher return to prison rates, it is entirely possible that higher return to prison rates are a function of the changing age composition of releases.

SOURCE: James Byrne and Linda Kelly, *Restructuring Probation as an Intermediate Sanction* (Final Report to the National Institute of Justice, Research Program on the Punishment and Control of Offenders, 1989).

Rico, and the Virgin Islands, are operating under court orders because of conditions relating to overcrowding.[55] There were over 76,000 inmates in California, 44,000 in New York, 40,000 in Texas and 35,000 in Florida. Inmates have begun to be housed two and three to a cell. Military bases and even tents have been used to house overflow inmates. In a move of great historical irony, New York City announced the purchase of two river barges that will be anchored offshore and hold 400 inmates each; more barges are planned for the future.[56] The skyrocketing number of drug-related arrests has pushed the daily count in New York City's jails to over 18,000, prompting a response similar to eighteenth-century London's use of abandoned ships.

In addition to detainees and misdemeanants, about 10,000 people convicted of felonies are being held in local jails because of prison crowding.[57] State correctional authorities have attempted to deal with prison overcrowding by building new facilities using construction techniques that limit expenditures, for example, by using modular or preassembled units that reduce costs.[58] Figure 16.2 illustrates one of these modules.

At the time of this writing, there is little evidence that the incarceration rate will decrease. The crime rate has been steadily increasing. Since it is likely that the current conservative outlook of state legislators and judges is more responsible for the explosion in the correctional population than any increase

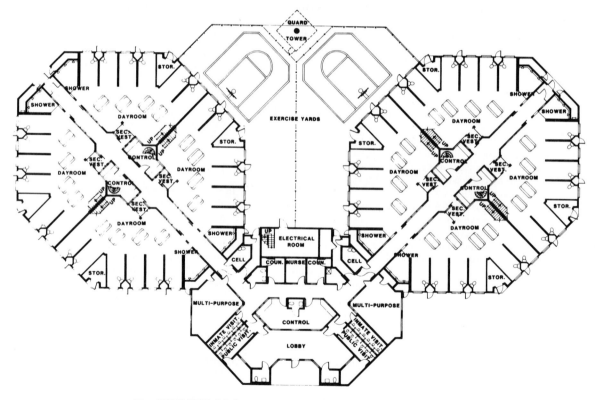

■ *FIGURE 16.2*

Modular Correctional Facility: Floorplan of Pinellas County (Florida) Jail

Floorplan shows Pinellas County Jail's two main housing wings, each consisting of 48 two-person cells arranged around the dayroom areas.

SOURCE: Charles DeWitt, National Institute of Justice, *Florida Sets Example with Use of Concrete Modules* (Washington: D.C.: National Institute of Justice, 1986), p. 3.

in the actual number of criminal defendants, it is likely that the prison population will continue to grow even if the crime rate should fall in the near future.

SUMMARY

Today's correctional institutions can trace their origins to European institutions. Punishment methods developed in Europe were modified and improved by American colonists, most notably William Penn. He replaced the whip and other methods of physical punishment with confinement in county institutions or penitentiaries.

Later, as their needs grew, the newly formed states created their own large facilities. Discipline was harsh, and most enforced a code of total and absolute silence. The Auburn System of congregate working conditions during the day and isolation at night has been perpetuated in our present penal system.

The current correctional population has grown dramatically in the past few years. Although the number of inmates diminished in the late 1960s and early 1970s, most recently the number of prison and jail residents has hit an all-time high. This development may reflect a toughening of sentencing procedures nationwide.

A number of different institutions currently house convicted offenders. Jails are used for misdemeanants and minor felons. The poor conditions in jails have made them a major trouble spot for the criminal justice system.

Federal and state prisons—classified as minimum, medium, and maximum security—house most of the nation's incarcerated felons. However, their poor track record of success has spurred the development of new correctional models, specifically the halfway house and community correctional center. Nevertheless, the success of these institutions has been challenged by research efforts that indicate that their recidivism rates are equal to those of state prisons. One recent development has been the privately run correctional institution. These are jails and prisons operated by private companies that receive a fee for their services. Used in a limited number of jurisdictions, they have been the center of some controversy: can a private company provide better management of what has traditionally been a public problem?

The greatest problem facing the correctional system today is overcrowding, which has reached a crisis level. To help deal with the problems of overcrowding, corrections departments have begun to experiment with modular prison construction and the use of alternative sanctions.

QUESTIONS

1. Would you allow a community correctional center to be built in your neighborhood?
2. Should pretrial detainees and convicted offenders be kept in the same institution?
3. What can be done to reduce correctional overcrowding?

4. Should private companies be allowed to run correctional institutions?
5. What are the drawbacks to shock incarceration?

NOTES

1. Allen Beck and Bernard Shipley, *Recidivism of Young Parolees* (Washington, D.C.: Bureau of Justice Statistics, 1987); see also John Wallerstedt, *Returning to Prison*, (Washington, D.C.: Bureau of Justice Statistics, 1984).
2. See David Fogel, *We Are the Living Proof*, 2d ed. (Cincinnati: Anderson Publishing Co., 1978); Andrew von Hirsch, *Doing Justice: The Choice of Punishments* (New York: Hill & Wang, 1976); R. G. Singer, *Just Deserts—Sentencing Based on Equality and Desert* (Cambridge, Mass.: Ballinger Publishing Co., 1979).

3. Ted Palmer, *Correctional Intervention and Research* (Lexington, Mass.: Lexington Books, 1978); Michael Gottfredson, "The Social Scientist and Rehabilitative Crime Policy," *Criminology* 20 (1982): 29–42. The most widely cited source on the failure of rehabilitation is Robert Martinson; see Robert Martinson, Douglas Lipton, and Judith Wilks, *The Effectiveness of Correctional Treatment* (New York: Praeger Publishers, 1975).
4. Among the most helpful sources for this section are David Duffee, *Corrections: Practice and Policy* (New York: Random House,

1989); Harry Allen and Clifford Simonsen, *Correction in America*, 5th ed. (New York: Macmillan, 1989); Benedict Alper, *Prisons Inside-Out* (Cambridge, Mass.: Ballinger Publishing Co., 1974); Harry Elmer Barnes, *The Story of Punishment*, 2d ed. (Montclair, N.J.: Patterson-Smith, 1972); Gustave de Beaumont and Alexis de Tocqueville, *On the Penitentiary System in the United States and Its Applications in France* (Carbondale, Ill.: Southern Illinois University Press, 1964); Orlando Lewis, *The Development of American Prisons and Prison Customs, 1776–1845* (Montclair, N.J.: Patterson-Smith, 1967); Leonard Orland, ed., *Justice, Punishment, and Treatment* (New York: Free Press, 1973); Julius Goebel, *Felony and Misdemeanor* (Philadelphia: University of Pennsylvania Press, 1976); Georg Rusche and Otto Kircheimer, *Punishment and Social Structure* (New York: Russell & Russell, 1939); Samuel Walker, *Popular Justice* (New York: Oxford University Press, 1980); Graeme Newman, *The Punishment Response* (Philadelphia: J. B. Lippincott Co., 1978); David Rothman, *Conscience and Convenience* (Boston: Little, Brown & Co., 1980).

5. Frederick Pollock and Frederic William Maitland, *History of English Law* (London: Cambridge University Press, 1952).

6. Margaret Wilson, *The Crime of Punishment*, Life and Letters Series, 64 (London: Jonathan Cape, 1934), p. 186.

7. John Howard, *The State of Prisons*, 4th ed. (1792; reprint ed., Montclair, N.J.: Patterson-Smith, 1973).

8. Lewis, *Development of American Prisons and Prison Customs*, p. 17.

9. Ibid., p. 29.

10. Michel Foucault, *Discipline and Punishment* (New York: Vintage Books, 1978).

11. Ibid., p. 16.

12. David Rothman, *The Discovery of the Asylum* (Boston: Little, Brown & Co., 1970).

13. Orland, *Justice, Punishment, and Treatment*, p. 143.

14. Ibid., p. 144.

15. Walker, *Popular Justice*, p. 70.

16. Ibid., p. 71.

17. Beverly Smith, "Military Training at New York's Elmira Reformatory, 188–1920," *Federal Probation* 52 (1988): 33–41.

18. Ibid.

19. See Z. R. Brockway, "The Ideal of a True Prison System for a State," in *Transactions of the National Congress on Penitentiary and Reformatory Discipline* (reprint ed.; Washington, D.C.: American Correctional Association, 1970), pp. 38–65.

20. This section leans heavily on Rothman, *Conscience and Convenience*.

21. Ibid., p. 23.

22. Ibid., p. 133.

23. 18 U.S.C. § 1761.

24. Barbara Auerbach, George Sexton, Franlin Farrow, and Robert Lawson, *Work in American Prisons: The Private Sector Gets Involved* (Washington, D.C.: National Institute of Justice, 1988), p. 72.

25. See, generally, Jameson Doig, *Criminal Corrections: Ideals and Realities* (Lexington, Mass.: Lexington Books, 1983).

26. Susan Kline, *Jail Inmates, 1987* (Washington, D.C.: Bureau of Justice Statistics, 1988).

27. John Irwin, *The Jail: Managing the Underclass in American Society* (Berkeley, Calif.: University of California Press, 1985).

28. Duffee, *Corrections*, p. 235.

29. Kline, *Jail Inmates, 1987*.

30. Cited in Ben Bagdikan and Leon Dash, *The Shame of the Prisons* (New York: Pocket Books, 1972), p. 32.

31. "Judge Won't Subject Man to Jail 'Brutalities,' " *Omaha World Herald*, 10 April 1981, p. 21.

32. "Jail Fire Blamed on Lit Cigarette," *Omaha World Herald*, 10 November 1982, p. 36.

33. *National Study of Jail Suicides: Seven Years Later* (Alexandria, Va.: National Center on Institutions and Alternatives, 1988).

34. Data in this section come from Kline, *Jail Inmates, 1987*.

35. "Overcrowding Crisis Forcing Extreme Measures in D.C.," *Criminal Justice Newsletter*, 1 April 1986, p. 3.

36. "Philadelphia Frees Defendants to Meet Goal on Jail Crowding," *Criminal Justice Newsletter*, 15 June 1988.

37. Fred Heinzlemann, W. Robert Burkhart, Bernard Gropper, Cheryl Martorana, Lois Felson Mock, Maureen O'Connor, and Walter Philip Travers, *Jailing Drunk Drivers, Impact on the Criminal Justice System* (Washington, D.C.: National Institute of Justice, 1984).

38. Ronald Corbett and Ellsworth Fersch, "Home as Prison: The Use of House Arrest," *Federal Probation* 49 (1985): 13–18; Richard Ball and J. Robert Lilly, "The Potential Use of Home Incarceration for Drunk Drivers," *Crime and Delinquency* 32 (1986): 224–47.

39. Billy Wayson, Gail Funke, Sally Hamilton, and Peter Beyer, *Local Jails: The New Correctional Dilemma* (Lexington, Mass.: Lexington Books, 1979), pp. 45–74.

40. W. Raymond Nelson, *Cost Savings in New Generation Jails: The Direct Supervision Approach* (Washington, D.C.: National Institute of Justice, 1988).

41. Ibid.

42. Dale Parent, *Shock Incarceration: An Overview of Existing Programs* (Washington, D.C.: National Institute of Justice, 1989). p. XI; See also, Bascom Ratliff, "The Army Model: Boot Camp for Youthful Offenders," *Corrections Today* 50 (1988): 98–102.

43. Bureau of Justice Statistics, *Prisons and Prisoners* (Washington, D.C.: U.S. Government Printing Office, 1982).

44. Correctional Research Associates, *Treating Youthful Offenders in the Community*, an evaluation conducted by A. J. Reiss (Washington, D.C.: Correctional Research Associates, 1966).

45. Kevin Krajick, "Not on My Block: Local Opposition Impedes the Search for Alternatives," *Corrections Magazine* 6 (1980): 15–27.

46. Andrew Scull, *Decarceration: Community Treatment and the Deviant: A Radical View* (Englewood Cliffs, N.J.: Prentice-Hall, 1977).

47. John Hylton, "Rhetoric and Reality: A Critical Appraisal of Community Correction Programs," *Crime and Delinquency* 28 (1982): 341–73.

48. "What Can We Learn From Recidivism Rates? Massachusetts Study Analyzes Trends, Patterns," *Corrections Digest* 16 (1985): 5.

49. For a review, see John DiIulio, *Private Prisons* (Washington, D.C.: U.S. Government Printing Office, 1988); Joan Mullen, *Corrections and the Private Sector* (Washington, D.C.: National Institute of Justice, 1984).

50. Ira Robbins, *The Legal Dimensions of Private Incarceration* (Chicago, Ill.: American Bar Foundation, 1988).

51. Lawrence Travis, Edward Latessa, and Gennaro Vito, "Private Enterprise and Institutional Corrections: A Call for Caution," *Federal Probation* 49 (1985): 11–17.

52. Patrick Anderson, Charles Davoli, and Laura Moriarty, "Private Corrections: Feast or Fiasco," *The Prison Journal* 65 (1985): 32–41.

53. Lawrence Greenfeld, *Prisoners in 1987* (Washington, D.C.: Bureau of Justice Statistics, 1988).

54. Data in this section come from Bureau of Justice Statistics, *Prisoners, 1925–1981* (Washington, D.C.: U.S. Government Printing Office, 1982).

55. *Status Report: The Courts and the Prisons*, (Washington, D.C.: National Prison Project, 1989).

56. Celestine Bohlen, "Jail Influx Brings Plan For 2 Barges," *New York Times*, 3 March 1989, p. B1.

57. Greenfeld, *Prisoners in 1987*, p. 4.

58. Charles DeWitt, *New Construction Methods for Correctional Facilities* (Washington, D.C.: National Institute of Justice, 1986).

17

Living in Prison

Part Four

Corrections

O n the night of April 21, 1989, a gang of youths swept into Central Park in New York City and went on a rampage. Among the atrocities committed was the rape and severe beating of a young woman who was left for dead. Outraged New Yorkers called for justice. New York's Mayor Edward Koch proclaimed that he did not want to know *why* these youths had committed the crimes but simply how *soon and severely* they would be punished for their acts.[1]

Considering incidents such as the Central Park assault, it is not surprising that the American public has called for a "get tough" policy on crime and an emphasis on community safety. The result has been an exploding correctional population and overcrowded prisons and jails. Correctional administrators have struggled to maintain security at the expense of treatment and rehabilitation. Despite their efforts, the crime rate has continued to climb. The public's demand that the justice system control drug- and gang-related violence has given criminal justice policymakers little choice but to place more antisocial people in secure correctional facilities. Although the new intermediate sanctions hold the promise of providing some relief, they are more appropriate for nonviolent criminals than for those who go on rampages in public parks and maim innocent victims.

To meet the needs of a growing inmate population, a vast and costly state and federal correctional system has developed. There are approximately 600 prison facilities in the United States.[2] A significant percentage of these facilities are old, decrepit, archaic structures: 25 were built before 1875, 79 between 1875 and 1924, and 141 between 1925 and 1949. In fact, some of the first prisons ever constructed such as New York's Auburn and Elmira facilities are still in operation.

Although a majority of prisons are classified as medium security, more than half of all inmates are being held in large, maximum security institutions. Despite the continuous outcry by penologists against the use of fortress-like prisons, institutions holding 1,000 or more inmates still predominate.[3]

Prison overcrowding currently presents a significant problem. The prison system now holds over 625,000 people. Some institutions are operating at two or three times stated capacity. For example, at the time of this writing, Concord Reformatory in Massachusetts, which contains cells for about 250 inmates, holds over twice that number. Recreation and workshop facilities have been turned into dormitories housing 30 or more inmates in a single room. Although most prison experts agree that a minimum of 60 square feet is needed for each inmate, many prisons fail to reach this standard. In fact, surveys show that not one state has avoided crowding inmates into less than adequate space. It is estimated that 58 percent of all one-person cells, 90 percent of all two-person cells, and 20 percent of all larger living units (dormitories) are overcrowded. In the states of Texas, North Dakota, West Virginia, Wyoming, and Mississippi, 97 percent of the cells designed for one person are considered overcrowded.[4]

This giant overcrowded system designed to reform and rehabilitate offenders is instead undergoing a crisis of epidemic proportions. Meaningful treatment efforts are often a matter of wishful thinking; recidivism rates are shockingly high. Inmates are resentful of the deteriorated conditions; correctional officers are fearful that the institution is ready to explode. This chapter presents a brief review of some of the most important issues confronting the United State's troubled correctional system.

Prison Inmates—A Profile

The Bureau of Justice Statistics conducts a survey of prison inmates every 5 to 7 years.[5] Although the composition of the prison population has changed since the last survey was conducted in 1986, surveys conducted during the past 10 years suggests that these data represent a reasonably accurate portrait of today's prison inmate.

As Table 17.1 shows, the personal characteristics of prison inmates reflect common traits of arrestees: inmates tends to be young, single, poorly educated, disproportionately male, and minority group members. The picture that emerges is that prisons hold those people who face the toughest social obstacles

TABLE 17.1 ■ **Characteristics of State Prison Inmates**

Characteristic	Percentage of Prison Inmates	
	1986	1979
Sex		
Male	95.6%	96.0%
Female	4.4	4.0
Race		
White	49.7%	49.6%
Black	46.9	47.8
Other	3.4	2.6
Ethnicity		
Hispanic	12.6%	9.9%
Non-Hispanic	87.4	90.1
Age		
Less than 18	.5%	.8%
18–24	26.7	35.6
25–34	45.7	42.4
35–44	19.4	13.8
45–54	5.2	5.1
55–64	1.8	1.7
65 or older	.6	.5
Marital status		
Married	20.3%	22.4%
Widowed	1.9	2.3
Divorced	18.1	16.9
Separated	6.0	6.6
Never married	53.7	51.9
Education		
Less than 12 years	61.6%	52.7%
12 years or more	38.4	47.3
Military service		
Served	20.2%	23.8%
Never served	79.8	76.2

SOURCE: Christopher Innes, *Profile of State Prison Inmates, 1986* (Washington, D.C.: Bureau of Justice Statistics, 1988), p. 3.

in society. Though a few middle-class, college-educated people wind up behind bars (and they are usually held in low security "country club" institutions), the typical offender is someone who was born into the underclass and has therefore failed to gain access to the economic benefits many Americans take for granted.

What did the inmates do to earn their present sentences? As Table 17.2 indicates, most inmates were serving time for violent crimes, though the percentage (55 percent) was lower than it was in 1979 (58 percent). The percentage of drug offenders in the inmate population increased about 35 percent between 1979 and 1986 (from 6.4 percent to 8.6 percent), reflecting the increased emphasis placed on controlling the drug trade and/or greater offender involvement in drug trafficking (arrests for drug offenses increased about 30 percent during the period). Over 80 percent of the inmates were recidivists who had previously been sentenced to probation or incarceration.

There is a considerable "gender gap" in the prison population. Women are actually underrepresented in prison, and not solely because they commit less

TABLE 17.2 ■ Current Offense of State Prison Inmates, by Sex, 1986 and 1979

| | Percent of Prison Inmates | | | | | |
| | | | 1986 | | 1979 | |
Current Offense	1986	1979	Male	Female	Male	Female
Violent offenses	54.6%	57.9%	55.2%	40.7%	58.3%	48.9%
Murder	11.2	12.3	11.2	13.0	12.2	15.5
Negligent manslaughter	3.2	4.0	3.0	6.8	3.8	9.8
Kidnapping	1.7	2.2	1.7	.9	2.2	1.4
Rape	4.2	4.3	4.4	.2	4.5	.4
Other sexual assault	4.5	2.0	4.7	.9	2.0	.3
Robbery	20.9	25.1	21.3	10.6	25.6	13.6
Assault	8.0	7.7	8.1	7.1	7.7	7.6
Other violent	.8	.3	.8	1.2	.3	.4
Property offenses	31.0%	31.4%	30.5%	41.2%	31.2%	36.8%
Burglary	16.5	18.1	17.0	5.9	18.6	5.3
Larceny/theft	6.0	4.8	5.6	14.7	4.5	11.2
Motor vehicle theft	1.4	1.5	1.4	.5	1.5	.5
Arson	.8	.7	.7	1.2	.6	1.2
Fraud	3.8	4.4	3.2	17.0	3.8	17.3
Stolen property	2.0	1.3	2.0	1.6	1.3	.9
Other property	.5	.7	.5	.4	.8	.4
Drug offenses	8.6%	6.4%	8.4%	12.0%	6.2%	10.5%
Possession	2.9	1.6	2.9	4.0	1.5	2.7
Trafficking	5.4	4.4	5.3	7.3	4.3	7.1
Other drug	.3	.4	.2	.7	.4	.7
Public-order offenses	5.2%	4.0%	5.2%	5.1%	4.1%	2.9%
Weapons offense	1.4	1.4	1.5	.9	1.4	.9
Other public-order	3.7	2.6	3.7	4.3	2.7	2.0
Other offenses	.7%	.3%	.7%	.9%	.3%	.9%

SOURCE: Christopher Innes, *Profile of State Prison Inmates, 1986* (Washington, D.C.: Bureau of Justice Statistics, 1988), p. 3.

TABLE 17.3 ■ **History of Pre-incarceration Use of Illegal Drugs by State Prison Inmates, 1986**

| | Percentage of Inmates Using Drugs | |
Type of Drug Use	1986	1979
Under the influence of drugs at time of the current offense	35.3%	32.3%
Ever used drugs on a regular basis	62.3	62.9
Ever used a major drug on a regular basis*	35.0	33.4
Used drugs on a daily basis in the month before the current offense	42.6	39.5
Used a major drug on a daily basis in the month before the current offense	18.5	14.0

*Major drugs include heroin, methadone, cocaine, LSD, and PCP.

SOURCE: Christopher Innes, *Profile of State Prison Inmates, 1986* (Washington, D.C.: Bureau of Justice Statistics, 1988), p. 6.

serious crimes. Although the FBI reports that women were arrested for about 20 percent of the index crimes in 1988, they made up only slightly more than 4 percent of the prison population.[6] While most (55 percent) male inmates were incarcerated for violent crimes, a majority (53 percent) of females committed property and drug offenses.

Drug and Alcohol Abuse

The survey also found that many inmates had engaged in a lifetime of drug and alcohol abuse. As Table 17.3 shows, more than one-third of all inmates report being under the influence of drugs when they committed their last offense. Another 19 percent claimed to have been under the influence of alcohol. About 42 percent used a major drug such as heroin, cocaine, PCP or LSD on a daily basis in the year prior to their arrest, while 62 percent claimed to be "regular" drug users.

These data support the view that a strong association exists between substance abuse and serious crime (unless one believes that only substance-abusing criminals are caught, convicted, and sent to prison). Considering that drug and alcohol abuse are rampant, it is not surprising that crime control strategies depending on general deterrence often fail to achieve their desired result: a majority of inmates may have been incapable of appreciating both the severity of the punishments they faced and the certainty of their capture. Substance abuse may be the single greatest obstacle to creating a successful deterrence-based crime control strategy.

In summary, the portrait of the prison inmate developed by the national survey is as follows: young, male, poor, drug-alcohol abuser, undereducated, recidivist, and violent.

■ Men Imprisoned

Prisons in the United States are **total institutions.** Inmates are locked within their walls, segregated from the outside world, kept under constant scrutiny and surveillance, and forced to obey a strict code of official rules or face formal sanctions. Their personal possessions may be taken from them, and they must conform to institutional dress and personal appearance norms. Many human functions are strictly curtailed—heterosexual activity, friendship, family relationships, society, education, and participation in groups become past events. As prison expert Robert Johnson observes:

> Imprisonment is a disheartening and threatening experience for most men. The man in prison finds his career disrupted, his relationships suspended, his aspirations and dreams gone sour. Few prisoners have experienced comparable stress in the free world, or have developed coping strategies or perspectives that shield them from prison problems. Although prisoners differ from each other, and may feel the pressures of confinement somewhat differently, they concur on the extraordinarily stressful nature of life in maximum security penal institutions.[7]

Inmates quickly learn what the term *total institution* really means. When they arrive at the prison, they are stripped, searched, shorn, and assigned living quarters. Their first experience will be in a **classification/reception center** where they are given a series of psychological tests and evaluated on the basis of their personality, background, offense history, and treatment needs. Based on this evaluation, they will be assigned to a permanent facility to serve the remainder of their sentence. Hard-core, repeat, and violent offenders will go to a maximum security unit; offenders with learning disabilities may be assigned to an institution that specializes in educational services; mentally disordered offenders will be held in a facility that can provide psychiatric care, and so on.

Once they arrive at the long-term facility, the inmates may be granted a short orientation period and then given a permanent cell assignment in the general population. Due to overcrowding they may be sharing a cell designed for a single person with one or more other inmates. All previous conceptions of personal privacy and dignity are soon forgotten. Gresham Sykes characterized these losses as the deprivation of liberty, goods and services, heterosexual relationships, autonomy, and security.[8]

Inmates in large, inaccessible prisons may find themselves physically cut off from families, friends, and former associates. Visitors may find it difficult to travel great distances to visit them; their mail is censored and sometimes destroyed.

The inmate may go through a variety of attitude and behavior changes, or cycles, as his sentence unfolds. During the early part of his prison stay, the inmate may become easily depressed while considering the long duration of the sentence and the loneliness and dangers of prison life. He must learn the ins and outs of survival in the institution: what persons can be befriended, and what persons are best avoided? Who will grant favors, and for what repayment? The inmate may find that some prisoners have formed cliques or groups based on ethnic backgrounds or personal interests; he will soon encounter Mafia-like or racial terror groups and must learn to deal with them. He may be the victim of homosexual attacks. The resident may find that power in the prison is being shared between terrified guards and inmate gangs; the only way to avoid being beaten and raped may be to learn how to beat and rape oneself.[9] If he is weak and unable to defend himself, the new inmate may find that he is considered a "punk"; if he asks a guard for help, he is labeled a "snitch." Thereafter he may spend the rest of his sentence in protective custody, sacrificing the "freedom of the yard" and rehabilitation services for personal protection.[10]

Adjusting to Prison

Despite these hardships, most inmates learn to adapt to the prison routine. Each prisoner has his own method of coping; he may remain alone, become friends with another inmate, join a group, or seek the advice of treatment personnel. The new inmate must learn to deal with the guards and other correctional personnel; these relationships will determine whether the inmate does "hard time" or "easy time." Regardless of adaptation style, the first stage of an inmate's prison cycle is marked by a growing awareness that he can no longer depend on his traditional associates for help and support and that for better or worse the institution is a new home to which he must adjust. Unfortunately for the goal of rehabilitation, the predominant emotion that an inmate confronts is boredom. As Kevin Wright suggests:

> The unmitigated absence of anything constructive to do, the forced idleness, is what is so distracting, so frustrating, and often so damaging.[11]

Part of an inmate's early adjustment involves becoming familiar with and perhaps participating in the black-market, hidden economy of the prison—**the hustle.** Hustling provides inmates with a source of steady income and the satisfaction of knowing that they are beating the system.[12] Hustling involves the sale of such illegal commodities as drugs (uppers, downers, pot), alcohol, weapons or illegally obtained food and supplies. A crackdown on hustled goods by prison officials merely serves to drive the price up—giving hustlers greater incentive to promote their black-market activities.[13]

The inmate must also learn to deal with the racial conflict that is a daily fact of life. Prisoners tend to segregate themselves and, if peace is to reign in the institution, stay out of each other's way. Often racial groupings are quite precise; for example, Hispanics will separate themselves according to their national origin (Mexico, Puerto Rico, Columbia, and so forth). Since sentencing disparity is a common practice in many U.S. courts, prisons are one area in which minorities often hold power; as sociologist James B. Jacobs observed, "Prison may be the one institution in American society that blacks control."[14]

The inmate may find that the social support of inmate peers can make incarceration somewhat less painful than he originally expected. He may begin to take stock of his situation and enter into educational or vocational training programs if they are available. From the inmate grapevine he learns what the parole board considers important in deciding whether to grant community release. He may become more politically aware due to the influence of other inmates, and the personal guilt he may have felt may be shifted to society at large. Why should the inmate be in prison when those equally guilty go free? He learns the importance of money and politics. Eventually, he may find that new arrivals look to him for help in adapting to the system.

Even in the harsh prison environment the inmate may learn to find a niche for himself by learning coping strategies.

Coping Behavior

Even in the harsh prison environment, the inmate may learn to find a **niche** for himself. According to Hans Toch, the inmate may be able to find a place, activity, or group in which he can feel comfortable and secure.[15] The inmate's niche is a kind of insulation from the pains of imprisonment; it enables him to cope and provides him with a sense of autonomy and freedom. As one prisoner says about his niche, a desirable work detail:

Now I have to deal with one officer, and I work a very short period each day. The rest of the day is mine to do as I choose with, which gives me a great deal of time for myself. . . . I don't have to lock in for some counts. . . . I'm pretty much free here.[16]

Corrections expert Robert Johnson argues that it is possible for inmates to adjust successfully to prison through a process of **mature coping.** This involves such tasks as:

> . . . dealing with problems . . . head-on, using all resources legitimately at one's disposal . . . addressing problems without resort to deception or violence, except where they are necessary for self-defense.
> . . . making an effort to empathize with and assist others in need, to act as though we are indeed members of a human community who can work together to create a more secure and gratifying existence.[17]

Mature coping strategies may be possible because, according to Johnson, many inmates reject the violent prison culture and are receptive to change. Even maximum security prisons can provide the opportunity for mature change, "and they must do just that if they are to play a viable role in the correctional process."[18]

Inmate Society

For many years it was popular for criminal justice experts to argue that inmates formed their own world with a unique set of norms and rules known as the **inmate subculture.**[19] One major aspect of the inmate subculture was a unique **social code,** unwritten guidelines that expressed the values, attitudes, and types of behavior that the older inmates demanded of younger inmates. Passed on from one generation of inmates to another, the inmate social code represented the values of interpersonal relations within the prison.

National attention was first drawn to the inmate social code and subculture by Donald Clemmer. In his *Prison Community*, Clemmer presented a detailed sociological study of life in a maximum security prison.[20] Drawing upon thousands of conversations and interviews, as well as inmate essays and biographies, Clemmer was able to identify a unique language (**argot**) that prisoners use. In addition, Clemmer found that prisoners tended to group themselves into cliques on the basis of such personal criteria as sexual preference, political beliefs, and offense history. He found that there were complex sexual relationships in prison and concluded that many heterosexual men will turn to homosexual relationships when faced with long sentences and the loneliness of prison life.

Clemmer's most important contribution may have been his identification of the **prisonization** process. This he defined as the inmate's assimilation into the existing prison culture through acceptance of its language, sexual code, and norms of behavior. Those who become the most "prisonized" will be the least likely to reform on the "outside."

Using Clemmer's work as a jumping-off point, a number of prominent sociologists set out to explore more fully the various roles in the prison community. For example, in one prominent analysis entitled *Society of Captives*, Gresham Sykes further defined prison argot and argued that prison rules exist because of the deprivations presented by the prison.[21] Later, writing with Sheldon Messinger, Sykes identified the following as the most important principles of the prison community:

1. *Don't interfere with inmates' interests.* Within this area of the code are maxims concerning the serving of the least amount of time in the greatest possible comfort. For example, inmates are warned . . . never [to betray another] inmate to authorities; . . . [in other words,] grievances must be handled personally. Other aspects of the noninterference doctrine include "Don't be nosy," "Don't have a loose lip," "Keep off [the other inmates' backs,]" and "Don't put [another inmate] on the spot."

2. *Don't lose you head.* Inmates are also cautioned to refrain from arguing, [quarreling, or engaging in] other emotional displays with fellow inmates. The novice may hear such warnings as "Play it cool" and "Do your own time."

3. *Don't exploit inmates.* Prisoners are warned not to take advantage of one another— "Don't steal from cons," "Don't welsh on a debt," "Be right."

4. *Inmates are cautioned to be tough and not lose their dignity.* While rule 2 forbids conflict, once it starts an inmate must be prepared to deal with it effectively and [thoroughly]. Maxims include "Don't cop out," "Don't weaken," "Be tough; be a man."

5. *Don't be a sucker.* Inmates are cautioned not to make fools . . . of themselves and support the guards or prison administration over the interest of the inmates—"Be sharp."[22]

According to Sykes and Messinger, some inmates violate the code and exploit their peers whereas the "right guy" is someone who personalizes the inmate social code as his personal behavior guide:

> A right guy is always loyal to his fellow prisoners. He never lets you down, no matter how rough things get. He keeps his promises. He's dependable and trustworthy. . . . The "right guy" never interferes with inmates who are conniving against the officials. He doesn't go around looking for a fight, but he never runs away from one when he is in the right . . . he acts like a man.[23]

THE IMPORTATION MODEL. Not all prison experts believed that the prison culture was a function of the harsh conditions existing in a total institution. In 1962 John Irwin and Donald Cressey published a paper in which they conceded that a prison culture existed but claimed that its principles were actually imported from the outside world.[24] In their **importation model,** Irwin and Cressey concluded that the inmate culture was affected as much by the values of newcomers as by traditional inmate values.[25] Irwin and Cressey found that the inmate world was actually divided into three groups, each corresponding to a role in the outside world. The *thief subculture* was made up of professional criminals who kept to themselves and adhered to the principle of always try to "do your own time." Members of the *convict subculture* tried to obtain power in the prison and control others for their own needs. The *conventional subculture* was made up of inmates who tried to retain legitimate elements of the outside world in their daily life (that is, they identified with neither of the deviant prison subcultures). Irwin and Cressey's research showed that the inmate culture could be influenced by outside events and that the values that inmates held on the "outside" could be imported into the prison setting.

The "New" Inmate Culture

Although the "old" inmate subculture may have been harmful because its norms and values insulated the inmate from pressures to change, it also helped create order within the institution and prevented violence among the inmates.

People who violated the code and victimized others were sanctioned by their peers. An understanding developed between guards and inmate leaders: the guards would let the inmates have things their own way; the inmates would not let things get out of hand and draw the attention of the administration.

In most institutions, however, the old system appears to be dying or is already dead. The change seems to have been precipitated by the Black Power movement in the 1960s and 1970s. Black inmates were no longer content to fill a subservient role and challenged the power of established white inmates. As the Black Power movement gained prominence, racial tension in prisons created divisions that severely altered the inmate subculture. Older respected inmates could no longer cross racial lines to mediate disputes. Predatory inmates could victimize others without fear of retaliation.[26] Consequently, more inmates than ever must be assigned to protective custody for their own safety.[27]

Sociologist James B. Jacobs is perhaps the most influential expert on the changing inmate subculture. His research has led him to conclude that the development of "black (and Latino) power" in the 1960s, spurred by the **Black Muslim** movement, significantly influenced the nature of prison life.[28] According to Jacobs, black and Latin inmates are much more cohesively organized than whites. Their groups are sometimes rooted in religious/political affiliations such as the Black Muslims; in groups created specifically to combat discrimination in prison, such as the Latin group La Familia; or in street gangs re-formed in prison, such as the Vice Lords, Disciples, or Blackstone Rangers in the Illinois prison system and the Crips in California. Only in California have white inmates successfully organized; their group takes the form of a neo-Nazi organization called the *Aryan Brotherhood*. Racially homogeneous gangs are so cohesive and powerful that they are able to supplant the original inmate code with one of their own. Consider the oath taken by new members of *Nuestra Familia* (Our Family), a Latin gang operating in California prisons: "If I go forward, follow me. If I hesitate, push me. If they kill me, avenge me. If I am a traitor, kill me."[29]

The racial polarity in today's prison system and its influence on the inmate culture have just begun to be explored in depth. Charles Stastny and Gabrielle Tyrnauer have documented the existence of racial cliques—the Black Prisoner's Forum Unlimited, the Confederated Indian Tribes, and United Chicanos—in the Washington State prison system. These groups not only provided protection to their members but also acted as a bloc to make demands on prison administrators.[30] Although group members might adhere to principles of the traditional inmate code (e.g., "don't inform"), allegiance was always directed toward members of one's own group.

It is evident that future research on prison culture will have to evaluate the role race plays in prison life and examine how inmate racism influences the "traditional" prisoner culture. This research is particularly important when we consider that it has been estimated that just four California gangs—Nuestra Familia, the Mexican Mafia, the Aryan Brotherhood, and the Black Guerilla Family—have reportedly killed more than a hundred inmates and wounded scores of others.[31] In fact, the situation is so bad and tensions so high that an authority as respected as James Jacobs has suggested that it may be humane and appropriate to segregate inmates along racial lines in order to maintain order and protect individual rights. Jacobs believes that in some prisons, administrators use integration as a threat to keep inmates in line; to be transferred to a racially mixed setting may mean beatings or death.[32]

■ Women Imprisoned

Approximately 33,000 women were incarcerated in the state and federal prison systems as of January 1, 1989.[33] Although their numbers have more than doubled since 1974, women have continued to make up about 5 percent of the total prison population. State jurisdictions have been responding to the influx of women offenders into the correctional system by expanding the facilities capable of housing and treating female offenders. New construction efforts include a 132-bed facility opened in Minnesota (1986), a 300-bed prison in Michigan (1985), and a 400-bed institution in California (1987); California has also begun construction on a 2,200-bed facility.[34] Other states such as New York, Georgia, Washington, and Florida have geared home confinement, restitution, and other alternative programs specifically toward women in an effort to relieve overcrowding.[35]

Women's prisons tend to be smaller than those housing male inmates. Similarly, most women's facilities are generally not the high security institutions commonly used for male inmates. Although some female institutions are strictly penal, with steel bars, concrete floors, and other security measures, the majority are nonsecure institutions similar to college dormitories and other group homes in the community. It is common for women's facilities, especially those in the community, to offer a great deal of autonomy to inmates and to allow them to make decisions affecting their daily life in the institution.

Like male institutions, women's prisons suffer from a lack of adequate training, health, treatment, and educational facilities. Psychological counseling often takes the form of group sessions conducted by lay people such as correctional officers. Most trained psychologists and psychiatrists restrict themselves to such activities as intake classification, court-ordered examinations, and the prescription of mood-controlling medication.

Educational programs usually offer only remedial education or occasional junior college classes. Of course, the small size of many women's prisons make large-scale educational programs difficult to maintain. In a similar vein, vocational training tends to stress what are considered to be "traditional" women's jobs: cosmetician, secretarial work, and food services. Relatively little effort has been made to update the programs to provide the types of educational and vocational skills needed for successful readjustment on release.

More than 30,000 women are currently incarcerated in state and Federal correctional institutions.

The Female Inmate

A number of efforts have been made to describe the female inmate; taken in sum, they provide an important picture of who the inmates are and what offenses they have committed.[36] Incarcerated women are young—two-thirds are under 30 years of age; the mean age is about 29. Black women are overrepresented in the inmate population (50 percent), as are native Americans; the proportion of Hispanic women, however, appears to be similar to their representation in the general population.

The family life of incarcerated women also appears to diverge from the norm. About half of incarcerated women came from two-parent homes, one-third had been on welfare as children, and over half (56 percent) had received welfare during their adult lives. Many incarcerated women exhibited a pattern of harsh discipline and physical abuse in their upbringing, which continued in their adult nuclear family life: although 60 percent had been married at least once, only 10 percent had actually been living with a husband prior to incarceration. Many female inmates had been the victims and perpetrators of domestic violence.

Another serious problem of women in prison is the disruption of their families. Many had children living at home prior to their incarceration. Who took care of the children while their mothers were incarcerated? It did not appear that children of incarcerated women were bound for foster homes. Some 85 percent of the time, the woman's parents or other relatives took the children. Husbands provided only 10 percent of all child-care arrangements. Ethnic differences in child care were significant, with whites and native Americans relying more on husbands and on nonrelatives, including agencies.

What offenses had these women committed? Misdemeanants serving one year or less had been convicted in the following proportions: 41 percent for property crimes (shoplifting, forgery, fraud); 20 percent for drug offenses; and 11 percent for violent crimes (usually assault, battery, or armed robbery). Convicted felons serving one year or more had been convicted for the following offenses: about 41 percent for violent crimes (murder, armed robbery); 41 percent for property crimes (forgery, fraud, some larceny); and 12 percent for drug offenses. Most unsentenced women had been charged with the following felony-type offenses: 30 percent for violent crimes; 22 percent for drug offenses; and 14 percent for forgery or fraud.

Nearly one-third of the women had been arrested for the first time at age 17 or younger. Another 49 percent were first arrested between the ages of 18 and 24. Almost one-third of the women had spent time in juvenile institutions.

Property offenders were most often recidivists; murderers were most likely to be first offenders. The women with the most extensive involvement with the criminal justice system were the habitual offenders—prostitutes, drug offenders, and petty thieves.

In addition to these offenses, a significant number of incarcerated females were involved with drugs, and their heroin use may actually be higher than that of male inmates. Some prison officials estimate that between 75 and 90 percent of female inmates have a drug or alcohol dependency problem.[37]

The Culture of the Female Prisoner

Daily life in the women's prison community also differs in some respects from that in male institutions. For one thing, women usually do not present the immediate, violent physical danger to staff and fellow inmates that many male prisoners do. Nor does there exist the rigid antiauthority inmate social code found in many male institutions.[38] Confinement for women, however, may produce severe anxiety and anger due to separation from families and loved ones and the inability to function in normal female roles. Unlike men, who direct their anger outward, female prisoners may revert to more self-destructive acts in order to cope with their problems. Female inmates are more likely than males to mutilate their own bodies and attempt suicide. For example, one common practice of female inmates is self-mutilation or "carving." This ranges from simple scratches to carving the name of their boyfriend or complex statements or sentences on their bodies ("To mother, with hate").[39]

Another form of adaptation to prison employed by women is the **make-believe family.** In this group women assume masculine and feminine roles and act as fathers and mothers; some even act as children and take on the role of either brother or sister. Formalized marriages and divorces may be conducted. Sometimes multiple roles are held by one inmate, so that a "sister" in one family may "marry" and become the "wife" of another inmate. In a highly detailed study of sex roles among young female inmates, Alice Propper found that about half were currently members of make-believe families (which she labels "quasi-kinship" groups).[40]

The primary female roles were "sister-sister" and "mother-daughter"; homosexual marriages were relatively rare, and most women did not wish to take on masculine roles. Nor were make-believe families unique to the female prisoners; when males were introduced into the institutions, they were included in the kinship groups.

Why do make-believe families exist? According to Propper and other experts, they provide the warm, stable relationships otherwise unobtainable in the prison environment:

> People in and out of prison have needs for security, companionship, affection, attention, status, prestige, and acceptance that can only be filled by having primary group relationships. Friends fill many of these needs, but the family better represents our ideal or desire for these things in a stable relationship.[41]

■ Institutional Treatment Programs

Almost every prison facility employs some mode of treatment for inmates.[42] This may come in the form of individual or group therapy programs, or educational or vocational training.

Despite good intentions, rehabilitative treatment within prison walls is extremely difficult to achieve. Trained professional treatment personnel usually command high salaries, and most institutions do not have sufficient budgets to staff therapeutic programs adequately. Usually, a large facility will have a single staff psychiatrist and/or a few social workers. A second problem revolves around the philosophy of **less eligibility,** which has been interpreted to mean that prisoners should always be treated less well than the most underprivileged law-abiding citizen. Translated into today's terms, less eligibility usually involves the question "Why should correctional system inmates be treated to expensive programs denied to the average honest citizen?" Enterprising state legislators use this argument to block expenditures for prison budgets, and some prison administrators may actually agree with them.

Finally, correctional treatment is hampered by the ignorance surrounding the practical effectiveness of one type of treatment program over another. It has not yet been determined what constitutes proper treatment, and studies evaluating treatment effectiveness have suggested that few if any of the programs currently employed in prisons actually produce significant numbers of rehabilitated offenders.

This section discusses a selected number of therapeutic methods that have been employed nationally in correctional settings and attempts to identify some of their more salient features.

Counseling-Oriented Programs

It is common for prison authorities to offer a wide range of group and individual **counseling** to inmates. In general, counseling therapy has the following goals:

The most common form of psychological rehabilitation within correctional institutions is group or individual counseling programs.

1. To help prisoners adjust to the frustrations that are an unalterable part of life in an institution and in society
2. To enable the clients to recognize the significance of emotional conflicts as underlying criminality
3. To provide the opportunity for the client to learn from his peers about the social aspects of his personality
4. To make possible a better understanding of make-believe, of fantasy, and of how costly may be behavioral responses to the antisocial content of daydreams
5. [To improve] the emotional climate of the institution.[43]

One of the most commonly used treatment techniques within the prison community is group counseling.[44] It has a number of beneficial features, not the least of which is the use of nonprofessional treatment personnel as group leaders. Group counseling does not depend on or attempt to make fundamental changes in the client's personality, but instead makes use of the group to stimulate the inmate's self-awareness and his or her ability to deal with everyday problems within the institution. Inmates may use the group to learn to understand how others view them and how they view themselves. Or, the group may be used to help inmates solve perplexing personal problems that they are incapable of dealing with alone, for example, forgoing deviant or violent sexual behavior patterns.[45] In addition to group counseling, many correctional systems employ a variety of more intensive individual and group techniques: behavior modification, aversive therapy, milieu therapy, reality therapy, transactional analysis, and responsibility therapy among other techniques.[46]

Although psychological counseling is a major component of correctional treatment policy, the personnel and resources needed to carry out effective programs are often lacking. For example, a national survey of mental health services in correctional settings found that 47 percent maintained a unit for the emotionally disturbed and 34 percent offered psychological services that were tied in with state hospitals and mental health services.[47] The survey also revealed, however, that only 352 master's level and 365 Ph.D. level psychologists and 129 psychiatrists were employed in the correctional system. This problem becomes even more acute when we consider that an estimated 10 percent of the prison population may be suffering from acute mental problems such as schizophrenia, that an additional 10–50 percent may suffer from adaptation problems marked by nervousness, sleeplessness, and depression, and that another 30 percent or more suffer from what is termed as character disorders or antisocial behavior.[48]

Treating the Special Needs Inmate

One of the challenges of correctional treatment is to care for the so-called **special needs inmate.**[49] These individuals can manifest a variety of social problems. Some are mentally ill but have been assigned to prison because the state has toughened its insanity laws. Others suffer mental problems developed during their prison experience. It is estimated that between 7 and 10 percent of all inmates suffer some form of emotional disorder.[50] Another special needs group are mentally retarded offenders who make up an estimated 1 to 6 percent of the inmate population.[51]

Restrictive crime control policies have also produced another special needs group, the elderly inmate who has health care, diet, work, and recreational needs that are quite different from those of the general population.

Other inmates are drug addicts who must receive special treatment if there is to be any chance of reducing future recidivism. Closely related to drug use is the AIDS-infected inmate. The HIV virus is spread among intravenous drug users who share needles and is also widespread among males engaging in homosexual behavior, two lifestyles common in the prison community. Though the numbers are constantly changing, more than 2,000 inmates have been diagnosed as having **AIDS,** and the numbers are rising daily. As the Criminal Justice in Review on page 566 explains, correctional administrators face a number of problems in managing the AIDS-infected inmate in the correctional system.

Educational Programs

In addition to treatment programs stressing personal growth through individual analysis or group process, inmate rehabilitation may also be pursued in programs emphasizing vocational training or educational training and/or rehabilitation. Although these two approaches may sometimes differ in style and content, they can also overlap when, for example, education is directed toward a practical area of job-related study.

The first prison treatment programs were in fact educational in nature. A prison school was opened at the Walnut Street Jail in 1784. Elementary courses were offered in New York's prison system in 1801 and in Pennsylvania's in 1844. An actual school system was established in Detroit's House of Corrections in 1870, and Elmira Reformatory opened a vocational trade school in 1876.[52]

Today most institutions provide some type of educational program. At some prisons, inmates are given the opportunity to obtain a high school diploma through equivalence exams or general educational development (GED) certificates. Other institutions provide an actual classroom education, usually staffed by full-time certified teachers or by part-time teachers who work at the institution after a full day's teaching in a nearby public school. The number of hours devoted to educational programs and the quality and intensity of these

AIDS in Prison

AIDS presents an important challenge to correctional administrators. In the following reading, Theodore Hammett discusses findings from a national survey of correctional practices being used to reduce the threat of AIDS and explains how these policies are affecting the correctional system.

CORRECTIONAL MANAGEMENT ISSUES: EDUCATION AND TRAINING

Because there is no vaccine or cure for the disease, education and training programs are the cornerstone of efforts to curb the spread of AIDS in prisons and jails, as well as in the population at large. Education and training programs also provide the opportunity to counteract misinformation, rumors, and fear concerning the disease. For example, the majority of systems responding to the questionnaire reported that inmates and staff worried about the possibility of contracting AIDS; many responses referred to fear of casual contact or types of contact not actually associated with transmission of the virus.

As a result, many correctional administrators feel strongly that education and training are not options but absolute requirements. Ninety-three percent of the responding jurisdictions currently offer or are developing AIDS educational programs for staff; 83 percent offer or are developing such programs for inmates.

Among respondents whose educational programs have operated for some time, the vast majority believe these programs to be effective in reducing the fears of staff and inmates. Several jurisdictions reported that timely educational efforts had successfully averted threatened job actions by correctional staff unions.

CORRECTIONAL POLICIES ON ANTIBODY TESTING

Only four state correctional systems (Nevada, Colorado, Iowa, and Missouri) have implemented or plan to implement mass screening programs for inmates; no city or county systems responding to the questionnaire have instituted or planned such programs. However, almost 90 percent of the responding jurisdictions do employ testing for more limited purposes. These include testing of risk-group members, testing in support of diagnoses of AIDS or ARC, testing in response to incidents in which the AIDS virus might have been transmitted, testing on inmate request, and testing carried out as part of anonymous epidemiological studies.

CORRECTIONAL HOUSING POLICIES

One of the most critical and difficult decisions for correctional administrators is where to house and treat inmates with AIDS or ARC. Of course, medical considerations dictate many

efforts vary greatly. Some are full-time programs employing highly qualified and concerned educators, while others are part-time programs without any real goals or objectives.[53]

Although worthwhile attempts are being made, prison education programs often suffer from inadequate funding and administration. The picture is not totally bleak, however. In some institutions, programs have been designed to circumvent the difficulties inherent within the prison structure. They encourage volunteers from the community and local schools to aid in tutoring willing and motivated inmates. Some prison administrators have arranged flexible schedules and actively encourage participation in these programs. In several states, such as Texas, Connecticut, and Illinois, statewide school districts serving prisons have been created.[54] The establishment of districts such as these can make better qualified staff available and provide the materials and resources necessary for meaningful educational programs.

Work Programs

Every state correctional system employs some sort of job-related services for inmates. Some have elaborate training programs within the institution while

of these decisions. Most jurisdictions place inmates with confirmed diagnoses of AIDS in a medical facility either within the correctional system or in the community, although the duration of such hospitalization varies considerably.

Preventing the spread of AIDS within the prison and protecting affected inmates from intimidation and violence are important considerations. Other factors in treatment and housing decisions include availability and location of facilities able to provide appropriate care, costs of any new construction or renovations necessary to prepare special units, and staffing of any special AIDS units (correctional as well as medical). The key options are the following:

■ Maintaining inmates in the general population;
■ Returning inmates to the general population when their illnesses are in remission;
■ Administratively segregating inmates in a separate unit or relying on single-cell housing;
■ Hospitalization; and

■ Case-by-case determination of all housing and treatment decisions.

Two-thirds of the federal and state systems and 70 percent of city and county systems have written policies in place or in development for managing inmates with AIDS or ARC. City and county jurisdictions are more likely to use segregation; 39 percent of responding city and county jail systems segregate all AIDS-related inmate categories, as opposed to only 16 percent of state and federal prison systems. Almost one-third of all responding systems have basic policies involving case-by-case determination of treatment and housing programs.

MEDICAL ISSUES

Perhaps the highest priority in the correctional response to AIDS is providing timely, professional, and compassionate medical care to inmates who become ill with the disease. As in society at large, prompt detection and diagnosis are needed to minimize spread of the disease and alleviate the suffering of patients.

LEGAL ISSUES

Suits on the quality of correctional medical care may be brought on the basis of federal constitutional standards, state law, or common law. There are three constitutional principles relevant to correctional medical care.

First, under the Eighth Amendment, inmates are entitled to a safe, decent, and humane environment. Second, in *Estelle v. Gamble*, "deliberate indifference to serious medical need" was held to violate the Eighth Amendment protection against "cruel and unusual punishment." Finally, the constitutional guarantee of "equal protection of the laws" applies to correctional medical care cases, and particularly to cases involving AIDS inmates, because of the segregation issues. ■

SOURCE: Theodore Hammett, *AIDS in Correctional Facilities* (Washington, D.C.: National Institute of Justice, 1988).

others have instituted pre- and postrelease employment services. A few of the more important work-related services are discussed below.

BASIC PRISON INDUSTRIES. Prisoners are normally expected to work within the institution as part of their treatment program. Aside from saving money for the institution, prison work programs are supposed to help inmates develop good habits and skills. Most prominent among traditional prison industries are those designed to help maintain and run the institution and provide services for other public or state facilities such as mental hospitals; such industries include the following:

1. *Food services.* Inmates are expected to prepare and supply food for the other prisoners and for the prison staff. These duties include baking bread, cooking and preparing meat and vegetables, and cleaning and maintaining kitchen facilities.
2. *Maintenance.* The buildings and grounds of most prisons are cared for by the inmate population. Electrical work, masonry, plumbing, and painting are all inmate activities. Less skilled work duties include garbage collection, gardening, and cleanup.

3. *Laundry.* Most prisons have their own inmate-run laundries. Quite often, prison laundries also furnish services to other state institutions.

4. *Agriculture.* In western and southern states, many prisons farm their own land. Inmates tend dairy herds, crops, and poultry, and the products are used in the prison and in other state institutions.

In addition to these basic tasks, many institutions run more sophisticated shops that manufacture such items as furniture and clothing for state use. For many years, however, prison industry has been criticized on the grounds that it employs relatively few inmates and that the jobs they do require skills with few applications in the outside world.

VOCATIONAL TRAINING. Most institutions provide **vocational training** programs. In New York State, for example, more than 42 different trade and technical courses are offered in organized training shops under qualified civilian instructors. Some of these courses not only benefit the inmate but also provide services for the institution.[55] For example, New York has trained inmates to become dental laboratory technicians; this program provides dentures for inmates and saves the state money. Another New York program trains inmates to become optical technicians and has the added benefit of providing eyeglasses for inmates. Other New York State correctional training programs include barber training, electronic computer programming, auto mechanics, auto body work, and radio and television repair. The products of most of these programs save the taxpayers money, and the programs themselves provide the inmates with practical experience. Similar vocational programs exist in many other states.[56]

Despite the promising aspects of such programs, they have been criticized on several grounds. Inmates often have difficulty finding skill-related, high-paying jobs on release; equipment in prisons is frequently secondhand, obsolete, and insufficient for the number of inmates; some programs are thinly disguised excuses for prison upkeep and maintenance; and unions and other groups resent the intrusion of prison labor into their markets.[57]

WORK RELEASE. To supplement programs stressing rehabilitation via in-house job training or education, a number of states have attempted to implement **work-release** or furlough programs. These allow deserving inmates to leave the institution and hold regular jobs in the community. Today almost every state has at least one institution that maintains a furlough program.

Inmates enrolled in work release may live at the institutions at night while working in the community during the day. However, security problems (e.g., contraband may be brought in) and the usual remoteness of prisons often make this arrangement difficult. More typical is the extended work release, where prisoners are allowed to remain in the community for significant periods of time. To help the client adjust, some states such as South Carolina operate community-based pre-release centers where inmates live while working. In some instances, inmates work at their previous jobs, while in others they do other work.

Like other programs, work release has its goods points and its bad points. Inmates are sometimes reluctantly received in the community and find that certain areas of employment are closed to them. Similarly, a number of states have reported that a few work-release inmates absconded while in the community.[58] Citizens who demand higher wages are often sensitive to prisoners "stealing" jobs or working for lower than normal wages; consequently, such practices are prohibited by the federal statute (Public Law 89–176), which controls the federal work-release program.[59]

At the same time, work release offers many benefits: it helps inmates maintain work-related skills and community ties and helps ease their transition from prison to the outside world. For those who have learned a skill in the institution, work release offers an excellent opportunity to test out a new occupation. For others, the job may be a training situation in which they acquire new skills.[60]

Despite such obvious benefits, an analysis of 40 work-release programs by Johnathan Katz and Scott Decker found that those that were scientifically evaluated showed little effectiveness in reducing recidivism and providing other social benefits.[61] Nevertheless, work-release programs have become a standard correctional format.

PRIVATE PRISON ENTERPRISE. Although opposition from organized labor ended the profitability of commercial prison industries, there have been a number of interesting efforts to vary the type and productivity of prison labor.[62] The impetus for the development came from former Chief Justice Warren Burger who long argued that prisons should be turned into "factories within walls" that could teach inmates marketable skills, allow them to earn money, and reduce idleness and boredom. The federal government helped implement Burger's ideas when it approved the **Free Venture** program in 1976.[63] Seven states including Connecticut, South Carolina, and Minnesota were given grants to establish private industries within the prison walls. This successful program led to the Percy Amendment (1979); this federal legislation allowed prison-made goods to be sold across state lines if the projects complied with strict rules that ensured that unions were consulted and prevented manufacturers from undercutting the existing wage structure.[64] The new law authorized a number of Prison Industry Enhancement (PIE) pilot projects. These were certified as meeting the Percy Amendment operating rules and were therefore free to ship goods out of state; by 1987 15 projects had been certified.[65]

Today private prison industries use a number of different models. One approach is to make the correctional system a supplier of goods and services for state-run institutions. New York State has long been a leader in creating productive prison industries. Today about 3,000 inmates (8 percent of the New York prison population) are working in various manufacturing jobs, earning an average of 50 cents per hour.[66] The New York Department of Corrections has actually created a brand name (Corcraft) for its product line and grosses over $30 million a year. Corcraft products include wire-mesh garbage cans, chairs, eyeglasses, clothing, mattresses, pillows, and auto body work.[67]

Other states have developed various types of partnerships with private industry that currently employ about 2,000 inmates in 55 different projects.[68] For example, La Pen, Inc., a sewing factory set up in a former gymnasium in the Nebraska State Penitentiary, employs 80 men in garment manufacture.[69] Other models call for private companies to set up manufacturing units on prison grounds and/or purchase goods made by inmates in shops owned and operated by the corrections department.

Despite widespread publicity, the partnership between private enterprise and the prison community has thus far been limited to a few experimental programs, one of which is discussed in the Criminal Justice in Review on page 571. Nevertheless, it is likely to grow in the near future.

POSTRELEASE PROGRAMS. A final element of job-related programing involves helping inmates obtain jobs before they are released and keep those jobs once they are on the outside. A number of correctional departments have set up employment services designed to ease the transition between the institution and the community. Employment program staff assess inmates' backgrounds to determine their abilities, interests, goals, and capabilities. They also consult with inmates to help them create job plans, which are essential to receiving early release (parole) and to being successfully reintegrated into the community. Some programs maintain community correctional placements in sheltered environments that help inmates bridge the gap between the institution and the outside world. Services include job placement, skill development, family counseling, and legal and medical attention.

Not all employment service programs show positive results, however. In a project conducted within the Pennsylvania correctional system, inmates in a noncounseled control group were as likely to be employed on release as inmates who were program clients. Moreover, job counseling neither helped releasees obtain more prestigious jobs nor lowered their recidivism rates (one-third of the clients were rearrested within one year).[70] An evaluation of nine ex-offender vocational programs found that the programs actually did serve thousands of clients (14,000 in one year), many of whom had little education or skills, and were generally successful in placing them in jobs, but the nine programs failed to reduce recidivism.[71]

Maintaining Conventional Ties

Research studies generally agree that inmates who are able to maintain family ties have a better chance for success on the "outside" after they have been released.[72]

Private Prison Enterprise

There have been a number of attempts to implement private prison enterprise in the correctional setting. The following reading discusses one of the most well-known efforts to date.

BEST WESTERN'S RESERVATIONS CENTER

In 1981 Best Western International, Inc., had a problem: its international marketing and reservations center in Phoenix needed a readily available work force of trained telephone reservations agents to handle the overflow of phone calls for room reservations during peak call volume periods and on holidays and weekends. Best Western staff approached the Arizona Department of Corrections with the idea of hiring prisoners. About six months later ACW (Arizona Center for Women) prisoners were booking Best Western rooms for guests calling from throughout the country on the chain's toll-free line.

The company has since installed additional computer terminals, and currently the ACW center has 30 work stations staffed by inmate employees. By November 1986 the center had processed more than 2.5 million calls representing more than $72 million in room reservation sales. On a given day the women at ACW process about 10 percent of Best Western's total domestic calls.

The ACW center operates from 5 A.M. to midnight or as needed according to call volume. Reservations agents work 20 to 40 hours per week and are supervised by a Best Western operations manager and three Best Western supervisors. The institution screens all applicants and maintains a pool of eligible candidates who are interviewed by Best Western Human Resource Management staff for job openings. Selection criteria for the ACW reservations agents are the same as those for agents at the main reservations center. Starting salaries are the same as those for reservations agents at the main center: $4.50 per hour, with an increase of up to 12 percent after nine months. ACW agents also are eligible for Best Western employee incentive programs. Employees at ACW are subject to the same policies and procedures as all Best Western employees, including those governing disciplinary actions and job requirements. Each ACW employee, in addition to paying federal, state, and social security taxes, contributes 30 percent of her net wage to offset the costs of incarceration. Since 1981 ACW agents have had $182,000 withheld in taxes and have paid over $187,000 to the state for room and board. Over $112,000 has been paid in family support.

Since start-up in 1981 Best Western has hired more than 175 women at ACW. The company also has hired 50 of its ACW employees upon their release from prison. Policies have been adjusted to treat postrelease employment as a lateral transfer rather than a new hire, thus preserving benefits earned prior to release. Twenty-four former ACW reservations agents currently are working at Best Western headquarters. Nine have been promoted to clerical positions in marketing, membership administration, and reservations.

Largely because of the manner in which Best Western has managed this operation, it represents one of the most positive illustrations of the potential of private-sector employment of inmates. The reservations center serves a demonstrable purpose for the company. Best Western staff have made a conscious commitment to treating inmate workers as employees in every sense of the word. Institution management has recongized the value of the program and has taken the necessary steps to ensure its success. The center serves as an incentive to the general inmate population, many of whom hope for a job here before release. In short, the institutional climate is positively affected by the presence of the center and the opportunities it offers. ∎

SOURCE: Barbara Auerbach, George Sexton, Franklin Farrow, and Robert Lawson, *Work in American Prisons, The Private Sector Gets Involved* (Washington, D.C.: National Institute of Justice, 1988).

A few correctional systems have developed programs that help inmates maintain their emotional stability by having closer ties with their families and living in an environment that is more "normal" than that provided in the typical correctional facility. For example, some women's prisons now allow pregnant inmates to keep their child in a nursery for up to a year and then maintain liberal visitation rights with the child thereafter. Others allow male and female inmates home visitation privileges if they show exemplary behavior in the institution. Others provide direct support to families, for example, by involving them in self-help groups, providing counseling, helping them obtain transportation to the prison, and finding them overnight lodging.[73] Two other well-known programs, conjugal visits and coed prisons are discussed in the next sections.

CONJUGAL VISITS. The **conjugal visit** is another mode of treatment that has received renewed emphasis from correctional administrators. During conjugal visits prisoners are able to have completely private meetings with wives and family on a regular basis. The explicit purpose of the program is to grant inmates access to normal sexual outlets and thereby counteract the pains of imprisonment.

Conjugal visitation is more frequently used in Latin America and Europe than in the United States. However, Mississippi has had such a program since 1900, and California began a program of family visits at its Tehachapi facility in 1971.[74] The New York prison system maintains a Family Reunion Program in seven of its facilities, but restricts participation to well-adjusted prisoners without histories of disciplinary problems. In 1980, Connecticut adopted a family visit program at its Somers and Enfield facilities. Similar programs have been established in Washington State, South Carolina, and Minnesota.[75]

Those who favor conjugal visitation argue that, if properly administered, it could provide a number of important benefits: inmate frustration levels would diminish, family ties would be strengthened, and normal sexual patterns would be continued. However, the many problems inherent in conjugal visitation have so far lessened its chances for implementation. As Donald Johns points out, conjugal visitation suffers for several reasons:

1. Such visits can serve only the minority of inmates who have wives or other female associates. Thus, there is a question of fairness.
2. Appropriate facilities are almost universally lacking.
3. Administrative problems abound: security, staff abuses of power, jealousy.
4. Administrative support is lacking.
5. Wives may feel embarrassment at openly sexual visits.
6. Children may be born to men who cannot support them.[76]

Johns concludes that these visits are feasible only in the following circumstances:

1. Facilities are available that could be converted satisfactorily and not too expensively to such use.
2. Administrative interest in such a program is reasonably high.
3. Opposition to such programs is neither strong nor actively organized.
4. The practical problems can be carefully recognized, planned for, and managed.[77]

After a careful analysis of the issue, Anne Goetting concludes that there is "no solid research support for the contentions that such programs reduce homosexuality, enhance social control, normalize prison life style, increase postrelease success or stabilize marriages."[78]

COED PRISONS. Another recent trend, though one with strong historical roots, has been the **coeducational prison**. Since 1973, prisons housing both men and women have proliferated throughout the United States. How popular are coed prisons? A recent survey by CONtact, Inc., a nonprofit correctional information center, found that 35 institutions around the country were operating as coed centers.[79] Although most were minimum security institutions, coed prisons were also found at the medium and maximum security levels, and some institutions operated with a mix of security levels. Officials reported that it was common for inmates to share food services, recreation, educational programs, and jobs. The typical coed prison is a small, low security institution, predominantly of one sex (either mostly male or mostly female) and populated by nonviolent, carefully screened offenders. In most instances males and females live in physically separate housing—either in different buildings or in separate cottages—but participate jointly in most institution activities such as work, recreation, and vocational and educational programs.[80]

The survey found that the benefits of coed prisons include the ease and cost-effectiveness of a joint operation, the more normal environment produced by heterosexual contact, expanded programs available to women because of joint participation, greater flexibility in staffing, alleviated overcrowding at male institutions, and the fact that some inmates could be housed closer to home.

Coed prisons are not without their drawbacks. The most important problems listed by administrators were illicit relationships, supervisory and disciplinary problems, staff attitudes, the need to develop similar and equal programs without joint participation, and security coverage.

Can Rehabilitation Work?

Despite the variety and number of treatment programs in operation, their effectiveness has been questionable. In their oft-cited early research, Robert Martinson and his associates found that a majority of treatment programs were failures.[81] Martinson's work was followed by studies that found that some high-risk offenders were more likely to commit crimes after they had been placed in treatment programs than before the onset of rehabilitation efforts.[82] Paul Lerman found that even California's highly touted community treatment program, which matched youthful offenders and counselors on the basis on their psychological profiles, exerted negligible influence on its clients.[83] As recently as 1988, a review published by Steven Lab and John Whitehead found that correctional treatment efforts aimed at youthful offenders provided little evidence that they could rehabilitate clients.[84]

The disparagement of correctional treatment has served to promote a more conservative view of corrections, which holds that prisons are places of incapacitation and punishment and should not be used for treatment.[85] Current policies stress eliminating the nonserious offender from the correctional system, but at the same time increasing the probability that serious, violent offenders will be incarcerated and serve longer sentences. This policy has resulted in the development of mandatory and determinate sentences for serious offenders and the simultaneous utilization of intermediate sanctions such as house arrest, restitution, diversion, and pretrial release programs to limit the nonserious offender's interface with the system.

Although the concept of correctional rehabilitation is facing serious challenges, many experts still believe strongly in the rehabilitative ideal. Others such as Elliott Currie believe that inadequate budgets and programs have prevented rehabilitation from being given a realistic chance.[86] Nevertheless,

Currie argues, we should not lose hope. Crime can be controlled if rational policies are created that focus on dealing with young offenders before they become enmeshed in the justice system. For example, intensive probation and restitution should be used as alternatives to incarceration. Every effort should be made to expand intensive rehabilitation services for youthful offenders at the local community level. This might include aid to the victims of family violence; neighborhood dispute resolution teams and community-based family support programs, especially those that respect cultural diversity; improved family planning services; assistance for teenage parents; and educational enrichment programs for youths. Other services that can help reduce youth crime include intensive job training, permanent private and public job creation, and income supports for families outside the job market.

In sum, if the correctional system is to bring about offender rehabilitation, the effort must be made early in an offender's criminal career. Rehabilitation services must be provided in the community before juveniles are immersed in the system at a very young age (and become **state raised**). Although institutional efforts can be successful, the odds favor intervention for high-risk offenders before a pattern of hard-core crime and repeat incarcerations has been developed.[87]

Systemwide Rehabilitation Efforts

Those who cling to the rehabilitation ideal argue that critical reviews such as Martinson's are methodologicially unsound and that interpretation of more recent data would show that many programs have resulted in significant improvements in the behavior and adjustment of both youthful and adult participants.[88] The truth of the matter is that correctional rehabilitation is flourishing around the United States.

A case in point can be found in the New York, Ohio, and Maryland correctional systems. The New York State correctional system recently underwent a $600 million expansion that added room for 8,800 more inmates. At the same time, New York provides about 14,000 inmates with educational programs, including 3,000 at the college level; in addition, about 17,000 inmates were enrolled in vocational training programs. The New York Department of Corrections is also sponsoring a number of other innovative treatment and guidance efforts. The Hispanic Needs Program is designed to bridge the cultural gap and give special support to Hispanic inmates within the system. The Family Reunion Program allows conjugal visits with families in trailers located on the prison grounds. Whereas the statewide recidivism rate is 30 percent, participants in the Family Reunion Program had only a 5 percent return rate. In an attempt to strengthen family ties, the Bedford Hills facility for women added a children's center so that mothers can spend more time with their children. Counseling programs include the sex offender treatment program at Elmira and the Network program, which brings inmates and correctional workers together in order to improve inmates' coping skills, to help them confront past mistakes, and to improve their lives. Medical care for inmates is also being improved. The Assessment and Program Preparation Unit is a 250-bed facility in Clinton, which is designed to help inmates whose emotional or physical characteristics make them prone to be victimized by other inmates and in need of special custody. The Unit for the Sensorially Disabled houses 28 inmates with sight or hearing impairments, and the Alcohol and Substance Abuse Treatment program at Coxsackie may serve as a model for substance abuse treatment in the system. There is even a dialysis unit at the Arthur Kill facility that treats inmates with kidney problems without the expense of taking them to private clinics.[89]

In 1987 the Ohio Department of Corrections began to link inmate education, training, and employment programs on a statewide basis (the TIE program).[90] Each inmate has a computerized file that contains information on his or her educational and work experience as well as reading and math proficiency test scores. All inmates who test below the sixth grade are required to take remedial reading classes for at least three months and are encouraged to stay in the program longer. Other inmates are placed in one of four tracks depending on their abilities, security profile, and the needs of the institution:

1. *Service track.* This includes unskilled jobs such as maintenance and cafeteria work.
2. *Vocational training track.* This includes more than 50 skill-related classes in areas ranging from electronics to computer skills.
3. *Prison industries.* These involve manufacturing furniture office supplies, or textiles.
4. *Special needs groups.* These serve the needs of handicapped and mentally impaired inmates.

Inmates usually start in the service track and move up to the more challenging tracks as positions open up. TIE hopes the track system will combine education with long-term job training while maintaining the service and security needs of the institution.

Maryland has established a program called "Partnerships," which has restructured the state's two oldest prisons and established a pre-release program that emphasizes private sector involvement in training and job placement.[91] Currently, the programs include vocational and college-level educational programs in which 3,000 inmates participate daily. More than 1,000 outside volunteers help by conducting religious services, organizing self-help groups, teaching, collecting money, and helping with the inmate newspaper. Maryland has also improved its systemwide industry capability and now sells $15 million worth of goods each year through a telemarketing sales force, merchandise catalog, and improved product line. The state has also adopted a Case Management System that ensures that inmates close to leaving the institution receive the highest priority for rehabilitation programming.

The systemwide correction efforts in these three states are not unique. Similar programs are being conducted in almost all state jurisdictions. Thus while skeptics have proclaimed the "death" of correctional rehabilitation, efforts to provide innovative services have continued unabated.

■ Guarding the Institution

Controlling a prison is a very complex task. On the one hand, a tough high security environment may meet the goals of punishment and control but fail to reinforce positive behavior changes. On the other hand, too liberal an administrative stance can lower staff moral and allow inmates to take charge of the institution.[92]

Caught up in the complexities of prison life is the guard staff. In 1989 over 122,000 correctional officers were working in the nation's state prison facilities, an increase of about 25 percent since 1986.[93] Correctional officers are generally low paid: the average starting salary is about $18,000. About 85 percent are male and 15 percent female, a ratio that has remained stable since 1986.

Most states require that the candidate for correctional officer meet an age requirement (usually 18 or 21) and have a high school education. Other common criteria are that the candidate should have a "clean" criminal record and a driver's license, be drug-free, and maintain good physical condition. Some states such as Oregon and Pennsylvania require either oral or written testing. After selection most correctional officer candidates receive between one and six weeks of training; Pennsylvania requires a two-year apprenticeship program including four weeks of academy training. About 26 states provide 40 hours a week of in-service training for correctional officers.[94]

For many years prison guards were viewed as ruthless people who enjoyed their positions of power over inmates, fought rehabilitation efforts, maintained a racist mentality, and had a "lock psychosis" developed from years of counting, numbering, and checking on inmates. In recent years this view of guards has changed. Pioneering research by Lucien X. Lombardo and others has painted a picture of prison guards as people who are seeking the security and financial rewards of a civil service position.[95] Most are in favor of rehabilitation efforts and do not hold any particular animosity toward the inmate population. The prison guard has been characterized by Lombardo as a "people worker" who must be prepared to deal with the human problems of inmates on a personal level. The guard is also a member of a complex bureaucracy who must be able to cope with its demands.

Guards play a number of roles within the institution. They supervise cell houses, dining areas, shops, and other facilities as well as patrolling the walls armed with rifles to prevent escapes and overseeing the yard. Guards also sit on disciplinary boards and escort inmates to hospitals and court appearances.

The greatest problem faced by prison guards is the duality of their role: they are at the same time maintainers of order and security and advocates of treatment and rehabilitation. Added to this basic dilemma is the changing inmate role. Whereas previously the guards could count on inmate leaders to help them maintain order, they are now faced with a racially charged atmosphere in which violence is a way of life. Today, guard work is filled with danger, tension, boredom; to make matters worse, there is little evidence that their efforts to help inmates lead to success. Furthermore, unlike police officers, there is little evidence that correctional workers form a close-knit subculture with unique values and a sense of intergroup loyalty. Correctional officers have been found to experience alienation and isolation from the inmates, correctional administration, and each other.[96] Interestingly, this sense of alienation seems greatest in younger officers, and evidence suggests that in the latter part of their careers, guards enjoy a revival of interest in their work and take great pride in providing human services to inmates.[97]

To aid the guards in their tasks, many state prison authorities have developed training programs to prepare them for the difficulties prison work entails. It has also become common for guard unions to be formed that negotiate with the corrections department on matters of wages and working conditions.

Female Correctional Officers

One issue that has come up repeatedly is the matter of female guards in male institutions. Today, an estimated 5,000 women are assigned to all-male institutions (out of a total of 77,000 correctional officers).[98] The employment of women raises many questions of privacy and safety, and there have been a number of legal cases questioning the use of women in close contact with male inmates. In one important case, *Dothard v. Rawlinson* (1977), the U.S. Supreme Court upheld Alabama's refusal to hire female correctional officers on the grounds that they would be in significant danger from the male inmates.[99] Despite such setbacks women now work side by side with men in almost every state, performing the same duties as their male counterparts. Research indicates that discipline has not suffered because of the inclusion of women in the guard force. Sexual assaults have been rare, and negative attitudes have been expressed more frequently by their male peers than by the inmate population.[100] Most commentators believe that the inclusion of female guards can have an important beneficial effect on the self-image of inmates and can improve the guard-inmate working relationship.[101] Interestingly, there has been little research on male correctional officers in female prisons. David Duffee reports that male officers are generally well received, that there is little evidence of sexual exploitation or privacy violations, and that female inmates feel that the presence of male correctional officers helps create a more natural environment and reduces tension levels.[102]

■ Prison Violence

Prison violence and brutality is a sad but ever-present aspect of institutional life. Violence can be individualistic (inmate versus inmate, or inmate versus guard and vice versa) or collective in the form of wide-scale prison riots like the famous Attica riot in 1971, which claimed 39 lives, and the more recent New Mexico State Prison riot of February 1980, in which the death toll was 33.

It is evident that prisons are highly volatile arenas ready to explode. Reports of violent deaths in prison are daily occurrences that American citizens have more or less learned to accept. About 100 inmates are killed by their peers each year in American prisons, about 6 or 7 staff members are murdered and about 120 suicides are recorded; these figures appear to be on the increase.[103]

What are the causes of prison violence? Although there is no single explanation for either collective or individualistic violence, a number of theories abound. One position holds that inmates themselves are often violence-prone individuals who have always used force to get their own way. In the crowded, dehumanizing world of the prison, it is not surprising that they resort to force to exert their dominance over others.[104]

A second view is that prisons convert people to violence by their inhuman conditions, including overcrowding, depersonalization, and threat of homosexual rape.[105] Social scientist Charles Silberman suggests that even in the most humane prisons, life is a constant put-down and prison conditions are a threat to the inmates' sense of self-worth; violence is not a surprising consequence of these conditions.[106]

Still another view is that prison violence stems from prison mismanagement, lack of strong security, and inadequate control by prison officials.[107] This view has contributed to the escalation of solitary confinement in recent years as a means of control. In a survey of 60 prisons conducted by Robert Freeman, Simon Dinitz, and John Conrad, 19 reported that the number of inmates in solitary confinement ranged from 250 to 600.[108]

Others view the fact that few prisons have effective grievance procedures for complaints against either prison officials or other inmates as a cause of prison violence. Prisoners who complain about other inmates are viewed as "finks" and marked for death by their enemies. Similarly, complaints or lawsuits filed against prison administration may result in the inmate being placed in solitary confinement—"the hole." The lack of communication is heightened by the diverse ethnic and racial backgrounds of the guards and inmates. The typical inmate at Attica Prison at the time of the riot was a 25-year-old black male from New York City, while the typical guard was a middle-aged white male from upstate rural New York. The frustration caused by living in a prison with a climate that promotes violence—that is, without adequate mechanisms for complaint, lack of physical security, and where the "code of silence" protects violators—is believed to promote both collective and individual violence by inmates who might otherwise be controlled.[109]

What form does prison violence take? One common threat is homosexual rape. Recent research has shown that prison rapes usually involve a weak victim and a group of aggressive rapists who can dominate the victim through their collective strength. Nonsexual assaults may involve an aggressor's desire to shake down the victim for money and personal favors, may be motivated by racial conflict, or may simply be used as a device to establish power within the institution.[110] Daniel Lockwood found that sexual harassment leads to fights, social isolation, racism, fear, anxiety, and crisis.[111]

Prison violence can also take the form of collective prison riots. A number of factors can spark these damaging incidents. According to criminologist Edith Flynn, they include poor staff/inmate communications, destructive ecological conditions, faulty classification, and promised but undelivered reforms.[112]

Overcrowding and Violence

Although revulsion over the violent riots in New Mexico and the earlier Attica riot in New York brought calls for prison reform, prison violence has continued unabated.[113] And as the following section suggests, the number of violent incidents may increase as prisons become more overcrowded.[114] Data from Texas indicate that a large increase in the prison population, unmatched by new space, was associated with increases in suicide, violent death, and disciplinary action rates. The largest prisons in Texas (with populations of over 1,600) demonstrated violence rates higher than the smaller prisons (800 or less).[115] Similar data on crowding and violent deaths from Oklahoma corroborate the Texas findings. One explanation is that high population in an institution exerts a negative influence that is associated with violence.

Other recent research efforts have reached similar conclusions. Paul Paulus and his associates found that feelings of crowding and blood pressure rates increased in cells occupied by more than one person.[116] E. I. Megargee found that crowding was associated with increased disciplinary infractions[117] P. L. Nacci and his associates found that the most overcrowded federal correctional institutions also had the highest disciplinary infraction rates.[118] A number of other studies have reached similar conclusions.[119]

It seems evident that as the prison population continues its upward climb, unmatched by expanded correctional capacity, prison violence may increase. Although judges in a number of states have ordered the mandatory release of prisoners because of overcrowded conditions, the problem of **overcrowding** may become even more acute in future years. Consequently, prison administrators have attempted to reduce tension levels by establishing inmate councils to help govern the institution (**self-governance**) and creating grievance mechanisms that take inmates' complaints into account. Such measures have been effective in some institutions.

■ Prisoners' Rights

Prior to the early 1960s, it was accepted that upon conviction an individual forfeited all rights not expressly granted by statutory law or correctional policy; inmates were "civilly dead." The U.S. Supreme Court held that convicted offenders should expect to be penalized for their misdeeds and that part of their punishment was the loss of freedoms free citizens take for granted.[120]

One reason that inmates lacked rights was because state and federal courts were reluctant to intervene in the administration of prisons unless the circumstances of a case clearly indicated a serious breach of the Eighth Amendment's protection against cruel and unusual punishment. This judicial policy is known as the **hands-off doctrine.** The courts used three basic justifications for their neglect of prison conditions:

1. Correctional administration was a technical matter to be left to experts rather than to courts ill-equipped to make appropriate evaluations.
2. Society as a whole was apathetic to what went on in prisons, and most individuals preferred not to associate with or know about the offender.
3. Prisoners' complaints involved privileges rather than rights. Prisoners were regarded as having fewer constitutional rights than other members of society.[121]

As the 1960s drew to a close, the hands-off doctrine began to erode. Federal district courts began seriously considering prisoners' claims concerning conditions in the various state and federal institutions and utilized their power to intervene on behalf of the inmate population. In some ways this concern reflected the spirit of the times, which saw the onset of the civil rights movement and was subsequently reflected in such areas as student rights, public welfare, mental institutions, juvenile court systems, and military justice.

Beginning in the late 1960s, activist groups such as the NAACP Legal Defense Fund and the American Civil Liberties Union's National Prison Project began to search for appropriate legal vehicles to bring prisoners' complaints before state and federal courts. The most widely used device was the **Federal Civil Rights Act** (42 U.S.C. 1983):

> Every person who, under color of any statute, ordinance, regulation, custom, or usage of any State or Territory subjects, or causes to be subjected, any citizen of the United States or other person within the jurisdiction thereof to the deprivation of any rights, privileges, or immunities secured by the Constitution and laws shall be liable to the party injured in an action at law, suit in equity, or other proper proceeding for redress.

The statute gave rise to the legal argument that as U.S. citizens, prison inmates could sue state officials if their civil rights were violated—if, for example, they were the victims of racial or religious discrimination.

The U.S. Supreme Court first recognized the right of prisoners to sue for civil rights violations in cases involving religious freedom brought by the Black Muslims. This well-organized group had been frustrated by prison administrators who feared their growing power and desired to place limits on their

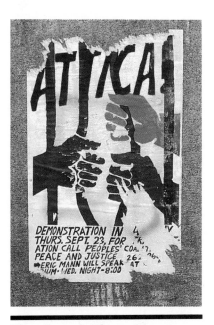

The prisoners' rights movement, which spanned from 1960–1980, paralleled the civil rights and women's movements.

recruitment activities. In the 1964 case of *Cooper v. Pate,* however, the Supreme Court ruled that inmates who were being denied the right to practice their religion were entitled to legal redress under the Civil Rights Act.[122] Although *Cooper* applied to the narrow issue of religious freedom, it opened the door to other rights for inmates. As James B. Jacobs states:

> It was not the breadth of the decision that mattered, but the Supreme Court's determination that prisoners have constitutional rights; prison officials were not free to do with prisoners as they pleased. And the federal courts were permitted, indeed obligated, to provide a forum where prisoners could challenge and confront prison officials.[123]

The subsequent prisoners' rights crusade, stretching from 1960 to 1980, paralleled the civil rights and women's movements. Battle lines were drawn between prison officials hoping to maintain their power and resenting interference by the courts and inmate groups and their sympathizers, who used state and federal courts as a forum for demanding better living conditions and personal rights. Each decision handed down by the courts was viewed as a victory for one side or the other; this battle continues today.

■ Substantive Rights of Inmates

Through a slow process of legal review, the courts have granted inmates a number of substantive rights that have significantly influenced the entire correctional system. The most important of these rights are discussed in the next sections.

Access to Courts, Legal Services, and Materials

Without the ability to seek judicial review of conditions causing discomfort or violating constitutional rights, inmates must depend for relief solely on the slow and often insensitive administrative mechanism within the prison system. Therefore the right of easy access to the courts gives the inmates hope that their rights will be protected.

In 1941 in *Ex parte Cleus Hull,* the U.S. Supreme Court declared that inmates have a basic constitutional right to access to the courts.[124] Although *Hull* granted inmates access to the courts, it was not uncommon for prison officials to use harsh disciplinary actions against inmates seeking legal remedies through court action. Most prisons lacked legal services, and in many situations the use of a **jailhouse lawyer** (an inmate possessing some legal skills who offers legal advice to other inmates) was restricted. Consequently, most prisoners found it virtually impossible to seek relief through the courts.

To help resolve this problem, the U.S. Supreme Court in the case of *Johnson v. Avery,* held that unless the state could provide some reasonable alternative to inmates in the preparation of petitions for postconviction relief, a jailhouse lawyer must be permitted to aid illiterate inmates in filing habeas corpus petitions.[125] Federal courts have expanded this right to include virtually all inmates with various legal problems:

1. *DeMallory v. Cullen* (1988). An untrained inmate paralegal is not a constitutionally acceptable alternative to law library access.[126]

2. *Lindquist v. Idaho State Board of Corrections* (1985). Seven inmate law clerks for a prison population of 950 were sufficient legal representation since they had had a great deal of experience.[127]

3. *Smith v. Wade* (1983). Inmates who have been raped can have access to state court in order sue a guard for failing to protect them from aggressive inmates.[128]

4. *Bounds v. Smith* (1977). State correctional systems are obligated to provide inmates either with adequate law libraries or with the help of people trained in the law.[129]

Freedom of the Press and of Expression

Correctional administrators traditionally placed severe limitations on a prisoner's speech and expression. For example, they have read and censored inmate mail and restricted their reading material. With the lifting of the hands-off doctrine, courts have consistently ruled that only when a compelling state interest exists can prisoners' First Amendment rights be modified; correctional authorities must justify the limiting of free speech by showing that granting it would threaten institutional security. The following cases related to prisoners' freedom of speech rights indicate current policy on the subject:

1. *Turner v. Safley* (1987). Prisoners do not have a right to receive mail from one another. Inmate-to-inmate mail can be banned if the reason is "related to legitimate penological interests." Unless it presents a threat to security, prisoners retain the right to marry.[130]

2. *Gregory v. Auger* (1985). Prison officials can restrict mail to those in temporary disciplinary detention as a means of increasing the deterrent value of this type of punishment.[131]

3. *Ramos v. Lamm* (1980). An institutional policy of refusing to deliver mail in a language other than English is unconstitutional.[132]

4. *Procunier v. Martinez* (1974). Censorship of a prisoner's mail is justified only when (1) there exists substantial government interest in maintaining the censorship in order to further prison security, order, and rehabilitation and (2) when the restrictions are not greater or more stringent than is demanded by security precautions.[133]

5. *Nolan v. Fitzpatrick* (1971). Prisoners may correspond with newspapers unless their letters discuss escape plans or contain contraband or other objectional material.[134]

6. *Saxbe v. Washington Post Co.* (1974). A federal prison rule forbidding individual press interviews with specific inmates was justified because there is no constitutional right to interview specific people; individual interviews would enhance the reputation of particular inmates and jeopardize the prison authorities' desire to treat everyone equally.[135]

Freedom of Religion

Freedom of religion is a fundamental right guaranteed by the First Amendment to the U.S. Constitution. The religious freedom clause has a dual purpose: (1) it protects an individual's rights to practice his or her religion freely, and (2) it prohibits the government from being partial to any particular religious group. In light of these two purposes, several issues pertaining to religious freedom within the context of the correctional setting have been brought to the attention of the courts. These include (1) religious discrimination, (2) the right to hold religious services, (3) access to ministers, (4) the right to correspond with religious leaders, and (5) the right to wear religious medals. In general, the courts have ruled that inmates have the right to assemble and pray in the religion of their choice, but that religious symbols and practices that interfere with institutional security can be restricted. Administrators can draw the line if religious needs become cumbersome or impossible to carry out for reasons of cost or security. Granting special privileges can also be denied on the grounds that they will cause other groups to make similar demands.

Some of the issues surrounding religious practices in prison and the manner in which some courts have handled cases concerning religious freedom are outlined below:

1. *Numin v. Phelps* (1988). If there is a legitimate penological interest, inmates can be denied special privileges to attend religious services.[136]
2. *O'Lone v. Shabazz* (1987). Prison officials can assign inmates work schedules that make it impossible for them to attend religious services as long as a reasonable alternative exists.[137]
3. *Rahman v. Stephenson* (1986). A prisoner's rights are not violated if the administration refuses to use his religious name on official records.[138]
4. *Abdullah v. Kinnison* (1985). Muslim inmates do not have the right to wear white prayer robes in their cells if it interferes with prison security.[139]
5. *Cruz v. Beto* (1972). Denying a Buddhist prisoner a reasonable opportunity to pursue his faith is discriminatory in that the more conventional religious practices of other inmates are permitted.[140]
6. *Kahane v. Carlson* (1975). An orthodox Jewish inmate has the right to a diet that can sustain him in good health without violating his or her religion, unless the government can show cause why it cannot be provided.[141]
7. *Chapman v. Pickett* (1978). A Black Muslim's right to religious freedom was violated when he was placed in segregation for refusing to handle pork while on a work detail.[142]
8. *Gallahan v. Hollyfield* (1981). A Cherokee Indian has the right to have long hair if that is a requirement of his sincere religious beliefs.[143]

Medical Rights

Until recently, the courts restricted inmates' right to medical treatment through the **exceptional circumstances doctrine.** Under this doctrine, the courts would hear only those cases in which the circumstances totally disregarded human dignity, while denying hearings to other less serious cases. The cases that were allowed access to the courts usually involved a situation in which medical care was denied altogether.

To gain their medical rights, prisoners have generally resorted to class actions (i.e., suits brought on behalf of all individuals governed by similar circumstances, in this case poor medical attention). In the most significant case, *Newman v. Alabama* (1972), the entire Alabama prison system's medical facilities were declared inadequate.[144] The court cited the following factors as contributing to inadequate care: insufficient physician and nurse resources; reliance on untrained inmates for paramedical work; intentional failure to treat the sick and injured; and failure to conform to proper medical standards.

Not until 1976, in *Estelle v. Gamble*, did the U.S. Supreme Court clearly mandate an inmate's right to have medical care.[145] Gamble had hurt his back in a Texas prison and filed suit contesting the type of treatment he received and also questioning the lack of interest prison guards had shown in his case. The Supreme Court established the following standard for judging future complaints:

Deliberate indifference to serious medical needs of prisoners constitutes the "unnecessary and wanton infliction of pain," . . . proscribed by the Eighth Amendment. This is true whether the indifference is manifested by prison doctors in their response to the prisoner's needs or by prison guards in intentionally denying or delaying access to medical care or intentionally interfering with the treatment once prescribed.[146]

Lower courts will now decide, on a case-by-case basis, whether "deliberate indifference" actually occurred.

Cruel and Unusual Punishment

The concept of **cruel and unusual punishment** is founded in the Eighth Amendment to the U.S. Constitution. To date, the term itself has not been specifically defined by the U.S. Supreme Court, but the Court has held that treatment constitutes cruel and unusual punishment when it

1. Degrades the dignity of human beings.[147]
2. Is more severe than the offense for which it has been given.[148]
3. Shocks the general conscience and is fundamentally unfair.[149]

In recent years, state and federal courts have placed strict limits on disciplinary methods that may be considered inhumane. Corporal punishment all but ended after the practice was condemned by then Eight Circuit Court of Appeals Judge Harry Blackmun in *Jackson v. Bishop* (1968).[150] Although the solitary confinement of disruptive inmates continues, its prolonged use under barbaric conditions has been held to be in violation of the Eighth Amendment. Courts have found that inmates placed in solitary have the right to adequate personal hygiene, exercise, mattresses, ventilation, and rules specifying how they can earn their release.

One issue relating to cruel and unusual punishment concerns overall prison conditions. In 1970 the district court of Arkansas in the case of *Holt v. Sarver* looked closely at the Arkansas prison system and found the conditions so deplorable that they were constitutionally unacceptable:

For the ordinary convict a sentence to the Arkansas Penitentiary today amounts to a banishment from civilized society to a dark and evil world completely alien to the free world, a world that is administered by criminals under unwritten rules and customs completely foreign to free world culture.[151]

Despite the court's demand for reform, little was done to improve conditions in the Arkansas prison system. More than seven years after the *Holt v. Sarver* decision, a federal court concluded that the inhumane conditions had not been substantially improved.

In a similar case, *Estelle v. Ruiz*, the Texas Department of Corrections was ordered to provide new facilities to alleviate overcrowding, to abolish the practice of inmate trustees, to lower the staff-to-inmate ratio, to improve treatment services such as medical, mental health, and occupational rehabilitation programs, and to adhere to the principles of procedural due process in dealing with inmates.[152] *Estelle v. Ruiz* illustrates the problems of achieving prison reform through court order. The case was filed in 1972, but the trial did not actually begin until 1978; the final court order took effect in 1981. Even with the final court decree, changes were slow in forthcoming. Geoffrey Alpert, Ben Crouch and C. Ronald Huff report that the final *Ruiz* decision created a crisis of control within the Texas Department of Corrections.[153]

In some cases, the courts have ruled that prisons such as this Georgia convict camp, photographed in 1941, constitute cruel and unusual punishment and violate due process.

While prisoner expectations rose, staff uncertainty also increased. A period of tension and violence followed the decision, which may be partially explained by the fact that the staff and administration felt that the court had undermined their authority.

Minimal Prison Conditions

From earliest times, prisoners have had the right to minimal conditions necessary for human survival, such as the food, clothing, shelter, and medical care necessary to sustain human life.[154] There have been a number of attempts to articulate reasonable standards of prison care and ensure that they are carried out. Federal judges have set forth minimum conditions that must be maintained in a prison and have appointed overseers to make sure their orders have been carried out. In a number of instances, courts have ordered improvement of the inmates' total living environment. For example, the U.S. District Court for the Eastern District of Oklahoma decreed in 1977 that living and dormitory space in the prisons within its jurisdiction must be 60 and 75 square feet, respectively. The court argued that although people are sent to prison for *punishment*, this does not mean that prison should be a *punishing experience*.[155] In a similar vein, a federal circuit court declared in *Wolfish v. Levi* (1979) that a prisoner's property must be accounted for, that inmates should be given commissary privileges, that food packages from the outside must be given to inmates, and that inmates must be allowed unmonitored calls.[156]

An important threat to overall prison conditions has been brought about by the recent overcrowding of the nation's prison system. In two decisions, the U.S. Supreme Court seems to have backed off from granting inmates an absolute right to adequate living conditions.

The first case, *Bell v. Wolfish* (1979), involved detainees awaiting trial. Louis Wolfish was incarcerated in the new Federal Metropolitan Correctional Center in New York.[157] This unit was designed to provide inmates with more privacy and better conditions than older jails. Although its 389 rooms were for single occupants only, the rising crime rate quickly filled the institution to overcapacity. As a result, many of the private rooms were converted to house two inmates (**double-bunking**), and some inmates were forced to sleep on cots in public areas. Inmates were also prohibited from receiving packages from friends and relatives (with the exception of Christmas), were allowed reading material only if it was sent directly from the publisher (thereby limiting the availability of reading material), and were subject to humiliating "strip" searches after every visitation. Inmate Wolfish filed a habeas corpus petition seeking his release because of these conditions, and the suit was quickly turned into a class action on behalf of all pretrial detainees in the jail.

After initial success for the plaintiffs in the lower courts, the U.S. Supreme Court accepted the case on appeal. When assessing the practices used in the jail, the Court found that "absent a showing of expressed intent to punish on the part of detention facility officials, that determination will turn on 'whether an alternative purpose . . . may rationally be (responsible for it).' " In other words, if there is a legitimate purpose for the use of government restrictions, they may be considered constitutional. In the present case, double-bunking was deemed an acceptable practice since it was not meant as a punishment; similarly, the restriction on reading material was upheld because other sources of printed matter were available (e.g., the prison library). Moreover, the Supreme Court upheld "strip" searches and the restriction on receiving outside packages as legitimate security measures.

In *Rhodes v. Chapman* (1981), the Supreme Court upheld the practice of placing more than one inmate in a single cell as an administrative solution to overcrowding.[158]

Despite the setbacks to inmates' rights in *Bell v. Wolfish* and *Rhodes v. Chapman*, a significant number of state courts have ordered that local prison conditions be improved and overcrowding reduced, even if it means closing prisons and releasing the excess inmate population. At the time of this writing, more than 30 states are under court order to reduce their prison populations.[159] Some courts have also refused to allow double-bunking of inmates if prison conditions were too deteriorated. An Indiana court refused to allow such measures at the Indiana Reformatory at Pendleton on the grounds that the facility was so cramped, dirty, inadequately ventilated, and poorly lit, that double-bunking under these conditions amounted to cruel and unusual punishment.

Some research indicates that court-ordered improvements have met with success. For example, G. Larry Mays and William Taggart found that lawsuits involving the prison conditions that gave rise to the New Mexico penitentiary riot of 1980 have helped improve correctional operations.[160]

Prisoners' Rights Today

There is little question that since 1980 a more conservative U.S. Supreme Court has curtailed prisoners' rights. While not rescinding all the gains made between 1960 and 1980, the Court has made it more difficult for prisoners to receive compensation or restitution if their rights have been violated. For example, in *Daniels v. Williams* the Court ruled that inmates do not have a constitutional right to collect damages if they are injured by another inmate due to a guard's negligence in protecting them from harm.[161] In order to receive damages, inmates must show that they were intentionally harmed by a correctional official. For example, if an inmate reports that another prisoner threatened him and a correctional officer does nothing about the threat, the inmate has no legal recourse if the threat is carried out and he is seriously injured.[162]

The Supreme Court has also placed limitations on an inmate's right to privacy. In *Hudson v. Palmer*, the Court ruled that inmates do not have a Fourth Amendment right to privacy over material contained in their cells.[163] Other rulings have denied inmates the right to contest their transfer to a more punitive institution[164] or to be eligible for classification and rehabilitation programs.[165] The Court has also made it easier to punish inmates by relaxing the administrative procedures required to place an inmate in segregation,[166] giving prison officials the right to use deadly force to put down a prison uprising,[167] and reducing the level of evidence required before officials can take away a prisoner's "good time" credit because of disciplinary violations.[168] In two recent (1989) cases, the Court ruled that it is not a violation of inmates' due process rights if correctional authorities restrict visitors who are considered to be a "security threat" or prevent inmates from receiving publications if banning them is related to reasonable penological interests such as maintaining institutional security.[169]

In sum, the Court has recently reverted to a hands-off approach to handling prisoners' rights cases.[170] Inmates must now make a powerful case to overcome correctional authorities' claim that restrictive conditions further prison security. Moreover, the *Turner* and *O'Lone* decisions, discussed earlier, indicate that even First Amendment rights such as the right to attend religious services or use the mails are no longer immune to control.

■ SUMMARY

On entering a major closed institution, the offender must make tremendous adjustments in order to survive. Usual behavior patterns or lifestyles are radically changed. Opportunities for personal satisfaction are reduced. Passing through a number of adjustment stages or cycles, the inmate learns to cope with the new environment.

An inmate also learns to obey the inmate social code, which dictates proper behavior and attitudes. If the code is broken, the inmate may be unfavorably labeled and punished by fellow inmates.

Once inside the institution, new inmates can avail themselves of a large number of treatment programs designed to help them readjust to the community. These include educational programs on the basic, high school, and even college levels, as well as vocational training programs. In addition, a number of treatment programs offer inmates individualized and group psychological counseling; work furlough programs, coed prisons, and conjugal visits have also been employed.

Despite such measures, prisons remain forbidding structures that house desperate men and women. Violence is a byword in prisons. Women often turn their hatred inward and hurt themselves, while male inmates engage in collective and individual violence against others. The Attica and New Mexico riots are examples of the most serious collective prison violence.

In years past, society paid little attention to the incarcerated offender. The majority of inmates confined in jails and prisons were deprived of the basic rights guaranteed them under the U.S. Constitution. Today, however, the judicial system is actively involved in the administration of correctional institutions. Inmates can now take their grievances to court and seek due process and equal protection under the law. The courts have recognized that persons confined in correctional institutions have rights, including access to the courts and legal counsel, the free exercise of religion, the right to correspondence and visitation, and the right to adequate medical treatment.

■ QUESTIONS

1. How might the prison experience be likened to living in a large university campus?
2. What steps could be taken to make prisons a more pleasant environment? Should these steps be taken?
3. What are the benefits and drawbacks of coed prisons? Of conjugal visits?
4. Should women be allowed to work as guards in male prisons? What about male guards in female prisons?

5. Should prison inmates be allowed a free college education while noncriminals are forced to pay tuition? Do you believe in less eligibility?
6. Do double bunking and other conditions relating to overcrowded prisons represent violations of inmates' constitutional rights?

■ NOTES

1. David Pitt, "Jogger's Attackers Terrorized at Least 9 in 2 Hours," *New York Times*, 22 April 1989, p. 1.
2. The data in this section are from Bureau of Justice Statistics, *Prisons and Prisoners* (Washington, D.C.: U.S. Government Printing Office, 1982).
3. Joan Mullen, *American Prisons and Jails*, vol. 1, *Summary Findings and Policy Implications* (Washington, D.C.: U.S. Government Printing Office, 1980), p. 56.
4. Bureau of Justice Statistics, *Prisons and Prisoners*, p. 5.
5. Christopher Innes, *Profile of State Prison Inmates, 1986* (Washington, D.C.: Bureau of Justice Statistics, 1988).
6. Federal Bureau of Investigation, *Crime in the United States, 1986* (Washington, D.C.: U.S. Government Printing Office, 1987), p. 181.
7. Robert Johnson, *Culture and Crisis in Confinement* (Lexington, Mass.: Lexington Books, 1976), pp. 1–2.
8. Gresham Sykes, *The Society of Captives* (Princeton, N.J.: Princeton University Press, 1958).
9. David Anderson, *Crimes of Justice: Improving the Police, Courts, and Prison* (New York: Times Books, 1988).
10. Robert Johnson, *Hard Time: Understanding and Reforming the Prison* (Monterey, Calif.: Brooks/Cole, 1987), p. 115.
11. Kevin Wright, *The Great American Crime Myth* (Westport, Conn.: Greenwood Press, 1985), p. 167.
12. Sandra Gleason, "Hustling: The 'Inside' Economy of a Prison," *Federal Probation* 42 (1978): 32–39.
13. Ibid., p. 39.
14. *Newsweek*, 18 February 1980, p. 75.
15. Hans Toch, *Living in Prison* (New York: Free Press, 1977), pp. 179–205.
16. Ibid., p. 192.
17. Johnson, *Hard Time*, pp. 55–60.
18. Ibid., p. 70.
19. John Irwin, "Adaptation to Being Corrected: Corrections from the Convict's Perspective," in *Handbook of Criminology*, Daniel Glazer, ed. (Chicago: Rand McNally & Co., 1974), pp. 971–93.
20. Donald Clemmer, *The Prison Community* (New York: Holt, Rinehart, & Winston, 1958).
21. Sykes, *The Society of Captives*.
22. Gresham Sykes and Sheldon Messinger, "The Inmate Social Code," in *The Sociology of Punishment and Corrections*, Norman Johnston et al., ed. (New York: John Wiley & Sons, 1970), pp. 401–8.
23. Ibid., p. 404.
24. John Irwin and Donald Cressey, "Thieves, Convicts, and the Inmate Culture," *Social Problems* 10 (1962): 142–55.
25. Ibid., p. 145.
26. See, generally, Wright, *The Great American Crime Myth*, p. 167.

27. Paul Gendreau, Marie-Claude Tellier, and J. Stephen Wormith, "Protective Custody: The Emerging Crisis within Our Prisons," *Federal Probation* 69 (1985): 55–64.
28. James B. Jacobs, *New Perspectives on Prisons and Imprisonment* (Ithaca, N.Y.: Cornell University Press, 1983); "Street Gangs behind Bars," *Social Problems* 21 (1974): 395–409; "Race Relations and the Prison Subculture," in *Crime and Justice*, Norval Morris and Michael Tonry, eds. (Chicago: University of Chicago Press, 1979), pp. 1–28.
29. Stanley Penn, "Prison Gangs Formed by Racial Groups Pose Big Problem in West," *Wall Street Journal*, 11 May 1983, p. 1.
30. Charles Stastny and Gabrielle Tyrnauer, *Who Rules the Joint?* (Lexington, Mass.: Lexington Books, 1982), pp. 143–45.
31. Penn, "Prison Gangs Formed by Racial Groups Pose Big Problems in West," p. 1.
32. Jacobs, *New Perspectives on Prisons and Imprisonment*, pp. 97–98.
33. Laurence Greenfeld, *Prisoners in 1988* (Washington, D.C.: Bureau of Justice Statistics, 1989).
34. Elaine DeCostanzo and Helen Scholes, "Women behind Bars, Their Numbers Increase," *Corrections Today* 50 (1988): 104–6.
35. Ibid., p. 106.
36. This section synthesizes the findings of a number of surveys of female inmates, including DeCostanzo and Scholes, "Women behind Bars, Their Numbers Increase," pp. 106–8 (1988); Ruth Glick and Virginia Neto, *National Study of Women's Correctional Programs* (Washington, D.C.: U.S. Government Printing Office, 1977); Anne Goetting and Roy Michael Howsen, "Women in Prison: A Profile," *The Prison Journal* 63 (1983): 27–46; Meda Chesney-Lind and Noelie Rodrigues, "Women under Lock and Key: A View from Inside," *The Prison Journal* 63 (1983): 47–65; CONtact, Inc., "Women Offenders," *Corrections Compendium* 7 (1982): 6–11.
37. DeCostanzo and Scholes, "Women behind Bars, Their Numbers Increase," pp. 104–6.
38. Edna Erez, "The Myth of the New Female Offender: Some Evidence from Attitudes toward Law and Justice," *Journal of Criminal Justice* 16 (1988): 499–509.
39. Robert Ross and Hugh McKay, *Self-Mutilation* (Lexington, Mass.: Lexington Books, 1979).
40. Alice Propper, *Prison Homosexuality* (Lexington, Mass.: Lexington Books, 1981).
41. Ibid.; see also Alice Propper, "Make-believe Families and Homosexuality among Imprisoned Girls," *Criminology* 20 (1983): 127–39.
42. For a review of rehabilitation techniques, see Ted Riggar and Jerome Lorenz, *Readings in Rehabilitation Administration* (New York: State University of New York Press, 1985).

43. Gene Kassebaum, David Ward, and Daniel Wilner, "Group Counseling," in *Legal Process and Corrections*, N. Johnston and D. Savitz, eds. (New York: John Wiley & Sons, 1982), p. 256.

44. Charles Tarr, "Group Counseling," *Corrections Today* 48 (1986): 72–75.

45. Marie Clark, "Missouri's Sexual Offender Program," *Corrections Today* 48 (1986): 84–89.

46. See, generally, William Glasser, *Reality Therapy* (New York: Harper & Row, 1965). For further use of this technique, see Richard Rachin, "Reality Therapy: Helping People Help Themselves," *Crime and Delinquency* 16 (January 1974): 143–45; Eric Berne, *Transactional Analysis in Psychotherapy* (New York: Grove Press, 1961). See also Richard Nicholson, "Transactional Analysis: A New Method for Helping Offenders," *Federal Probation* 34: (September 1970) 29–33; Gaylord Thorne et al., "Behavior Modification Techniques: New Tools for Probation Officers," *Federal Probation* 31 (June 1967): 21–25; Ralph Schwitzgabel, *Street Corner Research* (Cambridge, Mass.: Harvard University Press, 1967); J. T. Saunders and J. D. Reppucci, "Reward and Punishment: Some Guidelines for Their Effective Application in Correctional Programs for Youthful Offenders," *Crime and Delinquency* 18 (1972): 284–87.

47. Rafael Otero, Donna McNally, and Robert Powitzky, "Mental Health Services in Adult Correctional Systems," *Corrections Today* 43 (1981): 8–18.

48. Max Mobley, "Mental Health Services Inmates In Need," *Corrections Today* 48 (1986): 12–14; see also Edward Guy, Jerome Platt, Israel Swerling, and Samuuel Bullock, "Mental Health Status of Prisoners in an Urban Jail," *Criminal Justice and Behavior* 12 (1985): 17–29.

49. Richard Austin and Albert Duncan, "Handle with Care, Special Inmates, Special Needs," *Corrections Today* 50 (1988); 116–20.

50. Glenn Walters, Millard Mann, Melvin Miller, Leslie Hemphill, and Michael Chlumsky, "Emotional Disorder among Offenders," *Criminal Justice and Behavior* 15 (1988): 433–53.

51. Jean Spruill and Jack May, "The Mentally Retarded Offender," *Criminal Justice and Behavior* 15 (1988): 484–91.

52. Benedict Alper, *Prisons Inside-Out* (Cambridge, Mass.: Ballinger Publishing Co., 1974), pp. 43–94.

53. Sylvia McCollum, "New Designs for Correctional Education and Training Programs," *Federal Probation* 37 (June 1973): 6–8.

54. Ibid., p. 10.

55. Albert Roberts, *Readings in Prison Education* (Springfield, Ill.: Charles C. Thomas, 1973), p. 88.

56. Robert Walton, "New Jersey Places over 350 Trained Cooks, Bakers, and Meatcutters on Jobs during First 30 Months of Food Training," *American Journal of Corrections* 7 (November/December 1976).

57. Cited in Phyllis McCreary and John McCreary, *Job Training and Placement for Offenders and Ex-offenders* (Washington, D.C.: U.S. Government Printing Office, 1975), p. 10.

58. Paul Hahn, "Residential Alternatives to Incarceration," in *Order under Law*, R. Culbertson and M. Tezak, eds., (Prospect Heights, Ill.: Waveland Press, 1981), pp. 244–60.

59. Ibid., p. 13.

60. Ibid.

61. Johnathan Katz and Scott Decker, "An Analysis of Work Release: The Institutionalization of Unsubstantiated Reforms," *Criminal Justice and Behavior* 9 (1982): 229–50.

62. This section leans heavily on Barbara Auerbach, George Sexton, Franklin Farrow, and Robert Lawson, *Work in American Prisons, the Private Sector Gets Involved* (Washington, D.C.: National Institute of Justice, 1988).

63. United States Department of Justice, *Impact of Free Venture Prison Industries upon Correctional Industries* (Philadelphia: U.S. Department of Justice, 1981).

64. Public Law 96–157, § 827, codified as 18 U.S.C. 1761 (c).

65. Auerbach et al., *Work in American Prisons*, p. 11.

66. Leslie Boellstorff, "Private Industry Goes to Prison," *Corrections Compendium* 13 (1988): 1–8.

67. *Correctional Services News* 8 (March 1983): 1–8.

68. Figures cited are as of November 1988; Boellstorf, "Private Industry Goes to Prison," p. 5.

69. Ibid.

70. Pennsylvania Prison Society, "Employment Research Project," *Prison Journal* 60 (1980): 1–67.

71. Cicero Wilson, Kenneth Lenihan, and Gail Goolkasian, *Employment Services for Ex-offenders* (Washington, D.C.: U.S. Government Printing Office, 1981).

72. Barbara Bloom, "Families of Prisoners: A Valuable Resource," paper presented at the Academy of Criminal Justice Sciences, St. Louis, Mo., March 1987; Daniel Leclair, "Home Furlough Program Effects on Rates of Recidivism," *Criminal Justice and Behavior* 5 (1978): 249–59.

73. Creasie Finney Hairston, "Family Ties during Imprisonment: Do They Influence Future Criminal Activity?" *Federal Probation* 52 (1988): 48–53.

74. Anne Goetting, "Conjugal Association in Prison: Issues and Perspectives," *Crime and Delinquency* 24 (1982): 52–71.

75. Ibid.

76. Donald Johns, "Alternatives to Conjugal Visits," *Federal Probation* 35 (March 1971): 48–50.

77. Ibid., p. 49.

78. Goetting, "Conjugal Association in Prison" p. 70.

79. "Coed Prisons," *Corrections Compendium* 10 (1986): 7, 14–15.

80. Ibid.

81. D. Lipton, R. Martinson, and J. Wilks, *The Effectiveness of Correctional Treatment: A Survey of Treatment Evaluation Studies* (New York: Praeger Publishers, 1975).

82. Charles Murray and Louis Cox, *Beyond Probation: Juvenile Corrections and the Chronic Delinquent* (Beverly Hills, Calif.: Sage Publications, 1979).

83. Paul Lerman, *Community Treatment and Social Control* (Chicago: University of Chicago Press, 1975).

84. Steven Lab and John Whitehead, "An Analysis of Juvenile Correctional Treatment," *Crime and Delinquency* 34 (1988): 60–83.

85. See, generally, James Q. Wilson, " 'What Works?' Revisited: New Findings on Criminal Rehabilitation," in *Legal Process and Corrections*, N. Johnston and L. Savitz, eds. (New York: John Wiley & Sons, 1982).

86. Elliott Currie, *Confronting Crime: An American Challenge* (New York: Pantheon, 1985).

87. For an analysis of the early identification of serious offenders, see Todd Clear, "Statistical Prediction in Corrections," *Research in Corrections* (a publication of the National Institute of Corrections) 1 (1988): 1–41.

88. See, for example, Carol Garrett, "Effects of Residential Treatment on Adjudicated Delinquents: A Meta-Analysis," *Journal of Research in Crime and Delinquency* 22 (1985): 287–308.

89. Thomas Coughlin, "New York State Innovates in Prison Programming," *Corrections Today* 47 (1985): 68–74.

90. "Ohio Making Special Effort to Link Inmate Training and Jobs," *Criminal Justice Newsletter*, 1 September 1988, pp. 5–6.

91. Patricia Phelps Schupple and and H. David Jenkins, "Maryland's Division of Correction, Forming Partnerships for the Future," *Corrections Today* 50 (1988): 110–12.

92. Paul Keve, *Prison Life and Human Worth* (Minneapolis: University of Minnesota Press, 1974).

93. Emily Herrick, "Number of COs Up 25 Percent in Two Years," *Corrections Compendium* 13 (1988): 9–21.

94. Ibid., p. 9.

95. Lucien X. Lombardo, *Guards Imprisoned* (New York: Elsevier, 1981); James Jacobs and Norma Crotty, "The Guard's World," in Jacobs, *New Perspectives on Prisons and Imprisonment*, pp. 133–41.

96. David Duffee, *Corrections: Practice and Policy* (New York: Random House, 1989), p. 401.

97. John Klofas and Hans Toch, "The Guard Subculture Myth," *Journal of Research in Crime and Delinquency* 19 (1982): 238–54.

98. Peter Horne, "Female Correction Officers," *Federal Probation* 49 (1985): 46–55.

99. 433 U.S. 321, 97 S.Ct. 2720, 55 L.Ed.2d 786 (1977).

100. Horne, "Female Correction Officers," p. 53.

101. Robert Wicks, *Guard! Society's Professional Prisoner* (Houston: Gulf Publishing, 1980).

102. Duffee, *Corrections: Practice and Policy* p. 305.

103. "Prison Violence Survey," *Corrections Compendium* 10 (1986): 11.

104. For a series of papers on the position, see A. Cohen, G. Cole, and R. Bailey, eds., *Prison Violence* (Lexington, Mass.: Lexington Books, 1976).

105. See Hans Toch, "Social Climate and Prison Violence," *Federal Probation* 42 (1978): 21–23.

106. Charles Silberman, *Criminal Violence, Criminal Justice* (New York: Vintage Books, 1978).

107. Toch, "Social Climate and Prison Violence," p. 21.

108. Robert Freeman, Simon Dinitz, and John Conrad, "A Look at the Dangerous Offender and Society's Efforts to Control Him," *American Journal of Corrections* (January 1977): 30.

109. Toch, "Social Climate and Prison Violence," p. 23.

110. Lee Bowker, *Prison Victimization* (New York: Elsevier Books, 1980).

111. Daniel Lockwood, *Prison Sexual Violence* (New York: Elsevier, 1980).

112. Edith Flynn, "From Conflict Theory to Conflict Resolution: Controlling Collective Violence in Prison," *American Behavioral Scientist* 23 (1980): 745–76.

113. Michael Serrill and Peter Katel, "The Anatomy of a Riot: The Facts behind New Mexico's Bloody Ordeal," *Corrections Magazine* 6 (1980): 6–24.

114. "Reported Riots/Disturbances," *Corrections Compendium* 10 (1986): 13.

115. Cited in G. McCain, V. Cox, and P. Paulus, *The Effect of Prison Crowding on Inmate Behavior* (Washington, D.C.: U.S. Government Printing Office, 1981), p. vi.

116. Paul Paulus, V. Cox, G. McCain, and J. Chandler, "Some Effects of Crowding in a Prison Environment," *Journal of Applied Social Psychology* 5 (1975): 86–91.

117. E. I. Megargee, "The Association of Population Density, Reduced Space, and Uncomfortable Temperatures with Misconduct in a Prison Community," *American Journal of Community Psychology* 5 (1977): 289–98.

118. P. L. Nacci, H. Teitelbaum, and J. Prather, "Population Density and Inmate Misconduct Rates in the Federal Prison System," *Federal Probation* 41 (1977): 26–31.

119. D. D'Atri, "Psychophysiological Response to Crowding," *Environment and Behavior* 7 (1975): 237–52; D. D'Atri and A. Ostfeld, "Crowding: Its Effects on the Elevation of Blood Pressure in a Prison Setting," *Preventative Medicine* 4 (1975): 550–66; J. Freedman, *Crowding and Behavior* (San Francisco: W. H. Freeman, 1975); David Farrington and Christopher Nuttall, "Prison Size, Overcrowding, Prison Violence, and Recidivism," *Journal of Criminal Justice* 8 (1980): 221–31.

120. *Price v. Johnson*, 334 U.S. 266, 68 S.Ct. 1049, 92 L.Ed. 1356 (1948).

121. National Advisory Commission on Criminal Justice Standards and Goals, *Corrections* (Washington, D.C.: U.S. Government Printing Office, 1973, p. 18.

122. 378 U.S. 546, 84 S.Ct. 1733, 12 L.Ed.2d 1030 (1964).

123. James B. Jacobs, "The Prisoners' Rights Movement and Its Impacts, 1960–1980," in *Crime and Justice*, vol. 2, Norval Morris and Michael Tonry, eds. (Chicago: University of Chicago Press, 1980), p. 434.

124. 312 U.S. 546, 61 S.Ct. 640, 85 L.Ed. 1034 (1941).

125. 393 U.S. 483, 89 S.Ct. 747, 21 L.Ed.2d 718 (1969).

126. 855 F.2d 442 (7th Cir. 1988).

127. 776 F.2d 851 (9th Cir. 1985).

128. 461 U.S. 30, 103 S.Ct. 1625, 75 L.Ed.2d 632 (1983).

129. 430 U.S. 817, 97 S.Ct. 1491, 52 L.Ed.2d 72 (1977).

130. 482 U.S. 78, 107 S.Ct. 2254, 96 L.Ed.2d 64 (1987) at 2261.

131. 768 F.2d 287 (8th Cir. 1985).

132. 639 F.2d 559 (10th Cir. 1980).

133. 416 U.S. 396, 94 S.Ct. 1800, 40 L.Ed.2d 224 (1974).

134. 451 F.2d 545 (1st Cir. 1971); see also, *Washington Post Co. v. Kleindienst* 494 F.2d 997 (D.C. Cir. 1974).

135. 417 U.S. 843, 94 S.Ct. 2811, 41 L.Ed. 2d 514 (1974); see also *Pell v. Procunier* 417 U.S. 817, 94 S.Ct. 2800, 41 L.Ed.2d 495 (1974).

136. 857 F.2d 1055 (5th Cir. 1988).

137. 107 S.Ct. 2400 (1987).

138. 626 F.Supp. 886 (W.D. Tenn. 1986).

139. 769 F.2d 345 (6th Cir. 1985).

140. 405 U.S. 319, 92 S.Ct. 1079, 31 L.Ed.2d 263 (1972).

141. 527 F.2d 492 (2d Cir. 1975).

142. 586 F.2d 22 (7th Cir. 1978).

143. 516 F.Supp. 1004 (E.D. Va. 1981).

144. 349 F.Supp. 278 (M.D. Ala. 1972).

145. 429 U.S. 97, 97 S.Ct. 285, 50 L.Ed.2d 251 (1976).

146. 429 U.S. 97, 97 S.Ct. 285 at 291, 50 L.Ed.2d 251 (1976).

147. *Trop v. Dulles*, 356 U.S. 86, 78 S.Ct. 590, 2 L.Ed.2d 630 (1958); see also *Furman v. Georgia*, 408 U.S. 238, 92 S.Ct. 2726, 33 L.Ed.2d 346 (1972).

148. *Weems v. United States*, 217 U.S. 349, 30 S.Ct. 544, 54 L.Ed. 793 (1910).

149. *Lee v. Tahash*, 352 F.2d 970 (8th Cir. 1965).

150. 404 F.2d 571 (8th Cir. 1968).

151. 309 F.Sup. 362 (Ed.D. Ark, 1970); aff'd, 442 F.2d 304 (8th Cir. 1971).

152. 74–329 (E.D. Tex.) 1980.

153. Geoffrey Alpert, Ben Crouch, C. Ronald Huff, "Prison Reform by Judicial Decree: The Unintended Consequences of Ruiz v. Estelle," *Justice System Journal* 9 (1984): 291–305.

154. Fred Cohen, "The Law of Prisoners' Rights: An Overview," *Criminal Law Bulletin* 24 (1988): 321–50, at 322.

155. *Battle v. Anderson*, 447 F.Supp. 576 (1977); see also *Pugh v. Locke*, 406 F.Supp. 318 (M.D. Ala. 1976); *Palmigano v. Garrahy*, 443 F.Supp. 956 (D. R.I. 1977): *Jones v. Wittenberg*, 73 F.R.D. 82 (N.D. Ohio 1976).

156. 573 F.2d 118 (1979).

157. 441 U.S. 420, 99 S.Ct. 1861, 60 L.Ed.2d 447 (1979); see "*Bell v. Wolfish*: The Rights of Pretrial Detainees," *New England Journal of Prison Law* 6 (1979): 134.

158. 452 U.S. 337, 101 S.Ct. 2392, 69 L.Ed.2d. 59 (1981). For further analysis of *Rhodes*, see Randall Pooler, "Prison Overcrowding and the Eighth Amendment: The *Rhodes* Not Taken," *New England Journal on Criminal and Civil Confinement* 8 (1983): 1–28.

159. Bureau of Justice Statistics, *Data Report, 1987* (Washington, D.C.: Bureau of Justice Statistics, 1988), p. 60.

160. G. Larry Mays and William Taggart, "The Impact of Litigation on Changing New Mexico Prison Conditions," *The Prison Journal* 65 (1985): 38–53; see also Columbus Hopper, "The Impact of Litigation on Mississippi's Prison System," *The Prison Journal* 65 (1985): 54–63.

161. 474 U.S. 327, 106 S.Ct. 662, 88 L.Ed. 2d 662 (1986).

162. *Davidson v. Cannon*, 474 U.S. 355, 106 S.Ct. 662, 88 L.Ed.2d 662 (1986).

163. 468 U.S. 517, 104 S.Ct. 3194, 82 L.Ed.2d 393 (1984).

164. *Meachum v. Fano*, 427 U.S. 215, 96 S.Ct. 2532, 49 L.Ed.2d 451 (1976).

165. *Moody v. Daggett*, 429 U.S. 78, 97 S.Ct. 274, 50 L.Ed.2d 236 (1976).

166. *Hewitt v. Helms*, 459 U.S. 460, 103 S.Ct. 864, 74 L.Ed.2d 675 (1983).

167. *Whitley v. Albers*, 475 U.S. 312, 106 S.Ct. 1078, 89 L.Ed.2d 251 (1986).

168. *Superintendent v. Hill*, 472 U.S. 445, 105 S.Ct. 2768, 86 L.Ed.2d 356 (1985).

169. Kentucky Dept. of Corrections v. Thompson, No. 87-1815 (1989); Thornburgh v. Abbott No. 87-1344 (1989).

170. Cohen, "The Law of Prisoners' Rights: An Overview," p. 349.

Part Four

Corrections

■

18

Returning to Society

At the expiration of their prison term, most inmates return to society and try to resume life on the "outside." In some cases their reintegration into society comes by way of parole, the planned community release and supervision of incarcerated offenders prior to the actual expiration of their prison sentences. In states that have eliminated parole, offenders are released after having served their sentence less time off for good behavior and other credits designed to reduce their term of incarceration. In a few instances inmates are released after their sentence has been commuted by a board of pardons or directly by a state governor or even by the president of the United States. In addition, about 15 percent of prison inmates are released after serving their entire maximum sentence without any time excused or forgiven.[1] Regardless of the method of their release, former inmates face the formidable task of having to readjust to society. This means regaining legal rights they may have lost upon their conviction, reestablishing community and family ties, and gaining employment. After a prison stay, these goals are often difficult to achieve.

This chapter reviews the final stage of the justice system, release from prison and adjustment to society.

■ History of Prison Release

The practice of releasing inmates from prison prior to the expiration of their sentence has a long history. The term *parole* itself comes from the French word meaning "to promise," referring to the practice of releasing captured enemy soldiers if they promised not to fight again with the threat that they would be executed if recaptured.[2] The roots of early prison release, however, can be traced to one of the shifts in the history of punishment that occurred with the colonization efforts of the seventeenth century. In prior years, torture, mutilation, and death had been the standard forms of punishment for offenders convicted of a felony.[3] As early as the seventeenth century, however, it became common for English judges to spare the lives of offenders by banishing them to the new overseas colonies. In 1617 the Privy Council of the British Parliament standardized this practice by passing an order granting reprieves and stays of execution to convicts willing to be transported to the colonies. **Transportation** was viewed as an answer to labor shortages caused by war, disease, and the opening of new commercial markets.

By 1665, transportation orders were modified to include specific conditions of employment and to provide for reconsideration of punishment if the conditions were not met. For example, the offender might have returned to England before the expiration of the sentence.

In 1717 the British Parliament passed legislation creating the concept of **property in service.** Under this doctrine, control of prisoners was transferred to a contractor or shipmaster until the expiration of their sentences. When the prisoners arrived in the colonies, their services could be sold to the highest bidder. After sale, the offender's status changed from convict to **indentured servant.** Transportation quickly became the most common sentence for theft offenders.

The concept of early release and pardon underwent a series of transformations during the eighteenth century. In the American colonies, property in service had to be abandoned after the American Revolution. It was replaced in the North by European immigrant labor and a greater reliance on machinery.

In the South, the African slave system, which provided a long-term labor force and promised greater profits, proved to be a more lucrative substitute. Thereafter, Australia, established as a British colony in 1770, became the destination for most transported felons. From 1815 to 1850, large numbers of inmates were shipped to Australia to serve as indentured servants working for plantation owners, in mines, or on sheep stations.

In England, opposition to penal servitude and the deprivations associated with transportation gave rise to such organizations as the Society for the Improvement of Prison Discipline. This group asked the famous reformer **Alexander Maconochie** to investigate conditions in Australia. Maconochie condemned transportation and eventually helped end the practice. Later, when appointed director of the infamous Australian prison on Norfolk Island, Maconochie instituted reforms, such as classification and rehabilitation programs, which became models for the treatment of convicted offenders.

After Maconochie was recalled from Australia, he returned to England where his efforts led to the English Penal Servitude Act of 1853, which all but ended transportation and substituted imprisonment as a punishment. The act also made it possible to grant a **ticket-of-leave** to those who had served a sufficient portion of their prison sentence. This form of conditional release permitted former prisoners to be at large in specified areas. The conditions of their release, usually sobriety, lawful behavior, and hard work, were written on a license that the former inmates were required to carry with them at all times. Many releases violated their leave provisions, however, prompting criticism of the system. Eventually, prisoner aid society members helped supervise and care for releases.

In Ireland, *Sir Walter Crofton,* a disciple of Maconochie's reforms, liberalized Irish prisons. He instituted a mark system in which inmates could earn their ticket-of-leave by accumulating credits for good conduct and hard work in prison. Crofton also instituted a system in which private volunteers or police agents could monitor ticket-of-leave offenders in the community. Crofton's work is regarded as an early form of parole.

American Developments

In the United States, the concept of releasing inmates into the community before expiration of their sentence can be traced to the first "good-time laws," passed in New York in 1917. Today, all states have enacted statutes that enable prisoners to reduce their sentences through evidence of good behavior in prison.

In 1822 volunteers from the Philadelphia-based Society for Alleviating the Miseries of Public Prisons began to help offenders once they were released from prison. In 1851 the society appointed two agents to work with inmates discharged from Pennsylvania penal institutions. Massachusetts appointed an agent in 1845 to help released inmates obtain jobs, clothing, and transportation.

The real impetus for early release developed in the late nineteenth century when prison reformers, such as Z. R. Brockway, lobbied for passage of indeterminate sentences and advocated the rehabilitation of prisoners. Brockway became warden of the Elmira Reformatory in 1876 and succeeded in persuading New York to pass the first true indeterminate sentencing laws for adults. Using a carefully weighted screening procedure, Brockway selected "rehabilitated" offenders for early release under the supervision of citizen volunteers known as **guardians.** The guardians met with the parolees at least once a month and submitted written reports on their progress.

The parole concept spread rapidly. Ohio established the first parole agency in 1884. By 1901, as many as 20 states had instituted some type of parole agency. Parole quickly became institutionalized as the primary method of release for prison inmates.

■ Early Release Today

The practice of releasing inmates from prison before the expiration of their sentence continues today. Most inmates do not serve their entire sentence before returning to society. In fact, the average stay is usually less than half the original sentence.

A number of studies have attempted to determine the actual time inmates serve in prison. A recent national survey of sentencing practices found that inmates served about 41 percent of their original sentence behind bars. As Table 18.1 shows, those convicted of drug trafficking served the smallest percentage of their sentence (32 percent) while rapists did the most time behind bars (44 percent). The relationship between the original sentence and the actual time served can be startling: murderers who were originally sentenced to about 20 years in prison do "only" 7 years behind bars.

These data indicate that the average offender is back on the street in two years, violent offenders in three. Since most people arrested for serious felonies are under 24 years of age, and many are only teenagers, their return to society occurs while they still fall within the "peak" age for criminal activity.[4] Thus it should not come as a shock that a prison experience alone is unlikely to prevent recidivism. Inmates do too little time and are released before they are too old ("age out") to commit new crimes. One solution is to build more prison cells and incarcerate inmates for a greater portion of their sentence. An alternate approach is to devise more humane correctional treatment strategies that provide alternatives to crime.

The following sections review the administrative practices under which most inmates return to society before the completion of their prison sentence.

TABLE 18.1 ■ **Average Time Served in Prison**

Most Serious Conviction Offense	Percentage of Sentence Served in Prison	United States		75 largest counties	
		Mean Prison Sentence	Estimated Time to be Served in Prison	Mean Prison Sentence	Estimated Time to be Served in Prison
All	41%	81 mos.	33 mos.	75 mos.	31 mos.
Murder	39	221	86	220	86
Rape	44	151	66	164	72
Robbery	41	139	57	109	45
Aggravated assault	42	97	41	80	34
Burglary	41	75	31	60	25
Larceny	44	46	20	40	18
Drug trafficking	32	69	22	62	20
Other felonies	42	56	24	50	21

SOURCE: Patrick Lamgan, *Felony Sentences in State Courts* (Washington, D.C.: Bureau of Justice Statistics, 1989), p. 6.

■ Time Off for Good Behavior: "Good Time"

Most inmates do not serve their full sentence because they are awarded time off for good behavior or "good time." An inmate can accumulate **good-time credit** today in both the state and federal prison systems by obeying prison rules and/or by performing meritorious service such as volunteering for medical experiments, donating blood, or attending academic and/or vocational training programs.

The first good-time laws were passed in New York State in 1817 to reduce the overcrowding at Newgate Prison. Good-time laws permitted inmates a reduction of up to 25 percent of their sentence if they were first-time offenders who had worked hard and accumulated at least $15 while in prison.[5] The concept was spread by prison administrators who believed that rewards would control an inmate's behavior more effectively than punishments. In addition, the use of rewards for good behavior reflects the philosophy of the early reformers who worked throughout the nineteenth and early twentieth centuries to rehabilitate and reintegrate the offender into the community prior to the completion of the entire sentence.

Today, each correctional jurisdiction has its own method of dispensing good time. In about 20 states, all of which have indeterminate sentencing statutes, good-time credits are deducted from both the minimum and maximum terms. In other jurisdictions, such as New Hampshire, credit can be deducted from the maximum term only.[6]

The amount of good time granted an inmate also varies among jurisdictions. Some states allow good time on a flat basis per month or per year. This would mean, for example, that all eligible inmates would receive a reduction of three months per year during the period of their incarceration. Other states grant good time at an increasing rate for each additional year served. Thus, the offender would receive a reduction of two months for the first year served, three months for the second year, four months for the third, and so on. Still other states allow good time based solely on a rate determined by the length of the sentence: for a sentence of one to two years, allowable good time would be six days per month; for a sentence of four to six years, the inmate would be allowed seven days per month and so on. In some states that have adopted determinate sentencing statutes, such as California, as much as one-half of the inmate's sentence may be reduced by good time.

In most jurisdictions, the good-time allowance is applicable only to the time the inmate is incarcerated in a penal institution. In many instances, inmates do not receive credit for time spent in jail awaiting trial, in mental institutions pending psychiatric examinations, or while incarcerated pending an appeal. In *McGinnis v. Royster* (1973), the U.S. Supreme Court upheld the constitutionality of a New York correction law that did not require jail detention time to be counted for good-time credits when the inmate was transferred to a state prison.[7] The Court reasoned that the purposes of pretrial and posttrial incarceration differ and that offenders awaiting trial in jail should not be granted good-time credits because they are not yet participating in any state rehabilitation program. On the other hand, good-time programs exist not only to rehabilitate offenders but also to control and discipline them; why, then, should a defendant receive credit for prison time but not for the time spent in custody prior to sentencing or pending an appeal after the sentence has been imposed? This inconsistent logic has resulted in a haphazard approach to the development of statutory programs dealing with good-time credit.

Losing Good-Time Credits

Once good-time credit is gained, it can be forfeited. State and federal statutes that allow for good time include provisions governing the amounts of time that they may be lost, and by what methods. Ordinarily, the warden or superintendent of the institution, in conjunction with other prison officials, administers good-time credit programs. For minor prison infractions, the inmate may lose a month of good time; for serious violations of rules, such as an attempted escape, an inmate may lose all credit accumulated since incarceration.

Correctional authorities may not reduce good time because of institutional misconduct without giving the inmates the opportunity to defend themselves against the charges. The **procedural rights** accorded to inmates have varied from case to case and jurisdiction to jurisdiction; the following are some of the principal rights:

1. The right to notice of the nature of the complaint
2. The right to a fair hearing before an impartial official or panel
3. The right to an administrative review of the decision
4. The right to confront witnesses
5. The right to counsel or counsel substitute

In some cases, prisoners have been granted rights in excess of these; in others, the courts have taken a more restricted view.

In 1974 in *Wolff v. McDonnell*, the U.S. Supreme Court established the precise constitutional safeguards required at a disciplinary proceeding.[8] *Wolff* was a landmark decision because it recognized that inmates suffer a significant loss when their good time is eliminated and that they have the right to defend their accumulated release time benefits. This decision is highlighted in the Law in Review on page 597.

■ Parole

Most correctional administrations allow inmates to become eligible for parole after completing their minimum sentence less good time. Parole is considered a way of completing a prison sentence in the community under the supervision of the correctional authorities. It is not the same as a pardon; paroled offenders can be legally recalled to serve the remainder of their sentence in an institution if the parole authorities deem their adjustment inadequate or if they commit another crime while on parole.

The decision to parole is governed by statutory requirements and usually involves completion of a minimum sentence. In about 40 percent of all prison release decisions, parole is granted by a **parole board,** a duly constituted body of men and women whose task it is to review inmate cases and determine whether an offender has reached a rehabilitative level sufficient to deal with the outside world. The board also dictates the specific parole rules a parolee must obey.

Once community release has begun, the parolee is supervised by a trained staff of **parole officers,** who help with the parolee's adjustment to the community, help in the search for employment, and monitor the parolee's behavior and activities to ensure that he or she conforms to the conditions of parole.

Parolees are subject to a strict standardized and/or personalized set of rules that guide their behavior and set limits on their activities. If these rules are violated at anytime, the parolee can be returned to the institution to serve the

Wolff v. McDonnell (1974)

FACTS

In July 1970, Robert McDonnell, on behalf of himself and other inmates of the Nebraska Penal and Correctional Complex in Lincoln, Nebraska, filed a complaint in the form of a civil rights action under 42 U.S.C. § 1983 challenging as unconstitutional several of the practices in effect at the complex. In particular, McDonnell claimed that disciplinary proceedings did not comply with the due process clause of the U.S. Constitution, that the inmate legal assistance program did not meet constitutional standards, and that the regulations governing the inspection of inmates' mail to and from attorneys were unconstitutionally restrictive.

The U.S. Supreme Court granted the petition for a writ of certiorari because the case involved important issues dealing with the management of a state prison.

McDonnell requested relief in the form of the restoration of good-time credits, the development of a plan by the prison for hearing procedure in connection with good time, and damages for the deprivation of civil rights.

DECISION

In a 6 to 3 decision, the U.S. Supreme Court held that the due process clause of the Fourteenth Amendment provides inmates with procedural protections if they are facing a loss of good time or confinement because of an institutional disciplinary action. The Court ruled that a prisoner is not completely stripped of constitutional safeguards in prison. Even though prison disciplinary proceedings do not necessitate the full range of rights due a defendant in a criminal trial, such proceedings must be governed by an accommodation between prison needs and constitutional rights. Since prisoners under Nebraska law can only lose good-time credits if they are guilty of serious misconduct, the procedure for determining when this should occur requires due process of law.

In accommodating the interests of the state of Nebraska with those of the inmate, the Court concluded that due process requires the following in prison disciplinary proceedings for serious violations of conduct:

1. Advance written notice of the charges must be given to the inmate no less than 24 hours before the prisoner's appearance at the disciplinary committee hearing.
2. There must be a written statement by the factfinders listing the evidence relied on and the reasons for the disciplinary action.
3. The inmate should be allowed to call witnesses and present documentary evidence in his or her defense if this will not jeopardize institutional control.
4. The inmate has no constitutional right to confrontation and cross-examination in prison discipline proceedings.
5. Inmates have no right to retained or appointed counsel, although substitute counsel, such as a staff member or another inmate, may be provided in certain cases.
6. The record in this case did not show if the Adjustment Committee in the Nebraska Complex was impartial, but the inmate has the right to have an impartial group conduct disciplinary hearings.
7. In regard to regulations governing inmate mail, the Court held that the state may require that mail from an attorney to a prisoner be identified as such and that the attorney's name and address appear on the communication. In addition, as a protection against contraband, prison authorities may open mail in the inmate's presence.

In its decision, the Supreme Court rejected the state of Nebraska's assertion that disciplinary action against inmates is a matter of policy that raises no constitutional issues. At the same time, the Court did not adopt the prisoner's view that the full range of due process procedures should apply to disciplinary actions within an institutional setting. Instead, the Court addressed itself to the range of procedures applicable to a correctional institution.

SIGNIFICANCE OF THE CASE

Although the Court was faced with three major issues in this case (the adequacy of legal assistance, the confidentiality of the mail, and the loss of good time or confinement for prison infractions), primary emphasis was placed on the issue of procedural due process for prison misconduct. It represented a major breakthrough in the establishment of due process guidelines in prison disciplinary proceedings that will affect the practices of state and federal prison systems. On the other hand, the Court recognized the violent nature of the prison setting and did not want to restrict the ability of correctional administrators to ensure the safety of their prisons. Thus, the Court sought a formula that maintained both prison security and provided constitutional safeguards. As a result, disciplinary action against an inmate for a serious infraction resulting in loss of good-time credits or confinement must be accompanied by due process of law. ■

remainder of the sentence; this is known as a **technical parole violation.** Parole can also be revoked if the parolee commits a second offense while in the community. The offender may even be tried and sentenced for this subsequent crime.

Parole is generally viewed as a privilege granted to deserving inmates on the basis of their good behavior while in prison. There are two conflicting sides to parole, however. On one hand, the paroled offender is allowed to serve part of the sentence in the community, an obvious benefit for the deserving offender. On the other hand, since parole is a "privilege and not a right," the parolee is viewed as a dangerous criminal who must be carefully watched and supervised. The conflict between the treatment and enforcement aspects of parolee has not yet been reconciled by the criminal justice system, and the parole process still contains elements of both orientations.

In recent years the nation's parole system has come under increasing criticism from those who believe that it is both inherently unfair to inmates and that it fails to protect the public. The trend toward determinate and mandatory sentences has limited the attractiveness of parole and restricted the discretion of parole boards. The movement to abolish parole will be reviewed later in this chapter.

The Extent of Parole

According to the most recent statistics, approximately 362,192 adults are on parole in the United States.[9] In a given year (1987) about 240,000 people were newly released on parole, and about 204,000 parolees terminated their supervision, resulting in an increase of about 11 percent in the parole population.

The number of people on parole in a state is usually a function of the size of its prison population. For example, Texas, which has a relatively high prison population, has 57 people on parole per 10,000 population, while New Hampshire, with a relatively low prison population, has only 8 per 10,000 population on parole. However, some states, such as Louisiana, place few people on parole even though they have relatively high prison populations.

About 40 percent of those placed on parole in the United States were released at the discretion of correctional authorities. Another 31 percent were mandatory parole releasees, inmates whose discharge was required by determinate sentencing statutes or good-time reductions but whose release was still supervised by parole authorities. If they violate the conditions of their release, mandatory releasees can have their good time revoked and be returned to the institution to serve the remainder of their unexpired term. The remaining inmates were released for a variety of reasons, including expiration of their term, commutation of their sentence, and court orders to relieve overcrowded prisons.

There is little question that the movement to create mandatory and determinate sentencing statutes has had a significant impact on parole. The number of people leaving prison via parole has declined substantially in the past few years. Whereas at one time more than 70 percent of releasees were paroled, the number has declined to 40 percent; conversely, mandatory releases have increased from about 6 percent in the late 1970s to 30 percent today. Almost all the mandatory parole releases come from jurisdictions that rely heavily on determinate sentences: California, Illinois, Indiana, Texas, and New York. As various forms of determinate sentencing are adopted around the country, it is likely that the gap between the two forms of release will narrow further.

The Parole Board

In states that retain indeterminate sentences, the authority to grant parole is usually vested in the parole board. The American Correctional Association has suggested that state boards have four primary functions:

1. To select and place prisoners on parole
2. To aid, supervise, and provide continuing control of parolees in the community
3. To determine when the parole function is completed and discharge the parolee from parole
4. To determine whether parole revocation should take place if parole conditions are violated.[10]

As far as organization is concerned, there are three parole board models: boards that operate as independent agencies; boards that are part of corrections departments; and boards that are consolidated with corrections departments but act as independent agencies.[11]

Most state boards are relatively small, usually numbering under 10 individuals. Their size, coupled with their large caseloads and the varied activities they are expected to perform, can prevent board members from becoming as well acquainted with the individual inmate as might be desired. Advocates for locating the board within the department of corrections usually cite improved communications and the availability of more intimate knowledge about offenders as justifications for such an administrative arrangement. Vincent O'Leary and Joan Nuffield point out, however, that consolidated agencies may give more consideration to institutional needs than to those of the offender or the community.[12]

Nevertheless, O'Leary and Nuffield believe that a consolidated parole board structure may be the most appropriate type of organization, because it combines features of autonomy with the sensitivity to institutional activity that comes with being part of the correctional system.[13]

The manner in which parole board members are appointed differs from state to state. In most jurisdictions that use parole, governors are the appointing authorities; in a few jurisdictions, parole board members are chosen from civil service lists; and in the remaining jurisdictions, they are appointed by the commissioner of corrections or the governor and the governor's cabinet from

In states that retain indeterminate sentences, the authority to grant parole is usually vested in the parole board.

Prisoners have certain rights which ensure due process of law including the right to a hearing on the question of their release on parole. Here Sirhan Sirhan, the convicted assassin of Robert F. Kennedy, appears before the parole board. Sometimes the board will refuse to parole notorious criminals. Sirhan Sirhan has remained in prison for more than twenty years.

a prepared list.[14] Terms of appointment also tend to vary; depending on the jurisdiction, they range from a life term (4 states) to a term of two years (1 state; the average term is six years (16 states).[15]

Parole Hearings

The actual parole decision is made at a **parole grant hearing.** At this time the full board or a selected subcommittee reviews information, may meet with the offender, and then decides whether the parole applicant has a reasonable probability of succeeding outside prison. Candidates for parole may be chosen by statutory eligibility on the basis of time served in relation to their sentences. In most jurisdictions, the minimum sentence and accumulated good time regulates eligibility for parole; when no minimum sentence has been imposed, parole eligibility is based on the policy of the board and/or the corrections department.

Each parole board meets in a unique way and has its own administrative setup for reviewing cases. In some jurisdictions, the entire board meets with the applicant; in others only a few members are required to be present. In a number of jurisdictions, a single board member can conduct a personal investigation and submit the findings to the full board for a decision.

No specific national policy exists to govern the way in which inmates are informed of the board's decision. In some jurisdictions, the inmate is informed in writing by the board following the decision. A recent trend has been for the parole board to confront the offender with its decision immediately after the hearing. It is believed that this policy can give the offender a sense of participation in the correctional process and may also increase his or her perceptions of its fairness. By speaking directly to the applicant, the board can also indicate the specific types of behavior and behavior changes it expects to see if the inmate is to eventually qualify for or effectively serve parole.[16]

The inmate's specific rights at a parole grant hearing also vary from jurisdiction to jurisdiction. Approximately 20 states allow the inmate to have counsel, and 20 states also allow the inmate to present witnesses on his or her behalf; in other jurisdictions these privileges are not permitted. Because the federal courts have declared that the parole applicant is not entitled to any form of legal representation, the individual inmate may have to pay for legal services where this privilege is allowed.[17]

In almost all parole-granting jurisdictions, the reasons for the parole decision must be given in writing, while in about half the jurisdictions a verbatim record of the hearing is made.[18]

Presumptive Parole Dates

A new approach to selecting inmates for parole involves the **presumptive parole date.**[19] This procedure employs relevant information such as the seriousness of the offense and prior record of recidivism to determine when an inmate will be eligible for parole. The offender is notified of the presumed release date within a short period, about 120 days, after the start of his or her prison term. The prisoner's term may be extended for serious disciplinary infractions such as escape attempts. Similarly, parole release can be moved up if the inmate shows evidence of a superior record in prison rehabilitation programs.

Rather than being dependent on the whims of a parole board, inmates know that unless they misbehave in prison, they will be released in a set number of years or months. Correctional experts believe this method will cut down on prison misbehavior since inmates will be reluctant to lose a parole date they already know they have achieved.

About 15 states use **parole guidelines** to structure the release decision.[20] Parole guidelines are similar to those used in the sentencing and bail decisions. They employ a series of behavior categories and classify inmates on the basis of their personal characteristics. Typically, such factors as prior history of drug use, prior record, type of crime, and age at conviction are considered. Inmates who have positive profiles are considered better risks than those with negative scores and are therefore more likely to receive an early release recommendation.

In some jurisdictions such as Florida, parole guidelines are mandatory, while in other states such as Missouri and Oregon, their use is suggested as a systemwide policy.[21]

An analysis of presumptive parole dates and parole guidelines by Barbara Stone-Meierhoefer found that inmates with presumptive parole dates actually presented fewer disciplinary problems than inmates whose parole date was set at the normal time (after one-third of their sentence had elapsed).[22] Other differences, such as participation in prison treatment programs, were negligible. Some jurisdictions have been dissatisfied with the practice of removing discretion from parole boards, and one state, Colorado, recently initiated legislation that restored decision-making power to the board (Colorado is also developing guidelines to aid decision making).[23]

Due Process at Parole Grant Hearings

As noted previously, the due process rights of inmates at parole grant hearings vary widely. Some jurisdictions provide for counsel, allow witnesses and personal appearances, give reasons for decisions in writing, and allow appeals, whereas others provide none or only a few of these privileges.

The U.S. Supreme Court has considered the question of whether inmates are entitled to due process at parole grant hearings in two important cases, *Greenholtz v. Inmates of the Nebraska Penal and Correctional Complex* (1979)[24] and *Connecticut Board of Pardons v. Dumschat* (1981).[25] In *Greenholtz*, the Court held that early release on parole was a privilege and not a right and that this act of "grace" did not entitle inmates to receive a full complement of due process rights (under the Fifth and Fourteenth Amendments) at a parole hearing (for example, to have counsel or to call witnesses).

Thus, the Court suggested that an inmate does not have a right to due process merely because a state provides a possibility of parole. In this instance parole is only a "mere hope," and this hearing is therefore distinguishable from a proceeding for the revocation of parole (see the discussion of parole revocation later in this chapter). However, if the language of a particular state statute creates an "expectancy" of release, for example, by ordering parole for all inmates except those who violate prison rules, then inmates in that state have the right to due process at parole grant hearings.[26]

In *Dumschat* the Supreme Court considered whether the fact that the Connecticut Board of Pardons granted 75 percent of the applications it received for the commutation of life sentences created a "liberty interest" that entitled an inmate to written reasons if his or her request for an early parole date was turned down. The Court ruled that an inmate has only a "mere hope" of parole or pardon and therefore should not expect due process rights. The Court went on to state:

> No matter how frequently a particular form of clemency has been granted, the statistical probabilities standing alone generate no constitutional protections; a contrary conclusion would trivialize the Constitution. The ground for a constitutional claim, if any, must be found in statutes or other rules defining the obligations of the authority charged with exercising clemency.[27]

Thus, the Supreme Court has acted to limit the inmate's right at parole grant hearings.

Parole Board Discretion

A current trend in corrections is to fix release dates as part of determinate sentencing statutes. However, in states that retain parole, the decision to release an inmate into the community is a function of parole board discretion.

Parole board members meet regularly together or in subgroups to review cases of inmates who have met the statutory requirements for parole and are eligible for release. In deciding whether to grant parole, the state or federal board must take into account many important factors, some of which are discussed below.

Of primary concern to the board is whether the inmate can make an adequate adjustment to the community and refrain from further criminal activity. For example, the board must decide if it is the proper time to release

Sometimes a decision to grant parole meets with public opposition. One instance of this occurred in 1984 when demonstrators marched in San Francisco, California, to protest the parole of Dan White, who served five years in a Los Angeles prison for killing San Francisco mayor George Moscone and city supervisor Harvey Milk in 1979. Soon after his release, White committed suicide.

the offender or whether continued confinement will be beneficial. Parole board members whose primary concern is the protection of the community might argue that longer prison sentences help deter crime through incapacitation and at the same time increase the offender's awareness that the parole agency is a no-nonsense organization whose wishes must be respected. Other board members may be more concerned with the potential harm that continuation of a prison sentence might cause the inmate. Regardless of their orientation, most parole board members realize that the consequences of their decision can jeopardize the state's parole program if a too-hasty release turns out to have disastrous results for the community.[28]

Parole board members may also be concerned with the inherent justice and morality of their decision: Has the offender paid a debt to society? Should consideration be given to the victims of crime (or potential victims)? Should revenge be a motive for denying parole? The board members may also ponder the fairness of releasing one inmate into the community while returning another who has committed the same crime and has served the same amount of time.

Another consideration influencing the board's decision may be the condition and welfare of the prisoner's family. The family of a married man left on their own while the man is imprisoned may become wards of the state, receive public assistance, and have members placed in foster homes. As a result, his incarceration becomes a triple financial burden on the state and includes (1) the cost of imprisonment, (2) the cost of welfare and child support for his family, and (3) the lost tax dollars and revenue that would be acquired if the inmate were productively employed while on parole. Furthermore, the economic, social, and psychological burdens of having a family member incarcerated may help push other members of the family into crime. In the case of the female offender, the board may take into account the fact that she is a mother or has other dependents. Such considerations may work against the unmarried offender who has no dependents; again, the issue of fairness comes up.

Parole board members also base their decision on their perceptions of the values and attitudes of correctional personnel and other administrators of the criminal justice system. For example, if the parole board plans to release an inmate who has received a negative disciplinary report from prison authorities, its action may serve to notify other inmates that prison rules need not be taken seriously. A decision to parole a particular inmate must thus be balanced with the need to maintain a cordial working relationship with prison and correctional authorities. Early parole decisions may also be viewed with disappointment by judicial authorities within the state. If parole board and judicial attitudes are not similar, some judges may counteract the policies of the parole board by setting high minimum sentences where the statutory law allows them that discretion. Thus, consideration of the responses of criminal justice system personnel may influence the parole board members' decision to grant or deny parole or to set specialized and stringent conditions on parolees.[29]

The public's response to a parole grant may also influence the board's decision making. If, for example, a particularly well-known criminal, such as Charles Manson or Sirhan Sirhan, is up for parole, a positive finding on his behalf will receive widespread media coverage and possibly generate irate responses from the public. Conversely, in the case of public figures with well-defined sympathetic followings, such as battered women who kill their abusive spouses, the board may be swayed in a more lenient direction.[30]

Suing the Parole Board

Parole board members may also be influenced by their concern for the behavior of inmates in the outside world. It is possible that individual board members may be sued if they release an offender who injures someone. Traditionally, courts have ruled that parole board members have immunity for the actions of people they release. For example, in one Virginia case a 16-year-old offender was released after eight months in an institution although he could have been incarcerated for another five years. Three months after his release, he killed a robbery victim. The Virginia Supreme Court ruled that in their decision to discharge him, the correctional employees were (1) performing judicial functions, (2) within their jurisdiction, and (3) acting in good faith. After weighing the interests of the parolee and the state, the court concluded that it was a discretionary function and that the officials were immune from a lawsuit.[31]

The parole board's traditional immunity may be eroding, however. In an important case *Tarter v. State of New York*, the New York Supreme Court held that the parole board members could be sued if they failed to consider certain factors and criteria mandated by the New York parole guidelines. The court ruled that the decisions of the parole board amounted to carrying out government rules and standards in a prescribed manner and did not allow for personal discretion. In the case at hand, a person was rendered a paraplegic after being shot by a parolee who had been released after serving the minimum time for a crime that was identical to another for which he had been imprisoned four years earlier. The court ruled that the victim could challenge in court whether the rules and standards had been applied properly. Since no discretion was involved, there was no immunity from a lawsuit. The New York case may be the first to lift the mantle of immunity from parole board members and make them liable for the outcome of their decisions.[32]

Parole Rules

Before release into the community, a parolee is supplied with a standard set of rules and conditions that must be obeyed and conformed to. As with probation (see Chapter 14), the offender who violates these rules may have parole revoked and be processed back into the institution to serve the remainder of the sentence.

Parole rules may curtail or prohibit certain types of behavior while encouraging or demanding others. Some rules tend to be so moralistic or technical in nature that they severely inhibit the parolee's ability to adjust to society. By making life unnecessarily unpleasant without contributing to rehabilitation, such parole rules reflect the punitive side of community supervision. Rules such as these may prohibit marriage, ban the use of motor vehicles, or forbid the borrowing of money. Parolees must often check in and ask permission when leaving their residences, and the rules may bar them from associating with friends with criminal records, which, in some cases, severely limits their social life.

The way in which parole rules are stated, the kinds of things they forbid or encourage, and their flexibility vary among jurisdictions. Some states expressly forbid a certain type of behavior, while others will allow it with the permission of the parole officer.

Each item in the parole conditions must be obeyed lest the offender's parole be revoked for a technical violation. In addition, the parole board can impose specific conditions for a particular offender, such as demanding that the parolee receive psychiatric treatment.

A number of commentators have argued that the parole rules are sometimes so vague and restrictive that they interfere with the rehabilitation of the offender.[33] In a more recent analysis, Gray Cavender found that although rehabilitation is cited as the official goal of parole rules, operationally the control of the offender seems more important.[34]

It is apparent that parole rules must undergo modernization and standardization if they are to conform with the rehabilitative or due process framework of justice desired by the majority of criminal justice experts. As they exist today, parole rules are often vestiges of prior attempts to demean and shackle offenders, both within the institution and outside it. One controversial effort to reform standard rules has been made in Virginia where a "no read–no parole" rule is in effect. The question of whether individuals can be denied parole because they are illiterate will most likely be settled in the courts.

Parole Supervision

Once released into the community, the offender normally comes under the control of a parole officer, who enforces parole rules, helps the inmate gain employment, and meets regularly with the parolee for reasons of treatment and rehabilitation. Parole officers and their supervisors may be under the administrative control of the parole board, or they may comprise an autonomous branch of the department of corrections. In about 30 states and in the federal parole service, officers have combined caseloads of probation and parole clients.

Probation supervision and parole supervision are quite similar in some respects but differ in others. Both types of supervision attempt to help clients attain meaningful relationships in the community and use similar enforcement, counseling, and treatment skills to gain that end. However, there are some major differences between the official capacities of the two service roles.

The parole officers deal with more difficult cases. The parolee has been institutionalized for an extended period of time; to be successful on parole, the former inmate must make an adjustment to the community, which at first can seem a strange and often hostile environment. The parolee's family life has been disrupted, and he or she may find it difficult to resume employment. The paroled offender may have already been classified by probation officers (in a presentence report) as dangerous or as a poor risk for community adjustment. Furthermore, it would be overly optimistic to presume that a prison sentence substantially improves the offender's chances for rehabilitation. To overcome these roadblocks to success, the parole officer may have to play a much greater role in directing and supervising clients' lives than the probation officer. Moreover, the parole officer may have to be less flexible in accepting rule violations and may need to hold the client on a tighter rein. Richard McCleary argues that the typical parole officer is more concerned with the agency he or she works for, and with furthering his or her own career, than with the welfare of clients.[35] McCleary believes that parole officer decision making is usually based on the desire to remove from the community any offender who might be an embarrassment to the parole department. Consequently, more parolees are

Parole violations can result in a return to prison.

sent to prison for technical rule violations than for actually breaking the criminal law.

Parole supervision often begins in the institution when institutionally based agents help the inmate create a **parole plan.** This plan can include such activities as securing a promise of employment for the inmate, arranging for a residence, and developing community contacts. Often, the parole plan will require the inmate to spend time in a residential community treatment program such as a halfway house. The adequacy of the parole plan is an important element in the board's decision to grant community release.

Once in the community, a supervision program may develop in any number of ways. The parole officer may meet individually with the client or maintain contact in group sessions. Meetings may be weekly, biweekly, or monthly. The parole officer may check regularly with others who are in close, personal contact with the parolee, such as employers, teachers, neighbors, or family. Some agents may make unannounced spot checks to determine whether their clients are keeping regular hours, working steadily, and otherwise conforming to the parole contract.

To aid the supervision function, some jurisdictions are implementing systems that scientifically classify offenders on the basis of their supervision needs. Typically, these are point systems that divide parolees into three groups: (1) those who require intensive surveillance; (2) those who require social service rather than surveillance; (3) those who require limited supervision. In some jurisdictions, parolees in need of more restricted supervision may begin their term in a community correctional center or under electronic monitoring in their own home.

Returning to Prison: The Effectiveness of Parole

There is disagreement over the effectiveness of parole. It is popularly believed that recidivism rates are very high—approaching 70 percent.[36] Research efforts designed to study the effectiveness of parole systematically have produced a variety of results. For example, in one early study the National Council on Crime and Delinquency (NCCD) collected data from every adult parole authority and found that parole is actually more effective than had been believed. Their research on a sample of over 104,000 parolees indicated that success was quite high, ranging from homicide offenders (90.1 percent) to motor vehicle theft violators (64.9 percent).[37] Another NCCD survey of inmates released on parole found that after three years 12.8 percent had been returned to prison as **technical violators** and 12.3 percent had been reincarcerated for committing a new offense, a total failure rate of about 25 percent.[38] In both NCCD surveys, the relationship between commitment offense and parole success was remarkably similar. Offenders who had committed the most serious offenses were most likely to be successful on parole. Similarly, those with prior conviction records were more likely to violate parole than first offenders.

Not all research studies have found parole to be so successful, however, and today the consensus is that most released inmates are likely to recidivate. For example, Howard Sacks and Charles Logan compared parolees with inmates who were discharged outright from prison and found that after two years the recidivism rate for the parolees was 70 percent, and after three years it was 77 percent.[39] Of those simply discharged from prison, 82 percent recidivated after two years and 85 percent after three years. However, parolees who recidivated did manage to remain in the community longer (an average 12.8 months) than those who were discharged without supervision (8.3 months). Nevertheless, Sacks and Logan conclude that parole supervision has neither a long-term influence on the behavior of clients nor apparently much worth as a rehabilitation tool.

A recent federal study of 108,580 men and women released in 11 states (in 1983) found that within three years of release 63 percent had been rearrested for a felony or serious misdemeanor, 47 percent had been convicted of a new crime, and 41 percent had been sent back to prison.[40] Table 18.2 illustrates the most important findings from this survey of parole violations.

The spectre of recidivism is especially frustrating to the American public: apprehending and successfully prosecuting criminal offenders are so difficult that it seems foolish to grant them early release so they can prey upon more victims. This problem is exacerbated when the parolee is a chronic offender who has engaged in frequent and repeated criminal acts (parole for chronic offenders is discussed further in the Criminal Justice in Review on page 608).

TECHNICAL VIOLATIONS. Do many parolees return to prison because they violate the rules of parole such as failing to stay in the jurisdiction or failing to keep a job? A federal survey found that a significant number of returning parolees actually committed no new offense but were incarcerated for technical violations of parole. In some jurisdictions over 30 percent of the returnees had technical violations, and in one state more than half of the

---

TABLE 18.2 ■ **Recidivism of Parolees Released in 1983: A Six-Year Follow-up**

An estimated 68,000 of the released prisoners were rearrested and charged with more than 326,000 new felonies and serious misdemeanors, including approximately 50,000 violent offenses (of which 17,000 were robberies and 23,000 were assaults), more than 141,000 property offenses (of which 36,000 were burglaries), and 46,000 drug offenses.

Recidivism rates were highest in the first year—1 of 4 released prisoners were rearrested in the first 6 months and 2 of 5 within the first year after their release.

Approximately 5% of the prisoners had been charged with 45 or more offenses before and after their release from prison; 26% had been charged with at least 20 offenses.

More than 1 of every 8 rearrests occurred in states other than the state in which the prisoners were released.

Recidivism rates were higher among men, blacks, Hispanics, and persons who had not completed high school than among women, whites, non-Hispanics and high school graduates.

Recidivism was inversely related to the age of the prisoner at the time of release: the older the prisoner, the lower the rate of recidivism.

The more extensive a prisoner's prior arrest record, the higher the rate of recidivisim—over 74% of those with 11 or more prior arrests were rearrested, compared to 38% of the first-time offenders.

The combination of a prisoner's age when released and the number of prior adult arrests was very strongly related to recidivism: an estimated 94.1% of prisoners age 18 to 24 with 11 or more prior arrests were rearrested within 3 years.

More than 68% of the prisoners released for property offenses were rearrested within 3 years, compared to 59.6% of violent offenders, 54.6% of public-order offenders, and 50.4% of drug offenders.

Approximately 40% of the released prisoners had previously escaped from custody, been absent without leave (AWOL), or had a prior revocation of parole or probation. An estimated 73% of these prisoners were rearrested within 3 years of their release.

The amount of time served in prison did not systematically increase a prisoner's likelihood of rearrest. However, those prisoners who had served the longest, more than 5 years in prison, had lower rates of rearrest than other offenders during the followup period.

Released prisoners were often rearrested for the same type of crime for which they had served time in prison. Within 3 years, 31.9% of released burglars were rearrested for burglary; 24.8% of drug offenders were rearrested for a drug offense; and 19.6% of robbers were rearrested for robbery.

Released rapists were 10.5 times more likely than nonrapists to be rearrested for rape, and released murderers were about 5 times more likely than other offenders to be rearrested for homicide. An estimated 6.6% of released murderers were rearrested for homicide.

Nearly 1 in 3 released violent offenders and 1 in 5 released property offenders were arrested within 3 years for a violent crime following their release from prison.

SOURCE: Allen Beck and Bernard Shipley, *Recidivism of Prisoners Released in 1983* (Washington, D.C.: Bureau of Justice Statistics, 1989), pp. 1–2.

Releasing the Chronic Offender

The recent federally sponsored study of parole recidivism by Allen Beck and Bernard Shipley sheds some light on chronic offenders and the contribution they make to the overall crime problem. Beck and Shipley followed the offending careers of 108,850 inmates released in 11 states during 1983. Although their results are similar to those of other recidivism studies (62 percent of the parolees were rearrested within three years, and 41 percent returned to prison), they also developed data that help us understand the particular problems faced by chronic offenders as they attempt to readjust to society.

Table A shows the total number of arrest charges among the 108,850 inmates released in 1983. About 26 percent of the inmates had been arrested 20 or more times, and they accounted for almost 58 percent of all arrests experienced by the parolees. About 5 percent of the released inmates had been arrested 45 or more times in their lives. The total sample of inmates had been arrested 1,333,293 times before their current incarceration and 326,746 times after their release; the 1.7 million charges amount to an average of 15.3 arrests per offender since their first adult arrest.

It might seem startling to some people that inmates who have been arrested more than 15 times are still eligible for early release. How did these chronic offenders do once they were on the "outside"? As Table B shows, 82 percent of the inmates who had 16 or more prior arrests were rearrested within three years of their release. The survey found that within the first six months, released prisoners with 11 or more prior arrests were nearly four times more likely to be arrested for a new offense as those

TABLE A ■ Total Number of Arrest Charges among State Prisoners Released in 1983

Total Number of Arrest Charges	Percentage of All Released Prisoners	Cumulative Percentage of All Released Prisoners	Cumulative Percentage of All Arrest Charges
45 or more	5.0%	5.0%	19.4%
35–44	4.4	9.4	30.5
25–34	9.2	18.6	47.8
20–24	7.7	26.3	58.8
15–19	11.7	38.0	71.6
10–14	17.1	55.1	84.9
5–9	26.2	81.3	96.7
1–4	18.9	100.0	100.0

SOURCE: Allen Beck and Bernard Shipley, *Recidivism of Prisoners Released in 1983* (Washington, D.C.: Bureau of Justice Statistics, 1989).

returnees were technical violators[41] These data are supported by a study conducted by the National Center on Institutions and Alternatives (NCIA).[42] They surveyed 10 states including California, Florida, and Ohio and found that 15,400 people were incarcerated for technical parole violations, which amounted to 7 percent of the prison population; in some states technical violators made up 20 percent of the prison population.

In sum, many parolees are returned to prison for technical violations. If prison overcrowding is to be successfully dealt with, a more realistic parole violation policy may have to be developed in areas where the correctional system is under stress.

Legal Issues in Parole Revocation

Revocation proceedings in parole are similar to those in probation. When an offender violates a condition of probation or commits a new crime, the court

TABLE B ■ Rearrest Rates of State Prisoners Released in 1983, by Number of Prior Adult Arrests

Number of adult arrests prior to release	Percent of all releases	Percent of releasees who were rearrested	
		Within 3 years	Within 1 year
All released prisoners	100.0%	62.5%	39.3%
1 prior arrest	9.1	38.1	19.0
2	10.8	48.2	25.5
3	10.8	54.7	30.1
4	9.7	58.1	35.5
5	8.0	59.3	33.4
6	7.0	64.8	38.2
7–10	18.8	67.7	42.0
11–15	11.9	74.9	53.3
16 or more	14.0	82.2	61.5

SOURCE: Allen Beck and Bernard Shipley, *Recidivism of Prisoners Released in 1983* (Washington, D.C.: Bureau of Justice Statistics, 1989).

with 1 prior arrest and more than twice as likely as those with 2 or 3 prior arrests.

Other findings strongly support the conclusion that chronic offenders are not deterred by the threat or experience of punishment: those who began their offending career at a younger age (under 17) were significantly more likely to recidivate (72 percent) than offenders who were first arrested after they reached their thirtieth birthday (27 percent). In addition, those offenders who had started their career early and had 11 or more prior offenses had an 83 percent chance of being rearrested, higher than any other age and offending group (in contrast 40-year-olds with one prior offense had a 12 percent rearrest rate).

Beck and Shipley provide the following picture of the offender most likely to recidivate after a prison experience: released at age 24 or younger, more than 7 prior arrests, prior escape or revocation experience, committed robbery, burglary, or property offenses, first arrested at a relatively young age, and had a prior drug and violent crime arrest.

These data show that repeated contact with the criminal justice system has little specific deterrent effect on the chronic offender. If anything, Beck and Shipley's data suggest that the best way to reduce recidivism is to lengthen prison sentences, increase the time chronic offenders spend behind bars, and release them after they reach age 45. ■

SOURCE: Allen Beck and Bernard Shipley, *Recidivism of Prisoners Released in 1983* (Washington, D.C.: Bureau of Justice Statistics, 1989).

may revoke probation and impose a sentence of incarceration. Similarly, when a parolee violates his or her community status, the parole board has the authority to return the offender to prison.

The **parole revocation** process is almost always started by the parole officer when he or she believes that the parolee has violated a parole condition or when the parolee has been charged with a new crime. In the past, the statutory requirements and practices of parole agencies that applied once the parole officer initiated this process varied greatly. Some states provided informal hearings to determine if there was reason to believe that the parolee had violated a condition, while others held more formal revocation hearings. Few states, however, had established any minimum due process requirements. Parolees were often taken into custody and even returned to prison before any hearing was held on the violation of parole. This practice was not only unfair but resulted in undue hardships on parolees and their families.

In 1972, however, the U.S. Supreme Court caused an uproar in parole agencies throughout the nation when it handed down the landmark parole decision of *Morrissey v. Brewer*.[43] In this case the Court held that the Fourteenth Amendment requirement of due process of law applies to the parole revocation process. The Court's decision established specific due process guidelines that parole boards must follow before revoking an offender's parole. Because of its impact on the parole process, the case is summarized in the Law in Review on page 611.

Since the *Morrissey* decision, appellate courts have applied the Supreme Court's basic requirement for fairness and impartiality to various aspects of the revocation hearing process. For example, in *Drayton v. McCall* (1978), the U.S. Court of Appeals for the Second Circuit found that the due process clause mandates that certain procedural safeguards must be afforded to parolees before their community release may be rescinded.[44] The appellate court emphasized that a parolee has a right to a hearing before a detached and neutral hearing board, a right to advance written notice of charges, and a right to call witnesses. Moreover, the court expressed distress over the U.S. Parole Board's refusal of parolee Drayton's request for a lawyer to represent him at the hearing.

Nevertheless, in *Baldwin v. Benson* (1978), the Tenth Circuit Court rules that a federal parole violator lacks a statutory right to appointment of counsel at parole revocation proceedings.[45] In *Harris v. Day* (1981), a federal court ruled that a parole commission does not have to give a parolee credit against the sentence for time spent in the community.[46]

Abolish Parole?

Proponents of determinate sentencing have called for the abolition of parole. They believe that inmates should be sentenced by the trial judge to a fixed number of years and thereafter should serve their total sentence in a prison setting. Although parole would not be a release option, prisoners could in fact reduce their prison stay by amassing good-time credit. Some states (for example, California) have allowed inmates to eliminate four months of their sentence for every eight months served. Nevertheless, early release via parole would cease to exist.

The criticisms leveled against parole are threefold:

1. The procedures that control the parole granting decision are vague and are not controlled by due process considerations. Consequently, some inmates may be unfairly denied parole, while those who are undeserving may benefit.
2. It is beyond the capacity of parole authorities to predict who will make a successful adjustment on parole or to monitor parolees' behavior in the community accurately.
3. It is unjust to decide whether to release an individual from prison based on what we expect that person to do in the *future*. After all, we have no way of determining the future accurately.[47]

Above and beyond these considerations, the parole process has been criticized on the ground that it heightens the inmate's sense of injustice and powerlessness in the face of an omnipotent prison administration that has absolute control over the release date. As prison expert David Fogel suggests, "Parole board decisions are also unreviewable and are not hammered out in an adversary clash; rather they are five to fifteen minute sessions with members frequently using a combination of whim, caprice, and arbitrariness."[48]

Morrissey v. Brewer (1972)

FACTS

The petitioner, Morrissey, was convicted of falsely drawing checks in 1967 and pursuant to his guilty plea was sentenced to not more than seven years in prison. Morrissey was released on parole from the Iowa State Prison in June 1968. Seven months later, at the direction of his parole officer, he was arrested in his hometown as a parole violator and held in the county jail. One week later, after a review of the parole officer's written report, the Iowa Board of Parole revoked Morrissey's parole and returned him to prison.

Morrissey filed a writ of habeas corpus, claiming that his parole had been revoked without a hearing and that he had been deprived of his due process rights.

The parole officer's report on which the Board of Parole acted shows that the petitioner's parole was revoked on the basis of information that he had violated the conditions of parole by buying a car under an assumed name and operating it without permission, giving false statements to police concerning his address and insurance company after a minor accident, obtaining credit under an assumed name, and failing to report his place of residence to his parole officer. The report states that the officer inter-viewed Morrissey and that he could not explain why he did not contact his parole officer despite his effort to excuse this on the ground that he had been sick. Further, the report asserts that Morrissey admitted buying the car and obtaining credit under an assumed name, and also admitted being involved in the accident. The parole officer recommended that his parole be revoked because of "his continual violating of his parole rules."

DECISION

The major problem of this case had to do with the constitutionality of the parole revocation procedures. The U.S. Supreme Court was asked to decide whether due process requires that a state provide a parolee with a hearing and other safeguards before revoking parole.

1. Although the Supreme Court decided that parole revocation does not call for the full array of rights due a defendant in a criminal proceeding, a parolee's liberty involves significant values within the protection of the due process clause of the Fourteenth Amendment, and termination of that liberty requires an informal hearing to ensure that the finding of a parole violation is based on verified facts to support revocation.

2. Due process requires a reasonably prompt informal inquiry conducted by an impartial hearing officer near the place of the alleged parole violation or arrest to determine if there is reasonable ground to believe that the arrested parolee has violated a parole condition. The parolee should receive prior notice of the inquiry, its purpose, and the alleged violations. The parolee may present relevant information and question adverse informants. The hearing officer shall digest the evidence on probable cause and state the reasons for holding the parolee for the parole board's decision.

3. At the revocation hearing, which must be conducted reasonably soon after the parolee's arrest, the minimum due process requirements are (a) written notice of the claimed violations of parole; (b) a disclosure to the parolee of evidence against him or her; (c) the opportunity to be heard in person and to present witnesses and documentary evidence; (d) the right to confront and cross-examine adverse witnesses (unless the hearing officer specifically finds good cause for not allowing confrontation); (e) a "neutral and detached" hearing body such as a traditional parole board, members of which need not be judicial officers or lawyers; and (f) a written statement by the factfinders as to the evidence relied on and the reasons for revoking parole.

SIGNIFICANCE OF THE CASE

The *Morrissey* decision imposed dual procedures on state parole boards by which they are required to provide a preliminary inquiry at the time of the parolee's arrest, as well as a formal revocation hearing before termination of parole. The major issue left untouched by *Morrissey* was whether a parolee had the right to the assistance of counsel if indigent, and that was subsequently remedied in the case of *Gagnon v. Scarpelli*.

The principal effect of the *Morrissey* decision was to impose minimum procedural requirements on the parole revocation process. ■

At first it was thought that determinate sentencing statutes would spell the end of parole. At the time of this writing, however, only a few states, have *completely* eliminated *both* parole release and parole supervision though more than 10 jurisdictions including New York and the federal government have eliminated discretionary release by a parole board. A number of states that adopted determinate or presumptive sentencing models retain parole as a form of **postrelease aftercare.** California has retained parole supervision, but uses it as a one-year postrelease supervisory authority for inmates who have completed their prison sentences. Monitored by the Board of Prison Terms, released inmates can have up to one year of their good time revoked for behavioral indiscretions and therefore be returned to prison; under a similar arrangement in Indiana, the parole authority has the power to revoke all the good-time credits of released inmates and return them to prison. This can amount to half their original sentence. Even the federal government, which abolished discretionary parole, gives judges the right to order offenders to a three-year term of postrelease supervised aftercare. Offenders who violate the rules set for their release can be sent back to prison for the full period of the supervision order (without credit for time already served in the community).[49]

Similarly, in a survey of seven states (California, New Mexico, Illinois, Arizona, Indiana, Maine, and Colorado) that adopted determinate sentencing statutes, Frederick Hussey and Stephen Lagoy found that six actually retained some sort of parole supervision with the chance of good time being revoked.[50] Hussey and Lagoy conclude that far from abolishing parole and its release time uncertainties, determinate sentencing and parole now exist side by side. With the expansion of good-time credit and the reduction of parole board authority, however, determinate sentencing laws have placed release date authority into the hands of guards and other prison authorities who control the granting or reduction of good-time credit. Thus, the two most important reasons given for abolishing parole—ending uncertainty and disparity—may be circumvented by the new parole procedures.

To increase the effectiveness of parole, some jurisdictions have implemented experimental parole conditions such as limited caseload sizes, use of treatment facilities, matching of parolee and supervisor by personality, and **shock parole** (which involves immediate short-term incarcerations for violators to impress them with the seriousness of a violation). Data so far have indicated that these programs are not overly effective and may in fact produce a higher violation rate than traditional parole supervision. A possible explanation for this is that limiting caseload size enables parole officers to supervise their clients more closely and allows them to spot infractions more easily.

Parole will probably become more successful when the significant social, legal, and economic penalties levied on those convicted of crimes are removed and when the rules of parole become more humane and protect the basic rights of the parolee.

■ Making It on the Outside

Why do so many released inmates find their way back behind prison walls? For one thing the social-psychological-economic reasons that led them to crime probably have not been eliminated by a stay in prison. Despite rehabilitation efforts, typical "ex-cons" are still the same person—undereducated, unemployed, an addictive personality—they were when arrested. Being separated from friends and family, being cut off from conventional society, associating with dangerous people, and adapting to a volatile prison lifestyle probably have done little to improve their personality or behavior. And when they return to society, it may be to the same destructive neighborhood and peer group that prompted their original law-violating behavior. Some ex-inmates may have to prove that the prison experience has not changed them: taking drugs or being sexually aggressive may show friends that they haven't lost their "heart."

Ex-inmates may also find that going straight is an economic impossibility. Many employers are reluctant to hire people who have served time. Even if a criminal record does not automatically prohibit all chance of employment, why hire an ex-con when other applicants are available? If they lie about their prison experience and are later found out, ex-offenders will be dismissed for misrepresentation. "The wonder," claims Harry Allen and Clifford Simonsen, "is not that so many ex-offenders recidivate but that more do not."[51]

Losing Rights

One reason that ex-inmates find it so difficult to make it on the outside is the legal restrictions they are forced to endure. They may be barred from certain kinds of employment, their ability to obtain licenses may be limited, their freedom of movement may be restricted.

The practice of penalizing people even after they have served their sentence is grounded in the common law. In England during the Middle Ages, under the common law of **attainder,** convicted felons forfeited their land and possessions and their **civil rights** and suffered "corruption of blood," which prevented them from willing their land to heirs.[52] Although Article 1, Section 9 of the U.S. Constitution expressly forbids "bills of attainder," convicted felons still find that many of their activities are restricted once they are released from prison.

The degree to which these rights are lost varies from state to state and depends mainly on the judicial decisions of a particular jurisdiction. A list of rights that are or were once lost to the convicted offender follows:[53]

1. *The right to vote.* At one time this right was denied on the grounds of compelling state interest. It was believed that the purity of the voting process must be protected against immoral and dishonest elements of society. This thinking, however, has changed in most states, and today the restrictions on voting rights have been eliminated.
2. *The right to hold public office.* Denial of this right is based on the philosophy that the public must be protected.
3. *The right to public employment.* This restriction is gradually being lifted in the public sector. Now it is generally believed that the offense must be directly related to a job in order for employment to be denied.
4. *The right to an occupational license.* A "good moral character" is a requirement for more than 1,500 different licenses, which according to many licensing boards automatically bars ex-convicts from those fields.
5. *The right to serve on a jury.* Most states maintain that the "good character" qualification excludes a convicted offender from jury duty.
6. *The right to be a witness.* In most cases a convicted individual can serve as a witness; however, his or her criminal record can be used to discredit the testimony.
7. *The right to life and automobile insurance.* Obtaining insurance is often difficult, if not impossible, for an individual with a criminal record.

Inmate Self-Help

Recognizing that the probability of failure on the outside is greater than success, inmates have attempted to organize self-help groups to provide the psychological tools needed to prevent recidivism. In an impressive review of this issue Mark Hamm found that self-help groups could be divided into three distinct types. Some are chapters of well-known national organizations such as Alcoholics Anonymous. Membership in these programs is designed to improve inmates' self-esteem and help them cope with common problems such as alcoholism, narcotics abuse, or depression.

Other groups are organized along racial and ethnic lines. For example, chapters of the Chicanos Organizados Pintos Aztlan (COPA), the Afro-American Coalition, and the Native American Brotherhood can be found in prisons from California to Massachusetts. These groups try to establish a sense of brotherhood in order to work together for individual betterment. Members hold literacy, language, and religious classes and offer counseling, legal advice, and prerelease support. Ethnic groups seek ties with outside minority organizations such as the NAACP, Urban League, La Raza, and American Indian Movement as well as with religious and university communities.

A third type of self-help group has been developed specifically to help inmates find the strength to make it on the "outside." The most well-known are the Fortune Society, which claims 30,000 members, and the Seventh Step organization, which was developed by ex-offender Bill Sands. These groups try to raise inmates' self-esteem and help them find the inner strength to make it on the outside. The seven principles of the Seventh Step movement, whose first letters spell the word "freedom," are set out below:

1. **F**acing the truth about ourselves and the world around us, we decided we needed to change.
2. **R**ealizing that there is a Power from which we can gain strength, we have decided to use that Power.
3. **E**valuating ourselves by taking an honest self-appraisal, we examined both our strengths and weaknesses.
4. **E**ndeavoring to help ourselves overcome our weaknesses, we enlisted the aid of that Power.
5. **D**eciding that our FREEDOM is worth more than our resentments, we are using that Power to help FREE us from those resentments.
6. **O**bserving that daily progress is necessary, we set an attainable goal toward which we could work each day.
7. **M**aintaining our own FREEDOM, we pledge ourselves to help others as we have been helped.

Another organization the Self-Development Group (SDG), was founded in the 1960s by LSD advocate Timothy Leary. The group's creed advocates the following:

1. Trying to solve personal problems in an honest setting assisted by others of a similar purpose.
2. Learning to relate with each other and the world as reasonable, responsible persons.
3. Building a useful life structured on faith in God, in self, and in the ideals of the group.
4. Earning social respect and respecting society in return on the basis of mutual commitment to the objectives of the community.
5. Living as a power of example towards helping others in trouble.
6. Reviving commitment to SDG every day in compliance with the principles of the program.
7. Keeping SDG independent of ineffectual programs, yet open to assistance from any person or group who can help it in attaining its goals.

During the 1960s, Leary, a Harvard professor, conducted a self-awareness program on prison grounds. He was actually allowed to use psychedelic drugs in an attempt to forge a bond with the inmates. A number of current groups are the philosophical descendants of the SDG, including Inward Bound, Church of the New Sing, Ring of Keys, Human Potential Seminars, Wake up, and Discovery.

Hamm found that corrections authorities accept self-help groups that help inmates adjust to existing society and do not challenge authority. For example, prison authorities in some jurisdictions have formally sanctioned the Ring of Keys, whose goal is the "betterment of the individual through finding keys that will open many doors for a brighter and happier future," and Discovery, which tries to "challenge inmates to explore alternative decision-making and life styles." In a similar vein, the est programs developed by Werner Erhard have been paid for by corrections departments anxious to help inmates build the capacity for positive change.

Hamm concludes that nonthreatening organizations that embrace religious principles, which do not engage in activities foreign to the operations of corrections, and cultivate strong administrative and outside support will flourish in modern prison communities. ■

SOURCE: Mark Hamm, "Current Perspectives on the Prisoner Self-Help Movement," *Federal Probation* 52 (1988): 49–56.

8. *The right to marry and adopt children.* In most jurisdictions a record disqualifies an individual from adopting children; in a few states it prohibits one from marrying.

A recent survey by Velmer Burton, Francis Cullen, and Lawrence Travis found that a significant number of states still restrict the activities of former felons.[54] Their findings include the following:

1. Nineteen states prevent convicted felons from holding public office.
2. Almost every state prevents ex-cons from owning guns.
3. Twenty-eight states allow a husband or wife to obtain a divorce on the basis of a felony conviction and/or imprisonment of a spouse.
4. Sixteen states allow courts to terminate parental rights because of a felony conviction and/or imprisonment.
5. About 30 states bar ex-offenders from public employment.

Courts consider individual requests by convicted felons to have their rights restored on a case-by-case basis. Ordinarily, courts look at such issues as how recently the criminal offense took place and its relationship to the particular right before deciding whether to restore the right. For example, in *Carr v. Thompson*, a federal court ruled that a person could not be barred from a civil service job because of convictions on minor criminal charges that had occurred more than 10 years earlier.[55] In *Pordum v. N.Y. Board of Regents*, however, a U.S. Court of Appeals upheld the right of school officials to refuse to rehire a teacher who had been convicted and served time for bribery of public officials.[56]

A number of experts and national commissions have condemned the loss of rights of convicted offenders as a significant cause of recidivism. Consequently, courts have generally moved to eliminate the most restrictive elements of postconviction restrictions. Most important, when **civil death** statutes have been challenged, state and federal courts have ruled they deny due process and equal protection rights. In recent years, states such as Idaho, New York, and Montana have eliminated civil death statutes.[57]

In sum, it is both emotionally and legally difficult for the ex-inmate to make it on the outside. The problems of recidivism and self-destruction have prompted inmates to take matters into their own hands and form self-help groups to aid their adjustment. The work of these groups is discussed in the Criminal Justice in Review on page 614.

■ SUMMARY

Most inmates return to society before the completion of their prison sentence. The majority earn early release because of time off for good behavior or other sentence-reducing mechanisms.

In addition, about 40 percent of all inmates are paroled before the completion of their maximum term. Parole is the release of an offender into the community prior to the expiration of a prison sentence. Most state jurisdictions maintain an independent parole board whose members make the actual decisions to grant parole. Their decision making is extremely discretion-ary and is based on many factors such as their perceptions of the needs of society, the correctional system, and the client.

Once paroled, the client is subject to control by parole officers who ensure that the conditions set by the board (the parole rules) are maintained. These officers may also employ individual styles in their operations. For example, one may stress community protection and view parole as a law enforcement function, while another may believe in the social welfare aspects of parole and view the role as that of a treatment agent.

Parole can be revoked if the offender violates the rules of parole or commits a subsequent offense. In the past, revocation was purely an administrative function; however, recent decisions by the U.S. Supreme Court have granted procedural due process rights to offenders at parole revocation hearings, the most notable of which is the right to representation by an attorney. The effectiveness of parole has been questioned, and some experts call for its abolition.

Inmates have a difficult time adjusting on the outside, and the recidivism rate is disturbingly high. Inmates have formed self-groups to aid in their adjustment.

■ QUESTIONS

1. Define parole, including its purposes and objectives. How does it differ from probation?
2. What is the role of the parole board?
3. Identify the procedures involved in parole revocation. What are the rights of the parolee?

4. Should parole be abolished? How might this affect prison discipline?
5. Should a former prisoner have all the civil rights afforded the average citizen? Should people be further penalized after they have paid their debt to society?

■ NOTES

1. Stephanie Minor-Harper and Christopher Innes, *Time Served in Prison and on Parole, 1984* (Washington, D.C.: Bureau of Justice Statistics, 1987), p. 2.
2. David Duffee, *Corrections: Practice and Policy* (New York: Random House, 1989), p. 407.
3. These sections depend heavily on William Parker, *Parole: Origins, Development, Current Practices, and Statutes* (College Park, Md.: American Correctional Association, 1972); Gray Cavender, *Parole: A Critical Analysis* (Port Washington, N.Y.: Kennikat Press, 1982); Samuel Walker, *Popular Justice* (New York: Oxford University Press, 1980).
4. Edward Lisefski and Donald Manson, *Tracking Offenders, 1984* (Washington, D.C.: Bureau of Justice Statistics, 1988).
5. Harry Allen and Clifford Simonsen, *Corrections in America* (New York: MacMillan, 1989), p. 245.
6. American Bar Association, Commission on Correctional Facilities and Services, *Sentencing Computation: Laws and Practice, A Preliminary Survey* (Washington, D.C.: American Bar Association, 1974), p. 1.
7. 410 U.S. 263, 93 S.Ct. 1055, 35 L.Ed.2d 282 (1973).
8. 418 U.S. 539, 94 S.Ct. 2963, 41 L.Ed.2d 935 (1974).
9. Thomas Hester, *Probation and Parole, 1987* (Washington, D.C.: U.S. Government Printing Office, 1988).
10. Parker, *Parole*, p. 26.
11. Charles Johnson and Barry Smith, "Patterns of Probation and Parole Organization," *Federal Probation* 44 (1980): 43–51; American Correctional Association, *Directory of Juvenile and Adult Correctional Departments, Institutions, Agencies, and Paroling Authorities* (College Park, Md.: American Correctional Association, 1981), p. xx.
12. Vincent O'Leary and Joan Nuffield, *The Organization of Parole Systems in the United States* (Hackensack, N.J.: National Council of Crime and Delinquency, 1972), p. xiv.
13. Ibid., p. xv.
14. Parker, *Parole*, p. 26.
15. O'Leary and Nuffield, *The Organization of Parole Systems in the United States*, p. xxiv.
16. Ibid., p. xxix.
17. Vincent O'Leary and Kathleen Hanrahan, *Parole Systems in the United States: A Detailed Description of Their Structure and Procedures*, 3d ed. (Hackensack, N.J.: National Council on Crime and Delinquency, 1977), pp. 42–47.
18. Ibid.

19. Barbara Stone-Meierhoefer and Peter Hoffman, "Presumptive Parole Dates: The Federal Approach," *Federal Probation* 46 (1982): 41–56.
20. Todd Clear and George Cole, *American Corrections* (Monterey, Calif.: Brooks/Cole, 1986).
21. Peter Hoffman and Barbara Stone-Meierhoefer, "Post-release Arrest Experiences of Federal Prisoners: A Six Year Follow-up," *Journal of Criminal Justice* 7 (1979): 193–216.
22. Barbara Stone-Meierhoefer, "The Effect of Presumptive Parole Dates on Institutional Behavior: A Preliminary Assessment," *Journal of Criminal Justice* 10 (1982): 283–98.
23. Ray Enright, "Colorado Parole, Exacting and Imperfect Science," *Corrections Today* 50 (1988): 46.
24. 442 U.S. 1, 99 S.Ct. 2100, 60 L.Ed.2d 668 (1979).
25. 452 U.S. 458, 101 S.Ct. 2460, 69 L.Ed.2d 158 (1981).
26. 442 U.S. 1 at 12, 99 S.Ct. 2100, 60 L.Ed.2d 668 (1979).
27. 452 U.S. 458, 101 S.Ct. 2460 at 2464, 69 L.Ed.2d 158 (1981).
28. National Parole Institutes, "Selection for Parole," *Parole Resource Book–Part II* (April 1966): 168.
29. Franklin Zimring, "Making the Punishment Fit the Crime," in *Order Under Law*, R. Culbertson and M. Tezak, eds. (Prospect Heights, Ill.: Waveland Press, 1981), pp. 180–90.
30. Robert Carter, Richard McGee, and E. Kim Nelson, *Corrections in America* (Philadelphia: J. B. Lippincott Co., 1975), p. 206.
31. *Harlow v. Clatterbuck*, 230 Va. 490, 339, S.E.2d 181 (1986).
32. 68 N.Y. 2d 511, 511 N.Y.S. 2d 528, 503 N.E.2d 84 (1986).
33. President's Commission on Law Enforcement and the Administration of Justice, *Corrections* (Washington, D.C.: U.S. Government Printing Office, 1967), p. 86.
34. Cavender, *Parole: A Critical Analysis*, p. 55.
35. Richard McCleary, *Dangerous Men: The Sociology of Parole* (Beverly Hills, Calif.: Sage Publications, 1976).
36. "American Justice," *Newsweek*, 1 November 1982, p. 47.
37. Donald Gottfredson, M. G. Neithercutt, Joan Nuffield, and Vincent O'Leary, *Four Thousand Lifetimes: A Study of Time Served and Parole Outcome* (Hackensack, N.J.: National Council on Crime and Delinquency, 1973).
38. National Council on Crime and Delinquency, *Characteristics of the Parole Population* (Hackensack, N.J.: National Council on Crime and Delinquency, 1982).

39. Howard Sacks and Charles Logan, *Parole: Crime Prevention or Crime Postponement?* (Storrs, Conn.: University of Connecticut School of Law Press, 1980).

40. Allen Beck and Bernard Shipley, *Recidivism of Prisoners Released in 1983* (Washington, D.C: Bureau of Justice Statistics, 1989).

41. John Wallerstedt, *Returning to Prison* (Washington, D.C.: Bureau of Justice Statistics, 1984).

42. "Study Finds Many in Prison for Technical Parole Violation," *Criminal Justice Newsletter,* 16 January 1986, p. 5.

43. 408 U.S. 471, 92 S.Ct. 2593, 33 L.Ed.2d 484 (1972).

44. 584 F.2d 1208 (2d Cir. 1978).

45. 584 F.2d 953 (10th Cir. 1978).

46. 649 F.2d 755 (10th Cir. 1981).

47. Andrew von Hirsch and Kathleen Hanrahan, *Abolish Parole?* (Washington, D.C.: U.S. Government Printing Office, 1978).

48. David Fogel, *We Are the Living Proof* (Cincinnati: Anderson Publishing Co., 1979), p. 197.

49. 18 U.S.C. § 3583 (E) (1984).

50. Frederick Hussey and Stephen Lagoy, "The Determinate Sentence and Its Impact on Parole," *Criminal Law Bulletin* 19 (1983): 101–30.

51. Harry Allen and Clifford Simonsen, *Corrections in America*, 5th ed. (New York: Macmillan, 1989), p. 333.

52. See Sol Rubin, *United States Prison Law* (Dobbs Ferry, N.Y.: Oceana Publications, 1977), p. 1.

53. George Killinger, *Probation and Parole in the Criminal Justice System* (St. Paul, Minn.: West Publishing Company, 1976), pp. 126–44.

54. Velmer Burton, Francis Cullen, and Lawrence Travis, "The Collateral Consequences of a Felony Conviction: A National Study of State Statues," *Federal Probation* 51 (1987): 52–60.

55. Civ. No. 1973–93, U.S. District Court S.D. N.Y., 17 October 1974.

56. No. 279 Docket 73–1842, U.S. Court of Appeals, 2d Cir., 20 February 1974.

57. See, for example, *Bush v. Reid*, 516 F.2d 1215 (Alaska 1973); *Thompson v. Bond*, 421 F.Supp. 878 (W.D. Mo., 1976); *Delorem v. Pierce Freightlines Co.*, 353 F.Supp. 258 (D. Or. 2973); *Beyer v. Werner*, 299 F.Supp 967 (E.D. N.Y. 1969).

PART FIVE

MISSING KIDS

IF YOU HAVE ANY INFORMATION REGARDING
LOS ANGELES COUNTY SHERIFF'S
(213) 97

THESE CHILDREN WERE REPORTED MISSING

DORIA PAIGE YARBROUGH
WHITE FEMALE, 13 YEARS OLD
5'4", 105 LBS. BROWN HAIR & EYES.
LAST SEEN IN THE LANCASTER
AREA ON NOVEMBER 11, 1984.

The Nature and History
of the Juvenile Justice Process

19
Juvenile Justice

19

Juvenile Justice

*I*ndependent yet interrelated with the adult criminal justice system, the **juvenile justice system** is primarily responsible for dealing with juvenile and youth crime, as well as with incorrigible and truant children and runaways. When the juvenile court was originally conceived at the turn of the century, its philosophy was based on the idea of *parens patriae:* the state was to act on behalf of the parent in the interests of the child. In the 1960s, however, the theme changed when the U.S. Supreme Court began ensuring that juveniles would be granted legal rights. Today the emphasis of the juvenile justice system has shifted to chronically delinquent youths who must be controlled if society is to be protected.

The nation's juvenile justice system is in the midst of reexamining its fundamental operations and institutions. Although almost an entire century has passed since the first independent juvenile court was established, a comprehensive and comprehensible statement of its goals and purposes has yet to be developed. On the one hand, some authorities still hold to the social welfare origins of the juvenile justice system. They argue that the juvenile court is primarily a treatment agency that acts as a wise parent, dispensing personalized, individual justice to needy children who seek guidance and understanding. On the other hand, those with a law enforcement orientation suggest that the juvenile court's *parens patriae* philosophy has neglected the victims of delinquency and that serious offenders should be punished and disciplined rather than treated and rehabilitated. A third approach to juvenile justice takes the position that court processing has a potentially adverse effect on children, who are denied some of the constitutional rights afforded adult offenders. Advocates of this position believe that juvenile courts should dispense impartial justice and increase the due process rights of children who, depending on the outcomes of their trials, may be subjected to extended periods of confinement.

Ideologically, persons supportive of each of these positions appear unwilling to yield to the others. The concept of *parens patriae* is deeply rooted in the American system of juvenile justice and involves discretion, intervention, and treatment. Some experts believe that the principles underlying this concept have not been abandoned despite the new legal procedures.[1] Those arguing for an increase in the due process rights of juveniles maintain that the substantive intent of the law implies a mandate based on duty and morality and that the full protection of the U.S. Constitution should be applied to any person who comes before the national's tribunals at any time. To do otherwise, they contend, would abrogate the principle of equality under the law. Conflict over the proper role of the juvenile courts and the suspected negative impact of the stigma and delinquency labeling that follow a juvenile court appearance have also led some critics to advocate the total abolition of the juvenile court in favor of diversionary modes of justice.

These differing perspectives on juvenile court policy were reflected in the U.S. Supreme Court's reluctance to enter forcefully into the juvenile sphere until well into the 1960s. Since then, both the Warren and the Burger Courts have taken a due process approach to juvenile law; it remains to be seen what the Rehnquist Court will do.

This chapter reviews the history of juvenile justice and discusses the justice system's processing of youthful offenders.

Chapter 19
Juvenile Justice

■ History of Juvenile Justice

Originally, adults and juveniles who violated the law were subject to the same punishments—whipping, mutilation, banishment, and death.[2] Although a judge would sometimes treat a youth with leniency, there was no basis in law for clemency.

Foundations of the Juvenile Court

The modern practice of legally separating adult and juvenile offenders can be traced to two developments in English customs and law: the chancery court and the development of the poor laws. Both were designed to allow the state to take control of the lives of needy, but not necessarily criminal, children.

POOR LAWS. As early as 1535, the English passed statutes known as **poor laws.** These laws provided for the appointment of overseers to bind out destitute or neglected children as servants. Such children were forced to work during their minority for families who trained them in agricultural, trade, or domestic services. The Elizabethan poor laws of 1601 became a model for dealing with poor children for more than 200 years. These laws created a system of church wardens and overseers who, with the consent of the justices of the peace, identified vagrant, delinquent, and neglected children and took measures to put them to work. Often this meant placing them in poorhouses or workhouses or more commonly apprenticing them to masters. **Apprenticeship** in Great Britain had actually existed through almost the entire history of the country. Under this practice children were placed in the care of adults who taught them a trade. Voluntary apprentices were bound out by parents or guardians who wished to secure training for their children. Involuntary apprentices were compelled to serve by the authorities until they were 21 or older. The master-apprentice relationship was similar to the parent-child relationship in that the master had complete responsibility for and authority over the apprentice. If an apprentice was unruly, the master could complain to the authorities, and the apprentice could be punished. Even at this early stage, the conviction was growing that the criminal law and its enforcement should be applied differently to children.

CHANCERY COURTS. Chancery court existed throughout the Middle Ages. It was concerned primarily with protecting property rights, although its authority extended to the welfare of children in general. The major issues that came before the medieval chancery courts concerned guardianship, the uses and control of property, and the arrangement of people and power in relation to the monarchy. Agents of the chancery courts were responsible for settling problems involving rights to estates and guardianship interests in regard to the hierarchy of families and the state. These courts were founded on the proposition that children and other incompetents were under the protective control of the king. Thus, the Latin phrase *parens patriae* referred to the role of the king as the father of his country. As Douglas Besharov states, "The concept apparently was first used by English kings to justify their intervention in the lives of the children of their vassals—chidlren whose position and property were of direct concern to the monarch."[3] In the famous English case *Wellesley v. Wellesley*, a duke's children were taken from him in the name *parens patriae* because of his scandalous behavior.[4] Thus, the concept of *parens patriae* became the theoretical basis for the protective jurisdiction of the chancery courts acting on behalf of the crown.

As time passed, the crown increasingly used *parens patriae* to justify its intervention into the lives of families and children on the grounds of its interest in their general welfare. However, as Douglas Rendleman points out, "The idea of *parens patriae* was actually used to maintain the power of the crown and the structure of control over families known as feudalism."[5]

The chancery courts dealt with the property and custody problems of the wealthier classes. They never had jurisdiction over children charged with criminal conduct. Juveniles who violated the law were handled within the framework of the regular criminal court system. Nevertheless, the concept of *parens patriae*, which was established with the English chancery court system, came to refer primarily to the responsibility of the courts and the state to act in the best interests of the child. The idea that the state—and particularly the juvenile court—should act to protect the young, the incompetent, the neglected, and the delinquent subsequently became a major influence on the development of the American juvenile justice system in the twentieth century.

Care of Children in Early America

The forced apprenticeship system and the poor laws were brought from England to colonial America. Poor law legislation was passed in Virginia in 1646 and in Connecticut and Massachusetts in 1678. Forced apprenticeship of poor and destitute youths continued until the early nineteenth century. However, youths who committed serious criminal offenses continued to be treated in the same fashion as adults.

By the beginning of the nineteenth century, the apprenticeship system could no longer compete with the factory system. Yet the problems of how to deal effectively with growing numbers of dependent youths continued to increase. Early American settlers were firm believers in hard work, strict discipline, and education. These principles were viewed as the only reliable method for salvation and became the basis for the treatment of youths.

To accommodate groups of dependent and destitute youths, local jurisdictions developed systems of almshouses, poorhouses, and workhouses. In crowded, unhealthy conditions, they accepted the poor, the insane, the diseased, and vagrant and destitute children. The overseers who were responsible for them placed many children in institutions.

In addition, increased urbanization and industrialization led to the belief that certain segments of the population, namely youths in urban areas and immigrants, were particularly prone to criminal deviance and immorality. The children of these classes were regarded as persons who might be "saved" by state intervention. Such intervention, primarily by middle-class organizations and groups, became the basis of the **child-saving movement.** It became acceptable for wealthy, civic-minded citizens to help alleviate the burdens of the unfortunate urban classes and the immigrants. Such efforts included shelter care for youths, educational and social activities, and the development of settlement houses. Their main focus, however, was on extending government control over a whole range of youthful activities that had previously been left to private or family control, including idleness, drinking, vagrancy, and delinquency.

In 1874 Henry Bugh and Etta Angell Wheeler persuaded a New York court to take a child, Mary Ellen, away from her mother on the grounds of child abuse. This is the first recorded case in which a court was used to protect a child. These photos show Mary Ellen at age 9 when she appeared in court showing bruises from a whipping and several gashes from a pair of scissors. The other photograph shows her a year later.

Prominent among those interested in the problems of unfortunate children were penologist Enoch Wines, Judge Richard Tuthill, Lucy Flowers of the Chicago Women's Association, Sara Cooper of the National Conference of Charities and Corrections, and Sophia Minton of the New York Committee on Children.[6] These and other individuals became known as **child savers.** They believed that poor children presented a threat to the moral fabric of American society and should be controlled because their behavior could lead to the destruction of the nation's economic system. Thus, as a result of the process of industrialization and immigration, shortcomings in the existing criminal justice system, and the development of the child-saving movement, special institutions for children began to emerge. These factors eventually led various states to expand state jurisdiction over children.

The Child-Saving Movement

While various legislatures enacted laws giving courts the power to commit children who were runaways, who committed criminal acts, and who were out of the control of parents, specialized institutional programs were also created. One of the most concrete examples of institutional care was the **House of Refuge** in New York in 1825.[7] Its aim was to protect youths by taking potential criminals off the streets and reforming them in a familylike environment.

When the New York House of Refuge opened, the majority of children admitted were status offenders who were placed there because of vagrancy or neglect. The institution was run more like a prison, however, with a work schedule, study schedule, strict discipline, and absolute separation of the sexes. Such a harsh program led to runaways, with the result that the House of Refuge was forced to change its approach to a more lenient one. Children entered the house by court order, sometimes over parental objections, for vagrancy or delinquency. Their stay depended on need, age, and skill. Once there, youths were required to do piecework provided by local manufacturers or to work part of the day in the community.

Despite criticism of the program, the concept enjoyed widespread popularity. In 1826 the Boston City Council founded the House of Reformation for juvenile offenders in the city of Boston. Similar reform schools were opened in Massachusetts and New York in 1847.[8] To these schools, which were both privately funded and publicly supported, the courts committed children found guilty of criminal violations, as well as those beyond the control of their parents. Because the child-saving movement regarded convicted offenders and parents of delinquent children in the same light, they sought to have the reform schools establish control over the children. Robert Mennel argues that by training destitute and delinquent children, and by separating them from their natural parents and adult criminals, refuge managers believed they were preventing poverty and crime.[9]

The child savers influenced state and local governments, for example, to create institutions, called reform schools, exclusively devoted to the care of vagrant and criminal youths. State institutions opened in Westboro, Massachusetts, in 1848 and in Rochester, New York, in 1849.[10] These were soon followed by institutional programs in other states—Ohio in 1850 and Maine, Rhode Island, and Michigan in 1860.[11] Children lived in congregate conditions and spent their days working at institutional jobs, learning a trade where possible, and receiving some basic education. They were racially and sexually segregated, discipline was harsh and often involved whipping and isolation, and the physical care was of poor quality.

Some viewed houses of refuge and reform schools as humanitarian answers to poorhouses and prisons for vagrant, neglected, and delinquent youths, but many remained opposed to such programs. For example, as an alternative, New York philanthropist Charles Brace helped develop the **Children's Aid Society** in 1853. Brace's formula for dealing with neglected and delinquent youths was to rescue them from the harsh environment of the city and provide them with temporary shelter care. He then sought to place them in private homes throughout the nation. This program was very similar to foster home care programs today.

Establishment of the Juvenile Court: 1899

Although the child reformers provided services for children, they were unable to stop juvenile delinquency. Most reform schools were unable to hold youthful law violators and reform them. Institutional life was hard. Large numbers of children needing placement burdened the public finances supporting such programs. Thus, as state control over vagrant, delinquent, and neglected children became more widespread after the Civil War, it also become more controversial. As the nation grew, it became evident that private charities and public organizations were not caring adequately for the growing number of troubled youths.

The influence of the child savers prompted the development of the first comprehensive juvenile court in Illinois in 1899. The **Illinois Juvenile Court Act** set up an independent court to handle criminal law violations by children under 16 years of age, as well as to care for neglected, dependent, and wayward youths. The act also created a probation department to monitor youths in the community and to direct juvenile court judges to place serious offenders in secure training schools for boys and industrial schools for girls. The ostensible purpose of the act was to separate juveniles from adult offenders and provide a legal framework in which juveniles could get adequate care and custody. By 1925 most states had developed juvenile courts.

Although the efforts of the child savers were originally viewed as liberal reform, modern scholars commonly view their efforts as attempts at control and punishment. Justice historians such as Anthony Platt have suggested that the reform movement actually expressed the vested interests of a particular group. According to Platt:

> The child savers should not be considered humanists: (1) Their reforms did not herald a new system of justice but rather expedited traditional policies which had been informally developed during the nineteenth century; (2) they implicitly assumed the natural dependence of adolescents and created a special court to impose sanctions on premature independents and behavior unbecoming to youth; (3) their attitudes toward delinquent youth were largely paternalistic and romantic but their commands were backed up by force; (4) they promoted correctional programs requiring longer terms of imprisonment, longer hours of labor, and militaristic discipline, and the inculcation of middle class values and lower class skills.[12]

Thus, according to the revisionist approach, the reformers applied the concept of *parens patriae* for their own purposes, including the continuance of middle- and upper-class values, the control of the political system, and the furtherance of a child labor system consisting of lower-class workers with marginal skills.

Juvenile Justice Then and Now

The juvenile court movement quickly spread across the United States. In its early form, it provided youths with quasi-legal, quasi-therapeutic, personalized justice. The main concern was the "best interests of the child," not strict adherence to legal doctrine, constitutional rights, or due process of law. The court was paternalistic rather than adversarial.

For example, attorneys were not required. Hearsay evidence, inadmissible in criminal trials, was admissible in the adjudication of juvenile offenders. Verdicts were based on a "preponderance of the evidence" instead of being "beyond a reasonable doubt," and children were often denied the right to appeal their convictions. These characteristics allowed the juvenile court to function in a nonlegal manner and to provide various social services to children in need.

The major functions of the juvenile justice system were to prevent juvenile crime and to rehabilitate juvenile offenders. The function of the two most important actors, the juvenile court judge and the probation staff, was to diagnose the child's condition and prescribe programs to alleviate it. Until 1967, judgments about children's actions and consideration for their constitutional rights were secondary.

Juvenile corrections also underwent considerable change. Early reform schools were generally punitive in nature and were based on the concept of rehabilitation or reform through hard work and discipline. In the second half of the nineteenth century, emphasis shifted from massive industrial schools to the cottage system. Juvenile offenders were housed in a series of small cottages in a compound, each one holding 20 to 40 children. Each cottage was run by cottage parents, who attempted to create a homelike atmosphere. It was felt that this would be more conducive to rehabilitation than the rigid bureaucratic organization of massive institutions. The first cottage system was established in Massachusetts, the second in Ohio. The system was generally applauded for being a great improvement over the earlier industrial training schools. The general feeling was a movement away from punitiveness and toward rehabili-

Judge Benjamin Lindsey, left, specialized in the treatment of juvenile delinquents. Generally recognized as a founder of the U.S. juvenile court system, he is shown here in juvenile court in Denver, Colorado, where he presided from 1900 until 1927.

Part Five

The Nature and History of the Juvenile Justice Process

tation: "By attending to the needs of the individual and by implementing complex programs of diagnosis and treatment, known offenders could not only be rehabilitated, but crime among dependent and unruly children could be prevented."[13]

By the 1950s the influence of therapists such as Karen Horney and Carl Rogers promoted the introduction of psychological treatment in juvenile corrections. Group counseling techniques such as guided group interaction became standard procedure in most juvenile institutions.

In the 1960s and 1970s, the U.S. Supreme Court radically altered the juvenile justice system when it issued a series of decisions that established the right of juveniles to receive due process of law: *Kent v. United States* (1966), *In re Gault* (1967), *In re Winship* (1970), and *Breed v. Jones* (1975).[14] These cases will be discussed later in this chapter.

The 1970s also saw an alarming rise in juvenile crime and obvious inequities in the juvenile justice system. In addition to the legal revolution brought about by the Supreme Court, Congress passed the Juvenile Justice and Delinquency Prevention Act of 1974 (JJDP Act) and established the federal Office of Juvenile Justice and Delinquency Prevention (OJJDP).[15] This legislation was enacted to identify the needs of youth and fund programs in the juvenile justice system. As its centerpiece, the JJDP Act had two key compliance provisions:

1. Deinstitutionalization of status offenders
2. Separation and removal of juveniles from adult jail facilities[16]

After the "due process revolution," juvenile justice began to take on many of the characteristics of adult criminal justice. The provision of defense counsel for almost every juvenile offender signaled the end of the informal, nonadversarial juvenile justice system.

Today the distinctions between the adult and juvenile justice systems continue to blur. OJJDP has led the fight (through its ability to grant federal funds) to liberalize the system and diffuse its impact on young offenders. However, in the 1980s, the OJJDP has grown increasingly conservative and is now more concerned with the hardcore chronic offender than with aiding noncriminal youths; the role, and even the continued existence, of the OJJDP has been the subject of much debate in recent years.

The position of the federal government has not been lost on the states. Concern over serious juvenile crime has prompted a number of states to toughen their juvenile sentencing policies. It is also common for the juvenile court to waive jurisdiction over serious cases, allowing youths to be tried in adult courts. Yet the rehabilitation ideal still lives in juvenile justice, and community treatment and reducing the number of incarcerated youths still remain a top priority.

■ Juvenile Court Jurisdiction

The modern juvenile court is a specialized court for children. It may be organized as an independent statewide court system, as a special session of a lower court, or even as part of a broader family court. Juvenile courts are normally established by state legislation and exercise jurisdiction over two distinct categories of juvenile offenders—delinquents and status offenders.[17] Delinquent children are those who fall under a jurisdictional age limit, which varies from state to state, and who commit an act in violation of the penal code. **Status offenders,** on the other hand, include truants and habitually disobedient and ungovernable children. They are commonly characterized in state statutes as persons or children in need of supervision (PINS or CHINS), and their proscribed actions are in the nature of status offenses. Most states distinguish such behavior from delinquent conduct so as to lessen the effect of any stigma on the child as a result of his or her involvement with the juvenile court. In addition, juvenile courts generally have jurisdiction over situations involving conduct directed at (rather than committed by) juveniles, such as parental neglect, deprivation, abandonment, and abuse (see Table 19.1).

Today's juvenile court system embodies both rehabilitative and legalistic orientations; although the purpose of the court is therapeutic rather than punitive, children under its jurisdiction must be accorded their constitutional rights. The administrative structure of the court revolves around a diverse group of actors—a juvenile court judge, the probation staff, social workers, governmental prosecutors, and defense attorneys. Thus the juvenile court functions in a sociolegal manner. It seeks to promote the rehabilitation of the child within a framework of procedural due process.

Juvenile court jurisdiction is established by state statute and based on several factors, the first of which is age. The states have set different maximum ages below which children fall under the jurisdiction of the juvenile court. Many states include all children under 18, others set the upper limit at 17, and still others include children under 16.[18]

Juvenile court jurisdiction is also based on the nature of a child's actions. If an action committed by a child is a crime, this conduct normally falls into the category of delinquency. Definitions of delinquency vary from state to state, but most are based on the common element that delinquency is an intentional violation of the criminal law. The juvenile courts also have jurisdiction over status offenders, or children whose offenses involve some lack of parental supervision and are not the types of activity for which adults could be similarly prosecuted. Statutes attempting to define such conduct are marked by a vagueness that would most likely be impermissible in an adult criminal code. For example, terminology common to statutes of this kind includes designations such as unmanageable, unruly, and in danger of leading an idle, disolute, lewd, or immoral life. Understandably, statutory formulations such as these have been challenged as being unconstitutionally vague and indefinite.[19]

TABLE 19.1 ■ A Typical Status Offense Statute

Ohio Unruly Child Statute 2151.022 Unruly child defined
As used in sections 2151.01 to 2151.54, inclusive of the Revised Code, "Unruly child" includes any child:

■ Who does not subject himself to the reasonable control of his parents, teachers, guardian, or custodian, by reason of being wayward or habitually disobedient;

■ Who is an habitual truant from home or school;

■ Who so deports himself as to injure or endanger the health or morals of himself or others;

■ Who attempts to enter the marriage relation in any state without the consent of his parents, custodian, legal guardian, or other legal authority;

■ Who is found in a disreputable place, visits or patronizes a place prohibited by law, or associates with vagrant, vicious, criminal, notorious, or immoral persons;

■ Who engages in an occupation prohibited by law, or is in a situation dangerous to life or limb or injurious to the health or morals of himself or others;

■ Who has violated a law applicable only to a child.

SOURCE: Ohio Rev. Code Ann., sec. 2151.022.

However, most courts that have addressed this issue have upheld the breadth of the statutes in view of their overall concern for the welfare of the child.[20]

A juvenile court's jurisdiction is also affected by state statutes that exclude certain offenses from the court's consideration. Based on the premise that the rehabilitative resources and protective processes of the juvenile court are not appropriate in cases of serious criminal conduct, various states have excluded capital offenses, offenses punishable by death or life imprisonment, and certain other offenses from the juvenile court's jurisdiction. A more common exclusionary scheme involves **transfer** provisions, by means of which juvenile courts waive jurisdiction to the criminal courts (**waiver** is discussed later in this chapter). Having once obtained jurisdiction of a child, the juvenile court ordinarily retains it until the child reaches a specified age, usually the age of majority. Court jurisdiction terminates in most states when the child is placed in a public child-care agency. Figure 19.1 depicts the basic juvenile justice system.

■ Police Processing of the Juvenile Offender

For the past several years about 1.5 million youths under 18 years of age have been arrested each year.[21] When a juvenile is found to have engaged in delinquent or incorrigible behavior, police agencies are charged with the decision to release or to detain the child and refer him or her to juvenile court.[22] This discretionary decision—to release or to detain—has been found to be based not only on the nature of the offense but also on police attitudes and the social and personal conditions existing at the time of the particular arrest.[23] The following is a partial list of factors believed to be significant in police decision making regarding juvenile offenders:

1. The type and seriousness of the child's offense.
2. The ability of the parents to be of assistance in disciplining the child.
3. The history of the child's past contacts with police.
4. The degree of cooperation obtained from the child and parents and their demeanor, attitude, and personal characteristics.
5. Whether the child denies the allegations in the petition and insists on a court hearing.

After processing relevant information, the police may adjust a case by simply releasing the child at the point of contact on the street, giving an official warning and releasing the offender to the parents at the station house or the child's home, or referring the child to a social services program. Generally, cases involving violence, victim-related crimes, or serious property offenses are most often referred to court. On the other hand, police often attempt to divert from court action minor disputes between juveniles, school and neighborhood complaints, petty shoplifting cases, runaways, and ungovernable children.

When the police take a child into custody, the law of arrest requires that the police officer make a determination that probable cause exists that a crime has been committed and that the child may have committed it. Most states do not have specific statutory provisions distinguishing the arrest process for children from that for adults. Some jurisdictions, however, give broad arrest powers to the police in juvenile cases by authorizing the officer to make an arrest whenever it is believed that the child's behavior falls within the jurisdiction of the juvenile court.[24] Similarly, many states give the police authority to take a

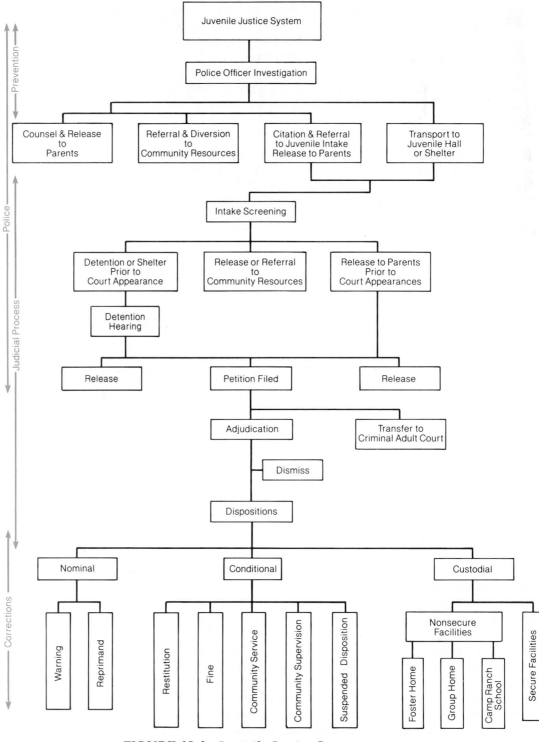

■ *FIGURE 19.1* **Juvenile Justice System**

SOURCE: National Advisory Commission on Criminal Justice Standards and Goals, *Report of the Task Force on Juvenile Justice and Delinquency Prevention* (Washington, D.C.: LEAA, 1976), p. 9.

child into custody if the child's welfare requires it. Because of the state's interest in the child, the police generally have more discretion in the investigatory and arrest stages of the juvenile process than they do when dealing with adult offenders. Although most juvenile arrests are warrantless, the requirements for the issuance of an arrest warrant for a juvenile are generally similar to requirements in adult cases.

Once a juvenile has been taken into custody, the child has the same Fourth Amendment right to be free from unreasonable searches and seizures as an adult does. The most common legal procedure used to exclude any incriminating evidence is for the child's attorney to make a pretrial motion to suppress inadmissible evidence, making it inadmissible in subsequent hearings.

School Searches

Educational officials often assume quasi police powers over children in school. School officials may search students in order to determine whether they are in possession of contraband such as drugs or weapons, search their lockers and desks, and question them about illegal activities. Such actions are comparable to the acts of the regular police. In *New Jersey v. T.L.O.* (1985), the U.S. Supreme Court held that a school official had the authority to search the purse of a student even though no warrant was issued nor was there probable cause that a crime had been committed; there was only the suspicion that T.L.O had violated school rules.[25]

This important case involved an assistant principal's search of the purse of a 14-year-old student observed smoking a cigarette in a school lavatory. The search was prompted when the principal found cigarette rolling papers as the pack of cigarettes was removed from the purse. A further search revealed marijuana and several items indicating marijuana selling; as a result, T.L.O. was adjudicated as a delinquent. The Supreme Court held that the Fourth Amendment protections against unreasonable searches and seizures apply to students, but said that the need to maintain an orderly educational environment modified the usual Fourth Amendment requirements of warrants and

Chapter 19

Juvenile Justice

probable cause. Thus, the Court relaxed the usual probable cause standard and found the search to be reasonable.[26] It declared that the school's right to maintain discipline on school grounds allowed it to search a student and his or her possessions as a safety precaution. Thus the Court, which had guarded the warrant requirement and its exceptions in the past, now permits warrantless searches in schools, based on the lesser standard of "reasonable suspicion." This landmark decision did not deal with other thorny issues, however, such as the search and seizure of contraband from a student's locker or desk.

Faced with increased crime by students in public schools, particularly illicit drug use, school administrators today are prone to enforce drug control statutes and administrative rules.[27] Some urban schools are using breathalyzers, drug-sniffing dogs, hidden video cameras, and routine searches of students' pockets, purses, lockers, and cars.[28] In general, courts consider such searches permissible when they are not overly offensive, and where there are reasonable grounds to suspect that the student may have violated the law.[29] School administrators are walking a tightrope between a student's constitutional right to privacy and school safety. Some schools have developed risk assessment models to evaluate the probable legality of a search and seizure situation.[30] The model considers the interaction of the focus, purpose, and occasion of the search, assigns point values to each factor, and calculates the degree of risk associated with conducting an illegal search. However, it remains for future court decisions to indicate how far the state may go in curbing school crime before privacy rights are violated.

Juveniles and the *Miranda* Decision

Another issue related to the exclusion of evidence in juvenile matters is the use of statements made by juvenile offenders to police officers. In years past, police often questioned juveniles in the absence of their parents or an attorney. Any incriminatory statements or confessions made by juveniles could be placed in evidence at their trials. As mentioned in Chapter 9, the U.S. Supreme Court in *Miranda v. Arizona* (1966) placed constitutional limitations on police interrogation procedures regarding adult offenders.[31] The *Miranda* warning, which lists the adult defendant's Fifth Amendment rights against self-incrimination, has been made applicable to children. The *In re Gault* decision—which gave juveniles procedural safeguards similar to those awarded adults at trial proceedings, including the right to counsel, the right to confront witnesses, and the privilege against self-incrimination—has indirectly influenced and reinforced juvenile *Miranda* rights. In other words, adjudicatory rights seem to require that the *Miranda* warning be given to all juvenile offenders who are questioned in custody if the police intend to admit their statements in subsequent proceedings. Most states have incorporated the *Miranda* decision into their juvenile statutes, and today a child's parents are usually contacted immediately after the child is taken into custody.

One of the most difficult problems involving self-incrimination is whether juveniles can waive their *Miranda* rights. This issue has resulted in considerable litigation. Some courts have concluded that it is not essential for the parent or attorney to be present for the child to effectively waive his or her rights. The validity of the waiver in this respect is based on the totality of the circumstances of a given case. This means that the court must determine whether the child is able to make a knowing, intelligent, and voluntary waiver. On the other hand, some jurisdictions will not accept a waiver of the juvenile's *Miranda* rights unless it is made in the presence of the child's parents or attorney.

The Supreme Court has clarified the rights of juveniles in two cases, **Fare v. Michael C.** and **California v. Prysock.**[32] In *Fare v. Michael C.* (1979) a young boy was arrested by police on suspicion of murder. After the *Miranda* warning was given, Michael requested to speak to his probation officer. This request was denied.

Michael then confessed to the crime and later appealed his conviction, charging that the police should have allowed him to speak to his probation officer. The Supreme Court found that the police were justified in refusing Michael's request and that considering the "totality of the circumstances" they had made a reasonable attempt to inform the suspect of his rights.

In *California v. Prysock* (1981), the Court was asked to rule on the adequacy of a *Miranda* warning given Randall Prysock, a youthful murder suspect. In upholding Prysock's conviction, the Court ruled that even though the *Miranda* warning was not given in the precise manner as the case decision, its meaning was plain and easily understandable, even to a juvenile. In light of these problematic cases, some legal experts believe that *Miranda* warnings used in juvenile settings should be modified to ensure that they are comprehensible to the youth suspect prior to custodial interrogation.[33]

Today almost as much procedural protection is generally given to children in juvenile justice as to adults tried in criminal courts. Table 19.2 describes the basic similarities and differences between the juvenile and adult justice systems.

TABLE 19.2 ■ Similarities and Differences between the Juvenile and Adult Justice Systems

Similarities

1. Discretion in decision making is used by police officers, judges, and correctional personnel in both adult and juvenile systems.
2. Search and seizure law and the Fourth Amendment apply to juvenile and adult offenders.
3. The right to receive the *Miranda* warning applies to juveniles as well as to adults.
4. Juveniles are protected, as are adults, from prejudicial lineups or other identification procedures.
5. Procedural safeguards similar to those of adults protect juveniles when they make an admission of guilt.
6. Prosecutors and defense attorneys play an equally critical role in juvenile and adult advocacy.
7. Juveniles, like adults, have the right to counsel at most key stages of the court process.
8. Pretrial motions are available in juvenile and criminal court proceedings.
9. Negotiations and plea bargaining are used with juvenile and adult offenders.
10. Children and adults have a right to a trial and appeal.
11. The standard of evidence in juvenile delinquency adjudications, as in adult criminal trials, is that of proof beyond a reasonable doubt.
12. Like adults, children waived from the juvenile court can receive the death penalty.

Differences

1. The primary purpose of juvenile procedures is protection and treatment; with adults, the aim is punishment of the guilty.
2. The jurisdiction of the juvenile court is determined chiefly by age; in the adult system, jurisdiction is determined primarily by the nature of the offense.
3. Juveniles can be held responsible for acts that would not be criminal if they were committed by an adult (status offenses).
4. Juvenile proceedings are not considered criminal, whereas adult proceedings are.
5. Juvenile court procedures are generally informal and private; those of adult courts are more formal and open to the public.
6. Courts cannot release identifying information to the press concerning a juvenile, but must do so in cases involving adults.
7. Parents are highly involved in the juvenile process; with adults, this would not be the case.
8. The standard of arrest is more stringent for adults than for juveniles.
9. As a practical matter, juveniles are released into parental custody, whereas adults are generally given the opportunity for bail.
10. Plea bargaining is used in most adult cases, whereas most juvenile cases are settled by open admission of guilt.
11. Juveniles have no constitutional right to a jury trial; adults do have this right.
12. Juvenile dispositional decisions are ordinarily based on indeterminate terms, whereas adults sentences include proportionality and definiteness.
13. The procedural rights of juveniles are based on the concept of "fundamental fairness"; those of adults are based on the constitutional right to due process under the Bill of Rights and the Fourteenth Amendment.
14. Juveniles have the right to treatment under the Fourteenth Amendment; adult offenders have no such recognized right.
15. A juvenile's record is sealed when the age of majority is reached; the record of an adult is permanent.

■ The Pretrial Stage of Juvenile Justice

After arrest and before trial, the juvenile defendant is processed through a number of important stages of the juvenile justice system. These may include intake, detention, bail, waiver hearing, and diversion programs. Each of these stages and processes is discussed in the following sections.

The Intake Process

As previously described, juveniles coming into contact with the police and juvenile courts generally may be categorized into two major groups: those accused of committing crimes that result in juvenile delinquency and those who commit acts of noncriminal behavior. Police officers who confront children committing a crime or behaving in a manner that could be dangerous to themselves or others must decide whether the situation warrants court attention or not. Thus the police role involves exercising a certain amount of discretion in dealing with children. If the police officer does not initiate court action, he or she may provide the child with a warning, advise the parents to refer the child to a welfare agency, or refer the situation to a social agency through the police department.

When the police department believes the child needs a court referral, the police become involved in the **intake** division of the court. The term *intake* refers to the screening of cases by the juvenile court system. It involves the review and initial screening of a child and family by intake probation officers to determine if the child needs to be serviced by the juvenile court. The intake stage is a time when the child can receive treatment in a most efficient and timely manner. It represents an opportunity to place a child in informal programs both within the court and in the community. Furthermore, the intake process is critically important because more than half the referrals to the juvenile courts never go beyond that stage.

Juvenile court intake—which seeks to screen out cases not within the court's jurisdiction or not serious enough for court intervention—is now provided for by statute in the majority of states.[34] Furthermore, virtually all the model acts and standards in juvenile justice suggest the development of juvenile court intake proceedings.[35]

Intake procedures in the juvenile court are desirable for a number of reasons including the following: (1) Filing a complaint against the child in a court may do more harm than good, since rehabilitation has often failed in the juvenile court system. (2) Processing a child in the juvenile court labels the child a delinquent, stigmatizes the juvenile, and may reinforce antisocial behavior. (3) Nonjudicial handling gives the child and the family a second chance and an opportunity to work with a voluntary social service agency. (4) Intake screening of children helps conserve resources that may not be available in already overburdened juvenile court systems. In addition, intake screening also provides for a wide range of nonjudicial decisions regarding the child, including the use of nonjudicial or informal probation, the provision of intake services by the intake department of the juvenile court, the additional dismissal of a complaint, and the referral to a community social service agency. Finally, intake screening allows juvenile courts to enter into a consent decree with the juvenile without the filing of a petition or formal adjudication. The consent decree is basically a court order authorizing the disposition of the case without a formal finding of delinquency, based on an agreement between the intake department of the court and the juvenile who is the subject of the complaint.

Notwithstanding all the advantages of intake, it does present some problems. Less than 50 percent of all juveniles who are arrested and brought to court actually proceed to trial. As a result, intake sections are constantly pressured to provide available services for the large group of children not handled by the court structure. In addition to being a link for court and community services, intake programs also need to be provided 24 hours a day in many urban courts, so that dispositions can be resolved quickly on the day the child is referred to the court. Furthermore, the key to good intake service is the quality of the intake probation staff in the court. Poorly qualified personnel in intake is a serious flaw in many court systems. A variety of legal problems are also associated with the intake process. These include whether the child has a right to counsel at this stage, whether the juvenile has a privilege against self-incrimination at intake, and to what degree the child needs to consent to nonjudicial disposition as recommended by the intake probation officer.

In some respects, juvenile intake can be compared to the adult plea-bargaining process. Both stages involve questions of due process, informal negotiations, discretionary justice, and issues of voluntarism.[36] Cases are generally resolved by making a deal and reaching a settlement rather than by making a formal determination of guilt or innocence.

Detention

After a juvenile is formally taken into custody, either as a delinquent or as a status offender, a decision is usually made whether to release the child to the parent or guardian or detain the child in a shelter pending trial. In the past, far too many children were routinely placed in **detention** while awaiting court appearances. Detention facilities were inadequate—in many parts of the country, county jails were used to detain juvenile offenders. Although this practice continues to some degree, the emphasis in recent years has been on reducing the number of children placed in detention.

Subsequent to arrest, and after being temporarily detained by the police, the child is usually released to the parent or guardian. Most state statutes ordinarily require a hearing on the appropriateness of detention if the initial decision is to keep the child in custody. At this hearing, the child has a right to counsel and may be given other procedural due process safeguards, notably the privilege against self-incrimination and the right to confront and cross-examine witnesses.

Most state juvenile court acts provide criteria to support a decision to detain the child. These include (1) the need to protect the child, (2) the question of whether the child presents a serious danger to the public, and (3) the likelihood that the juvenile will return to court for adjudication. Whereas in adult cases the sole criterion for pretrial release may be the offender's availability for trial, the juvenile may be detained for other reasons, including the child's own protection. Normally, the finding of the judge that the child should be detained must be supported by factual evidence. When a valid reason for a child's detention has not appeared on the record, courts have mandated release from temporary custody. In 1984 the U.S. Supreme Court upheld the right of the states to detain a child before trial in order to protect his or her welfare and the public safety.[37] The case, **Schall v. Martin,** is set out in the Law in Review on page 636.

Schall v. Martin (1984)

FACTS

Gregory Martin was arrested in New York City on December 13, 1977, on charges of robbery, assault, and criminal possession of a weapon. Since he was arrested at 11:30 P.M. and lied about his residence, Martin was kept overnight in detention and brought to juvenile court the next day for an "initial appearance" accompanied by his grandmother. The family court judge, citing possession of the loaded weapon, the false address given to police, and the lateness of the hour the crime occurred (as evidence of a lack of supervision), ordered him detained before trial under section 320.5(3)(6) of the New York State code. Section 320.5 authorizes pretrial detention of an accused juvenile delinquent if "there is a substantial probability that he will not appear in court on the return date or there is a serious risk that he may before the return date commit an act which if committed by an adult would constitute a crime." Later, at trial, Martin was found to be a delinquent and sentenced to two years probation.

Martin's attorney's filed a habeas corpus petition (demanding his release from custody) while he was in pretrial detention. Their petition charged that his detention denied him due process rights under the Fifth and Fourteenth Amendments. Their suit was a class action in behalf of all youths subject to preventive detention in New York. The New York appellate courts upheld Martin's claim on the grounds that because most delinquents are released or placed on probation, it is unfair to incarcerate them before trial. The prosecution brought the case to the U.S. Supreme Court for final judgment.

DECISION

The U.S. Supreme Court upheld the state's right to place juveniles in preventive detention. It held that preventive detention serves the legitimate objective of protecting both the juvenile and society from pretrial crime. Pretrial detention need not be considered punishment merely because the juvenile is eventually released or put on probation. And after all, there are procedural safeguards, such as notice and a hearing, and a statement of facts that must be given to juveniles before they are placed in detention. The Court also found that detention based on prediction of future behavior is not a violation of due process. Many decisions are made in the justice system, such as the decision to sentence or grant parole, which are based in part on a prediction of future behavior, and these have all been accepted by the Court as legitimate exercises of state power.

SIGNIFICANCE OF THE CASE

Schall v. Martin establishes the right of juvenile court judges to deny youths pretrial release if they perceive them to be "dangerous." It further distinguished practices of the adult justice system from the juvenile justice system; preventive detention is normally not legal for adults. However, the case establishes a due process standard for detention hearings, which includes notice and a statement of substantial reasons for the detention. ■

ISSUES IN JUVENILE DETENTION. The use of juvenile detention involves two important issues. The first has been the mostly successful effort to remove status offenders from lockups containing delinquents. After a decade of effort, almost all states have passed laws requiring that status offenders be placed in shelter care rather than detention facilities. An analysis of this effort found that one problem of deinstitutionalizing status offenders was that many had prior delinquent records; in addition, the recidivism rate was not improved by their removal from secure lockups.[38]

Another serious problem is removing youths from lockups in adult jails. This practice is quite common in rural areas where there are relatively few separate facilities for young offenders.

Although the federal government, through the Office of Juvenile Justice and Delinquency Prevention, has actively supported removal of detained youths from adult jails, the practice still continues. In fact, under the Juvenile Justice and Delinquency Prevention Act of 1974, states obtaining federal funds were compelled to revise their jail practices and separate juveniles from adults under its compliance provisions.[39] By 1980, amendments to the JJDP Act, mandating the absolute removal of juveniles from jails had been adopted. Despite such efforts, more than half the states are not complying with the jail removal provisions, and some experts estimate that over 100,000 youths are annually detained in adult jails.[40] Whatever the actual number jailed today, placing young offenders in adult jails continues to be a significant problem in the juvenile justice system.

Juveniles detained in adult jails often live in squalid conditions and are subjected to physical and sexual abuse. Furthermore, a federally sponsored study found that children confined in adult institutions were eight times as likely to commit suicide as those placed in detention centers exclusively for juveniles, and were 4.5 percent more likely to kill themselves as children in the general population.[41]

The Office of Juvenile Justice and Delinquency Prevention has given millions of dollars in aid to encourage the removal of juveniles from adult lockups.[42] These grants have helped many jurisdictions develop intake screening procedures, specific release or detention criteria, and alternative residential and nonresidential programs for juveniles awaiting trial.

Nevertheless, eliminating the confinement of juveniles in adult institutions remains a difficult task. In a recent comprehensive study of the jailing of juveniles in Minnesota, Ira Schwartz found that even in a state recognized nationally for juvenile justice reform, the rate of admission of juveniles to adult jails remains high.[43] His research also revealed that the rate of admission is not related to the seriousness of the offense, and that minority juveniles are spending greater amounts of time in jail for the same offenses than white offenders.[44]

In his report, Schwartz suggests (1) that government enact legislation prohibiting the confinement of juveniles in jail; (2) that appropriate juvenile detention facilities be established; (3) that funds be allocated for such programs; (4) that racial disparity in detention be examined; and (5) that responsibility for monitoring conditions of confinement be fixed by statutes and court decisions.[45] California, for example, has passed legislation ensuring that no minor under juvenile court jurisdiction can be incarcerated in any jail after July 1, 1989.[46] And in the recent landmark federal court case, *Hendrickson v. Griggs,* the court found that the State of Iowa had not complied with the juvenile jail removal mandate of the JJDP Act and ordered local officials to develop a plan for bringing the state into conformity with the law.[47] As a result, states will face increasing legal pressure to meet jail removal requirements in the future.

Bail

If a child is not detained, the question of bail arises. Federal courts have not found it necessary to rule on the issue of a constitutional right to bail since liberal statutory release provisions act as appropriate alternatives. Although only a few state statutes allow release on money bail, many others have juvenile code provisions that emphasize the release of the child to the parents as an acceptable substitute. A constitutional right to bail that on its face seems to benefit a child may have unforeseen results. For example, money bail might impose a serious economic strain on the child's family while simultaneously conflicting with the protective and social concerns of the juvenile court. Considerations of economic liabilities and other procedural inequities have influenced the majority of courts confronting this question to hold that juveniles do not have a right to bail.

Plea Bargaining

A child may plead guilty or not guilty to a petition alleging delinquency. Today state jurisdictions tend to minimize the stigma associated with the use of adult criminal standards by using other terminology, such as "agree to a finding" or "deny the petition." When the child makes an admission, juvenile court acts and rules of procedure in numerous jurisdictions require the following procedural safeguards: (1) that the child know of the right to a trial; (2) that the plea or admission be made voluntarily; and (3) that the child understand the charges and consequences of the plea. The same requirements for adult offenders have been established in a series of decisions by the U.S. Supreme Court.[48] Although such standards have not been established by constitutional law for juveniles, they carry equal weight in juvenile cases because the guilty plea constitutes a waiver of the juvenile's Fifth Amendment privilege against self-incrimination.

Open admission, as opposed to plea bargaining, seems to be the reason that the majority of juvenile court cases are not adjudicated. Unlike the adult system, where 70 to 90 percent of all charged offenders are involved in some plea bargaining, it is widely believed that little plea bargaining exists in the juvenile court. Most juvenile court legislation and rules of procedure do not provide rules governing the plea-bargaining process. The *parens patriae* philosophy of the juvenile court, the general availability of pretrial social services, and flexibility in the disposition of cases act to discourage the use of plea bargaining.

The practical application of plea bargaining in the juvenile court exists when the government—represented by the prosecutor, police officer, or probation officer—negotiates a guilty plea from the defense attorney in exchange for a disposition generally involving community supervision. Both parties may seek the judge's guidance in reaching an agreement and obtain judicial consent to the bargain. Efficient disposition of the case after plea bargaining is also an essential element of the process because it reduces the juvenile court caseload and enhances the rehabilitative prospects of the child.

The Waiver of Jurisdiction

Prior to the development of the first modern juvenile court in Illinois in 1899, juveniles were tried for violations of the law in adult criminal courts. The consequences were devastating; many children were treated as criminal offenders and often sentenced to adult prisons. Although the subsequent passage of state legislation creating juvenile courts eliminated this problem, the juvenile justice system did recognize that certain forms of conduct require that children be tried as adults. Today most jurisdictions provide by statute for waiver, or transfer of juvenile offenders to the criminal courts.

The transfer of a juvenile to the criminal court is often based on statutory criteria established by the state's juvenile court act, and waiver provisions generally vary considerably among jurisdictions. The two major criteria for waiver are the age of the child and the type of offense alleged in the petition. For example, some jurisdictions require that the child be over a certain age and be charged with a felony before being tried as an adult, while others permit waiver of jurisdiction to the criminal court if the child is above a certain age, regardless of the offense. Still other states permit waiver under any conditions.[49]

Because of the nature of the waiver decision and its effect on the child in terms of status and disposition, the U.S. Supreme Court has imposed procedural protections for juveniles in the waiver process. **Kent v. United States** (1966), the first major case before the Court on this issue, challenged the provisions of the District of Columbia code, which stated that the juvenile court could waive jurisdiction after a full investigation.[50] The Supreme Court in *Kent* held that the waiver proceeding is a critically important stage in the juvenile process and that juveniles must be afforded minimum requirements of due process of law at such proceedings (see the Law in Review on page 640).

In reaching this decision, Justice Abe Fortas declared:

> The Juvenile Court is theoretically engaged in determining the needs of the child and of society rather than adjudicating criminal conduct. The objectives are to provide measures of guidance and rehabilitation for the child and protection for society, not to fix criminal responsibility, guilt and punishment. The State is *parens patriae* rather than prosecuting attorney and judge. But the admonition to function in a "parental" relationship is not an invitation to procedural arbitrariness.[51]

In **Breed v. Jones** (1975), another significant decision on juvenile waiver proceedings, the U.S. Supreme Court held that the prosecution of a juvenile as an adult in the California Superior Court, following an adjudicatory proceeding in juvenile court, violated the double jeopardy clause of the Fifth Amendment as applied to the states through the Fourteenth Amendment.[52] The Court concluded that jeopardy attaches when the juvenile court begins to hear evidence at the adjudicatory hearing; this requires that the waiver hearing take place prior to any adjudication.

Youths in Adult Courts

Under certain circumstances, juveniles may be tried in criminal courts. The age at which the criminal court takes jurisdiction ranges from 16 to 19.

The problem of youths processed in adult courts is a serious one. An important federally sponsored survey found that in a single year 9,000 juveniles were waived to adult courts, 2,000 were prosecuted as adults because of concurrent jurisdiction, and 1,300 were prosecuted as adults because the offenses they committed were excluded from juvenile court jurisdiction.[53] In addition, since 12 states have low maximum ages for juvenile courts, about 250,000 youths, aged 16 and 17, are handled by adult courts each year. Among the other significant findings of the study were the following:

1. Most waived youths were not charged with violent crimes but with property and public-order (drug, alcohol) crimes.
2. Most of the youths tried in adult courts were convicted or pleaded guilty.
3. Youths were more likely to receive a probation sentence than confinement. However, 46 percent of the youths judicially waived were sent to adult correctional facilities.
4. Youths convicted as adults and sentenced to confinement did more time than they would have under juvenile court disposition.

Kent v. United States (1966)

FACTS

Morris Kent was arrested at the age of 16 in connection with charges of housebreaking, robbery, and rape. As a juvenile he was subject to the exclusive jurisdiction of the District of Columbia Juvenile Court. The District of Columbia statute declared that the court could transfer the petitioner "after full investigation" and remit him to trial in the U.S. District Court. Kent admitted his involvement in the offenses and was placed in a receiving home for children. Subsequently, his mother obtained counsel, and they discussed with the social service director the possibility that the juvenile court might waive its jurisdiction. Kent was detained at the receiving home for almost one week. There was no arraignment, no hearing, and no hearing for petitioner's apprehension. Kent's counsel arranged for a psychiatric examination, and a motion requesting a hearing on the waiver was filed. The juvenile court judge did not rule on the motion and entered an order stating, "after full investigation, that the court waives its jurisdiction and directs that a trial be held under the regular proceedings of the criminal court." The judge made no finding and gave no reasons for his waiver decision. It appeared that the judge denied motions for a hearing, recommendations for hospitalization for psychiatric observation, requests for access to the social service file, and offers to prove that the petitioner was a fit subject for rehabilitation under the juvenile court.

After the juvenile court waived its jurisdiction, Kent was indicted by the grand jury and was subsequently found guilty of housebreaking and robbery and not guilty by reason of insanity on the charge of rape. Kent was sentenced to serve a period of 30 to 90 years on his conviction.

DECISION

Petitioner's lawyer appealed the decision on the basis of the infirmity of the proceedings by which the juvenile court waived its jurisdiction. The U.S. Supreme Court found that the juvenile court order waiving jurisdiction and remitting the youth to trial in the district court was invalid. Its reasoning was based on the following:

1. The theory of the juvenile court act is rooted in social welfare procedures and treatments.
2. The philosophy of the juvenile court, namely, *parens patriae*, is not supposed to allow procedural unfairness.
3. Waiver proceedings are critically important actions in the juvenile court.
4. The juvenile court act requiring full investigation in the District of Columbia should be read in the context of constitutional principles relating to due process of law. The principles require at a minimum that the petitioner be entitled to a hearing, access to counsel, access by counsel to social service records, and a statement of the reason for the juvenile court decision.

SIGNIFICANCE OF THE CASE

The Supreme Court held that juvenile court waiver hearings must measure up to the essentials of due process and fair treatment. Furthermore, in an appendix to its opinion, the Court set up the following criteria concerning waiver of jurisdiction:

1. The seriousness of the alleged offense to the community.
2. Whether the alleged offense was committed in an aggressive, violent, or willful manner.
3. Whether the alleged offense was committed against persons or against property.
4. The prosecutive merit of the complaint.
5. The desirability of trial and disposition.
6. The sophistication and maturity of the juvenile.
7. The record and previous history of the juvenile.
8. Prospects for adequate protection of the public and the likelihood of reasonable rehabilitation.

As a result of the *Kent* decision, many jurisdictions have established specific rules for the waiver of a juvenile to the criminal court. In most jurisdictions that have waiver proceedings, the following are required by statute or court rule: a hearing, the presence of counsel, an investigation by the probation staff regarding whether the juvenile is amenable to treatment, evidence that reasonable grounds exist to believe that the child committed the delinquent act, and a statement of the reasons for the waiver. ■

Although the report did not recommend the abolition of waiver, it suggested that juveniles should always be kept out of adult correctional facilities and should be treated as juveniles as long as possible.

Today all states allow juveniles to be tried as adults in criminal courts in one of three ways:

1. *Concurrent jurisdiction.* The prosecutor has the discretion of filing charges for certain offenses in either juvenile or criminal court.
2. *Excluded offenses.* The legislature excludes from juvenile court jurisdiction certain offenses either very minor, such as traffic or fishing violations, or very serious, such as murder or rape.
3. *Judicial waiver.* The juvenile court waives its jurisdiction and transfers the case to criminal court (the procedure is also known as "binding over" or "certifying" juvenile cases to criminal court).

Today 12 states authorize prosecutors to bring cases in the juvenile or adult criminal court at their discretion; 36 states exclude certain offenses from juvenile court jurisdiction; 48 states, the District of Columbia, and the federal government have judicial waiver provisions.[54]

Barry Feld suggests that waiver to adult court should be mandatory for juveniles committing serious crimes.[55] He argues that mandatory waiver would jibe with the currently popular "just desert" sentencing policy and eliminate potential bias and disparity in judicial decision making.

In a recent extensive study of legislative changes in juvenile waiver statutes, Feld found that most states rely on the seriousness of the current offense in deciding whether to waive a youth to adult court. However, as Feld points out, youths transferred under excluded offenses statutes may not be as criminally responsible as their adult counterparts.[56]

Another recent trend has been to enact statutes giving original jurisdiction for juvenile crimes to the adult courts and then allowing judges to waive deserving cases back to the juvenile authorities. The most well-known of these statutes is New York's 1978 Omnibus Crime Act, which gives the adult courts jurisdiction over 13-year-olds accused of murder and 14- and 15-year-olds accused of serious crimes, such as murder, rape, and robbery.[57] The adult court judge is entitled to transfer these youths to juvenile court, but not vice versa. However, youths cannot be placed in adult correctional facilities until they reach age 16. New York's law has been criticized on several grounds:

1. Some 70 percent of the children arraigned in adult court are waived to juvenile court, wasting both time and money.
2. Some 40 percent of the juveniles tried in adult court are sentenced to probation.
3. Only 3 percent of the juvenile offenders tried in adult court received longer sentences than they would have if they had been tried in juvenile court.

THE EFFECT OF WAIVER. The key issue is what is accomplished by treating juveniles more like adults. Studies of the impact of the recent waiver statutes have yielded inconclusive results.[58] Some juveniles whose cases are waived to criminal court are sentenced more leniently than they would have been in juvenile court. In many states, even when juveniles are tried in criminal court and convicted on the charges, they may still be sentenced to a juvenile or youthful offender institution rather than to an adult prison. The laws may allow them to be transferred to an adult prison when they have reached a certain age. Some studies show that only a small percentage of juveniles tried as adults are incarcerated for periods longer than the terms served by young offenders convicted on the same crime in the juvenile court. Moreover, judges tend to sentence 16-year-olds appearing in adult court to probation rather than prison. In the end, what began as a "get tough" measure has had the opposite effect while costing taxpayers more money.

Critics view these new methods of dealing with juvenile offenders as inefficient, ineffective, and philosophically out of step with the original concept of the juvenile court. Supporters view the waiver process as a sound method of getting the most serious juvenile offenders off the streets while ensuring that rehabilitation plays a less critical role in the juvenile system.

■ The Juvenile Trial

Juvenile courts dispose of an estimated 1.3 million delinquency cases during a one-year period. The number of juvenile cases getting to court has stabilized in recent years, reflecting a downward trend in juvenile crime rates and the growth of alternative programs.[59]

During the adjudicatory or trial process, often called the fact-finding hearing in juvenile proceedings, the court hears evidence on the allegations stated in the delinquency petition. In its early development, the juvenile court did not emphasize judicial rule making similar to that of the criminal trial process. Absent were such basic requirements as the standard of proof, rules of evidence, and similar adjudicatory formalities.

Traditionally, the juvenile system was designed to diagnose and rehabilitate children appearing before the court. This was consistent with the view that the court should be social-service oriented. Proceedings were to be nonadversarial, informal, and noncriminal in nature. Gradually, however, the juvenile court movement became the subject of much criticism. This growing dissatisfaction was based primarily on the inability of the court to rehabilitate the juvenile offender, while at the same time failing to safeguard the offender's constitutional rights. Juvenile courts were punishing many children under the guise of being social service agencies, arguing that constitutional protections were not necessary because the juvenile was being helped in the name of the state. Under the *parens patriae* philosophy, the adjudicatory proceeding, as well as subsequent dispositions, was seen as being in the child's best interests. Thus, the philosophy of the juvenile court saw no need for legal rules and procedures, as in the criminal process, nor for the introduction of state prosecutors or defense attorneys. These views and practices have been changed by the U.S. Supreme Court. In 1966 with *Kent v. United States*, the Court began to consider the constitutional validity of juvenile court proceedings. This process culminated in the landmark case of **In re Gault** (1967).[60] In *Gault* the Court ruled that the concept of fundamental fairness is applicable to juvenile delinquency proceedings.

Gerald Gault was a 15-year-old boy on probation. He was arrested as the result of a complaint that he had made lewd telephone calls. After hearings before a juvenile court judge, Gault was ordered committed to the state industrial school as a juvenile delinquent until he reached his majority. The family brought a habeas corpus action in the state courts to challenge the constitutionality of the Arizona Juvenile Code on the ground that the boy was denied his procedural due process rights. The Court decided that the due process clause of the Fourteenth Amendment required that certain procedural guarantees were essential to the adjudication of delinquency cases. Justice Abe Fortas addressed this issue in the following manner:

> Due process of law is the primary and indispensable foundation of individual freedom. It is the basic and essential term in the social compact which defines the rights of the individual and delimits the powers which the state may exercise.[61]

The Court then specified the precise nature of due process by indicating that a juvenile who has violated a criminal statute and who may be committed to an institution is entitled to (1) fair notice of the charges, (2) the right to representation by counsel, (3) the right to confrontation by and cross-examination of witnesses, and (4) the privilege against self-incrimination.

Gault did not hold that the juvenile offender is entitled to all procedural guarantees applicable in the case of an adult charged with a crime. The Supreme Court did not rule, for instance, on such issues as whether the juvenile has the right to a transcript of the proceedings or the right to appellate review. Nor was it clear as to what extent the right to counsel should be provided for nondelinquent children. *Gault* specifically ruled that a juvenile is entitled to counsel in delinquency actions that may result in institutionalization. In this regard, many states have gone beyond *Gault* to provide juveniles with a right to counsel in all stages of court proceedings. However, the question of which juveniles have a right to guarantees under *Gault* has not been completely settled. Some jurisdictions specify that the right to counsel is applicable only in delinquency and status offenses, while other states go beyond *Gault* and provide counsel in neglect and dependency proceedings as well.

The *Gault* decision, particularly as it applies to the constitutional right of a juvenile to the assistance of counsel, has completely altered the juvenile justice system. Instead of dealing with children in a benign and paternalistic fashion, the court must process juvenile offenders within the framework of appropriate constitutional procedures. Although *Gault* was technically limited to the adjudicatory stage, it has spurred further legal reform throughout the juvenile system. Today the right to counsel, the privilege against self-incrimination, the right to treatment in detention and correctional facilities, and other constitutional protections are applied at all stages of the juvenile process, from investigation through adjudication to parole. Because of the significance of the *Gault* case, it is further described in the Law in Review on page 644.

After *Gault*, the Supreme Court continued its trend toward legalizing and formalizing the juvenile trial process with the decision in **In re Winship** (1970).[62] Relying on the "preponderance of the evidence" standard required by the New York Family Court Act, a judge found Winship, a 12-year-old boy, guilty of the crime of larceny. In *Winship*, however, the Supreme Court held that the standard of proof beyond a reasonable doubt, which is required in a criminal prosecution, is also required in the adjudication of a delinquency petition. The *Winship* decision did not settle whether this burden of proof is also applicable to nondelinquent forms of conduct. As a result, some state statutes require proof beyond a reasonable doubt only in delinquency matters. In these jurisdictions, such standards of proof as clear and convincing evidence or a preponderance of the evidence are used for incorrigibility, neglect, or dependency cases. Other jurisdictions, however, apply the reasonable doubt standard in all types of juvenile actions. In spite of these various statutory differences, *Winship* does impose the constitutional requirement of proof beyond a reasonable doubt during the adjudicatory stage of a delinquency proceeding. This case is discussed in detail in the Law in Review on page 645.

In re Gault (1967)

FACTS

Gerald Gault, 15 years of age, was taken into custody by the sheriff of Gila County, Arizona. His arrest was based on the complaint of a woman who said that he and another boy had made an obscene telephone call to her. Gerald was then under a six-month probation for stealing a wallet. Because of the verbal complaint, Gerald was taken to the children's home. His parents were not informed that he was being taken into custody. His mother appeared in the evening and was told by the superintendent of detention that a hearing would be held in the juvenile court the following day. On the day in question, the police officer who had taken Gerald into custody filed a petition alleging his delinquency. Gerald, his mother, and the police officer appeared before the judge in his chambers. Mrs. Cook, the complainant, was not at the hearing. Gerald was questioned about the telephone calls and was sent back to the detention home and then subsequently released a few days later.

On the day of Gerald's release, Mrs. Gault received a letter indicating that a hearing would be held on Gerald's delinquency a few days later. A hearing was held, and the complainant was not present. No transcript or recording was made of the proceedings, and the juvenile officer stated that Gerald had admitted making the lewd telephone calls. Neither the boy nor his parents were advised of any right to remain silent or to be represented by counsel or of any other constitutional rights. At the conclusion of the hearing, the juvenile court committed Gerald as a juvenile delinquent to the state industrial school in Arizona for the period of his minority.

This meant that Gerald at the age of 15 was being sent to a period of incarceration in the state school until age 21, or unless discharged sooner, whereas an adult charged with the same crime would have received a maximum punishment of no more than a $50 fine or two months in prison.

DECISION

Gerald's attorneys filed a habeas corpus writ, which was denied by the superior court of the state of Arizona; that decision was subsequently affirmed by the Arizona Supreme Court. On appeal to the U.S. Supreme Court, Gerald's counsel argued that the juvenile code of Arizona under which Gerald was found delinquent was invalid because it was contrary to the due process clause of the Fourteenth Amendment. In addition, the attorney argued Gerald had been denied the following basic due process rights: (1) notice of charges with regard to the timeliness and specificity of the charges, (2) right to counsel, (3) right to confrontation and cross-examination, (4) privilege against self-incrimination, (5) right to a transcript of the trial record, and (6) right to appellate review. In deciding the case, the Supreme Court had to decide whether procedural due process of law within the context of fundamental fairness under the Fourteenth Amendment applied to juvenile delinquency proceedings in which a child is committed to a state industrial school.

The Court, in a far-reaching opinion written by Justice Abe Fortas, agreed that Gerald's constitutional rights were violated. Notice of charges is an essential ingredient of due process of law, as is right to counsel, right to cross-examine and to confront witnesses, and the privilege against self-incrimination. The questions of whether a juvenile has a right to appellate review and a right to a transcript were not answered by the Court in this decision.

SIGNIFICANCE OF THE CASE

The *Gault* case established that a child has procedural due process constitutional rights as listed above in delinquency adjudication proceedings based on alleged misconduct where the consequences are that the child may be committed to a state institution. The case was confined to rulings at the adjudication stage of the juvenile process.

However, this decision was significant not only because of the procedural reforms, such as the right to counsel, but also because of its far-reaching impact throughout the entire juvenile justice process. *Gault* led to the development of due process standards at the pretrial, trial, and posttrial stages of the juvenile process. While recognizing the history and the development of the juvenile court, it sought to accommodate the motives of rehabilitation and treatment with children's rights. It recognized the principles of fundamental fairness of the law, for children as well as for adults. Judged in the context of today's juvenile justice system, *Gault* redefined the relationship between the juvenile, the parents, and the state. It remains the single most significant constitutional case in the area of juvenile justice. ■

In re Winship (1970)

Following the *Gault* case came the decision of *In re Winship*. This case expressly held that a juvenile in a delinquency adjudication must be proven guilty beyond a reasonable doubt.

FACTS

Winship, a 12-year-old boy in New York, stole $112 from a woman's pocketbook. The petition that charged Winship with delinquency alleged that this act, if done by an adult, would constitute larceny. Winship was adjudicated a delinquent on the basis of the preponderance of the evidence submitted at the court hearing. During a subsequent dispositional hearing, Winship was ordered placed in a training school in New York State for an initial period of 18 months, subject to extensions of his commitment until his eighteenth birthday—six years in total. The New York State Supreme Court and the New York Court of Appeals affirmed the lower court decision, sustaining the conviction.

DECISION

The question in the case was whether Section 744(b) of the New York State Family Court Act was constitutional. This section provided that any determination at the conclusion of an adjudicatory hearing must be based on a preponderance of the evidence. The State of New York argued that juvenile delinquency proceedings were civil in nature, not criminal, and the preponderance of evidence standard was therefore valid. The judge decided Winship's guilt on the basis of this standard and not on the basis of proof beyond a reasonable doubt, which is the standard in the adult criminal justice system. The issue in the case was whether proof beyond a reasonable doubt was essential to due process and fair treatment for juveniles charged with an act that would constitute a crime if committed by an adult.

SIGNIFICANCE OF THE CASE

Although the standard of proof beyond a reasonable doubt is not stated in the Constitution, the U.S. Supreme Court said that *Gault* had established that due process requires the essentials of fair treatment, although it does not require that the adjudication conform to all the requirements of a criminal trial. The Court went on to say that the due process clause recognized proof beyond a reasonable doubt as being among the essentials of fairness required when a child is charged with a delinquent act. The Court also indicated that the standard of proof beyond a reasonable doubt plays a vital role in the American criminal justice system and ensures a greater degree of safety for the presumption of innocence of those accused of a crime.

Thus, the *Winship* case required proof beyond a reasonable doubt as a standard for juvenile adjudication proceedings and eliminated the use of lesser standards such as a preponderance of the evidence, clear and convincing proof, and reasonable proof. ■

Although the traditional juvenile court was severely altered by *Kent, Gault,* and *Winship*, the trend for increased rights for juveniles was somewhat curtailed by the Supreme Court's decision in *McKeiver v. Pennsylvania* (1971).[63] In *McKeiver*, the Court held that trial by jury in a juvenile court's adjudicative stage is not a constitutional requirement. This decision, however, does not prevent the various states from giving the juvenile a trial by jury as a state constitutional right or by state statute. In the majority of states a child has no such right, but in a small number of jurisdictions a child is entitled to a jury trial. Because *McKeiver* is one of the major decisions signaling the Supreme Court's determination to further evaluate the adjudicatory rights of juvenile offenders, the case is highlighted in the Law in Review on page 646.

Once an adjudicatory hearing has been completed, the court is normally required to enter a judgment against the child. This may take the form of declaring the child delinquent, adjudging the child to be a ward of the court, or possibly even suspending judgment so as to avoid the stigma of a juvenile

Chapter 19

Juvenile Justice

■

McKeiver v. Pennsylvania (1971)

One of the most controversial issues in the area of children's rights at adjudication involves the jury trial. Although the Sixth Amendment guarantees the adult criminal defendant the right to a jury trial, the U.S. Supreme Court had not seen fit to grant this right to juvenile offenders. In fact, the Constitution is silent on whether all defendants, including those charged with misdemeanors, have a right to a trial by jury. In the case of *Duncan v. Louisiana*, the Supreme Court held that the Sixth Amendment right to a jury trial applied to all adult defendants accused of serious crimes in state and federal cases. However, no mention was made of the juvenile offender.

The case of *McKeiver v. Pennsylvania* deals with the right of the juvenile defendant to a jury trial.

FACTS

Joseph McKeiver, age 16, was charged with robbery, larceny, and receiving stolen goods, all of which were felonies under the Pennsylvania law. McKeiver was subsequently declared delinquent at an adjudication hearing and placed on probation after his request for a jury trial was denied.

In another case, Edward Terry, age 15, was charged with assault and battery on a police officer, misdemeanors under Pennsylvania law. He was declared a juvenile delinquent after an adjudication following a denial of his request for trial by jury.

In an unrelated case in North Carolina, a group of juveniles were charged with willful, riotous, and disorderly conduct, declared delinquent, and placed on probation. Their request for a jury trial was denied.

The Supreme Court heard all three cases together on the single issue of whether a juvenile has a constitutional right to a jury trial in the juvenile court system.

DECISION

The Supreme Court was required to decide whether the due process clause of the Fourteenth Amendment guarantees the right to a jury trial in the adjudication of a juvenile court delinquency case. It answered in the negative, stating that the right to a jury trial, which is guaranteed by the Sixth Amendment and incorporated into the Fourteenth Amendment, is not among the constitutional safeguards that the due process clause requires at delinquency adjudication hearings.

The Court's reasons were as follows:

1. A jury trial is not a necessary component of accurate fact-finding, as are the procedural requirements stated in the *Gault* case.

2. Not all the rights constitutionally assured to an adult are to be given to a juvenile.
3. Insisting on a jury trial for juvenile offenders could turn the adjudication into a fully adversary process.
4. Insisting on a jury trial would not remedy the problems associated with the lack of rehabilitation in the juvenile court.
5. The preferable approach would be to allow the states to experiment and adopt for themselves a jury trial concept in their individual jurisdictions.
6. The jury trial, if imposed in the juvenile court, would certainly result in delay, formality, and the possibility of a public trial, which at this point is not provided in most jurisdictions.

SIGNIFICANCE OF THE CASE

The *McKeiver* decision temporarily stopped the march toward procedural constitutional due process for juvenile offenders in the juvenile justice system. The majority of the Court believed that juvenile proceedings were different from adult criminal prosecutions. The case also emphasized the fact that, as Justice Harry A. Blackmun said, jurisdictions are free to adopt their own jury trial position in juvenile proceedings. The Court further noted that the majority of states denied a juvenile the right to a jury trial by statute. Thus, the Court believed that granting the juvenile offender the right to a jury trial would hinder rather than advance the system of juvenile justice in the United States. ∎

record. Once a judgment has been entered in accordance with the appropriate state statute, the court can begin its determination of possible dispositions for the child.

■ Disposition and Treatment

At the dispositional hearing the juvenile court judge imposes a sentence on the juvenile offender in light of his or her offense, prior record, and family background. Normally, the sentence is imposed by a juvenile court judge who has broad discretionary power to issue a range of dispositions from dismissal to institutional commitment. In theory, the dispositional decision is an effort by the court to serve the best interests of the child, the family, and the community. In many respects, this postadjudicative process is the most important stage in the juvenile court system because it represents the last opportunity for the court to influence the child and control his or her behavior.

Most jurisdictions have statutes that require the court to proceed with disposition following adjudication of the child as a delinquent or status offender. This is done as part of the adjudicatory process or at a separate dispositional hearing.

Statutory provisions that use a two-part hearing process are preferred, since different evidentiary rules apply at each hearing. The basic purpose of having two separate hearings is to ensure that only evidence appropriate to determining whether the child committed the alleged offense is considered by the court. If evidence relating to the presentence report of the child is used in the adjudicatory hearing, it would normally result in a reversal of the court's delinquency finding. On the other hand, the social history report is essential for court use in the dispositional hearing. Thus the two-part hearing process seeks to ensure that the adjudicatory hearing is used solely to determine the merits of the allegations, while the dispositional hearing determines whether the child is in need of rehabilitation.

In theory, the juvenile court seeks to provide a disposition that represents an individualized treatment plan for the child. This decision is normally based on the presentence investigation of the probation department, reports from social agencies, and possibly a psychiatric evaluation from the juvenile court clinic. The judge generally has broad discretion in dispositional matters but is limited by the provisions of the state's juvenile court act. The prevailing statutory model provides for the following types of alternative dispositions.

1. Dismissal of the petition
2. Suspended judgment
3. Probation
4. Placement in a community treatment program
5. Commitment to the state agency responsible for juvenile institutional care

In addition, the court may place the child with parents or relatives, make dispositional arrangements with private youth-serving agencies, or order the child committed to a mental institution.

One of the most complex problems in the juvenile system has been the limited number of alternative dispositions available for various types of juvenile offenders. Dismissal of the case only provides the court with legal authority to relinquish control over a juvenile. This occurs if allegations in the petition have not been sustained, or where the court does not want to stigmatize the child with a juvenile court record. Similar to dismissal is suspended judgment, where

Juvenile sentencing is designed to provide the care and treatment needed to rehabilitate youths and prevent them from becoming chronic offenders.

the court will continue the case without any formal finding of adjudication. In some instances, the child may also be placed under court supervision for a stipulated period of time. If the child responds well to treatment, the charges are generally dismissed. On the other hand, if the delinquent or incorrigible conduct continues, the court may impose greater supervision.

Juvenile Sentencing

Since the inception of the juvenile court over eight decades ago, its traditional goal and philosophy have been rehabilitation and treatment of the juvenile offender at disposition. Under the rehabilitative goal, the juvenile justice system operated to provide care for children "in their best interest," but often subjected them to harsh penalties without due process of law. In the mid-1960s, due process rights were granted to children, but the ideal of rehabilitation remained unfulfilled.

In order to achieve these traditional goals, juvenile court dispositional orders were based on totally indeterminate sentencing terms for juvenile offenders. The indeterminate sentence is often defined as a term of incarceration with a stated minimum and maximum period, or with no minimum. For instance, a sentence to prison for a period of from 3 to 10 years would constitute an indeterminate sentence. Based on the traditional belief that the indeterminate dispositional order should fit the child's needs, such sentencing provisions allow for individualized programs of treatment and provide for flexibility in sentencing. In some jurisdictions, the juvenile court judge could sentence the juvenile for an indeterminate period to a particular type of program. In other jurisdictions, the judge was required to send a child to a department such as a division of youth services within the given jurisdiction, and that agency would be responsible for the child's placement and treatment.

Over the past few years, juvenile justice experts and the general public have become aroused about the serious juvenile crime rate in general and about violent acts committed by children in particular. As a result, reform groups, especially law enforcement officials and legislators, have demanded that the juvenile justice system take a more serious stand with regard to dangerous juvenile offenders. Some state legislatures have responded by amending their juvenile codes and passing harsh laws that tighten up the juvenile justice system. For instance, in New York, children as young as 13 accused of murder may be tried in adult courts and sentenced to life terms.[64] California has lowered the age to 16 for transferring juvenile offenders to the adult court system.[65] The State of Washington has passed a determinate sentencing statute, which is discussed in detail later in this section. Other jurisdictions, including the District of Columbia, Colorado, Delaware, Florida, and Virginia, have passed mandatory or determinate prison sentences for juveniles convicted of serious felonies. The "get tough" approach even allows for the use of the death penalty in juvenile cases. Not all experts agree with this approach. Victor Streib, in *Death Penalty for Juveniles*, the most comprehensive text on the subject, concludes that there should be a court decision for a national constitutional prohibition against such executions.[66] But the U.S. Supreme Court disagrees. (See the Criminal Justice in Review on page 649.)

A second recent reform movement involves status offenders. This approach to the problem of disposition suggests that status offenders and other minor juvenile offenders be removed from the juvenile justice system and kept out of institutional programs that accept alleged juvenile delinquents. Because of the

Death Row Children— Executions for Juveniles Upheld

In more than half of the 36 states that provide for capital punishment, children who commit murder and who have been transferred to the adult court can be given the death penalty. In fact, more than 30 youths reside on death row today; some youths have been executed (though the executions occurred when they were in their 20s, after they had spent many years on death row).

The U.S. Supreme Court has ruled on this highly emotional issue. Two previous attempts to decide the issue left the justices closely divided. Bare majorities of the Court reversed the death sentences of both Monty Lee Eddings and William Wayne Thompson, but the justices could not agree on the fundamental question of whether it is "cruel and unusual" punishment to exact the penalty of death for murders committed by juveniles.[1]

However, the Court agreed to hear two other cases raising this issue,

Wilkins v. Missouri and Stanford v. Kentucky in 1989.[2] Wilkins was 16 when he committed murder, while Stanford was 17. The constitutional question raised by these two cases is basically the same as in the Thompson case: At what age does the Eighth Amendment ban the death penalty as punishment no matter what the crime? Critics of the death penalty believe that there is a consensus against executing young people in the United States. Supporters of capital punishment argue that juveniles after age 16 should be held fully responsible for murder. The Su-

preme Court concluded that states are free to impose the death penalty for murderers who committed their crimes while age 16 or 17. According to the majority opinion written by Justice Scalia, society has not formed a consensus that such executions constitute a cruel and unusual punishment in violation of the Eighth Amendment. Does this mean that the states will now execute juvenile offenders? Table A lists the minimum ages at which the death penalty can be imposed in the various states. ■

TABLE A ■ Minimum Age Authorized for Capital Punishment

10 years*	13 years*	14 years*	15 years*	16 years
Indiana	Georgia	Missouri	Arkansas	Connecticut
Vermont	Mississippi	North Carolina	Louisiana	Montana
			Virginia	Nevada

17 years	18 years	No minimum age specified	
New Hampshire	California	Federal	Oklahoma
Texas	Colorado	Alabama	Pennsylvania
	Illinois	Arizona	South Carolina
	Nebraska	Delaware	South Dakota
	New Jersey	Florida	Tennessee
	New Mexico	Idaho	Utah
	Ohio	Kentucky	Wyoming
	Oregon	Maryland	
	Washington		

SOURCE: *Capital punishment, 1985*, BJS Bulletin (November 1986); *Bureau of Justice Statistics* (Washington D.C.: U.S. Government Printing Office, 1988), p. 99.

[1] *Eddings v. Oklahoma*, 455 U.S. 104, S.Ct., L.Ed.2d (1982) and *Thompson v. Oklahoma*, 108 S.Ct 2687, L.Ed.2d (1988).

[2] *Stanford v. Kentucky* and *Wilkins v. Missouri*, 109 S.Ct. 2969.

*No longer legally permitted

development of numerous diversion programs, many children who are involved in truancy and incorrigible behavior, and who ordinarily would have been sent to a closed institution, are now being placed in community programs.

A third effort to reform juvenile justice, especially the sentencing process, emanates from the American Bar Association's development of standards for the juvenile justice system, in particular its work on dispositions, dispositional procedures, juvenile delinquency and sanctions, and corrections administration. Stanley Fisher suggests that these standards point to a shift in juvenile court philosophy from traditional rehabilitation to the concept of "just desert."[67] In other words, the standards recommend that juveniles be given determinate or "flat" sentences without the possibility of parole, rather than the indeterminate sentences that most juvenile offenders now receive. The standards further recommend that punishment be classified into three major categories: nominal, conditional, and custodial sanctions. Nominal sanctions consist of reprimands, warnings, or other minor actions that do not affect the child's personal liberty. Conditional sanctions deal with such regulations as probation, restitution, and counseling programs. Custodial sanctions, the most extreme, consider removal of the juvenile from his or her home into a nonsecure or secure institution. The National Advisory Commission on Criminal Justice Standards and Goals also recommended in 1976 that the dispositions available to the court for juveniles adjudicated delinquent include nominal, conditional, and custodial categories.[68]

The state of Washington has already adopted a determinate sentencing law for juvenile offenders.[69] All children convicted of juvenile delinquency are evaluated on the basis of a point system. Points are awarded to children based on their age, prior juvenile record, type of crime committed, and other factors. Minor offenders are handled in the community. Those committing more serious offenses are placed under probation. Children who commit the most serious offenses are subject to institutional penalties. Institutional officials, who had total discretion in the past for releasing children, now have limited discretion. As a result, juvenile offenders who commit crimes such as rape or armed robbery are being sentenced to periods of institutionalization for two, three, and four years. This approach is different from the indeterminate program of sentencing under which children who had committed a serious crime might be released from institutions in less than a year. Thus the use of presumptive sentencing provisions or proportionality in sentencing has become a factor in juvenile justice dispositional procedures.

Although this discussion indicates a change in traditional juvenile court sentencing, most jurisdictions continue to be preoccupied with rehabilitation as a primary dispositional goal. Joseph Goldstein, Anna Freud, and Albert Solnit, in their classic work *Beyond the Best Interests of the Child*, indicate that placements of children should be based on the "least detrimental alternative" philosophy available in order to safeguard the child's growth and development.[70] This goal applies to children involved in both delinquent behavior and noncriminal behavior and to those who may be neglected, abandoned, or abused. In reality today, most states apply custodial restrictions or institutionalization only to children who commit the most serious offenses.

In sum, rehabilitation and treatment remain the most realistic goals in the dispositional process. Proportionality in juvenile sentencing is being recognized and implemented by some jurisdictions. Whether the philosophy of "just desert" is the answer to juvenile criminality remains unclear. Some critics suggest that the ABA standards would "destroy the nation's juvenile court system and replace it with a junior criminal justice system."[71] There is no question that fitting the penalty to the child's behavior would effect a radical change in current juvenile justice sentencing philosophy. And the practical consequences can be tremendous—witness the increase in the number of institutionalized youth after a number of years of decline. The movement to toughen juvenile sentencing, like its adult counterpart, has produced an increased correctional population.

Juvenile Probation

Probation is the most commonly used formal sentence for juvenile offenders, and many states require that a youth fail on probation before being sent to an institution (unless the criminal act is quite serious). Probation involves placing the child under the supervision of the juvenile probation department for the purpose of community treatment. Conditions of probation are normally imposed on the child by either statute or court order and are of two kinds. Some are general conditions, such as those that require the child to stay away from other delinquents or to obey the law. Such conditions are often vague, but they have been upheld by the courts. More specific conditions of probation include requiring the child to participate in a vocational training program, to attend school regularly, to obtain treatment at a child guidance clinic, or to make restitution. Restitution can be in the form of community service—for example, a youth found in possession of marijuana might be required to work 50 hours in a home for the elderly. Monetary restitution requires delinquents to pay back the victims of their crimes. Restitution programs have proven quite successful and have been adopted around the country.[72]

In recent years, some jurisdictions have turned to a **balanced probation** approach in an effort to enhance the success of probation.[73] Probation systems that integrate community protection, the accountability of the juvenile offender, competency, and individualization incorporate the treatment values of this balanced approach. Some of these juvenile protection programs offer renewed promise for community treatment.

Once placed on probation, the child is ordinarily required to meet regularly with the probation officer for counseling and supervision and adhere to the conditions of probation established by the court. This plan may continue for a period of time, possibly six months to two years, depending on the duration of probation as established by the statutory law. Most states allow early release from probation if the child is making a good adjustment, or may permit an extension of the probationary period. If the child complies with the court order, probation is terminated. Proceedings to revoke probation occur if the child commits a new offense. Most states provide that the child be given notice, a hearing, the right to counsel, and other due process safeguards similar to those given adult offenders at such proceedings.

■ Institutionalization

The most severe of the statutory dispositions available to the juvenile court involves committing the child to a juvenile institution. The committed child may be sent to a state training school or private residential treatment facility. These are usually minimum security facilities with a small population and an emphasis on treatment and education. Some states, however, maintain facilities with a population of over 1,000.

Most state statutes vary when determining the length of the child's commitment. Traditionally, many jurisdictions would commit the child up to majority, which usually meant 21 years of age. This form of sentencing normally deprived the child of freedom for an extensive period of time—sometimes longer than an adult would be confined if sentenced for the same offense. As a result, some states have sought to circumvent this problem by passing legislation committing children for periods ranging from one to three years.

Profile of Incarcerated Youth

At last count approximately 55,000 youths were in public custody facilities, and 30,000 were in private facilities (see Table 19.3).[74] Most of the recent increase in population is accounted for by the growth in the number of delinquents held in public facilities from about 49,000 in 1979 to about 55,000 in 1987. The number of status offenders in public facilities has remained stable since 1979 at about 9,000.

According to the Children in Custody Census of Public Juvenile Facilities in 1987, of the more than 55,000 juveniles held in publicly run facilities, 86 percent were male, and 82 percent were between 14 and 17 years of age (see Table 19.4).[75]

TABLE 19.3 ■ Total Number of Juveniles in Public and Private Custody, 1985

	Number of juveniles in public and private facilities		Number of juveniles in public and private facilities
United States, total	83,402	South (continued)	
Northeast		Delaware	190
Connecticut	997	District of Columbia	417
Maine	467	Florida	3,335
Massachusetts	1,064	Georgia	1,300
New Hampshire	235	Kentucky	1,047
New Jersey	1,814	Louisiana	1,530
New York	5,396	Maryland	2,154
Pennsylvania	3,283	North Carolina	1,344
Rhode Island	316	Oklahoma	835
Vermont	137	South Carolina	762
		Tennessee	1,530
Midwest		Texas	4,122
Illinois	2,066	Virginia	1,724
Indiana	2,886	West Virginia	265
Iowa	1,090		
Kansas	1,363	West	
Michigan	3,369	Alaska	361
Minnesota	1,912	Arizona	1,799
Missouri	1,415	California	15,812
Nebraska	834	Colorado	1,096
North Dakota	207	Hawaii	210
Ohio	4,860	Idaho	261
South Dakota	439	Montana	247
Wisconsin	1,775	Nevada	542
		New Mexico	804
South		Oregon	1,179
Alabama	974	Utah	281
Arkansas	922	Washington	1,748

NOTE: Data on juveniles are for February 1, 1985. An additional 2,112 adults were held in juvenile facilities. Data from Mississippi and Wyoming are not shown to preserve confidentiality.

SOURCE: Bureau of Justice Statistics, *Report to the Nation on Crime and Justice*, (Washington, D.C.: U.S. Department of Justice, 1988).

TABLE 19.4 ■ **Number of Juveniles in Custody by Reasons Held and by Type of Public Facility (Census Classification), 1987**

	Total facilities	Short-term facilities			Long-term facilities		
		Short-term	Institutional	Open	Long-term	Institutional	Open
Total all juveniles	53,503	18,156	17,430	726	35,347	26,547	8,800
Total detained for:	16,176	15,403	14,730	673	773	479	294
Delinquent offenses[a]	14,649	14,006	13,883	123	643	454	189
Status offenses[b]	1,303	1,203	817	386	100	23	77
Abuse/neglect[c]	211	182	22	160	29	1	28
Offenses unknown[d]	13	12	8	4	1	1	0
Total committed for:	37,074	2,717	2,692	25	34,357	26,060	8,297
Delinquent offenses	35,620	2,620	2,606	14	33,000	25,632	7,368
Status offenses	1,220	76	71	5	1,144	353	791
Abuse/neglect	218	6	0	6	212	75	137
Offenses unknown	16	15	15	0	1	0	1
Voluntarily admitted	253	36	8	28	217	8	209

[a]Offenses that would be criminal if committed by an adult.
[b]Offenses that would not be criminal for adults, such as running away, truancy, or incorrigibility.
[c]Also includes dependency, emotional disturbance, and mental retardation.
[d]Includes unknown or unspecified acts.

SOURCE: *Children in Custody—Public Juvenile Facilities, Juvenile Justice Bulletin* (Washington, D.C.: U.S. Department of Justice, 1988), p. 3.

Minority youths—blacks, Hispanics, and other nonwhite ethnic groups—comprised more than half the juveniles in public facilities (see Table 19.5). The number of minority youths in custody has risen in recent years. The number of white juveniles held in public facilities decreased slightly between 1985 and 1987, while the number of black and Hispanic juveniles increased 15 percent and 20 percent, respectively.[76]

The disproportionate number of minority youths incarcerated in youth facilities may mean that blacks, Hispanics, and other minorities are more likely

TABLE 19.5 ■ **Juveniles in Custody by Minority Status and Type of Public Facility (Census Classification), 1987**

	Total facilities	Short-term facilities			Long-term facilities		
		Total short-term	Institutional	Open	Total long-term	Institutional	Open
Total juveniles	53,503	18,156	17,430	726	35,347	26,547	8,800
Nonminority[a]	23,375	8,077	7,589	488	15,298	10,785	4,513
Minority	30,128	10,079	9,841	238	20,049	15,762	4,287
Black[b]	20,898	6,777	6,583	194	14,121	11,033	3,088
Hispanic[c]	7,887	2,860	2,836	24	5,027	4,043	984
Other	1,343	442	422	20	901	686	215

[a]Includes whites not of Hispanic origin.

[b]Includes blacks not of Hispanic origin.

[c]Includes both blacks and whites of Hispanic origin. There were 159 black Hispanic juveniles held in public facilities; 73 in short-term institutions; 1 in short-term open; 38 in long-term open facilities.

SOURCE: *Children in Custody—Public Juvenile Facilities, Juvenile Justice Bulletin* (Washington, D.C.: U.S. Department of Justice, 1988), p. 4.

Youths line up in a boot camp style training school program.

to be arrested and charged with serious crimes than white youths.[77] However, some researchers such as Barry Krisberg question whether the seriousness of the offense alone can explain the differences in incarceration rates among racial groups.[78] With minority youths being incarcerated in U.S. training schools at a rate four times greater than their representation in the general population, it is appropriate to ask if we have a racist juvenile justice system.

Nine out of 10 (94 percent) of incarcerated juveniles were held for delinquent offenses—offenses that would be crimes if committed by adults. Forty percent were held for violent offenses, about 6 percent for drug offenses, and 7 percent for public-order crimes.[79] Just over 2 percent were confined for a juvenile status offense, such as truancy, running away, or incorrigibility. The efforts made in the 1970s and early 1980s to keep status offenders out of training schools seem to have paid off.

Over 43 percent of incarcerated juveniles have been arrested more than five times, and over 80 percent have been on probation previously. Over 97 percent of all incarcerated juveniles have committed prior violent offenses, and more than 80 percent have previously used illegal drugs.[80]

In summary, during the mid-1980s, despite the growth of alternative treatments, diversion, restitution, and the like, the number of delinquents under secure supervision has increased. Like their adult counterparts, juvenile offenders have been receiving incarceration sentences at a faster rate. In addition, nearly half of the juvenile offenders in custody were being held for violent crimes, and a very significant percentage (more than 60 percent) used drugs regularly. These percentages tend to explain why the juvenile justice system has become more formalized, restrictive, and punishment oriented in recent years—in spite of stabilized arrest rates.

Deinstitutionalization

Some experts in delinquency and juvenile law question the policy of institutionalizing juvenile offenders. Many believe that large institutions are too costly to operate and only produce more sophisticated criminals. Michigan, for example, projects a need for 2,000 more beds, at an annual cost of $60,000 per juvenile offender in the next decade. This dilemma has produced a number of efforts to remove youth from juvenile facilities and replace large units with smaller community-based facilities. For example, led by its former commissioner, Jerome Miller, a staunch opponent of incarcerating most youth, Massachusetts closed all its state training schools over a decade ago (subsequently, however, public pressure caused a few secure facilities to be reopened). Many other states have established small residential facilities operated by juvenile-care agencies to replace larger units.[81]

Despite the daily rhetoric on crime, public support of community-based programs for juveniles still exists. Although such programs are not panaceas, a recent survey in California, for instance, found that a majority of those surveyed supported more treatment and less incarceration for juvenile offenders. The states of Utah, Maryland, Vermont, and Pennsylvania, for example, have dramatically reduced their reform school populations while setting up a wide range of intensive treatment programs for juveniles. Many large, impersonal, expensive state institutions with unqualified staff and ineffective treatment programs have been eliminated.

WHAT TO DO WITH STATUS OFFENDERS. It has been almost 20 years since the movement to deinstitutionalize status offenders (DSO) began.[82] Since its inception, the DSO approach has been hotly debated. Some have argued that early intervention is society's best hope of forestalling future delinquent behavior and reducing victimization. Others have argued that legal control over status offenders is a violation of youth's rights. Still others have viewed status-offending behavior as a symptom of some larger trauma or problem that requires attention. These diverse opinions still exist today.

Millions of federal, state, and local dollars have been spent on the DSO movement under the Juvenile Justice and Delinquency Prevention Act of 1974. Vast numbers of programs have been created around the country to reduce the number of juveniles in secure confinement.

The twin concepts of "treatment" and "normalization" form the framework for the DSO approach. Since Congress passed the JJDP Act in 1974, 50 states have complied with some aspect of the deinstitutionalization mandate. What remains to be done, however, is to study the effect DSO has had on juveniles and the justice system. Previous research has focused on specific programs. Now DSO needs to be assessed as a reform movement of 25 years.

Treating the Chronic Offender

Chronic juvenile offenders are youths who are most likely to continue their law-violating behavior. One of the top priorities of recent years has been the treatment of hard-core chronic delinquents while removing nonviolent and noncriminal youths from the juvenile correctional system.

Juvenile courts currently concentrate their resources on youths who have appeared in court five or six times and are truly chronic offenders. A recent study of court careers of juvenile offenders has shed new light on this issue, however.[83] The study's major finding—that youths who were referred to juvenile court for a second time before age 16 were likely to continue their law-violating behavior—indicates that juveniles with two offenses may, in fact, be identified as chronic offenders (see Figure 19.2). This study argues that

■ FIGURE 19.2
Court Cases of Juvenile Offenders

SOURCE: U.S. Department of Justice, Office of Juvenile Justice and Delinquency Prevention, *Juvenile Justice Bulletin* (August 1988): 3.

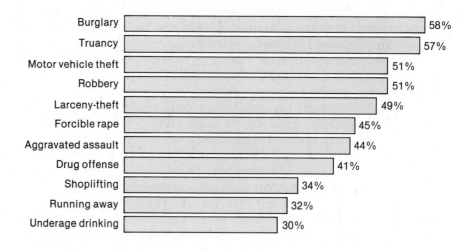

Percentage of youth who returned to juvenile court after a first referral for the following offenses

Offense	Percentage
Burglary	58%
Truancy	57%
Motor vehicle theft	51%
Robbery	51%
Larceny-theft	49%
Forcible rape	45%
Aggravated assault	44%
Drug offense	41%
Shoplifting	34%
Running away	32%
Underage drinking	30%

these juveniles should be treated the same as chronic offenders who have committed five or six offenses.

Thus the study suggests that juvenile courts have the opportunity to intervene in the lives of a large percentage of youths at a time when problems first become apparent. In addition, the study implies that courts should not wait until the youth has returned for the fourth or fifth time before taking strong remedial action.[84]

Programs around the country have attempted to use swift prosecution, high-security incapacitation, and intensive treatment to reduce serious juvenile crime. One such program, the Habitual Serious and Violent Juvenile Offender Program (HSVJOP), provided for prosecutors to target youths defined as chronic, serious, and violent offenders.[85] Undertaken in 13 locations nationwide from 1985 to 1987, the program resulted in speedier outcomes, more findings of guilt, more correctional commitments, and reduced plea-bargaining dispositions. The HSVJOP revealed that special targeting and prosecution of serious and habitual juvenile offenders may prove successful.

Related to the problem of the chronic offender is the juvenile court's response to violent youth crime. Violent crime represents a relatively small though significant part of a juvenile court's total delinquency caseload. In a recent 12-state sample, 6 percent of the youths referred to juvenile court for a criminal law violation were charged with a violent offense.[86] With such offenses as criminal homicides, violent sex offenses, robberies, and aggravated assaults, the juvenile court detains larger numbers of youths before trial, has more adjudicatory hearings, initiates more transfer petitions to adult courts, and orders significantly more serious dispositions.

Chronic and violent juvenile offenders represent a small proportion of the nation's juvenile population, but commit a disproportionate amount of juvenile crime. More dispositional alternatives aimed at this target population can increase the effectiveness of the juvenile court system.

■ Postdisposition: The Right to Treatment

The postdisposition stage of the juvenile process normally involves juvenile aftercare and provisions for appeal of cases disposed of in the juvenile court.

The question has been raised as to whether children committed to juvenile institutions have a constitutional or statutory right to treatment; those who support the right to treatment claim that the state must provide treatment for the juvenile offender if it intends to exercise control over the offender.

Once released from an institution, a juvenile may be placed on aftercare, usually involving parole under the supervision of a juvenile parole worker. The child completes the period of confinement in the community and receives assistance from the juvenile parole officer in the form of counseling, school referral, vocational training, and other services. If the conditions of parole are violated, the juvenile may have parole revoked and be returned to the institution. Unlike the adult postconviction process, where the U.S. Supreme Court has imposed procedural protections in revocation of probation and parole proceedings, juveniles have not yet received such due process rights. State courts have also been reluctant to litigate juvenile rights in this area, and those that have have generally refused to require the whole array of rights available to adult offenders. Since the *Gault* decision, however, many states have adopted administrative regulations requiring juvenile agencies to incorporate due process procedures such as proper notice, the hearing, and the right to counsel in postconviction proceedings.

Finally, there is the question of whether juveniles who are committed to institutions have a right to treatment. Because the system of dealing with juvenile offenders is similar to the system of commitment for the mentally ill in that both are based on the *parens patriae* philosophy, juveniles have also sought a right to treatment. In light of this similarity, the case of *Martarella v. Kelly* (1972) established that when juveniles judged to be "persons in need of supervision" are not furnished with adequate treatment, the failure to provide such treatment violates the Eighth and Fourteenth Amendments.[87] In **Inmates v. Affleck** (1972), the court recognized the right to treatment on statutory grounds and also required that minimum standards of treatment be implemented for juvenile offenders under institutional care.[88] The *Inmates v. Affleck* case illustrated the horrible conditions that exist in many juvenile institutions. Consider the following excerpt from the appellate court record in this case:

> Located on the floor above Annex C is a series of small, dimly lit, steel barred cells used for solitary confinement. Each cell is approximately eight feet by four feet, containing a metal slab bed and mattress, sink, and toilet. Boys confined there are released only to take showers, about twice a week. They get no exercise. The inmate's attorney, but not his family, is allowed to visit him there. Because windows on the wall opposite the cellblock are broken, the cells are cold. There is a small hole in the bars, through which meals, sometimes cold, are passed.[89]

Similar to Affleck was **Morales v. Turman** (1973), where the court specifically found that juveniles at a training school in Texas have a statutory right to treatment.[90] In accordance with these holdings, the Court of Appeals for the Seventh Circuit in **Nelson v. Heyne** (1974) upheld a constitutional right to treatment for institutionalized juveniles under the Fourteenth Amendment.[91] Supporting this position, the court said:

> Because children differ in their need for rehabilitation, individual need for treatment will differ. When a state assumes the place of a juvenile's parents, it assumes as well the parental duties, and its treatment of its juveniles should, so far as can be reasonably required, be what proper parental care would provide. . . . Without a program of individual treatment, the result may be that the juvenile "will not be rehabilitated, but warehoused. . . ."[92]

The *Nelson* case is significant because it was the first federal appellate court decision to affirm a constitutional right to treatment. Although the U.S. Supreme Court has not yet declared that juveniles do have such a right, these early decisions seem to indicate that juveniles do have a right, be it statutory or constitutional, to receive treatment and to be assured of a minimum standard of physical care if committed to a juvenile institution.

In recent years, however, progress in the legal right to treatment movement seems to have been curtailed. For example, in **Ralston v. Robinson** (1981), the Supreme Court held that a judge may modify the essential terms of treatment if he or she finds that such treatment was not consistent with the defendant's behavior.[93] Robinson, a 17-year-old youthful offender who had pleaded guilty to second-degree murder, was sentenced to 10 years' imprisonment under the Federal Youth Corrections Act (YCA). Subsequently, while incarcerated, he was found guilty of assaulting a federal officer, and the U.S. District Court, finding that he would not benefit from treatment under the YCA, imposed an adult sentence to be served consecutive by with the YCA sentence. Strongly endorsing the judge's discretionary power, the Supreme Court concluded that a trial court may convert a rehabilitative disposition into a more severe punitive sentence when it becomes apparent that the initial treatment decision will not help the offender further.

In 1987, the federal courts litigated a class action case dealing with minimum standards of care for adolescents in the McClaren School for Boys in Oregon (*Gary H. v. Hegstrom*).[94] The U.S. Court of Appeals ordered due process hearings prior to confinement in excess of 24 hours and minimum sanitary, health, educational, and medical resources for inmates, but wholesale adoption of various professional association concepts for model institutions was not constitutionally mandated. The court also held that it is not proper to order dispositions that are so expensive that other children may be deprived of services.

The future of the right to treatment for juveniles remains uncertain. Minimum standards of care and treatment have been mandated on a case-by-case basis, but some courts have limited the constitutional protections regarding the right to treatment. In light of the new hard-line approach to juvenile crime, it does not appear that the courts could be persuaded to expand this constitutional theory further.

The termination of aftercare marks the final stage of the formal juvenile justice process.

■ Children and Drugs: An American Crisis

For most of its history, the emphasis of the juvenile justice system has been on controlling juvenile crime and antisocial behavior. In recent years, however, these actions have become intertwined with the use of illegal drugs by children. Today, juvenile drug abuse has become a major problem in the United States, and the juvenile justice system is under great pressure to combat it.

The National Council of Juvenile and Family Court Judges estimates that drug abuse is a significant factor in 60 to 90 percent of all juvenile cases referred to their courts.[95] The problem is not limited to major urban areas, such as Miami, New York, and Los Angeles, but exists in many other urban as well as suburban areas of the country. It is further highlighted by regular television reporting of police raids on crack houses, cocaine distribution centers, and marijuana hangouts. Often those arrested are juveniles under 17 who have appeared in court previously. Unless the court can intervene early, it is safe to predict these juveniles will soon be chronic offenders, junkies, prostitutes, or drug dealing gang members. In addition, much of the drug-related crime and violence occurs in schools throughout the country and interferes with the teaching and learning process.

As the United States has become aware of the tremendous increase in drug-related juvenile arrests over the last decade, the juvenile justice system has become more important than ever before in combating the problem.[96] Attacking illegal drug use requires systemwide cooperation on both the enforcement and the prevention fronts. Law enforcement agencies have become involved in programs such as DARE (an acronym for Drug Abuse Resistance Education), which has been adopted by more than 790 school systems in 43 states.[97] Juvenile courts are placing offenders in secure facilities when drug abuse is a significant threat to the safety of the child or others. Community institutions, agencies, and social centers are being pressured to form active partnerships to develop and sustain local programs. Some jurisdictions have even considered the use of mandatory urine testing for adjudicated juvenile drug offenders. At all levels, the juvenile justice system is facing a major crisis of drug-related cases. It remains to be seen whether such programs as the Omnibus Drug Law of 1989 (discussed in Chapter 4) will have an impact in reducing substance abuse nationwide.

Police question a member of the "Florence" gang in California.

■ Youth Gangs

Another serious problem which is not of the magnitude of drug abuse although the two are related, is the reemergence of youth gangs. Gangs developed early in the nation's history and reached their heyday in the 1950s and early 1960s. After a lull of about 10 years, gang operations seem to be on the rise. Since the mid 1980s, youth gangs characterized as delinquent or violent have developed in many major urban areas, particularly Los Angeles, Miami, Chicago, and New York.

Most of these gangs are racially and ethnically homogeneous; there are black gangs known as the Crips, Bloods, and Vice Lords, Hispanic gangs, Asian gangs, Jamaican posses, and neo-Nazi groups, among others. Consisting of cohesive groups of youths, ages 14 to 20, these gangs seek monetary gain and act out aggressively against the general public. Often their actions erupt into newsworthy intragang warfare and violence. By virtue of their ages, many of the youths fall into the area of overlap between the juvenile and adult criminal jurisdictions and use this to their advantage.

In 1987, more than 350 gang-related killings occurred in Los Angeles County, an 80 percent increase over 1986.[98] In 1988, 59 homicides were attributed to youth gangs in Chicago, and the number of violent crimes ran into the thousands.

Traditionally, criminologists have offered a number of explanations of why gangs exist and why youths join them.[99] One view is that the gangs serve as a bridge between adolescence and adulthood in communities where adult control is lacking. Another view suggests that gangs are a product of lower-class social disorganization and that they serve as an alternative means of advancement for disadvantaged youths. Still another view is that some gangs are havens for psychotic and disturbed youths. Today's gangs, however, seem more commercial than culturally oriented. Profit from the drug trade is often the motive for gang activities. With little hope of offering conventional means of success, justice officials are finding it difficult to combat the lure of today's street gang.

■ Future Directions in Juvenile Justice

What does the future hold for the juvenile justice system? The following figures indicate the magnitude of the problem. Over 1.5 million youths under 18 are arrested each year; juvenile courts order over 1.3 million delinquency dispositions and hear almost 1 million status offense cases and 400,000 child abuse cases; drug abuse is a significant factor in from 60 to 90 percent of all cases referred to juvenile courts; and alcohol is the major substance abuse of youth throughout the country.[100]

These statistics present a disturbing picture of American youths who are not participating in traditional family, education, and community activities. Instead, many children are involved in disruptive behavior. Unfortunately, over the years few effective prevention and rehabilitation programs have been available for juvenile offenders.

In the 1980s the juvenile justice system has been torn between two concerns: on the one hand, noncriminal youths who can be salvaged during the early stages of their delinquent careers and status offenders who may be in court to cover up the sexual and physical abuse inflicted on them by their parents and, on the other hand, hard-core delinquents who are a threat to society and to themselves.

After many years in which attention was directed at such liberal reforms as removing status offenders from detention facilities and from institutions that housed delinquents, American society is now experiencing a period when the number of juveniles under lock and key is rising (although the number who are being arrested is declining). The supremacy of the crime control perspective is having an impact on the juvenile justice field. Yet considering the fact that so

Three members of an Hispanic youth gang in Los Angeles.

many adult offenders have had juvenile records, there is little to indicate that incarcerating youthful offenders is an answer to their criminal behavior.

The time is ripe for an attack on these problems. For years, the juvenile justice system has operated with ambiguous goals and limited resources. One suggestion is that we should develop a national commitment to children. Such a policy would seek to deter children from antisocial behavior during the early stages of their lives. Creating stronger family units, establishing better schools, and improving living conditions are all examples of sound delinquency prevention policies. Another recommendation is that the federal government should continue to focus on the problem of the serious, violent, and chronic offender, as it has done since 1986. This requires (1) prosecuting serious juvenile offenders more effectively; (2) preventing the victimization of children; and (3) maintaining the concept of responsibility in the juvenile system. Thirdly, state and local jurisdictions need to ensure that juvenile justice agencies are well organized and efficiently managed. This involves ensuring (1) that all children processed through the juvenile justice system are treated fairly and in accordance with due process of law; (2) that programs based on empirical data are developed to control chronic offenders; and (3) that diversion and the removal of status offenders from juvenile court jurisdiction are given further consideration.

Today, no single ideology dominates the juvenile justice system. As the liberal program of the 1970s has faltered, more restrictive sanctions have been imposed. Both the old and the new juvenile justice agendas will probably dominate the 1990s. However, as Supreme Court Justice Harry A. Blackmun stated in *McKeiver v. Pennsylvania:*

> The juvenile concept held high promise. We are reluctant to say that, despite disappointment of so grave dimensions, it still does not hold promise, and we are particularly reluctant to say, as do the Pennsylvania petitions here, that the system cannot accomplish its rehabilitative goals. So much depends on the availability of resources, on the interest and commitment of the public, on willingness to learn, and on understanding as to cause and effect and cure. In this field, as in so many others, one perhaps learns best by doing.[101]

■ SUMMARY

The juvenile justice system is concerned with delinquent children, as well as with those who are beyond the care and protection of their parents. Jurisdiction for juveniles involved in antisocial behavior exists in the juvenile or family court systems of each jurisdiction. Courts such as these belong to a system of agencies including law enforcement, child care, and institutional services.

When a child is brought to the juvenile court, the proceedings are generally nonadversarial and informal in nature. Representatives from different disciplines, such as lawyers, social workers, and psychiatrists, all play major roles in the judicial process.

In recent years, the juvenile court system has become more legalistic by virtue of U.S. Supreme Court decisions that have granted children procedural safeguards in these proceedings. However, neither rehabilitation programs nor the application of due process rights has stemmed the growing tide of juvenile antisocial behavior. Perhaps the answer lies outside the courthouse, in the form of job opportunities for juveniles, improved family relationships, and more effective school systems. How to cope with the needs of children in trouble remains one of the most controversial and frustrating issues in the justice system.

■ QUESTIONS

1. Should status offenders be treated by the juvenile court? Should they be placed in confinement for running away or cutting school?
2. Should a juvenile ever be waived to adult court and risk being incarcerated with adult felons?
3. Do you agree with the principle of a death penalty for children?
4. Should juveniles be given mandatory incarceration sentences for serious crimes as adults are?

5. Is it fair to deny juveniles a jury trial?
6. Do you think the trend toward treating juveniles like adult offenders is desirable?
7. What programs should communities develop to prevent juvenile drug abuse?
8. Discuss the recent increase in youth gangs in America. How can the juvenile justice system deal with this problem?

■ NOTES

1. Ralph Weisheit and Diane Alexander, "Juvenile Justice Philosophy and Demise of Parens Patriae," *Federal Probation* (December 1988): 56.
2. Material in this section depends heavily on Sanford J. Fox, "Juvenile Justice Reform: A Historical Perspective," *Stanford Law Review* 22 (1970): 1187–1205; Lawrence Stone, *The Family, Sex, and Marriage in England: 1500–1800* (New York: Harper & Row, 1977); Philipe Aries, *Century of Childhood: A Social History of Family Life* (New York: Vintage Press, 1962); Douglas R. Rendleman, "Parens Patriae: From Chancer to the Juvenile Court," *South Carolina Law Review* 23 (1971): 205–29; Wiley B. Sanders, *Some Early Beginnings of the Children's Court Movement in England*, National Probation Association Yearbook (New York: National Council on Crime and Delinquency, 1945); Anthony Platt, "The Rise of the Child Saving Movement: A Study in Social Policy and Correctional Reform," *Annals of the American Academy of Political and Social Science* 381 (1979): 21–38; Anthony M. Platt, *The Child Savers: The Invention of Delinquency* (Chicago: University of Chicago Press, 1969); Robert S. Pickett, *House of Refuge: Origins of Juvenile Reform in New York State, 1815–1857* (Syracuse, N.Y.: Syracuse University Press, 1969).
3. Douglas Besharov, *Juvenile Justice Advocacy: Practice in a Unique Court* (New York: Practicing Law Institute, 1974), p. 2.
4. *Wellesley v. Wellesley*, 4 Eng. Rep. 1078 (1827).
5. Rendleman, "Parens Patriae," p. 209.
6. Platt, *The Child Savers*, pp. 11–38.
7. Fox, "Juvenile Justice Reform," p. 1188.
8. Pickett, *House of Refuge*.
9. Robert Mennel, *Thorns and Thistles* (Hanover, N.H.: University Press of New England, 1973).
10. See U.S. Department of Justice, Juvenile Justice and Delinquency Prevention, *Two Hundred Years of American Criminal Justice: An LEAA Bicentennial Study* (Washington, D.C.: LEAA, 1976).
11. Ibid., pp. 62–74.
12. Platt, *The Child Savers*, p. 116.
13. LaMar T. Empey, *American Delinquency: Its Meaning and Construction* (Homewood, Ill.: Dorsey Press, 1978), p. 515.
14. *Kent v. United States*, 383 U.S. 541, 86 S.Ct. 1045, 16 L.Ed.2d 84 (1966): juveniles are entitled to minimum procedural safeguards in the waiver proceeding. *In re Gault*, 387 U.S. 1, 87 S.Ct. 1428, 18 L.Ed.2d 527 (1967): juveniles have the right to notice, counsel, confrontation, cross-examination, and the privilege against self-incrimination in juvenile court proceedings. *In re Winship*, 397 U.S. 358, 90 S.Ct. 1068, 25 L.Ed.2d 368 (1970): proof beyond a reasonable doubt is necessary for conviction in juvenile proceedings. *Breed v. Jones*, 421 U.S. 519, 95 S.Ct. 1779, 44 L.Ed.2d 346 (1975): jeopardy attaches in a juvenile court adjudicatory hearing, thus barring subsequent prosecution for the same offense as an adult.
15. Public Law 93-415.
16. Ibid.
17. For a comprehensive view of juvenile law, see, generally, Joseph J. Senna and Larry J. Siegel, *Juvenile Law: Cases and Comments* (St. Paul, Minn.: West Publishing Company, 1976).
18. *Lamb v. Brown*, 456 F.2d 18 (10th Cir. 1972): states cannot distinguish between males and females with respect to juvenile court age limits.
19. The effort to remove status offenders was pioneered by the nonprofit National Council on Crime and Delinquency.
20. See, for example, *District of Columbia v. B.J.R.*, 332 A.2d 58 (1975).
21. FBI, *Crime in the United States, 1987* (Washington, D.C.: U.S. Government Printing Office, 1988), p. 178.
22. *In re Gault*, 387 U.S. 1, 87 S.Ct. 1428, 18 L.Ed.2d 527 (1967).
23. See Dennis Sullivan and Larry Siegel, "How Police Use Information To Make Decisions," *Crime and Delinquency* 23 (1972): 253–62 for a discussion on the factors involved in police decision making.
24. See, generally, Donald Black and Albert Reis, "Police Control of Juveniles," *American Sociological Review* 35 (1960): 63.
25. 469 U.S. 325, 105 S.Ct. 733, 83 L.Ed.2d 720 (1985).
26. See D. A. Walls, "New Jersey v. T.L.O.: The Fourth Amendment Applied to School Searches," *Oklahoma University Law Review* 11 (1986): 225–41.
27. K. A. Bucker, "School Drug Tests: A Fourth Amendment Perspective," *University of Illinois Law Review* 5 (1987): 275.
28. See J. Hogan and M. Schwartz, "Search and Seizure in the Public Schools," *Case and Comment* 90 (1985): 28–32; see also M. Meyers, "T.L.O. v. New Jersey—Officially Conducted School Searches and a New Balancing Test," *Juvenile Family Journal* 37 (1986): 27–37.
29. For an interesting article suggesting that school officials should not be permitted to search students without suspicion that each student searched has violated the drug or weapons law, see J. Braverman, "Public School Drug Searches," *Fordham Urban Law Journal* 14 (1986): 629–84.
30. C. Avery and R. D. Simpson, "Search and Seizure: A Risk Assessment Model for Public School Officials," *Journal of Law and Education* 16 (1987): 403–34.
31. 384 U.S. 436, 86 S.Ct. 1602. 16 L.Ed.2d 694 (1966). *Miranda* held that accused individuals in police custody must be given the following warning: (1) that they have a right to remain silent; (2) that any statements made can be used against them; (3) that they have a right

to counsel; and (4) that if they cannot afford counsel, one will be furnished at public expense.

32. 442 U.S. 707, 99 S.Ct. 2560, 61 L.Ed.2d 197 (1979); 453 U.S. 355, 101 S.Ct. 2806, 69 L.Ed.2d 696 (1981).

33. Larry Holtz, "Miranda in a Juvenile Setting: A Child's Right to Silence," *Journal of Criminal Law and Criminology* 78 (1987): 552.

34. American Bar Association, *Standards Relating to Juvenile Probation Function* (Cambridge, Mass.: Ballinger Press, 1977), p. 23.

35. See, generally, National Council on Crime and Delinquency, *Standard Family Court Act* (New York: NCCD, 1965); National Conference of Commissioners on Uniform State Laws, *Uniform Juvenile Court Act* (Philadelphia: American Law Institute, 1968), sec. 9; William Sheridan, *Model Acts for Family Courts* (Washington, D.C.: Department of Health, Education, and Welfare, 1975), sec. 13.

36. Joyce Dougherty, "A Comparison of Adult Plea Bargaining and Juvenile Intake," *Federal Probation* (June 1988): 72–79.

37. *Schall v. Martin*, 467 U.S. 253 104 S.Ct. 2403 81 L.Ed.2d 207 (1984).

38. Solomon Kobrin and Malcolm Klein, *National Evaluation of the Deinstitutionalization of Status Offenders Programs, Executive Summary* (Washington, D.C.: U.S. Government Printing Office, 1982).

39. See Juvenile Delinquency and Prevention Act of 1974, 42 U.S.C. § 5633.

40. Phyllis Jo Baunach and Melissa Sickmund, Bureau of Justice Statistics, *Jail Inmates 1984* (Washington, D.C.: U.S. Government Printing Office, 1986).

41. Office of Juvenile Justice and Delinquency Prevention, News Release, 4 January 1981.

42. "$3.8 Million Awarded to Remove Juveniles from Adult Jails, Lockups," *Justice Assistance News* 3 (May 1982): 5.

43. Ira Schwartz, Linda Harris, and Laurie Levi, "The Jailing of Juveniles in Minnesota," *Crime and Delinquency* 34 (1988): 131.

44. See, generally, Ira Schwartz, ed., "Children in Jails," *Crime and Delinquency* 34 (1988): 131–228.

45. See Schwartz, Harris, and Levi, "The Jailing of Juveniles in Minnesota," p. 134.

46. David Steinhart, "California Legislation Ends Jailing of Children—The Story of a Policy Reversal," *Crime and Delinquency* 34 (1988): 150.

47. See Henry Swanger, "Hendrickson v. Griggs—A Review of Legal and Policy Implications for Juvenile Justice Policymakers," *Crime and Delinquency* 34 (1988): 209.

48. See Chapter 9.

49. See Bureau of Justice Statistics, *Report to the Nation on Crime and Justice* (Washington, D.C.: U.S. Department of Justice, 1988), p. 79.

50. 383 U.S. 541, 86 S.Ct. 1045, 16 L.Ed.2d 84 (1966).

51. Ibid, at 554–55.

52. 95 S.Ct. 1779, at 1785 (1975).

53. Donna Hamparian et al., *Major Issues in Juvenile Justice Information and Training, Youth in Adult Courts: Between Two Worlds* (Rockville, Md.: National Criminal Justice Reference Service, 1982).

54. Bureau of Justice Statistics, *Report to the Nation on Crime and Justice*, p. 79.

55. Barry Feld, "Delinquent Careers and Criminal Policy," *Criminology* 21 (1983): 195–212.

56. Barry Feld, "The Juvenile Court Meets the Principle of the Offense: Legislative Changes in Juvenile Waiver Statutes," *Journal of Criminal Law and Criminology* 78 (1987): 471–533.

57. Richard Allinson and Joan Potter, "Is New York's Tough Juvenile Law a 'Charade'?" *Corrections* 9 (February 1983): 40–45.

58. Peter Greenwood, *Juvenile Offenders* (Washington, D.C.: National Institute of Justice, 1986), p. 3.

59. Howard Snyder, Terrence A. Finnegan, Ellen Nimick, Melissa Sickmund, Dennis Sullivan, and Nancy Tierney, *Juvenile Court Statistics, 1984* (Pittsburgh: National Center of Juvenile Justice, 1987).

60. 387 U.S. 1, 87 S.Ct. 1428, 18 L.Ed.2d 527 (1967).

61. Ibid., at 20.

62. 397 U.S. 358, 90 S.Ct. 1068, 25 L.Ed.2d 368 (1970).

63. 403 U.S. 528, 91 S.Ct. 1976, 29 L.Ed.2d 647 (1971).

64. See the earlier discussion of New York's Omnibus Crime Act; see also S. Singer and C. Ewing, "Juvenile Justice Reform in New York State—The Juvenile Offender Law," *Law and Policy* 8 (1986): 463.

65. "Justice, Treating Kids Like Adults," *Newsweek*, 27 June 1979, p. 54; see also B. Benda and D. Waite, "Proposed Determinate Sentencing Model in Virginia," *Juvenile and Family Court Journal* 39 (1988): 55.

66. Victor Streib, *Death Penalty for Juveniles* (Bloomington, Ind.: Indiana University Press, 1987); see also Paul Reidinger, "The Death Row Kids," *American Bar Association Journal* (April 1989): 78.

67. Stanley Fisher, "The Dispositional Process under the Juvenile Justice Standards Project," *Boston University Law Review* 57 (1977): 732.

68. National Advisory Commission on Criminal Justice Standards and Goals, *Task Force Report on Juvenile Justice and Delinquency Prevention* (Washington, D.C.: LEAA, 1976), pp. 452–59.

69. See Michael Serrill, "Police Write a New Law On Juvenile Crime," *Police Magazine* (September 1979): 47; see also A. Schneider and D. Schram, *Assessment of Juvenile Justice Reform in Washington State*, vols. 1–4 (Washington, D.C.: U.S. Department of Justice, Institute of Policy Analysis, 1983); T. Castellano, "Justice Model in the Juvenile Justice System—Washington State's Experience," *Law and Policy* 8 (1986): 479.

70. See Joseph Goldstein, Anna Freud, and Albert Solnit, *Beyond the Best Interest of the Child* (New York: Free Press, 1973).

71. Fisher, "The Dispositional Process," p. 732.

72. Anne Schneider, U.S. Department of Justice, *Guide to Juvenile Restitution* (Washington, D.C.: U.S. Government Printing Office, 1985).

73. Dennis Mahoney, Dennis Romig, and Troy Armstrong, "Juvenile Probation: The Balanced Approach," *Juvenile and Family Court Journal* 39 (1988); see also Ted Pallmer and Robert Wedge, "California's Juvenile Probation Camps—Findings and Implications," *Crime and Delinquency* 35 (1989): 234.

74. Bureau of Justice Statistics, *Report to the Nation on Crime and Justice*, p. 102.

75. Office of Juvenile Justice and Delinquency Prevention, *Children in Custody, 1987* (Washington, D.C.: U.S. Government Printing Office, October, 1988).

76. Ibid., p. 3.

77. See Barry Krisberg, ed., "Minority Youth Incarceration and Crime," *Crime and Delinquency*, Special Issue 33 (1987).

78. See Barry Krisberg, Ira Schwartz, Gideon Fishman, Zvi Eisikovits, and Edna Guttman, *The Incarceration of Minority Youth* (Minneapolis: University of Minnesota, 1986).

79. See *Children in Custody—Public Juvenile Facilities, Juvenile Justice Bulletin* (Washington, D.C.: U.S. Department of Justice, 1988), p. 3.

80. Bureau of Justice Statistics, *Survey of Youth in Custody, 1987* (Washington, D.C.: U.S. Department of Justice, 1988).

81. I. Bakal, *Closing Correctional Institutions: New Strategies for Youth Services* (Lexington, Mass.: Lexington Books, 1973); see also Daniel Curran, "Destructuring, Prevailization, the Promise of Juvenile Diversion: Compromising Community-Based Corrections," *Crime and Delinquency* 34 (1988): p. 363.

82. Office of Juvenile Justice and Delinquency Prevention, *Assessing the Effects of DSO* (Washington, D.C.: U.S. Department of Justice, 1989).

83. Howard Snyder, *Court Careers of Juvenile Offenders* (Washington, D.C.: U.S. Department of Justice, Office of Juvenile Justice and Delinquency Prevention, March 1988).

84. Office of Juvenile Justice and Delinquency Prevention, "Study Sheds New Light on Court Careers of Juvenile Offenders," *Juvenile Justice Bulletin* (August 1988).

85. American Institute for Research, Evaluation of the Habitual Serious and Violent Juvenile Offender Program, (Washington, D.C.: U.S. Department of Justice, Office of Juvenile Justice and Delinquency Prevention, January 1988); see also U.S. Department of Justice, Office of Juvenile Justice and Delinquency Prevention, "Targeting Serious Juvenile Offenders Can Make a Difference," *Juvenile Justice Bulletin* (December 1988).

86. Office of Juvenile Justice and Delinquency Prevention, "Juvenile Courts Respond to Violent Crime," *Juvenile Justice Bulletin* (January 1989).

87. 349 F.Supp. 575 (1972).

88. 346 F.Supp. 1354 (1972).

89. Ibid., at 1361.

90. 364 F.Supp. 166 (1973).

91. 491 F.2d 352 (7th Cir. 1974).

92. Ibid., at 360.

93. 454 U.S. 201 102 S.Ct. 233, 70 L.Ed.2d 345 (1981).

94. 831 F.2d 1430 (9th Cir. 1987).

95. Metropolitan Court Judges Committee Report, "Drugs—The American Family in Crisis" (University of Nevada, National Counsel on Juvenile and Family Court Judges, 1988).

96. See "Kids Who Sell Crack," *Time*, 9 May 1988.

97. Office of Juvenile Justice and Delinquency Prevention, *Fighting Juvenile Drug Use* (Washington, D.C.: U.S. Department of Justice, December 1988).

98. Office of Juvenile Justice and Delinquency Prevention, *Safer Schools, Better Schools* (Washington, D.C.: U.S. Department of Justice, August 1988).

99. For a thorough review of gang theory, see Larry J. Siegel and Joseph J. Senna, *Juvenile Delinquency: Theory, Practice, and Law*, (St. Paul, Minn.: West Publishing Company, 1988), Chapter 10.

100. Metropolitan Court Judges Committee Report, National Council of Juvenile Court Judges, p. 1.

101. 403 U.S. 528, at 547.

Part Five

The Nature and
History of the
Juvenile Justice Process

■

Glossary

Academy of Criminal Justice Sciences A society whose purpose is to further the development of the criminal justice profession; its membership includes academics and practitioners involved in criminal justice.

accountability system A way of dealing with police corruption by making superiors responsible for the behavior of their subordinates.

actus reus An illegal act. The *actus reus* can be an affirmative act, such as taking money or shooting someone, or a failure to act, such as failing to take proper precautions while driving a car.

adjudication The determination of guilt or innocence; a judgment concerning criminal charges. Trial by jury is a method of adjudication; the majority of offenders charged plead guilty. Of the remainder, some cases are adjudicated by a judge without a jury and others are dismissed.

adversary system The procedure used to determine truth in the adjudication of guilt or innocence, which pits the defense (advocate for the accused) against the prosecution (advocate for the state), with the judge acting as arbiter of the legal rules. Under the adversary system, the burden is on the state to prove the charges beyond a reasonable doubt. This system of having the two parties publicly debate has proved to be the most effective method of determining the truth regarding a set of circumstances. (Under the accusatory, or inquisitorial, system which is used in continental Europe, the charge is evidence of guilt, which the accused must disprove; the judge takes an active part in the proceedings.)

administrative model Sentencing scheme in which control over sentence length is left to correctional authorities.

aging out The process in which the crime rate declines with age.

aggressive preventive patrol A patrol technique designed to suppress crime before it occurs.

alternatives to incarceration Various forms of community-based correctional treatment that replace traditional sentences to prison or jail.

anomie A condition produced by normlessness. Because of rapidly shifting moral values, a person has few guides to what is socially acceptable behavior.

appeal Review of lower court proceedings by a higher court. There is no constitutional right to appeal, although the "right" to appeal is established by statute in some states and by custom in others. All states set conditions as to the type of case or grounds for appeal that appellate courts may review. Appellate courts do not retry the case under review. Rather, the transcript of the lower court case is read by the appellate judges, and the lawyers for the defendant and for the state argue about the merits of the appeal—that is, the legality of lower court proceedings instead of the original testimony. Appeal is more a process for controlling police, court, and correctional practices than for rescuing innocent defendants. When appellate courts do reverse lower court judgments, it is usually because of "prejudicial error" (deprivation of rights), and the case is remanded for retrial.

appellate courts Courts that reconsider a case already tried to determine whether the measures used complied with accepted rules of criminal procedure and were in line with constitutional doctrines.

arbitrage The practice of buying large blocks of stock in companies that are believed to be the target of corporate buyouts or takeovers.

argot The unique language of the prison culture.

arraignment The step at which the accused is read the charges against him or her and is asked how he or she pleads. In addition, the accused is advised of his or her rights. Possible pleas are guilty, not guilty, *nolo contendere*, and not guilty by reason of insanity.

arrest The taking of a person into the custody of the law; the legal purpose is to restrain the accused until he or she can be held accountable for the offense at court proceedings. The legal requirement for an arrest is probable cause. Arrests for investigation, suspicion, or harassment are improper and of doubtful legality. The police have the responsibility to use only the reasonable physical force necessary to make an arrest. The summons has been used as a substitute for arrest.

arrest warrant A written court order issued by a magistrate authorizing and directing that an individual be taken into custody to answer criminal charges.

Aryan Brotherhood A white supremacist prison gang.

assembly-line justice The view that the justice process resembles an endless production line that handles most cases in a routine and perfunctory fashion.

atavistic According to Lombroso, the primitive physical characteristics that distinguish born criminals from the general population. According to Lombrosian theory, such characteristics represent throwbacks to animals or primitive people.

attainder Loss of all civil rights due to a conviction for a felony offense.

attorney general The senior U.S. prosecutor and cabinet member who heads the Justice Department.

Auburn system A prison system developed in New York during the nineteenth century that stressed congregate working conditions.

Augustus, John The individual credited with pioneering the concept of probation.

authoritarian A person whose personality revolves around blind obedience to a central authority that he or she considers infallible.

bail Monetary amount for or condition of pretrial release, normally set by a judge at the initial appearance. The purpose of bail is to ensure the return of the accused at subsequent proceedings. If the accused is unable to make bail, he or she is detained in jail. The Eighth Amendment provides that excessive bail shall not be required.

bail bonding The business of providing bail to needy offenders, usually at an exhorbitant rate of interest.

Bail Reform Act of 1984 Federal legislation that provides for both greater emphasis on ROR for nondangerous offenders and preventive detention for those who present a menace to the community.

basic car plan The patrol deployment system used in cities such as Los Angeles.

Beccaria, Cesare Eighteenth-century Italian philosopher who argued that crime could be controlled by punishments only severe enough to counterbalance the pleasure obtained from them.

behaviorism The branch of psychology concerned with the study of observable behavior rather than unconscious motives. It focuses on the relationship between the particular stimuli and people's responses to them.

bill of indictment A document submitted to a grand jury by the prosecutor asking them to take action and indict a suspect in a case.

blameworthiness The amount of culpability or guilt a person maintains for participating in a particular criminal offense.

blue curtain According to William Westly, the secretive, insulated police culture that isolates the officer from the rest of society.

booking Administrative record of an arrest; it involves listing the offender's name, address, physical description, date of birth, employer, time of arrest, offense, and name of arresting officer. Photographing and fingerprinting the offender are also part of booking.

bot Under Anglo-Saxon law, the restitution paid by the offender to the victim.

bourgeoisie In Marxist theory, the owners of the means of production; the capitalist ruling class.

broken windows A term used to indicate the role of the police as maintainers of community order and safety.

burglary Breaking and entering into a home or structure for the purposes of committing a felony.

capital punishment The use of the death penalty to punish transgressors.

career criminal A person who has repeated experiences in law-violating behavior and organizes his or her lifestyle around criminality.

challenge for cause Removal of a juror because he or she is biased, has prior knowledge about a case, or in some other way demonstrates the inability to render a fair and impartial judgment in a case.

chancery court Court created in fifteenth-century England to oversee the lives of high-born minors who were orphaned or otherwise could not care for themselves.

charge In a criminal case, the specific crime the defendant is accused of committing.

Chicago Crime Commission Citizens action group set up in Chicago to investigate problems in the criminal justice system and explore avenues for positive change. The forerunner of many such groups around the country.

child abuse Any physical, emotional, or sexual trauma to a child for which no reasonable explanation, such as an accident, can be found. Child abuse can also be a function of neglecting to give proper care and attention to a young child.

chronic offender According to Wolfgang, a delinquent offender who is arrested five or more times before the age of 18 and who stands a good chance of becoming an adult criminal; responsible for more than half of all serious crimes.

civil death The practice of revoking all civil rights of convicted felons such as the right to vote, marry, obtain a driver's license, and so on.

civil law All law that is not criminal; it includes torts (personal wrongs), contract law, property law, maritime law, commercial law, and so on.

civil rights The constitutional rights and privileges afforded all people under the protection of the law.

Civil Rights Division That part of the U.S. Justice Department that handles cases involving violations of civil rights guaranteed by the Constitution and the U.S. Code.

classical theory The theoretical perspective suggesting that (1) people have free will to choose criminal or conventional behaviors; (2) people choose to commit crime for reasons of greed or personal need; (3) crime can be controlled only by the fear of criminal sanctions.

classification The procedure in which prisoners are categorized on the basis of their personal characteristics and criminal history and then assigned to an appropriate institution.

clerk of court The individual charged with managing the court's case flow, docketing, and administrative functions.

Code of Hammurabi The first written criminal code; developed in Babylonia about 2000 B.C.

coeducational prison Institution that houses both male and female inmates, who share work and recreational facilities.

cohort study A study utilizing a sample whose behavior is followed over a period of time.

common law Early English law, developed by judges, which incorporated Anglo-Saxon tribal custom, feudal rules and practices, and the everyday rules of behavior of local villages. Common law became the standardized law of the land in England and eventually formed the basis of the criminal law in the United States.

community policing A policing strategy that stresses the development of community ties through foot patrol, ministations, community newsletters, and other decentralization policies. It emphasizes fear reduction, community organization, and order maintenance rather than crime fighting.

community service restitution An alternative sanction that requires an offender to work in the community at such tasks as cleaning public parks or working with handicapped children in lieu of an incarceration sentence.

community treatment The actions of correctional agencies that attempt to maintain the convicted offender in the community instead of in a secure facility. Includes probation, parole, and residential programs.

complaint A sworn allegation that an individual is guilty of some designated (complained of) offense, made in writing to a court or judge. This is often the first legal document filed regarding a criminal offense. The complaint can be "taken out" by the victim, the police officer, the district attorney, or another interested party. Although the complaint charges an offense, an indictment or information may be the formal charging document.

concurrent sentence Prison sentences for two or more criminal acts that are served simultaneously or run together.

conflict view The view that human behavior is shaped by interpersonal conflict and that those who maintain social power will use it to further their own needs.

conjugal visit A prison program that allows inmates to receive private visits from their wives for the purpose of maintaining normal interpersonal relationships.

consecutive sentence Prison sentences for two or more criminal acts that are served one after the other or follow one another.

consensus view The belief that the majority of citizens in a given society share common ideals and work toward a common good and that crimes are acts that are outlawed because they conflict with the rules of the majority and are harmful to society.

constable The peacekeeper in early English towns. The constable organized citizens to protect his territory and supervised the night watch to maintain order in the evening.

constructive intent The finding of criminal liability for an unintentional act that is the result of negligence or recklessness.

constructive possession In the crime of larceny, willingly giving up temporary physical possession of property but retaining legal ownership.

continuance A judicial order to continue a case without a finding in order to gather more information, begin an informal treatment program, and so on.

contract system (attorney) Providing counsel to indigent offenders by having an attorney(s) under contract to the county to handle all (or some) indigent matters.

contract system (convict) The system used earlier in the century by which inmates were leased out to private industry to work.

conviction A judgment of guilt; a verdict by a jury, a plea by a defendant, or a judgment by a court that the accused is guilty as charged.

convict subculture The separate culture that exists in prisons and has its own set of rewards and behaviors. The traditional culture is now being replaced by a violent gang culture.

corporal punishment The use of physical chastisement, such as whipping or electroshocks, to punish criminals.

corporate crime White-collar crime involving a legal violation by a corporate entity such as price fixing, restraint of trade, waste dumping, and so on.

corpus dilecti The body of the crime; made up of the *actus reus* and *mens rea*.

corrections The agencies of justice that take custody of offenders after conviction and are entrusted with their treatment and control.

counseling A form of treatment in which the client develops self-awareness through discussing his or her personality, behavior, and problems with a therapist on a one-to-one basis or in a group setting.

court administrator Individual who controls the operations of the court system in a particular jurisdiction. May be in charge of scheduling, juries, judicial assignments, and so on.

court of last resort Court that handles the final appeal on a matter. The U.S. Supreme Court is the official court of last resort for criminal matters.

courtroom work group The view that all parties in the adversary process work together in a cooperative effort to settle cases with the least amount of effort and conflict.

courts of limited jurisdiction Courts that handle misdemeanors and minor civil complaints.

crime A violation of existing societal rules of behavior as interpreted and expressed by a criminal code created by those holding social and political power.

crime control Model of criminal justice that emphasizes the control of dangerous offenders and the protection of society. Its advocates call for harsh punishments, such as the death penalty, to act as deterrents to crime.

crime fighter The police style that stresses dealing with hard crimes and arresting dangerous criminals.

Criminal Division Branch of the U.S. Justice Department that prosecutes criminal violations.

criminal justice process The decision-making points from the initial investigation or arrest by police to the eventual release of the offender and his or her reentry into society; the various sequential criminal stages through which the offender passes.

criminal law The body of rules that define crimes, set out punishments, and mandate the procedures to be followed in carrying out the criminal process.

criminal sanction The right of the state to punish a person if he or she violates the rules set down in the criminal code. The punishments are connected to commission of a specific crime.

criminology The scientific approach to the study of criminal behavior and society's reaction to it.

cruel and unusual punishment Physical punishment or punishment that is far in excess of that given to people under similar circumstances and is therefore banned by the Eighth Amendment. So far the death penalty has not been considered cruel and unusual if it is administered in a fair and nondiscriminatory fashion.

cultural transmission The concept that conduct norms are passed down from one generation to the next so that they become stable within the boundaries of a culture. Cultural transmission guarantees that group lifestyle and behavior is stable and predictable.

culture of poverty The view that people in lower-class society form a separate culture with its own values and norms that are in conflict with conventional society; the culture is self-maintaining and ongoing.

curtilage The fields attached to a house.

custodial convenience The principle of giving jailed inmates the minimum comforts required by law in order to keep down the costs of incarceration.

cynicism The belief that most people's actions are motivated solely by personal needs and selfishness.

deadly force The ability of the police to kill suspects if they resist arrest or present a danger to the officer or the community. The police cannot use deadly force against an unarmed fleeing felon.

decriminalize Reducing the penalty for a criminal act but not actually legalizing it.

defendant The accused in criminal proceedings; he or she has the right to be present at each stage of the criminal justice process except grand jury proceedings.

defense attorney Counsel for the defendant in a criminal trial who represents the defendant from arrest to final appeal.

degenerate anomalies According to Lombroso, the primitive physical characteristics that make criminals animalistic and savage.

deinstitutionalization The movement to remove as many offenders as possible from secure confinement and treat them in the community.

demystify The process by which Marxists unmask the true purpose of the capitalist system's rules and laws.

desert-based sentences The principle of basing sentence length on the seriousness of the criminal act and not the personal characteristics of the defendant or the deterrent impact of the law. Punishment is based on what people have done and not on what others may do or what they themselves may do in the future.

desistance The process in which the crime rate declines with age; synonymous with the aging out process.

detention Holding an offender in secure confinement before trial.

determinate sentence "Fixed" terms of incarceration, such as three years imprisonment. Many believe determinate sentences are too restrictive for rehabilitative purposes; the advantage is that offenders know how much time they have to serve, i.e., when they will be released.

detective The police agency assigned to investigate crimes after they have been reported, gather evidence, and identify the perpetrator.

deterrence The act of preventing crime before it occurs by means of the threat of criminal sanctions.

deviance Behavior that departs from the social norm.

differential association According to Edwin Sutherland, the principle that criminal acts are related to a person's exposure to an excess amount of antisocial attitudes and values.

directed verdict The right of the judge to direct a jury to acquit a defendant because the state has not proven the elements of the crime or otherwise has not established guilt according to the law.

direct examination The questioning of your own (prosecution or defense) witness during a trial.

discretion The use of personal decision making and choice in carrying out operations in the criminal justice system. For example, police discretion can involve the decision to make an arrest, while prosecutorial discretion can involve the decision to accept a plea bargain.

disposition For juvenile offenders, the equivalent of sentencing for adult offenders. The theory is that disposition should be more rehabilitative than retributive. Possible dispositions include dismissing the case, releasing the youth to the custody of his or her parents, placing the offender on probation, or sending him or her to an institution or state correctional institution.

district attorney The county prosecutor who is charged with bringing offenders to justice and enforcing the laws of the state.

diversion A noncriminal alternative to trial usually featuring counseling, job training, and educational opportunities.

double bunking The practice of holding two or more inmates in a single cell because of prison overcrowding; upheld in *Rhodes v. Chapman*.

drift According to Matza, the view that youths move in and out of delinquency and that their lifestyles can embrace both conventional and deviant values.

drug courier profile A way of identifying drug runners based on their personal characteristics; police may stop and question individuals whose characteristics fit the profile.

Drug Enforcement Administration (DEA) Federal agency that handles the enforcement of federal drug control laws.

due process A fundamental constitutional principle based on the concept of the primacy of the individual and the complementary concept of limitation on governmental power; a safeguard against arbitrary and unfair state procedures in judicial or administrative proceedings. Embodied in the due process concept are the basic rights of a defendant in criminal proceedings and the requisites for a fair trial. These rights and requirements have been expanded by appellate court decisions and include (1) timely notice of a hearing or trial that informs the accused of the charges against him or her; (2) the opportunity to confront accusers and to present evidence on one's own behalf before an impartial jury or judge; (3) the presumption of innocence under which guilt must be proven by legally obtained evidence and the verdict must be supported by the evidence presented; (4) the right of an accused to be warned of his or her constitutional rights at the earliest stage of the criminal process; (5) protection against self-incrimination; (6) assistance of counsel at every critical stage of the criminal process; and (7) the guarantee that an individual will not be tried more than once for the same offense (double jeopardy).

Durham Rule Definition of insanity that required that the crime be excused if it was a product of a mental illness; still used in New Hampshire.

economic crime An act in violation of the criminal law that is designed to bring financial gain to the offender.

electroencephalogram (EEG) A device that can record the electronic impulses given off by the brain, commonly called "brain waves."

embezzlement A type of larceny that involves taking the possessions of another (fraudulent conversion) that have been placed in the thief's lawful possession for safekeeping; for example, a bank teller misappropriating deposits or a stockbroker making off with a customer's account.

entrapment Criminal defense that maintains the police originated the criminal idea or initiated the criminal action.

exclusionary rule The principle that prohibits the use of illegally obtained evidence in a trial on the basis of the Fourth Amendment "right of the people to be secure in their persons, houses, papers, and effects, against unreasonable searches and seizures." The rule is not a bar to prosecution, since legally obtained evidence that may be used in a trial may be available.

excuse A defense to a criminal charge in which the accused maintains he or she lacked the intent to commit the crime (*mens rea*).

ex post facto laws Laws that make criminal an act that was not a crime when it was committed or retroactively increase the penalty for a crime. For example, an ex post facto law could change shoplifting from a misdemeanor to a felony and penalize people with a prison term even though they had been apprehended six months before; such laws are unconstitutional.

expressive crime A crime that has no purpose except to accomplish the behavior at hand, e.g., shooting someone, as opposed to committing a crime for monetary gain.

false pretenses Illegally obtaining money, goods, or merchandise from another by fraud or misrepresentation.

Federal Bureau of Investigation (FBI) The arm of the U.S. Justice Department that investigates violations of federal law, gathers crime statistics, runs a comprehensive crime laboratory, and helps train local law enforcement officers.

felony A more serious offense that carries a penalty of incarceration in a state prison, usually for one year or more. Persons convicted of felony offenses lose such rights as the right to vote, hold elective office, or maintain certain licenses.

fence A buyer and seller of stolen merchandise.

flat or fixed sentencing A sentencing model that mandates that all people who are convicted of a specific offense and sent to prison must be incarcerated for the same length of time.

folkways Generally followed customs that do not have moral values attached to them, such as not interrupting a person who is speaking.

fraud Taking the possessions of another through deception or cheating, such as selling an antique that is known to be a copy.

free venture Starting privately run industries in a prison setting in which the inmates work for wages and the goods are sold for profit.

functionalism The sociological perspective that suggests that each part of society makes a contribution to the maintenance of the whole. Functionalism stresses social cooperation and consensus of values and beliefs among a majority of society's members.

general deterrence A crime control policy that depends on the fear of criminal penalties. General deterrence measures, such as long prison sentences for violent crimes, are aimed at convincing the potential law violator that the pains associated with crime outweigh its benefits.

good faith exception Principle of law that holds that evidence may be used in a criminal trial even though the search warrant used to obtain it is technically faulty if the police acted in good faith and to the best of their ability when they sought to obtain it from a judge.

good-time credit Time taken off a prison sentence in exchange for good behavior within the institution; for example, 10 days per month. A device used to limit disciplinary problems within the prison.

grand jury A group (usually comprised of 23 citizens) chosen to hear testimony in secret and to issue formal criminal accusations (indictments). It also serves an investigatory function.

grass eaters Term used for police officers who accept payoffs when their everyday duties place them in a position to be solicited by the public.

guardian *ad litem* A court-appointed attorney who protects the interests of a child in cases involving the child's welfare.

Guardian Angels A self-help group begun by Curtis Siwa that patrols troubled neighborhoods and cooperates with the police to keep the peace.

habeas corpus *See* writ of habeas corpus.

habitual criminal statutes Laws that mandate long-term or life sentences for offenders who have multiple felony convictions.

halfway house A community-based correctional facility that houses inmates before their outright release so that they can gradually become acclimated to conventional society.

hands-off doctrine The judicial policy of not interfering in the administrative affairs of a prison.

hearsay evidence Testimony that is not firsthand but relates information told by a second party.

house of correction A county correctional institution generally used for the incarceration of more serious misdemeanants, whose sentences are usually less than one year.

hue and cry In medieval England, the policy of self-help used in villages; everyone was required to come to the aid of a citizen who raised a hue and cry.

hundred In medieval England, a group of one hundred families who had the responsibility of maintaining order and trying minor offenses.

incapacitation The policy of confining dangerous criminals to eliminate the risk that they will repeat their offense in society.

indeterminate sentence A term of incarceration with a stated minimum and maximum; for example, a sentence to prison for a period of from 3 to 10 years. The prisoner would be eligible for parole after the minimum sentence had been served. Based on the belief that sentences should fit the criminal, indeterminate sentences allow "individualized" sentences and provide for sentencing flexibility. Judges can set a high minimum to overcome the purpose of the indeterminate sentence.

index crimes The eight crimes that, because of their seriousness and frequency, have their reported incidence recorded in the annual FBI Uniform Crime Reports. Index crimes include murder, rape, assault, robbery, burglary, arson, larceny, and motor vehicle theft.

indictment A written accusation returned by a grand jury charging an individual with a specified crime after determination of probable cause; the prosecutor presents enough evidence (a *prima facie* case) to establish probable cause.

information A formal charging document like the indictment. The prosecuting attorney makes out the information and files it in court. Probable cause is determined at the preliminary hearing, which, unlike grand jury proceedings, is public and is attended by the accused and his or her attorney.

initial appearance The step at which the arrested suspect is brought before a magistrate for consideration of bail. The suspect must be taken for an initial appearance within a "reasonable time" after arrest. For petty offenses, this step often serves as the final criminal proceeding, either by adjudication by a judge or a guilty plea.

inmate social code The informal set of rules that govern inmates while in prison.

insider trading The illegal buying of stock in a company based on information provided by another who has a fiduciary interest in the company such as an employee or an outside attorney or accountant hired by the firm for management or legal purposes. Federal laws and the rules of the Securities and Exchange Commission require all profits to be returned and provide for both fines and a prison sentence.

interactionist perspective The view that one's perception of reality is significantly influenced by one's interpretations of the reactions of others to similar events and stimuli.

interrogation The method of accumulating evidence in the form of information or confessions from suspects by police; such questioning has been restricted because of concern about the use of brutal and coercive methods and because of the constitutional guarantee against self-incrimination.

investigation Inquiry concerning suspected criminal behavior for the purpose of identifying offenders or gathering further evidence to assist the prosecution of apprehended offenders.

jail Usually a part of the local police station or sheriff's office; used to detain people awaiting trial, to serve as a "lockup" for drunks and disorderly individuals, and to provide a place of short-term confinement for offenders serving sentences of less than one year.

just desert The philosophy of justice that asserts that those who violate the rights of others deserve to be punished. Severity of punishment should be commensurate with the seriousness of the crime.

justice model A philosophy of corrections that stresses determinant sentences, abolition of parole, and the view that prisons are places of punishment and not rehabilitation.

justification A defense to a criminal charge in which the accused maintains that his or her actions were justified by the circumstances and that therefore he or she should not be held criminally liable.

juvenile delinquency Participation in illegal behavior by a minor who falls under a statutory age limit.

juvenile justice process Court proceedings for youths within the "juvenile" age group that differ from the adult criminal process. Originally, under the paternal (*parens patriae*) philosophy, juvenile procedures were informal and nonadversary; they were invoked *for* the juvenile offender rather than *against* him or her. In such proceedings, a petition instead of a complaint is filed; courts make findings of involvement or adjudication of delinquency instead of convictions; and juvenile offenders receive dispositions instead of sentences. Recent court decisions (*Kent* and *Gault*) have increased the adversary nature of juvenile court proceedings. However, the philosophy remains one of diminishing the stigma of delinquency and providing for the youth's well-being and rehabilitation, rather than seeking retribution.

Kansas City study An experimental program that evaluated the effectiveness of patrol. The Kansas City study found that the presence of patrol officers had little deterrent effect.

Knapp Commission Led the investigation into police corruption in New York and uncovered a widespread network of payoffs and bribes.

labeling The process by which a person becomes fixed with a negative identity, such as "criminal" or "ex-con," and is forced to suffer the consequences of outcast status.

***male in se* crimes** Acts that are outlawed because they violate basic moral values; rape, murder, assault, robbery, and so on.

***male prohibitum* crimes** Acts that are outlawed by statute because they clash with current norms and public opinion; tax evasion, traffic violations, drug law violations, and so on.

mandamus *See* writ of mandamus.

mandatory sentence A statutory requirement that a certain penalty shall be set and carried out in all cases on conviction for a specified offense or series of offenses.

marital exemption The practice in some states of prohibiting husbands from being prosecuted for the rape of their wives.

***mens rea* Guilty mind.** The mental element of a crime of the intent to commit a criminal act.

***Miranda* warning** The result of two U.S. Supreme Court decisions (*Escobedo v. Illinois*, 378 U.S. 478, and *Miranda v. Arizona*, 384 U.S. 436), which require a police officer to inform individuals under arrest that they have a constitutional right to remain silent, that their statements can later be used against them in court, that they can have an attorney present to help them, and that the state will pay for an attorney if they cannot afford to hire one. Although aimed at protecting an individual during in-custody interrogation, the warning must also be given when the investigation shifts from the investigatory to the accusatory state, i.e., when suspicion begins to focus on an individual.

misdemeanor A minor crime usually punished by less than one year's imprisonment in a local institution, such as a county jail.

motion An oral or written request asking the court to make a specified finding, decision, or order.

National Crime Survey Ongoing victimization study conducted jointly by the Justice Department and Census Bureau that surveys victims about their experiences with law violation.

nolle prosequi The term used when a prosecutor decides to drop a case after a complaint has been formally made. Reasons for a *nolle prosequi* include insufficiency of evidence, reluctance of witnesses to testify, police error, office policy, and so on.

nolo contendere No contest. An admission of guilt in a criminal case with the condition that the finding cannot be used against the defendant in any subsequent civil cases.

obscenity According to current legal theory, sexually explicit material lacking a serious purpose, which appeals solely to the prurient interest of the viewer. Although nudity per se is not usually considered obscene, open sexual behavior, masturbation, and exhibition of the genitals are banned in many communities.

official crime Criminal behavior that has become known to the agents of justice.

parole The release of a prisoner from incarceration subject to conditions set by a parole board. Depending on the jurisdiction, inmates must serve a certain proportion of their sentences before becoming eligible for parole. Upon determination of the parole board, the inmate is granted parole, the conditions of which may require him or her to report regularly to a parole officer, to refrain from criminal conduct, to maintain and support his or her family, to avoid contact with other convicted criminals, to abstain from alcoholic beverages and drugs, to remain within the jurisdiction, and so on. Violations of the conditions of parole may result in revocation of parole, in which case the individual will be returned to prison. The idea behind parole is to allow the offender to be released under community supervision, where rehabilitation and readjustment will be facilitated.

particularity The requirement that a search warrant must state precisely where the search is to take place and what items are to be seized.

Peel, Sir Robert The British home secretary who in 1829 organized the London Metropolitan Police, the first local police force.

Pennsylvania system Prison system developed during the nineteenth century that stressed total isolation and individual penitence as a means of reform.

peremptory challenge Dismissal of a potential juror by either the prosecution or defense for unexplained discretionary reasons.

plea An answer to formal charges by an accused. Possible pleas are guilty, not guilty, *nolo contendere*, not guilty by reason of insanity. A "guilty" plea is a confession of the offense as charged. A "not guilty" plea is a denial of the charge and places the burden on the prosecution to prove the elements of the offense.

plea bargaining The discussion between the defense counsel and the prosecution in which the accused agrees to plead guilty for certain considerations. The advantage to the defendant may be in the form of a reduction of the charges, a lenient sentence, or (in the case of multiple charges) dropped charges. The advantage to the prosecution is that a conviction is obtained without the time and expense of lengthy trial proceedings.

police discretion The ability of police officers to enforce the law selectively. Police officers in the field have great latitude to use their discretion in deciding whether to invoke their arrest powers.

police officer style The belief that most police officers can be classified into ideal personality types. Popular style types include supercops, who desire to enforce only serious crimes like robbery and rape; professionals, who use a broad definition of police work; service oriented, who see their job as that of a helping profession; and avoiders, shirkers who do as little as possible. Whether ideal police officer types actually exist has been open to much debate.

population All people who share a particular personal characteristic, e.g., all high school students or all police officers.

positivism The branch of social science that uses the scientific method of the natural sciences and suggests that human behavior is a product of social, biological, psychological, and economic forces.

preliminary hearings The step at which criminal charges initiated by an "information" are tested for probable cause; the prosecution presents enough evidence to establish probable cause, i.e., a *prima facie* case. The hearing is public and may be attended by the accused and his or her attorney.

presentence report An investigation performed by a probation officer attached to a trial court after the conviction of a defendant. The report contains information about the defendant's background, education, previous employment, family, his or her own statement concerning the offense, prior criminal record, interviews with neighbors or acquaintances, and his or her mental and physical condition.

prison A state or federal correctional institution for incarceration of felony offenders for terms of one year or more.

probable cause The evidentiary criterion necessary to sustain an arrest or the issuance of an arrest or search warrant; less than absolute certainty or "beyond a reasonable doubt" but greater than mere suspicion or "hunch." A set of facts, information, circumstances, or conditions that would lead a reasonable person to believe that an offense was committed and that the accused committed that offense. An arrest made without probable cause may be susceptible to prosecution as an illegal arrest under "false imprisonment" statutes.

probation A sentence entailing the conditional release of a convicted offender into the community under the supervision of the court (in the form of a probation officer) subject to certain conditions for a specified time. The conditions are usually similar to those of parole. (*Note:* Probation is a sentence, an alternative to incarceration; parole is administrative release from incarceration.) Violation of the conditions of probation may result in revocation of probation.

procedural law The rules that define the operation of criminal proceedings. Procedural law describes the methods that must be followed in obtaining warrants, investigating offenses, effecting lawful arrests, using force, conducting trials, introducing evidence, sentencing convicted offenders, and reviewing cases by appellate courts (in general, legislatures have ignored postsentencing procedures). Given the substantive law, which defines criminal offenses, procedural law delineates how the substantive offenses are to be enforced.

proof beyond a reasonable doubt The standard of proof needed to convict in a criminal case. The evidence offered in court does not have to amount to absolute certainty, but should leave no reasonable doubt that the defendant committed the alleged crime.

psychopath A person whose personality is characterized by lack of warmth and affect, inappropriate behavior responses, and an inability to learn from experience. Some psychologists view psychopathy as a result of childhood trauma whereas others see it as a result of biological abnormality.

Racketeer Influenced and Corrupt Organizations Act (RICO) Federal legislation that enables prosecutors to bring additional criminal or civil charges against people whose multiple criminal acts constitute a conspiracy. RICO features monetary penalties that allow the government to confiscate all profits derived from criminal activities. Originally intended to be used against organized crime, RICO has also been employed against white-collar crime.

random sample A sample selected on the basis of chance so that each person in the population has an equal opportunity to be selected.

rationale choice The view that crime is a function of a decision-making process in which the potential offender weighs the potential costs and benefits of an illegal act.

relative deprivation The condition that exists when people of wealth and poverty live in close proximity to one another. Some criminologists attribute crime rate differentials to relative deprivation.

release on recognizance Nonmonetary condition for the pretrial release of an accused individual; an alternative to monetary bail that is granted after determination that the accused has ties in the community, has no prior record of default, and is likely to appear at subsequent proceedings.

restitution A condition of probation in which the offender repays society or the victim of crime for the trouble the crime caused. Monetary restitution involves a direct payment to the victim as a means of compensation. Community service restitution may be used in victimless crimes and involves volunteer work in lieu of more severe criminal penalties.

routine activities The view that crime is a "normal" function of the routine activities of modern living. Offenses can be expected if there is a suitable target that is not protected by capable guardians.

sample A limited number of persons selected for study from a population.

schizophrenia A type of psychosis often marked by bizarre behavior, hallucinations, loss of thought control, and inappropriate emotional responses. There are different types of schizophrenia: catatonic, which characteristically involves impairment of motor activity; paranoid, which is characterized by delusions of persecution; and hebephrenic, which is characterized by immature behavior and giddiness.

self-report study A research approach that requires subjects to reveal their own participation in delinquent or criminal acts.

sentence The criminal sanction imposed by the court on a convicted defendant, usually in the form of a fine, incarceration, or probation. Sentencing may be carried out by a judge, jury, or sentencing council (panel of judges), depending on the statutes of the jurisdiction.

Sherman Report National review of law enforcement education programs, which found that a liberal-arts-related curriculum was the most appropriate learning tool for police officers.

shield laws Laws designed to protect a rape victim by prohibiting the defense attorney from inquiring about her previous sexual relationships.

shire reeve In early England, the senior law enforcement figure in a county, forerunner of today's sheriff.

short-run hedonism According to Cohen, the desire of lower-class gang youths to engage in behavior that will give them immediate gratification and excitement, but which in the long run will be dysfunctional and negativistic.

shock probation A sentence that involves a short prison stay to impress the offender with the pains of imprisonment before he or she begins a probationary sentence.

social disorganization A neighborhood or area marked by culture conflict, lack of cohesiveness, transient population, insufficient social organizations, and anomie.

special needs inmates Inmates such as the mentally retarded, mentally ill, elderly, and AIDS patients who present special problems for the correctional system.

specific deterrence A crime control policy that suggests that punishment should be severe enough to convince previous offenders never to repeat their criminal activity.

specific intent The intent to accomplish a specific purpose as an element of crime, e.g., breaking into someone's house for the express purpose of stealing jewels.

split sentencing Legislation that allows judges to give convicted offenders a short prison stay followed by a longer term on probation. It is designed to give offenders a "taste of the bars" that will shock them into going straight.

stare decisis "to stand by decided cases." The legal principle by which the decision or holding in an earlier case becomes the standard with which subsequent similar cases are judged.

statutory law Laws created by legislative bodies to meet changing social conditions, public opinion, and custom.

sting An undercover police operation in which police pose as criminals to trap law violators.

stop and frisk The situation where police officers who are suspicious of an individual run their hands lightly over the suspect's outer garments to determine if he or she is carrying a concealed weapon. Also called a "patdown" or "threshold inquiry," a stop and frisk is intended to stop short of any activity that could be considered a violation of Fourth Amendment rights.

street crime Illegal acts designed to prey on the public through theft, damage, and violence.

strict liability crimes Illegal acts whose elements do not contain the need for intent or *mens rea*; usually acts that endanger the public welfare, such as illegal dumping of toxic wastes.

subculture A group that is loosely part of the dominant culture but maintains a unique set of values, beliefs, and traditions.

subpoena A legal document that requires the recipient to appear before the tribunal that is empowered to issue it, such as a court, grand jury or congressional committee.

substantive criminal law A body of specific rules that declare what conduct is criminal and prescribe the punishment to be imposed for such conduct.

summons An alternative to arrest usually used for petty or traffic offenses; a written order notifying an individual that he or she has been charged with an offense. A summons directs the person to appear in court to answer the charge. It is used primarily in instances of low risk, where the person will not be required to appear at a later date. The summons is advantageous to police officers in that they are freed from the time normally spent for arrest and booking procedures; it is advantageous to the accused in that he or she is spared time in jail.

team policing An experimental police technique that employs groups of officers assigned to a particular area of the city on a 24-hour basis.

technical parole violation Revocation of parole because conditions set by correctional authorities have been violated.

tort The law of personal wrongs and damage. Tort-type actions include negligence, libel, slander, assault, and trespass.

totality of the circumstances A legal doctrine that mandates that a decision maker consider all the issues and circumstances of a case before judging the outcome. For example, before deciding whether a suspect understood the *Miranda* warning, a judge must consider the totality of the circumstances under which the warning was given. The suspect's age, intelligence, and competency are examples of circumstances that the judge will consider.

transferred intent If an illegal yet unintended act results from the intent to commit a crime, that act is also considered illegal.

transitional neighborhood An area undergoing a shift in population and structure, usually from middle-class residential to lower-class mixed use.

Type I offenses Another name for index crimes.

Type II offenses All crimes other than index and minor traffic offenses. The FBI records annual arrest information for Type II offenses.

venire The group called for jury duty from which jury panels are selected.

victimization survey A crime measurement technique that surveys citizens in order to measure their experiences as victims of crime.

victimology The study of the victim's role in criminal transactions.

victim precipitated Describes a crime in which the victim's behavior was the spark that ignited the subsequent offense, e.g., the victim abused the offender verbally or physically.

voir dire The process in which a potential jury panel is questioned by the prosecution and defense in order to select jurors who are unbiased and objective.

waiver The act of voluntarily relinquishing a right or advantage; often used in the context of waiving one's right to counsel (e.g., *Miranda* warning) or waiving certain steps in the criminal justice process (e.g., the preliminary hearing). Essential to waiver is the voluntary consent of the individual.

warrant A written order issued by a competent magistrate authorizing a police officer or other official to perform duties related to the administration of justice.

watch system During the Middle Ages in England, men were organized in church parishes to guard at night against disturbances and breaches of the peace under direction of the local constable.

wergild Under medieval law, the money paid by the offender to compensate the victim and the state for a criminal offense.

white-collar crime Illegal acts that capitalize on a person's place in the marketplace. White-collar crimes can involve theft, embezzlement, fraud, market manipulation, restraint of trade, and false advertising.

Wickersham Commission Created in 1931 by President Herbert Hoover to investigate the state of the nation's police forces. The commission found that police training was inadequate and that the average officer was incapable of effectively carrying out his duties.

work furlough A prison treatment program that allows inmates to be released during the day to work in the community and return to prison.

writ of certiorari An order of a superior court requesting that the record of an inferior court (or administrative body) be brought forward for review or inspection.

writ of habeas corpus A judicial order requesting that a person detaining another produce the body of the prisoner and give reasons for his or her capture and detention. Habeas corpus is a legal device used to request that a judicial body review reasons for a person's confinement and the conditions of confinement. Habeas corpus is known as "the great writ."

writ of mandamus An order of a superior court commanding that a lower court or an administrative or executive body perform a specific function. It is commonly used to restore rights and privileges lost to a defendant through illegal means.

Table of Cases

Name Index

Subject Index

Abt Associates, 30
Acquired immune deficiency syndrome (AIDS), 149
    among prison inmates, 565, 566–67
Actus reus, 121, 122–23
Adjudication, 21, 416. *See also* Jury trial.
Adversary system, 323, 376–77, 384, 432
Age
    and capital punishment, 648, 649
    and crime rates, 46, 50–51, 60
    and criminal responsibility, 129
    and juvenile court jurisdiction, 628, 648
    police discretion and, 221
    of prison inmates, 553
    and sentencing, 467
AIDS. *See* Acquired immune deficiency syndrome.
Alcoholism (as defense), 129, 130–31, 165–66
American Bar Association, 4, 180, 301, 360, 363, 396, 440, 649–50
    Code of Professional Responsibility, 349, 363
    Grand Jury Policy and Model Act, 400
    Standards Relating to Court Organization, 343, 345–46
    Standards Relating to Pleas of Guilty, 407, 408
    Standards Relating to Sentencing Alternatives and Procedures, 468
    Standards Relating to Speedy Trial, 423, 426
    Standards Relating to the Prosecution Function and Defense Function, 350–51, 361
    Standards Relating to the Urban Police Function, 285–86
American Correctional Association, 599
American Law Institute, 180
    Model Code of Pre-Arraignment Procedures, 315
    Model Penal Code, 136, 137–38, 468, 490, 491
Appellate courts, 9, 15, 16, 22, 323, 326–27, 332–34, 340, 440–41, 469
Arraignment, 20, 366, 385, 406

Arrest, 223
    crimes cleared by, 45
    felony/misdemeanor distinction and, 119
    house, 512–14, 516–18
    in-presence requirement, 20, 119
    of juvenile offenders, 629–30
    power of police, 302–4
    probable cause and, 18
    searches incident to, 290–91, 292
    specific deterrent effect of, 225–27
    stage of criminal justice process, 18, 20
    trends, 45
    warrant, 291, 302, 630
Assault, 60, 63
    nonreporting of, 52

Bail, 20–21, 138, 143. *See also* Pretrial detention; Preventive detention; Release on recognizance.
    bondsmen, 389
    discriminatory effects of, 387–88
    guidelines, 390–92
    juvenile offenders and, 637–38
    reform, 389–90, 391
    release mechanisms, 387
    right to, 386–87
    success of, 388
Bail Reform Act
    of 1966, 390, 393
    of 1984, 390, 393–94, 395, 396, 397
Bargain justice. *See* Plea bargaining.
Bartley-Fox Law (Massachusetts), 170, 461
Battelle Institute, 30
Behavioral theory (of crime causation), 82–83
Bill of Rights. *See also* individual amendments.
    application to the states, 144–46, 147, 419–21
    and criminal procedure, 139–44
Biological theory (of crime causation), 79–81, 103
Blacks. *See also* Minority groups.
    arrest rate of, 48–49, 466
    deadly force and, 270

    death penalty and, 474–75
    jury selection and, 433–34
    as juveniles in custody, 653
    as offenders, 60
    police brutality against, 266–67
    police entrance exams and, 236–37
    as police officers, 255–56, 258–61, 262–63, 271
    in prison populations, 466–67, 553, 557
        Black Muslim movement, 560, 579–80
        women, 561
        sentencing and, 466–67
        as victims of crime, 59
Bureau of Justice Statistics (BJS), 31, 553

Capital punishment, 446, 447, 449, 526
    arguments for and against, 470–74
    current status of, 479–80
    death-qualified juries, 477
    jury selection and, 434
    of juveniles, 648, 649
    legality of, 475–77
    number of executions, 470
    racial bias in, 474–75
    research on, 477–79
Causes of crime
    behavioral theory, 82–83
    biological theory, 79–81, 103
    choice theory, 73–78, 103
    cognitive theory, 83
    control theories, 93–94, 104
    cultural deviance theory, 88, 103
    early theories of, 72–73
    ecological theory of, 90–91, 104
    female criminality, 97–99
    future developments in, 102
    labeling theory, 95–96
    physiological theory, 83–84
    psychoanalytic theory, 81–82, 103
    social conflict theory, 96–97
    social process theory, 91–96, 104
    social structure theory, 85–88, 91, 103
    sociological theories, 85–97
    strain theory, 88–89, 103

Photo Credits (continued from p. iv)